Commentary on John's Gospel

Commentary on John's Gospel

by

Frederic Louis Godet

KREGEL PUBLICATIONS
Grand Rapids, Michigan 49501

COMMENTARY ON JOHN'S GOSPEL
Copyright © 1978 by Kregel Publications
a division of Kregel, Inc. All rights reserved.

Printed in the United States of America

Library of Congress Cataloging in Publication Data

Godet, Frederic, 1812-1900.
   Commentary on John's Gospel.

   Translation of Commentaire sur l'Evangile de saint Jean.

   Reprint of the 1886 ed. published by Funk & Wagnalls, New York, in series: Bible Student's Library.
   1. Bible, N.T. John—Commentaries. I. Title. II. Series: Bible Student's Library.
  BS2615.G6   1978   226'.5'07   78-59145
  ISBN 0-8254-2714-2

CONTENTS

FOREWORD ix
Preface Third French Edition xiii
Preface to the Commentary to the Third French Edition xv

Preliminaries 1
  1. The Gospel Literature 3
  2. History of the Johannean Discussion 8
     The Adversaries 8
     The Defenders 20
     The Intermediate Positions 26
  THE APOSTLE JOHN 29
     In His Father's House 29
     As a Follower of Jesus 30
     At the Head of the Judaeo-Christian Church 35
     In Asia Minor 38
     His Death 51
  THE FOURTH GOSPEL 54
    1. Analysis 54
    2. Characteristics 66
      A. The Narrative 66
        1. The Governing Idea 66
        2. The Facts 68
        3. The Discourses 93
          a. Relation of the Idea of the Logos to
            the Discourses and Narrative 94
          b. Objections Against the Historical
            Character of the Discourses 97
            Internal Difficulties 98
            Relation of the Discourses to the Prologue and I John . . . 104

	Differences from the Synoptics	108
	c. The Person of Jesus	123
	Conclusion	127
B. Relation to the Old Testament		127
C. The Style		134

THE ORIGIN ... 139

1. The Time 140
   From 160-170 141
   From 130-155 147
   From 110-125 157
2. The Author 167
   1. Testimonies 168
   2. Objections 171
   3. Internal Proof 197
   4. Contrary Hypotheses 204
3. The Place 208
4. The Occasion and Aim 209

INTRODUCTION TO THE COMMENTARY ... 221

1. The Plan of the Gospel 221
2. The Preservation of the Text 230
3. The Title of the Gospel 238

PROLOGUE: John 1:1-18 ... 240

1. The Logos   John 1:1-4 243
2. Unbelief   John 1:5-11 253
3. Faith   John 1:12-18 263
4. General Considerations 283

FIRST PART: Birth of Faith   John 1:19-4:54 ... 299

First Cycle   John 1:19-2:11 300
1. The Testimonies of John the Baptist   John 1:19-37 300
   The Testimonies of the Forerunner 322
2. Beginnings of the Work of Jesus: Birth of Faith   John 1:28-82 .. 325
   The Son of Man 338
3. The First Miracle: Strengthening of Faith   John 2:1-11 .. 342

On the Miracle of Cana	352
Second Cycle John 2:12-4:54	355
1. Jesus in Judea John 2:12-3:36	355
The Brethren of Jesus	357
2. Jesus in Samaria John 4:1-42	415
3. Jesus in Galilee John 4:43-54	441

SECOND PART: Unbelief Develops in Israel   John 5-12 448
  First Cycle   John 5-8 451
    1. First Outbreak of Hatred in Judea   John 5:1-41 452
       Introductory Suggestions on the Internal Evidence 493
       Additional Notes on John 1-5 513
    2. The Great Messianic Testimony and the Crisis of
       Faith in Galilee   John 6:1-71 561
    3. The Conflict at Its Highest Stage of Intensity
       at Jerusalem   John 7:1-8:59 612
  Second Cycle   John 9 and 10 685
    1. The Miracle   John 9:1-41 685
    2. The First Discourse   John 10:1-21 699
    3. The Second Discourse   John 10:22-42 715
  Third Cycle   John 11 and 12 729
    1. The Resurrection of Lazarus   John 11:1-59 729
       On the Resurrection of Lazarus 756
    2. The Last Days of Jesus' Ministry   John 12:1-36 761
    3. Retrospective Glance at the Mysterious Fact of
       Jewish Unbelief   John 12:37-50 791

THIRD PART: The Development of Faith   John 13-17 801
  1. The Facts   John 13:1-30 802
  2. The Discourses   John 13:31-16:33 822
  3. The Prayer   John 17:1-26 883

FOURTH PART: The Passion   John 18, 19 908
  1. The Arrest of Jesus   John 18:1-11 909
  2. The Trial of Jesus   John 18:12-19:16a 914
  3. The Crucifixion of Jesus   John 19:16b-42 942
  4. On the Day of Jesus' Death   John 20:1-29 958

FIFTH PART: The Resurrection   John 20:1-29 972
    On the Resurrection   John 20:1-29 986

CONCLUSION: John 20:30,31 994

APPENDIX: John 21:1-25 997

  Additional Notes on John 6-21 1017
INDEX 1103

FOREWORD

THE Commentary on the Gospel of John which is now presented, in its third edition, to American readers, has been well known to New Testament scholars for twenty years. It was originally published in 1864–5, and immediately commanded attention. Ten or eleven years later an enlarged and greatly improved edition was issued, which was soon afterwards translated into English. The first volume of the third edition was given to the public in 1881; the second and third volumes have appeared during the present year (1885). Unlike most of the German commentators of recent days, Godet has, with each new edition, not simply revised what he had written at an earlier date, but, in large measure, prepared a new work. This is very strikingly true of the introductory volume of this latest edition of the original, which covers the first two hundred and nineteen pages of this translation. It is also true, as the reader who compares the two with minute study will perceive, that in the commentary properly so called every paragraph has been subjected to careful examination, and even where the matter is not altogether new, sentences have been very largely re-written, with changes sometimes of importance to the thought and sometimes apparently only for purposes of style. That the work has been greatly improved by these new labors of the author will be admitted by all who read the second and third editions in connection with each other. It may be almost said, that as great a service has been rendered by the additions and revisions since the book was first issued as was rendered by its original publication. Among the commentaries on this Gospel, this may be ranked as one of the best—a book which every student and minister may well examine, both for the light which it throws upon this most deeply interesting portion of the New Testament and for its suggestiveness to Christian thought.

When the proposal was first made to publish a new translation in this country, it was supposed that it would be ready for publication at a considerably earlier date. But soon after the work was undertaken, it was ascertained that the second and third volumes of the third edition would appear in Switzerland in 1885, and it was accordingly deemed best to await their issue. Advance sheets were kindly forwarded by the author as soon as they were printed—the preparation of this American edition being the result of consultation with him and having his approval. The present volume contains one half of the book, including the General Introduction (Vol. I.) of the original, and the Commentary as far as the end of the fifth chapter of the Gospel, or about four-fifths of Vol. II. The remainder of the translation, it is expected, will be published about the first of July, 1886.

Of the work of the American editor a few words may be said. With reference to the translation I may be allowed to state two things : 1. That my endeavor has been rather to place before the reader the exactness of the author's thought, than to make prominent the matter of English style. In this sense, I have sought to give a literal, rather than an elegant rendering of the original. I have, however, as I trust, not altogether failed in making a readable book, which may represent faithfully in all respects what Godet gave to his French readers. 2. A translation of the first volume of the third edition of the French work (pp. 1–219 of this vol.) was published in connection with the Edinburgh translation of the second edition about two years ago. It was not in my hands, however, until my own translation was finished. In the final revision of my work, as the volume was about to be printed, I compared it with this translation, and in a few instances, of no special significance, I allowed myself to be affected by it in the choice of a word. For anything of this kind as connected with the English work in its second or third edition, or with the German translation of the second edition which was in my hands, but which being not altogether on the plan of my own, I used very little, I would make whatever acknowledgment may be due. The statement already made, however, will show that my work was done independently, and that if correspondences in phraseology with the English translation occur, they are due to the fact that a substantially literal conformity to the French has been attempted both by the English translator and myself.

In the limited number of pages allowed me for additions to Godet's work, I have, at the end of the volume, inserted some introductory remarks on a certain part of the internal argument for the genuineness of the fourth Gospel, and also some additional annotations on the first five chapters. I would ask the reader's considerate attention to all the suggestions contained in these additional pages.

To the students and graduates of the Divinity School of Yale College I dedicate my part of this volume and the one which is to follow it, bearing with me always a most kindly feeling toward them and a most pleasant remembrance of their friendship for me.

TIMOTHY DWIGHT

New Haven.

PREFACE
TO THE THIRD FRENCH EDITION

I AM permitted for the third time to present to the Church this Commentary on the book which seems to me to be its most precious jewel, on the narrative of the life of Jesus in which His most intimate friend has included his most glorious and most sacred recollections. I feel all the responsibility of this office, but I know also the beauty of it; and I at once humble myself and rejoice.

God has blessed the publication of this Commentary beyond all that I was able to imagine when I wrote it for the first time. To do something, in my weakness, for the Church of France—the noblest branch, perhaps, which the tree that came from the *grain of mustard-seed* has put forth, but whose position seems to me more serious at this hour than in the days of bloody persecution,—this was all my ambition; it appeared to me even to border upon presumption. And now I receive from many quarters testimonies of affectionate sympathy and intimate communion of spirit, and I see this work translated into German, English, Dutch, Danish, Swedish, and exerting its influence far beyond the circle which I had proposed to myself to reach. God has done, according to the expression of the apostle, more than all that I was able to *ask* or even to *think*.

In the preceding edition, I had completely remodelled the treatment of the critical questions, by uniting all the discussions relative to the origin of the fourth Gospel in a special volume. This arrangement has been maintained; nevertheless, there is scarcely a page, scarcely a phrase of the preceding edition which has not been recast, and, as it were, composed anew. The reason of this fact is found, not only in the profound sense which I had of the imperfections of the previous work, but also in the appearance of recent works which I was obliged to take into the most special consideration. I allude particularly to the *Théologie johannique* of M. Reuss, in his great work on *La Bible* (1879), to the essay of M. Sabatier in the *Encyclopédie des sciences religieuses*, t. vii. pp. 173–195 (1879), to the sixth volume of M. Renan's book on the *Origines du christianisme* (1879), and to the last edition of Hase's work, *Geschichte Jesu* (1876).

The result of this renewed study has been in my case the ever more firm *scientific* conviction of the authenticity of the writing which the Church has handed down to us under the name of John. There is a conviction of a different nature which forms itself in the heart on the simple reading of such a book. This conviction does not grow up; it is immediate, and consequently complete, from the first moment. It resembles confidence and love at first sight, that decisive impression to the integrity of which thirty years of common life and mutual devotion add nothing.

Scientific study cannot form a bond like this; what it can do is only to remove the hostile pressure which threatens to loosen or to break it. Truly, I can say that I have never felt this scientific assurance so confirmed as after this new examination of the proofs on which it rests and the reasons recently alleged against it.

The reader will judge whether this is an amiable illusion; whether the conclusion formulated at the end of this volume is indeed the result of a profound and impartial study of the facts, or whether it has only been reached because it was desired in advance. It seems to me that I can, with yet more confidence than before, submit my book to this test.

May all that which passed from the heart of Jesus into the heart and the writing of John communicate itself abundantly to my readers, so that the wish of the Holy Apostle may be accomplished in them: "We write these things unto you, that your joy may be full."

Neuchâtel.

PREFACE TO THE COMMENTARY
IN THE THIRD FRENCH EDITION

It is not without a feeling of hope that I present to the Church the third edition of this Commentary, the introductory volume of which appeared in 1881. At the time when I first published this work, the two theories of Baur and Reuss held sway over scientific thought, one in Germany, the other in France. The former taught us to see in the Johannean narrative scarcely anything but a romance designed to illustrate the idea of the Logos and to cause it to pervade the Church. The other showed a little more respect to the history related in this book, but regarded the discourses inserted in this framework simply as the theology of the author himself, whoever he was, John or some one else ; theology which he had himself derived from the contemplation of Jesus and from his Christian experience.

When we follow attentively the progress of opinion, we are struck with the change which is gradually taking place in the estimate of this sacred writing. To speak only of points of most importance, Renan, in the masterly dissertation which he has placed at the end of the thirteenth edition of his *Vie de Jésus*, has, by the soundest analysis, demonstrated the indisputably historical character of the greater part of John's narratives, and the superiority to the Synoptic story which must be accorded to them in many respects. The following, moreover, is the way in which he expressed himself, last year, in a conversation reported in the *Christianisme au XIXᵉ siècle* (April, 1884): "The historical character of the Fourth Gospel is continually more impressive to me. When reading it, I say to myself : It is so." If *it is so*, what becomes of Baur's opinion !

Hase, in his *History of Jesus* (1876), has given in the Introduction a very careful study of the sources of this history, especially of the Gospel of John. He decides, it is true, for its non-authenticity, but after having laid down a series of preambles which lead directly to the opposite conclusion. One feels that he must have overcome by sheer force of will all the scientific reasons which were most fitted to justify the contrary conviction. And one is easily convinced that the ground of this decision, which is contrary to the premises, is nothing else than the rationalistic denial of the miraculous. A judgment can be formed from these words of the venerable writer : "Through the golden breastplate of the Logos-doctrine we feel (in the Jesus of the Fourth Gospel) the beating of a true human heart which is moved by joy and grief, and in this picture *we recognize the apostle* with all the fulness of his recollection." At what a distance we are from the estimates of Baur and Keim !

The two most considerable works, in relation to our subject, which have appeared in Germany in these most recent days, are the *Commentary on the Gospel of John* by Bernhard Weiss (in the collection of Meyer's Commentaries, sixth edition, 1880) and the *Life of Jesus* by the same author (1882). The historical verity of the entire narrative of John is fully recognized and proved. As to the discourses, Weiss no doubt makes partial concessions to criticism, which I cannot regard as sufficiently justified ; the readers will be able to judge of them for themselves. But the difference as compared with Reuss is nevertheless a difference *toto cœlo*, so that the few imported elements which Weiss allows do not in the least degree compromise, in his view, the authenticity of the book.

It may well be expected that this return movement will not be unanimous. The Tübingen school has not ceased to work in the direction which was given to it by the genius of its master. We will mention here only the writing in which this tendency has, so to speak, reached its climax. It is that of A. Thoma : *Die Genesis des Johannes-Evangeliums* (1882). On one point this author breaks with the tradition of the school : he acknowledges the close relations of our Gospel to Judaism and the Old Testament. But, on the other side, to what a phantasmagoria of allegorizing does the imagination of this writer surrender itself ! The discoveries of Baur and Reuss on this path are astonishingly surpassed. It is not a history of Jesus, it is that of Christianity itself that the author of our Gospel, an Alexandrian Christian of the second century, wished to write. From the condition of infancy described by the Synoptics, the new religion had arrived at the brilliant period of youth. Already all sorts of elements had arisen in the Church and were struggling in the midst of it. The personages who play a part in our Gospel are nothing else then personifications, freely created, of these different tendencies. Caiaphas is false prophecy ; the brethren of Jesus represent carnal Israel struggling against the Church. Pilate is the Roman despotism ; the Greek proselytes of ch. xii. personify paganism eager for truth. The different Christian parties are also represented, in particular by the family at Bethany ; the party of works, by Martha ; that of faith, by Mary ;

Christian Essenism, by Lazarus. The most skilful turn in this *jeu d'esprit* is the explanation of the person of James, the brother of Jesus. It is Judaism under its form which is hostile to Christianity. His name is designedly suppressed throughout the whole narrative, but is replaced by that of Judas ; nevertheless, allusion is made to its signification, *the supplanter*, in the passage, xiii. 18, where Jesus recalls to mind the words of Psalm xli. : "He that eats bread with me has *lifted up his heel* against me." One will form an idea of the author's critical method when he learns, for example, that the passage John i. 13 : "*Those who are born not of blood nor . . . but of God*," was composed by the Alexandrian author by means of the following three passages : Rom. viii. 29 ("the first-born among many brethren") ; Heb. ii. 13 ("with the children whom God has given me") ; 1 Cor. xv. 48 ("as the heavenly, . . . so the heavenly"). Such are specimens of what at the present day is called, by this party, the discovery of the genesis of the Fourth Gospel.

Happily these excesses, which may be called the Saturnalia of criticism, seem also to have contributed, according to their measure, to bring the minds of men back to sobriety and good sense. We gather together, with satisfaction, testimonies like the following :

Franke, a young scholar teaching at Halle, has recently published a work under the title : *Das alte Testament bei Johannes*, a work full of sagacity and sound erudition, in which he proves what I also have sought to prove, that the thought of the author of the Fourth Gospel penetrates with all its fibres into the soil of the Old Testament. The following is the way in which he expresses himself, as he closes his preface : "A continuous study of the writings of John has led me with ever-increasing force to the conviction that their interpretation cannot be undertaken with success except by decidedly maintaining their composition by John the apostle."

Another young scholar, Schneedermann, Professor at Basle, in his work : *Le judaisme et la prédication chrétienne dans les évangiles* (1884), writes the following lines : "When in the period of my academic course I came to the explication of the Fourth Gospel, I was uncertain respecting its origin, but determined to declare without mental reservation that I must remain undecided, and why I must remain so. . . . To my own surprise, the result of my work was the discovery, set forth in what precedes, that the cause of the Fourth Gospel and of the evangelic history is not in so bad a state as some would have us believe. . . . The impression to which I have been brought is, that there is nothing to oppose our seeing in the author of the Fourth Gospel a richly gifted Jewish thinker, of a powerful religious enthusiasm, and our recognizing in this author, conscious of his character as eye-witness, the apostle John."

These voices which rise in the midst of the younger generation and the concordant experiences which they express are of good augury; they announce a new phase of criticism. This is the reason why, as I began, I expressed a feeling of hope. Following upon this violent crisis, there is verified anew that old motto which has become that of the Gospel of John:

> Tant plus à me battre on s'amuse,
> Tant plus de marteaux on y use.

I hope that I have neglected nothing which could contribute to keep this Commentary at the height of the scientific work which is carried on at the present day, with so much solicitude, in relation to the Fourth Gospel. I have especially derived great advantage from the Commentaries of Weiss and Keil, which have appeared since my previous edition. There will scarcely be found a page in this book which does not present traces of work designed to improve it and to render it less unworthy of its object.

May the Lord give strength and victory to His Word in the midst of the Church and throughout the world!

F. GODET

Neuchâtel.

PRELIMINARIES

EVERY book is a mystery of which the author alone has the secret. The preface may, no doubt, lift a corner of the veil; but there are books without a preface, and the writer may not tell the whole truth. It belongs to literary criticism, as it is understood at the present day,[1] to solve the problem offered to the world by every work which is worthy of attention. For a book is not fully intelligible except so far as the obscurity of its origin is dissipated.

The science which is commonly called *Sacred Criticism* or *Introduction to the Old and the New Testament* was instituted by the Church, to fulfill this task with regard to the books which contain the object of its faith and the standards of its development. By placing in a clear light the origin of each one of these writings and thus revealing its primal thought, it has as its office to shed upon their whole contents the ray of light which illumines their minutest details.

According to Schleiermacher, the ideal of Sacred Criticism consists in putting the present reader in the place of the original reader,[2] by procuring for him through the artifice of science, the preliminary knowledge which the latter, as a matter of course, possessed. However valuable a result like this may be, it seems to me that criticism should propose to itself a yet more elevated aim. Its true mission is to transport the reader into the very mind of the author, at the time when he conceived or elaborated his work, and to cause him to be present at the composition of the book almost after the manner of the spectator who is present at the casting of a bell, and who, after having beheld the metal in a state of fusion in the furnace, sees the torrent of fire flow into the mold in which it is to receive its permanent form. This ideal includes that of Schleiermacher. For one of the essential elements present to the mind of the author at the time when he prepares his work, is certainly the idea which

---

[1] By Sainte-Beuve, for example. [2] *Einleitung ins N. T.*, herausg. von Wolde, p. 7.

2 / Preliminaries

he forms of his readers, and of their condition and wants. To identify oneself with him is, therefore, at the same time to identify oneself with them.

To attain this object, or, at least, to approach it as nearly as possible, Criticism makes use of two sorts of means: 1. Those which it borrows from the history, and especially from the literary history, of the time which witnessed the publication of the sacred writings, or which followed it; 2. Those which it derives from the book itself.

Among the former we rank, first of all, the positive statements which Jewish or Christian antiquity has transmitted to us respecting the composition of one or another of our Biblical writings; then, the quotations or reminiscences of any passages of these books, which are met with in subsequent writers, and which prove their existence and influence at a certain date; finally, the historical facts to which these writings have stood in the relation of cause or effect. These are the *external* data.

To the second class belong all the indications, contained in the book itself, respecting the person of its author, and respecting the circumstances in which he labored and the motive which impelled him to write. These are the *internal* data.

To combine these two classes of data, for the purpose of drawing from them, if possible, a harmonious result—such is the work of Criticism.

This is the task which we undertake with regard to one of the most important books of the New Testament and of the whole Bible. Luther is reported to have said that if a tyrant succeeded in destroying the Holy Scriptures and only a single copy of the Epistle to the Romans and of the Gospel of John escaped him, Christianity would be saved. He spoke truly; for the fourth Gospel presents the object of the Christian faith in its most perfect splendor, and the Epistle to the Romans describes the way of faith which leads to this object, with an incomparable clearness. What need of more to preserve Christ to the world and to give birth ever anew to the Church?

The following will be the course of our study. After having cast a general glance at the formation of our Gospel literature, we shall trace the course of the discussions relative to the composition of the fourth Gospel. These will be the subjects of two preliminary chapters.

Then, we shall enter upon the study itself, which will include the following subjects:

1. The life of the apostle to whom the fourth Gospel is generally ascribed.

2. The analysis and distinctive characteristics of this writing.

3. The circumstances of its composition:
    Its date;
    The place of its origin;
    Its author;
    The aim which the author pursued in composing it.

After having studied each of these points, as separately as possible from one another, we shall bring together the particular results thus obtained in a general view, which, if we have not taken a wrong path, will offer the solution of the problem.

Jesus has promised to His Church the Spirit of truth to lead it into all the truth. It is under the direction of this guide that we place ourselves.

1

A GLANCE AT THE FORMATION OF THE GOSPEL LITERATURE

OUR first three Gospels certainly have a common origin, not only in that all three relate one and the same history, but also by reason of the fact that an elaboration of this history, of some sort, was already in existence at the time of their composition, and has stamped with a common impress the three narratives. Indeed, the striking agreement between them which is easily observed both in the general plan and in certain series of identical accounts, and finally in numerous clauses which are found exactly the same in two of these writings, or in all the three—this general and particular agreement renders it impossible to question that, before being thus recorded, the history of Jesus had already been cast in a mold where it had received the more or less fixed form in which we find it in our three narratives. Many think that this primitive gospel type consisted of a written document—either one of our three Gospels, of which the other two were only a free reproduction, or one or even two writings, now lost, from which our evangelists, all three of them, drew. This hypothesis of written sources has been, and is still presented under the most varied forms. We do not think that in any form it can be accepted; for it always leads to the adoption of the view, that the later writer sometimes willfully altered his model by introducing changes of real gravity, at other times adopted the course of copying with the utmost literalness, and that while frequently applying these two opposite methods in one and the same verse; and, finally, at still other times, that he made the text which he used undergo a multitude of modifications which are ridiculous by reason of being insignificant. Let any one consult a Synopsis,[1] and the thing will be obvious. Is it psychologically conceivable that serious, believing writers, convinced of the supreme importance of the subject of which they were treating, adopted such methods with regard to it; and, above all, that they applied them to the reproduction of the very teachings of the Lord Jesus?—Common as, even at the present day, this manner of explaining the relation between our three Gospels is, we are convinced that Criticism will finally renounce it as a moral impossibility.

The simple and natural solution of the problem appears to us to be indicated by the book of Acts, in the passage where it speaks to us of the *teaching of the apostles*,[2] as one of the foundations on which the Church of Jerusalem was built (ii. 42). In this primitive apostolic teaching, the accounts of the life and death of Jesus surely occupied the first place. These narratives, daily repeated by the apostles, and by the evangelists instructed in their school, must speedily have taken a form more or less fixed and settled, not only as to the tenor of each account, but also as to the joining together of several accounts in one group, which formed ordinarily the subject-matter of a single teaching. What we here affirm is not a pure hypothesis. St. Luke tells us, in the preface of his Gospel (the most ancient document respecting this subject which we possess), of the first written accounts of the evangelic facts as composed " according to the story which they transmitted to us who were witnesses of them from the beginning, and who became ministers of the Word." These *witnesses* and *first ministers* can only have been the apostles. Their accounts conveyed to the Church by oral teaching had passed, therefore, just as they were, into the writings of those who first wrote them out. The pronoun *us* employed by Luke, shows that he ranked himself among the writers who were instructed by the oral testimony of the apostles.

The primitive apostolic tradition is thus the type, at once fixed, and yet within certain limits malleable, which has stamped with its ineffaceable imprint our first three Gospels. In this way a satisfactory explanation is afforded, on the one side, of the general and particular resemblances which make these three writings, as it were, one and the same narrative; and, on the other, of the differences which we observe among them, from those which are most considerable to those which are most insignificant.

These three works are, thus, three workings-over—wrought independently of one another—of the primitive tradition formulated in the midst of the Palestinian churches, and ere long repeated in all the countries of the

---

[1] An edition presenting the three texts in three parallel columns. [2] Διδαχὴ τῶν ἀποστόλων.

world. They are three branches proceeding from the same trunk, but branches which have grown out under different conditions and in different directions; and herein lies the explanation of the peculiar physiognomy of each of the three books.

In the first, the Gospel of St. Matthew, we find the matter of the preaching of the Twelve at Jerusalem preserved in the form which approaches nearest to the primitive type. This fact will appear quite simple, if we hold that this writing was designed for the Jewish people, and therefore precisely for the circle of readers with a view to which the oral preaching had been originally formulated. The dominant idea in the Palestinian preaching must have been that of the Messianic dignity of Jesus. This is also the thought which forms the unity of the first Gospel. It is inscribed at the beginning of the book as its programme.[1] The formula: *that it might be fulfilled*, which recurs, like a refrain, throughout the entire narrative, recalls this primal idea at every moment; finally it breaks forth into the full light of day in the conclusion, which brings us to contemplate the full realization of the Messianic destiny of the Lord.[2] With what purpose was this redaction of the primitive apostolic testimony published? Evidently the author desired to address a last appeal to that people, whom their own unbelief was leading to ruin. This book was composed, therefore, at the time when the final catastrophe was preparing. A word of Jesus (Matt. xxiv. 15) in which He enjoins upon His disciples to flee to the other side of the Jordan as soon as the war should break out, is reported by the author with a significant *nota bene*,[3] which confirms the date that we have just indicated.

Already twenty years before this, the preaching of the Gospel had passed beyond the boundaries of Palestine and penetrated the Gentile world. Numerous churches, almost all of them composed of a small nucleus of Jews, and a multitude of Gentiles grouped around them, had arisen at the preaching of the Apostle Paul and his fellow-laborers. This immense work could not in the end dispense with the solid foundation which had been laid at the beginning by the Twelve and the evangelists in Palestine and Syria: the connected narrative of the acts, the teachings, the death and the resurrection of Jesus. In this fact lay the imperative want which gave birth to our third Gospel, drawn up by one of the most

---

[1] Matt. i. 1: "Genealogy of Jesus *Christ* (*Messiah*)."

[2] xxviii. 18: "All power hath been given unto me in heaven and on earth."

[3] "When ye shall see the abomination of desolation . . . standing in the holy place—LET HIM THAT READETH UNDERSTAND! then let them that are in Judea flee unto the mountains."

eminent companions of the apostle of the Gentiles, St. Luke. The Messianic dignity of Jesus, and the argument drawn from the prophecies, had no more, in the estimation of the Gentiles, the same importance as with the Jews: all this is omitted in the third Gospel. It was as the Saviour of humanity that Jesus needed especially be presented to them; with this purpose, Luke, after having gathered the most exact information, sets in relief, in his representation of our Lord's earthly ministry, everything that had marked the salvation which He introduced as a *gratuitous* and *universal* salvation. Hence the agreement, which is so profound, between this Gospel and the writings of St. Paul. What the former traces out historically, the latter expounds theoretically. But, notwithstanding these differences as compared with the work of Matthew, the Gospel of Luke rests always, as the author himself declares in his preface, on the apostolic tradition formulated at the beginning by the Twelve. Only he has sought to complete it and to give it a more strict arrangement[1] with a view to cultivated Gentiles, such as Theophilus, who demanded a more consecutive and profound teaching.

Was a third form possible? Yes; this traditional type, preserved in its rigid and potent originality by the first evangelist with a view to the Jewish people, enriched and completed by the third with a view to the churches of the Gentile nations, might be published anew in its primitive form, as in the first Gospel, but this time with a view to Gentile readers, as in the third,—and such, in fact, is the Gospel of Mark. This work does not have any of the precious supplements which that of Luke had added to the Palestinian preaching; in this point it is allied to the first Gospel. But, on the other hand, it omits the numerous references to the prophecies and most of the long discourses of Jesus addressed to the people and their rulers, which give to the Gospel of Matthew its so decidedly Jewish character; besides, it adds detailed explanations respecting the Jewish customs which are not found in Matthew, and which are evidently intended for Gentile readers. Thus allied, therefore, to Luke by its destination and to Matthew by its contents, it is, as it were, the connecting link between the two preceding forms. This intermediate position is made clear by the first word of the work: "Gospel of Jesus, the *Christ* (Messiah), *Son of God*." The title of *Christ* recalls the special relation of Jesus to the Jewish people; that of *Son of God*, which marks the myste-

---

[1] i. 3: "I have thought it fit, after having accurately traced the course of all things, to write unto thee in order, that thou mightest know the certainty of the instructions which thou hast received."

rious relation between God and this unique man, raises this being to such a height that His appearance and His work must necessarily have for their object the entire human race. To this first word of the book answers also the last, which shows us Jesus continuing from heaven to discharge throughout the whole world that function of celestial messenger, of divine evangelist, which He had begun to exercise on the earth. Let us notice also a distinctive characteristic of this narrative: in each picture, so to speak, there are found strokes of the pencil which belong to it peculiarly and which betray an eye-witness. They are always, at the foundation, the traditional accounts, but evidently transmitted by a witness who had himself taken part in the scenes related, and who, when recounting them by word of mouth, quite naturally mingled in them points of detail suggested by the vividness of his own recollections.

As such do our first three Gospels present themselves to attentive readers—being called *Synoptic* because the three narratives may without much difficulty be placed, with a view to a comparison with one another, in three parallel columns. The date of their composition must have been nearly the same (between the years 60 and 70). Indeed, the first is, as it were, the last apostolic summons addressed to the people of Israel before their destruction; the third is designed to give to the preaching of St. Paul in the Gentile world its historical basis; and the second is the reproduction of the preachings of a witness carrying to the Gentile world the primitive Palestinian Gospel proclamation. If the composition of these three writings really took place at nearly the same time and in different countries, this fact accords with the opinion expressed above, that the writings were composed each one independently of the two others.

Did the Church possess in these three monuments of the primitive popular preaching of the Gospel that by which it could fully answer the wants of believers who had not known the Lord? Must there not have been in the ministry of Jesus a large number of elements which the apostles had not been able to introduce into their missionary preaching? Had they not, by reason of the elementary, and in some sort catechetical nature of that teaching of the earliest times, been led to eliminate many of the sayings of Jesus which reached beyond such a level and rose to a height where only the most advanced minds could follow Him? This is, in itself, very probable. We have already seen that a mass of picturesque details, which are wanting in Matthew, more vividly color the ancient popular tradition in Mark. The important additions in Luke prove still more eloquently how the richness of the ministry of Jesus

8 / Preliminaries

passed beyond the measure of the primitive oral tradition. Why may not an immediate witness of Jesus' ministry have felt himself called to rise once above all these traditional accounts, to draw directly from the source of his own recollections, and, while omitting all the scenes already sufficiently known, which had passed into the ordinary narrative, to trace, at a single stroke, the picture of the moments which were most marked, most impressive to his own heart, in the ministry of his Master? There was not in this, as we can well understand, any deliberate selection, any artificial distribution. The division of the evangelic matter was the natural result of the historical circumstances in which the founding of the Church was accomplished.

This course of things is so simple that it is, in some sort, its own justification. The apostolic origin of the fourth Gospel may be disputed, but it cannot be denied by any one that the situation indicated is probable, and the part assigned to the author of such a writing natural. It remains to be discovered whether in this case the probable is *real*, and the natural *true*. This is precisely the question which we have to elucidate.

2

THE DISCUSSIONS RELATING TO THE AUTHENTICITY OF THE FOURTH GOSPEL

IN the rapid review which is to follow, we might unite in a single series arranged chronologically all the writings, to whatever tendency they belong, in which the subject which occupies us has been treated. But it seems preferable to us, with a view to clearness, to divide the authors whom we have to enumerate into three distinct series: 1. The partisans of the entire spuriousness of our Gospel; 2. The defenders of its absolute authenticity; 3. The advocates of some intermediate position.[1]

The Adversaries

Until the end of the seventeenth century, the question had not even been raised. It was known that, in the primitive Church, a small sect, of which Irenæus and Epiphanius make mention, ascribed the fourth Gospel to Cerinthus, the adversary of the Apostle John at Ephesus. But the

---

[1] It is evident that this division cannot be fixed with absolute strictness, so varied are the different ways of viewing the subject.— In order to the revision and completion of this list we have, in this new edition, taken advantage of the excellent work of Mr. Caspar René Gregory (Leipsic, 1875), published as a supplement to Luthardt's Commentary.

science of theologians, as well as the feeling of the Church, confirmed the conviction of the first Christian communities and their leaders, who saw in it unanimously the work of that apostle.

Some attacks of little importance, proceeding from the English Deistic party, which flourished two centuries ago, opened the conflict. But it did not break out seriously until a century later. In 1792, the English theologian, *Evanson*, raised note-worthy objections, for the first time, against the general conviction.[1] He rested especially on the differences between our Gospel and the Apocalypse. He ascribed the composition of the former of these books to some Platonic philosopher of the second century.

The discussion was not long in being transplanted to Germany. Four years after Evanson, *Eckermann*[2] contended against the authenticity, while yet agreeing that certain Johannean redactions must have formed the first foundation of our Gospel. These notes had been amalgamated with the historical traditions which the author had gathered from the lips of John.—Eckermann retracted in 1807.[3]

Several German theologians continued the conflict which was entered upon at this time. The contradictions between this Gospel and the other three were alleged, also the exaggerated character of the miracles, the metaphysical tone of the discourses, the evident affinities between the theology of the author and that of Philo, the scarcity of traces in literature proving the existence of this writing in the second century.[4] From 1801, the cause of the authenticity seemed already so far compromised that a German superintendent, *Vogel*, believed himself able to summon the evangelist John and his interpreters to the bar of the last judgment.[5] However, it was yet only the first phase of the discussion, the time of the skirmishes which form the prelude of great pitched battles.

It was also a German superintendent who opened the second period of the discussion. In a work which became celebrated and was published in 1820, *Bretschneider* brought together all the objections previously raised and added to them new ones.[6] He especially developed with force the objection drawn from the contradictions in our Gospel as compared with the three preceding ones, both with reference to the form of the discourses and in respect to the very substance of the Christological teaching. The fourth Gospel

[1] *The dissonance of the four generally received evangelists*, etc.
[2] *Theologische Beiträge*, vol. v. 1796.
[3] *Erklärung aller dunkeln Stellen des. N. T.*
[4] Horst (1803), Cludius (1808), Ballenstädt (1812), etc.
[5] *Der Evangelist Johannes und seine Ausleger von dem jüngsten Gericht.*
[6] *Probabilia de evangelii et epistolarum Johannis apostoli indole et origine.*

10 / Preliminaries

must, according to his view, have been the work of a presbyter of Gentile, probably of Alexandrian origin, who lived in the first half of the second century. This learned and vigorous attack of Bretschneider called forth numerous replies, of which we shall speak later, and following upon which this theologian declared (in 1824) that the replies which had been made to his book were "more than sufficient,"[1] and (in 1828) that he had attained the end which he had proposed to himself: that of calling out a more searching demonstration of the authenticity of the fourth Gospel.[2]

But the seeds sown by such a work could not be uprooted by these rather equivocal retractions, which had a purely personal value. From 1824, the cause of the unauthenticity was pleaded anew by *Rettig*.[3] The author of the Gospel is a disciple of John. The apostle himself certainly was not so far wanting in modesty as to designate himself as "the disciple whom Jesus loved." *De Wette* in his *Introduction* published for the first time in 1826, without positively taking sides against the authenticity, confessed the impossibility of demonstrating it by unanswerable proofs. In the same year, *Reuterdahl*, following the footsteps of Vogel, assailed the tradition of John's sojourn in Asia Minor as fictitious.[4]

The publication of *Strauss' Life of Jesus*, in 1835, had, at first, a much more decisive influence upon the criticism of the history of Jesus than upon that of the *documents* in which this history has been transmitted to us. Evidently Strauss had not devoted himself to a special study of the origin of these latter. He started, as concerning the Synoptics, from the two theories of Gieseler and Griesbach, according to which our Gospels are the redaction of the apostolic tradition, which, after having for a long time circulated in a purely oral form, at length slowly established itself in our Synoptics (Gieseler); and this, first, in the redactions of Matthew and Luke, then, in that of Mark, which is only a compilation of the two others (Griesbach). As to John, he allowed as valid the reasons alleged by Bretschneider: insufficient attestation in the primitive Church, contents contradictory of those of the first three gospels, etc. And if, in his third edition, in 1838, he acknowledged that the authenticity was less indefensible to his view, he was not slow in retracting this concession in the following edition (1840). Indeed, the least evasion in regard to this point shook his entire hypothesis of mythical legends. The axiom which lies at its foundation: The ideal does not exhaust itself in one individual,

---

[1] In Tzschirner's *Magazin für christliche Prediger*.
[2] *Handbuch der Dogmatik*, pp. viii. and 268.
[3] *Ephemerides exegetico-theologicæ*, I., p. 62 ff.
[4] In his work *de Fontibus historiæ Eusebianæ*.

would be proved false, provided that the fourth Gospel contained, in however small a measure, the narrative of an eye-witness. Nevertheless, the immense commotion produced in the learned world by Strauss' work soon reacted upon the criticism of the Gospels.

Christian Hermann Weisse drew attention especially to the close connection between the criticism of the history of Jesus and that of the writings in which it has been preserved.[1] He contended against the authenticity of our Gospel, but not without recognizing in it a true apostolic foundation. The Apostle John, with the design of fixing the image of his Master, which, in proportion as the reality was farther removed from him, came to be more and more indefinite in his mind, and in order to give himself a distinct account of the impression which he had preserved of the person of Jesus, had drawn up certain "studies" which, when amplified, became the discourses of the fourth Gospel. To these more or less authentic parts, a historical framework which was completely fictitious was afterwards adapted. We can understand how, from this point of view, Weisse was able to defend the authenticity of the first Epistle of John.

At this juncture there occurred in the criticism of the fourth Gospel a revolution like to that which was wrought at the same time in the mode of looking at the first three. *Wilke* then endeavored to prove that the differences which distinguish the Synoptical narratives from one another were not, as had been always believed, simple involuntary accidents, but that it was necessary to recognize in them modifications introduced by each author, in a deliberate and intentional way, into the narrative of his predecessor or predecessors.[2] *Bruno Bauer* extended this mode of explaining the matter to the fourth Gospel.[3] He claimed that the Johannean narrative was not by any means, as the treatise of Strauss supposed, the depository of a simple legendary tradition, but that this story was the product of an individual conception, the reflective work of a Christian thinker and poet, who was perfectly conscious of his procedure. The history of Jesus was thus reduced, according to Ebrard's witty expression, to a single line: "At that time it came to pass . . . that nothing came to pass."

In the same year, *Lützelberger* attacked, in a more thoroughly searching way than Reuterdahl, the tradition as to the residence of John in Asia

---

[1] *Die evangelische Geschichte kritisch und philosophisch bearbeitet*, 1838. *Die Evangelien-Frage*, 1856.

[2] *Der Urevangelist*, 1838.

[3] *Kritik der evangel. Geschichte des Johannes*, 1840.

Minor.[1] The author of our Gospel was, in his view, a Samaritan, whose parents had emigrated to Mesopotamia, between 130 and 135, at the epoch of the new revolt of the Jews against the Romans, and he composed this Gospel at Edessa. The "disciple whom Jesus loved" was not John, but Andrew.—In a celebrated article, *Fischer* tried to prove, from the use of the term οἱ Ἰουδαῖοι in our Gospel, that its author could not be of Jewish origin.[2]

We arrive here at the third and last period of this prolonged conflict. It dates from 1844 and has as its starting-point the famous work published at that time by *Ferdinand Christian Baur*.[3] The first phase had lasted twenty and odd years, from Evanson to Bretschneider (1792–1820); the second, also twenty and odd years, from Bretschneider to Baur; the third has now continued more than thirty years. It is that of mortal combat. The dissertation which was the signal of it is certainly one of the most ingenious and brilliant compositions which theological science has ever produced. The purely negative results of Strauss' criticism demanded as a complement a positive construction; on the other hand, the arbitrary and subjective character of that of Bruno Bauer did not answer the wants of an era eager for positive facts. The discussion was, therefore, as it were, involved in inextricable difficulties.

Baur understood that his task was to withdraw it from that position, and that the only efficacious means was to discover in the progress of the Church of the second century a distinctly marked historical situation, which might be, as it were, the ground whereon was raised the imposing edifice of the fourth Gospel. He believed that he had discovered the situation which he sought in the last third of the second century. Then, indeed, *Gnosis* was flourishing, the borders of which the narrative of our Gospel touches throughout all its contents. At that time thinkers were pre-occupied with the idea of the *Logos,* which is precisely the theme of our work. The need was felt more and more of uniting in one great and single Catholic Church the two rival parties which, until then, had divided the Church, and which a series of compromises had already gradually brought near together; the fourth Gospel was adapted to serve them as a treaty of peace. An energetic spiritual reaction against the episcopate was rising: Montanism; our Gospel furnished strength to this tendency,

---

[1] *Die Kirchliche Tradition über den Apostel Johannes und seine Schriften in ihrer Grundlosigkeit nachgewiesen*, 1840.

[2] *Tübinger Zeitschrift für Theol.* II. 1840.

[3] In Zeller's *Theologische Jahrbücher* Hefte 1, 3, 4; reproduced and completed in the later writings of the same author: *Kritische Untersuchungen über die canonischen Evangelien,* 1847; and *Das Christenthum und die christliche Kirche der drei ersten Jahrhunderte*, 1853.

Authenticity - The Adversaries / 13

by borrowing from Montanism the truth which it contained. Then, finally, the famous dispute between the churches of Asia Minor and those of the West on the subject of the Paschal rite burst forth. Now, our Gospel modified the chronology of the Passion in just such a way as to decide the minds of men in favor of the occidental rite. Here, then, was the situation fully discovered for the composition of our Gospel. At the same time, Baur, following the footsteps of Bruno Bauer, shows with a marvelous skill the well-considered and systematic unity of this work; he explains its logical progress and practical applications, and thus overthrows at one blow the hypothesis of unreflective myths, on which the work of Strauss rested, and every attempt at selection in our Gospel between certain authentic parts and other unauthentic ones. In accordance with all this, Baur fixes, as the epoch of the composition, about the year 170—at the earliest, 160; for then it was that all the circumstances indicated meet together. Only he has not attempted to designate the "great unknown" to whose pen was due this master-piece of high mystical philosophy and skillful ecclesiastical policy, which has exercised such a decisive influence on the destinies of Christianity.

All the forces of the school co-operated in supporting the work of the master in its various parts. From 1841, *Schwegler* had prepared the way for it by his treatise on Montanism.[1] In his work on the period which followed that of the apostles, the same author assigned to each one of the writings of the New Testament its place in the development of the conflict between the apostolic Judæo-Christianity and Paulinism, and set forth the fourth Gospel as the crowning point of this long elaboration.[2] *Zeller* completed the work of his master by the study of the ecclesiastical testimonies,—a study whose aim was to sweep away from history every trace of the existence of the fourth Gospel before the period indicated by Baur.[3] *Koestlin*, in a celebrated work on *pseudonymous literature* in the primitive Church, endeavored to prove that the pseudepigraphical procedure to which Baur ascribed the composition of four-fifths of the New Testament was in conformity with literary precedents and the ideas of the epoch.[4] *Volkmar* labored to ward off the blows by which the system of his master was unceasingly threatened by reason of the less and less controvertible citations of the fourth Gospel in the writings of the second

---

[1] *Der Montanismus und die christliche Kirche des IIten Jahrhunderts.*

[2] *Das nachapostolische Zeitalter,* 1846.

[3] *Die aüsseren Zeugnisse über das Dasein und den Ursprung des vierten Evangeliums,* in the *Theologische Jahrbücher,* 1845 and 1847.

[4] *Ueber die pseudonymische Litteratur in der ältesten Kirche,* in the *Theol. Jahrbücher,* 1851.

14 / Preliminaries

century—in those of Marcion and Justin, for example, and in the *Clementine Homilies*.[1] Finally, *Hilgenfeld* treated, in a more profound way than Baur had done, the dispute concerning the Passover and its relation to the authenticity of our Gospel.[2]

Thus learnedly supported by this Pleiad of distinguished critics, devoted to the common work, although not without marked shades of difference, Baur's opinion might seem, for a moment, to have obtained a complete and decisive triumph.

Nevertheless, in the midst of the school itself a divergence became manifest which, in many respects, was detrimental to the hypothesis so skillfully contrived by the master. Hilgenfeld abandoned the date fixed by Baur, and consequently a part of the advantages of the situation chosen by him. He carried back the composition of the Johannean Gospel thirty or forty years. According to him, this work was connected especially with the appearance of the *Valentinian* heresy, about 140. The author of the Gospel proposed to himself to introduce this Gnostic teaching into the Church in a mitigated form. And as already about 150 "the existence of our Gospel could scarcely be any longer questioned," he put back its date even to the period from 130 to 140.[3]

In 1860, *J. R. Tobler*, discovering, side by side with the ideal character of the narrative, a mass of geographical notices or of narratives truly historical, conceived the idea of ascribing our Gospel to Apollos (according to him, the author of the Epistle to the Hebrews) who compiled it about the end of the first century from information obtained from John.[4]

Michel Nicolas advanced, in 1862, the following hypothesis: A Christian of Ephesus related in our Gospel the ministry of Jesus according to the accounts of the Apostle John; and this personage is the one who, in the two small Epistles, designates himself as the *Elder* (*the presbyter*), and the one whom history makes known to us under the name of John the Presbyter.[5]—*D'Eichthal* accepted Hilgenfeld's idea of a relationship between our Gospel and *Gnosis*.[6] The work which *Stap* published in the same year, in his collection of Critical Studies, is only a reproduction, without originality, of all the ideas of the Tübingen school.[7]

---

[1] Comp., in particular, *Ursprung unserer Evangelien*, 1866.

[2] *Der Passahstreit der alten Kirche*, 1860.

[3] *Das Evangelium und die Briefe Johannis nach ihrem Lehrbegriffe dargestellt*, 1849; die *Evangelien*, 1854; *das Urchristenthum*, 1855.

[4] *Ueber den Ursprung des vierten Evang.*, in the *Zeitschrift für wissensch. Theol.*, 1860.

[5] *Etudes critiques sur la Bible: Nouveau Testament*.

[6] *Les Evangiles*, 1863; t. I., pp. 25 ff., and elsewhere.

[7] *Etudes historiques et critiques sur les origines du christianisme*, 1863.

Authenticity - The Adversaries / 15

In 1864 two important books appeared. *Weizsäcker*, in his work on the Gospels,[1] sought to bring out from our Gospel itself the proof of the distinction between the editor of this writing and the Apostle John, who served as a voucher for him. The former wished only to reproduce in a free way the impressions which he had experienced when hearing the apostolic witness describe the life of the Lord.

The second book takes a more decided position : it is that of *Scholten*.[2] The author of the fourth Gospel is a Christian of Gentile origin, initiated in Gnosticism and desirous of rendering that tendency profitable to the Church. He seeks, also, to restrain within just limits the Marcionite antinomianism and the Montanist exaltation. As to the Paschal dispute, the evangelist does not decide in favor of the Western rite, as Baur thinks; he seeks rather to secure the triumph of Pauline spiritualism, which abolishes feast days in the Church altogether. According to these indications, the author wrote about 150. He succeeded in presenting to the world, under the figure of the mysterious personage designated as "the disciple whom Jesus loved," the ideal believer—the truly spiritual Christianity which was capable of becoming the universal religion.—*Réville* has set forth and developed Scholten's point of view in the *Revue des Deux-Mondes*.[3]

Let us also remind the reader here of the work of *Volkmar*[4] (page 19), directed against Tischendorf personally, as much as against his book, *When were our Gospels written?* However deplorable is its tone, this work exhibits with learning and precision the point of view of Baur's school. The author fixes the date of our Gospel between 150 and 160.

In 1867, appeared the *History of Jesus*, by *Keim*.[5] This scholar energetically opposes, in the Introduction, the authenticity of our Gospel. He lays especial stress upon the philosophical character of this writing; then upon the inconsistencies of the narrative with the nature of things, with the data furnished by the writings of St. Paul, and with the Synoptic narratives. But, on the other hand, he proves the traces of its existence as far back as the earliest times of the second century. "The testimonies," he says, "go back as far as to the year 120, so that the composition dates from the beginning of the second century, in the reign of Trajan, between 100 and 117."[6] The author was a Christian of Jewish

---

[1] *Untersuchungen über die evangelische Geschichte.*
[2] *Das Evangelium nach Johannes* (1864), translated into German, by H. Lang, 1867.
[3] *La question des évangiles*, May, 1866.
[4] *Der Ursprung unserer Evangelien*, 1866.
[5] *Geschichte Jesu von Nazara.*
[6] p. 146.

origin, belonging to the *Diaspora* of Asia Minor, in full sympathy with the Gentiles and thoroughly acquainted with everything relating to Palestine. In a more recent writing, a popular reproduction of his great work, Keim has withdrawn from this early date, stating as the ground of this change reasons which, we may say, have no serious importance. He now, with Hilgenfeld, fixes the composition about the year 130.[1] Of what consequence here is a period of ten years? It would follow from the one of these last mentioned dates as well as from the other, that, twenty or thirty years after the death of John at Ephesus, the fourth Gospel was ascribed to this apostle by the very presbyters of the country where he had spent the closing portion of his life and where he had died. How can we explain the success of a forgery under such circumstances? Keim felt this difficulty and made an effort to remove it. To this end he found no other means except to attach himself to the idea put forth by Reuterdahl and Lützelberger, and to rate the sojourn of John in Asia Minor as a pure fiction. By this course, he goes beyond even the Tübingen school. For Baur and Hilgenfeld did not call in question the truth of that tradition. Their criticism even rests essentially on the reality of John's sojourn in Asia, first, because the Apocalypse, the Johannean composition of which serves them as the point of support for their onset upon that of the Gospel, implies this sojourn, and, then, because the argument which they both draw from the Paschal controversy falls to the ground as soon as the sojourn of the Apostle John in that country is no longer admitted. Now, on the contrary, when the criticism hostile to our Gospel feels itself embarrassed by this sojourn, it rejects it unceremoniously. According to Keim, that tradition is only the result of a half-voluntary misunderstanding of Irenæus, who applied to John the apostle what Polycarp had related in his presence of another personage of the same name. *Scholten* reaches the same result by different means.[2] This error in the tradition is explained, according to him, by the confounding of the author of the Apocalypse, who was not the apostle, but who had taken advantage of his name, with the apostle himself; in this way the sojourn of John in Asia, where the Apocalypse appears to have been composed, was imagined. However this may be, and whatever may be the explanation of the traditional misunderstanding, the discovery of this error "removes," says Keim, "the last point of support for the idea of the composition of the Gospel by the son of Zebedee."[3]

---

[1] *Geschichte Jesu, nach den Ergebnissen heutiger Wissenschaft, für weitere Kreise*, 3d ed., 1873.

[2] *Der Apostel Johannes in Klein-Asien*, translated into German by Spiegel, 1872.

[3] P. 167.

We see that two of the foundations of Baur's criticism, the authenticity of the Apocalypse and John's sojourn in Asia, are undermined at this hour by the men who have continued his work—this denial appearing to them the only means of making an end of the authenticity of our Gospel.

In 1868, the English writer, *Davidson*, took his position among the opponents of the authenticity.[1] *Holtzmann*, like Keim, sees in our Gospel an ideal composition, but one which is not entirely fictitious. This book dates from the same epoch as the Epistle of Barnabas (the first third of the second century); it can be proved that the Church has given it a favorable reception since the year 150.[2] *Krenkel*, in 1871, defended the sojourn of John in Asia; he ascribes to this apostle the composition of the Apocalypse, but not that of the Gospel.[3]

The anonymous English work, *Supernatural Religion*, which has in a few years reached a very large number of editions, contends against the authenticity with the ordinary arguments.[4]

The year 1875 witnessed the appearance of two works of considerable importance. These are two Introductions to the New Testament—that of *Hilgenfeld*[5] and the third edition of Bleek's work, published with original notes by *Mangold*.[6] Hilgenfeld gives a summary, in his book, of the whole critical work of past times and of the present epoch. With regard to John, he continues in certain respects to defend the cause to which he had consecrated the first fruits of his pen:—the non-authenticity of the fourth Gospel, which was composed, according to him under the influence of the Valentinian Gnosticism. Mangold accompanies the paragraphs in which Bleek defends the apostolic origin of our Gospel with very instructive critical notes, in which in most cases he seeks to refute that scholar. The external proofs would seem to him sufficient to confirm the authenticity. But it has not been possible, in his opinion, at least up to the present time, to surmount the internal difficulties.

In 1876, a jurist, *d'Uechtritz*, published a book[7] in which he ascribes our Gospel to a Jerusalemite disciple of Jesus—probably John the Presbyter—who assumed the mask of the disciple whom Jesus loved and composed this work under his name. This critic does not find the opinion justified,

---

[1] *Introduction to the Study of the N. T.* Vol. II.

[2] *Schenkel's Bibellexicon;* Vol. II., art. *Ev. nach Joh.*, 1869.

[3] *Der Apostel Johannes*, 1871.

[4] *Supernatural Religion*, 1874.

[5] *Historisch-Kritische Einleitung in das N. T.*

[6] *Einleitung in das N. T.*, von Fr. Bleek, 3 Aufl., von W. Mangold.

[7] *Studien eines Laien über den Ursprung, die Beschaffenheit und die Bedeutung des Evang. nach Johannes.*

18 / Preliminaries

which is so widely spread, that the representation of Jesus traced in the Synoptics is less exalted than the idea which is given us of Him in St. John.

Four writers remain to be mentioned here—three French and one German, who, in our preceding edition, figured in the list of the defenders of the absolute or partial authenticity, and who have passed over into the opposite camp, *Renan, Reuss, Sabatier* and *Hase.*

The first from the outset manifested a marked antipathy to the discourses ascribed to Jesus by the fourth Gospel. Nevertheless, he always set forth prominently the remarkable signs of authenticity connected with the narrative parts of this same writing. He showed himself disposed, accordingly, in the first editions of his *Life of Jesus*, to recognize as the foundation of the historical parts not only traditions proceeding from the Apostle John, but even "precise notes drawn up by him." In the truly admirable dissertation which closes the thirteenth edition, and in which he thoroughly discusses the question, analyzing the Gospel—one narrative after another—from this point of view, he shows that the contradictory appearances almost exactly balance each other, and ends by positively affirming nothing but this alternative: either the author is John or he has desired to pass himself off as John. Finally, in his last book, entitled *l'Eglise chrétienne*,[1] he arrives at the result which might have been foreseen. The author was perhaps a Christian depositary of the traditions of the apostle, or, at least, of those of two other disciples of Jesus, John the Presbyter and Aristion, who lived at Ephesus about the end of the first century. We might even go so far, according to Renan, as to suppose that this writer is no other than Cerinthus, the adversary of John at Ephesus, at the same period.

Reuss and Sabatier have likewise just finished their evolution in the same direction. In all his previous works,[2] Reuss had maintained two scarcely reconcilable theses: the almost completely artificial and fictitious character of the discourses of Jesus in our Gospel and the apostolic origin of the work. It was not difficult to foresee two things: 1. That one of these theses would end in excluding the other; 2. That it would be the first which would prevail over the second. This is what has just happened. In his *Théologie Johannique*,[3] Reuss declares his final judgment on

---

[1] 1879.

[2] *Ideen zur Einleitung in das Ev. Joh.* (Denkschr. der theol. Gesellsch. zu Strasb.), 1840; *Geschichte der N. Tchen Schriften*, 1842: *Histoire de la théologie chrétienne au siècle apostolique*, 1852.

[3] *La Bible: Nouveau Testament*, VIe partie, 1879.

Authenticity - The Adversaries / 19

this subject: The fourth Gospel is not by the Apostle John. Nevertheless, Reuss is reluctant to allow that this work is by a forger. And it is not necessary to admit this, since the author expressly distinguishes himself from the Apostle John in more than one passage, and limits himself to tracing back to him the origin of the narratives contained in his book. We thus find again, point for point, the opinion of Weizsäcker mentioned above.

Sabatier, in his excellent little work on the sources of the life of Jesus,[1] had also maintained the authenticity of our Gospel. But, having once entered into the views of Reuss, with respect to the estimation of the discourses of Jesus, he was by a fatality obliged to follow him even to the end. He has just distinctly declared himself against the authenticity, in his article on the Apostle John, in the *Encyclopédie des sciences religieuses*:[2] An author whose constant inclination is to exalt the Apostle John cannot be John himself. It is one of his disciples who, believing that he was able to identify himself with him, has drawn up the Gospel history in the form which it had assumed in Asia Minor; he thus gives to the Church the *apocalypse of the Spirit*, a counterpart of the Apocalypse, properly so called, written by the apostle.

Since 1829, in the different editions of his Manual on the Life of Jesus,[3] Hase had supported the Johannean origin of the fourth Gospel. In 1866, he published a discourse in which he represented this work as the last product of the apostle's mind when it had reached its full maturity.[4] But this scholar has yielded to the same fatal law as the three preceding writers. In his History of Jesus,[5] published in 1876, he gives up the authenticity, though not without painful hesitation. "Let us cast a glance," he says in closing the discussion, "at the eight reasons alleged against the Johannean origin: they have not proved to be decisive;[6] nevertheless, it has not been possible to refute them all completely. . . . I thus see science driven to a conception fitted to reconcile the opposite reasons. A tradition different from that of the other Gospels, and already containing the notion of the Logos, had taken form in Asia Minor under the influence of the accounts given by John. It had remained in the purely oral state, so long as John lived." After his death (ten years afterwards, or perhaps more), this tradition was recorded by a highly gifted

---

[1] *Essai sur les sources de la vie de Jésus*, 1866.

[2] Vol. vii., 1879, pp. 181–193.

[3] *Das Leben Jesu.* Ein Lehrbuch für Academische Vorlesungen; 5th ed., 1865.

[4] *Das Evangelium des Johannes.* Eine Rede an die Gemeinde.

[5] *Geschichte Jesu.*

[6] "Sie haben sich nicht als entscheidend erwiesen."

disciple of the apostle. He wrote as if the latter himself were writing. In this way it is, that the evangelist is able to appeal at once to the testimony of his own eyes (i. 14) and to that of another, different from himself. "Who was the writer? The Presbyter John? This is possible. But it may be also an unknown person. The first Epistle may have proceeded from the same author, writing under the mask of John; but it may also have been from John himself and have served as a model for the style of the Gospel." This hypothesis is, according to this author, a compromise between the facts which are contradictory to each other. "I have not without a heavy heart," he adds, "broken away from the belief in the entire authenticity of the Johannean writing." Finally, a little further on, he also says: "The time is come in German theology when he who even ventures to recognize in the fourth Gospel a source possessing an historical value compromises his scientific honor.[1] It has not always been thus, even among those who are lacking neither in vigor nor in freedom of mind. But it may also change again:[2] the spirit of the times exercises a power even in science." What reflections do not these sad avowals of the veteran of Jena suggest!

The Defenders

This persevering contest against the authenticity of the Johannean Gospel resembles the siege of a fortress, and things have reached the point where already many think they see the standard of the besieger floating victoriously over the ramparts of the place. Nevertheless, the defenders have not remained inactive, and the incessant transformations which the onsets have undergone, as the preceding exposition proves, leave no room for questioning the relative success of their efforts. Let us rapidly enumerate the works devoted to the defence of the authenticity.

The oldest attack, that of the sectaries of the second century, called *Alogi*, did not remain unanswered; for it seems certain that the writing of Hippolytus (at the beginning of the third century), whose title appears in the catalogue of his works [3] as Ὑπὲρ τοῦ κατὰ Ἰωάννου εὐαγγελίου καὶ ἀποκαλύψεως, "*In behalf of the Gospel of John and the Apocalypse*," was directed against them.

The attacks of the English deists were repulsed in Germany and Hol-

---

[1] The author here quotes an expression of Keim.

[2] "Es kann aber auch anders kommen...." (p. 52).

[3] Catalogue engraved on the pedestal of his statue, discovered at Rome in 1561.

Authenticity - The Defenders / 21

land by *Le Clerc*[1] and *Lampe;* by the latter, in his celebrated Commentary on the Gospel of John.[2]

Two Englishmen, *Priestley*[3] and *Simpson*,[4] immediately answered Evanson. *Storr* and *Süskind* resolved the objections raised soon afterwards in Germany,[5] and this with such success that Eckermann and Schmidt declared that they retracted their doubts.

Following upon this first phase of the struggle, *Eichhorn* (1810), *Hug* (1808), and *Bertholdt* (1813), in their well-known Introductions to the New Testament, *Wegscheider* in a special work,[6] and others also, unanimously declared themselves on the side of the authenticity; so that at the beginning of this century the storm seemed to be calmed and the question settled in favor of the traditional opinion. The historian *Gieseler*, in his admirable little work on the origin of the gospels (1818), pronounced his decision in the same way, and expressed the idea that John had composed his book for the instruction of Gentiles who had already made progress in the Christian religion.[7]

The work of Bretschneider, which all at once broke this apparent calm, called forth a multitude of replies, among which we shall cite only those of *Olshausen*,[8] *Crome*,[9] and *Hauff*.[10] The first editions of the Commentaries of *Lücke* (1820) and *Tholuck* (1827) appeared also at this same period.

In consequence of the first of these publications, Bretschneider, as we have already said, declared his objections solved; so that once more the calm appeared to be restored, and *Schleiermacher*, with all his school, could yield himself, without encountering any opposition worthy of notice, to the predilection which he felt for our Gospel. From the beginning of his scientific career, Schleiermacher, in his *Reden über die Religion*, proclaimed the Christ of John to be the true historic Christ, and maintained that the Synoptic narrative must be subordinated to our Gospel. Critics as learned and independent as *Schott* and *Credner* likewise maintained at that time the cause of the authenticity[11] in their Introductions. De Wette alone at that moment caused a somewhat discordant voice to be still heard.

---

[1] *Annotationes ad Hammond. Nov. Test.,* 1714.

[2] *Commentarius in Evang. Johannis,* 1727.

[3] *Letters to a young man,* 1793.

[4] *An essay on the authority of the New Testament,* 1793.

[5] In Flatt's Magazine, 1798, No. 4, and 1800, No. 6.

[6] *Versuch einer vollständigen Einleit. in das Evang. des Johannes,* 1806.

[7] *Historisch-Krit. Versuch über die Entstehung und die frühesten Schicksale der schriftlichen Evangelien.*

[8] *Die Echtheit der vier canonischen Evangelien,* 1823.

[9] *Probabilia hand probabilia,* 1824.

[10] *Die Authentie und der hohe Werth des Evang. Johannes,* 1831.

[11] That of Schott in 1830; that of Credner in 1836.

The appearance of Strauss' *Life of Jesus,* in 1835, was thus like a thunderbolt bursting forth in a serene sky. This work called forth a whole legion of apologetic writings; above all, that of *Tholuck* on the credibility of the evangelical history,[1] and the *Life of Jesus* by *Neander.*[2] The concessions made to Strauss by the latter have been often wrongly interpreted. They had as their aim only to establish a minimum of incontrovertible facts, while giving up that which might be assailed. And it was this work which is so moderate, so impartial, and in whose every word we feel the incorruptible love of truth, which seems, for the moment, to have made upon Strauss the deepest impression, and to have drawn from him, with reference to the Gospel of John, the kind of retractation announced in his third edition.[3]

Gfroerer,[4] although starting from quite another point of view as compared with the two preceding writers, defended the authenticity of our Gospel against Strauss. *Frommann,*[5] on his side, refuted the hypothesis of Weisse. From 1837 to 1844, *Norton* published his great work on the evidences of the authenticity of the Gospels,[6] and *Guericke,* in 1843, his Introduction to the New Testament.[7]

In the following years appeared the work of *Ebrard* on the evangelical history,[8] the truth of which he valiantly defended against Strauss and Bruno Bauer, and the third edition of *Lücke's* Commentary (1848). But this last author made such concessions as to the credibility of the discourses and of the Christological teaching of John, that the adversaries did not fail soon to turn his work against the very thesis which he had desired to defend.

We reach the last period,—that of the struggle maintained against Baur and his school. *Ebrard* was the first to appear in the breach.[9] At his side a young scholar presented himself, who, in a work filled with rare patristic erudition and knowledge drawn from the primary sources, sought to bring back to the right path historical criticism, which, in the hands of Baur, seemed to have strayed from it. We mean *Thiersch,* whose work, modestly entitled an *Essay,* is still at the present day for beginners one of the most useful means of orientation in the domain of the history of the first two

---

[1] *Die Glaubwürdigkeit der evangel. Geschichte,* 1837.
[2] *Das Leben Jesu Christi,* 1837.
[3] Edition of 1840.
[4] *Geschichte des Urchristenthums,* 1838.
[5] *Ueber die Echtheit und Integrität des Evang. Joh.,* 1840.
[6] *The Evidences of the Genuineness of the Gospels.*
[7] *Historisch-Kritische Einleitung in das N. T.*
[8] *Wissenschaftliche Kritik der Evangel. Geschichte,* 1st ed., 1842; 3d ed., 1868.
[9] *Das Evang. Joh. und die neueste Hypothese über seine Entstehung,* 1845.

centuries.¹ Baur did not brook this call to order which was addressed to him—to him, a veteran in science—by so young a writer. In an excitement of irritation, he wrote that violent pamphlet in which he accused his adversary of fanaticism, and which had almost the character of a denunciation.² The reply of Thiersch was as remarkable for its propriety and dignity of tone as for the excellence of the general observations which are presented in it on the criticism of the sacred writings.³ The justness of some of Thiersch's ideas may be called in question, but it cannot be denied that his two works abound in ingenious and original points of view.

A strange work appeared at this time. The author is commonly quoted in German criticism under the name of *the Anonymous Saxon*; it is now known that he was a Saxon theologian, named *Hasert*, who was, at that time, one of the Thurgovian clergy. He defended the authenticity of our Gospels, but with the intention of showing, by this very authenticity, how the apostles of Jesus, the authors of these books, or rather of these pamphlets, had labored only to decry and traduce one another.⁴

The most able and most learned reply to the works of Baur and Zeller was that of *Bleek*, in 1846.⁵ By the side of this work, the articles by *Hauff* deserve to be specially mentioned.⁶

In the following years, *Weitzel* and *Steitz*, discussed with much care and erudition the argument drawn by Baur from the Paschal controversy, near the end of the second century.⁷ Following in the footsteps of *Bindemann* (1842), *Semisch* demonstrated the use of our four Gospels by Justin Martyr.⁸

The year 1852, saw the appearance of two very interesting works: that of the Dutch writer, *Niermeyer*, designed to prove by a subtle and thorough study of the writings ascribed to John, that the Apocalypse and the Gospel could and must have, both of them, been composed by him, and that the differences of contents and form, which distinguish them, are to be explained by the profound spiritual revolution which was wrought in

---

[1] *Versuch zur Herstellung des historischen Standpuncts für die Kritik der neutest. Schriften*, 1845.

[2] *Der Kritiker und der Fanatiker in der Person des Herrn H. W. J. Thiersch*, 1846.

[3] *Einige Worte über die Echtheit der neutest. Schriften, zur Erwiderung*, etc., 1847.

[4] *Die Evangelien, ihr Geist, ihre Verfasser, und ihr Verhältniss zu einander*, 1845.

[5] *Beiträge zur Evangelienkritik*.

[6] *Einige Bemerkungen über die Composition des Johann. Evangeliums*, in the *Studien und Kritiken*, 1846.

[7] Weitzel, *Die christliche Passahfeier der drei ersten Jahrhunderte*, 1848; Steitz in the *Studien und Kritiken*, 1856 and 1857.

[8] *Die apostolischen Denkwürdigkeiten des Märtyrers Justin*, 1848.

the apostle after the destruction of Jerusalem.[1] A similar idea was expressed, at the same time, by *Hase*.[2] The second work is the Commentary of *Luthardt* on the fourth Gospel, the first part of which contains a series of characteristic portraitures of the principal actors in the evangelical drama, according to St. John, designed to render palpable the living reality of all these personages. These portraitures are full of acute and just observations.

Ewald, like Hase, defends the authenticity, but does so, while according scarcely any historical credibility to the discourses which the apostle assigns to Jesus, and even to the miraculous deeds which he relates.[3] This is an inconsistency which Baur has severely criticised in his reply to Hase. Such defences of a gospel are almost equivalent to sentences of condemnation pronounced against it, or rather they destroy themselves. We can say almost the same of the opinion of *Bunsen*,[4] who regards the Gospel of John as the only monument of the evangelical history proceeding from an eye-witness, who declares even that otherwise "there is no longer an historical Christ," and who yet remits to the domain of legend so decisive a fact as that of the resurrection. *Bleek*, in his Introduction to the New Testament,[5] and *Meyer, Hengstenberg*, and *Lange*, in their Commentaries, have declared themselves in favor of the authenticity, as well as *Astié*[6] (who adopts Niermeyer's point of view), and the author of these lines.[7] The Johannean question, in its relation to that of the Synoptic Gospels, has been treated in an instructive way by *de Pressensé*.[8]

The study of the patristic testimonies has recently been made the object of two works, one of a popular character, and the other more exclusively scientific: the little treatise of *Tischendorf* on the time of the composition of our Gospels,[9] and the Academic programme of *Riggenbach*

---

[1] *Over die echtheid der Johanneischen Schriften*, etc., 1852. See the reviews of this work in the *Revue de théologie*, June, July and Sept., 1856. See also the articles *Jean le prophète* and *Jean l' évangéliste, ou la crise de la foi chez un apôtre*, by M. Réville (*Rev. de théol.*, 1854).

[2] *Die Tübinger-Schule.* Sendscreiben an Baur, 1855. *Vom Evangelium des Johannes*, 1866.

[3] *Jahrbücher der biblischen Wissenschaft*, 1851, 1853, 1860, 1865. *Die Johann. Schriften*, 1861.

[4] In his *Bibelwerk*.

[5] The chapters of Bleek relating to the Gospel of John have been translated into French by Bruston, under the title: *Etude critique sur l' évangile de Jean*, 1864. Translation of Bleek's Introduction into English, in Clark's For. Theol. Libr., 1869.

[6] *Explication de l'évangile selon saint Jean*, 1863.

[7] *Commentaire sur l' évangile de St. Jean*, 1864; translated into German by Wunderlich, 1869; the conclusion, since 1866, by Wirz, under the title: *Prüfung der Streitfragen über das 4te Evang.*—2d ed., 1876.

[8] In the first book of his *Vie de Jésus*.

[9] *Wann wurden unsere Evangelien verfasst?* 1865; 4th ed., 1866.

in 1866, on the historical and literary testimonies in favor of the Gospel of John.[1] The solidity and impartiality of this latter work have been recognized by the author's opponents.

We may add to these two writings that in which the Groningen professor, *Hofstede de Groot*, has treated the question of the date of Basilides and of the Johannean quotations, especially in the Gnostic writers.[2] The cause of the authenticity has also been maintained by the Abbé *Déramey* (1868).[3]

The tradition of the sojourn of John in Asia Minor has been valiantly defended against Keim by *Steitz*[4] and *Wabnitz*.[5] *Wittichen*, taking his position at a point of view which is peculiar to himself, gives up the sojourn of the Apostle John in Asia, but does this in order so much the better to support the authenticity of our Gospel, while he maintains that it was composed by the apostle in Syria for the purpose of combating the Ebionites who were of Essenic tendency. This work would thus date from the times which immediately followed the destruction of Jerusalem. As for the John of Asia Minor, he was the presbyter, the author of the Apocalypse.[6] We have here the antipode of the Tübingen theses.

In two works, one by *Zahn*, the other by *Riggenbach*, the question of the existence of John the Presbyter, as a distinct personage from the apostle, has been treated. After a careful study of the famous passage of Papias relative to this question, they come to a negative conclusion.[7] *Leimbach* likewise, in a special study,[8] does the same thing, and Professor *Milligan*, of Aberdeen, also, in an article in the *Journal of Sacred Literature*, entitled *John the Presbyter* (Oct. 1867).

The historical credibility of the discourses of Jesus in the fourth Gospel has been defended against modern objections by *Gess*, in the first volume of the second edition of his work on the Person of our Lord,[9] and more especially by *H. Meyer* in a very remarkable licentiate-thesis.[10] The English

[1] *Die Zeugnisse für das Evang. Johannis neu untersucht.*

[2] *Basilides am Ausgang des apostolischen Zeitalters;* German edition, 1868.

[3] *Défense du quatrième évangile.*

[4] *Studien und Kritiken,* 1869.

[5] In the *Bulletin théologique,* 1868.

[6] *Der geschichtliche Charakter des Evang. Joh.*, 1868.

[7] Zahn: *Papias von Hierapolis*, in the *Studien und Kritiken,* 1866, No. 2; Riggenbach: *Johannes der Apostel und Presbyter*, in the *Jahrbücher für deutsche Theologie,* 1868.

[8] *Das Papias-Fragment,* 1875 (reply to the work: *Das Papias-Fragment des Eusebius*, by Weiffenbach, 1874.)

[9] *Christi Person und Werk.* Neue Bearbeitung. Part I. *Christi Zeugniss*, etc., 1870.

[10] *Les Discours du 4ᵉ év. sont-ils des discours historiques de Jésus?* 1872.

work of *Sanday*[1] dates from the year 1872, and that of the superintendent *Leuschner*[2]—a brave little work which especially attacks Keim and Scholten.

We close this review by mentioning six recent and remarkable works, all of them devoted to the defense of the authenticity. Three are the products of German learning. The first is the critical study of *Luthardt*,[3] forming in a special volume the introduction to the second edition of his Commentary on the fourth Gospel. The second is the brilliant work of *Beyschlag* in the *Studien und Kritiken*,[4] which contains perhaps the most able replies to the modern objections. *Bernhard Weiss* (in the sixth edition of Meyer's Commentary) has treated, in a manner at once profound and concise, the question of the origin of our Gospel. He vigorously defends the authenticity, without, however, maintaining strictly the historical character of the discourses.[5]

The French work is that of *Nyegaard*.[6] It is a thesis devoted to the examination of the external testimonies relating to the authenticity. This same subject is specially treated by one of the two English works, that of *Ezra Abbott*, professor in Harvard University.[7] This work seems to me to exhaust the subject. A complete acquaintance with modern discussions, profound study of the testimonies of the second century, moderation and perspicuity in judgment—nothing is wanting. The other English work is the Commentary of *Westcott*, professor at Cambridge.[8] In the introduction all the critical questions are handled with learning and tact.

The Intermediate Positions

Pressed by the force of the reasons alleged for and against the authenticity, a certain number of theologians have sought to give satisfaction to both sides by having recourse to a middle position.

Some have attempted to make a selection between the truly Johannean parts and those which have been added later. Thus *Weisse*, to whom we have been obliged to attribute an important part in the history of the struggle against the authenticity (page 19), would be disposed, neverthe-

---

[1] *The authorship and historical character of the fourth Gospel.*

[2] *Das. Evang. Joh. und seine neuesten Widersacher.*

[3] *Der Johann. Ursprung des vierten Evang.*, 1874.

[4] 1874 and 1875.

[5] *Kritisch-exeget. Handbuch über das Evang. des Johann.*, 6th ed., 1880.

[6] *Essai sur les critères externes de l'authenticité du quatrième évangile*, 1876.

[7] *The authorship of the fourth Gospel.—External evidences*, Boston, 1880.

[8] *The Holy Bible*, commented upon by a company of English bishops and clergymen; N. T., vol. II., 1880.

less, to ascribe to John himself chap. i., 1-5 and 9-14, certain passages in chap. iii., and, finally, the discourses contained in chaps. xiv.-xvii. (while striking out the dialogue portions and narrative elements).

Schweizer has proposed another mode of selection.[1] The narratives which have Galilee as their theatre must, according to him, be eliminated from the Johannean writing; they have been added later to facilitate the agreement between the narrative of John and that of the Synoptics. Is not chap. xxi. for example, a manifest addition? *Schenkel* had formerly proposed to regard the discourses as forming the primitive work, and the historical parts as added subsequently.[2] But since the unity of the composition of our Gospel has been triumphantly demonstrated, the division in such an external way has been given up. We are not acquainted with any more recent attempts of this kind.

This long enumeration, which contains only the most noteworthy works, proves of itself the gravity of the question.[3] Let us sum up the preceding exposition. We may do this by making the following scale, which includes all the points of view which have been mentioned.

1. Some deny all participation, even moral and indirect, on the part of the Apostle John in the composition of the work which bears his name.

---

[1] *Das Evang. Joh. nach seinem inneren Werth kritisch untersucht*, 1841. The author has since then withdrawn his hypothesis.

[2] *Studien und Kritiken*, 1840 (review of the work of Weisse). In his later works he makes of the Gospel an ideal composition, dating from 110 to 120.

[3] Let us mention also various Review articles which are not without importance. First, three remarkable articles of Weizsäcker in the *Jahrb. für deutsche Theologie: Das Selbstzeugniss des Johann. Christus* (1857); *Beiträge zur Charakteristik des Joh. Ev.* (1859); *die Joh. Logoslehre* (1862). Then, four studies of Holtzmann in the *Zeitschrift für wissensch. Theol.: Barnabas und Johannes* 1871, in which the author proves that the epistle of Barnabas rests upon Matthew, but not upon John; *Hermas und Johannes* (1875), in which he seeks to prove, in opposition to Zahn, that Hermas does not depend on John, but John is posterior to Hermas; the *Shepherd* is an essay of a novice which the fourth Gospel has, at a later time, perfected (Harnack, in 1876, refuted Holtzmann in the same journal, but without accepting Zahn's thesis); *Johannes, Ignatius und Polycarp* (1877), in which he reduces to nothing the testimonies borrowed from the last two in favor of the Gospel of John; *Papias und Johannes* (1880), in which he seeks to show that the order of the apostles' names in the famous list of authorities in Papias does not rest, as Steitz has proved, upon the Gospel of John. The two works of Van Goens: *L'apôtre Jean est-il l'auteur du IVe évangile?* and of Rambert, in reply to the foregoing, in the *Revue de théologie et de philosophie*, Lausanne, 1876 and 1877.—The study of Weiffenbach on the testimony of Papias (p. 37) and the reply of Ludemann ("Zur Erklärung des Papiasfragments") in the *Jahrb. für protest. Theol.*, 1879. This last work closes with a general survey of the whole Johannean literature.—Finally, a critical article of Hilgenfeld on Luthardt's Introduction to the fourth Gospel and on my own, in the *Jahrb. für wissensch. Theol.*, 1880.

With the exception of certain elements borrowed from the Synoptics, this work contains only a fictitious history (Baur, Keim).

2. Others make our Gospel a free redaction of the Johannean traditions, which continued in Asia Minor after the sojourn of the apostle at Ephesus; the author thought that he could innocently pass himself off as the Apostle John himself (Renan, Hase).

3. A third party do not admit that the author wished to pass himself off as John; they think, on the contrary, that he has expressly distinguished himself from the apostle, whose stories served him as authorities (Weizsäcker, Reuss).

4. The partisans of a middle course go a little further. They discover in the Gospel a certain number of passages or notes which are due to the pen of John himself and which were amplified at a later time (Weisse, Schweizer).

5. Finally, there come the defenders of the authenticity properly so called, who are yet divided on one point; some recognize in the text as it exists more or less considerable interpolations (the incident of the angel at Bethesda, chap. v.; the story of the woman taken in adultery, chap. viii.), and the important addition of chap. xxi.; others adopt as authentic the common text in its entirety.

On which of the steps of this scale must we place ourselves in order to be with the truth? This is what the scrupulous examination of the facts alone can teach us.

THE APOSTLE JOHN

JOHN IN HIS FATHER'S HOUSE

It appears from all the documents that John was a native of Galilee. He belonged to that northern population, with whose lively, laborious, independent, warlike character Josephus has made us acquainted. The pressure exerted on the nation by the religious authorities having their seat at Jerusalem did not bear with equal weight upon that remote country. More free from prejudice, more open to the immediate impression of the truth, Galilean hearts offered to Jesus that receptive soil which His work demanded. Thus all His apostles, with the exception of Judas Iscariot, seem to have been of that province, and it was there that He succeeded in laying the foundations of His Church.

John dwelt on those shores of the lake of Gennesaret, which, in our day, present to the eye only a vast solitude, but which were then covered with towns and villages having in all, according to Josephus, many thousands of inhabitants. Did John, as is often said, have his home at Bethsaida? This is the conclusion drawn from Luke v. 10, where he is designated, along with his brother James, as a *partner* of Simon, and from John i. 44, where Bethsaida is called *the city of Andrew and Peter*. But, notwithstanding this, John may have dwelt at Capernaum, which could not have been far removed from the hamlet of Bethsaida, since on coming out of the synagogue of that city Jesus enters immediately into Peter's house (Mark i. 29).

The family of John contained four persons who are known to us: his brother James, who seems to have been his elder brother, since he is ordinarily named before him; their father Zebedee, who was a fisherman (Mark i. 19, 20), and their mother, who must have borne the name of Salome, for in the two evidently parallel passages, Matt. xxvii. 56, and Mark xv. 40, where the women are mentioned who were present at the crucifixion of Jesus, the name *Salome* in Mark is the equivalent of the title: *the mother of the sons of Zebedee* in Matthew. Wieseler has sought to prove that Salome was the sister of Mary, the mother of Jesus; from which it would follow that John was the cousin-german of our Lord.[1] We cannot regard this hypothesis as having sufficient foundation, either

---

[1] *Studien und Kritiken*, 1840.

30 / The Apostle John

exegetically or historically. The enumeration in John xix. 25, in which Wieseler finds four persons: 1. The mother of Jesus; 2. The sister of His mother; 3. Mary, the wife of Clopas, and 4. Mary Magdalene, appears to us to include only three, the words *Mary, the wife of Clopas* being quite naturally the explanatory apposition of the words, *the sister of His mother* (see the exegesis). And how is it possible in that case that our Gospels should not present some trace of so near a relationship between Jesus and John? Wieseler asks, it is true, how two sisters could, both of them, have borne the name of Mary. But there is nothing to prevent the word *sister* here from being taken, as it is so frequently, in the sense of *sister-in-law*. This sense is the more probable, inasmuch as, according to a very ancient tradition (Hegesippus), Clopas was the brother of Joseph, and consequently brother-in-law of Mary, the mother of Jesus.

John's family enjoyed a certain competency. According to Mark i. 20, Zebedee has day-laborers; Salome is ranked (Matt. xxvii. 56), in the number of the women who accompanied Jesus as He journeyed, and who (Luke viii. 3) *ministered* to Him and the Twelve *of their substance.* According to our Gospel (xix. 27), John possessed a house of his own, into which he received the mother of our Lord. Is it necessary to reckon, as some have done, among these indications of competency, the relation of his family to the high-priest, of which mention is made in xviii. 16? This conclusion has the less foundation since it cannot be proved that *the other disciple* mentioned in that passage was one of the sons of Zebedee, either John or James. The prosperous condition of the family was undoubtedly due to the then very lucrative business of fishing, and to the considerable commerce which was connected with it.[1]

Two points in the life of Salome betray a lively religious sentiment: the eagerness with which she consecrated herself, as we have just seen, to the service of Jesus, and the request which she had the boldness one day to present to the Lord on behalf of her two sons (Matt. xx. 20). Such a petition reveals an enthusiastic heart, and a piety which was ardent, yet imbued with the most earthly Messianic hopes. She had labored, no doubt, to exalt in the same direction the religious patriotism of her sons. So, as soon as the forerunner appeared on the scene, John hastened to his baptism. He even attached himself to him as his disciple (John i.); and it was in his presence that Jesus met him when he returned from the desert, whither he had betaken Himself after His baptism, with the design of beginning His work.[2]

JOHN A FOLLOWER OF JESUS

As John passed quietly from the paternal hearth to the baptism of the forerunner, he seems also to have passed without any violent crisis from the school of the latter to that of Jesus. In this progressive development

---

[1] See *Lücke's Commentary*, Introduction, p. 9.
[2] We refer for the justification of these data to the exegesis of John i.

there was no shock, and no rupture. He had only to follow the inward drawing, the Father's teaching, according to the profound expressions which he himself employs, in order to rise from step to step even to the summit of truth. It was the royal road described in that utterance of the Lord to Nicodemus: "He that doeth the truth cometh to the light, because his works are wrought in God" (John iii. 21). By this calm and continuous character of his development, John appears to be, in the spiritual world, the antipode of Paul.

The story of his call as a believer has been preserved to us in the first chapter of our Gospel; for everything tends to make us believe that the disciple who accompanied Andrew, at that decisive hour in which the new society was founded, was no other than John himself. From the banks of the Jordan, Jesus then returned, with him and the few young Galileans in the company of John the Baptist, whom He had attached to Himself, first to Cana and then to Nazareth, which He left soon afterwards in company with His mother and His brethren, to establish Himself with them at Capernaum (John ii. 12; comp. Matt. iv. 13). Jesus, as Himself still belonging to His family, had sent back these young men to the bosom of their own. But when, a few days afterwards, the moment arrived when He must enter upon His ministry in Judea, in the theocratic capital, He called them to follow Him in a permanent way and severed for them, as for Himself, the ties of domestic life. This new call took place on the shores of the lake of Gennesaret, near Capernaum. The account of it is given in Matt. iv. 18 and the parallel passages.

Subsequently, as the company of His disciples became more and more numerous, He chose twelve from among them, on whom He conferred the special title of *apostles* (Luke vi. 12 ff.; Mark iii. 13 ff.). In the first rank were the two brothers, John and James, with their two friends Simon and Andrew, who were also brothers. And soon among these four the two sons of Zebedee and Simon were honored by a more especial intimacy with Jesus. Thus we see them alone admitted to the raising of Jairus' daughter and to the two scenes of the transfiguration and Gethsemane. John was also, together with Peter, charged with the secret mission of preparing the Passover (Luke xxii. 8). It was, doubtless, this sort of preference of which he, as well as his brother, was the object, which emboldened Salome to ask for them the first places in the Messiah's kingdom.

Must we admit in favor of John a still closer degree of select friendship? Must we see in him that disciple whom Jesus had made His friend in the most peculiar sense of the word, and who, in the fourth Gospel, is several times designated as *the disciple whom Jesus loved* (xiii. 23; xix. 26; xx. 2; xxi. 7, 20 f.)? This was the unanimous opinion of the Church in the age which followed the time of the apostles. Irenæus says: "John, the disciple of the Lord, who rested upon His bosom, also published the gospel while he lived at Ephesus in Asia."[1] Polycrates, the bishop of Ephesus,

---

[1] Adv. Haer., iii. 1.

32 / The Apostle John

says expressly: "John who rested on the bosom of the Lord . . . is buried at Ephesus."[1] John even bore this title: *the disciple who rests on the bosom* of the Master (μαθητὴς ἐπιστήθιος).

Lützelberger was the first to call in question this application of the passages quoted to John, and to contend that the disciple loved by Jesus was Andrew, the brother of Peter. But why should this apostle, who, in the first part of the Gospel, is several times designated by his name (i. 41, 45; vi. 8; xii. 22) be, all at once, mentioned in the second part in this anonymous way? Späth has supposed that the beloved disciple was the one who is called Nathanael (John i. 46 ff.); and that this name, which signifies *gift of God*, designates this disciple as the normal Christian, the true gift of God to His Son.[2] But why, in that case, designate him sometimes by the name of Nathanael (i. 46; xxi. 2), and sometimes by this mysterious circumlocution.

Holtzmann likewise identifies the disciple whom Jesus loved with Nathanael, but does so while seeing in this personage only a fictitious being,—the purely ideal type of Paulinism.[3]

Scholten[4] also regards this unnamed disciple as a fictitious personage; he is, in the writer's intention, the symbol of true Christianity, in opposition to the Twelve and their imperfect conception of the gospel.

Is it worth our while to refute such vagaries of the imagination? In chap. xix., the author certainly makes of this disciple a real being, since it is he to whom Jesus entrusts His mother, and who receives her into his house; unless we are ready also to interpret in a symbolic sense this mother who was thus entrusted to him, and to see in her nothing else than the Church itself. This explanation of the sense would surpass in point of arbitrariness the master-pieces of allegorizing of which this passage has sometimes been the occasion among Catholic writers.

In reading the fourth Gospel, we cannot doubt that the disciple whom Jesus loved was, in the first place, one of the Twelve, and then, one of the three who enjoyed especial intimacy with the Saviour. Of these three, he cannot be Peter, for that apostle is named several times *along with* the beloved disciple. No more can he be James, who died too early (about the year 44, Acts xii.) for the report to have been spread abroad in the Church that he would not die (John xxi.). John is, therefore, the only one of the three for whom this title can be suitable. We reach the same result, also, by another way. In John xxi. 2, seven disciples are designated: "Simon Peter, Thomas, called Didymus, Nathanael, of Cana in Galilee, the sons of Zebedee, and two other disciples." Among these seven was the one whom Jesus loved, since he plays a part in the following scene (ver. 20 ff.) Now he cannot be Peter or Thomas or Nathanael, all three of whom are designated by name in the course of the Gospel and in this very passage, nor again one of the two last-mentioned disciples

---

[1] Eusebius, v. 24 (ἐν Ἐφέσῳ κεκοίμηται).
[2] Hilgenfeld's *Zeitschrift für wissenschaftliche Theologie*, 1868.
[3] Schenkel's *Bibellexicon*, vol. iv. art. *Nathanael*.
[4] In the brochure: *Der Apostel Johannes in Kleinasien*.

whom the author does not name, doubtless because they did not belong to the number of the Twelve. It only remains, therefore, to choose between the two sons of Zebedee; and between these two, as we have just seen, no hesitation is possible.

In the conduct of John, during the ministry of his Master, two features strike us; a modesty carried even to the extreme of reserve, and a vivacity reaching sometimes even to the point of violence. The fourth Gospel is fond of relating to us the striking sayings of Peter; it speaks of the conversations of Andrew and Philip with Jesus, of the manifestations of devotion or of incredulity in Thomas. In the Synoptics Peter speaks at every moment. But in the one narrative and the other John plays only a very secondary and obscure part. Three sayings only are ascribed to him in our Gospel, and they are all very remarkable for their brevity: "Master, where abidest thou?" (i. 38),—"Lord, who is it?" (xiii. 25),—"It is the Lord!" (xxi. 7).—Moreover, of these three expressions the first was probably uttered by Andrew; and the second came from the mouth of John only at Peter's suggestion. What significance, then, has this fact, which is apparently so little in accord with the altogether peculiar relation of this disciple to Jesus? That John was one of those natures which live more within themselves than without. While Peter occupied the foreground of the scene, John kept himself in the background, observing, contemplating, drinking in love and light, and satisfied with his character of silent personage which so well suited his receptive and profound nature. We can understand the charm which this character must have had for our Lord. He found in this relation, which remained their common secret, that complement which manly natures seek in family ties.

Along with this feature which reveals a character naturally timid and contemplative, we meet certain facts in which John betrays a vivacity of impression capable of rising even to passion; as when, with his brother, he proposes to Jesus to cause fire to descend from heaven on the Samaritan village which has refused to receive Him (Luke ix. 54), or when he is irritated at the sight of a man who, without joining himself to the disciples, takes the liberty of casting out demons in the name of Jesus, and forbids him to continue acting in this way (Luke ix. 49). We may bring into comparison with these two features that request for the first place in the Messianic kingdom, by which we discover the impure alloy which was still mingled with his faith.

How can we explain these two apparently so opposite traits of character? There exist natures which are at once tender, ardent and timid; which ordinarily confine their impressions within themselves, and this the more in proportion as these impressions are the more profound. But if it happens that these persons once cease to be masters of themselves, the long restrained emotions then break forth in sudden explosions which throw all around them into astonishment. Was it not to this order of characters that John and his brother belonged? If it was so, could Jesus better describe them, than by giving them the surname of *Boanerges, sons*

34 / The Apostle John

of thunder[1] (Mark iii. 17)? I cannot think, as the Fathers believed, that by this surname Jesus meant to mark the gift of eloquence which distinguished them. No more am I able to admit that He wished to perpetuate thereby the remembrance of their passion in one of the cases indicated (Luke ix. 54). But, as electricity is slowly accumulated in the cloud, until it suddenly breaks forth in the lightning and the thunderbolt, so Jesus observed in these two loving and passionate beings, how the impressions were silently stored within until the moment when, as the result of some outward circumstance, they violently broke forth; and this is what He meant to describe. St. John is often represented as a nature sweet and tender even to effeminacy. Do not his writings before and above all things insist upon love? Were not the last preachings of the old man: "Love one another?" This is true; but we must not forget the traits of a different nature which, both in the earlier and later periods of his life, reveal in him something decided, trenchant, absolute, and even violent?

In thus estimating the character of John we believe ourselves to be in accordance with the truth, rather than Sabatier, where he closes his judgment of the apostle with these words: "It is worthy of remark, that the name of John does not occur in the Synoptics except in connection with censure." But are we to forget that, in one case, he accused himself (Luke ix. 49); that, in another, it was by excess of zeal for the honor of Jesus that he drew upon himself a reprimand (Luke ix. 54); and that, in the third case, the jealous indignation of his fellow-disciples sprung from the same cause as the ambitious petition of the two sons of Salome (Mark x. 41, comp. 42 ff.)? Are we, above all, to forget the place which, according to the Synoptics themselves, Jesus had given to John, as well as to Peter and James, in His most intimate friendship? Comp. also the incident in Luke xxii. 8. The design of this manner of presenting the subject is explained by what follows: "There is here," continues the writer, "a singular contrast to the image of the beloved disciple who leans upon Jesus' bosom, of that ideal disciple who conceals and reveals himself at the same time in the fourth Gospel."[2] It was, then, a stepping-stone to something further! The biography was at the service of the criticism.

If we take account of all the facts which have been pointed out, we shall recognize in John one of those natures passionately devoted to the ideal which, at the first sight, give themselves without reserve to the being who seems to them to realize it. But the devotion of such persons easily takes on somewhat of exclusiveness and intolerance. Everything which does not answer in sympathy completely to their enthusiasm irritates them and excites their indignation. They have no comprehension of what a dividing of the heart is, any more than they know how to have such a divided heart themselves. The whole for the whole! Such is their motto. Where the complete gift is wanting, there is no longer anything to their view. Such affections do not exist without containing an alloy of egoism. A divine work is necessary to the end that the devotion which

---

[1] Bené régés (בני רגש). [2] *Encyclopédie des Sciences religieuses*, t. VII., p. 173.

forms their basis may at last come forth purified and may appear in all its sublimity. Such was John—worthy, even in his very faults, of the intimate friendship of the best of men.

JOHN AT THE HEAD OF THE JEWISH-CHRISTIAN CHURCH

John's part in the Church after the day of Pentecost was that which such antecedents lead us to expect. On that stage where Peter and James, the brother of John, the first martyr among the apostles, and where even mere assistants of the apostles, such as Stephen and Philip, and finally Paul and James, the Lord's brother, moved and acted, John appears only on two occasions:—when he goes up to the temple with Peter (Acts iii.), and when he accompanies this same apostle to Samaria, in order to finish the work begun by Philip (Acts viii.). And on each of these two occasions Peter is the one who plays the principal part; John seems to be only his assistant. As we have already seen, the disciple whom Jesus loved was not a man of action; he did not take the initiative as a conqueror; his mission, like his talent, was of a more inward character. His hour was not to strike until a later time, after the Church was founded. Meanwhile, a deep work, the continuation of that which Jesus had begun in him, was being wrought in his soul. That promise which he has himself preserved for us—"The Spirit shall glorify me in you" was finding its realization in his case. After having given himself up, he found himself again in his glorified Master, and he gave himself up still more fully.

But from this moment he had a particular task to fulfill—that which his dying Master had left as a legacy to him. To Peter, Jesus had entrusted the direction of the Church; to John, the care of His mother.

Where did Mary live? It is scarcely probable that she felt any attraction towards a residence in Jerusalem. Her dearest recollections recalled her to Galilee. Undoubtedly, it was there also, on the shores of the lake of Gennesaret, that John possessed that *home* where he received her and lavished upon her the attentions of filial piety. This circumstance likewise serves to explain why, in those earliest times, he took little part in missionary work. Had he lived at Jerusalem, Paul would undoubtedly have seen him, as well as Peter and James, at the time of his first visit to that city after his conversion (Gal. i. 18, 19).

Later traditions, yet traditions which nothing prevents us from regarding as well-founded, place the death of Mary about the year 48. After that time, John undoubtedly took a more considerable part in the direction of the Christian work. At the time of the assembly, commonly called the council of Jerusalem (Acts xv.), in 50 or 51, he is one of the apostles with whom Paul confers in the capital, and the latter ranks him (Gal. ii.) among those who were regarded as the *pillars* of the Church.[1] An important and much discussed question with respect to John presents itself at this point.

---

[1] Gal. ii. 9 : "James, Cephas and John, who were thought to be pillars."

36 / The Apostle John

The Tübingen school ascribes to these three personages, James, Peter and John, who represented the Jewish-Christian Church at that time over against Paul and Barnabas, an opinion opposed to that of these last as to the matter of maintaining legal observances in the Church. The only difference which it recognizes between the apostles and *the false brethren privily brought in,* of whom Paul speaks (Gal. ii. 4),—and it is not to the advantage of the former,—is this: the false brethren, the Pharisaical intruders, held their ground in opposition to Paul and attempted to make him yield, while the apostles, intimidated by his energy and by the eclat of his successes among the Gentiles, abandoned *in fact* their convictions, and agreed, in spite of these men, to divide with him the missionary work. Thus would be reduced to insignificance the import of that sign of co-operation which the apostles gave to Paul and Barnabas, in extending to them the right hand of fellowship at the moment when they separated from each other (ver. 9).

We can readily understand the interest which attaches to this question. If such was really the personal conviction of John, it is obvious that he could not be the author of the fourth Gospel, or that he could be so only on the condition of having previously passed through the crisis of a complete transformation. Schürer himself, who is independent of the Tübingen point of view, says:[1] "The John of the second chapter of Galatians, who disputes with Paul respecting the law, cannot have written our fourth Gospel."

But is it true that the abrogation of the law for the converted Gentiles was a concession which St. Paul was obliged to wrest from the apostles, contrary to their inward conviction? Is it true, in general, that there was on the question of the law a fundamental difference between Paul and the Twelve? This question has been discussed beyond measure during the last thirty years, and I do not think that, on the whole, the scale has turned in the direction of Baur's assertions. I will only take up here one decisive passage—the one which that school most habitually puts forward, and which, to the view of Hilgenfeld, is, as it were, its impregnable fortress. It is Gal. ii. 3, 4: "But Titus who was with me, being a Greek, was not compelled to be circumcised, and that because of ($\delta\iota\grave{\alpha}$ $\delta\acute{\epsilon}$) the false brethren brought in privily . . ." The following is the way in which Hilgenfeld reasons:—Paul does not say: I did not yield *to* the false brethren; but, I did not yield *because of them.* To whom, then, did he make resistance? Evidently to others than these. These others can only be the apostles. It was the apostles, therefore, who demanded the circumcision of Titus. Consequently they claimed, and John with them, the right to impose circumcision on the Gentiles. The observation from which Hilgenfeld starts is correct; but the conclusion which he draws from it is false. The apostles asked of Paul the circumcision of Titus, and he would not yield to them *because of the false brethren.* Such, indeed, is the fact. But what does it prove? That the false brethren demanded this circumcision in an alto-

---

[1] *Theol. Liter.-Zeit.*, 1876, No. 14.

gether different spirit from the Twelve. They demanded it as *an obligation*, while the apostles asked it of Paul only as a free concession in favor of the Christians of Jerusalem, who were offended at the thought of intercourse with an uncircumcised person. This is the reason why Paul was able to say: Apart from the false brethren, I might have yielded to the Twelve with *that compliance* (τῇ ὑποταγῇ, ver. 5) which every Christian should exhibit towards his brethren in the things which are in themselves indifferent. And this is what he really did every time that he put himself *under the law* with those who were under the law (1 Cor. ix. 20); comp. the circumcision of Timothy. But it was impossible for him at this time to act thus *because of the false brethren*, who were prepared to make use of that concession in order to turn it to account in relation to the Gentiles as an *obligatory* precedent. The Twelve understood this reason, and did not insist. If the case stands thus, the question is solved. As a matter of right, the Twelve did not impose the law upon the Gentiles. They personally observed it, with the Christians of Jewish origin, but not as a condition of salvation, since, in that case, they could not have exempted the Gentiles from it. They observed it until God, who had imposed this system upon them, should Himself put an end to it. Paul had anticipated them in knowledge on this point only: that to his view the cross was already for the Jews themselves the expected abrogation (Gal. ii. 19, 20). For those of the apostles who, like St. John, survived the fall of the temple, that event must naturally have removed the last doubt in relation to themselves and their nation.

This view does not force us to establish a conflict between the epistles of Paul and the narrative of the Acts. It is likewise in accord with our Synoptic gospels, which are filled with declarations of Jesus containing what involves the abolition of the law. That sentence: "It is not that which entereth into the man which defileth the man, but that which cometh out of *the heart of the man*,"[1] contains in principle the total abolition of the Levitical system. That other saying: "The Son of man is *Lord even of the Sabbath*,"[2] saps the foundation of the Sabbath ordinance in its Mosaic form, and thereby the entire ceremonial institution of which the Sabbath was the centre. By comparing His new economy to a new garment, which must be substituted *as a whole* for the old,[3] Jesus gives expression to a view of the relation between the Gospel and the law beyond which the apostle of the Gentiles himself could not go. And it is the apostles who have transmitted all these words to the Church; and yet they did this, it is said, without at all comprehending their practical application! Independently, then, of the epistles of Paul and the Acts, we are obliged to affirm that what is (wrongly) called Paulinism must have existed, as a more or less latent conviction, in the minds of the apostles from the time of Jesus' ministry. The death of Christ, the day of Pentecost, and the work of Paul could not fail to develop these germs.

Irenæus has very faithfully described this state of things in these words:

---

[1] Matt. xv. 18–20; Mark vii. 18–20.   [2] Mark ii. 28.   [3] Matt. ix. 16 and the parallels.

38 / The Apostle John

"They themselves (the apostles) persevered in the old observances, conducting themselves piously with regard to the institution of the law; but, as for us Gentiles, they granted us liberty, committing us to the Holy Spirit."[1]

JOHN IN ASIA MINOR

After the council of Jerusalem, we lose all trace of John until the time when tradition depicts him as accomplishing his apostolic ministry in the midst of the churches of Asia Minor. It is not probable that he repaired to those remote countries before the destruction of Jerusalem. He undoubtedly accompanied the Jewish-Christian Church when it emigrated to Perea at the time when the war against the Romans broke out. This departure took place about the year 67.[2] Only at a later period, when, in consequence of the death of Paul, and perhaps of the death of his assistants in Asia Minor, Titus and Timothy, the churches of that region, which were so important, found themselves deprived of every apostolic leader, John removed thither. He does not seem to have been the only apostle or apostolic personage who made choice of this place of residence. History speaks of the ministry of Philip, either the apostle or the deacon, at Hierapolis; we find, also, some indications of a sojourn of Andrew in Ephesus.[3] As Thiersch says, "The centre of gravity of the Church was *no longer* at Jerusalem, and it was *not yet* at Rome; it was at Ephesus." Like the circle of golden candlesticks,[4] the numerous and flourishing churches founded by Paul in Ionia and Phrygia were the luminous point towards which the eyes of all Christendom were directed. "From the fall of Jerusalem," says Lücke, "even into the second century, Asia Minor was the most living portion of the Church." What excited an interest on behalf of these churches was not merely the energy of their faith; it was the intensity of the struggle which they had to maintain against heresy. "After my departure," St. Paul had said to the pastors of Ephesus and Miletus (Acts xx. 29, 30), "ravenous wolves shall enter in among you not sparing the flock; and from among your own selves shall men arise speaking perverse things, to draw away the disciples after them." This prophecy was fulfilled. It is not surprising, therefore, that John, one of the last survivors among the apostles, should have gone to supply in those regions the place of the apostle of the Gentiles, and to water, as Apollos had formerly done in Corinth, that which Paul had planted.

The accounts of this residence of John in Asia are numerous and positive. Nevertheless, Keim and Scholten, after the example of Vogel, Reuterdahl, and especially Lützelberger, have in these latter days controverted the truth of this tradition. The former thinks that the personage, named John, whom Polycarp had known, was not the apostle, but the

---

[1] *Adv. Haer.* iii. 12.
[2] *Ewald, Gesch. des Volks Israel*, vol. vi., p. 642.
[3] So in the so-called Fragment of Muratori.
[4] Apoc. i. 12, 20.

presbyter of the same name, who must have lived at Ephesus about the end of the first century; and that Irenæus erroneously, and even with some willingness, imagined that this master of his own master was the apostle. This was the starting-point of the error which was afterwards so generally disseminated. Scholten believes, rather, that as the Apocalypse was falsely ascribed to the Apostle John, and as the author of that book appeared to have lived in Asia (Apoc. ii., iii.), the residence of the Apostle John in that region was inferred from these false premises.

Let us begin by establishing the tradition; we shall afterwards appreciate the importance of it.

Irenæus says: "All the presbyters who met with John, the disciple of the Lord, in Asia, give testimony that he conveyed to them these things; for he lived with them even to the time of Trajan. And some among them saw not only John, but also other apostles."[1] This whole passage, but especially the last sentence, implies that the person in question is the *apostle*, and not some other John. This is still more precisely set forth in the following words: "Afterwards, John, the disciple of the Lord, *he who leaned on His breast*, published the gospel while he dwelt at Ephesus, in Asia."[2] We read elsewhere: "The church of Ephesus, which was founded by Paul and in which John lived until the time of Trajan, is also a truthful witness of the tradition of the apostles."[3] And further: "Polycarp had not only been taught by the apostles, and lived with several men who had seen Christ, but he had been constituted bishop in the church of Smyrna *by the apostles* who were in Asia; and we ourselves saw him in our early youth, since he lived a very long time and became very aged, and departed this life after a glorious martyrdom, having constantly taught what he had heard from *the apostles*."[4] It cannot be doubted, therefore, that the following words, having reference to the Apocalypse, apply to the apostle: "This number (666) is found in all the accurate and ancient manuscripts, and it is attested by all those *who saw John face to face*."[5]

Thus speaks Irenæus in his principal work. Besides this, we have two letters of his in which he expresses himself in the same way. One of them is addressed to Florinus, his old fellow-pupil under Polycarp, who had embraced the Gnostic doctrines. Irenæus says to him: "These are not the teachings which the elders who preceded us and who lived after the apostles handed down to thee; for I saw thee, when I was still a child, in lower Asia with Polycarp. . . . And I could still show thee the place where he sat when he taught and gave an account of *his relations with John and with the others who saw the Lord*, and how he spoke of what he had heard from them respecting the Lord, His miracles and His doctrine, and how he recounted, in full accord with the Scriptures, all that which he had received from the eye-witnesses of the Word of life."[6] The other letter was addressed

---

[1] As far as the word *Trajan*, according to the Greek text preserved by Eusebius, H. E., iii. 23. 3; the last words according to the Latin translation: *Adv. Haer.*, ii. 22. 5.
[2] Irenæus, iii. 1. 1, (Eusebius, v. 8. 4).
[3] iii. 3. 4. (Eusebius, iii. 23. 4).
[4] iii. 3. 4. (Eusebius, iv. 14).
[5] v. 30. 1. (Eusebius, v. 8).
[6] Eusebius, v. 20.

by Irenæus to Victor, Bishop of Rome, on occasion of the controversy carried on with regard to the Passover:[1] "When the blessed Polycarp visited Rome in the time of Anicetus, slight differences of opinion having become manifest respecting certain points, peace was very soon concluded. And they did not even give themselves up to a dispute upon the principal question. For Anicetus could not dissuade Polycarp *from observing* [the 14th of Nisan, as the Paschal day], inasmuch as he had always observed it with John, the disciple of the Lord, and *the other apostles* with whom he had lived. And, on his side, Polycarp could not persuade Anicetus *to observe* [the same day], the latter replying that he must maintain the custom which he had received from his predecessors. This being the state of things, they gave each other the communion, and in the assembly Anicetus yielded the office of administering the Eucharist to Polycarp, by way of honor; and they separated in peace." Thus at Rome and in Gaul, no less than in Asia Minor, Polycarp was certainly regarded as the disciple of John *the apostle*, and the arguments of the bishops of Rome were rendered powerless twice in the second century—in 160 (or rather 155) and 190—as they met this fact which was, to the view of all, raised above all controversy.

We find in Asia Minor, about 180, another witness of the same tradition. Apollonius, an anti-Montanist writer, related, at that time, that John had raised a dead man to life at Ephesus. And it is to the apostle, certainly, that he attributed this act. For he is speaking here of the author of the Apocalypse, and we know that, at this period, the churches of Asia had no doubt as to the composition of that book by the apostle.

But, already before Irenæus and Apollonius, Justin has some words relative to John, which imply the idea of his residence in Asia.[2] He says: "A man among us, *one of the apostles of Christ*, has prophesied in the revelation which was given to him (ἐν ἀποκαλύψει γενομένῃ αὐτῷ)." As the fact of the composition of the Apocalypse in Asia is not doubtful (although Scholten seems desirous of disputing it), it follows from this statement of Justin that he had no doubt that the apostle had resided in Asia. This declaration is the more interesting since it is found in the account of a public discussion which Justin had to maintain at Ephesus itself with a learned Jew. This work [3] dates from 150–160.

We possess, finally, an official document, emanating from the bishops of Asia towards the close of the second century, which attests their unanimous conviction in regard to the matter with which we are engaged. It is the letter which Polycrates, bishop of Ephesus, addressed to Victor under the same circumstances which occasioned that of Irenæus quoted above (about 190). He—a man in whose family the office of bishop of that metropolis was, as it were, hereditary (since seven of his relatives had already filled it before him)—writes, with the assent of all the bishops

---

[1] Euseb., v. 24.
[2] Eusebius, v. 28: "He uses also testimonies derived from the Apocalypse of John, and relates that a dead man had been raised at Ephesus by the same John."
[3] *Against Trypho the Jew.*

of the province who surround him, the following words: "We celebrate the true day. . . . For some great lights are extinguished in Asia and will rise again there at the return of the Lord. . . . Philip, one of the twelve apostles, . . . and John, who reclined on the Lord's bosom, who was high priest and wore the plate of gold, and who was a witness and teacher, and who is buried at Ephesus. . . . All these celebrated the Passover on the fourteenth day, according to the gospel."[1]

Such are the testimonies proceeding from Asia Minor. They are not the only ones. We can add to them one coming from Egypt. Clement of Alexandria, about 190, in the preamble to the story of the young man whom John reclaimed from his errors, writes these words: "After the tyrant was dead, John returned from the island of Patmos to Ephesus, and there he visited the surrounding countries in order to constitute bishops and organize the churches."[2]

We omit the later witnesses (Tertullian, Origen, Jerome, Eusebius), who naturally depend on the older accounts.[3]

By what means is the attempt made to shake so ancient and widely established a tradition?

The Acts of the Apostles, says Keim, do not speak of such a residence of John in Asia. Is it a serious man who speaks thus? With such logic, answers Leuschner, it might also be proved that Paul is not yet dead even to the present hour. As if the book of Acts were a biography of the apostles, and as if it did not end before the time when John lived in Asia!

But the silence of the Epistles to the Ephesians and Colossians, and of the Pastoral Epistles? adds Scholten. As if the composition of these writings in the second century were a fact so thoroughly demonstrated that it could be made the starting point for new conclusions! Can critical presumption go further?

With more show of probability is the silence of the epistles of Ignatius and Polycarp alleged. Ignatius recalls to the Ephesians, Polycarp to the Philippians, the ministry of Paul in their churches; they are both silent with respect to that of John in Asia. As to Ignatius, these are the terms in which he recalls the Apostle Paul to the Ephesians: "You are *the place of passage* (πάροδος) of those who have been taken up to God, the co-initiated with Paul the consecrated one . . . , in whose footsteps may I be found![4]" The question is not of a residence of Paul in Ephesus in general, but quite specially of his last *passage* through Asia Minor, when, as he was repairing to Rome, he gave to the elders of those churches the farewell words reported in the Acts, and, in some sort, associated them with the consecration of his martyrdom. The analogy of

---

[1] Eusebius v. 24. 3 (comp. iii. 31. 3).
[2] Τίς ὁ σωζόμενος πλούσιος, c. 42 (comp. Eusebius iii. 24).
[3] We omit, with still stronger reason, the work of Prochorus, recently published by Zahn (*Acta Johannis*), of which a young scholar,—Max Bonnet, professor at Montpelier, is preparing a new edition. It is a book of pure imagination, without the least historical value, composed, according to Zahn, between 400 and 600. The Johannean fragments in the work of Leucius, which Zahn is disposed to carry back as far as 130, do not seem to have any greater value. See Overbeck in the *Theol. Liter. Zeit.*, 1881, No. 2.
[4] Ad Eph., c. 12.

42 / The Apostle John

that moment with the position of Ignatius, when he wrote to the Ephesians on his way to Rome, is obvious. There was no similar comparison to be made with the life of John. Moreover, the eleventh chapter of this same letter furnishes, perhaps, an allusion to the presence of John at Ephesus: "The Christians of Ephesus," says Ignatius, "have always lived in entire harmony (συνῄνεσαν) *with the apostles,* in the strength of Jesus Christ." Finally, we must not forget that Ignatius was from Syria, and that he had not been acquainted with John in Asia Minor.

Polycarp, writing to Macedonian Christians, had no particular reason for recalling to them John's ministry at Ephesus. If he speaks to them of Paul, it is because this apostle had founded and several times visited their church; and if he mentions Ignatius, it is because the venerated martyr had just passed through Philippi, at that very moment, as he was going to Rome.

The similar objection, derived from the account of the death of Polycarp, in the Acts of his martyrdom, by the church of Smyrna, is no more serious. Sixty years had passed since John's death, and yet that church could not have written a letter without making mention of him! Hilgenfeld, moreover, rightly notices the title of *apostolic teacher* given to Polycarp (chap. 18), which recalls his personal relations with one or with several of the apostles.

Keim and Scholten find the most decisive argument in the silence of Papias; they even see in the words of this Father the express denial of all connection with the apostle. Irenæus, it is true, did not understand Papias in this way. He thinks, on the contrary, that he can call him *a hearer of John* ('Ιωάννου ἀκουστής). But, it is said, precisely at this point is an error, which Eusebius has noticed and corrected by a more thorough study of the terms which Papias employed. The importance of the testimony of Papias in this question is manifest. Leimbach cites as many as forty-five writers who have treated this subject in these most recent times. We are compelled to study it more closely.

First of all, what is the epoch of Papias, and what the date of his work? Irenæus adds to the title of *hearer of John,* which he gives to him, that of *companion of Polycarp* (Πολυκάρπου ἑταῖρος). This term denotes a *contemporary.* Now, the most recent investigations place the martyrdom of Polycarp in 155 or 156,[1] and this date appears to be generally adopted at the present day (Renan, Lipsius, Hilgenfeld). As Polycarp himself declares that he had spent eighty-six years in the service of the Lord, his birth must be placed, at the latest, in the year 70. If Papias was his contemporary, therefore, he lived between 70 and 160; and if John died about the year 100, this Father might, chronologically speaking, have been in contact with the apostle up to the age of thirty. Irenæus, at the same time, calls Papias a man of Christian antiquity (ἀρχαῖος ἀνήρ); Papias belonged, then, like Polycarp, to the generation which immediately followed the

---

[1] Waddington, *Mémoires de l'Académie des Inscriptions et Belles-Lettres,* tome xxvi., 2ᵉ partie, p. 232 et suiv.

apostles. There is, finally, in the very fragment which we are about to study, an expression which leads us to the same conclusion. Papias says that he informed himself concerning "that which Andrew, and then Peter, Philip, etc., etc., *said* (εἶπεν), and that which Aristion and John the Presbyter, the disciples of the Lord, *say* (λέγουσιν)." This contrast between the past *said* and the present *say* is too marked to be accidental. It implies, as at the present day Keim, Hilgenfeld and Mangold acknowledge, that at the time when Papias wrote the two last-named personages were still living;[1] and, since they are both designated as *personal* disciples of Jesus, they can only, at the latest, have lived until about the year 110–120. It was, then, at this period also—at the latest—that Papias wrote. He was then thirty to forty years old.[2]

Now the following is the fragment quoted by Eusebius.[3] The question will be whether the personal relation of Papias with John the apostle is *affirmed*, as Irenæus thinks, or *excluded*, as Eusebius claims, by the terms employed in this much discussed passage.

"Now I shall not fail to add to my explanations also (συγκατατάξαι[4] ταῖς ἑρμηνείαις) all that which I have formerly very well learned and very well remembered from the elders (παρὰ τῶν πρεσβυτέρων), while guaranteeing to thee the truth of the same. For I did not take pleasure, like the great mass, in those who relate many things, but in those who teach true things; nor in those who spread abroad strange commandments, but in those who spread abroad the commandments given to faith by the Lord and that come[5] from the truth itself. And if, at times, also, one of those who accompanied the elders came to me (εἰ δέ που καὶ παρακολουθηκώς τις τοῖς πρεσβυτέροις ἔλθοι), I inquired about the words of the elders (τοὺς τῶν πρεσβυτέρων ἀνέκρινον λόγους) : what Andrew said, or Peter (τί Ἀνδρέας ἢ τί Πέτρος εἶπεν), or Philip, or Thomas, or James, or John,[6] or Matthew, or some other of the disciples of the Lord (ἤ τις ἕτερος τῶν τοῦ Κυρίου μαθητῶν); then about *what* Aristion and the presbyter John, the disciples of the Lord, say (ἅ τε[7] Ἀριστίων καὶ ὁ πρεσβύτερος Ἰωάννης, οἱ τοῦ Κυρίου μαθηταί, λέγουσιν), for I

---

[1] Zahn and Riggenbach think that this present *say* may denote merely the permanence of the *testimony* of these men; Leimbach: that it arises from the fact that Papias thinks that he still hears them speak.—All this would be possible only in so far as the contrast with the past tense *had said* did not exist.

[2] There must be a resolute determination to create a history after one's own fancy, to place, as Volkmar ventures to do, the work of Papias in 165!

[3] *H. E.* iii. 39.

[4] This reading, (and not συντάξαι), appears certain; see Leimbach.

[5] The ambiguity of our translation reproduces the possible meaning of the two readings (παραγινομένας and παραγινομένοις) according to which the words: *and that come* refer either to the commandments or to the individuals themselves.

[6] M. Renan has proposed to reject from the text the words: *or John*. This is absolutely arbitrary, and in that case the conclusion of Eusebius respecting the existence of a second John would lose its foundation.

[7] Papias here substitutes for the interrogative pronoun τί (employed in the preceding clause) the relative pronoun ἅ, because the idea of interrogation is remote. This ἅ is also the object of ἀνέκρινον, parallel with the preceding object λόγους (so also Holtzmann). No one, I think, will be tempted to accept Leimbach's translation : ". . . *or which* (τίς) of the disciples of the Lord [has related] that which Aristion or John says . . ." The position of the τε, placed as it is after ἅ, and not after Ἀριστίων, is sufficient to refute this.

did not suppose that that which is derived from books could be as useful to me as that which comes from the living and permanent word."

This passage is made up of two distinct paragraphs, of which the second begins with the words: *"And if at times* (now and then) *also."* Hilgenfeld and others think that the second paragraph is only the commentary on the first, and refers to the same fact. But this interpretation does violence to the text, as the first words prove: *And if at times also* (εἰ δέ που καί). This transition indicates an advance, not an identity. The two paragraphs, therefore, refer to different facts.

In the former paragraph, Papias evidently speaks of what he has favorably received and remembered *from the elders themselves*—that is to say, by a communication from them to him personally. This is implied by the use of the preposition παρά (*from*), the regular sense of which is that of direct communication; 2. By the adverb ποτέ (*formerly*), which, by placing these communications in a past already remote, shows that such a relation has for a long time been no more possible, and that it, consequently, belongs to the youth of the author.

The essential question in relation to the meaning of this first paragraph is the following: Who are these *elders* whom Papias heard in his youth? They cannot be, as Weiffenbach has maintained, the elders or *presbyters* appointed in the churches by the apostles. For how could Papias, the contemporary of Polycarp, one of the men of the older generation to the view of Irenæus, have been *formerly* (in his youth) instructed by these disciples of the apostles! The anachronism resulting from this explanation is a flagrant one. No more, on the other hand, can these elders be, as has been claimed, simply and exclusively the *apostles*. In that case Papias would have used this term, and not the term *elders*. The title elders (πρεσβύτεροι, *seniores*) has, with the Fathers, as Holtzmann has well remarked, a relative meaning. For Irenæus and the men of the third Christian generation, the *elders* are the men of the second, the Polycarps and the Papiases; for these latter, they are the men of the first—the apostles, first of all, and, besides them, every immediate witness and disciple of the Lord. This clearly appears from the second paragraph in which Papias gives an enumeration of those whom he calls the elders; it includes seven apostles and two *disciples of the Lord* who were not apostles, Aristion and the presbyter John. As the Apostle John has been named among the seven, it appears to me impossible to identify with the apostle this presbyter having the same name, notwithstanding the reasons given by Zahn and Riggenbach. He is a second John, who lived in Asia Minor, and whom the special surname of elder or presbyter was intended, perhaps, to distinguish from the apostle, who was called either simply John, or the Apostle John.[1]

And is it not evident that the words ἤ τις ἕτερος are the conclusion and, as it were, the *et cetera* of the preceding enumeration? Moreover, of what consequence is it *which* of the disciples said such or such a thing! Finally, the ellipsis of the verb is inadmissible.

[1] See the clear and precise setting-forth of this subject by Weiss: *Commentar zum Evangelium Johannis* (6th ed. of Meyer's Commentary).

It follows from this, that, in the first paragraph, Papias declares that he had in former years heard personally from the immediate disciples of Jesus (apostles or non-apostles). He does not name them; but we have no right to exclude from this number the Apostle John, and, because of this statement, to declare false, as Eusebius does in his History, the words of Irenæus: "Papias, a fellow-disciple of Polycarp and *hearer of John.*" And this even more, since Irenæus, a native of Asia Minor, had probably been personally acquainted with Papias, and since Eusebius himself, in his *Chronicon,* affirms the personal connection of Papias, as well as that of Polycarp, with St. John.[1]

In the second paragraph, Papias passes from personal to indirect relations. He explains how, at a later period, when he found himself prevented by distance or by the death of the elders from communicating with them, he set himself to the work of continuing to collect the materials for his book. He took advantage of all the opportunities that were offered him by the visits which he received at Hierapolis, to question every one of those who had anywhere met with the elders; and it is on occasion of this statement, that he designates the latter by name: " I asked him what Andrew, Peter . . John, etc., *said* " (when they were alive) respecting such or such a circumstance in the life of the Lord, "and what the two disciples of the Lord, Aristion and the presbyter John *say* " (at the present time). And why, indeed, even after having communicated directly in his youth with some of these men, may not Papias have sought to gather some indirect information from the lips of those who had enjoyed such intercourse more recently or more abundantly than himself? At all events, as it evidently does not follow from the first paragraph that Papias had not been acquainted with John, so it does follow with equal clearness, from the second, that he was not personally instructed by John the Presbyter; and thus a second error of Eusebius is to be corrected.

What becomes, then, of the modern argument (Keim and others), drawn from the passage of Papias, against the residence of John in Asia? " Papias himself declares," it is said, " that he was not acquainted with any one of the apostles, while he affirms that he was personally acquainted with John the Presbyter. Irenæus, therefore, in speaking of him as the hearer of the Apostle John, has confounded the apostle with the presbyter." The fact is: 1. That Papias affirms his having been acquainted with *elders* (among whom might be John the Apostle); 2. That he denies a personal acquaintance with John the Presbyter; and 3. That he *expressly* distinguishes John the Apostle from John the Presbyter. We see what is the value of the objection drawn from this testimony.

But, it is said, Irenæus may have been mistaken when alleging that the John known to Polycarp was the apostle, whereas this person was actually only the presbyter And this mistake of Irenæus may have led astray the whole tradition which emanates from him. Keim supports this assertion by the following expression of Irenæus in his letter to Florinus, when

---

[1] Comp. Zahn, *Patr. apost.* edition of Gebhardt, Harnack, etc.

he is speaking of his relations with Polycarp: "*When I was yet a child* (παῖς ἔτι ὤν)," and by that other similar expression, in his great work, on the same occasion: "*In our first youth* (ἐν τῇ πρώτῃ ἡλικίᾳ)." But every one acquainted with the Greek language knows well that such expressions, in particular the word translated by *child* (παῖς), often denote a young man;[1] and could the youngest Christian, who was of such an age as to hear Polycarp, in listening to his narratives, confound a simple presbyter with the Apostle John? Besides, Polycarp himself came to Rome, a short time before his martyrdom; he appealed in the presence of Anicetus to the authority of the Apostle John, in order to support the Paschal observance of Asia Minor. The misapprehension, if it had existed, would infallibly, at that time, have been cleared up. Finally, even if the testimony of Irenæus had been founded on an error, it could not have had the decisive influence on the tradition which is ascribed to it. For there exist other statements which are contemporaneous with his, and which are necessarily independent of it—such as those of Clement in Egypt and Polycrates in Asia Minor; or even anterior to his—such as those of Apollonius in Asia, Polycarp at Rome, and Justin. It is consequently to attempt an impossibility, when we try to make the whole tradition on this point proceed from Irenæus. Irenæus wrote in Gaul about 185; how could he have drawn after him all those writers or witnesses who go back in a continuous series from 190 to 150, and that in all parts of the world![2]

Scholten has acknowledged the impossibility of explaining the error in Keim's way.[3] He thinks that it arose from the Apocalypse, which was attributed to the Apostle John, and which *appeared* to have been composed in Asia.[4]

Mangold himself has replied, with perfect justice, that it is, on the contrary, only the certainty of John's residence in Asia which could have brought the churches of that region to ascribe to him the composition of the Apocalypse.[5] If Justin himself, while he resided at Ephesus, where he maintained his public dispute with Trypho, had not ascertained the certainty of John's residence in that country, could he have conceived the idea of ascribing to him so positively a book, the first chapters of which manifestly imply an Asiatic origin?

Moreover, this tradition was so widely spread abroad throughout the churches of Asia Minor, that Irenæus says that he had been acquainted

---

[1] John is called παῖς, by the Fathers, at the time when he becomes a disciple of Jesus.

[2] Against the testimony of Polycrates has been alleged the error contained in his letter to Victor, as to the *deacon* Philip, who, he says, was *one of the Twelve*. Steitz's hypothesis which regards the words, "*who was one of the seven*," as interpolated in the text of Acts xxi. 8, would overthrow the objection. But, in any case, if there is an error (which cannot be fully proved) there remains a great difference between an apostolic man, such as the evangelist Philip, who had played so great a part in the narrative of the Acts, and who, as a consequence, might be confounded with the apostle, and a man as obscure as the presbyter John.

[3] He decides in favor of Steitz, who has proved that the idea of John's residence in Asia *existed already* when Apollonius and Irenæus wrote.

[4] Keim does not altogether reject this explanation. He says, "The Apocalypse came in also as a help."

[5] Notes, in the 3d edition of Bleek's *Introduction*, p. 168.

with *several presbyters*, who, by reason of their *personal relations* with the Apostle John, testified to the authenticity of the number 666 (in opposition to the variant 616). Finally, how can we dispose of the testimony contained in the letter to Florinus? Scholten, it is true, has attempted to prove this document to be unauthentic. Hilgenfeld calls this attempt a *desperate undertaking*.[1] We will add: and a useless one, even in case it is successful; for the letter of Irenæus to Victor, which no one tries to dispute, remains and is sufficient. Besides, there is nothing weaker than the arguments by which Scholten seeks to justify this act of critical violence.[2] There is but one true reason—that which arises from the admission: If the letter were authentic, the personal relation of Polycarp to John the apostle could be no longer denied. Very well! we may say, the authenticity of this letter remains unassailable, and, by the admission of Scholten himself, the personal relation of Polycarp to John cannot be denied.

But it is claimed that, as the Apocalypse presupposes the death of all the apostles as an accomplished fact, and that in the year 68,[3] the Apostle John could not have been still living about the year 100. And what, then, are the words of the Apocalypse from which the death of all the apostles is inferred? They are the following, according to the text which is now established (xviii. 20): "Rejoice thou heaven and ye saints and apostles and prophets (οἱ ἅγιοι καὶ οἱ ἀπόστολοι καὶ οἱ προφῆται), because God has taken upon the earth the vengeance which was due to you." This passage assuredly proves that, at the date of the composition of the Apocalypse, there were in heaven a certain number of saints, apostles and prophets, who had suffered martyrdom. But these apostles are as far from being *all* the apostles as these saints are from being *all* the saints![4]

Thus the objections against the unanimously authenticated historical fact of the residence of John in Asia,[5] to which critical prejudices have given rise, vanish away.

Tradition does not merely attest John's residence in Asia in a general way; it reports, in addition, many particular incidents which may indeed

---

[1] *Einleitung*, p. 397.

[2] Thus he asks how Eusebius procured that letter; how the relation of Polycarp with John is compatible with his death in 168 (we ought to say 156); why Irenæus does not recall to Florinus his rank of presbyter of the Roman Church; and other arguments of like force.

[3] We do not here discuss this alleged date of the Apocalypse; we believe that we have elsewhere demonstrated its falsity. (*Etudes biblique*, tome ii. 5ᵉ étude.)

[4] On the objection derived from the account of the murder of John by the Jews, in the Chronicle of Georgius Hamartôlos, see page 51.

[5] In no question, perhaps, is the decisive influence of the will on the estimate of facts more distinctly observed. Hilgenfeld, Baur's disciple, and Baur himself have need of John's residence in Asia, for it is the foundation of their argument against the authenticity of our Gospel, which is derived from the Apocalypse and the Paschal controversy. What happens? They find the testimonies which attest this fact perfectly convincing. Keim, on the contrary, for whom that residence is a very troublesome fact (because the remote date which he assigns for the composition of our Gospel would be too near the time of that residence), declares these same testimonies valueless. What are we to think, after this, of the so much vaunted objectivity of historico-critical studies? It is plain:—each critical judgment is determined by a sympathy or an antipathy which warps the understanding.

have been amplified, but which cannot have been wholly invented. In any case, these anecdotes imply a well-established conviction of the reality of this residence.

There is, for example, the meeting of John with the heretic Cerinthus in a public bath, at Ephesus. "There are still living," says Irenæus (*Adv. Haer.* iii. 4), "people who have heard Polycarp relate that John, having entered a bath-house at Ephesus and having seen Cerinthus inside, suddenly withdrew, without having bathed, saying: Let us go out, lest the house fall down because Cerinthus, the enemy of the truth, is there." This well attested incident recalls the vividness of impressions in the young apostle, who refused the right of healing in the name of Jesus to the believer who did not outwardly walk with the apostles, or who desired to bring down fire from heaven on the Samaritan village which was hostile to Jesus. Or, again, there is the incident, related by Clement of Alexandria, of the young man who was entrusted by John to a bishop of Asia Minor, and whom the aged apostle succeeded in bringing back from the criminal course upon which he had entered.[1] This incident recalls the ardor of

---

[1] The following is the incident loaded with the rhetorical amplifications of Clement, as it is found in *Quis dives salvus*, c. 42:

"Listen to that which is related (and it is not a tale, but a true history) of the Apostle John: When he was on his return from Patmos to Ephesus, after the death of the tyrant, he visited the surrounding countries for the purpose of establishing bishops and constituting churches. One day, in a city near to Ephesus, after having exhorted the brethren and regulated the affairs, he noticed a spirited and beautiful young man, and, feeling himself immediately attracted to him, he said to the bishop: 'I place him on thy heart and on that of the Church.' The bishop promised the apostle to take care of him. He received him into his house, instructed him and watched over him until he could admit him to baptism. But, after he had received the seal of the Lord, the bishop relaxed in his watchfulness. The young man, set free too soon, frequented bad society, gave himself up to all sorts of excess, and ended by stopping and robbing passengers on the highway. As a mettlesome horse, when he has once left the road, dashes blindly down the precipice, so he, borne on by his natural character, plunged into the abyss of perdition. Despairing henceforth of forgiveness, he yet desired at least to do something great in this criminal life. He gathers together his companions in debauchery and forms them into a band of brigands, of whom he becomes the chief, and soon he surpasses them all in the thirst for blood and violence.

"After a certain lapse of time, John returned to this same city; having finished all that he had to do there, he asks the bishop, 'Well, restore now the pledge which the Lord and I have entrusted to thee in the presence of the Church.' The latter, dismayed, thinks that it is a matter of a sum of money which had been entrusted to him: 'Not at all,' answers John, 'but the young man, the soul of thy brother!' The old man sighs, and bursting into tears, answers: 'He is dead!'— 'Dead!' replies the Lord's disciple; 'and by what sort of death?' 'Dead to God! He became ungodly and then a robber. He occupies, with his companions, the summit of this mountain.' On hearing these words, the apostle rends his garments, smites his head and cries out: 'Oh, to what a guardian have I entrusted the soul of my brother!' He takes a horse and a guide, and goes directly to the place where the robbers are. He is seized by the sentinels, and, far from seeking to escape, he says: 'It is for this very thing that I am come; conduct me to your chief.' The latter, fully armed, awaits his arrival. But as soon as he recognizes in the one who is approaching the Apostle John, he takes to flight. John, forgetting his age, runs after him, crying: 'Why dost thou fly from me, oh my son, from me thy father? Thou in arms, I an unarmed old man? Have pity on me! My son, fear not! There is still hope of life for thee! I am willing myself to assume the burden of all before Christ. If it is necessary, I will die for thee, as Christ died for us. Stop! Believe! It is Christ who sends me!' The young man, on hearing his words, stops, with downcast eyes. Then he throws away his arms, and

In Asia Minor / 49

love in the young disciple who, at the first meeting with Jesus had given himself up wholly to Him, and whom Jesus had made *His friend*.

Clement says that the apostle returned from Patmos to Ephesus after the death of the tyrant. Tertullian (*De praescript. haer.* c. 36) relates that that exile was preceded by a journey to Rome; and he adds the following detail: "After the apostle had been plunged in boiling oil and had come out of it safe and sound, he was banished to an island." According to Irenæus it would seem that the tyrant was Domitian.[1] Some scholars claim that a reminder of this punishment undergone by John may be found in the epithet *witness* (or *martyr*) which is given him by Polycrates. But perhaps there is in that narrative simply a fiction, to which the words addressed by Jesus to the two sons of Zebedee may have given rise: "Ye shall be baptized with the baptism that I am baptized with," words the literal realization of which is sought for in vain in the life of John. As to the exile in Patmos, it might also be supposed that that story is merely an inference drawn from Apoc. i. Nevertheless, Eusebius says: "*Tradition states* (λόγος ἔχει);" and as history proves the fact of exiles of this sort under Domitian, and that precisely for the crime of the Christian faith,[2] there may well be more in it than the product of an exegetical combination. This exile and the composition of the Apocalypse are placed by Epiphanius in the reign of Claudius (from the year 41 to the year 54). This date is positively absurd, since at that epoch the churches of Asia Minor, to which the Apocalypse is addressed, had no existence. Renan has supposed[3] that the legend of the martyrdom of John might have arisen from the fact that this apostle had had to undergo a sentence at Rome at the same time as Peter and Paul. But this hypothesis is not sufficiently supported. Finally, according to Augustine, he drank a cup of poison without feeling any injury from it, and according to the anti-Montanist writer, Apollonius, (about 180), John raised to life a dead man at Ephesus (Eusebius, v. 18); two legends, which are perhaps connected with Matt. x. 8 and Mark xvi. 18. Steitz has supposed that the latter was only an alteration of the history of the young brigand rescued by John from perdition.

Clement of Alexandria thus describes the ministry of edification and organization which the apostle exercised in Asia: "He visited the churches, instituted bishops and regulated affairs." Rothe, Thiersch and Neander himself[4] attribute to the influence exerted by him the very stable constitution of the churches of Asia Minor in the second century,

---

begins to tremble and weep bitterly. And when the old man comes up, he embraces his knees and asks him for pardon with deep groanings; these tears are for him as if a second baptism; only he refuses and still conceals his right hand. The apostle becoming himself surety for him before the Saviour, with an oath promises him his pardon, falls on his knees, prays, and finally, taking him by the hand, which he withdraws, leads him back to the Church, and there strives so earnestly and powerfully, by fasting and by his discoursing, that he is at length able to restore him to the flock as an example of true regeneration."

[1] For in *Adv. Haer.* v. 33, he places the composition of the Apocalypse under Domitian.
[2] Eusebius, H. E. iii. 18.
[3] *L' Antéchrist*, p. 27 ff.
[4] *Geschichte der Pflanzung der christlichen Kirche*, Vol. II., p. 430.

of which we already find traces in the Apocalypse (*the angel* of the Church), and, a little later, in the epistles of Ignatius. History thus establishes the fact of a visit to these churches made by an eminent apostle, such as St. John was, who crowned the edifice erected by Paul. But the most beautiful monument of the visit of John in these regions is the maturity of faith and Christian life to which the churches of Asia were raised by his ministry. Polycrates, in his enthusiastic and symbolic language, represents to us St. John at this period of his life, as wearing on his forehead, like the Jewish high-priest, the plate of gold with the inscription, Holiness to the Lord. "John," he says, "who rested on the bosom of the Lord, and who became a priest wearing the plate of gold, both witness and teacher." The attempt has been made to find in this passage an absurdity, by taking it in the literal sense; but the thought of the aged bishop is clear: John, the last survivor of the apostolate, had left in the Church of Asia the impression of a pontiff whose forehead was irradiated by the splendor of the holiness of Christ. It is not impossible that, in these three titles which he gives him, Polycrates alludes to the three principal books which were attributed to him: in that of *priest* wearing the sacerdotal frontlet, to the Apocalypse; in that of *witness*, to the Gospel; in that of *teacher*, to the Epistle.

The hour for work had struck in the first place for Simon Peter; he had founded the Church in Israel and planted the standard of the new covenant on the ruins of the theocracy. Paul had followed: his work had been to liberate the Church from the restrictions of expiring Judaism and to open to the Gentiles the door of the kingdom of God. John succeeded them, he who had first come to Jesus, and whom his Master reserved for the last. He consummated the fusion of those heterogeneous elements of which the Church had been formed, and raised Christianity to the relative perfection of which it was, at that time, susceptible.

According to all the traditions,[1] John had never any other spouse than the Church of the Lord, nor any other family than that which he salutes by the name of "my children" in his epistles. Hence the epithet *virginal* (ὁ παρθένιος), by which he is sometimes designated (Epiphanius and Augustine).

We find in John Cassian an anecdote which well describes the memory which he had left behind him in Asia.[2]

---

[1] Tertullian, *De Monogamia*, c. 17; Ambrosiaster on 2 Cor. xi. 2: "All the apostles, except John and Paul, were married."

[2] We transcribe it here from Hilgenfeld's *Introduction* p. 405: "It is reported that the blessed Evangelist John one day gently caressed a partridge, and that a young man returning from the chase, on seeing him thus engaged, asked him, with astonishment, how so illustrious a man could give himself up to so trivial an occupation? What dost thou carry in thy hand? answered John. A bow, said the young man. Why is it not bent as usual? In order not to take away from it, by bending it too constantly, the elasticity which it should possess at the moment when I shall shoot the arrow. Do not be shocked then, young man, at this short relief which we give to our mind, which otherwise, losing its spring, could not aid us when necessity demands it. This incident is, in any case, a testimony to the calm and serene impression which the old age of John had left in the Church."

THE DEATH OF ST. JOHN

All the statements of the Fathers relative to the end of John's career, agree on this point, that his life was prolonged even to the limits of extreme old age. Jerome (Ep. to the Gal. vi. 10) relates that, having attained a very great age, and being too feeble to be able any longer to repair to the assemblies of the Church, he had himself carried thither by the young men, and that, having no longer strength to speak much, he contented himself with saying : " My little children, love one another." And when he was asked why he repeated always that single word, his reply was: "Because it is the Lord's commandment, and, if this is done, enough is done." According to the same Jerome, he died, weighed down by old age, sixty-eight years after the Lord's Passion—that is to say, about the year 100. Irenæus says " that he lived until the time of Trajan :" that is, until after the year 98. According to Suidas, he even attained the age of one hundred and twenty years. The letter of Polycrates proves that he was buried at Ephesus (οὗτος ἐν Ἐφέσῳ κεκοίμηται). There were shown also in that city two tombs, each of which was said to be that of the apostle, (Eusebius, *H. E.* vii. 25; Jerome, *de vir. ill.*, c. 9), and it is by means of this fact that Eusebius tries to establish the hypothesis of a second John, called *the presbyter*, a contemporary of the apostle. The idea had also been conceived, that John would be exempt from the necessity of paying the common tribute to death. The words that Jesus had addressed to him (John xxi. 22) were quoted : " If I will that he tarry till I come, what is it to thee ? " And we learn from St. Augustine that even his death did not cause this strange idea to pass away. In the treatise 124, on the Gospel of John, he relates that, according to some, the apostle was still living—peacefully sleeping in his grave, the proof of which was furnished by the fact that the earth was gently moved by his breathing. Isidore of Seville[1] relates that, when he felt that the day of his departure was come, John caused his grave to be dug; and, bidding his brethren farewell, he laid himself down in it as if in a bed—which, he says, leads some to allege that he is still alive. Some have gone even further than this, and alleged that he was taken up to heaven, as Enoch and Elijah were.[2]

A more important fact would be that which is related in a fragment of the chronicle by Georgius Hamartôlos (ninth century), published by Nolte.[3] "After Domitian, Nerva reigned during one year, who, having recalled John from the island, permitted him to dwell at Ephesus (ἀπέλυσεν οἰκεῖν ἐν Ἐφέσῳ). Being left as the sole survivor among the twelve disciples, after having composed his Gospel, he was judged worthy of martyrdom; for Papias, bishop of Hierapolis, who was a witness of the fact (αὐτόπτης τούτου γενόμενος), relates in the second book of the *Discourses of the Lord* that he was killed by the Jews (ὅτι ὑπὸ Ἰουδαίων ἀνῃρέθη), thus fulfilling, like his

---

[1] *De ortu et obitu patrum*, 71.
[2] Hilgenfeld cites as proof pseudo-Hippolytus, Ephrem of Antioch and the *Acta Johannis* in the collection of Apocryphal Acts, published by Tischendorf, 1851.
[3] *Theol. Quartalschrift*, 1862.

brother, the word which Christ had spoken respecting him: Ye shall drink the cup which I must drink. And the learned Origen, also, in his exposition of Matthew, affirms that John thus underwent martyrdom."

Keim and Holtzmann, at once regarding this event as established by evidence, and locating it without hesitation in Palestine because there is a reference to *the Jews,* have drawn from it an *unanswerable* proof as opposing John's residence in Asia Minor.[1] This proceeding proves only one thing: the credulity of science when the matter in hand is to prove what it desires. And, first of all, were there not then in Ephesus also Jews capable of killing the apostle?[2] Then, does not the fragment itself place the scene in Asia: "Nerva permitted John to return *to Ephesus.*" Still further, it is as having been a *witness* of the scene that Papias is said to have related it. Did Papias, then, live in Palestine? Finally, supposing that this account were displeasing to the critics and contradicted their system, they would certainly ask how it is possible, if the work of Papias really contained that passage, that none of the Fathers who had his book in their hands, should have been acquainted with this alleged martyrdom of John, or have made mention of it? They would tell us that the quotation which Hamartôlos makes from Origen is false, since that Father relates, indeed, the banishment to Patmos, but nothing more; etc., etc. And, in that case, their criticism would undoubtedly be well founded. All unprejudiced scholars have, in fact, admitted that the chronicler had a false Papias, or an interpolated Papias, in his hands. But in any case, if we accept this point in the account: *killed by the Jews,* it is only logical to see in the testimony given to this fact by Papias as an *eye-witness,* a sure proof of the personal relation which had existed between Papias and the apostle in Asia Minor. And yet Keim and Holtzmann find the means of seeing in it quite the opposite!

We conclude: If, as may be supposed, John was twenty to twenty-five years old, when he was called by Jesus about the year 30, he was from ninety to ninety-five about the year 100, three years after the accession of Trajan. There is nothing improbable in this. Consequently, he might have been in personal relations with the Polycarps and Papiases, born about the year 70, and with many other still younger presbyters who, as Irenæus says, *saw him face to face* while he was living in Asia until the time of Trajan.

THE CHARACTER OF JOHN

Ardor of affection, vividness of intuition,—such seem to have been, from the point of view of feeling and that of intelligence, the two dominant traits in John's nature. These two tendencies must have

---

[1] Keim, *Geschichte Jesu,* 3d ed., Vol. I., p. 42. "A testimony, newly-discovered, *which puts an end to all illusions.*"

[2] Those who have visited the tomb of Polycarp at Smyrna, and who have been received with a shower of stones from the hands of Jewish children when passing through the Jewish quarter, know something of the fanaticism of the Jews of Asia even at the present time. What was it then!

powerfully co-operated in bringing about the very close personal union which was formed between the disciple and his Master. While loving, John contemplated, and the more he contemplated, the more he loved. He was absorbed with this intuition of love and he drew from it his inner life. So he does not, like St. Paul, analyze faith and its object. "John does not discuss," says de Pressensé, "he affirms." It is enough for him to state the truth, in order that whoever loves it may receive it, as he has himself received it, by way of immediate intuition, rather than of reasoning. We may apply to the Apostle John, in the highest degree, what Renan has said of the Semite: "He proceeds by intuition, not by deduction." At one bound, the heart of John reached the radiant height on which faith has its throne. Already he feels himself in absolute possession of the victory: "He who is born of God sinneth not." The ideal appertains to him, realized in Him whom he loves and in whom he believes.

Peter was distinguished by his practical originating power, scarcely compatible with tender receptivity. Paul united to active energy and the most consummate practical ability the penetrating vigor of an unequalled dialectic. For, although a Semite, he had passed his earliest years in one of the most brilliant centres of Hellenic culture and had there appropriated the acute forms of the occidental mind. John is completely different from both. He could not have laid the foundations of the Christian work, like Peter; he could not have contended, like Paul, with dialectic subtlety against Jewish Rabbinism, and composed the Epistles to the Galatians and the Romans. But, in the closing period of the apostolic age, it was he who was charged with putting the completing work upon the development of the primitive Church, which St. Peter had founded and St. Paul had emancipated. He has bequeathed to the world three works, in which he has exalted to their sublime perfection those three supreme intuitions in the Christian life:—that of the person of Christ, in the Gospel; that of the individual believer, in the first Epistle; and that of the Church, in the Apocalypse. Under three aspects, the same theme:—the divine life realized in man, eternity filling time. One of John's own expressions sums up and binds together these three works:—*eternal life abiding in us.* That life appears in the state of full realization in the first, of progress and struggle in the two others. John, through his writings and his person, is, as it were, the earthly anticipation of the divine festival.

ANALYSIS AND CHARACTERISTICS OF THE FOURTH GOSPEL

Biedermann, in his *Christian Dogmatics* (p. 254), calls the fourth Gospel "the most wonderful of all religious books." And he adds: "From one end to the other of this work, the most profound religious truth and the most fantastic monstrosity meet not only with one another, but in one another." Neither this admiration nor this disdain can surprise us. For the Johannean conception possesses in the highest degree these two traits, one of which repels pantheism and the other attracts it: the transcendency of the divine personality and the immanence of the perfect life in the finite being.

1

ANALYSIS

WE do not intend to discuss here the different plans of the Johannean narrative proposed by the commentators.[1] We shall only indicate the course of the narrative as it becomes clear from an attentive study of the book itself.

I. The narrative is preceded by a *preamble* which, as interpreters almost unanimously acknowledge,[2] includes the first eighteen verses of the first chapter. In this introduction, the author sets forth the sublime grandeur and vital importance of the subject which he is about to treat. This subject is nothing less, indeed, than the appearance in Jesus of the perfect revealer,—the communication in His person of the life of God Himself to humanity. To reject this *word made flesh* will thus be the supreme sin and misfortune, as is shown by the example of the rebellious Jews; to receive Him will be to know and possess God, as already the experience of all believers, Jews and Gentiles, proves. The three aspects of the evangelical fact are, consequently, brought out in this prologue: 1. The *Word* as agent of the divine work; 2. The *rejection* of the Word, by the act of

---

[1] See at the beginning of the commentary.   [2] Reuss forms an exception; see at i. 1.

unbelief; 3. The *reception* given to the Word by the act of *faith.* The first of these three ideas is the dominant one in vv. 1–5; the second in vv. 6–11; the third in vv. 12–18.

But we must not regard these three aspects of the narrative which is to follow as being of equal importance. The primordial and fundamental fact in this history, is the appearance and manifestation of the Word. On this permanent foundation the two secondary facts are presented to view alternately—unbelief and faith—the progressive manifestations of which determine the phases of the narrative.

II. The *narrative* opens with the story of the three days, i. 19–42, in which the work of the Son of God began on the earth and in the heart of the evangelist, if it is true, as the greater part of the interpreters admit, that the anonymous companion of Andrew, vv. 35 ff., is no other than the author himself.

On the first day, John the Baptist proclaims before an official deputation of the Sanhedrim the startling fact of the actual presence of the Messiah in the midst of the people: "There is in the midst of you one whom you know not" (ver. 26). The day following, he points out Jesus personally to two of his disciples as the one of whom he had meant to speak; the third day, he lays such emphasis in speaking to them upon that declaration of the day before that the two disciples determine to follow Jesus. This day becomes at the same time the birthday of faith. Both recognize the Messianic dignity of Jesus. Then Andrew brings Simon, his brother, to Jesus; a slight indication, i. 42 (see the exegesis), seems to show that the other disciple likewise brings his own brother (James, the brother of John). The first nucleus of the society of believers is formed.

Three days follow (i. 43–ii. 11); the first two have as their result the adding of two new believers, Philip and Nathanael, to the three or four preceding ones; the third day, that of the marriage-feast at Cana, serves to strengthen the nascent faith of all. Thus faith, born of the testimony of the forerunner and of the contact of the first disciples with Jesus Himself, is extended and confirmed by the increasing spectacle of His glory (ii. 11).

Jesus, on His return to Galilee and still surrounded by His family, abandons Nazareth and comes to take up His abode at Capernaum, a city much more fitted to become the centre of his work (ii. 12).

But the Passover feast draws near. The moment has come for Jesus to begin the Messianic work in the theocratic capital, at Jerusalem, ii. 13–22. From this moment, He calls His disciples to accompany Him constantly (ver. 17). The purification of the temple is a significant appeal to every Israelitish conscience; the people and their rulers are invited by this bold act to co-operate, all of them together, for the spiritual elevation of the theocracy, under the direction of Jesus. If the people yielded themselves to this impulse, all was gained. Instead of this, they remain cold. This is the sign of a secret hostility. The future victory of unbelief is, as it were, decided in principle. Jesus discerns and by a profound saying reveals the gravity of this moment (ver. 19).

56 / The Fourth Gospel

Some symptoms of faith, nevertheless, show themselves in the face of this rising opposition (ii. 23–iii. 21); but a carnal alloy disturbs this good movement. It is as *a worker of miracles* that Jesus attracts attention. A remarkable example of this faith which is not *faith* is presented in the person of Nicodemus, a Pharisee, a member of the Sanhedrim. Like several of his colleagues, and many other believers in the capital, he recognizes as belonging to Jesus a divine mission, attested by His miraculous works (iii. 2). Jesus endeavors to give him a purer understanding of the person and work of the Messiah than that which he had derived from Pharisaic teaching, and dismisses him with this farewell which was full of encouragement (ver. 21): "He that doeth the truth cometh to the light." The sequel of the Gospel will show the fulfillment of this promise; comp. vii. 50 ff.; xix. 39 ff.

These few traces of faith, however, do not counterbalance the great fact of the national unbelief which becomes more marked. This tragic fact is the subject of a final testimony which John the Baptist renders to Jesus before he leaves the scene (iii. 22–36). They are both baptizing in Judea; John takes advantage of this proximity to proclaim Him yet once more as the Bridegroom of Israel. Then, in the face of the marked indifference of the people and the rulers towards the Messiah, he gives utterance to that threatening—the last echo of the thunders of Sinai, the final word of the Old Testament (ver. 36): "He that refuseth obedience to the Son shall not see life; but the wrath of God abideth on him."

On the occasion of this momentary contemporaneousness of the two ministries of Jesus and John, the evangelist makes the following remark which surprises us (ver. 24): "For John had not yet been cast into prison." Nothing in the preceding narrative could have given rise to the idea that John had already been arrested. Why this explanation without ground? Certainly the author wishes to correct a contrary opinion which he supposes to exist in the minds of his readers. The comparison with Matt. iv. 12 and Mark i. 14[1] explains for us this correction which is introduced by the way.

With this general unbelief, on the one hand, and this defective faith in some, is joyfully contrasted the spectacle of a whole city which, without the aid of any miracle, welcomes Jesus with faith, as all Israel should have received Him. And it is Samaria which gives this example of faith (iv. 1–42). It is the prelude of the future lot of the Gospel in the world.

Jesus returns to Galilee for the second time (iv. 43–54). The reception which He there meets from His fellow-countrymen is more favorable than that which He found in Judea; they feel themselves honored by the sensation which their fellow-citizen has produced in the capital. But it is always the worker of miracles, the *thaumaturgist*, whom they salute in Him. As an example of this disposition, is related the healing of the son of a prominent personage who hastens from Capernaum to Cana at the first report of the arrival of Jesus.

---

[1] "Jesus, having heard that John was delivered up, withdrew into Galilee." "After that John was delivered up, Jesus came into Galilee."

We meet here also with a remark (ver. 54) intended to combat a false notion for which the preceding narrative could not have given occasion: the confusion between the two returns to Galilee which had been previously mentioned (i. 44 and iv. 3). The author brings out the distinction between these two arrivals by means of the difference in the two miracles, both performed at Cana, which signalized them. The cause of the confusion which he labors to dispel is easily pointed out: it is found in the narrative of our Synoptics; comp. besides the passages already cited, Luke iv. 14 (together with the entire context which precedes and follows).

Up to this point we have seen the work of Jesus extend itself to all parts of the Holy Land in succession, and we have looked upon various manifestations either of true faith (in the disciples and the inhabitants of Sychar), or of faith mingled with a carnal alloy (in the believers of Jerusalem and Galilee), or of indifference or entire unbelief (at Jerusalem and in Judea), which it called forth. We think that it is in harmony with the evangelist's thought, to make here, at the end of the fourth chapter, a pause in the narrative. Till now we have had only a period of preparation, in which various moral phenomena have been announced, rather than distinctly emphasized. A change is made from chap. v. onward. The general movement, especially at Jerusalem, determines itself in the direction of unbelief; it goes on ever increasing as far as the end of chap. xii., where it reaches its provisional limit. Here the author arrests himself, to cast a glance backward, in order to search into the causes of this moral catastrophe and to point out the irremediable gravity of it. What is related, therefore, from chap. v. to the end of chap. xii., forms the third part of the book, the second part of the narrative properly so called.

III. The development of the national unbelief (chap. v.–xii.). Although Jesus had determined to leave Judea in consequence of a malevolent report made to the Pharisees respecting His work in that region (iv. 1, 3), from chap. v. onward we find Him again at Jerusalem. He desired to make a new attempt in that capital. For this purpose He takes advantage of one of the national feasts, probably that of Purim, which occurred a month before the Passover; His thought undoubtedly was to prolong His sojourn in the capital, if it were possible, until this latter feast. But the healing of the impotent man on a Sabbath caused the concealed hatred on the part of the rulers against Him to break forth; and when He justifies Himself by alleging His filial duty to labor in the work of salvation which His Father is accomplishing, their indignation knows no longer any limits; He is accused of speaking blasphemy in making Himself equal with God. Jesus defends Himself by showing that this alleged equality with God is, in fact, only the most profound dependence on God. Then, in support of this testimony which He bears to Himself, He cites not only that of John the Baptist, but especially that of the Father, first, in the miraculous works which He gives Him to perform, and then in the Scriptures—in particular, in the writings of Moses, in whose name He is accused. By this defense, to which the recently accomplished miracle gives an irresistible force, He escapes the present danger; but He sees Himself obliged immediately to leave Judea, which for a long time remains shut against Him.

In chap. vi. we find Him, therefore, again in Galilee.

The Passover is near (ver. 4). Jesus cannot go and celebrate it at Jerusalem. But God prepares for Him, as well as for His disciples, an equivalent in Galilee. He repairs with them to a desert place; the multitudes follow Him thither; He receives them compassionately and extemporizes for them a divine banquet (the multiplication of the loaves). The people are enraptured; but it is not the hunger and thirst for righteousness which excites them; it is the expectation of the earthly enjoyments and grandeurs of the Messianic Kingdom, which seems to them close at hand; they desire *to make Him a King* (vi. 15). Jesus measures the danger with which this carnal enthusiasm threatens His work. And as He knows how accessible His apostles still are to this spirit of error, and perhaps discerns in some one among them the author of this movement, He makes haste to isolate them from the people by causing them to recross the sea. He Himself remains alone with the multitudes, in order to quiet them; then, He commends His work anew to the Father in solitude, and thereafter, walking on the waters, He rejoins His disciples who are struggling against the wind; and on the next day, in the synagogue of Capernaum, where the people come to rejoin Him, He speaks in such a way as to cool their false zeal. He gives them to understand that He is by no means such a Messiah as the one whom they are seeking, that He is "the heavenly bread" designed to nourish souls that are spiritually hungry. He pushes so far His opposition to the common ideas that almost the whole body of His disciples who habitually follow Him break with Him. Not content with this purification, Jesus even wishes to make it penetrate further, even into the circle of the Twelve, to whom with boldness he gives the liberty of withdrawing also. We can understand that it was especially to Judas, the representative of the carnal Messianic idea among the Twelve, that He thus opened the door; the evangelist himself remarks this as he closes this incomparable narrative (vv. 70-71).

A whole summer passes, respecting which we learn nothing. The feast of Tabernacles draws near (chap. vii.). Jesus has an interview with His brethren; they are astonished that, having already failed to go and celebrate at Jerusalem the two feasts of the Passover and Pentecost, He does not seem disposed to repair to this one, in order to manifest Himself also to His adherents in Judea. He replies to them that the moment for His public manifestation as the Messiah has not yet come. This moment, indeed—He knows it well—will infallibly be that of His death; now His work is not yet finished. He repairs to Jerusalem, however, but secretly, as it were, and only towards the middle of the feast; He thus takes the authorities by surprise, and gives them no time to take measures against Him. On the last and great day of the feast, He compares Himself to the rock in the wilderness whose waters of old quenched the thirst of the fainting people. Lively discussions in regard to Him arise among His hearers. At every word which He utters He is interrupted by His adversaries, and while a part of His hearers recognize in Him a prophet, and some even declare Him to be the Christ, He is obliged to reproach others with cherishing towards Him feelings inspired by the one who is a liar and murderer from the beginning. All the discourses which fill chaps. vii. and viii. are summed up, as He Himself says, in these two words: *judgment* and *testimony;* judgment on the moral state of the people, testimony given to His own Messianic and divine character. A first judicial measure is taken against Him. Officers are sent out by the authorities to lay hold of Him in the temple where He is speaking (vii. 32). But the power of His word on their consciences and the power of the public sentiment, still favorable to Jesus, arrest them; they return without having laid hands upon Him (ver. 45). The rulers then take a new step. They declare every one excommunicated from the synagogue who shall recognize Jesus as the Messiah (comp. ix. 22); and in consequence of one of His sayings which seems to them blasphemous ("Before Abraham was, I am," viii. 58), they make a first attempt to stone Him.

Chapter ix. also belongs to this sojourn at the feast of Tabernacles. A new Sabbath miracle, the healing of the man who was born blind, exasperates the rulers. In the name of the legal ordinance, this miracle *should* not be, *cannot* have been. The blind man reasons in an inverse way: the miracle *is;* therefore, the Sabbath has not been violated. This unsettled conflict ends with the violent expulsion of the blind man. Jesus reveals to this man His divine character, and, after having cured him of his double blindness, receives him into the number of His own. Thereupon, in chap. x., He describes Himself as the divine Shepherd who brings His own sheep from the ancient theocratic sheepfold, in order to lead them to life, while the mass of the flock is led to the slaughter by those who have constituted themselves their directors and masters. Finally, he announces the incorporation in His flock of new sheep brought from other sheepfolds (ver. 16). On hearing this discourse, there is a still more marked division among the people, between His adversaries and His partisans (vv. 19–21).

Three months elapse; the evangelist does not speak of the use made of them. It cannot be supposed that, in the condition in which matters were, Jesus passed all this time at Jerusalem or even in Judea—He who, before the scenes of this character, had been able to reappear at Jerusalem only unawares. He undoubtedly returned into Galilee. At the end of December, Jesus goes to the feast of the Dedication (x. 22–39). The Jews surround Him, resolved to wrest from Him the grand declaration: "Tell us whether thou art the Christ?" Jesus, as always, affirms the thing while avoiding the word. ˙He emphasizes His perfect unity with the Father, which necessarily implies His Messianic character. The adversaries already take up stones to stone Him. Jesus makes them fall from their hands by this question (ver. 32): "I have shown you from my Father many good works; for which one do you stone me?" He well knew that it was His two previous miracles (chaps. v. and ix.) which had caused their hatred to overflow. Then He appeals, against the accusation of blasphemy, to the divine character attributed by the Old Testament itself to the theocratic authorities—a fact which should have prepared Israel to believe in the divine character of the supreme messenger, the Messiah.

From Jerusalem Jesus betakes Himself to Perea, into the regions where John had baptized, into that region which had been the cradle of His work (x. 40–42).

It is there (chap. xi.) that the appeal of the sisters of Lazarus reaches Him. We are surprised to see (ver. 1) Bethany designated as *the village of Mary and Martha*. As these two sisters have not yet been named, how can the mention of them serve to give the reader information respecting the village. It must, indeed, be admitted, here also, that the author makes an allusion to other narratives which he supposes to be known to the readers (comp. Luke x. 38–42; then also John xi. 2 with Matt. xxvi. 6–13 and Mark xiv. 3–9). The miracle of the raising of Lazarus completes that for which the two preceding ones had prepared the way. It brings to maturity the plans of Jesus' enemies. At the proposal of Caiaphas (xi. 49, 50), the Sanhedrim decide to rid themselves of the impostor. And while Jesus withdraws to the north, to the neighborhood of an isolated hamlet named Ephraim, the rulers determine at length to take a first public measure against His person. Every Israelite is called upon to tell the place where Jesus is to be found (ver. 57). At that time, perhaps, there sprang up in the heart of Judas the first thought of treachery. Shortly afterwards, six days before the Passover, Jesus sets out for Jerusalem; He stops at Bethany, and there, at a banquet which is offered Him by His friends, He detects the first manifestation of the murderous hatred of Judas (xii. 4, 5).

On the next day the royal entrance of Jesus into His capital takes place; this event realizes the wish which His brethren expressed six months before. His miracles—the raising of Lazarus, in particular—have excited to the highest degree the enthusiasm of the pilgrims who came to the feast; the rulers are paralyzed, as it were, and do nothing. Thus is accomplished the great Messianic act by which, once at least, Jesus says publicly to Israel: "Behold thy King." But, at the same time, the rage of His adversaries is pushed thereby to extremity (xii. 9–19). The resurrection of Lazarus and the public homage which resulted from it—these, therefore, according to the narrative of John, were the two immediate causes of the catastrophe which had long since been preparing.

Jesus was not ignorant of what was passing; He was not indifferent to it. The occasion was afforded Him of giving utterance in the temple itself to the impressions of His heart, in these days when He saw the end approaching. Certain Greeks asked that they might speak with Him (ver. 20). Like an instrument whose stretched strings become sonorous at the first contact with the bow, His soul responded to that appeal. The Greeks? Yes, certainly; the Gentile world is about to open itself; the power of Satan is about to crumble in this vast domain of the Gentile world and to give place to that of the divine monarch. But words cannot suffice for such a work; death is necessary. It is from the height of the instrument of punishment that Jesus will draw all men to Himself. And what anguish does not that bloody prospect cause Him! His soul is moved, even *troubled* by it. John alone has preserved for us the story of that exceptional hour. It was the close of His public ministry. After having yet once more invited the Jews to believe in the light which was about to be veiled from them, " He departed," he says, "and did hide Himself from them" (ver. 36).

Having arrived at this point, the evangelist casts a glance backward on the way which has been gone over,—on the public ministry of Jesus in Israel. He asks himself how the unbelief of the Jews has been able to resist so many and so great miracles (ver. 37 ff.), so many and so powerful teachings (ver. 44 ff.).

This general blindness, however, had not been universal (ver. 42). The divine light had penetrated into many hearts, even among the members of the Sanhedrim; the fear of the Pharisees alone prevented them from confessing their faith. In fact, even in this part of the Gospel which is devoted to tracing the progress of the national unbelief, the element of faith is not entirely wanting. Throughout the whole narrative, we can follow the steps of a development of faith parallel with, although subordinate to that of unbelief: thus, in the confession of Peter, chap. vi.; in the selection which is effected at Jerusalem (chaps. vii. viii.); in the case of the man born blind, in chap. ix., and in that of those sheep, in chap. x., who, at the shepherd's call, follow Him out of the theocratic sheepfold; finally, in the case of the numerous adherents in Bethany and in that of the multitudes who accompany Jesus on Palm Sunday. These are the hearts prepared to form the Church of Pentecost.

IV. As since chap. v., we have seen the tide of unbelief prevailing, so, from chap. xiii., it is faith in the person of the disciples which becomes the preponderant element of the narrative; and that even till this faith has reached its relative perfection and Jesus is able to give thanks for the finished work (chap. xvii.). This development is effected by manifestations, no longer of power, but of love and light. There is, first, the washing of the feet, intended to make them understand that true glory is found in serving, and to uproot from their hearts the false Messianic ideal which still hid from them, in this regard, the divine thought realized in Jesus. Then there are the discourses in which He explains to them in words that which He has just revealed to them in act. First of all, He quiets their minds with regard to the approaching separation (xiii. 31–xiv. 31); it will be followed by a near reunion, His spiritual return. For death will be for Him the way to glory, and if they cannot follow Him now into the perfect communion of the Father, they will be able to do so later in the way which He is about to open to them. In the meantime, by the strength which He will communicate to them, they will accomplish in His stead the work for which He has only been able to prepare. If they love Him, let them rejoice, therefore, in His departure, instead of sorrowing because of it, and let them, as a last farewell, receive His peace. After this,

Jesus transports them in thought to the moment when, by the bond of the Holy Spirit, they will live in Him and He in them, in the same manner as the branch lives when united to the vine (xv. 1–xvi. 15); He points out to them the single duty of this new condition, *to abide in Him* through obedience to His will; then He describes to them, without any reserve, the relation of hostility which will be formed between them and the world; but He reveals to them also the force which will contend by means of them, and by means of which they will conquer; the Spirit, *who shall glorify Him in them.* Finally, in closing (xvi. 16–33), He returns to that impending separation which so sorrowfully preoccupies their thoughts. He vividly portrays to them its brevity, as well as its grand results. And, summing up the object of their faith in these four propositions which answer to one another (ver. 28): " I came forth from the Father, and am come into the world; and now I leave the world, and go to the Father," He illuminates their minds with such a vivid clearness that the promised day, that of the Holy Spirit, seems to them to have arrived, and they cry out: "We believe that thou camest forth from God!" Jesus answers them: " *At last ye believe !* " And to this profession of their faith he affixes, in chap. xvii., the seal of the act of thanksgiving and prayer. He asks of the Father for Himself the reinstatement in His condition of glory which is indispensable to Him, in order that He may give eternal life to those who believe in Him on the earth. He gives thanks for the gaining of these eleven men; He prays for their preservation and their perfect consecration to the work which He entrusts to them. He intercedes, finally, for the whole world, to which their word is to bring salvation. This prayer of chap. xvii. recapitulates, in the most solemn form, the work accomplished in His disciples chaps. xiii.–xvii., after the same manner as the retrospective view at the end of chap. xii. summed up the development of unbelief in the nation and among its rulers (chaps. v.–xii.). Nevertheless, as the element of faith was not wanting in the part describing unbelief, so also the fact of unbelief is found in this picture of the development of faith. It is represented in the inmost circle of the disciples by the traitor, whose presence is several times recalled to mind in the course of chap. xiii. The departure of Judas (ver. 30), marks the moment when that impure element finally gives place to the spirit of Jesus.

The history of Jesus contains something more and other than the revelation of the character of God and the impressions of faith and unbelief to which that revelation gives rise among men. The essential fact in this history is the work of reconciliation which is accomplished, and which prepares the way for the communication of the life of God Himself to believers. Here is the reason why the history of Jesus includes, besides the picture of His ministry of teaching, the account of His death and resurrection.[1] It is by means of these last facts that faith will enter into

---

[1] It is easy to observe the embarrassment of those who, like Reuss, Hilgenfeld, etc., make of the idea of the *revelation of the Logos* the substance of the narrative of our Gospel. They cannot account for the two following parts.

complete possession of its object and will reach its full maturity, as it is by means of them, also, that the refusal will be consummated which constitutes final unbelief.

V. The whole story of the Passion, in chaps. xviii. and xix., is related from the point of view of Jewish unbelief, which is consummated in putting the Messiah to death. This part is connected with the previous one, in which the development of this unbelief was related (v.–xii.). At the very outset, we remark the complete omission of the scene in Gethsemane; but, after the numerous allusions to the Synoptical narratives which we have already established, these words: "Having said this, He went away with His disciples beyond the brook Cedron *into a garden, into which He entered with His disciples,*" can only be regarded as a reference to the account of that struggle which was known from the earlier writings. Then follows the deliverance of the disciples by reason of the powerful impression of the words: "I am he." On the occasion of the striking of the high priest's servant with the sword, Peter and Malchus are designated by name in this Gospel only. The story of the trial of Jesus mentions only the preliminary examination which took place in the house of Annas. But by expressly designating this appearance for trial as the *first* (ver. 13: "to Annas *first*"), even though a second one is not related, and by indicating the sending of Jesus to Caiaphas (ver. 24: "Annas sent Jesus bound to Caiaphas, the high priest"), the evangelist gives us to understand, as clearly as possible, that he supposes other accounts to be known, which complete what is omitted in his own. The three denials of St. Peter are not related in succession; but they are, as must in reality have been the fact, interwoven with the phases of the trial of Jesus (xviii. 15–27). The description of the appearance before Pilate (xviii. 28–xix. 16) reveals with an admirable precision the tactics of the Jews, at once audacious and crafty. The instinct of truth and the respect for the mysterious person of Jesus which restrain Pilate until he finally yields to the requirements of personal interest, the cunning of the Jews, who pass without shame from one charge to another, and end by wresting from Pilate through fear what they despair of obtaining from him in the name of justice, but who only obtain this shameful victory by renouncing their dearest hope and binding themselves as vassals to the heathen empire (xix. 15: "We have no king but Cæsar"),—all this is described with an incomparable knowledge of the situation. This is, perhaps, the master-piece of the Johannean narrative.

One feature of the story should be particularly noticed. In xviii. 28, the Jews are unwilling to enter into Pilate's palace—" that they might not be defiled, but might eat the Passover." The Paschal feast was therefore not yet celebrated on the day of Christ's death, according to our Gospel; it was to be celebrated only in the evening. It was, therefore, the 14th of Nisan, the day of *the preparation* of the Passover. This circumstance is so purposely made prominent in several other passages (xiii. 1, 29; xix. 31, etc.), that we are led to think of other narratives which placed the death of Christ only on the *following* day, the 15th of Nisan, and after the Paschal supper. Now this is what the Synoptical account seems to do. A new proof of the constant relation existing between the two narratives.

In the picture of the crucifixion, the disciple whom Jesus loved—that mysterious personage who had already played a quite peculiar part in the last evening—is found, as the only one among the disciples, near the cross. To him Jesus entrusts His mother. It is he, also, who sees the water and the blood flow from the pierced side of Jesus, and who verifies in this single fact the simultaneous accomplishment of two prophecies.

VI. The story of the resurrection (chap. xx.) includes the description of three appearances which took place in Judea: that which was granted to Mary Magdalene, near the sepulchre; that which, in the evening, took place in the presence of all the disciples, and in which Jesus renewed to the apostles their commission, and imparted to them the first-fruits of Pentecost; and, finally, that which occurred eight days afterwards, and in which the obstinate unbelief of Thomas was overcome. From this we see that, just as the element of faith was not entirely wanting in the scenes of the Passion (it is sufficient to recall to mind the parts played by the disciple whom Jesus loved, the women, Joseph of Arimathea, and Nicodemus), so the element of unbelief is no more wanting in the portion intended to describe the final triumph of faith. The exclamation of adoration uttered by Thomas, " My Lord and my God !" in which the faith of the most incredulous of the disciples suddenly takes the boldest flight and fully reaches the height of its divine object, as it is described in the prologue, forms the conclusion of the narrative. Thus it is that the end connects itself with the starting-point.

These three aspects of the evangelical fact already indicated in the prologue: the Son of God, Jewish unbelief, and the faith of the Church are, accordingly, now fully treated; the subject is exhausted.

VII. The last two verses of chap. xx. are the close of the book.[1] The author declares therein the aim which he set before himself. It is not a complete history that he has desired to relate; it is, as we have ourselves proved, the selection of a certain number of points designed to produce in the readers faith in the Messiahship and divinity of Jesus—a faith in which they will find life as he himself has found it.

VIII. Chap. xxi., in consequence of what precedes, is a supplement. Is it from the hand of the author? The affirmative and negative are still maintained. It is a matter of very little importance; for, even if it is from another writer, the latter has only written out a story which frequently came from the author's lips; so similar are the style and manner of narrating to those of the book itself. This appendix must have been added very early, and before the publication of the work, since it is not wanting in any manuscript or in any version. It completes the story of the appearances of Jesus by giving an account of one which took place in

---

[1] Hilgenfeld believes himself able to maintain, with some others, that the narrative continues even to the end of chap. xxi. But this is to come into collision with the evidence. Renan says, without hesitation, " With all critics, I make the first redaction of the fourth Gospel end at chap xx." (p. 534).

Galilee. Jesus gives to the disciples, by a symbolic act which connects itself with their former worldly occupation, a pledge of the magnificent success which they will obtain in their future apostleship (xxi. 1–14). Then He reinstates Peter in this office, and announces to him his future martyrdom by which he will completely efface the stain of his denial. The author takes advantage of this opportunity to restore the exact tenor of a saying which Jesus had uttered on that occasion with regard to the disciple whom He loved; He had been erroneously reported as saying that this disciple would not die.

In this appendix we easily remark a want of connection which is foreign to the rest of the Gospel. It is a desultory narrative, and one whose unity can only be established in a somewhat artificial way. It must be considered as an amalgam of various reminiscences, which came on different occasions from the lips of the narrator.[1]

Verses 24 and 25, which close this appendix, are unquestionably from another hand than that of the author of the Gospel. "*We know*," is said in the name of several. The singular, no doubt, returns in ver. 25: "*I suppose*." But he who speaks thus in his own name is none other than that member of the preceding collective body (ver. 24) who holds the pen for his colleagues. They bear witness, all of them at once (ver. 24), by means of his pen (ver. 25), that the disciple especially loved by Jesus is the one " who testifies these things and wrote these things." From the contrast between the present *testifies* and the past *wrote*, it naturally follows that the writers of these lines added them during the lifetime of the author and when his work was already finished.

The entire book, thus, is composed of *eight* parts, of which *five* form the body of the story, or the narrative properly so called; *one* forms the preamble: *one* the conclusion: the *eighth* is a supplement.

The permanent basis of the history which is related is the revelation of Jesus as the Messiah and Son of God (xx. 30, 31). On this basis there appear, at first in a confused way (i. 19–iv.), then more and more plainly, those two decisive moral facts: unbelief and faith; the unbelief which rejects the object of faith in proportion as it reveals itself more completely (v.–xii.), and the faith which apprehends it with an increasing eagerness (xiii.–xvii.); the unbelief which even goes so far as to try to destroy it (xviii.–xix.), and the faith which ends by possessing it in its glorious sublimity (xx.).

This exposition would, of itself, be sufficient to set aside every hypothesis which is opposed to the unity of the work. The fourth Gospel is indeed, according to the expression of Strauss, "the robe without seam for which lots may be cast, but which cannot be divided." It is the admirably graduated and shaded picture of the development of unbelief and of faith in the Word made flesh.

---

[1] "This conclusion resembles," says M. Renan, "a succession of private notes, which have a meaning only for him who wrote them or for the initiated " (p. 535). We do not subscribe to the last words.

2

CHARACTERISTICS OF THE FOURTH GOSPEL

BEFORE approaching the questions which relate to the way in which our Gospel was composed, it is fitting that we should give an exact account not only of the contents of the work, but also of its nature, of its tendency, and of its literary characteristics. This is the study to which we are now to devote ourselves. It is the more indispensable, since in modern times very different ideas on these various subjects have been brought out from those which were previously current.

Thus Reuss maintained even in his earliest works, and still maintains, that the tendency of the fourth Gospel is not historical, but that it is purely theological. The author has inscribed a speculative idea at the beginning of his book; we see from his own narrative, and from comparing it with that of the Synoptics, that he is not afraid to modify the facts in the service of this idea, and he develops it most prominently in the discourses which he puts into the mouth of Jesus, and which form the largest part of his book.

Baur shares in this view. The fourth Gospel is, according to him, an entirely speculative work. The few truly historical elements which may be found in it are facts borrowed from the Synoptical tradition. Keim also, in his *Life of Jesus*, denies all historical value to this work.

Another point which the two leaders of the schools of Strasburg and of Tübingen have sought to demonstrate, is the anti-Judaic tendency of our Gospel. It was generally believed that this work connected itself with the revelations of the Old Testament and with all the theocratic dispensations by a respectful and sympathetic faith. These two critics have endeavored to prove that, to the author's view, the bond between Judaism and the Gospel has no existence, and that there reigns in his book, on the contrary, a sentiment hostile to the entire Israelitish economy.

We shall seek, therefore, first of all to elucidate the following three points, so far as it shall be possible to do this without encroaching upon the questions of the authenticity and aim of the Gospel, which are reserved for the Third Book.

1. The distinctive features of the Johannean narrative and its relations to that of the Synoptic Gospels.
2. The attitude assumed by this work with reference to the Old Testament.
3. The forms of idea and style which are peculiar to it.

A. THE NARRATIVE OF THE FOURTH GOSPEL

Our examination here must bear upon three points: the general idea of the book; the facts; the discourses.

1. The ruling idea of the work

At the beginning of this narrative is inscribed a general idea, the notion of the *incarnate* Logos, which may indeed be called the ruling idea of the entire narrative. This feature, it is asserted, profoundly distinguishes our Gospel from the Synoptical writings. The latter are only collections of isolated facts and detached sayings accidentally united together, and their historical character is obvious; while this speculative notion, placed here at the beginning of the evangelical narrative, immediately betrays a dogmatic tendency and impresses on the whole book the stamp of a *theological treatise*. Reuss even goes so far as to claim that the term *gospel* cannot be applied to this work in the sense in which it is given to the other three, as designating a history of the ministry of Jesus. It is necessary to go back to the wholly spiritual sense which this term had at the beginning, when, in the New Testament, it denoted the message of salvation in itself considered, without the least notion of an historical setting forth of it.

This general estimate seems to me to rest upon two errors. A ruling idea, formulated in the prologue, certainly presides over the narrative which follows, and sums it up. But is this feature peculiar to the fourth Gospel? It is found again in the first Gospel, which is opened by these words, containing, as we have seen, an entire programme: "Genealogy of Jesus Christ, the son of David, the son of Abraham." It is unnecessary to show again how this notion of the Messianic royalty of Jesus and of the fulfillment by Him of all the promises made to Israel in David, and to the world in Abraham, penetrates into the smallest details of Matthew's narrative. The same is true of the Gospel of Mark, which opens with these words: "The beginning of the Gospel of Jesus Christ, the Son of God." This is the formula which sums up the whole narrative that is to follow: Jesus, realizing, in His life as Messiah-King, the wisdom and power of a being who has come from God. St. Luke has not himself expressed the idea which governs his book; but it is nevertheless easy to discover it: the Son of man, the perfect representative of human nature, bringing gratuitously the salvation of God to all that bears the name of man. If, then, the fourth Gospel also has its primal idea—that of the Son of God having appeared in the form of the Son of man—this feature by no means constitutes, as is claimed, a "capital difference" between this work and the other three. The central idea is different from those of these latter three: that is all. Each of them has its own idea, because no one of the four writers has told his story solely for the purpose of telling it. They tell their story, each one of them, in order to set in relief one aspect of the person of Jesus, which they present especially to the faith of their readers. They all propose, not to satisfy curiosity, but to save.

The second error connected with the estimate of Reuss is this: a general idea, placed at the head of a narrative, cannot fail to impair its historical character. This is not so. Would the description of the life and conquests of Alexander the Great become a didactic treatise, because the author gave as an introduction to the history that great idea which his hero was called to realize: the fusion of the East and the West, long separated and hostile, into one civilized world? Or would the author of a life of Napoleon compromise the fidelity of his narrative because he placed it under the control of this idea: the restoration of France after the revolutionary tempest? Or must one, in order to relate in conformity with the actual truth the life of Luther, give up bestowing upon him the title: The reformer of the Church? Every great historic fact is the expression, the realization of an idea; and this idea constitutes the essence, the greatness, even the truth of the fact. To make this prominent even at the beginning is not to render the fact suspicious; it is to render it intelligible. The presence of an idea at the beginning of a narrative does not, then, exclude its historical character. The only question is to determine whether this idea is the true one, whether it is evolved of itself from the fact, or whether it is imported into it. Hase expresses himself thus on this point: "The nerve of the objection would be cut if Jesus was really, in the metaphysical sense, that which our Gospel teaches (the Word made flesh). I dare not affirm it." And borrowing the avowal which Goethe puts in the mouth of Faust: "I know the message indeed," he says, "but I lack the faith." Well and good! This lack of faith is an individual matter. But the writer confesses that the beaming of an idea across a fact does not resolve it into a myth. A fact without an idea is a body without a soul. A notion like this has no place except in the materialist system.

The prologue of the Johannean gospel has, therefore, in itself nothing incompatible with the strictly historical character of the narrative which is to follow.

No, not necessarily, it is said; but is there not reason to fear that the idea, when once it has taken possession of the author's mind, will influence more or less profoundly the way in which he considers and sets forth the facts? Might it not even happen that, in all good faith, he should invent the situations and events which seemed to him most fitted to place in a clear light the idea which he has formed? Let us see whether it is thus in the case with which we are concerned.

2. *The facts*

Baur claimed that excepting the small number of materials borrowed from the Synoptics, the facts related here are only creations of the genius of the author, who sought to set forth in this dramatic form the internal dialectics of the idea of the Logos. Reuss, without going quite so far, regards the narrative sometimes as freely modified on behalf of the idea, sometimes as wholly created for its use. Nicodemus, the Samaritan woman, the Greeks of chap. xii., are only fictitious personages, placed on the scene by the author in order to afford the opportunity of putting into the mouth of Jesus the conception of His person which he has formed for himself. The history related in this Gospel has so little reality, that even from the beginning (chap. v.) it seems to have reached its end: the Jews wish already to put Jesus to death (v. 16)! The visits to Jerusalem, which form the salient points of the narration, are fictitious scenes, the theatre of which has been chosen with the design of contrasting the light (Jesus) with the darkness (the Jewish authorities), and of furnishing to

Christ the opportunity of testifying of the divinity of His person. For this same reason, the miracles of the fourth Gospel are made more wonderful than those of the Synoptics; and, besides, they are presented, no longer as works of compassion, but as signs of the divinity of Jesus. The author thus interweaves them into his theory of the Logos. The account of the Last Supper is omitted, because, from his idealistic point of view, the author is satisfied with having set forth the spiritual essence of it in chap. vi. The scene in Gethsemane is left out, because it would present the Logos in a state little worthy of His divine greatness. No healing of a demoniac is related, because the unclean spirits are too ignoble adversaries for such a being. No mention is made of the miraculous birth, because that prodigy is thrown into the shade by the greater miracle of the incarnation, etc., etc. It is thus that the study of the narrative, both in itself and in a comparison of it with that of the Synoptics, reveals at every step the alterations due to the influence of the idea upon the history.

In order to study this grave question with the scrupulous fidelity which it demands, we must begin by verifying the essential characteristics of the narrative which we have to estimate.

The first is certainly the potent *unity* of the story. The narration begins and ends precisely at the point determined by the plan of the work. The author, as we have seen, proposes to relate the gradual and simultaneous development of unbelief and faith under the sway of the increasing manifestations of the Christ as the Son of God. His narrative has, thus, as its starting-point the day on which, for the first time, Jesus was revealed as such by the testimony which John the Baptist, without naming Him as yet, bore to Him in presence of the deputation of the Sanhedrim—a day which was, as a consequence, also that of the first glimmering of faith in Jesus in the hearts of His earliest disciples. On the other hand, the end of the narrative places us at the moment when faith in Christ, fully revealed by His resurrection, attained its height, and, if we may so speak, its normal level in the profession: "My Lord and my God," coming from the lips of the least credulous of the disciples.

Between these two extreme points the history moves in a connected and progressive way, both on the side of Jesus, who, on each occasion and especially at each feast, adds to the revelation of Himself a new feature in harmony with a newly given situation (iii. 14: the brazen serpent; iv. 10: the living water; v. 19: the Son working with the Father; vi. 35: the bread of life; vii. 37: the rock pouring forth living water; viii. 56: the one in whom Abraham rejoices; ix. 5: the light of the world; x. 11: the good shepherd; xi. 25: the resurrection and the life; xii. 15: the humble king of Israel; xiii. 14: the Lord who serves; xiv. 6: the way, the truth and the life; xv. 1: the true vine; xvi. 28: He who has come from the Father and returns to the Father; xvii. 3: Jesus the Christ; xviii. 37: the king in the kingdom of truth; xix. 36: the true Paschal lamb; xx. 28: our Lord and God),—and with respect to faith, which increases by appropriating to itself each one of these testimonies in acts and words, and of which the progress is frequently marked by forms of expression such as this: "And his disciples believed on him" (ii. 11; comp. vi. 68, 69; xi. 15; xvi. 30, 31; xvii. 8; xx. 8, 29),—and with reference to Jewish unbelief, the hostile measures of which succeed each other with an increase of violence all whose stages we can verify (ii. 18, 19: refusal to participate in the Messianic reformation; v. 16–18: first explosion of hatred and desire for murder; vii. 32: first active measure, in the order given to the officers to arrest Jesus; viii. 59: a first attempt to stone Him; ix. 22: excommunication of every one who acknowledges Him as the Messiah; x. 31: new and more decided attempt to stone Him; xi. 53: meeting of the Sanhedrim in which the death of Jesus is in principle determined upon, so that there remains nothing further except to discover the ways of carrying it into execution; xi. 57: first official measure in this direction through the public summoning of witnesses against Jesus; xiii. 27: contract of the rulers with the traitor; xviii. 3: request for a detachment of Roman soldiers to effect the arrest; xviii. 13 and 24: sittings for examination in the house of Annas and for judgment in that of Caiaphas; xviii. 28: demand for execution addressed to Pilate; xix. 12: last means of intimidation employed to obtain his consent; xix. 16: the execution). —Such is the history which the fourth Gospel traces out. And yet Reuss can seriously put this question: "Is there anywhere the least trace of a progress, a development, in any direction?" (p. 23); and Stap can affirm that "the denouement might be found on the first page as well as on the last;" and, finally, Sabatier can speak of "shufflings about on one spot," which mark the course of our Gospel! Is not the Synoptic narrative, rather, the one against which this charge might be made? For in that narrative Jesus passes suddenly from Galilee to Jerusalem, and dies in that city after only five days of conflict. Is this a sufficient preparation for such a catastrophe?—Reuss takes offence at the fact that, in v. 16, it is said that they already seek to put Him to death. But he may read precisely the same thing in the Gospel of Mark—the one which, in his view, is the most primitive type of the narration—iii. 6: "Then the Pharisees took counsel with the Herodians against him *to put him to death.*" This is said after one of the first miracles, and at the beginning of the Galilean ministry.

The strong unity of the Johannean narrative appears, finally, in the precise and complete data by means of which the course of Jesus' ministry is, in some sort, marked out, so that, by means of this work, and this work only, can we fix its principal dates and make anew the outline of it. Here are the data which it furnishes us, ii. 12, 13: a first Passover, at which Jesus inaugurates His public work; it is followed by a working for several months in Judea, and finally by a return to Galilee by way of Samaria, about the month of December in that same year; chap. v.: a feast at Jerusalem, doubtless that of Purim, in the following spring and a month before the Passover; vi. 4: the second Passover, which Jesus cannot go to Jerusalem to celebrate, so great is the hostility towards Him, and which He passes in Galilee; vii. 2: the feast of Tabernacles, in the autumn of this second year, to which Jesus is only able to go *incognito* and, as it were, by surprise; x. 22: the feast of Dedication, two months later, in December, when, again, He makes but one appearance in Jerusalem; finally, xii. 1 : the third Passover, when He dies. Here is a series of dates outlined by a steady hand, with natural intervals, which gives us sufficient information as to the course and duration of our Lord's ministry, and which affords us the means of tracing out a rational delineation of it. The only story which does not enter organically into this so strongly united whole is that of the adulterous woman, which logically appertains neither to the development of unbelief, nor to that of faith, and which would thus be suspicious to a delicate ear, even if the external testimonies did not as positively exclude it as they do.

But, at the same time, this narrative, so thoroughly one, so consecutive, so graduated, forming such a beautiful whole, is found to be astonishingly *fragmentary*. It begins in the middle of John the Baptist's ministry, without having described the first part of it. It stops with the scene concerning Thomas, without any mention being made of the subsequent appearances in Galilee, or of the ascension itself.—In vi. 70: Jesus says to the apostles: "Have not I chosen you, the Twelve?" And yet there has not been up to this time a single word said of the foundation of the apostolate; the reader is acquainted with only five of the disciples, from the first chapter onward.—At ver. 71, Judas Iscariot is named as a perfectly well-known personage; and yet it is the first time that he is introduced on the scene.—xiv. 22; the presence of another Judas among the Twelve is supposed to be known; and yet it has not been mentioned.—xi. 1, Bethany is called *the village of Mary and Martha, her sister;* and yet the names of these two women have not as yet been given.—xi. 2, Mary is designated as she "who had anointed the Lord with ointment;" and yet this incident, supposed to be known to the reader, is not related until afterwards.—ii. 23, those are spoken of who believed at Jerusalem *on seeing the miracles which Jesus did;* iii. 2, Nicodemus makes allusion to these miracles, and iv. 45, it is said that the Galileans received Jesus on His return *because they had seen the miracles* which He did at Jerusalem; and yet not one of these miracles is related.

We have seen that from the first Passover to Jesus' return to Galilee, chap. iv., seven or eight months elapsed (from April to December). Now, of all that occurred during this time—in this long sojourn in Judea—with the exception of the single conversation with Nicodemus, we know only one fact: the continuance of the baptism of John the Baptist by the side of that of Jesus and the last testimony given by the forerunner (iii. 22 ff.). —From the return of Jesus to Galilee, chap. iv., to His new journey to Jerusalem, chap. v. (feast of Purim), three months elapsed, which the author sums up in this simple expression: *after these things,* v. 1.—Between this journey to Jerusalem and the second Passover. chap. vi., there is a whole month of which we know nothing except this single statement, vi. 2: "And a great multitude followed him, because they saw the miracles which he did on the sick." Of these numerous miracles which attracted

72 / The Fourth Gospel

the crowds not one is related!—Between this Passover, chap. vi., and the feast of Tabernacles, chap. vii.,—that is to say, during the six months from April to October,—many things certainly occurred; we have only these two lines thereupon, vii. 1: "And after that Jesus walked in Galilee; for He would not walk in Judea."—Between this feast and x. 22 (December), two months, and then, from that time to the Passover, three months, of which nothing (except the resurrection of Lazarus) is reported.—Thus, of two years and a half, we have twenty months touching which there is complete silence![1]

In xviii. 13, it is said that Jesus was led to the house of Annas *first;* this expression gives notice of a subsequent session in another place. The account of this session is omitted. It is indicated, indeed (ver. 24: "And Annas sent Jesus bound to Caiaphas, the high-priest"), but not related; and yet it is one of the most indispensable links of the history, since in the sitting in the house of Annas a simple examination was carried on, and in order to a capital execution an official session of the Sanhedrim was absolutely necessary, at which the sentence should be pronounced according to certain definite forms. The subsequent appearance before Pilate, when the Jews endeavored to obtain from him the confirmation of the sentence, leaves no doubt as to the fact that it had actually been pronounced. Now all this is omitted in our narrative, as well the session in the house of the high-priest Caiaphas as the pronouncing of the sentence. How are we to explain the omission of such facts?—In iii. 24, these words: "Now John had not yet been cast into prison," imply the idea in the mind of the reader that, at that moment, he had already been arrested. But there is not a word in what precedes which was fitted to occasion such a misapprehension.

Is not such a mode of narrating as this a perpetual enigma? On one side, a texture so firm and close, and on the other as many vacant places as full ones, as much of omission as of matter? Is there a supposition which can in any way explain two such contradictory features of one and the same narrative. Yes; and it is in the relation of our fourth Gospel to the three preceding ones that we must seek this solution, as we shall attempt to show.

The relation of the Johannean narrative to that of the Synoptic Gospels may be characterized by these two features: Constant *correlation,* on the one hand, and striking *independence,* and even *superiority,* on the other.

1. There is no closer adaptation between two wheels fitted to each other in wheelwork, than is observed, on a somewhat attentive study, between the two narratives which we are comparing. The full parts of the one answer to the blanks of the other, as the prominent points of the latter to the vacant spaces of the former. John begins his narrative with

[1] How, in the face of such facts, can a writer who respects himself, write the following lines: "John, we know(!), does not present any trace of gaps, or vacant spaces in which the materials furnished by the Synoptics might be placed." (Stap. *Etudes historiques et critiques,* p 259.)

Characteristics - The Facts / 73

the last part of the ministry of John the Baptist, without having described the first half of it, without even having given an account of the baptism of Jesus; just the reverse of what we find in the Synoptics. He relates the call of the first believers on the banks of the Jordan, without mentioning their subsequent elevation to the rank of permanent disciples on the shores of the lake of Gennesaret; again, the reverse of the Synoptic narrative. He sets forth a considerably long ministry in Judea, anterior to the Galilean ministry, which the Synoptics omit; then, when he reaches the period of the Galilean ministry so abundantly described by his predecessors, he relates, in common with them, only a single scene belonging to it—that of chap. vi. (we shall see with what motive he makes this exception), and, as for all the rest of these ten to twelve months of Galilean labor, he limits himself to indicating the framework and the compartments of it, without filling them otherwise than by the two brief summaries, ver. 1 of chap. vi. and ver. 1 of chap. vii. These compartments, left vacant, can only be naturally explained as references to other narratives with which the author knows his readers to be acquainted. But, while he passes on thus without entering into the least detail respecting the entire Galilean ministry, he dwells with partiality upon the visits to Jerusalem, which he describes in the most circumstantial way, and the omission of which in the Synoptics is so striking a blank in their narrative. In the last visit to Jerusalem, he omits the embarrassing questions which were addressed to Jesus in the temple, but he relates carefully the endeavor of the Greeks to see Him, which is omitted by all the other narratives. In the description of the last meal, he gives a place to the act of washing the disciples' feet, and omits that of the institution of the Lord's Supper; and in the account of the trial of Jesus, he takes notice of the appearance in the house of Annas, which is omitted by all the others, and, in exchange, passes over in silence the great session of the Sanhedrim in the house of Caiaphas, at which Jesus was condemned to death. In the description of the crucifixion, he calls to mind three expressions of Jesus, which are not reported by his predecessors, and he omits the four mentioned by them. Among the appearances of the risen Lord, those to Mary Magdalene and Thomas, omitted or barely hinted at by the Synoptics, are described in a circumstantial way; one only of the others is recalled, and it is given with quite peculiar details.

Could the closely fitting relation of this Gospel to the Synoptics which we have pointed out be manifested more evidently? We do not by any means conclude from this that John related his story *in order to complete them*—he set before himself, surely, a more elevated aim—but we believe we may affirm that he wrote *completing them;* that to complete was, not his aim, but one of the guiding principles of his narration. There was on the author's part a choice, a selection, determined by the narratives of his predecessors. If his work left us in any doubt on this point, the declaration which closes it must convince us: "*Many other* signs did Jesus in the presence of His disciples, which are not written *in this book* (ἐν τῷ βιβλίῳ

74 / The Fourth Gospel

τούτῳ).'' The expressions here employed signify two things: 1. That he has left aside a part of the facts which he might also have related; 2. That he has omitted these facts because they were already related in other writings than his own (*this book*, in contrast with others). What were these books? It is impossible not to recognize our three Synoptic Gospels, from the following indications: The choice of the Twelve, which John refers to in vi. 70, is related in Mark iii. 13–19 and Luke vi. 12–16. The two sisters, Martha and Mary, designated by name in John xi., as if persons already known, are introduced on the Gospel stage by Luke (x. 38–42). The confusion of the first two returns to Galilee (comp. John i. 44 and iv. 3), which John so evidently makes it a point to dispel (ii. 11 and iv. 54), is found in our three Synoptics (Matt. iv. 12 and parallels); and the idea that no activity of Jesus in Judea had preceded the imprisonment of John the Baptist—an idea which John corrects (iii. 24)—is found expressly enunciated in Matthew and Mark (passages already cited). How, then, can we doubt the close and deliberate correlation of John's narrative with that of the Synoptic Gospels? Renan has always recognized it.[1] And Reuss, after having more or less called it in question,[2] now consents to admit it. He goes even so far, as we all shall soon see, as to transform this correlation into a relation of dependence on the part of John with reference to the Synoptics. Baur and Hilgenfeld likewise recognize this relation, so that it may be regarded as a point which has been gained.

Starting from this fact, therefore, have we not the right to say: That two narratives which are in so close and constant relation to each other cannot be written from entirely different points of view, and that if the first, while seeking, in each of its three forms, to bring out one of the salient characteristics of the person of Jesus, pursues this end on a truly historical path, the same must be the case with the other, which, at every step, completes it and, in its turn, is completed by it?

It will be objected, perhaps, that the author of the Johannean narrative, being an exceedingly able man, labors, by means of all that he borrows from the earlier narratives, not to break with the universally received tradition, and at the same time, by all that he adds of new matter, attempts to make his dogmatic conception prevail, as M. Reuss says: in other words, to secure the triumph of his theory of the Logos.

This explanation must be examined in the light of the other two features which we have pointed out in the relation between our Gospel and the Synoptics. I mean, the complete independence and even the decided historical superiority of the former.

Baur had affirmed the dependence in which John stands with relation

---

[1] "The position of the Johannean writer is that of an author who is not ignorant of the fact that the subject of which he treats has been already written upon, who approves many things in that which has been said, but who believes that he has superior information and gives it without troubling himself about the others" (p. 531).

[2] He said previously: "One cannot discover, except with difficulty, in this Gospel the traces of a relation with the so-called earlier Gospels. The facts do not constrain us absolutely to hold that the author had any acquaintance with our Synoptic Gospels."

to the Synoptic narrative, as concerning all truly historical information; Holtzmann has sought to prove this in detail, and Reuss now declares himself, in spite of his previous denials, converted to this opinion.[1]

It is necessary, indeed, to distinguish here between the correlation which we have just proved and which, like every relation whatsoever, is a sort of dependence (but only as to the mode of narrating), and the dependence which has a bearing upon the very knowledge of the facts. As we affirm the first, so we are prepared to deny the second, and to affirm that the author of the Johannean narrative is in possession of a source of information which is peculiar to himself, and which, as to the matter of the narrative, renders him absolutely independent of the Synoptical tradition. Let us consult the facts.

It is not from the Synoptics that he knows the public testimony which the forerunner rendered to Jesus. For, before the baptism of Jesus, nothing of the kind is or could be attributed to him by them, and, after the baptism, the Synoptics do not mention anything beyond that single saying of John, which is rather an expression of doubt: "Art thou he that should come, or do we look for another?" And yet the answer of Jesus on occasion of the official inquiry of the Sanhedrim respecting His Messianic authority, (Matt. xxi. 23, and parallels), implies the existence of a public and well-known testimony of the forerunner, such as that which John relates in i. 19 ff.—It is not from the Synoptics that John has derived the account of the first relations of Jesus with His earliest disciples (chap. i.); and yet these relations are necessarily presupposed by the call of the latter to the vocation of fishers of men, on the shores of the lake of Gennesaret (Matt. v. 18 ff.).—It is not from the Synoptics that John has learned that Jesus inaugurated His public ministry by the purification of the temple, since they place this act in His last visit to Jerusalem. Now all the probabilities are in favor of the time assigned to this fact by John. Reuss himself acknowledges it, since according to him, if Jesus was at Jerusalem several times (a fact which he accepts), it is almost impossible to hold that He had been indifferent the first time to that which on a later occasion could excite His holy indignation.[2]—It is certainly not from the Synoptics that John borrows the correction which he brings to their own story, iii. 24, by recalling the fact that Jesus and His forerunner had baptized simultaneously in Judea at the beginning of the Lord's ministry, and iv. 54 (comp. i. 44 and iv. 3), by clearly distinguishing between the first two returns of Jesus to Galilee which are blended into one by the Synoptic narrative. And yet every one is obliged to admit that these corrections are well-founded rectifications and in harmony with the actual course of the history; for (1) if Jesus had not at first taught publicly in Judea, the imprisonment of John the Baptist would not have been a reason for His withdrawing and departing again for Galilee (Weizsäcker);

---

[1] "In my previous works, I believed myself able to maintain the independence of the fourth Gospel in regard to the Synoptic text. I am obliged to go over to the opposite opinion, which is at present shared even by those who in other respects adopt the traditional views." (*La Théologie johannique*, p. 76.)

[2] P. 139.

76 / The Fourth Gospel

and (2) there remains a manifest gap in the Synoptic narrative between the baptism of Jesus and the imprisonment of John the Baptist, a gap which the Johannean narrative exactly fills (Holtzmann).—Westcott with perfect fitness says: " Matt. iv. 12 and Mark i. 14 have a meaning only on the supposition of a *Judean* ministry of Jesus, which these books have not related."

It is not from the Synoptics that John borrows the account of the visits to Jerusalem; here is the feature which most profoundly distinguishes his narrative from theirs. And yet, if the Johannean narrative possesses a pronounced character of superiority to the other, we may say it is certainly in this point. Keim speaks very pathetically, it is true, of these "breathless journeys "[1] of Jesus to Jerusalem! Nevertheless, all are not agreed on this subject. Weiss expresses himself thus: "All the historical considerations speak in favor of John's narrative, and in the Synoptic narratives themselves there are not wanting indications which lead to this way of understanding the history."[2] Renan himself remarks that "persons transplanted only a few days before [the disciples, on the supposition that they also had not previously visited Jerusalem] would not have chosen that city for their capital . . . " And he adds, " If things had occurred as Mark and Matthew would have it, Christianity would have been developed especially in Galilee."[3] Hausrath and Holtzmann express themselves in the same way.[4] Without pursuing this enumeration, let us limit ourselves to quoting Hase, who, in a few lines, appears to us to sum up the question: " So far as we are acquainted with the circumstances of the time, it was natural that Jesus should seek to obtain the national recognition [of His Messianic dignity] at the very centre of the life of the people, in the holy city; and even the mortal hatred of the priests at Jerusalem would be more difficult to explain, if Jesus had never threatened them near at hand. But it is very natural that these journeys to Jerusalem, in so far as they are chronological determinations, should be effaced in the Galilean tradition and blended in the single and last journey which led Jesus to His death. In the Synoptic Gospels are preserved the traces of an earlier sojourn of Jesus in the capital and its neighborhood : ' Jerusalem, Jerusalem, thou that killest the prophets and stonest them that are sent unto thee, how often would I have gathered thy children together as a hen gathereth her chickens under her wings; and ye would not!' " This sorrowful exclamation which escaped from the deepest depths of the heart of Jesus, finds no satisfactory explanation in the visit of a few days which Jesus made in that city according to the Synoptics. The explanation of Baur is a subterfuge—he thinks that the children of Jerusalem are taken here as representatives of the whole people, while this exclamation is addressed in the most precise and local way to Jerusalem itself; as also it is a mere shift of Strauss to find here the quotation of a passage from a lost work (" The Wisdom of God "),—a passage which, in

---

[1] "Das athemlose Festreiseu."
[2] Introd., p. 35.
[3] *Vie de Jésus*, 13th ed., p. 487.
[4] *Neutest. Zeitgesch.* I., p. 386; *Gesch. des Volks Israel*, II., pp. 372, 373.

any case, could have been thus put into the mouth of Jesus only as the public mind remembered more than one visit to Jerusalem. Moreover, according to the Synoptics also, Jesus has hosts at Bethany, to whose house he returns every evening. . . ."[1] Sabatier calls to mind, besides, the owner of the young ass at Bethphage, the person at whose house Jesus caused the Passover supper to be prepared at Jerusalem, Joseph of Arimathea who goes to ask for His body. It is difficult to believe that all these relations of Jesus in Judea were contracted in the few days only which preceded the Passion. Finally, let us not forget the remarkable fact that Luke himself places at a considerably earlier period the first visit of Jesus at the house of Martha and Mary (x. 38 ff.).

Reuss cannot deny the weight of these reasons. While continuing to think that the choice of this theatre was dictated to the author " by the very nature of the antithesis, the antagonism between the Gospel and Judaism," that it is, consequently, the theological conception which created this framework, he is nevertheless obliged to admit "that there are evident traces of a more frequent presence of Jesus in Jerusalem" than that of which the Synoptics speak. But if historical truth is so *evidently* on the side of John, how can it be maintained, on the other hand, that "it is to the theological conception that this framework is due?"[2]

Reuss is likewise led by the facts to give the preference to the *chronological* outline of John's narrative, which assigns to the ministry of Jesus a duration of two years and a half, and not of a single year only, as the Synoptic narrative seems to do. "We do not think," he says, "that it can be affirmed that Jesus employed only a single year of His life in acting upon the spirit of those around Him."[3] Weizsäcker makes the same observation : "The transformation of the previous ideas, views and beliefs of the apostles must have penetrated even to the depths of their minds, in order to their being able to survive the final catastrophe and to rise anew immediately afterwards. In order to this, the schooling of a prolonged intercourse with Jesus was necessary. Neither instructions nor emotions were sufficient here; there was necessity of growing into the inner and personal union with the Master."[4] Renan also declares that the mention of the different visits of Jesus to Jerusalem (and, consequently, of His two or three years of ministry) "constitutes for our Gospel a decisive triumph."[5] Here is no secondary detail in the relation of John to the Synoptics. It is the capital point. How can it be maintained, after such avowals, that the fourth Gospel is dependent on its predecessors? How can we fail to recognize, on the contrary, the complete independence of the materials of which it disposes and their decided *historical* superiority to the tradition recorded in the Synoptics.

In the account of the last evening, the first two Synoptics divide the sayings of Christ into three groups : 1. The revelation of the betrayal and the betrayer; 2. The institution of the Holy Supper; 3. The personal

---

[1] *Geschichte Jesu, nach acad. Vorles*, p. 40.
[2] *Théol. johann.*, pp. 57–59.
[3] P. 58.
[4] *Untersuchungen*, p. 313.
[5] P. 487.

impressions of Jesus. Luke the same, but in the inverse order. There are always three distinct groups in juxtaposition. This arrangement was that of the traditional narration, which tended to group the homogeneous elements. But it is not that of real life: so it is not found again in John. Here the Lord reverts several times both to the betrayal of Judas and His own impressions. The same difference is seen in the account of Peter's denial. The three acts of denial are united in the Synoptics as if in one place and time; this narrative was one of the ἀπομνημονεύματα (traditional stories), which formed each of them a small, complete whole, in the popular narration. In John we do not find these three acts artificially grouped; they are divided among other facts, as they certainly were in reality ; the narrative has found again its natural articulations. This characteristic has not escaped the sagacity of Renan, who expresses himself thus : "The same superiority in the account of Peter's denials. This entire episode in the case of our author is more circumstantial, better explained."

We know that, according to John's account, the day of Christ's death was the 14th of Nisan, the day of the preparation of the Paschal supper, and not, as it seems, at the first glance, in the Synoptics, the 15th, the day after the supper. It has been claimed that this difference arose from the fact that the author of the fourth Gospel wished to make the time of Jesus' death coincide with that at which the Paschal lamb was sacrificed —a ceremony which took place on the 14th in the afternoon; and this in a purely dogmatic and typological interest. It is difficult to understand what the author would have gained by making so violent a transposition of the central fact of the Gospel,—that of the cross. For, after all, the typical relation between the sacrifice of the lamb and the crucifixion of Christ does not depend on the simultaneousness of these two acts. This relation had already been proclaimed by Paul (1 Cor. v. 7: "Christ, our Passover, has been sacrificed for us "); it was recognized by the whole Church, on the ground of the sacramental words: " Do this in remembrance of me," by which Jesus substituted Himself for the Paschal lamb. It is easier, on the other hand, to understand the loss which the author risked by subjecting the history to an alteration of this kind; he compromised in the Church the authority of his work and thereby (to put ourselves at the point of view of those who give this explanation) even that of his conception of the Logos, which, moreover, had nothing to do with typological and Judaic symbolism, and was even contrary to it. But more than this, we shall show, and that by the Synoptics themselves, that the Johannean date is the true one. Reuss cannot help admitting this, with ourselves, for the same reasons (the facts indicated Mark xiv. 21, 46 and parallels, which could not have occurred on a Sabbatical day, such as the 15th of Nisan was).[1] Here also, accordingly, it is John's account which brings to light again the true course of things, left in obscurity by the Synoptic narrative.

We shall not enter into the detailed study of the accounts of the Passion

---

[1] See *Théol. johann.*, p. 60.

Characteristics - The Facts / 79

and resurrection. I may limit myself to quoting this general judgment of Renan respecting the last days of Jesus' life: "In all this portion, the fourth Gospel contains particular points of information infinitely superior to those of the Synoptics." And with relation to the fact of the resurrection of Lazarus, he adds: "Now—a singular fact—this narrative is connected with the last pages [of the Gospel history] by such close bonds that, if we reject it as imaginary, the entire edifice of the last weeks of Jesus' life, so solid in our Gospel, crumbles at the same blow."[1] And, in fact, all things in the Johannean narrative are historically bound together: the resurrection of Lazarus determines the ovation of Palm Sunday; and this, joined with the treason of Judas, constrains the Sanhedrim to precipitate the denouement.

It is true that Hilgenfeld regards this explanation of the relation between John and the Synoptics as "a *degrading* of these last, they being nothing more than defective beginnings, of which John's work would be the censor."[2] Reuss several times expresses the same idea: "A singular way of strengthening the faith of the Christian—by suggesting the idea that what he may have previously read in Matthew or in Luke has great need to be corrected."[3] But to complete, is to confirm that which precedes and that which follows the gap which is filled up; and to correct an inaccuracy of detail in a narrative is not to unsettle the authority of the whole—it is, on the contrary, to strengthen it. The corrections and complements brought by John to the Synoptic story have been noticed since the first ages of the Church, but they have not in the least impaired the confidence which the Church has had in those writings.

We now have the necessary elements for resolving these two questions: Is the fourth Gospel, in the truth which it relates, dependent on the Synoptics? In the points where he differs from them, does the author modify the history according to a preconceived and favorite theory?

As to the first question, the facts, as rigidly examined, have just proved that the author of the fourth Gospel possesses a source of information independent of the Synoptic tradition. The negative solution of the second follows plainly from the fact that in case of a difference in the two narrations, it is, in every instance, the Johannean narrative which, *from the historical point of view*, deserves the preference. A narrative which is constantly superior, historically speaking, is secure from the suspicion of being the product of an idea.

What is urged in opposition to this result from facts, which are for the most part conceded by the objectors themselves? It is claimed, in spite of all, that there are found in the Johannean narrative certain traces of dependence on the Synoptic narrative. Holtzmann has exercised his critical adroitness in this domain. The following are some of his discoveries.[4] John says i. 6: "There was a man" ($\dot{\epsilon}\gamma\acute{\epsilon}\nu\epsilon\tau o\ \mathring{a}\nu\theta\rho\omega\pi o\varsigma$)." It is an imitation of: "There came a word ($\dot{\epsilon}\gamma\acute{\epsilon}\nu\epsilon\tau o\ \dot{\rho}\hat{\eta}\mu a$)," Luke iii. 2. John says (i. 7): "This one came;" he copies the: "And he came," Luke iii. 3.

[1] P. 514.
[2] *Zeitsch. für wissensch. Theol.*, I., 1880.
[3] P. 32.
[4] *Zeitschr. für wissensch. Theol.*, 1869.

The expression: "Lazarus our friend sleepeth" (John xi. 11), reproduces that of Mark v. 39 and parallels: "She is not dead, but sleepeth" (although Mark's term καθεύδει is different from John's, κεκοίμηται). The sickness of Lazarus (John xi.) is a copy of the representation of Lazarus covered with sores in the parable of Luke xvi. 20, and the whole account of the resurrection of Lazarus of Bethany is only a fiction created after that parable of the wicked rich man. According to Renan, the reverse is the case. The two assertions are of equal value. In Luke, Abraham refuses, as a useless thing, to send back Lazarus who is dead to the earth; in John, Jesus brings him back among the living: what an imitation! It is claimed also, from this point of view, that the representation of Martha and Mary, chap. xi., is an imitation of that in Luke x. 38 ff.; or that the two hundred denarii of Philip (vi. 7) are derived from the text of Mark vi. 37, as the three hundred of Judas (xii. 5) are borrowed from the text of Mark xiv. 5; or again that the strange term νάρδος πιστική (pure nard, trustworthy) in John (xii. 3) comes from Mark (xiv. 3). The comparison of the three accounts of the anointing of Jesus at Bethany has produced on Reuss so great an impression, that it has decided his conversion to the view of dependence, maintained by Holtzmann.[1] According to him, indeed, two different anointings are related by the Synoptics; that which took place in Galilee by the hands of a sinful woman, in the house of Simon the Pharisee (Luke vii.), and that which took place at Bethany on the part of a woman of that place, in the house of Simon the leper (Matt. xxvi.; Mark xiv.). "Well," says Reuss, "the author of the fourth Gospel gives us a third version," which can only be understood as an amalgam of the other two. He puts into the mouth of Jesus the same words as the narrative of Mark does. And at the same time he borrows from Luke this characteristic detail,—that the oil was not poured on His head (Mark and Matt.), but on His feet. Moreover, he thinks it good to deviate from the account of the first two Synoptics by transferring the scene from the house of Simon the leper to that of Lazarus, who has recently been raised from the dead. The truth is: 1. That John relates exactly the same scene as Mark and Matthew; but 2. That he relates it with more precise details; and 3. Without contradicting them in the least degree. He is more precise: he indicates exactly the day of the supper; it is that of the arrival of Jesus at Bethany from Jericho, the evening before Palm Sunday; in Matthew and Mark all chronological determination is wanting. He mentions the anointing of *the feet*, that of the head being understood as a matter of course, since it was an act of ordinary civility (comp. Ps. xxiii. 5; Luke vii. 46), while anointing *the feet* with a like perfume was a prodigality altogether extraordinary. It was precisely this exceptional fact which occasioned the murmuring of certain disciples and the following conversation. Then, John alone mentions Judas as the fomenter of the discontent which manifested itself among some of his colleagues. Matthew and Mark employ here only vague terms: *the disciples; some*. But these Gospels themselves, by the place which they

---

[1] *Théol. johann.*, p. 76, note.

assign to this story—making it an intercalation and, as it were, an episode in that of the treachery of Judas (comp. Mark xiv. 1, 2 and 10, 11, and the parallels in Matt.), indirectly bear testimony to the accuracy of this more precise detail of John's narrative. Tradition had assigned this place to the story of the anointing precisely because of the part of Judas on this occasion, which was as if the prelude to his treachery. It was an association of ideas for which John substitutes the true chronological situation. Finally, John's narrative does not, by any means, contradict the parallel narrative of the two Synoptics as to the house in which the supper took place. For the expression: "And Lazarus was one of those who were at table with him" (in John),—far from proving that the feast took place in the house of Lazarus,—is the indication of exactly the opposite. It would not have been necessary to say that Lazarus was at table in his own house, and that Martha served there. There remains the identical detail of the three hundred denarii and the common term πιστική. There would be no impossibility surely in the fact that, having the narrative of Mark under his eyes, John should have borrowed from it such slight details; his general historical independence would, nevertheless, remain intact. But these borrowings are themselves doubtful; for 1. John's narrative possesses, as we have seen, details which are altogether original; 2. The term πιστική was a technical term, which was used in contrast with the similarly technical one, *pseudo-nard* (see Pliny); 3. The two numbers, being certainly historical, might be transmitted in two accounts which were independent of each other. Moreover, in the narrative of the multiplication of the loaves, the parts ascribed to Philip and Andrew betray in John the same independence of information which we have just proved in that of the anointing in Bethany.

We come to the solution of the second question, the most decisive question: whether the philosophical idea of the Logos, which is believed to be the soul of the narrative, has not exerted an unfavorable influence on the setting forth of the facts, and whether it is not to this influence that we must attribute most of the differences which we notice between this narrative of the history of Jesus and that of the three Synoptics.

The facts which we have just proved contain, in a general way, the answer to this question. If in the cases of divergence previously examined, we have established, in every instance, the incontrovertible *historical* superiority of John's narrative, what follows from this fact? That the author had too much respect for the history which he was relating, to permit the idea which inspired him to be prejudicial to the faithful statement of the facts, or that this governing idea, belonging to the history itself, moved over the narrative, not as a cause of alteration, but as a salutary and conservative rule.

Let us, however, enter into details and take notice of the particular divergences which are cited as specimens of the unfavorable effect of the theological standpoint. The question is either of facts *omitted*, or of narratives *repeated*, with or without modifications, or finally of features *added*, by the Johannean story.

There are three facts, especially, the *omission* of which seems to several critics significant,—the temptation, the institution of the Holy Supper, and the agony in Gethsemane. The first and third of these facts, it is thought, appeared to the author unworthy of the Logos; as for the second, it was enough for him, from his spiritualistic point of view, to have unveiled the essence of it in the discourse of chap. vi.; after that, the outward ceremony had no more value to his view. Does he not proceed in the same way with respect to the baptism? He does not, any more than in the former case, give an account of its institution, but he sets forth its essence, iii. 5. We believe that John's silence respecting these two facts is to be explained in quite a different way. If the author was afraid to compromise the dignity of the Logos by placing Him in conflict with the invisible adversary, would he make Him say, xiv. 30: "I will no longer talk much with you, for the prince of the world cometh?" It must not be forgotten that the starting-point of John's narrative is later than the fact of the temptation. It is the same with the baptism of Jesus, which is also not related, but which the author does not dream of denying, since he distinctly alludes to it in the saying attributed to John the Baptist, i. 32: "I have seen the Spirit descending from heaven like a dove and abiding upon him." The scene of Gethsemane is omitted; but it is sufficiently indicated by that statement, which is really a reference to the Synoptical narratives, xviii. 1: "After that Jesus had said these things, he went forth with his disciples beyond the brook Cedron, *where there was a garden into which he entered, himself and his disciples.*" John takes precisely the same course here as he does with relation to the great session of the Sanhedrim, at which Jesus was condemned to death; that scene, which is necessarily presupposed by the appearance before Pilate, he nevertheless does not relate, but contents himself with indicating it by the words, xviii. 24, "And Annas sent him bound to Caiaphas, the high-priest" (comp. also the words "to Annas *first*," ver. 13). This tacit reference to the Synoptics belongs to John's mode of narrating. Limiting himself to a delicate hint, which should serve as a *nota bene*, he passes over the points with which he knows his readers to be sufficiently well acquainted. If he was afraid of compromising the dignity of the Logos, how should he have related in chap. xii., in a scene which he alone has preserved from oblivion, that inward struggle, the secret of which Jesus did not fear to betray to the people who were about him, ver. 27: "And now is my soul troubled; and what shall I say?" How should he make Him *weep* at the tomb of Lazarus (xi. 35) and represent him as *troubled in His spirit* in the presence of the traitor (xiii. 21)? The omission of the institution of the Holy Supper is no less easily explained. John was not writing the Gospel for neophytes; he was relating his story in the midst of Churches which had been long since founded, and in which the Holy Supper was probably celebrated every week. Far from wishing to describe the ministry of Jesus in its entireness, he set forth the manifestations in acts and words which had especially contributed to the end of revealing to himself the Christ, the Son of God; comp. xx. 30, 31. Now, this aim did not oblige him to take particular notice of the institution of the Supper; and as this ceremony was sufficiently well-known and universally celebrated, he could omit the institution of it without detriment. No more does he give an account of the institution of baptism, although he makes an allusion to it in iii. 5 and iv. 2.

Three examples ought to show to a cautious criticism how much it needs to be on its guard, when the question is of drawing from omissions like these conclusions as to the hidden intentions of the author. He omits the story of the selection of the twelve apostles; is this in order to disparage them? But he himself puts in the mouth of Jesus (vi. 70) this word: "Have not I *chosen* you, the *twelve?*" Let us suppose that this declaration were not found there, what consequences would not an impassioned criticism draw from the omission? The fourth Gospel does not give an account of the ascension; does it mean to deny it? But in vi. 62, we find these words in the mouth of Jesus: "How will it be, when you shall see the Son of man *ascending where he was before?*" The ground of the omission is, very simply, the fact that the close of the narrative, the scene connected with Thomas, is anterior to this event, which, besides, was suited in the best possible way to the idea of the Logos. If there was in the Synoptics a fact fitted to be used to advantage in behalf of this theory, it was, certainly, that of the transfiguration. Very well! it is omitted, no less than the scene of Gethsemane. Such examples should suffice to bring criticism back from the false path in which it has been wandering for the last forty years, and into which it is drawing after itself an immense public who blindly swear according to it.

But we are arrested in our course here. If the author of the fourth Gospel, they say to us, really proposed to himself to complete the two others, why does he relate a certain number of facts already reported by them: for example, the expulsion of the dealers and the multiplication of the loaves, the anointing by Mary at Bethany and the entrance into Jerusalem on Palm Sunday?

We have already said: the author does not write for the purpose of completing. He proposes to himself a more elevated aim, which he himself points out in xx. 30, 31. But in these same verses he also defines his method, which consists in *selecting*, among the things already written or not yet written, that which best suited the end which he is pursuing: to give the grounds of his faith in Christ the Son of God, in order to the reproduction of the same faith in his readers: "Jesus did many other signs . . . which are not written in this book; but *these are written in order that* . . ." This mode of selecting implies omissions—we have remarked them—but it also authorizes repetitions, on every occasion when the author judges them necessary or even useful to his purpose.

Thus the driving out of the dealers (chap. ii.) is related anew by him, because he knows that it played, in the ministry of Jesus and in the development of the national unbelief, a much more serious part than that which was attributed to it in the Synoptical narrative. The latter, by placing this fact at the end of Jesus' ministry, prevented it from being looked upon as the bold measure by which Jesus had called His people to join themselves with Him in beginning the spiritual reform of the theocracy; the refusal of the people and their rulers on that occasion ceased thus to be the first step in the path of resistance and rejection.

The multiplication of the loaves (chap. vi.) appeared in the Synoptics only as one among the numerous miracles of Jesus. The important part appertaining to the crisis in the history of Jewish unbelief which resulted from this fact, was in them almost completely effaced. It is this side of the event which John restores to full light. He shows the carnal and political character of the Galilean enthusiasm, which desires, on this occasion, to proclaim the royalty of Jesus, and which, immediately afterwards, is offended at the declarations by which He refuses to promise to His own anything else than the satisfaction of spiritual hunger and thirst. At the same time, the fact thus presented becomes a very conspicuous landmark in the history of faith, by displaying the contrast between the abandoning of Jesus by the greater part of His former disciples and the energetic profession of St. Peter: "To whom else shall we go . . . ? Thou art the Holy One of God."

The story of the anointing at Bethany (chap. xii., 1 ff.) is, on the one side, connected with the resurrection of Lazarus, which has just been related in the preceding chapter, and, on the other, with the treachery of Judas which is to play so important a part in the picture of the last supper. This twofold connection did not appear in the Synoptics, who gave no account of the resurrection of Lazarus, and who, by substituting for the name of Judas the vague expressions: *some* (Mark), *the disciples* (Matt.), prevented the connection between this malevolent manifestation and the monstrous act which was about to follow from being perceived.

The entrance into Jerusalem (xii. 12 ff.) is related so summarily by John that it is really nothing but a complement of the Synoptic narrative. Thus, when he says: "Having found a young ass," and when he adds that, after the ascension, "the disciples remembered that these things were written and *that they had done* these things," while in his own narrative they have done nothing at all to Him, it is evident that, for the complete picture of the scene, he refers to other narratives already known. Only he is obliged to recall the fact to mind, in order to present it, on the one hand, as the effect of the resurrection of Lazarus (vv. 17, 18), and, on the other, as the cause which forced the Sanhedrim to precipitate the execution of the judgment already given against Jesus (ver. 19).

We can easily see, therefore, how these narratives are, not useless repetitions, but essential features in the general picture which the author proposes to himself to trace. Take away these, and you have, not merely a simple omission, but a rent in the very texture of the narrative.

It remains for us to consider a last class of facts in which it is believed that one may detect, in a peculiarly sensible way, the influence exerted upon the narrative by the dogmatic conception which filled the mind of its author. These are the facts and particular features which John adds to the narrative of his predecessors.

One of the features which most profoundly distinguish this Gospel from the preceding ones is, certainly, the chronological framework traced out above. The question is, whether this framework is a product of the idea, or whether it belongs to the actual history. We have already shown that, by the admission of Reuss, the second answer is the true one. What significance would it have, moreover, for the idea of the Logos that the ministry of Jesus continued for one year, or for two years and more?— that He taught and baptized during a first year in Judea, before establishing Himself in Galilee, as John relates, or, on the contrary, that He betook Himself to that country immediately after His baptism by the forerunner, as appears to be indicated by the Synoptics (Matt. iv. 12 and parallels)? It seems rather, that the shorter the sojourn of the Logos on the earth was, the more magnificently does the power of the work accomplished by Him shine forth.—Or again, those large intervals, entirely destitute of facts, which extend from one to three, or even six months,—are they to be considered pure inventions of the author for the benefit of the Logos theory? But with justice, Sabatier asks, "if the author had invented this framework, how should he have neglected to fill it out?" (p. 188). Reuss thinks he cites a decisive fact against the historical tendency of the Johannean narration, when he says: "A single fact fills an entire season vi. 4–vii. 2."[1] But how is it that he does not see that this almost total silence of the author respecting the contents of these six entire months, between the Passover and the Feast of Tabernacles, is the unanswerable proof that he has not invented "this season" with a speculative end in view, and that he mentions it only with a truly historical purpose.

It is in the fact of the visits to Jerusalem that the influence of the idea on the Johannean narration can, as it is thought, be most clearly proved. The great conflict between the light and the darkness demanded the capital as its theatre. But those who reason thus, are themselves forced to recognize in these visits to Jerusalem related by John, an indispensable element of the history—a factor without which neither the tragical catastrophe at Jerusalem, nor the foundation of the Church in this same city, can be understood (see pages 76, 77). These visits are not, then, a product of the idea. All that can be claimed is that they have been *chosen* and made prominent by the author as the principal object of his narrative, because he has judged them particularly fitted to bring out the principal idea of his work. Let us add here, however, that this idea is, by no means, a metaphysical notion, like that of the Logos, but the fact of the development of faith and of unbelief towards Jesus Christ. Moreover, to this *ideal* explanation of the visits to Jerusalem, Sabatier rightly opposes the narrative of chap. vi.: "We may well be surprised," he says, "to see beginning in Galilee, in the synagogue at Capernaum, the crisis whose denouement is to come in Jerusalem. We cannot explain such partial annulling of the system "—we say, for ourselves: of the *alleged* system— " of the author, except by the very distinct recollection which he had of the Galilean crisis."

[1] P. 23.

At this point there arises, undoubtedly, a difficult question—the most obscure of all those which are connected with the relation between John and the Synoptics: that of the omission of the visits to Jerusalem in the latter. We have seen that their whole narrative supposes these visits and requires them; how is it that they give no account of them? This strange omission seems to us explicable only by means of these two facts: one, that our three Synoptics are the redaction of the popular tradition which took form at Jerusalem after the day of Pentecost; the other, that this tradition had, from the beginning, left these visits in the background for some reason which can only be conjectured. As we have seen that the various allusions to the treachery of Judas during the last supper (John xiii.) were blended into one in the traditional and Synoptic story, and that the narrative of John is necessary in order to restore them to their true places; that, in the same way, the story of the denials of Peter, which, in the Synoptics, form a single and unbroken cycle, has found again in John's Gospel its natural articulation—so a similar fact probably occurred with reference to the journeys to Jerusalem. In the popular narration, they all came to be mingled together in that last journey—the only one which really told decisively on the history of the Messianic work, and which consequently remained in the tradition. We readily notice, in studying the three accounts of the Galilean ministry in the Synoptics, that they are divided into certain groups or cycles, each containing the same series of stories; what Lachmann has called the *corpuscula historiæ evangelicæ*. The journeys to Jerusalem did not fall within any of these groups. And when the evangelical tradition thus divided and grouped was committed to writing, these journeys remained in the shade. The very contents of the discourses which Jesus had spoken in the capital might, likewise, contribute to this omission in the ordinary proclaiming of the Gospel. It was not easy to reproduce for the Jewish and Gentile multitudes who heard of the Gospel for the first time, discourses such as that of the fifth chapter of St. John, on the dependence of the Son as related to the Father, and on the various testimonies which the Father bears to the Son; or discussions such as those which are reported in chaps. vii. and viii., where Jesus can no longer say a word without being interrupted by evil-minded hearers. The discourse of chap. vi. held in Galilee, could not be reproduced for the same reason, while the fact of the multiplication of the loaves, which had given occasion to it, remained in the tradition. How much easier, more natural and more immediately useful it was to reproduce varied scenes, like those of the Galilean life, or moral discourses and conversations, like the parables or the Sermon on the Mount? For all these reasons, or for some other besides these which is unknown to us, this important part of the ministry of Jesus was omitted in the tradition and also, afterwards, in our Synoptics. But, as Hase so well says, "as it was in the natural order of things that those who, like Luke, desired to describe the life of Jesus without having lived with Him, should keep to that which was published and believed in the Church respecting that life;—so it was natural also that, if an intimate disciple of the Lord came to undertake this work, he should keep much less to the common matter which had been accidentally and involuntarily reduced to form, than to his own recollections. Then, such a man was less bound by pious regard for that sacred tradition; for he was also himself a living source of it. I am not at all surprised, therefore, that a Johannean Gospel, in its high originality, deviates from that common matter; much rather, if a Gospel published under the name of this disciple did nothing but repeat that collective inheritance, and did not differ from it more than the Synoptics differ from one another, should I in that case doubt the authenticity of that Gospel."[1]

An objection is also derived from the miraculous works, to the number of seven, which are related in our Gospel; it bears upon these four points: 1. These works have a more marvelous character even than those of the Synoptics; 2. They are presented as manifestations of the glory of the Logos, and no longer as the simple effects of the compassion of Jesus; 3. Several of these miracles are omitted by the Synoptics—a fact which, by reason even of their extraordinary greatness, renders them more suspicious; 4. No casting out of a demon is mentioned.

1. We think that it would be difficult to say wherein the change of the water into wine at Cana, chap. ii., is more extraordinary than the multiplication of the loaves and fishes, related by our four gospels alike. Is it more marvelous to transform the qualities of matter, than to produce it? Has not the latter act a greater analogy to the creative act?—If, in the healing of the son of the royal officer, chap. iv., the miracle is wrought at a distance, the fact is not otherwise in the case of the servant of the centurion at Capernaum, Matt. viii., and in that of the daughter of the Canaanitish woman, Matt. xv.—The impotent man of Bethesda, John v., was sick for thirty-eight years: but what do we know of the time during which the impotent man, whose healing the Synoptics relate with circumstantial particularity, was paralyzed?—If in the story of the walking on the water, John vi., the bark reaches the shore immediately after the arrival of Jesus, the story in Matthew presents a no less extraordinary detail—the person of Peter made to participate in the miracle accomplished in the person of Jesus.—Two miracles remain in which the narrative of John appears to go beyond the analogous facts related by the Synoptics: the healing of the one *born* blind, chap. ix., and the resurrection of Lazarus, who had been dead *four days*. By these two altogether peculiar circumstances, the author proposed, it is said, to glorify the Logos in an extraordinary way.—But how can we make such an intention accord with several sayings which the same author puts into the mouth of Jesus, and in which the value of miracles, as a means of laying a foundation for belief, is expressly combated or at least depreciated. "Unless ye see wonders and signs, ye will not believe" (iv. 48): it is with this reproach that Jesus receives the request of the royal officer. "If ye believe not me,

---

[1] *Geschichte Jesu*, pp. 39, 40. Let us remark that Hase, in this passage, is discussing the question of the authenticity. As for ourselves, we are as yet treating only that of the historical or speculative character of our narrative.

at least believe the works" (x. 38); comp. also xiv. 11. And yet the author who has preserved such declarations of Jesus, the authenticity and elevated spirituality of which every one recognizes, makes himself the flatterer of the grossest religious materialism, by inventing new miracles and giving them a more wonderful character!

2. Is it true that our Gospel forms a contrast with the Synoptics, in the fact that the latter present the miracles as works of compassion, while in the former they are the signs of the glory of the Logos?—But let us observe, first of all, that in the Gospel of John the miracles are not even ascribed to the power of Jesus. It is one of the characteristic features of this work, that it makes the miracles, so far as Jesus is concerned, acts of *prayer*, while the operative power is ascribed to the Father alone. "I can do *nothing* of myself," says Jesus, v. 30, after the healing of the impotent man. "The works which *God has given me* to do, these works testify for me," He adds, ver. 36. The miracles are an attestation of the Father only because it is the Father who accomplishes them on His behalf. In xi. 41, 42, Jesus says publicly, before the grave of Lazarus: "Father, I thank thee that *thou hast heard me* . . .; I know that *thou hearest me always.*" He must therefore ask, beg for His miracles, as one of us might do; and is it claimed that these acts are the glorification of *His own* divine power? No doubt, it is also said, ii. 11, after the miracle at Cana, that "he manifested *his glory*," and xi. 4, that "the sickness of Lazarus is for the glory of God,"—then it is added: "in order that the Son of God may be glorified thereby." If this glory is not that which He derives from His own power, what can it be? Evidently that which results from His compassion manifested in His prayer, as the glory of the Father results from His love manifested by hearing it. Here, indeed, is the glory "full of *grace and truth*," of which the author himself spoke in i. 14. It is, therefore, very easy to escape from the antithesis which Reuss establishes between the miracles of compassion (in the Synoptics) and those of revelation and of personal glorification (in St. John). The glory of the Son in the latter consists precisely in *obtaining* from the Father that which His compassion asks for. How, for example, is the resurrection of Lazarus introduced in our Gospel? By those words which overflow with tenderness, and which have nothing like them in the Synoptics: "And Jesus loved Martha and her sister and Lazarus" (xi. 5). In order to apprehend completely the manner in which the miracles are presented in our Gospel, it must, indeed, be considered that the true *aim* of these acts passed far beyond the relief of the suffering being who was the object of them. If Jesus was moved only by compassion for individual suffering, why, instead of giving sight to a few blind persons only, did He not exterminate blindness from the world? Why, instead of raising two or three dead persons, did He not annihilate death itself? He did not do it, although His compassion would certainly have impelled Him to it. It was because the suppression of suffering and death is a blessing for humanity only as a corollary of the destruction of sin. The latter must, therefore, precede the former; and the miracles were *signs*, intended to manifest Jesus as the one by whom sin

first, and then suffering and death, are to be one day radically exterminated. As collective love for humanity does not exclude compassion towards a particular individual, so the notion of miracles in John does not exclude the Synoptic point of view, but includes it, while subordinating it to a more general point of view.

3. But how does it happen that of the seven miracles related by John, five are omitted in the previous Gospels. That of Cana naturally fell out with the first year of the ministry which they omitted. That of Bethesda and that of the man who was born blind are omitted with the visits to Jerusalem of which they form a part. That of the son of the royal officer had nothing peculiarly striking in it and had its counterpart in a miracle which is related by the Synoptics, that of the healing of the centurion's servant, which many even identify—wrongly, in our view—with the miracle reported by John.

The omission of the resurrection of Lazarus in the Synoptics is the most difficult fact to explain. It is not enough to say that the miracle took place in Judea; for at the time when it occurred the Synoptics present the Lord to us as sojourning in Perea and in the southern districts. We have only one explanation: tradition remained silent with respect to this fact through consideration for Lazarus and his two sisters. This family lived within a stone's throw of Jerusalem and was thus exposed to the hostile stroke of the Sanhedrim. We read in John xii. 10 that "the chief priests took counsel that they might put Lazarus also to death" together with Jesus, because of the influence which the sight of this man who had been raised from the dead was exerting upon the numerous pilgrims arriving at the capital. The case might have been precisely the same after the day of Pentecost; and it is probable that it was found prudent, for this reason, to pass over this fact in silence in the traditional Gospel story. Either the names of Martha and Mary, in the story of the anointing (see Mark and Matthew), or the name of Bethany, when the two sisters were designated by their names (see the account of Luke x. 38), were likewise omitted. It was, undoubtedly, for a similar reason that, in the account of the arrest of Jesus in Gethsemane, the name of the disciple who drew the sword was suppressed in the tradition (see the three Synoptical narratives), while it is mentioned without scruple by John, who wrote at a time when no harm could any longer come to Peter from this precise indication. Objection is made, it is true, that the Synoptic narratives were drawn up after the death of Peter, and after that of the members of the Bethany family; to what purpose, then, these precautions (see Meyer)? But we too, do not, by any means, ascribe these precautions to the *authors* of these works; we ascribe them to the Gospel tradition, formed at Jerusalem *from the days which followed the day of Pentecost.* We see from the account of the ill treatment to which the Sanhedrim subjected the apostles, from the martyrdom of Stephen and of James, and from the persecutions of which Saul became the instrument, that, at that time, the power of the enemies of Jesus was still unimpaired, and that it was exercised in the most violent manner. Their hatred went on increasing with the progress of the Church; and there must have been an apprehension, that if any one should put publicly on the scene those who had played a part in that history, he would make them pay very dearly for such an honor. John, who composed his work at a time when there was no longer any Sanhedrim or Jewish people or temple, and who wrote under the sway, not of tradition, but of his own recollections, could, without fear, re-establish the facts in their integrity. This is the reason why he designates Peter as the author of the blow which was given in the scene in Gethsemane, while at the same time, at the suggestion of this name, he calls to mind that of Malchus, the one who was injured; this is the reason why he gives himself up to the happiness of tracing in all its details the wonderful scene of the resurrection of Lazarus.

4. We shall not dwell long upon the omission of the cures of demoniacs. Does not the author himself say that there are also in the history of Jesus *numerous* miracles, *different* from those which he has mentioned (xx. 30: πολλὰ καὶ ἄλλα σημεῖα)? Does not Jesus speak, xiv. 30, of "the prince of this world coming to Him"? There would be nothing, therefore, to prevent the evangelist from speaking of the victories of Jesus over his demoniacal agents. Cases of possession are mentioned only rarely in Greek countries (Acts xvi., xvii.). They were less known there.

The want of historical character, which criticism charges against the accounts of miracles in the fourth Gospel, it discovers again in *the personages* whom this book brings on the stage. They are not, it claims, living beings, but mere types. Nicodemus is the personification of learned Pharisaism. "We see him come, but we do not see him go away;" this is a favorite observation of Reuss; it passes from one of his works to another. He adds: "In any case there is no more question as to him." Finally, he asserts that the reply made by Jesus to this nocturnal visitor "ends in a theoretical exposition of the Gospel," and, consequently, is not at all addressed to him. The same estimate of the Samaritan woman, in chap. iv.; in this woman is simply personified "the artless and confident faith of the poor in spirit." And the same also of the Greeks of chap. xii.: they represent heathenism yearning for salvation. What meaning, indeed, would the mediation of Philip and Andrew have, to which they have recourse, and which was, by no means, necessary in the presence of a being whom every one could freely approach? These are, then, ideal figures, as suits the essential character of a book which is nothing but a treatise on theology.[1]

Reuss would wish, no doubt, that the account of the conversation with Nicodemus had been followed by this remark: And Nicodemus returned to his house. The narrator has not considered this detail necessary. He has judged it more useful to relate to us, in chap. vii., that, in a full session of the Sanhedrim, this same senator, who at the beginning came to Jesus *by night*, had the courage to take up His defense and to expose himself to insult from his colleagues. He has also preferred to show us, on the day

---

[1] Reuss, pp. 14, 15.

Characteristics - The Facts / 91

of deepest darkness, when the most intimate friends of Jesus were despairing of Him and His work, this same man offering to His dead body at the foot of the cross a royal homage, and publicly making known his faith in Him, in whom he recognized, at that hour, the true brazen serpent lifted up for the salvation of the world; comp. John iii. 14, 15. Here, it seems, are features which attest the reality of a man, and in presence of which it ought not to be said: "In any case there is no more question as to him." It is also wholly false to call the end of the conversation of Jesus with him, in chap. iii., "a theoretical exposition of the Gospel;" for every word of Jesus sets a feature of the true Messianic programme in direct opposition to the false Pharisaic programme which Nicodemus brought with him: The Messiah must be lifted up like the brazen serpent; which means: and not like a new Solomon. God so loved the world: and not only the Jews. The Son is come to save: and not to judge the uncircumcised. The one who is condemned is whoever does not believe: and not the Gentile as such. The one who is saved is whoever believes: but not the Jew as such. Through the addition of this last word: "He who does the truth *comes to the light,*" it is very clear, for every one who puts himself in the situation, that Jesus makes an encouraging allusion to the step which Nicodemus had taken; there is here a farewell full of kindness which is a guaranty for his future progress. Everything in this story, therefore, from the first word to the last, applies personally to Him. Is it possible to picture to oneself a scene more real and life-like than that at Jacob's well? That fatigue of Jesus carried to the extreme, even to exhaustion ($\kappa\epsilon\kappa o\pi\iota\alpha\kappa\omega\varsigma$); that malicious observation of the woman: "How dost thou ask drink of me, who am a Samaritan woman?" that water-pot which she leaves and which remains there as a pledge of her speedy return; those Samaritans hastening towards Jesus, whose eagerness makes upon Him the impression of a harvest already ripening, after a sowing which has just taken place at that very moment; that sower who rejoices to see, once in His life at least, His labor ending in the harvest feast, those people of Sychar who so artlessly attest the difference between their first act of faith, founded solely on the woman's story, and their present faith, the fruit of their contact with Jesus Himself ... What a painter is made of our author by attributing to his creative imagination such words, such a picture?—Can we say that the Greeks were really lost from sight in the answer which Jesus makes to the communication of Philip and Andrew? But to whom, then, does that expression of xii. 32 apply: "When I shall be lifted up from the earth, I will draw *all men* unto me?" Our Lord means: My teaching and my miracles will not suffice to extend the Kingdom of God over the earth and to make all peoples enter into it; my elevation upon the cross will be needed, followed by my elevation to the throne. Then only, "after it shall have been cast into the earth, will the grain of seed bear much fruit (ver. 24)." Then only will it be possible for the great fact of the fall of Satan's power and of the conversion of the Gentiles to be accomplished, which cannot yet at this moment be realized. The answer of Jesus, therefore, is equivalent, in its meaning, to that which He gave to the Canaanitish woman: "I am not sent (during my earthly career), except to the lost sheep of the house of Israel." It matters little to us, after this, to know whether the Greeks were admitted or not to a few moments of conversation with the Lord. It was the moral situation in itself and its gravity for Israel and for the world, which the narrator wished to describe, as Jesus Himself had so solemnly characterized it on that occasion; and what proves that it is, indeed, Jesus who spoke in this way, is the following picture of the profound emotion which this first contact with the Gentile world produces in Him: "And now is my soul troubled; and what shall I say? Father, save me from this hour? But for this cause came I unto this hour." Most certainly it may be said:—here are words which were not invented, and which, in any case, were not invented in the interest of the Logos-theory! Now if these words are historical, the entire scene cannot be otherwise. As for the mediation of Philip and Andrew, it is in truth more difficult to comprehend the objection, than to solve it.

After having given an account of the difficulties which have been raised, we ourselves proceed to raise some against this *ideal* explanation of the Johannean narrative. The historical differences between this Gospel and the preceding ones arise, it is said, from the influence exerted by the Logos theory which this work is designed to set forth. But a mass of details in John's narration are either wholly foreign or even opposed to this alleged intention.

We ask of what interest, from the point of view indicated, can be that *tenth hour* so expressly mentioned in i. 40, or that first sojourn of Jesus in Capernaum, indicated in ii. 12, but of which the author does not tell us the least detail; wherein is it of advantage to the Logos idea to mention, viii. 20, that the place where Jesus spoke was the place called *the Treasury* of the temple, or x. 23, that "it was winter" and that "Jesus was walking in Solomon's porch;" or, xi. 54, that after the resurrection of Lazarus, Jesus withdrew to a place named Ephraim and near the desert, without our learning anything of what He did and said there. What does the Logos idea gain from our knowing that the name of the servant whose right ear Peter cut off was called Malchus, and that he was the brother of a servant of the high priest; that it was the apostle Andrew who discovered the small lad carrying the two barley-loaves and the five fishes; or that the disciples had already gone twenty-five furlongs when Jesus overtook them on the sea (vi. 18, 19); or that in the scene at the tomb John moved more quickly than Peter, but Peter was more courageous than John; that it was Philip who said: "Show us the Father;" Thomas who asked: "Make known to us the way;" Judas, "not Iscariot," who wished to know why Jesus would reveal Himself only to believers and not to the world (chap. xiv.)? Is it fictitious realism which the author here indulges in as he introduces these names, these numbers, these minute details, or does he attach to them some symbolic meaning in connection with the theory of the Logos? The seriousness of the work does not allow the first explanation, common sense excludes the second.

More than this: a multitude of details in the narrative are in open contradiction to the notion of the Logos as it is ascribed to our author. The Logos wearied and thirsty! The Logos remaining in Galilee in order to escape the death with which He is threatened at Jerusalem, and going to that city only *secretly!* The Logos agitated in His soul and even in His spirit,—then, beginning to weep; praying and, at a given moment, troubled even to the point of not knowing how to pray! It is easy to see that in no one of our Gospels is the truly human side of Jesus' person so earnestly emphasized as in the story of the fourth. If the theme of the narrative is contained in these words : " The Word was made flesh," the predicate in this proposition is made prominent in the narrative at least as much as the subject.

But let us suppose, in spite of so many details which are foreign or contradictory to the philosophical notion of the Logos, that the intention of the author was to proclaim this new thesis and to win over the Church to it : what advantage was there for this end in introducing into the generally received narrative modifications which could only render the whole work suspicious? Why create, in some sort as a whole, a new history of our Lord's life, while it was so easy for him, as is shown by the discourse which follows the account of the multiplication of the loaves (chap. vi.), to connect his favorite theory with the facts already known and everywhere admitted.

Finally, can we, without an insurmountable psychological contradiction, hold either that the author believed his own fictions so far as to amalgamate them in one and the same narrative with the facts which were most sacred to him—those of the Passion and resurrection,—or that, not himself believing them, he presented them to his readers as real, with the purpose of strengthening and developing their faith (xx. 30, 31)? In particular, can we conceive that he founded on these miracles, invented by himself, the grand indictment which he draws up, in closing the part from v. to xii., against Jewish unbelief: "*Although he had done* so many signs before them, they believed not on him, that the word of Isaiah the prophet might be fulfilled . . ." (xii. 37, 38). And yet he who wrote thus knew perfectly that these signs, in the name of which he condemns his people, had never occurred! We reach here the limits of folly.

Thus more and more men like Weizsäcker, Hase and Renan feel themselves obliged to recognize in the fourth Gospel a real and considerable historical basis. They stop at the half-way point, no doubt; but the public consciousness will not rest there. The purely and simply historical character of the entire work will impress itself upon that consciousness, as soon as the present crisis shall have passed; and we await with confidence the moment when reparation will be made to the narrative which we have just been studying. This, as has been seen, will not be the first retractation which it will have wrested from science.

3. *The Discourses*

But if the narrative of the facts has not been altered by reason of the speculative idea, can the same thing be affirmed of the other part—and it is the more considerable part—of our Gospel, namely, the Discourses which it puts into the mouth of Jesus? According to the opinion of Baur, these discourses are only the evolution of the Logos idea presented in its various aspects. Reuss thinks that the author takes for his starting point certain authentic utterances of Jesus, but that he freely amplifies them, by giving them developments borrowed from his own Christian experience. In favor of this view, the glaring improbabilities are alleged, which are observed in the account given of most of these discourses; the singular conformity of thought and style between the way in which the author makes Jesus speak and the language which he ascribes to the forerunner, or his own language in the prologue and in his epistle; finally, and especially, the complete contrast in matter and form which exists between the discourses of Jesus in our Gospel and His teaching in the Synoptics.

In order to treat this important subject thoroughly, we shall study the following three questions:

1. Are the discourses of Jesus in this Gospel to be regarded as simple variations of the speculative theme which is placed by the author at the beginning of his book? Or, on the contrary, must we regard the prologue as a summing up, a quintessence, of the history and the teachings related in the following narrative?

2. Do the alleged difficulties render the historical character of the discourses inadmissible?

3. Can we rise to such a conception of the person of Jesus that the Johannean teaching shall flow from it as naturally as the Synoptic preaching?

a. *The relation of the prologue to the discourses and the narrative in general*

Let us determine, in the first place, the true import of what is called the theorem of the Logos. It is claimed that, in thus opening his book, the author places the reader, not on the ground of history, but on that of philosophical speculation.[1] This assertion can be sustained only on one condition, that of restricting the prologue, as Reuss, and he alone, does, to the first five verses. As soon as we extend it, as the sequel forces us to do, as far as ver. 18, we see that the author's thought is not to teach that *there is* in God a Logos—in this, indeed, there would be a speculative theorem—but that this Logos, this divine being, *has appeared* in Jesus Christ—which is not a philosophical idea, but a fact, an element of history, at least as the author understood it. And in fact John the Baptist, vv. 6-9, does not testify of the existence of the Logos, but of this historical fact: that in Jesus the true divine light has been manifested. John does not say, ver. 11, that the fault of the Jews consisted in refusing to believe in the existence of a Logos, but in not receiving, as their Messiah, this divine being when he had appeared in Jesus. The blessedness of the Church (vv. 14-18) does not, according to him, flow from the fact that it has believed in the theorem of the Logos, but from the fact that it has received Him and that it possesses Him, in Jesus Christ, as the Son, the

---

[1] Reuss, p. 11.

Characteristics - The Discourses / 95

source of grace and truth. The question in the prologue, therefore, is only of what Jesus is, the one whose history the author is about to relate. The tendency of this preamble is historical and religious, not metaphysical.

But more than this: the true notion of the person of Jesus is in itself only one of the essential ideas of the prologue. This passage contains two other ideas, which are no less important, and which belong still more manifestly to history. They are that of the rejection of Jesus by the Jews (ver. 11): "He came to his own, and his own received him not"—unbelief, with its consequence, perdition,—and that of the faith of the Church (ver. 16): "And of his fullness have we all received, grace upon grace"—the happiness and salvation of all believers, Jews and Gentiles. These two ideas are not metaphysical notions; they are, no less than the appearance of Christ, real facts, which the author had seen accomplished under his own eyes, and which he proposed to himself to trace out in his history. He contemplated them as realized, at the very moment when he was writing, so soon as he cast a glance on the world which surrounded him. Let us not be told, then, of "abstract formulas placed at the beginning of this book, as a kind of programme!"[1] It is the essence of the history itself which he is about to trace out, that the author sums up by way of anticipation in this preamble.

There is, to his view, such a correlation between the Gospel history which is to follow and the prologue, that the course of the latter has exactly determined the plan of the former. The narrative presents to us three facts which are developed simultaneously: the growing revelation of Jesus as the Christ and the Son of God (xx. 30, 31); the refusal of the Jewish nation, as such, to accept this revelation; and the faith of a certain number of individuals in these testimonies, consisting in acts and words. This course of the history is found again exactly in that of the prologue: vv. 1-5, the Logos; vv. 6-11, the Logos rejected; vv. 12-18, the Logos received. Now, who could hesitate for an instant as to the question whether the history was invented according to this plan, or whether this plan was conceived and traced out according to the history?

Let us remark, also, that the discourses of Jesus were one of the most important factors in the development of the history. What in a war the successive battles are which bring final victory or defeat, this same thing in the ministry of Jesus were those solemn encounters in which the Lord bore testimony of the work which God had just accomplished through Him, or in which there was formed in the people, on one side, that aversion and hatred, on the other, that sympathy and devotion which decided the result of His coming. If it is so, how could the discourses of Jesus which are related by the author be to his view only free theological compositions? Truly as the double result indicated by the prologue, the rejection by Israel and the foundation of the Church, are real facts, so truly must the discourses of Jesus, which so powerfully contributed to lead the history to this two-fold end, be facts no less real to his view.

[1] Reuss, p. 11.

96 / The Fourth Gospel

Finally, there is a quite singular and often noticed fact, which is absolutely opposed to the view that the discourses of Jesus in our Gospel are to be regarded as the developments of a speculative theory peculiar to the author; it is that the term Logos, or *Word*, which characterizes the prologue so strikingly, does not in a single instance figure, as taken in the same sense, in the discourses of Jesus. The expression *word of God* is frequently employed in them to designate the contents of the divine revelation. There was only one step more to be taken in order to apply this term to the revealer himself, as in the prologue. The author has not yielded to this temptation. He might have had, more than once, occasion to make Jesus speak thus, particularly in the conversation of x. 33 ff. The Jews accuse the Lord of blaspheming, because, being a man, He makes Himself God. He replies to them that, in the Old Testament itself, the theocratic judges receive the title of *gods;* comp. Ps. lxxii. 6: "I have said, ye are gods." It was in these terms that the Psalmist addressed himself to the members of the Israelitish tribunal, as organs of the divine justice here below. From these words Jesus draws the following argument: If the Scripture, which cannot blaspheme, calls men *to whom the word of God is addressed* gods, how say you that I blaspheme, I . . ., we almost infallibly expect here: I who am the Word itself. But no; the sentence closes with these words:—" I whom the Father hath sanctified and sent into the world." The author does not yield, then, to any theological allurement; he remains within the limits of the Lord's own language.

Other facts still attest the fidelity with which he can confine himself to his role as historian even in that which concerns the discourse-portion of his work. He had, in his prologue, attributed to the Logos the part of divine agent in the work of creation. He had done this, starting from the testimonies of Jesus respecting His pre-existence and completing them by the narrative of Genesis, and especially by that striking expression : " *Let us make* man in *our* image " (comp. also Gen. iii. 22). Nevertheless, he had not heard this notion of the creative Logos coming forth expressly from the lips of Jesus; therefore he does not bring it into any of His discourses. And yet it might very naturally have presented itself to him, as he wrote, on more than one occasion. Thus, when Jesus prays, saying: "Restore to me the glory which I had with thee before the world was made." How easy would it have been to substitute for these last words the following: Before I made the world, or: Before thou madest the world by me. In the prologue, the Logos is also presented as the illuminator of humanity during the ages previous to His coming (vv. 5, 9, 10). This idea, once expressed by the evangelist, has played a great part in theology since the earliest ages of Christianity. The author does not bring it out anywhere in the discourses of Jesus. And yet, in such a passage as x. 16, where Jesus declares that He has also *other sheep* which are not of this (Jewish) fold, and that He will ere long bring them, or in the discourse of chap. vi., where He several times expresses the idea, that there is needed a divine preliminary *teaching* and *drawing* in order to believe in Him, how natural it would have been to recur to the idea of the illumination of the human soul by the educating light of the Logos! No, surely, he who made Jesus say: "I say nothing except what my Father teaches me," did not allow himself to make Him speak after his own fancy. As he himself declares, 1 Ep. i. 1: "That which he announces to his brethren is only that which he has seen and *heard*." Far from the discourses of Jesus being only the development of a theorem placed at the beginning of the book, the prologue is to the entire work only that which the argument placed at the head of a chapter, and drawn from the contents of it, is to the chapter of a book of history. It is a forcible synthesis, freely formulated, of the history and teachings related in the work itself.

We should find a confirmation of this result in a fact frequently pointed out by Reuss, if this fact were as fully proved to our view as it is to his. According to this critic, we often meet in the Lord's discourses expressions which tend to establish a doctrine directly contrary to the speculative theory of the prologue. This doctrine is that of the subordination of Jesus in relation to God, which, it is urged, is contradictory to the notion of the perfect divinity of the Son, so clearly taught in the prologue. Reuss thinks that he finds in this very contradiction the proof of the fidelity with which the teachings of Jesus, on certain points, have been preserved by our evangelist, in spite of his own theology. But, for ourselves, we shall carefully refrain from using this argument, which rests on a completely false interpretation of the data of the prologue. For it is easy to prove that the subordination of the Logos to the Father is taught in this section, as well as in all the rest of the Gospel.

Before leaving this subject, let us bring forward a strange observation of the same writer. The question is as to the words of John xvii. 3. The distinction between *Jesus Christ* and *the only true God* is there very strongly emphasized—a fact which, according to Reuss, is also contradictory to the teaching of the prologue respecting the divinity of the Saviour. This judgment on his part would have nothing surprising in it, if, in his view, those words had been really uttered by Jesus; they would come into the category of those of which we have just spoken. But no; according to this critic, these words are invented by the author, as well as those of the prologue. The evangelist, then, would ascribe to Jesus, in this case, words contradictory to his own theology! We have been assured up to this point, that he freely composed the discourses in order to put *his* theology into them, and lo, now, he makes Jesus speak in order to combat Himself. In what a labyrinth of contradictions poor criticism here loses itself!

b. *The difficulties alleged against the historical character of the discourses*

There is a very prevalent opinion, at the present day, that Jesus could not have spoken as our evangelist makes Him speak. Renan regards the Johannean discourses as "pieces of theology and rhetoric to which we must not ascribe historical reality, any more than to the discourses which Plato puts into the mouth of his master at the moment of dying."

1. This opinion is, first of all, founded on the *improbabilities inherent in the discourses themselves.*

The argument is, first, from the *obscurity* of the teachings. It would have been a strange want of pedagogic wisdom on Jesus' part to teach in a way so little intelligible. "One would say that Jesus is anxious to speak in enigmas, to soar always in the higher regions inaccessible to the understanding of the common people." By such a mode of teaching He would never have "won hearts given birth to that enthusiastic faith which survived the catastrophe of Golgotha."[1] Assuredly not, if He had always spoken in this way, never otherwise. But our Gospel does not claim to be any more complete with regard to teachings, than with regard to facts. We have proved this: this work traces out only a score of occasions selected from a ministry of two years and a half. There were days—and they were the largest number—when Jesus led His hearers on the lower or middle slopes of the mountain which He wished to make humanity climb; but there were others when He sought to bring them near to the lofty summits and to give them a glimpse of their sublime beauties. Without the discourses of the first sort, no bond would have been formed between their souls and His own. Without those of the second, He would not have raised the Church to the height from which it was to conquer and rule the world. It is these last discourses which the fourth evangelist has especially reproduced, because this higher element of the Saviour's teaching had not found a sufficient place in the primitive tradition intended for popular evangelization. We can understand, indeed, that the life-like and brilliant parables, the very forcible moral maxims, and all the elements of this sort, would rather have supplied the material for the catechetical instruction of the earliest times, and that the teachings of a more elevated nature would have remained in the background in it, without, however, as we shall see, being altogether wanting.

With this first charge is connected that of a certain *monotony.* At bottom, there is in the whole Gospel, according to Sabatier, "only a single discourse;" Reuss would, indeed, find two of them. According to the first of these writers, it is throughout this same idea: "I am the way, the truth, the life." According to the second, this theme is developed, sometimes with regard to the unregenerate world, sometimes with regard to those who already belong to Jesus Christ.[2]

Do the facts, when seriously questioned, confirm this estimate? On the contrary, has not every discourse in this Gospel its originality, its particular point of view, as much as the teachings contained in the Synoptics? When Jesus reveals to Nicodemus the *spiritual nature* of the kingdom of God, in opposition to the earthly idea which the Pharisees formed of it; when He teaches the Samaritan woman the *universality* of the worship which He comes to inaugurate on the earth, in opposition to the local character of the ancient worships; when, at Jerusalem, He unfolds the mystery of the *community of action* between the Father and

---

[1] Reuss, *Théologie johannique*, p. 51.   [2] Sabatier, p. 185; Reuss, p. 28.

the Son, as well as the total dependence of the latter; when, at Capernaum, He sets forth His *relation to the lost world,* and offers Himself to His hearers as the bread from heaven which brings the life of God to mankind; when, in chap. x., He reveals to the people of Jerusalem the formation of the *new flock* which He is about to take out of the old one, and which He will fill up by the sheep brought from all the other folds; when, on the last evening, He announces to His disciples the commission which He entrusts to them of supplying His place on earth by *doing works greater* than His own; then, when He describes to them the *hatred of the world* of which they will be the objects, and when, finally, before saying a last farewell to them, and commending them to the Father in prayer, He promises the *new Helper,* by means of whom they will convince the world of sin, of righteousness and of judgment, and will obtain in His name a complete victory—can this be the teaching always of the same thing? Is there not some partisan interest in this judgment? There is monotony, if you will, in the light of the sun; but what variety in its reflections! There is the same in the boundless azure of the sky; but what richness in its contrasts with the varied lines of the earthly horizon! At the foundation of every Johannean discourse there is an open heaven, the heart of the Son in communion with that of the Father. But this living, personal heaven is in constant relation to the infinitely different individuals who surround it, and to the changing situations through which it moves along its life. The monotony which is charged upon the evangelist, is not that of uniformity, but of unity.

Offense is taken at the same monotony in the *method* employed by the evangelist to introduce the exposition of his theology. He regularly begins, by means of a figurative expression which he ascribes to Jesus, with making the hearer fall into a gross and absurd misapprehension; whereupon Jesus develops His thought and displays His superiority, and that, ordinarily, by pushing His thought even to the extreme of contradiction to that of His interlocutor. This is the fact in the case of Nicodemus, and in that of the Samaritan woman, in the case of the people after the multiplication of the loaves, and, finally, in the conflicts at Jerusalem. There is here a manner adopted by the author, and one which cannot, it is said, belong to the history. But if the people who surrounded Jesus were carnal in their aspirations, they must have been so also in their understanding; for in the moral domain it is from the heart that both light and darkness proceed; Jesus Himself says this, Matt. vi. 22. What then more natural than the constant repetition of this shock at every encounter between the thought of Jesus and that of His contemporaries? On one side, immediate intuition of things above; on the other, the grossest fleshly want of understanding. What point of spiritual development had the apostles reached, according to the Synoptics themselves, after two whole years, during which Jesus had sought, in the conversations of every day, to initiate them into a new view of things? He gives them this admonition: "Beware of the leaven of the Pharisees and of the Sadducees;" and they imagine that He means to reproach them with the forgetfulness into which they had fallen in respect to providing themselves with bread for their proposed journey! Jesus is obliged to say to them: "Have you no understanding, have you your heart still hardened, eyes not to see, and ears not to hear?" (Mark viii. 17, 18.) And yet the critic would declare a similar misunderstanding impossible in the case of Nicodemus, of the Samaritan woman, of His hearers in Galilee or in Jerusalem, who conversed with Him for the first time. And, moreover, it must not be forgotten that the thought of Nicodemus is simply this: "It is not, however, possible that . . ."—this is what the μή (negative interrogation), which begins his question, signifies; and that in other cases, such as John vii. 35 and viii. 22, the apparent misapprehension of the Jews is, in reality, only derisive bantering on their part. As to the misapprehension of the people of Capernaum, John vi., many others were deceived here, even afterwards, in spite of the explanation of Jesus, ver. 63: "It is the spirit that quickeneth, the flesh profiteth nothing." The phenomenon which is marked as suspicious is, therefore, simply a feature drawn from fact.

The same is true of the *dialogue-form* in which many of the teachings of Jesus are presented, especially in chaps. vii. and viii. and in chap. xiv. How could such minute details have been preserved, either in the individual recollection of the author, or traditionally? "These questions and objections," it is said, "do not belong to the history, but to the form of the redaction." They wonderfully depict the state of men's minds, as the *author* found it before him when he wrote, but by no means as it was when Jesus was preaching.[1] But are we then so exactly acquainted with the difference which the state of men's minds may have presented at the beginning of the second century or about the middle of the first? And how can it be seriously maintained that the questions and objections which follow suit better the state of mind in Asia Minor at the beginning of the second century, than the Palestinian prejudices in the time of Jesus? "Doth the Christ, then, come out of Galilee . . . ? Doth he not come from Bethlehem, the village where David was?" (vii. 41, 42.) "We know whence this man is; but when the Christ shall come, no one will know whence he is" (ver. 27). "Are we not right in saying that thou art a Samaritan?" (viii. 48.) "Art thou, then, greater than our father Abraham?" (ver. 53.) "We are Abraham's seed, and have never been in bondage to any one" (ver. 33). "How can this man give us his flesh to eat?" (vi. 52.) "Is not this Jesus, the son of Joseph, whose father and mother we know? How then doth he say: I came down from heaven?" (ver. 42.) If one desires to find a speaking proof of the truly historical character of the teaching of Jesus in our Gospel, it is precisely in these dialogues that it must be sought. To open a commentary is enough to convince us that we have here living manifestations of the Palestinian Judaism which was contemporary with Jesus. Besides, this dialogue-form is not constant; barely indicated in chaps. iii., iv., a little more developed in

---

[1] Reuss, *Théol. joh.*, p. 9.

Characteristics - The Discourses / 101

chap. vi., it is altogether dominant in chaps. vii., viii.—a thing which is perfectly suited to the situation, since here is the culminating point of the conflict between the Lord and His adversaries at Jerusalem. We find scarcely any traces of it in chap. x., where Jesus begins to withdraw from the struggle. It reappears in an emphatic way only in chap. xiv., where it is again rendered natural by the situation. It is the last moment of conversation between Jesus and His own; they take advantage of it to express freely the doubts which each one of them still has in his heart. Let one picture to himself a Christian of the second century crying out, with the simplicity of Philip: "Lord, show us the Father and it sufficeth us!" or, with the pretence of sharing in the ignorance of Thomas, setting himself to say: "We know not whither thou goest, and how shall we know the way?" or asking with Judas: "Why wilt thou make thyself known to us, and not to the world?" or murmuring aside like the disciples (xvi. 17): "What is this that he saith: A little while, and ye shall not see me; and again a little while, and ye shall see me? We cannot tell what he saith." The situation which gave rise to these questions and these doubts existed but for a moment, on that last evening in which John's narrative places them. From the days which followed all these mysteries had received their solution through the great facts of salvation which were from this time forward accomplished. These objections and questions, which it is claimed are to be placed in the second century, carry therefore their date in themselves and belong in their very nature to the upper chamber; it is, consequently, the same with the answers which correspond to them.

Certain *historical contradictions* are also alleged. The following are the two principal ones. Chap. x. 26, in the account of the visit of Jesus at the feast of the Dedication, in December, the evangelist places in His mouth this reproach: " Ye are not of my sheep, *as I said unto you*," which is supposed to be a quotation of the words addressed to the Jews, some months before, at the feast of Tabernacles (comp. the allegories of the Shepherd, the Door, and the Good Shepherd, in the first part of the same chapter). He forgets, therefore, as he makes Jesus speak thus, that the audience had entirely changed from the one feast to the other. But why changed? we will ask. It was not to pilgrims who were strangers, that Jesus had spoken so severely some months before. It was to a group of Pharisees who asked Him, mocking, (ix. 40): " And are we also blind?" They spoke thus in the name of their whole party, and this party, we know, had its seat at Jerusalem. I do not say certainly that at the feast of the Dedication it was the same *individuals* who found themselves again face to face with Jesus; but it was indeed the same class of persons, the Pharisees of Jerusalem, together with the population of that city which was entirely governed by their spirit. Besides, every one knows that the words: *as I said unto you*, on which all the complaint rests, are omitted in six of the principal majuscules, particularly in the *Sinaitic* and *Vatican*.

Another similar argument is drawn from the discourse of Jesus, reported in xii. 44 ff. It is "a recapitulation of the evangelical theology," says

102 / The Fourth Gospel

Reuss; and the author puts it into the mouth of Jesus here, without thinking that, according to his own narrative, Jesus has just "withdrawn and disappeared from the public view." Here is a fact, adds this critic, which is well fitted "to give us a just idea of the nature of the discourses of Jesus" in this work.[1] Baur had already concluded from this passage that the historical situations are for the author nothing but mere forms. It is not the evangelist's fault if his narrative is thus judged. He had counted on readers who would not doubt his common sense. He had just expressly concluded the narrative of the public ministry of Jesus by this solemn sentence: "And departing, he did hide himself from them" (ver. 36). And yet he is said to put into His mouth, immediately afterwards, a solemn address to the people! No; from ver. 37 the author has himself begun to speak; he gives himself up to the sorrowful contemplation of the unsuccessfulness of such an extraordinary ministry. He proves by the facts the inefficacy of the numerous miracles of Jesus to overcome the unbelief of the people (vv. 37–43). Then, in ver. 44, he passes, in this same recapitulation, from the miracles to the teachings, which, as well as the miracles, had remained inefficacious before such obduracy; and in order to give an understanding of what the entire preaching ministry accomplished by Jesus in Israel had been, he sums it up in the discourse, vv. 44–50, which is, in relation to the discourses of Jesus, what ver. 37 was to His miraculous activity, a simple summary: "And yet he cried aloud!" Then follows the summary, thus announced, of all the solemn testimonies which had remained fruitless. This passage, also, is distinguished from all the real discourses, in that it does not contain *a single* new idea; for every word, two or three parallels can be cited in the preceding discourses. Reuss, therefore, is unfortunate in proposing to draw from this discourse, which is not one in the intention of the evangelist himself, the true standard for the estimate of all those which, in this work, are put into the mouth of our Lord.

Finally, objection has also been made to the truth of the discourses by reason of the impossibility that the author should have retained them in memory up to the time, no doubt quite late in his life, when he wrote them out. Reuss abandons this objection. He thinks that the words of Jesus, so far as the author either heard them himself or borrowed them from the tradition, "must have been throughout his life the subject of his meditations, and must have been impressed the more deeply on his mind the longer he fed upon them."[2] In fact, if the question is of the earnest discussions carried on at Jerusalem (chaps. vii. viii.), how should they not have been distinctly impressed on the memory of the one who witnessed them with such lively anxiety? As for the discourses which are somewhat extended, like those of chap. v. and vi., x., xv.–xvii., the hearer's memory found, in every case, a point of support in a central idea which was clearly formulated at the beginning, and which unfolded itself afterwards in a series of particular notions subordinated to this primal idea.

[1] P. 50. [2] P. 44.

Thus in chap. v., the first part of the apologetic discourse of Jesus is contained, as if in its germ, in that very striking saying of ver. 17: "My Father worketh hitherto, and [consequently] I also work." This idea of the necessary co-operation of the Son with His Father is developed in a first cycle under two aspects: The Son beholding the Father, and the Father revealing His work to the Son, vv. 19, 20. Then, this first cycle, which is also very summary in its character, becomes the starting-point of a new, more precise development, in which is unfolded, even to its most concrete applications, the work of the Son in execution of the thought of the Father. This work consists in the two divine acts of *quickening* and *judging* (vv. 21-23), acts which are taken up each one of them successively, and followed out through all their historical phases even to their complete realization, at first spiritual, then external and material (vv. 24-29).—It is nearly the same in the second part of this discourse (vv. 30-47), in which everything is subordinated to this principal thought: "There is another [the Father] that beareth witness of me," and in which is set forth the three-fold testimony of the Father on behalf of the Son, with a final forcible application to the hearers.—In chap. vi., it is easy to see that everything—discourse and conversation—is likewise subordinated to a great idea,—that which naturally arises from the miracle of the preceding day: "I am the bread of life." This affirmation is developed in a series of concentric cycles, which end finally in this most striking and concrete expression: "Unless ye eat my flesh and drink my blood, ye will not have life in yourselves." In chap. xvii., in the second part of the sacerdotal prayer, which contains the intercession of Jesus for His disciples, His thought follows the same course. The general idea: "I pray for them," soon divides itself into those two more particular ones which become, each of them, the centre of a subordinate cycle: "*Keep them*" (τήρησον), ver. 11, that is to say: "Let not the work be impaired which I have accomplished in them," and: "*Sanctify them*" (ἁγίασον), ver. 17, that is to say: "Perfect and finish their consecration."—In these several cases, if the thoughts of Jesus really were unfolded in this form, which best suits the nature of religious contemplation, we can readily understand how it was not difficult for an attentive hearer to reproduce such sayings. It was enough for him to fix his attention strongly on the central thought, distinctly engraved upon his memory, and then inwardly to repeat the same process of evolution which, from this germ, had produced the discourse. He thus recovered again the subordinate ideas, from which he reached even the most concrete details. Jesus, however, did not always speak in this way; we have the proof of this in our Synoptics, and in the fourth Gospel itself. This method was natural when a theme of great richness was indicated to Him by the situation, as in chaps. v. and vi. But we do not find anything of the kind either in the conversation with Nicodemus, or in those of chap. xiv.—which proves that we need not see in this a style peculiar to the evangelist. The following is, probably, what happened in the last mentioned cases. The conversation with Nicodemus certainly continued much longer than the few moments which we use in reading

104 / The Fourth Gospel

it, and the last conversations of Jesus with the disciples, having filled a great part of the evening, must have lasted some hours. It must therefore be admitted (unless all this was invented) that a work of condensation was wrought in the mind of the narrator, in which the essential thoughts gradually became separated from the secondary thoughts and transitions, and then were directly, and without a connective, joined to one another, as they actually appear to us in the account given by John. There remain for us, therefore, of these conversations only the principal points. Nothing could be more simple than this process.

The conclusion of this study, therefore, is that there is no serious intrinsic difficulty to prevent us from admitting the historical truth of the teachings of Jesus contained in our Gospel.

II. But a more serious objection is drawn from the correspondence of these discourses with those of *John the Baptist,* and with the author's own teachings *in the prologue* and *in his first epistle.*

Jesus, in St. John, speaks just as John the Baptist does (comp. i. 15, 29, 30; iii. 27–36), just as the evangelist himself does in his own writings. Is there not here an evident proof that the discourses—those of Jesus, like those of John the Baptist—are his own composition? There can be no question here of style, as to its grammatical and syntactic forms; how, indeed, is it possible that the style should not be that of the evangelist? Neither Jesus nor John the Baptist spoke in Greek; and to reproduce their discourses in a tolerable way in that language, whose genius is precisely the opposite of that of the Aramæan language, in which the Saviour and His forerunner spoke, a literal translation was impossible. The author was obliged in any case, therefore, to go underneath the words to the thoughts, and then to clothe these again with a new expression borrowed from the language in which he was relating them. In such a work of assimilation and reproduction, why might not the language of John the Baptist have taken a coloring like that of the language of Jesus, and the language of both the coloring of the evangelist's style? The question here is not of the external forms of speech; it is of the faithful preservation of the thoughts. In translating the words of John and Jesus, is it to be supposed that the author altered their meaning? Was there anything of his own added? Or did he even compose with entire freedom? It is supposed that an affirmative answer can be given. First of all, the discourse of John the Baptist, iii. 27–36, is alleged. Reuss grants, no doubt, that two expressions of this discourse proceed from the forerunner —that which forms the opening of it: "I am not the Christ," and the word which is its centre: "He must increase, but I must decrease."[1] Moreover, continues the critic, "there is not in all the remainder a word which does not find a place quite as well, or rather a hundred times better, in the mouth of a Christian wholly imbued with the dominant ideas of this book, and which is not reproduced elsewhere, as to its essence, in the discourses ascribed to Jesus Himself."[2] But what! can it be that

---

[1] Reuss' Translation. [2] Pp. 48, 49.

Characteristics - The Discourses / 105

these words made up the whole of the Baptist's answer to his disciples, who were bitterly accusing Jesus of ingratitude! Let it be allowed us to believe that he developed them somewhat, and, in particular, to place in the number of the authentic expressions that word of inimitable beauty (ver. 29): "He that hath the bride is the bridegroom; the friend of the bridegroom who standeth and heareth him, rejoiceth greatly because of the bridegroom's voice; and this my joy is fulfilled." Men did not invent after this fashion in the second century, as our Apocryphal books bear witness! Let us go still further: if we admit the narrative of the Synoptics, according to which the forerunner had heard the voice of the Father saying to Jesus: "Thou art my beloved Son; in thee I am well pleased," is it impossible to admit that the same man should have uttered these words, which the evangelist puts into his mouth (ver. 35): "*The Father loveth the Son,* and hath put all things into his hand?" If it is also true—still according to the Synoptics—that John saw the Holy Spirit descending upon Jesus in the form of a dove, that is, in His organic and indivisible plenitude, is it incredible that he should have expressed himself with regard to Jesus as he does, according to John, in ver. 34: "He speaketh the words of God; for *God giveth him the Spirit* without measure (or: the Spirit giveth them to him without measure)?" And if John the Baptist expresses himself at the beginning of his ministry as the Synoptics make him speak: "Brood of vipers, who hath warned you to flee *from the wrath to come?* Every tree that bringeth not forth good fruit is cut down and cast into the fire!" (Matt. iii. 7–10), is it not very natural that he should close his public activity with this warning: "He that refuseth to obey the Son, the wrath of God abideth on him." Here is the last echo of the thunders of Sinai, which is in its appropriate place in the mouth of the last representative of the old covenant. But the objection falls back on the saying: "He testifieth of what he hath seen and heard, and no man receiveth his testimony," and it asks how it can be that John the Baptist should so literally repeat the declaration of Jesus Himself in His conversation with Nicodemus (ver. 11): "Verily, I say unto thee, we speak that which we know and testify that which we have seen, and ye receive not our testimony." He was not present, however, at that conversation! No; but it may well be that something of it had been reported to him; and, even if it was otherwise, what meaning would the words of the Baptist have which we were just now calling to mind: "The friend of the bridegroom who standeth and heareth, rejoiceth exceedingly *because of the bridegroom's voice;* and *this my joy* is fulfilled?" He hears the voice of the bridegroom! Some word of Jesus, then, has come to his ears. And is it not natural indeed, that, while John and Jesus were baptizing in each other's neighborhood (vv. 22, 23), those of the apostles who had been disciples of the forerunner should have taken a few steps to go and salute their former master, and should have reported to him what Jesus did and said? The discourse of John the Baptist is thus explained from beginning to end. And the word to which Reuss reduced it, ver. 30, was simply its central idea. Indeed, all that precedes (vv. 27–29), is the development of

106 / The Fourth Gospel

the second proposition: "I must decrease," and all that follows, vv. 31–36, is that of the first: "He must increase."

But is it possible to regard as historical the words put into the mouth of John the Baptist in the prologue, i. 15, and repeated afterwards in the narrative itself, i. 30: "He who cometh after me was before me?" Could John know and declare the divine pre-existence of Jesus? If this declaration had been mentioned only in the prologue, which is the composition of the evangelist, the doubt would be possible. But the author expressly places it again, at a little later point, in its historical context (ver. 30). He relates how it was at Bethany that the forerunner uttered it, on the day which followed that of the deputation of the Sanhedrim. There would be a singular affectation, not to say, palpable bad faith, in these subsidiary indications of time and place, if the words were the invention of the author. Besides they have a seal of originality and of mysterious conciseness which is foreign to the later fictions. And why should they not be authentic? When John the Baptist began his ministry, we know that the programme of his work was the double prophecy of Isaiah xl. 3: "A voice crying in the wilderness: Prepare ye the way of the Lord," and of Malachi iii. i: "Behold, I send my messenger, and he shall prepare the way before me" (Matt. iii. 3; x. 10; Mark i. 2, 3; Luke i. 17; vii. 27). Now, in the second of these two passages, always so closely bound together, He who *sends* the messenger (Jehovah) is none other than He who is Himself soon to *follow* him (Jehovah as Messiah); this is unanswerably proved by the words, *before me*, in the prophetic utterance. If John the Baptist was acquainted with this passage, could he not understand—what do I say?—could he fail to understand, that the one *coming after* him (the Messiah) was the one *sending* him, and consequently his *predecessor* on the scene of history, the invisible theocratic King. The question comes back, then, to this: Did John the Baptist know how to read?

The resemblance in matter and form between the *prologue* and the discourses of Jesus does not constitute a difficulty which is any more serious. For, on the one hand, we have seen that the matter of the teachings of the prologue is, in great part, only a résumé of these very discourses; and, on the other, it is impossible that, in translating them from Aramaic into Greek, the author should not, in a certain measure, have clothed them in his own style. The conformity indicated is, therefore, a fact which is easily explained.

Is the conformity between the discourses and *the first Epistle* to be considered more compromising for the authenticity of the former? As to the form, the resemblance is explained by the causes already pointed out, when speaking of the prologue. But even from this external point of view, H. Meyer has discovered a kind of impoverishment in the vocabulary of the epistle, as compared with that of the discourses.[1] Some thirty substantives, some twenty verbs—this is the whole linguistic fund of the epistle. What

---

[1] *Les discours du IV.ᵉ évangile*, p. 94.

Characteristics - The Discourses / 107

a difference from the discourses, so rich in living and original words, and in striking and varied images! There are also, on the other hand, certain particular expressions which appertain to the epistle and which are foreign to the Gospel, such as *to be born of God* (ii. 29; iii. 9; iv. 7; v. 1; comp. the prologue, Gosp. i. 13); the *anointing* of the Spirit (ii. 20, 27); the title of *Paraclete* applied to Jesus (ii. 1).

As to the matter, we discover even much more remarkable differences between the epistle and the Gospel, which prove that the author observed very carefully the line of demarcation between his own thoughts and the teachings of Jesus. We shall set forth three points, especially, which hold an important place in the epistle, and which are not mentioned anywhere in the discourses: 1. The expiatory value of the Lord's death (Ep. i. 7, 9; ii. 2; iv. 10; v. 6); 2. The coming of Antichrist (ii. 18, 22; iv. 1–3); 3. The expectation of the Parousia (i. 18, 28; iii. 2). These three notions, while connecting our epistle closely with the Synoptic Gospels, distinguish it profoundly from the Johannean discourses. The attempt has been, not long since, made to explain this difference by ascribing the epistle to another author than the Gospel. This hypothesis has not been able to maintain itself, even in the midst of the school in which it arose. The disciples of Baur, such as Hilgenfeld, Lüdemann, etc., are agreed in rejecting it. How then can we explain this singular difference? Several critics have been led to think that the author of the two works was still imbued with his old Jewish ideas when he composed the epistle, and that he rose only at a later time to the sublime spirituality which distinguishes the Gospel.[1] The epistle would, thus, be older than the Gospel. We do not believe that this hypothesis can be sustained. The discourses contained in the Gospel are distinguished from the teachings of the epistle by a force of thought and a vigor of expression, which indicate for them a date anterior to the composition of this latter work. Besides, the man who, in the epistle, addresses himself not only to *the children* and *young men*, but also to *fathers* of families and to all the members of the churches, calling them "my little children" (ii. 1, 18, 28; v. 21), cannot have been otherwise than far advanced in age. It is not under such conditions that a man rises from the style of the epistle to that of the Gospel, from the somewhat slow and even hesitating step of the one to the straightforward and powerful flight of the other.[2] A further proof that the composition of the discourses preceded that of the epistle, is the fact that all the ideas which in the discourses are presented in a form which is historical, occasional, actual, applicable to particular circumstances and hearers, reappear in the epistle in an abstract form as general Christian maxims, and, in some sort, as the elements of a religious philosophy. Jesus said in the Gospel: "God so loved the world," or "Thou didst love me before the foundation of the world." The epistle says: "God is love." Jesus said: "The Father whose offspring you are is

---

[1] Hilgenfeld, *Einleitung*, p. 738; Lüdemann, *zur Erklärung des Papias-Fragments*, in the *Jahrb. für prot. Theol.*, 1879.

[2] Sabatier himself acknowledges (p. 189) that the epistle is poorer, more feeble than the discourses in the Gospel.

the devil, and you do the works of your father." The epistle says: "He that commits sin is of the devil." Jesus said: "You have not chosen me, but I have chosen you." The epistle says: "It is not we who have loved God; it is He who has loved us." Jesus said: "I am the light of the world; he that followeth me shall not walk in darkness." The epistle says: "God is light ... the true light now shineth." Jesus said: "I have a witness greater than that of men." The epistle says: "If we receive the witness of men, that of God is greater." Is it not evident that these aphorisms of the second work are nothing but the generalization of the special affirmations, full of reality, which belong to the first? The Gospel is history; the epistle is the spirit of history. It is consequently contrary to all sound criticism to place the latter before the former.

The difference between these two works must, therefore, be explained in another way. It is an indisputable fact that the ideas which we have pointed out as clearly distinguishing the epistle from the Gospel, appertain to the Synoptic teaching, and consequently form a part of the apostolic beliefs and of the doctrine of the Church in general. Here, then, was the matter from which the author drew when writing the epistle. But when he wrote out the five or six discourses which he has preserved for us, he did not allow himself to go beyond their original purport, nor to introduce into them, as Reuss claims, *the whole* of his theology. He limited himself to that which he had *heard* on those particular occasions. The epistle forms thus a natural link of connection between the Johannean teachings and those of the Synoptics. And the more closely it attaches itself to the latter in the substance of the ideas, the more does it become a confirmation of the historical character both of the one and the other.

Far then from giving us grounds of suspicion, the comparison of the discourses with the author's own compositions is converted into a proof of the fidelity with which he has reproduced the former, and the author seems nowhere to have crossed the line of demarcation between what he had heard and what he himself composed.

III. We here reach the most difficult side of the question with which we have to do. We possess in the first three Gospels three documents, perfectly harmonious and of undisputed value, containing the teachings of Jesus. These teachings appear therein in a simple, popular, practical form; they are what they must have been in order to charm the multitudes and win their assent. How could the abstruse and theological discourses of the fourth Gospel have proceeded from the same mind and the same lips? "We must choose," says Renan: "if Jesus spoke as Matthew would have Him, He could not have spoken as John would have Him." "Now," he adds, "between the two authorities no critic has hesitated, or will hesitate."

Is the contrast thus indicated really as inexplicable as is asserted? It is to the study of this question that we are going to devote the following pages.

As to the *contents* of the teachings, three points, especially, appear to distinguish the discourses of John from those of the Synoptics: 1. The

Characteristics - The Discourses / 109

difference in the part assigned to the person of Jesus in the matter of salvation; 2. The Johannean notion of the existence of Jesus, as a divine being, anterior to His earthly life; 3. The omission in John of every expression relating to His visible return, as judge of the world.

With regard to the part of Jesus in the matter of salvation, it is alleged that, while the Christ of the Synoptics simply announces the kingdom of God—the *good tidings* of the near coming of that glorious state of things,— the Christ of John can only preach Himself, and tell what He is as related to God and what He is as related to the world. While the Synoptic teachings bear upon the most varied moral obligations, beneficence, humility, veracity, detachment from the world, watchfulness, prayer—in a word, upon *the righteousness of the kingdom,* according to the expression of Jesus Himself,—in John, on the contrary, every duty is reduced to the attaching of oneself to that being come from heaven, in whom God reveals and gives Himself. In the Synoptics, Jesus is the preacher of salvation; in John, He is salvation itself, eternal life, everything.

Is the difference thus pointed out as considerable as it is said to be, and is the contrast inexplicable? No, this cannot be; for the *central* position which the person of Christ occupies in the Johannean teaching is also decidedly ascribed to Him in that of the first three Gospels. The moral precepts which Jesus gives in the latter are placed in intimate relation with His own person; and among the duties of human life, that which takes precedence of all the rest is, in them as in John, faith in Christ the indispensable condition of salvation. Let the reader judge for himself.

"Sell that thou hast and give to the poor . . . , then *follow me,*" says Jesus to the rich young man (Matt. xix. 21). The second of these commands explains the first; the one is the condition, the other the end. "Verily I say unto you that, inasmuch as ye have done it unto one of these my brethren, ye have done it unto *me*" (Matt. xxv. 40). It is the sympathy for *Him,* Jesus, which constitutes the worth of this help, and which is, if we may so speak, the good work in the good work (comp. x. 42). Jesus adds (xxv. 41), as He turns towards the condemned: "Depart *from me,* ye cursed!" Perdition is the rupture of all union with *Him.* To receive *Him* is to receive God, He declares to His disciples (Matt. x. 40). The most indisputable proof that one possesses the humble disposition which is necessary in order to enter into the kingdom, is that of receiving a child *in the name of Jesus;* that is, as if one were receiving Jesus Himself; and the offense which will infallibly destroy him who has the unhappiness to occasion it, is this—that it is caused to *one of these little ones who believe in Him* (Matt. xviii. 5, 6); so true is it that the good in the good is love for *Him,* and the crime in the crime is the evil which one does to *Him.* The infallibly efficacious prayer is that of two or three persons praying *in His name* (Matt. xviii. 20). Real watchfulness consists in waiting for *Him,* the returning Lord, and the condition of the entrance with Him into His glory is the being ready to receive *Him* at His coming (Luke xii. 36). If the foolish virgins are rejected, it is for not having fulfilled their duty towards *Him* (Matt. xxv. 12). To confess *Him* here below is the way to be acknowledged by Him above, as also to deny *Him* is to pronounce one's own sentence (Matt. x. 32, 33; Mark viii. 38). The most intimate and sacred relations of human life must remain constantly subordinated to the bond which unites the believer to Jesus, so that the believer must be ready to break them, "to hate father, mother, child, wife, his own life," if the supreme bond requires this sacrifice (Matt. x. 37). Otherwise one would not be *worthy of Him*, which is equivalent to *being ranked among the workers of iniquity*, and being excluded with them (Matt. vii. 23; xxv. 12). Not to have turned to account the gifts entrusted by Him for working in *His cause*, for increasing *His* wealth here below,—to have been *His* unprofitable servant,—this is enough to cause one to be cast into the *outer darkness*, where there are only weeping and gnashing of teeth (Matt. xxv. 30). The most decisive act of the moral life, the indispensable condition to being able to *find* one's life again in the future,—to give oneself, to *lose* oneself—this act can be accomplished only *for His sake* (Matt. x. 39). Could Jesus describe otherwise the relation of man to God Himself?

There is one fact in the Gospel history omitted by John, but preserved by the three Synoptics, which shows, more clearly than all the sayings can do, how Jesus really made the whole religious and moral life of His own consist in personal union with Himself. It is the institution of the Holy Supper, together with those two declarations which explain it: "This is my blood which is shed for many for the remission of sins;" and, "The Son of Man came to give His life a ransom for many" (Matt. xxvi. 28; xx. 28). To incorporate Jesus into oneself, is to appropriate life to oneself. Jesus is not only the preacher of salvation; He is also, as in John, salvation itself. The part of Jesus in the matter of salvation, therefore, does not fundamentally differ in the two teachings; and so the Church has never experimentally felt the contrast indicated. Herein only, as it seems to me, is the difference and its origin. The Synoptics, with a partiality for them—we have seen the reason of this—traced out the popular and daily preachings of Jesus, in which He sought to awaken the moral life of His hearers and to stimulate the spiritual instincts which alone could lead them to Him. Now, these hearers were Jews, brought up from infancy in the expectation of the Messianic Kingdom. Jesus, like John the Baptist, takes, therefore, this glorious hope for the starting-point of His teaching, while endeavoring to spiritualize it and to set forth holiness as the essential characteristic of that future state of things. With this purpose, He emphasizes forcibly the moral qualities which its members must possess. But this was only the propaedeutic and elementary teaching, the general basis (which was common to Him with the law and the prophets) of the special and truly new preaching which He brought to the world. This preaching had reference to the part played by His person in the work of salvation and in the establishment of the kingdom. And when He comes to this subject in the Synoptics, He insists, no less than in the fourth Gospel, on the vital importance of faith in Him, and on the concentration of salvation in His person and work. Without the first form of teaching, He would have found His hearers only deaf. Without the second, He would never have carried them on to the point to which He desired to raise them. While describing to us particularly the first, the Synoptics have nevertheless faithfully preserved the second; and it is in this that we especially discover, as we have just now done, the common matter, as between them and John.

But there is a point on which the fourth Gospel seems to pass decidedly beyond the contents of the Synoptic teaching. It is that of the *divine pre-existence* of Jesus. Must we recognize here an idea imported by the author of the fourth Gospel into the Lord's teaching, or should we regard this notion as a real element in the testimony of Jesus respecting Himself?

Three sayings, in the Gospel of John, in particular, evidently contain this notion: "What will happen when you shall see the Son of man ascending up *where he was before*" (vi. 62). "Verily, verily, I say unto you, *Before* Abraham was, I *am*" (viii. 58). "And now, Father, glorify thou me with thyself, with the glory *which I had with thee* before the world was" (xvii. 5); or indeed, as Jesus says in ver. 24, "because thou lovedst me before the foundation of the world." Beyschlag, Weizsäcker, Ritschl, and others attempt to give to this pre-existence only an ideal sense: Jesus felt and recognized Himself as the man whom God had from eternity foreseen, loved, chosen, and destined to be the Saviour of mankind, and the feeling of this eternal predestination formulated itself in Him as the consciousness of His personal pre-existence. But this attempt at explanation stops far short of the meaning of the words which we have just quoted. "Where *He* was before" can only designate an existence as real, as personal, as the present existence of Him who thus speaks. And in the other two declarations, the comparison with Abraham ("before Abraham was," literally, *became*, γενέσθαι), and with the world ("before the world was"), two perfectly real beings, does not allow us to ascribe to Him who is compared with them, in the point of precedence, a less real existence than theirs. The sole question, consequently, is whether Jesus *Himself* spoke in this way, or whether some other person attributed to Him such assertions.

Let us, first of all, recall to mind the fact that the idea of the divinity of the Messiah was one of the fundamental points of the doctrine of the prophets. Only an exegesis thoroughly determined not to bow before the texts can deny this. If the critics will have it so, we will not insist upon the second Psalm, although, according to our conviction, the words: "Thou art my Son," and these: "Kiss the Son," cannot denote anything else than the participation of the Messiah in the divine existence, and the obligation on the part of men to worship Him. But what cannot be denied is the titles of *Mighty God* and *Eternal Father* which Isaiah gives to "the child who is born to us" (ix. 5); the contrast which Micah institutes (v. 2) between the earthly birth of the ruler of Israel, at *Bethlehem*, and His higher origin which is *from eternity;* the identification, in Zechariah, of Jehovah with the suffering Messiah, in that expression which is tortured in vain: "They shall look on *me* whom they have *pierced*" (xii. 10);

finally and above all, that promise which Malachi puts in the mouth—of whom? of Jehovah or of the Messiah? evidently of both, since it identifies them, as we have already seen: " Behold, *I send* my messenger (the forerunner), and he shall prepare the way *before me,* and the Lord whom ye seek, *the angel of the covenant* whom ye desire, shall suddenly enter into *his* temple; behold, he cometh, saith the Lord of hosts" (iii. 1). The coming of the Messiah is the coming of the Lord, of *Adonai,* a name which is given only to God; it is the coming of the *angel of the covenant,* of that angel of the Lord of whom the Pentateuch speaks many times, and whom Isaiah calls "the angel of his presence" (lxiii. 9), of that mysterious being in whom the Lord appears, ever since the earliest times, when He wishes to manifest Himself in a manner apprehensible to the senses, and of whom God says (Num. xxiii. 21): "*My name* (my manifested essence) is in Him." It is this mysterious being who, in these words of Malachi—which may be called the culminating point of Messianic prophecy—declares Himself to be at once the Messiah who is to follow the forerunner and the God who sends Him, and who is worshiped at Jerusalem. And let it not be said that we put into this passage things which are not in it, or which, at least, were not yet seen in it in the time of Jesus. We have already had the proof of the contrary. That saying of John the Baptist: " He who cometh after me was before me," was derived by him from this source through the illumination of the Spirit. But we possess yet another proof—it is the words which Luke puts into the mouth of the angel, when he announces to Zachariah the birth of John the Baptist: " He (John) shall turn many of the children of Israel to the Lord their God, and *he shall go before him* in the spirit and power of Elijah, to turn the hearts of the fathers to the children. . . ." He shall go before him . . . Before whom? The preceding words say expressly: "*before the Lord, their God.*" And if we could doubt that these words are a reproduction of those of Malachi, this doubt would fall away before the following words: " in the spirit and power of Elijah," which are literally taken from the following chapter of the same prophet (iv. 5, 6). No man in Israel, therefore, to whom the prophecies were familiar, could refuse to ascribe to the person of the Messiah a superhuman nature. There would be, consequently, even from the natural point of view, nothing surprising in the fact that Jesus, who proclaimed Himself the Messiah, should, at the same time, have affirmed His divine pre-existence.

A second instructive fact presents itself to us in the New Testament. The pre-existence of Christ is not only taught in the discourses of John; it is taught in the epistles of Paul. According to 1 Cor. viii. 6, as according to John's prologue, it is Christ who *created* all things. According to the same epistle, x. 4, the invisible rock which led Israel in the wilderness, and which delivered Israel, was Christ. According to Col. i. 15–17, He is "the first-born before the whole creation;" He is "before all things;" it is "by Him that all things are created, the heavenly and the earthly; all is by Him and for Him, all subsists in Him." And it is not only St. Paul who enunciates this idea. The epistle to the Hebrews which, by its destination even, testifies to the faith of the primitive Palestinian Church,[1] declares that it is Christ who made the world, whom the angels worship, who laid the foundations of the earth and the heavens, who is always the same, and is as much more exalted than Moses as the one who has built the house is greater than the house itself (i. 2, 6, 10, 12; iii. 3). More than this: the same idea is found again in the Apocalypse, that Judaizing book as it is claimed. Jesus is therein, as Jehovah Himself is in Isaiah, called *the first and the last;* that is to say, as the author himself explains it, the *beginning* and the *end* ($\dot{\alpha}\rho\chi\dot{\eta}$ καὶ τέλος) of the whole creation;[2] all creatures fall down before the Lamb seated on the throne, as well as before the Father. It is not then either to any individual (whether the true, or the pseudo-John), or to any school (that of Ephesus), or to any semi-Gnostic party, or to any Church of Asia Minor, that the doctrine of the divinity and pre-existence of the Christ belongs; it is to the Church represented in all its parts by the authors and the readers of the writings which we have just quoted.[3] If it is so, this idea, so generally received, of the person of Christ must have rested upon positive testimonies which proceeded from the mouth of Jesus, such as those which we find in the fourth Gospel.

The first three Gospels themselves, far from contradicting this result, confirm it. We have already shown that these writings attribute to the person of Christ absolutely the same central position, as related to the human soul, which the Old Testament ascribes to God. For whom were absolute trust and love reserved by Moses and the prophets? Jesus claims them for Himself in the Synoptics, and this even in the name of our salvation. Would Jewish monotheism, which was so strict and so jealous of the rights of God, have permitted Jesus to take a position like this, if He had not had the distinct consciousness that in the background of His human existence there was a divine personality? He cannot, as a faithful Jew, wish to be for us that which in the Synoptics He asks to be, except so far as He is what He declares Himself to be in John.[4]

A large number of particular facts in the same writings add their force to this general conclusion. We have just seen how, in Luke, He who comes after the forerunner is called, in the preceding words, *the Lord their God.* In

---

[1] We cannot allow any critical probability to the opinion which seeks in Italy or in any other country than Palestine the persons to whom this epistle was addressed.

[2] i. 17; ii. 8; xxii. 13. Hilgenfeld claims that the Jesus of the Apocalypse is only the first created among the *angels* (iii. 14). But comp. xxii. 9, 16, which positively excludes this idea; xxii. 11 proves that ἀρχή, Mi. 14, signifies not beginning, but origin, unless τέλος must signify that Jesus is the *end* of the existence of the universe, in the sense of de Hartmann!

[3] Here is what Weizsäcker himself says (p. 222): "At the time when the primitive apostolic tradition was still represented by a whole series of witnesses, the Apostle Paul taught respecting the person of Jesus a doctrine according to which He was the Son of God who had come from heaven to renew mankind, the one whom God made use of as His instrument in the creation of the world. And we do not find any trace of an opposition which this teaching had encountered in the primitive apostolic circles, and which gave it the character of a peculiar view."

[4] Schultz writes these words in his recent work on the divinity of Jesus Christ: "The sentiment of religious dependence is not admissible except before the *only* true God... We should not bow religiously except before that which is *really* divine." (*Die Lehre von der Gottheit Christi,* pp. 540, 541.)

114 / The Fourth Gospel

Mark, the person of the Son is placed even above the most exalted creatures: "Of that day knoweth no one, not even the angels who are in heaven, nor even the Son [during the time of His humiliation], but the Father only" (xiii. 32). In Matthew, the Son is placed between the Father and the Holy Spirit, the breath of God: "Baptize all the nations in the name of the Father and of the Son and of the Holy Spirit" (xxviii. 19). In the parable of the vine-dressers, Jesus Himself represents Himself, in contrast with the *servants* sent before Him, as the son and heir of the Master of the vineyard (Matt. xxi. 37, 38). It will be in vain to subject the question of Jesus (Matt. xxii. 45): "If David calls the Christ his Lord, how is he his son?" to all imaginable manipulations; the thought of Jesus will ever come forth simple and clear for him who does not try to find difficulties where there are none. If, on one side, the Christ is the son of David by His earthly origin, on the other side He is, nevertheless, his Lord, in virtue of His divine personality. This is what Micah had said already (v. 2). And how, if He did not have the consciousness of His divinity, could Jesus speak of *His* angels (Matt. xiii. 41), of *His* glory (xxv. 31), finally, of *His* name under the invocation of which believers are gathered together? The Old Testament did not authorize any creature thus to appropriate to himself the attributes of Jehovah. Now the notion of His pre-existence was for Jesus implicitly included in that of His divinity.

Undoubtedly, we do not find in the Synoptics any declaration as precise as those which we have just now quoted from the Johannean discourses. But do we not discover in the Gospel of Luke the immense quantity of materials which would be entirely wanting to us if we possessed only those of Matthew and Mark; for example, the three parables of grace (Luke xv.; the lost sheep, the lost drachma, the prodigal son); those of the unfaithful steward and of the wicked rich man (Luke xvi.); those of the unjust judge, and of the publican and the Pharisee (Luke xviii.); the story of Zacchæus; the incident of the converted thief, and so many other treasures which Luke has rescued from the oblivion where the other redactions of the tradition had left them, and which he alone has preserved to the Church? How, then, can we make of the omission of these few sayings in our first three Gospels an argument against their authenticity? If pictures so impressive, narratives so popular, as those which we have just recalled had not entered into the oral preaching of the Gospel, or into any of its written redactions, how much more easily could three or four expressions of a very elevated and profoundly mysterious character have been obliterated from the tradition, to reappear later as the reminiscences of a hearer who was particularly attentive to everything in the teaching of Jesus which concerned His person? The dogmatic interest which these declarations have for us did not exist to the same degree at that time; for the impression of the person of Jesus, contemplated daily in its living fullness, filled all hearts and supplied all special vacancies. Let us not forget, moreover, that of these three sayings one is found in the discourse which follows the multiplication of the loaves, a discourse which the Synoptics omit altogether; the second, in a discourse pronounced at Jerusalem, and which is

Characteristics - The Discourses / 115

likewise omitted in them, together with the entire visit of which it forms a part; the third, in the sacerdotal prayer of which they have also given no report. As to John, according to his plan he must necessarily call them to mind, if he wished, as appears from xx. 30, 31, to give an account of the signs by which he had recognized in Jesus the Christ, *the Son of God*, and which might contribute to produce the same assurance of faith in his readers. These culminating points of the testimony of Jesus respecting His person could not be wanting in such a picture.

There remains the difference in *the eschatological ideas*. In the Synoptics, a visible return of the Lord, a final external judgment, a bodily resurrection of believers, a reign of glory; in John, no other return of Christ than His coming into the hearts in the form of the Holy Spirit; no other resurrection than that of the soul through regeneration; no other judgment than the separation which is effected between believers and unbelievers through the preaching of the Gospel; no other reign than the life of the believer in Christ and in God. "This entire Gospel is planned," says Hilgenfeld, "so as to present the historical coming of Christ as His only appearance on the earth."[1]—But is this exclusive spiritualism which is attributed to the fourth Gospel indeed a reality? John certainly emphasizes the return of Jesus in the spirit. But is this in order wholly to supersede and to deny His visible return? No, according to him, the first is the preparation for the second: "I will come again," here is the spiritual return. Then he adds: "And I will take you unto myself, that where I am (in my Father's house, where there are many mansions, and where Jesus Himself is now going), you may be also with me," xiv. 3; here is, in some sense, a consummation. "If I will that he tarry till I come, what is that to thee?" (xxi. 23.) And in the first epistle: "My little children, abide in Him, to the end that, when he shall appear, we may have boldness" (ii. 28). "We know that, when he shall appear, we shall be like him" (iii. 3).—The spiritual judgment which John teaches is likewise, according to him, the preparation for the external judgment in which the economy of grace will end. "It is not I who will accuse you before the Father, it is Moses in whom you hope." "The hour is coming in which all who are in the tombs shall hear the voice of the Son of man, and shall come forth; those who have done good, to a resurrection of life; those who have done evil, to a resurrection of judgment" (v. 45 and 28, 29). Here, surely, an external judgment and a bodily resurrection are duly proclaimed. Scholten thinks, it is true, that these verses must be an interpolation. For what reason? They are not wanting in any manuscript, in any version. No; but the critic has decreed *a priori* what the fourth Gospel must be in order that it may be the antipode of the other three. And as these verses present an obstacle to this sovereign decision of *his* criticism, he takes his scissors and cuts them out. This is what at the present time is called *science*. Moreover, little is gained by these violent proceedings. Four times successively in chap. vi., indeed, Jesus returns to these troublesome

---

[1] *Einl.*, p. 728.

facts of the last day and the resurrection of the dead: "That I may not lose anything of what the Father hath given me, but that I may raise it up at the last day" (ver. 39); "that whosoever beholdeth the Son and believeth on Him may have eternal life, and I will raise him up at the last day" (ver. 40); "no man can come unto me, except the Father draw him; and I will raise him up at the last day" (ver. 44); "he who eateth my flesh and drinketh my blood . . .; I will raise him up at the last day" (ver. 54). It will be confessed that considerable boldness is needed to maintain that a book, in which such a series of affirmations is found, does not teach either a last judgment or the resurrection of the body. But the critics count, and unfortunately with good reason, upon a public which does not examine critically.

The truth is that, in conformity with his custom, the author of the fourth Gospel speaks less of external results than of spiritual preparations, because the popular preaching, and as a consequence the Synoptics, did just the reverse. Without omitting the coming of the Holy Spirit and His action in the heart (Luke xxiv. 48, 49; Matt. xxviii. 19; Luke xii. 11, 12, etc.), the first Gospels had transmitted to the Church, in all its details, the teaching of Jesus respecting the destruction of Jerusalem and His visible return at the end of time (Matt. xxiv., Mark xiii., Luke xxi. and xvii.). John had nothing to add on these various points. As for ourselves, in reading the conclusions which the critics draw from his silence, we cannot conceal a feeling of astonishment; here are men who maintain that the great discourse of Jesus on the end of time, in the Synoptics, was never spoken by Him; that it is only a composition of some Jewish or Jewish-Christian author in the year 67 or 68; and the same men dare to allege the absence in John of this unauthentic discourse, as a reason *against* the trustworthiness of this Gospel! Should criticism become a matter of jugglery?

It is impossible, then, to detect an *essential* difference, that is to say, one bearing on the matter of the teaching, between the Synoptics and the fourth Gospel.

But what is to be thought of the entirely different *form* in which Jesus expresses Himself in the Johannean discourses and the Synoptic preachings? Here, brief moral maxims, strongly marked, popular, easy to be retained; there, discourses of a lofty and in a sense theological, import. Here, as Keim says, "the jewel of the parable;" there, not a single picture of this kind. In a word, there the simple and practical spirit; here a mystic, exalted, dreamy hue.

As to the *parable*, it is in fact wanting in John, at least in the form in which we find it in the first Gospels; but we must recall to mind the fact, that nothing was more adapted than this kind of discourse to form the substance of the popular evangelization in the earliest times of the Church. All that could be recalled of such teachings was, therefore, successively put in circulation in the tradition, and passed from thence into the first evangelical writings. What could have been the object of the author of the fourth Gospel in suppressing these teachings with which he must have been acquainted, and which would have given credit to his book, on the supposition that his narrative was a fiction? But if he was simply recounting the history, what purpose would it serve to repeat that which every one could read in writings which were already within the reach of all? He could only have been led to take a different course if the parables had been a necessary land-mark in the history of the apostolic faith which he had it in mind to describe; but this was evidently not the case. Moreover, if we do not find in the fourth Gospel the parable in the form of a complete *story*, we do find it in a form closely allied to this, that of *allegory*.[1] Here is the analogue of what are called, in the Synoptics, the *parables* of the leaven or of the grain of mustard-seed; thus, the pictures of the Shepherd, the Door, and the Good Shepherd (chap. x.), or that of the woman who suddenly passes from the excess of grief to that of joy (xvi. 21), or again that of the vine and the branches (xv. 1 ff.). It is still the figurative and picturesque language of Him who, in the first Gospels, spoke to the people in these terms : "What went ye out into the wilderness to see? A reed shaken with the wind . . . . . ? (Matt. xi. 7.) This question very nearly recalls the saying of Jesus in our Gospel (v. 35); "John was a lamp which shineth and burneth; and ye were willing to rejoice for a season in his light." Let the following similitudes, also, be compared : The Spirit is like the wind which blows where it wills, and the presence of which we know only because we hear the sound of it (iii. 8). The unbeliever is like the evil doer who seeks the night to accomplish his evil works (vv. 19, 20). Spiritual emancipation is the formula of manumission which the son of the house pronounces upon the slaves (viii. 36), etc. Each of these figures is a parable in the germ, which the author could have developed as such, if only he had wished to do so.

As to the elevated, *mystical* character of the discourses of Jesus, the language forms a contrast, it is true, with the simple, lively, piquant cast of the Synoptic discourses. But let us notice, first of all, that this contrast has been singularly exaggerated. Sabatier himself acknowledges this: "A comparison of these discourses with those of the Synoptics proves that, at the foundation, the difference between them is not so great as it appears to be at the first view." How can we fail to recognize the voice which strikes us so impressively in the Synoptics, in those brief and powerful words of the Johannean Christ, which seem to break forth from the depths of another world? "My Father worketh hitherto and I also work." "Destroy this temple, and I will raise it up in three days." "Apart from me ye can do nothing." "Except the grain be cast into the earth and die, it abideth alone; but if it die, it beareth much fruit." "He who hath seen me, hath seen the Father." "The prince of this world cometh, but he hath nothing in me." There is a fact which is beyond dispute : we discover at least twenty-seven sayings of Jesus in John which are found in almost exactly

---

[1] It is remarkable that, in x. 6, John uses for characterizing this kind of comparisons the same word, παροιμία, which is so frequently employed in the Synoptics to designate the parables properly so-called.

118 / The Fourth Gospel

the same form in the Synoptics (see the list in the note).¹ Very well! no one can maintain that these sayings in the least degree harmfully affect either the texture of John's text or that of the Synoptic text. This fact proves, indeed, that the difference which has been pointed out has been singularly exaggerated. If, in fact, sayings of such an original cast as those of Jesus can, simultaneously and without surprising us in the least degree, occupy a place in the two sorts of documents, this fact proves that these documents are fundamentally homogeneous.

Several expressions are especially alleged by the critics which belong to John's style and which are foreign to the Synoptics,—for example, the terms *light* and *darkness;* or expressions in use in the latter which are wanting in the former, like *the kingdom of heaven* (or *of God*), for which John substitutes the less Jewish and more mystical term *eternal life.* But the contrast of *light* and *darkness* is found, also, in the Synoptics, as witness

¹ JOHN.

ii. 19: "Destroy this temple, and in three days I will raise it up."

iii. 18: "He that believeth on Him is not condemned: but he that believeth not is condemned already."

iv. 44: "For Jesus Himself testified, that a prophet hath no honour in his own country."

v. 8: "Jesus saith unto him, Arise, take up thy bed and walk."

vi. 20: "It is I; be not afraid."

vi. 35: "He that cometh to me shall not hunger; and he that believeth on me shall never thirst."

vi. 37: "All that the Father giveth me shall come to me; and him that cometh to me I will in no wise cast out."

vi. 46: "Not that any man hath seen the Father, save He which is from God, He hath seen the Father." Compare i. 18: "No man hath seen God at any time; the only-begotten Son, which is in the bosom of the Father, He hath declared Him."

xii. 8: "For the poor always ye have with you; but me ye have not always."

xii. 25: "He that loveth his life loseth it; and he that hateth his life in this world shall keep it unto life eternal."

xii. 27: "Now is my soul troubled; and what shall I say? Father, save me from this hour; but for this cause came I unto this hour."

xiii. 3: "Jesus knowing that the Father had given all things into His hands."

THE SYNOPTICS.

Matt. xxvi. 61 (xxvii. 40): "This man said, I am able to destroy the temple of God, and to build it in three days" (Mark xiv. 58 and xv. 29).

Mark xvi. 16: "He that believeth, and is baptized, shall be saved; but he that believeth not shall be condemned."

Matt. xiii. 57: "Jesus said unto them, A prophet is not without honour, save in his own country, and in his own house" (Mark vi. 4 and Luke iv. 24).

Matt. ix. 6: "Arise, take up thy bed, and go unto thine house" (Mark ii. 9; Luke v. 24).

Matt. xiv. 27: "It is I; be not afraid" (Mark vi. 50).

Matt. v. 6, Luke vi. 21: "Blessed are they that hunger and thirst: for they shall be filled."

Matt. xi. 28, 29: "Come unto me, all ye that labour and are heavy laden ... and ye shall find rest unto your souls."

Matt. xi. 27: "No man knoweth the Son, but the Father; neither knoweth any man the Father, save the Son, and he to whomsoever the Son will reveal him" (Luke x. 22).

Matt. xxvi. 11: "For ye have the poor always with you; but me ye have not always" (Mark xiv. 7).

Matt. x. 39: "He that findeth his life shall lose it; and he that loseth his life for my sake shall find it" (xvi. 25; Mark viii. 35; Luke ix. 24, xvii. 33).

Matt. xxvi. 38: "Then saith He unto them, My soul is exceeding sorrowful even unto death" (Mark xiv. 34 ff.).

Matt. xi. 27: "All things have been delivered unto me of my Father."

Characteristics - The Discourses / 119

Luke xi. 34–36 and Matthew vi. 22 and 23. Is it not already very common in the Old Testament? And as to the Johannean expression *eternal life,* it is employed in the Synoptics as the equivalent of the *kingdom of God,* absolutely as it is in John. We call to witness the examples quoted in the note, which have been very happily brought forward by Beyschlag.[1] John,

JOHN.	THE SYNOPTICS.
xiii. 16: "Verily, verily, I say unto you, A servant is not greater than his lord; neither one that is sent greater than he that sent him."	Matt. x. 24: "A disciple is not above his master, nor a servant above his lord."
xiii. 20: "He that receiveth whomsoever I send, receiveth me; and he that receiveth me, receiveth Him that sent me."	Matt. x. 40: "He that receiveth you, receiveth me; and he that receiveth me, receiveth Him that sent me" (Luke x. 16).
xiii. 21: "Verily, verily, I say unto you, that one of you shall betray me."	Matt. xxvi. 21: "Verily I say unto you, that one of you shall betray me" (Mark xiv. 18).
xiii. 38: "Verily, verily, I say unto thee, The cock shall not crow, till thou hast denied me thrice."	Matt. xxvi. 34: "Verily I say unto thee, that this night, before the cock crow, thou shalt deny me thrice" (Mark xiv. 30; Luke xxii. 34).
xiv. 18: "I will not leave you desolate; I will come to you;" and 23: "We will make our abode with him."	Matt. xxviii. 20: "I am with you alway, even unto the end of the world."
xiv. 28: "My Father is greater than I."	Mark xiii. 32: "That day knoweth no one, not even the angels which are in heaven, neither the Son, but the Father."
xiv. 31: "Arise, let us go hence."	Matt. xxvi. 46: "Arise, let us be going."
xv. 20: "If they persecuted me, they will also persecute you."	Matt. x. 25: "If they have called the Master of the house Beelzebub, how much more shall they call them of his household."
xv. 21: "But all these things will they do unto you for my name's sake."	Matt. x. 22: "Ye shall be hated of all men for my name's sake."
xvi. 32: "Behold, the hour cometh, yea, is come, that ye shall be scattered, every man to his own, and shall leave me alone."	Matt. xxvi. 31: "For it is written, I will smite the shepherd and the sheep of the flock shall be scattered abroad."
xvii. 2: "As Thou gavest Him authority over all flesh."	Matt. xxviii. 18: "All authority hath been given unto me in heaven and on earth."
xviii. 11: "Put up the sword into the sheath."	Matt. xxvi. 52: "Put up again thy sword into its place."
xviii. 20: "I ever taught in synagogues, and in the temple."	Matt. xxvi. 55: "I sat daily in the temple teaching."
xviii. 37: "Pilate therefore said unto Him: Art thou a king then? Jesus answered, Thou sayest that I am a king. To this end have I been born."	Matt. xxvii. 11: "And the governor asked him, saying, Art thou the king of the Jews? And Jesus said unto him, Thou sayest."
xx. 23: "Whose soever sins ye forgive, they are forgiven ...," etc.	Matt. xviii. 18 (xvi. 19): "What things soever ye shall bind on earth shall be bound in heaven ...," etc.

[1] The two verses placed in parallel lines are taken in each case from the same Gospel and from the same narrative:

Matt. xviii. 3: "Ye shall not enter *into the kingdom of heaven.*"	Matt. xviii. 8: "It is good for thee to enter *into life.*"
Matt. xix. 17: "If thou wouldest enter *into life.*"	Matt. xix. 23: "It is hard for a rich man to enter into *the kingdom of heaven.*"
Matt. xxv. 34: "Inherit *the kingdom prepared for you.*"	Matt. xxv. 46: "But the righteous into eternal life."
Mark ix. 45: "It is good for thee to enter *into life.*"	Mark ix. 47: "It is good for thee to enter *into the kingdom of God.*"

moreover, in the conversation with Nicodemus, twice uses (iii. 3, 5) the term *kingdom of God* (or *of heaven*, in the Sinaitic MS.).

What is there left, after all this, which suffices to establish, in respect to the form, an insoluble contrast between the words of Jesus in John and His language in the Synoptics? A certain difference remains; I do not deny this. It consists in that altogether peculiar tone of holy solemnity, and, if I may venture to speak thus, of heavenly suavity, which distinguishes not only our Gospel, but also the first Epistle of John, from all the other products of human thought, and which makes of these writings a literature by itself; with this difference, however, which has been already pointed out, that, while the course of thought is steady and of a strictly logical tenor in the Gospel, the subjects are treated in the epistles in a softer, more hesitating, and more diffuse way.—In order to explain the real contrast between the fourth Gospel and the preceding ones, we must first of all, as we have seen, take into account the influence exercised on the form of the discourses by the peculiar style of the translator, and by the work of condensation which was the condition of this reproduction. But, after this, there is still left a certain, in some sort, irreducible *remnant*, which demands a separate examination. It is said that *the unexplained remainders* in science are the cause of great discoveries. We are not ambitious of making a great discovery; but we would like, nevertheless, to succeed in giving, a little more clearly than has been given hitherto, an account of the difference with which we are concerned.

The question is whether this particular tone, which might be called the Johannean *timbre*, was foreign to Jesus, in such a degree that our evangelist was the real creator of it and, of his own impulse, attributed it to the Saviour; or whether it appertained to the language of Jesus Himself, at least in certain particular moments of His life. We have seen that the scenes related in our Gospel represent only a score of days, or even of moments, distributed over an activity of two years and a half. And it is consequently permitted us to ask whether these scenes, chosen evidently with a design, did not have an exceptional character which marked them out for the author's choice. He has made a selection among the facts, that is certain, and himself declares this (xx. 30, 31). Why might he not also have made one among the discourses? The selection in this case must have been with reference to the design of his work, which was to show that "Jesus is the Christ, the Son of God." If it is so, he was naturally obliged to choose, from among the numerous teachings of Jesus, the few words of an especially elevated character, which had, most of all, contributed to make him understand for himself the sublime richness of the being whom he had the happiness to see and to hear.

We have an expression which the author places in the mouth of Jesus, and according to which Jesus Himself distinguished between two sorts of discourses which were included in His teaching. He says to Nicodemus, iii. 12: "If I have told you *earthly things* (τὰ ἐπίγεια) and ye believe not, how shall ye believe when I tell you *heavenly things* (τὰ ἐπουράνια)?" In expressing Himself thus, Jesus recalled to Nicodemus the teachings which

He had given since His arrival in Jerusalem. What proved, indeed, that His hearers had not been laid hold of by them (*had not believed*), is the fact that Nicodemus himself was able to put forward, as the proof of the divine superiority of the Lord's teaching, only His miracles (ver. 2). What were those teachings of Jesus, in which He spoke of earthly things? His preachings in Galilee, such as we find them in the Synoptics, may give us an idea of them. It was the earth,—that is, human life, with all its different obligations and relations—considered from the heavenly point of view. It was, for example, that lofty morality which we find developed in the Sermon on the Mount: human life as related to God. But from this elementary moral teaching Jesus expressly distinguishes that which He calls the teaching of *heavenly things*. The object of the latter is no longer the earth estimated from the heavenly point of view; it is heaven itself with its infinite richness. This heaven—Jesus lived in it continually while acting upon the earth. He says this Himself in the following verse: "No man hath ascended to heaven but he who came down from heaven, the Son of man *who is in heaven*" (ver. 13). In the intimate and uninterrupted relation which He sustained to the Father, He had access here below to the divine thoughts, to the eternal purposes, to the plan of salvation, and He was able, in certain hours, to unfold to those who surrounded Him, friends or enemies, as He did in the progress of this nocturnal conversation with the pious councilor, the facts appertaining to this higher domain of the *heavenly things*. He would not have fully accomplished His mission, if He had absolutely concealed from the world what He was Himself for the heart of His Father, and what His Father was for Him. How could men have comprehended the infinite love of which they were the objects on heaven's part, if Jesus had not explained to them the infinite value of the gift which God made to them in His person. Does not love measure itself by the cost of the gift, by the greatness of the sacrifice? On the other hand, this revelation of the heavenly things could not be the *habitual* object of the Lord's teachings. Scarcely would one or two disciples have followed Him, if He had stayed upon these heavenly heights; the yet gross mass of the people who asked only for a Messiah after their own carnal heart—a king capable of every day giving them bread in the proper sense of the word (vi. 15, 34), would have remained strangers to His influence, and would soon have left Him alone with His two or three initiated ones.

It is undoubtedly for the same reason, that these teachings respecting the heavenly things remained, in general, outside of the limits of the first apostolical preaching and the oral telling of the Gospel story.

Nevertheless, even if this was the course of things, it is improbable that every trace of this mode of teaching, more lofty in matter and tone, would have completely disappeared from the Synoptic narrative. And, indeed, two of our evangelists—those who, along with John, have labored most to transmit to us the teachings of Jesus—Matthew and Luke, have preserved for us the account of a moment of extraordinary emotion in the Lord's life which presents us the example naturally looked for. It is in Luke especially, that we must seek the faithful representation of it (chap. x.). Jesus has sent into the fields and villages of Galilee seventy of His disciples, weak spiritual children, to whom He has entrusted the task of making the population understand the importance of the work which is being accomplished at this time, and the nearness of the kingdom. They return to Him filled with joy, and inform Him of the complete success of their mission. At this moment, the evangelist tells us, " Jesus rejoiced in His spirit, and said : I thank thee, Father, Lord of heaven and earth, that thou hast hid these things from the wise and prudent, and hast revealed them unto babes! Yea, Father, for so it seemed good in thy sight. All things have been delivered unto me by my Father, and no one knoweth who the Son is but the Father, nor who the Father is but the Son, and he to whom the Son willeth to reveal him." In reading these words, we ask ourselves whether it is indeed from St. Luke or St. Matthew that we are reading, and not from St. John. What does this fact prove? That, according to the Synoptics themselves, in certain exceptional moments of elevation, the language of Jesus really assumed that sweet tone, that *mystic* tinge, as it has been called—is it not more correct to say, *heavenly?*—of which we find in them but one single example, and of which six or seven discourses in John bear, in greater or less degree, the impress. This passage of Luke and Matthew has been called an erratic block of Johannean rock strayed into the Synoptic ground. The figure is quite just; what does it prove? The smallest fragment of granite deposited on the calcareous slopes of Jura, is for the geologist the undeniable proof that somewhere in the lofty Alpine summits the entire rock is in its place. Otherwise this block would be a monstrosity for science. The same is true of this fragment of Johannean discourse in the Synoptic Gospels. It is fully sufficient to prove the existence, at certain moments, of this so-called Johannean language in the teaching of Jesus. The real difference between John and the Synoptics, on this most decisive point, amounts to this : while these last have handed down to us but a single example of this form of language, John has preserved for us several examples selected with a particular purpose.

As, on the one hand, it is certain from the very nature of things, that the peculiar style of the translator has colored that of the Preacher whose discourses he reproduces, on the other hand, the passage of the Synoptics, which we have just quoted, places beyond doubt the fact that the language of the Lord Himself had stamped its impression deeply on the soul of the evangelist, and exercised a decisive and permanent influence on his style. There was here, therefore, if I may venture to express myself thus, a reflex action, the secret of which, undoubtedly, no one will ever completely disclose.

Moreover, the discourses of Jesus in the fourth Gospel bear in themselves, for every one who has eyes to see them, the seal of their true origin, and, notwithstanding all the assertions of learned men, the Church will always know what it should think of them. An intimate, filial, unchanging communion with the God of heaven and earth, like that which here reveals itself by the mouth of Jesus, must be lived in order to be thus expressed—what shall I say, in order to our having even a glimpse of it. The *inventor* of such discourses would be more than a genius of the first rank; he would need to be himself a Son of God, a Jesus equal to the true one. Criticism gains only one more embarrassment by such a supposition.

c. *The Johannean notion of the Person of Jesus*

Is it possible for us to go back even to the single source from which flow forth, like two diverging streams, the two forms of Jesus' teaching which we have just established. First of all, let us set aside the opinion, at present somewhat widespread, which holds that a dualism can be discerned even in the teaching of our Gospel. Two scholars, Baur and Reuss, have claimed that the author of this work did not hold a real incarnation of the Logos; that, according to him, the divine being continued in Jesus in the possession and exercise of His heavenly attributes, in such a way that His humanity was only a passing and superficial covering, which did not modify, in any respect, the state which He had possessed before coming to the earth. Starting from this point of view, Reuss finds in our Gospel a series of contradictions between certain words of Jesus, which he believes to be authentic, and that conception which is exhibited in the amplifications due to the pen of the evangelist. While in the former, Jesus distinctly affirms His inferiority to the Father, the author of our Gospel, filled with his own notion of the Logos, presents Him as equal with God. It is difficult to conceive a more complete travesty of the Johannean narrative. We have already shown that no Gospel sets forth with more pronounced features than this one the real humanity of Jesus, body, soul and spirit. The body is *exhausted* (iv. 6); the soul is overwhelmed in *trouble* (xii. 27); the spirit itself is *agitated* (xiii. 21) and *groans* (xi. 33). What place remains in such a being for the presence of an *impassible* Logos? More than this: according to the prologue, which is certainly the work of the evangelist, the Logos Himself, in His state of divine pre-existence, tends *towards God* as to His centre (i. 1); He dwells in God, as a first-born Son *in the bosom* of His Father (i. 18). Where in this representation is the place for a being *equal* with God? No; the subordination of the Son to the Father is affirmed by the evangelist as distinctly as it could have been by Jesus when speaking of Himself; and as for His real humanity, it is emphasized by this same evangelist more strongly than by any one of the Synoptics.

There is, then, no trace of a twofold contradictory theology in our Gospel.[1] This supposition is already, in its very nature, in the highest degree improbable. It implies a fact which it is very difficult to admit. This fact is, that so profound a thinker as the one who composed this work, the most powerful mind of his epoch, could, without being in the least degree

---

[1] As Beyschlag now claims; comp. also the thesis of Jean Réville, *La doctrine du Logos*, 1881.

aware of it, simultaneously teach two opposite conceptions respecting the subject which occupied the first place in his thoughts and in his heart.

The idea which the evangelist formed of the person of Christ, and which is in perfect accord with even the smallest historical or didactic details of the entire narrative, is clearly formulated by the author in the prologue: "The Word was made flesh,"—which evidently signifies that the being whom he calls the Word *divested* Himself of His divine state and of all the attributes which constituted it, in order to exchange it for a completely human state, with all the characteristics of weakness, ignorance, sensibility to pleasure and pain, which constitute our peculiar mode of life here below.[1] This mode of conceiving of the person of Christ during His sojourn on the earth is not peculiar to John; it is also that of Paul, who tells us in Philippians: "He who was in the form of God . . . emptied himself, taking upon him the form of a servant, and being made in the likeness of men" (ii. 6, 7); and also in Second Corinthians: "Ye know the grace of our Lord Jesus Christ, who, though he was rich, for your sakes became poor, that ye, through his poverty, might become rich" (2 Cor. viii. 9). The same teaching is found in the Epistle to the Hebrews and the Apocalypse, though it would require too much space to show this here.[2] Here is the key to all the Christological ideas of the New Testament. It is, in particular, the explanation of that double form of teaching which we find in the mouth of Christ, in John and in the Synoptics.

Up to His baptism, Jesus had lived in a filial communion with God; that saying of the child of twelve years is the proof of this: "Must I not be in that which belongs to my Father?" (Luke ii. 49.) But He had not as yet the distinct consciousness of His eternal, essential relation to the Father; His communion with Him was of a moral nature; it sprang from His pure conscience and His ardent love for Him. In this state, He must, indeed, have had a presentiment that He was the physician of sinful humanity, as the Messiah. But an immediate divine testimony was necessary, in order that He should be able to undertake the redemptive work. This testimony was given to Him at His baptism; at that moment the heavens were opened to Him; the heavenly things, which He was to reveal to others, were unveiled to Him. At the same time the mystery of His own person became clear to Him; He heard the voice of the Father which said to Him: "Thou art my beloved Son." From that day He knew Himself perfectly; and knowing Himself *as* the only-begotten *Son*, the object of all the Father's love, He knew also how greatly the Father loved the world to which He was giving Him: He knew fully, as man, the Father himself, *the Father* in all the riches of the meaning of this word. Thus it was that, from this day onward, He carried heaven in His heart, while living on the earth. He had, then, if we may so speak,

---

[1] The same expression is used (ii. 9), to express the change of the water into wine: one same substance, but clothed with different attributes.

[2] Comp. Heb. i. 3; ii. 17, 18; v. 6–8; Apoc. i. 1, 18; iii. 12, 21; v. 5.

two sources of information: one, the experience of the *earthly things* which He had learned to know during the thirty years of life which He had just passed here on earth as a mere man; the other, the permanent intuition of the *heavenly things* which had just unveiled themselves to Him at the hour of the baptism. How can we be surprised, therefore, that Jesus spoke alternately of the one and the other, according to the wants of His hearers, finding in the first the common ground which was needed by Him to excite their interest and gain their attention, deriving from the second the matter of the new revelation, by means of which He was to transform the world? On the one side, there were the moral obligations of man, his relations to things here below, treated from a divine point of view, as we see particularly in the Synoptics; on the other, the higher mystery of the relation of love between the Father and the Son, and of the love of both towards a world sunk in sin and death, a world to which the Father gives the Son and the Son gives Himself.

It seems to me that, by placing ourselves at this point of view, we may see springing up, as if by a sort of moral necessity, the two modes of teaching which fill science, but not the Church, with astonishment. Do we not know young persons or mature men who, after having led a perfectly moral life, see all at once opening before them, through the mysterious act of the new birth, the sanctuary of communion with Christ, the life of adoption, the inward enjoyment of the fatherly love of God? Their language assumes then, at certain moments, a new character which astonishes those who hear them speak thus, and ask themselves whether it is, indeed, the same man. There is in their tone something elevated, something sweet, which was previously strange to them. The words are, as it were, words coming from a higher region. We are tempted to cry out with the poet:

> Ah! qui n'oublierait tout à cette voix céleste!
> Ta parole est un chant . . .

but without adding, with him,

> où rien d'humain ne reste.[1]

For this divine language is, nevertheless, the most human language which can be spoken. Then, when this moment of exaltation has passed, and the ordinary life resumes its own course, the ordinary language returns with it, although ever grave, ever holy, ever dominated by the immediate relation with God which henceforth forms the background of the entire life. Such experiences are not rare; they serve to explain the mystery of the twofold teaching and the twofold language of the Word made flesh, from the moment when He had been revealed to Himself by the testimony of the Father.[2]

---

[1] Ah, who would not all forget in that celestial voice. Thy speech is a song . . . . where nothing of man remains.

[2] Regarded from this point of view, the fact of the incarnation, while still presenting to human reason profound mysteries, does not seem to us to contain unsolvable contradictions.

But, even if we cannot reach in thought the sublime point where, in the person of Christ, the two converging lines of the humanity which rises to the highest point, and the divinity which humbles itself most profoundly, meet together, do we not know that, in mathematics, no one refuses to acknowledge the reality of the point where the two lines called asymptotes meet when infinitely produced, and that the operations are carried on with reference to this point as with reference to a positive quantity? Weiss rightly says:[1] "It is necessary, indeed, to consider that the appearance of Jesus in itself, as the realization of a divinely human life, was much too rich, too great, too manifold, not to be presented in a different way according to the varied individualities which received its rays, and according to the more or less ideal points of view at which these rays were reflected; while, however, this difference could not be prejudicial to the unity of the fundamental impression, and of the essential character in which this personality made itself known."

Criticism has often compared the difference with which we are concerned to that which is presented by the two representations of the person of Socrates, traced by Plato and Xenophon. At the outset, the historians of philosophy turned to the side of Xenophon, thinking that they could recognize the true historical type in the simple, practical, varied, popular Socrates of the *Memorabilia*. At that time, the Socrates of Plato was regarded as only a mouth-piece chosen by that author in order to set forth his own theory of ideas. Xenophon was the historian, Plato the philosopher. But criticism has changed its mind; Schleiermacher, above all, has taught us that, if the teaching of Socrates had not contained speculative elements, such as Plato attributes to him, and elements as to which the other writer is completely silent, no account could be given either of the relation which so closely united the school of Plato to the person of Socrates, or of the extraordinary attractive power which the latter exercised over the most eminent and most speculative minds of his time, or of the profound revolution effected by him in the progress of Greek thought.[2] With Xenophon alone, there remains a vacancy—a vacancy which we cannot fill except with the aid of Plato. This fact arises, on the one hand, from the special aim of Xenophon's book, which was to make a moral defense of his master; on the other, from the circumstance that Xenophon, a practical man, lacked the philosophical capacity which was necessary for the apprehension of the higher elements of the Socratic teaching. Zeller also acknowledges that Xenophon did not comprehend the scientific value of Socrates; "that Socrates cannot have been that exclusive and unscientific moralist for which he was so long taken," while the starting-point for criticism was made from the work of Xenophon only. "There is," he says, "in the exposition of each of the two writers, a *surplus* (Ueberschuss) which can without difficulty be introduced into the common portrait." No doubt, Plato has put into the mouth of Socrates his

---

[1] Introduction to his Commentary on the Gospel of John, p. 33.

[2] Scholars like Brandis and Ritter hold this opinion.

own theory of ideas. But it was only the development of the teaching of Socrates himself; and it must be admitted that where he puts Socrates on the stage as an historical personage (in the *Apology* and the *Symposium*, for example), he does not take this course.[1]

This parallel presents, *mutatis mutandis*, several remarkable correspondences in detail. But it offers, above all, this fundamental analogy that, in the case of Socrates as in that of Jesus, we find ourselves in the presence of two portraits of an historical personage, the perfect synthesis of which it is impossible to make. Now, if philosophy is still seeking after the fusion of the two portraits of the wisest of the Greeks, are we to be surprised that theology has not yet succeeded in effecting that of the two pictures of Christ. Is the richness of the former, a man whose influence on the moral history of his people was so serious, but so transient, to be compared to the richness of Him whose appearance has renewed and is constantly renewing the world? And if there was in the former that which furnishes matter for two portraits, both of them true and yet not reducible to a single one, why should we be surprised to see the same phenomenon reappearing with regard to Him who could have exclaimed in Greece: "A greater than Socrates is here," as He did exclaim in Judea: "A greater than Solomon is here."

"No one knoweth *the Son* but *the Father*," says Jesus in the Synoptics. The point of convergence of the two representations—the Johannean and the Synoptic, is accordingly the consciousness which the Son had of Himself. We shall, undoubtedly, not be successful in reconstructing it perfectly here on earth.

We behold *one* sun in the arch of heaven; and yet what a difference between its burning reflection on the slopes of the Alpine glaciers and its calm and majestic image in the waves of the ocean! The source of light is one, but the two mirrors are different.

We conclude:

1. The primal idea of the Johannean work did not by any means necessarily impair its historical character.

2. The truthfulness of the narrative appears manifestly from the comparison of the story with that of the Synoptics, to which it is invariably superior in the cases where they differ.

3. The truthfulness of the account of the discourses, which is supported by such strong positive reasons, does not in fact encounter any insurmountable difficulty.

The fourth Gospel is, therefore, a truly historical work.

B. THE RELATION OF THE FOURTH GOSPEL TO THE RELIGION OF THE OLD TESTAMENT

Modern criticism believes itself able to prove a tendency in the fourth Gospel decidedly hostile to Judaism. Baur thinks that the author of this book desired to introduce anti-Jewish Gnosticism into the Church; that he

---

[1] *Philos. der Griechen*, IIter Th., 3d ed., pp. 85 ff.; 151, 155.

was a Docetist and dualist, professing the non-reality of the body of Jesus and the eternal contrast between darkness and light. Without going as far as this, Reuss says, "that he speaks of the Jews as of a class of foreigners, with whom he had no connection;" that "all that preceded Jesus belongs, according to him, to a past without any value, and can only serve to lead men astray and cause them to miss the gate of salvation" (x. 8).[1] Renan also attributes to the evangelist a "lively antipathy" to Judaism. Hilgenfeld, finally, is the one who has gone, and still goes, the farthest in the affirmation of this thesis. He originally ascribed our Gospel to some Gnostic writer of the second century; he has since softened this assertion; he thinks that the author, while belonging to the Church, "nevertheless goes a considerable distance along with Gnosticism." According to the fourth evangelist, "Judaism belonged, as much as paganism, to the darkness which preceded the Gospel;" the religion of the Old Testament possessed "only an imperfect and dim prefiguration of Christianity." The knowledge of the true God was wanting to it as much as to Samaritan paganism.[2]

What is alleged in justification of such judgments? In the first place, some particular *terms*, familiar to the evangelist, such as this: *the Jews*, an expression which he employs in a sense always hostile to that people; or that other expression: *your law*, a term in which a feeling of disdain for the Mosaic institution and the Old Testament betrays itself. But the unfavorable sense attached in our Gospel to the name, *the Jews*, to designate the enemies of the light, proceeds not from a subjective feeling of the evangelist, but from the fact itself—that is to say, from the position taken towards Jesus from the beginning (John ii.) by the mass of the nation and by their rulers. The author uses this term also, when there is occasion for it (which is rare), in an entirely neutral sense, as in ii. 6 ("the purification of the Jews") and xix. 40 ("the custom of the Jews to embalm bodies"); or even in a favorable sense, as in the passages iv. 22 ("salvation is from the Jews") and xi. 45 ("many of the Jews who came to Mary believed on him"). We may also cite here the use of the name *Israelite*, applied as a title of honor to Nathanael (i. 48). In the Apocalypse, which is affirmed to be an absolutely Judaizing work, the Jews who obstinately resist the Gospel are designated in a much more severe way: "Those who say they are Jews and who are not, but are *the synagogue of Satan*" (ii. 9; comp. iii. 9).[3] The great crisis which had cast Israel out of the kingdom of God, and which had made it henceforth a body foreign and even hostile to the Church, had begun already during the ministry of Jesus. This is what the author sets forth by this term: *the Jews*, which is contrasted in his narrative with the term: *the disciples*. In making Jesus say *your law*, the evangelist cannot have had the intention of disparaging the Mosaic institution, any

---

[1] *Théol. joh.*, pp. 82 and 19.
[2] *Das Evangelium und die Briefe Johannis*, 1849; comp. with his more recent article in the *Zeitschrift für wissenschaftliche Theologie* 1865, and *Einleitung*, pp. 722 ff.

[3] Ewald (*Comment. in Apoc. Joh.* ad. h. l.): "John, in a piquant way, calls the Jews an assembly, not of God, but of Satan, as Jesus Himself does (John viii. 37-44)."

more than in making Jesus say: "Abraham *your father*" (viii. 56), he dreamed of depreciating that patriarch. He exalts him, on the contrary, in that very verse, by setting forth the joyous sympathy which he experiences in a higher state of existence for Himself and His work : " Abraham rejoiced in expectation of seeing my day, and he saw it and was glad." In the same way, x. 34, after having used the expression: *your law*, He immediately adds, in connection with the passage of the O. T. which he has just quoted, these words: "And since the Scripture cannot be broken," making *the law* thus a divine and infallible revelation. Elsewhere He declares that "it is the Scriptures which testify of him" (v. 39); that the sin of the hearers consists in "not having the word of God abiding in them" (ver. 38), and even that the real cause of their unbelief towards Him is nothing else than their unbelief with respect to the *writings* of Moses (vv. 46, 47). The evangelist who makes Jesus speak thus evidently does not seek to disparage the law; the contradiction would be too flagrant. Jesus, therefore, in using the expression *your law*, means: "that law which you *yourselves* recognize as the sovereign authority," or: "that law which you invoke against me, and in the name of which you seek to condemn me." It must be remarked that He could not say "*our law*," because His personal relation to that institution was too widely different from that of the ordinary Jews to be included under the same pronoun; just as He could not say, when speaking of God: "*our* Father," but only "*my* Father," and "*your* Father" (xx. 17).

It has been remarked that Jesus never speaks in this Gospel of *the law* as the principle on which the life of the new community is to rest. This is true; but this is because He supposes the law to have become the *internal* principle of the life of believers through the fact of their communion with Him.

Critics also allege the freedom with which Jesus, in His cures, was ready to violate the *Jewish Sabbath*. Hilgenfeld even discovers the intention of abolishing that institution in the words of v. 17: "My Father worketh hitherto, and I also work." As to the Sabbath cures, they are found in the Synoptics as well as in John; and there, as here, it is these acts which begin to excite the deadly hatred of the Jews against Him (Luke vi. 11). But we formally deny the position that by these healings Jesus really violated the terms of the Mosaic command. He transgressed nothing else than that *hedge* of arbitrary statutes by which the Pharisees had thought fit to surround the fourth commandment. Jesus remained, from the beginning to the end, in our Gospel as in the others, *the minister of the circumcision* (Rom. xv. 8),—that is to say, the scrupulous observer of the law. As to the words of v. 17, they are by no means contrary to the idea of the Sabbath rest; they only mean: "As the Father labors in the work of the salvation of humanity—and this work evidently suffers no interruption at any moment whatsoever, still less on the Sabbath day than on any other—the Son cannot fold His arms and leave the Father to labor alone." This declaration does not contradict the Sabbatic rest when properly understood.

Hilgenfeld alleges also the two following passages: iv. 21, and viii. 44.

In the first, Jesus says to the Samaritan woman: "The hour cometh when ye shall no longer worship the Father either in this mountain or at Jerusalem," which proves, according to him, that Jesus wished to set Himself in opposition to the Jews no less than to the Samaritans, and that consequently, when he says in the following verse: "Ye worship that which ye know not," this judgment applies to the former as well as to the latter. The Jewish religion would therefore be, according to these words of Jesus, as erroneous as all the rest.—But there is enough in the following words: "because salvation comes from the Jews," to refute this explanation; for, instead of *because*, the author would have been obliged in that case to have said *although*: "*Although* the Jews are as ignorant as you and all the others, it has pleased God to make salvation come forth from the midst of them." The *because* (ὅτι) has no meaning unless Jesus in the preceding words had accorded to the Jews a knowledge of God superior to that of the Samaritans. This fact proves that the words: "*We worship* that which we know" apply not only to Him, Jesus, personally, but to Him conjointly with all *Israel*.[1] The true meaning of the words of ver. 21 is explained by ver. 23 (which resumes ver. 21): "Your worship, as for you Samaritans, will not be confined to this mountain Gerizim, nor will it, any more, be transported and localized anew at Jerusalem." Indeed, this second alternative must have appeared to the woman the only one possible, when once the first was set aside.

In the passage viii. 44, Jesus says to the Jews, according to the ordinary construction: "You are *of a father, the devil*." Hilgenfeld translates, as is no doubt grammatically possible: "You are *of the father of the devil*." This father of the devil is, according to him, the God of the Jews, the Creator of the material world, who in some of the Gnostic systems (Ophites, Valentinians) was actually presented as the father of the demon. This is not all; Jesus says at the end of the same verse: "When he speaketh a lie, he speaketh of his own, because he is a liar, *and his father*," which is ordinarily understood in this sense: because he is a liar and the father of the liar (or of the lie). But Hilgenfeld explains: because he (the devil) is a liar, *as also, his father* (is a liar). And he finds here a second time the father of the devil, who is called "a liar as well as his son," because, throughout the entire Old Testament, the God of the Jews made Himself pass for the supreme God, while He was only an inferior divinity.—The author of this explanation is astonished that it could have been regarded as monstrous, and claims "that no one has yet advanced the first reasonable word against it." He must, nevertheless, acknowledge the following facts: 1. The father of the devil is a personage totally foreign to the Biblical sphere, and the author of our Gospel would have greatly compromised the success of his fraud by introducing him on the stage. 2. The notion of two opposite and personal Gods, of whom the second is another being than the devil, is so opposed to the Israelitish and

---

[1] It was only through placing Himself in opposition to a foreign people (the Samaritans), that He could say *we* in speaking of Himself and the other Jews, as He does here.

Christian monotheism professed by the author (v. 44), that it is impossible to admit such a teaching here. 3. What Jesus, according to the entire context, wishes to prove to the Jews, is that they are the *children* of the devil, but not his *brothers*, as would follow from Hilgenfeld's translation: "You are born of the father of the devil." In this whole passage the matter in hand is that of contrasting filiation with filiation, father with father. "Ye do that which ye have seen with your father," Jesus said, ver. 38. The Jews replied to Him: "We have only one father, God" (ver. 41). And Jesus' answer is the echo of theirs: "Ye are born of a father, [who is] the devil." The first epistle offers a decisive parallel (iii. 10). "In this the *children of God* are manifest, and the *children of the devil*." 4. Finally, let us remark, that if the first words of the verse are applied to the *father of the devil*, it is necessary to apply to this same personage the whole series of the following propositions, even inclusive of the last. These words: "because he is a liar as well as his father," would signify, then (according to the explanation of Hilgenfeld): the father of the devil is a liar and his father none the less so. After having seen the father of the devil make his appearance, we should find ourselves here in the presence of his grandfather! All this phantasmagoria vanishes away before a single comma introduced between the two genitives πατρός (of a father) and τοῦ διαβόλου (of the devil), which makes the second substantive appositional with the former, and not its complement. The necessity of this explanation from the grammatical standpoint appears from the opposition to ver. 41: "We have one father [who is] God," and religiously from ii. 16, where the temple of the God of the Jews, in Jerusalem (which, according to Hilgenfeld, ought to be the house of the devil's father), is called by Jesus "the house of my Father." It is certainly, therefore, according to our Gospel, the *only true God* (xvii. 3) who is worshiped at Jerusalem.

Hilgenfeld and Reuss rest also upon the words of x. 8: "All those who came before me are thieves and robbers;" they think that Jesus meant to characterize by these two terms all the eminent men of the Old Covenant. Who then? The patriarchs and Moses, the psalmists and the prophets? And that in a book in which the author makes Jesus say, that to believe Moses is implicitly to believe in Him (v. 46, 47); in which He Himself declares that Isaiah beheld in a vision the glory of the Logos before His incarnation, and foretold the unbelief of the people towards the Messiah (xii. 38, 41); in which the words of a psalmist are quoted as the word of God which cannot be broken (x. 34, 35); in which Abraham is represented as rejoicing exceedingly at the sight of the coming of the Christ (viii. 56)! No; the quoted expression applies simply to the actual rulers of the nation, who already for a considerable period were in possession of power at the time when Jesus was accomplishing His work in Israel. This is clearly indicated by the present: εἰσί, *are*, and not, *were*, as the word has sometimes been rather thoughtlessly translated. "Those who came before me *are* thieves and robbers."

Reuss maintains that, in general, no expression in this work connects the Church in a more special way with Judaism: and Hilgenfeld affirms

132 / The Fourth Gospel

that this work "breaks every bond between Christianity and its Jewish roots." And yet the second of these scholars cannot help acknowledging what the first tries in vain to deny: that in the declaration of i. 11: "He came to his own, and his own received him not," the author really speaks of *the Jews,* considering them, he himself adds—" as the people of God or of the Logos."[1] No doubt, he endeavors afterwards to escape from the consequences of this conclusive fact, but by means of subterfuges which do not deserve even to be mentioned. Moreover, let the following facts be weighed: The temple of Jerusalem is "*the house of the Father*" of Jesus Christ (ii. 16); salvation comes from *the Jews* (iv. 22); the sheep whom Jesus gathers from the theocracy constitute the nucleus of the true Messianic flock (x. 16); the Paschal lamb slain at Jerusalem prefigures the sacrifice of the Messiah, even in the minute detail that the bones of both are to be preserved unbroken (xix. 36); the most striking testimony of the Father on behalf of Jesus is that which is given to Him by the Scriptures of the Old Covenant (v. 39). Finally, the author himself declares that he wrote his book to prove that Jesus is not only the *Son of God,* as he is so often made to say, but, first of all, *the Christ,* the Messiah promised to the Jews (xx. 30, 31).[2] The *Messianic* character of Jesus is expressly pointed out before His *divine* character. From end to end, our Gospel makes the appearance and work of Jesus the final evolution, the crowning of the Old Covenant.

As to all the passages which Hilgenfeld alleges with the design of proving that Jesus denies to Judaism all true knowledge of God (vii. 28; viii. 19; xv. 21; xvi. 25, etc.), they do not prove anything whatever; it is not to the Jewish religion as such, it is to the carnal and proud Jews who surround Him, that this often repeated reproach is addressed, that they did not know God, the God who nevertheless had revealed Himself to them. The prophets had all spoken in the same way, and had distinguished from the mass of the people (*this people,* Is. vi. 10) the elect, "the holy remnant" (vi. 13). They surely were not, for this reason, *anti-Jewish.*

The charge of *dualism,* directed against our Gospel by Hilgenfeld particularly, falls before this simple remark of Hase:[3] "A *moral* relation is thereby falsely translated into a *metaphysical* relation." Is it necessary to find a dualistic notion in that saying of Jesus: "To *you* it is given to know the mysteries of the kingdom; but to *them* it is not given" (Matt. xiii. 11)? or, in that other, ver. 38: "The good seed are the children of the kingdom; the tares are the children of the evil one?" or, again, in the contrast which St. Paul makes, 1 Cor. ii. 14, 15, between the *psychical* man who cannot understand spiritual things. and the *pneumatic* man who judges all things? Who ever dreamed, because of such words, of imputing to Jesus and to Paul the idea of two human *races,* one proceeding from God, the other from the devil. The Scriptures teach throughout that a holy power and

---

[1] *Einleitung,* p. 723.
[2] It is curious to observe how, in the citation of this passage, our critics are sometimes guilty of an inconsiderate inaccuracy in striking out this term, *the Christ;* comp. Sabatier, *Encyclop.*, p. 184. There are other examples of this.
[3] *Geschichte Jesu,* p. 44.

an evil power act simultaneously on the heart of man, and that he can freely surrender himself to the one or the other. The more emphatic the choice is in the one direction or the other, the more is the man given up to the moral current which bears him away, and thus it may happen that on the path of evil a man becomes incapable of discerning and feeling any longer the attraction of what is good. Here is the *incapacity* which Jesus so often charges upon the Jews; it is their own act; otherwise, why reproach them with it, and to what purpose call them again to repentance and to a renewal by faith? This hardness is only relative, because it is voluntary; Jesus declares this most expressly in that so profound explanation of Jewish unbelief (v. 44): "How can ye believe, ye who receive your glory one from another, and seek not the glory which comes from God only?" If, then, they *cannot* believe, it is because they *will not*, because they have made themselves the slaves of a good which is opposite to the benefits which faith procures,—*of human glory*. This dualism is moral, the effect of the will, not metaphysical or of nature. By teaching otherwise, the author would contradict himself; for has he not said in the prologue that "all things were made by the Logos, and that nothing, not even a single thing, came into being without Him?" Undoubtedly, Hilgenfeld claims that the existence of the darkness, i. 5, not having been explained as caused by anything, implies the eternity of the evil principle; but following upon that which precedes (the creation, the primitive state), it is altogether natural to find here the appearance of evil in humanity— the fall, as it is related after the creation in the story of Genesis, which the author follows, as it were, step by step.

Baur found in our Gospel the spirit of Gnostic *Docetism*, which would be, no less than dualism, in contradiction to the spirit of the Old Testament. But every one seems, at the present day, to have abandoned this opinion, and we believe that we can remit to exegesis the charge of proving the emptiness of it.[1] In order to maintain it, we must torture the meaning of that expression in which the whole work is summed up: "The Word *was made* flesh," and must reduce the force of it to this idea: The Word was *clothed* with a *bodily appearance*. The fourth Gospel throughout repels this mode of explaining the incarnation, which is also, up to a certain point, that which Reuss attributes to it. A being who is fatigued, who is thirsty, whose soul is troubled at the approach of suffering, and who must be preserved by extraordinary circumstances from the breaking of his bones; a being who rises from the dead, and who says: "Touch me not," or, again: "Reach hither thy finger," has certainly a real and material body, or the author does not know what he is saying.

Hilgenfeld discovers, finally, in the opposition of our Gospel to *Chiliasm* a proof of its anti-Judaic spirit. "The entire Gospel," says this writer, "is planned in such a way as to present the historical coming of Christ as His only appearance on the earth." But, first, it is false to regard Chiliasm, the expectation of a final reign of Christ over mankind, as the mark of a

---

[1] See on the passages vii. 10 and viii. 59.

Judaistic tendency. Hase rightly says: "This was the belief of nearly the whole Church in the second century, and even till far on in the third." But further, as the same author adds, "our Gospel, while turning the attention away from everything which delights the senses, does not contradict that hope." We have seen this, indeed; with many repetitions, mention is made of a glorious resurrection *of the body* which is promised to believers, and of a *last day*. But here, as in all things, John makes it his study to set forth the spiritual preparation on which the Synoptics had not dwelt, rather than the outward results described by the latter in so lively and striking a way.

We have, in this chapter, developed only the points which are related to the characteristics of our Gospel, without touching upon that which comes into the question of its origin,—of its composition by this author or by that. It is in studying this last subject that we shall seek for the origin of the notion and the term *Logos*. What concerned us at this point was to thoroughly establish the relation of our Gospel to the Old Covenant. This relation is a double one, as we have proved: on the one side, the Johannean Gospel fully recognizes the divinity of the Old Testament, law and prophets; on the other, it sees in the work and teaching of Christ a decided superiority to the old revelations. The God of Israel is the Father of our Lord Jesus Christ, but the patriarchal and prophetic revelations only made Him known imperfectly. It is the only-begotten Son, reposing in His bosom, who has come to reveal Him to us. "The law was given by Moses;" it prepared its faithful subjects to receive Jesus Christ; but it is only in Him that there is accorded to the believer a divine "fullness of grace and truth" (i. 16–18). The Word had in Israel His *home*, long since prepared on the earth; but the new birth through which a man obtains the life of God is impossible except through faith in the Word who has come in the flesh (i. 12, 13).

The evangelist began by recognizing in Jesus the promised Christ; thence he rose to the knowledge of the Son of God (i. 41; vi. 69; xvi. 28, 29). The expression in xx. 31, sums up this development.

C. THE STYLE OF THE FOURTH GOSPEL

It remains for us to study our Gospel from a literary point of view. Tholuck, in the introduction to his brief commentary, has well set forth the unique character of the evangelist's language. There is nothing analogous to it in all literature, sacred or profane; childlike simplicity and transparent depth, holy melancholy and vivacity no less holy; above all, the sweetness of a pure and gentle love. "Such a style could only emanate," says Hase, "from a life which rests in God and in which all opposition between the present and the future, between the divine and human, has wholly come to an end."

Let us try to state precisely the peculiarities of this style.[1]

---

[1] It is impossible to treat this subject with more acuteness and delicacy than Luthardt does in the Introduction to his Commentary, 2d ed., 1875, Vol. I., pp. 14–62.

1. The vocabulary, upon the whole, is *poor*. It is, in general, the same expressions which reappear from one end to the other: *light* (φῶς) twenty-three times; *glory, to be glorified* (δόξα, δοξάζεσθαι) forty-two times; *life, to live* (ζωή, ζῆν) fifty-two times; *to testify, testimony* (μαρτυρεῖν, μαρτυρία) forty-seven times; *to know* (γινώσκειν) fifty-five times; *world* (κόσμος) seventy-eight times; *to believe* (πιστεύειν) ninety-eight times; *work* (ἔργον) twenty-three times; *name* (ὄνομα) and *truth* (ἀλήθεια) each twenty-five times; *sign* (σημεῖον) seventeen times. Not only does the author not hesitate to repeat these words in his work, but he does this, and with reiteration, in sentences which are very closely allied to one another. At the first glance, this gives to his style a monotonous character; but only at the first glance. These expressions soon compensate the reader for their small number by their intrinsic richness. They are not at all, as one thinks at the first sight, purely abstract notions, but powerful spiritual realities, which can be contemplated under a multitude of aspects. If the author possesses in his vocabulary only a small number of terms, these words may be compared to pieces of gold with which great lords make payments. This feature is in harmony with the oriental mind, which loves to plunge into the infinite. The Old Testament already is familiar with these so rich expressions and their deep meaning: *light, darkness, truth, falsehood, glory, name, life, death*.

2. Certain favorite forms, which, without precisely offending against the laws of the Greek language, are nevertheless foreign to that language, betray a *Hebraistic* mode of thinking. Thus, to designate the most intimate spiritual union, the use of the term *to know;* to indicate moral dependence with respect to another being, the terms *to be in* (εἶναι ἐν), *to dwell in* (μένειν ἐν); to characterize the relation between a spiritual principle and the person in whom it is incarnated, the expression *son, the son of perdition* (υἱὸς τῆς ἀπωλείας); certain forms of a purely Hebrew origin: *to rejoice with joy* (χαρᾷ χαίρειν), *for ever* (εἰς τὸν αἰῶνα); finally, Hebrew words changed into Greek terms, as in the formula: *Amen, amen* (ἀμήν, ἀμήν), which is found only in John.

3. The construction is *simple;* the ideas are rather placed in juxtaposition, than organically fitted together after the manner of Greek construction. This peculiar feature is especially observed in some striking examples (i. 10; ii. 9; iii. 19; vi. 22–24; viii. 32; xvii. 25), where it would not have been difficult to compose a truly syntactical sentence, as a Greek writer certainly would have done. With this altogether Hebraic form are also closely connected the very frequent *anacolutha*, according to which the dominant idea is first placed at the beginning by means of an absolute substantive, and then repeated afterwards by a pronoun construed in accordance with the rules; comp. vi. 39; vii. 38; xvii. 2. We know that these cases are still more frequent in the Apocalypse.

4. Notwithstanding the abundance of particles belonging to the Greek language, the author only makes use of *now* (δέ), more frequently of *and* (καί), *then* (οὖν), and *as* (ὡς or καθώς). Μέν, which is so common, is almost unknown in his work. I think that it appears only once (xix. 24). The

and and *then* take the place of the *vav* conversive which is, in some sort, the only Hebrew particle. The *then* sets forth the providential necessity which in the author's view binds the facts together. The *and* is frequently used in cases where we should expect the particle of opposition *but;* thus: "The light shines in the darkness, *and* the darkness apprehended it not" (i. 5); or again: "And they have seen *and* have hated both me and my Father" (xv. 24). "We speak that which we know, *and* ye receive not our testimony" (iii. 11). Luthardt acutely observes that this form is the sign of a mind which has risen above the first emotion of surprise or indignation produced by an unforeseen result, and which has come to contemplate it for the future with the calmness of indifference, or with a grief which has no bitterness. The use of the particle *as* (comp. for example, chap. xvii.) is inspired by the necessity of setting forth the analogies; this feature is one of the most characteristic ones of the mind which created this style. This tendency goes even so far as to identify the earthly symbols of divine things with these latter: "I *am* the true vine; I *am* the good shepherd." To the eyes of him who writes thus, the reality is not the earthly phenomenon, but the divine, invisible fact; the sensible phenomenon is the copy.

The author also very frequently uses the conjuction *in order that* (ἵνα) in a weakened sense, and one which, as it seems, is tantamount to the simple notion of the Latin *ita ut, so that;* nevertheless, we think, with Meyer, that this is only apparently the case. The question in these cases is of a *divine* purpose. And here also there is revealed a peculiarity of the author's turn of mind: the teleological tendency, which belongs to the spirit of sacred historiography. That which, to the eyes of men, seems only an historical *result*, appears, from a more elevated point of view, as the realization of the design of God.

5. A singular contrast is observed in the narrative forms. On the one hand, something *slow*, diffuse,—for example, that form so frequent in the dialogues: "He answered and said;" or the repetition of proper names, John, Jesus, where a Greek writer would have used the pronoun (a thing which also appertains to the oriental stamp of style: Winer, Gram. N. T., § 65); or again that dragging construction, in virtue of which, after the statement of a fact, a participle with its dependent words comes in unexpectedly, with the purpose of bringing out in a clearer light one of the aspects of the fact mentioned (comp. i. 12; iii. 13; v. 18; vi. 71; vii. 50); or finally, instead of the finite verb, the heavier form of the verb *to be* joined with a participle, a form which, in certain cases, is undoubtedly founded on reasons, as in the classical style, but which is too frequently employed here not to be, as Thiersch has observed, a reproduction of the analogous form belonging to the Aramaic language;—and on the other hand, the frequent appearance of short clauses which break the sentence as if by an abrupt interruption: "And Barabbas was a robber" (xviii. 40); "now it was night" (xiii. 30); "it was the tenth hour" (i. 40); "it was the Sabbath" (v. 9); "Jesus loved Martha and Mary" (xi. 5); "Jesus wept" (xi. 35). Here are jets of an internal fire which, by its sudden outbursts,

breaks the habitual calmness of serene contemplation. Such indeed is the Semite; an exciting recollection may draw him all at once out of the majestic repose with which he ordinarily thinks it fit to envelop himself.

6. In the manner in which the ideas are connected together, we remark three characteristic features: Either, as we have seen, a brief, summary word is placed as a centre, and around it is unrolled a series of cycles, which exhaust more and more, even to its most concrete applications, the primary thought. Or there is a whole series of propositions without external connection, as in the first twenty verses of chap. xv., which all follow one another by *asyndeton;* it seems as if each thought had its whole value in itself and deserved to be weighed separately. Or, finally, there is a bond of a peculiar nature which results from the repetition, in the following clause, of one of the principal words of the preceding, for example, x. 11; xiii. 20; xvii. 2, 3, 9, 11, 15, 16; and, above all, i. 1–5. Each clause is, thus, like a ring linked with the preceding ring. The first two forms are repugnant to the Hellenic genius, the third is borrowed from the Old Testament (Psalm cxxi., and Gen. i. 1 ff.).

7. We have already called attention to the figurative character of the style; let us here add its profoundly *symbolic* character; thus the expressions *to draw, to teach,* in speaking of God; *to see, to hear,* in speaking of the relation of Christ to the invisible world; *to be hungry, thirsty,* in the spiritual sense. It is always the oriental and especially the Hebraic stamp.

8. We will only cite two more features; the *parallelism* of the clauses, which is known to be the distinctive mark of the poetic style among the Hebrews, and the *refrain,* which is likewise in use among them. At all times when the feeling of the one who speaks is elevated, or his soul is stirred by the contemplation of a lofty truth to which he is bearing testimony, these two forms appear in the Old Testament. It is exactly the same in John. For the parallelism, see iii. 11; v. 37; vi. 35, 55, 56; xii. 44, 45; xiii. 16; xv. 20; xvi. 28; for the refrain, iii. 15, 16; vi. 39, 40, 44; comp. Gen. i.: "And the evening was," etc.; Amos i. and ii.; and elsewhere, especially in the Psalms.

What judgment shall we pass, then, on the style and literary character of this work? On the one hand, Renan tells us: " This style has nothing that is Hebraic, nothing Jewish, nothing Talmudic." And he is right, if by style we understand only the wholly external forms of the language. We do not find in the fourth Gospel, as in certain parts of Luke (in the first two chapters, for example, after i. 5), Hebraisms, properly so called, imported just as they are into the Greek text (thus the *vav* conversive), nor, as in the translation of the LXX., Hebrew terms of expression roughly Hellenized. On the other hand, a scholar, who has no less profoundly studied the genius of the Semitic languages, Ewald, expresses himself thus: "No language can be, in respect to the spirit and breath which animate it, more purely Hebraic than that of our author." And he is equally right, if we consider the internal qualities of the style; the whole of the preceding examination has sufficiently proved this.

In the language of John, the clothing only is Greek, the body is Hebrew;

or, as Luthardt says, there is a Hebrew soul in the Greek language of this evangelist. Keim has devoted to the style of the fourth Gospel a beautiful page; he sees in it "the ease and flexibility of the purest Hellenism adapted to the Hebraic mode of expression, with all its candor, its simplicity, its wealth of imagery, and sometimes, also, its awkwardness. No studied refinement, no pathos; everything in it is simple and flowing as in life; but everywhere at the same time, acuteness, variety, progress, scarcely indicated features which form themselves into a picture in the mind of the reflective reader. Everywhere mysteries which surround you and are on the watch for you, signs and symbols which we should not take in the literal sense, if the author had not affirmed their reality, accidents and small details which are found, all at once, to be full of meaning; cordiality, calmness, harmony; in the midst of struggles, grief, zeal, anger, irony; finally, at the end, at the farewell meal, on the cross, and in the resurrection, peace, victory, grandeur."

From this study of the historiographical, theological and literary characteristics of our Gospel, it follows :
1. That the narrative of the fourth Gospel bears, both with respect to the facts, and the discourses, the seal of historical trustworthiness.
2. That, while marking the advance of the Gospel beyond the religion of the Old Testament, it affirms the complete harmony of the two covenants.
3. That though Greek in its forms, the style is, nevertheless, Hebrew in its substance.

THE ORIGIN OF THE FOURTH GOSPEL

WE come to the principal subject of this study, the mode of composition of the work which occupies our attention. This subject includes the following four points: 1. The *epoch* at which this book was composed; 2. The *author* to whom it is to be attributed; 3. The *place* where it had its origin; 4. The *purpose* which presided over its composition.

The means which we have at command for resolving these various questions are, besides the indications contained in the work itself, the information which we draw from the remains of the religious literature of the second century, from the canonical collections of the churches of that epoch, and from the facts of the primitive history of Christianity.

The remains of the literature of the second century are few in number; they resemble the fragments of a shipwreck. They are, first, the letter of *Clement* of Rome to the Church of Corinth, about the end of the first century or at the beginning of the second, and the so-called Epistle of *Barnabas*, belonging to the same period. After this come the letters of *Ignatius*, of the earlier part of the second century, provided we admit their authenticity either in whole or in part, and the letter of *Polycarp* to the Philippians, of a little later date, but with the same reservation. The *Shepherd of Hermas*, the letter to *Diognetus*, and a homily which bears the name of the Second Epistle of *Clement* follow next in order. The date of all these works is variously fixed. We come next to the writings of the Apologists about the middle of the century; *Justin Martyr* with his three principal works; *Tatian*, his disciple; *Athenagoras* with his apology, message addressed to Marcus Aurelius; *Theophilus* and his work addressed to Autolycus; *Melito* and *Apollinaris* with the few fragments which remain of their writings; finally, *Irenæus* of Lyons, *Clement* of Alexandria, and *Tertullian* of Carthage, who form the transition to the third century.

All these writers belong to the orthodox line. Parallel with them we find in the heretical line *Basilides* and his school; *Marcion;* then *Valentinus*, with his four principal disciples, *Ptolemy, Heracleon, Marcus, and Theodotus*, all of them authors of several works, some fragments of which we read in Irenæus, Clement and Hippolytus; the work of the last-mentioned author, recently discovered and entitled *Philosophumena*, is particularly important. Finally, let us mention the Jewish-Christian romance called *Clementine Homilies*.

140 / The Origin

The canonical collections of this epoch with which we are acquainted are three in number: That of the Syrian Church in the translation called *Peschito;* that of the Latin Church in the translation which bears the name of *Itala,* and the so-called fragment of *Muratori,* which represents the canon of some Italian or African Church about the middle of the second century.

It is by means of all these documents, as well as of the indications contained in the Gospel itself, that we must choose between the following four principal dates which at the present day are assigned by criticism to the composition of our Gospel.

1

THE TIME

THE traditional opinion, in attributing this book to the Apostle John, by this very fact places its composition in the first century, towards the end of the apostolic age.

At the opposite extreme to this traditional date is that for which Baur, the chief of the Tübingen school, has decided. According to him, our work was composed between 160 and 170; he places its origin in special connection with the Paschal controversy which broke out at that epoch.

The disciples of Baur have gradually moved back the date of the composition as far as the period from 130 to 155: Volkmar, about 155; Zeller and Scholten, 150; Hilgenfeld, 130–140; thus, a quarter of a century, nearly, earlier than Baur thought. This arises from the fact that several of these writers place the composition of our Gospel in connection with the efflorescence of Gnosticism, about 140.

Many critics, at the present day, make a new step backward. Holtzmann believes our Gospel to be contemporaneous with the Epistle of Barnabas; Schenkel speaks of 115–120; Nicolas, Renan, Weizsäcker, Reuss, Sabatier, all regarding the fourth Gospel as a product of the school in which the Johannean traditions were preserved at Ephesus, fix its composition in the first quarter of the second century. This was also the opinion of Keim, when he published, in 1867, his great work, *l'Histoire de Jésus de Nazara;* he indicated as the date the years 100–120 (p. 146), and more precisely 110–115 (p. 155). More recently, in his popular editions, he has come back to the date of Hilgenfeld (130).

Here are four situations proposed, which we must now submit to the test of facts. Shall we begin with that which is most advanced, or that which is most remote? In our preceding edition, we adopted the former of these two courses. A want of logic has been noticed in this, since, in short, the facts which speak against the earliest dates give proof *a fortiori* against the most recent ones, and yet they are not pointed out until after the discussion of the latter has already taken place.[1] This is true; but

[1] Review in the *Chrétien évangélique,* by Prof. Ch. Porret.

we have confidence enough in the logic of our readers to hope that they will themselves make this reckoning, and that when, for example, they reach, in the discussion of the date 140, a fact which proves it too late, they will not fail to add this fact to those by which the dates more recent than this had been already refuted. We continue to prefer the course which is chronologically regressive, because, as Weizsäcker has been willing to acknowledge, it gives more interest to the exposition of the facts. On the progressive path, every fact giving proof in favor of an earlier date renders the discussion respecting the more recent dates unnecessary.

160–170 —(Baur)

Eusebius declared, in the first part of the fourth century, "that the Gospel of John, well-known in all the churches which are under heaven must be received as in the first rank" (Hist. Eccl., iii. 24); and he consequently reckoned it among the writings which he calls Homologoumena, that is to say, universally adopted by the churches and their teachers. When speaking thus, he had before his eyes the entire literature of the preceding centuries collected together in the libraries of his predecessor Pamphilus, at Cæsarea, and of the bishop Alexander, at Jerusalem. This declaration proves that in studying these writings he had found no gap in the testimonies establishing the use of our Gospel by the Fathers and the churches of the first three centuries. It is necessary to recall to mind here with what exactness and what frankness Eusebius mentions the least indications of a wavering in opinion with regard to the Biblical writings; for example, he does not fail to mark the omission of any citation from the Epistle to the Hebrews in the principal work of Irenæus (an omission which we can ourselves also verify), although that epistle takes rank, according to him, among the fourteen epistles of St. Paul. Let us suppose that he had found in the patristic literature up to the date 160–170 an entire blank in relation to the existence and use of our Gospel, would he have been able in all good faith to express himself as he does in the passage quoted?

Origen, about 220, places the Gospel of John in the number of the four "which are alone received without dispute in the Church of God which is under heaven" (Euseb. H. E., vi. 25). Would this place have been thus unanimously accorded to it, if it had been known only after 170?

Undoubtedly, Eusebius and Origen are not the bearers of the tradition; but they are the founders of criticism who grouped the information from the preceding centuries and evolved from it the preceding summations of the case.

Clement of Alexandria, the master of Origen, is already in a little different position; he collected the items of information which were transmitted to him by the presbyters whose line of succession is connected with the apostles (ἀπὸ τῶν ἀνέκαθεν πρεσβυτέρων). In speaking thus, he is thinking especially of Pantænus, a missionary in India, who died in 189. The following is the information which had come to him through those venerable witnesses: "John received the first three Gospels, and observing that the corporeal things (the external facts) of our Lord's life had been recorded therein, he, being urged by the prominent men of the Church, wrote a spiritual Gospel" (Euseb. H. E., vi. 14). Could Clement, who wrote about 190, have spoken thus of a work which had been in existence only twenty or twenty-five years? He must, for this to be so, have invented this tradition himself. Let us add that in another passage (*Strom.* iii., p. 465), when quoting a saying of Jesus contained in an uncanonical gospel, called the Gospel of the Egyptians, he makes this reservation : "that we do not find this saying *in the four Gospels which have been transmitted to us*" (ἐν τοῖς παραδεδομένοις ἡμῖν τέτταρσιν εὐαγγελίοις). The contrast which Clement here establishes, clearly shows that, from the standpoint of tradition, there was a radical difference between the Gospel of John and a gospel such as that of the Egyptians.

Tertullian, born about 160, frequently cites our Gospel as being an authority in the whole Church. Would this be possible if this Father and this work were born in the same year, the one in Asia, the other in Africa? Let us notice that he quotes it according to a Latin translation of which he says (*Ad. Prax.*): "It is in use among our people (*In usu est nostrorum*)." And not only was it in use and so held in respect, that Tertullian did not feel free to turn aside from it, even when he was not in accord with it,[1] but also this Latin translation had already taken the place of another earlier one of which Tertullian says (*De Monogam*, c. 11) "that it has fallen into disuse (*In usum exiit*)." And yet all this could have occurred between the birth of this Father and the time when he wrote!

Irenæus wrote in Gaul, about 185, his great work *Against Heresies*. More than sixty times he quotes our Gospel in it with the most complete conviction of its apostolic origin. He who acts thus respecting it was born in Asia Minor about the year 130, and had spent his youth there in the school of Polycarp, the friend and disciple of St. John. How could he, without bad faith, have dated from the apostolic age a Gospel which had not been in existence more than fifteen to twenty years at the moment when he was writing, and which he had never heard spoken of in the churches where he had spent his youth and which must have been the cradle of this work? In 177, Irenæus drew up, on the part of the churches of Vienne and Lyons, a letter to the churches of Asia and Phrygia, for the purpose of giving them an account of the terrible persecution which had just smitten them under Marcus Aurelius. This letter has been preserved to us by Eusebius (H. E., v. 1). It says, speaking of one of the martyrs, "Having the Paraclete within him ;" and in another place : "Thus was the word uttered by our Lord fulfilled, that the time shall come when he who killeth you will think that he doeth God service." These are two quotations from John (xiv. 26 and xvi. 2). Thus, about ten years after the time of composition indicated by Baur, quotations were taken *in Gaul* from our Gospel as if from a writing possessing canonical authority!

About 180, Theophilus, bishop of Antioch, addresses to his heathen

---

[1] Rönsch, *Das Sprachidiom der urchristlichen Itala und der catholischen Vulgata*, 1869, pp. 2–4.

friend Autolycus an apology for Christianity; he quotes in it the prologue of John, expressing himself thus (ii. 22): "This is what *the holy writings* and all the men animated by the spirit teach us, *among whom John says*" (John i. 1 follows). Can it be admitted, that only fifteen to twenty years after the appearance of our Gospel, the bishop of Antioch spoke in this way? He so fully placed it in the rank of the other three, which were received everywhere and at all times, that he had published a *Harmony* of the Gospels, which Jerome describes to us (*De Vir.* 25) as "uniting in a single work the words of the four Gospels (*quatuor evangeliorum in unum opus dicta compingens*)." The adversaries of the authenticity bring forward the circumstance, it is true, that here is the first instance in which the author of our Gospel is designated by name. But what does so accidental a fact prove? Irenæus is the first ecclesiastical writer who names St. Paul as the author of the Epistle to the Romans. Would it be necessary to conclude, from this fact, that the belief in the apostolic authorship of the Epistle to the Romans began only at that moment to dawn on the mind of the Church? As it was not up to that time the custom to quote textually, so also it was not the custom to quote with a designation of the author.

Apollinaris, bishop of Hierapolis in Phrygia, about 170, contended against the opinion of persons who celebrated the Holy Passover Supper on the evening of the 14th of Nisan, at the same time that the Jews ate their Passover meal; for, as they alleged, according to the Gospel of Matthew, Jesus had eaten the Passover on that evening with His disciples, and He had not been crucified until the next day. Apollinaris made reply to this in two ways:[1] 1. That this view "was in contradiction to the law;" since, according to the law, the Paschal lamb was slain on the 14th, and not on the 15th; it was consequently on that day that the Christ must die; 2. That if this view was well founded, "the Gospels would contradict each other." This second remark can only refer to the account in the Gospel of John, which places the death of Jesus on the 14th, and not the 15th, as the Synoptics appear to do. Thus, in 170, Apollinaris rested upon the fourth Gospel as on a perfectly recognized authority, even on the part of his adversaries, and yet at this same epoch, according to Baur, it began to circulate as an altogether new work! This critic has endeavored, to be sure, to wrest this passage from its natural meaning; but this attempt has been unanimously discarded. Besides, the same Apollinaris in still another passage, also, adduces the fourth Gospel. He calls Jesus, "The one whose sacred side was pierced and who poured forth from His side water and blood, the word and the Spirit;"[2] comp. John xix. 34.

At the same period Melito, bishop of Sardis, wrote also on the same subject. Otto (in the *Corpus apologet.*, vol. ix.) has published a fragment from this Father, in which it is said that "Jesus, being at once perfect God and man, proved his divinity by his miracles in the *three years* which

---

[1] *Chronicon paschale* (ed. Dindorf I., p. 14): ὅθεν ἀσύμφωνός τε νόμῳ ἡ νόησις αὐτῶν καὶ στασιάζειν δοκεῖ κατ' αὐτοὺς τὰ εὐαγγέλια. [2] *Chron. pasch.*, p. 14.

144 / The Origin

followed his baptism, and his humanity during the thirty years which preceded it." Those three years of ministry can come only from the Johannean narration.

About the same time (in 176), Athenagoras thus expresses himself in his apology addressed to the Emperor Marcus Aurelius: "The Son of God is the Word of the Father; by him all things were made." Here is an undeniable quotation; Volkmar himself acknowledges it.

There is the same use of the fourth Gospel on the part of the *heretics* of this period, particularly on the part of the disciples of Valentinus. One of them, Ptolemy (in a fragment preserved by Irenæus), recalled in these words the passage in John xii. 27: "Jesus said: And what shall I say? I know not." He maintained (also according to Irenæus) that the Apostle John himself had taught at the beginning of his Gospel the existence of the first Ogdoad (the foundation of the doctrine of Valentinus). Irenæus and Epiphanius have preserved for us his letter to Flora, in which he cites John i. 3 in these words: "The apostle declares that the creation of the world belongs to the Saviour, inasmuch as all things were made by him and nothing was made without him." In the fragments of Theodotus preserved in the works of Clement of Alexandria, there are found seventy-eight quotations from the New Testament, of which number twenty-six are taken from the Gospel of John.[1] The fact most important to be cited here is the commentary which Heracleon wrote on the fourth Gospel. At what time? About the year 200, Volkmar asserts; but Origen, who refuted this work, calls its author *a familiar acquaintance* of Valentinus (Οὐαλεντίνου γνώριμος); now the latter taught between 140 and 160. Yes, replies Volkmar, but Heracleon is not at all mentioned by Irenæus, which proves that he lived after 185, the date at which the latter wrote against the heretics of his time. This assertion is, as Tischendorf has shown, an error of fact arising simply from the omission of the name of Heracleon in the registers of names in the editions of Massuet and Stieren, at the end of Irenæus' work. In fact, this Father expressly says ii. 4: "and all the other Æons of Ptolemy and *Heracleon*." This latter person lived and wrote, therefore, before Irenæus—at the latest, about 170 or even 160. And what did he write? A continuous commentary on the Gospel of John. This single fact implies that our Gospel enjoyed in the Church at that period an authority which was of long standing and general. For men do not comment except on a book which, up to a certain point, gives law to every one. How long a time must have elapsed, therefore, since this work was composed! Moreover, Irenæus (iii. 12, 12), testifies that the Valentinians "made abundant use of the Gospel of John" (*eo quod est secundum Johannem plenissime utentes*).

The Clementine Homilies which are located about the year 160,[2] express themselves thus (iii. 52): "This is the reason why the true prophet has said: I am the gate of life (ἡ πύλη τῆς ζωῆς); he who enters through me enters into life . . . My sheep hear my voice (τὰ ἐμὰ πρόβατα ἀκούει τῆς

---

[1] Hofstede de Groot, *Basilides*, p. 102. [2] Keim himself, I., p. 137.

ἐμῆς φωνῆς)." This is an evident quotation from John x. 3, 9, 27; but it is not enough to make Baur, Scholten, Volkmar, Hilgenfeld, etc., admit the use of the Johannean Gospel by the vehement Judaizing writer who composed this pamphlet against the doctrine and person of St. Paul. The discovery made by Dressel, in 1853, of the end of this book as yet unknown, was needed to cut short all critical subterfuges. In the nineteenth homily, chap. xxii., there is found this unquestionable quotation from the story of the man born blind related in the ninth chapter of John: "This is the reason why our Lord also replied to those who asked him: Did this man sin, or his parents, that he was born blind?—Neither did this man sin nor his parents, but that through him might be manifested the power of God healing the faults of ignorance." The slight modification which the author of the *Homilies* introduces into the last words of this Johannean saying is connected with the particular idea which he is endeavoring to make prominent in this passage. If Volkmar finds herein a reason for denial even in the presence of such a quotation, Hilgenfeld, on the contrary, frankly says (*Einl.*, p. 734): "The Gospel of John is employed without scruple even by the adversaries of the divinity of Christ, such as the author of the Clementines." What, then, must have been the authority of a book which even the adversaries of the teaching contained in the work used in this way! Here is what occurred in 160, and yet Baur tries to maintain that this work was composed between 160 and 170!

A heathen philosopher, Celsus, wrote a book entitled *The True Word* (λόγος ἀληθής), to controvert Christianity; he wished, he said, to slay the Christians "with their own sword," that is to say, to refute Christianity by the writings of the very disciples of its founder. He started in his work, therefore, from the universally acknowledged authenticity of our Gospels. Did he make use of the fourth Gospel also with this purpose? Certainly; for he recalls the demand which the Jews addressed to Jesus in the temple to prove by a sign that He was the Son of God (John ii. 18). He compares the water and the blood which flowed from the body of Jesus on the cross (John xix., 34), to that sacred blood which the mythological stories made to flow from the body of the blessed gods. He speaks of the appearance to Mary Magdalene (that πάροιστρος woman) near the sepulchre. He sets forth this contradiction between our Gospel narratives, that, according to some (οἱ μέν), two angels appeared at the tomb of Jesus, according to the others (οἱ δέ), on the contrary, only one. And in fact Matthew and Mark speak of only one angel, Luke and John mention two. The use of John in this passage, which Zeller still ventured to deny, is now acknowledged by Volkmar himself, but this avowal ends, as usual, in a subterfuge: "And who tells us that Celsus wrote before the beginning of the third century?" And by means of a passage of Origen the purport of which is incorrectly given, the attempt is made to prove that that Father spoke of Celsus as his contemporary.[1] Tischendorf has done full justice to this procedure. It was enough for him to quote Origen correctly, in

---

[1] *Ursprung uns. Evang.*, p. 80.

order to show that he said nothing of the sort. He has, in addition, recalled another passage of this Father, where he expressly designates Celsus as "a man already and long since dead (ἤδη καὶ πάλαι νεκροῦ)."[1] If we adopt the latest date for the work of Celsus, that of Keim (in 178), it still remains impossible that a heathen should have held a work published only eight years before to be composed by one of the disciples of Jesus. And how will it be if Celsus lived much earlier?

There remain to us three documents of the canonical collections of apostolic writings, already existing in the churches of the second century. In Syria, about the end of this century, a translation of the New Testament in the Syriac language was read, and our fourth Gospel certainly formed a part of it, for the only books of the New Testament which were wanting in this collection were, according to unquestionable data, four of the Catholic epistles and the Apocalypse. It even appears, from several fragments in the Syriac language which Cureton has published, that this translation which is called *Peschito,* and which contained the Old Testament as well as the New, had been already preceded by another more ancient one.[2] At the same period, at the opposite extremity of the Church, in Italy, in Gaul, and in the province of Africa, the Latin translation already existed of which we have spoken in connection with Tertullian. In this canonical collection, which also contained the Old Testament, the writings of the New Testament seem to have been divided into five groups: 1. The body of the four Gospels, *the evangelical instrument,* collection of documents; then, *the apostolical instruments,* to wit: 2. That of the Acts; 3. That of Paul; 4. That of John (Apocalypse and 1 John); 5. A group of disputed writings (1 Peter, Hebrews, Jude). Is it possible to suppose that in the last quarter of the second century, a work which did not appear until between 160 and 170, had already been translated into Syriac and into Latin, and had become possessed of canonical dignity in countries which, so to speak, formed the antipodes of the Church?

The famous document which was recovered in the last century by Muratori in the Library of Milan, and which bears the name of that scholar, is located between 160 and 170. It is a treatise on the writings which were said to have been read publicly in the churches. The author indicates in it the custom of the Church of Italy or of Africa to which he belongs. The Gospel of John is mentioned in it as the fourth. The author gives an account in detail of the manner in which it was composed by the Apostle John, and brings out some of its peculiarities. This is what was written in Italy or in Africa at the very date which Baur assigns to the composition of this Gospel!

It will not be surprising to any one, after the enumeration of these facts, that the so-called *critical* school has judged it impossible to maintain the position chosen by its master. It has effected its retreat movement throughout, and has sought, by going backward in the second century, a

---

[1] *Wann wurden unsere Evangelien verfasst?* pp. 73, 74.

[2] *Remains of a very ancient recension,* etc.; London, 1858.

more tenable situation. Before we follow it, let us note the fact that between 160 and 170 the fourth Gospel existed in the Greek, Latin and Syriac languages, and that it was publicly read in all the churches, from Mesopotamia even to Gaul. Facts like these imply, not only two or three decades of years, but at the least a half century of existence.

(130–155)

Volkmar, 155; Zeller, Scholten, 150; Hilgenfeld, 130–140; Keim (since 1875), 130

Instead of the fifty years which we ask for in order to explain the facts which we have just mentioned, only twenty or thirty are granted us. Let us see whether this concession is sufficient to account for the facts which we have yet to point out. Our means for guiding our course in the examination of this new date are the writings of Justin Martyr, the Montanist movement, and the two great Gnostic systems of Marcion and Valentinus.

Justin, born in Samaria, had traversed the Orient and then had come to Rome to establish a school of Christian instruction, about 140. There remain to us three generally acknowledged works of his : the *greater* and *smaller Apology*, which, since the labors of Volkmar, are ordinarily regarded as dating, the first from 147 ; the second, a supplement to the first, from one of the succeeding years; they are addressed to the emperor and the senate. The third work is the *Dialogue with Trypho the Jew;* it is the account of a public debate held at Ephesus. It is a little later than the Apologies. Justin was put to death in 166.

In these three works the author cites seventeen times, as the source of the facts of Jesus' history which are alleged by him, writings entitled, *Memoirs of the Apostles* (ἀπομνημονεύματα τῶν ἀποστόλων),[1] and the decisive question, in the matter which occupies us, will be whether the fourth Gospel was in the number of the writings comprised in this collection.

In order to understand the importance of the question here proposed, we must recall to mind the fact that the writings cited by Justin as his authorities were not only his private property. According to the famous passage of the first Apology (i. 67), in which Justin describes the worship of the Christians in the first half of the second century, the Memoirs of the Apostles were read every Sunday in the public assemblies of the Church, side by side with the books of the prophets;[2] and it is very evident that this description does not, in the writer's thought, apply only to the worship celebrated by the Church of Rome, but to that of Christendom generally ; this follows from the expressions used by him : "*All those who dwell in the towns and in the country* meet together in one place." Justin

---

[1] *Apol.* i. 33; 66; 67; *Dial.*, 88; 101; 102; 103 (twice); 104; 105 (3 times); 106 (3 times).

[2] " On the day called the day of the Sun, all those who dwell in the towns and in the country meet together in one place, and the Memoirs of the Apostles and the writings of the prophets are read, according as the time permits; afterwards . . . "

148 / The Origin

had visited Asia Minor and Egypt; he knew, therefore, how the worship was celebrated, as well in the East as in the West. Moreover, he defended before the emperor, not only the Christians of Rome, but the Church in general. Consequently, what he says in this passage of the celebration of public worship, and in several others of that of baptism (*Apol.* i. 61) and of the Holy Supper (*Apol.* i. 66), must be applied to the whole of the Christendom of that epoch.

What, then, were these Apostolic Memoirs which were venerated by the churches of the second century so far as to be read publicly in worship equally with the book which, according to the example of Jesus and the apostles, the Church regarded as the Divine Word, the Old Testament? Justin does not indicate to us the particular titles of these writings; it is our task to determine them.

1. First of all, let us note a probability which rises almost to certainty. We have seen above that Irenæus, who wrote thirty years after Justin (180–185), spoke, in Gaul, of our four canonical Gospels as the only ones received in the Church. This usage was already so fixed at his time, that he calls our evangelical collection the four-formed Gospel (τετράμορφον εὐαγγέλιον), and that he compares these four writings to the four Cherubim of the Old Covenant and to the four quarters of the horizon. They form for him an indivisible unity. Nearly at the same time, Clement, in Egypt, also calls our Gospels, as we have seen, "*the four* which alone have been *transmitted* to us" (p. 141). Theophilus, in Syria, at the same epoch, composes a Harmony of these four narratives (p. 142 f.). Finally, a little earlier still (about 160), the fragment of Muratori, enumerating the Gospels which are adopted for public reading, expresses itself thus: "*Thirdly*, the book of the Gospel according to Luke . . . ; *fourthly*, the Gospel of John . . . " Then there is nothing more with regard to writings of this kind; it passes to the Acts and Epistles. Can it be admitted that the Apostolic Memoirs, of which Justin tells us that they were generally read in the Christian worship twenty or thirty years before, were *other writings* than those which these Fathers and the churches themselves distinguished thus from all the other writings of the same kind, or that they did not, at least, make a part of the collection to which the Martyr already assigned a place in the worship by the side of the prophetic writings of the Old Testament? To this end there must necessarily have been wrought, during that short space of time, a revolution in Christian worship, a substitution of sacred writings for sacred writings, of which history does not present the least trace, and which is rendered absolutely impossible by the universality and publicity of the use of the Memoirs of which Justin speaks, and by the stability of the apostolic usages at that period. The Fathers, such as Irenæus, were at hand keeping watch over the matter, and they would not have permitted a change of the documents from which the Church derived its knowledge of the life of Jesus to be accomplished, without indicating it.

2. A special fact proves a still more direct connection between Justin, on the one side, and the Fathers of a little later date (Irenæus, etc.), on

the other. Justin had a disciple named Tatian, who had already, before
Theophilus, composed a work similar to his. Eusebius tells us (*H. E.* iv.
19) that this book was entitled *Diatessaron,* that is to say, *composed by
means of the four.*[1] Now, according to the report of the Syrian bishop
Bar Salibi (xii. cent.), who was acquainted with this work since he quotes
it in his Commentary on the Gospels, this writing began with these words
of John's prologue (i. 1): " In the beginning was the Word." According
to the same author, Ephrem, the well-known deacon of Edessa (died in
373), had composed a commentary on this same work of Tatian, an Armenian translation of which has been recently recovered and published
(Venice, 1876). This translation confirms everything which the Fathers
have reported respecting Tatian's Harmony. In a work of an apocryphal
character, the *Doctrine of Addæus* (of the middle of the third century), in
which the history of the establishment of Christianity at Edessa is related,
it is said: " The people meet together for the service of prayer and for
[the reading of] the Old Testament and [for that of the] New *in the Diatessaron.*"[2] This work of Tatian, therefore, was very widely spread abroad
in the East, since it was read in the East, even in the public worship,
instead of the four Gospels. This is confirmed by the report of the bishop
of Cyrus, in Cilicia, Theodoret (about 420). He relates that he had found
two hundred copies of Tatian's book in the churches of his diocese, and
that he had substituted for this Harmony, which was heterodox in some
points, "*the Gospels of the four evangelists* (τὰ τῶν τεττάρων εὐαγγελίστων ἀντεισήγαγον εὐαγγέλια)"—thus, our four separate Gospels, those which Tatian
had combined in a single one. If we recall to mind the relation which
united Tatian to Justin, the identity of the Apostolic Memoirs of the
master with the *four* blended in one by the disciple cannot be doubted.
Moreover, in his *Discourse to the Greeks* Tatian himself quotes Matthew,
Luke and John; from the last, i. 3: " All things were made by him " (the
Logos); iv. 24: "God is a spirit;" finally, i. 5, with that formula which
indicates a sacred authority : " This is that which is spoken (τοῦτό ἐστι τὸ
εἰρημένον): The darkness did not apprehend the light; . . . now the light
of God is the Word."

3. But why, if it is so, does Justin designate these books by the unusual
name of *Memoirs,* instead of calling them simply Gospels? Because he
addresses himself, not to Christians, but to the emperor and senate, who
would not have understood the Christian name of Gospels, which was
without example in profane literature. Every one, on the other hand,
was acquainted with the ἀπομνημονεύματα (*Memoirs*) of Xenophon. Justin
has recourse to this ordinary name, exactly as he substitutes for the
Christian terms *baptism* and *Sunday* the terms *bath* and *day of the Sun.*

---

[1] See also Epiphanius, *Haer.* xlvi. 1, and Theodoret, *Haer. Fab.* i. 20.

[2] In the Catena of Victor of Capua (545), the work of Tatian is called *Diapente* "*composed by means of five.*" But immediately before, the same author has described it as *unum ex quatuor.* There is, thus, here either a negligence of the author, or perhaps an allusion to quotations of Justin, which are foreign to our four Gospels, which seemed to him to imply the use of a fifth source.

150 / The Origin

Finally, Justin himself, in one of the passages where he quotes the Memoirs (*Apol.* i. 4, 66), adds expressly: "*which are composed by the apostles and called Gospels* (ἃ καλεῖται εὐαγγέλια)," and, in another passage (*Dial.* 103) he expresses himself thus: "*The Memoirs which I say were composed by the apostles and by those who accompanied them,*" which, whatever some critics may say, can only apply to our four Gospels, of which, as the fact is, two were composed by apostles and two by *apostolic helpers*. All the critical quibbles will not alter the evidence at all.

4. But let us, finally, consider the quotations taken by Justin from the Memoirs themselves. No one, at the present day, any longer denies the use of the three Synoptics by this Father. In 1848, Zeller conceded it with respect to Luke; in 1850, Hilgenfeld, with respect to Matthew; the same, in 1854, with respect to Mark; Credner in 1860, Volkmar in 1866, Scholten in 1867, have acknowledged it with respect to all the three. The Gospel of John remains. Keim, already in 1867 (vol. i., p. 138), wrote: "It is easy to show that the Martyr had under his eyes a whole series of Johannean passages," and Hilgenfeld said in 1875 (*Einl.* p. 734): "The first trace of the Gospel of John is found in Justin Martyr." Mangold, in the same year, formulates thus the result of all the discussions which have recently taken place respecting this point: "That Justin knew and used the fourth Gospel is certain, and it is also beyond doubt that he makes use of it as a work proceeding from the Apostle John."[1] And in fact John's doctrine of the Logos appears in all the writings of Justin; this is their fundamental peculiarity. Let us quote a single example taken from each of these writings: "His Son, the only one who may be properly called Son, the Logos who was begotten by him before created things, when he created all things by him, . . . is called Christ" (*Apol.* ii. 6). "The first power after God, the Father and Master of all, is the Son, the Word, who, having in a certain way been made flesh, became a man (ὃς τινα τρόπον σαρκοποιηθεὶς ἄνθρωπος γέγονεν)" (*Apol.* i. 32). *Dial.* 105: "Because he was the only begotten Son of the Father of all things (μονογενὴς ὅτι ἦν τῷ πατρὶ τῶν ὅλων)." The relation between Justin and John on this capital point is so evident that Volkmar has been obliged finally to acknowledge it; but he extricates himself by an expedient which not a little resembles a clown's trick. According to him, it is not Justin who has imitated John; it is a pseudo-John who, writing about 155, has imitated Justin, whose writings were in circulation since 147–150. Justin had drawn the first lineaments of the Logos theory; the false John has developed and perfected it. "But," answers Keim to this supposition, "who can seriously think of making out of the genial and original author of the fourth Gospel the disciple of a mind so mediocre, dependent, disposed to the work of compiling, and poor in style, as the Martyr?" We will add: The theology of the former is the simple expression of his religious consciousness, of the immediate effects produced on him by the person of Jesus, while, as Weizsäcker has clearly shown,[2] the characteristic trait of Justin is to serve

---

[1] *Gœtt. gelehrte Anzeigen*, 5 u. 12, Jan. 1881.   [2] *Jahrb. für deutsche Theol.*, 1867.

as an intermediary between Christian thought and the speculations which were prevailing at his epoch outside of Christianity. Justin teaches us that the Logos comes from the Father as a fire is kindled by another fire, without the latter being diminished; he explains to us that he differs from the Father in *number*, but not in *thought*, etc., etc. How can one venture to affirm that Justin surpasses John in simplicity? The truth is that John is the witness, and Justin the theologian. John's prologue—it is there only that there is any question of the Logos in our Gospel—is the primordial revelation, in its simple and apostolic form; the writings of Justin present to us the first effort to appropriate this revelation to oneself by the reason.

Besides, let us listen to Justin himself, *Dial.* 105: "I have previously shown that it was the only begotten Son of the Father of all things, his Logos and his power, born of him and afterwards made man by means of the Virgin, *as we have learned through the Memoirs.*" Justin himself tells us here from what source he had derived his doctrine of the Logos; it was from his Apostolic Memoirs. Hilgenfeld has claimed that Justin did not appeal to the Memoirs except for the second of the two facts mentioned in this passage: the miraculous birth; but the two facts indicated depend equally, through one and the same conjunction (ὅτι *that*), on the verbal ideas: *I have shown,* and *as we have learned.* Moreover, the principal notion, according to the entire context, is that of the *only begotten Son* (μονογενής) which belongs to the first of the two dependent clauses.[1] Our conclusion is expressly confirmed by what Justin says (*Dial.* 48); he speaks of certain Christians who were not in accord with him on this point, and he declares that, if he does not think as they do, it is not merely because they form only a minority in the Church, but "because it is not by human teachings that we have been brought to believe in Christ [in this way], but by the teachings of the holy prophets and by those of Christ himself (τοῖς διὰ τῶν προφητῶν κηρυχθεῖσι καὶ δι' αὐτοῦ διδαχθεῖσι)." Now, where can we find, outside of the Gospel of John, the teachings of Christ respecting His pre-existence? Comp. also *Apol.* i. 46: "That Christ is the first-born Son of God, being the Logos of whom all the human race is made participant—this is *what has been taught us* (ἐδιδάχθημεν)." We see from this *us,* which applies to Christians in general, and by the term *taught,* that Justin was by no means the author of the doctrine of the incarnation of the Logos, but that, when calling Jesus by this name, he feels himself borne along by the great current of the teaching given in the Church, and of which the source must necessarily be found in the writings, or at least in one of the writings, of the apostles of which he made use.

5. The use of our Gospel by Justin appears, finally, from several particular quotations, *Dial.* 88: "And as men supposed that he [John the Baptist] was the Christ, he himself cried out to them: I am not the Christ,

---

[1] This is clearly brought out by Drummond, *Theological Review* (vol. xiv. pp. 178-182, comp. Ezra Abbot, p. 43) by recalling the fact that all this development is occasioned by the expression μονογενής in Ps. xxii., of which Justin is here giving the explanation.

152 / The Origin

but I am the voice of one crying (οὐκ εἰμὶ ὁ Χριστὸς, ἀλλὰ φωνὴ βοῶντος)." Comp. John i. 20, 23. Hilgenfeld acknowledges this quotation. *Dial.* 69, Justin says that Jesus healed those who were blind *from birth* (τοὺς ἐκ γενετῆς πηρούς); the Gospel of John alone (ix. 1) attributes to Him a healing of this kind; the same term ἐκ γενετῆς is used by John. Another interesting passage is found in *Dial.* 88: "The apostles have written that, when Jesus came out of the water, the Holy Spirit shone above him like a dove." This is the only case where Justin uses the expression, *the apostles have written.* It evidently applies to the two Gospels of Matthew and *John.* *Dial.* 29, Justin proves that Christians are no more bound to the Jewish Sabbath, and he does this by calling to mind the fact that God governs the world on that day as well as on the others. In c. 27, he also points out the fact that infants are circumcised on the eighth day, even though it falls upon a Sabbath (κἂν ᾖ ἡμέρα τῶν σαββάτων). We easily recognize here the relation to John v. 17 and vii. 22, 23. *Apol.* i. 52, Justin quotes the words of Zach. xii. 10: "They shall look on Him whom they pierced (καὶ τότε ὄψονται εἰς ὃν ἐξεκέντησαν)." In this form it differs both from the terms of the Hebrew text ("they shall look *on me* whom they . . .") and from that of the LXX: "They shall look on me because they have mocked me." Now we read this same passage in the fourth Gospel exactly in the form in which Justin quotes it (John xix.): ὄψονται εἰς ὃν ἐξεκέντησαν. Some think, no doubt, that Justin may have derived this passage from the book of the Apocalypse, where it is likewise quoted, i. 7: "And every eye shall see Him, and they also who pierced Him." But Justin's text is more closely connected with that of the Gospel. Other grounds are alleged, it is true, such as the possibility of an ancient variation of text in the LXX.;[1] we shall, therefore, not insist much upon this fact.

Here, on the other hand, is an important, and even decisive passage. *Apol.* i. 61, Justin relates to the senate that when a man has been convinced of the truth of the Gospel, "he is led to a place where there is water, to be regenerated like the believers who (have) preceded him; and that he is bathed in the water in the name of God, the Father and Lord of all things, and of our Lord Jesus Christ, and of the Holy Spirit;" for Christ said: "Unless ye are born again (ἂν μὴ ἀναγεννηθῆτε), ye shall not enter into the kingdom of heaven. Now that it is impossible," continues Justin, "for those who have once been born to enter again into the womb of those who gave them birth, is evident to all." The relation to John iii. 3–5 is manifest; it appears especially from the last words, which reproduce, without any sort of necessity and in the most clumsy way, the meaning of the objection of Nicodemus in John's narrative (ver. 4). Many, however, deny that Justin wrote thus under the influence of John's narrative. They allege these two differences: instead of the term employed by John, ἄνωθεν γεννηθῆναι (*to be born from above* or *anew*), Justin says ἀναγεννηθῆναι (*to be born again*); then, for the expression *Kingdom of God*, he substitutes *Kingdom of heaven*. But these two changes do not have the importance

---

[1] See Abbott himself, p. 46.

which some critics attribute to them. As to the first, Abbot proves that it is found also in Irenæus, Eusebius, Athanasius, Basil, Ephrem, Chrysostom, Cyril of Alexandria, Anastasius Sin., as well as in most of the Latin authorities (*renasci*), all of whom made use of the Gospel of John and yet quote this passage as Justin does. Undoubtedly, it is because the term ἄνωθεν γεννηθῆναι was obscure, and subject to discussion, and because it is read only once in the Scriptures, while the other is clearer and more common (1 Pet. i. 3, 23; ii. 2). As to the expression *Kingdom of heaven*, it arises in Justin evidently from the Gospel of Matthew, which, from a mass of proofs, was much the most read in the earliest times of the Church, and in which this term is habitually employed. Abbot proves that this same change occurs in the quotation of this passage in the Greek and Latin Fathers, all of whom had John in their hands. But the following is a more serious objection, namely: that this same saying of Jesus is found quoted in the *Clementine Homilies* (ix. 26) with precisely the same alterations as in Justin, which seems to prove that the two authors borrowed from a common source other than John; for example, from the Gospel of the Hebrews. Here is the passage from the *Clementines;* the reader can judge: " This is what the true prophet has affirmed to us with an oath: Verily I say unto you that unless you are born again of living water (ἐὰν μὴ ἀναγεννηθῆτε ὕδατι ζῶντι), in the name of the Father, the Son and the Holy Spirit, you shall not enter into the kingdom of heaven." We see that the difference between Justin and the *Clementines*, as Abbot says, is much greater than that between these two works and John. The reason is, because the text of the *Clementines* is influenced not only, like that of Justin, by Matt. xviii. 3, but especially by Matt. xxviii. 19 (the formula of baptism).[1]

Let us, finally, recall a quotation from the first Epistle of John which is found in Justin. *Dial.* c. 123, he says: "All at once we are called to become sons of God, and we are so," which recalls 1 John iii. 1 (according to the reading adopted at the present day by many critics): " Behold, what love God has had for us, that we should be called children of God; and we are so." Hilgenfeld acknowledges this quotation.

How is it conceivable that, in the face of all these facts, Reuss can express himself thus (p. 94): " We conclude that Justin did not include the fourth Gospel among those which he cites generally under the name of Memoirs of the Apostles." What argument, then, is powerful enough to neutralize to his view the value of the numerous quotations which we have just alleged? "Justin," he says, " did not have recourse to our Gospel, as would have been expected, when he wished to establish the historical facts of which he was desirous to avail himself." But do we not know that there is nothing more deceptive in criticism than arguments

---

[1] The author of the *Recognitions* quotes thus: "Amen dico vobis, nisi quis denuo renatus fuerit ex aqua, non introibit in regna cœlorum." He quotes, combining the third and fifth verses of John; he only omits the expression *and of the Spirit*, to the end of glorifying so much the more the baptism of water, in conformity with the ritual tendency of that time.

154 / The Origin

drawn from what a writer should have said or done, and has not done or said? Abbot cites curious examples of this drawn from contemporary history. We have already recalled to mind the fact that the Gospel of Matthew was, in the earliest times of the Church, the source which was most generally used. This is also the case with Justin, who uses Luke much less frequently than Matthew, and Mark much less even than Luke. John is used more than Mark.[1]

For ourselves, we think we have proved: 1. That the fourth Gospel existed in the time of Justin and formed a part of his apostolic Memoirs; 2. That it was publicly read in the churches of the East and West as one of the authentic documents of the history and teachings of Jesus; 3. That, as a consequence, it possessed already at that period, conjointly with the other three, a very ancient notoriety and a general authority equal to that of the Old Testament. Now it is impossible that a work which held this position in the Church in 140, should have been composed only about the year 130.[2]

In the same year 140, when Justin came to settle at Rome, there also arrived in that city one of the most illustrious representatives of the Gnostic doctrines, Valentinus. After having carried on a school for quite a long time in that capital, he went away to end his career in Cyprus, about 160. We already know some of his principal disciples, Ptolemy, Heracleon, Theodotus, and we know how much favor the fourth Gospel had in their schools; history confirms this saying of Irenæus respecting them: "making use, in the most complete way, of the Gospel of John." It is, therefore, very probable that their master had given them an example on this point. Tertullian sets Valentinus in opposition to another Gnostic, Marcion, remarking that the former accepted the sacred collection as a whole, not making up the Scriptures according to his doctrine, but rather adapting his doctrine to the Scriptures.[3] We are acquainted with his system; he presented as emanating successively from the eternal and divine abyss pairs of Æons (principles of things), of which the first four formed what he called the *Ogdoad* (the sacred eight). The names of these Æons were: *Logos, Light, Truth, Grace, Life, Only begotten Son, Par-*

---

[1] The other general objections which are raised by A. Thoma in Hilgenfeld's *Zeitschrift* (1875), and by the work called *Supernatural Religion*, are refuted by Abbot (pp. 61-76). They do not concern us here, since Thoma himself admits that Justin was acquainted with and in almost every chapter used "the Gospel of the Logos;" he only claims that he did not recognize it as apostolic and truly historical. This is of little importance to us, since the question here is only whether the Gospel existed in Justin's time and was used by him.—As to the question whether the few facts of the evangelical history cited by Justin, which are not found in our Gospels, are borrowed from the oral tradition or from some lost work, the Gospel of the Hebrews for example, we have no reason to occupy ourselves with it here.

[2] To Justin is sometimes ascribed the *Letter to Diognetus*, in which the fourth Gospel has left its deeply marked imprint. In our view, as in that of Reuss, this letter must date approximatively from the year 130. But, independently of those who, like Overbeck, bring it down to the fourth century, others place it only under Marcus Aurelius, in the second half of the century. Comp. Draeseke, *Jahrb. für protest. Theol.*, 2 Heft., 1881. Under these conditions, we refrain from alleging the passages or expressions which are borrowed from John.

[3] *De praescr. haeret*, ch. 38.

aclete. The influence of John's prologue is easily recognized here, since all these names are found united together in that passage, with the exception of the last, which appears only later in the Gospel, and which is used in the epistle. It has been asked, it is true, whether perhaps it may not be the evangelist who composed his prologue under the influence of the Valentinian Gnosis, and Hilgenfeld has thought that his aim may have been to cause this new doctrine to penetrate the Church, by mitigating it. We have already seen to what forced interpretations (of John viii. 44, for example, and other passages), this scholar has been led from this point of view. Let us add that the terms by which Valentinus designates his Æons receive in his system an artificial, strained, mythological sense, while in the prologue of John they are taken in their simple, natural and, moreover, Biblical meaning; for they, all of them, belong already to the language of the Old Testament. It certainly is not John who has transformed the divine actors of the Gnostic drama into simple religious ideas; it is very evidently the reverse which has taken place: "Everything leads us to hold," says Bleek, "that the Gnostics made use of these expressions, which they drew from a work which was held in esteem, as points of support for their speculative system." "John," says Keim in the same line, "knows nothing of those Æons, of that Pleroma, of those masculine and feminine pairs, and of all that long line of machinery which was designed to bring God into the finite; it is he, therefore, undoubtedly, who is the earliest, and who, as Irenæus indicates, laid the foundation of the edifice." Hilgenfeld claims that the Logos of John is only a concentration of the series of Æons of Valentinus. Hase replies to him, that we can maintain, and with as good right at least, that it is the single Logos of John which was divided by the Gnostics into their series of Æons. In the *Philosophumena* (vi. 35), Hippolytus relates of Valentinus the following: "*He says* (φησί) that all the prophets and the law spoke according to the Demiurge, the senseless god, and that this is the reason why the Saviour said: "All those who came before me are thieves and robbers." This is an express quotation from John x. 8. Criticism replies: Perhaps it was not Valentinus himself who expressed himself thus, but one of his successors. Let us admit it, notwithstanding the very positive words *He says* of Hippolytus. The Ogdoad, with its Johannean names, which form the basis of the whole Valentinian system, remains nevertheless; and it would be very strange that the chief of the school should not have been the one who laid the foundation of the system. We do not think, therefore, that an impartial criticism can deny in the case of Valentinus himself the use of the fourth Gospel.[1]

Two years before Valentinus, in 138, Marcion arrived in Rome; he came

---

[1] The following is what Heinrici says in his well-known work, *Die Valentinianische Gnosis und die heilige Schrift:* "The Valentinians thus used the Scripture as a universally recognized authority; it possessed this authority, therefore, previously to the appearance of the system. The use which the Valentinians made of the Gospel of John and the Epistles to the Colossians and the Ephesians proves that these writings were recognized and used as apostolic writings already in the first half of the second century."

from Pontus, where his father was bishop, and where he had been brought up in the Christian beliefs. Tertullian makes an allusion to his Christian past, when he apostrophizes him thus (*De carne Christi*, c. 2): "Thou who, when thou wert a Christian, didst fall away, rejecting that which thou hadst formerly believed, as thou dost acknowledge in a certain letter." To what did this rejection (*rescindendo*) with which Tertullian reproaches him, and which had attended upon his spiritual falling away, refer? The answer is given us by two other passages from the same Father. In the work specially designed to refute the doctrines of Marcion, Tertullian relates (*Adv. Marc.* iv. 3), that Marcion, "in studying the Epistle to the Galatians, discovered that Paul charged the apostles with not *walking in the truth*, and that he took advantage of this charge to destroy the confidence which men had in the Gospels published under the name of the apostles and apostolic men, and to claim belief on behalf of his own Gospel which he substituted for these." We know, indeed, that Marcion had selected by preference the Gospel of Luke, and that, after having mutilated it in order to adapt it to his system, he gave it to his churches as the rule of their faith. Now, what does the conclusion which he drew from Galatians ii. prove? The apostles mentioned in that chapter are Peter and John. If Marcion inferred from that passage the rejection of *their* Gospels, it must be that he had in his hands a Gospel of Peter—was this Mark?—and a Gospel of John. He rejected from this time those books of the Canon which had been handed down to him by his father, the bishop of Sinope. In the *De carne Christi*, chap. 3, we read a second expression which leads to the same result as the preceding : " If thou hadst not *rejected* the writings which are contrary to thy system, the Gospel of John would be there to convince thee." In order that Marcion should reject this writing, it certainly must have been in existence, and Marcion must have previously possessed it. And let us notice, that he rejected it, not on the ground that it was not apostolic; but, on the contrary, that it was so. For to his thought the twelve apostles, imbued with Jewish prejudices, had not understood Jesus; so their Gospels (Matthew, Mark, John) must be set aside. Paul alone had understood the Master, and the Gospel of Luke, his companion, must alone be an authority.—Volkmar has made the author of the fourth Gospel a partisan of Marcion, who sought to introduce his doctrines into the Church. But what is there in common between the violent hatred of Marcion against the Jewish law and the God of the Jews, and a Gospel in which the Logos, in coming to Israel, comes *to His own*, and, in entering into the temple of Jerusalem, declares that He is in the house of *His Father?* And how can it be reasonably maintained that a writer whose thought strikes all its roots into the soil of the Old Testament, is the disciple of a master who rejected from the New everything that implied the divinity of the Old? In saying this, we have answered the question of the same author, who asks why, if John existed before Marcion, the latter did not choose to make his Gospel rather than Luke the Gospel of his sect. The ancient heretic was more clear-sighted than the modern critic; he understood that, in order to use John, he must mutilate it, in some sort, from one end to the other, and he preferred to reject it at one stroke *rescindendo*, as Tertullian says.

At the same period in which Justin, Valentinus and Marcion met each other in Rome, a fanatical sect arose in Asia Minor, Montanism. Its leader wished to make a reaction against the laxness of Christendom and the mechanical course of the official clergy. Montanus announced the near coming of the Christ, and pretended to cause the descent upon the Church of the Spirit who was promised for the last days, and whom he called the *Paraclete*, evidently in accordance with the promise of Jesus in John xiv. 16, 26, etc. He even identified himself with this Spirit, if it is true, as Theodoret affirms, that he gave himself the titles of *Paraclete, Logos, Bridegroom*. But it is not only these expressions, borrowed from John, it is the whole spiritualistic movement, it is that energetic reaction against the more and more prevailing ritualism, which implies the existence in the Church of a writing which was an authority, and was capable of serving as a point of support for so energetic a movement.

Thus, then, in 140, Justin, the martyr belonging to the orthodox Church, Valentinus, the Egyptian Gnostic, Marcion, who came from Pontus, Montanus, in Phrygia, are acquainted with and, excepting Marcion, use with one consent, the Gospel of John, in order to found upon it their doctrine and their churches; would all this be possible, if that work had only been in existence for a decade of years? The date 130–140 falls before these facts, just as the date 160–170 vanished in presence of those which were previously alleged.

Let us come to the third position attempted by criticism in our days.

110–125

(Reuss, Nicolas, Renan, Sabatier, Weizsäcker, Hase)

History offers us here four points for our guidance: The Gnostic Basilides, and the three apostolic Fathers, Papias, Polycarp, and Ignatius. Finally, we shall interrogate the appendix of our Gospel, chap. xxi., which, while connected with the work, does not properly form a part of it.

Basilides flourished at Alexandria about 120–125; he died a little after 132. Before teaching in Egypt, he is said to have labored in Persia and Syria. In the work *Archelai et Manetis disputatio*, it is said: "A certain Basilides, more anciently still, was a preacher among the Persians *a little after the time of the apostles*." According to Epiphanius (*Haer*. xxiii. 1–7; xxiv. 1), he had also labored at Antioch. His activity, consequently, goes back as far as the earliest period of the second century. He himself claimed that he taught only what had been taught him by the Apostle Matthias according to the secret instructions which he had received from the Lord. That this assertion should have any shadow of probability, it is certainly necessary that he should have been *able* to meet with that apostle somewhere; a fact which carries us back for the period of his birth to a quite early time in the first century.[1]

[1] See Hofstede de Groot, *Basilides und seine Zeit*.

158 / The Origin

In a homily on Luke, attributed to Origen, it is said that "Basilides had the boldness already to write a gospel according to Basilides."[1] The word *already* proves that Basilides was regarded as belonging to the earliest times of Gnosticism. As to the expression : *a gospel according to Basilides*, it is very doubtful whether it is necessary to understand thereby an evangelical narrative designed to come into competition with our Gospels. By this term, indeed, Basilides himself understood, not a simple narration, but "the knowledge of supersensible things" (ἡ τῶν ὑπερκοσμίων γνῶσις) (*Philos.* of Hippolytus, vii. 27). We are told, also, that his narrative of the birth of Jesus accorded entirely with that of our Gospels (*Philos.*, ibid.), and history does not present the least trace of an apocryphal Basilidian gospel. But we know from Eusebius (*H. E.* iv. 7. 7), that this Gnostic wrote *twenty-four books on the Gospel* (εἰς τὸ εὐαγγέλιον), which were refuted in a striking way by a Christian writer, named Agrippa Castor, whose work was still in the hands of Eusebius.[2] The real nature of this work of Basilides appears from a quotation which Clement of Alexandria makes from it in the *Stromata* (Bk. iv.), where he expresses himself thus : "Basilides says in the twenty-third book of his *exegetical dissertations*. . . . "[3] It was, therefore, a work of explanations; but on what text? The answer appears first, from the expression of Eusebius: "twenty-four books *on* (εἰς) the Gospel," and second, from the passage from the *Philosophumena* (vii. 22), according to which Basilides is said to have expressed himself as follows: "Here is what is said in the Gospels (τὸ λεγόμενον ἐν τοῖς εὐαγγελίοις)." From all this we conclude that this Gnostic set forth his theory respecting the origin of things in the form of exegetical explanations, having reference to the text of the Gospels which were received at his time in the churches. But the question for us to determine is whether he also worked upon the fourth Gospel. Now, we have two passages which seem to leave no doubt on this point; one is that we have just mentioned (*Philos.* vii. 22) : "Here, says he [Basilides], is what is said in the Gospels: It was the true light which lighteneth every man coming into the world ;" the other, a little further on, ch. 27 : "Let everything have its own appropriate time, says he [Basilides], is what the Saviour sufficiently declares when he says : My hour is not yet come."—These two quotations are evidently connected with John i. 8 and ii. 4.

The criticism which is opposed to the authenticity of our Gospel is obliged to make all efforts to escape the consequences of these Johannean quotations in Basilides; for they amount to nothing less than the carrying back of the composition of the fourth Gospel even into the first century. In fact, men only quote in this way a book which has already a recognized authority. It has been claimed, therefore, that, in mentioning these quotations from Basilides, Hippolytus did not distinguish the writings of the master from those of his later disciples. The term *he says*, it is claimed, related simply in his thought to the adversary, whoever he

---

[1] Ambrose and Jerome have repeated this statement.

[2] "There has come down even to us a work by Agrippa Castor," etc.

[3] Ἐν τῷ εἰκοστῷ τρίτῳ τῶν ἐξηγητικῶν.

was, Basilides or the Basilidians, Valentinus or the Valentinians; and in favor of this supposition, the alleged fact has been adduced, that Hippolytus sets forth the Basilidian system in a later form than that in which Irenæus still knew it. According to the latter, indeed, the system was dualistic; this was the earliest form; according to Hippolytus, on the contrary, it is rather pantheistic; there is here, therefore, a more recent form. Discussion can be carried on at great length respecting this difference. For ourselves, we are disposed to accept the explanation given by Charteris (*Canonicity*, p. lxiii.), according to which Irenæus did not, in his exposition of the system, go back to its first foundations. There was a hidden pantheism at the source of its apparent dualism, and Hippolytus who had examined even the writings of the master has, more completely than Irenæus, apprehended and set forth the original principles. However it may be with this explanation, it does not seem to us possible that a serious writer quotes a whole series of texts which he attributes to an earlier writer, repeating over and over again the formula *he says*, and even several times indicating the author by his name, without having his work under his eyes. Renan says, quite simply and frankly (*L'Eglise chrétienne*, p. 158): " The author of the Philosophumena undoubtedly made this analysis with reference to the original works of Basilides." And Weizsäcker, a few years ago, expressed himself also in the same way (*Unters.* p. 233): " It cannot be doubted that we have here quotations from a work of Basilides, in which the Johannean Gospel was used." At the present time, he has changed his opinion.[1] For what reason? Because these quotations ascribed to Basilides relate to Biblical writings whose composition is later than the time of Basilides himself. And what are these writings? They can only be the Epistles to the Colossians and the Ephesians, quoted many times by this Gnostic in the extracts from the Philosophumena, and perhaps the Gospel of John itself. Is it needful to call the attention of this scholar to the fact that he falls here into a vicious circle? For he rests his views precisely upon the point which is in question. If Weizsäcker reasons thus: The Basilides of Hippolytus quotes the letters to the Ephesians and the Colossians; therefore there is here a false Basilides, since those letters did not yet exist at the time of the true Basilides; have not we the right—we who believe in the authenticity of those epistles—to reason in an opposite way, and to say: Basilides quotes those writings: therefore in his time they existed and were acknowledged in the Church. This conclusion, valid for Colossians and Ephesians, is also valid for the Gospel of John.

Keim has also made a discovery which is said to prove that our Gospel is posterior to Basilides. This Gnostic writer asserted that the Jews by mistake had crucified Simon of Cyrene instead of Jesus, and that Jesus was all the time laughing at them. Here, says the author of the *Life of Jesus*, is that which explains the omission of the story of Simon bearing the cross in the fourth Gospel. Pseudo-John had noticed the abuse which

---

[1] *Jahrb. für deutsche Theol.*, 1868, p. 525.

Basilides made of this incident, and for this reason he suppressed it. We need not long discuss such an argument. We have treated in detail John's omissions and have shown that they are to be explained simply by the uselessness of such repetitions. To what purpose relate again what two or three widely-spread writings had already sufficiently related? It would be curious, certainly, to see one of our critics taking upon himself the task of explaining, by allusions to the Gnostic systems, all the gaps in the fourth Gospel!

Papias was a contemporary of Basilides. We have already seen (p. 43) that by this expression: "What Aristion and John the Presbyter *say*," he indicates clearly that these two men, immediate disciples of Jesus, were still living at the moment when he wrote. The years 110–120, are, therefore, the latest period to which we can assign the composition of his work. Already at that time, there was rising a whole literature which labored to falsify the meaning of the Gospel narratives. Papias also declares that "he does not take pleasure in the books in which many things are related, and in which the attempt is made to impose on the Church precepts that are strange and different from those which were given by the Truth itself."[1] It seems to me probable that in expressing himself thus he alludes to the first appearance of the Gnostic writings, such as those of Cerinthus, of the Ophites and the Sethians, of Saturninus, perhaps of Basilides himself.

It is quite generally affirmed in our days that all trace of the fourth Gospel is wanting in Papias, and this fact is regarded as the most decisive proof of the later composition of the Gospel of John. We pray the impartial reader carefully to consider the following facts:

Of Papias' work entitled *Explanations of the Words of the Lord* (in five books), there remain to us only some thirty lines, which Eusebius has preserved for us; they undoubtedly belonged to the preface. Papias explains therein the preference which he had thought himself obliged to give, for the end which he proposed to himself, to the text of Matthew over that of Mark; this, at least, is the meaning which we attribute to his words. He gives an account of the sources from which he had drawn the anecdotes respecting the life of Jesus, which were not contained in our Gospels, and by means of which he tried to explain His sayings. These sources, as we have seen, were of two sorts: they were first the accounts which the elders (the immediate disciples of the Lord) had formerly given to him himself; they were, next, the reports which he had gathered from the mouth of visitors who had also had the advantage of conversing with apostles and disciples of Jesus. He asked them "What Andrew had said to them, or Peter, or Philip, or Thomas, or James, or John, or Matthew, or any other of the Lord's disciples, and what Aristion and the Presbyter John, disciples of the Lord, say." This enumeration offers food for thought. Why is *Andrew* named at the beginning and before Peter himself? This order is contrary to the constant and in some sort stereotyped usage of the Synoptics; see all the apostolic catalogues (Matt. x.; Mark

---

[1] See the entire passage, pp. 43–45.

iii.; Luke vi.). The first chapter of John alone gives the answer to this question: Andrew (with John himself, who remains unnamed), was the first who came into the presence of the Saviour; he figures as the first personage in the evangelic history. After Andrew, Papias says: *Peter.* According to John i., Andrew, his brother, brought him, indeed, on the same day to Jesus. Then Papias says: *Philip;* he is precisely the one who immediately follows Andrew and Peter in the Johannean narrative (i. 43 ff.). Moreover, Andrew and Philip are the two apostles who are afterwards most frequently named in our Gospel (vi. 5-9; xii. 20-22). Then comes *Thomas.* Nathanael is here omitted (John i. 46 ff.), we know not why; he is included in the sort of *et cetera* with which the incomplete list closes: "or any other of the Lord's disciples." As for Thomas, he is the one among all the rest of the disciples who, together with the preceding ones, plays the most striking part in the fourth Gospel (xi. 16; xiv. 5; xx. 24 ff.). Afterwards, come *James* and *John.* Why so late, these who are always named in the Synoptics immediately after and with Peter? It is in the fourth Gospel also, that we must seek the explanation of this phenomenon. The two sons of Zebedee are not once named in the whole course of the narrative; they are not expressly designated, except in the appendix, xxi., where their names are found, as here, at the end of the list of the apostles who are mentioned in that passage. Among all the other apostles, *Matthew* only is further named by Papias; and it has been supposed, rightly no doubt, that it is the mention of the fourth evangelist which here leads to the mention of the first. It may be presumed also that these three names: James, John and Matthew, occupy this secondary position because the question in this passage was of the apostles as having furnished to Papias the oral traditions which he used. Now James had died too early to be able to give much information, and John and Matthew had consigned the greater part of theirs to their writings. Finally, Papias names two personages who were still living, *Aristion* and the *Presbyter John,* whom he calls "disciples of the Lord." It is exactly in the same way that the Johannean enumeration xxi. 2, closes: "And two others of his disciples" [not apostles]. If we add to these similarities, which are so striking, the fact that all these disciples named by Papias (except Peter, James and John), play no part whatever in the Synoptical narrative, we shall be led to acknowledge that the idea which this Father possessed of the evangelical history was formed on the foundation of the narrative of the fourth Gospel, even more than on that of the three others. Lüdemann, in his articles on the fragment of Papias,[1] does not call in question the similarity which we have just established. "It is a fact," he says, "that the fragment of Papias is closely related to the Johannean manner of speaking, both in the expressions ἐντολαί, *commandments,* and ἀλήθεια, *truth* (see the fragment, pp. 43-45), and in the beginning of the list of the apostolic names . . . The unexpected coming in of Thomas, in Papias, likewise does not allow us to think of anything but the fourth Gospel."

---

[1] *Jahrb. für protest. Theol.,* 1879, 3d *Heft.*

But after this frank declaration come the expedients which are never wanting. "There existed in the circle from which the Johannean writings came forth in Asia a mode of speaking and thinking, which, on the one hand, has left certain elements in the writings of Papias (between 120–140), and which, on the other, has found its full blossoming in the writings of pseudo-John, composed at nearly the same time." This explanation would be strictly admissible, if the question were of some fact of the evangelical history related simultaneously by the two authors, or of the use of some common terms such as *commandment* and *truth*. But it cannot account for an enumeration of proper names, such as those mentioned in the passage of Papias and in which the whole evangelical history is reflected. Holtzmann has perceived the injury to his cause which was involved in the admissions of his colleague; he has attempted to ward off the blow in another way.[1] He explains the order of the apostles in the fragment of Papias by the geographical situation of the countries in which they are thought to have labored as missionaries. This solution will remain the exclusive property of its author.

Two facts seem to us further to attest the existence of the fourth Gospel before the time of Papias. Eusebius attests that this Father quoted as evidence, in his work, passages from the first Epistle of John, as well as from the first Epistle of Peter. Now we have proved that that letter of John is by the *same* author as the fourth Gospel, and that it was composed *after* the latter. If, then, Papias was acquainted with and used the Epistle, how should he not have been acquainted with and have used the Gospel composed by the same author?—In the Vatican library there is found a Latin manuscript of the Gospels, of the ninth century, in which John's Gospel is preceded by a preface wherein it is said: "The Gospel of John was published and given to the churches by John while he was still living, as Papias of Hierapolis, the beloved disciple of John, relates in his five exoteric books, that is to say, the last ones." These last words evidently come from an incorrect copy, like so many of the sentences in the Muratorian fragment. Instead of exoteric, we must, at all events, read *exegetic;* comp. the title of Papias' book: "*Expositions* (ἐξηγήσεις) of the words of the Lord." Besides, this statement is followed by some legendary details,[2] which, however, are not ascribed to Papias himself. Notwithstanding all this, the fact that Papias spoke in his five books of the Gospel of John is yet attested by this passage.[3]

Irenæus sometimes quotes *the elders* who lived with John in Asia Minor until the time of Trajan. They were, thus, contemporaries of Papias and Polycarp. Here is an explanation which he ascribes to them (v. 36): "As the elders say: Those who shall be judged worthy of enjoying the heavenly abode will find their place there, while the rest will inhabit the city [the earthly Jerusalem]; and it is for this reason that the Lord said:[4]

---

[1] *Papias und Johannes*, in the *Zeitschrift für wissenschaftl. Theol.*, 1880, Heft 1.
[2] As the following for example: that it was Papias who wrote the Gospel at John's dictation.
[3] Comp. Tischendorf, *Wann wurden unsere Evangelien verfasst?* pp. 118, 119.
[4] Literally: "And for this reason the Lord to have said (εἰρηκέναι)." The infinitive serves to indicate that here is the saying of the elders themselves.

"In my Father's house there are many mansions." If it is the saying of Jesus related in John xiv. 2, which the elders interpreted in this way, as seems evident, then the Gospel of John was already in their hands. This appears, likewise, from the passage in Irenæus, ii. 22, where he attributes to them the idea that Jesus had attained the age of forty or fifty years—which can scarcely have arisen except through a misunderstanding of the words of the Jews, John viii. 57: "Thou art not yet fifty years old, and thou hast seen Abraham!"

Polycarp wrote, according to Irenæus, a very large number of letters, of which there remains to us but a single one consisting of only thirteen brief chapters. The fourth Gospel is not quoted in it; but we can prove, on the other hand, the truth of the statement of Eusebius, who declares that Polycarp, as well as Papias, borrowed testimonies from the first Epistle of Peter and the first Epistle of John; this is what induced him to place these works among the *homologoumena*. In fact, we read in Polycarp's Epistle to the Philippians (chap. 7) these words: "Whosoever does not confess that Jesus Christ is come in the flesh, is an antichrist." This is the principle laid down by John, 1 Ep. iv. 3: "Every spirit that confesseth not that Jesus Christ is come in the flesh, is not of God; and this is the spirit of antichrist." The coincidence of these two sentences cannot be accidental. The expedient devised by Baur and Zeller, who would find herein only a maxim circulating at this period in the Church, and that of Volkmar, who claims that it is John who copies Polycarp, and not the reverse, are destitute of probability. Ten lines of John read by the side of ten lines of Polycarp show on which side are the originality and priority. We must, therefore, conclude that if this letter of Polycarp is authentic, as Zahn[1] has with so much learning demonstrated, and if it dates, as appears from its contents, from the time which closely followed the martyrdom of Ignatius (in 110), the first Epistle of John, and consequently the Gospel, already existed at that period.

But it is asked how it happens, in that case, that Papias and Polycarp did not make more abundant use of such a work. Especially is the silence of Eusebius respecting any citation whatever from our Gospel, on the part of these two Fathers, set in contrast with the very express mention which he makes of the use of the first epistle, by both of them.—If Eusebius has expressly noticed this last fact, it is because the two epistles of Peter and John form a part of the collection of the Catholic Epistles, which, with the exception of these two, were all of them disputed writings. He was desirous, therefore, of marking their exceptional character as *homologoumena* in this collection, a character appearing from the use which was made of them by two such men as Papias and Polycarp. It was quite otherwise with the Gospel, which indisputably belonged to the class of books universally received. The use which these two apostolic Fathers might have made of it entered into the general usage. Eusebius himself gives an explanation respecting his general method (*H. E.* iii. 3, 3): "He wishes," he says, "to point out what ecclesiastical writings

---

[1] In his *Ignatius von Antiochien*.

made use of disputed books, and what ones among these books they made use of; then, what things, [or some of the things which][1] have been said respecting the universally received writings of the New Testament, and everything which has been said (ὅσα) respecting those which are not so received." To mention certain interesting details respecting the Homologoumena (as we know that he has done with regard to Matthew and Mark), then to report everything which he could gather respecting the Antilegomena—this was the end which he proposed to himself. It was therefore precisely because he, together with the whole Church, ranked John in the first class, that he did not think himself obliged expressly to point out the use which these Fathers made of this gospel. But, on the other hand, if he had discovered, in the case of such men, a complete blank with respect to this work, he could not have affirmed, as he does, its universal adoption. Still more: a word in the discussion of Eusebius respecting the fragment of Papias which he has preserved for us, clearly shows that he had found in that Father numerous passages relating to the fourth Gospel. On occasion of the mention of the name of *John* in the enumeration of the apostles by Papias, he remarks that this Father means evidently to designate thereby "the evangelist" (σαφῶς δηλῶν τὸν εὐαγγελιστήν). He might have said: *the apostle,* but he enters into the thought of Papias himself, and says: *the evangelist,* which clearly proves that he found in his work the constant evidence of the fact that John was the author of a Gospel. As to Polycarp, nothing obliged him, in precisely those eight pages of his which remain to us, to quote the Gospel of John. What preacher quotes in every one of his sermons all the writings of the New Testament which he recognizes as authentic?

The interminable discussions are well known, to which the letters of Ignatius, the bishop of Antioch at the beginning of the second century, have given rise. A nearly unanimous tradition, supported by the testimony of authors who wrote at Antioch itself, such as Chrysostom and Evagrius, declares that he perished at Rome, being devoured by wild beasts in the circus, in consequence of a sentence of the Emperor Trajan.[2] It was while on his way as a condemned person to that capital (between 107 and 116), that he is said to have written the seven letters which alone can claim authenticity.[3] These letters exist in a double form, one longer, the other more simple and concise. Zahn, in his book on *Ignatius of Antioch,* has clearly proved that the first of these two texts is the result of a deliberate work of interpolation; he has even very probably pointed out the author of this fraud.[4] He has, at the same time,

---

[1] Both translations are possible, according as we accent the Greek pronoun τίνα (*what things*), or τινά (*some* of the things).

[2] The chronicler John Malalas (8th cent.) places the martyrdom of Ignatius at Antioch itself. In that case, Ignatius could never have made the journey to Rome to which these letters refer. But how then can we explain so general a tradition? Would the Church of Antioch itself have so easily resigned in favor of Rome the honor of having seen such a martyrdom accomplished in its own midst?

[3] Eight others exist which are undoubtedly forgeries.

[4] One of the least honorable representatives of the semi-Arian party, Acacius, the successor of Eusebius at Cesarea.

demonstrated the authenticity of the seven letters, as they have been preserved for us in the briefer form. The historian Eusebius, already was acquainted only with these seven, and in this text. It is true that there have been recently discovered three among these seven, in Syriac, in a still briefer form;[1] and, at the first moment, the learned world was inclined to regard this text as the only faithful reproduction of the work of Ignatius. Zahn seems to us to have victoriously combated this opinion, and to have proved that this text is only an extract, made by some Syrian monk, from a more ancient translation in that language. There remains but one alternative; the authenticity of the seven letters, as Eusebius knew them, or their entire unauthenticity.—Two reasons especially are alleged in favor of this last opinion: 1. The Episcopal constitution, as it appears in these letters, belongs, it is said, to an epoch much later in the second century than the time of Ignatius; 2. The Gnosticism which is combated in them, betrays likewise a time posterior to Ignatius' death. These reasons do not seem to us decisive. The Episcopate, as its character is implied in these letters, is still a purely *parochial* ministry, as in the apostolic times, it is not the later *provincial* Episcopate. That which alone distinguishes it from the ministry of this name in the time of the apostles, is that it appears to be concentrated in a single person. But this is already the case in the Apocalypse, where *the angel* of the Church designates precisely the man who concentrates in himself the presbyterial power; and indeed long before this we meet already men like James, the Lord's brother, at Jerusalem, then his cousin and successor, Simeon, Anianus at Alexandria, Evagrius at Antioch, Linus at Rome, who occupy a position exactly similar to that which Ignatius ascribes to the bishop of his time. As to the heresy implied in these letters, it already had all its antecedent conditions in the first century; we can see this in the second Epistle to the Corinthians (xi. 3, 4), in the Epistle to the Colossians, and in the Apocalypse, where a form of Gnosticism is already clearly indicated (ii. 20, 24). The germs of heresy were sown abundantly in the East at the time of Ignatius. What in our view renders the hypothesis of the unauthenticity of these letters inadmissible, is that it seems impossible to invent, not only a style so original and a thought so strange, but especially such a character. There is a man in these letters, and a man who is not manufactured.

The following are some quotations from our Gospel which are contained in the seven letters, the text of which can lay claim to authenticity. *Rom.* (c. 7): "The living water which speaks in me says to me inwardly: Come to the Father; I take no pleasure either in corruptible food or in the joys of this life; I desire the bread of God which is the flesh of Jesus Christ . . . I desire as drink His blood which is incorruptible love." The entire Gospel of John is, as it were, included in this cry of the martyr; but comp. more specially the words iv. 14; xiv. 6; vi. 27, 32, 51, 55, 56. *Philad.* (c. 7): "The Spirit does not deceive, he who comes from God; for

---

[1] They were published for the first time by Cureton (1845).

he knows whence he comes and whither he goes, and he condemns secret things" (John iii. 8, 20). In the same epistle (c. 9): "He who is the door of the Father (θύρα τοῦ πατρός) by which Abraham, Isaac and Jacob, and the prophets and the apostles and the Church enter" (John x. 7–9). In the letter to the Ephesians (c. 7), Jesus is called (ἐν σαρκὶ γενόμενος θεός) *God come in the flesh:* and in that to the *Magnesians* (c. 8) the expression is used (αὐτοῦ λόγος ἀίδιος), *His eternal word.* The idea of spiritual *communion* (ἕνωσις), which forms the substance of these letters, as of that of Polycarp, rests on John xvii., as Riggenbach has remarked.

Hilgenfeld, who places the composition of these letters in 166, finds no difficulty in acknowledging that our Gospel (published according to him in 130) is really used in the passages quoted in the letters to the Romans and Philadelphians; he even affirms that "the entire theology of Ignatius' letters rests upon the Gospel of John." We welcome this declaration and conclude that, however little authentic matter there may be in the letters of this martyr, the existence and use of the Gospel of John are attested from the beginning of the second century.[1]

It remains for us to interrogate a final witness—the appendix placed at the end of the fourth Gospel, as the twenty-first chapter, in particular the twenty-fourth verse, the authenticity of which cannot be contested.[2] At the end of this account of one of the last appearances of Jesus after He rose from the dead, the exact text of a saying is restored which Jesus addressed to Peter with regard to John, and which circulated in the Church in an incorrect form. Jesus was made to say that John was not going to die. The author of the appendix, who is either John himself or one of those who surrounded him, and who had heard him relate this scene (see p. 64 f.), recalls the fact that Jesus had not expressed Himself thus, but that He had simply said: "If I will that He tarry till I come, what is it to thee?" At what time can we suppose that this correction was judged necessary? At the end of the second century, where Keim places the composition of this passage? But at that time, either the saying of Jesus was forgotten, or, if it was still repeated, it was somewhat late to remove the offence which it might cause. No, surely; there was but one period when this correction would have been in place. It was when men saw the aged apostle growing feeble, and asked themselves: Is he, then, going to die, in spite of the Lord's promise? Or when he had just died, and the offence was really occasioned. This passage, therefore, carries its date in itself; it comes either from the days which preceded, or from those which immediately followed John's death. The contrast between the *present* participle: "This is the disciple *who testifies* (ὁ μαρτυρῶν) of these things," and the *past* participle: "and who *wrote* them (καὶ γράψας)," appears to me to decide in favor of the former alternative. The disciple whom Jesus loved was still living and testifying when this passage was written. However

---

[1] We do not mention here either the *Testaments of the Twelve Patriarchs*, because of their numerous interpolations, nor the *Shepherd of Hermas* and the *Epistle of Barnabas*, in which the borrowings from our Gospel do not seem to us by any means evident.

[2] It is known that it is not the same with ver. 25, which is wanting in the *Sinaitic* MS.

this may be, this twenty-first chapter is necessarily later than the Gospel; hence it follows that this work dates even from the life of John.

We think we have thus proved that the third position attempted by criticism—that from 110–125—is as irreconcilable with the facts as the two others, and that we are forced to take a new step backward, and to place the composition of this work in the latest times of the first century. But we do not think that we can go back to an earlier date. Some writers—for example, Wittichen, Lange—have attempted to do this. The former dates our Gospel from 70–80 (see p. 25); the latter places it before the destruction of Jerusalem. A period so far back is incompatible with the knowledge of our three Synoptical Gospels, which the author not only himself possesses, but which he supposes, from beginning to end, to be in the possession of his readers. The dissemination of those three works, published either a little before or a little after the destruction of Jerusalem, requires a considerably long interval of time between their composition and that of our Gospel. The date of this latter, therefore, must probably —in accordance with the facts which we have just set forth—be placed between 80 and 90.

2

THE AUTHOR

MANGOLD formulates his judgment respecting the external testimonies relative to the fourth Gospel in these terms: "The external attestation is scarcely less strong than that for the Synoptical Gospels;" then he adds: "It would be sufficient to authenticate it, if the internal reasons did not oppose to the admission of its authenticity objections which, for me at least, remain up to this time insurmountable."[1] It is this second class of considerations which is now especially to occupy us. We approach the central and decisive question—the one for whose solution everything that precedes has only served to prepare the way. It has been sometimes claimed that our Gospel remains what it is, whoever may be its author. Those who maintain this proposition do not themselves seriously believe what they affirm; otherwise they would not be so zealous in contending against the Johannean origin of this work. And when Keim expresses himself thus: "The beauty of this book, its edifying quality, its saintliness . . . all this does not depend on a name," he will permit us to reply to him: You deceive others, or you deceive yourself; for you cannot conceal from yourself the fact that the discourses put into the mouth of Jesus, and the conception of His person which is set forth in this book, have for the Church an altogether different value, according as it is the beloved apostle of the Lord who gives us an account of what he has seen and heard, or a thinker of the second century who composes all this after his own fancy.

We have here four subjects to investigate: 1. The *ecclesiastical testimonies*

---

[1] Bleek-Mangold's *Einl.*, p. 281.

168 / The Origin

bearing more particularly on the person of the author; 2. The *objections* raised by modern criticism against the result of this tradition; 3. The *internal proof*, derived from the study of the book itself; 4. The examination of the principal *hypotheses* which are in our days set in opposition to the traditional opinion of the Johannean origin.

1. THE TRADITIONAL TESTIMONIES

Our point of departure is the period at which the general conviction of the Church expresses itself by a collection of indisputable testimonies, in the last third of the second century.

We find here Clement of Alexandria, who relates to us the origin of the fourth Gospel in the following manner: "*John*, the last, perceiving that the bodily things (τὰ σωματικά, the external facts) had been related in the Gospels, . . . composed a spiritual Gospel" (Eus. *H. E.*, vi. 14).

Polycrates of Ephesus, at the same time, expresses himself thus: " Illustrious men are buried in Asia, Philip . . . at Hierapolis; and, moreover, *John*, who rested on the bosom of the Lord, and who is buried at Ephesus" (Eus. *H. E.*, v. 31). This testimony proves that at Ephesus John was regarded as the author of the Gospel, since no one doubted that he was the beloved disciple who is spoken of in John xiii. 25.

Irenæus thus closes his report respecting the composition of the Gospels: "After that, *John*, the disciple of the Lord who rested on His bosom, also published the Gospel while he dwelt at Ephesus, in Asia" (*Adv. Haer.* iii. 1).

We have already quoted the testimony of Theophilus: "All the inspired men, among whom *John* says, In the beginning was the Word." The following is the way in which the Muratorian fragment relates the origin of our Gospel: "The author of the fourth among the Gospels is *John*, one of the disciples.[1] As his fellow-disciples and the bishops exhorted him [to write], he said to them: Fast with me these three days, and we will mutually relate to each other what shall have been revealed to each one. In that same night it was revealed to Andrew, one of the apostles, that John should relate everything in his own name, all the others revising [his narrative] . . . What is there, then, surprising in this, that John, in his epistles, sets forth these things in detail, saying in reference to himself: That which we have seen with our eyes, that which we have heard with our ears, and that which our hands have handled, we write unto you. Thus he declares himself successively eye and ear-witness, and, moreover, a redactor of the wonderful things of God." Hilgenfeld claims that we find in this report an allusion to doubts which existed at that time respecting the Johannean origin of our Gospel. Hesse, in his excellent work on the Muratorian fragment, has shown that this pas-

---

[1] This term is not opposed to the term *apostle*, as Reuss thinks. It is the translation of the term μαθητὴς τοῦ κυρίου which is applied by Papias to all the apostles, and many times by Irenæus to John himself (iii. 1, 3, 4).

sage betrays no such intention. The expression "what is there surprising?" applies not to the Gospel, but to the epistle.

Starting from this point, let us try to ascend the stream of tradition even to the apostolic times, and to search out the earliest indications of that conviction which shows itself so universally at the end of the second century. Between 140 and 150, it expresses itself, as it seems to us, in an unquestionable manner.

We have seen that Justin, according to the nearly universal admission at the present day, places our Gospel in the number of the Memoirs respecting the life of Jesus, of which he habitually made use. He calls these writings Memoirs *of the apostles*, and declares that some were composed by apostles and others by apostolic helpers. Consequently, if the fourth Gospel formed a part of them, Justin could ascribe it only to an apostle, and this apostle could only be John, since no one has ever attempted to ascribe this book to any other apostolic personage than John. And as, according to Justin, the Memoirs of the apostles already formed a collection, which was joined with that of the prophets and read, side by side with the latter, in the public worship of the Christians, it must have been at that period that the four identically-framed titles were placed at the beginning of the Gospels: " according to Matthew . . . according to John." This designation by titles—a work of the Church—accompanied the uniting of them in a canonical collection. The title, *according to John*, is, therefore, the expression of the general sentiment of the churches touching this book in the middle of the second century.

And it was not only the orthodox churches which, already at that period, had this thought; it was also the sects which were separated from the great body of the Church; witness, on one side, Marcion, who rejected our Gospel, not because it was not by an apostle of Jesus, but, on the contrary, inasmuch as it was composed by one of them, that is to say by John (see p. 156); witness also the most illustrious disciple of Valentinus, Ptolemy, who, in his letter to Flora, quoted our Gospel, saying: "The *apostle* declares" (p. 144). According to Irenæus, Ptolemy even went so far as to affirm, because of the prologue of the Gospel, that the true author of the Valentinian Ogdoad was *John* (p. 144).

Going still further back to a period from which only rare monuments remain to us, we discover always the same conviction.

We have already seen that, in the view of Papias, John was not only an apostle, but *an evangelist*, and that it is this quality of author of a Gospel which most naturally explains the position which he assigns to him in his famous list of apostles by the side of Matthew (see pp. 43, 160 f.).

If we do not possess any special testimony of Polycarp, there is a fact of much more considerable importance than any declaration whatever could have. Polycarp lived up to the middle of the second century; it was, then, during his activity as bishop of Smyrna, that our Gospel began to be circulated, and that it was spread throughout the whole Church as John's work. If he had not believed in the Johannean origin of this work, he would not have failed to deny it; for the use which the Gnostics made of this book rendered it very compromising for the Church, of which Polycarp was the most venerated leader; and the least denial on the part of such a man would have profoundly shaken the opinion of the Church. But nothing of the kind occurred. History does not indicate the least trace of hesitation, either in the case of Polycarp himself or among the members of the Church. No one of the presbyters of whom Irenæus speaks, and who "lived with John in Asia up to the time of Trajan," expressed a doubt—so that our Gospel was received without dispute, from one end of the world to the other, as the work of John. This absence of protestation is a negative fact of a very positive importance. We must not confound it with a mere literary silence which can be explained by accidental circumstances.

But from this period and from the circle even in which John lived, a positive testimony makes itself heard: "This disciple [the one whom Jesus loved] is he who testifieth of these things and who wrote these things; and we know that his testimony is true." This is what we read in John xxi. 24. Who are those who speak to us in this way, and who thus attest the composition of the fourth Gospel by the disciple whom Jesus loved? They are personally acquainted with him, since, in virtue of the knowledge which they have of him, they believe themselves able to guarantee the truth of his testimony. They do this during his life, since they say of him: "who *testifieth* and *wrote*" (p. 166). They live about him, therefore, and it is in their hands, undoubtedly, that he deposited his book; and, before giving it to the public, they supply this postscript, clearly perceiving that, by reason of the differences which exist between this work and its predecessors, it will have some difficulty in opening a way for itself. How can the force of such testimony be escaped? Reuss supposes that those who gave it were *bona fide* deceived, and that, living already quite a long time after John's death, they confounded with him the anonymous writer who had, by means of his narratives, composed the Gospel. But we have already seen that this twenty-first chapter can only have been written at a period very near to the death of John, when such an error was not possible. The use of the present: "he who *testifieth,*" confirms this remark. There would be only one possible supposition, namely: that the pseudo-John, in the course of the second century, had himself furnished this attestation. After having assumed the mask of St. John, he attempted to sustain his first fraud by adding to it a second. He imagined a circle of friends of the apostle, and himself composed, under their name, the postscript which we have just read. The composers of apocryphal works have often been excused by speaking of pious fraud. But here we should evidently have something more; we should even come to the borders of knavery. And he who imagined a course like this, is the man to whom we must attribute the qualities of moral purity, profound holiness, intimate communion with God, which were necessary for the composition of such a Gospel! The psychological and moral sense protests.

In the whole course of the second century, there exists, so far as our knowledge extends, but one single denial of the Johannean origin of the fourth Gospel. A party, to which Epiphanius gave the name *Alogi* (ἄλογοι, those who deny the Logos), maintained that the author of this work was, not the Apostle John, but the heretic Cerinthus, his adversary at Ephesus. This rejection was not founded on any traditional testimony. "The grounds on which those persons rested," says Zeller himself, "were, so far as we are acquainted with them, derived from internal criticism . . ." What follows from this fact—the only one which the adversaries of the authenticity can allege? Two things: first, that the Alogi lacked all support from tradition; secondly, that there did not exist a shadow of doubt respecting the fact that our Gospel was composed at Ephesus in the time of St. John, since Cerinthus, to whom they ascribed it, was the contemporary and rival of this apostle. The sole opponents are, thus, transformed into witnesses and defenders.

2. THE OBJECTIONS

It is in opposition to this result of a tradition which may be called unanimous, that many scholars rise up at the present day, and we have now to examine their reasons.

Hase, in his *History of Jesus*, enumerates eight objections against the authenticity; after having successively set them aside, he makes for himself a ninth which he does not succeed in solving, and which determines his negative vote. We shall follow him in this very clear exposition. Only of these nine objections we shall detach some which he unites with the others, and which it seems to us preferable to treat separately. The first seven, as we shall see, have already found their solution implicitly in the preceding pages.

I. The *silence* of the most ancient Fathers, particularly those of Asia Minor, respecting the fourth Gospel. It seems to us that the two preceding chapters have solved this objection. Hase justly observes that "nothing is more uncertain than this assertion: a writer must have spoken of a certain thing or a certain person." The Synoptical Gospels had been for a long time spread abroad; they had already for a generation formed the substance of the knowledge which the Church possessed of the history of Jesus. The Gospel of John, which was quite recent, had not yet made its way nor exerted its own influence; time must be allowed for it to take its place, before an appeal could be made to its narratives in the same way as to those of the earlier Gospels. We find this to be the fact only after the time of Justin.

II. John, being *Judaizing* as he was, cannot be the author of a Gospel as spiritual as that which bears his name. This, as it seems, is the strongest objection in the view of Schürer: "It is psychologically inconceivable that an apostle who, in his mature age, still disputed with Paul respecting the permanent value of the law, should have afterwards written a Gospel whose anti-Judaism surpasses even that of Paul."[1]—We think we have shown

[1] *Studien u. Kritiken*, 1876, iv., p. 774.

that this estimate of John's standpoint according to Gal. ii. is ill founded. The apostles personally observed the law, but not with the idea of its permanent value for salvation; otherwise they must have imposed it on the Gentiles; and instead of giving the hand of fellowship to Paul and Barnabas, they would have finally broken with them. The difference being a matter of *practice*, not of principle, the fall of Jerusalem must have resulted in the settlement of it, by breaking up the last remnant of solidarity between the apostles and their own people. Hase rightly remarks, that the residence of John in Asia Minor, his activity in the field which had been sowed by Paul, and the immense influence which he notoriously exercised in that country of Greek culture prove with what breadth, flexibility and freedom of mind he adapted himself to this new region, and knew how to become a Greek with the Greeks.

III. The Christianity of the churches of Asia Minor had a *legal* character. Now, if John was the author of such a teaching, he cannot have been the writer who composed our Gospel. But on what does this affirmation of the Judaizing character of the churches of Asia Minor rest? On their gross Chiliasm, it is answered. We have already seen that almost the whole Church of the second and of the greater part of the third century was devoted to Millenarianism; nevertheless it was not Judaistic. Moreover, the Paschal rite of these churches is alleged, in which their Judaistic sympathies are betrayed. The churches of Asia celebrated the Holy Supper of the Paschal feast on the 14th of Nisan in the evening, independently of the day of the week on which this monthly date fell, while the other churches, Rome in particular, celebrated the Holy Paschal Supper on the Sunday morning which followed Good Friday, whatever might be the day of the month on which that Sunday occurred. What were the reasons which had determined the rite which the churches of Asia had adopted? Either they wished thus to celebrate the evening of the day in the afternoon of which, according to the fourth Gospel, Christ died (the 14th of Nisan, the day before the Passover); in that case, whatever Baur may say, the Asiatic rite rests on the narrative of the Passion according to the fourth Gospel, and bears witness thereby to the authenticity of this work; this rite is, therefore, entirely independent of Jewish legality. Or the churches of Asia celebrated the Supper on the evening of the 14th, because it was on that evening that the Jews celebrated the Paschal feast,—and this is the explanation which certain expressions of the Fathers render most probable. Would this be a symptom of Jewish legality? But St. Paul himself saw in the Paschal lamb the symbol of Christ (1 Cor. v. 7); he very carefully regarded the Jewish feasts, particularly that of the Passover, as is proved by Acts xx. 6: "After the days of unleavened bread, we set sail from Philippi," and 1 Cor. v. 8, where, exactly at the time of the Passover feast (comp. xvi. 8), he represents the Christian life as a permanent feast of unleavened bread. It is probable, therefore, that it was Paul, and not John, who had originally introduced at Ephesus this Paschal rite which John merely continued. We find here the same symbolism in virtue of which Jesus, in the institution of the Holy Supper, had transformed the memorial of the deliverance from Egypt into a memorial of eternal redemption.

IV. The *divergences from the Synoptics*.—We have already treated this subject, and shown in detail that they are all to the advantage of the fourth Gospel, and evidently prove its historical superiority, so that, far from forming a point in the argument against the authenticity of this work, they are one of the most decisive proofs in favor of it.

V. The elevated, and, for the multitude, often even *incomprehensible*, contents of the discourses of Jesus. This subject has been treated at length; it is unnecessary to return to it.

VI. How could a Galilean fisherman have attained *such profound wisdom* as that which shines forth in many parts of our Gospel? But, we will ask in our turn, how can we estimate what an intimate and prolonged contact with the Lord may have produced in an ardent and profound soul, such as John's must have been? "If," says Hase, admirably, "the highest human wisdom has come from Christianity, must it not be allowed that, in proximity to a being like Jesus, a young man with a rich and profound soul may have been developed and, as it were, set on fire? A mind so powerful as that which, in any case, Jesus had, does not merely attach itself to a faithful and loyal heart, but also to a mind which has lofty aims and aspirations. Most certainly, if John, when he taught in Asia, had only possessed the apostolic simplicity and culture of the Galilean fisherman, he would not have produced in that country the enduring impression of admiration and veneration which he left there."

VII. The author of the fourth Gospel came forth from the *Gnostic* circles of the second century, not from the apostolic college. We have weighed this proposition, and it has been found to be too weak. There was certainly an elementary Gnosticism which dated from the apostolic times, and with which already the epistles of Paul and the letters in the Apocalypse contended; it is against this that the first epistle of John is directed. It has nothing in common with the great Gnostic systems of the second century, except the general tendency; and the fourth evangelist, far from having been formed under the influence of these latter systems, furnished in his book a part of the materials by means of which the leaders of those schools constructed their edifices on the very ground of Christianity.

VIII. We come to the decisive point, *the doctrine of the Logos*. The Judæo-Alexandrian origin of this idea and this term is historically proved; this alone is enough to prove that an apostle of Jesus cannot have written a book which rests altogether upon it. It must, therefore, be admitted that, as Philo, the principal representative of Alexandrianism at that period, made use of the ideas of Greek philosophy to give a rational account of the religious contents of his Jewish beliefs, in the same way the author of the fourth Gospel, in his turn, made use of Philo in order to appropriate to himself speculatively the contents of his Christian beliefs.[1]

---

[1] See *La doctrine du Logos dans le quatrième évangile*, etc., by Jean Réville, pp. 179, 180.

Two facts give an apparent support to this explanation of the Johannean teaching: 1. The *term* Logos inscribed at the beginning of our Gospel, which is precisely the one by which Philo expresses the fundamental notion of his philosophy; 2. The *idea* itself of an intermediate being between God and the world, by means of whom the absolute being communicates with finite beings. But it is to this point that the whole analogy is limited. And it remains to inquire whether what the two writers have in common in this relation is not explained by means of a higher source from which they both drew, or whether the fourth evangelist was really formed in the school of the Alexandrian philosopher.[1]

In this last case, there may be differences of detail between them, undoubtedly, but the same general tendency will necessarily be found in them both. Now, there is nothing of this. The notion of the Logos is for Philo a metaphysical theory; with John, a fact of Divine love. For the former, God, being raised above all particular determination, is not apprehensible by the human reason, and cannot communicate with matter except by means of the being in whom He manifests Himself; the Logos is the Divine reason, which conceives finite things and realizes them in the material world. With John, on the contrary, the idea of this being is a postulate of eternal love. "For thou didst love me before the creation of the world" (xvii. 24); and to this love of God for the Logos corresponds that of the Logos for God Himself: "In the beginning was the Word, and the Word was with God;" literally, tended to God, moved toward God. There is no secondary difference here; we are in the presence of two different tendencies;—on the one side, that of philosophical speculation, the need of knowing; on the other, that of piety, the need of salvation. Not that I would say that all piety is wanting to Philo, and all need of knowing to John. The question here is of the point of support of the two teachings in the souls of the two writers.

With this fundamental difference is connected the following fact: The doctrine of the Logos with Philo has its value in itself, as an idea indispensable to human speculation; with John, this idea is only at the service of an historical fact, a means of explaining the divine element which the author perceived in the person of Jesus Christ. Réville complains several times of the fact that the speculative data respecting the nature and activity of the Logos "are extremely limited in the prologue of John . . . A little more speculation, for the clearness of the narrative, would not have been misplaced" (pp. 37, 38). This charge is *naïve;* the young writer demands of the fourth Gospel that it should be what it ought to have been, assuredly, if it were that which he would desire it to be. He wishes to make of it a philosophical work, and, as it does not respond to this demand, he censures it instead of turning his criticism

---

[1] Let us recall to mind the fact that Philo lived in the first century of our era, and that he was a member of a rich Jewish family of Alexandria. He wrote a multitude of treatises on philosophical and religious subjects, in which he tries to show the relation between the Jewish beliefs and the Greek philosophies, especially those of Plato and the Stoics.

against his own theory. There is no philosophical speculation in the prologue; there is simply a conception of the person of Jesus expressed by means of a term which was current at that period in the philosophical language.

And further, this term is taken in a wholly different sense from that which it has in speculation generally, and in that of Philo in particular. With the latter, the word Logos is used in the sense of *reason;* it denotes the Divine reason, whether residing in God or as realized in the world of finite beings—in the sense in which the Stoics spoke of reason diffused through all beings (ὁ κοινὸς λόγος ὁ διὰ πάντων ἐρχόμενος). Thus Philo calls it sometimes the idea of ideas (ἰδέα ἰδεῶν) or the metropolis of ideas. It is the ideal of the finite world, in its whole and in its details, as existing in the divine understanding. With John, the term Logos is evidently taken in the sense of *word;* this is its constant meaning throughout the Gospel, where it denotes the divine revelation, and even in the prologue, where the creative word of Genesis is personified under this name. When Philo wishes to express this idea, he adds to the word Logos (reason) the term ῥῆμα (*word,* in the special sense of the word). Thus in this passage : " God creates the one and the other (the heaven and the earth) τῷ ἑαυτοῦ λόγῳ ῥήματι (by his own *Logos-word*)." Or he uses only the second term : " The whole world was made διὰ ῥήματος τοῦ αἰτίου (by the *word, the cause* of things)." This difference arises from the fact that Philo moves in the sphere of speculation, John in that of the divine action for the salvation of humanity.

How different, also, the part played by the Logos in the one and in the other! The Logos of Philo is a universal principle, the general law of things; it is not placed in any relation to the person of the Messiah ; while, with John, the Messiah is Himself this incarnate Word, the gift which the Father makes to the world and by means of which He comes to save it. The mere supposition of the incarnation of the Logos would be, whatever Réville may say, an enormity to the view of Philo. Does not sin arise from matter, and does not the defilement of the human soul result from its connection with a body? What blasphemy, therefore, would it not be, to represent the Logos as having appeared in a human person having a soul and body! The Messiah of Philo is, also, only a simple man who will bring back the Jews from their dispersion and will restore to them the glorious state to which they are entitled.

In the spiritual world itself the part sustained by the Logos differs entirely in the conception of Philo from what it is in that of John. With the latter, the Logos is the *light of men* (i. 4), and, if there is darkness in the world, it is because the world has not known Him—Him who continues to act in His creation by *illuminating every man* (vv. 9, 10). To the view of Philo, the Logos is indeed the interpreter of God, but not for the men who belong to the rank of *the perfect.* The true sage rises by the act of immediate contemplation even to the knowledge of God, without depending on the aid of the Logos. The Logos is the God of the imperfect, who, not being able to rise as far as the model, must be content to contemplate the portrait. The Logos of Philo, says Gess, is a guide who does not lead to the end, to God Himself; a God, in whom one does not possess the real God. To speculate is to work on the Logos, on the Divine reason manifested in the world; but, on this path, one will by no means reach God Himself; one comes to Him only by the way of immediate intuition, which passes one side of the Logos. Here is not the Logos of the fourth Gospel, in which Jesus says: " I am the way, the truth and the life; no one cometh to the Father but by me."

Finally, the intention of the theory of the Logos with Philo is to preserve God from all compromising contact with the material world. God is an absolutely transcendent being who cannot, without derogation, unite Himself with the finite world. Réville, indeed, cites a certain number of cases where God seems endowed with goodness and grace, and acts by Himself in the finite world. This is a remnant of the influence exercised on the thought of the Jewish philosopher by the living monotheism of the Old Testament. We might add such passages to the innumerable proofs of inconsistency which are found in the speculation of Philo; but it is also possible that he attributes these divine communications to the action of God confounded with that of the Logos. The Divine being, with John— He whom he calls absolutely *God*—is not an indeterminable essence; He is a person full of will, of activity, of love; He is *the Father*, who loves not only the Son whom He sacrifices, but also the world to which He gives Him; who, by an inward teaching and an attraction exercised on human individuals, *brings* them to the Son Himself; " No man," says Jesus, " can come to me except the Father who hath sent me *draw him* . . . All that the Father *giveth me*, shall come to me " (John vi. 44 and 37). This Father "Himself beareth witness to the Son " through acts wrought in the domain of matter, the miracles (v. 36). He even causes to resound in the temple an outwardly perceptible voice in answer to a prayer of Jesus (xii. 28). Thus the conception of John is so completely the opposite to that of Philo, that it makes of the Father an intermediate agent between Jesus and men, so that Jesus can utter those words, which would have been, for Philo, the height of absurdity: "Thine they were, and Thou gavest them me " (xvii. 6).[1]

The difference between John and Philo is so profound, that Gess, the one who has most thoroughly studied them both, has said: " He who believes that he can unite in one the thought of John and that of Philo, understands nothing either of John or of Philo."[2] It is not in certain details only, it is in the tendency itself, that they differ. And yet there are between the two, as we have seen, certain analogies of which it is necessary

---

[1] See Gess, II., p. 642 ff.

[2] The defenders of the theory which we contend against are so dominated by their preconceived idea, that they even fashion after their own fancy, without hesitation, the texts which they quote. Thus we have pointed out that error of Colani, who, quoting the prayer of Jesus, John xii. 28, makes him say: " Father, glorify *my* name," instead of " glorify *thy* name "(see our second ed., vol. III., p. 282). It happens that Réville commits a similar mistake in quoting the same verse: "A voice came from heaven and said: 'I have both glorified *thee*, and will also glorify *thee* [thee, Jesus],' while the actual voice said: ' I have both glorified *it*, and will also glorify *it* [my name].' "

to find the cause. But is it so difficult to discover it? Are not Philo and John, both of them, Jews, reared in the school of the law and the prophets?

Three converging lines in the Old Testament lead to a single end: 1. The notion of the *Word* of God, as a manifestation of His all powerful and creative will in the finite world. Very frequently this principle of action in God is even personified in the Old Testament. Thus when, in Ps. cvii. 20, it is said: "He sendeth His Word, and it healeth them," or Ps. cxlvii. 15: "He sendeth His Word on the earth, and it runneth swiftly;" or Is. lv. 11: "My Word shall do all the things for which I have sent it." There is evidently here, however, only a poetic personification. 2. The notion of *wisdom* in the book of Proverbs, especially in chap. viii. The author represents it as itself describing what it is for God: "He possessed me from the beginning of his way, before his works . . .; I was a workman with him, and I was his delight continually." Still a mere poetic personification, surely. The word is a power of action; wisdom, an intelligence and a conceived plan. 3. In several passages of Genesis, a being is spoken of in whom Jehovah Himself appears in the sensible world. He is sometimes distinguished from Him by the name *Angel of the Lord,* sometimes confounded with Him by the way in which He expresses Himself, saying: *I,* in speaking of Jehovah Himself. Some theologians see in him only an ordinary angel,—not always the same one, perhaps,—each time accomplishing a special mission. Others even deny Him personality, and see in Him only a sensible form, the passing mode of appearance of Jehovah Himself. These two interpretations are wrecked against the passage, Exod. xxiii. 21, where God, in speaking of this Angel of the Lord, says: "Beware! For he will not pardon your sin; *my name* is in him." The name is the reflection of the essence. Here this name is the reflection of the holy essence of God, inflexible towards the will which is obstinate in sinning. Such a quality implies personality. The question, therefore, is of a real person, having a divine character, and in whom God Himself manifests Himself (*my name—in him*). This angel is also called by Isaiah (lxiii. 9): "*The Angel of the Presence*" of Jehovah, and Malachi, at the end of the Old Testament, taking the final step, identifies him with the Messiah: "Suddenly the Lord whom ye seek and the Angel of the Covenant whom ye desire shall enter into his temple; behold, he cometh, saith the Lord of hosts." In this third idea we find no longer only the divine intelligence or force personified, but a living divine being, Him who should come to save his people as Messiah.—These so remarkable indications did not remain unnoticed by the ancient Jewish doctors. They appear to have early endeavored to bring together these three lines into a single idea; that of the being of whom God makes use on every occasion when He puts Himself in connection with the external world. They designate Him sometimes by the names *Shekinah* (*habitation*), or *Jekara* (*brightness*), sometimes, and most frequently, by the name *Memar* or *Memra di Jehovah* (*Word of the Lord*). The Chaldaic paraphrases of the Old Testament, called *Targums,* constantly introduce this being where the Old Testament speaks simply of the Lord. These writings, perhaps, date only from the third or fourth century of our era, it is true; but, as Schürer says, it is beyond doubt that these paraphrases rest upon more ancient works, and are the product of an elaboration for ages. Fragments of similar writings are preserved, dating from the second century *before* Jesus Christ, from the time of John Hyrcanus. Already before the fall of Jerusalem, mention is made of a Targum on the book of Job, and the Mischna (of the second century after Jesus Christ) already speaks of translations of the Bible into Chaldee.[1] It is infinitely improbable, moreover, that the Jewish theologians would have accepted from the Christians a notion so favorable to the religion of the latter. Now, the following are some examples of the manner in which these doctors paraphrase the Old Testament. It is said in Gen. xxi. 20, in speaking of Ishmael: "God was with the lad;" the paraphrase says: "The Word of Jehovah was with the lad." xxviii. 21, where Jacob says: "The Lord shall be my God;" the Targum makes him say: "The Word of Jehovah shall be my God." xxxix. 21, instead of "The Lord was with Joseph," . . . "the Memra (the Word) was with Joseph." Exod. xix. 17, instead of "And Moses brought forth the people to meet God" . . . "And Moses brought forth the people to meet the Word of Jehovah." Num. xxii. 20, instead of "God came unto Balaam." . . . "The Word of Jehovah came unto Balaam." Deut. iv. 24, instead of "God is a consuming fire." . . . "The Word of Jehovah is a consuming fire." Is. i. 14, instead of "My soul hateth your new moons." . . . "My Word hateth," . . . xlii. 1, instead of "My soul delighteth in him." . . . "My Word delighteth," . . . etc., etc. It is therefore indisputable that, at the time when John wrote, the Jewish theology had already, by the special name of *Word*, definitely expressed the idea of the God who enters into connection with the external world. It will have been noticed that this form is particularly used in the passages in which the Scriptures ascribe to God a human feeling, such as that of repenting, of aversion, of complacency, of hatred.

The question now is to determine whether these doctors represented this manifested God to themselves as a real person and distinct from the person of God Himself. There can be brought forward in relation to this point, just as in relation to the nature of the Logos of Philo, passages having opposite meanings. Gess regards as incompatible with the notion of a real person the passage 1 Kings viii. 15, in which the Targum substitutes for the expressions, *the mouth* and *the hand* of Jehovah, the following: *the Word (Memar)* and *the will* of Jehovah, the first as declaring, the second as executing. In the same way, Jer. xxxii. 41, or again Gen. xxii. 16, where the Targum makes the Lord say: "I swear by my Word," instead of: "I swear by myself." But is it necessary to suppose the paraphrasts systematically consistent with themselves in a region so mysterious and obscure? Besides, it appears to me much more difficult to explain how God should swear by His Word, if it is not a person like Himself, than if it is a personal being; and as to the first passage, the term

---

[1] Schürer, *Lehrbuch des neutest. Zeitgeschichte*, p. 479.

Word seems to regain its ordinary meaning, since the two terms *word* and *will* correspond to the two acts : speaking and acting. It is impossible not to find the idea of personality in all the following passages: " My Word *hates*," " My Word *has pleasure*," " the Word shall be *my God;* " " the Word shall contend for you; " " the Brightness of Jehovah arose *and said.*" So much the more, since in several passages, instead of the Word or the Brightness of Jehovah, it is the Angel of the Lord who is substituted for the simple name of Jehovah, for example, Exod. iv. 24, and Judges iv. 14. Gess objects that if this theory of a second divine person, called the Word of Jehovah, had been received in Palestine at that period, it could not be altogether wanting in the writings of St. Paul. But the teaching of that apostle is drawn from the revelation which he had received, and not from the lessons of his early masters. Paul may not have found in the region where he taught, and at the time when he taught, a call to use this term, while in the great centre, Ephesus, at the end of the first century, John found himself in circumstances which drew his particular attention to this term. The passages 1 Cor. viii. 6, where creation is attributed to Christ, and 1 Cor. x. 5, where Christ is represented as the leader of Israel in the wilderness, show in any case that the notion itself was as familiar to him as it was to John; and this is the essential point.

If the point is carefully considered, the paraphrasts, in denying to God all human emotions, in order to attribute them to the *Memar* (the Word), give in fact to this manifested God the seal of personality in even a much more pronounced way than to God Himself. But perhaps it is with them, as with Philo, whose idea respecting the personality of the Logos seems to be quite fluctuating. Zeller has clearly shown the cause of this oscillation in the mind of this philosopher. On one side, the Logos must appertain to the essence of God, which seems to make him a simple divine attribute (the divine reason or wisdom), and consequently to exclude personality; on the other side, he must be in relation with matter, in order to cause the particular types to penetrate it on which finite things are formed, and this function supposes a being distinct from God, and, consequently, personal. A similar observation may be made with regard to the oriental paraphrasts ; and this correspondence between them would have nothing surprising in it if, as Schürer thinks, Philo's philosophy exercised an influence on the exegesis of these latter.[1]

We may now conclude. Philo was formed, above all, in the school of the Old Testament; he had learned in it, through all the facts which we have pointed out above, the existence of a being, personal or impersonal, by means of whom God acts upon the world, when He puts Himself in connection with it. And he believed that he could philosophically interpret the idea of this being, through explaining it by means of the Logos, or divine reason, of the Greek philosophers. For this reason he calls him sometimes *Logos* or *second God* (δεύτερος θεός) when he speaks as a disciple

---

[1] Schürer, *Literatur-Zeitung*, 1878, No. 17.

of these schools, and sometimes *Archangel, High-priest, Son, First-born Son,* when he resumes the Jewish language. So true is it that the Porch and the Academy furnished him the key of his Judaism, that in one instance he even goes so far as to say: "the immortal *ideas* ($ἀθάνατοι\ λόγοι$) which we [Jews] call *angels*."

John, on his side, was also in the school of the Old Testament; he also learned from this sacred book the existence of that being, sometimes distinct from the Lord, sometimes confounded with Him, with whom God conversed when He said: "*Let us make* man in our image," who consequently participated in the creative act, who communicates life to all things, but who has especially marked with His luminous impress every human soul, who finally is the permanent agent in the theophanies of the Old Testament. John is so penetrated by this view, that in the person of Adonai, *the Lord,* who calls Isaiah (chap. vi.) to the prophetic ministry, he recognizes the same divine being who, at a later time, in Jesus Christ manifested His glory in a human life (John xii. 41);[1] exactly as St. Paul recognizes the divine being, manifested in Christ, in the leader of Israel through the wilderness (1 Cor. x. 4), and as the author of the Epistle to the Hebrews, finally, attributes to the Son the creation and preservation of all things, as well as the sacrifice of purification for our sins (Heb. i. 1–3).

But here is the difference between John and Philo: instead of going from the Old Testament to the schools of Plato and the Stoics, John passed to that of Jesus. And when he beheld in Him that unique glory, full of divine grace and truth, which he has described John i. 14—when he heard declarations such as these: "He who hath seen me, hath seen the Father;" "Thou didst love me before the foundation of the world;" "Before Abraham was, I am;" he comprehended what He whom he had before him was, and without difficulty accomplished, in his mind, that fusion between the eternal agent of God and the Christ, which had not entered into the mind of the Alexandrian philosopher. Philo is the Old Testament explained by Greek philosophy; John is the Old Testament completed and explained by Jesus Christ.[2]

As for the *term* Logos, on which John fixed in order to designate the divine being whom he had recognized in the person of Christ, it was offered to him, as we have seen, by the Old Testament; the part which the Word of God plays in that book, particularly in the account of the creation, was sufficient to make him prefer this term to every other. That of *Son,* as Gess rightly says, only expressed the personal relation between God and the divine being whom John wished to characterize. The

---

[1] "Isaiah said these things when he saw his glory and spake of him [Christ]."

[2] We see how many errors are included in the opinion of Jean Réville, which may be thus stated: "The Alexandrian theology is the synthesis of Judaism and Greek philosophy, and the doctrine of John is, in its turn, the synthesis of this Alexandrian theology with the Christian tradition." We believe that the Alexandrian theology is foreign to John's teaching, and that this teaching, instead of resting on the Christian tradition, is a personal testimony (John i. 14; 1 John i. 1–4).

term *Word*, on the contrary, expressed His double relation, on one side to the God who reveals Himself in Him, and on the other to the world to which He manifests Himself. And if this name of Word was already used in the Jewish schools (as seems to be shown by the paraphrases), we may so much more easily understand how it may have been the first one which presented itself to the apostle's mind. It is remarkable that this title is found as a designation of Christ in the three Johannean writings (Gosp. i. 1; 1 Ep. i. 1–3; Apoc. xix. 13), and in these three writings alone. It is, as it were, an indissoluble bond which unites them. The fact that this name is found even in the Apocalypse, whose author, assuredly, is not liable to the suspicion of Alexandrianism, completes the proof that its source is Jewish, and by no means Philonean. Finally, being established at Ephesus, that focus of religious syncretism, whither all the philosophical doctrines flowed in from Persia, from Greece and from Egypt, John might have often heard, in the religious and philosophical teachings or conversations, the term *Word* applied to the *manifested God*. When he inscribed it at the beginning of his narrative, therefore, it was as if he had said: "This Logos, respecting whom you are speculating, without coming to the real knowledge of Him, we possess, we Christians. We have seen and heard Him Himself, and He it is whose history we are about to relate to you."[1]

We see, consequently, that there is nothing compromising to the Johannean origin of the fourth Gospel in this term Logos, to which criticism clings with tenacity, and which it uses in a way that does little honor to its scientific impartiality.

IX. After having done justice to all these considerations, Hase avows himself overpowered by a ninth and last one, namely this: Certain incidents in our Gospel have a legendary stamp, and cannot have been related by an eye-witness; thus, the picture of John the Baptist and the first disciples of Jesus, the change of the water into wine and the multiplication of the loaves, finally, the appearances of Jesus after He rose from the dead. Hase, for a long time, believed that he could escape the force of this consideration by holding that John was not present when the facts occurred which gave rise to these legends. He now acknowledges that this was a forced expedient, and lays down his arms. The reply attempted by this theologian was, in fact, only a poor subterfuge, and he did well to renounce it. But the argument before which the veteran of Jena gives way, is of no more importance for that reason; for, however Hase may think he can affirm the contrary, it simply amounts to the question of the supernatural.

X. Baur has especially insisted upon the argument derived from the

---

[1] Neander, *Apost. Zeitalter*, ii. p. 549: "John wished to lead those who were occupying themselves too much with speculations about the Logos, from their idealism to a religious realism. . . Instead of exploring that which is hidden and cannot be attained, each one should come and behold Him who had manifested Himself in human nature;—to believe and test by experience, as John himself testified of what he had seen and experienced."

182 / The Origin

Paschal dispute at the end of the second century, but from a different point of view from that from which we have already treated this question (p. 172). He claims that in fixing on the 14th of Nisan as the day of Christ's death, which the Synoptics placed on the 15th, the author of the fourth Gospel sought to completely put an end to the Paschal rite of the churches of Asia, which celebrated the Passover on the 14th in the evening. In fact, he displaces thus the day of the last meal of Christ and carries it back to the evening of the 13th. Now, as it was at that meal that Jesus instituted the Passover, the author creates thereby a conflict between the Gospel history and the Asiatic rite. And as John must have been the author of that rite, he cannot have composed a Gospel designed to contest it. This argument rests on the idea that an annual commemorative festival is celebrated on the day on which that feast was *instituted*, and not the day on which the event that gave rise to it occurred. Every one at once perceives the falsity of this view. Besides, we have already shown that the narrative of John respecting this point is historically justified, and that by the Synoptics themselves (p. 78). It was not invented, therefore, in the service of ecclesiastical tactics. The rite of the churches of Asia probably depended, not on any date whatever in the history of the Passion, but on the day of the Paschal meal in the Old Covenant. In any case, if the evangelist had desired to favor the Roman Church, which celebrated the Holy Paschal Supper on the Sunday of the resurrection, and to combat the Asiatic rite which placed it on the evening of the 14th, it would have served no purpose to place the institution of the Holy Supper on the 13th, at evening;—to reach this end, it would have been necessary to place it on Sunday morning, and to make it the first act of Jesus after His resurrection! (See, for further details, the Commentary, at the end of chap. xix.)

XI. The difference of matter and form between the Gospel and the *Apocalypse*. The impossibility of referring these two works to the same author had formerly become a kind of axiom for criticism. Consequently, it was thought that, as the Apocalypse has in its favor earlier and more positive testimonies than the Gospel, it was just to give it the preference and to reject the Johannean origin of the latter. Thus even Baur, Hilgenfeld and many others reason. But the dilemma on which this conclusion rests is more and more doubted at present. It is positively set aside by Hase, who cites, as an analogy, the difference which is so marked between the first and second parts of Goethe's *Faust;* more than this, he thinks that the Apocalypse, bearing testimony to John's residence in Asia, rather confirms thereby the tradition relative to the Gospel.[1] Weizsäcker cannot help acknowledging that, notwithstanding the difference of author, the Apocalypse is "in organic connection with the spirit of the Gospel."[2] Baur himself has borne witness to the complete identity of the two works, by calling the Johannean Gospel "a spiritualized Apocalypse." If, indeed, it can be proved that it is necessary to interpret spiritually the poetic images and plastic forms of the Apocalypse, wherein, according to this declaration of Baur

---

[1] *Geschichte Jesu*, pp. 29–31.   [2] *Untersuch.*, p. 295.

himself, will it differ from the Gospel? Let us add that the superiority which is attributed to the testimony of tradition in relation to the Apocalypse is a fiction, which does not become more true for being continually repeated.¹ Keim and Scholten find the Apocalypse as insufficiently attested as the Gospel, and reject them both.

In our view, a choice between these works is by no means necessary, for they bear distinctly the seal of their composition by one and the same author.

And (1) from the standpoint of *style*. The charge made against the author of the Apocalypse of transgressing the rules of grammar or of Greek syntax, is one of those mistakes which it would be well not to repeat any further. The preposition ἀπό *from* is construed with the nominatives ὁ ὤν (*who is*) and ὁ ἐρχόμενος (*who is to come*). A barbarism! cries the critic. The Gospel, on the contrary, is written in correct Greek. But in the same verse, i. 4, we find this same preposition ἀπό *from*, construed regularly with the genitive τῶν ἑπτὰ πνευμάτων (*the seven spirits*). And the same is the case, without a single exception, throughout all the rest of the book! The construction which is found fault with, far from being a schoolboy's error, is, therefore, the bold anomaly of a master who wished to picture, by the immutability of the word, the immutability of the subject designated, namely God. Numbers of appositions in the nominative with substantives in the genitive or dative are charged. Comp. ii. 20 (Tisch.) iii. 12, etc. But constantly we find in the same book appositions in their regular cases (comp. i. 10, 11; iii. 10, etc.). In the cases of the opposite kind, the author, in setting grammar at defiance, has evidently desired to give a greater independence to the appositional substantive or participle. The Gospel, in several instances, offers us analogous irregularities (comp. vi. 39; xvii. 2, etc.).—It is remarked further that the Gospel uses abstract terms, where the Apocalypse is disposed to clothe the idea with a figure. The one will say *life*, where the other says *living fountains of waters;* the one *light*, where the other says *the lamp of the holy city;* the one *the world*, the other *the Gentiles;* the one *death*, the other *the second death*, etc., etc. It is sufficient, as a complete answer, to call to mind, with Hase, that "the Apocalypse employs the forms of poetry which are sensible (*sinnlich*)." Let us, also, not forget that the Apocalypse is the work of ecstasy and of vision, and that John conceived it ἐν πνεύματι (*carried away in the spirit*), while the Gospel is the calm and deliberate reproduction of simple historical recollections, and that it is written ἐν νοΐ (in an unexcited state of mind).²—The Aramaisms of the Apocalypse are also spoken of, which form a contrast with the Greek accuracy of the Gospel. Account must here be taken of a decisive fact. The Apocalypse is written under the constant influence of the prophetic pictures of the Old Testament, the coloring of whose style, as a conse-

---

¹ The question is especially of the testimony which Justin gives to the Apocalypse; now, we have seen what follows, in favor of the Gospel, from the testimony of the same Justin, from that of Papias and from that of the twenty-first chapter.

² Comp. respecting this difference, 1 Cor. xiv. 14, 15.

quence, comes out in its own style, while the Gospel simply relates the events of which the author was a witness, independently of every foreign model. Under these so very different conditions of redaction, as the Dutch critic Niermeyer justly observes,[1] the entire absence of difference between the two writings (on the supposition that they are both by the same author) would "afford ground for legitimate astonishment." Winer has remarked how the style of Josephus has a more Aramaic coloring when he relates the history of the Old Testament, and when he is under the influence of the sacred writings, than when he describes, in the *Jewish War*, the events which happened under his own eyes.—But with all this, what real and fundamental homogeneousness of style between these two works, to the view of every one who does not stop at the surface! We recommend, in this regard, the excellent study of Niermeyer (see p. 23 f). The same favorite expressions, *to make a lie, to do the truth; to keep the commandments*, or *the word; to hunger and thirst*, to designate the deep wants of the soul; the term *Amen, Amen*, which so often begins the declarations of Jesus in the fourth Gospel, becoming in the Apocalypse the personal name of Christ Himself; the figure of the *Lamb*, applied in the Gospel (with the term ἀμνός) to the victim burdened with the sin of the world, and used in the Apocalypse, with the neuter and more emphatic term ἀρνίον, in order to designate the glorified Lord and to form the counterpart of the term θηρίον, the Beast. Finally, the name Word or Word of God, given to Christ, which belongs only to the three Johannean writings in the entire New Testament, and unites them, as it were, by an indissoluble bond. To these analogies of expression let us add that of entire descriptions; for example, Apoc. iii. 20, where the author describes the intimate communion of Christ with the believer: "Behold, I stand at the door and knock; if any one hear my voice and open the door, I will come in to him, and will sup with him, and he with me." Let this expression be compared with John xiv., more particularly with the 23d verse: "We will come to him and make our abode with him." Or the description of the heavenly happiness of believers, Apoc. vii. 15–17: "And he that sitteth on the throne shall dwell with them. They shall hunger no more, and they shall thirst no more . . . . , because the Lamb who is in the midst of the throne shall feed them and shall lead them to living fountains of waters, and God shall wipe away every tear from their eyes." We find here brought together several characteristic expressions of the Johannean style: σκηνοῦν ἐν (*to dwell in a tent*), comp. John i. 14; πεινᾶν, διψᾶν (*to hunger, to thirst*), comp. vi. 35; ποιμαίνειν (*to feed*) x. 1–16; xxi. 16; ὁδηγεῖν (*to guide*) xvi. 13; and as to the last point, depicting God's tenderness, does it not recall the expression of Jesus, xiv. 21: "He that loveth me shall be loved of my Father?"—A final analogy, which sets the seal on the preceding, is found in the quotation from Zechariah (xii. 10), Apoc. i. 7, where the author corrects the translation of the LXX. precisely as the author of the Gospel does, in John xix. 37.

---

[1] Statement by Busken-Huet, *Revue de théologie*, Sept., 1856.

2. With regard to the *matter*, the agreement between the two writings is no less remarkable.

It has been sometimes said that the God of the Apocalypse is a God of wrath, while the God of the Gospel is all love. It seems to be forgotten that it is in the Gospel that this threatening is found: "He that obeyeth not the Son, the wrath of God abideth on him" (iii. 36), and that other threatening: "Ye shall seek me, but ye shall die in your sins" (viii. 24); and, on the other hand, that it is the author of the Apocalypse who twice reproduces (vii. 17 and xxi. 4) that promise of Isaiah—the most tender of all which the Scriptures contain: "God shall wipe every tear from their eyes." Love rules in the Gospel, because this book describes the first coming of the Son of God, as *Saviour;* severity in the Apocalypse, because it is the representation of the second coming of the Son, as *Judge.*

The Christology of the Apocalypse is identical with that of the Gospel. We have already shown (p. 113) that the designation of Christ as ἡ ἀρχή τῆς κτίσεως τοῦ θεοῦ, *the beginning of the creation of God* (iii. 14), must not be understood in the sense of a temporal beginning, as if Jesus Himself formed a part of the creation, but in the sense in which eternity may be called the beginning, that is to say, the principle of the creation. This sense follows from the passages in which the term *beginning* (ἀρχή) is completed by the term *end* (τέλος) and in which the parallel epithet, *the first,* is also completed by *the last.* We must recall to mind the fact that these expressions are borrowed from Isaiah, with whom they are, as it were, the insignia of the peculiar glory of Jehovah. If Jesus Himself formed part of the creation, according to the author of the Apocalypse, as Hilgenfeld claims, how could he call Him ὁ ζῶν, *the living one* (i. 18)? This word reminds one of the expressions of the Gospel, i. 4: "In him was life," and vi. 51: "I am the living bread," a term which, in the context, implies the sense of *life-giving.* The homage of worship from all creatures is addressed to the Lamb at the same time as to the Father (v. 15); a fact which may fitly be compared with xxii. 9: "Worship *God* (only)." But, at the same time, the Son is subordinate to the Father. As for the revelation "which He gives to His servants," in this very book, it is "God who gave it to Him" (i. 1). In the Gospel, Jesus declares also that it is "the Father who giveth the Son to have life in Himself" (v. 26), and that "His Father is greater than He" (xiv. 28). The terms *Word* and *Son,* which are common to the two works, both of them imply this double notion of dependence and community of nature.

The means of *justification* before God are absolutely the same in the two works; there is no question in the Apocalypse either of circumcision, or of any legal work. "Salvation" descends "from the throne of God and of the Lamb" as a divine gift (vii. 10). The same figure is applied to the *river of living water* (xxii. 1). It is "in the *blood of the Lamb* that the elect wash their robes" (viii. 14); it is "through this blood that they gain the victory over Satan" (xii. 11). Justification and sanctification are, therefore, the fruit of faith in the work of Christ. If the keeping of the *commandments of God* is frequently spoken of, the case is exactly the same in the Gospel (xiv. 21; xv. 10) and in the first epistle (v. 2, etc.). And it is very evident that this obedience is that which springs from faith. Critics especially urge the reproach addressed to the bishop of Pergamos, of tolerating persons who, "after the example of Balaam, teach men *to eat meats sacrificed to idols* and to commit fornication " (ii. 14). The teaching thus made the subject of accusation is none other, it is said, than that of St. Paul in First Corinthians (viii.-x.). Here, therefore, is a declaration of war made against Paulinism, and the evident indication of a Judaizing tendency; it is the antipode of the fourth Gospel. But one and the same thing may be said in two very different spirits. Paul in 1 Cor. begins by permitting, in the name of monotheism and the freedom of faith, the eating of the meats sacrificed to idols; the Christian should not be afraid of contracting defilement from material food; but afterwards he restricts this permission in two ways: 1. The exercise of this right is subordinate to the duty of charity towards brethren having conscientious scruples; 2. It must never be carried to the point of participation in the sacred feasts celebrated in the heathen sanctuaries, because such an act implies a close union with idolatry (x. 14–21), and because in such circumstances the believer "who thinks that he stands" may easily fall (1 Cor. x. 12). Evidently he means by this: fall into impurity—that vice which was so prevalent in Corinth and against which he had just put the members of the Church on their guard, in chap. vi. Now it is precisely against this second manner of eating the sacrificial meats that the author of the Apocalypse also raises his voice, as is shown by the close connection which is made between these two expressions: *to eat meats sacrificed to idols* and *to commit fornication.* What temptation to this latter vice could have resulted from the fact of eating such food at a private table, either that of the Christian himself, or at the house of a brother who had invited him! And this is the only thing which Paul authorizes (1 Cor. x. 25–27). We know, on the contrary, that, towards the end of the first century, and from the beginnings of Gnosticism, the heretics set about recommending the eating of meats sacrificed to idols, precisely in the sense in which Paul had prohibited it. They sought thereby to reconcile Christianity with Paganism. Irenæus says (i. 6) : "They eat without scruple the meats which have been sacrificed to idols, thinking that they do not defile themselves thereby, and whenever there is among the heathen a festival prepared in honor of the idols, they are the first to be there." We can understand the falls which resulted from this. Irenæus also immediately adds, "that these Gnostics give themselves up to the lusts of the flesh with greediness;" and when the Jew Trypho reproaches Justin with the fact that the Christians eat sacrificial meats, the latter replies, unhesitatingly, that "it is only the Valentinians and other heretics who act in this way." Basilides taught, according to the report of Eusebius (*H. E.*, iv. 7), that, in time of persecution, one might, in order to save one's life, eat sacrificial meats and deny the faith. The first of these acts was only the outward form of the second. These are the abominations against which the author of the Apocalypse protests. What have they in common with the case which is authorized by Paul? We have discussed this passage at considerable length, because it is one of the principal supports on which the opinion rests, which is so widely extended at the present day, as to the Judaizing character of the Apocalypse.

It has been maintained that when the author puts the Church of Ephesus on its guard "against those who say they are apostles and are not, and has found them liars," he means to designate St. Paul. But what! in a letter addressed to a Church which Paul had founded during a residence of three years, and from which Christianity had spread through all the countries of the neighborhood, a man dared to maintain that the apostleship of this man was an untruth! Was it not in that region of Asia Minor that there were found those multitudes of converts due to the labor of the apostle, whose triumph the author of the Apocalypse celebrates in chap. vii. and elsewhere? Luthardt simply says, in answer to such an assertion: "He who proves too much proves nothing." Volkmar has made another discovery: the false prophet, the beast with the horns of a lamb, the confederate of the antichrist, who seeks to bring the whole world under the power of the latter, is again St. Paul; for in the Epistle to the Romans (chap. xiii.), he teaches Christians the duty of submitting themselves to the superior powers, which is equivalent to binding them to assume the mark of the beast. Is not this a poor jest, rather than a serious argument? The way of submission marked out by Paul is that which the entire Scriptures teach with regard to earthly powers. It was that which Jeremiah marked out for the last kings of Judah towards Nebuchadnezzar. Jesus knows no other: "Put up thy sword into the sheath, for he that smiteth with the sword shall perish by the sword." The author of the Apocalypse himself recommends it to the Christians persecuted by the antichrist, for he sets in opposition to every desire for active resistance this threatening: "If any one leadeth into captivity, into captivity he shall go: if any one slayeth with the sword, he also shall be killed with the sword. Here is the *patience* and *faith* of the saints." The strength of the persecuted Church will be, as Isaiah already said, *to keep itself at rest*, relying upon God alone. The Reformed Church in France has carried this line of conduct even to heroism, and, when it has for a time departed from it, it has had no occasion to congratulate itself.

As to the conception of *the Church*, it is absolutely the same in the Apocalypse as in the fourth Gospel and with St. Paul; and it is a gross error to maintain, as Volkmar does, that the believing Gentiles are only *tolerated*, in this book, and constitute only a sort of *plebs* in the Holy City. As Hase says: "After the one hundred and forty-four thousand who are sealed from among the tribes of Israel, John sees an innumerable multitude from the twelve Gentiles, of every nation, of every tribe, of every tongue, clothed with white robes" (chap. vii.). "They are before the throne of God and serve him night and day in his temple," and "God dwells with them . . . and He wipes away every tear from their eyes" (vv. 15–17). Is this the reception given to a vile plebs? This assertion is so entirely false, that the one hundred and forty-four thousand Jews, who are previously spoken of, are not even yet believers. Their conversion is not related until chap. xiv. 1 ff. In chap. vii. they are merely *sealed* (reserved) in order to be consecrated afterwards. But, however it may be with this last point, and even if these one hundred and forty-four thousand formed the *élite* of the assembly of the Church, the Apocalypse in giving them this place would be in agreement with St. Paul, who, in the eleventh chapter of Romans, compares the converted Gentiles to wild branches grafted upon the patriarchal root in the place of the Jews, the natural branches; and also with the author of the fourth Gospel, who, in chap. x., makes the sheep taken from the Israelitish fold the centre of the Church and presents the sheep called from other nations as simply grouped about this primitive nucleus (ver. 16). The divine work which the author of the Apocalypse celebrates from the beginning to the end, when he puts into the mouth of all believers, without distinction, the song of the Lamb; when he gives to them all the titles of *kings* and *priests* of God the Father, which Israel had borne only typically; when to the twelve elders representing the twelve tribes of Israelitish Christianity, he adds twelve others perfectly equal to the first, and representing, together with them, before the throne the Christians of the Gentile world,—all this new creation which he beholds with rapture and which he glorifies, is nothing else than the work of St. Paul. And yet in this book, St. Paul is the false prophet in the service of the antichrist!

But do not the author's *eschatological* views condemn us perchance? Even Niermeyer feels himself embarrassed by that *Jerusalem* of the end of time, which seems to perpetuate the preponderance of Judaism even in the perfected state of the kingdom of God. "If," says he, "the *earthly* Jerusalem could be removed from the Apocalyptic picture, this book would be *spiritualized* throughout by this fact alone." It is not difficult to satisfy this demand. The author represents (xxi. 16) the wall of that future Jerusalem as having a height equal to its length and its breadth, and as forming, consequently, a perfect cube. This cube is of twelve thousand furlongs, which is nearly fifty leagues, in each dimension. Can it reasonably be believed that he is picturing to himself a real city of so monstrous a shape? But this image, grotesque if we take it in a material sense, becomes sublime as soon as it is spiritually understood. The Most Holy Place in the tabernacle and in the temple had the form of a perfect cube, while the Holy Place had that of a rectangle. What, then, does the author mean by this figure? That the New Jerusalem will be wholly what the Most Holy Place was in the former times: the dwelling-place of the Thrice Holy God. It is the realization of the last prayer of Jesus: "That they may be one in us, as we are one;" the state which Paul sets forth in 1 Cor. xv. 28: "God all in all." And if any one hesitates to believe that this glorious state of things applies, in the Apocalypse, to other believers than those of Jewish origin, let him read, xxi. 2, 3, these words: "I saw the holy city, the New Jerusalem coming down out of heaven from God, and I heard a great voice from heaven saying, Behold the tabernacle of God *is among men*." And as if to leave no doubt respecting the sense of the word *men*, the author adds: " And they [they who were not his people] *shall be his peoples*, and God Himself shall be with them, their God." In speaking of the *final* Jerusalem, Niermeyer simply forgets that that future Jerusalem is by no means a restoration of the ancient Jerusalem, and that the author describes it as a *new* Jerusalem *coming down out of heaven from God*. It is the Church in all its extent and all its perfection, comprehending all that which, throughout the whole of humanity, has been given to Christ. We find here the widest universalism. And if it is thus with the holy city itself, the same method of spiritual interpretation must, of course, be extended to all that which constitutes its beauty: the gates, the walls, the square, the river, the trees. And all these images, spiritually understood, lead us directly, if the Gospel is really a spiritualized Apocalypse (Baur), to this result: that the Apocalypse is fundamentally identical with the Gospel.

A general comparison of the Apocalyptic *drama* with the narrative contained in our Gospel leads us also to hold that their author was the same. True, the contrary is affirmed. It is said that the Apocalypse breathes the most intense hatred towards the Gentiles—it is by a Jewish author; the Gospel reserves all its hatred for the Jews—it is by a Gentile author. It is further said, that the Apocalypse moves amidst the scenes of the last times, which are unknown to the Gospel; the latter, on the contrary, treats only of the hostile relation of Jesus to the Jews during His sojourn on the earth. These two objections fall before a single observation. The work of Jesus is twofold. In the first place it concerned the Jews; then came *the times of the Gentiles* in which salvation was offered to these last. The Gospel gives an account of the first of these relations, the Apocalypse treats of the second; and the two works complete each other, as if the two halves of one and the same whole, which might have for its title: The substitution of the kingdom of God for that of Satan throughout the whole earth. The actors in the two dramas are also, at the foundation, the same. They are these three: *Christ, faith, unbelief.* In the Gospel: the Christ, as Christ *in humiliation;* faith, represented by *the disciples;* unbelief, represented by *the Jews*. In the Apocalypse, the Christ, as the *glorified Lord;* faith, represented by *the Bride*, or the Church; unbelief, by *the Gentiles*, the majority of whom reject the call of the Gospel, in the same way as the majority of the Jews had rejected it in the time of Jesus. There is, therefore, no partiality in this book. On the one side, believing Gentiles, an innumerable multitude, whom the author with rapture beholds triumphant before the throne, precisely as, during the life of Jesus, there had been believing Jews, raised into the most intimate communion with Him. On the other side, a mass of unbelieving Gentiles who draw upon themselves, more and more, the judgments of the glorified Lord (seals, trumpets, bowls), precisely as the mass of the Jews had been hardened and infuriated more and more against the Lamb of God in the midst of them. The sole difference between the two dramas, the Evangelic and Apocalyptic—and this difference appertains to the very nature of things—is that in the former the Passion and Resurrection, the foundations of the redemption of all, are related; in the latter, the second coming of Christ, as the consummation of salvation and judgment for all. This difference is one more bond of union between the two works; for thereby the Apocalypse all along supposes the Gospel behind itself, so to speak, and the Gospel, the Apocalypse before itself, in some sort; and thus we understand from what source comes the almost complete absence of the eschatological element in the Gospel. The *progress* and *phases* of the struggle, there with the Jews, here with the Gentiles, are also exactly similar. In both works the end seems near, even from the beginning. But, nevertheless, it is found to be deferred; we expect it in the Apocalypse after the sixth seal, after the sixth trumpet; nevertheless, it is again postponed, as in the Gospel where John repeats several times the phrase: "But his hour was not yet come." The *denouement*, also, is fundamentally the same, though under two different forms: outward victory of Satan over the kingdom of God: in the Gospel, by the murder of Jesus; in the Apocalypse, by the extermination of the Church under the Antichrist; but in both also, victory, at first spiritual, then soon afterwards external, of the champion of the cause of God; there, through the resurrection of Christ; here, through the glorification of the Church. We see that the two subjects only are different: on one side, the Christ *having come*, on the other, the Christ *coming*. But, nevertheless, the one of the two works seems to be made in imitation of the other, both in relation to the part of the actors and the progress of the action.

There is only one way by which these two works can be successfully placed in contradiction to each other: it is, as Luthardt says, to materialize the Apocalypse unduly, and unduly to spiritualize the Gospel. By this manœuvre the common crowd may be dazzled; but this is no longer science, it is fiction. The two works exist; and, sooner or later, the truth recovers its rights.

If the results of our study are well founded, all the external proofs in favor of the Johannean origin of the Apocalypse, to which Baur, Hilgenfeld and Volkmar attach so high a value, become so many confirmations of the Johannean origin of the Gospel.

XII. There is an objection which seems to have produced on the minds of our French critics, such as Renan and Sabatier, the decisive impression. John is called in the fourth Gospel *the disciple whom Jesus loved*: this is a marked superiority which is ascribed to him as related to his fellow apostles. This is not all; he is constantly exalted in such a way as to become fully the equal of Peter or even to surpass him, not only in agility, but also in intelligence and in readiness of faith. This spirit of jealousy and mean rivalry cannot have been the spirit of John himself: it must be acknowledged that the redaction of our Gospel, at least, is due to a disciple of this apostle, who wished at any cost to exalt the person and the role of the venerated master whose narratives and lessons he had gathered together. We find ourselves here evidently in the presence of a tendency-process. There are facts related; with what purpose are they related? One answers: because they happened in this way, the other searches after secret intentions and soon discovers them; he attributes the facts to the imagination of the narrator as being moved by some particular view. It is a serious thing to found conclusions, which may have decisive consequences for the Church, on such methods of interpretation. In this particular case, it happens that the supposed intention is in manifest contradiction to a very large number of facts. In chap. i. 43, Peter, it is true, only comes to Jesus as the third one. But if it were to exalt John at the expense of that disciple, the author, who does not trouble himself with the history, should have assigned to John himself the part of the one who introduced Peter to Jesus. This he does not do; he ascribes this honor to Andrew, Peter's *own brother*—by this expression he explains this part played by him, and assigns the cause of it historically. As for John, he is not directly designated in this scene, either by his name or by any paraphrase whatever. Not only this; but in ver. 41, even before Andrew brings Peter, when he is introduced for the first time on the scene, he is already designated as *the brother of Simon Peter*,—of that Peter who has not yet appeared, and who is thus presented, from the beginning, as the principal personage of the whole evangelical history by the side of Jesus. Finally, as if all this were not yet sufficient, in the view of the author, suitably to exalt the person and part of Peter, Jesus, at the first sight, discerns in him His principal auxiliary, and marks him by an honorable name, while he does nothing of the kind with regard to the four or five other disciples who were called at the same time. And yet in this scene it is that the critics are able to discover the intention of disparaging Peter or exalting John! Chap. vi. places us again in the midst of the apostolic circle. Who plays a part in this scene of friendship? It is Philip, it is Andrew, who is again designated as *the brother of Simon Peter* (vv. 5, 8). Then, at the end of the whole narrative, when, in presence of the defection of nearly all the Galilean disciples, one of the apostles begins to speak in reply to the question of Jesus: "Will ye also go away?" who is the one to whom the evangelist gives the post of honor, and who proclaims in the name of all his immovable faith in the Messiahship of Jesus? Is it John? Is it some little known disciple whose rivalry would be little dangerous to this apostle? It is Peter himself, he whom our evangelist wishes to disparage! At the last supper, Peter beckons to John, who is seated next to Jesus, to request him to make inquiry of the Master. But if the thing really happened in this way, what conclusion is to be drawn from it? And who would be able seriously to affirm the opposite? Is there here an impossibility? Does not the following story actually prove, by an insignificant circumstance, that Peter was not at Jesus' side (vv. 5, 6)? Finally, in the same passage, does not the evangelist attribute to Peter an expression in which all his devotion, all his faith, breaks forth; "Not only my feet, Lord, but also my hands and my head!" (xiii. 9). The conversations which follow the supper presented to the evangelist an admirable occasion for placing upon the scene his favorite disciple, the one whom Jesus loved. Questions of

Thomas, of Philip, of Judas are spoken of; but not the least allusion is made to the presence of this disciple. Peter's exclamation of devotion: "I will lay down my life for thy sake," is recalled to mind; can this be a piece of Machiavellism, for the purpose of more strikingly pointing out his presumption and afterwards making more prominent his denial? But as to this fall of Peter, John is precisely the one who relates it in the mildest way. No oath, no curse in Peter's mouth; this simple word—*He said*. Peter is introduced into the High-Priest's house by *another disciple*, who was an acquaintance of that personage; but nothing tells us that this disciple was John. And even if it were John, it would be a scanty honor, in a work whose tendency is said to be so strongly anti-Jewish, to have been in relation with the spiritual head of the nation. In Gethsemane, it is Peter who, in our Gospel, smites with the sword. When judged in relation to the thought of Jesus, this act is a fault, no doubt; but in contrast with the cowardice of the rest of the disciples, all of whom flee, it is assuredly an honor. Peter is not afraid to put into practice the profession of devotion which he had made. On the morning of the resurrection, when the two disciples run to the tomb, John reaches it *most quickly*, and this is said to be one of the deliberate claims on behalf of this apostle of superiority to his colleague. . . . Do the critics dare to write such puerilities! If it is so, let them abstain, at least, from calling such a work, with Hilgenfeld, "the Gospel with an eagle's flight!" Immediately afterwards, from the mere sight of the order which reigns in the sepulchre, John reaches the belief in the resurrection (xx. 8), while it is not said that this was the case with Peter. Here we have what seems a little more suspicious. But precisely here is one of the most decidedly autobiographical features of the fourth Gospel. The question is of the most internal fact, that of faith,—and John simply tells us how this fact was accomplished in himself. Could he tell so exactly what took place in his colleague?—whether the light came into his heart, also, *at that moment* and *in that way*? Perhaps he was always himself ignorant of it. But as Paul and Luke, both of them, speak to us of an appearance of Jesus after He rose, which was granted to Peter on that same day, this circumstance renders it probable that that apostle remained near the tomb with a confused presentiment, which was only transformed into real faith by means of that appearance. Let us remark, in passing, that no special appearance accorded to John is mentioned. There remains the scene of the twenty-first chapter. If the writer truly desired to establish a parallel between the two apostles, it must be acknowledged that the contrast is altogether in favor of Peter. John, it is true, discerns the Lord from the time when they were on the boat; but he does not stir from the place, while Peter immediately leaps into the water. John does not play the least part in the conversation which follows the meal; Peter is the sole object of the Lord's attention. Not only does Jesus reinstate him as an apostle; but He expressly entrusts to him the direction of the Church, and even that of the apostolate: "Feed my lambs! Lead my sheep!" And as the crown of his ministry, He promises him the honor of a bloody martyrdom. After this, it is he, and he only, whom He invites to follow Him, in order to receive, in a confidential conversation, the communications which He has still to make to him. The disciple whom Jesus loved allows himself, without having been summoned, to walk modestly behind them; it is Peter himself who puts him on the scene, by means of the question which he addresses somewhat indiscreetly to the Lord with regard to him. But, it is said, the superiority of John reappears even here; for the promise which is made to him, *that he should not die,* eclipses even that of martyrdom which had just been made to Peter. Let it be so, if one will; only it must be admitted that the following explanation of the evangelist, in that case, ought not immediately to invalidate the pretended promise! What a contrast between those two expressions, the one relative to John: "Now Jesus did not say, that he should not die;" the other relative to Peter: "Now he said this concerning the death by which Peter should glorify God."

There remains, in reality, only one expression that can be used to the advantage of the objection against which we are contending; it is the designation: *The disciple whom Jesus loved.* Weisse was the first, I believe, who was shocked at this expression, and saw in it a repulsive vainglory. Sabatier thinks that, if John had written it himself, "it would be difficult to place humility among his virtues." How much more delicate tact and more just a judgment does Hase show! He says: "Weisse did not comprehend this joyous pride of being in all humility the object of the most unmerited love." Among all the rays of the glory *full of grace and truth,* which the Word made flesh had displayed here below, there was one which had fallen upon John, and which he must reproduce in his work: the Son of God had carried condescension even to the point of having *a friend.* To recall to mind so sweet a remembrance was not pride: it was humble gratitude. To disguise his own name under this paraphrase was not to glorify the man; it was to exalt the tenderness of Him who had deigned to stoop so low. He knew himself no longer except as the pardoned believer knows himself—as the object of the most marvelous love. It is thus that Paul speaks of himself in 2 Cor. xii. 2–5.

XIII. We have long since expressed the conviction that the position of Reuss with regard to the fourth Gospel is untenable. To admit the apostolic origin of this work, and at the same time to regard the discourses which are contained in it as together forming a treatise of mystical theology, which the author, of his own will, has put into the mouth of Jesus— there is here an evident moral impossibility. Reuss was obliged to seek the means of extricating himself from this contradiction, and he has recently discovered it. It is the passage xix. 35.[1] Following the example of Weisse, Schweizer, Keim, and Weizsäcker, he thinks that he sees in this passage the perfectly clear distinction, established by the author of the Gospel himself, between his own person and that of the Apostle John, who orally furnished him the authentic materials of his narrative. Let us

---

[1] *Théologie johannique,* p. 103.

study this text more closely. It is composed of three propositions: "And he that hath seen, hath borne witness; and his witness is true; and he knoweth that he saith true, that ye may believe." Until now, it had been thought that it was the *witness* himself who spoke here. 1. He declares that his testimony respecting the fact related (the simultaneous accomplishment of the two prophecies by the thrust of the lance, apparently accidental, of the Roman soldier) is now given (the perfect μεμαρτύρηκε): it is a thing done, done by the story itself; comp. i. 34; 2. He attests the truth of this testimony; 3. He solemnly affirms the deep sense which he bears within himself of the reality of the fact related—and this, to the end that the readers (*you*) may fully believe it.

In this third clause *the author*, in speaking of the witness, uses the pronoun ἐκεῖνος, *that one*, and many find in this word the proof that he speaks of the witness as of a *different* person from himself and one who can be no other than the apostle. But, first, the author may with perfect propriety speak of himself in the third person, as Paul does in 2 Cor. xii. 2–5, or as Jesus Himself does, when He designates Himself habitually under the name *Son of man*, and consequently he may employ the pronoun of the third person in all its forms. The reason why he chooses here the pronoun ἐκεῖνος, *that one*, is because this word has a peculiar and constant signification in the fourth Gospel. It designates, in this book, a being who *exclusively* possesses a certain character, a certain function; consequently, not a person *remote* in contrast with another who is *nearer*, but a *single* person in contrast with *every* other; thus i. 18: "No one hath seen God at any time . . .; the only-begotten Son, *he* it is, (ἐκεῖνος), who hath declared him;" or xii. 48: "My word . . ., *it*, it alone (ἐκεῖνος), shall judge him;" comp. v. 39: "The Scriptures . . ., *they* are they (ἐκεῖνοι) which . . .;" xvi. 14: "The Spirit . . . *he* (ἐκεῖνος) shall glorify me," etc., etc. Jesus, also, in speaking of Himself, designates Himself by this pronoun; comp. ix. 37: "Thou hast seen him (the Son of God) and he that speaketh unto thee is *he* (ἐκεῖνος)."[1] It is exactly the same with xix. 35. He designates Himself by this pronoun as the one who, having been the only witness of the fact among the apostles, can alone attest it with the certainty of an eyewitnessing. There exists, therefore, no well founded logical or grammatical objection against the most generally admitted sense of the passage.

See now the sense which the before-mentioned writers endeavor to give to it.

1st proposition: The *redactor* of the Gospel declares that it is the *witness* (the apostle) who has informed him concerning the circumstance which he has just related. This meaning is not impossible, although we might be surprised to see suddenly appearing here the distinction between these two personages, of which the narrative does not, up to this point, offer the least trace.

2d proposition: The writer attests the truth of the story which he has

---

[1] Reuss objects that in the passage ix. 37, the pronoun ἐκεῖνος designates the predicate, while, in xix. 35, it refers to the subject of the clause. What matters this? In both cases it is still the same person, who is speaking, who designates himself by this pronoun.

from the lips of the witness. This is unnatural, for it would rather belong to the witness to attest the truth of the fact related by the evangelist. An unknown and anonymous redactor, presenting himself as guarantee for the story of the witness, and of a witness who is an apostle! This would be strange enough. Whence would he derive this right and this authority?

3d proposition: The redactor attests the deep sense which the witness bears within himself of the reality of the fact related. "He knoweth (the apostle-witness) that he saith true." This becomes altogether unintelligible; for how can a man testify of that which takes place in the inner consciousness of another individual? We might understand the redactor's saying, "And *I know* that he saith true." That would mean: Such an one as *I* know him to be,—I have the certainty that he cannot speak falsely. But with the form, "*he knows* (he) that he says true," the declaration has no meaning. Finally, the redactor adds: "to the end that ye may believe." If it is John who says this, to indicate the purpose of the story which he has just committed to writing, we understand what he means: "I, the witness, have the inward consciousness that what I relate to you is true, *to the end that you also* (who read) *may believe* (as well as I who have seen)." His testimony is to become for those who read, what the sight itself has been for him. But if the matter, on the other hand, is of the oral narrative which the apostle gave to the author a long time before, this statement has no longer any meaning; for there is no direct connection between such a testimony and the readers of the present work; the words "to the end that you may believe" have no longer any justification.

Finally, we must notice the two verbs in the present tense: "He *knows*" and "he *says true*." What do they prove? That, at the moment when these lines were written, the witness of the facts was still living. And in that case, what is gained by substituting for him, as a redactor, one of his disciples? The Gospel remains nevertheless, a narrative composed under the eyes and with the approbation of John himself.[1]

There is, moreover, another passage which absolutely condemns this sense given to xix. 35 by Reuss and by many others; it is the analogous declaration of xxi. 24. Here men, in a position which was recognized by the Church and respected, expressly affirm that which these critics deny on the foundation of xix. 35, to wit, the identity of the evangelist-redactor with the apostle witness: "This disciple (the one whom Jesus loved) is he *who testifieth* (ὁ μαρτυρῶν) of these things and *who wrote them* (ὁ γράψας), and we know that his testimony is true." Reuss claims, it is true, that these men fell into an error, and that, a certain time after John's death, they,

---

[1] Reuss, indeed, understands this serious difficulty and tries to find a way of removing it. He says that, if the author has said: *He knows*, it is because the Greek language did not offer him any special term for saying: *He knew*. But it was sufficient for the author to write instead of οἶδεν *he knows*, ᾔδει *he knew* (he knew when he was alive); and does not the following verb also, put in the present tense: "*that he saith true*," confute such a puerile evasion?

in good faith, confounded the apostle with the redactor. But these attestors, who had the power to provide the Gospel with a postscript which is not wanting in any manuscript or in any version, must have taken an active part in the publication of the work; they must, consequently, have been the first depositaries of it. Under these conditions, how could an error on their part be possible? Then, in order to their expressing themselves as they do, they must never have read the book which they themselves were publishing, at least the passage xix. 35, since, according to Reuss, the author declares, in the statement there made, precisely the opposite of what they solemnly affirm. Finally, when these two passages are compared, it must not be forgotten that the attestors of chap. xxi. say: *We know*, and not *he knows*, as the one who speaks in chap. xix. says. By the first person plural they distinguish themselves as clearly from the witness-apostle, as by the third person singular, *he knows*, the redactor of xix. 35 identifies himself with this witness. How, then, can Reuss say: "The sentence of xxi. 24 *recurs* in another place in the body of the Gospel; the analogy is patent." Yes, but the difference is none the less patent.[1]

Hilgenfeld has clearly perceived that it is impossible to find in xix. 35 the distinction, intentionally made by the writer, between himself and the witness. He admits, therefore, that the author, after having desired to pass himself off, throughout the whole work, as the Apostle John, forgot himself for a moment in the passage xix. 35, and that he inadvertently drops his disguise. There remains, in fact, only this expedient. But is it admissible? The reader will judge. In any case, if it is so, we must give up speaking of the supreme ability of an author to whom it is believed that such an oversight can be ascribed!

XIV. Will it be necessary to stop at a last objection, to which some critics seem to attach a certain importance? How, it is said, could a man have regarded Jesus as a divine being, after having lived on familiar terms with Him for three years? But this conviction formed itself in him only gradually. And precisely this familiar acquaintance of every day took away from it whatever overpowering element it might have had for dogmatic reflection. The Apocalypse, that work which, in the so-called critical school, is generally ascribed to the apostle, raises exactly the same problem. Jesus is there represented as *the first* and *the last;* He is called *the Holy One* and *the True*, just as Isaiah calls Jehovah; and yet it is ascribed to the apostle. The recognition of the Messianic dignity of Jesus was a first step, which rendered the transition easier to the recognition of His divinity.

Having reached the end of this long review of all the objections raised by modern criticism against the unanimous tradition of the Church, we may be permitted to bring forward a curious phenomenon which is not without psychological importance in the estimate of this discussion. Is it

---

[1] That we may not prolong this discussion, let us defer until the following section what we have to say respecting the beginning of the first Epistle of John (1 John i. 1–4).

not surprising that every adversary of the authenticity seems to be especially impressed by some one among these fourteen objections, which makes only a feeble impression on the rest of the critics, and in comparison with which he himself attributes to all the others only a slight importance? We leave to the reader the work of explaining this fact, which has more than once given us food for thought.

3. THE INTERNAL EVIDENCE

In his introduction to the New Testament (§ 93), Credner has summed up this evidence in the following manner: "If we had no historical statement respecting the author of the fourth Gospel, we should, nevertheless, be led to a positive result by the indications which the book itself affords. The nature of the language, the freshness and dramatic vivacity of the narrative, the exactness and precision of the statements, the peculiar manner in which the forerunner and the sons of Zebedee are mentioned, the love, the passionate tenderness, of the author for the person of Jesus, the irresistible charm diffused over the evangelical history as presented from this ideal point of view, the philosophical reflections with which this Gospel begins,—all this leads us to the following result: The author of this work can only be a man born in Palestine, only an eye-witness of the ministry of Jesus, only an apostle, only the beloved apostle; he can only be that John whom Jesus had bound to His own person by the heavenly charm of His teaching, that John who leaned upon His bosom, who stood near the cross, and who, during his residence in a city such as Ephesus was, not only felt himself attracted by philosophical speculation, but even prepared himself to hold his place among these Greeks who were distinguished for their literary culture."

We cannot do better than follow the course traced out in this admirable paragraph, in which we would only desire to change the two terms, *ideal* and *philosophical*, which seem to us not to give the true shade of thought. Taking this summary as a programme, we shall also make our beginning from the circumference, so as gradually to approach towards the centre.

I. The author is a Christian of *Jewish* origin.

This is proved by his style which, without Hebraizing, nevertheless, has the inward peculiarities of the Hebrew language (see p. 135 f.).

This follows also from the corrections which the author makes the translation of the LXX. undergo in accordance with the original Hebrew in a certain number of quotations. We believe, with Westcott[1], that the fact is beyond dispute in the three passages which follow: vi. 45 (Is. liv. 13); xiii. 18 (Ps. xli. 9); xix. 37 (Zech. xii. 10); and we will add, without hesitation, xii. 40 (Is. vi. 10). In no single instance, on the contrary, does the evangelist quote according to the LXX. in disagreement with the Hebrew.

The inner harmony of the teaching of Jesus with the Mosaic Law and the prophets, His constant references to the types of the Jewish history,

---

[1] *The Holy Bible*, St. John, p. xiv.

198 / The Origin

the perfect communion of spirit established between Abraham and Jesus, —all these features are brought out so forcibly that we must subscribe to Weizsäcker's judgment: Only a Jew who, in the foreign region where he was living, had preserved *the inheritance of his youth*, could relate his history in this way. The development of the author's personal faith has certainly passed through these two normal phases of Jewish-Christian faith: the recognition of Jesus as the Messiah, and faith in Him as the Son of God. Compare, for the first of these two steps, the profession of faith of the first disciples, i. 42, 46, and for the second, the whole sequel of the narrative. This course of development is again suggested in the expression which sums up the Gospel (xx. 31): "That ye may believe that Jesus is *the Christ, the Son of God.*"

A final and entirely decisive proof appears from the acquaintance which the author shows with Jewish usages. He is perfectly acquainted with the Jewish feasts (the Passover, the Feast of Tabernacles), and not only the greater ones, but also the minor ones, which the law had not instituted,—as the feast of *Purim*, v. 1 (see the Commentary), and that of the *Dedication*, x. 22. He knows of the addition of an eighth day to the Feast of Tabernacles (vii. 37) and the prohibition of all medical treatment on the Sabbath (ix. 14); the Jewish opinions, according to which the coming of the Messiah must be preceded by that of Elijah, and the Messiah must spring from an entirely obscure origin (i. 21; vii. 27). He is not ignorant either of the hostility prevailing between the Jews and the Samaritans, or of the more spiritual character of the Messianic expectation among the latter (iv. 9, 25, 26). The Jewish manner of embalming bodies, different from that of the Egyptians (xix. 40), the custom on the part of the Jews of purifying themselves on entering their dwellings (ii. 6), the synagogal excommunication (ix. 22), the custom of closing the sepulchral caves with great stones (xi. 38; xx. i.), the sale of animals and the money exchange established in the temple (ii. 14),—all these circumstances, several of which are not mentioned in the Synoptics, are familiar to him. He is acquainted with the scruples which the Jews feel, both as to entering into the house of a Gentile, and as to leaving the bodies of condemned persons publicly exposed beyond the very day of execution (xviii. 28; xix. 31). He knows that a Rabbi does not engage in conversation with a woman (iv. 27); that the religious leaders of the nation treat with the most profound disdain the portion of the people who have not received the Rabbinical teaching (vii. 49); and finally, that, in case of a conflict between the law of the Sabbath and that of circumcision on the eighth day, the latter takes precedence of the former (vii. 22, 23).

II. This Jew did not live in a foreign land; he is a *Palestinian* Jew.

He speaks of different places in the Holy Land as a man who is acquainted with them for himself and to whom all the topographical details of that country are familiar. He knows that there are other places of the name of Cana and Bethsaida than those of which he is speaking, and which he marks by the epithet: *of Galilee* (ii. 1; xii. 21). He knows that Bethany is fifteen furlongs from Jerusalem (xi. 18); that Ephraim is situated on the borders of the desert (xi. 54); that Ænon is near to Salim (iii. 23); that a distance of twenty-five or thirty furlongs is nearly equal to one-half of the breadth of the sea of Tiberias (vi. 19, comp. with Matt. xiv. 24); that the circuit of the northern shore of this sea can be easily made on foot (vi. 5, 22); that in order to go from Cana to Capernaum, one must *go down* (ii. 12); that Cedron must be crossed by a bridge in order to go from Jerusalem to the foot of the Mount of Olives (xviii. 1); that the pool of Siloam is very near to Jerusalem (ix. 7); and that there are intermittent springs in the neighborhood of the temple (v. 7). He also knows the place in the temple where the boxes designed to receive the offerings are found (viii. 20), and Solomon's porch (x. 23). The picture of the entrance to the valley of Sichem, in the scene of Jacob's well, can only have been traced by a man who had looked upon Mount Gerizim towering above the valley, and the magnificent fields of wheat which stretched to the right of the plain of Mukhna. Renan declares: "A Jew of Palestine, who had often passed through the entrance of the valley of Sichem, could alone have written this."

The author is no less well-informed as to the *historical circumstances* of the epoch in which the facts which he describes occur. He knows that the right of putting to death has been recently taken away from the Jews (xviii. 31); he knows that, at the moment when Jesus appears for the first time in the temple, the work of the reconstruction of that edifice has already continued for forty-six years (ii. 20). He is thoroughly acquainted with the relations of family and sympathy which unite the present high-priest with the former high-priest, and the influence which the latter continues to exercise upon the course of affairs (xviii. 13–28).

Baur believed that he had discovered in our Gospel a multitude of historical and geographical errors. This accusation is abandoned at the present day. "There is no reason," says Keim himself, "to believe in these alleged errors" (p. 133). Renan abounds in his expressions of this view: "The too often repeated opinion that our author was neither acquainted with Jerusalem nor with Jewish matters, seems to me altogether destitute of foundation" (p. 522).[1]

III. We can prove by a mass of details that this Palestinian Jew was a *contemporary* of Jesus and a *witness* of His history; let us even add, in order that we may not enter too much into detail and prolong the discussion too far, *an apostle*.

This appears from the mass of minute details, abounding in the narrative, which it is impossible to explain by a dogmatic or a philosophical idea, and which can only be the quite simple and almost involuntary expression of personal recollection.

And, first, with reference to times and occasions: "It was about the tenth hour" (i. 40); "It was about the sixth hour" (iv. 6); "And he abode there two days" (iv. 40); "Yesterday, at the seventh hour" (iv. 52); "It

---

[1] See, on the alleged mistakes imputed by Baur to the evangelist, this Commentary, at the following passages: i. 28 (*Bethany*); iii. 23 (*Ænon*); iv. 5 (*Sychar*); xviii. 1 (*Cedron*); vii. 52; xi. 49, etc.

was winter," or "It was stormy weather" (x. 22); "It was night" (xiii. 30); "In infirmity for thirty-eight years" (v. 5). As to the designation of places: the treasury of the temple (viii. 20); Solomon's porch (x. 23); Jesus stopped outside of the village (xi. 30). As to numbers: the six water-pots in the vestibule (ii. 6); the four soldiers (xix. 23); the hundred pounds of perfume (xix. 39); the two hundred cubits of distance, and the one hundred and fifty-three fishes (xxi. 8, 11). We are introduced by all sorts of details into the inmost circle of Jesus and His disciples. The author recalls the relations full of pleasantness, which Jesus sustained towards them—towards Philip, for example (vi. 5–7); the intervention of Andrew (vv. 8, 9); the small boy having the loaves; the indirect warning given to Judas (ver. 70); the name of the father of this apostle (ver. 71); the rough, but generous declaration of Thomas (xi. 16); his incredulous exclamation and his cry of adoration (xx. 25, 28); the questions of Thomas, Philip, and Judas, on the last evening (chap. xiv.); the decisive moment when the light finally came to them all, and when they proclaimed their faith (xvi. 30); the sudden invitation of Jesus: "Arise, let us go hence" (xiv. 31). Points such as these may also be noticed: "They had kindled a fire of coals . . . " (xviii. 18); "The robe was without seam, woven from the top throughout" (xix. 23); "Having put the sponge around the hyssop-stalk" (xix. 29); "The servant's name was Malchus" (xviii. 10), etc., etc. "So many precise details," says Renan, "which are perfectly understood if one sees in them the recollections of an old man of a wonderful freshness;" but, we will add, which become repulsive, in so serious a narrative, if they are only fictitious details designed to conceal the romance-writer under the mask of the historian. Only a profane charlatan could thus trifle with the person and character of the best-known actors in the evangelical drama, and with the person of the Lord Himself. Weitzel has properly noticed how this delicate narrative initiates us into all the varied shades of the inmost life of the apostolic circle.[1] The author designates the disciples, not according to their names as generally received in the Church—the ones which they bear in the apostolic catalogues, but according to that which they bore among their fellow-disciples; thus, instead of Bartholomew, he says: Nathanael (i. 46–50; xxi. 2), and three times he designates Thomas by the Greek translation *Didymus* (twin), as if it were for him a matter of personal reminiscence, dear to his heart (xi. 16; xx. 24; xxi. 2).

To all these details, let us add the great scenes in which, as if openly, the pencil of the eye-witness shows itself: the story of the calling of the first disciples (chap. i.); of the visit to Samaria (iv.); of the confidential scenes at the resurrection of Lazarus and at the washing of the disciples' feet (xi. and xiii.); and finally, the incomparable picture of the negotiations of Pilate with the Jews (xviii. and xix.).

If, after all these facts, any doubts could remain for us with reference to the author's having the character of an eye-witness, they would fall away

---

[1] *Studien und Kritiken*, 1849.

before his own testimony, which no one at the present day—neither Weizsäcker nor Reuss and Sabatier,—can bring themselves to charge with imposture, as the school of Baur did.

This testimony is expressed in the three following passages: i. 14; xix. 35, and 1 Ep. i. 1–4.

The author expresses himself thus in i. 14; "And the Word became flesh and dwelt among us, and we beheld his glory. . . ." It is at present claimed that the question here is only of the interior sight of faith, which is the appanage of every Christian. Does not Paul say, "We behold the glory of the Lord with unveiled face" (2 Cor. iii. 18); and John himself: "Whosoever sinneth hath not seen him" (1 John iii. 6)? Thus speak Keim and Reuss. There is a spiritual beholding of Jesus, it is true, to which the quoted words refer; but these words are not found, in the epistles from which they are taken, in connection with the representation of the fact of the incarnation, as in the passage John i. 14: "The Word *became* flesh, . . . it *dwelt*, . . . and we *beheld*. . . ." At the beginning of an historical work, which commences thus, and in which the earthly life of Jesus is to be related, such a declaration cannot have any other intention than that of solemnly *legitimizing* the narrative which is to follow. We cannot confound such a context with that of an epistle in which the author describes the spiritual state common to all Christians.

The passage xix. 35 has already been examined. The identity of the author of the Gospel with the apostle who was witness of the crucifixion of Jesus, is there positively affirmed. "This passage," Sabatier objects, "is of too similar a tenor to that of the appendix (xxi. 24), for us not to draw from it the same conclusion." But we have already shown (p. 185) that the tenor of the two passages is, on the contrary, entirely different, in chap. xix : (*he knows*), the witness affirms his identity with the redactor of the Gospel; in chap. xxi.: (*we know*), the friends of the author and witness affirm his identity with the disciple whom Jesus loved; thus each affirms fundamentally the same thing, but in a manner apposite to his particular position and role.[1]

There exists a second work, coming evidently from the same pen as the Gospel, and whose author likewise declares himself a witness of the facts and an apostle, with a clearness which leaves nothing to be desired on the part of any one who does not wish to close his eyes to the light. We read, 1 Ep. of John i. 1 ff.: "That which was from the beginning, which we have heard, which we have seen with our eyes, which we have beheld and our hands have handled of the Word of life, . . . we declare it unto you, that you may have fellowship with us; . . . and we write unto you these things, that your joy may be fulfilled; and this is the message which we have heard from him and declare unto you. . . ." How can we deny, in the face of expressions like these, that the author had the intention of giving himself out as an eye and ear-witness of the facts of the Gospel

---

[1] The ten lines of Sabatier on this subject (*Encycl. des sc. relig.*, p. 193), are for me an inexplicable enigma and one which cannot be discussed.

history? Let any one tell us what more forcible terms he could have used in order to designate himself as such. Reuss says: "The fact that Jesus lived the life of mortals is enough to enable every believer to say: We have seen, heard, touched Him."[1] Yes, but on the condition that, in speaking thus, he does not place himself in express contrast to other believers who have neither seen nor heard nor touched, and to whom for this reason he says: "*We* declare *unto you*, . . . *we* write *to you* these things, to the end that you may have part in them, and that your joy may be as complete as ours." Reuss says: "Every preacher who hands over the truth to a new generation will constantly be able to express himself in the same way." We leave in his happy quietude the man who can bring himself into tranquillity by such a subterfuge. There is evidently here the same contrast as in John xx. 29, between those who *have seen* and those who must *believe without having seen*, or, as in xix. 35, between the one who *has seen* and *you* who are to *believe*. Sabatier has recourse to another expedient. He thinks he can explain these words by the author's desire, "not to give an historical testimony, but to combat Docetism." There is nothing more in these words therefore, he says, than "the positive affirmation of the reality of the flesh of Jesus Christ" (p. 193). But, if it were so, to what purpose the commencing with these words: That which was *from the beginning*, which are developed in the second verse by the following: "And *the life which was with the Father* was manifested, and we have seen it, and we bear witness of it?" We see that the thought of the author is not to contrast the reality of Jesus' body with the idea of a mere appearance, but to bring out these two facts which seemed contradictory, and the union of which was of vital importance to his view: on one side, the *divine*, eternal being of Christ; on the other, the perfect reality, not of His body only, but of His *human* existence. It is the same thought as that which is formulated in the expression which is the theme of the Gospel: "The Word was made flesh." Moreover, the Docetae did not deny the sensible appearances in the life of the Lord, and the apostle would not have accomplished anything in opposition to them by affirming these.

It remains incontrovertible, therefore, for every one who is determined to take the texts for what they are, and not to make them say what he wishes, that the author expressly gives himself out in two of these texts, and that he is given out in the third by his friends who know him personally, as the witness of the facts related in this book; and if one refuses to admit this double testimony, one cannot escape the necessity of making him an impostor. We are thankful to the modern writers who, like Reuss and Sabatier, shrink from such a consequence; but we believe that it is impossible to do so except by sacrificing the exegetical conscience.

IV. If we endeavor, finally, to designate this apostle, at once the witness and redactor of the evangelical facts, we are forced to recognize in him the disciple whom Jesus loved, John himself.

---

[1] *Théol. johan.*, p. 106.

And first: *The disciple whom Jesus loved.*

The author declares himself, xix. 35, to be the one who saw with his own eyes two prophecies fulfilled at the same time by the thrust of the heathen soldier's spear. Now, his narrative mentions only one apostle as present at the crucifixion of the Lord—the one whom Jesus loved (ver. 26). It is evident, therefore, that he gives himself out as that disciple. We have already noticed the description of the way in which the disciple whom Jesus loved reached the belief in the resurrection (xx. 8, 9). The absolutely autobiographical character of this story leaves no doubt as to the identity of this disciple with the author. The same is the case with the confidential and entirely personal details which are given respecting the relation of Peter to him at the last supper (xiii. 24–27), and of the story of his last conversation with Jesus following upon His appearance in Galilee (xxi. 19–22). Let us add that no one ought to have been more anxious than the disciple whom Jesus loved to set right the meaning of a saying which concerned him, and which was circulating in a form that was compromising to the dignity of Jesus.

We say further: *John, the son of Zebedee.*

In all the apostolic catalogues, John and James are named in the first place after Simon Peter, and this rank which is constantly assigned to them is justified by the peculiar distinctions which they shared with that apostle. How does it happen that in the fourth Gospel, in the single case in which the sons of Zebedee are mentioned (xxi. 2), they are placed last among the five apostles who are named, and thus after Thomas and Nathanael? This circumstance can be explained only if the author of this narrative is precisely one of these two brothers. In the Synoptics, the forerunner of Jesus is constantly called: John *the Baptist;* this was the title which had been conferred upon him not only by the Christian, but also by the Jewish tradition, as we see from Josephus (*Antiq.* xviii. 5. 2.): "John, *surnamed Baptist,* whom Herod had killed." In our Gospel, on the contrary, he is always called simply John. It must naturally be inferred from this fact, that the author of this narrative had learned to know the forerunner before fame had added to his name, as an inseparable epithet, the title of Baptist, consequently from the beginning of his public activity. Then, if we have reasons for holding that the author himself bore the name of John, we can the more easily understand how he did not feel the need of giving to the forerunner a title suited to distinguish him from some other John, not less known in the Church. For the idea of a confusion between him and the one who had the same name with him must have been, as Hase says, "entirely remote from his consciousness." Finally, there remains a decisive circumstance: it is the absence from the narrative of any mention both of the name of John himself, and of the names of the other members of his family. His mother, Salome, who is mentioned in the Synoptics among the women present at the crucifixion of Jesus (Matt. xxvii. 56; Mark xvi. 1) is not named here in the parallel enumeration (John xix. 25). No more is James mentioned in the scene of the calling of the first disciples (chap. i.), where, however, a slight touch full of delicacy betrays his presence.¹ This way of proceeding is absolutely different from that of forgers. "The latter," says Reuss, "make it their study to lay emphasis upon the names which are to serve them as a passport."² This complete and consistent omission, from one end of the work to the other, of the names of three personages who occupied one of the first places in the company that surrounded Jesus, does not permit us to doubt that the author was in a peculiar relation to all the three.

We cannot deny ourselves the pleasure of quoting here, in closing, a beautiful paragraph from Hase (p. 48): "While the Apostle John is nowhere named, there passes across the entire Gospel an unknown and, as it were, veiled figure, which sometimes comes forth, but without the veil ever being raised. We cannot believe that the author did not himself know who this disciple *whom Jesus loved* was, who at the last supper rested on His bosom, who with Peter followed his Master when made a prisoner, to whom his Master left His mother as a charge, and who, running with Peter, came first to the tomb. There must have existed, therefore, a peculiar relation between the author and this personage, and a reason, personal to himself, for his not naming him. Why is it not natural to think that he is himself designated by this circumlocution which included in itself the sublimest contents and the whole happiness of his existence?"

4. THE CONTRARY HYPOTHESES

We shall occupy ourselves here only with the hypotheses which have a serious character. We set aside, therefore, without discussion, fancies such as those of Tobler and Lützelberger, who ascribe our Gospel, the former to Apollos, and the latter to a Samaritan emigrant at Edessa in Mesopotamia, about 135. We meet, in the first place, "*the great unknown*" of Baur and his school, who is said to have written, a little before or after the middle of the second century, the romance of the Logos; the man whom Keim calls "the most brilliant flower which followed the age of the apostles." One thing strikes us, at the first glance, in this hypothesis: it is precisely this title of unknown which the critics are obliged to give to the author of such a work. Every one knows the mediocrity of the personages and writers of the second century, as compared with those of the first. To the epoch of creative production that of tame reproduction had succeeded. What is that Epistle of Clement of Rome, to which Eusebius adjudges the epithets *great and wonderful* (ἐπιστολὴ μεγάλη τε καὶ θαυμασία)? A good, pious letter, such as an ordinary Christian of our day would write. Polycarp and Papias are in no way superior to Clement. Ignatius surpasses them in originality; but what strangeness and what eccentricity! Hermas is of the most oppressive dullness. The Epistle to Diognetus shows a certain superiority in a literary point of view; but as to the thoughts, and even as to what it has of a striking character in the expo-

---

¹ Chap. i. 42: "Andrew *first* finds *his own* brother Simon." This strange form is only explicable by the understood idea that the other disciple, also himself, sought his brother, but found him only at a later moment.
² *Théol. johannique*, p. 100.

sition of them, it rests absolutely on the epistles of Paul and the fourth Gospel. If what is borrowed from these writings is taken away from it, it falls back into the general mediocrity. And yet in the midst of this period of feebleness there rises a unique man, whose writings have so original a character that they form a class wholly by itself in the entire body of Christian and human literature; this man does not live as a hermit; he takes, according to Baur, an active part in the conflicts of his time; he pronounces the word of pacification respecting all the questions which disturb it; in an incomparable work, he lays the foundation of the Christianity and of the wisdom of future ages,—and this man, this "flower of his age" no one has seen blooming; the Church, the witness of his life and work, has forgotten even the trace of his existence. No one can tell where this extraordinary star rose and set. In very truth, a strange history! The critics say, it is true: "Are not also the author of the book of Job, and the author of the Epistle to the Hebrews "great unknown" persons? We answer: The remote antiquity from which the first of these works comes, remains for us buried in profound darkness; what a difference from that second century of the Church, respecting which we possess so many and so detailed points of information! The Epistle to the Hebrews is only a simple theological treatise, an important and original writing, no doubt; but what a difference as compared with a work containing a history, in many respects new, of Jesus, that chief of all subjects to the view of the Church! The author of the one is lost in the splendors of the apostolic period; while the author of the other ought to shine as a star of the first magnitude in the badly-lighted sky of the second century.

Let us add that at that epoch, when the image of Jesus was fixed by means of three universally disseminated narratives which were already distinguished from every other writing of the same kind, a pseudo-John would have carefully guarded himself against compromising the success of his fraud, by deviating from the generally received history of Jesus. Renan rightly says: "A forger, writing about the year 120 or 130 [how much more in the period from 130–160!] a gospel of imagination, would have contented himself with treating the received story after his own fancy, as the apocryphal gospels do, and would not have overturned from the foundation what were regarded as the essential lines of Jesus' life."[1] Or, as Weizsäcker also observes, "He who could have written this Gospel in order to introduce into the Church certain ideas, would never have ventured to invent an historical basis so different from that which the prevailing traditions presented."[2] The author who, with a sovereign and magisterial authority, has modified, rectified, completed the Synoptical narration, cannot have been a mere unknown person; he must have felt

---

[1] *Vie de Jésus*, 13th ed., pp. lxxv.-lxxvi.
[2] *Jahrb. für deutsche Theologie*, 1859, p. 698.—Reuss says, in the same line: "Is it to be believed that a forger, if he had desired to pass for one of the first disciples, would have dared to deviate so many times from the Synoptical narratives with respect to generally known facts, at the risk of immediately seeing his own charged with errors and falsehoods?" The fact here indicated is so manifest that de Wette himself was already struck by it: "A definitive critical judgment which

himself to be *recognized* as a master on this ground, and assured of finding credence for his narrative in the bosom of the Church.

Hase also justly calls attention to the point, that a writer removed from the facts and desirous of offering to the men of his time a picture of the person of the Logos, would not have failed, in this fictitious image, to reduce the human element to a minimum and to trace the absolutely marvelous history of a God, according to him only a mere earthly *form;* while the fourth Gospel presents to us precisely the opposite phenomenon: "Everywhere in Jesus the most complete and tender humanity; everywhere, under the golden breastplate of the Logos, the beating of the heart of a true man, whether in joy or in grief."[1]

Hilgenfeld thinks that the unknown author, in composing such a work, wished to bring back the churches of Asia from the Judaizing Christianity of the Apostle John to the pure spiritualism of St. Paul, which was originally established in those churches. Ordinarily, the course of forgers is justified by saying, that they make the alleged author speak as they think that he would have spoken in the circumstances in which they are themselves living. It is in this way that Keim also excuses the pseudo-John: "Our author has written in the just conviction that John would have written precisely so, if he were still living at his time." Let our two critics put themselves in accord, if they can! According to the second, the author aims at continuing the Johannean work in Asia; according to the first, he labors to overthrow it, and that by borrowing the mask of John himself! This second degree of pious fraud draws very near to impious fraud.

The expedient of pious fraud has been singularly abused in these last times, as if this device had been allowed without reluctance by the conscience of the Church itself. That it was frequently made use of, the facts indisputably prove; but that the Church ever gave its assent to it, the facts quite as positively deny. It was in vain for the author of the well-known book: *The Acts of Paul and Thecla,* to allege that he had composed that little story with a good intention and out of love for the Apostle Paul (*id se amore Pauli fecisse*); he was nevertheless obliged, after having confessed his faults, to give up his office of presbyter (*convictum atque confessum loco decessisse*). Here is what took place, according to the report of Tertullian, in a church of Asia Minor, in the second century.[2] And yet the question in the case of that writing was only of a harmless anecdote of which Paul was the hero, while, in the case of the fourth Gespel, the romance would be nothing less than a fictitious history of the person of the Lord!

This mysterious X of the Tübingen criticism is in truth only an *imag-*

---

denies to John any participation in this work, has against it not only the odiousness of the supposition of a forger, but also the improbability that Christian antiquity would have accepted a Gospel which deviated from the evangelical tradition respecting points which were so important, without feeling itself assured and quieted by its apostolic authority."
—*Einl.,* § 110 g.

[1] *Gesch. Jesu,* p. 47.
[2] Tertullian, *de baptismo.*

inary quantity. As soon as we place ourselves in the presence of the world of realities, we understand that this great unknown is no other than a great *unrecognized* one, John himself.

It was necessary, therefore, to make trial of a name. Nicolas has proposed *the presbyter John,* and it is for this personage that Renan seems disposed, at present, to decide.[1] But this hypothesis raises difficulties of no less magnitude than the preceding one. First of all, it cannot be supposed that such a man, an immediate disciple of Jesus and contemporary of John, would have tried to make himself pass for that apostle, by expressing himself as he makes the author do in the passage xix. 35. Moreover, with what other intention than that of disguising himself, could he have effaced so carefully from his narrative the names of this apostle, of his brother and his mother? Can such a role be attributed to the aged disciple of the Lord? Finally, this pious presbyter can only have been a man of the second rank. Papias, in the enumeration of his authorities, assigns to him the last place, even after Aristion. Polycrates, in his letter to Victor, in which he recalls to mind all the eminent men who had made the Church of Asia illustrious, the apostles Philip and John, Polycarp of Smyrna, Thrasias of Eumenia, Sagaris of Laodicea, Melito of Sardis, makes no mention of this personage. "We must therefore," says Sabatier rightly (p. 195), "leave him in the shade and in the secondary rank where the documents set him before us. He is of no assistance for the solution of the Johannean question."

And what do Reuss, Sabatier, Weizsäcker and others do? They take refuge in a sort of chiaroscuro. Not being able to deny the exactness, the precision, the historical superiority of the information on which our Gospel rests, and, on the other side, being thoroughly determined not to acknowledge the authenticity of the discourses of Jesus, they revert to an anonymous author, and are satisfied with finding in him one of the members of the school of Ephesus, a *disciple of the apostle,* who has mingled the tradition emanating from him with Alexandrian wisdom. But can this demi-authenticity suffice? Is it not, first of all, contrary to the testimony of the author himself, who, as we have seen, declares himself, in his epistle, a personal witness of the facts, and, in the Gospel, a witness of the facts, and the disciple whom Jesus loved? Is it not contrary, furthermore, to the testimony of his colleagues, the other members of the same school, who attest with one accord, xxi. 24, that the witness redactor is no other than the disciple whom Jesus loved? The more we find ourselves forced to carry back the composition of this work even to the epoch of John himself, the more are we obliged to acknowledge the improbability of the supposition of a fraud. It must have been concerted and executed, not by an individual only, but by the whole community who surrounded John. This supposition, which has so little probability, is, moreover, irreconcilable with the admirable originality of the discourses of Jesus. In fact: either these discourses are the work of

---

[1] *L'Eglise chrétienne,* 1879.

the Apostle John, and, in that case, there is no longer any reason to contest the Johannean composition of all the rest of the work; or they are the work of an anonymous disciple of this apostle, and, in that case, it is necessary to apply here what Sabatier says with reference to the hypothesis of the presbyter John: that "the disciple remains infinitely greater than he who served him as a patron." And how can we apply with any probability to an Ephesian disciple of John all that multitude of details by which we have proved the *Jewish* origin, the *Palestinian* home, the characteristics of *contemporary* and *witness*, of the author of this Gospel narration. The master might indeed have handed over to a *disciple-redactor* the great lines of the narrative; but that multitude of particular and minute details which distinguish this representation from one end to the other, can only be explained if the redactor and the witness are one and the same person.

We conclude by saying, with B. Weiss, that every hypothesis which is opposed to the authenticity strikes against even greater difficulties than the traditional opinion. Keim proudly says: "Our age has set aside the judgment of the ages." But is the school of Baur "our age"? And were it so, no age is infallible. There is quite enough of one proclaimed infallibility in our days, without adding also one of the left to that of the right.

3

THE PLACE OF COMPOSITION

IF John is indeed the author of the Gospel, and if this apostle fulfilled the second part of his apostleship in Asia Minor, nothing is more probable than the fact of the composition of this Gospel at Ephesus. This is the unanimous tradition of the primitive Church (see pp. 38 ff.); and that region is certainly the one in which we can most easily picture to ourselves the rise of such a work. A mass of details prevent us from thinking that it was composed for Palestinian readers. To what purpose to translate for the ancient Jews Hebrew terms, such as *Rabbi*, *Messiah*, and *Siloam*, to mark the term *Bethesda* as a Hebrew name, and to explain Jewish usages (i. 39, 42; iv. 25; v. 2; ix. 7; ii. 6; xix. 40, etc.)? Other points naturally direct our thoughts towards a Greek country: first, the language; then the complacency with which the author points out certain facts in the ministry of Jesus which have reference to the Greeks, as that ironical question of the Jews: "Will he go to those who are dispersed among the Greeks?" (vii. 35), or the request of the Greeks who, shortly before the Passion, desired to converse with Jesus (xii. 20). It is in an Hellenic sphere that these recollections would have their complete appropriateness. But there were Greek churches elsewhere than in Asia Minor; so some scholars have thought of different countries: Wittichen, of Syria; Baur, of Egypt. Very well! even independently of the tradition, we think that there would still be cause for making our choice in favor of Asia Minor. This country, says Renan, "was at that time the theatre of a strange movement of syncretic philosophy; all the germs of Gnosticism existed there already." We easily understand from this fact the use of the term Logos, which alludes to the discussions which were probably raised in such a theological and religious centre. Is it not, moreover, in this country that the influence of the Johannean Gospel makes itself quite peculiarly felt during the whole course of the second century? And is not the heresy against which the first Epistle of John seems especially to be directed that of Cerinthus, who taught at Ephesus in the latest period of the apostle's life? Let us add, that it is to the churches of Asia Minor that the epistles of St. Paul are addressed, which treat the subject of the person of Christ from precisely the same point of view as the fourth Gospel; we mean the Epistles to the Colossians and the Ephesians. It was in these regions, no doubt, that human speculations tended to lower the dignity of Christ, and that the churches had the most need of being enlightened on this subject. These indications seem to us sufficient, and even decisive.

4

THE OCCASION AND AIM OF THE FOURTH GOSPEL

THE tradition is not as unanimous on this point, as on the preceding ones. The statements of the Fathers agree undoubtedly in declaring that, if John determined to write, it was solely at the instance of those who surrounded him. In the Muratorian Fragment, it is said that "John was exhorted to write by his fellow disciples and by the bishops." Clement of Alexandria, states that he did it "at the instigation of the leading men and under the inspiration of the Spirit."[1] Eusebius expresses himself thus: "The apostle, being urged, it is said, by his friends, wrote the things which the first evangelists had omitted."[2] Finally, Jerome, in his emphatic style, declares that "he was constrained by almost the whole body of the bishops of Asia, and by deputations from numerous churches, to write something more profound respecting the divinity of the Saviour and to soar upwards even to the Word of God."[3] This circumstance, attested in so many ways, is interesting in that it accords with what we know of the essentially receptive character, and the absence of outward initiative, which distinguished the Apostle John. But the foreign impulse which induced him to take up his pen must itself have been called forth by some external circumstance; and the following is that which naturally presents itself to the mind. John had for a long period taught by the living voice in those churches. When the Synoptics reached those regions, his hearers noticed and appreciated the differences which distinguished

---

[1] Προτραπέντα ὑπὸ τῶν γνωρίμων, πνεύματι θεοφορηθέντα (Eus. *H. E.* vi. 14).

[2] *H. E.* iii. 24.

[3] *Comment. in Matth.* iv. *De vir. illustr.* c. 9.

the accounts given by their apostle from these other narrations; and it was the impression produced by this discovery which, no doubt, occasioned the solicitations that were thereafter addressed to him. This explanation is confirmed by the testimony of Clement. " John, the last, seeing that the external things (*corporeal*) had been described in the Gospels (the Synoptics), at the instigation of the leading men . . . composed a *spiritual* Gospel." Eusebius also says that " when Matthew, Mark and Luke had each published his Gospel, these writings having come into the hands of all, and into John's hands, he approved them, . . . and that, being urged by his friends, he wrote . . ." (see above). These friends of John, who had induced him to write, were undoubtedly the depositaries of his book and those who took charge of its publication; and it was they also who, in acquitting themselves of this duty, furnished it with the postscript which has accompanied it throughout the whole world and has reached even to us (xxi. 24).

But what *aim* did the apostle especially propose to himself in acceding to this desire? Here the ancient and modern writers differ. The author of the Muratorian Fragment does not seem to admit any other intention in the evangelist than that of instructing and edifying the Church. John had, according to him, the office of *relating;* the other apostles present (Philip, Andrew?) that of *criticising*. These expressions imply a purely *historical* and *practical* aim.

If, however, the Synoptical Gospels were already in the hands both of the author and of the readers, it is impossible that the new narrative should not have been designed to *complete*, or in certain respects to correct the earlier narratives. Else, to what purpose draw up a new one? So several of the Fathers do not hesitate to set forth this second aim, which is closely connected with the first. Eusebius declares that the apostle wrote the things which were omitted by the first evangelists, and, quite specially, that he supplied the omission of that which Jesus had done at the beginning of His ministry; then he adds that " if Matthew and Luke have preserved for us the *genealogy* of Jesus according to the flesh (γενεαλογία), John has taken as his starting-point His divinity (θεολογία)." "This," he adds, " was the part which the Divine Spirit had reserved for him as the most excellent of all" (iii. 24). Clement of Alexandria gives a very elevated and altogether spiritual import to John's intention of completing the Synoptics: " As the corporeal things were described in the Gospels, he was solicited to write a spiritual Gospel," that is to say, a Gospel fitted to set forth, by means of the discourses of Jesus preserved in this narrative, the *spirit* of the facts which are related by the Synoptics.

To this *historico-didactic* aim some Fathers add the intention to combat different errors which were beginning to come to light at the close of the first century. This *polemical* aim Irenæus attributes, if not to the whole Gospel as is frequently said, at least to the prologue: " John, the Lord's disciple, wishing to root out the seed which was scattered abroad in the hearts of men by Cerinthus, and already before him by the Nicolaitans . . . , and to lay down in the Church the rule of truth, began thus" (iii.

11, 1). Jerome expresses himself almost in the same way: "As John was in Asia and the seed of the heretics, such as Cerinthus, Ebion and others who deny that Christ has come in the flesh, was already multiplying . . . , he replied to his brethren who solicited him, that he would write if all fasted and prayed to God with him, which was done. After which, the revelation by which he was filled broke forth in this prologue: In the beginning was the Word." (*Ibid.*) Some modern writers have laid hold upon these suppositions, or have added new ones to them. Erasmus, Grotius and Hengstenberg adhere to the idea of a polemic against *Cerinthus*. Lessing, de Wette and others think, with Jerome, that it is especially the Ebionites whom the author had in mind. Semler, Schneckenburger and Ebrard believe that he had the Docetae in view; Grotius, Storr and Ewald; *the disciples of John the Baptist.*

Finally, the modern school, rejecting with a sort of disdain the different aims which we have just indicated, and thinking to rise to a higher conception of our Gospel, ascribe to it a purely *speculative* aim.[1] Lessing had already declared that John had saved Christianity—which would, without him, have disappeared as a Jewish sect—by teaching a loftier conception of the person of Christ.[2] Whence had he drawn this new notion of the Christ? Lessing did not enter into an explanation as to this point, through prudence no doubt. Modern criticism has undertaken to give the explanation in his place. Lücke thinks that John proposed to himself to raise the simple faith of the Church, threatened by the double heresy of Ebionitism and Gnosticism, to the state of *Gnosis*, of higher knowledge. Reuss attributes to the author of this work no other aim than that of publishing his own "evangelical theology founded on the idea of the divinity of the Saviour" (p. 29). Hilgenfeld, as we have seen, maintains that pseudo-John wrote in order to raise again in Asia Minor the standard of Paulinism, which had been overthrown and supplanted by the Judaic-Christianity of John. According to Baur, everything is fictitious, except some Synoptical materials, in this work which was designed to solve all the burning questions of the second century, apparently without touching them. The author brings Gnosis into credit in the Church by introducing the theory of the Logos into it; he moderates the Montanist exaltation; he resolves the question of the Passover at the expense of the churches of Asia, but in a way favorable to the other churches; he reconciles the two parties—the Pauline and the Judaic-Christian; and finally succeeds in founding the one and universal Church after which Christianity aspired from its origin; he consummates the apostolic work.

Our task is to examine these various conceptions and to discern the portion of truth or of error which each one of them may contain.

Our Gospels propose to themselves—all four of them—a single aim, that of giving rise to faith and strengthening it, by presenting to it historically its supreme object, Jesus Christ. But each one does this in its own

---

[1] Keim: "The evangelist is truly much too great to pursue the historical aim."

[2] *Neue Hypothese über die vier Evangelisten*, Lachmann's ed., vol. xi.

way,—that is to say, each one presents this object to the Church under a different aspect. Matthew *demonstrates*, with a view to the Jews and by means of the agreement between the history and the prophecies. Luke *expounds*, by setting forth for the Gentiles the treasures of the universal divine grace. Mark *depicts*, by making the Wonderful One live again as the witnesses beheld Him. If John relates, it is no more than in the other cases, merely for the purpose of relating. Altogether like the others, he relates for the sake of strengthening the faith of the Church, first in the Messiahship, then in the divinity of Jesus. This is what he declares in the often-quoted passage xx. 30, 31, where he himself gives an explanation respecting the aim of his book : to show in Jesus the Messiah (*the Christ*) first, and then *the Son of God*, to the end that every one may find in Him eternal life.

This declaration indicates nothing else than that *historical* and *practical* aim, which the author of the Muratorian Fragment implicitly ascribes to our Gospel; and its contents are fully confirmed by the contents of the book itself. How, indeed, does the author set about this? He relates the history of the development of his own faith and that of the other apostles, from the day when the two disciples of John the Baptist recognized in Jesus *the Christ* (chap. i.), even to the day when Thomas worshiped Him as his Lord and *his God* (chap. xx.). Here are the starting-point and the goal. The narrative included between these two limits only leads from the one to the other; and this fact alone is sufficient to enlighten us with respect to its aim. John wishes to present anew for his readers the path which his own faith had gone over in the company of Jesus ; he wishes by the entire series of facts and teachings which have enlightened himself, to enlighten the Church ; he wishes to glorify in its view the divine object of faith by the same means by which Jesus was glorified to his own view: by beholding and hearing the Word made flesh. In expressing ourselves thus, we do nothing but paraphrase the words of John himself at the beginning of his first epistle (i. 1–4), and comment upon that expression : *in presence of his disciples*, in the passage of the Gospel where he explains himself respecting his aim (xx. 30).

But by reason of the very fact that the history traced by him was already set forth in three works which he possessed and which his readers possessed, he inevitably places himself in connection with those earlier narratives. And herein is the reason why he gives up relating the totality of the facts, as if his redaction were the first or the only one. In the declaration xx. 30, 31, he expressly reminds us of the fact that "Jesus did many other things in the presence of His disciples which are not written in this book." It is natural also, as a consequence, that where he finds in those narratives gaps which seem to him of some importance, he should seek to supply them, or that, if some facts do not seem to him to be presented in a full light, he should endeavor to make the true rays fall upon them. As we have said, John certainly did not write *for the purpose of completing*, but he often completed or corrected, in passing, and without *losing* sight of his aim : to display the earthly glory of the Son of God to the view of faith. It is thus that he omits the Galilean ministry, abundantly described by his predecessors, and devotes himself particularly to the visits to Jerusalem, where the glory of the Lord had shone forth in an indelible manner for his heart, in the struggle with the power of darkness concentrated in that place. This intention of completing the earlier narratives, whether from an historical point of view, as Eusebius thought, or in a more spiritual relation, as Clement of Alexandria declared, is therefore perfectly well-founded in fact; we mention it as a secondary aim and, to express it in a better way, as a means subservient to the principal aim. Reuss thinks that this combination of certain secondary aims with the principal one "only betrays the weakness of these hypotheses." But is there in existence a single historical work, which really pursues only one end, and which does not allow itself, occasionally, to work towards some secondary result? Thiers, surely, did not write the history of the Consulate and the Empire with the purpose of completing earlier narratives. But will he refuse, when occasion calls, to notice particularly the facts which his predecessors may have omitted, or to correct those which, according to him, have been presented inexactly or incompletely? It is not, then, as "slaves of the most vulgar patristic tradition" that we maintain, as Reuss says, "so sorry a thesis."[1] It is because of the facts, the undeniable facts, respecting which Reuss himself, in his last work, has found himself at length compelled to open his eyes,[2] that we continue to maintain this view.

We persist even in a third opinion, no less opposed to the view of this critic. We maintain the truth, within certain limits, of the *polemic* aim attributed to our Gospel by several Fathers, and by a considerable number of modern scholars. The first epistle of John incontrovertibly proves that the author of our Gospel lived in a region in which many false doctrines had already arisen in the bosom of the Church. We are perfectly in accord with Keim and many others in recognizing that the principal heresy combated in this epistle was that of *Cerinthus*, known by the Fathers as the adversary of John at Ephesus. He taught that the true Christ, the Son of God, was not that poor Jew, the son of Joseph, called Jesus, who had died on the cross, but a celestial being who descended upon Him at His Baptism, who took Him temporarily as an organ, but who left Him to return to heaven before the Passion. Nothing gives a better account, than this teaching, of the polemic of 1 John ii. 22 : " Who is a liar, but he that denieth that Jesus is the Christ?" Comp. also iv. 1–3. Now, can it be denied that the central word of our Gospel: "The Word became flesh" cuts short this error by affirming, together with the fact of the incarnation, the organic and permanent union of divinity and humanity in the person of Jesus Christ? This same expression set aside, on the one hand, the ordinary heresy of the *Ebionites*, who, without falling into the subtleties of Cerinthus, simply denied the divinity of Christ, and, on the other, the *Gnostic* error, perhaps existing already in some, of

---

[1] *Hist. de la théol. chrétienne*, II. p. 312.   [2] See the note quoted, p. 75.

a divine Christ who had assumed nothing of humanity but the appearance. John thus placed a rock in the midst of the Church against which the waves of the most opposite false doctrines would have to break. This was an indirect polemic, the only one which was in harmony with an historical work, but one to which the more direct polemic of the epistle gave completeness and precise definition.

This epistle of John also does not allow us to deny, in certain passages of the Gospel, the intention to repel the claims of the disciples of John the Baptist, who from the first were ranked among the adversaries of the Lord. Where the apostle says, 1 Ep. v. 6: "This is He that came by water and blood, *even* Jesus Christ; not by water only, but by water and blood," is it not beyond dispute that he means to set aside the pretended Messiahship of John the Baptist, whom his disciples announced as the Christ, though he had offered to the world only the symbolic purification of the baptism of water, and not the real purification through the expiatory blood? If from this evidently polemical passage we come back to the declarations of the Gospel: "He [John] was not the light; but he came to bear witness to the light" (i. 8); "Who art thou?" "And he confessed and denied not, but confessed: I am not the Christ" (i. 19, 20); "And his disciples came to him and said unto him: Behold, He to whom thou hast borne witness, He baptizeth! . . . John answered: Ye are my witnesses that I said unto you: I am not the Christ" (iii. 26–28),—it will be necessary for us, nevertheless, to yield to the evidence and acknowledge that John had in view in these words and these stories early disciples of the forerunner who, impelled by jealous hatred of Christ and of the Gospel, went so far as to pronounce their old master to be the Messiah.[1]

The polemic aim, as a secondary aim, seems to us, therefore, to be justified by the facts. And what, indeed, could be more natural? When we establish a truth, especially a truth of the first importance, we establish it for itself, surely, and in consideration of its intrinsic importance; but not without desiring to set aside, at the same time, the errors which might supplant it or paralyze its beneficent effects.

There is but one aim, among those which have been pointed out, which we find ourselves forced to exclude absolutely; it is—we repeat it to the great offence of Reuss—the *speculative* aim, the only one which this critic allows. Let us explain. In the opinion of Reuss and many others, the fourth Gospel is intended to cause a new theory to prevail in the Church respecting the person of Jesus, which the author had personally formed through identifying Christ with the divine Logos, with which he had become acquainted through the teaching of the Alexandrian philosophy. We have shown that the facts, when seriously inquired into, are not in

---

[1] Apollos (Acts xviii.) and the twelve disciples of John (Acts xix.) did not go as far as this, surely. But it is not only the fact related in John iii. 25 ff., which shows us the secret hatred of a part of John's disciples, towards Jesus; there are also facts reported by the Synoptics; comp. Matt. ix. 14 and the parallels, and perhaps even xi. 2 ff., since the disciples must, by their statements, have called forth that procedure on John's part.

accord with this view, which, moreover, contradicts the author's own declaration (xx. 30, 31). For in that passage he does not speak of his intention to elevate faith to the condition of speculative knowledge, but simply of his desire to strengthen faith itself by presenting to it its object, Jesus the Messiah and Son of God, in His fullness and conformably to all the signs by which He had caused His matchless glory to shine forth in His own presence and in that of His disciples. There is no place in such a programme for a Christ who is only the fruit of the metaphysical speculations of the evangelist. Moreover, faith is never, in our Gospel, anything else than the assimilation of the testimony (i. 7); and the testimony relates to an historical fact, not to an idea. We may easily picture to ourselves Thiers writing the history of Napoleon with the design of displaying the greatness of his hero; we may also picture him to ourselves as occasionally completing and correcting the narratives preceding his own, or as indirectly justifying the political and financial measures of the great Monarch, by alluding to false theories which were spread abroad respecting these questions. But what the historian certainly would never have done, would be to make use of the person of his hero as a mouthpiece for disseminating in the world any theory whatever which pertained to himself, and to attribute to him with this aim acts which he had not performed or discourses which he had never spoken.[1]

To the end of confirming the theological and speculative aim attributed by him to our Gospel, Reuss asks "if this is not the book which served as the foundation and starting point for the formulas of Nicæa and Chalcedon" (p. 33). I answer: No; for the subject of those formulas was not the texts of John. It was the fact itself of the incarnation, of the union of the divine and human in the person of Christ, respecting the mode of which an understanding was sought for. Now, this fact is not taught only in the fourth Gospel. It is taught, as we have seen, in the Epistles of St. Paul (Col. i., Phil. ii., 1 Cor. viii. and x., etc.), in the Epistle to the Hebrews (chaps. i. and ii.), in the Apocalypse, in the Synoptics themselves. The Johannean Gospel has discovered the expression which best sets forth the union of the divine and human in Christ; but that union itself forms the basis of all the writings of the New Testament. It was not, therefore, the fourth Gospel, it was the Christian fact, which constrained the Fathers of Nicæa and Chalcedon to search out formulas fitted to give an account of

---

[1] In my first edition (p. 140), I expressed myself as follows: "The only aim which is positively excluded by what we have just gathered from the author's declaration (xx. 30, 31), is the speculative or didactic aim, the design of satisfying the understanding by giving to Christian dogma a new development." Reuss quotes this statement, suppressing the words: "The intention of *satisfying the understanding*." Now it is precisely these omitted words which explained what I here understood by a *didactic* aim. It is very clear that in narrating John proposed to himself to *teach;* the sole question is whether this instructive narrative had as its aim to confirm faith, as he claims himself and as I claim also, or was made with a view to *satisfy the understanding*. To suppress these last words, is to render my thought unrecognizable and absurd. In my second edition, I had already, to avoid all that was equivocal, entirely suppressed in this sentence the term *didactic*, and said: "The only aim excluded . . ., is the philosophical or speculative aim." (p. 360).

this contrast, which makes the supreme grandeur of Christianity, at the same time that it is its greatest mystery.[1]

I take pleasure in closing the study of this subject with the following lines from B. Weiss, in which I find my own opinion fully expressed: "To set forth the glory of the divine Logos as he had beheld it in the earthly life of Jesus (i. 14), as it had more and more magnificently revealed itself in conflict with unbelieving and hostile Judaism, and as it had led receptive souls to a faith ever more firm, to a contemplation ever more blessed,—this is what the evangelist desires. This fundamental idea of the narrative is in no degree detrimental to its historical character, because it is derived from the facts themselves which had been a living experience to the author, and because he confines himself to the demonstration of their realization in the history."[2]

Soon after the destruction of Jerusalem, the Apostle John, freed from all duty to his own people, came to Asia Minor to settle there. There the magnificent plantations which were due to the labors of the Apostle Paul were flourishing. But the prophecy of that same apostle: "I know that after my departure grievous wolves shall enter in among you, not sparing the flock" (Acts xx. 29), began to be fulfilled. An apostolic hand was needed to direct these churches. Around Ephesus was spread out the fairest field of Christian labor. We have already said, with a great writer: "The centre of gravity of the Church was no longer in Jerusalem; it was not yet in Rome; it was in Ephesus." Moreover, this city was not only the great commercial entrepot between Asia and Europe, but also the centre of a rich and active intellectual exchange between the religious and philosophical movements of the Orient and occidental culture. It was the rendezvous of the orators of all schools, of the partisans of all systems.

On such a theatre the Palestinian apostle must have grown daily, not, doubtless, in the knowledge of the person and work of Jesus, but in the understanding of the manifold relations, sympathetic or hostile, between the Gospel and the different tendencies of human philosophy. Those Christian populations to which St. Paul had opened the way of salvation by instructing them with respect to the contrast between the state of sin and the state of grace, and by showing them the means of passing from the one to the other, John now introduced into the full knowledge of the

---

[1] We do not return here to the aims set forth by Baur and Hilgenfeld. We think that the remarks, pp. 205 ff., may be sufficient.

[2] *Introduction to the Commentary on the Gospel of John*, p. 41. Among the recent hypotheses, we will further indicate, as an especially curious specimen, the system set forth by Noack in his work: *Aus der Jordan-Wiege nach Golgotha*, 1870: Jesus, the son of Mary and a Samaritan soldier, even in consequence of this dishonorable birth, came to regard God as his father. He lived in a continual state of ecstasy which he maintained by factitious means,—fasting, for example. After having kept himself at this artificial elevation, when he was no longer able to continue thus he sought death, and the one who aided him in the realization of this desire, and became accessory to this last act of his life was—Judas. He was *the disciple whom Jesus loved;* he was the author of the fourth Gospel, which was afterwards changed, but whose primitive sense Noack has re-established. Jesus died on Gerizim whither he had retired with his seven disciples, and where, by the aid of Judas, he fell into the hands of his enemies and was set free from life.

person of the Saviour Himself; he spread out before their eyes a great number of striking facts which, for one reason or another, tradition had left in obscurity, and many sublime teachings which had been deeply engraved on his heart, and which he alone had preserved; he described the relations, full of love and condescension, which the Lord had sustained towards His own friends, and the proofs which He had given them, in their intimate association, of His divine greatness and His filial relation to the Father. All these elements of the knowledge of Christ, which he brought with him, gain a new value through the connection in which they were placed, in such a region, with the speculations of all sorts which were there current.

The day came, after many years no doubt, when the churches said to themselves that the apostle, who was the depositary of such treasures, would not live always, and did not belong to them alone; and, measuring the distance between the teaching which they had enjoyed and that which they found recorded in the existing Gospels, they requested John to commit to writing what he had related to them. He consented, and he opened his work with a preamble in which, putting his narrative in connection with the efforts of human wisdom of which he was daily a witness, he fixed with a firm hand the central fact of the evangelical history, the incarnation, and reminded every reader of the vital importance of the history which he was about to read: The Christ, the subject of this narrative, would be for him *life*—as for the disciples—if he received Him; *death* —as for the Jews—if he rejected Him (John i. 1–18).

At a later time, the *first Epistle* of the same apostle proceeded from his apostolic working in the same churches, in which writing he addresses himself as a father to mature man, to young men and to children, and in which he makes allusion in the very first lines to the testimony which he bears unceasingly among them respecting that great fact of the incarnation which he has, as it were, *seen with his eyes* and *handled with his hands*. Some have been disposed to find in ver. 4: "And we write unto you" (comp. ii. 14, 21, 26, etc.), an allusion to the composition and sending of the Gospel. We do not think that we are authorized by the context to apply these expressions to any other work than the epistle itself.

The *two small epistles* were issued in the same surroundings. They seem to us, indeed, to belong to the same author. Independently of the identity of style, what other person than John could have designated himself simply by this title: *The Elder* (ὁ πρεσβύτερος), without adding to it his name? An official presbyter of the Church of Ephesus could not have done this, since he had colleagues, elders as well as himself; and if this word is taken here in the sense which it has in the fragment of Papias: *an immediate disciple of the Lord*, no other than the Apostle John could appropriate to himself this name in so absolute a way and as an exclusive title.

Finally, it was no doubt still later, during a temporary exile and under the impression of the recent persecution by Domitian, that John composed his last work: the *Apocalypse*, in which, beholding, as if from the summit of a mountain, the century which had passed away and those which were to follow, he completes the idea of the Christ *come* by that of the Christ *coming again*, and prepares the Church for the prolonged conflicts and for the final crisis which are to precede His return.[1]

One fact is fitted to excite the reflection of thinking men. St. Paul, the founder of the churches of Asia Minor, cannot fail to have left his type of doctrine deeply impressed on the life of those churches. And yet the Pauline imprint is, as it were, effaced in all the theological literature of Asia Minor in the second century. And this disappearance is by no means the effect of a weakening, of a decay : there is a substitution. There is the appearance of a new imprint, of equal dignity at least with that which preceded it,—the trace of another influence no less Christian, but of a different character. Another equally powerful personality has passed that way, and given a peculiar and altogether new stamp to the Christian life and thought of those countries. This phenomenon is the more remarkable, since the history of the Church of the West presents an entirely opposite one. Here the Pauline type continues; it reigns without a rival even to the third and fourth centuries; it is found anew at every moment in the conflicts of a purely anthropological character which agitate this portion of the Church. And when it is gradually effaced, it is not in order to give place to another quite as elevated, quite as spiritual, but it is by a way of gradual enfeeblement and a process of growing materialization and ritualism.

This grand fact ought to be sufficient to prove that the two Johannean books, which are the documents of the new type impressed on the churches of Asia—the fourth Gospel and the first Epistle—are not the works of a Christian of second rank, of some unknown disciple, but that they proceed from one of the *peers* of the apostle to the Gentiles, from one of those disciples who had drunk from the first source, from an immediate and peculiarly intimate heir of Christ.

We well understand what stays a certain number of excellent minds, at the moment of closing in the tribunal of their own consciousness the acts of this great process by a decision favorable to the apostolic origin of our Gospel. They are afraid that, by recognizing in Christ the appearance of a divine being, they will lose from Him the true man. This anxiety will vanish away as soon as they shall have substituted for the traditional notion of the incarnation the true Biblical notion of that supreme fact. From the truly Scriptural point of view, indeed, there are not in Christ two opposite and contradictory modes of being, which move together side by side in one and the same person. What the apostles show us in Him is a human mode of existence *substituted*, by the voluntary humiliation of the Saviour of men, for His divine mode of existence,—then transformed, by a holy and normal development, in such a way as to be able to serve as an organ for the divine life and to realize the original glory of the Son of God. And let us not forget that this transformation of our human existence into a

---

[1] See, for the reasons which do not allow us to place the writing of the Apocalypse earlier than this, my *Etudes bibliques*, 3d ed., vol. II., pp. 325-330.

glorified humanity is not accomplished in Christ alone; it is accomplished in Him only to the end of its realization through Him in all those who unite themselves to Him by faith: "To all who received Him gave he the power to become children of God, even to those who believe on His name; and [indeed] the Word became flesh" (i. 13, 14). If the Son for a time abandons the divine condition in order to descend into our human mode of being, it is to impel us to that upward movement which, from the day of His incarnation, He impresses, even in His own person, upon the history of humanity, which He communicates, from the day of Pentecost, to all believers, and the end of which is to be: *God all in all*, as its starting-point was: *God all in one*.

The domain of *being* passes infinitely beyond that of thought—not of absolute thought, but of ours. Do we not see, even in our human life which is so limited, the inspirations of love outrunning infinitely the calculations of the understanding? How much more when the question is of the inspirations of the divine love as related to the thoughts of the human mind.

To accept the living gift of eternal love by letting it descend through faith into the sphere of human life, is to accomplish three equally salutary things. It is to dethrone man in his own heart; for the Son of God, by voluntarily humbling Himself, impels us to the sacrifice of self (Phil. ii. 5 ff.). It is to open heaven to him; for such a gift is an indissoluble bond between the heart of God and that of every man who accepts it. It is to make the believer the eternal dwelling-place of God; for Christ in him is God in him. By this means, God reigns.

But suppress this gift by refusing or lessening it,—and this is the end for which those are laboring who make the fourth Gospel a theological treatise instead of a history,—the human sphere shuts in again upon itself; immediately man raises himself erect; he feeds no longer upon anything except himself; God withdraws. Man assumes the throne and reigns here on earth.

The thought of the gift of the only-begotten Son is not the fruit of human speculation; it bears in itself the seal of its divine origin. God alone can have had this thought, because God alone can love thus.

Let us enter now, with this certainty, upon the study of the pages in which this great fact of the divine love has been distinctly revealed on earth; and may those pages themselves speak with a louder voice than any pleader, and the moment come when they shall no more need an advocate!

INTRODUCTION
TO THE COMMENTARY

AFTER the General Introduction contained in the first part of this volume, it only remains for us, in the Special Introduction to the Commentary, to treat of the *plan* of the Gospel and of the most important *documents* in which the text of this writing has been preserved to us.

1

THE PLAN OF THE GOSPEL

THERE is a marked difference between the exegesis of the Fathers and modern works on the Gospel of John. With the former the thought of a plan, of a systematic arrangement, seems almost to have no existence, so completely is the historical character of the story assumed. The narrative is regarded as the simple reproduction of the history. It is no longer so in the modern conception. The agency of a governing idea is made to appear in the story. According to the view of which Baur's work is still the most remarkable expression, the *idea* plays even so decisive a part in this evangelical composition, that it not only determines its arrangement, but furnishes the substance of the story so far that, according to this critic, fact, as such, is almost annihilated, and that the allegorical exposition, the name of which until now recalled the worst days of exegesis, is again become the true method of interpretation. The fourth Gospel, a thoroughly systematic work, is as independent of real history as the Ethics of Spinoza can be of sensible reality.

This reversal of the point of view has been brought about gradually. The works of Lampe, de Wette, Schweizer and Baur seem to me to be the noteworthy points in this scientific elaboration.[1]

Lampe was the first, according to Lücke, to propose a general division of the Gospel. It was still very imperfect. Placed between a prologue

---

[1] For this exposition we are much indebted to the work of Luthardt, *Das Joh. Evang.* 2d ed., i. p. 200–222.

222 / Introduction

(i. 1–18) and an epilogue (xx. 30–xxi. 25), the narrative is subdivided into two parts: A. The public ministry of the Lord, i. 19–xii. 50. B. The last acts of His life, xiii. 1–xx. 29. Lampe had thus put his finger on one of the principal articulations of the Gospel. All those who, since his day, have effaced the line of division between ch. xii. and xiii. seem to me to have retrograded in the understanding of John's work.

Eichhorn made no change in this division. He merely designated the two principal parts of the narrative in a different way: 1. The first, i. 19–xii. 50, proves that Jesus is the promised *Messiah*; 2. The second, xiii.–xx., contains the account of the *last days* of His life. Here was no real improvement. What Eichhorn indicates as the contents of the first twelve chapters is really applicable only to the first four; and the subjects of the two parts, thus designated, are not logically co-ordinate with each other.

Before Eichhorn, Bengel[1] had attempted to found the division of the Gospel on another principle. After having ingeniously marked the correspondence between the initial week (i. 19–ii. 11) and the final week (xii. 1–xx. 31), he divided the intermediate history according to the journeys to the feasts: Passover, ii. 13; Pentecost (according to Bengel) v. 1; Tabernacles, vii. 2. But this arrangement evidently rests on a too external order of events; since it has the disadvantage of effacing the division, distinctly marked by the Evangelist himself and already pointed out by Lampe, between chs. xii. and xiii.

Bengel was, nevertheless, followed by Olshausen, who assumed, according to this principle of division, the following four parts; 1. i.–vi.; 2. vii.–xi.; 3. xii.–xvii.; 4. xviii.–xxi. Lücke himself, in his first two editions, despaired of reaching a more profound plan, and contented himself with endeavoring to improve the division which is founded on this principle.

De Wette, first of all, discerned and set forth the unfolding of a single idea in our Gospel. The *glory of Christ*,—such is, according to him, the central thought of the entire work: 1. The first chapter sets forth the idea in a summary way;—2. The first part of the narrative (ii.–xii.) exhibits it to us as translated into action in the ministry of Jesus, and that: A, by particular examples (ii.–vi.); B, by the preparation of the catastrophe during the last sojournings of Jesus in Judea (vii.–xii.);—3. The glory of the Lord manifests itself in all its splendor in the second part of the narrative (xiii.–xx.), and that: A, inwardly and morally, in His suf-

---

1. *Gnomon, N.T.*, 1742. Now reprinted as
  New Testament Word Studies, Kregel Publications, Grand Rapids, 1970.

ferings and death (xiii.–xix.); and B, outwardly and sensibly, by the triumphant fact of His resurrection (xx.).

This grand and beautiful conception, by means of which de Wette has certainly made an epoch in the understanding of our Gospel, governed exegesis for a certain period. Lücke yielded to its influence in his third edition; but he introduced into this plan a subdivision which must not be lost sight of. It is the separation between chs. iv. and v. Until ch. iv., indeed, the opposition to Jesus does not become distinctly noticeable. From ch. v., onward it is the governing element in the narrative, and goes on increasing up to ch. xii.

Baumgarten-Crusius, taking advantage of the conception of de Wette and of the subdivision introduced by Lücke, presented the following arrangement: 1. The works of Christ, i.–iv.; 2. His struggles, v.–xii.; 3. His moral victory, xiii.–xix.; 4. His final glory, xx. This was de Wette's idea, better formulated than it had been by de Wette himself. It was the first altogether rational division of the entire contents of our Gospel. Almost all the principal articulations of the narrative were established and pointed out: that between chs. iv. and v.; that between chs. xii. and xiii.; finally, that between xix. and xx.

This division, however, only took account of the divine and objective factor of the narrative, if we may so speak,—Christ and His manifestation. But there is another element in John's narration, the human, subjective factor—the conduct of men towards the Lord on occasion of His revelation, the faith of some and the unbelief of others.

Alexander Schweizer demanded a place for this human element in the arrangement of the narrative. He accorded to it even the decisive part, and this while especially laying emphasis on the side of unbelief. He adopted the following plan, which brings out precisely the leading articulations that we have just indicated. 1. The struggle makes itself known in the distance; i.–iv.; 2. It breaks forth in all its violence, v.–xii.; 3. The denouement, xiii.–xx. Understood in this way the Gospel becomes a drama, and assumes a tragic interest. But in the conduct of men towards the Lord, unbelief is only one side. Does not the element of faith remain too much in the background in this conception of Schweizer? The factor thus neglected could not fail to obtain its revenge.

Before coming to this point which was easy to be foreseen, we ought to mention some remarkable works which appear to us to connect themselves, if not historically, at least in principle, with the points of view already indicated. Like de Wette and Baumgarten-Crusius, Reuss makes the general arrangement of the Gospel rest upon the revelation of Christ.[1] He assumes three parts: 1. Jesus reveals Himself to *the world*, i.–xii.; (A) first, enrolling, i.–iv.; (B) then, selecting, v.–xii. 2. He reveals Himself to *His own*, xiii.–xvii., endeavoring to cause the speculative ideas, expressed in a dogmatic or polemical form in the first part, to penetrate their hearts, and to transmute these ideas into their inmost life. Up to this point the order is logical, and in this brief form of words are comprehended many of the ideas fitted to throw light upon the progress of the work of Christ in our Gospel. But here a difficulty presents itself, which arises from the general point of view at which Reuss takes his stand with regard to the work of John; the rational division is exhausted. There is no third term which can be logically placed beside the *world* and *the believers*. And yet the Gospel is not ended, and a place must be assigned to the three chapters which still remain. Reuss makes of them a third part, which he entitles: "The denouement of the two relations previously established;" xviii.–xx. It is difficult to understand how the narrative of the death and resurrection of Christ can undo the knot formed by the twofold relation of Jesus to the world and believers. Here is the reply of this author: "In that Jesus remains dead for the unbelievers, and rises victorious for the believers." If in a matter of this kind a clever phrase were sufficient, one might declare oneself satisfied. But can Reuss be so himself? Must he not perceive that this purely historical denouement is not consistent with a speculative Gospel, an *ideal* work such as *his* Gospel of John is? By this course we must reach the point of seeing in these last historical facts nothing but a religion or a system of ethics in action. And indeed how does Reuss close his analysis of the Gospel? By these words: "It is thus that the history, even to the end, is the mirror of religious truths." What! the events of the death and resurrection of the Saviour placed in the same rank with the metaphysics of John! But there remains no other way for Reuss to make of the Gospel a homogeneous whole, and logically to co-ordinate the third part with the two others. We see at what a price this higher conception must be purchased, according to which *the reflections of John* on the person of Christ form the substance of the fourth Gospel!

Ebrard returns to the plan of Bengel, and once more bases the order of our Gospel upon the feast-journeys. But he attaches a more profound meaning to this apparently quite external principle of division. He

---

[1] *Hist. de la Théol. chrét.*, 2d ed. t. ii., pp. 392–394. *Die Geschichte der heil Schr. N. T.*, 5th ed., 1874, § 221.

justly remarks that the journeys of Jesus to Judea are the natural turning points of the history, since, Jerusalem being the central point of opposition, each visit of Jesus to that capital, instead of being a step towards His glorious coming, became one towards the catastrophe. Nevertheless, we have already seen, and we shall see still further, the insufficiency of this division.

As de Wette had made everything rest upon the objective element, the manifestation of Jesus' glory, and as Schweizer had made especially conspicuous one of the two subjective factors, unbelief, it was natural that an interpreter should lay hold of the other, faith. This is what Baur has done. He sees in our Gospel the (ideal) history of the development of faith. Baur consecrated to this task the resources of a mind most sagacious and most fully determined not to recoil at the presence of any obstacle which the text presented to him; and he has thus powerfully contributed to demonstrate the unity of John's work. He divides the Gospel into nine sections, which, however, the prologue being set aside and certain secondary divisions passed without notice, can be reduced to five : 1. The first manifestations of the Word, and the first symptoms of faith and unbelief which resulted therefrom, i–vi.; 2. The (dialectic) victory of faith over its opposite, unbelief, vii.–xii.; 3. The positive development of faith, xiii.–xvii. Having reached this point, Baur meets the same difficulty as Reuss. How to pass from *idea* to history, from the dialectic development of faith to the positive facts of the death and resurrection of the Saviour? The idea demands nothing further. This is the way in which Baur continues; 4. The death of Jesus appears as the work of unbelief; 5. His resurrection, as the consummation of faith. Such is the meaning of xviii.–xx. But, from this author's point of view, this last part remains, nevertheless, a superfetation, as in the case of Reuss. The Passion and Resurrection are facts of too weighty a character to make it possible for them to have their place seriously assigned in the account of the dialectic development of faith, and to be made mere landmarks on the road which leads from the objection of Nathanael (ch. i.) to the cry of faith given by Thomas (ch. xx.). We must either idealize the fourth Gospel to its very end, or, by a retroactive conclusion, starting from the truly historical character of the last part, must recognize also that of the preceding parts.[1]

---

[1] We may see here the difficulty presenting itself, at a particular point, which attaches everywhere to the philosophical (Hegelian) view on which the theology of Baur rests. In virtue of what logical necessity does the idea pass out of its pure existence to translate itself into fact? The pure idea has no right to go out of itself, in order to transform itself into a real world. Only the world exists, and it is necessary to give it a place in the system.

226 / Introduction

Luthardt accepted almost wholly the results of the work of Baur in regard to the special point with which we are now concerned. Only he justly lays down as the basis of the development of faith the historic revelation of Christ, so properly emphasized by de Wette. The Son displays His glory; faith springs up, but at the same time unbelief awakes; and soon Jesus is unable to manifest further the divine principle which is in Him, except in conflict with the hostile elements which surround him. Nevertheless, in the midst of this conflict faith gathers strength among the disciples, and the moment arrives when Jesus, after having broken with the people and their rulers, gives Himself entirely to the faith of His own followers and impresses upon it the seal of completeness. Accordingly, Luthardt supposes the following three parts: 1. Jesus begins to reveal Himself as Son of God, i.–iv.; 2. Jesus continues to give testimony to Himself, while contending with Jewish unbelief, v.–xii.; 3. Jesus gives Himself completely to the faith of His own, xiii–xx.

Luthardt, in the footsteps of Baur, seems to me more successfully than any one else to have penetrated into the spirit of the book and into the inner thought which directed the course of the narrative. And yet the defective point in the plan which he proposes is obvious; it is found in the last section. How are we to find a place for the account of the Passion in the third section, entitled: *Jesus and His own?* Luthardt here mingles in one group elements which are altogether heterogeneous.

Meyer's division appears to me to be rather a retrograde step than an advance. On the one hand, it raises secondary parts to the position of principal parts; for example, in the first eleven chapters, which Meyer divides into four sections: 1. First revelations of the glory of the Son, i. 1.–ii. 11; 2. Continuation of this revelation in the presence of growing belief and unbelief, ii. 12–iv. 54.; 3. New revelations and progress of unbelief, v.–vi.: 4. Unbelief having reached its culmination, vii.–xi. On the other hand, Meyer unites quite distinct parts in one, when he joins together chaps. xii.–xx. in one group, entitled: 5. The supreme manifestation of the glory of Jesus before, in, and after the Passion.

Arnaud [1] has returned to the division of Bengel, Olshausen and Ebrard, according to the feast-journeys. Thus, between the prologue and the resurrection, he points out five parts corresponding with the five journeys indicated by the evangelist: 1. ii. 13, (Passover); 2. v., (a feast not designated); 3. vii. 2, (Tabernacles); 4. x. 22, (Dedication); 5. xii. 1, (Passover). In addition to the disadvantage already pointed out, of effacing

---

[1] *Commentaire sur le. N. T.*, t. ii. 1863.

the resting point of the narrative which is clearly marked by the evangelist at the end of ch. xii., this division has the further one of making an outside matter of that entire portion of the narrative,—so important nevertheless,—which precedes the first feast-journey, i. 19–ii. 12.

Lange discovers seven sections in the narrative : 1. The welcome given to Christ by the friends of the light, i. 19–iv. 54; 2. The conflict between Christ and the elements of darkness, v. 1–vii. 9; 3. The continually increasing fermentation, vii. 10–x. 21 ; 4. The complete separation between the heterogeneous elements, x. 22–xiii. 30; 5. The Lord among the friends of the light, xiii. 31–xvii. 26 ; 6. The Lord in the midst of His enemies, a conqueror in outward defeat, xviii. 1–xix. 42; 7. The victory accomplished, xx. This division seems to me a movement backward, rather than an advance.

F. de Rougemont, in his translation of *Olshausen's* Commentary, 1844, has traced the plan, which, so far as relates to the distinction and arrangement of the parts, seems to me to approach most nearly to the truth : 1. Jesus attracts to Himself the souls which do the truth, i.–iv.; 2. He reveals Himself to the world which rejects Him, v.–xii.; 3. He manifests Himself fully to His disciples, xiii.–xvii.; 4. After having accomplished everything, He dies, xviii.–xix.; 5. He rises from the dead and becomes through the Holy Spirit the source of life for believers, xx. The only defect in this arrangement appears to me to lie in the designation of the contents of certain parts and in the absence of a distinct logical relation established between them.

The foregoing review has made evident, in succession, the three principal factors in the narrative of our Gospel : 1. Jesus and His manifestation ; 2. Faith; 3. Unbelief; or to state it more precisely, the manifestation of Jesus as Messiah and as Son of God; the birth, growth, and completing of faith in the disciples; the parallel development of the national unbelief. De Wette, Schweizer and Baur have shown us in their plans the most remarkable examples of three divisions founded solely or mainly on one of these factors. But we have seen the impossibility of making either one or another part of the narrative find its place in the frame-works proposed by these three men. This fact has an easy explanation, if our Gospel is a work of a really historical character. A purely rational framework applied to history must always retain something of artificiality, and betray its insufficiency on some side. Fact must always go beyond the idea, because it includes the incalculable element of freedom. Let us, then, renounce synthetical divisions which are more or less connected with the opinion that the fourth Gospel is a work essentially speculative, and, without bringing to this question any preconceived idea, let us allow the narrative to act upon us and reveal to us its own secret. It seems to me that we shall, without difficulty, discern five groups which have a natural gradation and which the efforts already indicated have successively brought to light.

1. i. 19–iv. 54: *Jesus* reveals Himself as the Messiah. With this fundamental facts are connected, on the one side, the birth and the first growths of faith; on the other, the first scarcely perceptible symptoms of unbelief.

2. v.–xii.: The national *unbelief* develops itself rapidly and powerfully, and that on the foundation of the growing revelation of Jesus manifesting Himself ever more clearly as the Son of God; at the same time, there is wrought out, subsidiarily, the development of faith in the disciples, by means of those very struggles.

3. xiii.–xvii.: *Faith* develops itself and reaches its highest point of strength and light in the disciples during the last hours which they spend with their Master; and this development is wrought by means of the last revelations of Jesus, and in consequence of the expulsion of the faithless disciple in whose person unbelief had gained a foothold, even in the bosom of the apostolic college.

4. xviii.–xix.: The national *unbelief* consummates its work by the murder of the Messiah, while the calm radiance of the glory of the latter penetrates that gloomy night, and the silent growth of faith continues in the few disciples whose eyes are still open to receive these divine splendors.

5. xx. (xxi.): The *Resurrection*, that supreme revelation of Jesus as the Son of God, completes the victory of *faith* over the last remnants of unbelief in the company of the Twelve.

Exegesis will show whether this summary of the narrative is in conformity with the text and the spirit of the writing. If it is, the three principal elements, which we have pointed out are met with again, and are developed simultaneously and face to face in all parts of the narrative, but with this difference, that the first, the revelation of Jesus, forms the continuous basis of the narrative, and that the two others unfold themselves alternately, the one with an ever clearer brightness, the other in more and more sombre colors, on this permanent basis. To sum up: From i. 18–xx. 29 we see Jesus revealing Himself continuously as the Christ and the Son of God; under the influence of this growing manifestation, faith is born and unbelief awakes, i.–iv.; the latter gets the mastery in the midst

Plan of the Gospel / 229

of the nation, v.–xii.; the former attains its relative perfection in the last conversations of Jesus with His disciples, xiii.–xvii.; finally, unbelief is consummated, xviii.–xix.; and faith reaches its completeness, xx. (xxi.).

There is in this arrangement nothing systematic, nothing factitious. It is the photography of the history. If exegesis proves that this plan, at once so natural and so profound, is indeed that of this book, we shall find in this fact an important confirmation of the truly historical character and the seriously practical aim of our Gospel.

Of the plans which have been proposed since the publication of this commentary, we mention only the following:

That of Milligan and Moulton [1] is absolutely the same with the one which we have just sketched, with the exception of the last two parts, the Passion and the Resurrection, which they combine in a single one under this title: the apparent victory and real defeat of unbelief. It does not seem to us that this is an advance. The element of faith is thereby too far effaced.

Westcott [2] accepts the grand division of Reuss: revelation of Christ to the world (i.–xii.); revelation of Christ to the disciples (extending this latter even to the end) xiii.–xx. But it is not possible to place the story of the Passion under the general title of the revelation to the disciples.

In 1871, in the *Zeitschrift für wissenschaftliche Theologie*, Hönig, presented the following plan: The manifestation of the Logos in the person of Jesus—this is the general idea. It unfolds itself in three phases: 1. i.–vi.: the manifestation of the Logos; 2. vii.–xii.: the selection between the opposite elements; 3. xiii.–xx.: The catastrophe resulting from this selection and issuing in the victory of the Logos. But we do not altogether see the reason of the opposition thus established between the first two parts. The selection between the opposite elements has begun from the first chapter; and the revelation of Jesus continues after chap. vi., as before. The same is the case in the last part. The revelation of the Logos remains even to the end the groundwork of the narrative, and that as the principle of a selection the description of which also fills the whole book.

As on a day in spring the sun rises in a serene sky; the ground, moistened by the snows, absorbs greedily his warm rays; everything which is susceptible of life awakens and revives; nature is in travail. Nevertheless, after some hours vapors rise from the moist earth; they unite and form an obscure canopy; the sun is veiled; the storm threatens. The

---

[1] *Popular Commentary*, Edinburgh, 1880.   [2] *The Gospel according to John*, London, 1882.

plants under the impulse which they have received, nevertheless accomplish their silent progress. At length, when the sun has reached the meridian, the storm breaks forth and rages; nature is abandoned to destructive forces; it loses for a time the star which gives it life. But at evening the clouds are scattered; the calm returns, and the sun reappearing with a more magnificent splendor than that which accompanied its rising, casts on all these plants—children of his rays—a last smile and a sweet adieu; thus, as it seems to us, the work of St. John unfolds itself. This plan, if it is real, is not the work of theological reflection; it is the product of history, long meditated upon. Conceived in the calmness of recollection and the sweetness of possession, it has nothing in common with the combinations of metaphysical effort or the refined calculations of ecclesiastical policy, except what a criticism which is foreign to the spirit of this book tries to ascribe to its author.

2

THE PRESERVATION OF THE TEXT

THE text of our Gospel has come down to us in three sorts of documents; *Manuscripts*, ancient *Versions* and citations of the *Fathers*.

The Manuscripts

The manuscripts (MSS.) are divided as is well-known, into two great classes: those which are written in uncial letters, called *majuscules* (Mjj.), and those in which we find the rounded and cursive writing in use since the tenth century of our era, *the minuscules* (Mnn.).[1] The text of our Gospel is contained, in whole, or in part, in 31 Mjj. and about 500 Mnn. which are now known.

I. The majuscules, of which the most ancient have acquired in some sort an individual value in critical science, can be divided into three groups: 1. The *vetustissimi*, *i. e.* those which date from the fourth and fifth centuries, eight in number. 2. The *vetustiores*, going back to the sixth and seventh centuries, six in number. 3. The *vetusti*, or simple veterans, which proceed from the eighth, ninth and tenth centuries, seventeen in

---

[1] We shall not speak here of the *Evangelistaria* and *Lectionaria*, containing only the collection of the portions of the gospels and epistles which were appointed to be regularly read in public worship.

number. They are designated, since Wetstein's time, by means of the capital letters of the Latin, Greek or even Hebrew alphabets.[1]

The first group at present includes four MSS., more or less complete, and four documents more or less fragmentary.

1. *Cod. Sinaiticus* (א) ; at St. Petersburg ; discovered by Tischendorf, Feb. 4th, 1859, in the monastery of St. Catherine on Mount Sinai ; dating, according to this scholar, from the first part of the fourth century ; according to others, Volkmar for example, from the end of the fourth or the beginning of the fifth century ; written probably at Alexandria ; retouched by several correctors. It contains our Gospel without any lacuna. Published by Tischendorf, Leipsic, 1863.

2. *Cod. Vaticanus* (B) ; dating, according to Tischendorf, from the middle of the fourth century ; according to most, earlier than the preceding and the most ancient of all ; probably written in Egypt ; containing our Gospel without any lacuna ; published by Tischendorf, *Nov. Testam. Vaticanum, Lipsiæ*, 1871.

3. *Cod. Ephraemi* (C), No. 9 of the Imperial Library of Paris, *rescriptus ;* according to Tischendorf, of the first part of the fifth century ; written probably in Egypt ; retouched in the sixth and ninth centuries. In the twelfth century, the text of the New Testament was effaced to make room for that of the works of Ephrem, a father of the Syrian Church. The ancient writing has been restored by chemical means, but this manuscript presents still considerable lacunae. Of our Gospel, only the following eight passages have been recovered : i. 1–41 ; iii. 33–v. 16 ; vi. 38–vii. 3 ; viii. 34–ix. 11 ; xi. 8–46 ; xiii. 8–xiv. 7 ; xvi. 21–xviii. 36 ; xx. 26 to the end of the Gospel.

4. *Cod. Alexandrinus* (A) ; at London ; of the second half of the fifth century ; written probably at Alexandria. One lacuna only in our Gospel : vi. 50–viii. 52.

5. Seven palimpsest fragments (I) found by Tischendorf in Egypt ; dating from the fifth and sixth centuries, and in John containing some passages of chaps. iv., xi., xii., xv., xvi. and xix.

6. Fragments brought from an Egyptian monastery (I^b) ; at London ; dating from the fourth or fifth century, according to Tischendorf; containing in John some verses of chaps. xiii. and xvi.

7. A palimpsest fragment (Q) ; of the fifth century (according to Tischendorf) ; found in the Wolfenbüttel Library ; containing in our Gospel the two following passages : xii. 3–20 ; xiv. 3–22.

8. Some fragments of a *Cod. Borgianus* (T) ; at Rome ; fifth century (Tischendorf), containing, with the Egyptian translation, called the Sahidic, on the opposite page, the two passages : vi. 28–67 ; vii. 6–viii. 31.

The *second* group is more meagre. It includes only one manuscript, and five fragments, or collections of fragments.

9. *Cod. Cantabrigiensis* (D) ; at Cambridge ; of the middle of the sixth century (Tischendorf) ; although presenting certain Alexandrian forms, it was, no doubt, written in the West, and probably in Southern Gaul (see Bleek, *Einl.*, 3d ed., publ.

---

[1] We shall employ the signs adopted by Tischendorf in his eighth and last edition, Vol. I., 1869, and Vol. II., 1872.

232 / Introduction

by Mangold, p. 816). Parallel with the Greek text a Latin translation is found, earlier than that of Jerome. Two large lacunae in our Gospel: i. 16–iii. 26; xviii. 13–xx. 13.

10. A palimpsest fragment (P); at Wolfenbüttel; of the sixth century; containing three passages of our Gospel; i. 29–41; ii. 13–25; xxi. 1–11.

11. Fragments of a splendid manuscript (N), four leaves of which are found at London, two at Vienna, six at Rome, thirty-three at Patmos; of the end of the sixth century (Tischendorf); containing of John's Gospel only xiv. 2–10; xv. 15–22.

12. Fragments obtained by Tischendorf from the *Porphyric* Library (Θ^c and ε); of the sixth century; passages from chaps. vi. and xviii.

13. Some fragments (T^b); at St. Petersburg; of the sixth century; passages from chaps. i., ii. and iv. of our Gospel.

14. Marginal annotations (F^a) in the *Cod. Coislinianus* of the Epistles of Paul (H—202 of the National Library of Paris); containing some verses of John from a text of the seventh century (v. 35, and vi. 53, 55).

The third group is the most considerable; it contains eleven manuscripts, more or less complete, and fragments of six others.

15. *Cod. Basileensis* (E); at Basle; of the eighth century; it appears to have been used in public worship in one of the churches of Constantinople; it contains the entire Gospel of John.

16. The beautiful Cod. of Paris (L); of the eighth century; it wants only xxi. 15 to the end.

17. Fragments of a Cod. in the Barberini Library (Y); of the eighth century; containing, of our Gospel: xvi. 3–xix. 41.

18. *Cod. Sangallensis* (Δ); written in the ninth century by the Scotch or Irish monks of the monastery of St. Gall; complete, with the exception of xix. 17–35. This Cod. contains an interlinear Latin translation, which is neither that of Jerome nor the version anterior to this Father.

19. *Cod. Boreeli* (F) at Utrecht; of the ninth century; containing the portion of our Gospel from i. 1–xiii. 34; but with numerous lacunae.

20. *Cod. Seidelii* (G); brought from the East by Seidel; at London; of the ninth or tenth century; two lacunae: xviii. 5–19, and xix. 4–27.

21. A second *Cod. Seidelii* (H); at Hamburg; of the ninth or tenth century; some lacunae in chaps. ix., x., xviii. and xx.

22. *Cod. Kyprius* (K); at Paris; of the ninth century; brought from the island of Cyprus to the Colbert Library; complete.

23. The Cod. of *des Camps* (M); at Paris; of the ninth century; a gift to Louis XIV. from the Abbé des Camps in 1706; complete.

24. Fragments of a Cod. from Mount Athos (O); at Moscow; of the ninth century; containing i. 1–4, and xx. 10–13.

25. A fragment belonging to the Library of Moscow (V); of the ninth century; containing i. 1–vii. 39.

26. A Cod. brought from the east by Tischendorf (Γ); at Oxford and St. Petersburg; ninth century; containing iv. 14–viii. 3, and xv. 24–xix. 6.

27. A Cod. brought by the same from the East (Λ); at Oxford; ninth century; complete.

28. Fragments of a Cod. (X) in the University Library at Munich; containing passages from chaps. i., ii., vii.--xvi.

29. A Cod. brought from Smyrna by Tischendorf (Π); ninth century; complete.

30. A Cod. of the Vatican (S); of the year 949; complete.

31. A Cod. at Venice (U); of the tenth century; complete.

It is well known that the oldest of these MSS. bear almost no trace of accentuation, punctuation, or separation between words and periods. These different elements were only gradually introduced into the text; and herein we have one of the means which are employed in estimating the age of the manuscripts. To these elements of the text, therefore, we should not allow any sort of authority.

II. Of the five hundred *minuscules* deposited in the various libraries of Europe, a large number have not yet been collated. Although they are all of more recent origin than the *majuscules*, many of them occasionally offer interesting readings.

The Ancient Versions

The translations (Vss.) have the disadvantage of not directly furnishing the text of the New Testament, but leaving it to be conjectured. Nevertheless, they may render important service for the criticism of the text, especially when the question is as to the omission or interpolation of words and passages, and the more so as some of them are much earlier than our most ancient manuscripts.

There are two of them which, for critical importance, surpass all the others; the ancient Syriac translation called *Peschito*, and the ancient Latin translation to which the name *Itala* has been given from a passage in Augustine.

I. *Peschito* (Syr.).

This translation (whose name apparently signifies the *simple*, the *faithful*[1]) goes back, according to the common opinion, as far as the second century of our era; according to *Westcott* and *Hort*, it must in its present form be placed between 250 and 350. It seems to have had, at first, an ecclesiastical destination. It is what its name indicates, faithful without servility. The principal edition, according to which it is cited by Tischendorf, is that of Leusden and Schaaf, 1709 and 1717 (Syr. sch.). Cureton published in 1858, from a Syriac manuscript of the fourth century, dis-

---

[1] Tischendorf has a different view. See Bleek, *Einl.*, 3d ed., p. 729, and J. B. Glaire, *Intr. hist. et. crit.*, 1862, t. p. 187.

covered in an Egyptian convent, fragments of a Syriac translation of the Gospels, which more recently have been still further increased by some others. They contain the following parts of John: i. 1–42; iii. 6–vii. 37; xiv. 11–28 (Syr. cur.). Another Syriac version exists, which was made at the beginning of the sixth century; it is called the *Philoxenian* translation (Syr. p.). It is absolutely literal.

II. *Itala* (It.).

Much earlier than St. Jerome, probably even from the middle of the second century, there existed a Latin translation of the New Testament. It certainly came from proconsular Africa, where the Greek language was less widely extended than in Italy. It was servile to excess and of an extreme rudeness, but it existed in very varied forms. We possess several copies of these ancient Latin versions, either in the bilingual manuscripts —the Cod. D, for example, which contains the Latin translation designated by d—or in particular manuscripts, such as the *Vercellensis*, of the fourth century, (a); the *Veronensis*, of the fourth or fifth century, (b); the *Colbertensis*, of the eleventh century, (c), etc.

Near the end of the fourth century St. Jerome revised this primitive translation, according to ancient Greek manuscripts. This new version, the *Vulgate* (Vg.) has been preserved to us in several documents of a high antiquity, but quite different from each other; thus the Cod. *Amiatinus* (am.), and the *Fuldensis* (fuld.), both of the sixth century.

Among the other ancient translations, the most interesting for critical use are the three *Egyptian* versions; the fragments of the *Sahidic* translation (Sah.), in the dialect of Upper Egypt; the *Coptic* translation (Cop.), in that of Lower Egypt, and the *Baschmuric* translation (Bas.), in a third dialect, which the younger Champollion supposed to be that of Fayoum (of John, only iv. 28–53). What gives these versions a special interest is, first, their date (the third, or even, according to Bishop Lightfoot, the second century), and, then, their intimate relation to the text of our most ancient Greek manuscripts.

The Fathers

The quotations from the New Testament in the writings of the Fathers have, with reason, been called "fragments of ancient manuscripts." Only it must be remembered that very frequently the Fathers cite merely from memory and according the sense. But their citations, nevertheless, remain in a multitude of cases an important critical means of establishing the condition of the text at an epoch to which our MSS. do not go back. The most important are Irenæus (Ir.), Clement of Alexandria (Clem.), Tertullian (Tert.), Origen (Or.), Chrysostom (Chrys.). The readings of the heretics have, also, a certain value, particularly for the Gospel of John, those of Heracleon, a Gnostic of the second century, of the school of Valentinus; he is the author of the oldest commentary on this writing. Origen has preserved for us some parts of this interesting work.

The Text in general

These suggestions, as much abridged as possible, will be sufficient to place the readers in a condition to comprehend the portion of our commentary which relates to the criticism of the text, and to render accessible to them the eighth edition of Tischendorf, in the notes of which the result of the immense labors of that scholar is concentrated.

Since the time of Bengel, it began to be established that the critical documents have a tendency to group themselves, in case of variants, after a more or less regular manner. Thus, in the Epistles of Paul, if we run over several pages of a list of variations, together with an indication of their respective authorities, it will be sufficient to lead us to remark very soon that the documents separate themselves frequently into three more or less fixed groups. In the Gospels, these opposing camps tend, rather, to reduce themselves to two. But the conflict is permanent. It is natural to suppose that these two or three groups of manuscripts represent the different forms of text which were spontaneously formed in the principal regions of the Church from the second and third centuries. As the writings of the N. T. were copied by hand in Syria, in Greece, in Asia Minor, in Egypt, in the Roman province of Africa and in Italy, why should not various readings have been introduced, and then perpetuated and fixed in each of these regions where the Church flourished? Three principal original homes of our textual documents have up to these most recent times been admitted, and as a consequence three principal courses of variations: 1. Egypt, with its great manufacture of manuscripts at Alexandria; 2. The West, particularly Italy and proconsular Africa, with the two centres, Rome and Carthage; 3. Palestine and Syria, whose capital, Antioch, was superseded from the beginning of the fourth century by the new capital of the world, Byzantium; and with these three ecclesiastical regions the three principal families of manuscripts are made in greater or less degree to correspond: 1. The *Alexandrian* group, composed especially of B. C. L., then also of א and finally A, although these last two, especially the second, partake in large measure of other texts:[1] 2. The *Western* or *Greco-Latin* group, including principally the Majuscules which are a little less ancient, D. F. G., etc., whose Western origin is easily recognized by the Latin translation which accompanies the Greek text; 3. The *Byzantine* or *Syrian* group, containing nearly all the later Majuscules of the eighth, ninth and tenth centuries and almost all the Minuscules. To the first the Egyptian Versions belong; to the second the Old Latin Version, the Itala; to the third the Syriac Version, named Peschito. The most ancient Syriac translation of which Cureton recovered fragments, reproduces especially the Alexandrian text. Among the Fathers, Clement of Alex. and Origen present more the Alexandrian readings; the Latin Fathers, the Western readings; Chrysostom and Theodoret, the Byzantine readings. Although criticism and exegesis appear, more and more, disposed openly to prefer the Alexandrian text, the documents pertaining to which are evidently the most ancient, to the two others, yet there is no denial of all authority to these last two. Tischendorf, in particular, in his seventh ed., and up to the discovery of the Sinaitic MS., believed that he ought to readmit into the text many Byzantine readings, which he had before set aside.

But *Hort* and *Westcott*, after immense labors, have arrived at quite a different view of the history of the text;[2] and one which, if it should come to be accepted, would modify completely this earlier mode of judging. According to them we must distinguish, on one side, the Syrian or Byzantine text and, on the other, three texts anterior to that. The first dates only from the earliest part of the fourth century, while the formation of these last goes back even to the second century. They are: 1. The Alexandrian text; 2. The Western text; and 3. A text which they call *neutral*, that is to say, which has neither the Alexandrian peculiarities, nor the Western peculiarities; which consequently approaches most nearly to the Apostolic text. This last has been preserved for us in the most faithful manner in the Vatican MS., then, in a less degree of purity, in the Sinaitic, so that, where these two manuscripts are in accord, there is scarcely any room for discussion, even when all the other authorities are on the other side. As for the Syrian text, it is a simple compilation, made by means of the three others, which does not have any reading

---

[1] The Egyptian origin of all these manuscripts has received a recent confirmation through the study of two fragments (Luke vii. 36-44; x. 38-42) belonging to an Evangelistarium of Lower Egypt (of the sixth century). These fragments which were found in a private library in Vienna, present all the readings peculiar to the manuscripts indicated. See the account by Karl Wessely in the *Wiener-Studien* of 1882.

[2] *The New Testament. Introduction*, 1881.

The Principal Documents / 237

which is original and of a date anterior to the three preceding ones. Its own readings are only the product of a work of revision cleverly accomplished at the end of the third century. There is, therefore, no reason to take the least account of this text, even when the others are not in agreement. It is absolutely without authority. Thus the revolution begun by Mill and Bentley, continued by Griesbach, Lachmann, Tischendorf and Tregelles, is at last consummated. The Byzantine text, which, under the name of *Received Text*, had reigned as sovereign from the time of Erasmus to the eighteenth century, has received its complete and final dismissal.

Let me be allowed, however, not to accept this verdict as a sentence without appeal. I can hardly believe that the Church in Syria, the first established in a heathen country, did not preserve a text for itself, as well as the other countries of Christendom, and that it was obliged to borrow wholly from foreign documents the text of its official translation, the Peschito. I am not ignorant that the Syriac of Cureton, which seems to present a more ancient text than that of the Peschito, approaches more nearly to the Alexandrian. And more learned persons than myself give up the attempt to explain, with our present means, the relation between this text and that of the Peschito. But how can we believe that such a man as Chrysostom would have adopted that of the Peschito for the purpose of making it the foundation of his sermons, if that text had been only the product of a quite recent compilation, not resting on any sort of local authority.[1] To these reasons is to be added that which exegetical experience appears to me to furnish. As there are cases where in my opinion the Greco-Latin text is certainly preferable to the so-called neutral text of B and ℵ, and in general to the reading of all the others, there are also cases, and in considerable numbers, where the texts called ante-Syrian by Hort and Westcott are decidedly inferior, when weighed in the balance of the context, to the Byzantine readings. Meyer himself is obliged to acknowledge this very frequently.

I ask, then, simply that we should keep the protocol open, that the documents should not be used according to an altogether external and mechanical method, and that in each particular case the casting vote should be accorded to exegetical good sense and tact.[2]

---

[1] See the development of these reasons in the *Revue théologique* of Montauban: *Une nouvelle édition du N. T.*, 1882, i.

[2] I am happy to find myself in agreement in this view with the most learned and one of the most sagacious among the American critics, Ezra Abbot, the recent loss of whom science deplores. See his excellent article on

THE TITLE OF THE GOSPEL

This title appears in the MSS. in different forms. The simplest is that which we find in ℵ B D : κατὰ 'Ιωάννην (*according to John*). The majority of the Mjj. and ℵ (at the end of the book) : εὐαγγέλιον κατὰ 'Ιωάννην, *Gospel according to John*. T. R., with a large number of Mnn. : τὸ κατὰ 'Ι. εὐαγγ., *The Gospel according to John*. Stephen's third edition adds ἅγιον (*holy*) before εὐαγγ., with several Mnn. Some Mnn. read: ἐκ τοῦ κ. 'Ι. εὐαγγ. The Vss. vary also : evang. Johannis (Syr.); ev. per Joh. (Goth.); ev. secundum Joh. (Cop.); ev. sanctum prædicationis Joh. præconis (according to certain edd. of the Syriac).

All these variations seem to prove that this title did not proceed from the hand of the author or the editors of the Gospel. Had it belonged originally to the body of the work, it would be the same, or nearly the same, in all the documents. It was doubtless added when the collection of the Gospels was made in the churches, which formation of a collection was brought about more or less spontaneously in each locality, as is shown by the different order of our four Gospels and of the New Testament writings in general in the canons of the churches. The differences in the titles are, doubtless, explained by the same cause.

But what is the exact sense of this formula : "*according to John?*" From the time of the Manichean Faustus (Augustine, *contra Faustum*, xxxii. 2) even to our day, scholars have been found who have given to κατά, *according to*, a very broad sense : Gospel drawn up according to the type of preaching of Matthew, John, etc. It is thus that Reuss (*Gesch. der heil. Schr. N. T.*, § 177) and Renan (*Vie de Jésus,*, p. xvi.),[1] appear to understand the word. The result of this would be that these four formulas, instead of attesting the fact of the composition of our Gospels by the four men

---

the variant in John i. 18 in the *Unitarian Review*, June, 1875. This is what he says of our ancient Alexandrian manuscripts: "All these documents, or the greater part of them, often agree in readings which are either clearly false or exceedingly improbable or very doubtful." Thereupon he gives a list of passages for which I would, from my own exegetical experience, substitute the following, borrowing some examples from his list: Matt. xxvii. 49 (the Alex. addition taken from John xix. 34)—Mk. vi. 22 (αὐτοῦ for αὐτῆς) —Luke i. 17 (προσελεύσεται instead of προελ- εύσεται)—John i. 18 (θεός instead of υἱός). Acts xii. 25 (εἰς Ἱερ. instead of ἀπὸ Ἱερ.)—xx. 28 (τοῦ θεοῦ instead of τοῦ κυρίου)—Rom. v. 1. (ἔχωμεν instead of ἔχομεν)—1 Cor. ix. 10 (the Western reading only admissible)—xiii. 3 (καυχήσωμαι !)—Jas. i. 17—2 Pet. ii. 13, etc. In all these cases, as in many others which I omit, it seems to me that a sound exegesis cannot hesitate.

[1] " These formulas merely signify that these were the traditions which proceeded from each one of these apostles, and which were clothed with their authority."

designated in the titles, would, on the contrary, exclude it. But no one in the primitive church ever dreamed of assigning other authors to these four writings than those who are named in the titles; the thought of those who formulated these titles cannot therefore, have been that which is thus ascribed to them. Moreover, this sense of *according to* cannot be at all suitable to the second or the third Gospel; since Mark and Luke have never been regarded as the founders of an independent personal tradition, but only as the redactors of narrations proceeding from Peter and Paul. The title of these two writings should therefore have been: Gospels *according to Peter* and *according to Paul*, if the word *according to* had really had in the thought of the authors of the titles, the meaning which the learned authorities whom we are opposing give to it. The error of these authorities arises from the fact that they give to the term *Gospel* a sense which it did not have in the primitive Christian language. In that language, in fact, this word did not at all designate a *book*, a writing relating the coming of the Saviour, but the good-tidings of *God* to mankind, that is to say, that coming itself; comp. e. g. Mark i. 1; Rom. i. 1. The meaning of our four titles, then, is not: "Book compiled according to the tradition of," but: "The blessed coming of Jesus Christ, related by the care or the pen of. . ." We find the preposition κατά frequently employed as it is here, to designate an author himself; so in Diodorus Siculus, when he calls the work of Herodotus "The history according to Herodotus (ἡ καθ' Ἡρ. ἱστορία)" or in Epiphanius (Haer. viii. 4), when he says "The Pentateuch according to Moses (ἡ κατὰ Μωϋσέα πεντάτευχος)." Reuss presents by way of objection the title of the apocryphal Gospel, εὐαγγ. κατὰ Πέτρον. But it is very evident that the one who wished to make this Gospel pass under the name of Peter *intended* to attribute the redaction to this apostle, and so gave to the word *according to* the same sense which we give. As for the well-known phrases εὐαγγ. κατὰ τοὺς δώδ. ἀποστόλους, καθ' Ἑβραίους, κατ' Αἰγυπτίους (*according to* the twelve Apostles, the Hebrews, the Egyptians), it is clear that κατά designates, in these cases, the ecclesiastical circle from which these writings were supposed to proceed, or that in the midst of which they were current.[1]

[1] We think we may understand that in the passage of his work *Histoire évangélique*, which we read on page 14, Reuss intended to retract his former explanation.

PROLOGUE

John 1:1-18

EACH evangelist begins his book in a manner appropriate to the aim of his narrative. Matthew proposes to prove the *right* of Jesus to the Messianic throne. He opens his story with His genealogy. Mark desires quite simply to collect *memorials* fitted to give a comprehension of the greatness of the personage whose active work he describes; he throws himself *in mediam rem*, by relating, without an exordium, the beginning of the public ministry of John and of Jesus. Luke proposes to write *a history* in the proper sense of the word: he introduces his narrative, after the manner of the Greek historians, by a preface in which he gives an account of his sources, his method, and his aim. The prologue of John is likewise in close connection with the aim of his narrative. We shall be brought to the understanding of this fact by the study of this remarkable passage which has exercised so decisive an influence on the conception of Christianity even to our own day.

How far does this prologue extend? Only to ver. 5, answers Reuss. The words: *There was a man called John*, in ver. 6, are the beginning of the narrative; this is continued in ver. 14, by the mention of the incarnation of the Word; in ver. 19 by the account of the ministry of the Baptist, and finally with ver. 35 it reaches the ministry of Jesus.

But a glance at the whole passage vv. 6–18 shows that this arrangement does not correspond with the thought of the evangelist. The appearance of the Messiah is already mentioned before ver. 14; since vv. 11–13 directly relate to it; then, if the narrative had really commenced with the mention of John the Baptist in ver. 6, why should his testimony be placed much later (in ver. 15)? The quotation made in ver. 15 comes either too early, if it should be placed in its historical situation which will be exactly described in vv. 27, 30, or too late, if the author wishes to connect it with the mentioning of the appearance of the forerunner in ver. 6. No more can we understand, on Reuss' view, the appropriateness of the religious reflections contained in vv. 16–18, which would strangely interrupt the narrative already begun. It is evident that ver. 18 forms the pendant of ver. 1, and thus closes the cycle which is opened by that verse. The narrative, then, does not begin till ver. 19, and vv. 1–18 form a whole of a peculiar character.

What is the course of the ideas expressed in this preamble? For it is clear that we do not have here a mere pious effusion without any fixed plan.

Lücke supposes two parts: The first, vv. 1–5, describing the *primordial* existence of the Logos; the second, vv. 6–18, tracing summarily His *historical* appearance. This division does not explain the two-fold mention of the historical appearance of the Word ver. 11 (*came*) and ver. 14 (*was made flesh*). It is alleged, no doubt, that the fact is taken up, the second time, more profoundly than the first. But if the progress is to be historical, this does not solve the difficulty.

Olshausen and Lange suppose three sections: 1. vv. 1–5, The *primordial* activity of the Logos; 2. vv. 6–13, His activity during the course of the *Old Covenant;* 3. vv. 14–18, His incarnation; then, His activity in *the Church*. There would be here an historical plan which is complete and rigorously followed. But the question is whether the idea of this progress is truly derived from the text, or whether it is not imported into it. In vv. 6–8 John the Baptist is named alone; there is no indication that he is intended to represent all the prophets, and still less the Old Covenant in general. Besides it would be necessary, according to this plan, to refer the coming of the Logos, described in ver. 11, to the revelations of the Old Covenant, and its regenerating effects which are spoken of in vv. 12, 13, to the spiritual blessings bestowed upon faithful Jews before the coming of Christ. Now it is manifest that the terms employed by John reach far beyond any such application.

Luthardt and Hengstenberg, rejecting the idea of an historical progress, suppose a series of *cycles* which have each of them reference to the totality of the Gospel-history, but reproducing it under different aspects. The first, vv. 1–5, embodies in a summary way, the activity of the Logos up to His coming in the flesh, comprehending therein the general unsuccessfulness of His ministry here on earth. The second cycle, vv. 6–13, takes up the same history again, calling to mind especially the part of the forerunner, with the purpose of coming thereby to the fact of the Jewish unbelief. The third, finally, vv. 14–18, decribes a third time the work of Jesus Christ, and that from the point of view of the extraordinary blessings which it has brought to believers. This plan certainly approaches more nearly to the truth than the preceding ones. Nevertheless, it would be a quite strange procedure to open a narrative by making a threefold summation of it. Moreover, if these three cycles are really intended to present each time the same subject, how does it happen that they have points of departure and ending-points which are altogether different. The starting point of the first is the eternal existence of the Logos; that of the second, the appearance of John the Baptist (ver. 6); that of the third, the incarnation of the Logos (ver. 14). The first ends in the unbelief of the world (ver. 5); the second, in the Israelitish unbelief (ver. 11); the third, in the perfect revelation of God in the person of the Son (ver. 18). Three paragraphs beginning and ending so differently can scarcely be three summaries of the same history.

Westcott divides into two parts: I. The Logos in His eternal existence (ver. 1); II. The Logos in His relation to the creation (vv. 2–18). This second part contains three subdivisions: 1. The fundamental facts (vv. 2–

5); 2. The historical manifestation of the Word in general (vv. 6-13); 3. The incarnation as the object of individual experience (vv. 14-18). This subdivision presents a fair progress, but the great disproportion between the two principal parts does not prepossess one in favor of this outline. And its chief difficulty is that of not sufficiently setting in relief the central idea, the fact of the incarnation of the Logos, and of establishing between the coming of Christ in general and His coming as the object of individual experience, a distinction which is scarcely natural and is not sufficiently indicated in the text.

The Commentary of Milligan and Moulton proposes the following plan: 1. The Word in Himself and in His general manifestations (vv. 1-5); 2. The Word appearing in the world (vv. 6-13); 3. The Word fully revealed by His incarnation (vv. 14-18). But the difference between the last two parts does not distinctly appear.

Gess[1] supposes four parts: 1. The primordial relation of the Logos to God and to the creation (vv. 1-4); 2. The behavior of the darkness towards Him (vv. 5-13); 3. His dwelling as Logos incarnate among men (vv. 14, 15). 4. The happiness which faith in Him procures (vv. 16-18). There would be, according to this view, a correspondence between the first and the third part (the Logos before and after the incarnation) and in the same way also between the second and the fourth (unbelief and faith). This arrangement is ingenious. But does it correspond well with the divisions which are marked in the text itself, especially so far as the last part is concerned? It seems not. Besides, it would appear that the Logos before His incarnation met nothing but unbelief, and as incarnate nothing but faith, which is certainly not the evangelist's thought.

Let us mention finally the arrangement presented by Düsterdieck; 1. The Logos and the critical nature of His appearance (vv. 1-5); 2. The Logos from His divine existence down to His historical appearance (vv. 6-13); 3. The Logos since His historical appearance, as the object of experience and of the testimony of the Church. This plan is broad and simple. But where do we find in the prologue the mentioning of the Old Covenant which answers to the second part? The person of John the Baptist is mentioned on account of his personal role, and not as the representative of the entire Israelitish epoch. Besides, no account is given, according to this course, either of the double mention of the appearance of the Logos (vv. 11, 14), or of the quotation of the testimony of John the Baptist, in ver. 15.

In spite of the criticism of which the arrangement of the prologue which I have proposed has been the object, I can do no otherwise than reproduce it here, as that which, according to my view, corresponds most exactly with the thought of the evangelist. It is summed up in these three words: the Logos, unbelief, faith. The first part presents to us the eternal and creative Logos, as the person who is to become in Jesus Christ the subject of the Gospel-history (vv. 1-4). The second describes human

---

[1] *Christi Person und Werk* (2d ed.), in the volume: *Das apostolische Zeugniss*, p. 562 f.

unbelief with reference to Him, as it was realized in the most tragic manner in the midst of the people best prepared to receive Him (vv. 5–11). Finally, the third glorifies faith, by describing the blessedness of those who have recognized in Christ the Word made flesh, and have thus gained re-entrance into the communion with the Logos and recovery of the life and the truth which man derived from Him before he separated himself from Him (vv. 12–18).

We shall see, by studying the Gospel, that these three fundamental ideas of the prologue are precisely those which preside over the arrangement of the entire narrative, and which determine its grand divisions.

It is undoubtedly difficult, to tell whether we must assign to ver. 5 its place in the first or in the second passage. This verse is the transition from the one to the other, and, at the foundation, it appertains to both. The twelfth and thirteenth verses occupy an analogous position between the second and the third passage. Let us notice, however, that at the beginning of ver. 12 a δέ (*but*) is found, the only adversative particle of the prologue. The apostle seems to have wished, by this means, to mark clearly the opposition between the picture of unbelief and that of faith. This is a point which seems to me not to be taken into account by the numerous interpreters who, like Weiss and Gess, connect vv. 12, 13, with the second part, in order to begin the third at ver. 14; this circumstance induces us rather to begin the third part (that of faith) at ver. 12.

As the overture of an oratorio causes all the principal themes to be sounded which will be developed in the sequel of the work, and forms a prelude thus to the entire piece, so John in this preamble has brought out at the outset the three essential factors of the history which he is going to trace: *the Logos*, then *the unbelief* and *the faith* of which his appearance has been the object.

The general questions to which this passage gives rise will be treated in an appendix following upon the exegesis.

1. THE LOGOS
John 1:1-14

It would be difficult not to recognize in these first verses an allusion to the beginning of Genesis. The first words of the two writings manifestly correspond with each other. The *beginning* of which John here speaks can only be that which Moses had made the starting-point of his narrative. But, immediately afterwards, the two sacred writers separate from each other. Starting from the fact of the creation, Moses descends the stream of time and reaches the creation of man (ver. 26). John, having started from the same point, follows the reverse course and ascends from the beginning of things to eternity. It is because his end in view is more remote and because in order to reach farther he must start from a point farther back. The Jewish historian has in view only the foundation of the theocratic work in Abraham, while the evangelist would reach the redemption of humanity by Jesus Christ. To find Him who shall be the agent of this second creation, instead of descending the course of things, he must ascend even beyond the beginning of the first creation.

At ver. 1, John finds in eternity the subject of the history which he is going to relate, the Logos; at ver. 2, he takes his place with Him at the beginning of time; in the 3d verse, he shows Him to us coöperating in the work of creation, which is the condition of that of Redemption; finally, in the 4th verse, he unveils the relation which from all time has existed between that divine being and humanity, down to the moment when He Himself appeared as a member of this race.

Ver. 1. *In the beginning was the Word, and the Word was with God, and the Word was God.*[1] These three propositions follow each other like oracles; they enunciate, each of them, one of the features of the greatness of the Logos before His coming in the flesh. The ascending progression which binds them together is indicated, after the Hebrew manner, by the simple copula καί, καί, *and, and*. The ἐν ἀρχῇ, *in the beginning*, manifestly is a reproduction of the first word of Genesis (beréschith). It therefore naturally designates the beginning of the existence of created things. Some Fathers applied it to that divine *wisdom* which the book of Proverbs describes as the *principle* of the universe; but nothing could justify such an extraordinary sense. Several modern writers, such as *Olshausen, de Wette, Meyer*, understand by this beginning *eternity*. In fact, eternity is, not the temporal beginning, but the rational principle, of time. And it is in this sense that the word ἀρχή seems to be taken in Prov. viii. 23: "In the beginning, before creating the earth," perhaps also in 1 John i. 1: "That which was from the beginning (ἀπ' ἀρχῆς)." Indeed, as *Weiss* observes,[2] the absolute beginning can be only the point from which our *thought* starts. Now such a point is not found in time, because we can always conceive in time a point anterior to that which we represent to ourselves. The absolute beginning at which our minds stop can therefore only be eternity *a parte ante*. It is none the less true, however, that, as this same author acknowledges, the allusion to Gen. i. 1 determines the word ἀρχή as the temporal beginning of things. But if the notion of eternity is not found in the word itself, it is nevertheless implied in the logical relation of this dependent phrase to the verb ἦν, *was* (see farther on; comp. *Keil*). The Socinians, in the interest of their doctrine, have applied this word ἀρχή to the beginning of the *Gospel preaching*, as Mk. i. 1; Luke i. 2. This sense is evidently incompatible with all that follows; no one any longer defends it at the present day.—
The imperfect ἦν, *was*, must designate, according to the ordinary meaning of this tense, the simultaneousness of the act indicated by the verb with some other act. This simultaneousness is here that of the *existence* of the Word with the fact designated by the word *beginning*. "When everything

---

[1] L and Gregory of Nyssa read ο before θεος.

[2] *Lehrbuch der biblischen Theologie*, 4th ed., p. 619.

which has begun began, the Word *was.*" Alone then, it did not begin; the Word *was* already. Now that which did not begin with *things,* that is to say, with time, the form of the development of things, belongs to the eternal order. *Reuss* objects, it is true (*Hist. de la théol. chrétienne,* p. 439), that, "if we infer from these words the eternity of the Word, we must infer also from the beginning of Genesis the eternity of the world." This argument is without value. Since in Genesis we do not have the imperfect *was,* but the perfect definite *created.* When John passes to the act of creation (ver. 3), he also abandons the imperfect to make use of the aorist (ἐγένετο). The notion of eternity, as we have seen, is not in the term *in the beginning,* but only in the relation of this term to the imperfect *was.* The term *Word,* no less than the term *in the beginning,* serves to recall the narrative in Genesis; it alludes to the expression: *and God said,* repeated eight times, which is as it were the refrain of that magnificent poem. All these *sayings* of God John gathers as if into one single, living word, endowed with intelligence and activity, from which emanates each one of those particular orders. At the foundation of all those spoken divine words, he discovers the divine speaking Word. But while those resound in time, this exists above and beyond time. The idea of this first proposition is, therefore, that of the *eternity* of the Logos.

The salient word of the second proposition is the preposition πρός, which, with the objective word in the accusative, denotes the movement of approach towards the object or the person serving to limit it. The meaning is, therefore, quite different from what it would have been, if John had said μετά, *in the society of,* or σύν, *in union with,* or ἐν, *in the bosom of,* or παρά, *near to* (xvii. 5). This preposition is chosen in order to express under a local form, as the prepositions in general do, the direction, the tendency, the moral movement of the being called the Word. His aspiration tends towards God. The form, apparently incorrect, by which John connects a preposition of motion (*towards*) with a verb of rest (*was*), signifies that this motion was His permanent state, that is to say, His essence. Comp. 2 Cor. v. 8; Gal. i. 18. This use of the preposition πρός has evidently no meaning except as it is applied to a personal being. We believe that we hear in this an echo of that plural of Genesis which indicates intimate communion (i. 26): "Let *us* make man in *our* image." So in the 18th verse the term *Son* will be substituted for *Word,* as *Father* will take the place of *God.* It is not of abstract beings, of metaphysical principles, that John is here pointing out the relation, but of persons. The end to which the Logos incessantly tends is τὸν θεόν, *God* (with the article); God is thereby designated as a being complete in Himself, independently of the Word Himself. It is not the Logos who makes Him God, even though He is inseparable from His Logos. Hence it results that the existence of the Logos rests on another principle than that of a metaphysical necessity. The idea of this second proposition is that of the *personality* of the Logos and of His intimate communion with God. But thus there is found lying in the Divine existence a mysterious **duality.** This duality is what the third proposition is designed to resolve.

In this third proposition we must not make θεός (*God*) the subject, and ὁ λόγος (the Word) the predicate, as if John meant to say: And God was the Word. John does not propose in this prologue to explain what God is, but what the Word is. If the word θεός (*God*), although the predicate, is placed at the beginning of the proposition, it is because in this word is contained the progress of the idea relatively to the preceding proposition. An anonymous English writer[1] has recently proposed to place a period after ἦν *was*, and to make ὁ λόγος, *the Word*, the subject of ver. 2. The meaning would thus be: "The Word was in relation with God and was God." Then would follow in ver. 2: "And *this Word* (ὁ λόγος οὗτος) was in the beginning with God." He has not perceived that the threefold repetition of the word ὁ λόγος, *the Word*, in these three first propositions was intentional, and that this form has a peculiar solemnity; comp. the similar repetition of the word κόσμος, ver. 10 and iii. 17. We find here the same grammatical form as in iv. 24 (πνεῦμα ὁ θεός), where the predicate is also placed at the beginning of the clause. The word θεός, *God*, is used without an article, because it has the sense of an adjective and designates, not the person, but the quality. Undoubtedly we must guard against giving it, for this reason, the meaning *divine*, which is the signification of the word θεῖος. The apostle does not mean to ascribe to the Logos that which this adjective would express, a quasi-divinity, a condition intermediate between God and the creature. This idea would be incompatible with the strict monotheism of the Scriptures. The Logos is something different from the most perfect of men or the most exalted of angels; He partakes of θεότης (*deity*). It is when this proposition is thus understood, that it answers its purpose, that of bringing back to unity the duality posited in God in the preceding clause. The idea contained in the third proposition is thus that of the essential *divinity* of the Word.

To the plenitude of the divine life, therefore, there appertains the existence of a being *eternal* like God, *personal* like Him, *God* like Him; but dependent on Him, aspiring towards Him, living only for Him. And this being it is whom John has recognized in that Jesus whom he knew as the Christ, and who is to be the subject of the following narrative (ver. 14).

We have given to the word Logos the meaning *Word*, and not *reason* which it ordinarily has with the Greek philosophers. This word signifies two things: 1, the reason, as being by its very nature in the line of manifestation; and 2, the word, as the instrument of the reason. But the first of these two meanings is foreign to the N. T. Besides, it is excluded in this passage by the relation to Gen. i. 1. We cannot therefore, as has sometimes been attempted, give to this word here the philosophical sense of divine *reason* and apply it to the consciousness which God has of Himself. *Storr* and others have taken it in the sense of ὁ λέγων, *he who speaks*, the supreme interpreter of the thought of God; others (*Beza*, etc.) in that of ὁ λεγόμενος, *the one announced, the one promised*. These two senses are grammatically inadmissible. *Hofmann* and *Luthardt*, with the desire

---

[1] *The Prologue of St. John's Gospel (Plymouth).*

of removing from John's Prologue every element of philosophical speculation, have taken this word in the sense which the expression *Word of God* ordinarily has in the N. T.: the message of salvation. According to Hofmann, Jesus is thus designated because He is the true subject of all the divine messages; according to Luthardt, as being the personified proclamation, the message and the messenger identified. But what becomes of the allusion to Gen. i. 1, according to these two views? Then, in the following verses the work of creation is spoken of, not that of redemption. Finally, if the term *Word* had this sense, could the proposition of ver. 14: *the Word was made flesh*, be any longer understood? Is it allowable to suppose that John meant thereby: The contents or the agent of the gospel proclamation was made flesh? The fact is that Jesus did not become these contents or this agent except as following upon and by means of the incarnation. The anonymous English writer of whom we spoke, who evidently belongs to a party professing the Unitarian (anti-Trinitarian) doctrine, gives to the word Logos the sense of divine *declaration*. This is, in fact, the divine decree proclaimed as a command which produced the universe (vv. 1–5), then the prophetic revelations (vv. 6–13), finally, the Christian redemption (ver. 14). All personality of Jesus anterior to His earthly appearance is thus eliminated from the text of John. But how, with this sense of the term *Word*, is the ἦν, *was*, of ver. 1 to be explained? The *declaration* of the divine will is not eternal; ἐγένετο must have been used, as in ver. 3; since this is an historical fact. No more comprehensible are the second and third propositions of ver. 1. They would signify, according to this view, that the creative command has relation to God (πρός), in the sense that the creation is designed to reveal God, and other strange ideas of the same kind. *Beyschlag*, and several others after him, recognized clearly in ver. 1 the idea of the eternity of the Logos; but they deny to this being personality and would see in Him only an abstract principle, pre-existing in the divine understanding, and which is realized in time in the person of Jesus Christ. To this sense the Socinian explanation comes, according to which the Logos pre-existed only in the divine decree; also that of *Ritschl* and his school, which reduces the pre-existence of Christ to the eternal *election* of His person as the agent in the establishment of the kingdom of God on earth. Exegetically speaking, all these explanations come into collision with the second and third propositions of our verse, which, as we have seen, both of them imply the personality of the Logos. They are equally in contradiction to the words of Jesus, reported by our evangelist, from which he has also himself derived the idea formulated in this Prologue,—particularly that of vi. 62: "When ye shall see the Son of man ascending where he was before," viii. 58: "Before Abraham was, I am," xvii. 5: "Restore to me the glory which I had with thee before the world was." Either Jesus used this language or the evangelist ascribed it to Him. In the first case, Jesus gave a false testimony respecting His person, even as the Jews accused Him of doing. In the second, the apostle allowed himself to make Him speak according to his own fancy, and this on a subject of capital importance. For ourselves, we regard both of these suppositions alike morally impossible. *Meyer* has modified the preceding view by supposing that the Logos, essentially impersonal, assumed the character of a person at the moment of creation and for the purpose of performing that act. This view has no basis in the text of the Prologue and none in the rest of the Scriptures. The three ἦν, *was*, of ver. 1 much rather indicate a permanent condition and one identical with itself. Finally, *Neander* saw in the Logos the organ by which God reveals Himself, as in the Holy Spirit he saw the force by which He communicates Himself. We do not contest the relative truth of this conception; we only find it incomplete. And for this reason: The second proposition of ver. 1 shows us the Logos turned primordially, not *ad extra*, towards the world in order to reveal God, but *ad intra* towards God Himself. The Logos reveals God to the world only after being immersed in God. He interprets in time the revelation of God which he receives or rather which He Himself *is* eternally.

To the divine essence, then, there appertains a being who is for God that which the word is for the thought, that which the face is to the soul. A living reflection of God within, it is He who reveals Him outwardly. This relation implies at once the most intimate personal communion and the most perfect subordination. How can these two facts be reconciled? Only on one condition: That this eternal existence of the Logos is a matter, not of metaphysical necessity, but of the freedom of love. "God is love." Now what He is, He is altogether, freely and essentially. It is the same with the Logos. His existence is a matter of eternal essence, and of free divine will, or, what unites these two ideas, of moral necessity (comp. xvii. 24). It becomes one to remember that word of Christ Himself: "No one knoweth the Father except the Son" (Luke x. 22; Matt. xi. 27), and that other word of the Apostle Paul: "We see now only darkly and as in a mirror; then we shall know as we have been known." (See further the General Considerations on the Prologue, at the end of ver. 18.)

Ver. 2. "*This Word was in the beginning with God.*"—With this Logos which John has in a manner just discovered in eternity, he takes his place at that beginning of time (ver. 1) from which he went backward even to what was before time, and now he comes down the course of the ages, to the end of showing the Logos operating in the history of the world as the organ of God, before the moment when He is Himself to appear on the earth. The pronoun οὗτος, *this Logos*, reproduces more particularly the idea of the third proposition of ver. 1: *this Word-God;* but the apostle joins with it that of the first two, in such a way as to resume in this verse the substance of the three propositions of ver. 1, and thus to explain the part of Creator which he is about to ascribe to the Logos in ver. 3. There is, therefore, no contrast in the pronoun οὗτος to any other being whatever, as Meyer supposes, and as the translation of Rilliet would indicate: "*It is he who* was . . ." The allusion to the account in Genesis in the words: *with God*, is no less evident here than in ver. 1; comp. Gen. i. 26 (*let us make, . . . our* image, *. . . our* likeness).

Ver. 3. "*All things were made through Him, and not one of the things which exist*[1] *was made without Him.*"—The work of creation was the first act of the divine revelation *ad extra*. The preposition διά, *through*, does not lower the Logos to the rank of a mere instrument. For this preposition is often applied to God Himself (Rom. xi. 36; Gal. i. 1; Heb. ii. 10). Neverthe-

---

[1] D, some Fathers and some Gnostics read ουδεν (*nothing*), instead of ουδε εν (*not even one thing*).—The Gnostics, Heracleon, Ptolemy, etc., the Alex. Fathers, Clem., Orig., as well as C D L It. Vulg., place a period after εν and connect ο γεγονεν (*that which has been made*) with the following clause.

less it has as its object to reserve the place of God beside and above the Logos. This same relation is explained and more completely developed by Paul, 1 Cor. viii. 6: "We have but one God, the Father *from* whom (ἐκ) are all things, and we are *for* him (εἰς); and one Lord, Jesus Christ, *through* (διά) whom are all things, and we are *through* him." So, then, no being has come into existence without having passed through the intelligence and will of the Logos. But, also, the Logos derives everything from the Father, and refers everything to the Father. This is what is at once indicated by διά, *through*, which leaves room for ἐκ with relation to the Father.—The word πάντα, *all things*, differs from τὰ πάντα all *the* things, in that the second phrase can designate a particular totality which must be determined according to the context (comp. 2 Cor. v. 18), while the first indicates the most unlimited universality.—The term γίνεσθαι, *to become*, forms a contrast with εἶναι, *to be*, in vv. 1, 2; it indicates the passage from nothing to existence, as opposed to eternal existence; comp. the same contrast, viii. 58: Before Abraham became, I *am*.

The second proposition repeats in a negative form the idea which is affirmatively stated in the first. This mode of expression is frequently found in John, especially in the first Epistle; it is intended to exclude any exception. The reading οὐδέν, *nothing*, instead of οὐδὲ ἕν, *not even one thing*, is not sufficiently supported. It is, undoubtedly, connected with the explanation which places a period immediately after this word ἕν (see on ver. 4).—Some modern writers, *Lücke, Olshausen, de Wette, Bäumlein*, suppose that by this expression: *Not even one thing*, John meant to set aside the Platonic idea of eternal matter (ὕλη). But eternal matter would not be a ἕν, *one* thing; it would be the foundation of everything. It is no less arbitrary to claim, as has been claimed, that in this passage the apostle aims to make the world proceed from an eternally pre-existing matter. Where in the text is the slightest trace of such an idea to be found? Far from holding that a blind principle, such as matter, co-operated in the existence of the universe, John means to say, on the contrary, that every existence comes from that intelligent and free being whom he has for this reason designated by the name *Word*. There is not an insect, not a blade of grass, which does not bear the trace of this divine intervention, the seal of this wisdom.—"The foundation of the universe," as Lange says, "is luminous." It is the Word!

We have, in the translation, joined the last words of the Greek phrase: ὃ γέγονεν (*which exists*) to ver. 3, and not, as many interpreters, to ver. 4 (see on that verse). These words seem, it is true, to mak a useless repetition in connection with the verb ἐγένετο (*became*). This apparent repetition has been explained by a redundancy peculiar to the style of John. But it must not be forgotten that the Greek perfect is, in reality, a present, and that the sense of ὃ γέγονεν is consequently, not: nothing of what has *come to be*, has come to be without Him; but nothing of what *subsists*, of what now *is* (γέγονε), came to be (ἐγένετο) without Him. There is here, therefore, neither redundance nor tautology. The apostle here has nothing to do with theological speculation; his aim is practical. He has in view the redemptive work (ver. 14); he wishes to make it understood that He who is become our Saviour is nothing less than the divine and personal being who was associated with God in the work of creation. But the Word has not been the organ of God simply for bringing all beings from nothing into existence; it is He, also, who, when the world is once created, remains the principle of its conservation, and of its ulterior development, both physical and moral.

Ver. 4: "*In Him there was life,*[1] *and the life was the light of men.*"[2] A large number of authorities join with this verse the words ὃ γέγονεν (*that which subsists*), which we have united with the preceding verse; so already the Gnostic *Heracleon*, then *Origen*, the Syriac versions, the MSS. A C D (ℵ B, have no punctuation), and the Latin Fathers. Several modern editors (*Wetstein, Lachmann, Westcott*, etc.), do the same. On this view, we can translate in three ways. Either, with Cyril of Alexandria: "That which exists . . . there was life in him" (in that existing being); or: "That which exists in him was living" (placing the comma after αὐτῷ); or finally: "That which exists, had life (was living) in him" (the comma before αὐτῷ). The first meaning is grammatically forced; the thought, moreover, is an idle one. Of the other two constructions, the simplest, the one also which gives the most natural meaning, is certainly the second. For the idea which needs to be determined and explained by the defining words ἐν αὐτῷ (*in him*), is not the subject, *that which subsists*, which is made sufficiently plain by ver. 3, but the predicate *was life*. This last interpretation, however, is also inadmissible. With this meaning, John would have said, not: *was life* (a far too strong expression), but: "*had life in him.*" The expression ζωὴν ἔχειν is familiar to him in the sense of participating in life (iii. 15, 16; v. 24; vi. 47, etc.). The words ὃ γέγονεν, therefore, cannot in any way belong to ver. 4; and the subject of the first proposition of this verse is, consequently, the word ζωή, *life:* "Life was in Him." But what meaning is to be given to these words? Must we, with *Weiss*, apply the term *life* to the life of the Logos Himself. The Logos had life, as unceasingly in communication with the Father (ver. 1). But why return to the description of the nature of the Logos, already described in vv. 1, 2, and after His first manifestation, the act of creation, had already been mentioned? Weiss answers that, as vv. 1, 2, had prepared the way for the mentioning of the creative work (ver. 3), ver. 4 returns to the nature of the Logos in order to prepare for that which is about to be said in ver. 5 of His illuminating activity. But this alleged symmetry between ver. 4 and ver. 1 is very forced. There is constant progress, and no going backward. It is an altogether simple course to regard ver. 4 as continuing the description of the *work* of the Logos. The world, after having received *existence* through Him (ver. 3), gained in Him the *life* which it enjoyed. There is here a double gradation: first, from the idea of *existence* to that of *life*, then from "*through* Him" to "*in* Him." Compare an analogous

---

[1] ℵ D, It. plerique; Syr^{cur}.; read εστιν (*there is*), instead of ην (*there was*).

[2] B omits in the text των ανθρωπων (*of men*), afterwards supplied in the margin.

double gradation in Col. i. 16, 17 : "All things have been created *through Him* (δι' αὐτοῦ ἔκτισται) . . . ; and they subsist *in Him* (ἐν αὐτῷ συνέστηκε)." Life, indeed, is more than existence. It is existence saturated with force, existence in its state of normal progress towards the perfect destination of being. And this first gradation is connected with the second : It is *through* the Logos that the world exists; it is *in* intimate relation with Him ("in Him") that it receives the life-giving forces by means of which it subsists and is developed. With the same meaning, *Gess* says : "The creation has not been abandoned by the Logos subsequently to the act of creation; but He penetrated it with forces which were able to make it prosper, make it move onward with success." Some interpreters apply the term *life* here solely to the physical life (*Calvin*, etc.); others, to the spiritual life (*Origen, Hengstenberg, Weiss*). But this distinction is out of place in this passage. For, as the question in hand is as to what the Logos was for created beings, it follows from this fact that He communicates life to each one of them in a different measure, and in a form appropriate to its aspirations and capacities; to some, physical life only; to others, that life, and besides one or another degree of the higher life, Thus, the want of the article before the word ζωή (*life*), is very fully explained; the purpose being to leave this word in its most unlimited and most variously applicable sense. The reading ἐστι (*is*), instead of ἦν (*was*), in the Sinaitic and Cambridge manuscripts, has been wrongly adopted by Tischendorf, in his eighth edition; it is incompatible with the ἦν of the following clause. It is, undoubtedly, a correction arising from the interpretation of those who connect the words ὃ γέγονε with ver. 4; since this perfect γέγονε, being in sense a present, demands in the verb of the principal clause the present (*is*), and not the imperfect (*was*).

To what moment of history must we refer the fact declared in this proposition ? *Hengstenberg* and *Brückner* think that the question is of a purely ideal relation; the first, in this sense : "The Logos *must* one day (at the moment of His incarnation) become the life, that is to say, the salvation of the world;" the second: "The Logos *would have been* the life of the world, had it not been for sin, which has broken the bond between the world and Him." But these two explanations violate the sense of the word *was*, which must express a reality, as well as the *was* in vv. 1, 2.

In the first editions of this Commentary, suffering myself to be guided by the connection between ver. 3 and ver. 4, I referred ver. 4, with *Meyer*, to the time which immediately followed the creation, to that moment of normal opening to life when the Word, no longer meeting any obstacle to His beneficent action in nature and in humanity, poured forth abundantly to every being the riches of life; these words designated thus the paradisaical condition. In this way, ver. 4 answered to Gen. ii., as ver. 3 to Gen. i., and ver. 5 to Gen. iii. (the fall). The two imperfects *was*, in this verse, are in harmony with this view. I am obliged, however, to give up this view now, in consequence of a change which I have felt compelled, since the second edition, to make in my interpretation of ver. 5 (see on that verse). If the 5th verse is referred, as I now refer it, not to the fall and the condition which followed it, but to the appearance of the Logos at His coming in the flesh, and to the rejection of Him by mankind, the interval between ver. 4 (Paradise) and ver. 5 (the rejection of Christ) would be too considerable to be included in the simple καί, *and*, at the beginning of ver. 5. We must therefore necessarily extend the epoch described in ver. 4 to the whole time which elapsed from the creation (ver. 3) to the coming of Christ (ver. 5). During all that period of the history of humanity, the world subsisted and was developed only by virtue of the life which was communicated to it by the Logos. The Logos was, as *Schaff* says, "the life of every life." Not only all existence, but all force, all enjoyment, all progress in the creation were His gift.

The meaning of the second proposition naturally follows from that which has been given to the first. If, as *Weiss* thinks, the first referred to the life which the Logos possesses in Himself, the second would signify that this same Logos, in so far as He possesses the spiritual life through the perfect knowledge which He has of God, became *the light* of men by communicating it to them. But John does not say in ver. 4 that the Logos was Himself the light of men; he makes the light proceed from *the life* which the Logos communicated to them. And this is the reason why he limits the word *life* in the second proposition by the article: *That* life, which the world received from the Logos become light *in men*, it opened itself in them and in them alone, in virtue of their inborn aptitudes, in the form of light.

Light, with John, is one of those extremely rich expressions which it is difficult accurately to define. It does not designate an exclusively moral idea, *salvation*, as *Hengstenberg* thinks, or *holiness*, the true mode of being, as *Luthardt* says; for in these two senses it could not be sufficiently distinguished from life. No more is it a purely intellectual notion: *reason* (*Calvin, de Wette*), for John could not say, in this sense: *God is light*, (1 Ep. i. 5). In this last passage, John adds: "And there is in him no *darkness*." If he means by this last term moral evil, the depravity of the will uniting with it the inward falsehood, the darkening of the intelligence which results from it, the light will be, to his thought, moral good, holiness, together with the inward clearness, the general intuition of the truth which arises from a good will; let us say: the distinct consciousness of oneself and of God in the common sphere of good, the possession of the true view-point with respect to all things through uprightness of heart, holiness joyously contemplating its own reality and thereby all truth. This inward light is an emanation of the life, of the life as moral life. Here is the explanation of the objective phrase: *of men;* for men alone, as intelligent and free beings, as moral agents, are capable of the enjoyment of such light. This word would certainly have a very natural application to the primitive state of man in paradise. But it can be extended to the human condition in general, even after the fall. God has continued to reveal to man "the end and the way" (*Gess*). From existence, as it appeared in man, determined by the consciousness of moral obligation, there has sprung up in all times and in all places a certain light concerning man, concerning his relations with God, concerning God Himself, and concerning the world; comp. as to the Jews vii. 17, and as to the Gentiles x. 16; xi. 52; so also in Paul: Rom. i. 19, 21; 1 Cor. i. 21; Acts xiv. 17. The various forms of worship and the indisputable traces of a certain moral sense, even among peoples the most degraded, are the proofs of this universal light emanating from the Logos. All the rays of the sentiment of the beautiful, the true and the just which have illuminated and which ennoble humanity, justify the expression of John (comp. ver. 10). It is this fundamental truth which was formulated by the Fathers (Justin, Clem. Alex.) in their doctrine of the λόγος σπερματικός. There is nothing more contrary to the idea of an original dualism which *Baur* and his school ascribe to John, than this expression: *of men*, which embraces all humanity without any distinction.

2. UNBELIEF
John 1:5-11

This Logos, light of the world, appears in the world buried in the darkness of sin; He is not recognized and is rejected (ver. 5). And yet God had taken all precautions to prevent such a result (vv. 6–8). But the impossible is realized (vv. 9–11).

Ver. 5: *"And the light shines in the darkness, and the darkness apprehended it not."*[1]—What, then, is this *darkness* (σκοτία) which all at once fills the scene of the world created and enlightened by the Word? It is impossible, with some interpreters of Baur's school, to think of eternal darkness, of a kingdom of evil co-eternal with that of good. Ver. 3 is positively opposed to this: everything that is, without exception, is the work of the Logos. But John, as vv. 3, 4 have proved, wrote for readers who were acquainted with the account in Genesis. We must also explain ver. 5 according to this account. The darkness of which the evangelist speaks is the subjection to sin and falsehood in which humanity lives in consequence of the fact of the fall, narrated in Gen. iii. As the Logos was the principle of life and light for the world, moral obscurity invaded it, as soon as humanity had ceased to live *in Him* (ver. 3); there was *darkness*. The Logos, however, none the less perseveres in His office of illuminator (ver. 4), and He ends by appearing Himself on this theatre which He has never ceased to enlighten. Formerly, I referred the present φαίνει, *it shines*, to the beneficent action of the Logos before His incarnation: this is the thought which I have just shown to be contained in the second clause of ver. 4. This view approaches the explanation of *de Wette*, who refers the φαίνει, *shines*, to the revelations of the O. T., and that of the interpreters who apply it to the moral light granted to the heathen by means of reason and conscience. Three reasons have made me give up this explanation: 1. The present φαίνει, *shines*, is only naturally explained, especially in con-

---

[1] B and 5 Mnn. read αυτον (the Logos) instead of αυτο (the light).

trast to the two past tenses of ver. 4, if we refer it to a present fact; now this fact contemporaneous with the moment when the evangelist writes can only be the earthly appearance of Christ and of the Gospel proclamation which perpetuates the glory of it here on earth. 2. The very striking parallel passage, 1 Ep. ii. 8: " Because the darkness is passing away, and the true light already shineth " (ἤδη φαίνει), can apply only, according to the context, to the Gospel era, and it thus determines the meaning of the same expression in the Prologue. 3. The truly decisive reason, to my view, is the significant *asyndeton* between ver. 5 and ver. 6. The absence of a logical particle most frequently indicates, in Greek, a more emphatic and more developed reaffirmation of the thought already expressed. Now, it does not appear to me possible to interpret otherwise this form of expression in this passage. The historical fact so abruptly introduced in ver. 6 by the words: "There appeared a man . . . . ," can only be thus mentioned with the design of giving through history the proof of the thought declared in ver. 5; and as the development which opens at ver. 6 and closes in ver. 11 relates wholly to the rejection of Christ by Israel, it follows that the second part of ver. 5, the theme of this development, can only relate to this same fact. Thus the φαίνει, *shines*, is understood by *Ewald, Hengstenberg, Luthardt, Weiss*. Some interpreters think that the act of *shining* can apply to the action of the Logos alike *before* and *during* His earthly life; so *Olshausen, Meyer, Westcott*,—the last writer extending the meaning of the present *shines* from the moment of the creation even to the consummation of things. But the two modes of illumination, internal and external, which would be thus attributed to the Logos here, are of too heterogeneous a nature to make it possible to unite them in the same term. We have, moreover, already seen that the present *shines* cannot naturally apply to the time which preceded the incarnation.

The καί, *and*, simply indicates the calm continuity of the work of the Logos throughout these different stages; the office which He accomplished in the depths of the human soul (ver. 4) has ended in that which He has just accomplished as Messiah in the midst of the Jewish people (vv. 5–11). *Weiss* and *Gess* object to this explanation, that it forces us to give to the word τὸ φῶς, *the light*, a different sense in ver. 4 and ver. 5 : there, the light as a *gift* of the Logos; here, the light as being the Logos Himself. But in ver. 4 the question is of a light emanating from the life, and consequently impersonal, while in ver. 5, John speaks of the light as visibly and personally present. This, then, is his meaning: that that moral good the ideal of which the Logos caused to shine in the human soul, He has come to realize in Himself here on earth, and thus to display it in all its brightness (ver. 5). John uses this notion of light with great freedom. We find the same two senses united in the same verse in viii. 12: "I am the light of the world "—this is the sense of the light in our ver. 5—and " He that followeth me shall have the light of life "—this is the sense of the word in ver. 4. The active form φαίνει, *shines*, is purposely employed rather than the middle φαίνεται, which would signify : *appears*, shows itself. John means, not that it has appeared, but that from this time forward it pours forth its brilliancy in the darkness of humanity, striving to dissipate the darkness.

The second part of ver. 5 is explained in two opposite ways, according to the two opposite meanings which are given to the verb, κατέλαβεν. This verb, which signifies to lay hands on, to seize, may denote a hostile act: to seize in order to restrain, to overcome, or a friendly act: to seize in order to appropriate to oneself, to possess. The first of these meanings is that which the ancient Greek interpreters (*Origen, Chrysostom,* etc.), adopt: for a long time abandoned, it is now again preferred by some modern writers (*Lange, Weiss, Westcott*) ; " And the darkness did not succeed in restraining, in extinguishing this light." In favor of this meaning the expression in xii. 35 is cited : " Walk while you have the light, lest the darkness *overtake* you (καταλάβῃ in the hostile sense)." But even in that passage, the meaning of this verb is not *overcome ;* Jesus speaks of the night, not as *restraining* the day, but as *overtaking* the traveler who started on his journey too late. This single example which is cited, therefore, is not really one. Besides, this meaning is excluded by the context when properly understood. We have seen that the *asyndeton* between vv. 5 and 6, implies a very close relation of thought between them. Now, this relation exists only as ver. 5 states a fact which already refers, like all that which follows, to the development of unbelief, not of faith. This it is which prevents us from translating : " and the darkness did not restrain it." In order to find in what follows the evidence of a similar idea, we must pass beyond the entire development of vv. 6–11, and proceed to discover it in the fact mentioned in vv. 12, 13 : "To all those who received him . . . ; " which is, of course, impossible, and the more so as ver. 12 is connected with ver. 11 by the adversative particle δέ. Besides, if the apostle wished to express the idea which is attributed to him, he had for this purpose the very natural word κατέχειν, to check, to repress : comp. Rom i. 18. It is fitting, therefore, to apply to the word here the other meaning which is the prevailing one throughout the whole New Testament. Comp. Phil. iii. 12, 13 (to attain the end) ; 1 Cor. ix. 24 (to lay hold of the prize) ; Rom. ix. 30 (to obtain the righteousness of faith). In the same sense it is also used in Sirach xv. 1–7 : καταλαμβάνειν σοφίαν (to attain to wisdom). I lay stress only on the passages where the verb is used, as it is here, in the active. The sense of *comprehend* in which it is taken in the middle (Acts iv. 13 ; x. 34 ; Eph. iii. 18) rests also on the meaning of the verb which we here adopt. John means, accordingly, that the darkness did not suffer itself to be penetrated by the light which was shining in order to dissipate it. To understand this somewhat strange figure, we must recall to mind the fact that the word *darkness* here denotes, not an abstract principle, but living and free beings, corrupted humanity. Understood in this sense, this second proposition is the summary statement which is developed in the following passage, vv. 6–11 ; it has its counterpart in the second proposition of ver. 11. The choice of the slightly different term παρέλαβεν *received* (ver. 11), in order to express nearly the same idea as κατέλαβεν of ver. 5, will be easily explained. The καί, *and,* which joins this proposition to the preceding one, takes the place, as is often the case, of a *δέ, but*. John presents the course of things, not from the point of view of the changing conduct of mankind towards God, but from that of the faithful and persevering conduct of the Logos towards mankind. The aorist κατέλαβεν stands out in relief on the general basis of the present φαίνει, as a particular and unique act, an attitude taken once for all. To the view of the evangelist, the refusal of the mass of mankind to allow themselves to be enlightened by the Gospel is already an accomplished fact. Comp. the saying of Jesus in iii. 19, which is, as it were, the text from which are derived the present words: "The light is come into the world, and men *loved* the darkness *rather* than the light, because their works were evil." The apostle passes now to the account of the manner in which this decisive moral fact stated in ver. 5 was accomplished and how it was consummated in Israel. And that he may make the gravity of it thoroughly apprehended, he begins by calling to mind the extraordinary means which God adopted, in order, as it would seem, to render it impossible, vv. 6–8.

Ver. 6. "*There appeared a man sent from God; his name was John.*"— The forerunner is not mentioned here as representing, either the whole of the Jewish economy, or prophetism in particular, as is thought by the interpreters who endeavor to find an historical plan in the Prologue. The apostle speaks of the forerunner only with respect to his personality and from the point of view of his relation to that of the Saviour.—The mention of the forerunner in this place with such particularity is, as *Weiss* observes, characteristic of the Apostle John, to whom the Baptist had served as a guide to conduct him to Christ.—The word ἐγένετο, *became, appeared*, points to an historical fact, and might thus form a contrast with the verbs ἦν, *was*, which in ver. 1 designated the eternal existence of the Word; but between them the two ἦν of ver. 4 have intervened. The word ἄνθρωπος, *a man*, might also be the antithesis to the divine subject who has alone been brought forward up to this point; yet there is nothing which indicates this with sufficient positiveness.—The analytic form ἐγένετο ἀπεσταλμένος sets forth the importance of the person of John in a better way than the simple ἀπεστάλη, which would have reference only to his mission. He was the first prophetic person raised up by God since a time long past. On the word *sent*, comp. iii. 28: "Because I am *sent* before him," as well as Mal. iii. 1, from which passage this expression is certainly drawn. The name John (*God shows grace*) marked the character of the era which was about to open. Yet it is not for this reason that the evangelist mentions the name here. He means simply to say: "This man, of whom I speak to you, is the one who is known by you all under the name of John." It is remarkable that our evangelist uses simply the name John, without adding the epithet *Baptist*, which had early become inseparable from this name, as we see from the Synoptics, and even from the Jewish historian, Josephus.[1] Does not Meyer reasonably conclude from this omission (Introd. p. 31), that the author of our Gospel must have known the forerun-

---

[1] "John surnamed the Baptist." *Antiq.* xviii. 5, 2.

ner otherwise than through the general tradition of the Church? If he had really known him before the public voice had given him this title, it was very natural that he should designate him simply by his name. *Credner* thought that, inasmuch as the title *Baptist* served in the Church to distinguish the forerunner from another person of the same name (John the apostle), the latter omitted the title in order that he might not attract attention to himself by the contrast; an ingenious observation, but, perhaps, less well-founded than the preceding. After having introduced this personage, the author describes his role:

Ver. 7. " *This one came as a witness, to bear witness to the light, that all might believe through him.*"—The pronoun οὗτος, *this one*, sums up all the statements of the preceding verse, as οὗτος of ver. 2 summed up all those of ver. 1. The verb ἦλθε, *came*, indicates a more advanced step than the ἐγένετο, *appeared*, of ver. 6; the entrance of John upon his public activity. —This character of witness has such importance, in the view of the evangelist, that he presents it, the first time, without an object: as a *witness* or (more literally), *for testimony;* the second time, with an indication of the object of the testimony. The first expression makes prominent the *quality* of witness in itself (in contrast to the superior dignity of the personage who is to follow). The second completes the idea of this testimony.

This idea of *testimony* is one of the fundamental notions of our Gospel. It is correlative to and inseparable from that of faith. Testimony is given only with a view to faith, and faith is impossible except by means of testimony. The only faith worthy of the name is that which fastens itself upon a divine testimony given either in act or in word. Testimony resembles the vigorous trunk of the oak; faith, the slender twig which embraces this trunk and makes it its support. But did the light need to be attested, pointed out? Does not the sun give its own proof of itself? Certainly, if the Word had appeared here below in the glory which belongs to Him (*the form of God*, Phil. ii. 6), the sending of a witness would not have been necessary. But He was obliged to appear enveloped in a thick veil (*the flesh*, ver. 14); and, in the condition of blindness into which sin had plunged man (ver. 5, *the darkness*), he could not recognize Him except with the help of a testimony. The evangelist adds: *That all might believe through him;* evidently: Believe on Christ through John, and not on God through Christ, as *Grotius* and *Ewald* thought. The question in this verse is not of the office of Christ, but of that of John. When the critics of Baur's school charge our author with setting up, in agreement with the Gnostics, two kinds of men, of opposite origins and destinies, the psychical and the pneumatical, they seem to be forgetful of these words: "That *all* might believe through him."—We find here a new indication of the part which the forerunner had played in the development of the writer's own faith. To the affirmation of the fact, John adds, as in ver. 3, a negative proposition, designed to exclude every opposite idea.

Ver. 8. " *He was not the light; but [he came] to bear witness to the light.*"— The emphasis is not, as *Meyer* and *Weiss* think, on the verbal idea, *was*, but on the subject *He*, in contrast with the other personage (ver. 9).

258 / Prologue

Hence the choice of the pronoun ἐκεῖνος, which has always with John a strongly emphatic and even oftentimes exclusive sense. It is in vain, as it seems to me, that *Weiss* denies this special use of the pronoun ἐκεῖνος in our Gospel. In a multitude of cases, this commentator is obliged to have recourse to veritable feats of skill in order to maintain that this pronoun always designates a subject or an object which is *more remote*, in opposition to one that is nearer; comp. e. g. i. 40; v. 39; vii. 45, and many other passages which we shall notice, and where the sense which is claimed by Weiss is not applicable. The ἵνα, *in order that*, depends, according to *Meyer* and *Weiss*, on an ἦλθε (*came*) understood, or it is even, according to *Luthardt*, independent of any verb, as often in John (ix. 3; xiii. 18; xv. 25). But this independence can never be other than apparent; a purpose must always depend on some action. And it is unnatural to go very far in search of the verb ἦλθε, *came*, while the verb ἦν, *was*, can easily take the sense of "was *there*" (*aderat*) and serve as a point of support for the *in order that;* comp. vii. 39, where Weiss himself renders ἦν by *aderat*.

It appears to me scarcely admissible that by this remark John desires simply to set forth the absolute superiority of Jesus to John the Baptist, (*Meyer, Hengstenberg*); or that, as *Weiss* thinks, we have here again a point merely describing the experience of the author himself as an old disciple of the forerunner. The negative form is too emphatic to be explained thus, and the analogous passages i. 20; iii. 25 ff., compared with Acts xiii. 25, and with the remarkable fact related in Acts xix. 3, 4, lead us rather to suppose a polemic design in opposition to persons who attributed to the forerunner the dignity of Messiah (comp. *Introd.* pp. 213, 214).

The testimony of John should have opened the door of faith to all, and rendered unbelief impossible. And yet the impossibility is realized, and even under the most monstrous form. This is what is developed in vv. 9-11.

Ver. 9. "*The true light, which enlightens every man, came into the world.*" I think I must positively decide for this interpretation, making the participle ἐρχόμενον, *coming*, the predicate of the verb ἦν, *was: was coming*, for : *came*. This analytic form implies an idea of continuance. At the moment when John bore witness of the light, it was in course of coming; it was properly coming; thus *Bengel, Lücke, de Wette, Weiss, Westcott*. This verse, thus understood, leaves to the expression *to come into the world* the ordinary, and in some sort technical, sense which it has in John (iii. 19; vi. 14; ix. 39; xviii. 37, etc.). Some interpreters, while adopting the same construction, refer this term : *came into the world* to the long coming of the Logos through the ages, by means of His revelations during the whole course of the Old Covenant (*Keim, Westcott*). But this sense would lead, as we shall see, to a tautology with the first proposition of the following verse. Other meanings given to ἦν ἐρχόμενον by *Tholuck:* "He was going to come," and by *Luthardt*, "He was to come," are hardly natural. *Meyer*, with some ancient and modern interpreters (*Origen, Chrysostom, Augustine, Calvin, Beza, etc.*), adopts an entirely different construction; he joins the ἐρχόμενον with the substantive ἄνθρωπον: "which enlightens *every man coming into the world."* In this case τὸ φῶς, *the light*, is taken as the subject of ἦν, which is translated in the sense of *aderat* "was present." "The true light, which enlightens every man coming into the world, was present;" or τὸ φῶς is made the predicate of ἦν, by giving to this verb as its subject a φῶς to be supplied from the preceding verse: "This light (to which John bore witness, ver. 8) was the true light which enlightens every man coming into the world." The uselessness of this appended phrase, which is self-evident, has been often alleged against this connection of ἐρχόμενον, *coming*, with the substantive *every man;* but wrongly, as I showed in my first edition, where I adopted this explanation. For these words thus understood would signify that the light of the Logos is a divine gift which every man brings with him when he is born, —that the matter in question is, accordingly, an innate light. This idea, however, is not lost in the other construction; it is still found in the words: *which enlightens every man*. The two constructions of ἦν, either in the sense of *was present*, or by supplying with it a subject derived from the preceding verse, are not very natural. Finally, the logical connection with ver. 8 is closer with the first meaning: John came to testify of the light (ver. 8): for at that very moment it was on the point of appearing in the world (ver. 9). In my second edition, I attempted a third, or even a fourth construction, by attaching the participle ἐρχόμενον, not to ἦν, nor to ἄνθρωπον, but to φωτίζει, *to enlighten,* making it a sort of Latin gerundive: "which *enlightens* every man *by coming* (itself) into the world." But this use of the participle can scarcely be justified by sufficient examples.

The word ἀληθινός, *veritable*, appears here for the first time. It is one of the characteristic terms of John's style. Of twenty-eight passages in which we meet with it in the N. T., twenty-three belong to John, nine in the Gospel, four in the first Epistle, and ten in the Apocalypse (*Milligan*). It is also used in the classics. It designates the fact as the adequate realization of the idea. It contrasts, therefore, not the true with the false, but the normal appearance with the imperfect realization. The light of which John speaks, consequently, is characterized by it as the *essential* light, in opposition to every light of an inferior order. The expression: *which enlightens every man*, if applied to the Gospel revelation, would designate the universalistic character of the Gospel; the present *enlightens* would be that of the idea. It is more natural, however, to find here again the notion which was expressed in ver. 4: the Logos, as the internal light, enlightening every man, illuminating him by the sublime intuitions of the good, the beautiful and the true. The term *every man* gives again a formal contradiction to the assertion of Baur's school which makes John a dualistic philosopher.

The Logos when coming into the world did not arrive there as a stranger. By profound and intimate relations with humanity, He had prepared for His advent here on earth, and seemed to be assured of a favorable reception:

Ver. 10. "*He was in the world and the world had been made by Him, and the world knew Him not.*" A contrast is evidently intended between the first words of this verse and the last words of ver. 9. This contrast is the occasion of the *asyndeton.* "The Logos came into the world" (ver. 9); "and *yet* he had long been there" (ver. 10 a); "and also the world was His work" (ver. 10 b). The first two propositions set forth that which is incredible, apparently impossible, in the result which is stated in the third (10 c): "and the world did not know him." *Weiss* regards the *being in the world* (10 a) as the consequence of *coming into the world* indicated in ver. 9. But the *asyndeton* between the two verses 9 and 10 does not suit this logical relation (see *Keil*); and, in this case, to what fact does the expression: "He was in the world" refer? It must necessarily be to a fact posterior to the birth of Jesus. This is held, indeed, by *de Wette, Meyer, Astié, Weiss,* and others; they apply the first proposition (10 a) to the presence of Jesus *in Israel* at the moment when John the Baptist was carrying on his ministry, and the third (10 c) to the ignorance in which the Jews still were at that moment of the fact—so important—of the presence of the Messiah; so, in the same sense, where John himself says to them (ver. 26): "There is present in the midst of you *one whom you do not know.*" I do not believe it possible to suggest a more inadmissible interpretation. In the first place, that ignorance in which the people then were with regard to the presence of the Messiah had nothing reprehensible in it, since this presence had not yet been disclosed to them by the forerunner; it could not therefore be the ground of the tone of reproach which attaches to this solemn phrase: "And the world knew him not!" Then, the imperfect would have been necessary: "And the world *was not knowing* him," and not the aorist, which denotes an accomplished and definite fact. Moreover, it would be necessary to give to the word *world* an infinitely narrower meaning than in the preceding clause, where it was said: "and the world (the universe) had been made by him." Finally, how are we to justify the juxtaposition of two facts so heterogeneous as that of the creation of the world by the Word (10 b) and that of His presence, then momentarily unknown, in Israel! There is no harmony between the three clauses of this verse except by referring the first and the third to facts which are no less cosmic and universal than that of the creation of the world, mentioned in the second. This is the reason why we do not hesitate to refer the first to the presence and action of the Logos in humanity before His coming in the flesh, and the third to the criminal want of understanding in humanity, which, in its entirety, failed to recognize in Christ the Logos, its creator and illuminator, who had appeared in its midst. This return backward to that which the Logos is for the universe (comp. ver. 3), and especially for man (comp. ver. 4), is intended to make conspicuous the unnatural character of the rejection of which He was the object here on earth. The world was His work, bearing the stamp of His intelligence, as the master-piece bears the stamp of the genius of the artist who has conceived and executed it; He was filling it with His invisible presence, and especially with the moral light with which He was enlightening the human soul . . . and behold, when He appears, this world created and enlightened by Him did not recognize

Him! One might be tempted to apply the words: "*did not know him,*" to the fact indicated in Rom. i. 21–23; Acts xiv. 16; xvii. 30; 1 Cor. i. 21, the voluntary ignorance of the *heathen* world with respect to God as revealed in nature and conscience. In that case we should be obliged to translate: "*had not* known him," and to see in this sin of the heathen world the prelude to that of the Jewish world, indicated in the following verse. But the non-recognition and rejection of the Logos *as such* cannot be made a reproach to the world before His personal incarnation in Jesus Christ. The matter in question, then, is the rejection of the Logos in His earthly appearance. This general and cosmic rejection was already regarded by Jesus as a consummated fact in the time of His ministry (iii. 19; xv. 18); how much more must it have seemed so at the moment when John was writing! The Church formed among mankind only an imperceptible minority, and this proportion between the true believers and the unbelievers has remained the same in all times and in all places.

The masculine pronoun αὐτόν, *him*, refers to the neuter term τὸ φῶς, *the light*, which proves that αὐτοῦ also must be taken as masculine. This grammatical anomaly arises from the fact that the apostle has now in view the light in so far as it had personally appeared in Jesus. This is, likewise, the reason why he substitutes the word ἔγνω *knew*, for κατέλαβε *laid hold of* (ver. 5), although the idea is fundamentally the same. One *lays hold of* a principle, one *recognizes* a person.

The failure to recognize the Logos as He appeared in Jesus is stated at first, in the third proposition of ver. 10, in an abstract and summary way as a general fact. Then, the fact is described in ver. 11 under the form of its most striking historical and concrete realization.

Ver. 11. "*He came to His own and they that were His own received Him not.*" A relation of gradation might be established between this verse and the preceding, if this verse were applied to the rejection of the natural revelation by the heathen: "And there was something still worse!" But the *asyndeton* is unfavorable to this sense, which we have already refuted. It leads us rather to find here a more emphatic reaffirmation of the fact indicated in ver. 10: "The world did not know Him." Yes; that rejection took place, and where it seemed the most impossible—in the dwelling-place which the Logos had prepared for Himself here below! The words *His home, His own,* by setting forth the enormity of the Jewish crime, characterize it as the climax of the sin of humanity. The word ἦλθε, *came,* refers to the public ministry of Jesus in Israel. Τὰ ἴδια, literally: *His home* (comp. xix. 27). Before coming to the earth, the Logos prepared for Himself there a dwelling-place which peculiarly belonged to Him, and which should have served Him as a door of entrance to the rest of the world. Comp. Ex. xix. 5, where Jehovah says to the Jews: "*You shall be my property among all peoples,*" and Ps. cxxxv. 4: "*The Lord hath chosen Jacob for Himself.*" Malachi had said of Jehovah, in describing the Messianic advent as His last appearance: "And the Lord whom ye seek shall suddenly come *to His temple;* behold, he cometh" (iii. 1). But this door was closed to Him, and even by those who should have opened it to Him: οἱ ἴδιοι, *His own*, His servants, the dwellers in His house, which He had Himself established. In the same way as τὰ ἴδια *His home* designates Canaan together with the entire theocratic institution, οἱ ἴδιοι, *His own*, designates all the members of the Israelitish nation. Paul also calls them οἰκεῖοι, *members of the household, domestici, familiares,* in contrast with ξένοι and πάροικοι, strangers and sojourners. Never, it seems, had the Jews better deserved that title of honor from Jehovah, "His people," than at the moment when Jesus appeared. Their monotheistic zeal and their aversion to idolatry had reached at that epoch the culminating point. The nation in general seemed to form a Messianic community altogether disposed to receive " Him who should come," as a bride welcomes her bridegroom. The word παραλαμβάνειν, *receive to oneself* (xiv. 3), well expresses the nature of the eager welcome which the Messiah had a right to expect. That welcome should have been a solemn and official reception on the part of the whole nation hailing its Messiah and rendering homage to its God. If the home prepared had opened itself in this way, it would have become the centre for the conquest of the world. Instead of this, an unheard of event occurred. Agamemnon returning to his palace and falling by the stroke of his faithless spouse—this was the tragic event *par excellence* of pagan history. What was that crime in comparison with the theocratic tragedy! The God invoked by the chosen nation appears in His temple, and He is crucified by His own worshipers. Notice the finely shaded difference between the two compound verbs, καταλαμβάνειν, *to apprehend,* ver. 5, which corresponds with *the light* as a principle, and παραλαμβάνειν, *to welcome,* which characterizes the reception given to the master of the house. Respecting the καί, *and,* the same observation as in vv. 5 and 10. The writer has reached the point of contemplating with calmness the poignant contrast which the two facts indicated in the two propositions of this verse present.

Two explanations opposed to that which we have just been developing have been offered. Some interpreters, *Lange,* for example, refer the *coming* of the Word indicated in this verse, to the manifestations of Jehovah and the prophetic revelations in the Old Testament. Others, as Reuss, while applying the words "*He came,*" just as we do, to the historical appearing of Jesus Christ, think that the ἴδιοι, *His own,* are not the Jews, but "men in general, as creatures of the pre-existent Word" (*Hist. de la théol. chrét t.* II., p. 476). Reuss even describes the application of the words τὰ ἴδια, οἱ ἴδιοι, to the Jews, as "a strange error of the ordinary exegesis." He is, however, less positive in his last work; he merely says: "An interpretation *may be maintained* according to which there is no question here of the Jews. So far as the first view is concerned, it is excluded by the word ἦλθε, *He came,* which can only designate, like the same word in ver. 7, an historical fact, the coming of Christ in the flesh. We shall see, moreover, that the following verses cannot be applied to the time of the Old Covenant, as must be the case according to the sense which Lange gives to ver. 11. Reuss' interpretation seems to him to be required, first, by a difficulty which he finds in the ὅσοι, *all those who*, of ver. 12, if by *His own*, of ver. 11, the Jews are to be understood—we shall examine this objection in its proper place—and then, by the general fact that, according to our Gospel, "there are no special relations between the Word and the Jews as such." We believe that we can prove, on the contrary, that the fourth Gospel, no less than the first, establishes from the beginning to the end an organic relation between the theocracy and the coming of Christ in the flesh. The following are some of the principal passages which do not allow us to question this: ii. 16, "The house *of my Father;*" iv. 22, "Salvation is from *the Jews;* " v. 39, " The scriptures *bear witness of me;* " v. 45–47 ; viii. 35, 56; x. 2, 3; xii. 41; xix. 36, 37. All these sayings are incompatible with the thought of Reuss and prove that the expressions *His abode, His own*, are perfectly applicable to the land of Israel and the ancient people of God.

3. FAITH
John 1:12-18

The appearance of the Word, therefore, did not succeed in scattering the darkness of mankind and overcoming the resistance of Israel as a nation. Nevertheless, His mission could not fail. At the moment when the people which He had prepared for Himself turns away from Him, a family of believers, divinely begotten, appears and clusters about Him. This is the contrast pointed out by vv. 12 and 13. Ver. 14 a explains the regenerating power of this faith: it is that its object is nothing less than the absolutely unique fact of the incarnation of the Word. And the sequel proves that this fact, wonderful as it is, is nevertheless *certain;* certain, because He was beheld with rapture by *eye-witnesses*, to whose number the author belongs (ver. 14 b); —certain, because He was pointed out by a *divine herald*, who had received the mission to proclaim Him (ver. 15); certain, because He is an object of experience for the *whole Church*, which through all the heavenly gifts which it receives from this unique man, called Jesus Christ, verifies in Him all the characteristics of the Divine Logos (vv. 16–18). This triple testimony of eye-witnesses, of the official witness, and of the Church itself is the immovable foundation of faith. This third part of the Prologue, then, is indeed the demonstration of the certainty and the riches of faith. The majority of the commentators make this third part begin only at ver. 14, with the words: "And the Word was made flesh." But this way of separating the sections has two serious difficulties: 1, vv. 12, 13 become a dragging appendage to the preceding section into which they do not enter logically, since the dominant idea of that section is the unbelief which the Logos encountered here on earth; and 2, this third mention of the coming of the Word (comp. vv. 5 and 11), not having any introduction, has somewhat of an abrupt and accidental character. It is quite otherwise when vv. 12, 13 are joined with the following section, which treats of faith. They form the antithesis to ver. 11 and thus the transition from the first to the second section of the Prologue. Thus the third and principal mention of the fact of the incarnation is occasioned by the expression of the idea of faith in vv. 12, 13.

Ver. 12. *But,*[1] *to all those who received Him, to them He gave the power of becoming children of God, to those who believe on His name.*—Δέ, *but*, expresses not merely a gradation, but an opposition. This is confirmed by the antithesis of the verb ἔλαβον, *received*, to οὐ παρέλαβον, *did not welcome* (ver. 11); as well as by that of the subject ὅσοι (literally, *as many as there are who*), to οἱ ἴδιοι, *His own* (ver. 11). This last term designated the nation as a body; the pronoun ὅσοι indicates only individuals. By its official representatives, the nation, as such, refused to welcome Jesus; from that moment faith took on the character of a purely individual and, so to speak, sporadic act. This is expressed by the pronoun ὅσοι, *all those who*. But the ὅσοι are not, therefore, only the few members of the Jewish people who did not share the national unbelief; they are *all believers* (τοῖς πιστεύουσιν ver. 12b), whether Jews or Greeks, whom John contemplates as united into one family of the children of God (ἡμεῖς πάντες, *we all*, ver. 16). Reuss (*Hist. de la théol. chrét.* t. ii., p. 475) thinks that if the term *His own* (ver. 11), designates the Jews, and not men in general, we must also conclude from this fact that the believing ὅσοι are only Jews. But John does not say ὅσοι ἐξ αὐτῶν, all those *from among them*, but: *all those who*, in general. When the Messiah is once rejected by unbelieving Israel, there is henceforth only *humanity*, and in it *individual* believers or unbelievers. This substitution of individual faith for the collective and national welcome of the chosen people, which was wanting, is precisely that which occasions, in this verse, the use of the simple verb ἔλαβον, *received*, instead of the compound παρέλαβον, *welcomed* (ver. 11). The compound had in it something grave and solemn, which was suited to an official reception, such as the Israelitish authorities should have given in the name of the entire theocratic nation joyously introducing its divine King into His palace, the temple at Jerusalem; while the simple λαμβάνειν, which signifies *to take*, to seize in passing and, as it were, accidentally, is perfectly apposite to the notion of individual faith. In this verse, therefore, John substitutes, in the same manner as St. Paul does in all his epistles, the great idea of Christian individualism, with its universal and human character, for Jewish nationalism, with the narrow particularism in which it remained confined. By marking the contrast (δέ, *but*) between the unbelief of the Israelite nation and the faith of individual believers, whoever they may be, Jews or heathen, the apostle would succeed in making the greatness of the blessings understood of which the rebellious people were deprived, although they had been called first of all to enjoy them. Through rejecting the Word, they were deprived of a participation in the life of God which He brought in Himself. In fact, this divine guest, the Logos, conferred on those who received Him

---

[1] Δέ is omitted by D and some Fathers.

two privileges worthy of Himself: first, a new position in relation to God, and then, by reason of this position, the power to participate in His divine life.

The word ἐξουσία, *authority, competency,* denotes more than a simple possibility, and less than a power properly so called. What is meant is a new position, that of being reconciled, justified, which the believer gains through faith, and through this it is that he receives the power of asking for and receiving the Holy Spirit, by means of which he becomes *a child of God.* The expression τέκνον θεοῦ (*child of God*), which is used by John, includes more than υἱός (*son*), which is used by Paul. The meaning of this latter word does not go beyond the idea of *adoption* (υἱοθεσία), the right of sonship which is accorded to the believer, while the word τέκνον (*child*), from τίκτειν (*to beget*), implies the real communication of the divine life. Comp. Gal. iv. 6: "*Because ye are sons, God sent forth the Spirit of His Son into your hearts;*" a sentence which is equivalent to saying: "Because you are *sons* (υἱοί)—by adoption—God has made you *children* (τέκνα) by regeneration." This ὅτι (*because*), of Paul, expresses precisely the relation of the idea contained in the word ἐξουσία in John. How can Hilgenfeld venture, in the face of the word γενέσθαι (*become*), to impute to John the dualistic system, according to which the children of God are such by nature, and before all faith in the historical Christ!

The idea of *child of God*, in the concrete sense in which it here appears, is foreign to the Old Testament. The words *father* and *child*, in the rare cases in which they are there employed (Ps. ciii. 13; Is. lxiii. 16; Jer. xxxi. 20; Hos. xi. 1), express only the sentiments of affection, tenderness, compassion. This observation is sufficient to set aside the opinion of the interpreters, who, like Lange, with the purpose of reserving the idea of the incarnation for ver. 14, refer these verses 12 and 13 to the faithful ones of the Old Covenant. The expressions *receive the Word* and *become children of God* are far too strong to be applied to the Israelitish saints and would be in flagrant contradiction to the declaration of Jesus (Matt. xi. 11, 12); and to the reflections of John himself (i. 17 and vii. 39).

The figurative, and consequently, somewhat vague, term *receive,* required to be explained, precisely defined; for the readers must know accurately the means by which they may place themselves among the number of the ὅσοι (*all those who*). Hence the appended phrase: τοῖς πιστεύουσιν . . . , (*to those who believe on His name*). *To believe*—this is the means of the λαμβάνειν, the mode of this individual reception. Only, instead of connecting this explanation with the verb, *they received,* the author unites it with the persons of the ὅσοι (*to those who*). "It is one of the peculiarities of John's style," *Luthardt* observes, to define the moral condition by means of which an act is accomplished, by an explanatory appendix added to one of the words which depend on the principal verb. As a point of style, this is perhaps heavy; but as an expression of thought, it is forcible. See the same construction in iii. 13; v. 18; vii. 50, etc. We have sought to give the force of this turn in the translation. The relation between these two acts, *to receive* and *to believe,* is a close one; the first is accomplished by the very fact of the second. But why, then, is an act of faith necessary for the reception of the Word? Because His divine character is hidden from sight by the veil of the flesh which envelops it. It can only be discerned, therefore, by a perception of a moral nature. Made attentive by the testimony, the man fixes his gaze upon Christ, and, discerning in Him the divine stamp of holiness, he surrenders himself personally to Him. This is faith.

The object of faith, as here indicated, is not the Logos; it is *His name*. *The name*, the normal name of the being, is the true expression of His essence, the perfect revelation of His peculiar character. This name is thus the means which other beings have of knowing Him, of forming their idea of His person. Hence it is that this *idea* is sometimes called *the name*, in a relative and secondary sense, as in the prayer: *Hallowed be thy name.* In our passage, John means: those who believe in the revelation which He has given of Himself, as Logos, who have discerned under the veil of the flesh the manifestation of that divine being, the *only-begotten Son* (vv. 14, 18), and have, because of this perception, surrendered themselves to Him. After having thus explained the term *received*, the apostle develops in ver. 13 the idea of the expression *children of God*.

Ver. 13. "*Who were born*,[1] *not of blood, nor of the will of the flesh, nor of the will of man, but of God.*" It seems, at the first glance—because of the past verb: *who were born*—that the apostle places regeneration before faith, which is, of course, impossible. But, as *Meyer* rightly observes, the relative οἵ (*who*), does not refer to the words τοῖς πιστεύουσιν (*those who believe*), but, by a *constructio ad sensum*, to the neuter substantive τέκνα θεοῦ (*children of God*). Ver. 13 unfolds this term: *children of God*, first in a negative relation, by means of three cumulative phrases which have a somewhat disdainful and even contemptuous character. Does John mean thereby to stigmatize the false confidence of the Jews in their character as children of Abraham? This does not seem to me probable. Three expressions to set forth the idea of the theocratic birth would be useless. Besides, the Prologue has too lofty a flight, too universal a bearing, to admit of so paltry a polemic. John means rather to set forth with emphasis the superiority of the second creation which the Logos comes to accomplish on the foundation of the first. There are two humanities, one which propagates itself in the way of natural filiation; the other, in which the higher life is communicated immediately by God Himself to every believer. It is, therefore, ordinary birth, as the basis of natural humanity, which John characterizes in the first three expressions. The first phrase: *not of blood*, denotes procreation from the purely physical point of view; the blood is mentioned as the seat of natural life (Lev. xvii. 1). The plural αἱμάτων has been applied either to the duality of the sexes, or

---

[1] Irenæus cites this passage three times in the form: *Qui natus est*, etc., applying these words, thus, to Christ Himself; and Tertullian so firmly believes in the authenticity of this reading, that he attributes the opposite reading—that of our text—to a falsification of Gnostic (Valentinian) origin. But the received reading is found in all our critical documents without exception.

to the series of human generations. It should rather be interpreted as the plural γάλαξι, in the words of Plato (Legg. x., p. 887, D): ἔτι ἐν γάλαξι τρεφόμενοι—the plural suggesting the multiplicity of the elements which form the blood (see *Meyer*). The two following phrases are not subordinate to the first, as St. Augustine thought, who, after having referred the latter to the two sexes, referred the two others, the one to the woman and the other to the man. The disjunctive negative, *neither . . . nor* (οὔτε . . . οὔτε), would be necessary in that case. The last two expressions designate, like the first, the natural birth; but this, while introducing, in the one phrase, the factor of the will governed by the sensual imagination (*the will of the flesh*), in the other, that of a will more independent of nature, more personal and more manlike, the will of man. There is a gradation in dignity from one of these terms to the other. But, to whatever height the transmission of natural life may rise, this communication of life-power cannot pass beyond the circle traced out at the first creation—that of the physico-psychical life. *That which is born of the flesh*, even in the best conditions, *is*, and remains *flesh*. The higher, spiritual, eternal life is the immediate gift of God. To obtain it, that divine begetting is needed by which God communicates His own nature. The limiting phrase, ἐκ θεοῦ (*of God*), contains, in itself alone, the antithesis to the three preceding phrases. By its very conciseness it expresses the beauty of that spiritual birth which is altogether free from material elements, from natural attraction, from human will, and in which the only coöperating forces are God acting through His Spirit on the one side, and man's faith on the other.

But how are we to explain the virtue of this faith which fits the man to be begotten of God? Does it have in itself, in its own nature, the secret of its power? No, for it is only a simple receptivity, a λαμβάνειν, *receive*: its virtue comes from its object. The apostle had already intimated this by the words: "who believe *on His name;*" and he now expressly declares it:

Ver. 14. "*And the Word became flesh and dwelt among us—and we beheld His glory, a glory as of the only-begotten Son coming from the presence of the Father—full*[1] *of grace and truth.* The connection between this verse and the preceding, which is involved in καί, *and*, is expressed in the following thought: If faith can make of a man born of the flesh a child of God, it is because it has for its object *the Word made flesh*. The coming of Christ upon earth in the flesh had been already mentioned in ver. 11, from the point of view of its relation to Israel, and of the unbelief by which it had been met. John proclaims again the great fact, the subject of his narrative, from the point of view of all mankind, and as the object of the faith of the Church. There is, therefore, no tautology in this repetition. It even reflects very faithfully the phases of the development of faith in the heart of those who were formerly Jews, like John and the apostles. They first witness the appearance of the Messiah in Israel

---

[1] D and some Fathers read: πληρη (agreeing with δοξαν), and Augustine: pleni (according to a variant πληρους??) to be referred to *unigeniti*.

(*to His own*) ver. 11, and they see Him ignominiously rejected. But far from joining in this rejection, they receive Him as the promised Messiah, and through their faith in Him find the privileges of adoption and regeneration (vv. 12, 13). Then sounding in all its depths the object of a faith which is capable of effecting such wonders, they cry out: " This is the Word who has been made flesh ! " The idea of the national Messiah was thus gradually transformed in them into that of the Son of God, the Saviour of mankind. The καί, *and*, is not, therefore, here a simple connecting copula. How, indeed, can we connect with one another by an *and* or an *and also* two ideas which are as unlike as those of 13b and 14a: " They are born of God," and (and *also*): " the Word became flesh." We do not think that the thought of the evangelist is any more successfully apprehended by paraphrasing this καί, as Luthardt does, "and *to tell the whole truth*," or, as Brückner, "and *in these circumstances*." The paraphrase of *Weiss-Meyer:* " And *this is the way in which* faith in Him was able to take form and produce such happy fruits . . . . ," amounts to nearly the same thing with our own explanation, which was already that of *Chrysostom, Grotius,* etc. The emphasis is not on the subject: *the Word;* this noun is repeated (instead of the simple pronoun) only with the purpose of better emphasizing the contrast between the subject and the predicate *became flesh.* The Word to which everything owes its existence, which created us ourselves, became a member of the human race. The word *flesh* properly denotes, in its strict sense, the soft parts of the body, as opposed either to the hard parts, the bones; thus when it is said, " Flesh of my flesh, bone of my bones" (Gen. ii. 23),—or to the blood (vi. 54). From this more restricted sense, a broader one is derived: the entire body, regarded from the view-point of its substance, the animated matter; so 1 Cor. xv. 39. Finally, as the flesh is properly the seat of physical sensibility, this word, by metonymy, often designates the entire human being, in so far as he is governed in his natural state by sensibility with respect to pleasure and pain. " *For also they are but flesh,*" is said of men before the deluge, Gen. vi. 3. Comp. John xvii. 11; Ps. lxv. 1; Rom. iii. 20: *all flesh, no flesh,* for: every man, no man. Undoubtedly, the desire of enjoyment and the dread of suffering are not in themselves criminal instincts. They are often the precious means by which man escapes from a multitude of losses and injuries of which he would otherwise not be conscious. Still more: without this double natural sensibility, man would never be able to offer to God anything but "sacrifices which cost him nothing." He could not himself become "a living sacrifice, holy, acceptable to God" (Rom. xii. 1), and thereby fulfill his noblest destiny, that of glorifying God by the sacrifice of himself. But, on the other hand, it cannot be denied that in these two natural propensities lies the possibility of temptation and sin. Human nature in this critical condition: such is the form of existence which the Word has consented to take for himself. The expression *became flesh,* accordingly signifies, first of all, that the Word left the immaterial state of divine being to assume a body, and to confine Himself, like the creature, within the limits of time and space. But the word *flesh* expresses much more than this. Since the work of *Zeller* (*Theol. Jahrb.* 1842), the Tübingen school makes John say that the Logos borrowed from humanity only the material body, while He Himself filled, in Jesus, the office of the *spirit* in every other man (the old theory of Apollinaris). But John does not dream of any such thing. We have just proved that the word *flesh* often designates the entire human person (*spirit, soul and body*, 1 Thess. v. 23). This is certainly the case in this passage. The expression: "*the* Word became body," would have no meaning. It would have been necessary to say: took a body. Jesus sometimes speaks in our Gospel of *His soul*, and of His soul as *troubled* (xii. 27). It is related of Him that He groaned or that He was troubled in *His spirit* (xi. 33; xiii. 21), that He *gave up His spirit* (xix. 30); all this implies that the Logos does not play the part of the spirit in the person of Jesus. The spirit of Jesus is, as in every man, one of the elements of the human nature, like the soul and the body. It follows from this that *the flesh* denotes, in our passage, complete human nature. Consequently, this term *flesh* is not intended to describe merely the visibility or corporeity of Jesus (*de Wette, Reuss, Baur*), or even the poverty and weakness of His earthly manifestation (*Olshausen, Tholuck*). It designates the *reality* and *integrity* of the human mode of existence into which Jesus entered. In virtue of this incarnation, He was able to suffer, to enjoy, to be tempted, to struggle, to learn, to make progress, to love, to pray, exactly *like us;* comp. Heb. ii. 17. The phrase ἄνθρωπος ἐγένετο, *became man*, would have expressed nearly the same idea; only it would have described Jesus as a particular personality, as a definite representative of the human type, and it might have been imagined that *this* man had reserved for Himself an exceptional position in the race. The term *flesh*, which denotes only the state, the mode of existence, more clearly affirms the complete homogeneity between His condition and ours. Moreover, Jesus does not hesitate to apply to Himself the word ἄνθρωπος, *man*, John viii. 40; and the name by which in preference to all others He described Himself, was *Son of man* (see on i. 52).

The word which fills the interval between the subject, *the Word*, and the predicate, *flesh*, is the verb ἐγένετο, *became*. The word *become*, when it has a substantive for its predicate, implies a profound transformation in the subject's mode of being. Thus ii. 9: "The water *became* wine" (τὸ ὕδωρ οἶνον γεγενημένον). When a person is in question, this word *become*, without implicating his identity, indicates that he has changed his condition; for example, in the expression: The king become a shepherd. *Baur* and *Reuss* affirm that, in the evangelist's thought, the Logos, though becoming flesh, remained in possession not only of His consciousness, but also of His attributes as Logos. He clothed Himself, indeed, with a body, according to them, but as if with a temporary covering. "This incarnation was for Him only something accessory" (Reuss, ii., p. 456). Yet this scholar cannot help saying (p. 451): "There is nothing but the word *become* which positively affirms that, in coming, He changed the form of His existence." Certainly! And we affirm nothing more, but nothing less. The word *become* shows, indeed, that this change reached even the foundation of the existence of the Logos. This natural sense of the word *become* is not invalidated by the expression *is come in the flesh*, 1 John iv. 2, in which Reuss finds the affirmation of the preserving of His original nature with all its attributes, but which really involves only the continuity of His personality. The personal subject in the Logos remained the same when He passed from the divine state to the human state, but with the complete surrender of all the divine attributes, the possession of which would have been incompatible with the reality of the human mode of existence. And if He ever recovers the divine state, it will not be by renouncing His human personality, but by exalting it even to the point where it can become the organ of the divine state. This, as it seems to us, is the true Christological conception, as it appears in the Scriptures generally, and in our passage in particular.

The content of John's declaration, therefore, is not: Two natures or two opposite modes of being co-existing in the same subject; but a single subject passing from one mode of being to another, in order to recover the first by perfectly realizing the second. The teaching of John, as thus understood, is in complete harmony with that of Paul. That apostle says, indeed, Phil. ii. 6–8: "He who was in the form of God . . . emptied (divested) Himself, having taken the form of a servant and having become like to men;" and 2 Cor. viii. 9: "Though He was rich, He *became poor*, that ye through His poverty might be rich." These passages express, in a form which is completely independent of that of John, a conception which is identically the same: The incarnation by means of a divesting (κένωσις). We shall see that the whole Gospel history, and especially the picture of Jesus which is traced by our evangelist, accords perfectly, notwithstanding all the contrary assertions of *Reuss*, with the thesis of the Prologue as thus understood.

After having entered the human life, the Word took up His abode there and appropriated it to Himself even to the end; this is expressed by the following clause. The word σκηνοῦν, literally, *to dwell in a tent*, contains, according to *Meyer, Reuss*, etc., an allusion to a technical word in the religious philosophy of the later Jews, Shechinah (*the dwelling-place*), which denoted the visible forms by which Jehovah manifested His presence in the midst of His people. We might see thus in this word σκηνοῦν, *to live in a tent*, especially with the limiting phrase ἐν ἡμῖν, *among us*, an allusion to the Tabernacle in the wilderness, which was, as it were, the tent of Jehovah, Himself a pilgrim among His pilgrim people. To this conformity between the sort of habitation which Jehovah had and that of His people answers the complete community in the mode of existence between the incarnate Word and men, His brethren. Perhaps, these allusions are somewhat refined and John's thought is merely that of comparing the flesh of Jesus (His humanity) to a tent like ours (2 Cor. v. 1). This word σκηνοῦν, *to camp*, denotes, in any case, all the familiar relations which He sustained with His fellow-men; varied relations like those which a pilgrim sustains towards the other members of the caravan. It is as if John had said: "We ate and drank at the same table, slept under the same roof, walked and journeyed together; we knew Him as son, brother, friend, guest, citizen. Even to the end, He remained faithful to the path on which He entered when He became a man." This expression, therefore, calls to mind all the condescension of that divine being, who thus veiled His majesty in order to share in the existence of the companions of His journey. —The limiting phrase ἐν ἡμῖν, *among us*, does not refer to men in general, nor even to the Church in its totality. In connection with the word σκηνοῦν, *to live in a tent*, and with the following phrase, *we beheld*, it can only designate the immediate witnesses of the earthly existence of Jesus, who sustained towards Him the familiar relations comprised in the notion of life in common. The expression of the general feeling of the Church will come later, vv. 16–18.

According as this spectacle presents itself to the thought of the evangelist, and assumes, in the words *among us*, the character of the most personal recollection, it becomes to him the object of delightful contemplation. The phrase is broken. The word *us*, of the limiting phrase, suddenly becomes the subject, while the subject, the Word and His glory, passes into the position of the grammatical object: *"And we beheld His glory."* How easily may this change of construction be understood in the writing of an eye-witness! We observe the reverse change in the first verses of 1 John: *"That which we have heard, that which we beheld of the Word of life . . . , for the life was manifested and we have seen it, this it is which we declare unto you."* Here, the apostle begins with the impression received —it is a letter—to pass from this to the fact itself. But in the Gospel, where he speaks as a historian, after having started from the fact, he describes the ineffable joy which the witnesses experienced in this sight. The word θεᾶσθαι (*to behold*), is richer than ὁρᾶν (*to see, to discern*); it is the *restful seeing*, as Luthardt says, with an idea of satisfaction, while to ὁρᾶν attaches rather the idea of knowledge. *Baur, Keim, Reuss*, apply this word *behold* here to a purely spiritual act, the inward sight of Christ which is granted to every believer; comp. 1 Ep. iii. 6: "He that sinneth hath not seen him;" and 2 Cor. iii. 18. We may understand the design of this interpretation. These critics refuse to recognize in the evangelist a witness, and yet they would not wish to make him an impostor. This expedient, therefore, alone remains. But this expedient involves inextricable difficulty, as we have shown in the Introduction (pp. 201–202). How could there be a question here of the glorified Christ, as an object of the spiritual contemplation of believers? Are we not at the opening of the narrative of the earthly life of Christ, at the moment when the coming of the Logos in the flesh and His condescension towards the companions of His earthly career have just been pointed out? To attribute to the word *behold* in such a context a purely spiritual sense, is to set at nought the evidence. Undoubtedly, the witnesses had more than the sight of the body. This beholding was an internal perception. But the first was the means of the second.

The object of the beholding was *the glory* of the Word. The glory of

God is the beaming forth of His perfections before the eyes of His creatures. This glory is really unique; every glory which any being whatsoever possesses is only the participation in some measure of the splendor which is sent forth by the perfection of God Himself. The glory which the witnesses of the earthly life of the Logos beheld in Him could not be the splendor which He enjoyed in His pre-existent state. For this glory Jesus asks again in xvii. 5: "And now, Father, glorify thou me with thyself, with the glory which I had with thee before the world was." One does not ask again for what one still possesses. *Reuss* claims that it is only "the most arbitrary harmonistic," which can ascribe to John the idea that the Logos divested Himself of the divine attributes when he became incarnate (*Théol. johann.*, p. 120). But as for this harmonistic, it is John himself who suggests it in the prayer of Jesus which we have just quoted, and this is in full harmony with Paul (Phil ii. 6 ff.). What must we understand, then, by that glory of Jesus, of which John here speaks, and which is not that of the pre-existent Logos? In Chap. ii., ver. 11, after the miracle of Cana, John says: "And he manifested his glory." We might conclude from this that, as *Weiss* thinks, the earthly glory of the Logos consisted in the works of omnipotence, as well as in the words of omniscience, which the Father gave Him to do and to utter. Nevertheless, in chap. xvii. 10, Jesus says: "I am glorified *in them,*" and this expression leads us to a more spiritual idea of the glory which He possessed here on earth. Even in our verse, the words: *full of grace and truth*, describe the Word and give us a much more moral notion of His glory than the explanation of Weiss implies. The essential character of this earthly glory of the Logos was, as it appears to me, the stamp of sonship impressed upon the whole human life of Jesus, the intimate communion with the Father which so profoundly distinguished His life from every other. Jesus puts us upon the right path when, before uttering the words: "I am glorified in them," He says (xvii. 10): "All things that are mine are thine, and all things that are thine are mine." Such a relation with God is the most complete glory which can irradiate the face of a human being. It comprehends, of course, all the manifestations of such a relation, thus works of power, words of wisdom, the life of holiness and charity, all of divine grandeur and beauty, that the disciples beheld in Jesus. This explanation agrees with that of John himself in the following words: "A glory as of the only-begotten from the Father." The conjunction ὡς, *as*, does not certainly express here a comparison between two similar things, but, as is often the case, the absolute agreement between the fact and the idea: a glory as (must be) that of the Son coming from the presence of the Father. *Weiss* urges against this explanation the absence of the article τοῦ, *of the*, before the words: *only-begotten Son* and *Father;* and further, the most natural sense of ὡς, *as*, which is that of comparison. He translates accordingly, "A glory like to that of *an* only-begotten Son coming from *a* father," in the sense that every only son inherits the rank and fortune of his father. Thus in this case it was seen that God had conveyed *all* His glory to Jesus. But this explanation would imply that every father, who has an only son, possesses also a great fortune to convey to him, which is by no means true. The absence of the article, which leads Weiss to an explanation which is so forced, is much better explained by the fact that the terms *only Son* and *Father* are treated here, as proper names, or at least as substantives designating single beings of their kind (*Winer's Grammar*, § 18). Indeed, the Father in question is *the Father*, in the absolute sense, the one from whom every one who is called *father* in heaven and on earth derives his paternal character (Eph. ii. 15); and this *only Son* is the only one, not merely as the sole son of this father, but inasmuch as He is the absolute model and prototype of every one who among the sons of men bears the name of only son. With reference to ὡς, *as*, used to indicate the complete agreement of the fact with the idea, comp. the quite similar ὡς in Matt. vii. 29; 1 Cor. v. 3; 2 Cor. ii. 17; Gal. iii. 16, etc. The glory of the incarnate Logos was undoubtedly, therefore, a humbler glory than that of his pre-existent state, but a glory which, nevertheless, marked Him as united to God by the bond of an unparalleled filial intimacy. There was seen in Him, as never in any man, the assurance of being loved paternally by God, of the power of asking everything of Him with the certainty of being heard, and at the same time the most perfect filial fidelity towards Him. This unique glory of the Word made flesh the apostle describes, when he characterizes the entire earthly manifestation of the Word by that last stroke of his pencil: *Full of grace and truth.* We refer these words to the principal subject of the whole sentence, the Word. This is the simple and correct construction of the nominative πλήρης, *full;* it is also that which gives the best sense. Undoubtedly, this adjective might be made a nominative absolute, with *Grotius, Meyer, Luthardt, Weiss* and others, by referring it either to δόξαν: "*glory full* of grace . . ." (hence the reading πλήρη in D), or rather to αὐτοῦ *of him*, "His glory, *His who was full* of grace . . ." (hence the reading *pleni* in *Augustine*). But these explanations, which are grammatically possible, appear to me to misconceive the true movement of the sentence. Carried away by the charm of the recollection, the evangelist interrupted the historical description of the relations which the Word sustained to those who surrounded Him; he now takes up again the picture which remained unfinished,—not that a parenthesis must be supposed including the words from καί to πατρός; there is no deliberate interruption; the ardor of feeling caused the break in the sentence, which is now completed. In the Old Testament, the two essential features of the character of God were *grace* and *truth* (Ex. xxxiv. 6): "*abundant in grace and truth.*" These are also the two features which, in John's view, distinguished the human life of the Word made flesh, and which served to reveal to Him His filial relation to the Father. *Grace:* the divine love investing the character with affableness towards friends, with condescension towards inferiors, with compassion towards the wretched, with pardon towards the guilty; God consenting to *give Himself.* And as it is from grace that *life* flows forth, the Word became anew for believers, by reason of this first characteristic, what He had been originally for the world (ver.

4), the source of life. The second feature, *truth*, is the reality of things adequately brought to light. And, as the essence of things is the moral idea which presides over the existence of each one of them, truth is the holy and good thought of God completely unveiled; it is God *revealed*. Through this attribute the incarnate Word also became anew what He originally was, the *light* of men (vv. 4, 5). By these two essential attributes of Jesus' character, therefore, the witnesses of His life were able to recognize in Him the only Son coming from the presence of the Father. Their feeling was this: This being is God *given*, God *revealed* in a human existence.

As a man who has made an important discovery recalls with satisfaction the suggestions which caused the first awakening of his thought and set his mind on its way forward, so from this experience, which he had had, the apostle transports himself to the decisive moment when he heard the first revelation of the fact of the incarnation. Not understood at the beginning, but afterwards made clear. For it is to this divine fact that the word of the forerunner which he is about to cite refers. John detaches this testimony from the historical situation in which it was declared, and which will be expressly recalled in ver. 30; and he makes use of it, at this time, simply with a didactic purpose, confirming by its means the capital fact of the incarnation, set forth in ver. 14. It is the second testimony, that of the official divine herald, following after that of the eye-witnesses.

Ver. 15. *John bears witness of him, and cries, saying :*[1] *This is he of whom I spoke when I said,*[2] *He who comes after me hath preceded me, because he was before me."* The present, *bears witness* is ordinarily explained by the *permanent* value of this testimony; but perhaps it is due rather to the fact that the author transports himself in a life-like way backward to the moment when he heard this mysterious saying coming from such lips; he seems to himself to hear it still. The perfect κέκραγε is always used in Greek in the sense of the present: *he cries ;* this declaration was made with the solemnity of an official proclamation. According to the reading of B. C. and Origen, we must, in order to give sense to these words : *it was he who spake,* put them in a parenthesis, as Westcott and Hort do, and thus ascribe to the evangelist the most inept of repetitions. See where these critics lead us by the critical system which they have once for all adopted ! The reading of ℵ is equally inadmissible. According to ver. 30, the forerunner uttered this saying on the next day after the deputation of the Sanhedrim had officially presented to him the question relating to his mission. After having expressly declined the honor of being the Messiah in the presence of these delegates, he had added in mysterious words, that that personage was already present and was immediately to succeed him, although in reality He had been already present before him (vv. 26, 27). The next day, he made this declaration again before the people, but this

---

[1] ℵ D^b omit λεγων.
[2] B. C. Or. (once) read ο ειπων (*he who spake*) instead of ον ειπον (*of whom I spake*). ℵ omits these words and adds ος after ερχομενος (*he who cometh after me was the one who was,* etc.).

time designating Jesus positively as the one of whom he had spoken on the preceding day, and adding an explanation with reference to that previous existence which he attributed to Him as compared with himself (ver. 30). This second more full declaration the evangelist quotes in ver. 15; because it was the first which referred personally and intelligibly to Jesus,—Jesus not being present on the previous day. It may be asked why there is this slight difference between the cited declaration and that of ver. 15, that there John the Baptist says οὑτός ἐστι, "this *is* he," while, in ver. 15, the evangelist makes him say: οὑτος ἦν, "this *was* he." The first form seems more in harmony with the immediate presence of the one to whom the testimony refers: "This *is* he of whom I was saying yesterday . . . You see him there!" This form perfectly suits the original testimony. The form: This *was*, might have been also suitable in the Baptist's mouth. It only called up the fact that it was He of whom he had thought on the preceding day, when speaking as he had done. But it proceeds rather from the evangelist; for it is natural from the standpoint more remote from the fact, at which he now is.

The testimony here reproduced by the apostle has a paradoxical cast in harmony with the original character of John the Baptist: "He who follows me has preceded me." There was something in the apparent contradiction of these two verbs to excite the attention and stimulate the mental activity of those to whom the saying was addressed. Many interpreters, as if making a point of depriving this saying of what in fact gives it its point, have assigned to the word *has preceded me* the sense of *has surpassed me* (*Chrysostom, Tholuck, Olshausen, de Wette, Lücke, Luthardt*). But what is there surprising in the fact that he who comes afterward should be superior to the one who goes before him? Is it not so in ordinary life? Does not the herald precede the sovereign? A platitude, therefore, is ascribed to John the Baptist. *Hofmann* has felt this. And instead of referring one of these verbs to *time* and the other to *dignity*, he applies them both to *dignity*, in this sense: "He who was at first inferior to me (who went behind me as my disciple) has become my superior (goes before me now as my master)." But Jesus was never in the position of a disciple with relation to John, and no more did He become his master. Besides, the words μείζων and ἐλάσσων would have presented themselves much more naturally for the expression of this idea. Let us remember that the evangelist has as his aim to prove by the testimony of the forerunner the dignity of the Logos incarnate, which is attributed to Jesus; now it is precisely the *temporal* sense which is adapted to this aim, and if one of the two prepositions refers to time, the other must refer to it also: for the apparent contradiction of the two terms is what gives this saying all its meaning. "He who is my successor preceded me" (*Luther, Meyer, Bäumlein, Weiss, Keil*, etc.). *My successor:* as to the Messianic work; Jesus appeared on the stage after John. And yet *He was before Him.* How so? By His presence and activity in the whole period of the Old Covenant. The Christ really preceded His forerunner in the world; comp. xii. 41; 1 Cor. x. 4, and the passage in Malachi (iii. 1), where John the Baptist found this idea, as we shall see. The perfect γέγονε does not mean *existed*, but *was there* (in fact); comp. vi. 25.

On repeating this enigmatical word on the next day, John added to it the phrase which should give a glimpse of the solution of the enigma: *because he was before me*, or more literally, *" my first."* Here also, many refer the word *first* to superiority of *rank*, not of *time*, (*Chrysostom, Beza, Calvin, Hofmann, Luthardt*); but the imperfect *was* is opposed to this sense; *is* would have been necessary. Objection is made to the tautology between this proposition and the preceding one, if both refer to time. But it is forgotten that there is a difference between γέγονε, which places us on the ground of history: *was there*, and ἦν, *was*, which refers to the essence of the Logos, to the eternal order to which He by nature belongs. He did not pass from nothingness into being, like His forerunner. If He preceded the latter on the field of history, it was because, in reality, He belonged to an order of things superior to that of time. Many interpreters (*Meyer, Bäumlein*), who take the word *first* in the same sense as ourselves, say that the superlative πρῶτος is put here for the comparative πρότερος, *anterior to*, and they cite as an example xv. 18. But John avoids the comparative because it would refer to the relation of two persons, who both belonged to the same order of things, and consequently might be compared with each other. Now it is not so in this case; and any comparison is impossible. Jesus is not only anterior to John; He is, speaking absolutely, *first* with relation to him and to everything that is in time. Hence the expression: *my first*. And such, indeed, is also the meaning in xv. 18. For Jesus was not merely persecuted before the disciples, as their equal; He it is who in them is the real object of the persecution. This last clause contains, accordingly, the solution of the apparent contradiction presented by the two preceding clauses. It was possible for Him to be the predecessor of His forerunner, since He appertains to the eternal order.

It is alleged that John the Baptist cannot have uttered such a saying, which already implies knowledge of the divinity of the Messiah, a knowledge which was developed only afterwards in the Church. It is the evangelist, then, who puts it into his mouth (*Strauss, Weiss, de Wette*), or who, at least, modifies in this way some expression which he had heard from his mouth, and in which the forerunner proclaimed the superior dignity of Jesus (*Weiss*). On the other hand, *Lücke, Meyer, Brückner* and others, defend the historical accuracy of this saying. And, in fact, the preexistence of the Messiah already forms a part of the teaching of the Old Testament; comp. Is. ix. 5; Micah v. 1; Dan. vii. 13, 14. *Bertholdt*, in his *Christologia Judæorum*, p. 131, has demonstrated the presence of this idea in the Rabbinical writings. It is found in the book of Enoch and in the fourth book of Esdras (Schürer, *Lehrb. der N. T. Gesch.*, § 29, 3). Far from having borrowed it from the Christians, the Jewish theology turned away from it rather, in its struggle with Christianity (Schürer, *ibid.*). If this saying were, either in whole or in part, a composition of the evangelist, it would be sufficient for him to place it in his Prologue; he would not allow himself to return to it again twice in the course of the following narrative, in order to point out the historical situation in which John had uttered it, fixing exactly the place, the moment, the occasion (vv. 26, 27, 30), and marking the progress in its terms from one occasion to the other. Besides, the original and enigmatical form in which it is presented would be enough to guarantee its authenticity. In this respect, it offers a full analogy to the indisputably authentic saying of the forerunner in iii. 30. Let us not forget that there was in the Old Testament a passage which, more than any other, contained, as it were, the programme of John the Baptist's mission, a passage which he must have read again and again, and which was the text of the declaration which occupies our attention. It is Mal. iii. 1 : " Behold, I send my messenger before me, and he prepares my way." If the Messiah sends His messenger before Him, that is, in order Himself soon to follow him, and if this sending consists in a birth, it is clear that the Messiah must necessarily exist before His successor. Simple common sense forces upon us this conclusion, which John the Baptist well knew how to draw. Finally, even independently of all this, the forerunner had received special revelations, instructions relative to his mission : " He who *sent* me to baptize with water, he *said to me ;* " thus he expresses himself, alluding to a direct communication, a sort of theophany which had been granted to him (i. 33). It is impossible, therefore, that, with the vision of the baptism to crown this special prophetic preparation, he should not have had his eyes open to understand fully the superior dignity of the One whom God Himself saluted with the title of His *well-beloved Son*.

The evangelist has made us hear the testimony of the immediate witnesses of the life of Christ (ver. 14), then, that of the herald sent to prepare the way for Him (ver. 15); it only remains for him to formulate that which comes forth from the experience of the whole Church.

Ver. 16. "*And*[1] *of his fullness we have all received, and grace for grace.*" By that first feature of the divine character, *grace*, the Church recognized in Jesus the Word made flesh. The two words, χάρις (*grace*), and πλήρωμα (*fullness*), closely connect this sentence with the last words of ver. 14. The experience which the Church has had, has come to set the seal upon the testimony of those who surrounded Jesus when on earth. Since *Heracleon* and *Origen*, many (*Luther, Melanchthon*, etc.), have made ver. 16 the continuation of John the Baptist's discourse (ver. 15). And it is possible that from this explanation the reading ὅτι (*because*), arose, which the Alexandrian authorities, Origen, and some other documents substitute for καί (*and*) read by T. R. at the beginning of the verse. The *we all* of ver. 16, which implies the existence of the Church, in any case excludes the supposition that John the Baptist is still speaking in ver. 16. As to ὅτι (*because*), if it were the true reading, it would be necessary to make it relate either to the testimony of the apostles in ver. 14, or to that of the Baptist in ver.

---

[1] Instead of και, which is the reading of T. R. with A E F G H Γ Δ Λ Π, Syr^{cur}.; Syr^{sch}.; Syr.; It^{aliq}.; and most of the Mnn., οτι is read in ℵ, B C D L X, It^{aliq}. Cop. Some Mnn and some Fathers, in particular Origen (3 times).

15. The first reference is not possible, since it would force us to make ver. 15 a simple parenthesis, which is inadmissible; the second is no more possible; since it would be necessary in that case to refer this *because*, as *Weiss* attempts to do, not to the contents of John's testimony (ver. 15), but to the very *act* of the testimony, and thus to the verb *he testifies:* "John testifies thus of Jesus, because indeed we have all received . . ." A connection which is, grammatically and logically speaking, more unnatural cannot be imagined. Nothing is more natural, on the contrary, than the connection through καί (*and*) in the T. R.; this *and* expresses very simply the addition of the third testimony, that of the Church, to the two others. This reading, therefore, is certainly the true one; it is found already in the oldest Syriac version, the Curetonian Syriac. The other is due to Heracleon's false interpretation, which was followed by Origen.

The word πλήρωμα which properly denotes that which serves to fill an empty space, refers to the inexhaustible fullness of grace and truth by which the person of the Logos is filled and with which it overflows. This word πλήρωμα is used here in the most simple and natural way, in the same sense as in Rom. xv. 29 (πλήρωμα εὐλογίας, *fullness of blessing*), and without the least analogy to the mythological sense, which the Gnostics of the second century gave to it in their systems. In the words *we all* are included all the believers mentioned in ver. 12, the Church already extended through every country of the East and the West at the time when John wrote this Prologue. The verb: *we have received* is left without an object. The question at first is not of such or such a gift received, but only of *the act* of *receiving*. "We have all drawn, richly drawn from this invisible source." The witnesses had *beheld* (ver. 14); the Church *has received*. In the following words, John states precisely what it has received. First, *grace*—that first sign by which it had recognized in Him the divine Logos; then, *truth;* this second sign will be noticed in vv. 17, 18. The καί, *and*, signifies here: "and this is the way." The words "grace for grace" are ordinarily translated "grace *upon* grace." That would simply mean, grace added to previous grace. But, with this sense, would not John rather have used the preposition ἐπί (Phil. ii. 27)? In the following verse, grace is opposed to the law. It must, therefore, be supposed that John has this antithesis already present to his mind, and that this is the reason why he seeks to bring out with emphasis in ver. 16 the peculiar character of the grace. Under the rule of the law each new grace must be obtained at the cost of a new work. In the economy of grace which faith in the Word made flesh opens, the gift already received is the one title to the obtaining of a new gift: "To him who hath, more is given." There is enthusiasm in this paradoxical formula which exalts the system of grace by setting it in such complete opposition to that of the law. No one defends any longer, at the present day, the explanation of the ancient Greek interpreters, who thought they saw here the supplying the place of the gift of the Old Covenant by the superior gift of the New Covenant. The following verse, where grace, as such, is opposed to the law, would be sufficient to exclude such an interpretation. That of

Calov, who imagined he could see here the grace of *salvation* replacing the happy state which man possessed before the fall, is still more unfortunate.

Ver. 16 describes *grace;* ver. 18 will describe *truth;* ver. 17 which connects them, unites grace and truth:

Ver. 17. " *For the law was given by Moses; grace and truth came by Jesus Christ.*" John, who had reached the light of the new revelation through the preparatory system of the old, could not fail to point out in this Prologue, at least summarily, the relation between the two; and he does it naturally in this place, where the mention of the two divine gifts obtained through Jesus Christ summons him to a comparison with those which the ancient people of God had received, especially with the law. The *for* refers to the idea of grace, which has been so forcibly expressed in ver. 16 : " grace upon grace; *for* the legal system has given place henceforth to that of free grace which is, at the same time, that of truth." We meet again, in this verse, the parallel construction peculiar to the Hebrew; a Greek writer would not have failed to mark the antithesis between the two clauses of this verse by the particles $\mu\acute{\epsilon}\nu$ and $\delta\acute{\epsilon}$. The office of the *law* is to command and to demand; the peculiarity of grace, the essence of the Gospel, is to offer and to give. The law connects salvation with a work which it exacts; Christ gives gratuitously a salvation which is to become the cause of works. Now this whole manifestation of grace fully reveals at last the *true* character of God, which remained veiled in the law, and consequently it reveals *truth* which is the perfect knowledge of God. *Bengel* explains the opposition between the law and the two following terms by this ingenious formula : *lex iram parans et umbram habens;* but perhaps this is the mark of Paul rather than of John. *Weiss* makes grace consist in the revelation of truth; that is to say, of God as love. *Keil*, in the opposite way, makes the truth of God consist in the revelation of His grace, which is more true. But John seems to me rather to place these two gifts in juxtaposition and to regard them as distinct from each other; grace is God possessed; truth is God known. These two gifts are joined together, but they are distinct. So John, after having developed the first in ver. 16, sets forth the second in ver. 18.

The term *was given*, $\dot{\epsilon}\delta\acute{o}\theta\eta$, recalls the positive and outward institution of the law, its official promulgation. The expression *came*, literally *became*, suits better the historical manifestation of grace and truth in the person and in the ministry of Jesus Christ. Moses may disappear; the law given by him remains. But take away Jesus Christ, and the grace and truth manifested in Him disappear. " John," says Bengel on this point, " chose his expressions with the strictness of a philosopher." Let us rather say, with the emphatic precision which is the characteristic of inspiration.

It is at this point of the Prologue that the apostle introduces, for the first time, the name so long expected, *Jesus Christ*. He descends gradually from the divine to the human : the Logos (ver. 1), the only-begotten Son (ver. 14), finally, Jesus Christ, in whom the heavenly world fully assumes for us life and reality. The apostle now passes to the second characteristic of the divine glory of Jesus Christ: truth, ver. 18.

280 / Prologue

Ver. 18. "*No one has ever seen God; the only-begotten Son,*[1] *who is in the bosom of the Father, he has revealed him to us.*"—The absence of a particle between vv. 17 and 18 is the proof of a very intimate relation of thought or feeling between the two. The second becomes thus, as it were, an energetic reaffirmation of the preceding. And in fact, what is this *truth* born for the earth in the person of Jesus Christ, according to ver. 17, if it is not the perfect revelation of God described in ver. 18?—The true knowledge of God is not the result of philosophical investigation; our reason can seize only some isolated rays of the divine revelation shed abroad in nature and in conscience. It does not succeed in making of them a whole, because it cannot ascend to the living focus from which they emanate. The theocratic revelations themselves, which were granted to the saints of the Old Covenant, contained only an approximate manifestation of the divine being, as the Lord caused Moses to understand, at the very moment when He was about to make him behold something of His glory: "Thou shalt see my back; but my face shall not be seen" (Ex. xxxiii. 23). This central and living knowledge of God which is the only true knowledge, and which has as its symbol *sight*, was not possessed by any man, either within or outside of the theocracy, not even by Moses. The word *God* is placed at the beginning, although it is the object, because it is the principal idea. One can know everything else, not God! The perfect ἑώρακε, *has seen*, denotes a result, rather than an act, which would be indicated by the aorist: "No one *is in possession* of the sight of God, and consequently no one can speak of Him *de visu.*" The full truth does not exist on earth before or outside of Jesus Christ; it truly *came* through Him. The Alexandrian reading *God only-begotten,* μονογενὴς θεός, or, according to ℵ, *the* (ὁ) *only-begotten God,* long since abandoned, has found in Hort[2] a learned and sagacious defender, who has gained the assent of two such scholars as *Harnack*[3] and *Weiss.*[4] The received reading has been defended, with at least equal erudition and skill, by the American critic, *Ezra Abbot*, in an article in the *Bibliotheca Sacra*, Oct., 1861, and in a more recent essay in the *Unitarian Review*, 1875. The result of these studies with reference to the external testimonies, is: 1. That the two readings must have already co-existed in the second century. It is probable that both of the two are found already in *Irenæus.* The received reading was read in the *Itala* and by Tertullian; the other, that of the Alexandrian authorities, by Clement of Alex.;[5] 2. That the latter is found only in the

---

[1] T. R. reads ο μονογενης υιος (*the only-begotten Son*) with 24 Mjj., from the fifth to the tenth cent., A E F G . . . X Γ Δ Λ, etc., almost all the Mnn. It. Syr^cur.; Syr^hare.; Iren. (twice), Orig. (once), Tert., Eus. (six times), Athan. (four times), the emperor Julian (twice) Chrys., Theod., etc. The reading μονογενης θεος (ℵ ο μονογ. θ.) (*God only-begotten*) is found in ℵ B C L 33 Syr^sch. Ir. (once), Clem. (twice), Orig. (twice), Epiph. (three times).—D has a vacancy here.

[2] *Two dissertations on* μονογενὴς θεός, Cambridge, 1875.

[3] *Schürer's Literatur-Zeitung*, 1876, No. 21.

[4] Sixth ed. of *Meyer's Commentary.*

[5] It has been wrongly believed that among the witnesses for the latter reading, the Valentinian Ptolemy could be ranked, in accordance with a fragment from this Gnostic quoted by Irenæus (i. 8, 5). It does not follow from this quotation that Ptolemy read in his copy θεός instead of υἱός, nor that the quotation refers to John i. 18. (See Keil, p. 101.)

John 1:17 / 281

Egyptian documents (Fathers, versions and manuscripts), and that the documents of all other countries present the received reading; thus for the West, the *Itala, Tertullian* and all the Latin Fathers without exception, —the only exception which has been cited, that of *Hilary*, is only apparent, as *Abbot* proves:—in Syria and Palestine, the ancient *Syriac* translation of Cureton, *Eusebius, Chrysostom, Theodoret,* etc.; and, what is more surprising, in Egypt *Athanasius* himself, the most inflexible defender of the divinity of Christ. Does it not seem to follow from this, that the Alexandrian reading is due to a purely local influence, which goes back even to the second century? As to internal reasons, as favoring the Alexandrian reading, stress may be laid upon its unique and wholly strange character; for it is said to be more improbable that it should be replaced by the received reading, which has a more simple and common character, than that the contrary could have taken place. But it may also be asked whether a reading which does not find its counterpart in any writing of the New Testament, and in any passage of John himself, does not become by reason of this fact very suspicious. To account for its rejection it is enough that an explanation be given as to how it may have originated and been introduced, and *Abbot* does this by reminding us how early readings like the following were originated : *the Logos-God*, which is found in the second century in Melito and Clement of Alexandria, and the epithet θεοτόκος, *mother of God*, given to Mary. Hence, readings like these: *the body of God*, instead of *the body of Jesus*, John xix. 40, in A ; or *all were waiting for God*, instead of *all were waiting for Him* (Jesus), Luke viii. 40, in ; or *the Church of God which He purchased with His own blood*, instead of *the Church of the Lord*, etc. (Acts xx. 28), in ℵ and B. It is curious that it is precisely these same two MSS., which especially support the reading *God*, instead of *Son*, in our passage. It would be difficult, on the other hand, to explain the dogmatic reason which could have substituted here the word *Son* for *God*. The Arians themselves, as Abbot has well shown, had no interest in this change; for they were able to make use of the Alexandrian reading to prove that the word *God* could be taken in a weakened sense, and designate a divine being of second rank, inferior to the Father; it was for them the best means of getting rid of the word *God* applied to the Word in ver. 1. So Athanasius himself does not hesitate to use the received reading; as for ourselves, we cannot hesitate. The absence of any parallel to the Alexandrian reading and its very pronounced doctrinal savor seem to us, independently of external criticism, sufficient reasons for rejecting it. It is true that *Hort* and *Weiss* urge against the received reading the article ὁ, *the*, before the title *only-begotten Son*, for the reason that Jesus, not having been yet called by this name in the Prologue, could not be thus designated with the definite article. This objection falls to the ground through the true explanation of ver. 14, where the words *only-begotten Son* cannot denote *an* only-begotten Son in general, as Weiss will have it, and can only be applied to the Word made flesh. Moreover, even without this preceding expression, no reader, when reading the words: "The only-begotten Son has revealed him to us" could for an instant doubt concerning whom John meant to speak.

The character of complete revelator ascribed here to Jesus is explained by His intimate and personal relation with God Himself, such as is described in the following words: *who is in the bosom of the Father.* The participle ὁ ὤν, *who is*, is connected in a very close logical relation with the following verb: *He has revealed.* As *Bäumlein* says, it is equivalent to ὅτι ὤν, *inasmuch as He is;* thereupon rests His competency to reveal.— The figure which John employs might be derived from the position of two nearest guests at a banquet (xiii. 23); but it seems rather to be borrowed from the position of a son seated on his father's knees and resting on his bosom. It is the emblem of a complete opening of the heart; he who occupies this place in relation to God must know the most secret thoughts of the Father and His inmost will. The word κόλπος, *bosom,* would by itself prove that the mystery of the Son's existence is a matter, not of metaphysics, but of love, comp. xvii. 24: "Thou didst love me before the foundation of the world." The omission of the words ὁ ὤν in ℵ is a negligence condemned by all the other MSS. Must we, with *Hofmann, Luthardt* and *Weiss,* refer the words: "who is in the bosom of the Father" to the present glorified condition of Jesus? But the heavenly state which Jesus now enjoys cannot explain how He was able to reveal the Father perfectly while He was on the earth. We must then, in that case, refer the revealing act of Jesus to the sending of the Holy Spirit on the day of Pentecost, which is implied by nothing in the text. Or is John thinking especially of the divine condition of the Logos before His coming to the earth? But that would be to say, that the knowledge of God which Jesus communicated to men was drawn from the recollections of His anterior existence. We cannot admit this. In fact, everything which Jesus revealed on earth concerning God passed through His human consciousness (see on iii. 13, vi. 46). I agree, therefore, in opinion rather with *Lücke,* that this present participle ὁ ὤν, *who is,* refers to the permanent relation of the Son to the Father through all the stages of His divine, human and divine-human existence. He ever presses anew with an equal intimacy into the bosom of the Father, who reveals Himself to Him in a manner suitable to His position and His work at every moment. The form εἰς κόλπον, instead of ἐν κόλπῳ (the prep. of motion, instead of that of rest), expresses precisely this active and living relation. The bosom of the Father is not a place, but a life; one *is there* only in virtue of a continual moral act. If John substitutes εἰς here for πρός of ver. 1, this arises simply from the difference between the object κόλπος, *the bosom,* which denotes a thing, and the object θεόν, *God,* which designated a person. The word τοῦ πατρός, *of the Father,* is not merely a paraphrase of the name of God; this term is chosen in order to make the essential contents of the revelation brought by the Son understood. He manifested God *as Father,* and for this He did not need to give speculative teaching; it was enough for Him to show Himself *as Son.* To show in Himself the Son, was the simplest means of showing in God the Father. Thus, by His filial relation with God, Jesus has initiated earth into the most profound secret of heaven, a secret which the angels themselves perchance did not yet sound completely. Outside of this revelation of the divine character, every idea which man forms of God is incomplete or imaginary—in a certain measure, an *idol*, as John says (1 Ep. v. 20). The pronoun ἐκεῖνος, *he*, has here, as ordinarily in John, a pregnant and even exclusive sense: "he and he alone!" It is impossible to explain the use of this pronoun, as *Weiss* would do, by the contrast with a nearer subject, which would be the Father Himself. The employment of the word ἐξηγεῖσθαι to *explain*, to *make known*, is often explained by the technical use of it which was made by the Greeks, with whom it denoted the explanation of divine things by men charged with this office, the ἐξηγηταί. The simplicity of John's style hardly harmonizes with this comparison, which, besides, is not necessary in order to the explanation of the word. The apostle uses it absolutely, without giving it any complement. It is to the act, rather than its object, that he desires to draw attention, as in the first clause of ver. 16 (*we have received*): "He has declared; really declared!" Every one understands what is the object of this teaching: God first, then in Him all the rest. To reveal God, is to unveil everything.

With this 18th verse we evidently come back to the starting-point of the Prologue, to the idea of ver. 1. Through faith in Christ as only-begotten Son, the believer finds again access to that eternal Word from whom sin (*the darkness*, ver. 5) had held him apart. He obtains anew, in the form of *grace* and *truth* (vv. 16–18), those treasures of life and light, which the Word has spread abroad in the world (ver. 4). Sin's work is vanquished; the communion with heaven is re-established. God is possessed, is known; the destiny of man begins again to be realized. The infinite dwells in the finite and acts through it; the abyss is filled up.

At the same time, these last words of the Prologue form, as *Keil* says, the transition to the narrative which is about to begin. How did Jesus Christ reveal the Father? This is what the story to which the apostle passes from ver. 19 onward is to relate.

4. GENERAL CONSIDERATIONS

1 THE PLAN

Three thoughts sum up this remarkable passage and determine its progress: The *Logos* (vv. 1–4); the Logos *unrecognized* (vv. 5–11); the Logos *received* (vv. 12–18). Between the first and second subjects ver. 5 forms the transition, in the same manner as vv. 12, 13 form that between the second and third. Finally, the last verses of the Prologue bring back the mind of the reader to the first words of the passage.

This plan seems to us the only one which is harmony with the apostle's thought. We shall convince ourselves of this by recognizing, in the sequel of this study, the fact that the entire narrative is founded upon the three factors which have been indicated and that its phases are determined by the appearance, and the successive preponderance of these three essential elements of the history.

2 The Intention of the Prologue

There are three very different ways of viewing this subject.

1. The *Tübingen School* think that the author proposed to himself to acclimate in the Church the doctrine of the Logos. Finding that speculative idea in the systems of his time, he wished to build the bridge between the Church and the reigning philosophy. And as, in his whole narrative, he had no other aim except to realize this design by illustrating this dominant idea of the Logos, by means of certain acts and discourses more fictitious than real, he did not hesitate to inscribe at the beginning of his book the great thought which forms its synthesis—namely, that of an eternal being intermediate between the infinite God and the finite world.

If it is so, it must be acknowledged that the theorem of the Logos is the end of the work, and that the person of Jesus is nothing more than the means. Is this, indeed, the meaning of this Prologue? Who can think, in comparing ver. 1 and ver. 14, that the second of these verses is there for the sake of the first, and not the reverse? No; the author does not wish to take us on a metaphysical walk in the depths of Divinity, in order to discover there the being called Logos; he wishes to make us feel all the grandeur and all the value of the person and work of Jesus Christ, by showing us in this historical personage the manifestation of the divine Logos. It is not the fact of the incarnation (ver. 14) which is at the service of the thesis of the Logos (ver. 1); it is this thesis which prepares the way for the account of this capital fact of human history. By nothing is the opposition between the speculative intention which Baur ascribes to the Prologue (as to the whole Gospel) and the real aim of this passage, better indicated, than by the explanation which that scholar is obliged to give of ver. 14. To that verse, which is the centre of the whole passage, Baur gives an altogether subordinate place. John does not mean that the Logos becomes incarnate, but simply that He is made visible by a kind of theophany. This fact, according to Baur, has no value for the accomplishing of salvation; it serves only to make us perceive more clearly all its sweetness. This explanation is sufficient to show the contradiction between the thought of the Tübingen professor and that of the evangelist.

II. *Reuss* avoids such an exaggeration; he understands that the historical person of Jesus is the end and that the theory of the Logos can, in any case, be only a means. The author, in possession of the Gospel faith, seeks to give a rational account to himself of his new belief, and for this purpose he undertakes to draw, outside of the Gospel, from the contemporary philosophy an idea capable of becoming for him the key of Jesus' history, and of raising his faith and that of his readers to the full height of religious speculation. Our Prologue is the initiation of the Church into the true Gnosis. This is also the result of *Lücke's* study. To explain the Prologue thus, whether one wills it or not, is to give up the authenticity of the entire work. For it is impossible to ascribe to an apostle of Jesus such an amalgam of contemporary metaphysics with the conception of the person of his Master. So the author of this explanation has ended, after much hesitation, by placing himself in the number of the adversaries of the authenticity. By a fatality he was obliged to come to this point. There was, indeed, for the Apostle John, if he was really desirous to deposit in a written work the theory of the Logos, which had thrown a clear light for him upon his own faith, a simple means of establishing for the Church this new view. It was that of setting it before the Church in an epistle; there was no need of using for this purpose the means—very equivocal in a moral point of view—of a Gospel narrative.

Reuss regards the procedure which he attributes to the author as unconscious on his part and, consequently, as innocent. But the fact that the author all along avoids putting the word Logos into the mouth of Jesus, clearly proves that he acted with reflection, and that he had the consciousness of not having this name from the lips of Him to whom he applied it. As to the innocence of this matter, history has passed judgment, and its judgment is severe. History says, indeed, that among all the writings of the New Testament, the Gospel of John and particularly the Prologue have especially contributed to establish in the Church *Jesus-worship*, that is to say—from the standpoint of those who think after this manner—a remnant of paganism. Julian the Apostate could well say: "This John who declared that the Word was made flesh must be regarded as the source of all the evil."[1] This is the result of John's speculative desires; he has thrown into the Gospel the leaven of idolatry, corrupted the worship in spirit and truth, and even troubled at its source the purity of the Christian life, for eighteen centuries. Only at the present day does the Church awake from this long infatuation of which he was the author, and return to a sound mind. Thus so far as he is concerned has the Master's promise been verified: "He who heareth you, heareth me!"

When we penetrate the thought of the Prologue we see clearly that the doctrine of the Logos is not to the author's mind superimposed upon his faith, but that it forms the foundation and essence of it. If Jewish unbelief with regard to Jesus was something so monstrous, it is because He was not only the Messiah, but the Word who had come into the midst of His own. If the faith of the Church is so great a privilege for itself, it is because, by uniting it with Jesus, it puts the Church again in communication with the divine source of life and light, with the Word Himself. This Logos-idea, then, belongs to the essence of John's faith; it is no longer for him a *means*, as *Reuss* claims, but an *end*, as *Baur* would have it.

III. This idea was simply a *result*. It was evolved for John from the sum of his reflections on the person of Jesus. He himself describes to

---

[1] *Cyril, contra Julianum.*

us in ver. 14 the way in which this work was accomplished in him. The Son of God was revealed to him in the person of Jesus through the glory full of grace and truth which distinguished this man from every other man; and he inscribed this discovery at the beginning of his narrative, in order that he might make the reader understand the decisive importance of the history, which was about to pass under his eyes; here is not one of those events which we leave after having read it, that we may pass on to another: "These things have been written, that you may believe, and that believing you may have life" (xx. 31). The question in this history is of eternal life and death; to accept, is to live; to reject, is to perish. This is the *nota bene* by which John opens his narrative and guides the reader.

But why employ so singular a term as Logos?

3 THE IDEA AND TERM LOGOS

We have here to study three questions: 1. Whence did the evangelist derive the *notion* of the Logos? 2. What is the origin of this *term?* 3. What the reason of its *use?* Having discussed these questions in the Introduction (pp. 173–181), we will notice here only that which has a special relation to the exegetical study which we are about to undertake.

1. First of all we establish a fact: namely, that the Prologue only sums up the thoughts contained in the testimony which Christ bears to Himself in the fourth Gospel. *Weiss*[1] mentions two principal points in which the Prologue seems to him to go beyond the testimony of Christ: 1. The notion of *the Word* by which John expresses the pre-historic existence of Christ; 2. The function of *creator* which is ascribed to Him (ver. 3).

Let us for a moment lay aside the *term* Logos, to which we will return. The creative function is naturally connected with the fact of the eternal existence of the Logos in God. He who could say to God: "*Thou didst love me before the creation of the world*," certainly did not remain a stranger to the act by which God brought the world out of nothing. How is it possible not to apply here the words of v. 17: "As the Father . . . I also work," and v. 19, 20: "The Father showeth the Son all that he doeth . . . ," and: "Whatsoever things the Father doeth, these doeth the Son in like manner." Add the words of Gen. i. 26: "Let *us* make man in *our* image," to which John certainly alludes in the second clause of ver. 1 of the Prologue. All the other affirmations of this passage rest equally on the discourses and facts related in the Gospel; comp. ver. 4: "*In Him was life* . . . ," with v. 26: "*As the Father hath life in himself, so hath he given to the Son to have life in himself;*" ver. 9: "*There was the true light,*" with viii. 12 and ix. 5: "*I am the light of the world* . . . *He that followeth me shall have the light of life;*" ver. 7: "*John came to bear witness,*" with i. 34: "*And I have seen, and have borne witness that this is the Son of God,*" and ver. 33: "*Ye have sent unto John, and he hath borne witness to the truth;*"

[1] *Johanneischer Lehrbegriff*, 1862.

what is said of the presence and activity of the Logos in the world in general (ver. 10), and in the theocracy in particular (*to His home, His own,* ver. 11), previous to His incarnation, with what Jesus declares in chap. x. of the Shepherd's voice which is immediately *recognized* by *His sheep,* and this not only by those who are already in the fold of the Old Covenant (ver. 3), but also by those *who are not of that fold* (ver. 16), or what is said of the children of God *scattered throughout the whole world* (xi. 52); the opposition made in the Prologue (ver. 13) between the fleshly birth and the divine begetting, with the word of Jesus to Nicodemus (iii. 6): "*That which is born of the flesh is flesh; that which is born of the Spirit is spirit;*" the notion of Christ's real humanity, so earnestly affirmed in the Prologue (ver. 14), with the perfectly human character of the person and affections of the Saviour in the whole Johannean narrative; He is *exhausted* by fatigue (iv. 6); He *thirsts* (iv. 7); He *weeps* over a friend (xi. 35); He is *moved,* even *troubled* (xi. 33, xii. 27); on the other hand, His glory, *full of grace and truth,* His character as *Son who has come from the Father* (vv. 14–18), with His complete dependence (vi. 38 f.), His absolute docility (v. 30, etc.), His perfect intimacy with the Father (v. 20), the divinity of the works which it was given Him to accomplish, such as: to give life, to judge (v. 21, 22); the perfect assurance of being heard, whatsoever He might ask for (xi. 41, 42); the adoration which He accepts (xx. 28); which He claims even as the equal of the Father (v. 23); the testimony of John the Baptist quoted in ver. 15, with the subsequent narrative (i. 27, 30); the gift of the law, as a preparation for the Gospel (ver. 17), with what the Lord says of His relation to Moses and his writings (v. 46, 47); ver. 18, which closes the Prologue with the saying in vi. 46: "*Not that any one hath seen the Father, except He that is from the Father, He hath seen the Father;*" the terms *Son* and *only-begotten Son,* finally, with the words of Jesus in vi. 40: "*This is the Father's will, that He who beholds the Son . . . ;*" iii. 16: "*God so loved the world, that He gave His only-begotten Son,*" and iii. 18: "*Because he hath not believed on the name of the only-begotten Son of God.*" It is clear: the Prologue is an edifice which is constructed wholly out of materials furnished by the words and the facts of Jesus' history. It contains of what is peculiar to John only the idea and term Logos applied to His pre-existent state. It is certainly this term, used in the philosophical language of the time, which has led so many interpreters to transform the author of the Prologue into a disciple of Philo. We shall limit ourselves here to the mentioning of the essential differences which distinguish the God of Philo from the God of John, the Logos of the one from the Logos of the other. And it shall be judged whether the second was truly at the school of the first.

1. The word λόγος, in John, signifies, as in the whole Biblical text, *word.* In Philo, it signifies, as in the philosophical language of the Greeks, *reason.* This simple fact reveals a wholly different starting-point in the use which they make of the term.

2. In Philo, the existence of the Logos is a metaphysical theorem. God being conceived of as the absolutely indeterminate and impersonal being, there is an impassable gulf between Him and the material, finite, varied

world which we behold. To fill this gulf, Philo needed an intermediate agent, a *second God*, brought nearer to the finite; this is the Logos, the half-personified divine reason. The existence of the Logos in John is not the result of such a metaphysical necessity. God is in John, as in all the Scriptures, Creator, Master, Father. He acts Himself in the world, He loves it, He gives His Son to it; we shall even see that it is He who serves as intermediate agent between men and the Son (vi. 37, 44), which is just the opposite of Philo's theory. In a word, in John everything in the relation of the Logos to God is a matter of liberty and of love, while with Philo everything is the result of a logical necessity. The one is the disciple of the Old Testament interpreted by means of Plato and Zeno; the other, of the same Old Testament explained by Jesus Christ.

3. The office of the Logos in Philo does not go beyond the divine facts of the creation and preservation of the world. He does not place this being in any relation with the Messiah and the Messianic kingdom. In John, on the contrary, the creating Logos is mentioned only in view of the redemption of which He is to be the agent; everything in the idea of this being tends towards His Messianic appearance.

4. To the view of Philo, as to that of Plato, the principle of evil is matter; the Jewish philosopher nowhere dreams, therefore, of making the Logos descend to earth, and that in a bodily form. In John, on the contrary, the supreme fact of history is this: "*The Logos was made flesh,*" and this is also the central word of the Prologue.

The two points of view, therefore, are entirely different, and are even in many respects the antipodes of each other. Nevertheless, we notice in Philo certain ideas, certain terms, which establish a relation between him and John. How are we to explain this fact?

The solution is easy: it is not difficult to find a common source. John and Philo were both Jews; both of them had been nourished by the Old Testament. Now three lines in that sacred book converge towards the notion of an intermediate being between God and the world.[1] 1. The appearances of *the Angel of the Lord* (*Maleach Jehovah*), of that messenger of God, who acts as His agent in the sensible world, and who sometimes is distinguished from Jehovah, sometimes is identified with Him; comp. e. g. Gen. xvi. 7 with ver. 13; again, Gen. xxxii. 28 with Hos. xii. 4, 5. God says of this mysterious being, Exod. xxiii. 21: "*My name* (my manifested essence) *is in him*." According to the Old Testament (comp. particularly Zech. xii. 10, and Mal. iii. 1), this divine personage, after having been the agent of all the theophanies, is to consummate His office of mediator by fulfilling here on earth the function of Messiah. 2. The description of *Wisdom*, Prov. viii. 22–31; undoubtedly this representation of Wisdom in Proverbs appears to be only a poetic personification, while the Angel of the Lord is presented as a real personality. 3. The active part ascribed to the *Word of the Lord*. This part begins with the creation and continues in the prophetic revelations

---

[1] See Introd. p. 177.

comp. Ps. cvii. 20; cxlvii. 15, and Is. lv. 11, where the works accomplished by this divine messenger are described.

From the time of the Babylonish captivity, the Jewish doctors united these three modes of divine manifestation and activity in a single conception, that of the permanent agent of Jehovah in the sensible world, whom they designated by the name of *Memra* (Word) *of Jehovah* (מימרא דיהוה).[1] It cannot be certainly determined whether these Jewish learned men established a relation between this Word of the Lord and the person of the Messiah.[2]

This idea of a divine being, organ of the works and the revelations of Jehovah in the sensible world could not, therefore, fail to have been known both by John and by Philo. This is the basis common to the two authors. But from this starting-point their paths diverge. John passing into the school of Jesus, the idea of the Word takes for him a historical significance, a concrete application. Hearing Jesus affirm that He is before Abraham; that the Father loved Him *before the creation of the world*, . . . he applies to Him this idea of the *Word* which in so many different ways strikes its roots into the soil of the Old Testament, while Philo, living at Alexandria, becomes there the disciple of the Greek philosophers, and seeks to interpret by means of their speculations and their formulas the religious ideas of the Jewish religion. We thus easily understand both what these two authors have in common, and what distinguishes them and even puts them in opposition to each other.

---

[1] Introd. pp. 177, 178.—Along with this expression the terms *Shekinah* (*habitation*) and *Jekara* (*splendor*) are used in the *Targums*, or Chaldaic paraphrases of the O. T. The two oldest, those of Onkelos and Jonathan, were generally regarded as dating from the middle of the first century of our era. Recent works seem to bring the redaction of them down to the third or fourth century; but only the redaction. For a great number of points prove that the materials go back to the apostolic times. We have even proofs of the existence of redactions going back as far as the time of John Hyrcanus. With the Jews everything is a matter of tradition. The redaction in a case like this is only "the completion of the work of ages." Comp. Schürer, *Lehrb. d. neutest. Zeitgesch.* pp. 478, 479.

[2] Perhaps in Palestine there was, from the early times, more inclination to blend together the notion of the Word and the Messianic idea, than at Alexandria. There is in the book of Enoch (of the last part of the second century before Jesus Christ) and in one of the very parts of it which are almost unanimously recognized as the oldest, a remarkable passage, which, if the form in which we have it is the exact reproduction of the original text, would allow no further doubt on this point. The Messiah is there represented (chap. xc. 16–38) as a white bull, which, after having received the worship of all the animals of the earth, transforms all these races into white bulls like itself; after which the poet adds: And the first bull "*was the Word*, and *this word* was a powerful animal which had great black horns on its head [the emblem of the divine omnipotence]" . . . It is thus that Dillmann in his classic work on this book, translates these words. Comp. the remarkable article of M. Wabnitz, *Rev. de Théolog.* July, 1874. The Messianic application of this passage cannot be doubted (see Schürer, *Lehrbuch der neutest. Zeitgesch.*, p. 568). There seems, then, clearly to be an indication here of the relation established in Palestine, from the time anterior to Jesus Christ, between the divine being called *Memra* or *Word* and the person of the Messiah. There is no doubt of the Palestinian origin of the Book of Enoch. The Book of *Wisdom*, which was composed at Alexandria a century before Jesus Christ, speaks of *Wisdom*, personifying it with great emphasis. But it is impossible to discover here (even in chap. vii.) the notion of a real personality, or to recognize in the representation of the persecuted just man in chap. ii. the least allusion to the person of the Messiah.

II. With respect to the term *Word*, frequently used, as it already was, in the Old Testament, then employed in a more theological sense by the Jewish doctors, it must have presented itself to the mind of John as very appropriate to designate the divine being in the person of his Master. What confirms the Palestinian, and by no means Alexandrian, origin of this term, is that it is used in the same sense in the Apocalypse, which is certainly by no means a product of Alexandrian wisdom; comp. Acts xix. 13: " And his name was *the Word of God.*" Philo, as he laid hold of this Jewish term Logos, in order to apply it to the metaphysical notion which he had borrowed from Greek philosophy, could not do so without also modifying its meaning and making it signify *reason* instead of *word*. This is what he did in general with regard to all the Biblical terms which his Jewish education had rendered familiar to him, such as *archangel, son, high-priest,* which he transferred to speculative notions according to the method by which he applied the word *angels* to the *ideas* of Plato.

We see, therefore: it is the same religion of the Old Testament, which, developed on one side in the direction of Christian realism, on the other in that of Platonic idealism, produced these two conceptions of John and of Philo, who differ even more in the central idea than they resemble each other in that which envelops it.

In applying to Jesus the name Word, John did not dream, therefore, of introducing into the Church the Alexandrian speculative theorem which had for him no importance. He wished to describe Jesus Christ as the *absolute revelation* of God to the world, to bring back all divine revelations to Him as to their living centre, and to proclaim the matchless grandeur of His appearance in the midst of humanity.

III. But can the *employment* of this extraordinary term on his part have occurred without any allusion to the use which was made of it all about him in the regions where he composed his Gospel?[1] It seems to me difficult to believe this. Asia Minor, particularly Ephesus, was then the centre of a syncretism in which all the religious and philosophical doctrines of Greece, Persia and Egypt met together. It has been proved that in all those systems the idea of an intermediate divine being between God and the world appears, the *Oum* of the Indians, the *Hom* of the Persians, the *Logos* of the Greeks, the *Memar* of the Jews.[2] If such were the surroundings in the midst of which the fourth Gospel was composed, we easily understand what John wished to say to all those thinkers who were speculating on the relations between the infinite and the finite, namely: "That connecting link between God and man, which you are seeking in the region of the idea, we Christians possess in that of reality, in that of history; we have seen, heard, touched this celestial mediator. Listen and believe! And by receiving Him, you will possess, with us, *grace upon grace.*" In introducing this new term into the Christian language, therefore, John had the intention, as *Neander* thought, of opposing to the empty

---

[1] Comp. Introd., p. 180 f.
[2] Comp. Baumlein, *Versuch die Bedentung des joh. Logos zu entwickeln,* Tübingen, 1828.

(We take our position on the general results of this essay, with pretending to vouch for all its particular citations.)

idealism on which the cultivated and unchristian persons around him were feeding, the life-giving realism of the Gospel history which he was proposing to set forth.[1]

4 THE TRUTH AND IMPORTANCE OF THE TEACHING OF THE PROLOGUE RESPECTING THE PERSON OF JESUS CHRIST.

If the Prologue is the summary of the testimonies which Jesus bore to Himself in the course of His ministry, the teaching of John in this passage can no longer be regarded as the last term of a series of phases by means of which the Christological conception passed into the midst of the Church; it is at once the most normal and the richest expression of the consciousness which Jesus had of His own person. *Renan* is not indisposed to accept this result. Only in this estimation of Himself which Jesus allowed Himself to indulge, he sees the height of self-exaltation. But this explanation is incompatible with the moral character of Jesus. If He overrated Himself even to folly, how are we to understand that inward calm, that profound humility, that unalterably sound judgment, that so profoundly true appreciation of all the moral relations, whether between God and man, or between man and man, which Renan himself recognizes in Him? The kingdom of truth and holiness which has come from the appearance of Jesus is enough to set aside the suspicions of His modern biographer and to decide in the evangelist's favor.

The critic might limit himself to calling in question the historical accuracy of the discourses which John puts into the mouth of Jesus. But we think that we have demonstrated the full confidence which we are obliged to accord to them (Introd., pp. 93–134). They cannot be separated from the facts with which they are closely connected, and these facts are as well, not to say better, guaranteed than those of the Synoptics (Introd., pp. 68–93).

Reuss urges, as an objection, a contradiction between the Prologue, in which the perfect *equality* of the Father and Son (such as ecclesiastical orthodoxy professes) is taught, and the authentic words of Jesus in the Gospel, starting from the idea of the *subordination* of the Son.[2] The exegesis of the Prologue has proved that this contradiction does not exist, since subordination is taught in the Prologue, as clearly as in the discourses. Let us recall the expressions: "*he was with God,*" ver. 1; "the only-begotten Son," ver. 14; "*who is in the bosom of the Father,*" ver. 18; these expressions imply subordination as much as any saying related in the Gospel. Reuss' mistake is that of wishing by all means to identify the conception of the Prologue with the Nicene formulas.

Baur[3] does not believe in the possibility of reconciling the notion of the incarnation with that of the miraculous birth taught in the Synoptics. But if we take this expression, *became flesh*, seriously,—as Baur does not— the alleged contradiction is solved of itself. As in this case the subject of the Gospel hisory is not longer, as Baur claims, the Logos continuing in

---

[1] *Gesch. d. Pflanzung d. christl. Kirche*, ii. p. 549.
[2] *Hist. de la théol. chrét.*, II., p. 440 f.
[3] *Theol. Jahrb.* 1844, III., p. 24 f.

His divine state, but a true man, the fact of a real birth of this man, whether miraculous or natural, becomes a necessary condition of his human existence.

The most serious objection is derived from the difficulty of reconciling the pre-existence of Christ with His real humanity. Thus *Lücke*,[1] while fully recognizing that there is something dangerous in the rejection of the pre-existence, thinks, nevertheless, that this dogma implies a difference of *essence* between the Saviour and His brethren, which seriously compromises both His character as Son of man, and His redemptive function. *Weizsäcker* takes his position at the same point of view.[2] He acknowledges that the communion of the Son with the Father is not simply moral; that Jesus did not gain His dignity as Son by His fidelity; but that it is, much rather, the presupposition of all that He did and said; that His moral fidelity maintained this original relation, but did not produce it; that, it is the unacquired condition of the consciousness which He had of Himself. On the other hand, he maintains that the superior knowledge which Christ possessed, could not be the continuation of that which He brought from above; for that origin would take away from it the progressive character, limited to the task of each moment, which we recognize in it and which makes it a truly human knowledge. And, as for the moral task of Jesus, it would also lose its truly human character; for where would be the moral conflict in the Son, if He still possessed here below that complete knowledge of the divine plan which He had had eternally in the presence of the Father? There are, therefore, in the fourth Gospel according to this critic, two Christs placed in juxtaposition: the one, truly man, as Jesus Himself teaches in harmony with the Synoptics; the other, divine and pre-existent—the Christ of John. In attempting to resolve this difficulty, we do not conceal from ourselves that we are entering upon one of the most difficult problems of theology. What we shall seek after, in the lines which follow, is not the reconciliation of Scripture with any orthodoxy whatever, but the agreement of Scripture with itself.

The Scriptures, while teaching the eternal existence of the Word, do not, by any means, teach the presence of the divine state and attributes in Jesus during the course of His earthly life. They teach, on the contrary, the complete renouncing by Jesus of that state, with a view to His entrance into the human state. The expression: *the Word was made flesh* (i. 14), speaks of the divine subject only as reduced to the human state; it does not at all, therefore, suppose the two states, divine and human, as co-existent in Him. The *impoverishment* of Christ of which Paul speaks 2 Cor. viii. 9, and His voluntary *emptying of Himself* described in Phil. ii. 6, 7, have no meaning except as we see in this renunciation of the divine state and the entrance into the human mode of existence two facts which were coincident. The Gospel history confirms these declarations. Jesus does not on earth any longer possess the attributes which constitute the divine state. Omniscience He does not have. He Himself declares His

---

[1] p. 378

[2] *Jahrb. für deutsche Theol.* VII. 4, p. 639 and 655–664.

ignorance on a particular point (Mark xiii. 32). In our Gospel, also, the expression: "*When he heard* that the Jews had cast him out. . . " (ix. 35), proves the same thing. In general, every question put by Him would have been only a pretence, if He had still possessed omniscience. He possessed a superior prophetic vision, undoubtedly (John iv. 17, 18); but this vision was not omniscience. And I do not think that the facts by any means confirm the opinion of *Weizsäcker*, that John's narrative ascribes to Jesus a knowledge which was a reminiscence of His heavenly knowledge. The exegesis will show that Jesus never enunciated anything whatsoever which did not pass through His human consciousness. No more does He possess omnipotence. For He prays and is heard (xi. 42); as for His miracles, it is the Father who works them on His behalf (v. 36). He is equally bereft of omnipresence. He rejoices in His absence at the time of the sickness of Lazarus (xi. 15). His love, perfect as it is, is nevertheless not divine love. This is immutable; but who will maintain that Jesus in His cradle loved as He did at the age of twelve, and at the age of twelve, as He did on the cross? Relatively perfect, at each given moment, His love increased from day to day, both in intensity and with reference to voluntary self-sacrifice, and in extent and with reference to the circle which it embraced, at first His family, then His people, then the whole of mankind. It was a truly human love. For this reason, St. Paul says: "The grace of one *man*, Jesus Christ" (Rom. v. 15). His holiness was, also, a human holiness; for it was realized at every moment only at the cost of a struggle, through renouncing lawful enjoyment and the victory over the no less lawful dread of pain (xii. 25, 27; xvii. 19 a.). This holiness is so human that it is to pass into us and become ours (xvii. 19 b.). All these texts clearly prove that Jesus did not possess, while on earth, the attributes which constitute the divine state. And, indeed, how could He otherwise terminate His earthly career by asking back again the glory which He had before His incarnation (xvii. 5)?

Can we conceive of such an emptying of Himself on the part of a divine being? *Keil*, while acknowledging that there is here a problem which has not yet been solved, thinks that the emptying of the divine attributes took place through the very fact of the entrance of the subject who possessed them into a more limited nature. *Steinmeyer*, likewise says: The very fact of the entrance into a material body had the effect of reducing to the condition of latency the qualities which befit an absolute personality. We might carry back to this idea the saying of Paul (Phil. ii. 7): "He divested himself (*emptied*), having taken the form of a servant," by making the act expressed in the participle *having taken* the antecedent and condition of that which is expressed by the finite verb: "*he divested himself.*" But we may also conceive of the act of voluntary divesting as preceding the entrance into the human state, and as being the condition of it. And it is rather to this idea, as it seems to me, that the passage in Philippians leads us. However this may be, Scripture does not, by any means, teach that He came to earth with His divine attributes—a fact which implies that He had renounced not only their use, but also their possession.

Even the consciousness of His anterior existence as a divine subject would have been incompatible with the state of a true child and with a really human development. The word which He uttered at the age of twelve years (Luke ii. 49) is alleged; but it simply expresses the feeling which Jesus had already at that age of being entirely devoted to the cause of God, as a well-disposed son is to the interests of his father. With a moral fidelity like His, and in the permanent enjoyment of a communion with God which sin did not impair, the child could call God His Father in a purely religious sense, and without resulting in a consciousness within Him of a divine pre-existence. Certainly the feeling of His redemptive mission must have developed itself from his early age, especially through the experience of the continual contrast between His moral purity and the sin by which He saw all those who surrounded Him affected, even the best of them such as Joseph and Mary. The only one in health in this caravan of sick persons with whom He made His journey, He must early have had a glimpse of His task as physician and have inwardly consecrated Himself wholly to it. But there is in the Gospel history not a word, not an act attributed to Jesus which leads us to suppose in the child or the youth the consciousness of His divine nature, and of His previous existence. It is to the apocryphal gospels that we must go to seek this contra-natural and anti-human Jesus. It was, if we mistake not, on the day of His baptism, when the moment arrived at which He was to begin to testify of Himself, of what He was for God and of what God was for Him and for the world, that God thought it fit to initiate Him into the mystery of His life as Son anterior to His earthly existence. This revelation was contained in the words: "Thou art my Son," which could not refer only to His office as Messiah, since they were explained by the following words: "In thee I am well-pleased." He recovered at that time that *consciousness* of Sonship which He had allowed to become extinguished in Him, as at night, as we surrender ourselves to sleep, we lose self-consciousness; and He was able from that moment to make the world understand the greatness of the gift which was made to it and of the love of which He was the object on God's part.

The following, therefore, as it seems to me, are the constituent elements of this mysterious fact:

1. As man was created *in the image* of God and *for the divine likeness*, the Logos could, without derogation, descend even to the level of a human being and work out His development from that moment in truly human conditions.

2. Receptivity for the divine, aspiration towards the divine, being the distinctive feature of man among the other natural beings, the essential characteristic of the life of the Logos made man must be incessant and growing assimilation to the divine in all its forms.

3. This religious and moral capacity of the Logos having entered into human existence is not to be measured by that which each particular man possesses. Through the fact of His miraculous birth, He reproduces

not the type of a determinate father, but that of the race itself which He represents a second time, as it had been represented the first time by the father of all mankind. In Him, therefore, is concentrated the aspiration of the whole race, the generic and absolute receptivity of humanity for the divine. Hence the incomparable character of this personality, to which all are forced to render homage.

4. Having arrived at the consciousness of His eternal relation to God, the Logos can only aspire to recover the divine *state* in harmony with the consciousness which He has of Himself; but, on the other hand, He is too closely connected with humanity to consent to break the bond which unites Him to it. There remains, therefore, only one thing: to raise humanity with Himself to His glory and thus to realize in it the highest thought of God, that which St. Paul calls "the purpose of the wisdom of God for our glory" (1 Cor. ii. 7), the elevation of man, first, to communion with Christ, and then, in Him, to the possession of the state of the Man-God. This is the accomplishment of the eternal destiny of believers, as St. Paul also states it in Rom. viii. 29, 30.

The course of the development of the earthly life of Jesus is easily understood when we place ourselves at this point of view. By His *birth* as a member of the race, as *Son of man*, humanity finds itself replaced in Him at its normal starting-point; it is fitted to begin anew its development, which sin had perverted. Up to the age of thirty, Jesus accomplishes this task. He elevates humanity in His own person, by His perfect obedience and the constant sacrifice of Himself, from innocence to holiness. He is not yet conscious of Himself; perhaps, in the light of the Scriptures, He begins to have a presentiment of that which He is in relation to God. But the distinct consciousness of His dignity as Logos would not be compatible with the reality of His *human development* and with the accomplishment of the task assigned to this first period of His life. This task being once fulfilled, the conditions of His existence change. A new work opens for Him, and the consciousness of His dignity as well-beloved Son, far from being incompatible with the work which He has still to accomplish, becomes the indispensable foundation of it. Indeed, in order to bear witness of God as Father, He must necessarily know Himself as Son. The *baptism* is the decisive event which opens this new phase.[1] Meeting the aspirations and presentiments of the heart of Jesus, the Father says to Him: "*Thou art my Son.*" Jesus knows Himself from this moment as the absolute object of the divine love. He can say now what He could not have said before: "*Before Abraham was, I am.*" This consciousness of His dignity as Son, the recompense for His previous fidelity accompanies Him everywhere from this hour. It forms the background of all His manifestations in acts and words (see Weizsäcker's fine passage,

---

[1] Since the time when the Gnostics falsified the meaning of the baptism by making it the epoch of the descent of the divine Æon upon the man Jesus, de Rougemont is the first who has ventured to give to this fact its full significance in the personal development of the Lord (see *Christ et ses témoins*, 7e, 8e, and 9e *lettres*; t. i., pp. 229-296; particularly, pp. 250-255).

pp. 120, 121). Heaven is opened to *Him* and *He testifies of what He sees there.*

The baptism, however, while giving to Jesus His *consciousness* of Sonship, did not give back to Him His *state* of Sonship, His *form of God.* There is still an immense disproportion between that which He *knows* Himself to be and that which He really *is.* Herein, especially, there is for Him the possibility of temptation : " *If thou art the Son of God . . .* " Master of all, He disposes of nothing, and must at every moment address Himself with a believing and filial heart to the paternal heart of God. It is only through the *resurrection* and the *exaltation* which follows it, that His position is placed on the level of the consciousness which He has of Himself, and that He recovers the divine state. Henceforth, *all the fullness of the divinity dwells in Him,* and that humanly, and even, as Paul says, *bodily* (Col. ii. 9). Finally, ten days after His personal assumption into the divine glory, He begins from the day of Pentecost to admit believers to a participation in His state of sonship. He thus prepares the day on which, by His *Parousia,* He will consummate outwardly their participation in His glory, after having re-established in them the perfect holiness which was the basis of His own exaltation. Living images of the Logos from our creation, we shall then realize that type of divine-human existence which we at present behold in Him. Such was the divine plan, such was the last wish of Jesus Himself (John xvii. 24) : " *Father, I will that where I am, they also may be with me."*

The true formula of the incarnation, according to our Gospel, would, therefore, be the following : *That filial communion with God which the Logos realized before His incarnation in the glorious and permanent form of the divine life, He has realized in Jesus since His incarnation in the humble and progressive form of human existence.*[1]

The school of Baur think that they discover an essential difference between John's conception and that of Paul respecting this point. The latter could have seen in the pre-existent Christ only the prototypic *man,* but not a divine being. This view is rested upon 1 Cor. xv. 47 : " The first man, derived from the earth, is earthy ; the second *man* is from heaven." But this conclusion, which is founded upon no other passage, has really no support in this one. The whole fifteenth chapter of First Corinthians has an eschatological bearing, for it treats of the resurrection of the body. The words cited, therefore, apply to the now glorified Christ, and not to the pre-existent Christ; this is also proved by the words which immediately follow : " *As is the earthly* (Adam), *such are they also that are earthly* (men in their present state): *as is the heavenly* (Christ), *such are they also*

---

[1] We would not wish to make Gess jointly responsible with us for all the ideas which we here express. We are aware that on some points we are not entirely in accord with him. But the view which we present is nevertheless, in general, that which he has developed in his fine work, *Lehre von der Person Christi,* 1856, which I had the honor of reviewing at the time of its appearance, in a series of articles, *Revue chrétienne,* 1857 and 1858. The first two volumes of the second edition have been already published. Let us hope that the closing part of the work will soon appear.

that are heavenly (the believers risen from the dead). *For as we have borne the image of the earthly, we shall also bear the image of the heavenly.*" Certainly, Paul does not mean to say that we shall bear the image of the pre-existent Christ, but that of the Christ as man raised from the dead and glorified. Even the term *second* (*man*) would be sufficient to prove this; since the pre-existent Christ would be the *first* Adam, the *Adam Kadmon* of Jewish theology. The idea which Baur finds in this passage is, moreover, incompatible with two other expressions of the same epistle, in which two divine functions, the creation of the universe and the leading of Israel through the wilderness, are ascribed to the pre-existent Christ (viii. 6 and x. 4). These functions surpass the idea of a mere heavenly *man*.

When Paul calls Christ "*the image* of the invisible God," "the first-born before every creature," the one "in whom all things have been created and all things subsist" (Col. i. 15, 16), he says exactly what John says, when he calls Him *the Word* (the image of the invisible thought), and when he adds: "All things were made by Him, and nothing which has been made was made without Him." The two terms, *image* and *Word*, express, under two different figures, the same notion: God affirming with an affirmation which is not a simple *verbum volens*, but a living person, all that He thinks, all that He wills, all that He loves that is most perfect, giving thus in this being the word of His thought, the reflection of His being, the end of His love, almost *His realized ideal*. Let us picture to ourselves an artist capable of giving life to the master-piece of his genius, and entering into personal relation with this child of his thought; such is the earthly representation of the relation between God and the Word. This word is *divine;* for the highest affirmation of God cannot be less than God Himself. It is *eternal;* for God cannot have begun at any time to affirm Himself. It is *single;* for it is His absolute *saying*, the perfect enunciation of His being, consequently His primordial sovereign utterance, in which are included, in advance, all His particular sovereign utterances which will re-echo successively in time. It is, accordingly, this Word who, in his turn, will call forth all beings. They will be His free affirmation, as He is Himself that of God. He will display in the universe, under the forms of space and time, all the riches of the divine contents which God has eternally included in Him. The creation will be the poem of the Son to the glory of the Father.

This notion of the Word, as a creative principle, has the greatest importance as related to the conception of the universe. The universe rests thereby on an absolutely luminous basis, which secures its final perfection. Blind and eternal matter, fatal necessity, are banished from a world which is the work of the Word. The ideal essence of all things is absolutely protected by this view.[1]

---

[1] See *Lange, Leben Jesu*, iv. pp. 553–556. We do not think it necessary here to treat of the questions which are raised, with regard to the internal relations of the divine persons, by the view which we have just set forth touching the fact of the incarnation. Precisely because the existence of the Son is a matter of love, and not of necessity (as with

298 / Prologue

The notion of the person of Christ which is contained in the Prologue is of decisive importance for the Church.

If the supreme dignity ascribed to Jesus is denied Him, however worthy of admiration this Christ may be, humanity may and should always "*look for another;*" for the path of progress is unlimited. The gate thus remains open for one who comes afterward: " I am come in my Father's name, and ye receive me not; another shall come in his own name, and him ye will receive" (v. 43).

But if in Jesus the Word was really made flesh, there is no higher one to be looked for. The perfect revelation and communication of God are accomplished; eternal life has been realized in time; there is nothing further for every man but to accept and live, or to reject and perish.

We understand, therefore, why John has placed this preamble at the head of his narrative. Faith is not faith—that is to say, absolute, without reserve—except so far as it has for its object that beyond which it is impossible to go.

Philo), there is nothing, when the Word descends to the world to become Himself one of the beings of the universe, to prevent the Father's ability to enter directly into relation with the world, and to exercise in it the functions of creator and preserver which He ordinarily exercises by the intermediate agency of the Word. No doubt, the Word has life in Himself and communicates it to the world, but because the Father *has given Him* this privilege; thus everything proceeds always from the Father (John v. 26).

FIRST PART

FIRST MANIFESTATIONS OF THE WORD—BIRTH OF FAITH—
FIRST SYMPTOMS OF UNBELIEF

John 1:19-4:54

As compared with the two parts which are to follow, of which one specially traces out the development of *unbelief* (v.-xii.), the other, that of *faith* (xiii.-xvii.), this First Part has a character which may be called neutral. It serves as the starting-point for the two others. It contains the first revelations of the *object* of faith and unbelief, of Jesus as *Son of God*. Jesus is declared to be the Messiah and Son of God by John the Baptist; a first group of disciples is formed about Him. His glory beams forth in some miraculous manifestations within the circle of His private life. Then He inaugurates His public ministry in the temple, at Jerusalem. But this attempt having failed, He limits Himself to teaching, while performing miracles and collecting about Himself adherents by means of baptism. Finally, observing that, even in this more modest form, His activity gives umbrage to the dominant party at Jerusalem, He withdraws into Galilee, after having sowed by the way the germs of faith in Samaria. This summary justifies the title which we give to this First Part, and the more general character which we ascribe to it as compared with those which follow.

The evangelist himself seems to have wished to divide it into two cycles by the distinctly marked correlation between the two remarks, ii. 11 and iv. 54, which are placed, one at the end of the story of the wedding at Cana: "*This was the beginning of Jesus' miracles which took place at Cana in Galilee; and He manifested His glory, and His disciples believed on Him;*" the other, which closes this whole Part, after the healing of the nobleman's son, "*Again, Jesus did this second miracle when He came from Judea into Galilee.*" By the manifest correlation of these two sentences the evangelist calls attention to the fact that there were, in this first period of Jesus' ministry, two sojournings in Judea, each of which terminated with a return to Galilee, and that both of these returns were alike marked by a miracle performed *at Cana*. This indication of the thought of the historian should be our guide. Accordingly, we divide this Part into two cycles—the one comprising the facts related i. 19-ii. 11; the other, the narratives ii. 12-iv. 54. In the first, Jesus, introduced into His ministry by

John the Baptist, fulfills it without as yet going out of the inner circle of His first disciples and His family. The second relates His first steps in His public ministry.

First Cycle
John 1:19-2:11

This cycle comprises three sections: 1. The testimonies borne by John the Baptist to Jesus, i. 19–37; 2. The first personal manifestations of Jesus and the faith of His first disciples, i. 38–52; 3. His first miraculous sign, ii. 1–11. The facts related in these three sections fill a week which forms, as *Bengel* has remarked, the counterpart of the final Passion-week. The one might be called the week of the betrothal of the Messiah to His people; the other the time of the absolute rupture long since announced by Jesus: "*When the bridegroom shall be taken away, then shall the friends of the bridegroom fast.*"

1
John 1:19-37
THE TESTIMONIES OF JOHN THE BAPTIST

These testimonies are three in number and were given on three successive days (see vv. 29, 35, "*the next day*)." These three days, eternally memorable for the Church, had left on the heart of the evangelist an ineffaceable impression. On the first he had heard that solemn declaration made before a deputation of the Sanhedrim: The Messiah is present! (ver. 26); and this word, no doubt, had thrilled him as it had the multitude who were there. The next day, the forerunner, pointing out Jesus, had changed his first declaration into that still more important one: Behold Him! and faith in Jesus, prepared for on the preceding day, had illuminated with its first ray the heart of John and that of the Baptist's hearers. Finally, on the third day, by repeating his declaration of the day before, the Baptist evidently meant to say: *Follow Him!* John immediately leaves the Baptist, to attach himself to the new Master whom he points out to him.

Why did the author make the first of these three days the starting-point for his narration? If his intention was to make us witness the opening, not only of his own faith and that of the apostles, but of faith itself in the midst of mankind, he could not choose another starting-point. The Messiah *announced*, then *pointed out*, then *followed;* this certainly is the normal beginning of such a narrative.

First Testimony: vv. 19–28

In unfolding in the Prologue the contents of faith, the apostle had adduced two testimonies of John the Baptist (vv. 6–8 and ver. 15); the second contains, as *Baur* well says, "the idea of the absolute pre-existence of the Messiah," and consequently the true thought of the author—that of the divinity of Christ. But when was the testimony, cited at ver. 15, given? This is what the apostle proceeds to relate.

Ver. 19. "*And this is the testimony which John gave when*[1] *the Jews sent*[2] *priests and Levites from Jerusalem to ask him, Who art thou?*" It is quite strange to see a narrative beginning with the word *and*. This fact is explained by the relation which we have just indicated between ver. 19 and ver. 15. What gives an especial importance to this declaration of John the Baptist, is its official character. It was uttered in presence of a deputation of the Sanhedrim, and as a reply to a positive inquiry emanating from that body, the religious head of the Jewish nation. The Sanhedrim, of whose existence we find the first traces only in the times of Antipater and Herod (Josephus, *Antiq.* xiv. 9, 4), was undoubtedly the continuation or renewal of a very ancient institution. We are reminded of the tribunal of the seventy-two elders established by Moses (Num. xi. 16). Under Jehoshaphat (2 Chron. xix. 8), mention is also made of a supreme tribunal sitting at Jerusalem and composed of a certain number of Levites, priests and fathers of Israel. Comp., perhaps, also Ezek. viii. 11 f., "*seventy men of the elders of Israel.*" In Maccabees (1 Macc. xii. 5; 2 Macc. i. 10; iv. 44, etc.), the body called γερουσία, *senate*, plays a part analogous to that of these ancient tribunals, yet without the possibility of establishing a historic continuity between these institutions. At the time of Jesus, this senate, called *Sanhedrim*, was composed of 71 members, including the president (Tract. *Sanhedr.* i. 6). These members were of three classes: 1. The *chief-priests* (ἀρχιερεῖς), a term which probably designates the high-priests who had retired from office, and the members chosen from the highest priestly families; 2. The *elders* of the people (πρεσβύτεροι, ἄρχοντες τοῦ λαοῦ), a term which undoubtedly comprehends the other members in general, whether lay members or Levites; 3. The *scribes* (γραμματεῖς), a term designating especially the experts in the law, the jurists by profession. The high-priest was *ex-officio* the president.[3] The Sanhedrim had up to this time closed its eyes to John the Baptist's work. But observing that things were daily taking a more serious turn, and that the people were beginning even to ask themselves whether John were not the Christ (comp. Luke iii. 15), they felt at length that they must use their authority and officially present to him the question respecting his mission. Jesus alludes to this step (v. 33); afterwards, He Himself answered a similar inquiry with a refusal (Matt. xxi. 23 f.). The Mishna says expressly: "The judgment of a *tribe*, of a *false prophet* and of a *high-priest* belongs to the tribunal of the seventy-one." *Sanh.* i. 5. We meet here, for the first time, the title, "*the Jews*," which plays an important part in the fourth Gospel. This name,

---

[1] Origen reads τοτε (*then*) once, elsewhere οτε (*when*).

[2] B. C. It^{aliq} Syr. and other Vss. add after απεστειλαν: προς αυτον (*to him*), words which A X place after λευιτας.

[3] The old opinion, according to which the Sanhedrim had an elective president and vice-president (the *Nasi* and the *Av-Beth-Din*), seems now to have been thoroughly refuted by *Kuenen* and *Schürer*. See Schürer's *Lehrbuch der Zeitgesch.*, § 23.

by its etymology, properly designates only the members of the tribe of Judah; but after the return from the captivity it is applied to the whole people, because the greater part of the Israelites who returned to their own land belonged to this tribe. It is in this general sense that we find it in ii. 6, "*After the Jews' manner of purifying;*" ii. 13, "*The passover of the Jews;*" iii. 1, "*One of the rulers of the Jews.*" In this purely political sense, this term may even include the Galileans (vi. 52). But the name has most frequently in our Gospel a religious coloring. It designates the nation as an unbelieving community, which, in the majority of its members and through its authorities, had rejected the Messiah. This particular sense is explained by the history; for the focus of the hatred and rejection of Jesus was found at Jerusalem and in Judea. This unfavorable sense attached to the name *the Jews* in our Gospel, has been adduced for the purpose of proving that the author of this book could not have been himself of Jewish origin.[1] But after the fall of Jerusalem the Jewish nation had ceased to exist as a political body; this name of Jews thus became a purely religious title; and as John himself belonged to a different religious community, it is quite natural that he speaks of them as people who were henceforth foreigners to him. The Jewish-Christian author of the Apocalypse expresses himself still more severely with respect to his old fellow-countrymen, when he calls them "the Synagogue of Satan" (iii. 9); and Mark, in spite of his Jewish origin, also designates them by this word, the Jews, absolutely as John does (vii. 3). The words: *from Jerusalem* depend, not on the substantive *the Jews*, but on the verb *sent*. The design of this limiting phrase is to make the solemnity of the proceeding appear; it had an official character, because it emanated from the centre of the theocracy. *Levites* were joined with the priests. It has been often supposed that they merely played the part of bailiffs. But, in several passages of the Old Testament (2 Chron. xvii. 7–9; xxxv. 3; Neh. viii. 7), we see that it was the Levites who were charged with instructing the people in the law, from which fact *Hengstenberg* has, not without reason, concluded, that the scribes, so frequently mentioned in the New Testament, generally belonged to this order, and that it is in this character, and consequently as members of the Sanhedrim, that some of their number figured in the deputation. The question which they address to John the Baptist relates to the expectation, prevailing at that epoch in Israel, of the Messiah and of the extraordinary messengers who, according to the popular opinion, were to precede His coming. "*Who art thou?*" signifies in the context, Art thou one of these expected personages, and what one? We shall see in ver. 25 what embarrassment this question was preparing for John, in case he refused to declare his title.

Origen thought that with the second clause of ver. 19 ($\ddot{o}\tau\epsilon\ \dot{a}\pi\dot{\epsilon}\sigma\tau\epsilon\iota\lambda\epsilon\nu$) a new testimony of John the Baptist began. The first was, according to him, that of ver. 15 f, to which ver. 19 *a* refers. Consequently, he appears

---

[1] *Fischer, Tübingen Zeitschrift*, 1840, and so *Hilgenfeld*. We have refuted this objection in the Introd.

to have read τότε, *then*, instead of ὅτε (*when*). To complete this series of misconceptions, he only needed to find further on a third testimony addressed to a new deputation; he succeeded in this through his interpretation of ver. 24 (see on that verse). *Cyril* and some modern writers begin with the *when* of ver. 19 a new sentence, of which the principal clause is found in ver. 20: "When the Jews sent. ... he declared." But the καί, *and*, before the verb ὡμολόγησε, *he declared*, renders this construction inadmissible. The particle καί, *and*, is never in John the sign of the apodosis, not even in vi. 57. The words πρὸς αὐτόν, *to him*, which are added by a portion of the Alexandrian authorities, and which two Mjj. place after λευίτας, are probably interpolated. *Meyer* and *Weiss* wrongly make καὶ ὡμολόγησε, *and he declared*, depends on ὅτε, *when;* this construction makes the sentence a dragging one. It is better to translate: "And this is the testimony ... (ver. 19) ... and he declared."

Ver. 20. *"And he confessed, and denied not, and confessed:*[1] *I am not the Christ."*[2] Before pointing out the contents of the response of John the Baptist, the evangelist sets forth its characteristics: it was ready, frank, categorical. The first *he confessed*, indicates spontaneity, eagerness. By the negative form: *he denied not*, the evangelist means to say he did not for an instant yield to the temptation which he might have had to deny. The second *he confessed* is added in order to connect with it the profession which is to follow. This remarkable form of narrative (comp. i. 7, 8) seems to us, whatever *Weiss* may say of it, to be more naturally explained if we suppose an allusion to people who were inclined to give to the person of John the Baptist an importance superior to his real dignity. According to the reading of the Alexandrian authorities and Origen, we must translate: "*It is not I* who am the Christ (ἐγὼ οὐκ εἰμί)." This reply would have been suitable, if the question had been, "*Is it thou* who art the Christ?" But the question is merely, "*Who art thou?*" and the true response is consequently that which is found in the T. R. following the Byzantine authorities: "I am not *the Christ* (οὐκ εἰμὶ ἐγώ)," that is, "I am indeed something, but not the Christ."

Ver. 21. *"And they asked him: what then?*[3] *Art thou*[4] *Elijah? And he said I am not. Art thou the prophet? And he answered, No."* Some interpreters understand the question τί οὖν (*what then?*) in the same or nearly the same sense as the preceding: "If thou art not the Christ, *what art thou then?*" But the two following questions: "*Art thou Elias ... ?*" would imply τίς rather than τί in this sense. *De Wette* sees in these words an adverbial expression: "*What then!*" This sense is pointless. We must, rather, supply ἐστί, with *Meyer:* "What then is the case? What extraordinary thing, then, is happening?" This form of question betrays impatience. There was, indeed, in the unprecedented behavior of John the Baptist something which seemed to indicate an exceptional condition.

[1] D omits και, and א Syr^cur Or. the second και ωμολογησεν.

[2] א A B C L X Δ It^plerique Cop. Or. (3 times) read εγω ουκ ειμι, while Γ Δ and 9 other Mjj. Syr^sch and T. R. place ουκ ειμι before εγω.

[3] B reads συ ουν τι (*what art thou then?*), instead of τι ουν (*what then?*)

[4] א B L reject συ after ει.

Malachi had announced (iv. 5) the coming of Elijah as the one preparing for the great Messianic day, and we know from Justin's *Dialogue* with Trypho the Jew, that, according to a popular opinion, the Messiah was to remain hidden until he had been pointed out and consecrated by this prophet. Several passages of the Gospels (Matt. xvi. 14; Mk. vi. 15) prove that there was, besides this, an expectation of the reappearance of some other prophet of the ancient times, Jeremiah for example. Among these expected personages, there was one who was especially called *the prophet*. Some distinguished him from the Messiah (John vii. 40, 41); others confounded him with the Messiah (vi. 14). The question was, evidently, as to the personage announced by Moses (" a prophet like unto me "), in the promise in Deut. xviii. 18. Of course, the people did not picture to themselves a second Elijah or a new Moses in the spiritual sense, as when the angel says of John the Baptist (Luke i. 17), " *He shall go in the spirit and power of Elijah.*" It was the person himself who was to reappear in flesh and bones. How could John the Baptist have affirmed, in this literal sense, his identity with the one or the other of these ancient personages? On the other hand, how could he enter into the domain of theological distinctions? Besides, this mode of discussion would be scarcely in accordance with his character. His reply, therefore, must be negative.

Vv. 22, 23. " *They said then to him, Who art thou? that we may give an answer to those who sent us. What sayest thou of thyself? 23. He said, I am a voice crying in the wilderness: Make straight the way of the Lord, as said the prophet Isaiah.*" The deputies have now exhausted the suppositions which were furnished by the accepted Messianic programme of their time. Nothing remains for them but to propose to John again the question which shall make him abandon the negative attitude to which he is limiting himself: "*Who art thou?*" that is to say, " *What personage art thou?*" For his extraordinary conduct must be occasioned by an exceptional mission. John replies to it by a passage from Isaiah, which contains at once the explanation asked for and the guarantee of his mission. The sense of the prophetic passage is this: Jehovah is on the point of appearing in order to manifest His glory. At the moment which precedes His appearance, without the appearing of any person on the scene, a voice is heard which invites Israel to make straight the way by which the Lord is to come. The question in this description is not of the return from the captivity, but of the *Messianic* appearance of Jehovah. As in the East, before the arrival of the sovereign, the roads are straightened and leveled, so Israel is to prepare for its divine King a reception worthy of Him; and the function of the mysterious voice is to engage her in carrying out this work of preparation, lest the signal grace of which she is to be the object may turn into judgment. John applies to himself so much more willingly these words of Isaiah, because it fully accords with his desire to put his own person into obscurity and to let nothing but his message appear: "*A voice.*" The words *in the wilderness* can be referred, in Hebrew as in Greek, either to the verb *to cry*, or to the verb *to make straight*. As regards the sense, it amounts to the same thing, since the order sounds forth in the place where it is to be executed. The reference to the preceding verb is more natural, especially in the Greek. The *wilderness* designates in the East uncultivated lands, the vast extents of territory which serve for pasturage, and which are crossed by winding paths, and not by roads worthy of a sovereign. Such is the emblem of the moral state of the people; the royal way by which Jehovah is to enter is not yet prepared in their hearts. The feeling of national repentance is still wanting. The sojourning of the forerunner in the wilderness indicated clearly, through this literal conformity to the prophetic emblem, the *moral* accomplishment of the prophecy. Does the formula of citation, "*as said*," also belong to the reply of the Baptist? Or is it a remark of the evangelist? What makes us incline to the first alternative is, that the forerunner had more need of legitimating himself than the evangelist had of legitimating him so long afterwards. To reply as John does was to enunciate his commission, and to declare his orders. It was to say, in fact, to these deputies, experts in the knowledge of the law and the prophets, that, if he was not *personally* one of the expected ancient personages, his mission was, nevertheless, in direct connection with the approaching manifestation of the Messiah. This was all which the Sanhedrim and the people practically needed to know.

The inquiry had borne, at first, upon the *office* of John the Baptist. The deputation completed it by a more special interrogation respecting the rite of *baptism*, which he is allowing himself to introduce into the theocracy without the authorization of the Sanhedrim. The evangelist prepares the way for this new phase of the conversation by a remark having reference to the religious character of the members of the deputation.

Ver. 24. "*And those who*[1] *were sent were of the Pharisees.*" We translate according to the T. R., which is in conformity with the majority of the Mjj., with the Mnn., and with the greater part of the Vss. According to this reading, the participle $ἀπεσταλμένοι$, sent, is defined by the article $οἱ$, *the;* it is the subject of the sentence. The design of this remark added here by John is easily understood; it is to explain the question which is to follow. John likes to supply in this way, as a narrative progresses, the circumstances, omitted at first, which serve gradually to explain it; comp. i. 41, 45; iv. 30; ix. 14; xi. 5, 18; xiii. 23, etc. The Pharisees were the ultra conservatives in Israel; no one could have been shocked more than they by the innovation which John the Baptist had taken it upon himself to make in introducing baptism. Lustrations undoubtedly formed a part of the Jewish worship. It is even maintained that the pagan proselytes were subjected to a complete bath, on occasion of their passing over to Judaism. But the application of this symbol of entire pollution to the members of the theocratic people was so strange an innovation, that it must have awakened in the highest degree the susceptibility of the authorities who were guardians of the rites, and very particularly that of the party most attached to tradition. The Pharisaic element also was the

---

[1] ℵ A B C L and Orig. reject $οἱ$ (*the*) before $ἀπεσταλμένοι$ (*sent*).

main one in the deputation which the Sanhedrim had chosen. We see how skillfully the plan of the examination had been laid; first of all, the question relative to the mission; then, that which concerned the rite; for the latter depended on the former. Nothing can be more simple than the course of the narrative, as thus understood. This mode of explaining the intention of the remark in ver. 24 appears to me more natural than that of *Weiss* and *Keil*, according to which John would thereby characterize the spirit of unbelief which animated the interrogators of the Baptist. The fact of their unbelief not being noticed in the narrative, did not demand explanation. Opposed to the reading of the T. R. there is another supported by the Alexandrian authorities and by Origen, and adopted by *Tischendorf*, and *Westcott and Hort*, which rejects the article οἱ before ἀπεσταλμένοι; the meaning is: "and they had been sent from the Pharisees," or, as Origen understood it: "and there were persons sent (come) from the Pharisees," as if the question were of another deputation than that of ver. 19. Neither the one nor the other of these meanings is possible. For the Pharisees did not form an officially constituted body, from which a proceeding like this which is here spoken of could have started. The Alexandrian reading is, therefore, indefensible, as, in this instance, *Weiss* and *Keil* themselves acknowledge. It is, probably, as is so frequently the case, an arbitrary correction by Origen, to serve his false interpretation of this whole passage, from the end of the Prologue. *Weiss* and *Keil* see here a mere case of negligence of a copyist arising from the preceding καί, in which the οἱ was lost. But how many similar errors should we not have, in that case, in the New Testament!

Ver. 25. "*And they asked him and*[1] *said unto him; why baptizest thou then, if thou art not the Christ, nor*[2] *Elijah, nor*[2] *the prophet.*" The strictest guardians of rites conceded, indeed, to the Messiah or to one of His forerunners the right of making innovations in the matter of observances; and if John had declared himself one of these personages, they would have contented themselves with asking for his credentials, and would have kept silence respecting his baptism, sufficiently legitimated by his mission. In fact, it seems to follow from this verse itself that, on the foundation of words such as those of Ezek. xxxvi. 25, 26, and Zech. xiii. 1, a great national lustration was expected as an inauguration of the kingdom of the Messiah. But John the Baptist having expressly declined the honor of being one of the expected prophets, the deputation had the right to say to him: "Why *then* dost thou baptize?" According to the reading of the T. R. *nor, nor,* the thought is this: "The supposition that John is the Christ is set aside; there remains, therefore, no other way of explaining his baptism except that he is *either* the one *or* the other of the two expected forerunners; now he declares that he is *neither* the one *nor* the other; why then . . . etc. This delicate sense of the *disjunctive* negative was not understood; hence, in our view, the Alexandrian reading οὐδέ, οὐδέ, *nor*

---

[1] ℵ rejects ηρωτησαν αυτον και (the copyist has confounded the two και).

[2] Instead of ουτε ουτε, which the T. R. reads after most of the Mjj. and Mnn., ουδε ουδε is read in A B C L and Orig. (6 times).

even, which puts the three cases on a common level. The partisans of the Alexandrian text (*Weiss, Keil, Westcott*, etc.), judge otherwise. The position of John the Baptist, in presence of this question and after his previous answer, became a difficult one. His interrogators, indeed, had counted on this result.

Vv. 26, 27. "*John answered them saying, Yea, I baptize with water;*[1] *in the midst of you*[2] *there standeth*[3] *one whom you know not; 27. He*[4] *who comes after me—but who was before me*[5]—*the latchet of whose sandal I am not worthy to loose.*" This reply has been regarded as not very clear and as embarrassed. *De Wette* even thinks that it does not correspond altogether with the question proposed. The generally adopted explanation is the following: " My baptism with water does not, in any case, encroach upon that of the Messiah, which is of an altogether superior nature; it is only preparatory for it." John would in some sort excuse his baptism by trying to diminish it, and by reminding them that beyond this ceremony the Messianic baptism maintains the place which belongs to it. But, first of all, this would be to evade the question which was put; and the criticism of de Wette would remain a well-founded one. For the baptism of John was attacked in itself and not as being derogatory to that of the Messiah. Then, the words ἐν ὕδατι, *with water*, should be placed at the beginning: " It is *only with water* that I baptize," and the baptism of the Spirit would necessarily be mentioned in the following clause, as an antithesis. Finally, it would scarcely be in harmony with the character of the Baptist to shelter himself under the insignificance of his office and to present his baptism as an inoffensive novelty. This reply, properly understood, is, on the contrary, full of solemnity, dignity, even threatening; it makes apparent the importance of the present situation, into the mystery of which John alone, until now, is initiated. " The Messiah is present: this is the reason why I baptize!" If the Messianic time has really come, and he is himself charged with inaugurating it, his baptism is thereby justified (see ver. 23). This feeling of the gravity of the situation and of the importance of his part is expressed in the ἐγώ, *I*, placed at the beginning of the answer, the meaning of which, as the sequel proves, is this: "*I* baptize with water, and in acting thus I know what I do: for *He* is present who . . ." We have given the force of this pronoun by the affirmation *Yea!* The ἐγώ, *I*, is ordinarily contrasted with the Messiah, by making an antithesis between the baptism of water and the baptism of the Spirit. But this latter is not even mentioned, and this interpretation results from a recollection of the words of the Baptist in the Synoptics. Hence also probably came the introduction of the particle δέ, *but* (in what follows

---

[1] ℵ alone: εν τω υδατι instead of εν υδατι.

[2] After μεσος the T. R. reads δε (*but*) with all the authorities, except ℵ B C L and Orig. (10 times) who reject this word.

[3] B L T^b στηκει (*stat*); ℵ G: εστηκει (*stabat*); T. R. with all the rest εστηκεν (*stat*).

[4] T. R. reads after οιδατε, αυτος εστιν (*it is he*) with 13 Mjj., the Mnn., It.Vg. Syr. Orig.(once);

these words are rejected by ℵ B C L T^b Syr^{cur} and Orig. (6 times). The art. ο before ερχομενος is omitted by ℵ B Orig.

[5] After ερχομενος T. R. adds ος εμπροσθεν μου γεγονεν (*who has become before me*) with the same authorities as above; these words are rejected by the authorities which reject αυτος εστι (*it is he*).

after the word μέσος), which is rightly omitted by the Alexandrian authorities. It is precisely *because* he knows that the Messiah is present among them, that he baptizes with water and that he has the right to do so. This reply, accompanied as it undoubtedly was, with a significant look cast upon the crowd, in which the mysterious personage of whom he was thinking could be found, must have produced a profound sensation among his hearers. The two readings ἔστηκεν and στήκει, although one is in the perfect and the other in the present, have the same sense: *He stands there.* The important words are these: *Whom you know not.* The word *you* contrasts John's hearers, who are still ignorant, with John himself, who already knows. This expression necessarily assumes that, at the time when the forerunner was speaking, the baptism of Jesus was already an accomplished fact. For it was by means of that ceremony that, in conformity with the divine promise (ver. 33), the person of the Messiah was to have been pointed out to him. In vv. 31 and 33, He Himself affirms that, up to the moment of the baptism, he did not know Him. It is impossible, then, to place the baptism of Jesus, with *Olshausen* and *Hengstenberg*, on this same day or the next, with *Bäumlein*, between ver. 28 and ver. 29, or, with *Ewald*, between ver. 31 and ver. 32. Moreover, this testimony, whatever *Weiss* may say of it, is wholly different from the preachings of John which are reported in the Synoptics, and which had preceded the baptism of Jesus. The very terms which the forerunner here employs contain a very clear allusion to previous declarations in which he had announced a personage who was to follow him; this is especially evident if we read ὁ before ὀπίσω μου ἐρχόμενος, "*the one coming after me* whom I have announced to you." This testimony has an altogether new character: "The Messiah is *present*, and I *know* him." This is the first declaration which refers personally to Jesus; it is for his hearers the true starting-point of faith in *Him.* The words *it is he* (αὐτός ἐστιν), omitted by the Alexandrian authorities, sometimes omitted and sometimes read by Origen, are not indispensable, and may have been added either by copyists who wrongly identified this testimony with that of ver. 15 (οὗτος ἦν), or by others who wished to bring out better the allusion to the previous testimonies related by the Synoptics.

It is otherwise with the words, *who was before me,* which the Alexandrian authorities, Origen and the Curetonian Syriac omit, but which 15 Mjj. and the two ancient versions, *Itala* and *Peschito*, read. The relation between this testimony and that of ver. 30, which will follow, renders these words indispensable in ver. 27. For in ver. 30, John reproduces expressly ("*he it is of whom I said* [yesterday]"), the testimony of ver. 27, and not, as is imagined, that of ver. 15, which is itself only a quotation of our ver. 30 (see on ver. 15). The first day, John uttered, without yet designating Jesus, the declaration of vv. 26, 27; the second day, he repeated it, as it is related in ver. 30, this time applying it to Jesus as present. *Gess* rightly says, "If the *shorter* reading of ver. 27 were the true one, the evangelist would refer in ver. 30 to a fact which had not been related by him" (i. p. 345). These words: *who was before me*, are, in ver. 27, a sort of parenthesis inserted by the forerunner: "Come after me? Yes, and yet in reality, my predecessor!" (See on ver. 15). By the expression "to loose the latchet of the sandals," John means to designate the humble office of a slave. On the pleonasm of οὐ and αὐτοῦ Bäumlein rightly says: "imitation of the Hebrew construction." Philologues discuss the question whether the form ἄξιος ἵνα implies a weakening of the sense of the conjunction ἵνα, which becomes here, according to some, a simple paraphrase of the infinitive (*worthy to loose*), so Bäumlein, or whether this conjunction always retains the idea of purpose (*Meyer*). Bäumlein rests upon the later Greek usage and on the νά of the modern Greek, which, with the verb in the subjunctive mood, supplies the place of the infinitive. Nevertheless, we hold, with Meyer, that the idea of purpose is never altogether lost in the ἵνα of the New Testament; he who is worthy of doing a thing, is, as it were, intended *to* do it.

Ver. 28. "*These things were done at Bethany,[1] beyond the Jordon,[2] where John was baptizing.*" The notice of ver. 28 is certainly not suggested to John by a geographical interest; it is inspired by the solemnity of this whole scene, and by the extraordinary gravity of this official testimony given in presence of the representatives of the Sanhedrim as well as of the entire nation. It was, indeed, to this declaration that the expression of the Prologue applied: "*in order that all might believe through him.*" If the people had been ready for faith, this testimony coming from such lips, would have been enough to make the divine fire break forth in Israel.—As for the two readings *Bethany* and *Bethabara*, Origen relates that nearly all the ancient MSS. read *Bethany*, but that, having sought for a place of this name on the banks of the Jordan, he had not found it, while a place was pointed out called Bethabara (comp. Judg. vii. 24), where tradition alleged that John had baptized. It is, therefore, certain that the reading *Bethabara* was substituted for the primitive reading *Bethany* in a certain number of documents, and that it was under the influence of Origen; as the Roman war had caused a large number of ancient places to disappear even as to their names, we may easily understand the disappearance of Bethany at the time of Origen. We must, therefore, conclude from the text which is established by evidence, that there existed in the time of Jesus, in the vicinity of the Jordan, a place by the name of Bethany, which was consequently different from the city of this name near Jerusalem. As there were two Bethlehems, two Antiochs, two Ramas, two Canas, why should there not have been, also, two Bethanies? Perhaps this name had, in the two cases, different etymologies. *Bethany* may signify, indeed, either place of dates, or place of poverty, etc., a meaning which suits Bethany near Jerusalem; or *place of the ferry-boat* (*Beth-Onijah*), a meaning which would well suit the Bethany which is here in question.[3]

---

[1] The reading Βηθανια is found in almost all the Mjj.; the large part of the Mnn.; It.; Vg.; Cop.; Syr^sch, etc. Only the Mjj. K T^b Y Λ Π; some Mnn.; Syr^cur read, with T. R., Βηθαβαρα.

[2] ℵ, Syr^cur add ποταμου (*the river*), after Ιορδανου.

[3] Lieutenant Conder, in one of his reports

310 / Birth of Faith

Second Testimony: vv. 29-34

How can we comprehend the fact that the deputies of the Sanhedrim left John without asking him who the person was of whom he intended to speak? Either they did not care to know, or they affected to despise the declaration of the one who spoke to them in this way. In both cases, here is their first positive act of unbelief. After their departure, the forerunner remained with his disciples and the multitude who had been present at this scene; and from the next day his testimony assumed a still more precise character. He no longer merely said, "He is there," but seeing Jesus approaching him, he cries out: "There He is." He characterizes first the *work* (ver. 29), then the *person* of Christ (ver. 30); afterwards, he relates how he attained the knowledge of Him, and on what foundation the *testimony* which He gives to Him rests (vv. 31-33); finally, he sets forth the importance which the act that he has just performed in disburdening himself of such a message in their presence has for his hearers (ver. 34).

Ver. 29. "*The next day he*[1] *sees Jesus coming to him, and he says: Behold the Lamb of God who takes away the sin of the world.*" The very next day after the day when John had proclaimed the presence of the Messiah in the midst of the people, Jesus approaches His forerunner, who recognizes Him and declares Him to be the Messiah. The words, *coming to Him*, have troubled the interpreters. Some have understood that He came to be baptized, which is impossible, since the following verses (31-33), and even ver. 26, imply that the baptism was already accomplished. *Baur* thinks that Jesus came to John for the purpose of receiving his testimony, and he, of course, finds in this fact, thus understood, a proof of the purely ideal character of the narrative. But this detail implies simply that Jesus, after having been baptized, had, previously to this meeting, separated Himself from John for a certain time, and that after this interval He, on this very day, returned to the presence of His forerunner, hoping to find in His presence those whom God should give to Him in order to begin His work. And we know, in fact, from the Synoptical account, that Jesus, after His baptism, had withdrawn into the solitude of the desert, where He had passed several weeks; it was now the moment, therefore, when He reappeared to take up His work as Redeemer. Nothing is more natural than that, with this design, He should return to the presence of John. Was not he the one who had been sent to open the way for Him to Israel? Was it not at his hands that He could hope to receive the instruments which were indispensable to Him for the accomplishment of

---

on the discoveries of the English expedition in Palestine, thinks he has proved the existence, on the east of the Jordan, of a district named *Bethany*, which already bore this name in the time of Eusebius, and which, according to Ptolemy, extended even to the Jordan.

[1] The words ὁ Ἰωαννης of the T. R., which are omitted in a large number of Mjj. and Mnn., both Alexandrian and Byzantine, and in several Vss. are one of those additions, especially frequent in the Byzantine text, which were introduced by the necessities of reading in public worship.

His task? Jesus Himself (x. 3) designates John as *the porter* who opens to the Shepherd the door of the sheepfold, so that He does not have to climb over the wall of the inclosure like the robber, but can enter without violence into the sheepfold. *Lücke* also places this return of Jesus in connection with the narrative of the temptation.

We may be surprised that for the purpose of designating Jesus as the Messiah John does not employ one of the titles which were commonly used for this end: Christ, Son of God, or King of Israel. The term *Lamb of God* is so original that, if it is historical, it must have its ground in some particular impression which the Baptist had received at the time of his previous meeting with Jesus. And indeed, we must remember that when an Israelite came to have himself baptized by John, he began by making confession of his sins (Matt. iii. 6; Mk. i. 5). Jesus could not have dispensed with this preparatory act without arrogating to Himself from the first an exceptional position, and nothing was farther from His thought than this: He wished to "fulfill all righteousness" (Matt. iii. 15). What, then, could His confession be? Undoubtedly a collective confession, analogous to that of Daniel (Dan. ix.), or that of Nehemiah (Neh. ix.), a representation of the sin of Israel and of the world, as it could be traced by the pure being who was in communion with the perfectly holy God, and at the same time the tenderly loving being, who, instead of judging His brethren, consecrated Himself to the work of saving them. If, as we cannot doubt, this was the spirit in which Jesus spoke and perhaps prayed at that moment, we may understand that the expression which the forerunner uses here to designate Him, is indeed the reflection of what he had experienced when hearing and seeing this unique man, who, by His tender sympathy and His intercession, took upon Himself the burden of the sin of the world. On the other hand, in order that the title of which the Baptist made use might be intelligible for his hearers, it was indispensable that it should connect itself with some well-known word or some well-known fact of the Old Covenant, which was generally referred to the Messiah. This is implied by the article ὁ, *the*, before the term *Lamb of God*, an article which signifies the Lamb known and expected by the hearers. The thought which presents itself most naturally to the mind is that of seeing here an allusion to the *Servant of the Lord* described in Is. liii., under the figure of a lamb which allows itself "to be led to the slaughter without opening its mouth." On the preceding day, the Baptist had already appealed to a saying of the same prophet (Is. xl. 3). Before the polemic against the Christians had driven the Jewish interpreters to another explanation, they did not hesitate to apply that sublime representation (Is. lii. 13–liii. 12) to the Messiah. *Abarbanel* says expressly: "Jonathan, the son of Usiel, referred this prophecy to the Messiah who was to come, and this is also the opinion of our sages of blessed memory." (See Eisenmenger, *Entdeckt, Judenth*, II. Th. p. 758; *Lücke*, I. p. 406).[1]

---

[1] Comp. Wünsche, *die Leiden des Messias*, 1870, p. 55 ff. By a multitude of Rabbinical sayings, he furnishes proof that the passages Is. lii. 13–liii. 12, Zech. ix. 9 (*lowly, riding upon an ass*), and xii 10 ("*on me whom they pierced*"), were always and unanimously re-

312 / Birth of Faith

We need not here prove the truth of this explanation of Is. liii. and the insoluble difficulties in which every contrary interpretation is involved. The fact is sufficient for us that it was the prevalent one among the ancient Jews. From this it follows that the allusion of John the Baptist could be easily understood by the people who were present. Some interpreters have claimed that the term, *Lamb*, represents, in the mouth of the forerunner as well as in the book of Isaiah, only the meekness and patience of the just one suffering for the cause of God. Thus *Gabler*: "Here is the man full of meekness who will support patiently the evils which human perversity shall occasion him;" and *Kuinoel*: "Here is the innocent and pious being who will take away wickedness from the earth." But these explanations do not account for the article ὀ, *the well-known, expected, Lamb,* and they entirely efface the manifest relation which the text establishes between the figure of *lamb* and the act of taking away sin. *Weiss* explains, almost as the preceding writers do, by emphasizing the allusion to Is. liii. 7, but without finding here the least notion of sacrifice. This last view seems to us not defensible. The idea of sacrifice is at the foundation of the whole passage Is. liii.; comp. especially, vv. 10–12: "When his soul shall have offered the expiatory sacrifice *ascham*)," and : "He shall bear their iniquities," words to which precisely John the Baptist alludes in these last words: "*who takes away the sin of the world.*" The Lamb of God designates Jesus, therefore, as realizing the type of the Servant of Jehovah, Is. liii., charged with delivering the world from sin by His sacrifice. Some interpreters, especially *Grotius, Lampe, Luthardt* and *Hofmann*, believe that the Baptist is thinking only of the sacrifices of the Old Covenant in which the lamb was used as a victim, specially of that of the Paschal lamb. It is, indeed, indisputable that, among the clean animals used as victims, the lamb was the one which, by its character of innocence and mildness, presented the emblem most suited to the character of the Messiah as John the Baptist here describes Him (comp. Lev. iv. 32; v. 6; xiv. 12; Num. vi. 12), and that, in particular, the sacrifice of the Paschal lamb really possessed an expiatory value (comp. Ex. xii. 13). It appears to me indubitable, therefore, notwithstanding all that *Weiss* and *Keil* still say, that, in expressing himself as he does here, the forerunner is thinking of the part of the lamb, not in the daily Jewish worship, but in the Paschal feast. And this allusion seems to me to be perfectly reconcilable with the reference to that saying of Is. liii. since in this chapter Isaiah represents the Servant of the Lord precisely under the

---

ferred to the Messiah and His expiatory sufferings. The very attempt to distinguish between two Messianic personages, the one *the son of Joseph*, or of Ephraim who had the lot of suffering, and the other *the son of Judah*, to whom is ascribed the glory, is only a later endeavor (from the second century, comp. Wünsche, p. 109) to reconcile this undisputed interpretation with the idea of the glorious Messiah. In the book, *The assumption of Moses*, written probably at the time of Jesus' childhood, the author also represents the Messiah as passing through death with all mankind during the space of eight days, and then returning to life with the elect and founding His Kingdom. The idea of the death of the Messiah was, therefore, by no means strange to the popular Israelitish opinion at the time when John the Baptist spoke.

figure of the lamb sacrificed as an expiatory and delivering victim. The complement θεοῦ, *of God*, is the genitive of possession, and at the same time of origin. In this sacrifice, indeed, it is not man who offers and slays, it is God who gives, and gives of His own. Comp. 1 Pet. i. 19, 20; Rom. viii. 32. It is remarkable that this title of *lamb*, under which the evangelist learned to know Jesus for the first time, is that by means of which the Saviour is by preference designated in the Apocalypse. The chord which had vibrated, at this decisive hour, in the deepest part of John's heart resounded within him even to his latest breath.

Exegetes are not agreed as to the sense which the word αἰρων, *who takes away*, has here. The verb αἰρειν sometimes signifies to *raise a thing* from the ground, to lift it, sometimes *to take it away*, to carry it away. For the first sense, comp. viii. 29 (stones); Matt. xi. 29 (the yoke): xvi. 24 (the cross). For the second: John xi. 39, 48, xv. 2, xvii. 15, etc., and especially 1 John iii. 5: "Jesus Christ appeared to take away our sins." The second sense would lead rather to the idea of the destruction of sin; the first, to that of expiation, as in some expressions of the fifty-third chapter of Isaiah. But if John had thought especially of expiation, he would probably have employed the term βαστάζειν, to bear, which the LXX. used in the words quoted from Is. liii. He is probably, therefore, thinking of the taking away of sin. Let us not forget, however, that, in accordance with Is. liii. and the Israelitish worship in general, this end cannot be attained except by means of expiation. In order to take away sin, it was necessary that Christ should begin by taking upon Himself the burden of it, to the end that he might be able afterwards to remove it by the work of sanctification. The idea of removing includes, therefore, implicitly that of bearing. The present participle αἰρων might be referred to the *idea* of the mission of Jesus. But it is more simple to see in it an historical present; since the first act of His ministry, Jesus has labored for the taking away of sin on earth.

The burden to be taken away is designated in a grand and sublime way: *the sin of the world.* This substantive in the singular presents the sinful error of humanity in its profound unity. It is sin *in the mass*, in which all the sins of all the sinners of the world are comprehended. Do they not all spring from the same root? We must guard against understanding by ἁμαρτία, as *de Wette* does, *the penalty* of sin. This idea, "the sin of *the world*," has been judged too universal for the Baptist's mouth. So *Weiss* ascribes it solely to the evangelist. *Reuss* says: "We have here an essentially Christian declaration." But in Is. lii. 13–15, it was already said that the sight of the suffering Servant would startle *many peoples* (*rabbim*) and would strike their kings with astonishment. And who, then, were these *many* individuals (*rabbim*) whom, according to liii. 11, this same Servant was to *justify*, after Israel had rejected Him (ver. 1)? Comp. also the wonderful prophecy, Is. xix. 24, 25, where the Assyrians, the Egyptians and Israel are represented as forming the three parts, perfectly equal in dignity, of the kingdom of God. Could Isaiah have surpassed in clearness of vision the Baptist, who was not only a prophet, but the greatest of the prophets?

314 / Birth of Faith

This expression *the world* says no more, in reality, than that threatening or promise which the Synoptics put into the mouth of the forerunner: "Even of these stones God will raise up children to Abraham." Let us also recall that first word of the Lord to Abraham (Gen. xii. 3): "All the families of the earth shall be blessed (or shall bless themselves) in thee."

The forerunner, after having described the work of Jesus, designates Him Himself as the one to whom, notwithstanding His humble appearance, his declaration of the day before applies:

Ver. 30. "*This is he*[1] *concerning whom I said: After me cometh a man who has preceded me, because he was before me.*" This saying, while applying to Jesus as *present* (*this is he*) the testimony uttered on the preceding day in His absence (vv. 26, 27), is designed to solve the enigma which that declaration contained: "He who *follows* me was *before* me." The last clause explains it; see on ver. 15. It is difficult to decide between the two readings περί, *in respect to,* and ὑπέρ, *on behalf of,* both of which are suitable. The word ἀνήρ (a *man* in the strength of his age) which is not found in the quotation of this saying in ver. 15, is suggested to the forerunner by the sight of Jesus present before his eyes. *Lücke, Meyer, Keil* think that in ver. 30 the Baptist refers, not to the testimony of the day before (vv. 26, 27), but to some other previous saying which is not mentioned, either in our Gospel or in the Synoptics. They are condemned to this absurd supposition by their servile dependence on the Alexandrian text, which in ver. 27 omitted the words: *who has preceded me.* *Weiss* attempts to escape this difficulty by making the formula of quotation: *he of whom I said,* ver. 30, relate simply to the words: *cometh after me,* and not to those which follow, *who has preceded me,* an unfortunate expedient which cannot satisfy any one. For the emphasis, as the end of the verse shows, is precisely on the words which *Weiss* thus treats as insignificant. The systematic partisans of the Alexandrian text must, therefore, bring themselves to acknowledge, in this case also, that that text is no more infallible than the Byzantine or the Greco-Latin.

But how can John the Baptist have the boldness to give such a testimony to this mere Jew, like all the rest whom he had before him there, and to proclaim Him as the Redeemer of men, the being whom God had drawn forth from the depth of eternal existence that He might give Him to the world? He explains this himself in vv. 31–33:

Ver. 31. "*And neither did I know him; but that he might be manifested to Israel, I am come baptizing with water.*[2] The word κἀγώ, *and neither I,* placed at the beginning and repeated, as it is in ver. 33, has necessarily an especial emphasis. The meaning is obvious; he has just said to his hearers: "*He whom you know not.*" When, therefore, he adds: "And neither did I know him," it is clear that he means: "And neither did I, when he came to present himself to me to be baptized, know him any more than you now know him." *Weiss* and *Keil* object to this meaning, that it can-

---

[1] Instead of περι (*touching*), ℵ B C and Orig. (twice) read ὑπέρ (*on behalf of*).

[2] B C G L P T⁵ Δ Or. reject τω before υδατι.

not be applied to the two κἀγώ of vv. 33, 34. We shall see that this is not correct. According to these interpreters the "*and I*" signifies: "*I*, for my part, that is, according to my mere human individuality, and independently of the divine revelation." But it is this meaning which is inapplicable to ver. 34; and besides, it is very far-fetched. John means: I did not know him absolutely when he came to present himself to me; I did not know, therefore, that He was the Messiah. But we must not neglect to draw from this only natural meaning the important consequence which is implied in it: that John also did not know Jesus *as a man*, as the Son of Mary; for, if he had known Him as such, it would have been impossible for him not to know Him also as the Messiah. He could not be ignorant of the circumstances which had accompanied his own birth and that of Jesus. If, therefore, he did not know Jesus as Messiah, no more did he know Him personally. And this can be understood: having lived *in the wilderness* up to the time of his manifestation to Israel (Luke i. 80), he might indeed have heard the marvelous circumstances of his own birth and of the birth of the Son of Mary related by his parents, but without having ever seen Him. It *must necessarily*, even, have been so, in order to his not recognizing Jesus *as the Messiah*, when He presented Himself to Him for baptism. And it is only in this way that the testimony given by him to Jesus is raised above all suspicion of bias. This is the reason why John brings out this circumstance with so much stress by the three successive κἀγώ. Here is the guarantee of the truth of his testimony. But, in this case, how can we explain the word which John addresses to Jesus in the narrative of Matthew (iii. 14): "I have need to be baptized of thee." To resolve this difficulty, it is not necessary to resort to the expedient, which was found already in the Gospel of the Hebrews and which Lücke has renewed,—that of placing this conversation between John and Jesus *after* the baptism of the latter. We have already recalled the fact that, according to Matt. iii. 6 and Mk. i. 5, the baptism of John was preceded, on the part of the neophyte, by an act of confession of sins. The confession which the forerunner heard proceeding from the mouth of Jesus might easily convince him that he had to do with a more holy being than himself, who had a deep sense of sin and condemned it, as he had never felt and condemned it himself, and could thus extort from him the exclamation which Matthew relates. Not knowing Jesus personally, John received Him as he did every other Israelite; after having heard Him speak of the sin of the world, he caught sight of the first gleam of the truth; finally, the scene which followed completed his conviction.

The logical connection between this clause and the following one is this: "And that I might bring to an end that ignorance in which I still was, even as you are now, is the very reason why God has sent me to baptize." The Baptist's ministry had undoubtedly a more general aim: to prepare the people for the Kingdom of God by repentance, or, as he has said himself in ver. 22: "to make straight the way of the Lord." But he makes prominent here only that which forms the culminating point of his ministry, the testimony borne to the person of the Messiah, without which all

316 / Birth of Faith

his labor would have been useless. The article τῷ before ὕδατι (*the water*) appears to me to have been wrongly rejected by the Alexandrian authorities; there is something dramatic in it: "I am come to baptize with *that water*" (pointing to the Jordan). Without the article, there would be a tacit contrast between the *baptism of water* and another (that of the Spirit), which is not in the thought of the context. John now explains how that ignorance ceased for him on the occasion of the baptism which he began to solemnize by the command of God.

Ver. 32. "*And John bore witness saying : I have seen the Spirit descending as* [1] *a dove, and it abode* [2] *upon Him.*" This declaration is introduced with a peculiar solemnity by the words: "*And John bore witness.*" Here, indeed, is the decisive act, as *Hengstenberg* calls it, the *punctum saliens* of the entire ministry of John the Baptist, his Messianic testimony properly so called. With what sense had John *seen?* With the bodily eye, or with the inner sense? This is to ask whether the fact mentioned here took place only in the spiritual world, or also in the external world. According to the narratives of Mark (i. 10, 11), and of Matthew (iii. 16, 17), it was the object of the perception of Jesus only. "And behold, the heavens were opened, and *he saw* the Spirit . . ." (Matt.): "And straightway coming out of the water *he saw* . . ." (Mark). In Luke the narrative is completely objective: "*It came to pass that* . . . . . *the heaven was opened*" (iii. 21, 22). But the narrative in Matthew makes the Baptist also participate in this heavenly manifestation by the form of the declaration of God: "*This is* my Son;" not as in Mark and Luke: "*Thou art* my Son." The divine declaration in Matthew addresses itself, therefore, not to Jesus who is the object, but to him who is the witness of it, namely, John. Now, if it was perceived simultaneously by Jesus and by John, it must have had an objective reality, as the narrative of Luke says. The following is, perhaps, the way in which we can represent to ourselves the relation between the perception of Jesus and that of John: The divine communication, properly so called (the declaration of the Father and the communication of the Spirit), was given from God to Jesus, and the latter had knowledge of the fact at once by the impression which He received, and by a vision which rendered it sensible to him. As to John, he was associated in the perception of this symbolic manifestation, and thereby initiated into the spiritual fact, of which it was as if the covering. Thus the voice which said to Jesus: "*Thou art* my Son," sounded within him in this form: "*This is* my Son." *Neander* cannot admit that a symbolic communication, a vision, could have found a place in the relation between Jesus and God. But this rule is applicable only to the time which followed the baptism. It has been wrongly concluded from the expression, *I have seen*, that, according to the fourth Gospel, the vision was only perceived by John, to the exclusion of Jesus. It is forgotten that the forerunner, in his present account, has no other aim

---

[1] Instead of ωσει which T. R. reads with 8 Mjj., ℵ A B C and 8 Mjj. read ως.

[2] ℵ reads μενον instead of εμεινεν.

but to justify his testimony. For this purpose he does not have to speak of anything else than that which he has himself seen. This is the reason why he relates the fact of the baptism only from the point of view of his own perception.

In the fact here described, we must distinguish the real gift made to Jesus, which is indicated by the narrative in these words: *the Spirit descending and abiding* upon Him; and the symbolic representation of this gift intended for the consciousness of Christ and for that of John: the visible form of the dove. The *heaven* as we behold it with the bodily eye, is the emblem of the state perfect in holiness, in knowledge, in power, in felicity. It is, consequently, in the Scriptures the symbol of the place where God manifests His perfections, in all their splendor, where His glory shines forth perfectly, and from which the supernatural revelations and forces proceed. John sees descending from the sky, which is rent, a luminous form like a *dove*, which rests and abides upon Jesus. This symbol is nowhere employed in the Old Testament to represent the Holy Spirit. In the Syrian religions, the dove was the image of the force of nature which broods over all beings. But this analogy is too remote for the explanation of our passage. The words of Matt. x. 16: " *Be ye harmless as doves,*" have no direct relation to the Holy Spirit. We find some passages in the Jewish Rabbis, where the Spirit who *hovered over the waters* (Gen. i. 3) is connected with the Spirit of the Messiah, and compared to a dove, which hovers over its young without touching them (see Lücke, p. 426). Perhaps this comparison, familiar to the Jewish mind, is that which explains for us, most naturally, the present form of the divine revelation. This emblem was admirably adapted to the decisive moment of the baptism of Jesus. It was a matter, indeed, of nothing less than the new creation, which was to be the consummation of the first creation. Humanity passed at that instant from the sphere of the natural or psychical life to that of the spiritual life, with a view to which it had been created at the first, 1 Cor. xv. 46. The creative Spirit which had of old brooded with His life-giving power over chaos, to draw from it a world full of order and harmony, was going, as if by a new incubation, to transform the first humanity into a heavenly humanity. But that which must here be observed is the *organic* form which the luminous apparition assumes. An organism is an indivisible whole. At Pentecost, the Spirit descends in the form of "*cloven tongues* (διαμεριζόμεναι γλῶσσαι)" which distribute themselves among the believers. This is the true symbol of the way in which the Holy Spirit dwells in the Church, *distributing to each one His gifts according as He pleases* (1 Cor. xii. 11). But at the baptism of Jesus, the fact is another and the emblem is different. The Spirit descends upon Christ in His fullness. " *God,*" it is said in iii. 34, "*gives not to Him the Spirit by measure.*" Comp. Is. xi. 1, 2, where the seven forms of the Spirit, enumerated in order to designate His fullness, come to rest upon the Messiah. We must notice, finally, the term *to abide*, which is a precise allusion to the word נוח in this passage of Isaiah (xi. 2). The prophets received occasional inspirations: *the hand of the Lord was upon*

318 / Birth of Faith

them; then, withdrawing Himself, the Spirit left them to themselves. It was thus, also, with John the Baptist. But Jesus will not only be visited by the Spirit; the Spirit will dwell in Him, and will even one day be poured forth from Him, as if from His source, upon believers; this is the reason why in ver. 33 the idea of *abiding* is placed in close connection with that of *baptizing with the Holy Spirit.* The reading ὡσεί emphasizes more strongly even than the simple ὡς the purely symbolic character of the luminous appearance. The μένον of the Sinaitic MS. is a correction arising from the καταβαῖνον which precedes. The proposition is broken off designedly (καὶ ἔμεινεν), in order to make more fully apparent the idea of *abiding,* by isolating it from what precedes. The construction of the accusative ἐπ' αὐτόν, *upon Him,* with the verb of rest *to abide,* springs from the living character of the relation, (comp. ver. 1 and 18). But had John the Baptist properly interpreted the vision? Had he not ascribed to it a meaning which it did not have? This last possible doubt is answered by the fact related in the following verse.

Ver. 33. *"And neither did I know him; but he who sent me to baptize with water, he said to me: The man on whom thou shalt see the Spirit descend and abide, is he who baptizeth with the Holy Spirit."* Not only was a sign given (ver. 32); but this sign was that which had been promised, and the meaning of which had been indicated beforehand. No human arbitrariness can, therefore, mingle itself with this testimony which John renders to Jesus. Κἀγώ: And I repeat it to you: When He presented Himself, I did not know Him any more than you now know Him. I have then placed here nothing of my own. The expression ὁ πέμψας, *He who sent me,* has something solemn and mysterious in it; John evidently means to designate thereby God Himself who had spoken to him in the desert and given him his commission. This commission included: 1. The command to baptize; 2. The promise to reveal to him the Messiah on the occasion of the baptism; 3. The indication of the sign by which He should be manifested to him; 4. The command to bear testimony to Him in Israel. The emphatic resumption of the subject by the pronoun ἐκεῖνος, *he,* with its meaning which is so emphatic in John, makes prominent this idea: That everything in this testimony proceeds from Jehovah, and Jehovah only. *Weiss,* who is not willing to acknowledge the special and commonly exclusive sense which this pronoun has in the fourth Gospel, thinks that it serves here to place God, as the more remote subject, in contrast with Jesus, as the nearest object. But to what purpose mark a contrast between Jesus and God? The pronoun indisputably signifies: "He and not another." The sign had been announced by God Himself. The words ἐφ' ὃν ἄν (*on whom*), indicate the most unlimited contingency: Whoever he may be, though he be the poorest of the Israelites. The act of *baptizing with the Holy Spirit* is indicated here as the peculiar work of the Messiah. By the baptism of water, John gives to the repentant sinner the pledge of pardon and the promise of sanctification; by the gift of the Holy Spirit, the Messiah realizes this last promise, and accomplishes thereby the highest destiny of the human soul.

The Gift made to Jesus in the Baptism

Vv. 32, 33, suggest an important question: Did Jesus really *receive* anything at His baptism? *Meyer* denies this, alleging that this idea has no support in our Gospel, and that, if the Synoptics say more, it is because they contain a tradition which had been already altered. The real fact was solely the vision granted *to John* in view of the testimony which he was to render to Jesus. This vision was transformed by tradition into the event related by the Synoptics. The idea of the real communication of the Holy Spirit to Jesus would be incompatible with that of the incarnation of the Logos. *Lücke* and *de Wette* think, also, that Jesus received nothing new at that moment. John was only instructed, by means of the vision, as to a permanent fact in the life of Jesus, His communion with the Holy Spirit. *Neander, Tholuck* and *Ebrard* think that there was simply progress in the *consciousness* which Jesus had of Himself. *Baumgarten-Crusius, Kahnis, Luthardt, Gess,* allow a real communication, but only with reference to the *task* which Jesus had to fulfill, that of His own ministry, and of the communication of the Holy Spirit to other men. The opinion of *Meyer,* as well as that of *Lücke,* sacrifices the narrative of the Synoptics, and even that of John to a dogmatic prejudice; for John saw the Spirit not only *abiding,* but *descending,* and this last feature must correspond to a reality, as well as the other. The view of *Neander* is true, but inadequate. There was certainly wrought, at that moment, a decided advance in the consciousness of Jesus, as is indicated by the fact of the divine address: *Thou art my Son;* but the symbol of the *descent* of the dove must also correspond to a real fact. Finally, the view which admits an actual gift, but only in relation to the public activity of Jesus, appears to me superficial. In a life so completely *one* as that of Jesus, where there is nothing purely ritual, where the external is always the manifestation of the internal, the beginning of a new activity supposes a change in His own personal life.

When we lay hold of the idea of the incarnation with the force with which it is apprehended and presented by Paul and John (see ver. 14, and the Appendix to the Prologue), when we recognize the fact that the Logos divested Himself of the divine state, and that He entered into a really human state, in order to accomplish the normal development originally assigned to every man, there is nothing further to prevent us from holding that, after having accomplished the task of the first Adam on the pathway of free obedience, He should have seen opening before Him the sphere of the higher life for which man is destined, and that, as the first among the violent who take the kingdom of heaven by force, He should have forced the entrance into it for Himself and for all. Undoubtedly, His entire existence had passed on under the constant influence of the Holy Spirit which had presided over his birth. At every moment, He had obeyed this divine guide, and each time this docility had been immediately rewarded by a new impulse. The vessel was filled in proportion as it enlarged, and it enlarged in proportion as it was filled. But to be under the operation of the Spirit is not to possess the Spirit (xiv. 17). With the hour of the baptism, the moment came when the previous development was to be transformed into the definite state, that of *the perfect stature* (Eph. iv. 13). "First, that which is psychical," says Paul, in 1 Cor. xv. 46, "afterwards that which is spiritual." If the incarnation is a verity, this law must apply to the development of Jesus, as much as to that of every other man. Till then, the Spirit was *upon* Him ἐπ' αὐτό [τὸ παιδίον] Luke ii. 40; He increased, under this divine influence, in wisdom and grace. From the time of the baptism, the Spirit becomes the principle of His psychical and physical activity, of His whole personal life; He can begin to be called *Lord-Spirit* (2 Cor. iii. 17, 18); *life-giving Spirit* (1 Cor. xv. 45).

The baptism, therefore, constitutes in His interior life as decisive a crisis as does the ascension in His external state. The *open heaven* represents His initiation into the consciousness of God and of His designs. The voice: *Thou art my Son*, indicates the revelation to His inmost consciousness of His personal relation with God, of His eternal dignity as Son, and, at the same time, of the boundlessness of divine love towards Him, and towards humanity on which such a gift is bestowed. He fully apprehends the name of Father as applied to God, and can proclaim it to the world. The Holy Spirit becomes His personal life, makes Him the principle and source of life for all men. Nevertheless, His glorification is not yet; the natural life, whether psychical or physical, still exists in Him, as such. It is after the ascension only that His soul and body will be completely spiritualized ($\sigma\tilde{\omega}\mu\alpha$ $\pi\nu\epsilon\upsilon\mu\alpha\tau\iota\kappa\acute{o}\nu$, 1 Cor. xv. 44).

But, it is asked, does not the gift of the Holy Spirit form a needless repetition of the miraculous birth? By no means; for in this latter event the Holy Spirit acts only as a life-giving force in the stead and place of the paternal principle. He wakens into the activity of life the germ of a human existence deposited in the womb of Mary, the organ prepared for the Logos that He may realize there a human development; in the same way as, on the day of creation, the soul of the first man, breath of the creating God, came to dwell in the bodily organ prepared for its abode and for its earthly activity (Gen. ii. 7).

Some modern theologians, in imitation of some of the Fathers, think that the Logos is confounded by John with the Spirit. But undoubtedly every one will acknowledge the truth of this remark of Lücke: "No more could we say, on the one hand, 'The Spirit was made flesh,' than we could say, on the other, 'I have seen the Logos descend upon Jesus.'" The distinction between the Logos and the Spirit, scrupulously observed by John, even in chaps. xiv.-xvi., where Reuss thinks it is sometimes wholly effaced (*Hist. de la th. chrét.* ii., p. 533 f.), is the following: The Logos is the principle of *objective* revelation, and, through his incarnation, the culminating point of that revelation, while the Spirit is the principle acting internally by which we assimilate to ourselves that revelation subjectively. Hence it results that, without the Spirit, the revelation remains for us a dead letter, and Jesus a simple historical personage with whom we do not enter into any communion. It is by the Spirit alone that we appropriate to ourselves the revelation contained in the word and person of Jesus. Thus, from the time when the Spirit begins to do His work in us, it is Jesus Himself who begins to live within us. As, through the Spirit, Jesus lived on earth by the Father, so, through the Spirit, the believer lives by Jesus (vi. 57). This distinction of offices between Christ and the Spirit is steadily maintained throughout our whole Gospel.[1]

This solemn testimony being given, the forerunner expresses the feeling of satisfaction with which this grand task accomplished inspires him, yet

---

[1] Hilgenfeld, identifying the descent of the Holy Spirit at the baptism with the coming of the Æon Logos into the man Jesus (according to the Valentinians), finds here a trace of Gnosticism. This idea has not the least support in the text.

so as, at the same time, to make his hearers understand that their own task is beginning.

Ver. 34. "*And I have seen and have borne witness that this is the Son of God.*"¹ The ἐγώ, *I*, in κἀγώ, distinguishes, as in vv. 31, 33, him who alone was to *see*, and who *also* (καί) has seen, from all the others who were to *believe* on the ground of his testimony. The perfects: *I have seen* and *I have testified* indicate facts accomplished once for all and abiding for the future. The ὅτι, *that*, depends on the second verb only; the verb *to see* is without an object; it is the act which is of importance, as the condition of that of testifying. The term *Son of God* characterizes a being as a representative of the divinity in a particular function. It is applied in the Old Testament to angels, to judges, to kings, and, finally, to the Messiah: "*Thou art my Son; to-day have I begotten thee*" (Ps. ii. 7, 12); but there is a difference in the mode of representation in each case. An ambassador represents his sovereign, but otherwise than does the son of the latter, for the son, while representing the sovereign, represents in him also his father. Ver. 30 proves that John the Baptist takes the word *Son* here in the loftiest sense which can be attached to it; the being whose existence is united to that of God by an incomparable bond, and who comes to fulfill here on earth the function of Saviour.

Third Testimony: vv. 35–37

Vv. 35, 36. "*On the next day, John was again standing there, and two of his disciples with him; 36, and fixing his eyes upon Jesus as he passed he saith: Behold the Lamb of God.*" Holy impressions, great thoughts, an unutterable expectation doubtless filled, even on the following day, the hearts of those who had heard the words of the forerunner. The next day, John is at his post ready to continue his ministry as the Baptist. We are not at all authorized to suppose, with *de Wette*, that the two disciples who were with him had not been present at the scene of the preceding day. Far from favoring this idea, the brevity of the present testimony leads us rather to suppose that John confines himself to recalling that of the day before to persons who had heard it. The expression ἐκ τῶν μαθητῶν, *of his disciples*, intimates that he had a very considerable number of them. Of these two disciples, one was Andrew (ver. 40); it is difficult to suppose that the other was not the author of the narrative which is to follow. All the subsequent details have no special importance except for the one to whom they recalled the most decisive and happiest hour of his life. The fact that his person remains anonymous, while the four others who play a part in the narrative are all named, confirms this conclusion (*Introd.* p. 203). We may notice a certain difference between this day and the day before in the relation of Jesus to John. The day before, Jesus came *to John*, as to the one who was to introduce Him

---

¹ Instead of ο υιος του θεου, א reads ο εκλεκτος του θεου. It is the only document which presents this plainly indefensible reading.

to future believers. On this day, the testimony is officially given; He has only in a sense to receive *from the hands of* His forerunner the souls which His Father has prepared through him. Like the magnet which one moves through the sand to attract metallic particles, He simply approaches the group which surrounds the Baptist, for the purpose of deciding some of those who compose it to follow Him. The conduct of Jesus is, therefore, perfectly intelligible. It is regulated according to the natural course of the divine work. The Church is not torn, it is gathered, from the tree of the theocracy. This easiness in the course is the seal of God.

As Jesus enters into the plan of God, John the Baptist enters into the thought of Jesus. A tender and respectful scruple might detain the two disciples near their old master. John the Baptist himself frees them from this bond, and begins to realize that saying, which from this moment becomes his motto: "*He must increase, but I must decrease.*" The word ἐμβλέψας indicates a penetrating look which searches its object to its depths (see ver. 42). The practical meaning of this new declaration of John was evidently this: "Go to Him." Otherwise, to what purpose this repetition which adds nothing to the testimony of the day before, which, on the contrary, abridges it? Only this invitation is expressed in an indirect form, that of an affirmation *respecting* the person of Jesus, because, as *Luthardt* says, attachment to Jesus was to be on their part an act of freedom based upon a personal impression, not a matter of obedience to their old master.

Ver. 37. "*And the two disciples heard him speak*[1] *thus, and they followed Jesus.*" John's word, which was an exclamation, was understood. It is very evident that, in the thought of the evangelist, these words: "*And they followed Jesus,*" conceal, under their literal sense, a richer meaning. This first step in following Jesus decided their whole life; the bond, apparently accidental, which was formed at that hour, was, in reality, an eternal bond.

The Testimonies of the Forerunner

We have still to examine three questions which criticism has raised in regard to these testimonies.

I. *Baur* and *Keim*[2] maintain that the narrative of the fourth Gospel denies, by its silence, the fact of the Baptism of Jesus by John; and this for the dogmatic reason, that it would have been contrary to the dignity of the Logos to *receive* the Holy Spirit.—*Hilgenfeld* himself rejects this view (*Einl.* pp. 702 and 719): "The baptism of Jesus," he says, "is *supposed*, not related." The second testimony of John vv. 31 f., mentions it as an accomplished fact, and vv. 32, 33 imply it, since their meaning can only be this: "Among the Israelites who shall come to thy baptism, there shall be found one on whom, when thou shalt baptize him, thou shalt see the Spirit descend. . . . " *Holtzmann* has recognized the indisputable bearing of this passage.[3] But if the fact is not *related*, it is simply, because, as we

---

[1] ℵ and B place αυτου before λαλουντος. John."
[2] *Keim* (I., p. 520): "The fourth Gospel is wholly ignorant of a baptism of Jesus by John."
[3] Hilgenfeld's *Zeitschr. f. wiss. Theol.*, 1872 p. 156 f.

have discovered, the starting point of the narrative is chosen subsequently to the baptism. If the Logos-theory in our Gospel were to play the part which, in this case, Baur and Keim attribute to it, it would exclude from the history of Jesus many other facts which are related at full length by our evangelist.

II. It has been regarded as inconceivable, that, after such a sign and such declarations, the Baptist could have addressed to Jesus, from the depths of his prison, this question: *"Art thou he that should come, or are we to look for another"* (Matt. xi. 3)? *Strauss* has derived from this proceeding of John, a ground for denying the whole scene of the baptism. Some of the Fathers supposed that the forerunner wished thereby only to strengthen the faith of his disciples by calling forth a positive declaration, on Jesus' part, respecting His Messianic character. But the terms of the Synoptical account do not allow this meaning. Two circumstances may be alleged which must have exercised an unfavorable influence upon John's faith; first, his imprisonment (*Meyer*), then the malevolent disposition of his disciples with regard to Jesus (iii. 26), which might have reacted at length on the already depressed spirit of their master. These two circumstances undoubtedly prepared the way for the shaking of faith produced in John; but they cannot suffice to explain it; we must add, with *Bäumlein*, the fact that there was in John, besides the prophet, the natural man who was by no means secure from falling. This is what Jesus gives us to understand when, in His reply, He said, evidently thinking of John: *"Blessed is he who is not offended in me"* (Matt. xi. 6 comp. with ver. 11). *Lücke* has explained this fall by the striking contrast between the expectation, which John had expressed, of a powerful and judicial activity of the Messiah in order to purify the theocracy, and the humble and patient labor of Jesus. A comparison of the reply of the latter to the messengers of John (Matt. xi. 4–6) with the proclamations of John (Matt. iii. 10, 12) is enough to convince us of the justice of this observation. But to all this we must still add a last and more decisive fact. It is this: John did not for an instant doubt concerning the divine mission of Jesus and concerning this mission as higher than his own. This follows, first, from the fact that it is to Jesus Himself that he addresses himself in order to be enlightened, and then, from the very meaning of his question: "Art thou he that should come or are we to look for another (literally, a second)?" We must recall to mind here the prevailing doubt, at that time, in relation to the *prophet*, like to Moses, whose coming was to prepare the way for that of the Messiah (according to Deut. xviii. 18). Some identified him with the Messiah himself; comp. John vi. 14, 15: "It is of a truth the prophet. . . . They were going to take him by force, to *make him king.*" Others, on the contrary, distinguished this prophet *par excellence*, from the Messiah properly so-called; comp. vii. 40, 41. They attributed, probably, to the first of these personages the *spiritual* side of the expected transformation, and to the Messiah, as King descended from David, the *political* side of this renovation. John the Baptist had, at first, united these two offices in the single person of Jesus. But learning in his prison that the work of Jesus limited itself to working miracles of healing, to giving forth the preachings of a purely prophetic character, he asks himself whether this anointed one of the Holy Spirit would not have as His part in the Messianic work only the spiritual office, and whether the political restoration and the outward judgment announced by him would not be devolved upon a subsequent messenger; to the divine prophet, the work of pardon and regeneration; to the King of a Davidic race, the acts of power which were des-

324 / Birth of Faith

tined to realize the external triumph of the Kingdom of God. This is precisely what the form of the question in Matthew expresses: ἕτερον, not ἄλλον: *a second* (Messiah); not: *another* (as Messiah): this expression really ascribes to Jesus the Messianic character, only not exclusively.[1] At the foundation, this distinction which was floating before the eyes of the Baptist had in it nothing erroneous. It answers quite simply to the two offices of Jesus, at His first and second coming. At the first coming, pardon and the Spirit; at the second, judgment and royalty. The Jewish learned men were led by the apparently contradictory prophecies of the Old Testament, to an analogous distinction. Buxtorf (*Lexic. Chaldaic.* p. 1273) and *Eisenmenger* (*Entdeckt, Judenth.* pp. 744 f.) cite a mass of rabbinical passages which distinguish two Messiahs,—the one, whom they call *the son of Joseph*, or of Ephraim, to whom they ascribe the humiliations foretold respecting the Messiah; the other, whom they name *the son of David*, to whom they apply the prophecies of glory. The first will make war, and will perish; for him the sufferings; the second will raise the first to life again and will live eternally. "Those who shall escape from the sword of the first, will fall under that of the second." "The one shall not bear envy against the other, *juxta fidem nostram*," says Jarchi (ad. Jes. xi. 13). These last words attest the high antiquity of this idea.

III. *Renan* (*Vie de Jésus*, pp. 108 f.) draws a poetic picture of the relation between "these two young enthusiasts, full of the same hopes and the same hates, who were able to make common cause and mutually to support each other." He describes Jesus arriving from Galilee with "a little school already formed," and John fully welcoming "this swarm of young Galileans," even though they do not attach themselves to him but form a separate band around Jesus. "We have not many examples, it is true," observes Renan, "of the head of a school eagerly welcoming the one who is to succeed him;" but is not youth capable of all self-abnegations? Behold the romance: the history shows us Jesus arriving alone and receiving from John himself these young Galileans who are for the future to accompany Him. We can understand how there is in this story a troublesome fact for those who are unwilling to explain the history except by natural causes.

The manner in which John the Baptist, at the height of his ascendant and his glory, throws himself immediately and voluntarily into the shade that he may leave the field free for one younger than himself, who until then was completely obscure, cannot be explained by the natural generosity of youth. Conscious, as he was, of the divinity of his mission, John could not thus retire into the shade except before a divine demonstration of the higher mission of Jesus. The conduct of John the Baptist, as attested by our four evangelists, remains for the historian, who does not recognize here the work of God, an insoluble problem. Before closing, one word more on a fancy of *Keim*. This scholar alleges (cf. p

---

[1] The expectation of a great prophet, who is not expressly designated as Messiah, may be proved from the work entitled *The Assumption of Moses*, composed in the years which followed the death of Herod the Great (comp. Wieseler, *Stud. u. Kritiken*, 1868, and Schürer, *Lehrbuch*, etc., p. 540). In this work, which contains the most faithful description of the spiritual state of the Jewish people at the very time of the birth of Jesus, there is announced (chap. 14, Latin transl. published by Ceriani), the coming of a *supreme messenger*, *nuntius in summo constitutus*, whose *hands shall be filled*, in order to effect the deliverance of the people. Moses himself receives only the name of *great messenger*, *magnus nuntius* (c. 18). This messenger will, therefore, be the final prophet, a Moses of the second power; but no royal and Messianic title is ascribed to him.

525) that, in opposition to the Synoptical account (comp. especially Luke iii. 21), our Gospel makes Jesus *the first* of all the people to come to the baptism of John.[1] Where do we find in John's narrative a word which justifies this assertion? But: *sic volo, sic jubeo!*

IV. We are now able to embrace the Messianic testimony of the Baptist in its totality. First, the calling of the people to repentance and baptism, with the vague announcement of the nearness of the Messiah. He comes! (See the Synoptics.) Then, the three days which form the beginning of the narrative of John: He is present! Behold Him! Follow Him! Finally, the last summons: Woe unto you, if you refuse to follow Him! (iii. 28–36.) This totality is so much the more remarkable as the particular elements of it are scattered in several writings and different narratives.

2

John 1:38-52

BEGINNINGS OF THE WORK OF JESUS — BIRTH OF FAITH

Testimony is the condition of faith. For faith is, at the outset, the acceptance of a divine fact on the foundation of testimony. But there is here only an external relation between the believer and the object of faith. In order to become living, faith must enter into direct contact with its object. In the case which occupies our thought, this contact demanded personal manifestations of Jesus, fitted to change believers into witnesses, and to form a direct connection between their hearts and Jesus. This is precisely what the following narratives describe to us. They are divided into two groups; the first comprising that which relates to the three earliest disciples, Andrew, John and Peter (vv. 38–43); the second, that which concerns Philip and Nathanael (vv. 44–52).

First Group: vv. 38–43

We have just mentioned John. Almost all the adversaries of the authenticity themselves acknowledge that the author, in relating his story as he does here, wishes to pass himself off as one of the apostles. Even *Hilgenfeld* says: "Andrew and an unnamed person who is assuredly John."

Vv. 38, 39. "*Then*[2] *Jesus turned and saw them following and saith unto them, What seek ye?* 39. *They said unto Him: Rabbi (which is to say, Master) where dwellest thou?*" Jesus, hearing footsteps behind Him, turns about. He sees these two young men who are following Him with the desire to accost Him, but who do not venture to begin the conversation by addressing Him. He anticipates them: "*What seek ye?*" He who thus interrogates them knows full well what they are seeking after. He knows to whom the desire of Israel and the sighing of humanity tend; He is not ignorant that He is Himself their object. By their answer, the disci-

---

[1] "Das vierte Evangelium kehrt die Dinge um und lässt Jesum zuerst auf der Stelle sein."

[1] Mjj. and 30 Mnn. omit δε.

326 / Birth of Faith

ples modestly express the desire to speak with Him in private. The title *Rabbi* is undoubtedly quite inferior to that which the testimony of John had revealed to them concerning Jesus. But discretion prevents them for the moment from saying more. This title, at the same time, expresses indirectly the intention to offer themselves to Him as disciples. The translation of this term, which is added by the evangelist, proves that the author is writing for Greek readers.[1]

Ver. 40. "*He saith unto them: Come, and you shall see.*[2] *They came*[3] *and saw where he abode: and they remained with him that day; it was*[4] *about the tenth hour.*" The disciples made inquiries as to His dwelling, that they might afterwards visit Him there. Jesus invites them to follow Him at once: "Come *immediately.*" This is, indeed, what the present ἔρχεσθε indicates: the continuance of the going. It has been said that this sense would require the aorist. This is an error. The aorist would signify: *set about* going. Is the reading of the *Vatican* MS.: "Come and *you shall see,*" preferable to that of the greater part of the other documents? We may suppose that the latter comes from ver. 47. Where was Jesus dwelling? Was it in a caravansary, or in a friend's house? We do not know. No more do we know what was the subject of their conversation. But we do know the result of it. Andrew's exclamation in ver. 42 is the enthusiastic expression of the effect produced on the two disciples. When we remember what the Messiah was to the thought of a Jew, we understand how powerful and profound must have been the impression produced upon them by Jesus, to the end that they should not hesitate to proclaim as Messiah this poor and unostentatious man. In the remark: "*And they remained with Him that day,*" all the sweetness of a recollection still living in the heart of the evangelist at the moment of his writing, finds expression. The *tenth hour* may be understood in two ways: either as four o'clock in the afternoon; John would thus reckon the hours as they were generally reckoned among the ancients, beginning from six o'clock in the morning,—we shall see that this is the most natural interpretation in iv. 6, 52, and also in xix. 14;—or as ten o'clock in the morning; he would, thus, adopt the mode of reckoning of the Roman Forum, which has become that of modern nations, and according to which the reckoning is from midnight. *Rettig, Ebrard, Westcott,* etc., think that the author of our Gospel reckons throughout in this way. It would give a satisfactory account of the expression *that day.* But this expression is also very well explained, if the question is of four o'clock in the afternoon; and that by the contrast with the idea of the mere visit which the two youths had thought of making. Instead of continuing a few moments, the interview was prolonged until the end of the day. Comp. the remarks iv. 6,

---

[1] Vv. 38, 39 (in the Greek text) are united in our version. Ver. 40 thereby becomes ver. 39, and so on.

[2] T. R. reads ιδετε (*see*), with ℵ A and 13 other Mjj., almost all the Mnn., It. Vg. Cop., while B C L some Mnn. Syr. and Orig. read οψεσθε (*you shall see*).

[3] T. R. with 13 Mjj. omits the ουν (*therefore*) here, which is read by ℵ A B C L X A.

[4] T. R. reads δε (*now*) after ωρα with some Mnn. only.

iv. 52, xix. 14.¹ This indication of the tenth hour has sometimes been applied, not to the moment when the disciples arrived, but that when they left Jesus. In this case, however, John would undoubtedly have added a limiting expression, such as ὅτε ἀπῆλθον, *when they departed*. It is the hour when he *found*, not that when he *left*, that the author wished to indicate. Faith is no sooner born of testimony, than it extends itself by the same means:

Vv. 41, 42. " *Andrew, Simon Peter's brother, was one of the two who heard John's words and followed Jesus. 42. As the first, he* ² *findeth his own brother Simon, and saith to him: We have found the Messiah (which means: the Christ).*" At this point of the narrative, the author names his companion Andrew. It is because the moment has come to point out his relationship to Simon Peter, a relationship which exercised so decisive an influence on the latter and on the work which is beginning. The designation of Andrew as *Simon Peter's brother*, is so much the more remarkable, since Simon Peter has not as yet figured in the narrative, and since the surname *Peter* did not as yet belong to him. This future apostle, is, therefore, treated from the first as the most important personage of this history. Let us remark, also, that this manner of designating Andrew assumes a full acquaintance already on the part of the readers with the Gospel history. Did Peter's visit to Jesus take place on the same evening? *Weiss* and *Keil* declare that this is impossible, because of the expression *that day* (ver. 40), which leaves no place for this new visit. *Westcott*, on the contrary says: "All this evidently happened on *the same* day." This second view, which is that of *Meyer* and *Brückner*, seems to me the only admissible one. It follows, by a kind of necessity, from the exact enumeration of the days in this passage. See: *the next day*, vv. 29, 35, 44, and also ii. 1. Towards evening, the two disciples left Jesus for some moments, and Peter was brought by Andrew to Him while it was not yet night.

How are we to explain the expressions "*first*" (or *in the first-place*) and "*his own* brother"? These words have always presented a difficulty to interpreters. They contain, in fact, one of those small mysteries with

---

¹ We owe to the kindness of M. André Cherbuliez the following points of information: Ælius Aristides, a Greek sophist of the second century, a contemporary of Polycarp, with whom he may have met in the streets of Smyrna, relates in his *Sacred Discourses* (book v.), that on his arrival in that city, he had, during the night, a dream in which the sun, rising over the public square, ordered him to hold, on that same day, a seance for declamation in the Council-hall at the *fourth* hour. This hour, according to the customs of the ancients, could only be ten o'clock in the morning,—the hour which Xenophon calls that of the πλήθουσα ἀγορά, when the whole population frequents the public square. So he found the hall quite full. In the first book, the deity having ordered him to take a bath, he chose the *sixth* hour as the most favorable to health. Now it was winter, and it was a cold bath which was in question. The hour was, therefore, that of *noon*. What leaves no doubt on this point, is the fact that he says to his friend Bassus who keeps him waiting: "Seest thou, the shadow is already turning." The ordinary reckoning in Asia, therefore, was from six o'clock in the morning. *Langen* has alleged in favor of the opposite usage a passage from the *Acts* of the martyrdom of Polycarp (c. 7). But this passage appears to us insufficient to prove the contrary of that which follows so plainly from the words of the Greek rhetorician.

² Instead of the received reading πρωτος, which is in א L Γ Δ Λ and 8 other Mjj., A B M T♭ X Π some Mnn. Syr. read πρωτον.

328 / Birth of Faith

which John's narrative, at once so subtle and so simple, is full. The Mjj. which read the adverb or the accusative πρῶτον, are six in number, among them the *Vatican:* "He finds his own brother *first* (or *in the first-place*)." But with what brother would he be contrasted by this *first?* With the disciples who were found later, Philip and Nathanael? But it was not Andrew who found these; Jesus found Philip, and Philip Nathanael. And yet this would be the only possible sense of the accusative or the adverb πρῶτον. The nominative πρῶτος, therefore, must necessarily be read, with the Sinaitic MS. and the majority of the Mjj.: "As the first, Andrew finds his own brother." This might strictly mean that they both set about seeking for Simon, and that Andrew was the first to find him, because, Simon being his brother, he knew better where to seek him; this would in a manner explain the τὸν ἴδιον, *his own,* but in a manner very far-fetched. As it is impossible to make this very emphatic expression a mere periphrasis of the possessive pronoun *his,* the author's thought must be acknowledged to have been as follows: "On leaving, each one of them seeks his own brother: Andrew seeks Simon, and John his brother James; and it is Andrew who first succeeds in finding *his own.*" The πρῶτον may have been substituted for πρῶτος under the influence of the four following words in ov.

The term *Messiah,* that is, the *Anointed,* from *maschach, to anoint,* was very popular; it was used even in Samaria (iv. 25). The Greek translation of this title, Χριστός, again implies Greek readers. John had twice employed the Greek term in the preceding narrative (vv. 20 and 25); but here, in this scene of so personal a character, he likes to reproduce the Hebrew title (as he had done at ver. 39, as he is to do again in iv. 25), in order to preserve for his narrative its dramatic character. If we have properly explained this verse, we must conclude from it that James, the brother of John, was also among the young Galilean disciples of John the Baptist, and that John is not willing to name him any more than he is to name himself, or afterwards to name his mother, xix. 25.

Ver. 43. "*And*[1] *he brought him to Jesus. Jesus, looking upon him fixedly, saith, Thou art Simon, son of Jonas,*[2] *thou shalt be called Cephas (which means: Peter).*" The pres. *he finds* and *he says* (ver. 42) were descriptive; the aor. *he brought* indicates the transition to the following act: the presentation of Peter. The word ἐμβλέπειν denotes a penetrating glance which reaches to the very centre of the individuality. This word serves to explain the following apostrophe; for the latter is precisely the consequence of the way in which Jesus had penetrated the character of Simon, and had discovered in him, at the first look, the elements of the future Peter. It is not necessary to suppose that Jesus in a *miraculous* way knew the names of Simon and his father; Andrew, in presenting his brother, must have named him to Jesus. Instead of *Jona,* the three principal Alexandrian

---

[1] ℵ B L reject και (*and*) before ηγαγεν.
[2] ℵ B L Italiq Cop. read Ιωαννου instead of Ιωνα which is read in all the other Mjj. and in almost all the Vss.

authorities read *John*. The received reading is, perhaps, a correction according to Matt. xvi. 17 (*son of Jonas*), where there is no variation of reading and where the name Jonas might be itself an abbreviation of Ἰωάννου (*John*), as *Weiss* supposes. A change of name generally marks a change of life or of position. Gen. xvii. 5: " *Thy name shall be no more Abram (exalted father), but Abraham (father of a multitude).*" Gen. xxxii. 28: " *Thy name shall be no more Jacob (supplanter), but Israel (conqueror of God, in honorable combat).*" The Aramaic word *Képha* (Hebrew, *Keph*), denotes a piece of rock. By this name, Jesus characterizes Simon as a person courageous enough and decided enough to become the principal support of the new society which He is about to found. There was surely in the physiognomy of this young fisherman, accustomed to brave the dangers of his profession, the expression of a masculine energy and of an originating power. In designating him by this new name, Jesus takes possession of him and consecrates him, with all his natural qualities, to the work which He is going to entrust to him.

Baur regards this story as a fictitious anticipation of that in Matt. xvi. 18; the author, from his dogmatic standpoint hastens to show forth in Jesus the omniscience of the Logos. But the ἐμβλέψας, *having regarded him fixedly*, is by no means consistent with such an intention; and as for the expression: " *Thou art Peter,*" Matt. xvi., it implies precisely a previous expression in which Jesus had already conferred this surname upon him. Jesus starts, in each case, from that which is, to announce that which is to be; here: " *Thou art* Simon; thou shalt be Peter; " in Matthew: *thou art* Peter; thou shalt really become what this name declares. Availing himself of the fact that Peter is mentioned here third, *Hilgenfeld* draws up his argument as prosecutor against the author, and says : " Peter is thus deprived by him of the position of the first-called ! " And he finds here a proof of the evangelist's ill will towards this apostle. *Reuss* says, with the same idea, " Peter is here very expressly put in the second place." But the designation of Andrew as *Peter's brother* (ver. 41), before the latter has appeared on the scene, and the magnificent surname which Jesus confers upon him at first sight, while no similar honor had been paid to his two predecessors—are there not here, in our narrative, so many points designed to exalt Simon Peter to the rank of the principal personage among all those who formed the original company, who surrounded Jesus? And if this narrative had been invented with the purpose of depreciating Peter, in order to give the first place to John, why make Andrew so prominent and place him even before the latter? And besides, of what consequence is the *order* of arrival here? Does not every unprejudiced reader feel that the narrative is what it is, simply because the event happened thus. Comp., moreover, vi. 68 and xxi. 15–19 for the part ascribed to Peter in this Gospel.

A contradiction has been found between this account and that of the calling of the same disciples in Galilee, after the miraculous draught of fishes (Matt. iv. 18–22; Mark i. 16–20; Luke v. 1–11). *De Wette, Brückner, Meyer* himself, regard

330 / Birth of Faith

any reconciliation as impossible, and give preference to the narrative of the fourth Gospel. To the view of *Baur*, on the contrary, it is our narrative which is an invention of the author. *Lücke* thinks that the two narratives can be harmonized; that of John having reference to the call of the disciples to *faith*, that of the Synoptics, to their calling as *preachers* of the Gospel, in conformity with the words: "*I will make you fishers of men.*" The first view cannot positively explain how the Synoptical narrative could arise from the facts related here by John and altered by the oral tradition. Everything is too completely different in the two scenes; the place: here, Judea; there, Galilee; the time: here, the first days of Jesus' ministry; there, a period already farther on; the persons: in the Synoptics, there is no reference either to Philip or Nathanael; on the other hand, James, who is not named here, is there expressly mentioned; the situation: here, a simple meeting; there, a fishing; finally, the mode: here, a spontaneous attachment; there, an imperative summons. The view of Baur, on the other hand, cannot explain how the author of the fourth Gospel, in the face of the Synoptical tradition received throughout the whole Church, could attempt to create a new history in all points of the calling of the principal apostles, and a history which positively glorifies Jesus much less than that of the Synoptics. For instead of gaining His disciples by the manifestation of His power, He simply receives them from John the Baptist. The view of *Lücke* is the only admissible one (see also *Weiss*, *Keil* and *Westcott*). Having returned to Galilee (ver. 44), Jesus went back for a time to the bosom of His own family, which transferred its residence, probably in order to accompany Him, to Capernaum (Matt. iv. 13; John ii. 12; comp. Mark iii. 31). In these circumstances, He naturally left His disciples also to return to the bosom of their families (Peter was married); and He called them again, afterwards, in a complete and decisive manner when the necessities of His work and of their spiritual education for their future task required it. The very readiness with which these young fishermen followed His call at that time (Synoptic account),—leaving, at His first word, their family and their work to unite themselves with Him, implies that they had already sustained earlier relations to Him. Thus the account of the Synoptics, far from excluding that of John, implies it. Let us remember that the Synoptic narratives had for their essential object the *public* ministry of Jesus, and that, consequently, these writings could not omit a fact of such capital importance as the calling of the earliest disciples to the office of preachers. The fourth Gospel, on the contrary, having as its aim to describe the development of apostolic faith, was obliged to set in relief the scene which had been the starting point of this faith. We shall prove in many other cases this reciprocal relation between the two writings, which is explained by their different points of view and aims.

Second Group: vv. 44–52

The following narrative seems to be contrived for the purpose of driving to despair, by its conciseness, the one who attempts to account for the facts from an external point of view. Does ver. 44 express merely the *intention* of setting out for Galilee? Or does it indicate an actual departure? Where and how did Jesus find Philip and Nathanael? Were they also in Judea among the disciples of John the Baptist? Or did He meet them on His arrival in Galilee?—Evidently, a narrative like this could proceed only from a man pre-occupied above all with the spiritual element in the history which he relates, and who, in consequence, simply sketches as slightly as possible the external side of the facts related. This is the general character of the narrative of the fourth Gospel.

Vv. 44, 45: "*The next day he*[1] *resolved to set out for Galilee, and finds Philip; and Jesus says to him: Follow me.* 45. *Now Philip was of Bethsaida, of the city of Andrew and Peter.*" The aorist, $\dot{\eta}\theta\acute{\epsilon}\lambda\eta\sigma\epsilon\nu$ (*wished*), indicates quite naturally, a realized wish. The words: "*He wished to set out and He finds,*" are thus, equivalent to: "*At the moment when* He *decides* to set out, He *finds.*" Here is the juxtaposition of propositions which is so frequent in John (*Introd.*, p. 135). This mode of expression is irreconcilable with the idea that Jesus only met Philip at a later time in Galilee; the latter was, therefore, in the same region with Andrew, John and Peter, and for the same reason. It was of importance to Jesus to surround Himself particularly with young men who had gone through with the preparation of the ministry and baptism of John the Baptist. The notice of ver. 45, intercalated here, gives us to understand that it was through the intervention of the two brothers, Andrew and Peter, that Philip was brought into connection with Jesus. On the other hand, the expression: *He finds,* is incompatible with the idea that they had positively brought him to Him. At the time of His setting out, Jesus probably found him conversing with his two friends; whereupon He invited him to join himself to them. The words, "*Follow me,*" merely signify, "Accompany me on this journey." But Jesus well knew what must result from this union once formed; and it is impossible that this invitation should not have had in His thought a higher import. The verb $\dot{\eta}\theta\acute{\epsilon}\lambda\eta\sigma\epsilon\nu$ (*wished*), denotes a deliberate wish, and leads us to inquire what was the motive of the resolution, which Jesus formed, of setting out again for Galilee. *Hengstenberg* thinks that He wished to conform to the prophecies which announced that Galilee would be the theatre of the Messianic ministry. This explanation would give to the conduct of Jesus somewhat of artificiality. According to others, He desired to separate His sphere of action from that of John the Baptist, or also to withdraw from the seat of the hierarchy which had just shown itself unfavorably disposed towards the forerunner. The subsequent narrative (ii. 12–22) appears to me to lead to another solution. Jesus must inaugurate His Messianic ministry at Jerusalem; but, in order to this, He desired to wait for the solemn season of the Passover feast. Before this time, therefore, He decided to return to His family, and to close, in the days which remained until the Passover, the period of His private life.

Ver. 46: "*Philip finds Nathanael and says to him: We have found Him of whom Moses, in the law, and the prophets did write, Jesus, the son of Joseph, of Nazareth.*[2] Philip's part in the calling of Nathanael is like that of Andrew in

---

[1] T. R. reads here: ο Ιησους with 5 byz., and omits it with 4 of them in the following clause.
[2] T. R. with E F G H K M U V Γ Δ Π: Ναζαρεθ; ℵ A B L X: Ναζαρετ; Δ: Ναζαραθ e: Ναζαρα (see *my Comment. sur l'év. de Luc.*, 2d. ed., t. I., pp. 107, 108.

the calling of Peter, and that of Peter and Andrew in his own. One lighted torch serves to light another; thus faith propagates itself. *Luthardt* sets forth finely the heavy and complicated form of Philip's profession; those long preliminary considerations, that full and formal Messianic certificate, which is in contrast with the lively and unconstrained style of Andrew's profession (ver. 42). The same traits of character are met with again in the two disciples in vi. 1–13, and perhaps also in xii. 21, 22. From the fact that Philip designates Jesus as the *son of Joseph*, and as a native of *Nazareth, Strauss, de Wette*, and others, conclude that the fourth evangelist either was ignorant of, or did not admit, the miraculous origin of Jesus and His birth at Bethlehem; as if it were the evangelist who was here speaking, and not Philip! And that disciple, after exchanging ten words with Jesus, must have been already thoroughly acquainted with the most private circumstances of His birth and infancy! Is it Andrew and Peter who must have informed him of them? But whence could they have got the knowledge of them themselves? Or Jesus? We must suppose, then, that this was the first thing that Jesus hastened to communicate to them: that He was not the son of the man who was said to be His father, that He was miraculously born! How criticism can become foolish, through its desire of being sagacious! The place where Nathanael was met by Jesus and His disciples, when returning to Galilee, is not pointed out. The most probable supposition is, that they met each other in the course of the journey. Philip, who was his fellow-citizen—Nathanael was also of Cana (xxi. 2)—became the connecting-link between him and Jesus. We may suppose that Nathanael was returning home from the presence of John the Baptist, or that, like all his pious fellow-countrymen, he was going to be baptized by him. At all events, he had just rested for a few moments in the shade of a fig-tree, when he met Jesus and His companions (comp. ver. 48). Ewald wrongly supposes the meeting to have taken place at Cana. The circumstantial account of the calling of Nathanael leads us to believe that he afterwards became one of the apostles: for this is the case with all the disciples mentioned in this narrative. It appears, moreover, from xxi. 2, where the apostles are distinguished from the mere disciples, and where Nathanael is placed among the former. As this name does not figure in the apostolic catalogues (Matt. x. 3; Mark iii. 18; Luke vi. 14; Acts i. 13), it is generally admitted that Nathanael is no other than Bartholomew, whose name is connected with that of Philip in almost all these lists. Bartholomew being only a patronymic (son of Tolmai or Ptolemy), there is no difficulty in this supposition. As for the hypothesis of *Späth*, that Nathanael is a symbolic name (this word signifies *gift of God*), invented by the later author to designate the apostle John, it is one of those fancies of the criticism of the day, which, if it needed any refutation, would be refuted by its insoluble inconsistency with xxi. 2.

Ver. 47: "*And Nathanael said unto him: Can anything good come out of Nazareth? Philip says to him: Come and see.*" According to *Meyer*, Nathanael's answer alludes to the reputation which the town of Nazareth had had for immorality; according to *Lücke* and *de Wette*, to the smallness of the place. But there is nothing in history to prove that Nazareth was a place of worse fame, or less esteemed than any other village of Galilee. Nathanael's answer does not at all require such suppositions. Is it not more simple to connect this reply closely with the words of Philip? Nathanael, not recollecting any prophetic passage which asscribes to Nazareth so important a part, is astonished; the more so, since Cana is only at the remove of a league from Nazareth, and it is difficult for him to imagine this retired village, near his own, raised all at once to so high a destiny. We are well aware of the paltry jealousies which frequently exist between village and village. The expression, *anything good*, signifies, therefore, in this case : " anything so eminent as the Messiah ! " We notice here, for the first time, a peculiarity of the Johannean narrative : the author seems to take pleasure in mentioning certain objections raised against the Messianic dignity of Jesus, to which he makes no reply because every reader instructed in the Gospel history could dispose of them on the spot (comp. vii. 27, 35, 42, etc.). At the time when John wrote, every Christian knew that Jesus was not actually from Nazareth. The answer of Philip : " *Come and see*," is at once the most simple and the most profound apologetic. To every upright heart Jesus proves Himself by showing Himself. This rests on the truth expressed in ver. 9. (Comp. iii. 21.)

Ver. 48. "*Jesus saw*[1] *Nathanael coming to him and says of him : Behold a true Israelite, in whom there is no guile.*" Nathanael is one of those upright hearts who have only to see Jesus in order to believe in Him; Philip is not mistaken. Jesus Himself, as He sees him, also signalizes in him this quality. Penetrating him, as He had penetrated Simon, he utters aloud this reflection *with regard to him* ($\pi\epsilon\rho\grave{\iota}$ $\alpha\dot{\upsilon}\tau o\tilde{\upsilon}$) : "Behold. . . ." We can make the adverb $\dot{\alpha}\lambda\eta\vartheta\tilde{\omega}\varsigma$, *truly*, qualify ἴδε, Behold *really* an Israelite without guile ;" in this case, the idea *without guile* is not placed in connection with the national Israelitish character; it is applied to Nathanael personally. But we can make the adverb $\dot{\alpha}\lambda\eta\vartheta\tilde{\omega}\varsigma$ qualify the word *Israelite :* a true (*truly*) Israelite, and that as being without guile." In that case, it is the national character, as well as that of Nathanael, which Jesus signalizes, and there may be, perhaps, an allusion to the name *Israel* (*conqueror of God*) which was substituted for *Jacob* (*supplanter*), after the mysterious scene, Gen. xxxii., where the new way of struggling took the place, in the patriarch's case, of the deceitful methods which were natural to him. However, vi. 5 and viii. 31, where the adverb qualifies the verb *to be*, must not be cited for this meaning.

Ver. 49. " *Nathanael says to Him : whence knowest thou me ? Jesus answered and said to him : Before Philip called thee, when thou wert under the fig-tree, I saw thee.*" This reply by which Nathanael seems to appropriate to himself the eulogy contained in ver. 48 has been criticised as not modest. But he wishes simply to know on what grounds Jesus, who sees him

---

[1] ℵ alone reads ἰδών . . . λεγει.

334 / Birth of Faith

for the first time, forms this judgment of him. Certainly, if we take account of the extraordinary effect which Jesus' answer produced upon Nathanael (ver. 50), it must contain to his view the indubitable proof of the supernatural knowledge which Jesus has of him. *Lücke* thinks that this knowledge applies only to the inward moral state of Nathanael; *Meyer*, on the contrary, that it applies only to the external fact of his sitting under the fig-tree. But thoroughly to comprehend the relation of this saying of Jesus, on the one side, to his previous declaration (ver. 48), and, on the other, to the exclamation of Nathanael (ver. 50), it is indispensable to unite the two views. Not only does Nathanael note the fact that the eye of Jesus had followed him in a place where His natural sight could not reach him, but he understands that the eye of this stranger has penetrated his interior being, and has discerned there a moral fact which justifies the estimate expressed by Jesus in ver. 48. Otherwise, the answer of Jesus does not any the more justify that estimate, and we cannot understand how it can call forth the exclamation of Nathanael in ver. 50, or be presented, in vv. 51, 52, as the first of the Lord's miraculous works. What had taken place in Nathanael, at that moment when he was under the fig-tree? Had he made to God the confession of some sin (Ps. xxxii. 1, 2), taken some holy resolution, made the vow to repair some wrong? However this may be, serious thoughts had filled his heart, so that, on hearing the word of Jesus, he feels that he has been penetrated by a look which participates in the divine omniscience. The words: *before Philip called thee*, are connected by *Weiss* with what follows, in this sense: "When thou wert under the fig-tree before Philip called thee." But they much more naturally qualify the principal verb: *I saw thee*. And the same is true of the second limiting phrase: "*when thou wert under the fig-tree,*" which refers rather to what follows than to what precedes. For the situation in which Jesus *saw him* is of more consequence than that in which Philip *called him*. The construction of ὑπό, with the accusative (τὴν συκῆν), with the verb of rest, is owing to the fact that to the local relation there is joined the moral notion of shelter. *I saw* denotes a view such as that of Elisha (2 Kings v.). In Jesus, as in the prophets, there was a higher vision, which may be regarded as a partial association with the perfect vision of God. At this word, Nathanael feels himself, as it were, penetrated by a ray of divine light:

Ver. 50. "*Nathanael answered and said to him:*[1] *Master, thou art the Son of God; thou art the King of Israel.*" By the title *Son of God*, he expresses the thrilling impression which was made within his mind by the intimate relation between Jesus and God, of which he had himself just had experience. *Lücke*, *Meyer*, and most others maintain that this title is here equivalent to that of Messiah. They regard this as proved by the following expression: *the King of Israel*. But it is precisely this juxtaposition which implies a difference of meaning. At all events, if the two titles had exactly the same sense, the second would be joined to the first as a

---

[1] B. L. reject και λεγει αυτω; ℵ reads και ειπεν.

simple apposition, while the repetition of the pronoun σύ, *thou*, and of the verb εἶ, *art*, before the second title, absolutely excludes this synonymy. Besides, the title which Nathanael here gives must be the vivid and fresh expression of the moral agitation which he has just experienced, and not, like that of Messiah, the result of reflection. If the latter is added afterwards, it is to do justice to the affirmation of Philip (ver. 46); but still, it can only come in the second place. In general, we believe that the equivalence of the term, Son of God, with that of Messiah, even in the form in which *Weiss* makes it out, who understands by Son of God the man well-beloved of God, never wholly corresponds with reality. In this passage, in particular, the title Son of God, can only be connected with the proof of supernatural knowledge which Jesus has just given, and consequently, it contains the feeling of an exceptional relation between Jesus and God. Undoubtedly, it is a vague impression; but it is, nevertheless, rich and full, as is everything which is a matter of feeling, even more than if it were already reduced to a dogmatic formula. As *Luthardt* observes: "Nathanael's faith will never possess *more* than that which it embraces at this moment" (the living person of Jesus), it will only be able to possess it more distinctly. The seeker for gold puts his hand on an ingot; when he has coined it he has it better, but not more. The two titles complete each other: *Son of God* bears on the relation of Jesus to God; *King of Israel* on His relation to the chosen people. The second title is the logical consequence of the first. The personage who lives in so intimate a relation with God can only be *the King of Israel*. This title is undoubtedly the response to that of *true Israelite*, with which Jesus had saluted Nathanael. The faithful subject has recognized and salutes his King. Jesus feels indeed, that he has just taken the first step in a new career—that of miraculous signs, of which His life had been completely destitute up to this time; and His answer breathes the most elevated feeling of the grandeur of the moment.

Ver. 51. "*Jesus answered and said to him: Because I said unto thee that*[1] *I saw thee under the fig-tree, thou believest; thou shalt see*[2] *greater things than these.*" Since Chrysostom, most interpreters (*Lücke, Meyer*, etc.), editors and translators (*Tischendorf, Rilliet*), give to the words: *Thou believest*, an interrogative sense. They put into this question either the tone of surprise (*Meyer*) because of a faith so readily formed, or even that of reproach (*de Wette*), as if Nathanael had believed before he had sufficient grounds for it. I think, notwithstanding the observations of *Weiss* and *Keil*, that there is a more serene dignity in the answer of Jesus, if it is taken as an affirmation. He recognizes and approves the nascent faith of Nathanael; He congratulates him upon it; but He promises him a succession of increasing miraculous manifestations, of which he and his fellow-disciples will be witnesses, and which from this moment onward will develop their nascent faith. This expression proves that from that day Nathanael re-

---

[1] ℵ A B G L Syr., etc., read ὅτι before εἶδόν.

[2] The T. R. reads ὄψει (Attic form). All the Mjj. with the exception of U Γ read ὄψῃ.

mained with Jesus. Up to this point, Jesus had spoken to Nathanael alone: "*Thou believest . . . thou shalt see.*" What He now declares, although also promised to him, concerns, nevertheless, all the persons present.

Ver. 52. "*And he says to him: Verily, verily, I say unto you, From this time onward*[1] *you shall see the heaven opened and the angels of God ascending and descending upon the Son of man.*" We meet for the first time the formula *amen, amen*, which is found twenty-five times in John (*Meyer*), and nowhere else in the New Testament. Matthew says *amen* (not repeated) thirty times. This expression *amen*, serving as an introduction to a declaration which is about to follow, is found nowhere either in the Old Testament, or in the Rabbinical writings. It belongs exclusively to the language of Jesus. Hence is the fact more easily explained that Jesus is Himself called the Amen in the Apocalypse (iii. 14). This word (coming from the Hebrew *aman, firmum fuit*) is properly a verbal adjective, *firm, worthy of faith*; it is used as a substantive in Is. lxv. 16: *Elohé amen*, "the God *of truth*." It also becomes an adverb in a large number of passages in the Old Testament, to signify: that remains sure; or: let it be realized! This adverb is doubled, as in St. John, in the two following passages: Num. v. 22: "*Then the woman* (accused of adultery) *answered: Amen, amen;* Nehem. viii. 6: *All the people answered: Amen, amen.*" This doubling implies a doubt to be overcome in the hearer's mind. The supposed doubt arises sometimes, as here, from the greatness of the thing promised, sometimes from a prejudice against which the truth affirmed has to contend (for example, John iii. 3, 5).

The words ἀπ' ἄρτι, *from now on*, are rejected by three of the ancient Alexandrian authorities; they were, in general, adopted by the moderns, and by Tischendorf himself who said in 1859 (7th ed.): *cur omissum sit, facile dictu; cur additum, vix dixeris*. But the omission in the Sinaitic MS. has caused him to change his opinion (8th ed.). The rejection can be easily understood, as the Gospel history does not contain any appearance of an angel in the period which followed these first days. It would be very difficult, on the contrary, to account for the addition. *Weiss* and *Keil* allege the words of Matt. xxvi. 64. But there is no resemblance either in situation or thought between that passage and this one, which can explain such an importation; and I persist in thinking, with the Tischendorf of 1859, that the rejection is much more easily explained than the addition. Jesus means to say that heaven, which was opened at the time of His baptism, is not closed. The communication re-established between heaven and earth continues, and the two regions form for the future only one, so that the inhabitants of the one communicate with those of the other; comp. Eph. i. 10 and Col. i. 20. The expression *ascend and descend* is a very clear allusion to the vision of Jacob (Gen. xxviii. 12, 13). There it represented the continual protection of divine providence, and of its invisible agents assured to the patriarch. What the disciples are about to

---

[1] ℵ B L It. Cop. Orig. omit απ' αρτι, which is read by T. R. with all the other Mjj., the Mnn., Syr., etc.

behold from now on will be a higher realization of the truth represented by that ancient symbol. Jesus certainly does not mean to speak of certain appearances of angels which occurred at the close of His life. The question is of a phenomenon which from this moment is to continue uninterruptedly. Most moderns, putting themselves at the opposite spiritualistic extreme to the literal interpretation, see here only an emblem of the heavenly and holy character of the daily activity of Jesus and, as *Lücke* and *Meyer* say, of the living communion between God and His organ, in which the divine forces and revelations are concentrated. *Reuss* says, with the same meaning: "Angels are the divine perfections common to the two persons . . . ," together with this observation: "The literal explanation would here be as poor as it is absurd." *Luthardt* (following *Hofmann*): "the (personified) forces of the Divine Spirit." If the explanation of the Fathers was too narrow, that of the moderns is too broad. There is no passage where the spiritual activity of Jesus is referred, even symbolically, to the ministry of angels. It is derived from the Spirit (ver. 32; iii. 34), or, still more commonly, from the Father dwelling and acting in Jesus (vi. 57). Angels are the instruments of the divine force in the domain of nature (see the angel of *the waters*, Apoc. xvi. 5; of the *fire*, Apoc. xiv. 18). This expression refers, therefore, to phenomena, which, while taking place in the domain of nature, are due to a causality superior to the laws of nature. Could Jesus characterize His miracles more clearly without naming them? It is also the only sense which connects itself with what has just passed, even at this moment, between Nathanael and Himself: "Thou believest because of this wonder of *omniscience;* this is only the prelude of more remarkable signs of the same kind." By this Jesus means the works of *power* of which the event that follows, the miracle of Cana, will be the first example (*from now on*). This explanation is confirmed, moreover, by the remarkable parallel, Matt. viii. 9, 10. It is difficult to explain why the angels *who ascend* are placed before those *who descend*. Is it simply owing to a reminiscence of Genesis? But there, there was a special reason: Jacob must understand that the angels were already near him at the moment when he was receiving that revelation. According to *Meyer* and *Lücke*, Jesus would here also mean that, at the moment when the "*you shall see*" shall take place, this relation with heaven shall be already in full activity. I think, rather, that the angels are here presented by Jesus as an army grouped around their chief, the Son of man, who says to one, *Go*, and to another, *Do this*. These servants ascend first, to seek power in the presence of God; afterwards, they descend again to accomplish the work.

Were not these two allusions, one to the name of Israel (ver. 48), the other to the dream of Jacob, suggested by the sight of the very localities through which Jesus was, at this moment, passing? He was going from Judea to Galilee, either by the valley of the Jordan or by one of the two plateaus which extend along that valley on the east and the west. Now *Bethel* was on the eastern plateau, the very locality in which Jacob's dream had occurred, and whose name perpetuated the remembrance of that

338 / Birth of Faith

event; on the eastern plateau *Mahanaim* was situated (the *double camp* of angels) and *the ford of Jabbok*, two places which equally recalled appearances of angels (Gen. xxxii. 1, 2 and 24 ff.). It is possible that, in passing through these places which were classic for every Israelitish heart, Jesus conversed with His disciples concerning those scenes precisely which they recalled, and that this circumstance was the occasion of the figure which He makes use of at this moment.

What are the purpose and meaning of the expression : *Son of man*, by which Jesus here describes Himself? We examine this question here only in its relation to the context (see the following appendix). It is manifest that this title has a relation to the two titles which Nathanael has just given to Jesus. This is intended to make His disciples sensible of the fact that, besides His particular relation to God and to Israel, He sustains a third no less essential one, His relation to the whole of humanity. It is to this last that this third title refers. By making this designation His habitual title and by avoiding the use of the title of *Christ*, which had a very marked political and particularistic hue, Jesus wished from the first to establish His ministry on its true and broad foundation, already laid by that saying of His forerunner: "who takes away the sin *of the world.*" His task was not, as Nathanael imagined, to found the Israelitish monarchy: it was to save the world. He did not come to complete the theocratic drama, but to bring to its consummation the history of man.

This title, thus, completes *the two* others; the three relations of Jesus to *God*, to *men*, and to the *people of Israel* exhaust, indeed, His life and His history.

The Son of Man

Jesus designates Himself here, for the first time, by the name *Son of man*, and it is quite probable that this occasion was really the first on which He assumed this title. We find it thirty-nine times in the Synoptics (by connecting the parallels: most frequently in Matt. and Luke); ten times in John (i. 52; iii. 13, 14; v. 27 (without the article); vi. 27, 53, 62; viii. 28; xii. 23, 34; xiii. 31). Three very different opinions prevail respecting the meaning, the origin and the purpose of this designation. We can, however, arrange these in two principal classes.

I. Some think that Jesus here borrows from the Old Testament a title in some measure technical, which was adapted to designate Him either as *prophet*—there would thus be an illusion to the name *son of man* by which God often designates Ezekiel, when addressing His word to him—or as *Messiah*, in allusion to Dan. vii. 13: "And I saw one *like unto a son of man* coming on the clouds of heaven." This Messianic prophecy had become popular in Israel, to such an extent that the Messiah had received the name *Anani*, עֲנָנִי, the man of the clouds. It would thus be natural to suppose that Jesus made choice of this term as in a popular way designating his Messianic function; the more so, as there exists a saying of Jesus, in which He solemnly recalls this description of Daniel, applying it to Himself, Matt. xxvi. 64: "Henceforth ye shall see *the Son of man* seated at the right hand of power and coming on the clouds of heaven." Of these two alleged allusions, the first cannot be sustained. For it is not as a prophet that God calls Ezekiel son of man, but as a creature completely powerless to perform the divine work of which he is inviting him to become the agent—thus, as *a man*. Would it not be contrary to all logic to maintain that, because God on one occasion has called a prophet son of man, it follows that this name is the equivalent of the title prophet.[1]

The allusion to Daniel, as the foundation of this peculiar name of Jesus, is admitted by almost all modern interpreters, *Lücke, Bleek, Ewald, Hilgenfeld, Renan, Strauss, Meyer, Keil, Weiss*, etc. This is also, apparently, the opinion of M. *Wabnitz*.

If the question were this: Did Jesus, in designating Himself thus, bring together in His own mind this name and the: *as a son of man*, of Daniel? it would seem difficult to deny it, at least as to the time when He proclaimed Himself the Messiah in reply to the high-priest before the Sanhedrim. But this is not the question. The point in hand is to determine whether, in choosing this title as His habitual name, as His title by predilection, Jesus meant to say: "I am the Messiah announced by Daniel." As for myself, I think that this name is rather an immediate creation of His own heart, with which He was inspired by the profound feeling of what He was for humanity. The following are the reasons which impel me to reject the first view; and to prefer the second to it: 1. The borrowings of Jesus from the O. T. have, in general, a character of formal accommodation rather than that of a real imitation. The idea always springs up as perfectly original from His heart and mind; and if He connects it with some saying of Scripture, it is that He may give it support with His hearers, rather than that He may cite it as a source. How, then, could the name of which Jesus, by preference, makes use to designate His relation to humanity be the product of a servile imitation? If anything must have come forth from the depths of His own consciousness, it is this name. 2. Throughout the whole course of the Gospel of John, Jesus, as we shall see, carefully avoids proclaiming Himself as the Messiah, Χριστός, before the people, because He knows too well the political meaning commonly attached to this term, and that the least misunderstanding on this point would have been immediately fatal to His work. He makes use, therefore, of all kinds of circumlocutions to avoid designating Himself as the Messiah: comp. viii. 24, 25; x. 24, 25, etc. Comp. also, in the Synoptics, Luke iv. 41; ix. 21, where he forbids the demons and His disciples to declare Him to be the Christ. And in direct contradiction to this procedure, He would have chosen, for His habitual name, a designation to which the popular opinion had attached this sense of Messiah! 3. Two passages in John prove, moreover, that the name *Son of man* was not generally applied to the Messiah: xii. 34, where the people ask Jesus who this personage is whom He designates by the name Son of man (see the exegesis); and v. 27, where Jesus says that the Father has committed the judgment to Him because He is *Son of man*. Certainly, if this expression had here meant: the Messiah, the article *the* could not have been wanting. It was necessary, in that case, since the question was of a personage well-known and designated under this name. Without the article, there is here a mere indication of *quality*:

---

[1] This explanation presented by *Vernes*, and up to a certain point by *Weizsäcker*, has been well refuted in the article of *Wabnitz*, *Revue théol.*, Oct. 1874, pp. 165 f.

God makes Him judge of men as having the quality of man. Besides, let us not forget that in Daniel judgment is exercised, not, as *Renan* wrongly says, by the Son of man, but by Jehovah Himself; and it is only after this act is wholly finished, that the Son of man, to whom the title is given, appears on the clouds.[1]

4. In the Synoptics, also, there are passages where the meaning Messiah does not suit the term Son of man. It is sufficient to cite Matt. xvi. 13, 15, where Jesus asks His disciples: " Who do men say that I, the Son of Man, am? . . . And you, who do you say that I am?" Had this term been equivalent to Messiah, would not the first question contain an intolerable tautology, and would not *Holtzmann* have ground for asking how Jesus, after having designated Himself a hundred times as Son of Man, could still propose to His disciples this question, " Whom do you take me to be?" 5. The appearance of the Son of man in the prophecy of Daniel has an exclusively eschatological bearing. The question is of the glorious establishment of the final kingdom. Now one cannot comprehend how from such a representation, especially, Jesus could have derived the title of which He makes use to designate His person during the period of His earthly abasement. But one can easily understand that, when this title had once been adopted by Him for other reasons, He should have made express allusion to this term employed by Daniel, at the solemn moment when, before the Sanhedrim, He wished to affirm His glorious return and His character as judge of His judges. Let us add, finally, that Daniel had not said: I saw the Son of man, or even a Son of man, but vaguely: *like* [the figure of] a son of man; and could Jesus have derived from such a vague expression His title of Son of man? 6. If we believe the common exegesis, the term Son of God had the sense of Messiah. Now, according to the same exegesis, this also is the meaning of the term Son of man, and it would follow from this that these two titles, which are evidently antithetic, would both have the same sense [2]—a thing which is impossible. They do not, either the one or the other, properly designate the office of the Messiah, but rather two aspects of the Messianic personage, which are complementary of each other.

II. We are led thus to the second class of interpretations, that which finds in this title a spontaneous expression of the consciousness which Jesus had of Himself—some finding the feeling of His greatness expressed in it, and others, the feeling of His humiliation.

1. There is no longer any need of refuting the explanation of *Paulus* and *Fritzsche*, according to which Jesus simply meant to say: This individual whom you see before you: *homo ille quem bene nostis*. Jesus would not, by so exceptional a term, have paraphrased more than fifty times the simple pronoun of the first person.

2. *Chrysostom, Tholuck* and others explain this title by a deliberate antithesis to the feeling which Jesus had of His own essential sonship to God. To choose, as His characteristic name, the title of descendant of the human race, He must feel

---

[1] Undoubtedly, in the passage of the *Book of Enoch* (c. 37–71) the Messiah is several times called Son of man, but not the Son of Man; comp. *Westcott*. Besides, this passage is suspected of Christian interpolations (Oehler, art. *Messias*, in Herzog's *Encycl.* (1st ed.); Keim, *Gesch. Jesu* (p. 659). But in any case, if these passages were entirely authentic, the passages in John prove that this designation was not yet a popular one.

[2] To this impossible identification all the efforts tend which *Keim* makes to attenuate the difference between these two terms, (p. 948).

Himself a stranger by nature to that race. This explanation is ingenious: but only too much so for the simplicity of the feeling of Jesus.

3. *Keerl* thought that Jesus meant to designate Himself thereby as *the eternal man*, pre-existent in God, of whom the Rabbis spoke, the Messiah differing from that heavenly man only through the flesh and blood with which He clothed Himself when He came to the earth. But no others than the Scribes could have attached such a sense to this title which Jesus habitually used, and nothing in His teaching indicates that He Himself shared in that Rabbinical opinion. Moreover, the term Son of man would be very ill adapted to a heavenly man.

4. *Gess* expresses an analogous idea,[1] but less extra-Biblical. According to him, Jesus wished to express thereby the idea of "the divine majesty as having appeared in the form of human life." He rests upon the passages in which divine functions are ascribed to the Son of man, *as such ;* thus the pardon of sins (Matt. ix. 6, and parallels), lordship over the angels (Matt. xiii. 41), judgment (Matt. xvi. 27, xxv. 31, John v. 27). But, if the destiny of man is to be exalted even to participate in the functions and works of God, there is nothing in the acts cited which surpasses that sublime destiny, and consequently the limits of the *human* life when it has reached the summit of its perfection. Besides, is the idea of the *Kenosis*, which *Gess* adopts, compatible with that of the divine majesty realized in Jesus—in Jesus in the form of the human life?

5. *De Wette* and others think, on the contrary, that by this name Jesus meant to make prominent the weakness of His earthly state. It seems to us that the words of v. 27 are altogether opposed to this sense. It is not because of the meanness of His earthly state, that the judgment is committed to Christ.

6. Only one explanation remains for us, in itself the most simple and natural one, which in various forms has been given by *Böhme, Neander, Ebrard, Olshausen, Beyschlag, Holtzmann, Wittichen, Hofmann, Westcott, Schaff,* etc., which we have already set forth in the first edition of this work, aud which we continue to defend. Jesus meant to designate by this title, in the first place, His complete participation in our human nature. *A* son of man is not the son of such or such a man, but an offspring of the human race of which He presents an example; a legitimate representative. It is in this sense that this expression is used in Ps. viii. 5: "What is man that thou art mindful of him, and the son of man that thou visitest him?" The same is true in the frequent addresses of the Lord to Ezekiel. It is also the same in Dan. vii. 13, where the being who appeared like a Son of man represents the human, gentle, holy character of the Messianic kingdom, just as the wild beasts, which preceded him, were figures of the violent, harsh, despotic character of earthly empires. Jesus, therefore, above all, obeyed the instinct of His love in adopting this designation of His person, which expressed the feeling of His perfect homogeneousness with the human family of which He had made Himself a member. This name was, as it were, the theme of which those words of John: "*the Word was made flesh,*" are the paraphrase. But Jesus does not merely name Himself: *a* son of man; *a* true man; He names Himself *the* Son of man; He declares Himself, thereby, *the* true man, the only normal representative of the human type. Even in affirming, therefore, His *equality* with us, He affirms, by means of the article, *the*, His *superiority* over all the other members of the human family, who are simply sons of men; comp.

[1] *Christi Zeugniss von seiner Person*, 1870.

342 / Birth of Faith

Mk. iii. 28; Eph. iii. 5. To designate Himself thus was, indeed, to affirm, yet only implicitly, His dignity as Messiah. He expressed the idea, while yet avoiding the word whose meaning was falsified. Without saying: "I am the Christ," He said to every man: "Look on me, and thou shalt see what thou oughtest to have been, and what, through me, thou mayest yet become." He succeeded thus in attaining two equally important ends: to inaugurate the pure Messianism separated from all political alloy, and to present Himself as the chief of a kingdom of God, comprehending, not only Israel, but all the human race. This is what has led Böhme to say (*Versuch das Geheimniss des Menschensohns zu enthüllen*, 1839), that the design of Jesus in choosing this designation was to *de-judaize* the idea of the Messiah.

We see with what admirable wisdom Jesus acted in the choice of this designation, the creation of His own consciousness and of His inner life. It was His love which guided Him wonderfully in this matter, as it did in everything. Perhaps His inward tact was directed in this choice by the recollection of the most ancient of all the prophecies—the one which was the germ of the tree of the Messianic revelations: "The seed of the woman shall bruise the serpent's head." As the term ἄνθρωπος, *man*, refers equally to the two sexes, and as the woman represents the human *nature*, rather than the human *individuality*, the term Son of man is not far removed from the term *seed of the woman*. Jesus would designate Himself, thus, as the normal man, charged with accomplishing the victory of humanity over its own enemy and the enemy of God.[1]

3

John 2:1-11

THE FIRST MIRACLE.—STRENGTHENING OF FAITH

Jesus, after having been declared by John to be the Messiah, manifested Himself as such to His first disciples; an utterance of miraculous knowledge, in particular, had revealed the intimate relation which united Him with God. He now displays His glory before their eyes in a first act of omnipotence; and their faith, embracing this fact of an entirely new order, begins to raise itself to the height of its new object. Such is (according to ver. 11), the meaning of this passage.

His first miracle takes place in the family circle. It is, as it were, the

---

[1] In the idea which we have just set forth all the explanations of the authors mentioned above, who are different from one another in certain unimportant points, as it seems to me, converge. *Baur:* "A simple man, to whom cling all the miseries which can be affirmed of any man whatever." *Schenkel:* "the representative of the poor." *Holtzmann:* "the one to whom may be applied, in the highest degree, everything which can be said of all other men," or, "the indispensable organic centre of the kingdom of God in humanity." *Wittichen:* "the perfect realization of the idea of man, with the mission of realizing it in humanity." *Colani:* "That man who is the Messiah, but who does not wish to designate himself expressly as such." *Hofmann:* "the man in whom all the history of humanity must have its end." *Neander:* "He who realizes the idea of humanity." *Böhme:* "the universal Messiah." *Westcott:* "a true man and, at the same time, the representative of the race in whom are united the virtual powers of the whole of humanity." I am astonished to see this explanation lightly set aside by *Wabnitz* in these words: "It will be desirable thus to set aside from the immediate historical sense of our title . . . etc."

point of connection between the obscurity of the private life, to which Jesus has confined Himself until now, and the public activity which He is about to begin. All the sweet and amiable qualities by which He has, until now, adorned the domestic hearth, display themselves once more, but with a new brightness. It is the divine impress which His last footstep leaves in this inner domain; it is His royal farewell to His relation as son, as brother, as kinsman.

Ver. 1: *"And the third day there was a marriage in Cana of Galilee, and the mother of Jesus was there."* A distance of somewhat more than twenty leagues, in a straight line, separates the place where John was baptizing, from Nazareth, to which Jesus was probably directing His course. This journey requires three days' walking. *Weiss, Keil*, and others, think that the first of these three days was the day after that on which Jesus had taken the resolution to depart (i. 44). But the resolution indicated by ἠθέλησεν has certainly been mentioned in i. 44 only because it was executed at that very moment. The first day, according to the natural interpretation of the text, is, therefore, that which is indicated in i. 44 as the day of departure. The second is understood; it was, perhaps, the one on which the meeting with Nathanael took place. On the third, the travelers could arrive at a quite early hour in the region of Cana and Nazareth. It was the *sixth* day since the one on which John had given his first testimony before the Sanhedrim (i. 19).—It is affirmed that there are at the present time in Galilee, two places of the name of Cana. One is said to be called *Kana-el-Djêlil* (*Cana of Galilee*), and to be situated about two hours and a half to the north of Nazareth; the other is called *Kefr-Kenna* (*village Cana*); it is situated a league and a half eastward of Nazareth. It is there, that, ever since the eighth century, tradition places the event which is the subject of our narrative. Since *Robinson* brought the first into vogue, the choice has been ordinarily in its favor (*Ritter, Meyer*); this is the view of *Renan* (*Vie de Jésus*, p. 75). *Hengstenberg* almost alone, has decided for the second, for the reason that the first, as he says, is nothing but a ruin, and has no stable population, capable of preserving a sure tradition respecting the name of the place. What if the name were itself only a fable.[1] In any case, the situation of Kefr-Kenna answers better

---

[1] Robinson (*Biblical Researches*, ii. pp. 194, 195, 204, f.), relates that he was guided by a Christian Arab named *Abu Nasir*, from Nazareth to the height of the Wely Ismail, whence one has a magnificent view of all the surrounding regions, and that this Arab showed him, from that point, at three leagues' distance towards the northwest, a place called *Kana-el-Djêlil*, in the name of which he recognized the *Cana of Galilee* of our Gospel. On the other hand, here are the contents of a note which I made at Nazareth itself, Sept. 26, 1872, after a conversation with a competent European who accompanied us to the Wely Ismail. He declared to us that the real name of the place pointed out to Robinson is *Khurbet-Cana*, and that it was only *from Arabian politeness* (aus arabischer Höflichkeit), that Robinson's guide, yielding at length to the pressing questions of the celebrated traveler, pronounced the desired name of *Kana-el-Djêlil*, which does not at all exist in the region. Such is also the result of the work published in the *Palestine Exploration Fund*, No. III., 1869, by J. Zeller, missionary at Nazareth, who gives a very precise description of the two localities in dispute. He shows how the Christian tradition has always connected itself with Kefr-Kenna, where considerable ruins are found,

to our narrative. The date: "*the third day*," covers in fact, the whole of the following passage, as far as ver. 11; consequently, the miracle must have taken place on the very day of the arrival. Now even if he did not arrive at Nazareth until towards evening of the third day, Jesus might still have repaired before night to the very near village of Kefr-Kenna—this would have been impossible in the case of the Cana of Robinson—or even, what is more probable, He reached Kefr-Kenna directly from the south, without having passed through Nazareth. If Nathanael was coming from Cana (xxi. 2) at the time when Philip met him, he might inform Jesus of the celebration of the wedding, and of the presence of His family in that place—a circumstance which induced Jesus to betake Himself thither directly. Let us add that the defining object *of Galilee*, which recurs in iv. 46 and xxi. 2, must have been a standing designation, intended to distinguish this Cana from another place of the same name, situated outside of Galilee (comp. Josh. xix. 28, the place of this name situated on the borders of Phœnicia). This designation would have meaning only as there was but *one* place of this name in Galilee.

The name of the mother of Jesus is not indicated, yet not precisely because John supposes the name to be known to the readers by tradition. It might have been added, even in that case, but because it is in her character of *mother* of Jesus that Mary is to play the principal part in the following narrative. There is no well-founded reason to suppose, with *Ewald*, *Weiss*, and *Renan*, that Mary had already for a long time been settled with her sons at Cana. How, in that case, should not Nathanael, who was of Cana, and Jesus, have been acquainted with each other before their recent meeting? How should the sisters of Jesus have been still dwelling in Nazareth (Mk. vi. 3)? The fact that it is not said that Mary and her sons had repaired from Nazareth to Cana because of the wedding evidently cannot prove anything. The expressions of ver. 1, much more naturally imply that Mary was at Cana only *because of the wedding;* (comp. besides, Philip's word to Nathanael, i. 46: "*of Nazareth*").

Ver. 2. "*Now Jesus also was bidden to the marriage, as well as His disciples.*" There is a contrast between the imperfect, *was there*, which is used in speaking of Mary, and the aorist *was bidden*, applied to Jesus and His disciples. Jesus was bidden only on His arrival, while Mary, at that time, was already there. It appears from all these points that the family in question was quite closely related to that of the Lord; this is likewise proved by the authoritative attitude which Mary assumes in the following scene. The singular, *was bidden*, is owing to the fact that the disciples were not bidden except in honor, and, as it were, in the person of their Master. *Rilliet*, with some commentators, translates: *had been bidden*. But when? Before going to His baptism (*Schleiermacher*), or later, through a

which are altogether wanting at Khurbet-Cana; then, how a statement of the chronicler Seawulf (1103), and, finally, the whole account of Josephus (*Vita*, 15 and 16), correspond only with Kefr-Kenna. On the other side, Robinson and Raumer cite Quaresmius, and some other chroniclers, in favor of the hypothesis of Khurbet-Cana. But it is a certain fact that the name *Kana-el-Djêlil* no longer exists at the present day.

messenger? Two very improbable suppositions. Moreover, the added words: *as well as His disciples*, are incompatible with this meaning. For they could not have been invited before it was known that Jesus had disciples.

Ver. 3. "*And when the wine failed*,[1] *the mother of Jesus saith to Him: They have no wine.*"[2]—The marriage feasts sometimes continued several days, even a whole week (Gen. xxix. 27; Judg. xiv. 15; Tob. ix. 12; x. 1). The failure of the wine is commonly explained by this circumstance. However this may be, it is scarcely possible to doubt that this failure was connected with the unexpected arrival of six or seven guests, Jesus and His disciples. The reading of the *Sinaitic MS.*: "And they had no more wine, for the wine of the wedding-feast was entirely consumed," is evidently a diluted paraphrase of the primitive text?—What does Mary mean by saying to Jesus: "*They have no wine?*" Bengel and Paulus have thought that Mary wished to induce Jesus to withdraw and thus to give the rest of the company the signal to depart. The reply of Jesus would signify: "What right hast thou to prescribe to me? The hour *for leaving* has not yet come for me." Such an explanation has no need to be refuted. The expression "*my hour*," always used, in our Gospel, in a grave and solemn sense, would be enough to make us feel the impossibility of it. The same thing is true of *Calvin's* explanation, according to which Mary wished "to admonish Jesus to offer some religious exhortation, for fear that the company might be wearied, and also courteously to cover the shame of the bridegroom." This expression, "*They have no wine*," has a certain analogy to the message of the sisters of Lazarus: "*He whom thou lovest is sick.*" It is certainly a tacit request for assistance. But how does it occur to Mary to resort to Jesus in order to ask His aid in a case of this kind? Does she dream of a miracle? *Meyer, Weiss* and *Reuss* think not; for, according to ver. 11, Jesus had not yet performed any. Mary, thus, would only think of natural aid, and the reply of Jesus, far from rejecting this request as an inconsiderate claim, would mean: "Leave me to act! I have in my possession means of which thou knowest not, and whose effect thou shalt see as soon as the hour appointed by my Father shall have struck." After this, the order of Mary to the servants, "*Do whatsoever He shall say to you*," presents no further difficulty. But this explanation, which supposes that Mary asks *less* than what Jesus is disposed to do, is contradictory to the natural meaning of the words "*What is there between me and thee?*" which lead rather to the supposition of an encroachment by Mary on a domain which Jesus reserves exclusively to Himself, an inadmissible interference in His office as Messiah. Besides, by what means other than a miracle could Jesus have extricated the bridegroom from his embarrassment? *Meyer* gives no explanation of this point. *Weiss* thinks of friends (like Nathanael) who had relations at Cana, and by means of whom Jesus could

---

[1] א reads instead of υστερησαντος οινου: και οινον ουκ ειχον οτι συνετελεσθη ο οινος του γαμου ειτα λεγει, a reading which is found in some documents of the *Itala* (a. b. ff²) and adopted by Tischendorf in the 8th ed.

[2] א οινος ουκ εστι, instead of οινον ουκ εχουσιν.

provide a remedy for the condition of things. But even in this sense we cannot understand the answer of Jesus, by which He certainly wishes to cause Mary to go back within her own bounds, beyond which she had, consequently, just passed. What she wished to ask for, is therefore a striking, miraculous aid worthy of the Messiah. Whence can such an idea have come to her mind? *Hase* and *Tholuck* have supposed that Jesus had already wrought miracles within the limits of His family. Ver. 11 excludes this hypothesis. *Lücke* amends it, by saying that He had simply manifested, in the perplexities of domestic life, peculiar gifts and skill: one of those convenient middle-course suggestions which are frequently met with in this commentator and which have procured for him such vigorous censure on the part of Baur. It affirms, in fact, too much or too little. It seems to me that the state of extraordinary exaltation is forgotten in which, at this moment, that whole company, and especially Mary, must have been. Can it be imagined for an instant, that the disciples had not related everything which had just occurred in Judea, the solemn declarations of John the Baptist, the miraculous scene of the baptism proclaimed by John, the proof of supernatural knowledge which Jesus had given on meeting Nathanael, finally that magnificent promise of greater things impending, of an open heaven, of angels ascending and descending, which their eyes were going *henceforth* to behold? How should not the expectation of the marvelous—that *seeking after miracles*, which St. Paul indicates as the characteristic feature of Jewish piety—have existed, at that moment, in all those who were present, in the highest degree? The single fact that Jesus arrived surrounded by disciples, must have been sufficient to make them understand that a new phase was opening at that hour, that the time of obscurity and retirement had come to its end, and that the period of Messianic manifestations was about to begin. Let us add, finally, with reference to Mary herself, the mighty waking up of recollections, so long held closely in her maternal heart, the return of her thoughts to the marvelous circumstances which accompanied the birth of her son. The hour so long and so impatiently waited for had, then, at last struck! Is it not to her, Mary, that it belongs to give the decisive signal of this hour? She is accustomed to obedience from her Son; she does not doubt that He will act at her suggestion. If the words of Mary are carried back to this general situation, we easily understand that what she wishes is not merely aid given to the embarrassed bridegroom, but, on this occasion, a brilliant act fitted to inaugurate the Messianic royalty. On the occasion of this failure of the wine, she sees the heaven opening, the angel descending, a marvelous manifestation exhibiting itself and opening the series of wonders. Any other difficulty in life would have served her as a pretext for seeking to obtain the same result: "Thou art the Messiah: it is time to show thyself!" As to Jesus, the temptation in the wilderness is here seen reproducing itself in its third form (Luke iv. 9). He is invited to make an exhibition of His miraculous power by passing beyond the measure strictly indicated by the providential call. It is what He can no more do at the prayer of His mother than at the suggestion of Satan or at the demand of the Pharisees. Hence the tone of Jesus' reply, the firmness of which goes even to the point of severity.

Ver. 4. "*Jesus saith to her : What is there between me and thee, woman ? My hour is not yet come.*" Jesus makes Mary sensible of her incompetency in the region into which she intrudes. The career on which He has just entered, is that in which He depends only on His Father; His motto henceforth is: My Father and I. Mary must learn to know in her son the *servant of Jehovah,* of Jehovah only. The expression " *What is there between me and thee ?* " is a frequent one in the Old Testament. Comp. Judg. xi. 12; 2 Sam. xvi. 10; 1 Kings xvii. 18; 2 Kings iii. 13. We even meet it, sometimes, in profane Greek; thus the reply of a Stoic to a jester is quoted, who asked him, at the moment when their vessel was about to sink, whether shipwreck was an evil or not: " What is there between us and thee, O man? We perish, and thou permittest thyself to jest! " This formula signifies, that the community of feeling to which one of the interlocutors appeals is rejected by the other, at least in the particular point which is in question. Mary had, no doubt, well understood that a great change was being wrought in the life of her son; but, as often happens with our religious knowledge, she had not drawn from this grave fact the practical consequence which concerned her personally. And thus, as *Bäumlein* says, Jesus finds Himself in a position to reject the influence which she presumes still to exercise over Him. The address γύναι, *woman,* is thereby explained. In the language in which Jesus spoke, as well as in the Greek language, this term involves nothing contrary to respect and affection. In Dio Cassius, a queen is accosted by Augustus with this expression. Jesus Himself uses it in addressing His mother at a moment of inexpressible tenderness, when, from His elevation on the cross, He speaks to her for the last time, xix. 26. Here this expression, entirely respectful though it may be, gives Mary to understand, that, in the sphere on which Jesus has just entered, her title of *mother* has no longer any part to play.

"Here for Mary," as Luthardt well observes, "is the beginning of a painful education." The middle point of this education will be marked by the question of Jesus, " *Who is my mother, and who are my brethren?* " (Luke viii. 19 f.) The end will be that second address: *Woman* (xix. 26), which will definitely break the earthly relation between the mother and the son. Mary feels at this moment, for the first time, the point of the sword which, at the foot of the cross, shall pierce through her heart. After having made her sensible of her incompetency, Jesus gives the ground of His refusal. The words: " *My hour is not yet come* " have been understood by *Euthymius, Meyer, Hengstenberg, Lange* and *Riggenbach* (*Leben des Herru Jesu,* p. 374), in a very restricted sense: "the hour for performing the desired miracle." The following words of Mary to the servants, according to this view, would imply two things: the first, that Jesus received a little later from His Father an inward sign which permitted Him to comply with His mother's wish; and the second, that by a gesture or a word, He

348 / Birth of Faith

made known to her this new circumstance. This is to add much to the text. Besides, how could Jesus, before having received any indication of His Father's will, have said: "not *yet*," a word which would necessarily mean that the permission will be granted Him later. Finally, this weakened sense which is here given to the expression "*my hour*" does not correspond with the solemn meaning which is attached to this term throughout our whole Gospel. If it were desired to hold to this weakened meaning, it would be still better to give to this clause, with *Gregory of Nazianzum*, an interrogative turn: "Is not the hour (of my emancipation, of my autonomy) *come?*" Let us remark that the expression "*my hour*" is here connected with the verb *is come*, as in all the passages in John where it is taken in its weightiest sense: "*His hour was not yet come*" (vii. 30; viii. 20, comp. xiii. 1); "*The hour is come*" (xii. 23; xvii. 1). His hour, in all these passages, is that of His *Messianic manifestation*, especially through His death and through the glorification which should follow it. The analogous expression *my time*, vii. 6, is also applied to His Messianic manifestation, but through the royal entry into Jerusalem. This is the meaning which seems to me to prevail here. Jesus makes known to Mary, impatient to see Him mount the steps of His throne, that the hour of the inauguration of His Messianic royalty has not yet struck. It is in His capital, Jerusalem, in His palace, the Temple, and not in the centre of His family, that His solemn manifestation as Messiah must take place (Mal. iii. 1: "*And then He shall enter into His temple*"). This sense of the expression "*my hour*" could not be strange to the mind of Mary. How many times, in her conversations with Jesus, she had doubtless herself used this expression when asking Him: Will thine hour come at last? That hour was the one towards which all her desire as an Israelite and a mother moved forward. Jesus rejects Mary's request, but only so far as it has something of ambition. How often in His conversations, He replies less to the question which is addressed to Him than to the spirit in which it is put (comp. ii. 19; iii. 3; vi. 26). He thus lays hold of the person of His interlocutor even in his inmost self. Mary desires a brilliant miracle, as a public sign of His coming. Jesus penetrates this ambitious thought and traces a boundary for Mary's desires which she should no more attempt to cross. But this does not prevent His understanding that along with this, there is something to be done in view of the present difficulty.

Ver. 5. "*His mother says to the servants, Whatsoever he says to you,*[1] *do it.*" Something in the tone and expression of Jesus gives Mary to understand that this refusal leaves a place for a more moderate granting of the desire. Perhaps in this narrative, which is so summary, there is here the omission of a circumstance which the reader may supply for himself from what follows (precisely like that which occurs in xi. 28), a circumstance which gives occasion to the charge of Mary to the servants: "*Do whatsoever He shall tell you.*" How, at this moment of heavenly joy, when Jesus was receiving His Spouse from the hands of His Father, could He have

---

[1] The MSS. are divided between λεγη and λέγει.

altogether refused the prayer of her who, during thirty years, had been taking the most tender care of Him, and from whom He was about to separate Himself forever? Jesus, without having need of any other sign of His Father's will, grants to the faith of His mother a hearing analogous to that which, at a later time, He did not refuse to a stranger, a Gentile (Matt. xv. 25). If criticism has found in the obscurities of this dialogue an evidence against the truth of the account, it is an ill-drawn conclusion. This unique conciseness is, on the contrary, the seal of its authenticity.— By the expression: *Whatsoever He says to you*, Mary reserves full liberty of action to her Son, and thus enters again within her own bounds, which she had tried to overstep.

Ver. 6. "*Now there were there*[1] *six water-pots of stone, according to the usual manner of purifying among the Jews, containing two or three measures apiece.*" Ἐκεῖ, *there*, denotes, according to *Meyer*, the banqueting room itself. Is it not more natural to imagine these urns placed in the court or in the vestibule at the entrance of the hall? The ninth verse proves that all this occurred out of the bridegroom's sight, who was himself in the room. These vases were designed for the purification either of persons or utensils, such as was usual among pious Jews, especially before or after meals (Matt. xv. 2; Luke xi. 38; particularly, Mk. vii. 1–4.)—Κατά, not *with a view to*, but according to its natural sense, *in conformity with*. This preposition has reference to the complement τῶν Ἰουδαίων: *conformably* to the mode of purification customary *among the Jews*. John expresses himself thus because he is writing among Gentiles and as no longer belonging to the Jewish community. Ἀνά has evidently, considering the very precise number. *six*, the distributive sense (*singulae*), not the approximative meaning (*about*). The measure which is spoken of was of considerable size; its capacity was 27 *litres* (*Rilliet*) or even 38 (*Keil*) or 39 (*Arnaud*). The entire contents might, therefore, reach even to about 500 *litres*. [The litre is a measure nearly corresponding with the English quart.] This quantity has seemed too considerable, it has even scandalized certain critics (*Strauss*, *Schweizer*), who have found here an indication of the falsity of the account. *Lücke* replies that all the water was not necessarily changed into wine. This supposition is contrary to the natural meaning of the text; the exact indication of the capacity of the vessels certainly implies the contrary. Let us rather say that when once Jesus yields to the desire of His mother, he yields with all His heart, as a son, a friend, a man, with an inward joy. It is His first miraculous sign; it must give high testimony of His wealth, of His munificence, of the happiness which He has in relieving, even in giving gladness; it must become the type of the fullness of grace, of joy and of strength which the only-begotten Son brings to the earth. There is, moreover, nothing in the text to lead us to suppose that all the wine must have been consumed at this feast. It was the rich wedding gift by which the Lord honored this house where He with his attendants had just

---

[1] Κειμεναι placed by T. R. after ἐξ according to the majority of the MSS. and Vss., is put after Ιουδαιων in B C L, and is altogether wanting in ℵ.

350 / Birth of Faith

been hospitably received. Perhaps the number *six* was expressly called to mind, because it corresponded precisely with the number of persons who accompanied Jesus. This gift was thus, as it were, a testimony of the gratitude on the part of the disciples themselves to their host; it was, at all events, the enduring monument of the Master's benediction upon the youthful household formed under His auspices. How can criticism put itself in collision with everything that is most *truly human* in the Gospel? Moreover, what a feeling of lively pleasure is expressed in the following words! Jesus foresees the joyous surprise of His host:

Vv. 7, 8. "*Jesus says to them, Fill the water-pots with water. And they filled them up to the brim.* 8. *And he says to them, Draw out now and bear unto the ruler of the feast. And they bore it.*"[1] We should not understand γεμίσατε, *fill*, in the sense of *filling up*, nor allege in support of this meaning the words ἕως ἄνω, *up to the brim*; the matter thus understood has something repugnant in it. Either the urns were empty in consequence of the ablutions which had taken place before the repast, or they were beginning by emptying them, in order to fill them afterwards anew. The: *up to the brim* serves to make the ardor with which the work was done apparent. The moment of the miracle must be placed between vv. 7 and 8; since the transformation is presupposed as accomplished by the word *now* of ver. 8. This *now*, as well as the words: *bear it*, breathes a spirit of overflowing joy and even gaiety. The person here called *ruler of the feast* was not one of the guests; he was the chief of the servants: it belonged to his office to taste the meats and drinks before they were placed upon the table. He ordinarily bears in Greek the name τραπεζοποιός.

Vv. 9, 10. "*When the ruler of the feast had tasted the water which was made wine—and he knew not whence it came, but the servants who had drawn the water knew—the ruler of the feast calls the bridegroom,* 10, *and says to him, Every one serves first the good wine, and when men have become drunken, then*[2] *that which is worse; thou*[3] *hast kept the good wine until now.*" The words ὕδωρ οἶνον γεγεννημένον, *the water become wine*, admit of no other sense than that of a miraculous transformation. The natural process by which the watery sap is transformed every year in the vine-stock (*Augustine*), or that by which mineral waters are formed (*Neander*), offers, indeed, a remote analogy, but not at all a means of explanation. The parenthesis which includes the words καὶ οὐκ . . . ὕδωρ presents a construction perfectly analogous to that of i. 10 and vi. 21–23. This parenthesis is designed to make the reality of the miracle apparent, by reminding the reader, on the one hand, that the servants did not know that it was wine which they were bearing, and on the other, that the ruler of the feast had not been present when the event occurred. *Weiss* makes the clause καὶ οὐκ ᾔδει πόθεν ἐστίν also depend on ὡς, and commences the parenthesis only with οἱ δέ . . . This is undoubtedly possible, but less natural as it seems to me. He calls the bridegroom; the latter was in the banqueting hall.

---

[1] Instead of καὶ ἤνεγκεν, ℵ B K L some Mnn. Cop. read οἱ δὲ ἤνεγκαν.

[2] ℵ B L some Mnn. omit τότε (*then*).

[3] ℵ G Δ some Mnn. and Vss. read σὺ δέ instead of σύ.

Some have desired by all means to give a religious import to the pleasantry of the ruler of the feast, by attributing to it a symbolic meaning; on one side, the world, which begins by offering to man the best which it has, to abandon him afterwards to despair; on the other, God, always surpassing Himself in His gifts, and, after the austere law, offering the delicious wine of the Gospel. There was by no means anything of this sort in the consciousness of the speaker, and no indication appears that the evangelist attached such a sense to the words. This saying is simply related in order to show with what entire unreservedness Jesus gave Himself up to the common joy, by giving not only abundantly but excellently. There is here, also, one of the rays of His δόξα (*glory*). For the rest, it is not at all necessary to weaken the sense of μεθυσθῶσι, *to be drunken*, in order to remove from the guests at the wedding all suspicion of intemperance. This saying has a proverbial sense, and does not refer to the company at Cana.

Ver. 11. " *This first*[1] *of his miracles Jesus did in Cana of Galilee*[2], *and he manifested his glory, and his disciples believed on him.*" John characterizes under four important relations the miracle which he has just related. 1. This was *the first*, not only of the miracles performed at Cana, but of all the miracles of Jesus. As here was a decisive moment in the revelation of the Lord and in the faith of the disciples, John brings out this fact with emphasis. The Alexandrian authorities have rejected the article τήν before ἀρχήν, without doubt as being superfluous on account of ταύτην. But, as is frequently the case with them, when desiring to correct, they spoil. Without the article, the attention is rather drawn to the *nature* of the miracle: " It was by this prodigy that Jesus began to work miracles." By the article the notion itself of a beginning is more strongly emphasized: " *That fact* . . . was the true beginning . . . " The second of these ideas is as thoroughly an essential element in the context, as we shall see, as the first is foreign to it. 2. John recalls a second time, in closing, the *place* where the event occurred. The design of this repetition cannot be purely geographical. We shall see, in iii. 24 and iv. 54, how anxious John was to distinguish between the two returns of Jesus to Galilee (i. 44 and iv. 1–3), which had been united in one by tradition, and this is the reason why he expressly points out how the *one* and the *other* of these two returns was signalized by a miracle accomplished at Cana. According to *Hengstenberg*, the defining words *of Galilee* recall the prophecy of Is. viii. 23–ix. 1, according to which the glory of the Messiah was to be manifested in Galilee. This aim would be admissible in Matthew; it seems foreign to the narrative of John. 3. John indicates the *purpose* of the miracle. He uses here, for the first time, the term *sign* (σημεῖον) which is in harmony with the following expression: " *He manifested His glory.*" The miracles of Jesus are not mere wonders (τέρατα), designed to strike the imagination. A close relation exists between these marvelous acts and

---

[1] The T. R. reads with the majority of the Mjj. among them ℵ, and the Mnn., την before αρχην. A B L T^b Λ and Orig. reject this article.
[2] ℵ adds πρωτην after Γαλιλαιας.

the person of Him who performs them. They are visible emblems of what He is and of what He comes to do, and, as *Reuss* says, "radiant images of the permanent miracle of the manifestation of Christ." The glory of Christ is, above all, His dignity as Son and the eternal love which His Father has for Him. Now this glory is, in its very nature, concealed from the eyes of the inhabitants of the earth; but the miracles are the brilliant *signs* of it. They manifest the unlimited freedom with which the Son disposes of all things, and thus demonstrate the perfect love of the Father towards Him: "*The Father loveth the Son and hath given all things into His hands*" (iii. 35). The expression "*His* glory" makes a profound distinction between Jesus and all the divine messengers who had accomplished like wonders before Him. In the miracles of the other divine messengers the glory of Jehovah is seen (Exod. xvi. 7); those of Jesus reveal His own, by bearing witness in concert with His words, to His filial position. The expression *His glory* contains, moreover, all of His own that Jesus puts into the act which He has just performed, the love full of tenderness with which He makes use of divine omnipotence in the service of His own. (4.) John, finally, sets forth the *result* of this miracle. Evoked at first by testimony, faith was strengthened by personal contact with Jesus, its object. Now in the course of this personal relation, it makes such experience of the power and goodness of Him to whom it is attached, that it finds itself thereby immovably confirmed. Doubtless it will grow every day in proportion as such experiences shall multiply; but from this moment it has passed through the three essential phases of its formation: testimony, personal contact and experience. This is what John expresses by the words: "*And his disciples believed on him.*" These glorious irradiations from the person of Jesus, which are called miracles, are, therefore, designed not only, as apologetics often assume, to strike the eyes of the still unbelieving multitude and to stimulate the delaying, but, especially, to illuminate the hearts of believers, by revealing to them, in this world of suffering, all the riches of the living object of their faith.

What took place in the minds of the other witnesses of this scene? John's silence leads us to suppose that the impression produced was neither profound nor enduring. This is because the miracle, in order to act efficaciously, must be understood *as a sign* (vi. 26), and because to this end certain moral predispositions are necessary. The impression of astonishment which the guests experienced, not connecting itself with any spiritual need, with any struggle of conscience, was soon effaced by the distractions of life.

On the Miracle of Cana

Objections of two sorts are raised against the reality of this event: the one class bear on miracles in general; the other, on this one in particular. We do not concern ourselves with the first. We think there is nothing more opposed to the sound method—the method called experimental—than to begin by declaring, as a principle, the impossibility of a miracle. To say that *there has never been* a miracle until now,—be it so. This is a point for examination. But to say that there *cannot* be one, is to make metaphysics, not history; it is to throw oneself into the *à priori*, which is repudiated.[1]

The objections which relate especially to the miracle of Cana are:

1. Its *magical* character (*Schweizer*). The difference between the magical and the miraculous is, that, in the former, the supernatural power works *in vacuo*, dispensing with already existing nature, while in the second, the divine force respects the first creation and always connects its working with material furnished by it. Now, in this case, Jesus does not use His power to create, as Mary undoubtedly was expecting; He contents Himself with transforming that which is. He remains, thus, within the limits of the Biblical supernatural.

2. The *uselessness* of the miracle is made an objection. It is "a miracle of luxury," according to Strauss. Let us rather say with *Tholuck*, "a miracle of love." We think we have shown this. It might even be regarded as the payment of a double debt: to the bridegroom, for whom the Lord's arrival had caused this embarrassment, and to Mary, to whom Jesus, before leaving her, was paying His debt of gratitude. The miracle of Cana is the miracle of filial piety, as the resurrection of Lazarus is that of fraternal affection. The symbolic interpretations, by means of which it has been desired to explain the purpose of this miracle, seem to us artificial: to set the Gospel joy in opposition to the ascetic rigor of John the Baptist (*Olshausen*); to represent the miraculous transformation of the legal into spiritual life (*Luthardt*). Would not such intentions betray themselves in some word of the text?

3. This miracle is even charged with *immorality*. Jesus, it is said, countenanced the intemperance of the guests. "With the same right one might demand," answers *Hengstenberg*, "that God should not grant good vintages because of drunkards." The presence of Jesus and, afterwards, the thankful remembrance of his hosts would guarantee the holy use of this gift.

4. The *omission* of this story in the Synoptics seems to the adversaries the strongest argument against the reality of the event. But this miracle belongs still to the family life of Jesus; it does not form a part of the acts of His public ministry. Moreover, as we have seen, it has its place in an epoch of the ministry of Jesus, which, by reason of the confusion of the first two returns to Galilee, had disappeared from the tradition. The aim of John in restoring this event to light was precisely to re-establish the distinction between these two returns and, at the same time, to recall one of the first and principal landmaks of the development of the apostolic faith (comp. ver. 11).

Do not a multitude of proofs demonstrate the fragmentary character of the oral tradition which is recorded in the Synoptics? How can we explain the omission in our *four* Gospels of the appearance of the risen Jesus to the five hundred? And yet this fact is one of the most solidly attested (1 Cor. xv. 6).

If we reject the reality of the miracle as it is so simply related by the evangelist, what remains for us? Three suppositions:

1. The *natural* explanation of *Paulus* or of *Gfrörer*: Jesus had agreed with a tradesman to have wine brought secretly, during the feast, which He caused to be served to the guests *mixed with water*. By His reply to Mary, ver. 4, He wishes to induce her simply not to injure the success of the entertainment which He has

---

[1] On miracles in general, comp. *Introd.*, p. 37 and the author's Conferences on the *Miracles of Jesus Christ*, and on the *Supernatural*.

354 / Birth of Faith

prepared, and *the hour* for which *has not yet come*, through an indiscretion. "The glory of Jesus (ver. 11), is the exquisite humanity which characterizes His amiable proceeding (*Paulus*). Or it is to Mary herself that the honor of this attention is ascribed. She has had the wine prepared, in order to offer it as a wedding present; and at the propitious moment she makes a sign to Jesus to cause it to be served (*Gfrörer*). *Renan* seems not far from adopting the one or the other of these explanations. He says in vague terms: "Jesus went willingly to marriage entertainments. One of His miracles was performed, it is said, to enliven a village wedding" (p. 195). *Weiss* adopts a form of the natural explanation which is less incompatible with the seriousness of Jesus' character (see above on ver 3): nevertheless, he acknowledges that John believed that he was relating a miracle and meant to do so. But could this apostle, then, be so completely deceived respecting the nature of a fact which he himself related as an eye-witness? Jesus must, in that case, have intentionally allowed an obscurity to hover over the event, which was fitted to deceive His nearest friends. The seriousness of the Gospel history protests against these parodies which end in making Jesus a village charlatan. 2. The *mythical* explanation of *Strauss:* Legend invented this miracle after the analogy of certain facts related in the Old Testament, e. g. Exod. xv. 23 ff., where Moses purifies bitter waters by means of a certain sort of wood; 2 Kings ii. 19, where Elisha does something similar. But there is not the least real analogy between these facts and those before us here. Moreover, the perfect simplicity of the narrative, and even its obscurities, are incompatible with such an origin. "The whole tenor of the narrative," says *Baur* himself (recalling the judgment of de Wette), "by no means authorizes us to assume the mythical character of the account." 3. The *ideal* explanation of *Baur, Keim,* etc. According to the first, the pseudo-John made up this narrative as a pure invention, to represent the relation between the two baptisms, that of John (the water) and that of Jesus (the wine). According to the second, the evangelist invented this miracle on the basis of that saying of Jesus: "Can the friends of the *bridegroom* fast while the bridegroom is with them. . . . They put *new wine* into new bottles" (Matt. ix. 15, 17). The water in the vessels represents, thus, the insufficient purifications offered by Judaism and the baptism of John. The *worse* wine, with which ordinarily the beginning is made, is also Judaism, which was destined to give place to the better wine of the Gospel. The delay of Jesus represents the fact that His coming followed that of John the Baptist. His *hour* is that of His death, which substitutes for the previous imperfect purifications the true purification through the blood of Christ, in consequence of which is given the joyous wine of the Holy Spirit, etc. . . . In truth, if our desire were to demonstrate the reality of the event as it is simply related by John, we could not do it in a more convincing way than by explanations like these, which seem to be the parody of criticism. What! shall this refined idealism, which was the foundation and source even of the narrative, betray itself nowhere in the smallest word of the story! Shall it envelop itself in the most simple, prosaic, sober narrative which carries conciseness even to obscurity! To our view, the apostolic narrative, by its character of simplicity and truth, will always be the most eloquent defender of the reality of the fact.[1]

---

[1] We refrain here from answering *Schweizer*, who attacked the authenticity of this passage, but has withdrawn his hypothesis. (See Introd. p. 27).

Before leaving this first cycle of narratives, we must further take notice of a judgment of *Renan* respecting this beginning of our Gospel (p. 109): "The first pages of the fourth Gospel are incongruous notes carelessly put together. The strict chronological order which they exhibit arises from the author's taste for apparent precision." But exegesis has shown, on the contrary, that if there is a passage in our Gospels where all things are linked together and are strictly consecutive, not only as to time, but also as to substance and idea, it is this one. The days are enumerated, the hours even mentioned: it is the description of a continuous week, answering to that of the final week. More than this: the intrinsic connection of the facts is so close that *Baur* could persuade himself that he had to deal with an ideal and systematic conception, presented under an historic form. The farther the Gospel narrative advances, the more does Renan himself render homage to its chronological exactness. He ends by taking it almost exclusively as a guide for his narration. And the beginning of such a story, whose homogeneity is evident, is nothing but an accidental collection of " notes carelessly put together! " This, at all events, has little probability.

Second Cycle
John 2:12-4:54

This second cycle is naturally divided into three sections: 1. The ministry of Jesus in *Judea*, ii. 12–iii. 36; 2. The return through *Samaria:* iv. 1–42; 3. The settling in Galilee, iv. 43–54. We shall see that to these three geographical domains three very different moral situations correspond. Hence the varied manner in which Jesus reveals Himself and the different reception which he meets.

1
John 2:12-3:36

JESUS IN JUDEA

Here again, as in the preceding story, the course of the narrative is steadily continuous and its historical development accurately graduated. Jesus first appears in the *temple* (ii. 12–22); later He teaches in the *capital* (ii. 23–iii. 21), finally, He exercises His ministry in the *country* of Judea (iii. 22–36).

Jesus in the Temple: ii. 12–22

Ver. 12. "*After this, he went down to Capernaum,*[1] *he and his mother and his brethren*[2] *and his disciples,*[3] *and they abode there not many days.*"[4] From Cana Jesus undoubtedly returned to Nazareth. For it was the latter place

---

[1] א B T⁰ X It^pler.: Καφαρναουμ, instead of Καπερναουμ which T. R. reads with the 19 other Mjj.

[2] B L T⁰ It^aliq. Orig. omit αυτου after αδελφοι.

[3] א It^pler. omit και οι μαθηται αυτου (confusion of the two αυτου).

[4] Instead of εμειναν, A F G Δ Cop. read εμεινεν (*he abode*).

which He had in view when returning from Judea, rather than Cana to which He was only accidentally called. *Weiss* finds this hypothesis arbitrary. He prefers to hold that the family of Mary had already before this left Nazareth to settle in Cana. It seems to me that this is the supposition which merits precisely the name of an arbitrary one (see on ver. 1). From Nazareth Jesus and His family removed at that time to Capernaum, as is related also by Matthew, iv. 13: "*Having left Nazareth, He came and dwelt at Capernaum.*" It is only necessary to recognize the fact that Matthew unites in one the first two returns to Galilee (John i. 44 and iv. 1–3), which John so accurately distinguishes. From his point of view, *Weiss* is obliged to see in our twelfth verse only the account of a mere visit, which was made by Jesus' family from Cana to friends at Capernaum. But what purpose does it serve to mention a detail so insignificant and one which would not have had any importance? Jesus' *mother* and *brethren* accompanied Him. No doubt, under the impression produced by the miracle of Cana, and by the accounts of the disciples, His family were unwilling to abandon Him at this moment. They all desired to see how the drama which had just opened would unfold. This detail of John's narrative is confirmed by Mark vi. 3, from which it appears that the sisters of Jesus, probably already married, had *alone* remained at Nazareth, and by Mark iii. 21–31, which is most naturally explained if the brothers of Jesus were settled with Mary at Capernaum. As for Jesus, He had not, for the time, the intention of making a prolonged stay in that city. It was only later, when He was obliged to abandon Judea, that He fixed His ordinary residence at Capernaum, and that that place became His own city (Matt. ix. 1). We may discover in the words of Luke iv. 23 an indication of this brief visit, previous to His settlement in that city. Thus a considerable difficulty in the narrative of Luke would be resolved and the accuracy of his sources would be verified in respect to one of the points most assailed in his narrative. Capernaum was a city of considerable commerce. It was located on the route of the caravans which passed from Damascus and from the interior of Asia to the Mediterranean. There was a custom-house there (Luke v. 27 f.). It was, in some sort, the *Jewish* capital of Galilee, as Tiberias was its Gentile or Roman capital. Jesus would have less narrow prejudices to meet there than at Nazareth, and many more opportunities to propagate the Gospel. The word κατέβη, *went down*, is due to the fact that Cana and Nazareth were situated on the plateau, and Capernaum on the shore of the lake.[1] The

---

[1] It does not seem that authorities are near to an agreement on the question of the site of Capernaum. The old opinion named *Tell Hum* at the northern extremity of the lake. There are ruins there, undoubtedly, but by no means a copious spring of water such as that which Josephus mentions and to which he even gives the name Capernaum, Κεφαρναώμη (*Bell. Jud.* iii. 10, 8). *Keim*, following *Robinson*, pleads energetically in favor of *Khan-Minyêh*, about a league south-west of *Tell-Hum*. But at that place there is no abundant spring, for the little neighboring fountain, *Ain-et-Tin*, which issues from the base of the rock a few paces from the lake, cannot answer to the description of Josephus, and cannot have served to irrigate the country. *Caspari* and *Quandt* have good grounds, therefore, for proposing the site of *Ain-Mudawara*, a magnificent basin of water

silence preserved respecting Joseph leads to the supposition that he had died before this period. Before calling His disciples to follow Him definitely, Jesus, no doubt, granted them the satisfaction of finding themselves once more, like Himself, in the family circle. It was from that circle that he called them again. (See p. 361.)

What is the true meaning of the expression: *the brethren of Jesus?* This question, as is well known, is one of the most complicated ones of the Gospel history. Must we understand by it brothers, in the proper sense of the word, the issue of Joseph and Mary and younger than Jesus? Or sons of Joseph, the issue of a marriage previous to his union with Mary? Or, finally, are we to hold that they are not sons either of Joseph or of Mary, and that the word *brother* must be taken in the broad sense of *cousins?* From the exegetical point of view, two reasons appear to us to support the first of these three opinions: 1. The two passages, Matt. i. 25: " He knew her not *until she* brought forth her *first-born* son " (or, according to the Alexandrian reading " *her son* "), and Luke ii. 7: "she brought forth her *first-born* son." 2. The proper sense of the word *brothers* is the only natural one in the phrase: *his mother and his brethren.* The following appendix will give a general exposition of the question.

The Brethren of Jesus

The oldest traditions, if we mistake not, unanimously assign *brothers* to Jesus, and not merely cousins. They differ only in this point, that these brothers are, according to some, sons of Joseph and Mary, younger brothers of Jesus; according to others, children of Joseph, the issue of a first marriage. The idea of making the brothers of Jesus in the New Testament *cousins,* seems to go no further back than Jerome and Augustine, although *Keim* (I., p. 423) claims to find it already in Hegesippus and Clement of Alexandria. (Comp. on this question, the excellent dissertation of *Philip Schaff: Das Verhältniss des Jacobus, Bruders des Herrn, zu Jacobus Alphaei,* 1843.) Let us begin by studying the principal testimonies: *Hegesippus,* whom Eusebius (ii. 23) places " in the first rank in the apostolical succession," writes about 160: "James, the Lord's brother, called the Just from the times of Christ even to our days, then takes in hand the administration of the Church with the apostles ($\mu\varepsilon\tau\grave{\alpha}$ $\tau\tilde{\omega}\nu$ $\dot{\alpha}\pi o\sigma\tau$.)." It clearly follows from these words: *with the apostles,* that Hegesippus does not rank James, the Lord's brother, among the apos-

in the centre of the plain of Gennesaret, half a league west of Khan-Minyeh. *Renan* objects that Capernaum must have been situated on the lake-shore ($\pi\alpha\rho\alpha\theta\alpha\lambda\alpha\sigma\sigma\iota\alpha$, Matt. iv. 13). But Ain-Mudawara is only a quarter of a league distant from the shore of the lake (comp. Mark v. 21, Matt. ix. 9). Only we do not find ruins in this district. Are we then to think of *Ain-Tabigah,* between Tell-Hum and Khan-Minyeh? This is the opinion expressed in *Heydenheim's Vierteljahrschrift,* 1871, pp. 533–544. A powerful spring is found there which may have served the purpose of irrigating the country by aqueducts, such as one which supplies, at the present time, the mill which is placed on this spot. But here also no ruins have been discovered up to the present hour. As for *Bethsaida,* there is the same uncertainty. Some think of *Ain-Tabigah,* others of *Et-Tin. Quandt* even expresses an opinion in favor of *El-Megdil (The Tower),* which is ordinarily regarded as the *Magdala* of the Gospel. In this case, we must, with this writer, locate Magdala, together with the district of *Dalmanutha,* southward of Tiberias. —Comp. my Comment *sur l' évang. de Luc,* I. p. 301 f.; Eng. Trans. I., p. 365.

358 / Birth of Faith

tles, and consequently distinguishes him from the two *apostles* of this name, the *son of Zebedee*, and *the little* (*less*), son of Alphæus. Now, if Alphæus is the Greek form of the Aramæan name *Clopas* (חלפי = Κλωπᾶς), a name which, according to Hegesippus, was that of the brother of Joseph, it follows from this, that, this last James being the cousin of the Lord, the first could be only His brother, in the proper sense.

The distinction which Hegesippus established between the three Jameses is confirmed by an expression quoted from him in the same chapter of Eusebius: "For there were *several* persons called James (πολλοὶ Ἰάκωβοι)." The word πολλοί (*several*), implies that he supposed there were more than two Jameses.

Eusebius relates (iii. 11), that after the martyrdom of James the Just, the first bishop of Jerusalem, "Simeon, *the son of Clopas*, who was the Lord's *cousin* (ἀνεψιός), was chosen as his successor." For, Eusebius adds: "Hegesippus relates that Clopas was the brother of Joseph." By this expression: *the son of Clopas*, Simeon's relationship to Jesus is evidently distinguished from that of James; otherwise, Eusebius would have said: who was *also* the son of Clopas, or at least: who was the brother *of James*. Hegesippus did not, therefore, consider James as the son of Clopas, nor, consequently, as the Lord's *cousin*; he regarded him, therefore, as His brother in the proper sense of the word.

Eusebius (iii. 32), quotes, also, the following words of Hegesippus: "Some of these heretics denounced Simeon, the son of Clopas . . . In the time of Trajan, the latter, *son of* the Lord's *uncle* (ὁ ἐκ τοῦ θείου τοῦ κυρίου . . .), was condemned to the cross." Why designate Simeon by the expression: *son of the Lord's uncle*, while James was always called, simply, *the Lord's brother*, if they were brothers, one of the other, and related to the Lord in the same degree? The principal passage of Hegesippus is cited by Eusebius (iv. 22): "After James had suffered martyrdom, like the Lord, Simeon, born of *His* uncle (θείου αὐτοῦ), son of Clopas, was appointed bishop, having been chosen by all as a second cousin of the Lord (ὄντα ἀνεψιὸν τοῦ κυρίου δεύτερον)." If we refer the pronoun αὐτοῦ (*His* uncle), to James, the question is settled: Simeon was the son of James' uncle, consequently, James' cousin, and not his brother; and James was, therefore, not the cousin, but the brother of Jesus. If we refer the αὐτοῦ to the Lord Himself, it follows, as we already know, that Simeon was the son of Jesus' uncle, that is to say, His cousin. The last words of Hegesippus carry us still further. Simeon is called the *second* cousin of Jesus; who was the *first?* It could not be James the Just, as Keim thinks. Everything that precedes prevents our supposing this. As constantly as Simeon is called *cousin* of Jesus, so constantly is James the Just designated as His *brother*. How would this be possible, if they were brothers to each other? It appears to me that the *first* cousin of Jesus (the eldest son of Clopas), could have been only the apostle James (the little) the son of Alphæus. He, as an apostle, could not be head of a particular flock, or consequently, bishop of Jerusalem. This was, then, the second cousin of Jesus, to whom they turned after the death of James the Just. Thus, everything is harmonious in the account of Hegesippus, and the identification of the name Alphæus and Clopas, which is at the present day called in question, is confirmed by this ancient testimony.[1] This result is

---

[1] The identification of the two names Alphæus and Clopas is, at the present day, called in question again for different reasons. Holtz- mann, for example, prefers to derive the second of these names from the Aramaic word *culba*—hammer (*Jacob der Gerechte und seine*

also confirmed by the words of Hegesippus respecting Jude, *the brother of James* (Jude ver. i.): "There existed, also, at that time, grandsons of Jude, called *His brother* (brother of the Lord) *according to the flesh*" (Euseb. iii. 20). This expression: *brother of the Lord according to the flesh*, applied to Jude, clearly distinguishes his position from that of Simeon.[1]

The opinion of *Clement of Alexandria* may appear doubtful. This Father seems (Euseb. ii. 1) to know only two Jameses: 1. The son of Zebedee, the brother of the Apostle John; 2. The Lord's brother, James the Just, who was at the same time the son of Alphæus, and the *cousin* of Jesus. "For there were two Jameses," he says, "one, the Just, who was thrown from the pinnacle of the temple . . . , the other, who was beheaded (Acts xii. 2)." Nevertheless, Clement may very well have passed in silence James, the son of Alphæus, of whom mention is only once made in the Acts, and who played no part in the history of the Church with which this Father here occupies himself. Clement, moreover, seems to derive his information respecting James from Hegesippus himself (Schaff, p. 69). Now we have just ascertained the opinion of the latter.[2] Tradition recognizes, therefore, the existence of *brothers of Jesus*, and particularly of these two: James and Jude. But are they children of Joseph, the issue of an earlier marriage, or sons of Joseph and Mary?

The former opinion is that of the author of an apocrypal writing, belonging to the first part of the second century, the *Protevangelium Jacobi*. In chap. ix. Joseph says to the priest who confides Mary to him: "I have *sons*, and am old." At chap. xvii.: "I have come to Bethlehem to have *my sons* registered," etc. Origen accepted this view. In his Homily on Luke vii., translated by Jerome, he says: "For these sons, called sons of Joseph, were not born of Mary." (See the other passages in Schaff, p. 81 f.) It follows, however, from his own explanations that this opinion rested, not on an historical tradition, but on a double dogmatic prejudice: that of the moral superiority of celibacy to marriage, and that of the exceptional holiness of the mother of Jesus (comp. especially the passage *ad Matth.* xiii. 55). Several apocryphal Gospels—those of Peter, Thomas, etc., as well as several Fathers, Gregory of Nyssa, Epiphanius, etc., spread abroad this opinion. But Jerome charges it with being *deliramentum apocryphorum*.

The other view is found in the following authorities: *Tertullian* evidently admits brothers of Jesus in the strict and complete sense of the word. For he says, *de Monog.* c. 8: "The virgin was not married until after having given birth to the Christ." According to *Jerome* (adv. Helvid.), some very ancient writers spoke of sons of Joseph and Mary, and they had already been combated by Justin; a fact, which proves to what a high antiquity this opinion goes back.[3]

Brüder, in the *Zeitschr. f. wiss. Theol.*, 1880). The philological scruples, however, which are raised, do not seem to me sufficient to overthrow what results from the simple and plain tradition of Hegesippus.

[1] Before these facts, *Keim's* affirmation (I., p. 423) falls to the ground: "Hegesippus makes James and Simeon . . . cousins of Jesus." (Comp. the same assertions: Schenkel's *Bibellexic.*, I., p. 482.)

[2] *Eusebius* himself certainly distinguished James, the Lord's brother, from James, the son of Alphæus, since in his Commentary on Is. xvii. 5 (Montfaucons *Coll. nova patr.*, II., p. 422), he reckons *fourteen* apostles: the well-known twelve . . . , then Paul . . . , then James, the Lord's brother, first bishop of Jerusalem. But respecting the manner in which the latter was related to the Lord, the passage ii. 1, leaves us in doubt (see the various reading). The thought of Eusebius on this subject does not seem to me to be clear.

[3] We do not here allege testimonies of so late a time as that of the letter of the pseudo-Ignatius to the Apostle John, or that of the *Apostolical Constitutions*, viii. 35 (see Schaff).

Whatever preference should be given to the one or the other of these two relationships, the difference between the *brothers* and *cousins* of Jesus remains established from the historical point of view.

This now is the difficulty which it raises: The names of Jesus' brothers, mentioned in Matt. xiii. 55; Mark vi. 3, are *James, Joses* (according to the various readings, *Joseph* or *John*), *Simon* and *Judas.* Now, according to John xix. 25, comp. with Matt. xxvii. 56 and Mark xv. 40, Mary, the wife of Clopas, aunt of Jesus, had two sons, one named *James* (in Mark, James *the little*), the other *Joses,* who were, consequently, two cousins of Jesus. Moreover, Hegesippus makes Simeon, the second bishop of Jerusalem, a *son of Clopas;* he was, therefore, also a cousin of Jesus. Finally, Luke vi. 14–16 speaks of an apostle *Judas* (son or brother) of *James* who is mentioned as son of *Alphœus* (or *Clopas*). He would, thus, be a fourth cousin of Jesus, and the two lists would coincide throughout! Four brothers and four cousins with the same names! Is this admissible? But 1. As to the Apostle Judas, the natural ellipsis in Luke's passage is not *brother*, but *son* of James—consequently of some James unknown to us. This designation is designed merely to distinguish this apostle from the other Judas, Iscariot, whose name follows. Jesus had then, indeed, a brother named Judas, but not a cousin of this name. 2. The statements of Hegesippus certainly force us to admit a cousin of Jesus by the name of Simon. 3. If, for the second brother of Jesus, we adopt the reading *Joseph*, the identity of name with that of the third cousin falls to the ground of itself. 4. As to the name James, it is undoubtedly found in the two lists. The actual result, therefore, is this: In these two lists, that of the *brothers*, and that of the *cousins* of Jesus, there are two names in common: those of James and Simon. Is this sufficient to prove the identity of these two categories of persons? Even in our day, does it not happen, especially in country places, that we find families related to one another, in which, among several children, one or two bear certain very familiar names in common?

Notice, on the other hand, two positive exegetical reasons in favor of the distinction between the brothers and the cousins of Jesus: 1. Without doubt, assuming the premature death of Clopas, we could understand how his widow and her sons might have been received by Joseph and Mary, and the latter brought up with Jesus, and in this way their designation as *brothers of Jesus* could be explained. But is it conceivable that, in presence of the fact that the mother of these young persons was still living (Matt. xxvii. 56 and parall.), the expression would have been used in speaking of Mary and her nephews, " *His mother and His brethren,*" as it is used in our Gospels (Matt. xii. 46; Mark iii. 31; Luke viii. 19)? 2. The surname, *the little*, given to James, the cousin of Jesus (Mark xv. 40), must have served to distinguish him from some other member of his family, bearing the same name. Is it not probable that this other James was precisely James, his cousin, the brother of Jesus?

We conclude, therefore, that Jesus had four brothers strictly so called: James, surnamed the Just, Joseph, Simon and Judas,—and three cousins: James, the little, Simon and Joses.

No one of His brothers was an apostle; a fact which accords with vii. 5: "*Not even did his brethren believe on him.*" Being converted later, after His resurrection (1 Cor. xv. 5), they became, one of them (James), the first bishop of Jerusalem (Gal. i. 19; ii. 9; Acts xv; xxi. 18 ff.); the others, zealous missionaries (1 Cor. ix. 5). James and Judas are undoubtedly the authors of our two canonical

Epistles. As for the cousins of Jesus, one only was an apostle, James (the little); the second, Simon, was the second bishop of Jerusalem. Of Joses, the third, we know nothing.[1]

It is perhaps not impossible to place in this first visit at Capernaum some of the facts appertaining, according to the Synoptical narratives, to the first period of the Galilean ministry. The calling of the disciples, following upon the miraculous draught of fishes, takes its place naturally here. At the time of His setting out for Jerusalem, Jesus called them to follow Him for ever. He was going to inaugurate His work, and He must have desired to be surrounded from that time by those whom He had the design of associating in it. This twelfth verse is not, therefore, the close of the preceding narrative, as *Weiss* thinks. It is, at the same time, the indication of the moment when Jesus passed from private life to His public ministry. Like His disciples, He separates Himself from His family in order to begin the Messianic work. Moreover, this narrative is so summary, that if the whole of Jesus' life were not presupposed as known to the readers, it would resemble an enigma.

We have to consider in the following event: 1. The act of the Lord: vv. 13–16; 2. The effect produced: vv. 17–22.

Vv. 13–16

It was at Jerusalem and in the temple, that the Messiah's ministry must open. "The Lord whom ye seek," Malachi had said (iii. 1–3), "shall enter *into his temple* . . . . he *shall purify* the sons of Levi . . ." That prophecy said to Israel that her King would announce Himself, not by a miracle of power, but by an act of holiness.

The moment of this inauguration was naturally indicated. The feast of the Passover, more than any other, assembled the whole people in the holy city and in the courts of the temple. This was *the hour* of Jesus (ver. 4). If the people had entered into the reformatory movement which He sought, at that time, to impress upon them, this entrance of Jesus into His temple would have become the signal of His Messianic coming.

The temple had three particularly holy courts: that of the *priests*, which enclosed the edifice of the temple properly so-called (ναός); more to the eastward, that of the *men*, and finally, to the east of the latter, that of the *women*. Around these courts a vast open space had been arranged, which was enclosed on four sides by colonnades, and which was called the *court of the Gentiles*, because it was the only part of the sacred place (ἱερόν) into which proselytes were permitted to enter. In this outermost court there were established, with the tacit consent of the temple authorities, a market and an exchange. Here were sold the different kinds of animals intended for the sacrifices; here Greek or Roman money, brought from

---

[1] Why is Mary, the wife of Clopas (Mark xv. 40), called the mother of James and Joses, and not of Simon? This is a fact not easy to explain.

362 / Birth of Faith

foreign regions, was exchanged for the sacred money with which the capitation-tax determined by Exod. xxx. 13 for the support of the temple (the half-shekel or double-drachma = about 31 cents) was paid.

Until this day, Jesus had not risen up against this abuse. Present in the temple as a simple Jew, He did not have to judge the conduct of the authorities, still less to put himself in their place. Now, it is as the Son of Him to whom this house is consecrated, that He enters into the sanctuary. He brings to it, not merely new rites, but new duties. To keep silence in the presence of the profanation of which religion is the pretext, and at which His conscience as a Jew and His heart as the Son revolt, would be to belie, at the outset, His position as Messiah. The word of Malachi, which we have just quoted, traces His course for Him. It is to misconceive gravely the meaning of the act which is about to be related, to see in it, with *Weiss*, only a simple attempt at reform, such as any prophet might have allowed himself. The single expression: "*My Father's* house" (ver. 16), shows that Jesus was here acting in the full consciousness of His Messianic dignity; comp. also ver. 19. Vv. 19–21, make us appreciate the true bearing of this act; it is an appeal to the conscience of Israel, a demand addressed to its chiefs. If this appeal is heard, this act of purification will inaugurate the general reform of the theocracy, the condition of the Messianic kingdom. If the people remain indifferent, the consequences of this conduct are clear to the view of Jesus; all is over with the theocracy. The rejection of the Messiah, His death even; this is the fatal end of such conduct. Comp. an analogous ordeal at Nazareth, Luke iv. 23–27. The power in virtue of which Jesus acted, was by no means, therefore, the alleged *right of the zealots* of which the act of Phineas (Num. xxv.; Ps. cvi. 30) is thought to have been the type, but which never really existed in Israel.

Ver. 13. "*And*[1] *the Passover of the Jews was near, and Jesus went up to Jerusalem.*" John says: *of the Jews*, with reference to his Gentile readers, with whom he identifies himself in the feeling of Christian communion.

Ver. 14. "*And he found in the temple those who sold oxen and sheep*[2] *and doves, and the money-changers sitting.*" The article *the* before the terms designating the sellers and money-changers, which *Ostervald* omits with other translators, sets forth this office as a known one; they are *the* habitual, and in a sense licensed sellers and money-changers. The three sorts of animals mentioned were the ones most habitually used for the sacrifices.—Κερματιστής, *money-changer*, from κέρμα, *piece of money*.

Ver. 15. "*And having made*[3] *a small scourge of cords, he drove them all out of the temple, both the sheep and the oxen; and he poured out the changers' money*[4] *and overthrew*[5] *their tables.*" This scourge was not an instrument, but an emblem. It was the sign of authority and of judgment. If it

---

[1] ℵ alone reads δε instead of και.
[2] ℵ alone reads και τα προβ. και βοας.
[3] ℵ alone reads εποιησεν . . . και (*he made and . . .*)
[4] B L T^b X Orig. read τα κερματα, instead of το κερμα.
[5] Instead of ανεστρεψεν, B X: ανέτρεψεν: ℵ: κατεστρεψεν.

had been a matter of performing a physical act, the means would have been disproportionate to the end, and the effect would be even more so to the cause. The material use of the scourge had no place. The simple gesture was enough.—Πάντας, *all*, includes, according to many (comp. Bäumlein, Weiss, Keil), only the two following objects connected by τε καί, "all, both *sheep* and *oxen*." But it is more natural to refer πάντας to τοὺς πωλοῦντας, *the sellers*, which precedes, and to make of the following words a simple apposition: "He drove them all out, *both sheep and oxen*." The design of the τε καί, *as well as*, is certainly not to indicate by a lifeless disjoining of parts the contents of the word *all*, but to express the sort of bustle with which men and animals hastened off at His command and at the gesture which accompanied it. *He overturned*, with His own hand.— Κολλυβιστής, *money-changer*, from κόλλυβος, *nummus minutus*.—τὸ κέρμα, singular taken in the collective sense.

Ver. 16. "*And he said to those that sold the doves: take these things hence; make not my Father's house a house of merchandise.*" With regard to the sellers of doves Jesus limits Himself to speaking. He cannot drive out the doves, as one drives oxen or sheep; and He does not wish to overturn the cages, as He has overturned the tables of the money-changers. He is perfectly master of Himself. If He had really struck the dealers in oxen and sheep, we cannot see why He should have spared the sellers of pigeons. The command "*take away*" is addressed only to these last; the following words, "*make not*, . . ." to all the traffickers. The defining phrase, "*of my Father*," contains the explanation of Jesus' act. He is a son who avenges the honor of the paternal house. When He was in the temple at the age of twelve, it was already the same filial feeling which animated Him; but on this day He is sustained by the distinct consciousness of His duty as Messiah, involved henceforth for Him in His position as Son. It is very remarkable that in the Synoptics (the scene of the baptism), no less than in John, the feeling of His filial relation to God takes the lead in Jesus of that of His office as Messiah. He does not feel Himself to be Son because He is Christ; He knows Himself to be Christ because He is Son (comp. *my Comment. on Luke* I., p. 235). Here is an indication which is incompatible with the opinion of Renan, who represents Jesus as exalting Himself by degrees and raising Himself by degrees from His Messianic consciousness to the consciousness of His divinity.

The outward success of this judicial act is explained by the majesty of Jesus' appearance, by the irresistible ascendency which was given to Him by the consciousness of the supernatural force which He could exert at need, by the feeling of His sovereignty in that place, as it betrays itself in the expression "*my Father*," and, finally, by the bad conscience of those who were the objects of such a judgment.

Vv. 17–22

The effect is described in vv. 17–22. We meet here a fact, which will repeat itself at every manifestation of the Lord's glory; a twofold impres-

364 / Birth of Faith

sion is produced, according to the moral predisposition of the witnesses; some find in the act of Jesus nourishment for their faith; for others the same act becomes a subject of offense. It is the pre-existing moral sympathy or antipathy that determines the impression.

Ver. 17. "*His disciples remembered*[1] *that it was written: The zeal of thy house shall eat me up.*"[2] This recollection took place immediately; comp. ver. 22, where the opposite fact is expressly pointed out. Ps. lxix., the ninth verse of which presents itself at this moment to the remembrance of the disciples, is only indirectly Messianic—that is to say, the subject contemplated by the Psalmist is not the person of the Messiah (comp. ver. 6: "*Thou knowest my foolishness, and my sins are not hid from thee*"), but the theocratic righteous person, suffering for the cause of God. The highest realization of this ideal is the Messiah. *Weiss* claims that this quotation finds an explanation only so far as this Psalm was, at that time, exclusively, and through an error, referred to the Messiah. But in order to this, the reading of ver. 6 must have been forgotten. The unanimity of the Mjj. decides in favor of the reading καταφάγεται. This verb is a future; the evangelist substitutes it for the past κατέφαγε, *hath eaten up*, of the LXX. which is in conformity with the Hebrew text. The disciples are thinking, not of Jesus' last sufferings, which were at that time beyond the thoughts which occupied their minds, but on the consuming force of His zeal, on that living holocaust, the first act of which they beheld at this moment. This also is the meaning of the word *hath eaten up*, in the Psalm.

While the disciples compare the Scriptures, and this remembrance strengthens their faith, the Jews reason and object, just as the inhabitants of Nazareth do, Luke iv. 22. Instead of letting the act of Jesus speak, as every manifestation of holiness should, to their conscience, they demand the external sign which should legitimate this act, as if it did not contain in itself its own legitimation!

Ver. 18. "*The Jews, therefore, answered and said unto him: What sign showest thou unto us, that thou doest these things?*" The particle, *therefore*, connects again with ver. 16, after the interruption in ver. 17. The expression "*the Jews*" designates here especially the authorities charged with the care of the temple, with the shade of hostility which attaches to this term in our Gospel (see i. 19). *Riggenbach* ("*Leben des Herrn Jesu*," p. 382) observes that "it is, indeed, the method of Pharisaism to demand a σημεῖον, an external sign, to legitimate an act which commends itself to the conscience by itself alone, because, once on this path, one can cavil about the nature and value of the sign, can move on indefinitely from demand to demand, and can ask finally, after a multiplication of loaves: *What sign doest thou then?* Ἀποκρίνεσθαι does not signify here, any more than elsewhere, *to take up the discourse* (*Ostervald, Rilliet, Arnaud*). This word always contains the idea of *reply;* only the reply is sometimes addressed to the conduct or the feeling of the interlocutor. Here the Jews' question is

---

[1] ℵ B L T^b X Cop. Orig. omit δε after ἐμνήσθησαν.
[2] The T. R. reads κατεφαγε (*hath eaten up*) with several Mnn. It., instead of καταφαγεται (*shall eat up*) which all the Mjj. read

an answer to the act of Jesus; Jesus had just addressed an appeal to the religious sentiment of the people. The attitude of the people, thus called upon to declare themselves, in some sort decided fatally their future. The reply was significant. The nineteenth verse will show us that Jesus immediately penetrated its whole meaning.—Ὅτι: "What sign showest thou (to explain) *that* thou art doing . . . " Meyer: εἰς ἐκεῖνο ὅτι.

Ver. 19. "*Jesus answered and said unto them: Destroy this temple, and in three days I will raise it up.*" This answer of Jesus is sudden, like a flash of lightning. It springs from an immeasurable depth; it illuminates regions then completely unexplored by any other consciousness than His own. The words: *Destroy this temple*, characterize the present and future conduct of the Jews in its innermost significance, and the words: *In three days I will raise it up*, display all the grandeur of the person and of the future work of Jesus. This mysterious saying involves the following difficulty: on the one hand, the connection with what precedes prompts us to refer the words, *this temple*, to the temple properly so called, which Jesus had just purified; on the other, the evangelist's interpretation (ver. 21) obliges us to apply them to the body of Jesus. Some, as *Lücke* and *Reuss*, cut the Gordian knot by declaring that there is a conflict which cannot be settled between scientific exegesis and the apostle's explanation, and by determining that there is an advance of the first beyond the second. *Baur* administers a severe lecture to Lücke for irreverence towards the apostolic exegesis, of which this view gives evidence. In fact, according to Baur, this saying being partly the creation of the evangelist himself, he must know better than any one, better than Lücke, what is its true meaning!

The *historical* truth of this saying of Jesus is guaranteed: 1. By the declaration of the false witnesses (Matt. xxvi. 61; Mark xiv. 57, 58), which proves that, although the recollection of the circumstances in which it was pronounced may have been effaced, the expression itself had remained deeply engraved on the memory, not only of the disciples, but of the Jews. 2. By Acts vi. 14, where Stephen's accusers said: "*We have heard him say that this Jesus of Nazareth shall destroy this place and shall change the customs which Moses gave to us.*" Stephen could not have spoken thus except on the foundation of a positive declaration of Jesus. 3. By the originality, the conciseness, and even the obscurity of the saying.

The first clause cannot contain an invitation to the Jews directly to destroy the temple, not even in the hypothetical sense of *de Wette*: "If you should destroy." This supposition would be absurd; no Israelite would have thought of laying his hand on the sacred edifice. The word *destroy* should, therefore, be taken in the indirect sense: to bring about, by continuing in the course which you are following, the destruction of the theocracy and that of the temple. But what is the offense by which Israel can provoke this final chastisement? Modern interpretation,— "scientific exegesis," as *Lücke* says,—answers: By continually increasing moral profanations, such as that against which Jesus had just protested. This answer is insufficient. Simple sins of this kind could prepare, but not decide, this catastrophe. The Old Testament assigns a more positive cause for the final ruin of Israel; it is the rejection and murder of the Messiah. Zechariah announces this crime, when describing (xii. 10) the mourning of the Israel of the last days, lamenting the murderous sin against Jehovah *whom they have pierced.* Daniel, chap. ix., says: "*The Messiah shall be cut off. . . . and the people of a prince who shall come shall destroy the city and the sanctuary;*" a passage which Matthew (xxiv. 15, 16) applies to the circumstances of his time. The means for Israel of destroying its temple, are, to the view of Jesus, to put the Messiah to death. The appearance of the Messiah is the purpose of the theocratic institution. The Messiah being once cut off, it is all over with Israel and consequently with the temple. The people and the priesthood may indeed still exist for a while after this; but all this is nothing more than *the carcase over which the eagles of the divine judgment gather themselves* (Matt. xxiv. 28). Why, at the moment when Jesus expires, is the veil of the temple rent? It is because, in reality, there is no longer a Most Holy place, no longer a Holy place, no longer courts, sacrifice, priesthood; the temple, as Jehovah's temple, has ceased to exist.

When He says "*Destroy this temple,*" therefore, it is, indeed, of the temple properly so called, that Jesus speaks; but He knows that it will be *in His own person,* that this destruction, so far as it depends on the Jews, will be consummated. It is *on His body* that they will cause the blow to fall, which will destroy their sanctuary. The imperative λύσατε is not, then, merely concessive: "If it happens that you destroy." It is of the same kind with that other imperative, "*What thou hast to do, do quickly*" (xiii. 27). When the fruit of perversity, collective or individual, is ripe, it *must* fall. Comp. also the πληρώσατε, Matt. xxiii. 32.

The meaning of the second clause follows from that of the first. If the death of Jesus is the real destruction of the temple, the restoration of the latter can consist only in the resurrection of Jesus Himself. Jesus once said: "*Here is more than the temple*" (Matt. xii. 6). His body was the living and truly holy dwelling of Jehovah; the visible sanctuary was the anticipatory emblem of this real temple. It is, therefore, really, in Him, in *His body,* that this supreme crisis will be effected. The Messiah perishes; the temple falls. The Messiah lives again; the true temple rises again; in a new form, beyond doubt. For in the Kingdom of God, there is never a simple restoration of the past. He who speaks of rising anew speaks of progress, reappearance in a higher form. The word ἐγείρειν, *to waken up, to raise up,* is perfectly suitable here. For it may be applied at once to a resurrection and a construction (see *Meyer*). The expression: *in three days,* the authenticity of which is guaranteed in a very special way by the statement of the false witnesses (διὰ τριῶν ἡμερῶν, Matt. xxvi. 61; Mark xiv. 58), receives in our explanation its natural meaning; for, in an historical situation so solemn as this, it is impossible to see only a poetic or proverbial form for saying: "in a very short time," as Hos. vi. 2, or Luke xiii. 31. A demonstrative miracle has been demanded of Jesus, as a sign of His competency. We know from the Synoptics that Jesus always rejected such demands, which renewed for Him the third temptation in the wilderness.

But there was a miracle, one only, which He could promise, without condemning Himself to the role of a wonder-worker, because this miracle entered as a necessary element into the very work of salvation: it was His resurrection. Thus it is to this sign that He in like manner appeals, in similar cases, in the Synoptics (Matt. xii. 38–40; xvi. 4). We come also here upon one of those profound analogies which, beneath the difference of the forms, blend into one whole the representation of the Synoptics and that of John. It is by the *reparative* power which He will display, when the Kingdom of God shall have sunk down, in a sense, even to nothing, that Jesus will prove the competency for *reformation* which He has just arrogated to Himself at this hour. This explanation answers thus to the natural meaning of the expressions of the text, to the demands of the context, and finally to the evangelist's interpretation.

The following is the meaning at which modern exegesis has arrived, by following, as *Lücke* says, "the laws of philological art." It is best set forth, as it seems to us, by *Ewald* (*Gesch. Christi*, p. 230): "All your religion, resting upon this temple, is corrupted and perverted; but He is already present, who, when it shall have perished as it deserves, shall easily restore it in a more glorious form, and shall thus work, not one of those common miracles which you ask for, but the grandest of miracles." In this explanation, the temple destroyed is Judaism; the temple raised up is Christianity; the act of raising it up is Pentecost, not the resurrection. We shall not say that this sense is absolutely false; it is so only so far as it is given as the exact expression of the thought of Jesus at this moment. What condemns it is: 1. That the transformation of the economy of the letter into that of the Spirit is not *a sign*, but the work itself. It is necessary that the event indicated by Jesus should have an external character, in order to be adapted to the demand which was addressed to Him; 2. It is impossible, from this point of view, to interpret naturally the words: *in three days*. The passages (Hos. vi. 2 and Luke xiii. 31) do not sufficiently justify the figurative sense which must, in that case, be given to them here; 3. The temple raised up would be entirely different from the temple destroyed; but the pronoun αὐτόν (*it*), demands that there should, at least, be a relation between the one and the other (the body of Jesus destroyed and raised again). Objection is made to the meaning which we have proposed, that the Jews could not have understood so mysterious a reply. Assuredly, they did not see in the temple, of which Jesus spoke, anything but the material edifice, and they represented to themselves the sign promised by Him as the magical appearance of a new and supernatural temple (Mark xiv. 58). But we shall see that, in dealing with evil-disposed persons, the method of Jesus is to throw out enigmas and to reveal the truth only while veiling it; comp. the explanation of Jesus respecting the use of parables (Matt. xii. 11–16). Here is a secret of the profoundest pedagogics.

Objection is also made, that Jesus could not, so long beforehand, know of His death and resurrection. But in the Synoptics, also, He very early announces the tragical end of His Messianic ministry. It is during the first days of His activity in Galilee, that He speaks of the time "when the *bridegroom will be taken away*, and when the disciples will fast" (Mark ii. 19, 20). Had Jesus, then, never read Is. liii., Dan. ix., Zech. xii., etc.? Now, if He foresaw His death, He must have been assured also of His resurrection. He could not suppose that the bridegroom would be taken away, not to be restored.

Finally, it is objected, that, according to the Scriptures, it is not Jesus who raised Himself. But the receptivity of Jesus, in the act of His resurrection, was not that of passivity. He says Himself (x. 17, 18): "*I give up my life, that I may take it again . . . I have the power to give it up, and I have the power to take it again.*" He lays hold, as in all His miracles, of the divine omnipotence, and this becomes thereby active in Him.

Renan has seen in this utterance, so original and so profound, only a whim: "One day," he says, "His ill-humor against the temple drew from Him an imprudent word." He adds: "We do not know, indeed, what sense Jesus attached to this word, in which His disciples sought forced allegories" (*Vie de Jésus*, p. 367). Where Renan sees a proof of the ill-humor of Jesus against the temple, the immediate witnesses found one of the zeal for the house of God, which devoured their Master. Which has better understood Jesus? As for the explanation given by John (ver. 21), we shall hope that every serious reader will find in it something else than a "forced allegory."

Weiss does not think it is possible to defend the complete authenticity of the expression of Jesus, as it has been preserved for us by John. If Jesus expressed Himself thus, he must, at the same time, have pointed to His body with His finger, and this gesture would have been sufficient to render the misapprehension of the Jews (ver. 20) impossible. Besides, the interpretation which Mark gives of the saying of Jesus (xiv. 58), leads one to suppose that its real meaning was a little different from that which we find in John. To the demand of the Jews relative to His *competency* to purify the temple (ver. 18), Jesus is said to have answered, that for the outward temple He would substitute the habitation of God in the spirit. It was John, according to *Weiss*, who introduced afterwards into the quite simple answer of Jesus, the two ideas of His death and His resurrection. This hypothesis could be taken into consideration only if the difficulty presented by the saying of Jesus, as we have it, were insurmountable. But we believe that we have shown that it is not so. At the foundation, the true ground of this supposition is, that according to this author, Jesus must not have predicted beforehand His death and resurrection.

How did Jesus discover in this question, apparently so innocent: "*What sign showest thou?*" the prelude of the catastrophe which was to put an end to His own life, and, by that means, to the theocracy itself? We know from ii. 3, 4, with what penetration Jesus seized upon the moral bearing of the words which were addressed to Him. We have also cited Luke iv. 22, where it was enough for Jesus to hear the critical reflection on the part of the inhabitants of Nazareth: "*Is not this the son of Joseph?*" in order to His announcing to them His near rejection, not only on their part (ver. 23), but on the part of the whole people (vv. 24–27).

In the most fugitive impression of His interlocutors, the perspicacious eye of Jesus discerned the principle of the great final decision. By this characteristic feature, also, we verify in the Jesus of the Synoptics and of John, one and the same Jesus.

Ver. 20. " *The Jews said, therefore : Forty-six years was this temple in building, and wilt thou raise it up in three days ?* " The restoration of the temple by Herod had begun in the eighteenth year of his reign, according to Josephus (*Antiqq.* xv. 11, 1). In the *Jewish War*, the same historian, by an error, mentions the fifteenth. The first year of the reign of this prince was that from the first of Nisan 717 U. C. to the first of Nisan 718; the eighteenth would consequently be the year included between the first of Nisan 734 and the first of Nisan 735 : it was about the autumn of that year that the work began (Jos. *Ant.* xv. 11, 1). The time indicated, forty-six full years (ᾠκοδομήθη), brings us, therefore, as far as to the autumn of the year 780. The present Passover, consequently, must be that of the year 781, and as it was divided from the year in which Jesus died by the one alluded to in vi. 4, it follows therefrom, that Jesus died in 783. Now for many other reasons, that year seems really to have been the year of His death. *Weiss* objects that the expression : *was built*, does not necessarily imply that it was still in the course of building at that moment. But the work continued still for many years, until in 64 it was finished under Agrippa II. What reason could there be to suppose an interruption at the time in which our narrative places us?

Ver. 21. " *But he spoke of the temple of his body.*" By ἐκεῖνος, *ille vero*, he opposed to every other, John strongly contrasts the thought of Jesus with the interpretation of the Jews and the want of understanding of the apostles. Only He comprehends perfectly the true sense of His own saying.

Ver. 22. " *When, therefore, he was risen from the dead, his disciples remembered that he had said this,*[1] *and they believed the Scripture and the word which Jesus had said.*" Into docile hearts the light came, although slowly. The event explained the word, as in its turn the word contributed to disclose the deep meaning of the event. It is surprising to meet here the limiting words τῇ γραφῇ, *the Scripture;* for the Scripture had not been quoted by Jesus, unless we think, with *Weiss*, of ver. 17, which is unnatural in view of the formal opposition established by ver. 22 between the time of the one and that of the other reminiscence. The evangelist undoubtedly wishes to intimate that the first point on which the light fell, in the hearts of the apostles, after the resurrection, was the prophecies of the Old Testament which announced that event (Ps. xvi.; Is. liii.; Hos. vi.; the prophet Jonah), and that it was by the intermediate agency of the interpreted prophecies that the present word of Jesus came back to their remembrance and was also made clear to them.

This little point which belongs to the inner biography of the apostles, stamps the narrative with the seal of historical reality. Let the reader

---

[1] T. R. wrongly adds αυτοις (*to them*), with K and some Mnn.

picture to himself, with *Baur*, a pseudo-John, in the second century, inventing this momentary want of intelligence in the disciples with regard to a saying which he had himself ascribed to Jesus! The moral impossibility of such a strange charlatanism as this is obvious. This remark applies to the similar points, iv. 32, 33; vii. 39; xi. 12; xii. 16, 33; xiii. 28, etc.

The Synoptics relate an act of Jesus similar to this; which they place at the beginning of the week of the Passion, either on Palm-day (Matt. xxi.; Luke xix.), or more exactly on the next day after that (Mark xi.). We might naturally enough suppose that these three evangelists, having omitted all the first year of Jesus' ministry, were led thereby to locate this event in the only visit to Jerusalem of which they relate the story. This is the opinion of *Lücke, de Wette, Ewald, Weiss*, etc. *Keim* goes much further; he claims that it would have been the grossest want of tact on Jesus' part thus at the start to advertise His Messiahship, and to break with the old Judaism as He does in John. But what gives to the corporeal act its meaning and its character is the words with which Jesus accompanies it. Now these words, which constitute the soul of the narrative, are very different in the Synoptics and in John, to such a degree that it would be impossible to unite them in one consecutive discourse. In the Synoptics, Jesus claims, on the ground of Is. lvi. 7 (*" My house shall be called a house of prayer for all peoples "*), the right of the Gentiles to the place which, from the beginning, had been conceded to them in the temple (1 Kings viii. 41–43). In John, there is no trace of this intention; Jesus has in view Israel itself and only Israel. This difference, as well as the characteristic reply, John ii. 19, argues two distinct events. If, as we may not doubt, the abuse which is in question really existed at the moment when Jesus presented Himself for the first time as Messiah, and as Son of God, it was impossible that He should tolerate it. It would have been to declare Himself Messiah and abdicate the Messianic office by one act. Thus John's narrative is self-justified. But it is, also, wholly true that if, after having been reduced during more than two years to the simple activity of a prophet, Jesus wished to reassume on Palm-Sunday His office as Messiah-King, and thus to take up again a connection with His beginnings, He could not do so better than by repeating that act by which He had entered upon His career, and by repressing again that abuse which had not been slow in reproducing itself. By the first expulsion He had invited the people to the reformation which could save them; by the second, He protested against the profane spirit which was about to destroy them. Thus the narrative of John and the Synoptic narrative equally justify themselves. This contrast between the two situations agrees with the difference between the words uttered. In John, seeing His appeal repelled, Jesus thinks of His death, the fatal limit of that first rejection; in the Synoptics, seeing the fall of Israel consummated, He proclaims the right of the Gentiles, who are soon going to be substituted for the Jews. As for *Keim's* objection, this author forgets that, by acting in this way, Jesus made an appeal precisely to that which was deepest in the consciousness of every true member of the theocracy, respect for the temple. *Beyschlag* has justly called this proceeding on the part of Jesus, "the most profoundly conservative Jewish act." It was precisely the wonderful character of this act, that it inaugurated the revolution which was preparing, by connecting it with that which was most vital in the Israelitish past.

Jesus at Jerusalem: ii. 23–iii. 21

Jesus, not having been welcomed in the temple, does not force matters forward. The use of violence, even though by divine means, would have led Him to the career, not of a Christ, but of a Mahomet. In presence of the cold reserve which He meets, He retreats; and this retrograde movement characterizes, for a time, the course of His work. The palace has just shut its doors to Him; the capital remains open. Here He acts, yet no longer in the fullness of that Messianic sovereignty with which He had presented Himself in the temple. He confines Himself to teaching and miracles, the two prophetic agencies. Such is the admirable elasticity of the divine work in the midst of the world; it advances only as far as faith permits; in the face of resistance it yields; it retires even to its last entrenchment. Then, having reached this, it all at once resumes the offensive, and, engaging in the last struggle, succumbs externally, to conquer morally.

Vv. 23–25 are a preamble. It is the general picture of the activity of the Lord at Jerusalem, following after His undertaking in the temple. Then, in the following passage, iii. 1–21, John gives the remarkable example of the teaching of Jesus and of His Messianic testimony, in this earliest period, in presence of those whom He found disposed to faith.

Ver. 23. "*As he was in Jerusalem, at the Passover, at the feast, many believed on his name, seeing the miracles which he did.*"—The first clause of the verse contains three designations. One is that of *place : in Jerusalem*, at the centre of the theocracy, the normal theatre of His work. The second is that of *time : at the Passover*, in those days when the whole people were assembled in the capital, in greater numbers than on any other occasion in the year. The third designation is that of *the mode : at the feast*, in the midst of the solemn impressions which the daily ceremonies of that Paschal week awakened. The pronoun πολλοί, *many*, denotes nothing more than individuals; they form a contrast with the nation which should have collectively believed. Comp. the contrast between οἱ ἴδιοι, *His own*, and ὅσοι, *all those who*, i. 11, 12. But a still more sorrowful contrast is pointed out by the evangelist; it is that which existed between the faith of these believers and true faith. Their faith, to the view of Jesus, was not faith. No doubt, it had for its object His revelation as Christ and Son of God (*His name*); but it rested only upon the external fact of His miracles. The logical relation between this aorist *believed* and the present participle *seeing*, is expressed by the conjunction *because*. This faith had nothing inward and moral; it resulted solely from the impression of astonishment produced upon them by these wonders. *Signs* may, indeed, strengthen and develop true faith, where it is already formed, by displaying to it fully the riches of its object (ii. 11). They may even, sometimes, excite attention; but not produce real faith. Faith is a moral act which attaches itself to the moral being in Jesus. The last words: *which He did*, depict, indeed, the nature of this faith; it was the material operation which impressed these persons. These miracles were, undoubtedly, numerous; allusion is made to them in iv. 45. John relates, however, only one of them; so far different is His aim from that of the Synoptics. He wishes only to describe here a spiritual situation.

Ver. 24, 25. "*But Jesus did not trust himself to them, because he knew all men,* 25, *and because he had no need that any one should testify of man ; for he knew of himself what was in man.*" Jesus is no more dazzled by this apparent success, than He had been discouraged by the reverse which He had undergone in the temple. He discerns the insufficient nature of this faith. There is a sort of play upon words in the relation between οὐκ ἐπίστευεν, *He did not believe*, did not trust Himself, and ἐπίστευσαν, *they believed*, ver. 23. While they considering only the external facts, the miracles, *believed*, He (αὐτὸς δέ) not stopping with appearances, *did not believe;* He did not have *faith in their faith*. It is because He did not recognize in it the work of God. Consequently, He did not any more treat them as believers. How was this attitude of distrust manifested? It is difficult to state precisely. Probably the point in John's thought was rather a certain reserve of a moral nature, than positive external acts, such as reticence respecting His doctrine or the solitude in which He shut Himself up. *Luthardt*, "As they did not give themselves morally to Him, He did not give Himself morally to them." It is a profound observer initiated into the impressions of Jesus' mind,—this man who has laid hold of and set forth this delicate feature of His conduct. If he was himself one of the disciples whose call is related in chap. i., he must indeed have felt the difference between the conduct of Jesus towards these persons, and the manner in which He had deported Himself towards himself and his fellow-disciples. Let one picture to himself such a feature invented in the second century! Nothing in the text obliges us to identify this superior knowledge of Jesus with divine omniscience. The evangelist undoubtedly knew for himself that clear and penetrating look (ἐμβλέπειν) which read in the depth of the heart as in an open book. This superior knowledge of Jesus is the highest degree of the gift of the *discerning of spirits* (1 Cor. xii. 10; 1 John iv. 1).

The clause: *and because* . . . . etc., generalizes the statement of ver. 24. It signifies that, *in any case*, Jesus did not need to have recourse to information, in order to know what He had to think of such or such a man. This faculty of discernment was inherent in His person (*He Himself*) and, consequently, permanent (imperfect, *knew*). Ἵνα, *in order that*, is here no more than elsewhere the simple periphrasis for the infinitive (in opposition to *Weiss*). The idea of purpose, which remains always attached to this word, is explained by the tendency, which is inherent in the need of knowledge, to satisfy itself. The article τοῦ before ἀνθρώπου, "*the* man," may be explained either in the generic sense : *man* in general, or, what is perhaps more correct, in an altogether individual sense : the man with whom He had to do in each given case (*Meyer*). But even in this last explanation, the generic sense can be applied to ἐν τῷ ἀνθρώπῳ, *in the man*, in the following clause. The *for* would mean that He knew thus each representative of the type, *because* He knew thoroughly the type itself. However, it is more simple to give to this expression : *in the man*, the same individual sense as in the preceding clause, and to explain the *for* by the word : *Himself.* He had no need of information; for *of Himself* He knew . . .

On the foundation of this general situation, there is brought out separately, as a particular picture, the scene of the conversation with Nicodemus. Is this incident quoted as an *example* of that Jewish faith which is nothing but a form of unbelief ii. 23 (comp. ver. 2), as *Baur* thinks, or, on the contrary, as an *exception* to the attitude full of reserve which was assumed by Jesus and described vv. 24, 25 (*Ewald*)? The opinion of Baur strikes against the fact that Nicodemus later became a believer (chaps. vii. and xix.), so that the example would have been very badly chosen. On the other hand, the text gives no more indication that the following occurrence is related as a deviation from the line of conduct traced in ii. 24; and ver. 2 even makes Nicodemus belong in the class of persons described in vv. 23–25. *Lücke* sees in this narrative only an example of the supernatural knowledge of Jesus, but this idea does not correspond sufficiently with the very grave contents of the conversation. In *Reuss'* view, Nicodemus is a type, created by the evangelist, of that "literary and learned Judaism whose knowledge is nothing, and which has everything to learn from Jesus." But Nicodemus reappears twice afterwards, playing a part in the history of Jesus (chs. vii. and xix.); he was not, therefore, created only in order to give Jesus here the opportunity to convince him of ignorance. If the author inserted this incident in his narrative, it is because he saw in it the most memorable example of the *revelation* which Jesus had given, in the first period of His ministry, of His person and His work; comp. *Weiss* and *Keil.*

The part of this conversation in our Gospel may be compared with that of the Sermon on the Mount in the Gospel of Matthew : these two passages have an inauguratory character. As for Nicodemus, he is at once an example and an exception : an example, since miracles were the occasion of his faith; an exception, since the manner in which Jesus treats him proves that He hopes for the happy development of this faith. The faith characterized vv. 23–25, as *Luthardt* observes, is not real faith; but none the more is it unbelief. From this point there may be falling back or advance.—How did the evangelist get the knowledge of this conversation? May Jesus or Nicodemus have related it to him? The first alternative (*Meyer*) has somewhat of improbability. In the second, it is asked whether Nicodemus understood well enough to retain it so thoroughly. Why could not John himself have been present at the interview, even though it took place at night? Comp. ver. 11.

But this question is subordinate to another. Is not this conversation itself, as we have it before us, a free composition of the author in which he has united different elements of the ordinary teaching of his master, or even, as *Keim* says, put into His mouth a highly spiritual summary of his own semi-Gnostic dogmatics? Finally, without going so far, can it not be supposed, at least, that the subjectivity of the author has, without his having a suspicion of it himself, influenced this account more or less, especially towards the end of the conversation? This is what we shall have to examine. For this purpose, what shall be our touch-stone? If the direct, natural application of the words of Jesus to Nicodemus *the Pharisee* is sustained even to the end, we shall recognize by this sign the authenticity of the account. If, on the contrary, the discourse loses itself, as it advances, in vague generalities, without appropriateness and without direct relation to the given situation, we shall find in this fact the indication of a more or less artificial composition.

Ver. 1. "*There was a man of the Pharisees, whose name was Nicodemus, one of the rulers of the Jews.*" The name Nicodemus, though of Greek origin, was not unusual among the Jews. The Talmud mentions several times a person of this name (*Nakedimon*), called also *Bounai*, reckoned in the number of Jesus' disciples. He was one of the four richest inhabitants of the capital. His family fell into the greatest destitution. He must have been alive also at the time of the destruction of Jerusalem. This last circumstance, connected with the great age of Nicodemus at the time of Jesus' ministry, renders the identity of the latter with the personage of whom the Talmud speaks, doubtful. *Stier* saw in the word ἄνθρωπος, *a man*, an allusion to ii. 25; John would remind us thereby that Nicodemus was an example of that human type which Jesus knew so well; this is far-fetched. Before naming him, John points out his quality as *Pharisee*. This characteristic signifies much more, indeed, than his name, for the understanding of the following conversation. The most narrow and exalted national particularism had created for itself an organ in the Pharisaic party. According to the ideas of that sect, every Jew possessing the legal virtues and qualities had a right of entrance into the Messianic kingdom. *Universo Israeli est portio in mundo futuro*, said the Rabbis. The Messiah Himself was only the perfect and all-powerful Jew, who, raised by His miracles to the summit of glory, was to destroy the Gentile power and place Israel at the head of humanity. This Messianic programme, which the imagination of the Pharisaic doctors had drawn out of the prophecies, was that which brought with it Nicodemus to the presence of Jesus. The title ἄρχων, *ruler*, denotes, undoubtedly, one of the lay members of the Sanhedrim (vii. 50), in contrast to the ἀρχιερεῖς, *chief priests* (vii. 50; Luke xxiii. 13).

Ver. 2. "*He came to him*[1] *by night and said: Master, we know that thou art a teacher come from God; for no one can do these miracles which thou doest,*

---

[1] 6 Byz. Syr^sch. read προς τον Ιησουν instead of προς αυτον (a correction with a view to public reading).

except God be with him."—What was the purpose of this visit? These first words of Nicodemus are only a preamble; it would be idle to seek here the revelation of the purpose of his procedure. *Koppe* has supposed that he came to act as a spy on the Lord. But Jesus treats him as an honest person, and Nicodemus shows himself sincere during the course of the conversation, and also afterwards. *Meyer* has supposed that he came to inquire about the way to be saved. But as a good Jew and pious Pharisee, he by no means doubted as to his own salvation. We must, rather, suppose that he had discerned in Jesus an extraordinary being, and as he must have known the answer of the forerunner to the deputation of the Sanhedrim, he asked himself seriously whether Jesus might not be the Messiah announced by John as already present. In that case he would try to sound His plans respecting the decisive revolution which His coming was to involve. This supposition appears to me more natural than that of *Weiss*, who, because of the title of *teacher* with which Nicodemus salutes Jesus, thinks that he wished to question Him concerning what new teaching He had just given. But Nicodemus evidently could not salute Jesus by any other title than that of *teacher*, even if, as he must have had from the testimony of John the Baptist and in consequence of the expulsion of the traders, he had a presentiment that there was in Him something still greater. The plural οἴδαμεν, *we know*, proves that He did not take this step solely in his own name, but that a certain number of his colleagues entertained the same thoughts with himself.—He comes *by night*. This circumstance, noticed expressly in xix. 39 and perhaps also in vii. 50, is easily explained by the fear which he had of compromising himself before the other members of the Sanhedrim, and even before the people. Perhaps, also, he wished to avoid further increasing, through a step taken in broad daylight, the reputation of the young teacher. Nicodemus gives Him the title of ῥαββί, *Master;* this is saying very much on his part; since Jesus had not passed through the different degrees of rabbinical studies which gave a right to this title. Comp. vii. 15 : " *The Jews were astonished, saying : How does this man know the Scriptures, not being a man who has studied?* " It is precisely this extraordinary course of the development of Jesus which Nicodemus characterizes by saying : *a teacher come from God.* Ἀπὸ θεοῦ, *from God*, is placed at the beginning as the principal idea, opposed to that of a regular doctorate. The same contrast is found in vii. 16 in the mouth of Jesus Himself. This designation : *from God*, depends neither on the verb, *come*, nor on the word *teacher*, separately, but on the complex phrase; the sense is : "come as a teacher from God." The argument is consonant with theocratic precedents (Exod. iv.). Miracles prove divine assistance, and this proves the divine mission. But this formal demonstration, intended to prove to Jesus a truth which he does not doubt, is somewhat pedantic and must have shocked the ear of Him to whom it was addressed. So Jesus cuts short the discourse thus commenced by a sudden apostrophe, intended rather to answer the inmost thoughts of His interlocutor than his spoken words.

Ver. 3. " *Jesus answered and said unto him : Verily, verily, I say unto you,*

Except a man be born anew, he cannot see the kingdom of God."—The relation of this answer to the words of Nicodemus has been differently understood, for the very reason that He was not able to finish the expression of His thought. *Meyer*, in conformity with his supposition indicated above, interprets this answer thus: "Every particular work is unfitted to open the door of the kingdom of God; there must be a radical regeneration." But we have seen that Nicodemus, the Pharisee, could not have come with the thought which Meyer supposes. *Baumgarten-Crusius* and *Weiss*, starting from the title of *teacher* which he had given Him, think that Jesus means to say: "It is not a new teaching only that you need, it is a new birth." According to our previous remarks, we think, rather, with *Luthardt*, that, on hearing the first words of Nicodemus, the whole Pharisaic programme with relation to the kingdom of God presented itself vividly to the mind of Jesus, and that He felt the need of directly opposing to it the true divine plan touching this capital subject. Nicodemus believes that he discerns in the appearance of Jesus the dawn of the Messianic kingdom, such as he conceived it; Jesus reveals to him an altogether spiritual conception of that kingdom, and, consequently, of all other moral conditions for entrance into it: "It is not a glorified earthly life; it is not a matter of expelling the Roman legions and of going to conquer the Capitol! The true kingdom of God is a state of the soul, the submission of the heart to the Divine will; to enter it, there must be wrought within the man a work at once spiritual and individual, which has nothing in common with the great political drama which thou hast in view." It is, then, the full security in which Nicodemus is living with regard to his participation in the kingdom of the Messiah, that Jesus wishes to break up, by answering him in this way. We have in Luke xvii. 20, 21, a parallel which offers the best commentary on our passage. "*When cometh the kingdom of God?*" a group of Pharisees ask of Jesus. "The kingdom of God cometh not with observation," Jesus answers; "it is within you." The coincidence could not be more complete. The formula *amen, amen,* implies a doubt in the hearer's mind (see i. 52); the doubt implied here is that which naturally arises from the Pharisaic prejudices of Nicodemus. "The pious Jew, the honored Pharisee, the powerful ruler, Nicodemus is prostrated," says *Hengstenberg*, "at the shock of this, *verily.*" The solemn expression: "*I say unto thee,*" or "I declare to thee," recalls to Nicodemus that dignity of divine teacher which he has himself just attributed to Jesus. By the indeterminate formula: *if any one,* Jesus avoids the harshness which the direct application to such an old man would have involved. The word ἄνωθεν has, in the three other passages where John uses it (ver. 31; xix. 11, 23) the local meaning: *from above,* that is to say, *from heaven.* The passages, also, may be compared in which he makes use of the expression: *to be born of God;* for example, i. 13, and in the 1st Epistle ii. 29, iii. 9, etc.; nine times in all. These parallel passages seem decisive and have determined a large number of interpreters (*Origen, Erasmus, Lücke, de Wette, Meyer, Bäumlein, Reuss,* etc.) to adopt this meaning here. But may we not also conclude from the last passages cited that if this were the idea which John wished to express, he would rather have employed the expression ἐκ θεοῦ, *of God?* The misunderstanding of Nicodemus (ver. 4) is more easily explained, if Jesus said in Aramaic: *anew*, than *from above*, since even in this latter case, also, Nicodemus might have spoken of a *second* birth. At all events, it follows from the expressions: *a second time* (δεύτερον) and *his mother's womb*, that, if he thought of a birth coming *from above*, he understood this term in the sense in which it can be applied even to the natural birth,—that is to say, that every child who is born comes from God, descends from heaven. However, if the word ἄνωθεν expressed here such a striking idea, the emphasis would be laid upon this word, and, in that case, it ought to be placed before the verb. Placed after the verb, ἄνωθεν only *strengthens* the idea of beginning connected with that of being born, which leads us to give to this adverb the temporal, rather than the local sense: *from the beginning*. We have three striking examples of this sense of ἄνωθεν. Josephus says (*Antiqq.* i. 18, 3): φιλίαν ἄνωθεν ποιεῖται; he contracts friendship with him, *going back to the beginning*, that is, as if they entered for the first time into mutual relations. Tholuck cites, the following passage of Artemidorus (*Oneirocriticon* i. 14): A father dreaming that his wife gives birth to a child exactly like himself, says: "that he seems to himself ἄνωθεν γεννᾶσθαι; to be born from the beginning, to recommence his own existence." In the *Acta Pauli*, Jesus says to Peter, who is flying from martyrdom and to whom He presents Himself: ἄνωθεν μέλλω σταυρωθῆναι, "I am going to begin anew my crucifixion." Compare also in the New Testament, Luke i. 3; Acts xxvi. 5; and Gal. iv. 9. In this last passage ἄνωθεν is completed by πάλιν: "entering from the beginning into a state of slavery which will be the second." This sense of ἄνωθεν can scarcely be given in French. The expression *tout à neuf* would best answer to it. The sense is: to place in the course of the earthly life a beginning as new as birth itself. There is nothing to oppose this sense, philologically, according to the examples cited. And it makes the answer of Nicodemus more easily understood. The word *to see* is perhaps connected with *to be born;* a new sight implies a new life. Sight is often the symbol of enjoyment, as well as of suffering (viii. 51). In the old covenant, the *kingdom of God* was realized in a politico-religious form. From this temporary envelopment, Jesus freed the spiritual principle which forms the true foundation of that state of things, the submission of the human will to the divine will, in one word, holiness (comp. the Sermon on the Mount); and from this principle He derives a new order of things which is first realized in individuals, and which brings about thereby the renewal of society, and finally is to transform nature itself. For it is false to exclude, as *Reuss* does (*Hist. de la théol. chrét.* t. II., pp. 555 f.), the social and final consequences of the notion of the kingdom of God in the sense of our Gospel. The eschatological hopes attached to this term in the Old and New Testaments are found again in full in v. 28, 29; vi. 39, 40, 44, 54. *Meyer* calls attention to the fact that the term *kingdom of God* does not again appear anywhere else in John, and rightly finds in this fact a proof of the truly historical character of the narrative which occupies our attention. If, as *Renan* thinks, Jesus had been only a young enthusiast, obedient to a mission which He had assumed for Himself, would He not have been flattered by seeing such considerable personages as Nicodemus and those whom he represented (ver. 1) as well as the colleagues in whose name he spoke, ranked among the number of his adherents, and would not this feeling have borne Him on, at this moment, to entirely different language? The assured feeling of the divinity and holiness of His missson alone could, in the face of this success, keep Him from a false step.

Ver. 4. "*Nicodemus says to him: How can a man be born when he is old? He cannot enter a second time, can he, into his mother's womb and be born?*" This saying, to the view of several modern critics, is a master-piece of improbability. *Reuss* thinks that "it is indeed, wrong to try to give to this answer a meaning even in the smallest degree plausible or defensible." *Schleiermacher* proposes to explain thus: "It is impossible, at my age, to recommence a new *moral* life." *Tholuck, Bäumlein* and *Hengstenberg*, nearly the same: "What thou askest of me is as impossible as that a man should enter again. . . ." These explanations evidently weaken the meaning of the text. *Meyer* thinks that the embarrassment into which the saying of Jesus throws Nicodemus, leads him to say something absurd. *Lange* finds rather a certain irritation in this answer: The Pharisee would attempt to engage in a rabbinical discussion in order to show Jesus the exaggeration of His demands. These suppositions have little probability. Would Jesus speak as He does in the sequel to a man so narrow-minded or so irritable? *Lücke* explains: "Thou canst not, by any means, mean that . . .?" This explanation is philologically accurate; it faithfully renders the meaning of the negative μή (comp. our translation). As *Weiss* observes, Nicodemus does not answer thus as a man wanting in understanding; but he is offended at seeing Jesus propose to him such a condition; he refuses to enter into His thought, and, holding firmly to the literal sense, he limits himself to a setting forth of its absurdity. The manner in which he expresses this impression does not seem even to be entirely free from irony. It is because in truth, he cannot conceive how the beginning of another life can be placed in the womb of the natural existence. The kingdom of God has always appeared to him as the most glorious form of the earthly existence itself. To what purpose a new birth, in order to enter into it? The Old Testament spoke, no doubt, of the force from above, of the divine aid necessary to sanctify the man, but not of a new birth (see *Luthardt*).

The words: "*when he is old,*" prove that Nicodemus did not fail to apply to himself the: "*If any one*" of Jesus. The word δεύτερον, *a second time*, undoubtedly reproduces only partially the meaning of ἄνωθεν, *from the beginning*, in the mouth of Jesus. This is because Nicodemus does not comprehend the difference between a beginning anew and a *different* beginning. A radical moral renewal seems to him impossible without a simultaneous physical renewal. Thus the explanation which Jesus gives him bears on the absolute *difference* between the natural birth and the new birth which He demands:

Ver. 5. "*Jesus answered: Verily, verily, I say unto thee that except a man is born of water and of spirit, he cannot enter into the kingdom of God.*"[1] The words, *of water and spirit*, substituted for ἄνωθεν (*from the beginning*) indicate to Nicodemus the new factors, and consequently the totally different nature of this second birth. The first term: *of water*, agrees better with the idea of a *new* birth, than with that of a *heavenly* birth. Spiritualism, embarrassed by the material character of this first means, has often sought to unite it with the second. Thus *Calvin* paraphrases the expression *of water and spirit* by the term *aquae spiritales;* he finds support in the expression *baptism of the Spirit and of fire* (Luke iii. 16). But the spiritual sense of the word *fire* could not be questioned in that phrase. It was otherwise with the word *water* in the saying with which we are occupied, especially at the time when Jesus was speaking thus. The baptism of John was producing at that time an immense sensation in Israel, so that the thought of Nicodemus, on hearing the words, *birth by water*, must have turned immediately to that ceremony; as it was celebrated in the form of a total or partial immersion, it quite naturally represented a birth. Jesus, moreover, at the moment when He thus expressed Himself, was in a sense coming out from the water of baptism; it was when completing this rite that He had Himself received the Holy Spirit. How, in such circumstances, could this expression: *Born of water*, have possibly designated on His lips anything else than baptism? Thus, also, is explained the negative and almost menacing form: *Except a man* . . . Nicodemus was a Pharisee, and we know that the Pharisees had refused to submit to John's baptism (Luke vii. 30); this saying contained, therefore, a very real admonition addressed to Nicodemus. *Weiss*, laying stress upon the absence of the article before the word *water*, rejects this special allusion to the rite of baptism. He sees in the water only an image of the purification of sin effected by the new spiritual birth. But the absence of the article simply makes prominent the *quality* of the means, and does not prevent us from thinking of the special practical use which was made of it by John at that time. Nicodemus must learn that the acceptance of the work of the forerunner was the first condition of entering into the new life. This first term, therefore, contained a positive invitation to break with the line of conduct adopted by the Pharisaic party towards John the Baptist. But what is the relation between baptism and the new birth (ver. 3)? *Lücke* makes prominent in baptism the subjective element of repentance (μετάνοια). He thinks that Jesus meant to say: First of all, on the part of man, repentance (of which baptism is the emblem); afterwards, on the part of God, the Spirit. But the two defining words are parallel, depending on one and the same preposition; the one cannot represent something purely subjective and the other something purely objective. The water also contains something objective, divine; this divine element in baptism is expressed in the best way by *Strauss*. "If baptism is, on the part of man," he says, "the declara-

---

[1] א reads ιδειν την βασιλειαν των ουρανων (*the kingdom of heaven*), a reading which Tischendorf adopts (8th edition).

380 / Birth of Faith

tion of the *renunciation* of sin, it is, on the part of God, the *declaration of the pardon* of sins." The baptism of water, in so far as offered and administered on the part of God and in His name, contains the promise of pardon, of which it is the visible pledge, in favor of the sinner who accepts it. In this sense, Peter says on the day of Pentecost, Acts ii. 38: "Be baptized, every one of you, in the name of Jesus Christ *for the pardon of sins;* and [following upon this pardon] you shall receive the gift of the Holy Spirit." And it must, indeed, be noticed that he says: "The pardon of *sins*," and not of *his sins*. For it is the idea of baptism *in itself*, and not that of its individual efficacy, which Peter wishes to indicate. Baptism is, indeed, the crowning-point of the symbolic lustrations of the Old Testament; comp. Ps. li., 4, 9, "*Wash me from mine iniquity . . . Cleanse me from my sin with hyssop; wash me and I shall be whiter than snow.*" Ezek. xxxvi. 25, "*I will sprinkle upon you clean water, and you shall be clean.*" Zech. xiii. 1, "*In that day there shall be a fountain opened to the house of David and to the inhabitants of Jerusalem for sin and for uncleanness.*" Water is, in all these passages, the emblem of the expiatory blood, the only real means of pardon. Comp. 1 John v. 6, where *the water, the blood* and *the Spirit* are placed in connection with one another; the water, on the one hand, as the symbol of the blood which reconciles and, on the other, as the pledge of the Spirit which regenerates. To accept the baptism of water administered by John was, therefore, while bearing witness of one's repentance, to place oneself under the benefit of the promise of the Messianic pardon. The condemnation being thus taken away, the baptized person found himself restored before God to his normal position, that of a man who had not sinned; and consequently he found himself fitted to receive from the Messiah Himself the gift of the Spirit. The *Spirit:* Here is the active, efficient principle of the new birth, of the renewal of the will and of the dispositions of the heart, and thereby even of the whole work of sanctification. Jesus sums up, therefore, in these two words: *Of water and spirit*, the essential principles of the Christian salvation, pardon and sanctification, those two conditions of entrance into the divine kingdom.

In the following verses, no further mention of water is made, precisely because it has in the new birth only a negative value; it removes the obstacle, the condemnation. The creative force proceeds from the Spirit. The absence of the article with the word *spirit*, is explained in the same way as with the word *water*. The question is of the *nature* or *quality* of the factors co-operating in this supernatural birth. The expression, εἰσελθεῖν (*to enter*), is substituted here for the term ἰδεῖν (*to see*), of ver. 3. The figure of *entering into*, is in more direct correspondence with that of *being born*. It is by *coming forth from* (ἐκ) the two elements indicated, in which the soul is plunged, that it *enters into* (εἰς), the kingdom. The reading of the Sinaitic MS.: "the kingdom *of heaven*," is found also, according to Hippolytus, among the Docetæ of the second century; it is found in a recently discovered fragment of *Irenæus*, in the *Apostolical Constitutions*, and in *Origen* (transl.). These authorities are undoubtedly not sufficient to authorize us to substitute it for the received reading, as *Tischen-*

dorf does. But this variant must be extremely ancient. At all events, it overthrows the objection raised against the reality of the quotation of our passage in Justin, *Apol.* i. 61. (See *Introd.*, p. 152, 153.)

In speaking thus to Nicodemus, Jesus did not think of making salvation depend, either in general or in each particular case, on the material act of baptism. The example of the thief on the cross proves that pardon could be granted without the baptism of water. But, when the offer of this sign has been made and the sinner has rejected it, the position is different; and this was the case with Nicodemus. By the two following sentences, Jesus demonstrates the *necessity* (ver. 6a), and the *possibility* (ver. 6b), of the new birth, by leaving aside the water, to keep closely to the Spirit only.

Ver. 6. " *That which is born of the flesh is flesh, and that which is born of the Spirit is spirit.*" The logical transition from ver. 5 to ver. 6 is this understood idea: "The Kingdom of God can only be of a spiritual nature, as God is Himself." In order to enter it, therefore, there must be, not *flesh*, as every man is by his first birth, but *spirit*, as he becomes by the new birth. The word *flesh* (see pp. 268–269), taken in itself, does not necessarily imply the notion of sin. But it certainly cannot be maintained, with *Weiss*, that the question here is simply of the *insufficiency* of the natural birth, even in the state of innocence, to render man fit for the divine kingdom. Nevertheless, we must not forget that the question here is of humanity in its present constitution, according to which sin is connected with the fact of birth more closely than with any other of the natural life (Ps. li. 7).[1] The expression: *the flesh*, seems to me, therefore, to denote here humanity in its present state, in which the flesh rules the spirit. This state is transmitted from generation to generation in such a way that, without renewal, no man can come out of that fatal circle. And hence the *necessity* of regeneration. How does this transmission of the carnal state accord with individual culpability? The last words of this conversation will throw some light on this difficult question. According to this saying, it is impossible to suppose that Jesus regarded Himself as born in the same way as other men (ver. 7, *you*). The substantive *flesh*, as a predicate (*is flesh*), has a much more forcible meaning than that of the adjective (*carnal*) would be. The state has, in some sort, become nature. Hence, it follows that it is not enough to cleanse or adorn outwardly the natural man; a new nature must be substituted for the old, by means of a regenerating power. We might also see in the second clause a proof of the *necessity* of the new birth; it would be necessary, in that case, to give it the exclusive sense: " *Nothing except* what is born of the Spirit is spir-

---

[1] The opposition which *Weiss* makes to appear between Paul and John as to the use of the word *flesh*, as if the notion of sin were connected more closely to this term by the first than by the second, is only relatively well-founded. This is what the difference amounts to: in Paul, of eighty-eight cases in which the word *flesh* is used, there are thirty-two where the term has a morally indifferent sense; in John (Gospel and Epistle), there is, beyond our present passage, only one case among fifteen (1 John ii. 16), where the notion of sin seems to be attached to the word *flesh*.

itual (and can enjoy, in consequence, the Kingdom of the Spirit)." But the clause has rather a positive and affirmative sense : " That which is born of the Spirit is really spirit, and consequently cannot fail to enjoy the Kingdom of the Spirit." The idea, therefore, is that of the *reality* of the new birth, and consequently, of its *complete possibility.* This is the answer to the question : " How *can* a man ? " Let the Spirit breathe, and the spiritual man exists ! The word *Spirit*, as subject, denotes the Divine Spirit, and, as predicate, the new man. Here, again, the substantive (*spirit*), is used instead of the adjective (*spiritual*), to characterize the new essence. This word *spirit*, in the context here, includes not only the new principle of spiritual life, but also the soul and body, in subjection to the Spirit. The neuter, τὸ γεγεννημένον (*that which is born*), is substituted in the two clauses for the masculine (*he who is born*), for the purpose of designating the *nature* of the product, abstractedly from the individual ; thus, the generality of the law is more clearly brought out. *Hilgenfeld* finds here the Gnostic distinction between two kinds of men, originally opposite. *Meyer* well replies : "There is a distinction, not between two classes of men, but between two different phases in the life of the same individual."

Jesus observes, that the astonishment of Nicodemus, instead of diminishing, goes on increasing. He penetrates the cause of this fact : Nicodemus has not yet given a place in his conception of divine things to the action of the Holy Spirit ; this is the reason why he is always seeking to represent to himself the new birth as a fact apprehensible by the senses. Recognizing him, however, as a serious and sincere man, He wishes to remove from his path this stumbling-stone. Here is not a fact, He says to him, which one can picture to himself ; it can be comprehended only as far as it is experienced.

Vv. 7, 8. " *Marvel not at that which I have said unto thee : ye must be born anew. The wind bloweth where it listeth, and thou hearest the sound thereof, but knowest not whence it cometh nor* [1] *whither it goeth. So is every one that is born of the Spirit.*[2]—By the expression : " Ye must *be born*," Jesus exempts Himself from this general condition. It was necessary for Him to *grow spiritually*, no doubt, (Luke ii. 40, 52) ; but He did not need to be born again. The gift of the Holy Spirit at His baptism was not a regeneration, but the crowning of a perfectly normal previous development under the constant influence of the Spirit.—Jesus directs the attention of Nicodemus to a fact which, like the new birth, escapes the observation of the senses, and which is proved only by its effects, the blowing of the wind.—The Greek word πνεῦμα has, as well as the Hebrew word רוּחַ, the twofold meaning of *wind* and *spirit.* As it appears from the following *so that there is a* comparison, this term is certainly taken here in the sense of *wind.* Tholuck (first edition) supposed that, at that very moment, the wind was heard blowing in the streets of Jerusalem. This supposition gives more of reality to the words : *and thou hearest the sound thereof.*—When he says : *thou*

---

[1] The Mjj. Mnn. and Vss. read και που, and not η που (A. It. Vg.)

[2] א alone reads εκ του υδατος και του πνευματος.

knowest not . . . Jesus does not speak of the explanation of the wind in general. He calls to mind only that, in each particular case, it is impossible to determine exactly the point where this breath is formed and the one where it ends. Perhaps there is an allusion to Eccles. xi. 5: " As thou knowest not the way of the wind . . . " While the development of all natural life connects itself with an organic visible germ and ends in a product which falls under the senses, the wind appears and subsides as if a free irruption of the infinite into the finite. There is, therefore, in nature no more striking example of the action of the Spirit. The operation of the regenerating principle is not bound to any rule appreciable by the senses; it is perceived only by its action on the human soul. But the man in whom this action works does not understand either from whence these new impressions which he feels proceed, nor whither they lead him. He is only conscious of a profound work which is wrought within him and which radically renews him. The adverb of rest ποῦ, with the verb of motion ὑπάγει, is a frequent construction in Greek. It is, as it were, the anticipation of the state of rest which will follow the motion when it has reached its end. The application of the comparison, in the second part of the verse, is not expressed altogether correctly. It would have been necessary to say : so it takes place *in every man* who is born . . . But it is not in the genius of the Greek language to make a comparison and its application correspond symmetrically; comp., in the New Testament, Matt. xiii. 19 f., xxv. 1, etc.—The perfect participle γεγεννημένος denotes the completed fact: The eye has seen nothing, the ear has heard nothing. And yet there is a man born anew and one who has entered into the eternal kingdom? All is done, and nothing has been visible! What a contrast with the noisy and pompous appearance of the divine kingdom according to the Pharisaic programme!

Vv. 9, 10. " *Nicodemus answered and said unto him : How can these things be?* 10. *Jesus answered and said unto him : Thou art the teacher of Israel, and thou knowest not these things !*"—Nicodemus does not deny; but he acknowledges himself a stranger to all experience of the action of the Spirit. It is Jesus' turn to be astonished. He discovers with surprise such spiritual ignorance in one who, at this moment, represents before Him the teaching of the old covenant. Something of bitterness has been found in this reply; it expresses nothing but legitimate astonishment. Ought not such passages as Jer. xxxi. 33; Ezek. xxxvi. 26-28; Ps. cxliii. 10, 11, to have prepared Nicodemus to understand the power of the divine breath? But the Pharisees set their hearts only on the *glory* of the kingdom, rather than on its *holiness*.—The article ὁ before διδάσκαλος, "*the* teacher" has been interpreted in the sense: "the well-known, illustrious teacher" (*Winer, Keil.*) The irony would, thus, be very strong. This article, rather, designates Nicodemus as the representative of the Israelitish teaching office, as the official διδασκαλία personified. Comp. the ὁ ἐσθίων Mk. xiv. 18.

The tenth verse forms the transition to the second part of the conversation. That which externally marks this part is the silence of Nicodemus.

As *Hengstenberg* observes, he seems to say, like Job before Jehovah: "*I am too small; what shall I answer? I have spoken once; but I put my hand upon my mouth.*" On His part, Jesus treats him with a touching kindness and condescension; He has found him humble and docile, and He now opens Himself to him without reserve. Nicodemus came, as we have seen, to interrogate Him respecting His Messianic mission and the mode of the establishment of the divine kingdom so long expected. He did not by any means preoccupy his thoughts with the moral conditions on which he might himself enter into that state of things. A faithful Jew, a pious Pharisee, a holy Sanhedrist, he believed himself saved by the very fact that he was such. Jesus, as a consummate educator, began by reminding him of what he forgot,—the practical question. He taught him that which he did not ask for, but that which it was more important for him to know. And now He reveals to him kindly all that which he desired to know: He declares to him what He *is* (vv. 11–13); what He comes to *do* (vv. 14–17); and what will *result* for humanity from His coming (vv. 18–21).

The first part of the conversation is summed up thus: What will take place? Answer: Nothing, in the sense in which you understand it. The second means: And yet something really takes place, and even a thing most unheard of: The supreme revelator is present; redemption is about to be accomplished; the universal judgment is preparing. Such are the divine facts which are displayed before the eyes of Nicodemus in the second part of the conversation. The conduct of Jesus with this man is thus in complete contrast with that which had been mentioned in ii. 24. He *trusts Himself to him;* for He has recognized his perfect uprightness; comp. ver. 21.

The positive teaching does not, properly, begin until ver. 13. Vv. 11, 12, are prefatory to it.

This passage vv. 11–13 is clearly joined to ver. 2; Nicodemus had spoken in the name of several: "*We know* . . ." (ver. 1); Jesus addresses himself to these absent interlocutors: "*You* receive not . . . ; if I told *you* . . ." (v. 11b and 12a). Nicodemus had called Jesus a teacher "*come from God*" (ver. 1). Jesus shows him that he has spoken more truly than he thought; He reveals Himself to him as the Son of man, descended from heaven to bear witness of heavenly things (ver. 13). This relation between ver. 1 and vv. 11–13 proves that the whole of the beginning of the conversation, vv. 3–10, was called forth accidentally, and is in reality but an episode; and that now only do the revelations, which Nicodemus had come to seek, properly speaking, begin.

Vv. 11–13. In opposition to the doctorate of the letter, devoid of all spiritual intuition, Jesus announces to him the coming of a teaching, which will rest on the immediate knowledge of the truth (ver. 11). In order that Nicodemus may profit by this higher teaching, Jesus invites him to faith (ver. 12). Finally He displays to him, in His own person, the perfect revealer (ver. 13). *Weiss* and *Keil* think that Jesus wishes now to point out the way to attain regeneration, and, consequently, also to understand it. But the setting forth of salvation given in the sequel is far too considerable for it possibly to be caused by so special a relation to that which precedes.

Ver. 11. "*Verily, verily, I say unto thee, We speak that we do know and bear testimony of that we have seen; and ye receive not our testimony.*" The formula *amen, amen* ("*in truth*"), declares, as always, a truth which Jesus is about to draw from the depths of His consciousness, and which, presenting itself as a revelation to the mind of His interlocutor, must triumph over his prejudices or his doubts. The rabbinical teaching worked upon the letter of the Scriptures, but did not place itself in contact with the essential truth which it contained (v. 39). Jesus proclaims with an inward satisfaction the coming of a wholly different teaching of holy things, which will have the character of certainty: "*that which we know;*" because it will spring from immediate intuition: "*that which we have seen.*" The two subordinate verbs, *we speak*, and *we testify*, are in correspondence with the two principal verbs: one *speaks* (declares) that which one *knows;* one *testifies* of what one *has seen*. There is, moreover, evident progress between each verb and the corresponding verb of the following clause: *Knowledge* rises to the clearness of *sight*, and *speaking* assumes the solemn character of *testimony*. The contrast marked here by Jesus between the rabbinical teaching and His own struck even the people; comp. Matt. vii. 28, 29.

But of whom, then, does Jesus speak when He says "*We*"? What is this college of new teachers whom He contrasts with the caste of the scribes and sages of this age which passes away (1 Cor. i. 20)? These plurals "*we speak . . . we testify*" have been explained in a variety of ways. *Beza* and *Tholuck* understand by *we*: "I and the prophets." *Bengel*: "I and the Holy Spirit." *Chrysostom* and *Euthymius*: "I and God." The impossibility of these explanations is manifest. *De Wette* and *Lücke* see in this *we* a plural of majesty; *Meyer* and *Keil*, the plural of category: "teachers such as I." These explanations are less untenable. But this first person of the plural, used for the designation of Himself, is unexampled in the mouth of Jesus. And why return afterwards to the singular (vv. 12, 13): "*I* tell thee . . . if *I* have told you . . . if *I* tell you." Just as the *you* is addressed to other persons besides Nicodemus (comp. ver. 2: *we know*), so the *we* must be applied not only to Jesus, but to a plurality of individuals which He opposes to that of which Nicodemus is the representative. We must, therefore, suppose that Jesus here announces to Nicodemus the existence of a certain number of men who already represent the new mode of teaching. According to *Knapp, Hofmann, Luthardt, Weiss*, etc., Jesus, when speaking thus, thinks only of Himself and *John the Baptist*. He alludes to that which John and He beheld in the scene of the baptism. But the idea of regeneration to which it is claimed that this *seeing* and *knowing* refer is totally foreign to the scene of the baptism, and even in our chapter, vv. 31, 32, the forerunner expressly places himself outside of the limits of the new teaching inaugurated by Jesus. We believe, therefore, with *Lange, Hengstenberg* and *Westcott*, that Jesus is thinking of Himself and *His disciples*, of whom one

386 / Birth of Faith

or several were at that moment with Him; and who were beginning already to become the organs of this new teaching-office inaugurated by Him. In the person of Jesus, then, through His acts and His words, heaven is constantly opened before their eyes (i. 52); already they truly *see* and *know;* their gaze pierces to the essence of things: "*He who hath seen me, hath seen the Father.*" On this foundation, they already testify. What vivacity, what freshness, in the declaration of John and Andrew, i. 42, in that of Philip, i. 47, in the exclamation of Nathanael, i. 50, in the profession of Peter, vi. 68, 69! There are here, no doubt in a weak measure, sight and testimony. Jesus feels Himself no more alone. Hence the feeling of profound joy which breathes in these plurals: *we speak, we know*, etc., and which betrays itself even in the form of His language. Indeed, *Luthardt* has observed, with reason, that we see appearing here that form of parallelism which constitutes the poetic rhythm of the Hebrew language. This feature of style betrays emotion and always marks a moment of peculiar exaltation (v. 37; vi. 35, 55, 56; xii. 44, 45). The language resembles chant. Nicodemus must learn that things are more advanced than he thinks! This passage recalls the one in the Synoptics where Jesus declares the preference which God gives to *little children*, to His humble and ignorant disciples, over the intelligent and learned rabbis of Jerusalem (Matt. xi. 25; Luke xi. 21). While his colleagues and himself are still waiting for the solemn hour of the advent of the kingdom, that kingdom is already present without their knowledge, and others participate in it before them! *Meyer, Astié* and others refer the expression "*we have seen*" to the knowledge possessed by Christ in His pre-existent state. But *Weiss* himself rejects here this explanation which he thinks himself obliged to adopt in other analogous cases (see on ver. 13). It would be altogether incompatible with the interpretation which we have given to the word *we*.

Before unfolding to Nicodemus what He knows and what He sees of the things above, Jesus sadly reverts to the manner in which His testimony has been received by the leaders of the theocracy: "*And ye receive not our testimony.*" Καί, *and*, has the meaning here of *and yet* (i. 10). This copula brings out better than would the particle καίτοι, *yet* (which John never uses), the contradiction between two facts which should be exclusive of each other and which nevertheless move on together (hearing and rejecting the testimony). Jesus was conscious, as every living preacher is, of the inward resistance which His appearance and His teaching met in the hearts of the people and their rulers. A presentiment of this might have been had already at the time of the deputation of the Sanhedrim to John (i. 19 ff.). The conduct of the people and the authorities, with regard to the solemn procedure of Jesus in the temple (ii. 12 ff.), had given Him the measure of that which awaited Him. The words of Nicodemus himself (iii. 2), in which he had called Him teacher in consideration of His miracles, not of His teaching itself (ver. 2), showed how little His word had found access to hearts. The want of spiritual receptivity, which the misunderstanding of Nicodemus had just betrayed, will, as Jesus perceives, render very difficult the acceptance of the heavenly revelations which he brings to the world:

Ver. 12. "*If I have told you earthly things and ye believe*[1] *not, how shall ye believe if I tell you*[2] *of heavenly things?*" When a teacher says to his pupil: "If you do not understand me on this point, how will you understand me on that?" we must suppose that the disciple expects to be instructed respecting this latter point. We must, therefore, conclude from this word of Jesus, that *the heavenly things* are to Jesus' view those which preoccupy Nicodemus, and with reference to which he had come to interrogate Him: the person of the Messiah, the nature of His kingdom, the way in which He will lay the foundation of, and complete this great work, both in Israel and in the Gentile world. And, indeed, these are precisely the questions which Jesus answers in the second part of the conversation, which is to follow. The contrast between the past, "if I *have told* you" and the present "if I *tell* you" proves that Jesus had not yet set forth publicly what He calls the *heavenly things*. This conversation was the first communication of Jesus concerning the nature of the Messianic kingdom and the mode of salvation, outside of the innermost circle of His own friends. The public teaching of Jesus had, therefore, up to that time related to what He calls *the earthly things*. This expression cannot denote things which appertain to earthly interests: for Jesus did not occupy Himself with these things before this, any more than He did afterwards. If by the heavenly things we must of course understand the designs of God, inaccessible to the human mind, for the establishment of His kingdom, we must include in the domain of *earthly things* all that which appertains to the *moral* nature of man; outside of the region of redemption and regeneration; thus, everything which Jesus comes to declare respecting the carnal state of the natural man and the necessity of a radical transformation. Jesus is thinking, no doubt, of the contents of His first preachings, analogous to those of John the Baptist, and which Mark sums up (i. 15) in these words: "*Repent ye, and believe the Gospel: for the kingdom of heaven is at hand;*" those preachings of which we possess the most remarkable example in the Sermon on the Mount. What a difference as compared with the revelations which Jesus makes to Nicodemus! The conversation with him is the first step in a region infinitely elevated above that elementary preaching. We understand now why it has been preserved to us by John; it had been of marked importance in the development of his own faith.

According to *Lücke* and *Reuss* the earthly things are the things easy to be understood, and the heavenly "the most elevated ideas of the Gospel, less accessible to an intelligence which was not yet enlightened by it." This sense is true from the standpoint of consequences, but not from that of explanation strictly so-called. There is no example to prove that heavenly can signify difficult, and earthly, easy. *Ewald* makes of εἶπον a

---

[1] E H 10 Mnn.: ουκ επιστευσατε (*ye did not believe*), instead of ου πιστευετε (*ye do not believe*).

[2] The second υμιν is wanting in E H 9 Mnn. It^{aliq}.

third person plural: "*If they* (the prophets) have spoken to you of earthly things and you *have not believed* (the reading: ἐπιστεύσατε)." But a subject of this sort could not be understood, and an ἐγώ could not be omitted in the following clause (*Meyer, Bäumlein*). In this remarkable saying, Jesus contrasts the facts which pertain to the domain of the human consciousness, and which man can verify by observation of himself, with the divine decrees which cannot be known except by means of a revelation. This is the reasoning: "If, when I have declared to you the things whose reality you can, by consulting your own consciousness, discover, you have not believed, how will you believe when I shall reveal to you the secrets of heaven, which must be received solely on the foundation of a word?" There, the testimony of the inner sense facilitates faith; here, on the contrary, everything rests upon confidence in the testimony of the revealer. This testimony being rejected, the ladder, on which man may raise himself to the knowledge of heavenly things, is broken, and the access to the divine secrets remain, closed.

This saying of Jesus should teach apologetics to place the supporting point of faith in the declarations of the Gospel which are most immediately connected with the facts of consciousness and the moral needs of the soul. Its truth being once recognized in this domain where it can be verified by every one, it is already half-demonstrated in relation to those declarations which are connected with the purely divine domain. It will be completely so, as soon as it shall be established that these two parts, divine and human, of the Gospel, are adapted to one another as the two parts of one whole; that the moral needs of man which are proved by the one find their full satisfaction in the divine plans revealed in the other. The moral truth of the Gospel is the first guarantee of its religious truth.

Ver. 13. "*And no one hath ascended up to heaven except he who descended from heaven, the Son of man who is in heaven.*"[1] The question, "*how will you believe?*" (ver. 12) implied, in the thought of Him who proposed it, the necessity of faith. Ver. 13 justifies this necessity. The intermediate idea is the following: "Indeed, without faith in my testimony, there is no access for you to those heavenly things which thou desirest to know." Καί: *and yet. Olshausen, de Wette, Lücke, Luthardt* and *Meyer* find in ver. 13 the proof, not of the necessity of *faith* in the revelation contained in the teaching of Jesus, but of that in *revelation* in general. But this thesis is too purely theoretical to find a place in such a conversation. *Hengstenberg* thinks that Jesus here wishes to reveal *His divinity* as the first among the heavenly things which Nicodemus has need to know. *Meyer* rightly answers that the negative form of the proposition is inconsistent with this intention. Besides, Jesus would have employed, in that case, the expression *Son of God*, rather than *Son of man*. The general meaning of this saying is as follows: "You do not believe my word . . . And yet no one has ascended to heaven so as to behold the heavenly things and make them known to you, except He who has descended from it to

---

[1] ℵ B L T^b Orig. (once) Euseb. omit the words ο ων εν τω ουρανω (*who is in heaven*).

live with you as a man, and who, even while living here below, abides there also; so that He alone knows them *de visu*, and so that, consequently, to believe in His teaching is for you the only means of knowing them." But how can Jesus say of Himself that He ascended to heaven? Did He speak of His ascension by way of anticipation (*Augustine, Calvin, Bengel, Hengstenberg*)? But His future ascension would not justify the necessity of faith in His earthly teaching. *Lücke, Olshausen, Beyschlag*, after the example of *Erasmus, Beza*, etc., think that heaven is here only the symbol of perfect communion with God—a communion to which Jesus had morally risen, and by virtue of which He alone possessed the adequate knowledge of God and of the things above. This sense would be admissible if the word *ascended* had not as its antithesis the term *descended*, which refers to a positive fact, that of the incarnation; the corresponding term *ascend* must, therefore, refer to a fact no less positive, or rather—since the verb is in the perfect and not the aorist—to a *state* resulting from a fact quite as positive. *Meyer* and *Weiss*, following *Jansen*, think that the idea of *ascending* may be regarded as applying only to men in general and that an abstraction from it can be made with reference to Jesus. Ascending is here only as if the indispensable condition *for all other men* of dwelling in heaven: "No one . . . except he who (without having ascended thither) has descended from it, he who is there essentially (*Meyer*), or who *was* there previously (*Weiss*)." This is an attempt to escape the difficulty of the εἰ μή, *except ;* the fact of *being* in heaven is reserved for Jesus, while suppressing, so far as He is concerned, that of *ascending;* comp. the use of εἰ μή in Matt. xii. 4; Luke iv. 26, 27; Gal. i. 19. However, the case is not altogether the same in those passages. We might try to take the εἰ μή in the sense of *but*, like the Hebrew *ki im;* but in that case John must have written κατέβη instead of ὁ καταβάς: "No one has ascended, *but* the Son of man *descended*." The Socinians, perfectly understanding the difficulty, have had recourse to the hypothesis of a carrying away of Jesus to heaven, which was granted to Him at some time or other of His life before His public ministry. As for ourselves, we have no occasion to have recourse to such an hypothesis; we know a positive fact which is sufficient to explain the *has ascended* when we apply it to Jesus Himself; it is that which occurred at His baptism. Heaven was then opened to Him; He penetrated it deeply by His gaze; He read the heart of God, and knew at that moment everything which He was to reveal to men of the divine plan, the *heavenly things*. In proportion as the consciousness of His eternal relation as Son to the Father was given to Him, there necessarily resulted from it the knowledge of the love of God towards mankind. Comp. Matt. xi. 27.—*Heaven* is a state, before being a place. As *Gess* says: "To be in the Father is to be in heaven." Subsidiarily, no doubt, the word *heaven* takes also a local sense; for this spiritual state of things is realized most perfectly in whatever sphere of the universe is resplendent with all the glory of the manifestation of God. The moral sense of the word *heaven* prevails in the first and third clauses; the local sense must be added to it in the second. "No one has ascended

390 / Birth of Faith

. . . " signifies thus: "No one has *entered into* communion with God and possesses thereby an intuitive knowledge of divine things, in order to reveal them to others, except He to whom heaven was opened and who dwells there at this very moment."

And by virtue of what was Jesus, and Jesus alone, admitted to such a privilege! Because heaven is His original home. He alone has ascended thither, because He only descended thence. The term *descended* implies in His case the consciousness of having personally lived in heaven (*Gess*). This word denotes, therefore, more than a divine mission; it implies the abasement of the incarnation, and consequently involves the notion of pre-existence. It is an evident advance upon Nicodemus' profession of faith (ver. 2). The filial intimacy to which Jesus is exalted rests on His essential Sonship, previous to His earthly life. If the word *descended* implies pre-existence, the term, *Son of man*, brings out the *human* side in this heavenly revealer. The love of mankind impelled Him to become one of us, in order that He might speak to us as a man, and might instruct us in heavenly things in a manner intelligible to us. The recollection of Prov. xxx. 4 seems not to be foreign to the expression which Jesus makes use of: "Do I know the knowledge of the holy ones? Who ascendeth to heaven and descendeth from it?"—The last words: *who is in heaven* are preserved in the text by *Tischendorf* (8th ed.) and by *Meyer*, notwithstanding the Alexandrian authorities; *Westcott* rightly says: "They have against them the ancient MSS., and for them the ancient versions." But according to this critic, the testimony of the versions is in this case remarkably weakened by the contrary testimony of the Sinaitic MS. which so often accords with them. The rejection may have been the result of an accidental omission or of the difficulty of reconciling this addition with the idea of the preceding clause;—that of having *descended*. On the other hand, we can understand how these words may have been interpolated, in order to resolve the apparent contradiction between the idea of *being* in heaven in order to have ascended thither, and that of having *descended*. At all events, the idea which these words express, that of the actual presence of Christ in heaven, is already very positively contained in the *perfect ἀναβέβηκεν, has ascended*. This tense indeed does not signify: has accomplished at a given moment the act of ascending (this would be the sense of the aorist), but He is there, He lives there, as having ascended thither. Thus the preceding antithesis is resolved. Jesus lives in heaven, as a being who has re-ascended thither after having descended in order to become Son of man (xvi. 28). The Lord led two lives parallel to each other, an earthly life and a heavenly life. He lived in His Father, and, while living thus with the Father, He gave Himself unceasingly to men in His human life. The teaching *in parables*, in which the heavenly things take on His lips an earthly dress, is the true language answering to that existence which is formed of two simultaneous lives, the one penetrating the other.

Some interpreters (*Luthardt, Weiss*), understand the participle (ὁ ὤν), in the sense of the imperfect *who was* (before the incarnation); this word, according to them, expresses the idea of pre-existence as a condition of the καταβαίνειν, of the act of *descending*. But this participle (ὁ ὤν), if it is authentic, is rather in relation with the principal verb: *has ascended*, than with the participle (ὁ καταβάς). "He lives in heaven, having re-ascended thither, inasmuch as He has descended thence." To express, without ambiguity, the idea of the imperfect, the periphrasis (ὃς ἦν) would have been necessary; *Lücke* sees in ὁ ὤν a perpetual present. This idea may be applied to i. 18, where the question is of the Son of God, but not to our passage, where the subject is the *Son of man*.

Meyer, *Weiss* and *Keil* maintain that Jesus explains here the knowledge which He has of divine things by His pre-existence. Such an idea can be found in these words only on condition of denying any application of the idea of *ascending* to Jesus, a thing which is impossible. The higher knowledge of Jesus is, much rather, presented here as the result of an initiation (*has ascended*), which took place for Him during the course of His human existence, and through which He received at a certain time the immediate and constant, though truly human, intuition of divine things. And, in fact, this is the impression which every word of Jesus produces: that of a man who perceives the divine directly, but who perceives it with a human consciousness like our own. It is impossible for me to understand how *Weiss* can, on the one hand, make this higher knowledge proceed from a recollection of His anterior existence, and maintain, on the other, that such knowledge "does not go beyond the limits of a truly human consciousness." The Son of man, living in heaven, so as to have re-ascended thither after having descended, is the sole revealer of divine things: this is the first of the ἐπουράνια, the heavenly secrets, which Jesus communicates to Nicodemus. The second is the salvation of men through the lifting up of this same Son of man, not on a throne, but on a cross, the supreme wonder of divine love to the world: vv. 14–16. This is the *essential contents* of the revelation which Jesus announced to him in ver. 13.

Vv. 14, 15. "*And as Moses lifted up the serpent in the wilderness, so must the Son of man be lifted up, 15, that whosoever believeth on him,[1] may have eternal life.*" The commentators give more or less forced explanations of καί (*and*). *Lücke*: "I *can* reveal (vv. 11–13), and I *must* do so" (vv. 14–16). *Olshausen*: "I give not only my *word*, but my *person*." *De Wette*: "Jesus passes from the theoretical to the practical." *Meyer* and *Luthardt*: "He has spoken of the *necessity* of faith; He speaks now of its *sweetness*." *Weiss*: "There is here a new motive to believe. The elevation of Jesus will give salvation only by means of *faith*." All this is too artificial. From our point of view, the connection is more simple: the καί *and*, and also, adds a second divine mystery to the first, the decree of *redemption* to that of *revelation*.

The central idea of this verse is that of the lifting up of the Messiah.

---

[1] Instead of εἰς αυτον, which T. R. reads with 14 Mjj. (among them ℵ), nearly all the Mnn.: It.plur.; Vg; Chrys.; επ' αυτον is read in A, επ' αυτω in L, εν αυτω in B Tᵇ. ℵ B L Tᵇ; some Mnn.; Syrᶜᵘʳ.; Itᵃˡⁱᑫ., omit the words μη απολητας αλλ'.

392 / Birth of Faith

Three principal explanations have been given of the word ὑψωθῆναι (*to be lifted up*). It has been applied either to the spiritual glory which the moral perfection which He will display in His sufferings will procure for Jesus in the hearts of men (*Paulus*), or to His elevation to heavenly glory which will take place as following upon His death (*Bleek*), or finally, to the very fact of His suspension on the cross; this last interpretation is the one most generally received. And indeed, in the one or the other of the first meanings, Jesus would rather have used the term δοξασθῆναι (*to be glorified*). For the third, the following points decide the case: 1. The comparison with the serpent raised to the top of the pole, which certainly had nothing glorious in it; 2. The naturally material sense of the word ὑψωθῆναι (*to be lifted up*); finally, 3. The relation of this word to the corresponding Aramaic term *zekaph*, which is applied to the suspension of malefactors. Only we must take account of the allusion which Jesus, in using this term (*being lifted up*), certainly made to the ideas of Nicodemus, according to which the Messiah was to ascend the throne of Solomon and rule the world. And the voluntary and ironical amphibology of this expression will be understood as in connection with the Messianic expectation of the Pharisees. To perceive this shade, we must strongly emphasize the οὕτως: (*it is thus*)—and not as you picture it to yourselves—that the *lifting up* of the Son of man will take place. This word (*will be lifted up*), intimates indeed that by this strange elevation the Son of man will attain not only to the throne of David, but to that of God. Such is the full meaning of the word: *to be lifted up*. We must not, as *Meyer* does, refuse to follow the thought of Jesus in this rapid evolution, which instantaneously brings together the greatest contrasts, if we would understand all the depth and all the richness of His words. We find here again the same enigmatical character as in ii. 19. The fact related in Num. xxi. 9, is one of the most astonishing in sacred history. Three peculiarities distinguish this mode of deliverance from all the other analogous miracles: 1. It is *the plague itself*, which, represented as overcome, becomes, by its ignominious exposure, the means of its own defeat; 2. This exposure takes place, not in a *real* serpent—the suspension in that case would have proclaimed only the defeat of the individual exposed—but in a typical copy, which represents the entire species; 3. This expedient becomes efficacious through the intervention of a moral act, the look of faith on the part of each injured person. If this is the type of salvation, it follows from this fact that this salvation will be wrought in the following way: 1. Sin will be exposed publicly as vanquished, and for the future powerless; 2. It will not be in the person of a real sinner—which would proclaim only the particular defeat of *that* sinner—but in the person of a holy man, capable of representing, as a living image, the condemnation and defeat of sin, *as such ;* 3. This exhibition of sin as one who is vanquished, will save each sinner only by means of an act on his part, the look of faith upon his spiritual enemy condemned and vanquished. Here, Jesus declares, is the salvation on which the establishment of the Kingdom will be founded; here is the second heavenly decree revealed to men. What a reversal of the Messianic programme of

Nicodemus! But, at the same time, what appropriateness in the choice of this Scriptural type, designed to rectify the ideas of the old doctor in Israel!

"*Must*," says Jesus; and first, for the fulfillment of the prophecies; then, for that of the divine decree, of which the prophecies were only an emanation (*Hengstenberg*); let us add, finally; and for the satisfaction of certain moral necessities, known to God only. The designation, *Son of man*, is here, as at ver. 13, chosen with a marked design. It is on the complete homogeneousness of His nature with ours, that the mysterious substitution rests, which is proclaimed in this verse, precisely as it was on this same community of nature that the act of revelation rested, which was announced in the preceding verse.

Ver. 15 finishes the application of the type. To the look of the dying Israelite the faith of the sinner in the crucified one corresponds; to the life restored to the wounded one, the salvation granted to the believer.— Πᾶς, *whosoever* extends to the whole of humanity the application of the Israelitish type, while emphatically individualizing the act of faith (ὁ).— The reading of the T. R. εἰς αὐτόν, *to* or *on Him*, is the one which best suits the context (the look turned *towards* . . .); faith looks *to* its object. If we consider how little the Alexandrian authorities agree among themselves, the received reading will be acknowledged as, on the whole, the best supported one. *Tischendorf* (8th ed.) reads ἐν αὐτῷ, after the Vatican MS.; in that case, this limiting phrase may be connected with ἔχῃ, as *Weiss* and *Keil* connect it, rather than with πιστεύων. But, in this context, the connection with πιστεύων remains, nevertheless, the most natural relation. The Alexandrian authorities reject the words μὴ ἀπόληται ἀλλά *should not perish, but;* they may certainly have been introduced here from ver. 16. Even in that case we are struck with the rhythmic relation between the last words of these two verses; it is the sign of the stirring of feeling and elevation of thought (Introd., p. 137). We comprehend, indeed, what an impression this first revelation of His future suffering of punishment must have produced on Jesus Himself; comp. xii. 27. As for Nicodemus, we also account for what he experienced when on the Holy Friday he saw Jesus suspended on the cross. That spectacle, instead of being for him, as for others, a stumbling-block, a ground of unbelief and despair, causes his latent faith to break forth (xix. 39). This fact is the answer to *de Wette's* question, who asks if this anticipatory revelation of the death of the Messiah was not contrary to the pedagogic wisdom of Jesus. *Weiss*, who is not willing to admit that Jesus so early foresaw and predicted His death, thinks that Jesus did not express Himself in so precise a way, but that he spoke vaguely of some lifting up which would be accorded to Him during His earthly life, to the end that He might be recognized as Messiah by the Jews. But, in that case, it is necessary to suppose: 1. That John positively falsified the account of the words of Jesus; 2. That Jesus spoke of something which was never realized, for we know not what that supposed lifting-up can be; 3. There no longer remains, in this case, any relation between the prophecy of Jesus and the matter of the brazen serpent. From the cross Jesus ascends to God, from whose love this decree emanates (δεῖ *must*, ver. 14).

Ver. 16. "*For God so loved the world that he gave his only-begotten Son, that whosoever believeth on Him should not perish, but should have eternal life.*"—Here is the ἐπουράνιον, the heavenly mystery, *par excellence;* Jesus displays the source of the redemptive work, which He has just described; it is the love of God itself. The *world*, that fallen humanity of which God in the Old Testament had left the largest part outside of His theocratic government and revelation, and which the Pharisees devoted to wrath and judgment, Jesus presents to Nicodemus as the object of the most boundless love: "*God so loved the world . . .*" The gift which God makes to it is *the Son*,—not only the Son of man, as He was called vv. 13, 14 in relation to His humanity, but His *only-begotten Son*. The intention, in fact, is no longer to make prominent the homogeneity of nature between this Redeemer and those whom He is to instruct and save, but the boundlessness of the love of the Father; now this love appears from what this messenger is for the Father Himself. It has been claimed that this term, only-begotten Son, was ascribed to Jesus by the evangelist. For what reason? Because, both in his Prologue (i. 14–18), and in his Epistle (iv. 9) he himself makes use of it. But this term is, in the LXX., the translation of the Hebrew יחיד (Ps. xxv. 16; xxxv. 17; Prov. iv. 3). Why should not Jesus have employed this word if He was, as we cannot doubt (Matt. xi. 27; xxi. 37), conscious of His unique relation to God? And how should the evangelist have been able to render it in Greek otherwise than the LXX. had rendered it? Man had once offered to God his only son; could God, in a matter of love, remain behind His creature?—The choice of the verb is equally significant; it is the word for *giving*, and not only for sending; to give, to surrender, and that, if necessary, even to the last limits of sacrifice.—The last clause produces the effect of a musical refrain (comp. ver. 14). It is the homage rendered by the Son to the love of the Father from which everything proceeds. The universality of salvation (*whosoever*), the easiness of the means (*believeth*), the greatness of the evil prevented (*should not perish*), the boundlessness, in excellence and in duration, of the good bestowed (*eternal life*): all these heavenly ideas, new to Nicodemus, are crowded into this sentence, which closes the exposition of the true Messianic salvation.—According to this passage, redemption is not extorted from the divine love; it is its thought, it is its work. It is the same with Paul: "*All things are of God, who reconciled us unto Himself by Jesus Christ*" (2 Cor. v. 18). This spontaneous love of the Father for the sinful world is not incompatible with the wrath and the threatenings of judgment; for here is not the love of communion, which unites the pardoned sinner to God; but a love of compassion, like that which we feel towards the unfortunate or enemies. The intensity of this love results from the very greatness of the unhappiness which awaits him who is its object. Thus are united in this very expression the two apparently incompatible ideas which are contained in the words: *so loved* and *may not perish*. Some theologians, beginning with *Erasmus* (*Neander, Tholuck, Olshausen, Bäum-*

lein) have supposed that the conversation of Jesus and Nicodemus closes with ver. 15, and that, from ver. 16, it is the evangelist who speaks, commenting with his own reflections on the words of his Master. This opinion finds its support in the past tenses, *loved* and *were*, ver. 19, which seem to designate a more advanced period than that at which Jesus conversed with Nicodemus; in the expression μονογενής, *only-begotten Son*, which belongs to John's language; finally, in the fact that, from this point, the dialogue-form wholly ceases. The *for* of ver. 16, is, on this view, designed to introduce John's explanations; and the repetition in the same verse of the words of ver. 15 are, as it were, the affirmation of the disciple answering to the Master's declaration.—But, on the other hand, the *for* of ver. 16 is not a sufficient indication of the passing from the teaching of Jesus to the commentary of the disciple. The author must have marked much more distinctly such an important transition. Then, how can we imagine that the emotion which bears on the discourse from ver. 13 is already exhausted in ver 15? The increasing exaltation with which Jesus successively presents to Nicodemus the wonders of divine love, the incarnation (ver. 13) and redemption (vv. 14, 15), cannot end thus abruptly; the thought can rest only when it has once reached the highest principle from which these unheard of gifts flow, the infinite love of the Father. To give glory to God, is the goal to which the heart of Jesus always tends. Finally, who could believe that He would have dryly sent Nicodemus away after the words of ver. 15, without having given him a glimpse of the effects of the salvation announced, and without having addressed to him for himself a word of encouragement? Would this be the affectionate sympathy of a truly human heart? The part of Jesus, in that case, would be reduced to that of a cold catechist. The difficulties which have given occasion to this opinion do not seem to us very serious. The past tenses of ver. 19 are justified in the mouth of Jesus, like the reproach of ver. 11: " *You receive not our testimony*," by the attitude, which the population and authorities of the capital had already taken (ii. 19). We have justified by the context the term *only-begotten Son*, and have seen that it would hardly be natural to refuse it to Jesus Himself. The terms *new birth, birth of water* and *birth of the Spirit* (vv. 3, 5) are also not found in the rest of Jesus' discourses; must we, for this reason, doubt that they are His? In a kind of discoursing so original as His, does not the matter, at each moment, create an original form? When we remember that the ἅπαξ λεγόμενα (words employed only once) are counted by hundreds in the Epistles of St. Paul (two hundred and thirty in the first epistle to the Corinthians, one hundred and forty-three in the epistles to the Colossians and Ephesians taken together, one hundred and eighteen in the Ep. to the Hebrews), how can we conclude from the fact that a term is found only once in the discourses of Jesus which have been preserved to us, that it does not really belong to His language? Finally, the cessation of the dialogue-form results simply from the increasing surprise and humble docility with which Nicodemus, from this point onwards, receives the revelation of the heavenly things. In reality, notwithstanding this silence, the dialogue none the less continues.

For, in what follows, as in what precedes, Jesus does not express an idea, does not pronounce a word, which is not in direct relation to the thoughts and needs of His interlocutor, and that as far as ver. 21, where we find, at last, the word of encouragement which naturally closes the conversation, and softens the painful impression which must have been left in the heart of the old man by the abrupt and severe admonition with which it had begun.—*De Wette* and *Lücke*, while maintaining that the author makes Jesus speak even to the end, nevertheless think that, without himself being conscious of it, he mingled more and more his own reflections with the words of his Master. Nearly the same is also the opinion of *Weiss*, who thinks that, in general, John has never given an account of the discourses of Jesus except by developing them in his own style. If, in what follows, we find any expression wanting in appropriateness, any thought unconnected with the given situation, it will indeed be necessary to accept such a judgment. If the contrary is the fact, we shall have the right to exclude this last supposition also.

One idea is inseparable from that of redemption,—it is that of *judgment*. Every Pharisee divided man into the saved and the judged, that is to say, into circumcised and uncircumcised, into Jews and Gentiles. Jesus, who has just revealed the redeeming love towards the whole world, unfolds now to Nicodemus the nature of the true judgment. And this revelation also is a complete transformation of the received opinion. It will not be between Jews and Gentiles, it will be between *believers* and *unbelievers*, whatever may be their nationality, that the line of demarcation will pass.

Ver. 17. "*For God sent not his*[1] *Son into the world to judge the world, but that the world might be saved through him.*" *For:* the purpose of the mission of the Son, as it is indicated in this verse, proves that this mission is indeed a work of love (ver. 16). The word, *world*, is repeated three times with emphasis. Nicodemus must hear in such a way as no more to forget that the divine benevolence embraces all humanity. The universalism of Paul, in its germ, is in these verses 16, 17. The first clause, by its negative form, is intended to exclude the Jewish idea, according to which the immediate purpose of the coming of the Messiah was to execute the judgment on the Gentile nations. Our versions translate, κρίνειν, in general, with the meaning *condemn; Meyer* himself still defends this meaning. It is explained thus: "Jesus did not come to execute a judgment *of condemnation* on the sinful world." But why should not Jesus have said κατακρίνειν, to condemn, if He had this thought? What He means to say is, that His coming into the world has for its purpose, not an act of judgment, but a work of salvation. *Reuss* concludes from this saying that "the idea of a future and universal judgment is repudiated" in our Gospel. But the future judgment is clearly taught in vv. 27, 28. The idea which Jesus sets aside in this saying, is only that the present coming of the Messiah has for its purpose a great external judicial

---

[1] א B L T^b and some Mnn. omit αυτου.

act, like that which the Pharisee Nicodemus was certainly expecting. If a judgment is to take place as a personal act of the Messiah, it does not appertain to this coming. However, although the *purpose* of His coming is to save, not to judge, a judgment, but an altogether different one from that of which the Jews were thinking, was about to be effected because of that coming: a judgment of a moral nature, in which it is not Jesus who will pronounce the sentence, but every man will himself decide his own salvation or perdition.

Ver. 18. "*He that believeth on him is not judged; but*[1] *he that believeth not is judged already, because he hath not believed on the name of the only-begotten Son of God.*" The idea of this verse is as follows: "I do not judge any one, for the reason that he who believes is not judged, and he who does not believe has already judged himself." As has been well said: "Here is justification by faith, and condemnation by unbelief."[2] Jesus does not judge the believer, because he who accepts the salvation which He brings is no longer a subject of judgment. *Meyer, Hengstenberg*, etc., and our translators [A. V.] render the word κρίνειν here also by *condemn. Weiss, Keil, Westcott* acknowledge that this sense is arbitrary. The passage in v. 24 shows that it is contrary to the true thought of Jesus. *To judge* is, after a detailed investigation of the acts, to pronounce on their author a judicial sentence deciding as to his innocence or his guilt. Now the Lord declares that the believer, being already introduced into eternal life, will not be subjected to an investigation of this kind. He will appear before the tribunal, indeed, according to Rom. xiv. 10; 2 Cor. v. 10, but to be recognized as saved and to receive his place in the kingdom (Matt. xxv.). If faith withdraws man from the judgment, there is in this nothing arbitrary. This follows precisely from the fact that, through the interior judgment of repentance which precedes and follows faith, the believer is introduced into the sphere of Christian sanctification which is a continual judgment of oneself, and consequently the free anticipation of the judgment (1 Cor. xi. 31). The present οὐ κρίνεται, *is not judged*, is that of the idea. Jesus does not judge the unbeliever, because he who refuses to believe finds his judgment in this very refusal. The word ἤδη, *already*, and the substitution of the perfect (κέκριται) for the present (κρίνεται) show clearly that Jesus is thinking here of a judgment of a spiritual nature, which is exercised here below on him who rejects the salvation offered in Christ. Such a man has pronounced on himself, by his unbelief, and without any need on the part of Jesus of intervening judicially, his own sentence. It is self-evident that this sentence is a sentence of condemnation. But the word does not say this. The meaning is: The one is not to be judged; the other is judged already; consequently, the Son does not have to intervene personally in order to judge. The use here of the subjective negative (the first μή) belongs, according to *Bäumlein*, to the decline of the language. According to *Meyer*, this form has, on the contrary, its regular sense: *in not* believing," or "*because* he does not believe." The title of *only-begotten*

---

[1] א B It^{aliq}. Orig.: ο μη, for ο δε μη in all the rest.   [2] H. Jacottet.

Son sets forth the guilt of those who reject such a being and the work which He accomplishes. The more glorious the Saviour is, the more grave a matter it is to turn away from Him. The more holy He is, divine in His entire manifestation, the more does unbelief towards Him bear witness of a profane sentiment. *His name:* the revelation which He gives us of His essence (see i. 12). The perfect μὴ πεπίστευκεν, *has not believed,* denotes not the *act* of not believing, but the *state* which results from it. "Because he is not in the favorable position of a man who has given his confidence to such a being." The μή is used here as among the later Greeks (e. g. Lucian) to denote the cause *in the thought* of the speaker. The moral separation between men, described in ver. 18, constitutes the judgment in its essence; this is the idea developed in vv. 19-21. By the position which men take with regard to Jesus, they class themselves as reproved (vv. 19, 20) or saved (ver. 21). Thus far, Jesus has proved that He does not judge, but He does this by contrasting with the outward judgment, which was expected, a moral judgment of which no one dreamed. This judgment it is which He now explains.

Ver. 19. "*Now this is the judgment, that the light is come into the world, and men loved the darkness rather than the light; for their works were evil.*" In rejecting Jesus, man judges himself. The strictest inquiry into his whole life would not *prove* his disposition, as opposed to what is good, better than does his unbelief. The final judicial act will have nothing more to do than to ratify this sentence which he pronounces on himself (vv. 28, 29). In order to make the matter understood, the Lord here calls Himself *the light,* that is to say, the manifested good, the divine holiness realized before the human conscience. It follows from this, that the attitude which the man takes in relation to Him, reveals infallibly his inmost moral tendency. To the view of Jesus, the experiment has been already made for the world which surrounds Him: "*Men loved rather . . .*" There is in every servant of God, in proportion to his holiness, a spiritual tact which makes him discern immediately the moral sympathy or antipathy which his person and his message excite. The visit of Jesus to Jerusalem had been for Him a sufficient revelation of the moral state of the people and their rulers. They are *the men* of whom He speaks in this verse, but with the distinct feeling that they are in this point the representatives of fallen humanity. The expression *loved rather* is not designed, as *Lücke* thinks, to extenuate the guilt of unbelievers, by intimating that there is still in them an attraction, but a weaker one, towards the truth. As has been well said, the word μᾶλλον does not mean *magis, more,* but *potius, rather.* This word, therefore, aggravates the responsibility of the Jews, by bringing out the free preference with which, though placed in presence of the light, they have chosen the darkness (comp. ver. 11). What is, indeed, the ground of this guilty preference? It is that *their works are evil.* They are determined to persevere in the evil which they have hitherto committed; this is the reason why they flee from the light which condemns it. By displaying the true nature of their works, the light would force them to renounce them. The term τὸ σκότος, *the darkness,* includes with the love of evil the inward falsehood by which a man seeks to exculpate himself. The aorist ἠγάπησαν, *loved*, designates the preference as an act which has just been consummated recently, while the imperfect ἦν, *were*, presents the life of the world in evil as a fact existing long before the appearance of the light. The word ἔργα, *works*, denotes the whole moral activity, tendency and acts. In the following verse, Jesus explains, by means of a comparison, the psychological relation between immorality, gross or subtle, and unbelief.

Ver. 20. "*For, every one who practiseth evil hateth the light and doth not come to the light,*[1] *that his works may not be condemned.*" Night was reigning at the moment when Jesus was speaking thus. How many evil-doers were taking advantage of the darkness, to pursue their criminal designs! And it was not accidental that they had chosen this hour. Such is the image of that which takes place in the moral world. The appearance of Jesus is for the world like the rising of the sun; it manifests the true character of human actions; whence it follows, that when any one does evil *and wishes to persevere in it*, he turns his back upon Jesus and His holiness. If his conscience came to be enlightened by this brightness, it would oblige him to renounce that which he wishes to keep. He denies therefore, and this negation is for him the night in which he can continue to sin: such is the genesis of unbelief. The expression ὁ φαῦλα πράσσων, *he who does evil*, denotes not only the tendency to which the man has hitherto surrendered himself, but also that in which he desires to persevere. This is what the *present* participle πράσσων (instead of the past πράξας) expresses. For the word πονηρά (*perverse things*) is substituted the word φαῦλα (*things of nought*) of ver. 19; the latter is taken from the estimate of Jesus himself, while the former referred to the intrinsic nature of the acts, to their fundamental depravity. We must also notice a difference between the two verbs πράττειν and ποιεῖν: the first indicates simply labor—the question is of works of nought—the second implies effective realization, in the good the product remains. But we need not believe that the term *practise evil* refers only to what we call immoral conduct. Jesus is certainly thinking, also, of a life externally honorable, but destitute of all serious moral reality, like that of the greater part of the rulers in Israel, and particularly of the Pharisees: the exaltation of the *I* and the pursuit of human glory, as well as gross immorality, belong to the φαῦλα πράττειν, "*practise things of nought*" in the sense in which Jesus understands it.— Μισεῖ, *he hates*, expresses the instinctive, immediate antipathy; οὐκ ἔρχεται, *he comes not*, denotes the deliberate resolution. The verb ἐλέγχειν (perhaps from πρὸς ἕλην κρίνειν, to hold to the light in order to judge) signifies: to bring to light the erroneous or evil nature of an idea or a deed.

The reason of unbelief, therefore, is not intellectual, but moral. The proof which Jesus gives, in ver. 20, of this so grave fact is perfectly lucid. All that Pascal has written most profoundly on the relation between the

---

[1] ℵ alone omits και ουκ ερχεται εις το φως (*and he does not come to the light*) evidently by reason of a confounding of the two φως on the part of the copyist.

will and the understanding, the heart and the belief, is already in advance contained in this verse and the one which follows. But that which is true of unbelief is equally true of faith. It also strikes its roots into the moral life; here is the other side of the judgment:

Ver. 21. "*But he that doeth the truth cometh to the light, that his works may be made manifest*[1] *because they are wrought in God.*" Sincere love of moral good predisposes to faith; for Jesus is the good personified. There are in humanity, even before the appearance of Christ, men who, although like others affected by inborn evil, react against their evil inclinations, and pursue with a noble ardor the realization of the moral ideal which shines before them. Jesus here calls them *those who do the truth*. St. Paul, also in accord with St. John on this point, describes them as those who *by persevering in well-doing seek for glory, honor and incorruption* (Rom. ii. 7). This earnest aspiration after the good, which the theocratic discipline stimulates and protects in Israel, forms a contrast to the mummeries of the Pharisaic righteousness. It can be present in a penitent publican, no less than in an irreproachable Pharisee. The same idea is found again in the expressions *to be of God, to be of the truth* (viii. 47, xviii. 37). This disposition is the condition of all real faith in the Gospel. The adherence of the will to the preparatory revelation of God, whether in the law of conscience or in that of Moses, is the first condition of the adherence to the higher revelation of divine holiness in Jesus Christ. The expression *to do the truth* denotes the persevering effort to raise one's conduct to the height of one's moral consciousness, to realize the ideal of the good perceived by the conscience; comp. Rom. vii. The soul which, it may be, in consequence of the bitter experience of sin, longs after holiness, recognizes in Jesus its realized ideal and that by which it will itself attain to the realization of it. The figurative expression *to come to the light* signifies to draw near to Jesus, to listen to Him with docility, to surrender oneself to Him; comp. Luke xv. 1, 2. Is there not, in the choice of this figure, a delicate allusion to the present course of Nicodemus? As truly as this night which reigns without is the figure of the unbelief in which the lovers of sin envelop themselves, so really is this light around which these few interlocutors meet, the emblem of the divine brightness which Nicodemus came to seek for. And so it will come to pass. It is the farewell of Jesus: Thou desirest the good; it is this which brings thee here. Take courage! Thou shalt find it!

If the upright hearts come to the light, it is because they do not, like those spoken of before, dread the manifestation of the true character of their conduct; on the contrary, they desire it: To the end, says Jesus, "*that their works may be manifested because they are done in God.*" I return thus to the ordinary translation of the close of this verse. I had previously preferred the following: That they may be manifested as being done in God; comp. for this Greek construction, iv. 35. But the first construction

---

[1] ℵ omits almost the whole of this verse as far as οτι (confusion of the two εργα αυτου, vv. 20, 21, a portion of the authorities in ver. 21 placing αυτου after εργα).

John 3:21 / 401

is more natural here. The truly righteous man seeks, as Nicodemus did, to come into contact with Christ, the living holiness, because he has within him nothing which impels him to withdraw himself from the light of God; on the contrary, the nature of his works is the cause of his being happy to find himself fully in that light. The expression *wrought in God* seems very strong to characterize the works of the sincere man before he has found Christ. But let us not forget that, both in Israel and even beyond the theocratic sphere, it is from a divine impulse that everything good in human life proceeds. It is the Father who draws souls to the Son, and who gives them to Him (vi. 37, 44). It is God who causes to resound in the sincere soul the signal for the strife, ineffectual though it be, against inborn evil (Rom. vii.). Wherever there is docility on the part of man towards this divine initiative, this expression *works wrought in God* is applicable, which comprehends as well the sighs of the humbled publican and the repentant believer as the noble aspirations of a John or a Nathanael. Such a man, conscious of his sincere desire for the good, does not fear to expose himself to the light and consequently to come to Christ. The more he acts *in God*, the more he desires to see clearly within himself, to the end of attaining a still more perfect obedience. In the previous editions, I had referred the *in order that* to the need of a holy approbation. *Weiss* sees in it the desire to show that the good works accomplished are those of God and not those of the man. I think that the question is rather of a need of *progress*. *Luthardt* seems to me to have completely perverted the meaning of this verse and to have lost the very profound teaching which it contains, by explaining: "He who practices the moral truth *manifested in Christ* soon attaches himself to Christ by the religious bond of faith." But does not the practice of the holiness revealed in Christ necessarily imply faith in Him? The saying of Jesus in vii. 17 has a striking analogy to this.

"In humanity anterior to Christ," says *Lücke* rightly, "two kinds of men are mingled together. With the appearance of Jesus, the separating begins;" αὕτη ἡ κρίσις. "Under the trees of the same forest," observes *Lange*, "all sorts of birds find shelter together during the night. But in the morning, as soon as the sun sheds forth his rays, some close their eyes and seek the darkest retreat, while others clap their wings and salute the sun with their songs. Thus the appearing of Christ separates the lovers of the day from those of the night, mingled together until then in the mass of mankind." We must not, however, understand this idea in the sense which the Tübingen school ascribes to the evangelist: That there are two kinds of men opposite in their nature. All the expressions used by John: "They *loved rather*," "*to practise* evil things," "*to do* the truth," are, much rather, borrowed from the domain of free choice and deliberate action. (Comp. Introd., pp. 132 f.).

It is with this word of hope that Jesus takes leave of Nicodemus. And we can easily understand why, in contrast with John the Baptist's course (ver. 36), Jesus spoke, in the first place, of those who reject the light (vv. 19, 20), and, in the second place, of those who seek it (ver. 21). He wished to terminate the conversation with a word of encouragement addressed to His interlocutor. He had recognized in him one of those righteous souls who will one day believe and whom faith will lead to the baptism of water, and thereby to the baptism of the Spirit. Henceforth Jesus waits for him. *Reuss* deems the silence of John respecting his departure surprising. "We have, indeed, seen him come; but we do not see him go away. We are wholly ignorant of the result of this interview." Then this scholar boldly draws therefrom a proof against the historical reality of the personage of Nicodemus and his conversation with Jesus. Is this objection serious? The evangelist should then have told us expressly, that Nicodemus, on leaving Jesus, returned to his own home and went to bed! Does not the effect produced upon him by the conversation appear plainly from the later history? Comp. vii. 50, 51; xix. 39. John respects the mystery of the inner working which had just begun, and leaves the facts to speak. It is the revelation of Jesus to Nicodemus which is the subject of this narrative, and not the biography of this Pharisee. No more does Matthew mention the return of the Twelve after their first mission (chap. x.); does it follow from this that their mission is not historical? The narrative of our Gospels is wholly devoted to the religious end and does not entertain itself with empty details.

We are now in a condition to give a judgment respecting this interview. It seems to me that its historical character follows from the perfect appositeness, which we have established, in all the words of Jesus and in their exact appropriateness to the given situation. The statement of ver. 1, "A man *of the Pharisees*" is found to be the key of the whole passage. Every word of Jesus is like a shot fired at close quarters with such an interlocutor. He begins by bringing home to this man who approaches Him, as well assured of his participation in the divine kingdom as of his very existence, a sense of all that which he lacks, and by saying, although in other terms: "*Unless thy righteousness surpasses that of the Scribes and Pharisees, thou shalt not enter the kingdom of heaven.*" After having thus made a void in this heart full of itself and its own righteousness, he endeavors to fill this void in the positive part of the conversation, in which He answers the questions which Nicodemus had proposed to present to Him. In this answer, He opposes, from the beginning to the end, programme to programme: first, Messiah to Messiah, then, salvation to salvation, finally, judgment to judgment, substituting with regard to each of these points the divine thought for the Pharisaic expectation. There is enough, as it seems to me, in this direct application, this constant fitness, and this unshaken steadiness of course in the conversation to guarantee its reality. An artificial composition of the second century would not have succeeded in adapting itself so perfectly to the given situation. In any case, the cohesion of all the parts of the conversation is too evident to allow of the distinction between the part belonging to Jesus and that belonging to the evangelist. Either the whole is a free composition of the latter, or the whole also must be regarded as the summary of a real conversation of Jesus. We say: the summary; for we certainly do not possess a complete report. The visit of Nicodemus, of course, continued longer than the few minutes necessary for reading the account of it. John has transmitted to us in a few salient words the quintessence of the communications of Jesus at this juncture. This is what the quite vague transitions by means of a simple *and,* καί, indicate. We have before us the principal mountain peaks, but not the whole of the chain (comp. *Introd.,* p. 99).

Jesus in the Country of Judea: III. 22–36

The previous testimonies of John the Baptist were appeals to faith. That which is to follow assumes the character of a threatening protest against the generally hostile attitude and the rising unbelief of Israel. This discourse appertains, therefore, to the picture of the manifestation of Jesus and its general result in Israel.

After the feast of the Passover, Jesus did not immediately return to Galilee; the reason of this course of action will be pointed out in iv. 43–45. He repaired to the country region of Judea, where He set Himself to preach and baptize almost as John the Baptist was doing. Vv. 25, 26, lead us to suppose that the place where Jesus set Himself to the exercising of this ministry, was not far removed from that in which the forerunner was working.

How are we to explain this form, which the activity of Jesus assumes at this time? The temple was closed to Him and He had gone over the holy city, without meeting in it any other man of note disposed seriously to prefer the light to darkness, except Nicodemus; then he removes still further from the centre, and establishes Himself in the province. To this local retreat corresponds a modification in the character of His activity. He had presented Himself in the temple with full authority, as a sovereign who makes his entrance into his palace. That summons not having been accepted, Jesus cannot continue His Messianic activity; He restricts Himself to the work of prophetic preparation; He is obliged to become again, in some sort, His own forerunner, and by this retrogade step He finds Himself placed, for a moment, at the same point which John the Baptist had reached at the termination of his ministry. Hence the simultaneousness and the sort of competition which appeared between the two ministries and the two baptisms. After His return to Galilee, Jesus will Himself renounce this rite, and as the single element of Messianic organization He will only preserve the apostolate. He will no longer aim at anything except to awaken faith by the word. The foundation of the Church, with which the re-establishment of baptism is connected, will be deferred to the epoch when, by His death and resurrection, the bond between Him and the unbelieving people shall have been completely broken and the foundation of the new society prepared.

These changes in the mode of Jesus' activity have not escaped the notice of the rationalists; they have seen in them nothing else than the result of a growing miscalculation. Yet Jesus had announced all from the first day: "*Destroy this temple;*" and the final success of His work proves that there was something better here than the result of a deception. Faith, on

404 / Birth of Faith

the contrary, admires, in this so varied course, the elasticity of the divine plan in its relations to human freedom, and the perfect submissiveness with which the Son can yield to the daily instructions of the Father. Thereby the absence of plan becomes the wisest and most wonderful of plans; and the divine wisdom, accepting the free play of human freedom, can make even the obstacles which the resistance of men opposes to it, the means of realizing its designs. This glance at the situation explains the momentary juxtaposition of these two ministries, the one of which, as it seemed, must succeed the other.

The following passage contains: 1. The general picture of the situation (vv. 22–26); 2. The discourse of John the Baptist (vv. 27–36).

1. Vv. 22–26

Ver. 22. "*After this Jesus came with his disciples into the country of Judea; and he tarried there with them and baptized.*" Μετὰ ταῦτα (*after this*), connects this passage, in a general way, with ii. 23–25: "*Following upon* this activity of Jesus at Jerusalem." Ἰουδαία γῆ (*the land of Judea*), denotes the *country*, as opposed to the capital. The imperfect *he was tarrying*, and *he was baptizing*, indicate that this sojourn was of some duration. The expression, *he was baptizing*, is more exactly defined in iv. 2: "*Yet Jesus himself baptized not, but his disciples.*" The moral act belonged to Jesus; the material operation was wrought by the disciples. If these two passages were found in two different Gospels, criticism would not fail immediately to see in them a contradiction, and would accuse of harmonistic bias the one who should seek to explain it. The intention of the narrator in our passage is only to place this baptism under the responsibility of Jesus Himself.

Ver. 23. "*Now John also was baptizing in Ænon, near to Salim, because there was abundance of water there; and they came and were baptized.*" *Æn*, from which *Ænon*, denotes a *fountain*. We may also, with *Meyer*, make of the termination *on* an abridgment of the word *jona, dove;* this word would thus signify *the fountain of the dove*. This locality was in the vicinity of a town called *Salim*. The situation of these two places is uncertain. *Eusebius* and *Jerome*, in the *Onomasticon*, place Ænon eight thousand paces south of Bethsean or Scythopolis, in the valley of the Jordan, on the borders of Samaria and Galilee, and Salim, a little further to the west. And indeed there has recently been found in these localities a ruin bearing the name of *Aynûn* (*Palestine Exploration Report*, 1874). From this, therefore, it would be necessary to conclude that these two localities were in Samaria. But this result is incompatible with the words of ver. 22: *in the country of Judea* (on the supposition, at least, that the two baptisms were near each other). And, above all, how should John have settled among the Samaritans? How could he have expected that the multitudes would follow him into the midst of this hostile people? *Ewald, Wieseler, Hengstenberg*, and *Mühlau*, because of these reasons, suppose an altogether different locality. In Josh. xv. 32 three towns are spoken of: *Shilhim, Ain,* and *Rimmon,* situated towards the southern frontier of the tribe of Judah, on the borders of Edom (comp. xv. 21). In Josh. xix. 7 and 1 Chron. iv. 32, Ain and Rimmon again appear together. Finally, in Neh. xi. 29 these two names are blended in one: *En-Rimmon.* Might not Ænon be a still more complete contraction? This supposition would do away with the difficulty of the baptism in Samaria, and would give a very appropriate sense to the reason: *because there was abundance of water there.* Indeed, as applied to a region generally destitute of water and almost desert, like the southern extremity of Judah, this reason has greater force than if the question were of a country rich in water, like Samaria.

Jesus would thus have gone over all the territory of the tribe of Judah, seeing once in His life Bethlehem, His native town, Hebron, the city of Abraham and David, and all southern Judea even as far as Beersheba. This remark has excited the derisive humor of *Reuss;* we do not at all understand the reason of it. In the Synoptical Gospels, we see Jesus making a series of excursions as far as the northern limits of the Holy Land, once even to Cæsarea Philippi, in the vicinity of the ancient Dan, at the foot of Hermon, at another time as far as into the regions of Tyre and Sidon. He would thus have visited all the countries of the theocratic domain from Dan to Beersheba. Is not this altogether natural? *Hengstenberg* has taken advantage of this sojourn of Jesus in the vicinity of the desert, to place the temptation at this time. This opinion is chronologically untenable.

Ver. 24. *"For John had not yet been cast into prison."* This remark of the evangelist is surprising, because there is nothing in what precedes which is adapted to occasion it. The fact of the incarceration of John the Baptist, as already accomplished, was not, in any way, implied in the preceding narrative. It is therefore elsewhere than in our Gospel that we must seek for the reason why the evangelist thinks that he must correct a misapprehension existing on this subject, as he evidently does by the remark of ver. 24. This reason is easily discovered in the narrative of our first two Synoptics: Matt. iv. 12: *" Jesus, having heard that John was delivered up, withdrew into Galilee."* Mark i. 14: *"After that John was delivered up, Jesus came into Galilee."* These words immediately follow the account of the baptism and temptation; they would necessarily produce on the reader the impression that the imprisonment of John the Baptist had followed very closely upon the baptism of Jesus, and preceded—even occasioned—His *first* return to Galilee; thus precisely the opinion which the remark of John sets aside. The account in Luke iii. 19, 20 is different; the imprisonment of the Baptist is there evidently mentioned only by way of anticipation. *Hengstenberg* thought that the narrative of Matthew and Mark might be explained by the fact that the first return of Jesus to Galilee—the one which John relates in i. 44—was simply omitted by them. But we have seen (ii. 11) that the first visit of Jesus to Capernaum coincided with certain scenes of the very first period of the Galilean ministry related by the Synoptics. It only remains, therefore, to acknowledge that frequently in the primitive oral tradition the first two re-

406 / Birth of Faith

turns from Judea to Galilee (i. 44 and iv. 1–3) were blended together. From this identification would, naturally, result the suppression of the entire interval which had separated them—that is to say, of almost a whole year of Jesus' ministry. To recover this ground which had disappeared, John was thus obliged expressly to restore the distinction between the two returns. He was especially obliged to do this on reaching the fact which he is about to relate, a fact which falls precisely in this interval. *Hilgenfeld* himself, speaking of this passage, says: "Involuntarily the fourth evangelist bears witness here of his acquaintance with the Synoptical narrative." There is nothing to criticise in this remark except the word *involuntarily*. For the intentional character of this parenthesis, ver. 24, is obvious. We have already proved in John the evident intention of distinguishing these two returns to Galilee by the manner in which he spoke of the miracle of Cana, ii. 11; we shall have occasion to make a similar remark of the same character, with reference to iv. 54. As for the way in which this confusion arose in the tradition written out by the Synoptics, we may remember that it was only after the *second* return to Galilee that Jesus began that uninterrupted prophetic ministry which the first three Gospels portray for us very particularly and which was the beginning of the foundation of the Church. However important were the attempts made in Judea, up to this time, in the description of the development of Jewish unbelief which John traced, they could just as easily be omitted in the narrative of the actual establishment of the kingdom of God, and of the foundation of the Church which was the result of the Galilean ministry, related especially by the Synoptics.

We can draw from this twenty-fourth verse an important conclusion with respect to the position of the author of the fourth Gospel in the midst of the primitive Church. Who else but an apostle, but an apostle of the first rank, but an apostle recognized as such, could have taken in his writing a position so sovereign with regard to the tradition received in the Church, emanating from the Twelve, and recorded in the Gospels which were anterior to his own? By a stroke of the pen to introduce so considerable a modification in a narrative clothed with such authority, he must have been, and have felt himself to be, possessed of an authority which was altogether incontestable.

Ver. 25. " *There arose therefore a dispute on the part of John's disciples with a Jew,*[1] *touching purification.*" The occasion of the following discourse was a discussion provoked by the competition of the two neighboring baptisms. Οὖν, *therefore*, marks this relation. The expression *on the part of the disciples*, shows that John's disciples were the instigators. The reading of the greater part of the Mjj. Ἰουδαίου, *a Jew*, instead of Ἰουδαίων, *some Jews*, is now generally preferred. I accept it, without being able to convince myself altogether of its authenticity. Should not the substantive Ἰουδαίου have been accompanied by the adjective τινός? And would an altercation

---

[1] The T. R. reads Ιουδαιων (*Jews*) with ℵ Mnn. It. Syr^cur. Cop. Orig. All the rest read Ιουδαιου (a *Jew*).

with a mere unknown individual have deserved to be so expressly marked? The three most ancient Versions agree in favor of the reading Ἰουδαίων, *Jews*. The Sinaitic MS. also reads in this way. The two substantives in ων, before and after this word, might have occasioned an error. The subject of the discussion was the true mode of purification. Of what purification? Evidently of that which should prepare the Jews for the kingdom of the Messiah. *Meyer* thinks that the Jew ascribed to the baptism of Jesus a greater efficacy than to that of John. *Chrysostom*, followed by some others, holds that the Jew had had himself baptized already by the disciples of Jesus. *Hofmann* and *Luthardt* suppose, on the contrary, because of the term *Jew*, that he belonged to the Pharisaic party, hostile both to Jesus and to John, and that he had maliciously recounted to the disciples of John the successes of Jesus. The use of this term scarcely allows us, indeed, to suppose in this man kindly feelings, either towards Jesus or towards John. Perhaps in response to the disciples of John who invited him to have himself baptized, reminding him of the promises of the Old Testament (Ezek. xxxvi. 25, etc.), he answered ironically that one knew not to whom to go: "Your master began; here is a second who succeeds better than he; which of the two says the truth?" The question was embarrassing. The disciples of John decide to submit it to their master. This historical situation is too well defined to have been invented.

Ver. 26. "*And they came to John and said to him: Master, he that was with thee beyond the Jordan, to whom thou hast borne witness, behold, he baptizeth, and all men come to him.*" There is something of bitterness in these words. The words: "*to whom thou hast borne witness*" make prominent the generosity which John had shown towards Jesus: "See there, how thou hast acted, thou (σύ); and see here, how He is acting, He (οὗτος). Ἴδε, *behold*, sets forth the unexpected character of such a course: "He baptizes, quite like thyself; thus, not content with asserting Himself, He seeks to set thee aside." Baptism was a special rite, introduced by John, and distinguishing his ministry from every other. By appropriating it to Himself, Jesus seemed to usurp the part peculiar to His predecessor and to desire to throw him altogether into the shade. And what is more poignant in this course of action is, that it succeeds: "*All men come to him.*" This exaggeration, *all*, is the result of spite. Matt. ix. 14 shows us John's disciples in Galilee, after the imprisonment of their master, animated by the same hostile disposition and combining more or less with the adversaries of Jesus.

2. Vv. 27–36

John does not solve the difficulty raised by the Jew or the Jews. He goes directly to the foundation of things. After having characterized the relation between the two personages of whom it is desired to make rivals, he shows that all opposition, even all comparison between them, is out of place. The solution of the pending question follows of itself from this general explanation. The discourse has two parts which are very distinct and the idea of which evidently answers to the given situation: "*I*" and "*He*," or, to use John's own expressions, the friend of the bridegroom (vv. 27–30), and the bridegroom (vv. 31–36). The first must be thrown into the shade and decrease; the second must increase. Each of the two, therefore, is in his place; that which grieves his disciples fills him with joy. It will be asked why the forerunner did not at that moment abandon his particular position, in order to go and join himself, with his disciples, to the retinue of Jesus. The answer to this question, often proposed, is not difficult. Summoned to prepare Israel for the kingdom of the Messiah, John was like the captain of a vessel, who must be the last to abandon the old ship, when all its company are already safely in the new one. His special part, officially marked out, continued so long as the end was not yet attained, that is, so long as the whole people were not yet given to Jesus.

Vv. 27–30. "*I.*"

Ver. 27. "*John answered and said: A man can receive nothing except that which hath been given him from heaven.*" As far as ver. 30, which is the centre of this discourse, the dominant idea is that of the person and mission of the forerunner. Accordingly, it seems natural to apply the general sentence of ver. 27 specially to John the Baptist. He is urged to defend himself against Jesus who is despoiling him. "I cannot take," he answers, "that which God has not given me"—in other words, "I cannot assign to myself my part: make myself the bridegroom, when I am only the friend of the bridegroom." So *Bengel, Lücke, Reuss, Hengstenberg*, I myself (first ed.). I abandoned this application in the second edition, for that of *Olshausen, de Wette, Meyer, Weiss*, according to which this maxim refers to Jesus: "He would not be obtaining such success, if God Himself did not give it to Him." With this meaning, this saying must be regarded as the summary of the two parts of the discourse (*I* and *He*), and not only of the first part. Yet I ask myself whether it is not proper, as I did originally, to refer this maxim to the *mission* conferred, rather than the *success* obtained; comp. Heb. v. 4. Then the asyndeton between vv. 26 and 27 is more consonant with the application to John only, since he announces the following verse as an energetic reaffirmation of the thought of ver. 26.

Ver. 28. "*Ye yourselves bear me*[1] *witness that I said: I am not the Christ, but I am sent before him.*" John expressly applies to himself the maxim of ver. 26. He has informed his disciples, from the beginning, of the fact of which they are complaining. He has always said to them, that it was not given to him to be the Christ, that his mission went no further than to open the way for Him. He appeals, with respect to this point, to their own recollection and discharges Himself thus from all responsibility for their jealous humor towards Jesus. The words: "*Ye bear me witness*," seem to allude to their own expression, in ver. 26, where they had recalled

---

[1] The Mjj., ℵ E F H M V, and 60 Mnn. omit μοι (*me*).

the conduct of John with reference to Jesus. Then, he explains to them, by a comparison, the feeling which he experiences and which is so different from theirs.

Ver. 29. "*He that hath the bride is the bridegroom, and the friend of the bridegroom, who standeth and heareth*[1] *him, rejoiceth greatly because of the bridegroom's voice; this, my joy, therefore, is now perfect.*" His position is subordinate to that of Jesus, but it has also its privileges and its own joy, and that joy perfectly satisfies him. Νύμφη (the *bride*), is the Messianic community which John the Baptist was to form in Israel that he might lead it to Jesus; νύμφιος (the *bridegroom*), designates the Messiah, and, if we may so speak, the *betrothed* of this spiritual bride. The name Jehovah signifies precisely : *He who shall be* or *shall come*. According to the Old Testament, indeed, the Lord would not confide this part of bridegroom to any other than Himself, and the coming of the Messiah is to be the highest manifestation of Jehovah Himself (p. 276); comp. Is. liv. 5; Hos. ii. 19; Matt. ix. 15; xxv. 1 f.; Eph. v. 32; Apoc. xix. 7, etc. The functions of the marriage friend were, first, to ask the hand of the young woman, then to serve as an intermediary between the betrothed couple during the time of betrothal, and finally, to preside at the marriage-feast; a touching image of the part of John the Baptist : ὁ ἑστηκώς *he who standeth*. This word expresses, as *Hengstenberg* says, " the happy passivity " of him who beholds, listens and enjoys. While he fulfills his office in presence of the betrothed, the marriage-friend hears the noble and joyous accents of his friend, which transport him with joy. John speaks only of hearing, not of seeing. Why? Is it because he is himself removed from Jesus? But then, how can he even speak of *hearing?* If this term has a meaning apphcable to John the Baptist, it implies that certain words of Jesus had been reported to him, and had filled his heart with joy and admiration. And how, indeed, could it have been otherwise? Could Andrew, Simon Peter, John, these former disciples of the Baptist, be in his neighborhood without coming to him, to give an account of all which they heard and saw? This is *the bridegroom's voice,* which causes the heart of his friend to leap for joy. The phrase, χαρᾷ χαίρειν (*to rejoice with joy*), corresponds to a Hebrew construction (the infinitive placed before the finite verb to strengthen the verbal idea) ; comp. שוש איש, Is. lxi. 10 (and the LXX); Luke xxii. 15. This expression describes the joy of John as a joy reaching to the full, and, consequently, as excluding every feeling of a different sort, such as that which the disciples were attempting to awaken in him. The words : *this joy which is mine*, contrast his joy as the marriage-*friend* to that of the *bridegroom*. John alludes to those words of the disciples : *all go to him;* in this spectacle is *his joy* as friend. Πεπλήρωται, not : *has been accomplished* (*Rilliet*), the aorist would be necessary, but : *is*, at this very moment, *raised to its highest point*. He means : "that which calls forth vexation in you is precisely the thing which fulfills my joy."

Ver. 30. "*He must increase, but I must decrease.*" Here is the expres-

---

[1] א places αυτου after εστηκως.

sion which forms the connecting link between the two parts of the discourse, announcing the second and summing up the first. The friend of the bridegroom had, at the beginning of the relation, the principal part; it was he alone who appeared. But, in proportion as the relation develops itself, his part diminishes he must disappear and leave the bridegroom to become *the sole person*. This is the position of John the Baptist; he accepts it, and desires no other. No one could have invented this admirable saying, a permanent motto of every true servant of Christ.

At this point, *Bengel, Tholuck, Olshausen* and others, make the discourse of the Baptist end, and the reflections of the evangelist begin. They rest principally on the Johannean character of the style in what follows, and on the reproduction of certain thoughts of the conversation with Nicodemus (see, especially, vv. 31, 32). To pronounce a decision, we must study the discourse even to the end. But, in itself, it would be scarcely natural that the words of ver. 30, *he must increase*, should not be developed in what follows, as the other words, *and I must decrease*, have been in what precedes.

Vv. 31-36 "*He*"

The bridegroom, He must increase, while the friend decreases, for He is superior to him, first, through His origin (ver. 31), then, through the perfection of His teaching (vv. 32-34), finally, through His dignity as Son, and the absolute sovereignty which belongs to Him as such (ver. 35). The discourse closes with a practical conclusion (ver. 36).

Ver. 31. "*He that cometh from above is above all;*[1] *he that is of the earth,*[2] *is of the earth, and speaketh as being of the earth; he that cometh from heaven is above all.*"[3] With his own earthly nature John contrasts the heavenly origin of Jesus. Ἀνωθεν, *from above*, is applied here, not to the mission—for that of John is also from above—but to the *origin* of the person. The *all* denotes the divine agents in general. All, like John himself, are to be eclipsed by the Messiah. The words three times repeated: *of the earth*, forcibly express the sphere to which John belongs and beyond which he cannot go. The first time they refer to the origin (ὢν ἐκ): a mere man; the second, to the mode of existence (ἐστί): as being of the earth, he remains earthly in his whole manner of being, feeling and thinking (comp. the antithesis ver. 13); the third time, to the teaching (λαλεῖ): seeing the things of heaven only from beneath, from his earthly dwelling-place. This is true of John, even as a prophet. No doubt, in certain isolated moments and as if through partial openings, he catches a glimpse of the things from above; but even in his exstacies he speaks of God only as an earthly being. So, while inviting to repentance, he does not introduce into the kingdom. This estimate of John by himself is in harmony with the judgment of Jesus, Matt. xi. 11: "*The least in the kingdom of heaven is greater than he.*" And the shaking of his faith, which followed so soon,

---

[1] ℵ D Italiq: και before ο ων.
[2] ℵ: επι instead of εκ; D: απο.
[3] ℵ D some Mnn. a b Syr^sur. omit επανω παντων εστι (*above all*) the second time.

was not long in demonstrating the justice of it. After having thus put in their proper place, as contrasted with Jesus, all the servants of heaven, John returns to the principal theme: *He.* If, with some of the Mjj., we reject the last words of this verse: *is above all,* the words *he that cometh from heaven* must be made the subject of the verb *bears witness,* ver. 32 (rejecting the καί). But the fullest and richest reading is also the one most accordant with the spirit of the text. By the last words, John returns to the real subject of this part of his discourse, Jesus, from which he had turned aside, for a moment, in order to make more prominent His superiority by the contrast with himself.

Ver. 32. " *What*[1] *he hath seen and heard, of that*[2] *he beareth witness; and no man receiveth his witness.*" The καί, *and,* is omitted by the Alexandrian authorities, and no doubt rightly; *asyndeta* are frequent in this discourse. From the heavenly origin of Jesus follows the perfection of His teaching. He is in *filial* communion with the Father. When He speaks of divine things, He speaks of them as an immediate witness. This saying is the echo of that of Jesus in ver. 11. In reproducing it, the forerunner declares that Jesus has affirmed nothing respecting Himself which is not the exact truth. But how could he know this? We think we have answered this question in the explanation of ver. 29. By the last words, John confirms the severe judgment which Jesus had passed upon the conduct of the people and their rulers (ver. 11). However, while declaring, as Jesus had done, the general unbelief of Israel, John does not deny individual exceptions; he brings them out expressly in ver. 33. What he means here by the word *no one,* is that these exceptions which seem so numerous to the view of his disciples that they make the whole ("*all*" ver. 26), are to his view only an imperceptible minority. To the exaggeration of envy, he opposes that of zeal: " Where you say: all, as for me, I say: no one." He would not be satisfied unless he saw the Sanhedrim in a body, followed by the whole people, coming to render homage to the bridegroom of the Messianic community. Then, he could, himself also, abandon his office as friend of the bridegroom, and come to sit, as spouse, at the Messiah's feet. We should notice the verbs in the present tense, "*he testifies . . . no one receives,*" which place us in the time of the ministry of Jesus, and do not permit us to put this part of the discourse in the evangelist's mouth.

Vv. 33, 34. " *He that hath received his testimony hath set his seal that God is true; 34, for he whom God hath sent speaketh the words of God; for he giveth*[3] *not the Spirit by measure.*" There are, nevertheless, some believers, and what is the grandeur and beauty of the part which they act! Σφραγίζειν, *to seal,* to legalise an act by affixing one's seal to it. This is what the believer does in relation to the testimony which Christ gives; in ranging himself among those who accept it, he has the honor of associating, once for all, his personal responsibility with that of God who speaks

---

[1] Καί (*and*) is omitted by ℵ B D L T^b It^{aliq} Syr^{cur} Cop. Orig.

[2] ℵ D omit τοῦτο.

[3] T. R. 15 Mjj. Syr. read, after δίδωσιν, ὁ θεός (*God*) omitted by ℵ B C L T^b.

by His messenger. Indeed, this certification of truth, adjudged to Jesus by the believer, rises even to God Himself. This is what is explained by ver. 34 (*for*). The utterances of Jesus are to such a degree those of God, that to certify the truth of the former is to attest the veracity of God Himself. Some think that the idea of the divine veracity refers to the fulfillment of the prophecies which faith proclaims. But this idea has no connection with the context. According to others, John means that to believe in Jesus is to attest the truth of the declaration which God gave on His behalf at the time of His baptism. This sense would be natural enough in itself, but it does not accord well with ver. 34. The profound thought contained in this expression of John is the following: In receiving the utterances of Jesus with faith in their divine character, man boldly declares that what is divine cannot be false, and proclaims thus the incorruptible veracity of God. We must notice the aorist ἐσφράγισεν, *set his seal:* it is an accomplished act. And what an act! He affixes His private signature by his faith to the divine testimony, and becomes thus conjointly responsible for the veracity of God Himself. There is evidently somewhat of exaltation in this paradoxical form, by which John expresses the grandeur of the act of faith. The expression *whom he hath sent* (which recalls ver. 17), must be taken in the most absolute sense. The other divine messengers merit this name only in an inexact sense; they are, in reality, only raised up; to be sent, in the strict sense of the word, one must be from above (ver. 31). The same absolute force should be given to the expression: *the words of God:* He alone possesses the complete, absolute divine revelation. This is what the article τά, *the*, indicates; all others, John the Baptist himself, have only fragments of it. And whence comes this complete character of His revelation? From the fact that the communication which is made to Him of the Spirit is *without measure*. The T. R. reads, after δίδωσιν, ὁ θεός: "*God* gives the Spirit . . ." The Alexandrian authorities unanimously reject this subject, *God;* and it is probable that it is a gloss, but a gloss which is just to the sense. It is derived from the first clause of the verse. No doubt *the Spirit* might be made the subject, as I myself tried to do formerly. The position of the word τὸ πνεῦμα, *the Spirit*, however, is not favorable to this sense. And it is more simple to understand the subject of the preceding clause. The present δίδωσιν *gives*, as well as the expression: "*not by measure*," are explained by the recollection of the vision of the baptism: John saw the Spirit in the form of a dove, that is to say, in its living *totality*, descending *and abiding* upon Him. Meyer, offended by the ellipsis of the pronoun αὐτῷ, *to him*, makes a general maxim out of this saying, with the following sense: "God is not obliged always to give the Spirit, only in a definite measure, as He formerly did in the case of the prophets. He may, if He pleases, give it once without measure in its fullness," from which this application is understood: "And this is what He has done with respect to the Son." But thus precisely the thing would be understood which ought to be expressed, and expressed which might very well have been left to be understood. Perhaps, the ellipsis of the pronoun αὐτῷ, *to Him*, arises from the fact that the gift of the Spirit to Jesus is in reality of a universal bearing. God does not give it *to* Him *for* Himself only, but for *all*. It is a permanent, absolute gift.

Ver. 35. "*The Father loveth the Son and hath given all things into his hand.*"—The *asyndeton* between this verse and the preceding may be rendered by this emphatic form: "Because also the Father loveth . . ." This absolute communication of the Spirit results from the incomparable love which the Father has for the Son. These words are, as it were, the echo of that divine declaration which John had heard at the baptism: "*This is my beloved Son.*" The term ἀγαπᾷ, *loves*, is taken in the absolute sense, like the expressions: *sent* and *the words*. Jesus had used the term *Son*, when speaking with Nicodemus, vv. 16–18; the second Psalm already applied it to the Messiah in vv. 7, 12 (where every other explanation seems to us untenable); Isaiah and Micah had expressed themselves in a similar way (Is. ix. 5; Micah v. 2, 3). John himself had heard it at the baptism. It is not surprising, therefore, that he uses it here. From this love of the Father flows the gift of *all things*. Some interpreters, starting from ver. 34, have applied this expression solely to spiritual gifts, to the powers of the Holy Spirit. But the expression *into His hand* does not accord with this sense. There is rather an advance upon the idea of ver. 34: "*Not only* the Spirit, but *all things*." By the Spirit, the Son reigns in the heart of believers; this is not enough; the Father has, moreover, given Him universal sovereignty, that He may be able to make *all things* serve the good of His own. This is exactly the thought which Paul expresses in Eph. i. 22 by that untranslatable phrase: αὐτὸν ἔδωκεν κεφαλὴν ὑπὲρ πάντα τῇ ἐκκλησίᾳ. The *hand* is the symbol of free disposal. Thereby John meant to say: "I complain of being despoiled by Him! But He has a right to everything and can take everything without encroachment." And from this follows the striking application which he makes to his disciples, in closing, of the truth which he has just proclaimed:

Ver. 36. "*He that believeth on the Son hath eternal life; but he that obeyeth not the Son shall not see*[1] *life, but the wrath of God abideth on him.*" This is the practical consequence to be drawn from the supreme greatness of the Son. These last words present a great similarity to the close of Ps. ii: "*Do reverence to the Son, lest he be angry, and ye perish in the way when, in a little time, his wrath will be kindled; but blessed are they that put their trust in him.*" Only John, the reverse of the Psalmist and of Jesus Himself (iii. 19–21), begins with believers, to end with unbelievers. It is because he would give a stern and last warning to his disciples and the entire nation. John declares, as Jesus had said to Nicodemus, that all depends for every man on faith and unbelief, and that the absolute value of these two moral facts arises from the supreme dignity of Him who is the object of them: the Son. This name is sufficient to explain why faith gives life, why unbelief brings wrath. The phrase ὁ ἀπειθῶν, *he who disobeys*, brings out the voluntary side in unbelief, that of revolt. The Son is the legitimate sovereign; unbelief is the refusal to submit. The words: *the wrath abides*,

---

[1] ℵ reads ουκ εχει (*hath not*), instead of ουκ οψεται (*shall not see*).

have often been understood in this sense: The *natural* condemnation abides, because the act which alone could have removed it, that of faith, has not taken place. But this sense seems to us weak and strained, and is only imperfectly connected with what precedes. The question is rather of the wrath called forth by the very refusal of obedience, and falling upon the unbeliever *as such.* Is it not just that God should be angry? If faith seals the veracity of God (ver. 33), unbelief *makes God a liar* (1 John v. 10).—The future *shall see* is opposed to the present *has.* Not only does he not have life now, but when it shall be outwardly revealed in its perfect form—that of glory—he shall not behold it; it shall be for him as though it were not. Here is a word which shows clearly that the ordinary eschatology is by no means foreign to the fourth Gospel. The verb $\mu\varepsilon\nu\varepsilon\iota$, *abides,* in spite of its correlation with the future $\check{o}\psi\varepsilon\tau\alpha\iota$, *shall see,* is a present, and should be written $\mu\acute{\varepsilon}\nu\varepsilon\iota$. The present *abides* expresses, much better than the future *shall abide,* the notion of permanence. All other wrath is revocable; that which befalls unbelief abides forever. Thus the epithet *eternal* of the first clause has its counterpart in the second.

Respecting the fact which we have just been studying, the following is *Renan's* judgment: "The twenty-second and following verses, as far as ver. 2 of chap. iv., transport us into what is thoroughly historical. . . . This is extremely remarkable. The Synoptics have nothing like it" (p. 491).—As to the *discourse,* it may be called: the last word of the Old Covenant. It recalls that threatening of Malachi which closes the Old Testament: "*Lest I come and smite the earth with a curse.*" It accords thus with the given situation: In view of the unbelief which was emphatically manifested even among his disciples, the forerunner completes his previous calls to faith by a menacing warning. All the details of the discourse are in harmony with the character of the person of the Baptist. There is not a word which cannot be fully explained in his mouth. Vv. 27, 29, 30 have a seal of inimitable originality; no other than the forerunner, in his unique situation, would have been able to create them. Ver. 35 is simply the echo of the divine declaration which he had himself heard at the moment of the baptism. In ver. 34 there is formulated no less simply the entire content of the vision which was beheld at that same moment. Ver. 28 is the reproduction of his own testimony in the Synoptics (Matt. iii. and parallels). Ver. 36 also recalls his former preachings on the *wrath to come* (Matt. iii. 7) and that *axe already laid unto the root of the trees* (iii. 10) with which he had threatened Israel. There remain only vv. 31, 32. We believe we have indicated the very probable origin of these verses (see on ver. 32). Will any one find an objection in the Johannean coloring of the style? But we must recall to mind the fact that we have here the Greek reproduction by the evangelist's pen of a discourse given in Aramaic (see Introd. pp. 172–175). It is entirely impossible to imagine a writer of a later epoch carrying himself back thus into the midst of the facts, drawing all the words from the given situation, and, above all, adapting to it with so much precision the progress of the discourse (John and Jesus), and binding together the two parts of it by the admirable saying of ver. 30. *Weizsäcker* himself cannot refrain from acknowledging (p. 268) "that there are in this discourse elements of detail which distinctly mark the Baptist's own point of view" (vv. 27, 34, 35, 36).

We have already replied to the objection derived from the special and independent position which John the Baptist keeps, instead of going to rank himself among the disciples of Jesus. As long as the aim of his mission—to lead Israel to Jesus,—was so far from being attained, that preparatory mission continued, and the Baptist was not free to exchange it for the position of a disciple which would have been more satisfactory to him (ver. 29). It is asked how, after such a discourse of their Master, John's disciples could have subsequently formed themselves into an anti-Christian sect? But a small number from among the innumerable multitude of those baptized by John were present at this scene, and it would, in truth, be much to expect of a discourse—to suppose that it could have extirpated a feeling of jealousy which was so deep that we even find the traces of it again in the Synoptics (Matt. ix. 14 and parallels). On the point in Matt. xi. 2, also alleged in opposition to the authenticity of this discourse, see on i. 34.

Weiss holds, like *Reuss*, that this discourse contains authentic elements, but worked over by the evangelist, and that he has fused them into one whole with his own ideas. Thus, he proves the authenticity of the saying of ver. 34 by this argument: The perfection of Jesus' teaching is here ascribed by the forerunner to the action of the Holy Spirit, while John the Evangelist ascribes it to the remembrance which He had of His knowledge of the Father in His pre-existent state. This difference between the idea of the evangelist and that of the Baptist must prove the historical character of the discourse, at least in this point. But we have seen hitherto and we shall continue to discover that this way of conceiving of the higher knowledge of Jesus, which Weiss attributes to the evangelist, is by no means in harmony with the text and with the thought of our fourth Gospel. This alleged difference between his conception and that of the Baptist does not exist.

Our Gospel does not give an account of the imprisonment of John the Baptist. But the saying of Jesus (v. 35) implies the disappearance of the forerunner. This took place, therefore, very shortly after this last testimony uttered by him in Judea (see at iv. 1). The fact of John's death was omitted here, like so many other facts with which the author knows that his readers are well acquainted, and the mention of which does not fall within his plan.

I cannot believe (see p. 258) that the account which occupies our attention was written without some allusion to the disciples of John, who were moving about in considerable numbers in Asia Minor; not, surely, that I would wish to claim, that the entire fourth Gospel owes its existence to this polemical design, but it has entered as a factor into its composition (comp. Introd., pp. 213, 214).

2

John 4:1-42

JESUS IN SAMARIA

The first phase of the public ministry of Jesus is ended. Unbelief on the part of the masses, faith on the part of a few, public attention greatly aroused, such is the result of His work in Judea. Nevertheless the uneasiness which He sees appearing among the leaders of the people with relation to Himself, is for Him the signal for retreat. He does not wish to engage prematurely in a conflict which He knows to be inevitable. He abandons Judea therefore to His enemies and, returning to Galilee, He makes that retired province, from this time onward, the ordinary theatre of His activity.

The direct road from Judea to Galilee passed through Samaria. But was it the one which was followed by the Jews, for example the Galilean caravans which went to the feasts at Jerusalem? Writers ordinarily answer in the affirmative, resting upon the passage of Josephus *Antiq.* vi. 1: "It was the custom of the Galileans to pass through Samaria in order to go to the feasts at Jerusalem." But *R. Steck*[1] has concluded, not without reason, from a passage in the *Life of Josephus* (chap. 52): "Those who wish to go quickly from Galilee to Jerusalem must pass through Samaria," that the custom of which that author speaks in the *Antiquities* was not so general as the first passage seems to imply. Perhaps this road was that of the festival caravans; but it was not that of the Jews who were of strict observance, at least in private life. As to Jesus it has been claimed that by following this road in this case, He would have put Himself in contradiction to His own word in Matt. x. 5, where, on sending them out to preach, He said to the apostles: "*Go not into the way of the Gentiles and enter not into any city of the Samaritans; but go ye rather to the lost sheep of the house of Israel.*" But, between *passing through Samaria* (διὰ τῆς Σαμαρ., ver. 4) and making the Samaritan people the object of a mission, there is an easily appreciable difference. We should much rather acknowledge, with Hengstenberg, that it might be befitting for Jesus to give once, during His earthly life, an example of largeness of heart to His apostles which might afterwards direct the Christian mission throughout the whole world. Luke ix. 51 proves that Jesus really did not fear to approach the Samaritan soil.

The fact which is to follow has a typical significance. Jesus Himself acutely feels it (ver. 38). This Samaritan woman and these inhabitants of Sychar, by the readiness and earnestness of their faith, and by the contrast of their conduct with that of the Israelitish people, become in His eyes the first-fruits, as it were, of the conversion of the Gentile world. There is therein a sign for Him of the future destiny of the kingdom of God on earth. Must we from this conclude, with *Baur*, that this whole account is only an *idea* presented in action by the author of our Gospel? Certainly not. If the Samaritan woman was nothing but a personification of the Gentile world, how would the author have put into her mouth (ver. 20 f.) a strictly monotheistic profession of faith, as well as the hope of the near advent of the Messiah (ver. 25; comp. ver. 42)? Because a fact has an ideal and prophetic significance, it does not follow that it is fictitious. If there is a story of the Saviour's life which, by reason of the vivacity and freshness of its totality and its details, bears the seal of historic truth, it is this. *Renan* himself says: "Most of the circumstances of the narrative bear a strikingly impressive stamp of truth." (*Vie de Jésus*, p. 243.)

[1] *Jahrb. f. prot. Theol.*, 1880, IV., (Der Pilgerweg der Galiläer nach Jerusalem).

As an example of faith, this incident is connected with the two preceding representations: that of the faith of the apostles (i. 38 ff.) and that of the visit of Nicodemus (iii. i.–21). These are the luminous parts of the narrative which alternate with the sombre parts, representing the beginning of unbelief (i. 19 ff.; ii. 12 ff.; iii. 25 ff.).

We distinguish in this narrative the following three phases: 1. Jesus and the Samaritan woman: vv. 1–26; 2. Jesus and the disciples: vv. 27–38; 3. Jesus and the Samaritans: vv. 39–42.

Jesus and the Samaritan Woman: vv. 1–26

In this first phase we see how Jesus succeeds in awaking faith in a soul which was a stranger to all spiritual life. The historical situation is described in vv. 1–6.

Vv. 1–3. " *When therefore the Lord*[1] *knew that the Pharisees had heard that Jesus made and baptized more disciples than*[2] *John,—2, though Jesus did not himself baptize, but his disciples,—3, he left Judea, and departed again*[3] *into Galilee.*" Ver. 1. explains the motive which leads Jesus to leave Judea: A report has reached the Pharisees respecting Him, according to which this new personage may become more formidable than John himself. Οὖν, *therefore:* because of this great concourse of people, mentioned in iii. 23–26. The title: *the Lord* (in the larger part of the MSS.), is but rarely applied to Jesus during His earthly life (vi. 23; xi. 2). It pre-supposes the habit of representing Jesus to the mind as raised to glory. It is frequent in the epistles. If it is authentic in this passage (see the various reading of three MSS., which read: *Jesus*), it is occasioned either by the feeling of the divine greatness of Jesus, which manifests itself in the preceding section, or, more simply, by the desire of avoiding the repetition of the name of Jesus, which occurs again a few words further on. The expression *had heard* excludes a supernatural knowledge. We see in what follows that the tenor of the report made at Jerusalem is *textually* reproduced; comp. the name of Jesus instead of the pronoun *He,* and the present tenses ποιεῖ and βαπτίζει, *makes* and *baptizes.* Jesus must have appeared more dangerous than John, first, because of the Messianic testimony which John had borne to Him, and, then, because of His course of action which was much more independent of legal and Pharisaic forms; finally, because of His miracles; with relation to John, comp. x. 41. The reading of the five Mjj., which omit ἤ, *than,* could only have this meaning: "that the Pharisees had heard that Jesus is making more disciples, and *that* (on his side) John is baptizing." This meaning is strange, and even absurd. The term *disciples,*which here denotes the baptized, will be found again in vii. 3 in this special sense.

The practical conclusion which Jesus draws from this report may lead

---

[1] ℵ Δ Λ some Mnn. Itplerique Vg. Syr. Cop. read ο Ιησους (*Jesus*) instead of ο κυριος (*the Lord*).

[2] A B G L Γ reject η (*than*).

[3] Παλιν (*again*) is found in ℵ C D L M Tᵇ some Mnn. Itplerique Vg. Cop. Syrsch. It is omitted by all the other documents.

us to suppose that John had been already arrested and that, as *Hengstenberg* thinks, the Pharisees had played a part in this imprisonment; comp. the term παρεδόθη, *was delivered up*, Matt. iv. 12; it was, he says, by the hands of the Pharisees, that John had fallen under the power of Herod. But it will be asked why Jesus retires into Galilee, into the domain of Herod; was not this running in the face of danger? No; for this prince's hatred to John was a personal matter. As to His religious activity, Jesus had less hindrance to fear on the part of Herod than on that of the dominant party in Judea.

The remark of ver. 2 is designed to give precision to the indefinite expression used by the evangelist himself, iii. 22: that *Jesus is baptizing*. Nothing is indifferent in the Lord's mode of acting, and John does not wish to allow a false idea to be formed by his readers, respecting one of His acts. Why did Jesus baptize, and that without Himself baptizing? By baptizing, He attested the unity of His work with that of the forerunner. By not Himself baptizing, He made the superiority of His position above that of John the Baptist to be felt. He recalled to mind that which the latter had said: "I baptize you with water, there cometh another who will baptize you with the Spirit and with fire," and reserved expressly for Himself that higher baptism. The first of these observations makes us understand why, at the end of a certain time, He discontinued the baptism of water, and the second, why He re-established it later as a type of the baptism of the Spirit which was to come. At all events, we must not compare this course of action with that of Paul (1 Cor. i. 17) and of Peter (Acts x. 48), which had quite another aim. If He gave up this rite in the interval, this fact stands in relation to that other: that Jesus ceased taking a Messianic position in Galilee, to content Himself with the part of a prophet, up to the moment when He presented Himself again in Judea as the Son of David and the promised Messiah (chap. xii.). At the same time, He gave up transforming into a Messianic community, by means of baptism, that Israel whose unbelief emphatically manifested itself towards Him. There are therefore three degrees in the institution of baptism: 1. The baptism of John: a preparation for the Messianic kingdom by repentance; 2. The baptism of Jesus, at the beginning of His ministry: a sign of attachment to the person of the Messiah, with the character of disciples; 3. The baptism re-instituted by Jesus after His resurrection: a consecration to the baptism of the Spirit. Those who had received the first of these three baptisms (e. g. the apostles) do not seem to have submitted afterwards to the second or third. Jesus made use of them to administer these two latter baptisms (ver. 2; Acts ii.). It is not without reason that *Beck* has compared the baptism of infants in the Christian Church with the second of these three baptisms.

The departure from Judea is pointed out, ver. 3, as a distinct act of *return* to Galilee; and this because, according to ver. 1, the real object of Jesus was much less to go thither than to depart thence. The word πάλιν, *again*, which is read by six Mjj., alludes to a previous return to Galilee (i. 44). John avails himself of each occasion to distinguish these two returns which had been identified by the Synoptic tradition (see on iii. 24). This adverb is, therefore, authentic, notwithstanding the numerous MSS. and critics that omit it or reject it.

Vv. 4, 5. "*Now he must needs pass through Samaria. He cometh thus to a city of Samaria called Sychar,*[1] *near to the parcel of ground which Jacob gave to his son Joseph.*" Ἔδει, *it was necessary*: if one would not, like the very strict Jews, purposely avoid this polluted country (comp. p. 416); Jesus did not share this particularistic spirit. The name *Sychar* is surprising; for the only city known in this locality is that which bears the name of *Shechem*, and which is so frequently mentioned in the Old Testament. Can there be an error here of a writer who was a stranger to Palestine, as the adversaries of the authenticity of our Gospel claim? We think the solutions scarcely probable which make the name Sychar a popular and intentional corruption of that of Shechem, deriving it either from *Schéker, falsehood* (city of falsehood, that is to say, of heathenism), or from Schékar, *liquor* (city of drunkards; comp. Is. xxviii. 1, *the drunkards of Ephraim*). We might rather hold an involuntary transformation through an interchange of liquid letters which was frequent (as e. g. that of *bar* for *ben, son*). But the most natural solution is that which is offered by the passages of Eusebius and Jerome, in which two neighboring localities bearing these two distinct names are positively distinguished. Eusebius says in the *Onomasticon*: "Sychar *before* Neapolis." Neapolis, indeed, is nothing else then the modern name of Shechem. The Talmud speaks also of a locality called *Soukar*, of a *spring* Soukar, of the *plain* of Soukar. At the present day also, a hamlet exists very near Jacob's well and situated at the foot of Mount Ebal, which bears the name *El-Ascar*, a name which very much resembles the one which we read in John and in the Talmud. *Lieut. Conder* and *M. Socin*[2] also give their assent to this view. It seems certain, moreover, that the ancient Shechem was situated somewhat more to the east than the present city of Nablous. This is proved by the ruins which are discovered everywhere between Nablous and Jacob's well (see Félix Bovet, *Voyage en Terre-Sainte*, p. 363). Petermann (art. *Samaria* in Herzog's *Encyclop*. xiii. p. 362) says: "The emperor Vespasian considerably enlarged the city on the western side." In any case, to see, with *Furrer*, in this name Sychar an indication of the purely ideal character of the account, one must be thoroughly preoccupied by a preconceived theory (*Bibellex.*, iii., p. 375). It is at Nablous that the remnant of the Samaritan people who are reduced to the number of about one hundred and thirty persons live at the present day.

According to *de Wette, Meyer*, and others, the gift of Jacob to Joseph, mentioned in this fifth verse, rests on a false tradition, even arising from a misunderstanding of the LXX. Gen. xlviii. 22, Jacob says to Joseph: "*I give thee one portion* (Schekem), *above thy brethren, which I took from the Amorites with my sword and my bow.*" As the patriarch has just adopted as

---

[1] All the MSS.. with the exception of some Mnn., and all the ancient Versions read Συχαρ and not Σιχαρ.

[2] *Zeitschrift des Deutschen Palästina-Vereins*, I. Heft. p. 42.

his own the two children of Joseph, it is natural for him to assign to this son *one portion above all his brethren*. But the Hebrew word (*Schekem*) which denotes a portion of territory (strictly *shoulder*) is at the same time the name of the city, Shechem; and it is claimed that the LXX., taking this word in the geographical sense (as the name of a city), gave rise, through this false translation, to the popular legend which we find here, and according to which Jacob left Shechem as a legacy to Joseph. But it is incontestable that when Jacob speaks " of the portion of country which he had taken from the Amorites *with his bow and his sword*," he alludes to the bloody exploit of his two sons, Simeon and Levi, against the city of Shechem (Gen. xxxiv. 25–27): "*Having taken their sword, they entered the city of Shechem, and slew all its inhabitants and utterly spoiled it.*" This is the only martial act mentioned in the history of the patriarch. Notwithstanding its reprehensible character, Jacob appropriates it to himself in these words, as a confirmation of the purchase which he had himself previously made (Gen. xxxiii. 19) of a domain in this district of Shechem, and he sees therein, as it were, the pledge of the future conquest of this whole country by his descendants. Thus, then, by using in order to designate the *portion* which he gives to Joseph, the word *schekem*, it is the patriarch who makes a play upon words, such as is found so frequently in the Old Testament; he leaves to him a portion (*Schekem*) which is nothing else than *Shechem*. His sons so well understood his thought, that, when their descendants returned to Canaan, their first care was to lay the bones of Joseph in Jacob's field near to Shechem (Josh. xxiv. 32), then to assign, as a *portion*, to the larger of the two tribes descended from Joseph, that of Ephraim, the country in which *Shechem* was located. The LXX. not being able to render the play upon words in Greek, translated the word *schekem* in the geographical sense; for it was the one which had most significance. There is here, therefore, neither a false translation on their part, nor a false tradition taken up by the evangelist.

Ver. 6. "*Jacob's well was there; Jesus therefore, wearied by his journey, sat thus*[1] *by the well; it was about the sixth hour.*" This well still exists; for "it is probably the same which is now called *Bir-Jakoub*" (Renan, *Vie de Jésus*, p. 243). It is situated thirty-five minutes eastward of Nablous, precisely at the place where the road which follows the principal valley, that of Mukhna, from south to north, turns suddenly to the west, to enter the narrow valley of Shechem, with Ebal on the northeast and Gerizim on the southwest. The well is hollowed out, not in the rock, as is commonly said, but rather, according to Lieutenant Anderson, who descended into it in 1866, in alluvial ground; the same person has ascertained that the sides are for this reason lined with rude masonry. It is nine feet in diameter. In March, 1694, Maundrell found the depth to be one hundred and five feet. In 1843, according to Wilson, it was only seventy-five feet, owing, doubtless, to the falling in of the earth. Maundrell found in it fifteen feet of water. So also Anderson, in May, 1866. Robinson and

---

[1] Ουτως (*thus*), is omitted by some Mnn.; It^{alla}., and Syr.

Bovet found it dry. Schubert, in the month of April, was able to drink of its water. Tristram, in December, found only the bottom wet, while, in February, he found it full of water. At the present day, it is blocked up with large stones, five or six feet below the aperture; but the real opening is found several feet lower. A few minutes further to the north, towards the hamlet of Askar, the tomb of Joseph is pointed out. Robinson asks with what object this gigantic work could have been undertaken in a country so abounding in springs—as many as eighty are counted in Nablous and its environs. There is no other answer to give but that of Hengstenberg: "This work is that of a man who, a stranger in the country, wished to live independently of the inhabitants to whom the springs belonged, and to leave a monument of his right of property in this soil and in this whole country. Thus the very nature of this work fully confirms the origin which is assigned to it by tradition."

The caravan, leaving the great plain which stretches towards the north, directed its course to the left, in order to enter the valley of Shechem. There Jesus seated Himself near the well, leaving His disciples to continue their journey as far as Sychar, where they were to procure provisions. He was oppressed by fatigue, κεκοπιακώς (*wearied*), says the evangelist; and the Tübingen school ascribes to John the opinion of the Docetæ, according to which the body of Jesus was only an appearance! Οὕτως (*thus*), is almost untranslatable in our language; it is doubtless for some such reason that it is omitted in the Latin and Syriac versions. It signifies: without further preparation; taking things as He found them. According to the meaning given by *Erasmus, Beza*, etc., "wearied *as He was*," the adverb would rather have been placed before the verb; comp. Acts. xx. 11; xxvii. 17 (*Meyer*). The imperfect (ἐκαθέζετο), is descriptive; it does not mean: *He seated Himself*, but: *He was seated;* (comp. xi. 20; xx. 12; Luke ii. 46, etc.). The word refers not to what precedes, but to what follows. "He *was there seated* when a woman came . . . " The *sixth hour* must denote mid-day, according to the mode of reckoning generally received at that time in the East (see at i. 40). This hour of the day suits the context better than six o'clock in the morning or evening. Jesus was oppressed at once by the journey and the heat. The first part of the conversation extends as far as ver. 15; it is immediately connected with the situation which is given.

Vv. 7–9. "*A woman of Samaria comes to draw water. Jesus says to her: Give me to drink.* 8. *For his disciples had gone to the city to buy food.* 9. *The Samaritan woman therefore says to him: How is it that thou, being a Jew, dost ask drink of me who am a Samaritan woman. (For the Jews have no dealings with the Samaritans.*"[1]) How was it that this woman came so far to seek water, and at such an hour? She had undoubtedly been working in the fields, and was coming to draw water on her return to her home at the hour of dinner (see at ver. 15). It has been thought that this feature suits an evening hour better, since that is ordinarily the hour when the women go to the well. But in that case this woman would undoubtedly not have been found here alone (*Meyer, Weiss*).

[1] This parenthesis is wholly omitted by ℵ.

The objective phrase: *of Samaria*, depends on the word *woman*, and not on the verb *comes;* for, in the latter case, Samaria would mean the city of that name; an impossible meaning, since that city was situated three leagues to the northeast. The request of Jesus must be understood in the most simple sense, and regarded as serious. There is no allegory in it; He is really thirsty; this follows from the word *wearied*. But this does not prevent Him, in beginning a conversation with the woman, from obeying another necessity than that of thirst—namely, of saving (vv. 32, 34). He is not unaware that the way to gain a soul is often to ask a service of it; there is thus conceded to it a kind of superiority which flatters it. " The effect of this little word was great; it began to overturn the wall which had for ages separated the two peoples," says *Lange*. The remark of ver. 8 is intended to explain that, if the disciples had been present, they would have had a vessel, an ἄντλημα, to let down into the well. Indeed, in the East, every caravan is provided with a bucket for drawing from the wells which appear on the road (see ver. 11). This explanation given by the evangelist, proves the complete reality, in his view, of the need which called forth the request of Jesus. There is no longer here anything of docetism! Does the expression, *the disciples*, denote all the disciples without exception? Might not one of them, John, for example, have remained with Jesus? It would be strange enough that Jesus should have been left there, absolutely alone, in the midst of a hostile population; and twelve men were not necessary to procure provisions! *Meyer's* prudery is offended at such a simple supposition, and *Reuss* goes so far as to say : " The luminous idea has been formed of leaving John at the place to take notes."—The Jewish doctors said : " He who eats bread with a Samaritan is as he who eats swine's flesh." This prohibition, however, was not absolute; it did not apply either to fruits or to vegetables. As to corn and wine, we are ignorant. Uncooked eggs were allowed; whether cooked, was a question (*Hausrath, Neutest. Zeitgesch.*, I., p. 22). It is proved, however, that the most strict Rabbinical regulations belong to a later epoch.

How did the Samaritan woman recognize Jesus as a Jew. By His dress or His accent? *Stier* has observed that in some words which Jesus had just spoken the letter ש occurred, which, according to Judg. xii. 6, distinguished the two pronunciations, the Jewish (*sch*), and the Samaritan (*s*); תני לשחת (*teni lischechoth;* Samaritan: *lisechoth*).—The last words (οὐ γὰρ συγχρῶνται) are a remark of the evangelist, with a view to his Gentile readers who might be unacquainted with the origin of the Samaritan people (2 Kings xvii. 24 ff.). It was a mixture of five nations transported from the East by Esarhaddon to re-people the kingdom of Samaria, the inhabitants of which his predecessor had removed. To the worship of their national gods, they united that of the divinity of the country, Jehovah. After the return from the Babylonish captivity, they offered the Jews their services for the rebuilding of the temple. Being rejected, they used all their influence with the kings of Persia, to hinder the re-establishment of the Jewish people. They built for themselves a temple on Mount Gerizim. Their first priest was Manasseh, a Jewish priest who had married a Persian wife. They were more detested by the Jews than the Gentiles themselves were. Samaritan proselytes were not received. It has been thought that the woman, in frolicsomeness, exaggerated somewhat the consequences of the hostility between the two peoples, and that in submitting to Jesus this insignificant question, she wished to enjoy for a moment the superiority which her position gave her. This shade of thought does not appear from the text. The Samaritan woman *naively* expresses her surprise.

Ver. 10. "*Jesus answered and said unto her: If thou knewest the gift of God and who it is who says unto thee: Give me to drink, thou wouldst have asked of him thyself, and he would have given thee living water.*" To this observation of the woman Jesus replies, not by renewing His request, but by making her an offer by means of which He reassumes His position of superiority. To this end, it is enough to raise this woman's thoughts to the spiritual sphere, where there is no more anything for Him but to give, and for her but to receive. The expression: *The gift of God*, may be regarded as an abstract notion, whose concrete reality is indicated by the following words: *who it is that says to thee* (so in our first edition). The words of Jesus in iii. 16 : " *God so loved the world, that he gave his only-begotten Son*," favor this sense, according to which Jesus is Himself the gift of God. But as Jesus distinguishes Himself from the living water, in the following words, it is better to see in the words: *He who says to thee*, the agent through whom God makes this gift to the human soul. God gives Jesus to the world, and Jesus gives to it the living water. *Living water*, in the literal sense, denotes spring-water, in contrast with water of a cistern, or stagnant water. Gen. xxvi. 19: " *Israel's servants dug in the valley, and found there a well of living water*," that is, a subterranean spring of which they made a well; comp. Levit. xiv. 5. In the figurative sense, living water is, therefore, a blessing which has the property of incessantly reproducing itself, like a gushing spring, like life itself, and which consequently is never exhausted. What does Jesus mean by this? According to *Justin* and *Cyprian*, baptism; according to *Lücke*, faith; according to *Olshausen*, Jesus Himself; according to *Calvin, Luthardt, Keil*, the Holy Spirit; according to *Grotius*, the evangelical doctrine; according to *Meyer*, truth; according to *Tholuck, Weiss*, the word of salvation ; according to *Westcott*, eternal life, consisting in the knowledge of God and of His Son Jesus Christ (xvii. 3); this scholar cites as analogous the Rabbinical proverb: " When the prophets speak of water, they mean the law." *Lange*, according to ver. 14: The interior life, especially with reference to peace in the heart. It seems to me that, according to Jesus Himself (vv. 13, 14), it is, as Westcott thinks, eternal life, salvation, the full satisfaction of all the wants of the heart and the possession of all the holy energies of which the soul is susceptible. This state of soundness of the soul can only be the result of the dwelling of Jesus Himself in the heart, by means of His word made inwardly living by the Holy Spirit (chaps. xiv.–xvi.). This explanation includes, therefore, all the others up to a certain point.

Vv. 11, 12. "*The woman*[1] *says to him: Sir, thou hast nothing to draw with, and the well is deep; from whence, then,*[2] *hast thou that living water?* 12. *Art thou greater than our father Jacob, who gave us the well, and who drank of it himself, as well as his sons and his cattle?*" The Samaritan woman takes the expression *living water* in its literal sense. She means: "Thou canst *neither* (οὔτε) draw from the well the living water which thou offerest to me—for thou hast no vessel to draw with—*nor* (καὶ), because of its depth, canst thou reach by any other means the spring which feeds it." Unable to suppose that He is speaking spiritually, she cannot understand that He offers her what He has Himself asked from her (*Westcott*). The term κύριε, Sir, expresses, however, profound respect. She calls Jacob *our father*, because the Samaritans claimed descent from Ephraim and Manasseh (Joseph. *Antiqq.* ix. 14, 3). Θρέμματα: servants and cattle, everything requiring to be supported. It is the complete picture of patriarchal nomad life which appears here.

Vv. 13, 14. "*Jesus answered and said to her: Whoever drinks of this water shall thirst again; but he that shall drink*[3] *of the water that I shall give him, shall never thirst; but the water that I*[4] *shall give him*[4] *shall become in him a fountain of water springing up unto eternal life.*" It is to no purpose that the water of the well is spring-water; it is not that which Jesus means by living water; it has not the power of reproducing itself in him who drinks it; so, after a certain time, the want revives and the torment of thirst makes itself felt. "A beautiful inscription," says Stier, "to be placed upon fountains." Such water presents itself to the thought of Jesus as the emblem of all earthly satisfactions, after which the want reappears in the soul and puts it again in dependence upon external objects in order to its satisfaction.

Jesus defines in ver. 14 the nature of the true living water; it is that which, reproducing itself within by its own potentiality, quenches the soul's want as it arises, so that the heart cannot suffer a single moment of inward torment of thirst. Man possesses in himself a satisfaction independent of earthly objects and conditions.—Ἐγώ; yes, *I*, (in opposition to Jacob).—With *Reuss*, I formerly referred the words εἰς ζωὴν αἰώνιον, *unto eternal life*, not to time, but to the effect produced, to the *mode* of appearance: in the form of eternal life. The parallel term, however, εἰς τὸν αἰῶνα *for ever*, favors rather the temporal sense, "*even to the life without end.*"

Ver. 15. "*The woman says to him: Sir, give me this water, that I may not thirst, neither pass this way*[5] *to draw.*"—This woman's request has certainly a serious side. The respectful address, *Sir*, is sufficient to prove this. It follows likewise from the grave character of the answer of Jesus. Even though the absence of spiritual wants causes her not to understand, she is

---

[1] B rejects η γυνη. ℵ reads εκεινη.
[2] ℵ D Syr., omit ουν.
[3] ℵ D read ο δε πινων, instead of ος δ' αν πιη.
[4] ℵ D M, some Mnn., and It., read εγω before δωσω. ℵ rejects αυτω which follows this same word.
[5] Instead of ερχομαι or ερχωμαι, between which the other three Mjj. are divided, ℵ reads διερχωμαι, B διερχομαι.

impressed; can this man indeed have the power of working such a miracle? Nevertheless, the expression of the desire which she experiences to have her life made more comfortable has in it something *naive* and almost humorous. —The last words reproduce the promise of Jesus: "shall not thirst." The reading of the two oldest MSS.: "that I *pass* no more this way," instead of: *that I come hither no more*, should undoubtedly be adopted. No one would have substituted this for the received reading. It confirms the idea that we have expressed: namely, that the woman was merely *passing* that way, as she returned to her house.

The first phase of the conversation is closed. But Jesus has raised a sublime ideal in this woman's imagination—that of eternal life. Could he abandon her before having taught her more on this subject, since she had thus far shown herself teachable.

Vv. 16–18. "*Jesus says to her: Go, call thy husband, and come hither.* 17. *The woman answered and said: I have no husband. Jesus says to her: Thou hast well said: I have*[1] *no husband.* 18. *For thou hast had five*[2] *husbands, and he whom thou now hast is not thy husband. In this thou hast said truly.*"[3]— Westcott observes that the natural transition to this invitation, which is apparently so abrupt, is perhaps to be found in the last words of the woman: "that I pass no more this way to draw," which suggest persons of her family for whom she is performing this duty.—Must we seek the object of this request in the moral *effect* which it should produce on the woman, by giving Jesus the opportunity to prove to her his prophetic knowledge (*Meyer, Reuss*, etc.)? Certainly not, for there would then be a miracle of exhibition, which would not be in harmony with the ordinary simplicity of Jesus. The invitation must be its own justification. Others think that Jesus proposed to Himself to awaken in this woman the sense of her life of sin (*Tholuck, Luthardt, Bonnet, Weiss*, etc.). But under this form of supposition also, the means used have something of indirectness, which does not seem to be in entire conformity with the perfect sincerity of the Lord. The true reason of it seems to me rather to be this: Jesus did not wish to act upon a dependent person without the participation of the one to whom she was bound, and the more because the summoning of the latter might be the means of extending His work. *Meyer* makes the nature of the relation which united them an objection. But the arrival of this woman, at so unusual an hour, had undoubtedly been for Jesus the signal of a work to be done; and there is nothing to show that, when addressing this invitation to the woman, Jesus had her antecedents already present to His mind. Might not the term, *thy husband*, indeed, be completely justified by this supposition? The prophetic insight may not have been awakened in Him till He heard the answer which struck Him: "*I have no husband:*"—She had been married five times; and now, after these five lawful unions, she was living in an illicit relation. The fact that she did not venture to call the man with whom she is living *her husband*, shows in this woman a certain element of right character.

[1] ℵ It^{aliq}.; Heracleon: $\varepsilon\chi\varepsilon\iota\varsigma$ (*that thou hast not*) instead of $\varepsilon\chi\omega$ (*I have not*).

[2] Heracleon: $\varepsilon\xi$ (*six*) instead of $\pi\varepsilon\nu\tau\varepsilon$ (*five*).

[3] ℵ E: $\alpha\lambda\eta\theta\omega\varsigma$ instead of $\alpha\lambda\eta\theta\varepsilon\varsigma$.

The reply of Jesus is not free from irony. The partial assent which He gives to the woman's answer, has something sarcastic in it. The same is true of the contrast which Jesus brings out between the number *five* and the: " I have no ! "—The emphatic position of the pronoun σοῦ before ἀνήρ implies, perhaps, the following understood antithesis: "Not thine own, *but the husband of another*." From this it would follow that she had lived in adultery. It is not absolutely necessary, however, to press so far the meaning of this construction.—Modern criticism, since the time of *Strauss* (see especially *Keim* and *Hausrath*), connects this part of the conversation with the fact that the Samaritan nation was formed of five eastern tribes which, after having each brought its own God, had adopted, besides, Jehovah, the God of the country (2 Kings xvii. 30, 31). The woman with her five husbands and the man with whom she was now living as the sixth, are, it is said, the symbol of the whole Samaritan people, and we have here a proof of the ideal character of this story. The view rests especially on this statement of Josephus (*Antiq.* ix. 14, 3): " Five nations having brought each its own God to Samaria." But 1, in the O. T. passage (2 Kings xvii. 30, 31), there is, indeed, a question of *five* peoples, but, at the same time, of *seven* gods, two peoples having introduced two gods. 2. These seven gods were all worshiped simultaneously, and not successively, up to the moment when they gave place to Jehovah; a fact which destroys the correspondence between the situations. 3. Is it conceivable that Jehovah would be compared to the sixth husband, who was evidently the worst of all in the woman's life ? If the reading *six* of Heracleon, has reference to the ancient Samaritan religion, it does not refer to the addition of Jehovah to the other five gods, but rather to 2 Kings xvii. 30, where there is an allusion to six or seven gods brought in by the Eastern Gentiles.

Vv. 19, 20. " *The woman says to him: Sir, I see that thou art a prophet. 20. Our fathers worshiped in this mountain;*[1] *and you say that in Jerusalem is the place*[2] *where men ought to worship.*" Some see in this question of the woman only an attempt to turn aside the disturbance of her conscience, " a woman's ruse " (*de Wette*) with the design of escaping from a painful subject. "She diverts attention from her own life by proposing a point of controversy " (*Astié*). But would Jesus reply, as He does, to a question proposed in such a spirit ? *Besser* and *Luthardt* go to the opposite extreme: This question is, in their view, the indication of a tortured conscience, which, sighing for pardon, desires to know the true sanctuary to which it can go to make expiation for its faults. This is still more forced. *Reuss*, with an irony which assails the evangelist himself, says: " If she asks the question thus, it is only for the purpose of bringing out the declaration of the Lord which we are about to read." Westcott says rightly: " Here is the very natural inquiry of a soul which finds itself face to face with an interpreter of the divine will." This woman has recognized in Jesus a

---

[1] All the Mjj.: εν τω ορει τουτω, instead of εν τουτω τω ορει which T. R. reads with Mnn. [2] ℵ omits ο τοπος.

prophet; she has at the same time found in Him largeness of heart. The two answers, vv. 17, 19, have proved that, notwithstanding her faults, she is not altogether wanting in right character. It follows even from ver. 25 that religious thoughts are not strange to her, that she is looking for the Messiah and that she waits to receive from Him the explanation of the questions which embarrass her. The fact of a *Jewish* prophet, present before her eyes, inspires her with doubts as to the religious claim of her nation. Is it not an altogether simple thing, that, in her present situation, after her conscience has been so profoundly moved, her thoughts should turn to the great religious question which separates the two peoples, and that she should ask the solution of it? It is an anticipation of the more complete teaching which she expects from the Messiah. By the term: *our fathers*, she perhaps understands the Israelites of the time of Joshua, who, according to the reading of the Samaritan Pentateuch (Deut. xxvii. 4), raised their altar on Mount Gerizim, and not on Ebal; in any case, she understands by this expression all the Samaritan ancestors who had worshiped on Gerizim, from the period when a temple was built there in Nehemiah's time. This temple had been destroyed by John Hyrcanus one hundred and twenty-nine years before Christ. But even after this event, the place had remained a sacred spot Deut. xi. 29, as it still is at the present day. It is there that the Samaritans even now celebrate the feast of the Passover every year. Jerusalem not being named anywhere in the law, the preference of the Samaritans for Gerizim found plausible reasons in the patriarchal history. The superiority of the Jewish sanctuary could be justified only from the standpoint of the later books of the Old Testament. But we know that the Samaritans admitted only the Pentateuch and the Mosaic institution. When she said: *on this mountain*, she pointed to it with the finger. For Jacob's well is situated directly at the foot of Gerizim. She confines herself to setting forth the antithesis, thinking indeed that Jesus will understand the question which follows from it.

Ver. 21. " *Jesus says to her: Woman, believe me;* [1] *the hour cometh when neither on this mountain nor at Jerusalem shall ye worship the Father.*" The position of Jesus is a delicate one. He cannot deny the truth, and He must not repel this woman. His reply is admirable. He has just been called a prophet, and He prophesies. He announces a new economy in which the Samaritans, having become children of God, will be set free from that local sanctuary which the woman points out to Him on the summit of Gerizim, but without being compelled for this reason to go to Jerusalem. The filial character of this new worship will free it from all the external limitations by which all the old national worships were burdened. If the privilege of Gerizim passes away, it will not be that it may be assigned to Jerusalem. " You will not bring the Jews hither; but they shall no more force you to go to them. You shall meet each other,

---

[1] T. R. reads γυναι πιστευσον μοι with 14 Mjj. It^{aliq}. Syr. while ℵ B C D L 3 Mnn. b Orig. read πιστευε μοι γυναι (D πιστευσον).

both parties alike, in the great family of the Father's worshipers." What treasures cast to such a soul! What other desire than that of doing His Father's will could inspire in Jesus such condescension!—The aorist πίστευσον in the T. R. signifies: " Perform an act of faith." We can understand the prefixing of the apostrophe: *woman*, in this reading which makes such an earnest appeal to her will. The present πίστευε in the Alexandrian documents simply signifies: " Believe from this moment and for the future." Both the readings may be sustained. This summons to faith answered to this woman's profession: "Thou art a prophet." The subject *you* of *shall worship* might denote the Samaritans and Jews (*Hilgenfeld*), or men in general (so in my 2d ed.), in contrast to Jesus Himself or to Jesus and His own. But this woman could not regard herself as the representative either of humanity in general, or of the Samaritans and Jews together. The subject of *you shall worship* must rather be derived from those words of her question in ver. 20: *Our fathers worshiped*. It is the Samaritans only.

Ver. 22. " *Ye worship that which ye do not know ; we worship that which we know, because salvation comes from the Jews.*" The antithesis, which is so clearly marked between *ye* and *we* proves, whatever *Hilgenfeld* may say, who wrongly cites *Hengstenberg* as being of his opinion (comp. the Commentary of the latter, I. pp. 264–269), that the *ye* denotes the Samaritans and the *we* Jesus and the Jews. After having put His impartiality beyond suspicion by the revelation of the great future announced in ver. 21, Jesus enters more closely into the question proposed to Him and decides it, as related to the past, in favor of the Jews. "It is at Jerusalem that the living God has made Himself known; and that because it is by means of the Jews that He intends to give salvation to the world." God is known only so far as He gives Himself to be known. The seat of the true knowledge of Him can, therefore, only be where He makes His revelation; and this place is Jerusalem. By breaking with the course of theocratic development since the time of Moses, and rejecting the prophetic revelations, the Samaritans had separated themselves from the historic God, from the living God. They had preserved only the abstract idea of the one God, a purely rational monotheism. Now the *idea* of God, as soon as it is taken for God Himself, is no more than a chimera. Even while worshiping God, therefore, they *do not know* what they worship. The Jews, on the contrary, have developed themselves in constant contact with the divine manifestations; they have remained in the school of the God of revelation, and in this living relation they have preserved the principle of a true knowledge. And whence comes this peculiar relation between this people and God? The answer is given in what follows. If God has made Himself so specially known to the Jews, it is because He wished to make use of them, in order to accomplish the salvation of the world. It is salvation which, retroactively in some sort, has produced all the previous theocratic revelations, as it is the fruit which, although appearing at the end of the annual vegetation, is the real cause of it. The true cause of things is their aim. Thus is the ὅτι, *because*, explained.

This passage has embarrassed rationalistic criticism, which, making the Jesus of our Gospel an adversary of Judaism, does not allow that He could have proclaimed Himself *a Jew*, and have Himself united in this *we* His own worship and that of the Israelitish people. And indeed if, as *d'Eichthal* alleges (*Les Evangiles* I. p. xxviii.), the Jesus of the fourth Gospel, "from one end to the other of His preaching, seems to make sport of the Jews," and consequently cannot "be one of them," there is a flagrant contradiction between our passage and the entire Gospel. *Hilgenfeld* thinks that, at ver. 21, Jesus addresses the Jews and the Samaritans taken together, as by a kind of prosopopoeia, and that at ver. 22, by the words: *we worship that which we know*, he designates *Himself*, (with the believers) in opposition to these Jews and Samaritans. We have already seen at ver. 21 that this explanation cannot be sustained, and this appears more clearly still from the words of ver. 22: "Because salvation comes from *the Jews*," which evidently prove that the subject of "*we worship*" can only be the Jews. *D'Eichthal* and *Renan* make use here of different expedients. The enigma is explained, says the first, when it is observed that this expression is only "the annotation, or rather the protest, which a Jew of the old school had inscribed on the margin of the text, and of which an error of the copyist has made a word of Jesus" (p. xxix., note). And this scholar is in exstacies over the services which criticism can render to the interpretation of the sacred writings! Renan makes a similar hypothesis. "The 22d verse, which expresses an opposite thought to that of vv. 21 and 23, seems an awkward addition of the evangelist alarmed at the boldness of the saying which he reports" (p. 244, note). Arbitrariness could not be pressed further. The critic begins by decreeing what the fourth Gospel must be; an anti-Jewish book. Then, when he meets an expression which contradicts this alleged character, he rejects it with a stroke of the pen. He obtains, thus, not the Gospel which *is*, but that which he *would have*. But is it supposed that the first Jew whom one might meet was in possession of the authentic copy of our Gospel, to modify it according to his fancy; or that it was very easy for any chance foreigner, when this writing was once spread abroad, to introduce an interpolation into all the copies which were in circulation among the Churches? As for Renan's hypothesis, it supposes that the evangelist thought he knew more than the Master whom he worshiped; which is not very logical. The alleged incompatibility of this saying with vv. 21, 23, and with spirit of the fourth Gospel in general, is an assertion without foundation. (See Introduction, p. 127–134.)

At ver. 21 Jesus has transferred the question to the future, when the *localized* worship of ancient times should no longer exist. In ver. 22, He has justified the Jews, historically speaking. At ver. 23 He returns to the future announced in ver. 21, and describes all its grandeur.

Vv. 23, 24. "*But the hour cometh and now is, when the true worshipers shall worship the Father in spirit and in truth; for also the Father seeketh such worshipers. 24. God is spirit, and they that worship him*[1] *must worship him in spirit and in truth.*"[2] *But:* in contrast with the period of Israelitish prerogative now ended. The words, *and now is*, added here, serve to arouse more strongly the already-awakened attention of the woman. It

---

[1] ℵ D d Heracleon Orig. omit αυτον after προσκυνουντας.

[2] ℵ reads: εν πνευματι αληθειας (*in the spirit of truth*).

430 / Birth of Faith

is as if the first breath of the new era were just passing across this soul. Perhaps Jesus sees in the distance His disciples returning, the representatives of this nation of new worshipers which in a few moments will be recruited by the first-fruits of the Samaritan people. He brings out the two characteristics of the future worship: spirituality and truth. *Spirit* denotes here the highest organ of the human soul, by means of which it has communion with the divine world. It is the seat of contemplation, the place of the soul's meeting with God, the sanctuary where the true worship is celebrated; Rom. i. 9: "*God, whom I serve in my spirit*" (ἐν τῷ πνεύματί μου); Eph. vi. 18: *praying in the spirit* (ἐν πνεύματι). This *spirit*, in man, the πνεῦμα ἀνθρώπινον, remains a mere potentiality, so long as it is not penetrated by the Divine Spirit. But when this union is accomplished, it becomes capable of realizing the true worship of which Jesus speaks. This first feature marks the *intensity* of the new worship. The second, *truth*, is the corollary of the first. The worship rendered in the inner sanctuary of the spirit is the only true worship, because it alone is conformed to the nature of God, its object: "*God is spirit.*" The idea of *sincerity* does not fill out the meaning of the word *truth;* for a Jewish or Samaritan prayer might evidently be sincere. The truth of the worship is its inward character, in opposition to every demonstration without spiritual reality. Though these words exclude all subjection of Christian worship to the limitations of place or time, it is nevertheless true that by virtue of its very freedom, this worship can spontaneously accept conditions of time and place. But, as Mme. Guyon says, the external adoration is then "only a springing forth of the adoration of the Spirit" (quoted by *Astié*). The two defining words: *in spirit* and *in truth* are formal; the concrete character of the new worship is expressed by the word: *the Father*. The worship of which Jesus is speaking is the converse of a son with his father. We know from what source Jesus drew this definition of spiritual and true worship. "*Abba (Father)*" such was the constant expression of His inmost feeling. By adding that the Father, at this very moment, is *seeking* such worshipers, Jesus gives the woman an intimation that He is Himself the one sent by the Father to form this new people and that He invites her to become one of them.

The 24th verse justifies, from the essential nature of God, what He has just said of the spiritual and true nature of the worship now demanded by God Himself. Jesus does not give the maxim "*God is spirit*" as a new revelation. It is like an axiom from which He starts, a premise admitted by His interlocutor herself. The Old Testament taught, indeed, the spirituality of God in all its sublimity (1 Kings viii. 27), and the Samaritans certainly held it, like the Jews (see *Gesenius, de Samarit. theol.* p. 12, and *Lücke*). What is new in this saying is not the truth affirmed, but the consequence which Jesus draws from it with reference to the worship which was to come. He calls forth from it the idea of the people of the children of God offering throughout the whole world constant adoration; comp. Mal. i. 11. Thus to a guilty woman, perhaps an adulteress, Jesus reveals truths which He had probably never unfolded to His own disciples.—The reading of the Sinaitic MS. ἐν πνεύματι ἀληθείας, *in the spirit of truth*, is derived from xiv. 17; xv. 26, etc., and arises from the false application of the word πνεῦμα to the Holy Spirit.

Ver. 25. "*The woman says to him, I know*[1] *that Messiah cometh* (*he who is called Christ*); *when he is come, he will declare unto us*[2] *all things.*"[3] The woman's answer bears witness of a certain desire for light. Her Spirit yearns for the perfect revelation. This is the reason why we were not wrong in interpreting vv. 15, 20 in a sense favorable to her character. According to modern accounts, the Samaritans actually expect a Messiah, to whom they give the name *Assaëf* (from שׁוּב, *to return*); this word signifies, according to *Gesenius*, *he who brings back*, who converts; according to *de Sacy* and *Hengstenberg*, *he who returns*, in the sense that, as the expectation of the Samaritans was founded on Deut. xviii. 18: "*God will raise up for you another prophet from among your brethren, like unto me*," the Messiah to their view is a Moses who returns. At the present day, they call him *el-Muhdy*. There is a striking contrast between the notion of the Messiah, as it is expressed by the mouth of this woman, and the earthly and political notions on this subject which Jesus encountered in Israel. The Samaritan idea was imperfect, no doubt; the Messiah was a prophet, not a king. But it contained nothing false; and for this reason Jesus is able to appropriate it to Himself, and *here* declare Himself the Christ, which He did in Israel only at the last moment (xvii. 3; Matt. xxvi. 64). The translation ὁ λεγόμενος Χριστός, *who is called Christ*, belongs to the evangelist. He repeats this explanation, already given in i. 42, unquestionably because of the complete strangeness of this word Μεσσίας to Greek readers. It has been said that the Jewish term Messiah could not have been ascribed by John to this foreign woman. But this popular name might easily have passed from the Jews to the Samaritans, especially in the region of Shechem, which was inhabited by Jewish fugitives (Joseph. *Antiq*. xi. 8. 6). Perhaps, the very absence of the article before the word Μεσσίας, indicates that the woman uses this word as a proper name, as is done in the case of foreign words (comp. i. 42). The word ἔρχεται (*comes*) is an echo of the two ἔρχεται of vv. 21, 23; she surrenders herself to the impulse towards the new era which Jesus has impressed on her soul. The pronoun ἐκεῖνος, *he*, has, as ordinarily with John, an exclusive sense; it serves to place this revealer in contrast with all others; to that very one whom she had before her. The preposition in the verb ἀναγγελεῖ marks the perfect *clearness*, and the object, πάντα or ἄπαντα, the *complete* character of the Messiah's expected revelation.

Ver. 26. "*Jesus says to her : I who speak unto thee am he.*" Jesus, not having to fear, as we have just seen, that he would call forth in this woman a whole world of dangerous illusions, like those which, among the Jews, were connected with the name of Messiah, reveals Himself fully to her. This conduct is not therefore, as *de Wette* claims, in contradiction with

---

[1] G L A some Mnn. Syr. read οιδαμεν (*we know*).

[2] ℵ D (but not d) read αναγγελλει instead of αναγγελει (the present instead of the future).

[3] ℵ B C Orig. (four times) read απαντα instead of παντα.

such words as Matt. viii. 4; xvi. 20, etc. The difference in the soil explains the difference in the seed which the hand of Jesus deposits in it.

How can we describe the astonishment which such a declaration must have produced in this woman? It expresses itself, better than by words, in her silence and her conduct (ver. 28). She had arrived, a few minutes before, careless and given up to earthly thoughts; and lo, in a few moments, she is brought to a new faith, and even transformed into an earnest missionary of that faith. How did the Lord thus raise up and elevate this soul? When speaking with Nicodemus, He started from the idea which filled the heart of every Pharisee—that of the kingdom of God, and he drew from it the most rigorous moral consequences; for He knew that He was addressing a man accustomed to the discipline of the law. Then, He unfolded to him the truths of the divine kingdom, by connecting them with a striking Old Testament type and putting them in contrast with the corresponding features of the Pharisaic programme. Here, on the contrary, conversing with a woman destitute of all Scriptural preparation, He takes His point of departure from the commonest of things, the water of this well. Then, by a bold antithesis, He wakens in her mind the thought, in her heart the want, of a supernatural gift which may forever quench the heart's thirst. The aspiration for salvation once awakened becomes in her an inward prophecy to which He attaches His new revelations. By the teaching with reference to the true worship, He responds to the religious prepossessions of this woman, as directly as by the revelation of the heavenly things He had responded to the inmost thoughts of Nicodemus. With the latter He reveals Himself as the only-begotten Son, while still avoiding the title of *Christ*. With the Samaritan He boldly uses this latter term; but without dreaming of initiating into the mysteries of the incarnation and of redemption this soul which is yet only in the first rudiments of the moral life. Certain analogies have been observed in the outward course of these two conversations, and an argument has been drawn from them against the truth of the two stories. But this resemblance naturally results from what is analogous in the two meetings: on both sides, a soul wholly earthly finding itself in contact with a heavenly thought, and the latter trying to raise the other to its own level. This similarity in the situations sufficiently explains the correspondences of the two conversations, the diversity of which is, moreover, quite as remarkable as the resemblance.

Jesus and the Disciples: vv. 27–38

Ver. 27. *Upon this*[1] *his disciples came, and they were astonished*[2] *that he was speaking with a woman; yet no one of them said:*[3] *What seekest thou? or, Why speakest thou with her."* There existed a rabbinical prejudice, according to which a woman is not capable of receiving profound religious instruc-

---

[1] א D read εν τουτω instead of επι τουτω.
[2] T. R. reads εθαυμασαν with E S U V Δ Λ the larger part of the Mnn. Sah. etc. But א A B C D G K L M It. Vulg. Cop. Orig. read εθαυμαζον (*were marveling*).
[3] א D add αυτω (*to him*) after ειπεν.

tion: "Do not prolong conversation with a woman; let no one converse with a woman in the street, not even with his own wife; let a man burn the words of the law, rather than teach them to women" (see *Lightfoot* on this verse). Probably the apostles had not yet seen their Master set Himself above this prejudice.—We may hesitate between the two readings *marvelled* (ἐθαύμασαν) and *were marvelling* (ἐθαύμαζον). The first gives to the astonishment the character of a momentary act, the second makes of it a continuing state. Μέντοι: *However*, the astonishment did not extend so far in any one of them as to lead to ask Him for an explanation. Ζητεῖν, *to seek*, ask, refers to a service which He had requested, like that of ver. 10; λαλεῖν *to speak*, to a given instruction.

Vv. 28, 29. "*The woman therefore left her water-pot and went away into the city and says to the men: 29. Come, see a man who hath told me all the things that*[1] *I have done; can this be the Christ?*" *Therefore:* following upon the declaration of ver. 26, she does not speak, she acts, as one does when the heart is profoundly moved. She leaves her water-pot: this circumstance, apparently insignificant, is not without importance. It is the pledge of her early return, the proof that she goes to seek her husband and those whom she will find. She constitutes herself thereby a messenger, and, as it were, a missionary of Jesus. What a contrast between the vivacity of this conduct and the silent and meditative departure of Nicodemus! And what truth in the least details of this narrative!—Τοῖς ἀνθρώποις (*to the men*), to the first persons whom she met in the public square.—There is great simplicity in the expression: *All the things which I have done*. She does not fear to awaken by this expression recollections which are by no means flattering to herself. She formulates her question in a way which seems to anticipate a negative answer (μήτι, *not however?*). "This is not, however, the Christ, is it?" She believes more than she says, but she does not venture to set forth, even as probable, so great a piece of news. What can be more natural than this little touch.

Ver. 30. "*They went out*[2] *of the city, and were coming towards him.*" The Samaritans, gathered by her, arrive in large numbers. The imperfect, *they were coming*, contrasted with the aorist, *they went out*, forms a picture; we see them hastening across the fields which separate Sychar from Jacob's well. This historical detail gives the key to Jesus' words, which are to follow. The *therefore* must be rejected from the text; the attention is wholly turned to the *they were coming*, which follows.

Vv. 31, 32. "*In the mean while, the disciples prayed him, saying: Master, eat. 32. But he said unto them, I have meat to eat which ye know not.*" Ver. 31 (after the interruption of vv. 28, 29), is connected with ver. 27. The words, ἐν δὲ τῷ μεταξύ (*in the mean while*), denote the time which elapsed between the departure of the woman and the arrival of the Samaritans. Ἐρωτᾶν (*to ask*) takes here, as often in the New Testament, and as שאל does

---

[1] Instead of παντα οσα, א B C; It^{aliq}.; Cop., read παντα α.
[2] T. R. reads ουν (*therefore*), after εξηλθον,

with א A.: several Mnn.; It^{aliq}.; Sah. This particle is rejected by all the other Mjj.; Vss.; Orig.

434 / Birth of Faith

in the Old Testament, the sense of *pray*, without, however, losing altogether its strict sense of *interrogate*: ask whether he will eat.

Since the beginning of His ministry, Jesus had perhaps had no joy such as this which He had just experienced. This joy had revived Him, even physically. "You say to me: eat! But I am satisfied; I have had, in your absence, a feast of which you have no suspicion." Ἐγώ (*I*), has the emphasis; this word places His person in strong contrast to theirs (ὑμεῖς, *you*): "You have your repast; I have mine."—Βρῶσις, strictly the act of eating, but including the food, which is its condition. The abstract word better suits the spiritual sense of this saying, than the concrete βρῶμα, (*food*).

Vv. 33, 34. "*The disciples therefore said one to another: Has any one brought him anything to eat?* 34. *Jesus says unto them: My meat is to do*[1] *the will of my Father and to accomplish his work.*" Μήτις introduces a negative question: "No one indeed has brought Him . . . ?" Jesus explains the profound meaning of His answer. Here He uses βρῶμα, in connection with the gross interpretation of the disciples. We need not see in the conjunction ἵνα, as *Weiss* would have us, a mere periphrasis for the infinitive. That which sustains Him is His *proposing to Himself* continually *to do . . . to accomplish . . .* The present ποιῶ—this is the reading of the T. R.—refers to the permanent accomplishment of the divine will at each moment, and the conjunctive aorist τελειώσω (*to accomplish, to finish*), refers to the end of the labor, to the perfect consummation of the task which will, of course, depend on the obedience of every moment (xvii. 4). The reading (ποιήσω), of the Vatican MS., Origen, and the Greco-Latin authorities spoils this beautiful relation; it is rejected by *Tischendorf* and *Meyer*. This ποιήσω arose from an assimilation to τελειώσω. The relation between the two substantives θέλημα (*will*), and ἔργον (*work*), corresponds with that of the two verbs. In order that the *work* of God may be accomplished at the last moment, His *will* must have been executed at every moment. Hereby Jesus makes His disciples see that, in their absence He has been laboring in the Father's work, and that it is this labor which has revived Him. This is the idea which He is about to develop, by means of an image which is furnished Him by the present situation.

Vv. 35, 36. "*Say ye not that there are yet*[2] *four months,*[3] *and the harvest cometh. Behold I say unto you: Lift up your eyes, and look on the fields, for they are white for the harvest.* 36. *Already even*[4] *he that reapeth receiveth wages, and gathereth fruit unto eternal life, that both*[5] *he that soweth and he that reapeth may rejoice together.*" The following verses (35–38) have presented such difficulties to interpreters, that some have supposed that they should be transposed by placing vv. 37, 38 before ver. 36 (*B. Crusius*). Weiss has

---

[1] Instead of ποιω which T. R. reads with 11 Mjj. [including ℵ], Mnn.; Vss., ποιησω is read in B D K L T^b, Orig. (three times).

[2] Ετι is wanting in D L II, 60 Mnn.; Syr^{cur}; Orig. (sometimes).

[3] T. R.: τετραμηνον with Π only, instead of τετραμηνος.

[4] T. R. reads και before ο θεριζων with 13 Mjj., omitted by ℵ B C D L T^b, It^{aliq.}; Orig.

[5] The και after ινα is rejected by B C L T^b U, Orig. (four times).

supposed that ver. 35 originally belonged to another context. It must be admitted that the interpretations proposed by *Lücke, de Wette, Meyer,* and *Tholuck* are not adapted to remove the difficulties. Some see in them a prophecy of the conversion of the Samaritan people, related in Acts viii.; others apply them even to the conversion of the entire Gentile world, and especially to the apostolate of St. Paul. In that case, it is not surprising that their authenticity should be suspected! If the words of vv. 36 ff., have no direct connection with the actual circumstances, how can we connect them with those of ver. 35, which, according to *Lücke* and *Meyer* themselves, can only refer to the arrival of the inhabitants of Sychar in the presence of Jesus? From a word stamped with the most perfect appropriateness, Jesus would suddenly pass to general considerations respecting the propagation of the Gospel. So de Wette, perceiving the impossibility of such a mode of speaking on Jesus' part, has, contrary to the evidence, resolutely denied the reference of ver. 35 to the arrival of the inhabitants of Sychar. This general embarrassment seems to us to proceed from the fact that the application of Jesus' words to the actual case has not been sufficiently apprehended and kept in mind. They have thus been despoiled of their appropriateness. A friendly and familiar conversation has been converted into a solemn sermon.

Ver. 35 is joined with ver. 30 precisely as ver. 31 is with ver. 27. Jesus gives His disciples to understand, as already appeared from His answer (ver. 34), that a scene is occurring at this moment of which they have not the least idea: while they are thinking only of the preparation of a meal to be taken, behold a harvest already fully ripe, the seeds of which have been sown in their absence, is prepared for them. Jesus Himself is, as it were, the point of union between the two scenes, altogether foreign to each other, which are passing around His person: that in which the disciples and that in which the Samaritans are, with Himself, the actors.—*Lightfoot, Tholuck, Lücke, de Wette* find a general maxim, a proverb, in the first words of ver. 35: When a man has once sowed, he must still wait four months for the time when he can reap—that is to say, the fruits of any work whatever are not gathered except after long waiting (2 Tim. ii. 6). But in Palestine not four, but six months separate the sowing (end of October) from the reaping (middle of April). Besides, the adverb ἔτι (there are *yet*) would not suit a proverb; the words: since the sowing, would have been necessary. Finally, why put this proverb especially into the mouth of the Apostles (*you*), rather than in that of men in general? There is then here a reflection which Jesus ascribes to His disciples themselves.—Between Jacob's well, at the foot of Gerizim, and the village of Aschar, at the foot of Ebal, far on into the plain of Mukhna, there stretch out vast fields of wheat. As they beheld the springing verdure on this freshly sown soil, they no doubt said to one another: we must wait yet four months till this wheat shall be ripe! From this little detail we must conclude that this occurred four months before the middle of April, thus about the middle of December, and that Jesus had consequently remained in Judea from the feast of the Passover until the close of the year, that is, eight full months.—The words: *You say*, contrast the domain of nature to which this reflection of the disciples applies, to the sphere of the Spirit in which Jesus' thought is moving. In that sphere, indeed, the seed is not necessarily subject to such slow development. It can sometimes germinate and ripen as if in an instant. The proof of this is before their eyes at this very moment: ἰδού (*behold*)! This word directs the attention of the disciples to a spectacle which was wholly unexpected and even incomprehensible to their minds, that of the Samaritans who are hastening across the valley towards Jacob's well.—*I say unto you:* I who have the secret of what is taking place. The act of *raising the eyes* and *looking*, to which He invites them, is, according to *de Wette*, purely spiritual ; Jesus would induce them to picture to themselves beforehand through faith, the future conversion of this people (comp. Acts viii.). But the imperative, θεάσασθε (*look*), must refer to an object visible at that very moment. And what meaning is to be given to the figure of *four months?* The fact to which these words refer, therefore, can only be the arrival of the people of Sychar. We understand, then, the use of the imperfect *they were coming* (ver. 30), which formed a picture and left the action incomplete. These eager souls who hasten towards Him disposed to believe— this is the spectacle which Jesus invites His disciples to behold. He presents these souls to them under the figure of a ripening harvest, which it only remains to gather in. And, as He thinks of the brief time needed by Him to prepare such a harvest in this place, until now a stranger to the kingdom of God, He is Himself struck by the contrast between the very long time (five to six months), which is demanded by the law of natural vegetation, and the rapid development which the divine seed can have in a moment, in the spiritual world ; and, as an encouragement for His disciples in their future vocation, He points out to them this difference. The ἤδη (*already*), might be regarded as ending ver. 35. "They are white for the harvest *already*." This word would thus form the counterpart of ἔτι (*yet*), at the beginning of the verse; comp. 1 John iv. 3, where ἤδη is placed, in the same way, at the end of the sentence. This word, however, becomes still more significant, if it is placed, as we have placed it in the translation, at the opening of the following verse : ἤδη καί (*already even*). This is acknowledged by *Keil*, who rightly observes that in this way also *already* forms a contrast to *yet*.

There is, indeed, between ver. 35 and ver. 36, a climactic relation which betrays an increasing exaltation. "It is true," says Jesus, "that already the harvest is ripe, that at this very hour the reaper has only to take his sickle and reap, in order that both the sower and the reaper may in this case, at least, celebrate together the harvest-feast." If such is the meaning, the authenticity of καί, *and* (after ἤδη), is manifest, and Origen, with the Alexandrian authorities in his train, is found, once more, to have been an unfortunate corrector. After having connected ἤδη (*already*), with the preceding sentence, he rejected the καί (*and* or *even*), in order to make of ver. 36, instead of an expression full of appropriateness and charm, a general maxim. The reaper, according to ver. 38, must denote the apostles.

The expression, μισθὸν λαμβάνειν (*to receive wages*), describes the joy with which they are to be filled when gathering all these souls and introducing them into the kingdom of heaven. This expression (*receive wages*) is explained by συνάγειν καρπόν (*to gather fruit*). Perhaps there is a reference to the act of baptism (ver. 2), by which these new brethren, the believing Samaritans, are about to be received by the disciples into the Messianic community. And why must the reaper set himself at work without delay? Because there is something exceptional to happen on this day, ἵνα (*in order that*). God has intended in this circumstance to bring to pass a remarkable thing, namely: that both the sower and the reaper may once rejoice together. Those who apply the figure of the harvest to the future conversion of the Samaritans by the apostles, or to that of the Gentile world by St. Paul, are obliged to refer the common joy of the sower (Jesus), and the reaper (the apostles), to the *heavenly triumph* in which the Lord and His servants will rejoice together in the fruit of their labor. But, first, this interpretation breaks all logical connection between ver. 35 and ver. 36. How pass directly from this spectacle of the Samaritans who hasten to Him to the idea of the future establishment of the Gospel in their country or in the world? Then, the present χαίρῃ (*may rejoice*), refers naturally to a present joy, contrary to *Meyer*. *Luthardt* seeks to escape the difficulty by giving to ὁμοῦ (*together*), the sense, not of a *simultaneous* joy, but of a *common* joy, which is, of course, impossible. This sense of the adverb would, moreover, suppress the idea which constitutes the beauty of this expression, the simultaneousness of the joy of the two laborers. Jesus recognizes in what takes place at this moment, a feast which the Father has prepared for Him, and which He, the sower, is about to enjoy at the same time with His disciples, the reapers. In Israel Jesus has sowed, but He never has had the joy of being Himself present at a harvest. The ingathering will one day take place, no doubt, but when He will be no longer there. Here, on the contrary, through His providential meeting with this woman, through her docility and the eagerness of this population which hastens to Him, He sees the seed spring up and ripen in a moment, so that the harvest can be gathered, and He, the sower, may, at least once in His life, participate in the harvest-feast. This simultaneousness of joy, altogether exceptional, is strongly brought out by the ὁμοῦ (*together*), but also by the double καί ("*both* the sower *and* the reaper"), and by the ἤδη (*already*), at the beginning of the clause. To understand fully the meaning of this gracious expression, we must remember that the Old Testament established a contrast between the function of the sower (united with that of the laborer), and the office of the reaper. The first was regarded as a painful labor; Ps. cxxvi. 5, 6: "Those who sow *with tears* . . . He who puts the seed in the ground shall go *weeping* . . . " The reaper's task, on the contrary, was regarded as a joyous thing. "They shall reap *with a song of triumph* . . . He shall return *with rejoicing*, when he shall bring back his sheaves." On this day, by reason of the rapidity with which the seed has germinated and ripened, the labor of the seed sowing meets the joyous shouts of the harvest. Herein is the explanation of the construction by which the verb χαίρῃ is much more closely connected, in the Greek sentence, with the first subject ὁ σπείρων, *the sower*, than with the second ὁ θερίζων, *the reaper :* " that the sower *may rejoice* at the same time with the reaper."

Weiss refers the *in order that* to the intention of the reaper, who, being in the service of the same landholder as the sower, wishes that the latter also may rejoice with him. The idea, if we thoroughly understand him, is that the disciples were to reap in their future ministry, and this in order that Jesus may rejoice in heaven, at the same time that they rejoice on earth. But where has Jesus ever given to His disciples such a motive as this? And in what connection would this expression stand with the present case?

Vv. 37, 38. *" For herein is the saying*[1] *true : The sower is one and the reaper another.* 38. *I sent*[2] *you to reap that whereon ye have not labored ; other men labored, and ye are entered into their labor."* According to *Tholuck*, Jesus is grieved at the thought that He is not Himself to be present at the conversion of the Gentiles, after having prepared the way for it, and to this point it is that the proverb refers. *Astié* appears to be of the same opinion. *Westcott* thinks that Jesus prepares the apostles for the future disappointments in the apostleship. They would then be the sowers who do not reap, while the whole context proves that only Jesus can be so. *Weiss :* In this region of the spiritual harvest it is not as in ordinary harvests, where the sower is often the same as the reaper. But then the origin of the common maxim which Jesus quotes is not explained, for it expresses just the contrary of what would most frequently be the case in life. Then, this sense of ἐν τούτῳ, " in the spiritual domain," is hardly natural. This form of expression has rather a logical sense : " *In this*," that is, " in that you reap to-day what has been sown in your absence and without your knowledge " (ver. 36) : thus is the common saying verified. *For if* this proverb is false in the sense which is ordinarily assigned to it, namely, that he who does the main part of the labor is rarely the one who gathers the fruit of it (an accusation against Providence), it is nevertheless true in this respect, that there is a distinction of persons between him who has the charge of sowing and him who has the mission of reaping. This distinction was at the foundation (*for*) of the saying in ver. 36, since the *community* of joy declared in that verse rests upon the duality of persons and offices affirmed by the proverb ver. 37 : " *one* . . . *another.* . . . "— Ἀληθινός, not in the sense of ἀληθής, veritable, which says truth, but in the ordinary Johannean sense : which answers to the idea of the thing ; thus : *The* or (without the ὁ) *a* saying which is the true maxim to be pronounced. This distinction, of which they have this day the evidence, between him who sows and him who reaps—on this it is that the whole activity to which Jesus has called them will rest : such is the idea of ver. 38.

Ver. 38. As preachers, the apostles will do nothing but reap that which

---

[1] The article ο before αληθινος is rejected by B C K L Δ some Mnn. Heracleon, Orig.

[2] ℵ D read απεσταλκα, instead of απεστειλα.

has been painfully sown by *others*. These last are, undoubtedly, John the Baptist and Jesus Himself, those two servants who, after having painfully ploughed the furrow, have watered with their blood the seed which they had deposited in it. Only there is ordinarily a misapprehension of the allusion which Jesus makes to the particular fact which has given occasion to these words, and which is, as it were, an illustration of them. " That will happen in all your career which is occurring to-day." *I have sent you to reap:* Jesus had done this by calling them to the apostleship (vi. 70; Luke vi. 13).—*That on which you have not labored:* This harvest in Samaria —they have not prepared it, any more than they have prepared that which they will reap afterwards in preaching the Gospel. *Others have labored:* in the present case, Jesus and the Samaritan woman—the one by His word, the other by her eager hastening. What an enigma for the disciples—this population hastening to Jesus to surrender themselves to His divine influence,—and, what is more, Samaritans! What has taken place in their absence? Who has prepared such a result? Who has sown this sterile ground? Jesus seems to rejoice in their surprise. And it is, no doubt, with a friendly smile that He throws out to them these mysterious words: *Others labored.* They may see here an example of what they will afterwards experience: In all their ministry nothing different will occur. Commentators discuss the question whether, by this word *others*, Jesus designates *Himself* alone (*Lücke, Tholuck, de Wette, Meyer* and *Weiss*), taking *others* as the plural of category; or *Himself* and *the prophets*, including *John the Baptist* (*Keil*); or all these personages except Jesus (*Olshausen*). *Westcott* applies this word *others* to all the servants of God in the Old Testament (perhaps with an allusion to Josh. xxiv. 13). The disciples have entered into the work of their predecessors through their fruitful ministry in Judea (ver. 2). But to what end say all this precisely in Samaria? The two most curious explanations are certainly those of *Baur* and *Hilgenfeld*. According to the first, by the term *others*, Jesus designates the evangelist Philip (Acts viii.), and by the *reapers*, the apostles, Peter and John, in the story in Acts viii. 15. To the view of the second, the term *others* designates St. Paul, and the reapers are the Twelve, who seek to appropriate to themselves the fruit of his labor among the Gentiles. On these conditions, one might wager that he could find anything in any text whatever. These forced meanings and the grave critical consequences which are drawn from them, arise in large measure from the fact that the wonderful appropriateness of these words of Jesus, as He applied them to the given situation, has not been apprehended.

Jesus is thinking undoubtedly on His own work and that of John, and the perfect: *you are entered*, is indeed that which is ordinarily understood by it, a prophetic anticipation; but this form can be well explained only by means of a present fact which suggests it. We discover here, with *Gess*, the contrast between the manner in which Jesus regarded His work and the idea which the forerunner had formed of it beforehand. "For the latter the time of the Messiah was the harvest; Jesus, on the contrary, here regards the days of His flesh as a mere time of sowing."

440 / Birth of Faith

We can understand how it must have been more and more difficult for John to bring his thought into accord with the work of Jesus.

The heavenly joy which fills the Lord's heart throughout this section has its counterpart only in the passage, Luke x. 17–24. Here it even assumes a character of gaiety. Is it John's fault, if *Renan* finds in the Jesus of the fourth Gospel only a heavy metaphysician?

Jesus and the Samaritans: vv. 39–42

Vv. 39–42. "*Now many of the Samaritans of that city believed on him*[1] *because of the word of the woman who testified: He told me all things that*[2] *I have done.* 40. *When, therefore, the Samaritans came unto him, they besought him to abide with them; and he abode there*[3] *two days.* 41. *And many more believed on him because of his word.* 42. *And they said to the woman: No longer because of thy saying*[4] *do we believe; for we have heard him ourselves,*[5] *and we know that this is indeed the Saviour of the world.*"[6] Here now is the harvest-feast announced in ver. 36: The sower rejoices with the reapers. This time passed at Sychar leaves an ineffaceable impression on the hearts of the apostles, and the sweetness of this recollection betrays itself in the repetition of the words *two days*, in the fortieth and forty-third verses. $\Delta\acute{\epsilon}$, *now*, resumes the course of the narrative after the digression in vv. 31–38. What a difference between the Samaritans and the Jews! Here a miracle of knowledge, without éclat, is enough to dispose the hearts of the people to come to Jesus, while in Judea eight months of toil have not procured for him one hour of such refreshment.

The thirty-ninth verse has shown us the first degree of faith: The *coming to Jesus*, as the result of testimony. The fortieth and forty-first verses present the higher degree of faith, its development through personal contact with Jesus.

Ver. 41 marks a two-fold advance, one in the number of believers, the other in the nature of their faith. This latter advance is expressed in the words: *Because of His word*, contrasted with the words: *Because of the woman's story* (ver. 39); it is reflectively formulated in the declaration of ver. 42. The Samaritans reserve the more grave term $\lambda\acute{o}\gamma o\varsigma$ for the word of Jesus; they apply to the talk of the woman the term $\lambda a\lambda\acute{\iota}a$, which has in it, undoubtedly, nothing contemptuous (viii. 43, where Jesus applies it to His own discourses), but which denotes something more outward, a mere *report*, a *piece of news*. The verb $\dot{a}\kappa\eta\kappa\acute{o}a\mu\epsilon\nu$, *we have heard*, has in the Greek no object; the idea is concentrated in the subject $a\dot{\nu}\tau o\acute{\iota}$: "We have *ourselves* become hearers;" whence follows: "And *as such* we know." The reading of the Sinaitic MS.: "We have heard *from him* (from his mouth)

---

[1] ℵ It^{aliq} Orig., omit εις αυτον (*on him*).
[2] ℵ B C L It^{aliq} Syr. Cop. read α instead of οσα.
[3] ℵ Syr.: παρ' αυτοις (*with them*), instead of εκει (*there*).
[4] Instead of σην λαλιαν B: λαλιαν σου; ℵ D It^{aliq} σην μαρτυριαν.
[5] ℵ Syr^{cur} add παρ αυτου (*from him*).
[6] 16 Mjj., most of the Mnn., It^{aliq} Syr^{sch} add, with the T. R., ο χριστος. These words are rejected by ℵ B C T^b., some Mnn., It^{plerique} Vulg. Cop., Syr^{cur} Orig. Iren. Heracleon.

and we know that . . . ," would give to the following profession the character of an external and slavish repetition, opposed to the spirit of the narrative. The expression: *The Saviour of the world* seems to indicate an advance in the notion of the Messiah in these Samaritans. The question is of salvation, and no longer merely of teaching as in ver. 25. This expression is, perhaps, connected with the word of Jesus to the woman (ver. 22), which Jesus must have developed to them: "*Salvation* is from the Jews." *Tholuck* and *Lücke* suspect the historical truth of this term *Saviour of the world*, as too universalistic in the mouth of these Samaritans. By what right? Did not these people possess in their Pentateuch the promise of God to Abraham: "*All the families of the earth shall be blessed in thy seed*," to which Jesus might have called their attention? And had they not just been, during those two days, in direct contact with the love of the true Christ, so opposite to the particularistic arrogance of Jewish Pharisaism? The Alexandrian authorities reject the words ὁ χριστός, *the Christ*. Undoubtedly there might be seen in them the seal of the union announced by Jesus (vv. 23, 24) between the Samaritans (the *Saviour of the world*) and the Jews (the *Christ*). But it is easier to understand how this term may have been added, than how it could have been rejected.

The eager welcome which Jesus found among the Samaritans is an example of the effect which the coming of Christ should have produced among His own. The faith of these strangers was the condemnation of Israel's unbelief. It was, undoubtedly, under this impression that Jesus, after those two exceptional days in His earthly existence, resumed His journey to Galilee.

3

John 4:43-54

JESUS IN GALILEE

In Judea, unbelief had prevailed. In Samaria, faith had just appeared. Galilee takes an intermediate position. Jesus is received there, but by reason of His miracles accomplished at Jerusalem, and on condition of responding immediately to this reception by new prodigies. The following narrative (comp. ver. 48) furnishes the proof of this disposition of mind. Such is the import of this narrative in the whole course of the Gospel.

Vv. 43–45 describe the general situation. Then, on this foundation there rises the following incident (vv. 46–54). We may compare here the relation of the conversation with Nicodemus to the general representation in ii. 23–25, or that of the last discourse of the forerunner to the representation in iii. 22–24.

1. Vv. 43–45

Vv. 43–45. "*After these two days, he departed thence and went away*[1] *into Galilee. 44. For Jesus Himself had declared that a prophet has no honor in*

---

[1] ℵ B C D T^b It^{plerique} Syr^{cur} Cop. Orig. omit the words και απηλθεν (*went away*) after εκειθεν.

his own country. 45. *When*[1] *therefore he came into Galilee, the Galileans received him, because they had seen all the things that he*[2] *did in Jerusalem, at the feast; for they also went*[3] *to the feast."* This passage has from the beginning been a *crux interpretum*. How can John give as the cause (*for*, ver. 44) of the return of Jesus to Galilee this declaration of the Lord "that no prophet is honored in his own country!" And how can he connect with this adage as a consequence (*therefore*, ver. 45) the fact that the Galileans gave Him an eager welcome? 1. *Brückner* and *Luthardt* think that Jesus *sought* either conflict (*Brückner*) or solitude (*Luthardt*). This would well explain the *for* of ver. 44. But it would be necessary to admit that the foresight of Jesus was greatly deceived (ver. 45), which is absolutely opposed to the particle οὖν (*therefore*), which connects ver. 45 with the preceding. Instead of *therefore*, *but* would have been necessary. Moreover, Jesus did not seek conflict, since He abandoned Judea in order to avoid it; still less solitude, for He wished to work. 2. *Weiss*, nearly like Brückner: Jesus leaves to His disciples the care of reaping joyously in Samaria afterwards; He Himself goes to seek the hard labor of the sower in Galilee. But the thought of the future evangelization of Samaria is altogether foreign to this passage (see above); and ver. 45 is opposed to this sense; for it makes prominent precisely the fact that Jesus found in Galilee the most eager welcome. Weiss escapes this difficulty only by making the *therefore* of ver. 45 relate to ver. 43 and not to ver. 44, and by making it a particle designed to indicate the *resumption* of the narrative. But after the *for* of ver. 44, *therefore* has necessarily the argumentative sense. 3. According to *Lücke*, *de Wette* and *Tholuck*, the *for* of ver. 44 is designed to explain, not what precedes, but the fact which is about to be announced, ver. 45.[4] The sense would, thus, be: "Jesus had *indeed* declared . . . ;" this *indeed* relating to the fact mentioned in ver. 45, that the Galileans no doubt received Him, but only because of the miracles of which they had been witnesses. But this very rare use of γάρ is foreign to the New Testament. This interpretation is hardly less forced than that of *Kuinoel*, who gives to *for* the sense of *although*, as also *Ostervald* translates. 4. *Origen, Wieseler, Ebrard, Baur* and *Keil* understand by ἰδία πατρίς (*his own country*), *Judea*, as the place of Jesus' birth. By this means, the two difficulties of the *for* and the *therefore* pass away at once. But common sense tells us that, in the maxim quoted by Jesus, the word *country* must denote the place where the prophet has lived and where he has been known from infancy, and not that where he was merely born. It is, therefore, very evident that, in the thought of John, His own country is Galilee. 5. *Calvin, Hengstenberg* and *Bäumlein* understand by *his own country* especially *Nazareth*, in contrast with the rest of Galilee, and with Capernaum in particular where He went to make His abode. He came, not to Nazareth, as might have been expected, but to Capernaum. (Comp. Mark vi.

---

[1] ℵ D read ὡς instead of ὅτε (probably according to ver. 40).
[2] A B C L Orig. (4 times) read ὅσα for α.
[3] ℵ It. read ἐληλυθεισαν for ηλθον.
[4] Comp. *Tholuck*, Commentary on the Ep. to the Rom. 5th ed. chap. ii. ver. 1.

1; Matt. xiii. 54–57; Luke iv. 16, 24.) *Lange* applies the term *country* to the whole of lower Galilee, in which Nazareth was included, in opposition to upper Galilee where Jesus went to fix His abode from this time. But how could Nazareth, or the district of Nazareth, be thus, without further explanation, placed outside of Galilee, or even in contrast with that province? It might still be comprehensible, if, in the following narrative, John showed us Jesus fixing His abode at Capernaum; but it is to Cana that He betakes Himself, and this town was very near to Nazareth. 6. *Meyer* seems to us quite near the truth, when he explains: Jesus, knowing well that a prophet is not honored in his own country, began by making Himself honored *outside of it*, at Jerusalem (ver. 45); and thus it was that He returned now to Galilee with a reputation as a prophet, which opened for Him access to hearts in His own country. *Reuss* is disposed to hold the same relation of thought: " In order to be received in Galilee, He had been obliged first to make Himself acknowledged outside of it."

The complete explanation of this obscure passage follows, as in so many cases, from the relation of the fourth Gospel to the Synoptics. The latter make the Galilean ministry begin immediately after the baptism. But John reminds us here, at the time of Jesus' settlement in Galilee, that Jesus had followed a course quite different from that which the earlier narratives seemed to attribute to Him. The Lord knew that the place where a prophet has lived is the one where, as a rule, he has most difficulty in finding recognition. He began, therefore, by working at Jerusalem and in Judea for quite a long time (almost a whole year: ver. 35), and it was only after this that He came in the strict sense to begin His ministry in Galilee, that ministry with which the narrative of the other Gospels opens. The meaning, therefore, is: It was then, and only then, (not immediately after the baptism), that He commenced the Galilean work with which every one is acquainted. We find in this passage, as thus understood, a new confirmation of our remarks on iii. 24. If the *for*, ver. 44, indicates the cause of Jesus' mode of acting, the *therefore*, ver. 45, brings out in relief the joyful result and serves thus to justify the wisdom of the course pursued. The Galileans who had seen Him at work on the grand theatre of the capital, made no difficulty now in welcoming Him. The words καὶ ἀπῆλθεν, *and went away*, are rejected by the Alexandrian authorities; perhaps they were added from ver. 13.

Ver. 44. Αὐτός, *he*, the same who apparently was acting in an opposite way. The solution of the contradiction is given in ver. 45. Ἐμαρτύρησεν, *testified*, can here, whatever *Meyer*, *Weiss*, etc., may say, have only the sense of the pluperfect, like ἐποίησεν and ἦλθον which follow. It is difficult to believe, indeed, that John quotes here, for the purpose of explaining the conduct of Jesus, a declaration which was uttered at an epoch much farther on, like that of Mark vi. 4. Comp. Luke iv. 24, which assigns to this saying a much earlier date. The idea of the quoted proverb is that one is less disposed to recognize a superior being in a fellow countryman, very nearly connected with us, than in a stranger who is clothed, to our view, in a veil of mystery. But after that this same man has brought

444 / Birth of Faith

himself to notice elsewhere and on a wider theatre, this glory opens the way for Him to the hearts of His own fellow-citizens. That moment had arrived for Jesus; this is the reason why He now braves the vulgar prejudice which He had Himself pointed out; and of which we have seen an instance in the reply of Nathanael, i. 47. And the success justifies this course. The words πάντα ἑωρακότες, *having seen* . . . , explain the ἐδέξαντο, *they received:* there is undoubtedly an allusion to ii. 23–25. This verse finds its commentary in Luke iv. 14, 15: "*And Jesus returned to Galilee in the power of the Spirit, and his fame spread abroad through all the region round about; and He taught in their synagogues, being glorified by all.*"

2. Vv. 46–54

Vv. 46, 47. "*He came,*[1] *therefore, again to Cana of Galilee where he had changed*[1] *the water into wine. And*[2] *there was at Capernaum*[3] *a king's officer, whose son was sick.* 47. *He, having heard that Jesus had come from Judea into Galilee, went unto him and besought him*[4] *that he would come down and heal his son; for he was at the point of death.*" *Therefore* connects with ver. 3 and ver. 45. Jesus directed His course towards Cana, not, as Weiss thinks, because His family had settled there (comp. ii. 12 with Matt. iv. 13), but undoubtedly because it was there that He could hope to find the soil best prepared, by reason of His previous visit. This is perhaps what St. John means to intimate by the reflection, "*where he had changed the water into wine.*" His coming made a sensation, and the news promptly spread as far as Capernaum, situated seven or eight leagues eastward of Cana. The term βασιλικός, in Josephus, denotes a public functionary, either civil or military, sometimes also an employé of the royal house. This last meaning is here the most natural one. Herod Antipas, who reigned in Galilee, had officially only the title of tetrarch. But in the popular language that of King, which his father had borne, was given him. It is not impossible that this nobleman of the king's household may have been either Chuza, "Herod's steward" (Luke viii. 3), or Manaen, his "foster-brother" (Acts iii. 1). By its position at the end of the clause, the defining expression *at Capernaum* (which refers, not to *was sick*, but to *there was*) strongly emphasizes the notoriety which the return of Jesus had speedily acquired in Galilee.

Ver. 48. "*Jesus therefore said to him: Unless ye see signs and wonders ye will in no wise believe.*" This reply of Jesus is perplexing; for it seems to suppose that this man asked for the miracle to the end of believing, which is certainly not the case. But the difficulty is explained by the plurals, *ye see, ye will believe,* which prove that this expression is not the reply to the father's request, but a reflection which He makes on occasion of that request. It is true, He addresses the remark to the man who is the occa-

---

[1] ℵ reads ηλθαν, εποιησαν; "*They came, they had changed.*" (!)

[2] ℵ D L T^b lt.: ην δε instead of και ην.

[3] ℵ B C D T^b It^{pleriq}: Καφαρναουμ.

[4] ℵ B C D L T^b It^{aliq}. omit αυτου.

sion of it (πρὸς αὐτόν), but He speaks thus, with reference to all the Galilean people, whose moral tendency this man represents, to His view, at this moment. Indeed, the disposition which Jesus thus meets at the moment when He sets foot again on Israelitish soil, is the tendency to see in Him only a thaumaturge (worker of miracles); and He is so much the more painfully affected since He has just passed two days in Samaria, in contact with an altogether opposite spirit. There, it was as the Saviour of souls that He was welcomed. Here, it is bodily cures which are immediately asked of Him. He seems to be fit for nothing but to heal. And He is obliged to confess—such is the true meaning of His word—that if He refuses to play this part, there is reason to fear that no one will believe, or rather, according to the slightly ironical turn of expression of which He makes use (οὐ μή), "that it is not to be feared that any one will believe." There is likewise the expression of a painful feeling in the accumulation of the two nearly synonymous terms σημεῖα and τέρατα, *signs* and *wonders*. The first designates the miracle as related to the fact of the invisible world which it manifests; the second characterizes it as related to external nature, whose laws it sets at defiance. The latter term, therefore, brings out with more force the sensible character of the supernatural manifestation. The meaning, therefore, is : " You must have signs; and you are not satisfied unless these signs have the character of wonders." Some have found in ἴδητε, *ye see,* an allusion to the request which is addressed to Him to go personally to the sick person, which proves, it is said, that the father wishes to *see* the healing with his own eyes. But in that case ἴδητε ought to stand at the beginning; and the meaning is forced.

Vv. 49, 50. " *The officer says to him: Sir, come down ere my child die.*[1] *50. Jesus says to him: Go thy way, thy son liveth. And* [2] *the man believed the word which Jesus had* [3] *said to him, and he went his way.*" The father has well understood that the remark of Jesus is not an answer, and consequently not a refusal. He renews his request, employing the term of affection τὸ παιδίον μου, *my little child*, which renders his request more touching. Jesus yields to the faith which breathes in his prayer, but in such a way as immediately to elevate the faith to a higher degree. There are at once in this answer : " *Go thy way, thy son liveth,*" a granting of the request and a partial refusal, which is a test. The healing is granted; but without Jesus leaving Cana; He wishes this time to be believed on His word. Until now the father had believed on the testimony of others. Now his faith is to rest on a better support, on the personal contact which he has just had with the Lord Himself. For the term παιδίον Jesus substitutes υἱός, *son*. This is the term of dignity; it exalts the worth of the child, as representing the family. The father lays hold by faith upon the promise of Jesus, that is to say, on Jesus Himself in His word; the test is sustained.

Vv. 51–53. "*As he was now going down, his servants met* [4] *him, and told* [5]

---

[1] A and some Mnn. read υιον instead of παιδιον; ℵ παιδα.
[2] Και is wanting in ℵ B D It^{aliq} Vulg.
[3] ℵ : του Ιησου instead of ω .... Ιησους.
[4] Instead of απηντησαν, ℵ B C D K L 20 Mnn. read υπηντησαν.
[5] ℵ D read ηγγειλαν for απηγγειλαν.

446 / Birth of Faith

him saying :[1] *Thy son liveth.*[2] 52. *So he inquired of them the hour when he began to mend. They said to him: yesterday,*[3] *at the seventh hour, the fever left him.* 53. *The father, therefore, knew that it was at that hour*[4] *in which Jesus had said to him:*[5] *Thy son liveth. And he believed, himself and all his house.*" The servants, in their report, use neither the term of affection (παιδίον), which would be too familiar, nor that of dignity (υἱός), which would not be familiar enough, but that of family life : παῖς, *the child*, which the T. R. rightly gives. The selected term κομψότερον, suits well the mouth of a man of rank. It is the expression of a comparative improvement; as we say, *finely*. The seventh hour, according to the ordinary Jewish mode of reckoning, denotes one o'clock in the afternoon (see on i. 40). But if it was at that hour that Jesus had given his answer to the father, how was it that he did not return to his home on the same day? For seven leagues only separate him from his house. Those also who, like *Keil, Westcott*, etc., think that John used, in general, the mode of reckoning the hours which was usual in the Roman courts, support their view, with a certain probability, by our passage. Nevertheless, even on the supposition that Xθές, *yesterday*, proves that it was really the following day, in the ordinary sense of the word, this delay may be explained either by the necessity of letting his horses rest or by the fear of traveling by night. But the term *yesterday* does not even compel us to suppose that a night has elapsed since the healing of the child. For as the day, according to the Hebrews, closed at sunset, the servants might, some hours after this, say *yesterday*.

At this moment the faith of this man rises, at last, to a higher degree, that of personal experience. Hence the repetition of the word : *and he believed;* comp. ii. 11. The entire household is borne on by this movement of faith impressed on the heart of their head.

Ver. 54. " *Jesus did, again, this second sign, on coming out of Judea into Galilee.*" The word δεύτερον cannot be an adverb: *for the second time;* this would be a useless synonym for πάλιν, *again*. It is, then, an adjective, and, notwithstanding the absence of an article, a predicative adjective. " He did *again* (πάλιν) this miracle, and that as a *second* one." There is evidently something strange in this somewhat extreme manner of expressing himself : *again* and as a *second*. There is an indication here which betrays one of those disguised intentions which are so frequent in the fourth Gospel. The expression employed here can only be explained by closely connecting the verb *did* with the participle *coming into*, which follows. Other miracles in large numbers had occurred between the first act at Cana, ii. 11 and this one ; this was not therefore the second, speaking absolutely. Two ideas are united in this clause : He did a *second* miracle at Cana, and He did it *again on coming* from Judea into Galilee. In other terms: Also this second time Jesus signalized His return to Galilee, as the first time, by a new miracle done at Cana. It will be in vain to refuse to

---

[1] ℵ D b omit λεγοντες.
[2] D K L U 11. Syr. read υιος instead of παις.
ℵ A B C: αυτου instead of σου.
[3] Xθες in 11 Mjj., εχθες in 8.
[4] ℵ B C reject the first εν.
[5] ℵ A B C L omit οτι.

acknowledge this intention of the evangelist. It is a fact, that John shows himself concerned to distinguish these first two returns which the tradition had confounded. He makes prominent the miracle of chap. ii. and this one as the two enduring monuments of that distinction.

Irenæus, Semler, de Wette, Baur, Ewald, Weiss, unhesitatingly identify this miracle with the healing of the Gentile centurion's servant, Matt. viii. 5 and Luke vii. 3. As to the differences of details, they give the preference, some to the account of the Synoptics, others to that of John. In the two cases, the cure is wrought at a distance; this is all that the two events have in common. The charge of unbelief which, in the view of *Weiss*, is another common feature, on the contrary profoundly distinguishes them. For, in John, it is addressed to the people including the father, while in the Synoptics it applies only to the nation from which the father is distinguished as the example of the most extraordinary faith of which Jesus has yet been witness. And yet here is the same story! Moreover, all the details are different, even opposite. Here a father and his son, there a master and his servant. Here a Jew, there a Gentile. Here it is at Cana, there at Capernaum, that the event occurs. Here the father wishes Jesus to travel to the distance of six leagues; there the centurion absolutely denies the intention of making Him come to his house, and this in the same city. Finally, as we have said; here is a sample of the sickly faith of the Galileans; there an incomparable example of faith given by a Gentile to the whole people of Israel. If these two narratives refer to the same event, the Gospel history is thoroughly unsound. *Weiss* so clearly sees this alleged identity melt away in his hands, that he is obliged to bring in a third story, that of the healing of the epileptic child (Matt. xvii.), with which John blended the one which occupies our attention.

This 54th verse closes the cycle began at ii. 12, as its counterpart ii. 11 closed the cycle opened by i. 19. Of these two cycles, the first recounts the manner in which Jesus passed from private life to His public ministry: the latter relates the beginnings of His work.

The first contains three groups of narratives: 1. The testimonies of John the Baptist; 2. The coming to Jesus of His first disciples; 3. The wedding at Cana. The second shows us Jesus: 1. In Judea; 2. In Samaria; 3. In Galilee. Each particular narrative is preceded by a short preamble in which the general situation is sketched (ii. 12, 13; ii. 23–25; iii. 22–24; iv. 1–3 and iv. 43–45). The revelation of Jesus goes forward in a continuous way: at the Jordan, at Cana, in the temple, with Nicodemus, in Samaria, in Galilee. But the national unbelief manifests itself: before it, He is obliged to retire from the temple to the city, from the city to the country, from Judea to Galilee. But, at the same time, faith comes to light and is developed: in all its integrity in the disciples; as a feeble glimmering in Nicodemus; dimmed by an intermingling of carnal elements in Galilee.

# SECOND PART

THE DEVELOPMENT OF UNBELIEF IN ISRAEL

John 5:1-12:50

Up to this point, decided faith and unbelief have been only exceptional phenomena; the masses have remained in a state of passive indifference or of purely outward admiration. From this time, the situation assumes a more determinate character. Jesus continues to make known the Father, to manifest Himself as that which He is for humanity. This revelation meets with increasing hostility; the development of unbelief, becomes the predominating feature of the history. Faith indeed still manifests itself partially. But, in comparison with the powerful and rapid current which bears on the leaders and the entire body of the nation, it is like a weak and imperceptible eddy.

It is in Judea especially that this preponderant development of unbelief is accomplished. In Galilee opposition is, no doubt, also manifested; but the centre of resistance is at Jerusalem. The reason of this fact is easy to be understood. In this capital, as well as in the province of Judea which depends on it, a well-disciplined population is found, whose fanaticism is ready to support its rulers in every most violent action which their hatred may undertake. Jesus Himself depicts this situation in the Synoptics by that poignant utterance: "It cannot be that a prophet perish out of Jerusalem" (Luke xiii. 33).

This observation explains the relatively considerable place which the journeys to Jerusalem occupy in our Gospel. The general tradition, which forms the basis of the three Synoptical Gospels, was formulated with a view to the popular preaching, and to serve the ends of the apostolic mission; consequently it set in relief the facts which were connected with the foundation of faith. What had not this issue had little importance for a narrative of this kind. Now, it was in Galilee, that province which was relatively independent of the centre, that the ministry of Jesus had especially displayed its creative power and produced positive results. In this generally simple and friendly region, where Jesus found Himself no more in the presence of a systematic and powerfully organized resistance, He could preach as a simple missionary, give free scope to those discourses inspired by some scene of nature, to those happy and most appropriate words, to those gracious parables, to those teachings in connection with the immediate needs of human consciousness; in a word, to all those forms of discourse which easily become the subject of a popular tradition. There was little engaging in discussion, properly so-called, in this region, except with emissaries coming from Judea (Matt. xv. 1–12; Mark iii. 22; vii. 1; Luke v. 17, and vi. 1–7).

At Jerusalem, on the other hand, the hostile element by which Jesus found Himself surrounded, forced Him into incessant controversy. In this situation, no doubt, the testimony which He was obliged to give for Himself took more energetic forms and a sterner tone. It became more theological, if we may so speak; consequently less popular. This character of the Judean teaching, connected with the almost complete failure of its results, was the occasion of the fact that the activity displayed at Jerusalem left scarcely any trace in the primitive oral tradition. It is for this reason, undoubtedly, that the visits to that capital almost entirely disappeared from the writings which contain it, our Synoptics. The Apostle John, who afterwards related the evangelical history, and who had in view, not the practical work of evangelization, but the preservation of the principal testimonies which Jesus bore to Himself, as well as the representation of the unbelief and faith which these testimonies encountered, was necessarily led to draw the journeys to Jerusalem out of the background where they had been left. It was these visits in the capital which had prepared the way for the final catastrophe, that supreme event the recollection of which alone the traditional narrative had preserved. Each one of these journeys had marked a new step in the hardening of Israel. Designed to form the bond between the Messianic bridegroom and bride, they had served, in fact, only to hasten that long and complete divorce between Jehovah and His people, which still continues to this hour. We can understand that, from the point of view of the fourth Gospel, the journeys to Jerusalem must have occupied a preponderant place in the narrative.

Let us cast a glance at the general course of the narrative in this part. It includes three cycles, having, each one, as its centre and point of departure, a great miracle performed in Judea: 1. The healing of the impotent man at Bethesda, chap. v.; 2. That of the one who was born blind, chap. ix.; 3. The resurrection of Lazarus, chap. xi. Each of these events, instead of gaining for Jesus the faith of those who are witnesses of it, becomes in them the signal of a renewed outbreaking of hatred and unbelief. Jesus has characterized this tragic result by the reproach, full of sadness and bitterness (x. 32): *"I have showed you many good works from my Father; for which of them do ye stone me?"* These are the connecting links of the narrative. Each one of these miraculous deeds is immediately followed by a series of conversations and discourses in connection with the *sign* which has given occasion for them; then, the discussion is suddenly interrupted by the voluntary removal of Jesus, to begin again in the following visit. Thus the strife which is entered upon in chap. v., on occasion of the healing of the impotent man, is resumed in the visit of Jesus at the feast of Tabernacles (chaps. vii. and viii.); thus also, the discourses which are connected with the healing of the one born blind are repeated, in part, and developed at the feast of dedication, in the second

450 / Unbelief Develops in Israel

part of chap. x. This arises from the fact that Jesus is careful, each time, to leave Jerusalem before things have come to the last extremity. Herein is the reason why the conflict which has broken out during one visit re-echoes also in the following one.

The following, therefore, is the arrangement of the narrative: First cycle: In chap. v., the strife, which had been vaguely hinted at in the first verses of chap. iv., commences in Judea in consequence of the healing of the impotent man; after this, Jesus withdraws into Galilee and allows the hatred of the Jews time to become calm. But in Galilee also, He finds unbelief, only in a different form. In Judea, they hate Him, they desire to put Him to death; in Galilee, His discontented adherents confine themselves to going away from Him (chap. vi.). There did not exist there the stimulant of active hatred, jealousy: unbelief arose only from the carnal spirit of the people, whose aspirations Jesus did not satisfy. With the journey to the feast of Tabernacles (chap. vii.), the conflict begun in chap. v. is resumed in Judea, and reaches in chap. viii. its highest degree of intensity. Such is the first phase (chaps. v.–viii.). Chap. ix. opens the second cycle. The healing of the one born blind furnishes new food for the hatred of the adversaries; nevertheless, in spite of their growing rage, the struggle already loses somewhat of its violence, because Jesus voluntarily withdraws from the field of battle. Up to this time, He had sought to act upon the hostile element; from this moment onward, He gives it over to itself. Only, in proportion as He breaks with the ancient flock, He labors to recruit the new one. The discourses which are connected with this second phase extend as far as the end of chap. x. The third cycle opens with the resurrection of Lazarus; this event brings to its highest point the rage of the Jews, and impels them to an extreme measure; they formally decree the death of Jesus; and, soon afterwards, His royal entrance into Jerusalem, at the head of His followers (chap. xii.), hastens the execution of this sentence. This last phase includes chaps. xi.–xii. 36. Here Jesus completely abandons Israel to its blindness, and puts an end to His public ministry: "*And departing, He hid himself from them.*" The evangelist pauses at this tragical moment, and, before continuing his narrative, he casts a retrospective glance on this mysterious fact of the development of Jewish unbelief, now consummated. He shows that this result had in it nothing unexpected, and he unveils the profound causes of it: xii. 37–50.

Thus the dominant idea and the course of this part, are distinctly outlined—

1. v.–viii.: The outbreak of the conflict;
2. ix., x.: The growing exasperation of the Jews;
3. xi., xii.: The ripe fruit of this hatred: the sentence of death for Jesus.

The progress of this narrative is purely historical. The attempt, often renewed—even by *Luthardt*—to arrange this part systematically according to certain *ideas*, such as *life, light* and *love*, is incompatible with this course of the narrative which is so clearly determined by the facts. It is no less excluded by the following observations: The idea of life, which, according to this system, must be that of chaps. v. and vi., forms again the basis of chaps. x. and xi. In the interval (chaps. viii., ix.), the idea of *light* is the dominant one. That of *love* does not appear till chap. xiii., and this in an entirely different part of the Gospel. Divisions like these proceed from the laboratory of theologians, but they do not harmonize with the nature of apostolic testimony, the simple reflection of history. The real teaching of Jesus had in it nothing systematic; the Lord confined Himself to answering the given need, which was for Him, at each moment, the signal of the Father's will. If in chap. v. He represents Himself as the one who has the power to raise from the dead, spiritually and physically, it is because He has just given life to the limbs of an impotent man. If in chap. vi., He declares Himself the bread of life, it is because He has just multiplied the loaves. If in chaps. vii. and viii., He proclaims Himself the living water and the light of the world, it is because the feast of Tabernacles has just recalled to all minds the scenes of the wilderness, the water of the rock and the pillar of fire. We must go with Baur, to the extent of claiming that the facts are invented in order to illustrate the ideas, or we must renounce the attempt to find a rational arrangement in the teachings of which these events are, each time, the occasion and the text.

First Cycle

John 5-8

This cycle contains three sections:
1. Chap. v. The beginning of the conflict in Judea;
2. Chap. vi. The crisis of faith in Galilee;
3. Chaps. vii., viii. The renewal and continuation of the conflict in Judea.

From chap. v. to chap. viii. we must reckon a period of seven or eight months. Indeed, if we are not in error, the event related in chap. v. occurred at the feast of Purim, consequently in the month of March. The story of the multiplication of the loaves, chap. vi., transports us to the time of the Passover, thus to April; and ch. vii. to the feast of Tabernacles, thus to October. If to this quite considerable period we add some previous months, which had passed since the month of December of the preceding year, when Jesus had returned to Galilee (iv. 35), we arrive at a continuous sojourn in that region of nearly ten months (December to October), which was interrupted only by the short journey to Jerusalem in chap. v. It is strange that of this ten months' Galilean activity, John mentions only a single event: the multiplication of the loaves (chap. vi.). Is it not natural to conclude from this silence, that, in this space of time left by John as a blank, the greater part of the facts of the Galilean ministry related by the Synoptics are to be placed. The multiplication of the loaves is, as it were, the *connecting link* between the two narratives.

1

John 5:1-47

FIRST OUTBREAK OF HATRED IN JUDEA

1. The miracle, occasion of the conflict: vv. 1–16; 2. The discourse of Jesus, commentary and defense of the miracle: vv. 17–47.

The miracle: vv. 1–16

Ver. 1. "*After these things, there was a feast*[1] *of the Jews, and Jesus went up to Jerusalem.*" The connecting phrase μετὰ ταῦτα, *after these things*, does not seem to us to indicate, notwithstanding the examples cited by *Meyer*, as immediate a succession as does μετὰ τοῦτο, *after this*. Whatever may be the feast to which we refer the event which is about to be related, it must have been separated by quite a long interval from the previous return. In fact, the feast which followed next after that return (in the course of December), that of the Dedication, at the end of this month, cannot be the one in question here. Jesus would not have returned to Judea so soon after He had left it for the reason indicated in iv. 1. After this came the feast of Purim in March, then that of the Passover in April. If the article ἡ before ἑορτή, "*the* feast," is read, the meaning is not doubtful; the latter feast is the one in question; for it was the principal one among the Jewish festivals, and the one best known to Greek readers (vi. 4). But why should such a large number of documents have omitted the article, if it was authentic? We can much more easily understand the reason for its addition; it was supposed that the question was precisely of the Passover. If the article is rejected, not only is there no further evidence in favor of this feast, but it is even positively excluded. More than this, it would be excluded even with the article. For why should not John, who elsewhere names it distinctly, do the same here? Comp. ii. 13; vi. 4; xi. 55, etc. Moreover, immediately afterwards, the narrative speaks to us, vi. 4, of a Passover during which Jesus remains in Galilee. We should, therefore, be obliged to suppose that between chaps. v. and vi. a whole year elapsed, of which John does not say a single word—a very improbable supposition. Besides, in chap. vii. (vv. 19–24), Jesus reverts to the healing of the impotent man which is related in chap. v., for the purpose of justifying it; would He have proceeded thus with respect to it after an interval of more than a year? Chap. iv. (ver. 35) placed us in the month of December; chap. vi. (ver. 4) points to the month of April. Between these two dates, it is quite natural to think of the feast of Purim, which was celebrated in March. This feast had reference to the deliverance of the Jews by queen Esther. It was not, it is true, of Divine institution, like the three great

---

[1] T. R. reads εορτη (*a* feast) with A B D G K S U V Γ Λ Mnn. Ir. Or. Chrys. and Tisch. (ed. of 1859); the article η before εορτη (*the* feast) is read by ℵ C E F H L M Δ Π 50 Mnn. Cop. Sah. some Fathers, Tisch. (8th ed.)

feasts; but why should this fact have prevented Jesus from going to it, as He did to the feast of Dedication (chap. x.) which was in the same case? And the expression: *a feast*, is exactly explained by this circumstance. As it was much less known than the others, outside of the Jewish people, and as by reason of its political character it had lost all importance for the Christian Church, it was needless to name it. Against this feast is alleged that it was not specially celebrated at Jerusalem. It consisted, in fact, in the reading of the book of Esther in every synagogue, and at banquets which took place throughout the country. But Jesus may have gone to Judea at that time with the intention of remaining there until the Passover feast, which was to be celebrated soon afterwards. The conflict that occurred on occasion of the healing of the impotent man was that which forced Him to return sooner to Galilee. Although, therefore, *de Wette* pronounces his verdict by declaring, "that there is not a single good reason to allege in favor of the feast of Purim," it appears to me that everything speaks in favor of this interpretation, which is that of *Hug, Olshausen, Wieseler, Meyer, Lange, Gess, Weiss*, etc. *Irenæus, Luther, Grotius, Lampe, Neander, Hengstenberg*, etc., decide in favor of the Passover. *Chrysostom, Calvin, Bengel, Hilgenfeld*, etc., give the preference to Pentecost. The absence of the article and of a precise designation speak against the second supposition, as well as against the first. Besides, between v. 1 (Pentecost) and vi. 4 (Passover of the following year), a period of more than ten months would have to be placed, respecting which John kept complete silence. *Ebrard, Ewald, Lichtenstein, Riggenbach* (doubtfully), pronounce for the feast of Tabernacles. This supposition is quite as improbable; for this feast is expressly named vii. 2: ἡ ἑορτὴ τῶν Ἰουδαίων, ἡ σκηνοπηγία. Why should it not be named here, as well as there? *Westcott* thinks of the feast of trumpets, on the first of the month *Tisri*, which opened the civil year of the Hebrews. It is on this day that the Rabbis fix the creation of the world and the last judgment. This day was solemnly announced by the sound of the sacerdotal trumpets. But can we suppose that a whole year elapsed between chap. v. and chap. vii., where we find ourselves again in the month of October? *Lücke, de Wette, Luthardt*, regard any determination of the point as impossible.

This question has more importance than appears at the first glance. If we refer v. 1 to the feast of Purim, as we believe we should, the framework of the history of Jesus is contracted: two years and a half are sufficient to include all its dates: ii. 13 Passover (1st year); iv. 35, December (same year); v. 1, Purim, March (2d year); vi. 4, Passover (April); vii. 1, Tabernacles (October); x. 22, Dedication (December); xii. 1, Passover, April (3d year). If, on the other hand, v. 1 designates a Passover feast, or one of those which followed it in the Jewish year, we are necessarily led to extend the duration of Jesus' ministry to three years and a half. *Gess* places this journey of Jesus at the time of the mission of the Twelve in Galilee (Matt. xi. 1; Mark vi. 7); this circumstance would explain why Jesus repaired to Judea alone or almost alone. This combination has nothing impossible in it (see on ver. 13). Has not Beyschlag good grounds for

454 / Unbelief Develops in Israel

alleging in favor of John's narrative the very naturally articulated course of the history of Jesus which appears in it: Judea, chap. i.; Galilee, chap. ii.a; Judea, chap. ii.b. iii.; Samaria, chap. iv.a; Galilee, chap. iv.b; Judea, chap. v.; Galilee, chap. vi.; Judea, chap. x., etc., in opposition to the strongly-marked contrast, without transition, which the Synoptical narrative presents: Galilee, Judea?

Ver. 2. "*Now there is at Jerusalem, by*[1] *the sheep-gate,*[2] *a pool called*[3] *in Hebrew, Bethesda,*[4] *having five porches.*" The Sinaitic MS. rejects the words ἐπὶ τῇ, *by the*, and thus makes the adjective προβατικῇ, *pertaining to sheep*, the epithet of κολυμβήθρᾳ: *the reservoir* or *the pool for sheep*. This reading is too weakly supported to be adopted, even in the view of *Tischendorf*. We must, therefore, understand as the substantive belonging with the adjective προβατικῇ, *pertaining to sheep*, one of the substantives, πύλη, *gate*, or ἀγορᾷ, *market*. The passages in Nehemiah, iii. 1–32; xii. 39, where a *sheep-gate* is mentioned, favor the former of these two ellipses. In Neh. iii. 3, mention is made of a *fish-gate* as near the preceding; it is probable that these two gates derived their names from the adjacent markets. The sheep-gate must have been situated on the side of the valley of Jehoshaphat, on the east of the city. As *Bovet* says, "the small cattle which entered Jerusalem came there certainly by the east; for it is on this side that the immense pastures of the wilderness of Judea lie." *Riehm's* Dictionary also says: "Even at the present day, it is through this gate that the Bedouins lead their flocks to Jerusalem for sale." The *sheep-gate*, as *Hengstenberg* observes, according to Neh. xii. 39, 40, must have been quite near the Temple; for it is from this that, in the ceremony of the inauguration of the walls, the cortege of priests entered immediately into the sacred inclosure. The gate, called at the present day St. Stephen's, at the northeast angle of the Haram, answers to these data. *M. de Saulcy* (*Voyage autour de la mer Morte*, t. II. pp. 367, 368) holds, according to some passages of St. Jerome and of authors of the Middle Ages, that there were in this place two neighboring pools, and supplying, in thought, κολυμβήθρᾳ, he explains: "Near the *sheep-pool*, there is *the pool* called Bethesda." In spite of the triumphant tone [5] with which this explanation is proposed, it is inadmissible. The expression of the evangelist, thus understood, would suppose this alleged *sheep-pool*, which is nowhere mentioned in the Old Testament, to be known to his Greek readers. *Meyer*, accepting the reading of the Sinaitic MS. τὸ λεγόμενον ἑβραιστὶ Βηθζάθα, explains: "There is near the *sheep-pool the place* called in Hebrew, Bethzatha." But a place so com-

---

[1] Instead of επι, A D G L read εν.
[2] ℵ Vulg^{aliq}. some Mnn. reject επι τη. Syr^{cur}. Syr^{sch}. Cyr. omit επι τη προβατικη.
[3] Instead of η επιλεγομενη, ℵ reads το λεγομενον, D V Mnn. λεγομενη.
[4] Instead of Βηθεσδα, ℵ L 1 Mnn. read Βηθζαθα Eus. Βηζαθα, B. Vulg. Βηθσαιδα, D Βελζεθα.
[5] The following are his expressions: "It is very curious to see how the commentators have made incredible efforts to understand this verse.... They have all been equally happy in their suppositions; it was the word κολυμβήθρα which needed to be understood, and all became clear." M. de Saulcy holds that, according to Brocardus, the second pool was situated west of the first. But the passage quoted would rather prove that it must have been to the north.

pletely unknown as the sheep-pool could not be indicated as a determining-point to Greek readers. The feminine ἔχουσα which follows is, besides, hardly favorable to this reading, which is only an awkward correction, like so many others which are met with in this manuscript. *Weiss* makes κολυμβήθρᾳ, a dative, and thinks that the best subject to be supplied is οἰκίᾳ, *the building Bethesda;* this ellipsis seems to me very unnatural. *Bengel* and *Lange* have concluded from the present ἐστι, *there is,* that the Gospel was written before the destruction of Jerusalem. But this present may be inspired by the vividness of recollection. Besides, an establishment of this kind belongs to the nature of the place and may survive a catastrophe. *Tobler* (*Denkblätter*, pp. 53 ff.), has proved that, in the fifth century, the porches here spoken of were still pointed out. *Hengstenberg* concludes from the ἐπί, *upon,* in the word ἐπιλεγομένη, "*sur*named," that the pool bore also another name. But it is more simple to suppose that John regards the word *pool* as the name, and *Bethesda* as the *sur*name. The expression: *in Hebrew,* denotes the Aramaic dialect, which had become the popular language since the return from the captivity. The most natural etymology of the word *Bethesda* is certainly *beth-chéseda, house of mercy,* whether this name alludes to the munificence of some pious Jew who had had these porches constructed to shelter the sick, or whether it refers to the goodness of God, from which this healing spring proceeded. *Delitzsch* has supposed that the etymology may be *beth-estaw* (אסטו׳) *peristyle. Beth-Aschada* (אשדא) *place of outpouring* (of the blood of victims), has also been thought of. The Alexandrian and Greco-Latin variants are only gross corruptions (see those of B and D). It might be supposed that these porches were five isolated buildings, arranged in a circle around the pool. But it is more simple to imagine a single edifice, forming a pentagonal peristyle, in the centre of which was the reservoir. There are still known at the present day, in the eastern part of the city of Jerusalem, some springs of mineral water; among others, on the west of the inclosure of the Temple, in the Mahometan quarter, the baths of *Aïn-es-Schefa* (*Ritter,* 16th part, p. 387). *Tobler* has proved that this spring is fed by the large chamber of water situated under the mosque which has replaced the temple. Another better known spring is found at the foot of the southeastern slope of Moriah; it is called *the Virgin-spring.* We have two principal accounts respecting this pond, those of *Tobler* and *Robinson.* The spring is very intermittent. The basin is sometimes entirely dry; again, the water is seen springing up between the stones. On the 21st of January, 1845, Tobler saw the water rise four and a half inches, with a gentle undulation. On the 14th of March, it rose for more than twenty minutes to the height of six or seven inches, and in two minutes sank again to its previous level. Robinson saw the water rise a foot in five minutes. A woman assured him that this movement is repeated at certain times, two or three times a day, but that in summer it is often observed only once in two or three days. These phenomena present a certain analogy to what is related of the spring of Bethesda. *Eusebius* also speaks of springs existing in this locality whose water was reddish. This color, which evidently arises from mineral elements, was, according to him, due to the infiltration of the blood of victims. Tradition places the pool of Bethesda in a great square hollow, surrounded by walls and situated to the north of the Haram, southward of the street which leads from St. Stephen's gate. It is called *Birket-Israïl;* it has a depth of about twenty-one meters, a breadth of about forty, and a length more than twice as great. The bottom is dry, filled with grass and shrubs. Robinson supposed that it was a fosse, formerly belonging to the fortifications of the citadel of Antonia. This supposition is rejected by several competent authorities. However this may be, Bethesda must have been nearly in this locality, for it is here that the sheep-gate (see above) was situated. As it is impossible to identify the pool of Bethesda with any one of the thermal springs of which we have just spoken, it must have been covered with débris, or have disappeared, as happens so frequently with intermittent fountains. The springs which are found at the present day merely prove how favorable the soil is to this kind of phenomena.[1]

Vv. 3, 4. " *In these porches lay a great number of sick persons, blind, lame, withered,*[2] *[waiting for the movement of the water.*[3] *4. For an angel descended from time to time into the pool and troubled the water; whosoever then first entered in after the troubling of the water, was healed of whatever disease he had].*"[4] The spectacle which this portico surrounding the pool presented is reproduced in some sort *de visu* by *Bovet,* describing the baths of Ibrahim, near Tiberias: "The hall where the spring is found is surrounded by several porticos, in which we see a multitude of people crowded one upon another, laid upon pallets or rolled in blankets, with lamentable expressions of misery and suffering. . . . . The pool is of white marble, of circular form and covered by a cupola supported by columns; the basin is surrounded on the interior by a bench on which persons may sit." Ξηροί, *impotent,* properly denotes those who have some member affected with atrophy, or, according to the common expression, *wasting away.* The end of ver. 3 and the 4th verse are wanting in the larger part of the Alexandrian MSS., and are rejected by *Tischendorf, Lücke, Tholuck, Olshausen, Meyer.* The large number of variants and the indications of doubt by which this passage is marked in several MSS., favor the rejection. The defenders of the authenticity of the passage, for example *Reuss,* explain the omission of it by the Alexandrian authorities by a dogmatic antipathy which, they hold, betrayed itself in the similar omission Luke xxii.

[1] Josephus *Bell. Jud.* (not *Antiqq.*, as Meyer says through an error), x. 5. 4, speaks of two pools called *Strouthion* and *Amygdalon;* the former near the citadel of Antonia on the northwest of the temple; the latter at the north of the temple. Bethesda must have been situated not far from these, towards the northeast corner.

[2] D a b add to ξηρων; παραλυτικων.

[3] א A B C L Syr^cur Sah. some Mnn. omit the ending of ver. 3 from εκδεχομενον (*waiting*) inclusively. This ending is read in D I Γ Δ Λ Π and nine other Mjj. Mnn. It. Syr^sch.

[4] The whole of ver. 4 is rejected by א B C D It^aliq Syr^cur Sah. some Mnn. Besides this, the text presents in the other MSS. an exceptional number of variants; instead of γαρ: και (L It^aliq); instead of αγγελος: αγγελος κυριου (A K L It^aliq Vulg. 30 Mnn.); instead of κατεβαινεν: ελουετο (A K Π): instead of εταρασσε: εταρασσετο (several Mjj.); etc.

43, 44 (the appearance of the angel at Gethsemane). This supposition would not, by any means, apply either to the *Sinaitic* MS., which has the passage in Luke entire, or to the *Alexandrian* which, in our passage, reads the fourth verse. The *Vatican* MS., alone presents the two omissions together; which evidently is not enough to justify the suspicion expressed above. I held with Ewald, in my earlier editions, that the true reading is the one presented by the *Cambridge* MS., and by numerous MSS. of the *Itala*, which preserve the close of ver. 3 while omitting the whole of ver. 4. The words: *waiting for the movement of the water*, if they are authentic, may indeed easily have occasioned the gloss of ver. 4. And ver. 7 seems to demand, in what precedes, something like the last words of ver. 3. Still it seems to me difficult to understand what should have occasioned the omission of these words in so large a number of documents, if they had originally formed part of the text. I am inclined, therefore, to hold with *Weiss, Keil*, etc., that they, as well as ver. 4, were added. The whole was at first written on the margin by a copyist; then this marginal remark was introduced into the text, as is observed in so many cases. This interpolation must be very ancient, for it is found already in one of the Syriac Versions (Syr[sch]), and *Tertullian* seems to allude to it (*de Bapt.*, c. 5). It was the expression of the popular opinion respecting the periodical movement of the water. According to the authentic text, there is nothing supernatural in the phenomenon of Bethesda. The whole is reduced to the intermittence which is so frequently observed in thermal waters. It is known that these waters have the greatest efficacy at the moment when they spring up, set in ebullition by the increased action of the gas, and it was at this moment that each sick person tried to be the first to feel its influence. *Hengstenberg*, who admits the intervention of the angel, extends the same explanation to all thermal waters. But it would be necessary, in this case, to hold a singular exaggeration in the terms of ver. 4. For after all no mineral water instantaneously heals the sick and all the kinds of maladies which are here mentioned.

Vv. 5-7. " *There was a man there*,[1] *held by his*[2] *sickness for thirty-eight years.* 6. *When Jesus saw him lying*,[3] *and knew that he had been already sick for a long time, he said unto him : Dost thou wish to be healed ?* 7. *The sick man answered him : Sir*,[4] *I have no one, when the water is troubled, to put*[5] *me into the pool; and while I am coming, another goes down before me.*" The long continuance of the malady is mentioned, either to set forth how inveterate and difficult to heal it was, or rather, according to ver. 6, to explain the profound compassion with which Jesus was moved on beholding this unhappy man. Ἔχων might be taken in the intransitive sense (ἀσθενῶς ἔχειν); but the construction is so similar to that of ver. 6, where χρόνον is the object of ἔχει, that it is preferable to make ἔτη the

---

[1] ℵ alone omits εκει.
[2] ℵ B C D L Itplerig some Mnn. read (after ασθενεια) αυτου, which is omitted by T. R. with A I Γ Δ Λ Π and 9 other Mjj.
[3] ℵ alone reads ανακειμενον.
[4] E F G H Syr[sch] some Mnn. read ναι (*yes*) before κυριε.
[5] T. R. reads βαλλη with some Mnn. only; all the Mjj. read βαλη.

object of ἔχων: "Having thirty-eight years in this condition of sickness." One has what one suffers. It is not necessary to connect ἔχων closely with ἦν ἐκεῖ, as if John meant to say that the sick person *had been there* for thirty-eight years.

Jesus appears here suddenly, as it were coming forth from a sort of *incognito*. What a difference between this arrival without éclat and His entrance into the Temple at the first Passover, ii. 13 ff.! Here it is no longer the Messiah; it is a simple pilgrim. *Meyer* translates γνούς: *having learned*, as if Jesus had received information. *Weiss* thinks that he heard the fact from the lips of the sick man himself. This meaning is possible; γνούς may, however, indicate one of those instantaneous perceptions by which the truth revealed itself to Jesus in the degree which was demanded by His task at the moment. Comp. i. 49; iv. 17. The 14th verse will show that the entire life of the sick man is present to the view of Jesus. The *long time* recalls the thirty-eight years of ver. 5: in this way is the identity of construction explained. The feast of Purim was celebrated among the Jews by works of beneficence and mutual gifts. It was the day of largesses. On Purim-day, said a Jew, nothing is refused to children. Jesus enters into the spirit of the feast, as He does also in chaps. vi. and vii., as regards the rites of the feasts of the Passover and of Tabernacles. His compassion, awakened by the sight of this man lying ill and abandoned (*lying on a couch*), and by the inward contemplation of the life of suffering which had preceded this moment (*already*), impels him to bestow largess also and spontaneously to accomplish for him a work of mercy. His question: "*Dost thou wish to be healed?*" is an implicit promise. Jesus endeavors thus, as *Lange* says, to draw the sick man from the dark discouragement in which this long and useless waiting had plunged him, and to reanimate hope within him. At the same time, Jesus by means of this question wishes to turn away His thought from the means of healing on which it was exclusively fixed, and to give him a perception of a new means, the living being who is to become for him the true Bethesda. Comp. the similar words of Peter to the impotent man, Acts iii. 4: "*Look on us.*" Faith, awakened by his look fixed upon Him who is speaking to him, will be, as it were, the channel through which the force from above will penetrate within him. The answer of the sick man does not imply the authenticity of ver. 4, nor even necessarily that of the end of ver. 3. It is sufficiently explained by the fact, known or easy to understand, of the intermittent ebullition of the spring. We see by the words: *I have no one*, that he was solitary and poor.

Vv. 8, 9. "*Jesus saith unto him: Arise,[1] take up thy bed,[2] and walk. 9. And immediately[3] the man was healed,[4] and he took up his bed, and walked. Now that day was a Sabbath.*" The word κράββατος comes from the Macedonian dialect (*Passow*); it is written in different ways. The imperfect *he walked* dramatically paints the joy in the recovered power.

[1] T. R. reads εγειραι with U V Γ Δ Mnn.; the rest: εγειρε.
[2] T. R. with V and several Mnn.: κραββατον;
[17] Mjj.: κραβαττον; ℵ: κραβακτον; E: κραβατον.
[3] ℵ D only omit ευθεως.
[4] ℵ It^{aliq} add here και ηγερθη (*and arose*).

Vv. 10–13. "*The Jews therefore said unto him who had been healed: It is the Sabbath; it is not lawful for thee to carry thy bed.* 11. *He answered*[1] *them: He that healed me said unto me: Take up thy bed, and walk.*[2] 12. *They asked him therefore: who is the man who said unto thee: Take up thy bed and walk?* 13. *But he that was healed*[3] *knew not who it was; for Jesus had disappeared*[4] *as there was a multitude in the place.*"[5] The act of carrying his bed seemed to the Jews a violation of the Sabbath rest. The Rabbis distinguished three sorts of works interdicted on the Sabbath, among them that of carrying a piece of furniture. The Rabbinical statute also prohibited treating a sick person medically, and perhaps the term τεθεραπευμένος (*cared for, treated*), contains an allusion to this other no less heavy grievance. But the fault of the Jews was in identifying the rabbinical explanation of the fourth commandment with its real meaning. The sick man very logically places his action under the protection of Him who miraculously has given him the power to perform it. The question of the Jews (ver. 12) is very characteristic. It is reproduced with much accuracy and nicety. They do not ask: "Who healed thee?" The fact of the miracle, though surprising enough, affects them very slightly. But the contravention of their Sabbatic statute, this is what is worthy of attention. Here is, indeed, the spirit of the Ἰουδαῖοι (ver. 10). The aorist ἰαθείς (*healed*), differing from τεθεραπευμένος (*cared for*), sets forth prominently the moment when the sick man, having gained the consciousness of his cure, looked about for His benefactor without being able to find Him. The reading adopted by *Tischendorf* (ὁ ἀσθενῶν) has no intrinsic value, and is not sufficiently sustained. The design of Jesus in withdrawing so speedily was to avoid the noise and the flocking together of a multitude; He feared the carnal enthusiasm which His miracles were exciting. But it does not follow from this, that the last words: "*as there was a crowd in the place,*" are intended to express this motive. They rather set forth, as *Hengstenberg* thinks, the possibility of escape. Jesus had easily disappeared in the midst of the crowd which was thronging the place. This is, undoubtedly, the meaning which the reading of the *Sinaitic* MS. is designed to express: ἐν μέσῳ (*in the midst of*); it is inadmissible, as well as the other variant of the same MS. in this verse (ἔνευσεν).—Ἐκνεύω, strictly: *to make a motion of the head* in order to avoid a blow, hence: to escape. The aorist has certainly here the sense of the pluperfect (against *Meyer* and *Weiss*). From this slight detail, *Gess* concludes that Jesus was not accompanied by His disciples in this visit to Jerusalem, and that they were at this time accomplishing their mission in Galilee.

Vv. 14, 15. "*Afterward, Jesus finds him*[6] *in the temple and said to him: Behold, thou art made whole; sin no more, lest a worse thing befall thee.* 15. *The*

---

[1] Instead of απεκριθη, A B: ος δε (C G K L Δ: ο δε) απεκριθη; ℵ: ο δε απεκρινατο.

[2] Instead of αρον and περιπατει, ℵ reads in this verse and the following αραι and περιπατειν. ℵ B C L omit τον κραββατον σου.

[3] Instead of ιαθεις, Tisch. reads ασθενων with D It.[2] only.

[4] ℵ D read ενευσεν (*made a sign*) instead of εξενευσεν.

[5] ℵ alone: μεσω instead of τοπω

[6] ℵ Syr^cur τον τεθεραπευμενον instead of αυτον.

460 / Unbelief Develops in Israel

man went away and told[1] *the Jews that it was Jesus who had healed him."* The sick man had, undoubtedly, come into the temple to pray or offer a thank-offering. The warning which Jesus addresses to him certainly implies that his malady had been the effect of some particular sin; but we need not infer from this that every malady results from an individual and special sin; it may have as its cause, in many cases, the debasement of the collective life of humanity by means of sin (see on ix. 3). By *something worse* than thirty-eight years of suffering, Jesus can scarcely mean anything but damnation.

In the revelation which the impotent man gives to the Jews, we need not see either a communication dictated by thankfulness and the desire to bring the Jews to faith (*Chrysostom, Grotius,* etc.), nor an ill-disposed denunciation (*Schleiermacher, Lange*), nor an act of obedience to the Jewish authorities (*Lücke, de Wette, Luthardt*), nor, finally, the bold desire of making known to them a power superior to their own (*Meyer*). It is quite simply the reply which he was not able to give, at ver. 13, and which he now gives to discharge his own responsibility; for he remained himself under the complaint so long as he could not refer it to the author of the act, and this violation of the Sabbath might draw upon him the penalty of death (vv. 16, 18); comp. Num., xv. 35.

Ver. 16. *"For this cause did the Jews persecute Jesus,*[2] *because he did these things on the Sabbath day."* Διὰ τοῦτο (*for this cause*), resumes what precedes, and, at the same time, is explained by the phrase which closes the verse: *because . . .* The word διώκειν (*persecute*), indicates the seeking of the means to injure. In favor of the authenticity of the following words in the T. R.: *and they sought to kill him,* the μᾶλλον (*yet more*), of ver. 18, can be alleged. But it is still more probable that it is these words in ver. 18 which have occasioned this interpolation. The imperfect ἐποίει (*He did*), malignantly expresses the idea that the violation of the Sabbath has henceforth passed with Him into a rule: He is accustomed to do it. This idea is entirely lost in the inaccurate translation of Ostervald and of Rilliet: *"because He had done this."* The plural ταῦτα (*these things*), refers to the double violation of the Sabbath, the healing and the bearing of the burden.

Let us notice here two analogies between John and the Synoptics: 1. In the latter also, Jesus is often obliged to perform His miracles as it were by stealth, and even to impose silence on those whom He has healed. 2. It is on occasion of the Sabbatic healings wrought in Galilee, that, according to them also, the conflict breaks out (Luke vi. 1–11).

The discourse of Jesus: vv. 17–47

In this discourse which is designed to vindicate the act which He has just performed, the three following thoughts are developed:

---

[1] Instead of ανηγγειλε, D G U Δ 20 Mnn. read απηγγειλε; א C L Syr Cop ειπεν.
[2] T. R. adds here και εζητουν αυτον αποκτειναι with 12 Mjj.; the larger part of the Mnn.; It², Syrsch. These words are omitted in א B C D L Itplerique; Vulg.; Syrcur; Cop.

1. Jesus justifies His work by the *perfect subordination* which exists between His activity and that of His Father: vv. 17–30.

2. The reality of this relation does not rest solely on the personal affirmation of Jesus; it has as its guarantee the *testimony of God Himself*: vv. 31–40.

3. Supported by this testimony of the Father, Jesus passes from defense to attack and unveils to the Jews the moral *cause* of their unbelief, the absence of the true spirit of the law: vv. 41–47.

The Son the Father's workman: vv. 17–30

Ver. 17. " *Jesus answered them: My Father worketh until now, and I work.*" The aorist middle ἀπεκρίνατο is found only here and in ver. 19; perhaps also xii. 23. Its use may be occasioned by the personal, apologetic character of the following discourse. This utterance, like that of ii. 19 (comp. Luke ii. 49), is like a flash of light breaking forth from the inmost depths of the consciousness of Jesus, from the point of mysterious union where He inwardly receives the Father's impulse. These sudden and immeasurably profound outbreakings of thought distinguish the language of Jesus from all other language.

These words are ordinarily explained in this sense: " My Father works *continually* (that is without allowing Himself to stop on the Sabbath), and, for myself, I work in the same way, without being bound by the legal statute; " either in that this declaration is applied to the work of God in the preservation of the universe, when once the creation is finished, (*Reuss*), or in that it is referred to the work of the salvation of humanity, which admits of no interruption (*Meyer*). In both cases, Jesus would affirm that He is no more subjected, as a man, to the obligation of the Sabbatic rest, than is God Himself. But if this were, indeed, His thought, He would not have said: *until this very hour* (ἕως ἄρτι), but *always, continually* (ἀεί). This objection is the more serious, because, according to the position of the words, this adverb of time, and not the verb, has the emphasis. Then, in the second member of the sentence, Jesus could not have refrained from either repeating the adverb or substituting for it the word ὁμοίως, *in the same way;* "And I also work continually, or likewise." Besides, it would have been very easy to answer to this argument that the position of a man with regard to the Sabbatic commandment is not the same with that of God. Finally the declaration of Jesus, thus understood, would contradict the attitude of submission to the law which He constantly observed during His life. Born a Jew, He lived as a faithful Jew. He emancipated Himself, undoubtedly, from the yoke of human commandments and Pharisaic traditions, but never from that of the law itself. It is impossible to prove in the life of Jesus a single contravention of a truly legal prescription. Death alone freed Him from this yoke. Such is the impression which He left, that St. Paul says of Him (Gal. iv. 4): " *born under the law,*" and characterizes His whole life by the expression (Rom. xv. 8) : " *minister of the circumcision.*" *Luthardt* has fully per-

462 / Unbelief Develops in Israel

ceived the special sense which the adverb ἕως ἄρτι, *until this hour*, must have. He has had the idea of contrasting it, not with the Sabbatic institution, but with the final Sabbath yet to come: "Since up to this time the work of salvation has not been consummated, as it will be in the future Sabbath, and consequently my Father works still, I also work." This sense is certainly much nearer to the thought of Jesus; only the antithesis between the present Sabbath and the Sabbath to come is not indicated by anything in the text.

To apprehend thoroughly the meaning of this utterance, let us for a moment set aside the words ἕως ἄρτι, until this hour. Jesus says: "My Father works, and I also work." The relation between these two propositions is obvious. We easily understand that it is necessary to combine logically what is grammatically in juxtaposition, and that it is as if it were: "*Since* my Father works, I also work." The Son cannot remain idle when the Father is working. We find again here that paratactic construction which is conformed to the genius of the Hebrew language, and which expresses by the simple copula, *and*, one of the numerous logical relations which the genius of the Greek states with precision by means of some other conjunction; comp. i. 10, ii. 9, etc. Nothing is changed in this relation by the addition of the adverb ἕως ἄρτι, *until this hour*. The meaning becomes the following: "Since my Father works *up to this moment*, I also work." *Passow*, in his Dictionary, remarks that in Greek, especially in the later writers, ἄρτι following καί, as is the case here, serves to indicate the immediate and rapid succession of two states; thus in this sentence: ἄρτι ἀπείργαστο τὸ ἄσμα καὶ ἀπῆλθεν (*the song was no sooner finished than he departed*). This is precisely the relation of immediate succession which Jesus affirms here as the law of His activity, as the true relation between His Father's work and His own, from which He draws the justification of the miracle which had been made the subject of incrimination. *Westcott, Weiss* and *Keil* are unwilling to see here an idea of *subordination;* they claim that the work of the Son is much rather *co-ordinated* with that of the Father. But this alleged co-ordination would not justify Jesus; for, as we have already said, the position of a man cannot be compared to that of God. We must reach the point of *dependence* in order that the argument may avail. And this relation of dependence it is, indeed, which appears from the relation between the two propositions: "Since my Father works until this moment, I also work." In order to grasp the meaning of this word, at once simple and profound, it is sufficient to imagine Jesus working with Joseph in the carpenter's shop at Nazareth. Can we not readily understand the reply which He would have addressed to the one who wished to turn Him aside from the work: "My Father works until now, and I also [consequently] cannot cease to work." Jesus finds Himself now with His Heavenly Father in a vaster workshop; He sees God at work in the theocracy and in the whole world, occupied with working for the salvation of mankind, and He suits His own local and personal working to this immense work. This is what He has just done in healing the impotent man; this modest healing is a link in the great chain suspended from His Father's hand, a real factor in the work which God is accomplishing here on earth. The development of this thought will follow in vv. 19, 20.

The meaning, therefore, is not: "I, as truly as God, have the right to work on the Sabbath;" but: "I have done nothing but obey the signal which God gave me at the moment . . . " Jesus sets forth, not the continuity of His working, but his filial and devoted adaptation to the work of the Father. And if objection is made that this amounts to the same thing, since God might direct Him to work even on the Sabbath, the answer is easy. God will not direct him to do anything which is contrary to the position of Jew, which He has imposed upon Him for the time of His earthly life. And He has done this none the more in this case, since neither the way in which Jesus healed the impotent man, nor the return of the latter to His dwelling, carrying his bed, really fell under the prohibition of the Mosaic law, as rightly understood. *Hilgenfeld* has gone even so far as to see in this saying of the Gospel an *intentional* contradiction of the idea of the rest of God in Genesis. But the rest in Genesis refers to the work of God in the sphere of nature, while the question here is of the divine work for the salvation of the human race. Is there here, as is affirmed, pretentious metaphysics? No. It is the deepest foundation of the peculiar filial life of Jesus, which all at once appears in this marvelously concise saying. The life of Socrates presents a phenomenon which has some analogy to that of which we have just had a glimpse. His *genius* arrested him when he was on the point of acting contrary to the will of the gods. But what a distance between this purely negative action and the positive divine impulse to which Jesus attaches His whole work! And what an appropriateness in this saying, what an imposing apology! It was to say to His adversaries: In accusing me, it is the Father whom you accuse. It is the legislator Himself whom you reproach with the transgression of the law; for I only act on a signal received from Him. We can understand, however, how this saying, instead of pacifying the adversaries, was only like the drop of oil thrown upon the fire, and caused their rage to overflow.

Ver. 18. "*For this reason*[1] *the Jews sought the more to kill him, because he not only broke the Sabbath, but called God his own Father, making himself equal with God.*" The διὰ τοῦτο (*for this reason*), is explained by the ὅτι (*because*), which follows. We have seen, that according to the genuine text in ver. 16, the intention *to kill* Jesus had not yet been ascribed to His enemies; it was only implicitly contained in the word ἐδίωκον (*they persecuted*). This suffices to explain the μᾶλλον (*yet more*) of ver. 18. Let us notice here the singular exaggerations of *Reuss:* "Let one read," he says, "the discourse, ver. 18 ff., many times interrupted by the phrase: *They persecute him, they seek to kill him.* According to the common and purely historical exegesis, we reach the picture of the Jews running after Jesus in the streets and pursuing Him with showers of stones "(t. ii., p. 416). The

---

[1] ℵ D It.: δια τουτο ουν; the rest omit ουν.

464 / Unbelief Develops in Israel

fact is, that the simple historical exegesis, which does not of set purpose go into error, does not find in these expressions: "*They persecuted Him*" (ver. 16), "*they sought to kill Him*" (ver. 18), anything else than the indication of some hostile secret meetings in which the rulers asked themselves, even then, how they could get rid of so dangerous a man. The Synoptics trace back also to this epoch the murderous projects of the adversaries of Jesus (Luke vi. 7, 11; Mark iii. 6; Matt. xii. 14). The anxious look of John was able to discern the fruit in the germ.—Ἔλυε, not: *He had violated* (*Ostervald*); but (imperfect): *He broke*, strictly: *dissolved*. His example and His principles seemed to annihilate the Sabbath. Besides this first complaint, the declaration of Jesus in ver. 17 had just furnished them a second—that of blaspheming. It was, first of all, the word μοῦ (*my* Father), which shocked them because of the special and exclusive sense which this expression assumed in the mouth of Jesus. If He had said *Our Father*, the Jews would have accepted the saying without displeasure (viii. 41). It was, in addition, the practical consequences which he seemed to draw from the term, making the working of God the standard of His own, and thus making Himself equal with God.

The 17th verse contains the primal idea of the whole following discourse: the relation of subordination between the activity of the Father and that of the Son. Vv. 19, 20, set forth this idea in a more detailed way; in ver. 19, the relation of the Son's action to that of the Father; in ver. 20, the relation of the Father's action to that of the Son. We might say: the Son who puts himself with fidelity at the service of the Father (ver. 19), and the Father who condescends to direct the activity of the Son (ver. 20).

Ver. 19. "*Jesus therefore answered and said unto them*[1]: *Verily, verily,*[2] *I say unto you: the Son can do nothing of himself, but what he seeth the Father doing. For the things which he doeth, these doeth the Son also in like manner.*" The interpreters who find a speculative idea in ver. 17, such as that of continuous creation, see in vv. 19, 20, the unfolding of the metaphysical relation between the Father and the Logos. But if one gives to ver. 17, as we have done, a sense appropriate to the context, vv. 19, 20 do not have this more or less abstract theological character; they, as well as ver. 17, have a practical application to the given case. Jesus means to say, not: I am this or that for my Father; I sustain to Him such or such a relation; but: "Whatever work you see me do, though it should give offence to you, like that for which I am now accused, be well assured that, as a submissive Son, I have done it only because I saw my Father acting in this way at the same time." There is no theology here; it is the explanation of His work which had been charged as criminal and of all His working in general, starting from the deepest law of His moral life, from His filial dependence with relation to His Father. This answer resembles the "I cannot do otherwise " of Luther, at Worms. Jesus puts His work under

---

[1] א begins the verse thus: ελεγεν ουν αυτοις ο Ιησους. B L: ελεγεν instead of ειπεν.

[2] א alone omits one of the two αμην.

John 5:19 / 465

the guarantee of His Father's, as the impotent man had just put his own under the guarantee of the work of Jesus (ver. 11).

The first proposition of ver. 19 presents this defense in a negative form: Nothing by myself; the second, in an affirmative form: Everything under the impulse of the Father. The expression: *can do nothing*, does not denote a metaphysical impossibility or one of essence, but a moral, that is absolutely free, powerlessness. This appears from ver. 26 and from the very term *Son*, which Jesus intentionally substitutes for the pronoun *I* of ver. 17. For it is in virtue of His filial—that is to say, His perfectly submissive and devoted—character, that Jesus is inwardly prevented from acting *of Himself*, at any moment whatever. He would indeed have the power of acting otherwise, if He wished; and here is the idea which gives to the expression ἀφ' ἑαυτοῦ, *of Himself*, a real and serious meaning. In all the phases of His existence, the Son has a treasure of force belonging to Himself which He might use freely and independently of the Father. According to ver. 26, He could, as Logos, bring forth worlds out of nothing and make Himself their God. But *He is wholly with God*, here on earth as in heaven, (John i. 1); and rather than be the God of a world for Himself, He prefers to remain in His position as Son and not to use His creative power except in communion with His Father. This law of the Son in His divine life is also His law in His human existence. He possesses as man all the faculties of man, and besides, after the baptism, all the Messianic forces. Therewith He could create, of His own impulse, in the sense in which every man of talent creates—create by and for Himself, and could found here below a kingdom which should be His own, like men of genius and conquerors. Was it not to this very real power that the various suggestions of Satan appealed in the wilderness? But He voluntarily refused to make any such use of His human and Messianic powers, and, invariably connecting His work with that of His Father, He thus freely remains faithful to His character as Son. The clause ἐὰν μή τι ... *unless He sees* ... *doing it*, or rather: if He does not see the Father *doing it*, does not restrict the idea to: *do of Himself*. It is rather an epexegetical explanation of ἀφ' ἑαυτοῦ, *of Himself*: "Of Himself, *that is to say*, if He does not see ..." The present participle ποιοῦντα, *doing*, answers to ἄρτι, *now*, of ver. 17: The Son sees the Father *acting*, and associates Himself, *at the same instant*, with His action. The figurative term βλέπειν, *see*, denotes the look of the mind constantly fixed upon the Father to watch for His will and to discern the point where His working actually is, in order to adapt His own to it. In fact, this *cannot*, of which Jesus has just spoken, is only the negative side of His filial devotion. But love, while preventing His acting *by Himself*, causes Him to co-operate actively in the work of the Father. Contemplating it as already accomplished in the thought of God, He immediately executes it on the earth. He can only act on this condition.

This is the idea contained in the second part of ver. 19. It is united by *for* to the preceding. In fact, if every work of His own is impossible for the Son, it is because He devotes Himself *entirely* to the work of the

Father. The sum of His activity being absorbed in this voluntary dependence, there remains for Him neither time nor force for acting by Himself. Ἃ γὰρ ἄν, *the things, whatever they may be.* This word includes eventualities without number, and, as a consequence, many other infractions of their Pharisaic statutes besides the one which they have just seen and which gives them so much offense. But He has no change to make for this reason; for every work of the Father, whatever it may be, must reproduce itself in His work. The word *in like manner,* ὁμοίως, does not denote a mere *imitation,* for the Father's work is still to be done, since the Son sets Himself to the execution of it; it is rather, as *Reuss* says, "an application of the Son's work to the Father's." The Father's work becomes that of the Son, in so far as the latter is capable of containing the former. The Son connects Himself at each moment with the work of the Father, in order to continue it in the measure in which His intelligence can embrace it and His power realize it. In this saying, we know not which is the more astonishing, the simplicity of the form or the sublimity of the idea. Jesus speaks of this intimate relation with the Being of beings, as if the question were of the simplest thing in the world. It is the saying of the child of twelve years: "*Must I not be in that which belongs to my Father?*" raised to its highest power. But this perfect subordination of the Son's work to the Father's cannot exist except on one condition: that the Father consents to initiate the Son incessantly into the course of His working. This is also what He deigns to do.

Ver. 20. The relation of the Father to the Son: *For the Father loveth the Son, and showeth him all things that he himself doeth, and he will show him greater works than these, that ye may marvel."* The co-operation of the Son in the divine work rests (*for*) upon the infinite love of the Father, which conceals nothing from the Son. The term φιλεῖν expresses tenderness (*to cherish*), and suits perfectly the intimacy of the relation here described. It was otherwise in iii. 35, where the word ἀγαπᾶν, which indicates the love of approbation and, in some sort, of admiration (ἄγαμαι), was found; because the question there was of the communication of omnipotence. The *showing* of the Father corresponds to the *seeing* of the Son (ver. 19), and is, at once, its condition and consequence; the condition: for the Father unveils His work to the Son, to the end that He may be able to know it and co-operate in it; the consequence: for it is this constant and faithful co-operation of the Son which causes this revelation incessantly to renew itself.

But the initiation and co-operation of the Son in the Father's work are subjected to a law of *progress,* as is suitable to the truly human state of this latter. This is what the end of the verse expresses: *And he will show him greater works than these.* The expression: *whatsoever things,* in ver. 19, gave a hint already of that gradual extension of the domain of the works which the Father entrusts to the Son. *Reuss* thinks that the question is of two different kinds of works, those of the Father appertaining to the outward domain, and those of the Son to the spiritual domain, and that the term *greater* refers to the superiority of the second to the first. But the bodily resurrection is also the work of the Son (vv. 28, 29), and Jesus could not, in any case, say that the Son's works are greater than the Father's. The word ὁμοίως, *in like manner*, would suffice to refute this explanation. Τούτων, *than these*, evidently refers to the healing of the impotent man and to the miracles of the same sort which Jesus had performed and of which the Jews were then witnesses. This is only the beginning. In proportion as the work of Jesus grows in extent and force, the Father's work will pass more completely into it; and thus will the saying of Isaiah be realized : " *The pleasure of the Lord shall prosper in His hand.*" The word *will show* declares that the Father will give Him at once the signal and the power to accomplish these greater and still greater works. Comp. Apoc. i. 1: " the revelation which the Father gave to Him."

The words which close the verse: *to the end that ye may marvel*, are carefully weighed. Jesus refrains from saying: to the end that ye may believe. He knows too well to whom He is speaking at this moment. The question here, as *Weiss* says, is of a surprise of confusion. We might paraphrase thus : " And then there will truly be something at which you may be astonished." The Jews opened their eyes widely as they saw an impotent man healed : How will it be when they shall one day, at the word of this same Jesus, see mankind recovering spiritual, and even corporeal life! One cure astonishes them : What will they say of a Pentecost and a resurrection of the dead! This somewhat disdainful manner of speaking of miracles would be strange enough on the part of an evangelist who was in the whole course of his narrative playing the part of an inventor of miracles.—Ἵνα, *in order that*, expresses not only a result (ὥστε), but a purpose. This astonishment is willed by God; for it is from it that the conversion of Israel will issue at the end of time. In view of the wonders produced by the Gospel among mankind, Israel will finally render to the Son that homage, equal to what it renders to the Father, of which ver. 23 speaks.

These two verses are one of the most remarkable passages of the New Testament in the Christological point of view. *De Wette* finds in the expression, *of Himself* (ver. 19), an exclusive and scarcely clear reference to the *human* side of the person of Jesus; for, after all, if Jesus is the Logos, His will is as divine as that of the Father, and there can be no contrast between the one and the other, as the expression, *of Himself*, would imply. This defect in logic is found, according to his view, again in the words of xvi. 13, where this same expression, *of Himself*, is hypothetically applied to the Holy Spirit. According to *Lücke*, it is only a popular way of presenting the human appearance of Jesus, excluding the divine element. *Reuss* (t. II., pp. 438 ff.) brings out in this passage heresy upon heresy, if the Logos theory, as it has been presented in the Prologue, is taken as the norm of the Johannean thought. According to him, indeed, God is conceived, in the Prologue, as a purely abstract being, who does not act in space and time except through the intermediation of the Logos, who is perfectly equal to the Father, " the essence of God reproduced, so to speak, a second time and by itself." According to our passage, on the contrary, the Father does a work for Himself (ἃ αὐτὸς ποιεῖ), which He reveals to the Son, and in which He gives Him a share, which is entirely contradictory. According to this latter view indeed, the Father acts directly in the world without making use of the Logos, and the Son is relatively to the Father in a condition of subordination, which is incompatible with "the equality of the two divine persons" taught in the Prologue.

The judgment of Lücke and de Wette undoubtedly strikes against the conception of the person of Jesus which is called orthodox, but not that of the New Testament and of John in particular. John does not know this Jesus, *now* divine, *now* human, to which the traditional exegesis has recourse. He knows a Logos who, once deprived of the divine state, entered fully into the human state, and, after having been revealed to Himself at the baptism as a divine subject, continued His human development, and only through the ascension recovered the divine state. By His human existence and His earthly activity, He realized in the form of *becoming*, the same filial relation which He realized in His divine existence in the form of *being*. This is the reason why all the terms employed by Jesus—the *showing* of the Father, the *seeing* of the Son, the expressions "*cannot*" and "*of Himself*"—apply to the different phases of His divine and human existence, to each one according to its nature and its measure. To understand the "*of Himself*," in our passage and xvi. 13, it is only necessary to take in earnest, as the Scripture does, the distinction of persons in the divine being; if each one of them has His own life, from which He may draw at will, there is no inconsequence between the passages cited.

As to the judgment of Reuss, the idea, which he finds in the Prologue, of an abstract divinity, purely transcendental and without any possible relation to the world, is not that of John; it is only that of Philo. On the contrary, God is, in the Prologue, a Father full of love both for His Son (ver. 18) and for the children whom He Himself begets by communicating to them His own life (ἐκ θεοῦ ἐγεννήθησαν, *were begotten of God*, ver. 13). He can thus act directly in the world and, consequently, associate His Son, made man, in His work on the earth. Vv. 19, 20 are in contradiction to the theory of Philo, but not to the conception of the evangelist. It is exactly the same with regard to the subordination of the Son. The true thought of the Prologue is exactly that of our two verses, 19, 20; the dependence, and free dependence, of the Son (ἦν πρὸς τὸν θεόν, ver. 1). This conception of the Logos undoubtedly, also, contradicts that of Philo, a fact which only proves one thing: that it is an error to make the evangelist the disciple of that strange philosopher, while he is simply the disciple of Jesus Christ. (Introd., pp. 127 ff.)

If we wish to form a lively idea of the relation of the work of Jesus to that of the Father, as it is presented here, the best way is to enter ourselves into a similar relation to the Lord Jesus Christ. We shall then have this experience: that the more the faithful servant heartily participates in the work of his Master, the more also does the latter give him understanding in respect to the totality and the details, and the more does He make him capable of realizing it. The agent grows with the work, as the work grows with the agent. The following are well-known examples of each of the two things: Oberlin, his eyes fixed upon Christ as Christ had His eyes fixed upon the Father, discerning the point which the divine work has reached among the inhabitants of Ban-de-la-Roche and what the continuation of this work demands; John Bost, contemplating so many sufferings unrelieved on the soil of France; Felix Neff, shocked at the sight of the deserted Churches of the High Alps; Wilberforce, feeling the chains of his enslaved brethren weigh upon his heart; Antoine Court, weeping over the ruins of the Reformed Church of France; Zinzendorf, finding himself suddenly in the presence of the persecuted Moravian emigrants who arrive in troops in his own lands . . . ; in all these cases, the faithful workman applies his ear to the heart of his Master, discerns its beating, and then, rising up, acts. Christ's work, that work which He wishes to do, passes then, in a certain portion of it, into the hands of His servant. Thus it is, no doubt, that Christ gradually entered into possession of the divine work, even till it became His own in its totality (John iii. 35). And having come to this point He gradually gives His own a part in it, who become the free sharers in His working, and He makes real to them that promise which is not without analogy to the saying which we are explaining: "Verily, verily, I say unto you, that he who believeth in me, he also shall do the works which I do; he shall do even *greater works than these* (μείζονα τούτων), because I go to my Father" (xiv. 12).

Jesus has just spoken of works, greater than His present miracles, which He will one day accomplish at the signal of His Father. He now explains what these works are; they are *the resurrection* and *the judgment* of mankind, vv. 21–29. This difficult passage has been very differently understood. I. Several Fathers, *Tertullian*, *Chrysostom*, later *Erasmus*, *Grotius*, *Bengel*, finally in recent times *Schott, Kuinoel, Hengstenberg*, etc., have applied the whole of the passage (except ver. 24) to the resurrection of the dead, *in the strict sense*, and to the last judgment. II. A diametrically opposite interpretation was held already by the Gnostics, then, among the moderns, by *Ammon, Schweizer, B. Crusius*,—it is that which refers the whole passage, even vv. 28, 29, to the *spiritual* resurrection and the moral judgment which the Gospel effects; (see also *Reuss*, in some sort). III. Finally, a third group of interpreters unite these two views in this sense, that they refer vv. 21–27 to the *moral* action of the Gospel, and vv. 28, 29 to the resurrection of the dead in the proper sense. These are, *Calvin, Lampe*, and most of the moderns, *Lücke, Tholuck, Meyer, de Wette*, etc. IV. By taking account, with greatest care, of the shades of expression, we arrive at the opinion that the true progress of ideas is the following: In a first cycle, the thought of ver. 17 has been quite summarily developed (vv. 19, 20). Then, the works of the Father which the Son is to accomplish are precisely stated in a second cycle (vv. 21–23); those of *making alive* and *judging*. Finally, in a third cycle (vv. 24–29) the thought makes a final advance, which brings it to its end, in the sense that vv. 24–27 apply to the resurrection and the spiritual judgment, and vv. 27–29 to the final judgment and the resurrection of the dead. This last view is, as it seems to me, nearly that of several modern commentators, such as *Luthardt, Weiss* and *Keil*.

Ver. 21. " *For, as the Father raiseth the dead and giveth them life, so doth the Son also make alive whom He will.*" To raise the dead is a greater work than to heal an impotent man; hence the *for*. This work, as well as the particular miracles, is the reproduction of the Father's work. The great difficulty here is to determine whether, as the greater part of the interpreters seem to think (for many do not explain themselves sufficiently on this point), the work of resurrection ascribed to the Father is to be identified with that which the Son accomplishes, or whether it is specifically different, or, finally, whether they combine with one another by a process, the formula of which must be sought after.[1] According to the first explanation, the ζωοποιεῖν, *give life*, ascribed to the Father, would remain in a purely ideal state until the Son, yielding to the divine initiative, caused the design of the Father to pass into the earthly reality. Thus *Luthardt* says: " The work belongs to God, in so far as it proceeds from Him; to the Son, in so far as it is accomplished by Him in the world " (p. 444). *Gess:* " It is not that the resurrection of the dead was until now the work of the Father, to become now the work of the Son; the resurrection of the dead is not yet an accomplished fact. No more is it that one part of the dead are raised by the Father, another by the Son. . . . But the Son is regarded as *the organ* by which the Father raises from the dead." *Bäumlein:* " The Son is the bearer and mediator of the Father's activity." This sense is very good in itself; but does it really suit the expression: *like as?* Was this indeed the proper term to designate a single divine impulse, an initiative of a purely moral nature? Jesus, in expressing Himself thus, seems to be thinking, rather, of a *real* work which the Father accomplishes and to which His own corresponds. According to the second sense, adopted by *Reuss*, we must ascribe the *bodily* resurrection to the Father and the resurrection in the spiritual sense, *salvation*, to the Son. Reuss finds the proof of this distinction in the οὓς θέλει, *whom he wills*, which indicates a selection and refers consequently to the moral domain only. This solution is untenable. How could vv. 28, 29, which describe the consummation of the Son's work, be applied to the spiritual resurrection? Comp. likewise vi. 40, 44, etc., where Jesus expressly ascribes to Himself, by an ἐγώ, *I*, several times repeated, the resurrection of the body—a fact which entirely destroys the line of demarcation proposed by Reuss. Jesus seems to me rather to speak here of the divine action, at once creative, preservative and restorative, which is exercised from the beginning of things in the sphere of nature, and which has broken forth with a new power in the theocratic domain. Comp. Deut. xxxii. 39: " I kill and *make alive*, I wound and *heal*." 1 Sam. ii. 6: " It is the Lord who killeth and *maketh alive*, who bringeth down to the grave and *bringeth up* from it." To this work of moral and physical restoration, till now accomplished by God, Jesus now unites His own; He becomes the agent of it in the particular sphere in which He finds Himself at each moment; this sphere will extend itself ever more widely; His capacity, in Himself, for performing it will increase in the same measure,

---

[1] As if (to take up anew the comparison of the common work of Jesus and Joseph) we had to decide for one of these three forms: Either Jesus executing the plans traced out by Joseph; or each of the two having a distinct part in the work; or, finally, Jesus seconding Joseph more and more, in proportion as He grows, and ending by charging Himself with the whole of the work.

until this domain is the universe and the power of the Son is omnipotence (comp. Matt. xxviii. 18). The steps of this growth are the following: He begins to perform isolated miracles of corporeal and spiritual resurrection, samples of His great future work. From the time of His elevation to glory, He realizes, through the communication of the Holy Spirit, the moral resurrection of mankind. Finally, on His return, by the victory which He gains over the last enemy, death (1 Cor. xv. 26), He effects, in the physical domain, the resurrection of believers, and afterwards also the universal resurrection. At that moment only will the work of the Father have passed entirely into His hands. The work of the Son is not, therefore, different from that which the Father acccomplishes. Only the Son, made man, becomes the agent of it only by degrees. The present, *makes alive*, in the second member, is a present of competency. Comp. indeed vv. 25 and 28 ("the hour *cometh* that . . . "), which show that the reality is yet to come. Nevertheless, even now, the word of Christ possesses a life-giving force (*the hour even now is*, ver. 25). We may connect the object *the dead* with the first verb only (*raiseth*), and give to the second verb (ζωοποιεῖ, *gives life*), an absolute sense. But perhaps it is more natural to make the words, *the dead*, the object of both of the verbs (see *Weiss*). Ἐγείρειν, strictly *to awake*, refers to the passage from death to life; ζωοποιεῖν, *to give life*, to the full restoration of life, whether spiritual or bodily. Nothing forces us, with *Reuss*, to restrict the application of the word *make alive*, in the second member, to spiritual life The restriction: *to whom he wills*, undoubtedly indicates a selection. But will there not be a selection, also, in the bodily resurrection? In ver. 29, Jesus distinguishes, in fact, two bodily resurrections, one of *life*, the other of *judgment*. The first alone truly merits the name of making alive.

By saying: *those whom he wills*, Jesus does not contrast His will as Son with that of the Father. This meaning would require οὓς αὐτὸς θέλει. He contrasts those whom He feels Himself constrained to make alive (believers) with those on behalf of whom it is morally impossible for Him to accomplish this miracle. These words, therefore, are the transition to ver. 22, where it is said that *the judgment*, that is to say, the selection, is committed to Him. In effecting the selection which decides the eternal death and life of individuals, Jesus does not cease for an instant to have His eyes fixed upon the Father, and to conform Himself to His purpose. According to vi. 38, 40, He discerns those who fulfill the divinely appointed condition: *he that believeth;* and immediately He applies to them the life-giving power which the Father has given to Him, and which has now become His own. Might there not be in this οὓς θέλει, *those whom he wills*, an allusion to the spontaneity with which Jesus had offered healing to the impotent man, without being in any way solicited by him, choosing him freely among all the sick persons who surrounded the pool? *Reuss* finds, in these words: *those whom he wills*, a contradiction to the idea of the dependence of the Son's work as related to that of the Father. But the inward feeling which makes Jesus *will* in such or such a way, while forming itself in Him spontaneously, is none the less in accord with that of God. Jesus wills of *His own* will, as He loves of *His own* love. But this love and this will have the same objects and the same end as the love and will of the Father. Comp. the formula, in the Apostolic Epistles : " Grace and peace *from* God, and the Lord Jesus Christ." Liberty is no more arbitrariness in Jesus, than in God. In the same sense it is ascribed to the Spirit (iii. 8 and 1 Cor. xii. 11), and to the God of nature (1 Cor. xv. 38). What Jesus meant to express here is not, therefore, as *Calvin* and formerly *Reuss* have supposed, the idea of predestination, it is the glorious competency which it pleases God to bestow upon Jesus for the accomplishment of the common work. He is a source of life like the Father, morally at first, and then, one day, corporeally. While affirming His voluntary dependence, Jesus allows a glimpse to be gained of the magnificence of His filial prerogative.

Vv. 22, 23. "*For also the Father judgeth no man; but he hath committed all power of judging unto the Son, 23, to the end that all may honor the Son as they honor the Father. He that honoreth not the Son honoreth not the Father who sent him.*" Two particles connect ver. 22 with the preceding ! γάρ, *for*, and οὐδέ (translated by *also*), which literally signifies : *and no more*. The meaning is, therefore : " For the Father *no more* judges any one (no more than He raises from the dead, when once He has committed to the Son the charge and power of raising from the dead," ver. 21). The *for* presents the second fact (the passing over of judgment to the Son) as the explanation of the first (the passing over of the power to raise from the dead). Indeed, to make alive is to absolve ; to refuse to make alive is to condemn. The power of making alive those whom one wills implies, therefore, the dignity of a *judge*. *Meyer* understands *judge* here, as in chap. iii., in the sense of *condemn*. But in ver. 21, the question is expressly of making alive, saving, and not of the opposite ; and the expression τὴν κρίσιν πᾶσαν, *judgment in all its forms* (ver. 22), shows that the term *judge* should be taken in the most general sense. H. *Meyer* (*Discourses of the Fourth Gospel*, p. 36) is shocked because this term is taken in ver. 22 in the *spiritual* sense (present moral judgment), in ver. 29 in the *external* sense (the final judgment), and finally in ver. 30 in a sense purely *subjective* (the individual judgment of Jesus), and hence he concludes that the tenor of the discourse has not been, in this case, exactly reproduced. But in ver. 22 the question is of judgment in the most *general* sense, without definite application (*all judgment*). It is only in the following cycle, vv. 24–29, that the meaning of this term is precisely stated, and that it is taken, first, in the spiritual sense, then, in the external sense. Everything is, therefore, correct in the progress of the thought.

Ver. 23. And what is the Father's will in transferring to Jesus the two highest attributes of divinity, *making alive, judging?* He wills that the homage of adoration which humanity renders to Him should be extended to the Son Himself. " The Father loveth the Son " (iii. 35) ; this is the reason why He wishes to see the world at the feet of the Son, even as at His own. " The equality of honor," says *Weiss*, " must correspond with the equality of action." The word τιμᾶν, *to honor*, does not directly express the act of adoration, as *Reuss* remarks. But in the context (καθώς *as*), it certainly denotes the religious respect of which the act of adoration is the expression. And in claiming for His person this sentiment, in the same sense in which it is due to the Father, Jesus authorizes, as related to Himself, worship properly so called, comp. xx. 28; Phil. ii. 10 " that every knee *should bow* at the name of Jesus;" and the Apocalypse throughout. The Father is not jealous of such homage. For it is He whom the creature honors in honoring the Son because of His divine character; as also it is to God that honor is refused, when it is refused to the Son. There is a terrible warning for the accusers of Jesus in these last words of the verse. Jesus throws back upon them the charge of blasphemy; they must learn—these zealous defenders of the glory of God—that when they accuse Him, Jesus, as they are doing, because of the miracle which He has performed in the midst of them, it is God to whom the outrage which they inflict upon Him is addressed, and that the treatment to which they subject this weak and poor man touches the Father Himself, who places Himself in closest union with Him. This menacing close of ver. 23 is an anticipation of the severe application which is to terminate the discourse (vv. 41–47).

The second cycle vv. 21–23 was a still very general development of the abridged cycle vv. 19, 20. In the third cycle, vv. 24–29, Jesus now shows the progressive *historical* realization of these two works of *making alive* and *judging*, which the Father has conferred upon Him. Until this point (vv. 21–23) He has attributed them to Himself only under the abstract form of mere competency. Now we behold this twofold power of saving and judging really in exercise, first in the spiritual sphere, vv. 24–27; then, in the *outward* domain, vv. 28, 29.

Vv. 24–27. First phase: the *spiritual* resurrection and *moral* judgment of humanity by the Son.

Ver. 24. " *Verily, verily, I say unto you, He that heareth my word, and believeth him that sent me, hath eternal life; and he cometh not into judgment, but is passed from death into life.*" Divine things are present to the mind of Jesus; He speaks that which He sees (iii. 11); hence this energetic affirmation: " *Verily, verily, I say unto you* " (vv. 24, 25). These words set forth, at the same time, the greatness of the fact announced. It is really unheard of: For him who receives with confidence His word, the two decisive acts of the eschatological drama, the resurrection and the judgment, are completed things. The simple word of Jesus received with faith has accomplished everything. This fact is indeed the proof of the qualities of life-giver and judge which Jesus ascribed to Himself (vv. 21, 22). Ἀκούειν, *to hear*, denotes not, as *Weiss* thinks, the outward hearing only, in contrast to the inward reception, which would come afterwards (*and believeth* . . .); it is the spiritual hearing, at the same time with the physical, in the sense of Matt. xiii. 43. For the verb *believe* has a new object (*Keil*); it is *the Father* as the one who has sent the Son. To surrender oneself to the word of Jesus in faith in the divine character of His being and word, is to render homage not only to the Son. but also to **the**

Father. The meaning of ἔχει ζωήν, *has life*, can be fully rendered here only by saying "has life *already*." It is the proof of ver. 21: "The Son makes alive." Is it not, indeed, His word which works this miracle? Καί, *and*, signifies: *and in consequence*. The exemption from judgment follows naturally from the entrance into life. The place of judgment is at the threshold of life and death. Ἔρχεται, *comes*, is the present of idea. The word *judgment* is by no means equivalent to *condemnation*, κατάκρισις, as *Meyer* will have it and as *Ostervald* translates. A judgment deciding on eternal destiny, says *Weiss*, is no longer possible with regard to the man who has in fact already obtained salvation. By the word of Jesus, received into the inner man, the believer undergoes this moral judgment here on earth to which unbelievers will be subjected at the last day. The revelation of the hidden things (1 Cor. iv. 5) is made in the inner forum of his conscience, where everything is condemned in succession which will be condemned for the rest before the tribunal at the last judgment. The judgment, is thus for him, an accomplished thing. If therefore the word received with faith frees the believer from the judgment, it is because it anticipates it; comp. xii. 48, where it is said that the judge, at the last day, will be no other than this same word. What a feeling of the absolute holiness and of the perfection of His word do not such expressions imply in the consciousness of Jesus! The reconciliation of this passage with Rom. xiv. 10 and 2 Cor. v. 10 has been given at iii. 18. The last words: *But he hath passed from death unto life*, contrast (*but*) the condition of him who has entered into life with the fate of the one who will have to pass through the judgment. The terms *death* and *life* are taken in the spiritual sense. *Westcott* thinks that, in this verse, the idea of the physical resurrection is still united with that of the spiritual resurrection. The combination of these two ideas seems to me impossible. The question is of the effects of the *word* of Jesus in the sense of His word of teaching. It is altogether arbitrary to explain the μεταβέβηκεν, with *Bäumlein*, in the sense of "*has the pledge of being able* to pass from death to life."

Ver. 25. "*Verily, verily, I say unto you, The hour is coming, and now is,*[1] *when the dead shall hear*[2] *the voice of the Son of God,*[3] *and they that*[4] *hear shall live.*"[5] A new affirmation, which Christ draws from the depths of His consciousness. An immense perspective opens before Him. The great act of the spiritual resurrection of humanity dead in its sins, dead to God, is to begin at this hour, and it is through Him that it will be wholly accomplished! The identity of the formula which begins these two verses, 24 and 25, "*verily, verily, I say unto you*" as well as the *asyndeton*, which makes the second the energetic reaffirmation of the first, would suffice to prove that ver. 25 cannot refer to a fact essentially differ-

---

[1] ℵ a b omit the words και νυν εστιν.
[2] Instead of ακουσονται, ℵ L some Mnn. read ακουσωσιν, and B some Mnn. ακουσουσιν.
[3] Instead of θεου, K S and some other authorities read ανθρωπου (*of man*).
[4] ℵ rejects οι (*and having heard, they* . . .).
[5] T. R. with 11 Mjj. and nearly all the Mnn. ζησονται; ℵ B D L: ζησουσιν.

ent from the preceding, and how wrong it is for *Keil* to find included here at once the physical and the spiritual resurrection. Jesus has passed, at ver. 24, from the general idea of resurrection to that of the spiritual resurrection in particular; He does not return backward. Only in order to make a picture, He borrows from the physical resurrection the images by which He wished to depict the spiritual work which is to prepare the way for it. He seems to allude to the magnificent vision of Ezekiel, in which the prophet, standing in the midst of a plain covered with dry bones, calls them to life, first, by his word, and then, by the breath of Jehovah. Thus Jesus abides here below the only living one in the midst of humanity plunged in the death of sin, and the hour is approaching in which He is going to accomplish with reference to it a work like that which God entrusted to the prophet with regard to Israel in captivity. There is here a feeling analogous to that which leads Him to say in the Synoptics: " *Let the dead bury their dead.*" The expression: *The hour cometh, and is now come*, is intended (comp. iv. 23) to open the eyes of all to the grandeur of this epoch which is passing and of that which is in preparation. Jesus says: *the hour cometh ;* what He means is the sending of the Holy Spirit (vii. 37–39). But he adds: *and is now come ;* for His word, which is spirit and life (vi. 63), is already preparing the hearts to receive the Spirit. Comp. xiv. 17. For the expression: *my word*, Jesus substitutes: *the voice of the Son of God.* The teaching of Christ is thus presented as the personal voice of Him who calls sinners to life. The article οἱ before ἀκούσαντες (*those who* have heard), distinctly separates the spiritually dead into two classes: those who hear the voice without understanding it (comp. xii. 40), and those who, when hearing it, *have ears to hear*, hear it inwardly. Only these last are made alive by it. It is the function of *judging* which is accomplished under this form.

Those who apply this verse to the resurrection of the dead in the strict sense, are obliged to refer the words: *and now is*, to a few miraculous resurrections wrought by Jesus in the course of His ministry, and to explain the words οἱ ἀκούσαντες in this sense: *and after having heard . . .* But all *Hengstenberg's* efforts have not succeeded in justifying this grammatically impossible interpretation of οἱ ἀκούσαντεις. According to *Olshausen*, ver. 24 refers to the spiritual resurrection, and ver. 25 to the *first* bodily resurrection—that of believers at the Parousia (1 Cor. xv. 23). Vv. 28, 29, finally, designate the final, universal resurrection. The words: *and now is*, must, in that case, refer to the resurrection of the few believers who appeared after the resurrection of Christ (Matt. xxvii. 52, 53). Undoubtedly, Jesus admits a distinction between the first resurrection and the universal resurrection (Luke xiv. 14: *to the resurrection of the just;* comp. Apoc. xx. 6); but the explanation which Olshausen gives of the words: *and now is*, is not open to discussion. Nothing in the text authorizes us to see here the indication of a resurrection different from that of ver. 24. The following verse explains the secret of the power which the voice of Christ will display in the hour which is about to strike for the earth.

Ver. 26. "*For, as*[1] *the Father hath life in himself, so hath he also given to the Son to have life in himself.*" The emphasis is on the twice-repeated words ἐν ἑαυτῷ (*in himself*), which terminate the two clauses. The Son not only has a *part* in life, like the creature: He possesses it in Himself, and He is thereby the source of it, like the Father Himself—hence His voice can give or restore life (ver. 25; comp. i. 3, 4). But, on the other hand, this divine prerogative the Son does not possess except as a gift of the Father. Here is the boldest paradox which it is possible to declare. Life in Himself, what in theology is called *aseity*, self-existence, *given* to the Son! We could not get an insight into the solution of this contradiction, unless we saw an analogous contradiction resolved in ourselves. We possess, as *a thing given*, the faculty of determining for ourselves, that is, of ourselves morally creating ourselves. We draw at each instant from this faculty moral decisions which appertain peculiarly to ourselves, for which we are seriously responsible before God, and which are transmuted into our permanent character. It is through making us a gift of this mysterious privilege of free action, that God has placed us in the rank of beings made in His *image*. What freedom is for man, this the divine faculty of living in Himself is for the Son. It is by this means, also, that the *subordination* of the Son to the Father becomes an act of divine freedom, and consequently, of divine love. By the gift of divine independence to the Son, the Father has given Him everything; by His perfect and voluntary subordination, the Son gives back everything to the Father. To give everything, to give back everything, is not this perfect love. *God is love.* Thus, not only does God love divinely, but He is also divinely loved. The act expressed by the word, ἔδωκεν (*gave*), is regarded by *Tholuck, Luthardt, Weiss*, etc., as a fact falling within the earthly life of Jesus: Jesus possesses, here on earth, spiritual life abiding in Him, and can communicate it to men. But if this were the full meaning of this word, how would it harmonize with vi. 57, where Jesus declares that in His earthly condition "*He lives only by the Father*," just as we, believers, live only by Him. It must, therefore, be acknowledged, that He is speaking of an eternal gift, of a unique prerogative appertaining to His divine state and entering into His essential Sonship. The spiritual resurrection of mankind through Him, this is the work which He wishes to explain in this passage; this work is yet to come; it implies the re-instatement of Christ in His divine state (xvii. 1, 2, 5). This expression must, consequently, be applied to Him in so far as raised, as man, to the supreme position which He enjoyed, as Logos[1], before the incarnation. It is from the midst of this glory that He will accomplish the resurrection described in vv. 24, 25 (*the hour cometh*); for it is then only that He can pour out the Spirit (vii. 39; xvii. 2). With the spiritual resurrection and judgment is closely connected, as a second divine act, the judgment together with the external resurrection, which is the condition of it.

Ver. 27. "*And he hath given him power also*[2] *to execute judgment, because*

---

[1] ℵ D: ως, instead of ωσπερ. [2] A B L It^pleriq Syr^cur Cop. Orig. (twice) omit the second και.

he is son of man." Jesus had said in ver. 22, in an indefinite way, that *all* judgment is committed to Him. This word *all judgment* included, of course, both the present moral, internal judgment and the final, external judgment. It is under these two aspects, taken together, that this idea is reproduced in ver. 27, which thus forms the transition from the work of the spiritual resurrection and judgment (vv. 24–26), to that of the outward resurrection and judgment (vv. 28, 29). Jesus adds to the idea of ver. 22 a new limitation: that the function of judge is committed to Him inasmuch as He is *Son of man.* The second καί *also,* although omitted by B, is perhaps authentic. It emphasizes the relation between the character of judge and that of Son of man. What is this relation? It has been understood in a great variety of ways. According to *Lücke* the meaning is: Because He is the *Messiah* and judging is (according to Dan. vii.) a Messianic function. But in that case the article before the words *Son of man* could not be wanting. Without the article, this expression signifies simply: *a son of man. Keil* denies this and thinks that the absence of the article may be explained by the fact that the words are here the predicate, designating a quality, rather than a person. He explains therefore: Because He is mediator between God and man, author of salvation and consequently judge; for judgment forms a part of the salvation. But the absence of the article is not justified by this, and the idea of salvation is arbitrarily introduced here. *Beyschlag* understands: Because He is the perfect man, the ideal man, fitted to serve as the standard for the moral worth of all others. But the article could not, any more than in the other case, be wanting with this meaning. The term, Son of man, without the article sets forth simply the quality of *man* which He shares with all other men. *Lange:* Because, as a son of man, He can have compassion on our weakness. But this would be to deny to God the feeling of compassion, while the Scriptures say expressly: "Like as a Father pitieth . . . ., so the Lord pitieth . . . . for *he knoweth our frame* " (Ps. cii. 13). Heb. ii. 18 cannot be cited as parallel, since the question there is of intercession, not of judgment. *De Wette:* Because the Father, as being the hidden God, cannot judge. *Reuss,* nearly the same: "In the system, God, in Himself, does not place Himself in contact with the world which He is to judge; He makes Himself man for this."[1] This reason would apply to the God of Philo, not to the God of Jesus Christ and of St. John; the latter is a Father, who is in direct relations with the world and humanity; He begets children for life (i. 13); He *loves* the world (iii. 16); He even *testifies* by outward miracles in favor of the Son; He *draws* souls to Christ, etc. Such a God might also, if He wished, judge the world. Besides, as *Luthardt* observes, the opposite of the hidden God would not be the Son *of man,* but the revealed God, the Word, the Son *of God,* or, speaking absolutely, the Son. *Meyer* and *Weiss:* Because Jesus is, as man, the

---

[1] Reuss, in his last work (*Théol. johann.*), quotes without remark this very different explanation: "God was obliged to *delegate* judgment to Him, because He in His quality as man could not Himself exercise it." But the special relation between the *has given* and the *because,* would, in that case, need to have been more distinctly marked.

executor and proclaimer of salvation, on which depends the decision of each man's destiny. There is the same reason against this explanation, as against that of *Keil*. The quality of man is made prominent here for the purpose of explaining, not the dignity of *Saviour*, but that of judge. *Holtzmann*: Because He can make the revelation of the divine holiness shine forth before the eyes of men through the fact of His human appearance. But God is able directly to manifest His holiness to the human conscience, as is many times seen in the Old Testament. *Hengstenberg*: to recompense Him for becoming man. Strange reward! In this embarrassment, the *Peschito* (Syr^sch), some Mjj. (E. M Δ.), and *Chrysostom* have recourse to a desperate expedient; they connect these words: "because he is son . . ." with the following verse: "Because He is a Son of man, marvel not." But what is there in the context leading us to suppose an astonishment respecting this point? Is it then so difficult to grasp the thought of Jesus? The judgment of humanity is a homage rendered to the holiness of God; but this homage, in order really to make reparation for the outrage committed, must proceed from the race itself which has committed the offense. Judgment, in this view, is exactly on the same line with expiation, of which it serves as the complement. Expiation is the reparation freely offered by believing humanity; judgment is the satisfaction which God takes from humanity which has refused Him this reparation. In the one, as in the other, of these acts, a man must preside.

Vv. 28, 29. "*Marvel not at this: for the hour is coming when all who are in the tombs shall hear his voice and shall come forth, 29, those who have done good, unto a resurrection of life, those who have done evil, unto a resurrection of judgment.*" The Lord reaches here the more outward domain, both as to the resurrection (ver. 28), and as to the judgment (ver. 29). It is impossible, indeed, not to refer ver. 28 to the resurrection of the dead, in the proper sense. 1. The question is of a wholly future event; for Jesus purposely omits here the words: καὶ νῦν ἐστί, *and now is*, of ver. 25. 2. He does not merely say, *the dead* (as in ver. 25); He uses the expression: *those who are in the tombs*, an expression which must, of course, be taken in the strict sense. 3. No more does He say: *those who shall hear* (ver. 25), an expression which implies a selection between two classes, but: *All those who are in the graves shall hear;* that is to say, the whole number of the dead. 4. Finally, He does not speak, as previously, of a single result: life; but of two opposite results which that resurrection will have (ver. 29). Jesus rises, therefore, from the highest act *of authority* (ἐξουσία), the judgment, to the highest act of *power* (δύναμις), the resurrection of the body; and this is the way in which He reasons: "*Marvel not* because I attribute to myself the right of judging (ver. 27), for behold the display of divine power which it shall one day be given me to make: to bring all mankind out of the grave." *Lücke* gives quite another turn to the thought of Jesus: "You will cease to be astonished that judgment is given to me, if you call to mind that as Son of man (as Messiah), it is I who accomplish the resurrection." Jesus according to his view, makes

His starting point, as from a thing well known and acknowledged, from an article of Jewish theology, according to which the Messiah is the one who is to raise mankind from the dead. But it is still doubtful whether, at the time of Jesus, the work of the resurrection was ascribed to the Messiah. Even the later Jewish theology shows itself very much divided on this point. Some ascribe this act to the omnipotent God, others to the Messiah (Eisenmenger, *Entdeckt, Judenth.* Th. II. pp. 897–899). This mechanical appeal to a Jewish doctrine is, moreover, little in accord with the ever original character of the testimony of Jesus. Finally, the meaning given by Lücke implies a false interpretation of the term *son of man,* ver. 27. There is great force in the words: shall hear *His voice.* "This voice which sounds in your ears at this moment, will be the one that shall awake you from the sleep of death and cause you to come forth from the tomb. Marvel not, therefore, that I claim to possess both the authority to judge and the power to raise from the dead spiritually." Thus the last convulsion of the physical world, the universal resurrection, will be the work of that same human will which shall have renewed the moral world —that of the Son of Man. "*Since death came by man,*" says St. Paul with precisely the same meaning, "*the resurrection of the dead comes also by man*" (1 Cor. xv. 21). No doubt, it might be said to Jesus: All these are only assertions on thy part. But we must not forget that behind these affirmations there was a fact—namely, "*Arise and walk,*" immediately followed by a result, which was at once the text of this discourse and its point of support. The twenty-ninth verse concludes this whole development by the idea of the final judgment, of which the resurrection of the body is the condition. To be judged, the dead must be revived in the fullness of their consciousness and of their personality, which implies their restoration to bodily existence. We must not translate: "Those who shall have done good, evil works," but: "*the* good, *the* evil works." In these two expressions is declared, as *Keil* says, the *total* result of the life in good or evil. In the former of these expressions are included the moral sincerity which leads to faith (iii. 21), the act of faith itself, when the hour of calling for it has come, finally, all the fruits of sanctification which result from faith. The latter comprehends the natural inward depravity which alienates from faith, unbelief which voluntarily takes sides with sin against the light (iii. 19, 20), finally, all the inevitable, immoral consequences of such a choice. On the use of the word ποιεῖν with ἀγαθά and πράσσειν with φαῦλα, see on iii. 20. The expression *resurrection of life* is explained by the opposite term: *resurrection of judgment.* The latter can only signify: resurrection leading to judgment; the former, only; resurrection introducing to the fullness of life, and that without any further necessity of a judgment in order to decide this favorable result. *Luthardt* and *Weiss* take the genitive ζωῆς, *of life,* as a limiting word of cause or quality: a resurrection which results from life (spiritual) already possessed (vv. 24, 25), or which is appropriate to that life. But there are degrees in the development of life, and if this resurrection, on the one hand, presupposes life, it may also, on the other hand, have life as its result. Here also we must avoid translating κρίσις, with *Osterwald, Arnaud,* etc., by *condemnation.*

Reuss maintains that the spiritual resurrection is in this passage declared to be "greater and more important than the physical resurrection" (see on ver. 20); and in his attempt to make this idea accord with the: "*Marvel not,*" of ver. 28, which implies the opposite, the following is the meaning which he gives to these words: "Marvel not that I speak to you, as I have just been doing, of a moral resurrection which must precede the physical resurrection. For you hold yourselves that the Messiah is to accomplish the latter; and this is in your eyes the more astonishing." But these words *in your eyes* are an importation of the commentator, intended to justify his system, according to which he has been able to write respecting the fourth Gospel that line, in manifest contradiction to the reality (vv. 28, 29): "The idea of a future and universal judgment is repudiated as something superfluous" (II., p. 559). *Scholten,* feeling the powerlessness of every exegetical expedient to reach the end which is pursued, that of causing every trace of the ordinary eschatology to disappear from our Gospel, declares vv. 28, 29 to be unauthentic, which verses, nevertheless, are not wanting in any document. He reasons thus: the activity of Jesus extending, according to pseudo-John, only to men *who are in this life* . . . , vv. 28, 29, must be interpolated." Convenient method! When they do not find the Gospel such as they *wish,* they make it such! *Hilgenfeld* (*Einl.,* p. 729), does not hesitate to affirm that our passage excludes all the Judæo-Christian eschatology, the outward coming of Jesus, a first resurrection, etc. But even though our passage does not contain all the elements of the picture, it does not absolutely exclude any one of them. Much more, the glorious coming of the Messiah is implied in ver. 28, and the entire eschatological drama, which the Parousia is to inaugurate, is summed up in ver. 29, so far as relates to the *final result,* which alone is of importance here, the resurrection and the judgment as works of Jesus.

After this passage (vv. 19–29), the development of the idea of ver. 17: "My Father worketh until now and I also work," is completely unfolded and Jesus returns to the starting-point.

Ver. 30. "*I can do nothing of myself; as I hear, I judge; and my judgment is just, because I seek not mine own will, but the will of him who sent me.*"[1] Can ver. 30 be connected with what immediately precedes, by the idea of judgment which is common to this verse and ver. 29? But the *present* tense: *I judge* (ver. 30) does not suit the idea of the future judgment (ver. 29); and the first clause: *I can do nothing of myself,* impresses at once on the thought of ver. 30 a much more general bearing. We are evidently brought back to the idea of ver. 19, which served as the starting-point of the preceding development: the infallibility of the Son's work finding its guarantee in its complete dependence on that of the Father. As *Reuss* well says: "The last verse reproduces the substance of the first; and the discourse thus is rounded out even externally." After having ascribed to Himself the most wonderful operations, Jesus seems to feel the need of

---

[1] T. R. adds πατρος at the end of the verse, with E G H M S U V Mnn., It^{aliq}; this word is rejected by ℵ A B D K L Δ Λ 12 Mnn. It^{pleriq} Vulg. Syr. Cop. Orig. (three times).

sinking again, as related to the Father, into a sort of nothingness. He who successively accomplishes the greatest works, is powerless to accomplish by Himself the humblest act. The pronoun ἐγώ (*I*), positively applies to that visible and definite personality which they have before their eyes the unheard of things which He has just affirmed, in a more abstract way, of *the Son*. This is the first difference between ver. 30 and ver. 19; the following is the second: In order to describe the total subordination of His work to that of the Father, Jesus made use of figures borrowed from the sense of sight: the Father *shows*, the Son *sees*. Here He borrows His figures from the sense of hearing: the Son *hears*, evidently from His Father's lips, the sentences which He is to pronounce, and it is only thus that He *judges*. Moreover, of the two divine works which He accomplishes, *raising from the dead* and *judging*, it was especially the first which Jesus had in view in ver. 19, in relation to the miracle wrought on the impotent man; He here makes the second prominent, in connection with the supreme act indicated in ver. 29. The sentences of which He speaks are the acts of absolution or of condemnation, which He accomplishes here on earth, by saying to one: " *Thy sins are forgiven thee*," to the other: " *Thy works are evil.*" Before declaring Himself thus, Jesus meditates in Himself; He listens to the Father's voice, and only opens His mouth after He has heard. It is upon this perfect docility that He rests the infallibility of His judgments, and not upon an omniscience incompatible with His humanity: "*And*—that is, and thus—*my judgment is just.*" But there is a condition necessary for listening and hearing in this way; it is to have no will of one's own; hence the ὅτι (*because*), which follows. No doubt, Jesus, Himself also, has a natural will distinct from that of God; His prayer in Gethsemane clearly proves it: " *Not my will, but thine be done.*" But, in a being entirely consecrated to God, as Jesus was, this natural will (*my* will), exists only to be unceasingly submitted or sacrificed to the Father's will: " *I seek not* mine own will, but the will of Him that hath sent me." From the ontological point of view, the Monothelites, therefore, well deserved to be condemned; for in denying to Jesus a will distinct from that of God, they suppressed the human nature in Him. And yet morally speaking, they were right. For all self-will in Jesus was a will continually and freely sacrificed. It is on this unceasing submission that the absolute holiness of His life rests, and from this holiness it is that the infallibility of His knowledge and His words results. He declares this here Himself.—The τοῦ πέμψαντός με of *Him who sent me*, is not a mere paraphrase of the name of God. It is argumentative: the one sent does the work of the sender.

What an existence is that of which this passage, vv. 19–30, traces for us the type! Such a relationship with God must have been lived, in order to be thus described: to act only after having seen, to speak only after having heard, what a picture of filial consciousness, of filial teaching, of filial activity! And all this attaching itself to a mere healing, accomplished on the initiative of the Father! Do we not see clearly that the essential idea of ver. 17 is that of the relation of dependence of the Son's work towards the Father's, and by no means that of the Sabbath, of which not the least mention is made in all this development? At the same time, this passage gives us, so to speak, access even to the inner laboratory of our Lord's thought and allows us to study the manner in which His word was produced. The miracle performed and the accusations which He excites awaken His reflection. He collects Himself, and the profound relation of His work to that of His Father formulates itself in His consciousness in the form of that simple, summary, oracle-like thesis of ver. 17. This is the theme which He develops afterwards. At the first moment (vv. 19, 20), He remains in the highest generalities of the paternal and filial relation. Then there are precisely formulated in His thought the two essential works which result from this relation: *making alive, judging* (vv. 21–23); finally, those two works themselves are presented to His mind in a more and more concrete form, in their progressive historical realization; first in the *moral* domain (vv. 24–27), then in that of *external* realities (vv. 28, 29). Where in this incomparable passage is what is called *religious metaphysics?* From the first word to the last, everything breathes that sentiment of filial abnegation which is the heart of Jesus' heart.

The testimony of the Father, in support of that which the Son renders to Himself: vv. 31–40

Jesus had just ascribed to Himself marvelous works. Such declarations might provoke an objection among His hearers: "All that which thou affirmest of thyself has no other guaranty than thine own word." Jesus acknowledges that His testimony has need of a divine sanction (vv. 31–35); and He presents it to His adversaries in a double testimony of the Father: 1. That of His miracles (ver. 36); 2. And that which is found from old time in the Scriptures (vv. 37–40).

Vv. 31, 32. "*If I bear witness of myself, my witness is not true. 32. There is another that beareth witness of me; and I know*[1] *that the witness which he witnesseth of me is true.*" Perhaps ver. 31 is the answer to an objection which was actually made to Jesus, in consequence of the preceding words. Similar interruptions abound in the much more circumstantial narratives of the following chapters. No doubt, the testimony which a person bears on his own behalf may be perfectly true. But in the sphere of sinful men, such a testimony is always suspected of partiality or falsehood. Jesus speaks here from the point of view of His hearers, who regard Him as an ordinary man. In the saying of viii. 14, on the contrary, He resumes His normal position and will claim distinctly the exceptional authority which His perfect holiness confers upon Him. The ἐγώ, *I*, might signify here: "*I alone* (apart from every other witness)." It is better to understand it: "I myself, bearing witness of my own person." Everything which follows proves that this *other*, whose testimony Jesus is about to allege, is God, and not John the Baptist, as *de Wette* thought. Vv. 33–35 are intended precisely to set aside the application of this saying

---

[1] ℵ D It^aliq Syr^cur read οιδατε (*ye know*), instead of οιδα (*I know*).

to the forerunner. In the second clause of ver. 32, this word: *I know:* signifies: "I bear in myself the inward consciousness of that filial relation of which my Father bears witness." He means to say that for Himself He has no need of any testimony. The reading οἴδατε, *you know*, probably arises from the false application of these words to the testimony of John the Baptist. The expressions περὶ ἐμοῦ, περὶ ἐμαυτοῦ, *concerning me, concerning myself,* repeated three times (vv. 31, 32) do not mean: *in my favor, for me* (*Rilliet*), but quite simply: *respecting me.* Before saying who *this other* is, whose testimony serves to support His own, Jesus removes the supposition that it is to the testimony of the forerunner that He means to appeal.

Vv. 33–35. "*Ye have sent unto John, and he hath borne witness unto the truth.* 34. *But the witness which I receive, is not from man; and what I say unto you here, is to the end that ye may be saved.* 35. *He was the lamp that burneth and shineth; and ye were willing to rejoice for a season in his light.*" The testimony of John the Baptist had made so much noise that Jesus might suppose that, at the moment when He was saying: "I have another witness," every one would think of that personage. Jesus rejects this supposition, but does so while calling attention to the fact that, from His hearers' standpoint, the testimony of John should certainly be regarded as valid; for it was they themselves who had called it forth (an allusion to the deputation, i. 19 ff.). The word *you,* ὑμεῖς, at the beginning of the verse, places the hearers in contrast to Jesus, who does not ask for human testimonies and contents himself with being able to allege that of the Father. The perfect μεμαρτύρηκε, *hath borne witness,* declares that the testimony of John preserves its value notwithstanding the disappearance of the witness (ver. 35: he *was,* etc.). On this *truth* to which John bore witness, comp. i. 20, 27, 29. The ἐγὼ δέ, *but I,* of ver. 34 forms an antithesis to the *you* of ver. 33. This human testimony which they demanded, is not that by which Jesus supports the truth of His own, even though it was favorable to Him. But does Jesus regard the testimony of John the Baptist as purely human? Some interpreters escape the difficulty by translating οὐ λαμβάνω in the sense: "I do not seek" or "I am not ambitious of." This is to strain the meaning of the expression, which merely means: I do not make use of it. It is enough if we take account of the article τήν before the word *testimony;* "*the* testimony," means here: "that of which I have need, the only one which I would allege as confirmation of my own." John's testimony was designed to direct their eyes to the light; but, when once the light had appeared, it gave place to the direct testimony of God Himself. That testimony was, indeed, the fruit of a revelation; but, as *Keil* says, this inspiration, passing through human lips, might be called in question. Nevertheless, Jesus recalls, in passing, this testimony of John. It is the care which He has for their souls, which does not permit Him to pass it over in silence: "If I recall it, it is to the end that *you* (ὑμεῖς) may profit by it unto salvation. It is, then, for you, not for me."

The 35th verse expresses the transitory character of the appearance of John the Baptist. John was not *the light,* the sun (i. 8); but he was *the torch,* lighted by God for giving light before the day came. The article *the* before the word *torch* has been explained in many ways. *Bengel* finds here an allusion to Sirach xlviii. 1 : *" the word* (of Elijah) *shone as a torch."* *Luthardt* believes that John is compared to *the* well-known torch-bearer, who ordinarily preceded the bridegroom in the marriage feasts. *Meyer, Weiss, Keil,* understand: *the true* torch which is designed to show the path. Perhaps there is an allusion to that *single* light which was lighted at night to illumine the house (Mark iv. 21). We might see in the two epithets : *which burneth and shineth,* only this one idea: which is consumed in shining. But it is more simple to find here the two conditions of the usefulness of the light: to be lighted and not to be covered (Weiss). The imperfect ἦν, *was,* proves that, at the moment when Jesus was speaking, the light was already covered. For there is evidently an allusion in this past tense to the imprisonment of John the Baptist. The second part of the verse: *Ye were willing* . . . . , continues the figure. Jesus compares the Jews to children who, instead of making use of the precious moments during which the light shines, do nothing but frolic in its brightness. *To rejoice* is contrasted with *to be saved,* ver. 34. It was impossible better to characterize the vain and puerile curiosity, with which the people were infatuated by an appearance so extraordinary. Comp. Luke vii. 24: *" What went ye out into the wilderness to see ? " Weiss* thinks that Jesus meant to indicate the hopes which had at first been excited in the rulers by this appearance. Can this be in accordance with Luke vii. 30 ?—Ἠθελήσατε: *you pleased yourselves with . . .*

Ver. 36. *" But I have the*[1] *witness which is greater*[2] *than [that of] John : for the works which the Father hath given*[3] *me to accomplish, these very works that I do*[4] *bear witness of me, that the Father hath sent me."* The passage relating to John the Baptist was only a remark thrown in in a passing way, an argument *ad hominem ;* Jesus now develops the fact announced at first, ver. 32: the testimony of the Father. The ἐγώ, *I,* is like that of ver. 34, the antithesis of *you,* ver. 33 ; it completes the preceding by adding the affirmation to the negation. For the article *the,* see on ver. 34: the absolute witness, the only one to which I wish to appeal here.

The absence of the article before μείζω is explained thus: *" the* true testimony, which is *a* testimony greater than." In the genitive τοῦ Ἰωάννου, *of John,* is ordinarily found the abbreviated form of comparison : "greater than *that* of John." May it not be explained more literally : "greater *than John,"* that is to say, than John testifying in my favor : John identified with his testimony. *Meyer, Weiss, Keil, Reuss,* etc., understand by the ἔργα, *the works* of which Jesus speaks, His whole activity in general, and not only His miracles. *Weiss* alleges for this meaning the whole passage vv. 20–27 on the spiritual resurrection of humanity. But the spiritual works of Jesus do not come under the perception of the

---

[1] ℵ omits την before μαρτυριαν.
[2] A B E G M Λ read μειζον (evidently a mistake).
[3] ℵ B L Γ read δεδωκεν, instead of εδωκεν.
[4] ℵ A B D L some Mnn. reject εγω before ποιω.

John 5:36,37 / 485

senses; in order to believe them, they must have been experienced; they are not, therefore, a *testimony* for the unbeliever. Moreover, at the moment when Jesus was speaking, they were still to come. Finally, we must not forget the starting-point of this whole discourse, which is a miracle properly so called. Jesus certainly alludes to the healing of the impotent man and to all the similar works which He is accomplishing every day. *Meyer* concedes this explanation in the passages vii. 3, 21 and elsewhere; but the context demands it here as well as there. The miracles are designated, on the one side, as *gifts* of the Father to Jesus; on the other, as *works* of Jesus Himself. And it is, in fact, by this double right, that they are a testimony of God. If the Son did them by His own force, they would not be a declaration of God on His behalf; and if God performed them directly, without passing through the Son as an organ, the latter could not derive from them a personal legitimation.—We may hesitate between the readings ἔδωκε and δέδωκε, both of which are compatible with the following ἵνα τελειώσω. The object of this verb *hath given* is: *the works;* God makes a gift to Jesus of His miracles. Then this object is developed by these words: (literally) *that I may accomplish them.* For these miracles are not given to Him in the form of works *done,* but of works *to be done.* This is brought out forcibly by the repetition of the subject in the words: *these very works which I* (ἐγώ) *do.* The expression *give in order that* includes both permission and power. As it is from this double character of the miracle, as a *gift* of God and a *work* of Jesus, that the testimony results, it is necessary to keep in the text the word ἐγώ, *I,* before ποιῶ, which is rejected by some Alexandrian authorities, and which well sets forth the second of these two characteristics. But this testimony of the miracles is still indirect, as compared with another which is altogether personal (ver. 37):

Ver. 37. "*And the Father who sent me, himself*[1] *hath borne witness of me. Ye have neither heard his voice at any time, nor seen his form.*" It is clear, whatever *Olshausen, Baur* and others may say, that Jesus here speaks of a *new* testimony of the Father: otherwise, why should He substitute for the present *beareth witness* (ver. 36), which applies to the miracles which Jesus at present performs, the perfect *hath borne witness,* which can only denote a testimony given and completed.—The pronoun αὐτός, *Himself,* emphasized as it is, strongly sets forth the *personal* character of this new testimony: God has spoken *Himself.* This is the reason why the reading αὐτός seems to me preferable to the ἐκεῖνος, *he,* of the Alexandrian authorities. What is this personal testimony? *De Wette* and *Tholuck,* understand by it the inner voice by which God testifies in *the heart* of man in favor of the Gospel, "*the drawing of the Father* to the Son." But it is impossible from this point of view to explain the perfect *hath borne witness,* and very difficult to account for the following expressions, *His voice, His form,* which so evidently refer to a personal manifestation. *Chrysostom, Grotius, Bengel* (I myself, in the former editions), refer this expression to the testimony of

---

[1] ℵ B L. am. read εκεινος, instead of αυτος; D: εκεινος αυτος.

God at the *baptism* of Jesus, which very well answers to this condition. But objection is rightly made because of the οὐ . . . πώποτε, *never*, in the following words: and it would be to return to the testimony of John the Baptist, which Jesus had set aside, since the voice of God had not been heard except by the forerunner and everything rested, therefore, upon his testimony. We must, accordingly, take our position rather with the explanation of *Cyril, Calvin, Lücke, Meyer, Luthardt, Weiss, Keil,* who refer ver. 37 to the testimony of God *in the Old Testament,* the book in which He manifests Himself and Himself speaks. Vv. 38, 39 confirm this view. But how, from this point of view, can we explain the following clause? A reproach has been found here (*Meyer, Luthardt, Keil*); "You are miserably deaf and blind, that is, incapable of apprehending this testimony; you have never inwardly received the divine word." This sense suits the context. But the expression: "*You have not seen his face*" would be a strange one to designate moral insensibility to the Holy Scriptures. Others see rather in these words a *concession* made to the hearers: for example, *Tholuck:* "You have, no doubt, neither heard . . . nor seen . . . , for that is impossible; it is not this with which I reproach you (ver. 37); but you should at least have received the testimony which God gives in the Scriptures" (ver. 38). If this were the thought, however, an adversative particle could not be wanting at the beginning of ver. 38. But the expression: *and you have not in you,* on the contrary, continues the movement of the preceding clause. The expressions *to hear the voice, see the form of God,* denote an immediate personal knowledge of God (i. 18). Jesus uses the former in vi. 46, to characterize the knowledge of God which He has Himself, in contrast with all purely human knowledge: "*Not that any one hath seen the Father, save He that is of the Father; he hath seen the Father.*" This declaration ought to serve as a standard for the explanation of the one before us. We shall say with *Weiss:* There is not here either a reproach or a concession; it is the simple authentication of a fact, namely, the natural powerlessness of man to rise to the intuitive knowledge of God. The thought of Jesus is, therefore: "This personal testimony of God (ver. 37a) has not reached you, first because no divine revelation or appearance has been personally given to you, as to the prophets and men of God in the Old Testament (ver. 37b); and then because the word to which those men of God consigned their immediate communications with God, has not become living and abiding in you (ver. 38)." Consequently the personal testimony of God, that which Jesus here means, does not exist for them. God has never spoken to them directly, and the only book, in which they could have heard His testimony, has remained for them, through their own fault, a closed book. We can well understand why in ver. 37 Jesus employs the term φωνή, the personal *voice,* the symbol of immediate revelation, while in ver. 38 He makes use of the word λόγος, *word,* the term in use to denote the *revelation* handed down to the people. The direct connection of ver. 37 with ver. 38 by καί, *and,* presents no more difficulty from this point of view.

Vv. 38–40. "*And his word ye have not abiding in you, for ye believe* **not** *him whom he hath sent.* 39. *Ye search the Scriptures, because ye think that in them ye have eternal life; and these are they which bear witness of me.* 40. *And ye will not come to me that ye may have life.*" The written word might have supplied the place of the personal revelation; they have had it in their hands and on their lips, but not in the heart. They have studied the letter, but have not appropriated to themselves the contents, the thought, the spirit. Thus it has not become a light lighted within them to guide them, a power to bear sway over them. Jesus gives a proof of this inward fact—it is their unbelief towards Him, the divine messenger. Undoubtedly, there is no *argument* here; for the reality of His divine mission was precisely the point in question. It is a *judgment* which Jesus pronounces, and which has its point of support, like the entire discourse, in the miracle which He had wrought.

The 39th verse may be regarded as a concession: No doubt, you study the Scriptures with care. But we must rather see herein the indication of a fact which Jesus is about to contrast with another. "You search the Scriptures with so much care; you scrutinize the externals of them with the most scrupulous exactness, hoping to make eternal life spring forth from this minute study; and at the same time you obstinately reject the one to whom they bear testimony!" We take the verb ἐρευνᾶτε, therefore, as an indicative: *you search;* as do *Cyril, Erasmus, Bengel, Lücke, Westcott,* and now also *Luthardt.* A large number of commentators and translators (*Chrysostom, Augustine, Luther, Calvin, Stier, Hofmann, Keil, Ostervald,*) make this verb an imperative: *Search.* Jesus would exhort them to a profound study of the Scriptures. But, in that case, He should not have said, "because you *believe* you have in them . . .," but "because you will have in them;" or at least "because you *yourselves* think you have in them." And then He should have continued, in order to give a ground for the exhortation, by saying: "*For* these are *they.*" The verb ἐρευνᾶν, *search,* is very suitable as characterizing the Rabbinical study of the Scriptures, the dissection of the letter. Ἐκεῖναι, *they,* still with the emphatic and exclusive meaning which this pronoun has in John: and it is precisely *they.*

The copula καί, *and,* in ver. 40, sets forth, as so often in John, the moral contradiction between the two things which unbelief succeeds in causing to move on together: to study the Scriptures which testify of Christ, *and,* at the same time, not to come to Christ! They seek life, *and* they reject Him who brings it! The words: *ye will not,* mark the voluntary side of unbelief, the moral antipathy which is the real cause of it. We find again in this passage the sorrowful tone of that saying preserved in the Synoptics: "*Jerusalem, Jerusalem, how often would I . . . . But ye would not!*" This passage clearly shows how Jesus recognized Himself in the Old Testament. He beheld there so fully His own figure, that it seemed to Him impossible to have sincerely studied that book and not *come to Him* immediately.

But whence *arises,* then, the not willing pointed out in ver. 40, and what will be its *result?* These are the two questions which Jesus answers in the words which close the discourse, and which are, as it were, the practical application of it.

The condemnation of Jewish unbelief: vv. 41–47

In vv. 41–44, Jesus unfolds the cause of the moral antipathy which keeps them away from Him; in vv. 45–47, the terrible consequences of this refusal to believe.

Vv. 41–44. "*I receive not my glory from men.* 42. *But I know you,* [*and I know*] *that ye have not the love of God in yourselves.* 43. *I am come in my Father's name, and ye receive me not; if another shall come in* [1] *his own name, him ye will receive.* 44. *How can ye believe, ye who receive your glory from one another, and seek not* [2] *the glory which cometh from God* [3] *only.*"—On one side, a Messiah who has no care for the good opinion of men and the homage of the multitude, and on the other, men who place their supreme good in public consideration, in an unblemished reputation for orthodoxy, in a high renown for Scriptural erudition and for fidelity to legal observances (comp. the description of the Pharisees, Matt. vi. 1–18; xxiii. 1–12): how could this opposition in tendency fail to put an obstacle in the way of the birth of faith in these latter? *Weiss* thinks that, if this were the sense of ver. 41, an ἐγώ, *I*, would be necessary, in contrast with *you* (ver. 42). In the same manner with *Westcott*, he understands in this way: Do not think that I am speaking thus "in order to glorify myself in your eyes" (*Weiss*); or: "as the result of spite which my disappointed hopes cause me" (*Westcott*). But the ἐγώ would be necessary only if the case of Jesus were placed second. If Jesus had meant to reply to such a supposition on the part of His adversaries, He would, no doubt, have said: μὴ δοκεῖτε, "*think not that* I seek . . . . ."—The perfect ἔγνωκα means: "I have studied you, and I know you." Jesus had penetrated the depth of vanity which these fine exteriors so much admired among the rulers covered.—*The love of God* denotes the inward aspiration towards God which may be found in the Jew and even in the sincere Gentile. Rom. ii. 7: "Those who seek for honor, glory and immortality." (Comp. ver. 44.) This divine aspiration it is, which leads to faith, as the absence of it to unbelief. Jesus states precisely here the thought which is expressed in an indefinite way in iii. 19–21. *In yourselves:* not only on the lips, but in the heart.

Ver. 43. The result of this contrast between His moral tendency and theirs. While they reject Him, the Messiah, whose whole appearance bears the seal of dependence on God, they will receive with eagerness every false Messiah who will act from his own wisdom and his own force, glorifying man in his person. All glorious with the glory of this world will be the one welcomed by these lovers of human glory. *In the name of God:* coming by His authority and as His delegate. *In his own name:* representing only himself, his own genius and power. Ἔλθῃ, *comes*, in

---

[1] א omits ἐν. [2] א 10 Mnn. It^{aliq}. read ζητοῦντες, instead of ζητεῖτε. [3] B a b. omit θεοῦ.

its relation to ἐλήλυθα, *I have come*, can only denote a pseudo-Messianic appearance. According to the Synoptics also, Jesus expected false Christs (Matt. xxiv. 5, 24 and the parallels). History has confirmed this prophecy; it speaks of sixty-four false Messiahs, who all succeeded in forming a party among the Jewish people in this way. See Schudt, *Jüdische Merkwürdigkeiten* (cited by Meyer). *You will* receive him; comp. 2 Thess. ii. 10, 11. The application of this expression; *another* to the false Messiah Bacochebas (about 132), which some critics have desired to make for the purpose of proving that the composition of our Gospel belongs to the second century (*Hilgenfeld, Thoma*), is an absolutely gratuitous supposition, which has no authorization in the text.

This vicious tendency with which Jesus reproaches His adversaries went so far as even to destroy in them the faculty, the *possibility* of believing: ver. 44. The pronoun, ὑμεῖς, *you*, signifies: men such as you are (vv. 42, 43). In the last words, the adjective μόνον, *only*, may be connected with the idea of θεοῦ: God who is *the only God*. Jesus would, in this case, characterize God as having, as *only God*, the right to bestow the true glory. This is the meaning ordinarily given to this expression. I think that it is more in the spirit of the context to understand, with *Grotius* and *de Wette*: the glory which is received from *God alone*, from God only, and not from men. The idea of these verses is that nothing renders men more unfit for faith than the seeking for human glory. But as necessarily as the current of Pharisaic vainglory bears the rulers of the people far away from faith, so infallibly would the spirit of love for God which inspires the books of Moses have directed them to Jesus and led them to faith.

Vv. 45–47. "*Think not that I will accuse you to the Father: there is one that accuseth you,*[1] *Moses, on whom ye have set your hope. 46. For if ye believed Moses, ye would believe me; for he wrote*[2] *of me. 47. But if ye believe not his writings, how shall ye believe*[3] *my words.*" After having unveiled to them the moral *cause* of their unbelief, Jesus shows to His hearers the *danger* to which it exposes them,—that of being condemned in the name of that very law, on the observance of which they have founded their hopes of salvation. It is not He, the Messiah rejected by them, it is Moses himself, in whose name they condemn Him, who will demand their condemnation. Jesus pursues them here on their own ground. His word assumes an aggressive and dramatic form. He causes to rise before them that grand figure of the ancient deliverer, to whom their hopes were attached (εἰς ὅν), and transforms this alleged advocate into an accuser. The words: *that I will accuse you*, show that, already at that time, a sentiment of hostility to His own people was imputed to Jesus. It was His severe discourses which gave rise to this accusation. Ἔστι, is very solemn: "*He is there*, he who . . . " The words: *on whom you hope*, allude to the zeal for the law, which the adversaries of Jesus had manifested on this very

---

[1] B adds πρὸς τὸν πατέρα (*to the Father*).
[2] ℵ: γεγραφεν instead of εγραψεν.
[3] Instead of πιστευσετε, B V It^{aliq} Syr^{cur} read πιστευετε and D G S Δ some Mnn. πιστευσητε.

day; this zeal was their title, in their eyes an assured title, to the Messianic glory. " It will be found that this Moses, whom you invoke against me will testify *for* me *against* you." What an overturning of all their ideas! *Meyer* and *Weiss* claim that the words: *who will accuse you* cannot refer to the *last judgment*, since Jesus will then fill the office, not of accuser, but of judge. But Jesus does not enter into this question, which would have had no meaning with people who did not recognize Him as the Messiah. *To the* Father: who will judge by means of Christ.

The two verses, 46 and 47, prove the thesis of ver. 45, by showing, the first, the connection between faith in Moses and faith in Christ; the second, the no less necessary connection between the two unbeliefs in the one and in the other. In other words: Every true disciple of Moses is on the way to becoming a Christian; every bad Jew is on that towards rejecting the Gospel. These two propositions are founded on the principle that the two covenants are the development of one and the same fundamental thought and have the same moral substance. To accept or reject the revelation of salvation at its first stage, is implicitly to accept or reject it in its complete form. This is exactly the thesis which St. Paul develops in Rom. ii. 6–10 and 26–29. The words: *wrote of me*, allude to the Proto-gospel, to the patriarchal promises, to the types such as that of the brazen serpent, to the Levitical ceremonies which were *the shadow of things to come* (Col. ii. 17), more especially to the promise Deut. xviii. 18: " *I will raise up unto them a prophet like unto thee;* "—this last promise, while including the sending of all the prophets who followed Moses, finds its consummation in Jesus Christ.—*Ye would believe on me:* in me as the one whom Moses thus announced. In truth, many of the prophecies had not yet found in Jesus their fulfillment. But we must think especially of the spirit of holiness in the law of Moses and the theocratic institutions, which found in Jesus its full realization. Moses tended to awaken the sense of sin and the thirst for righteousness, which Jesus came to satisfy. "To give access to this spirit, was to open one's heart in advance to the great life-giver " (*Gess*).

Ver. 47. On the other hand, unbelief towards Moses carries naturally in its train the rejection of Jesus. The essential antithesis is not that of the substantives, *writings* and *words*, but that of the pronouns, *his* and *my*. The former is only accidental; it arises only from the fact that the Jews knew Moses by his *writings* and Jesus by His *words*. This charge of not believing Moses, addressed to people whom the alleged violation of one of the Mosaic commandments threw into a rage, recalls that other saying of Jesus, so sorrowful and so bitter (Matt. xxiii. 29–32): "*Ye build the tombs of the prophets, and ye bear witness thus that ye are children of those who killed them.*" The rejection of a sacred principle shelters itself sometimes under the appearances of the most particular regard and most ardent zeal for the principle itself. From this coincidence, there result, in the religious history of humanity, those tragic situations, among which the catastrophe of Israel here announced certainly holds the foremost place.

As regards the historical reality of this discourse, the following appear to us to be the results of the exegesis:

1. The *fundamental thought* is perfectly suited to the *given situation*. Accused of having done an anti-Sabbatical work, and even of ascribing to Himself equality with God, Jesus justifies Himself in a way at once the most lofty and the most humble, by averring, on the testimony of His consciousness, the absolute dependence of His work, relatively to that of the Father.

2. The *three* principal *parts* of the discourse are naturally *linked together*, as they start from the central idea which we have just indicated: 1. Jesus affirms the constant adapting of His activity to that of the Father, and declares that from this relation of dependence between Him and God will proceed yet far more considerable works. 2. He proves this internal relation, which it is impossible for men to test, by a double testimony of the Father: His miracles, a specimen of which is at this very moment before their eyes, and the Scriptures. 3. He closes by showing them, in their secret antipathy to the moral tendency of His work, the reason which prevents them from trusting the divine testimony, and by declaring to them their future condemnation in the name of that Moses whom they accuse Him of despising.

Instead of the abstruse metaphysics which has been charged upon the discourses in John, there remains for us only the simple expression of the filial consciousness of Jesus. This latter displays itself gradually in a series of views of imposing grandeur, and of an unique elevation. What renders this feature more striking, is the *naive* and almost child-like simplicity of the figures employed to describe this communion of the Son with the Father. Such a relation must have been *lived*, in order to be expressed, and expressed in this way.

Strauss has acknowledged, up to a certain point, these results of exegesis. "There is not," he says, "in the tenor of the rest of the discourse, anything which causes difficulty, anything which Jesus could not Himself have said, since the evangelist relates, in the best connection, things . . . which, according to the Synoptics also, Jesus ascribes to Himself."[1] The objections of Strauss bear only on the analogies of style between this discourse, that of John the Baptist (chap. iii.), and certain passages of the first Epistle of St. John (Introd., pp. 106, 107). Strauss concludes by saying: "If, then, the form of this discourse should be ascribed to the evangelist, it might be that the substance of it belonged to Jesus." We believe that we may conclude by saying: Jesus must have really spoken in this way. The principal theme bears the character of most perfect appropriateness. The secondary ideas are logically subordinated to this theme. No detail turns aside from the idea of the whole, or goes beyond it; finally, the application is of a thrilling solemnity, as it should be in such a situation, and closes by impressing on the whole discourse the seal of reality.

Renan considers that the author of this narrative must have derived the substance of his account from tradition, which is, he says, *extremely weighty*, because it proves that a part of the Christian community really attributed to Jesus miracles performed at Jerusalem. As to the discourse in particular, see his summary judgment respecting the discourses of the fourth Gospel (p. lxxviii.): "The

---

[1] *Leben Jesu*, I., 2d part. The expression "in the rest of the discourse" is not intended to limit this favorable judgment given respecting the whole of the discourse; it applies to an exception which Strauss had himself just set aside.

theme cannot be without a certain degree of authenticity; but in the execution, the fancy of the artist gives itself full play. We feel the factitious action, the rhetoric, the studied diction." But *factitious action* betrays itself by commonplaces without appropriateness; have we met with them? *Rhetoric*, by emphasis and inflation; have we found a redundant word, a word which does not express an original thought? *Studied diction*, by the ingenious antithesis or the striving after piquancy; has the discourse which we have just studied offered us anything like this? The substance and the force equally exclude the idea of an artificial work, of a composition in cold blood.

Finally, let us notice an assertion of *Réville*, trenchant and bold like those which so often come from the pen of this critic: "This book," he says, in speaking of the fourth Gospel, "in which Judaism, the Jewish law, the Jewish temples, are things as foreign, as indifferent, as they could be to a Hellenistic Christian of the second century . . . "[1] And one ventures to write words like these in the face of the last verses of this chapter, in which Jesus so identifies His teaching with that of Moses, that to believe the one is implicitly to believe the other, and to reject the second, is virtually to reject the first, because Jesus is in reality nothing but Moses completed. The agreement of the law and the Gospel does not appear more clearly from the Sermon on the Mount, than from the passage which we have just studied. But we know that the Sermon on the Mount is universally regarded as that which has most authenticity in the Synoptic tradition.

[1] *Revue germanique*, I., Dec. 1863, p. 120, note.

INTRODUCTORY SUGGESTIONS
ON
THE INTERNAL EVIDENCE
BY TIMOTHY DWIGHT

The intelligent reader of the New Testament, when he comes to the Fourth Gospel, is at once impressed by the difference between it and the three narratives of the life of Jesus which precede it. Each of these earlier writings, though having certain peculiarities of its own which distinguish it from the other two, is, in some prominent sense, a biography written for the purpose of telling the story itself. If there is a further end in view, as undoubtedly there may be, it is rather secondary than primary, or, to say the least, it is left to the reader to discover, without any direct statement of it on the author's part. But one cannot open the Fourth Gospel and read the verses of its first chapter without realizing that the book has a new character. The writer is evidently moving in the sphere of great thoughts, and not merely of a biographical narrative. He is evidently intending to relate his story for an end which is beyond the mere record. He does not mean to commit his book to those who may chance to receive it, and then let them find in the works or words of Jesus whatever idea of His person or influences for their own spiritual life they may be able to discover for themselves. He has, on the other hand, a thought of his own. He has studied the life of the Master for himself, and he would impress, if possible, upon the mind of his reader the conviction which has been impressed upon his own.

What is this conviction? What is this purpose? These are the questions which immediately present themselves. The phenomena brought before us in the book, and the direct statements, if there be any such, which it contains, must furnish the answer. If we look for these—reading carefully from the beginning to the end—we discover, first of all, the remarkable declarations of what is commonly called the Prologue, and the equally striking words of xx. 30, 31, which close the work. What is, if possible, still more remarkable, we find that, while the words and propositions which evidently hold the most prominent place in the Prologue disappear altogether after it reaches its termination, the last verses of the twentieth chapter, just alluded to, have a manifest connection with these propositions and words. These last verses, also, clearly set forth the purpose of the book. The phenomena of this Gospel are, therefore, the great thoughts of the introductory verses respecting the Logos, the story of Jesus which forms the substance and contents of the book, and the formal declaration, at the end, that the author's object in writing is to induce the readers to believe with regard to Jesus that which, as he cannot doubt, will give them the true life of the soul. In a word, he is moved to write a new Gospel narrative, not merely to tell once more, or in a somewhat different way, a story which had been told before, but in order that, by telling it, he may prove to his readers the truth of his own conception of his Master, and that they, by this means, may attain to the highest good.

Let us consider the Prologue briefly with reference to the plan of the work.[1] There can be little doubt that the two leading ideas of the first eighteen verses are those of ver. 1 and ver. 14: The Logos was in the beginning, was with God, and was God; and the Logos became flesh and tabernacled among us. In connection with the first of these statements, certain additional declarations, evidently of a subordinate character, are made in vv. 3, 4; The Logos was the instrumental agent in creation; with reference to the living part of created things He was the life; and with respect to the part capable of intelligence and spiritual life He was the light. He was thus the source of all existence, of any sort, which any portion of the creation is able to possess. That there is a steady movement and progress here in the line of the idea of revelation seems evident. The movement is towards the spiritual region, and naturally so, because it is in that region that the author's mind is dwelling. These earliest verses, therefore, indicate what the word Logos in itself indicates, whatever may be its origin—whether the Old Testament or the Jewish-Alexandrian philosophy—namely, that the thought of John is of God as revealing Himself to and in the world, as distinguished from God in His unrevealed state or His hidden being. The Logos is the revealer. This revealer was working in the world, from the beginning, to the end of giving the true light, but the world did not fully lay hold of what He offered to it.

---

[1] For a more detailed setting forth of the ideas of the Prologue and the meaning of its leading words, see additional notes.

"The light shineth in the darkness; and the darkness apprehended it not." Some clearer mode of manifesting Himself as manifesting also the light became, therefore, a necessity; and, accordingly, the Logos became flesh. Without attempting to determine, at this point, precisely what the author's idea, in the use of these words, is, we cannot doubt that he intends to represent the Logos as, in some way, coming into human life in the person of a man. This is made clear, not only by the contrast of the words σάρξ ἐγένετο with the propositions of the first verse, but also by the peculiar phrase ἐσκήνωσεν ἐν ἡμῖν and by the words *we beheld his glory, glory as of the only begotten from the Father*. Finally, the immediate connection of vv. 17, 18 with ver. 14, through the words *grace and truth* and the verb ἐξηγήσατο which carries in it the idea of revelation, show that the person in whom the Logos, in some sense, took up His abode for the purpose of giving the clearer light which men needed was Jesus Christ. The substance of the statement of the Prologue is, accordingly, that—in some way, which it is not necessary at this point of our discussion to discover and definitely establish—Jesus Christ is the Logos who was in the beginning with God and was God, and who, at a later period, became flesh. The narrative of the earthly life of Jesus which occupies the space intervening between the Prologue and the closing verses—that is, which really forms the substance of the work—is the means which the author adopts for the accomplishment of his purpose. The story is the proof. Instead of establishing his proposition that Jesus is the Logos incarnate by arguments appropriate to a doctrinal treatise, he simply gives the narrative of what He did and said, evidently believing that the life will bear the strongest testimony to the doctrine.

That he should have adopted this method of proof was natural, because the establishment of the doctrinal proposition in itself considered was not the final end which he had in view. This end was, as he himself states, a practical one, to be realized in the life of his readers. They were to have life in the name of this incarnate Logos. But this life (ζωή) was not merely to the view of this writer a thing of the future, to be experienced in eternity. It was a present experience of the individual soul— the life of Jesus transferred, as it were, to the believing disciple and made a possession of his own. There could be no better way, therefore, of accomplishing his twofold purpose—the doctrinal and the practical— than to lead the reader to believe the truth that Jesus is the Christ, the Son of God, by giving the narrative of His earthly career.

There are, however, two peculiar elements in the narrative which further distinguish it from the narratives of the Synoptical Gospels. The first of these is immediately connected with the doctrinal character of the book. As the story is told for the purpose of proving the truth just mentioned, it is viewed everywhere by the author in the light of testimony. The Greek word which conveys the idea of testimony occurs in this Gospel in its verbal form thirty-three times, and in its substantive form fourteen times. It is found in almost every chapter, and almost universally with reference to Jesus. Very singularly it appears in two places in the Prologue as bringing out the witness borne by John the Baptist—once, immediately after the first leading statement respecting the Logos (vv. 1–4), and again, after the second leading statement (ver. 14). Then, at the opening of the historical section of the first chapter, it is introduced a third time with a detailed setting forth of what the Baptist said. It is plain that the biography is, as we may say, founded upon testimony; and the simplest, or even the only explanation which can be given, as regards the Prologue, is that the author desired to connect each of His two great propositions with that witness of the forerunner which was, in a sense, the accrediting word from God Himself. We find the word, also, in those central and vital chapters of the first main division of the book—the fifth and the eighth,—in which the evidences for His claims to Divine Sonship are given by Jesus Himself, and pressed upon the attention of His adversaries. Testimony turns the minds and footsteps of the earliest disciples to Jesus. The believer becomes immediately a witness, as we see, for example, in the case of the Samaritan woman. The apostolic work in the present and the future is to be that of testifying. The words and works which Jesus speaks and does bear testimony to Him. The Spirit who shall appear after He is glorified shall be always giving His divine witness. The author himself writes his book as one who has seen and testified. When we discover this idea thus filling the book, and observe at the end that the writer has evidently selected his materials, excluding much that he might have inserted ("many other signs, etc., which are not written in this book"), we may not doubt that his principle of selection was connected with this idea.

The second of the two elements referred to appears first in the verses which follow the Prologue and which extend as far as the middle of the second chapter. This passage may be called the historical introduction of the Gospel. It will be noticed by the attentive reader that the entrance of Jesus on His public ministry, as given in this book, is described in ii. 13 ff. The passage i. 19–ii. 12 contains only an account of the coming of five or six persons to Jesus while He was still continuing in His private and family life. The story, as related to these persons, opens with the mention of two, one of whom only is named, who were directed to Jesus by John the Baptist and apparently came to Him at John's suggestion. If we observe closely the record of John's testimony, we shall see that there are not three independent statements of it (i. 19–28; 29–34; 35 f.), which are given merely for the purpose of making known what he said. But, on the contrary, there is a manifest movement from the first to the third, in such a way as to show that it is for the sake of the last that the other two are introduced. When John says to the two disciples in ver. 36, " Behold the Lamb of God," the absence of all further words makes it evident that he must have given a more full explanation of the term on a previous occasion. The mind of the reader is thus carried back immediately to the preceding day (ver. 29), when he said: " Behold the Lamb of God, who taketh away the sin of the world," and then added the account of the way in which he came to know at the baptism of Jesus that He was indeed the Lamb of God. This was the declaration and this the explanation which they needed to make them ready, when they saw Him again, to go to Him and form His acquaintance. But, as John tells the company around him on that second day that Jesus whose office is to take away sin is the one of whom he had said, After me cometh a man who is etc., and that he had himself come baptizing with water in order that this greater one might be made manifest to Israel, the thought is again carried back to the witness which had been borne on the first day (ver. 26, comp. also ver. 15). The first day is thus preparatory to the second, and the second to the third. The whole story centres upon the two disciples, and the Baptist's testimony is given because of its bearing upon them. The writer, indeed, suggests this even by the careful marking of the successive days, which, as related to the testimony considered in itself alone, could scarcely have any importance. The result of the testimony in the life of those who receive it is thus distinctly brought before us; and, as in the μαρτυρία of ver. 19, which is unfolded in the following verses, we have the beginning of the proof that Jesus is the Christ the Son of God, xx. 31a, so in the case of these disciples we find the first beginning of that gaining of life in His name through faith which is the practical end to be secured by the proof, xx. 31b. Answering to the element of testimony, therefore, we discover that of experience.

But this experience is confined to five or six persons. Indeed, in the verses for which the record of John's testimony prepares the way (35–40), it is limited to two. There can be no doubt that the story of these two persons is the starting-point from which the whole narrative of the life of Jesus is developed. Instead of beginning, as Matthew and Luke do, with an account of Jesus' birth and genealogy, or as Mark does, with His baptism and entrance upon His public work, this writer takes his departure from a brief interview which these two disciples of John the Baptist had with Him, and the first impressions produced upon their minds by what they heard Him say. They communicate their impressions to one or two others and persuade them to come to Jesus. Two more are gained as disciples on the next day, and then the little company go to the wedding-feast at Cana, where their faith is strengthened by a miracle. Then the public life and work of Jesus begin. But there is abundant evidence that the record of this public life and work, as given by the author, has constant reference to the disciples, and, at the end, he sums up the whole book by the statement, that, while Jesus did many other signs in the presence of His disciples which are not written here, these signs—these σημεῖα (or miraculous proofs of what He was) which He did in their presence—are written, etc. The plan of this Gospel in relation to this point is certainly very remarkable, as compared with that of the Synoptics or with the ordinary plan of a biography. No reasonable explanation can be given of it, except as we hold that the writer intended to connect the evidences that Jesus was the Logos with the new life and faith of these disciples. But, more than this,—the opening story points to *individual* experience. How are we to account for the placing of such a little narrative at the beginning of the whole biography—for the development, in a certain sense, of everything out of it? The narrative seems so insignificant in itself as to make it improbable that an ordinary historian would find it even arresting his attention. It is presented with little or no detail. One of the characters in it is, so far as the reader discovers from the words of the story itself, unknown even by name. Andrew and some one else, we know not who, went to Jesus on a certain afternoon and spent two hours with Him, and began to believe in Him as the Messiah. This is all. But on this the future narrative, the entire book, is founded. How impossible it seems, that a writer of another century, or removed entirely from the experience and life of the apostles, should have opened his work in this way. If, now, the author was himself the unnamed disciple, if that brief conversation with Jesus was the beginning of his own faith, if the new life came into being in his soul on that afternoon and thus the event here mentioned was the deciding point of his personal history, everything is made clear. The little story rises into marked significance. It may well be the foundation for all that follows. The author gives the record of the life of Jesus *as he had known it*. He says to his readers, Let me tell you of that wonderful man whom I lived with years ago, of what I heard Him say and saw Him do. Let me carry you back to the hour when I first became acquainted with Him, and take you along with me through the subsequent history. Let me show you how I came to believe and how I grew in my belief, and I hope that the story as I give it may lead you also to believe with an earnest and saving faith. But, if the writer was not the unnamed disciple, if, on the other hand, he had never seen Jesus or the apostles, and knew only the life of a hundred years later, this story has no meaning and its insertion is inexplicable. The whole book, as related to its beginning, is a mystery, if this meeting with Jesus was not a vital thing in the author's own life. It breaks forth into clearness and light and has a wonderful naturalness and power, so soon as we find the writer of the narrative in the disciple whose name is not given.

The fact that the element of personal experience is an important one in the book, and indeed that it is centered, as it were, upon the experience of the writer himself, is made evident also by other indications. Among these the following may be particularly mentioned.

1. The great prominence given to the word πιστεύειν. This word which occurs only thirty-five times in the three Synoptic Gospels, and one hundred and three times from the beginning of Acts to the end of Revelation (excluding John's first Epistle), is found ninety-eight times in this Gospel. Around it the whole narrative turns. As the words and works of Jesus, the declarations of John, the preaching of the Apostles, the work of the Spirit, the Scriptures and the voice of God, are all viewed in the light of testimony, so everywhere the attitude of men towards this testimony is marked by the verb πιστεύειν. If they receive the witness which is borne to Christ, they are said to believe. If they reject it, they do not believe. If they are partly influenced by it, but yet not affected in the inmost principle of their life, they are described as believing (ἐπίστευσαν), but not so that Jesus could trust Himself to them (οὐκ ἐπίστευεν αὐτὸν αὐτοῖς, ii. 23, 24, comp. viii. 31 ff.). If they grow in faith, as in the case of the Twelve, they are repeatedly spoken of as believing—the indications of the context being, with each repetition, that the word has a growing fullness of meaning. If the final blessing of Jesus is recorded,

it is a blessing on those who have not seen and yet have believed. If the author wishes to express the purpose of his writing, it is that the readers may believe. If he desires to tell them the way of securing eternal life, it is in the words "that believing you may have life." Moreover, this ever-repeated word, in which all that is most vital to the human soul rests, is the *verb*, which expresses action, and not the *noun*. The substantive πίστις, the doctrinal word, which is so frequently used by Paul (nearly one hundred and fifty times in his Epistles), and which even occurs twenty-four times in the Synoptic Gospels, is not found in this book. The author is not moving in the sphere of doctrine, so far as the human side of truth is concerned, but of life. Indeed, as we have already seen, the very argument to prove the Divine doctrine is the life of Jesus. What can be the meaning of this striking feature of this Gospel, except that, to the author's mind, the living experience of the soul was the thing of all importance? And how exactly do the closing words, which give the object and purpose of the book (xx. 30, 31), answer to this thought—I write that you may believe the doctrine because, and only because, I know that believing is the gate-way of life.

2. Again, if we look at this verb as the author uses it with reference to the apostles, how plainly is the same thing indicated. No attentive student of this Gospel can fail to see that, as the disciples are said, again and again, at different points of the history, to believe in view of what they had seen or heard, the word *believe* gains a new fullness of meaning. There is a steady progress from the first day to the last, from the time when Andrew and his unnamed companion went to Jesus for a two hours' conversation to the day when Thomas exclaimed " My Lord, and my God," and was addressed by the Master as believing. One can almost see the growth of the word in significance as the successive stories are read. Moreover, the same thing is marked, in a very incidental and yet striking way, by the statements which occur with regard to certain things, that the disciples only came to understand and believe after Jesus rose from the dead. What more vivid picture of developing faith, and thus of inmost personal experience, could be given than that which is suggested by this word, which means on each new day more than it did on the day before, and which has its limits during the Lord's earthly life so carefully pointed out, by the declaration that this or that mysterious thing did not become clear to the believing soul until after His earthly life was ended. And finally this word is connected with the author himself, if we hold him to be the companion of Andrew in chap. i. and the one who ran with Peter

to the tomb of Jesus on the morning of the resurrection. Evidently, like Andrew, he was led to believe in the hours of that first interview. Evidently, he is included among the disciples who believed in consequence of the first miracle at Cana. But what progress had been made, when (xx. 8), on entering into the tomb on that Sunday morning, he saw and believed.

3. The same thing is shown by all the indications which prove that the disciple whom Jesus loved, and the one who is alluded to, but not named, in different parts of the book, is the author. It will be unnecessary to enter in this matter at length, for Godet has dwelt upon it largely in his Introduction. But we would give a brief presentation of a few points. The phenomena of the book, in this regard, are the following: first, that, while the other principal characters in the story are mentioned by name, and always thus mentioned, there is a prominent disciple who is only alluded to, or is set before us simply by means of a descriptive phrase; secondly, that, while it is not made so plain as to be beyond the possibility of questioning, that this unnamed person is always one and the same, yet in the doubtful cases, which are only two in number (i. 35 ff., xviii. 15, 16), the probabilities strongly favor the identification of the person referred to with the disciple whom Jesus loved, who is mentioned in all the others. Godet seems to question this in the second case (see p. 30 and note on xviii. 15). But the argument, even in this case, is a strong one: (*w*) The very fact that elsewhere there is but one disciple who takes an active part in any scene, such as this one here takes, and yet is not named, makes the supposition probable, that here also the same person is intended. (*x*) The fact that this "other disciple" (if he was the author of the Gospel) was known to Annas, will easily account for the report of the examination before that dignitary which he gives, while he omits the judicial trial before Caiaphas of which the other Gospels speak. He was an acquaintance of Annas, and so was admitted to his house. But not being on the same terms with Caiaphas, he was not present at the trial.[1] (*y*) The relation of this other disciple to Peter corresponds with that which is set forth elsewhere as existing between Peter and the disciple whom Jesus loved. (*z*) If the disciple whom Jesus loved was the author of the book, and therefore familiar with the scenes of the time and with Peter, it is scarcely possible that he should not have known who this other disciple was, and have given his name (unless, indeed, he was him-

---

[1] That Annas was the high priest referred to in xviii. 19, and so also in xviii. 15, is altogether probable.

self the person). Or, on the other hand, if the author was of a later time, we may ask whether it is probable that the name of Peter's companion on this occasion could have been forgotten? The story of Peter's denials certainly belonged to the widest circle of tradition, and the whole scene connected with them was a marked and impressive one. The only objection which may be urged on the other side is the omission of the article ὁ before ἄλλος μαθητής. But, in view of the writer's care in concealing the name of this beloved disciple, this omission can scarcely be regarded as having such weight as to overbalance the considerations mentioned. As to the other case (i. 35 ff), the points already alluded to are sufficient to show that the companion of Andrew was the disciple whom Jesus loved. But it may also be remarked that this companion of Andrew stood apparently in the same relation to him and Peter in which John stood, as represented by the other gospels, and that their acquaintance or association before the permanent call to discipleship, which is indicated here, corresponds to that which is hinted at in Mark i. 16–20, i. 29; Lk. iv. 38; v. 1 ff.

But, if the person alluded to in xviii. 15 and i. 35, is the same with the one called the disciple whom Jesus loved, we find the direct statement in xxi. 24, that he is the author—a statement either from himself, or from others who declare that they know his testimony to be true, and who, by reason of the present μαρτυρῶν as distinguished from the aorist γράψας, must have written their postscript, as Godet has pointed out, during his lifetime; we also find the direct declaration of xix. 35 that the author was present at the crucifixion; and we find, once more, bearing to the same end, all those incidental things which mark the narrative of an eye-witness; comp., for example, the story in i. 35 ff., that of the supper in chap. xiii., that of the early part of chap. xviii., etc. With reference to xix. 35, Godet has sufficiently shown the untenableness of the position of those who deny that the author is speaking of himself. But we may add, in a single word, that the introduction of an entirely new person, at this point in the story, with no description except that he saw the scenes, is wholly improbable, and also wholly unlike the author's course elsewhere. As the disciple whom Jesus loved has been mentioned, ten verses earlier, as present at the crucifixion, it is infinitely more probable that he is the person referred to. If he is not so, the writer attempts to give emphasis and force to a statement of the facts mentioned by citing for them a witness utterly unknown to his readers, and then attempts to confirm his testimony—this man whom they knew nothing of—by saying: he knows that he tells the truth. Who is he, is the question of all questions, if his testimony is to be of any value. But no answer to this question is given. Moreover, this unknown man is declared to know that he says the truth, that *you* (the readers) *also may believe*. Certainly, no intelligent writer would ever write such a sentence, or bring forward such testimony. Let us remember that this book was to meet adversaries and the advocates of other systems, and was to exhibit proofs to them. What would such a proof be worth? If, on the other hand, the " one who hath seen " is the beloved disciple, how far greater the emphasis, and how far more probable the insertion of the verse, in case the author is making a solemn declaration of *his own* knowledge and truthfulness, than if he is simply assuring the readers that that disciple (who was another person than himself and who had lived many years before this writing) knew the truth of what he said. There is but one difficulty in the passage, if he means himself—namely, the use of the third person of the pronoun. This, however, belongs with the other expression: the disciple, etc., which is also in the third person, and is occasioned by his desire to keep himself in a sense concealed. But against the other views of the sentence every difficulty, which the nature of the case allows, arises, and improbability can scarcely reach a higher point than it does as related to them. The verse loses, largely or wholly, its emphasis and its significance, unless the author is the one who makes the declaration. It may be added that the present tenses and the correspondence in thought with the verses expressing the purpose of the book (xx. 30, 31) should not be overlooked—and they give their evidence for the same conclusion.

Testimony and inward experience—testimony originally coming to the writer and his fellow disciples, and their own personal inward experience as they received and believed the testimony; these are the two essential elements of the author's plan. In the light which we gain in connection with them, we may explain the peculiarity of the Prologue. Why does the writer open his book with the word Logos, giving no explanation of its meaning and, after the few introductory verses are ended, making no further allusion to it? The use of this term with no explanation must indicate that it was so familiar to his readers as to be readily understood. The laying it aside at the close of the Prologue suggests that it was only intended to connect the book with inquiries or discussions, which were occupying the minds of thoughtful men in the region where the author was living. If the subject represented by this word was a wholly new one to the original readers, we may safely say that the phenomena of the Prologue could not be what they are. Whatever, therefore, may have been the origin of the term Logos as here used, we may believe that it was employed in the philosophical disputations of the time—that learned and intelligent men were asking for an answer to their questions which were represented by this term. We may, also, believe that these questions had reference to the possibility and manner of God's revealing Himself to or in the world. The writer found such men considering this great subject and giving what explanations or theories they could. He found them in uncertainty or in darkness, inquiring with no answer or wandering off into the gross errors of which Paul speaks in the Epistle to the Colossians and errors which even passed beyond these. He desired to connect his book with their inquiries and to tell them that he had discovered the answer which they needed. The man with whom he had lived was the Logos. He was the full and final revelation of God. The Logos was in the beginning with God and was God, but had now become incarnate in Jesus Christ. Let me prove this to you, he says, as it were. But let me accomplish this end, not as I might do by setting before you a mere collection of evidences or arguments, which have no immediate personal connection with myself, and none even with Him as a part of the daily life which He led among men. Let me do it, rather, by giving you the picture of the living man as He walked with His contemporaries, and especially with his earliest followers, along the pathway of His earthly career. In this way I can place Him before you as He was, and you can see the evidences as they were given by Himself. You can live with Him, as it were, and hear Him speak of the heavenly things. To these readers the term Logos may have come from the Jewish-Alexandrian philosophy, while to him it came directly from the Old Testament. To him it may have had a different meaning, in some degree, from that which it had for them, and a far deeper one. But it served, nevertheless, as a connecting-link between his answer and their questionings, and having made it useful to this end, he leads them away from fruitless discussion to the contemplation of Jesus as he had known Him. At the same time, his book would have its adaptation to every chance reader, in whose way it might fall, and would call his mind, if possible, through the testimony and the experience to the life.

If we explain the Gospel in this way, everything becomes plain, and the book comes forth, as its rich, deep thoughts would indicate, from the depths of a meditative soul in personal union with Christ when He was on earth. But if we locate the writer in the second century, what must we believe? We must believe that out of a few notes made by the Apostle John, or, apart from anything of his, out of the Synoptic narratives, the writer manufactured a history of Jesus' life which he represented as moving along with his disciples and gradually influencing their characters and their living. Yes, even more than this; that he did this so successfully, so far as relates to the person of the disciple whom Jesus loved, that the great majority of the Church in all ages have believed the author to be that disciple. To accomplish such a result, a century after the history was ended, would require an imagination of a high order, a power of transferring oneself to the life of a remote past period such as even men of genius rarely have. Such a power belongs only to the higher order of poets or writers of fiction. But this author, whoever he may have been, did not possess this faculty. We may not know his name, but the peculiar characteristics of his mind and soul are exhibited so clearly in his writings, that he stands before us with distinctness and with individuality. He was no writer of fiction or poet of the order mentioned. He was a man who, beyond any other in the New Testament history, or, indeed, almost any other of any age, dwelt within himself, in the region of contemplation, and that not the contemplation of intellectual themes, but of the growth of the soul's life. Introvertive, meditating upon himself and his own character, thinking deep thoughts only as they took hold upon the relation of his soul to God and brought the inward man into the light, picturing to himself the glory of heaven only as that likeness to God which should come from seeing Him as He is—such a man would be the last of all to transfer his experience to the life of another, or either to desire or be able to picture another as himself. To such a man, the inward life is too precious and too personal to be represented as if it were not his own. It is too intensely individual to pass beyond the one to whom it belongs as the central thing of his being.

We may add, that it would have been no easy thing for any man, as near even to the life of Jesus as Paul or Apollos were—and surely not for one living in the second century—to represent his own Christian life as if it had grown up in a personal association with Him when He was on earth. The sorry failures of all attempts, in our day even, to give a lifelike picture of those apostolic scenes may show us how hard a task it must have always been to do such a work successfully. But, in some respects, it must have been more difficult for the early Christians to do it, for the dividing line between the apostles and themselves, as those who had seen the Lord and those who had not, was a broad one and one of which they never lost sight. But here is a success which has deceived the ages, and a success accomplished by a man who had great thoughts, yet not at all the genius of fiction—who lived in his friendship with the Lord, but could not have pictured it to himself or others as growing up under different conditions from those which actually belonged to it.

We venture, also, to maintain that *the motive* of a speculative or theological character, which has led some to believe that the story is told by the author as if he were the apostle when he was not, did not exist. The evidences as to the mental character of the writer of the Gospel, which we find in his works, are not that he was a speculative philosopher, that he dwelt upon propositions or truths for their own sake, that he was ready to construct a theological system for the purpose of teaching it, or to introduce new theories into the Church. His thoughts relate only to character and life. He cares nothing for them except as they enrich the soul. He even writes his story of Jesus for the purpose of proving His Divine nature and work, only because he is assured that belief in the truth will bring life eternal to the believer. And these thoughts which grow into character are, first of all, interesting to him for the reason that they take hold of and beautify his own character.

If we examine the First Epistle in connection with the Gospel, we find what these thoughts were, and where the writer first received them into his mind. The great truth is that God is light, and in Him is no darkness at all. This absolute and perfect spiritual light, is what the human soul, according to the measure of its capacity, must participate in, if it is to have its highest life. The life of the soul is light. Comp. 1 Ep. i. 5, Gosp. i. 4. How is this life to be secured? This is the question with which his mind is wholly occupied. How shall it be secured by himself and by all other men? The day which brought him into communication with Jesus Christ answered the question. The years and the meditations which followed from that first meeting to his latest age, only made the answer more full and more satisfying. Thought, therefore, moves along this line. The relation of the personal Jesus, full of grace and truth, to his individual soul is the starting-point of all thinking, and the nature of Jesus, His work, and everything respecting Him centre, in their all-absorbing interest, around this relation. Friendship with Jesus was the atmosphere in which he lived. The meditations of friendship and the study, in experience, of its power to develop the inward man—not the speculations of philosophy or theology—were what occupied his life. Hence we find him, when he comes to write for the world, telling first, in the Gospel, the simple story of what Jesus did and said, and afterwards, in the Epistle, saying at the outset, "That which we have heard, seen, handled of the

Word of life, which was with the Father and was manifested unto us, declare we unto you." The end in view, in the latter case, is also the same as in the former: "that you (the readers) may have fellowship with us whose fellowship is with the Father and with his Son Jesus Christ."

No writer in the New Testament was more unfitted by the peculiar characteristics of his nature to find interest in creating a history for the purpose of developing an idea. No class of thinking men in any age turn with less readiness to mere speculations for their own sake than those who, like this writer, are ever studying with intense delight the progress of their own souls in true living. Let us try to imagine a speculative philosopher, of earlier or later times, coming before his readers with a manufactured history, told in the simple style of the Gospel, and then saying: That which I have heard and seen and handled I declare to you, that you may have fellowship with me in God and Christ, and these things I write that my joy may be fulfilled. The inmost nature of the two classes of men is different. The author of the fourth Gospel was not a philosopher of the schools, nor a contemplative mystic. He lived in the experience and recollections of a personal friendship and found in that friendship the eternal life. He could not have created the story of his life with Jesus by his imagination, if he would, for his nature was such that it must rest on reality. The deepest souls, of his peculiar order, as we have already said, do not and cannot picture their own experience as that of another; much less, if possible, can they make a fictitious narrative contradicting the supremest facts of their personal life, for the purpose of impressively presenting to the world a theological idea.

Among the personages of the apostolic history who live and move before us on the pages of the New Testament, the writer of this Gospel takes his place as truly as any other. Paul and Peter, even, do not stand forth as living characters more clearly than he does. He comes forward, indeed, as if in his bodily presence, in several of the narratives, and by reason of the familiar acquaintance which he shows with the details of the history and with the geography, the customs, the men of the region which he describes. But with far greater distinctness even, does he appear to us in his character and inward personality. The testimony of thousands of men who have communed with him in spirit, as they have given themselves up to the contemplation of his deep thoughts, bears witness as to what he was, and their testimony, in all the ages, is the same. The book which he has written gives evidence with regard to him as truly and as fully as the Pauline Epistles do for their author. It shows as plainly that he was one of apostolic company who attended Jesus in the years of His ministry, as the writings of the apostle to the Gentiles prove that he was not.

The external testimonies for the authenticity of the Gospel, as Godet and many other writers have shown, are exceedingly strong. That of Irenæus, given so abundantly, is in itself sufficient, for he knew Polycarp, who had known John. But we are persuaded that the book carries *within itself* its strongest evidence. And this evidence is inwoven into its whole texture, and is the more powerful in its impressiveness because it is so incidental and undesigned. We have given a few suggestions with regard to it, which may, in a measure, supplement what Godet has presented in his excellent introduction. The subject might be set forth with much greater detail and with more of completeness in the plan of presentation. But in the limited space allowed us, we have desired only to move along one line of thought, and have been able, even in this line, to do no more than indicate what may open a wide field of study for the thoughtful reader of this Gospel. Before concluding these introductory remarks upon the book, however, we will call attention to two or three scenes in the story related by the author, in which the reality of a past experience is what gives them all their life and power. The scene recorded in i. 35 ff. is one of these. Of this we have already spoken. But it is by no means the only one. In the narrative of the last evening of the life of Jesus, the author represents Him as comforting the hearts of the disciples in view of His approaching death by the promise of a future reunion in heaven. He begins by assuring them that there are many mansions in His Father's house, and adds the declaration that He is going to prepare a place for them there. But between the two statements there is a word inserted, which has been to many difficult of explanation: "If it were not so, I would have told you." Whence does the force of this expression come? Where does it get its significance? Surely, from the past life with the disciples, and from that alone. As spoken by a stranger, or by another than a friend, the words would have had little or no meaning. But as taking hold upon every day of those three years of their life together, as recalling all that He had been to them and done for them, as opening the depths of His love and friendship so wonderfully revealed to their inmost experience, they became the strongest testimony to the truth of what He said at the parting hour. Your experience in the past may bear witness that I would not deceive you—may prove to you that there is a place for you in the Father's house, for, if it were not so, I would not have failed to tell you. But they are of that peculiar character which makes it improbable, almost to the extent of impossibility, that a writer of another generation would have dreamed of inserting them. To the soul of the beloved disciple they would be a precious memory for a lifetime, a word of love to be often recalled with tenderest recollection. They speak of living friendship and appeal to a past. But the one to whom they spoke thus must have known the past and have shared in the living friendship. Stories created for the presentation of a theological idea do not move in the sphere of such expressions. The Christian author of the third or fourth generation of believers might, perhaps, have put into the mouth of Jesus the promise that He would prepare a place for His followers, or the assurance that there was room for them in Heaven, but this little sentence would never have found place in his thought or his narrative. It belongs to the evening on which it is said to have been uttered and to the experience of one who heard it from the Lord Himself. It testifies of the authorship of the book by an ear-witness.

Or again, in the same scene of the last evening, who but one who was present and witnessed the changing thoughts of successive moments could have recorded those words of xvi. 5, 6 : "But now I go unto him that sent me; and none of you asketh me whither goest thou," after having related in the earlier part of the conversation, that one of the disciples had suggested this very question, xiv. 5 ? To one, however, who remembered the scene as himself participating in it, these words had a living freshness and recalled the grief and disappointment of their hopes, which so filled the hearts of all that they thought only of their own future, and not of the blessedness which should come to Jesus. How completely does this place us in the midst of the apostolic company and tell us of the living experience of the hour. It is not the effort of the advocate of some intellectual conception or theory that we find here, but the thought of a loving friend who always bore with him, even to his latest life, what he had felt and what Jesus had said in one of the supreme moments of the past.

Or, if we look at the story of the morning of the resurrection, the striking way in which the faith of the disciple whom Jesus loved is represented as confirmed by what he saw in the tomb, while that of Peter is not spoken of, points to such knowledge of the inner history of the former as indicates that the writer was referring to himself. The same is true of the life-like picture presented before us in the twenty-first chapter. Not only is it wholly improbable that a writer, who had never stood at the standpoint of the event related, and who was writing after the death of the beloved disciple, would have taken this method of correcting the error alluded to; but the story, by its inimitable naturalness as answering to the feeling of the two participants in the last part of the scene with Jesus, carries us into the heart of the writer as he remembers all that happened.

Or, finally—to refer only to one more passage—how are we to account for the touching incident in xix. 25–27, where Jesus entrusts his mother to the care of the beloved disciple? She had children of her own who could care for her, or, if not children, nephews who were to her as if sons. Why does not Jesus commit her to their care? The fact that they were unbelievers at the time will not explain this peculiar act, for they were to become believers within a few days after the death of Jesus (comp. Acts i. 14), and He must have foreseen this. The only answer to the question which the verses suggest is that, at the final hour, Jesus rose above the power of earthly relationships, and, in view of His separation from them both, joined the two friends, to whom He was most closely bound in affection, as son and mother. But, if this was the reason of His giving the one of the two to the other, the act bears within itself the result of a long-continued and real life of the soul in all the three as related to one another. It is wholly dependent on a living experience. And whose experience is to be found in the unnamed sharer in this scene? Is it the originator of a system, the defender of an idea, the meditative philosopher, who brings into a fictitious narrative a little incident like this, which could have no interest as compared with many things that might have directly emphasized his doctrine of the Logos? Is it not, on the other hand, the man who, in the later years of his life, goes over once more the facts of his own association with his Master and finds in them all the power of a holy friendship for his own soul?

All these things—if any judgment of what is true can be formed in the case of any man's utterance or writing—testify of reality. They depend on the reality of that which is related for their significance. And the only satisfactory explanation of their appearance in the book is that the author was bearing witness of what he had seen and heard. The supposition that such stories were told for the purpose of maintaining a theory or of glorifying one of the apostles at the expense of another is little less than absurd. They are not fitted in any considerable measure for either purpose. They take hold upon the tenderest feelings of the heart, and are foreign to the sphere of rivalry or discussion. And the fact that their full meaning is to be sought and found only beneath the surface adds to the evidence that the writer and the apostle of whom he wrote were one and the same person.

It is often said that the student of the Bible must be in sympathy with it, if he would reach the deepest understanding of what it is and what it teaches. This is no doubt true, for the unsympathetic mind never reaches the perfect light in any line of study. But, in a peculiar sense, it is necessary for one who comes to the investigation of the fourth Gospel, that he should have some comprehension of the inner life of a Christian believer who grows into the likeness of Christ by personal communion with Him —who abides within the region of his own spirit, and moves upward and onward in the sphere of a divine friendship. It is not enough to dissect the sentences, or consider the theological doctrine, or attempt to fit the narrative to an idea, or trace the possible development of thought under certain influences on the foundation of the Synoptic story. The man himself who wrote the book must be understood, for he is, after all, in his own inner life, the greatest factor in it. The student of his writings must see him himself. He must be in sympathy with him, if he would be prepared to appreciate the evidence which he has furnished as to his personality. It is the want of this sympathy, arising from the want of that peculiar belief which gave him his truest life, that has placed many writers on his Gospel quite outside of its central and inmost part. They have dissected the book, but they have not known the man.

But when we know the man, we comprehend the book—and we recognize in the book not a poem or a work of fiction; the author did not live in the region of the imagination :—not the writing of one who created a doctrine or system for himself by means of his own reflection; his musings were of a far different order from this :—not the effort of a man who tries to save Christianity from the influence of Judaism, or to reconcile parties and unify the Church, or to elevate or depreciate one or another of the apostolic company; he is neither a partisan nor a professed peacemaker :— but the simple story of what a man of the richest inward life, who had lived with Jesus, learned of His nature and His wonderful spiritual power, both in his association with Him and in the meditations of the years that followed.

The Christian system is not dependent on the genuineness of the fourth Gospel, so that, if the latter could be disproved, the former would fail. But there is no doubt that the author of this Gospel penetrated in his thought into the centre of the Christian system, as it has been understood by the Church. The question of the authorship becomes, therefore, one of gravest importance. If the author was that most intimate disciple of Jesus of whom the book speaks so frequently, he gained his conception of Christ and the new faith from the Lord Himself, and he could not be mistaken. His book is the flower and consummation of the apostolic thought. It is in the truest and highest sense inspired of God. The attempt to deny the system is a hopeless one, so soon as this Gospel is established on a firm foundation. In view of this fact, it may well seem divinely ordered that the book should stand in the world as it has ever done, bearing within itself its own evidence. The writer of it, in addressing the readers for whom his first Epistle was intended, says that he writes that which he has seen and heard, in order that they may have fellowship, as he himself has, with the Father and with his Son Jesus Christ. It is a wonderful fact in the history of the centuries which have passed since he wrote, that those who have been persuaded by his story to believe and who have been conscious, as the result of their faith, that they had fellowship with God, have had an abiding confidence that he told of what he had heard and seen, and that it is those who have rejected the doctrine and the peculiar life, who have questioned the reality of the author's experience as the disciple whom Jesus loved. The past may give us confidence in the future; and we may safely predict that, until the inner life of the author ceases to bear this witness, he and his Gospel will be among the unshaken pillars of the Church.

ADDITIONAL NOTES BY THE AMERICAN EDITOR

1

John 1

THE leading thoughts respecting the Logos which are presented in the Prologue are those of ver. 1 and ver. 14. The former verse sets forth what He was antecedent to the time of His incarnation, and in the beginning; the latter declares that He became flesh.

A. With reference to the first verse the following points may be noticed:—1. The object of the whole Prologue being to make certain declarations respecting the Logos, there can be no doubt that ὁ λόγος is the subject in all the three clauses of which the verse is composed—in the third, no less than in the other two. This is indicated also by the parallelism, with slight variation, which seems to belong to the rhetorical style of this author. The clauses are parallel, but the predicate stands first in two of them, while in the intermediate one the subject has its natural position. 2. In the third clause, the predicate θεός, being different from that in the second, ὁ θεός, must be intended to suggest to the reader a different idea. This different idea, however, being expressed by the same substantive, cannot reasonably be held to be of an entirely different order. The word without the article must move in the same sphere with that which has it. The Logos, according to the statement of the writer, must be *God* in a similar sense to that in which the one *with whom He is* is God, and yet not in precisely the same sense. So far as the book may properly be regarded as an unfolding, in any degree, of the thoughts of the Prologue, we may naturally expect to find in the chapters which follow, the answer to the question thus presented: in what sense are the words to be understood, when it is said that the Logos is θεός and not ὁ θεός? 3. In the verses (2–4), which are immediately connected with ver. 1, the last of the three clauses of that verse does not appear, but the other two are repeated. The explanation of this fact is, doubtless, to be found in the purpose of these verses. The author is moving, in these verses, along the line of revelation. This line is presented in the three terms: creation, life and light. The Logos was the instrumental agent through whom all created things were brought into being. To that portion of creation which is animate or rational, as contrasted with the inanimate or irrational part, He is the life-principle, which gives it life. To that part which has the higher element, the πνεῦμα, and thus has the capacity for the action of the life-principle in the higher region, He is the light. What the idea of light is may best be understood by the use of the word in 1 John i. 5, where it is said that God is light, and it is added, with the same contrast of φῶς and σκοτία which we have here, that in Him is no darkness at all. The divine Spiritual illumination for man comes in and through the Logos. 4. As the world of beings capable of receiving spiritual light failed, by reason of their moral darkness, to see and take to themselves the enlightening revelation, which the Logos was ever making to all even from the hour of creation, some clearer mode of making the light known to them was necessary, and for this purpose the Logos became incarnate (ver. 14). 5. The person in whom He became incarnate is Jesus Christ, ver. 17.—Such is the development of the thought connected with the Logos as the revealer of God. The Logos was in the beginning with God. Thus He is the one by means of whom God gives the true light to men. That they may have it as fully as is needful in order to their possessing it in the soul's life, He enters into a human mode of existence and appears in Jesus. The first and second clauses of ver. 1, repeated in ver. 2, are the starting-point of this development, and are all that are essential to its beginning. 6. It cannot be doubted, however, that the statement of the third clause, which is added to the other two, and which must have a deeper meaning than the others because it declares *what* the Logos was, while they only, as it were, tell *where* and *when* He was, is intended by the writer to hold even a more prominent place than they. They are repeated, and the thought for which they open the way is unfolded, because the discussions and questionings which occasioned the writing of the book required the idea of revealing God to be presented. But that this revelation of which the book is to speak is and must be the true one, the only true one, is a point of greatest importance to the end which the author has in view. For thus only can it exclude every other and become the undoubted answer to the question which all were raising. To the completeness of His power to reveal, He must be, not only πρὸς τὸν θεόν, but θεός. Since He is θεός, He must, in some sense, become ἄνθρωπος in order that the revelation may be perfectly apprehended by men. He must be the θεὸς ἄνθρωπος. In this view of the author's thought, the third clause of ver. 1 unites itself with the suggestion of ver. 14, and then these two leading ideas pass on to ver. 17; and, joining that verse with themselves, they find their full expression in the words: Jesus Christ is the θεὸς-ἄνθρωπος. Hence it is, as we may believe, that the Prologue closes with the last statement of the 18th verse: The only-begotten Son (or—if that be the true reading—God only begotten) who is in the bosom of the Father, He hath declared Him. 7. While, therefore, in one view of the Prologue and the whole Gospel, this final proposition of ver. 1 may hold only a secondary place in the plan, or even, perhaps, be unessential to it, in another and a most important sense, these words are the primary words of the entire book, to which everything else is subordinate. That he may prove that Jesus is the Son of God, and thus that that life which is the living of the human soul in the light of God, having in it no darkness at all, may be realized by every reader through faith in Him, is the object and purpose of his writing his story of Jesus. 8. It is on this third clause, not on the first two only, that the expressions

Additional Notes on John 1 / 515

in the Gospel which have the deepest meaning rest. As being θεός and in the bosom of the Father, He has life in Himself, even as the Father has life in Himself; He is the living bread and the life-giving bread; He and His Father are one; to know Him is to know God and to have the eternal life of the soul. This deepest meaning must be gathered from all the words of the book which have any teaching in them with reference to it, and they must all be centered in this word θεός, if we are in any true sense to comprehend its significance.

B. With respect to ver. 14, it may be said: 1. That the word σάρξ must be interpreted in connection, not only with its use in the writings of this author, and, as would also seem probable, with that of the other authors of the New Testament, but with the words or clauses in the context which evidently belong in the same circle of thought. The Logos, as He became flesh, is said to have tabernacled among us; to have been beheld by the writer and others; to have imparted from His own fullness that grace which came through Jesus Christ; apparently, in some true conception of the words, to have become Jesus Christ (see ver. 17 in its relation to ver. 14 and ver. 16, on the one hand, and to ver. 18 on the other). Σάρξ must, therefore, in some sense, be the equivalent of ἄνθρωπος; and, as in the case of θεός of ver. 1, already alluded to, every indication which the book presents before us points to the end that we should make our attempt to determine in what sense it is thus equivalent, by means of the representation given in subsequent chapters respecting Jesus.—The term Logos is laid aside by the author immediately at the close of the Prologue, but we cannot fail to see that he never loses sight of the two statements as to what the Logos was and became. Jesus—the friend and master of whom he writes—is not merely a messenger of God to the world to bring to it a revelation, but he is the one in whom the Logos, who was θεός, has become ἄνθρωπος, the one who is able perfectly to reveal because of the θεός side or relation of His being, and to make His revelation understood by those around Him because of the ἄνθρωπος side or relation. Thus, and thus only, is He the true light of the world, bringing it into the actual experience of the eternal life.

2

In what relation to the leading ideas of the Prologue do the statements respecting grace and truth stand? The answer to this question may be sought in connection with ver. 17 and the contrast with the law which is there presented. It will be noticed that these words are first introduced at the end of ver. 14, that immediately after them follows the second reference to the testimony of John the Baptist, and that then they are taken up again as if for further explanation. From these peculiar characteristics of the passage, it would seem not improbable that the writer was thinking of John the Baptist, who, as the last of the prophets, was also, in a certain sense, the one who brought the Old Testament legal system to its end, and, by turning the minds of the people to the righteousness which the true idea of the law required, as opposed to that which its Pharisaic expounders preached, prepared them for the new system which was about to be introduced. The office of John the Baptist, as he proclaimed the advent of the Messiah, was to set forth the necessity of a radical change of character (μετάνοια), to make known with a new power and impressiveness the vital importance of being, not merely externally, but internally right, to demand on behalf of the kingdom of God a new life. Repentance and reformation were the burden of his message. This message, as we may say, was the final word of the legal system, as it passed away and opened the door for the faith-system. The work of Jesus was to make this reformation and new life possible, through the proclamation of the fullness of Divine truth, the revealing and imparting of Divine grace, the teaching of the way of salvation through forgiveness and that righteousness which grows up in the pardoned soul by means of faith. This revelation made by Jesus Christ was that which justifies the expression used in ver. 18. The law, even in its spiritual application to the inner life, might be revealed through a man, like Moses or John the Baptist. But, in order to reveal the fullness of God's grace and truth, the appearance of a greater than man was needed. To this end one must have seen God, in the highest sense of that word—as *no man* has ever seen Him. The only-begotten Son who is in the bosom of the Father, the Logos who was with God in the beginning and was God, and who, by becoming flesh, brings God into closest communion with men, can alone make this revelation.

3

Why is the testimony of John the Baptist referred to and made so prominent in the Prologue? We find it alluded to not only after the verse (14) in which the incarnation is set forth, but even in ver. 5 f. immediately following the statements respecting the Logos in His pre-existent state. The distinct presentation of its contents, however, is evidently deferred until the beginning of the historical introduction (ver. 19 ff.). The true explanation of this peculiar fact may, not improbably, be suggested by the plan of the book, as already indicated in the Introductory Remarks on the internal evidence for the fourth Gospel. As the earliest disciples, according to the representation of the book, were brought to Jesus by the testimony of John the Baptist, and the object of the book is to induce the readers to believe on the same grounds on which these disciples believed, it was natural to give a peculiar prominence to John's testimony at the beginning. His testimony was, in a certain sense, the foundation of all that followed, and hence it was not unsuitable—it was, on the other hand, especially impressive—to place it in connection with the great fundamental propositions which were designed to arrest the attention of those for whom the book was primarily written. That the testimony of John is regarded by the author as having a very prominent place, in its direct bearing upon Jesus' position and His relation to God,

Additional Notes on John 1 / 517

is shown by the reference to it in v. 33, 34. In the author's selection, in that chapter, of the expressions of Jesus which set forth the evidence for His claims respecting Himself, he chooses for his narrative this one which points to John. And though Jesus in the surrounding words declares that He has a higher and greater testimony, the witness of John is pressed upon the thought of the hearers.

John's testimony, as it is introduced in ver. 6 f., has immediate reference to the Logos as the light, and thus to the last point in the statements of vv. 1–4. We may believe, however, that, though not directly, yet in an indirect way, it is mentioned in just this place in order to carry the mind of the reader back to the first great propositions of ver. 1, which lie at the foundation of the declaration that He is the light.

The second mention of John's testimony (after ver. 14) evidently bears upon that verse. As it includes the words "He was before me," and as these words are even the ones which have special emphasis, so far at least as relates to the depth of the meaning of the sentence, the suggestion just made with regard to the previous allusion, in ver. 6 ff., may also be applicable here. That John the Baptist comprehended fully, when He bore witness to Jesus, all that John the Apostle knew of His Divine nature, we need not affirm. But that the witness which he gave was a significant element in the proof that Jesus Christ is the Logos, of whom what is said in ver. 1 and what is said in ver. 14 are both true, we alike believe; and this is the reason for including what John had testified in the Prologue.

4

The reference of ver. 5, by reason of the position which the verse holds—in immediate connection with vv. 1–4 and before the allusion to the testimony of John—is probably to the general and permanent illuminating power of the light before the incarnation. The Logos was with God and was God; as being thus, He was the source of existence to the creation, of life to creatures endowed with life, of light to those having the spiritual faculty. So far vv. 1–4. It is now declared that this light permanently shines—from the beginning ever onward—but that the darkness did not apprehend it in the earlier times, and hence the necessity is suggested of a clearer shining or revelation (that of ver. 14). The past tense of the verb *apprehended* seems to show that the permanent present (which would hold true of all time) is limited, so far as the thought of this verse is concerned, to the time indicated by its associate verb. We may hold, therefore, with reasonable confidence, that the entire passage vv. 1–5 has reference to the Logos before His incarnation, as vv. 14–16 relate to Him as incarnate.

But what shall we say of vv. 6–13? The intermediate position of this passage suggests a pointing in both directions. The antecedent probabilities, also, as to what the writer would do in moving from ver. 5 to ver. 14 indicate the same thing. Finally, the proper interpretation of different individual verses in the passage may, not improbably, confirm us in the conclusion. Certainly, ver. 11 must be taken as referring to the period following the incarnation, as of course the actual witness-bearing of John must be located in this period. But ver. 9, by reason of the emphatic ἦν and also by reason of the correspondence in the permanent present φωτίζει of this verse with φαίνει of ver. 5, is most naturally interpreted as preceding the ἐγένετο of ver. 14. There seems, also, to be a natural progress in vv. 10–12, of such a nature that, within the sphere of the general present φωτίζει, ver. 10 points to what was before the earthly appearance of the Logos, and vv. 11, 12 point to what followed after that appearance. John *was* not the light, but He *came* to *testify* of it. The true light *was* always— in the early ages, bearing witness for itself and shining through and in the creation, physical and spiritual, which He had brought into existence; and in the later time, through His manifestation of Himself as a man of the Jewish race. In both periods alike, however, the darkness in which men were, because of evil, prevented His being known and received. The presence of faith was needed in order to the receptivity of the soul for the light, and that it might be secured, so far as to bring men to look to Jesus as the revealer of God in the highest sense, John the Baptist had appeared as a divinely-appointed witness-bearer. He came, that all might believe through him.

5

Following upon this intermediate passage, which has thus a progressive movement from the pre-existent to the incarnate period, the second great idea of the entire Prologue is distinctly stated, in a proposition standing in a parallelism with those in ver. 1. The Word became flesh. The Logos entered into human life. The light which had previously been shining in creation and, in some sense, in the soul of every man, but which had not been apprehended, is now revealed in the clearest possible manner by means of the indwelling of the Logos in a man, and by thus bringing God and man into immediate communication. The word *light* now passes away, but it gives place to the expressions: We beheld His glory; full of grace and truth. The idea is therefore preserved, though the mode of presenting it changes. The change, however, is in sympathy with the advance movement of the thought. The revelation of the Logos is now so perfect that those who see it behold His glory. The darkness has passed, and He is looked upon face to face. And, moreover, the revelation is of grace and truth—it is of that deepest part of God's nature which He alone who was with Him in the beginning, and who is in His bosom as the Son with the Father, can make known. The light thus shines from the beginning to the end, only more clearly at last than at first. It is apprehended, as it shines, by the souls that are susceptible to it. But the susceptibility comes always through faith, and only through faith. And at the end the believers behold, with undimmed vision, the glory of the light. To this more glorious manifestation John the Baptist bears testimony, and, pointing to the man in whom the Logos is revealed, he says " He that cometh after me is become before me, for He was before me." This man is Jesus Christ.

6

If this view of the Prologue, which has been set forth in the preceding notes, is correct, the plan of the author, so far from presenting serious difficulties, becomes a thoroughly artistic one—the different lines of thought being most carefully interwoven with one another; the progress is plain, not only from ver. 1 to ver. 14, but from ver. 1 to ver. 4 and ver. 5, from ver. 6 to ver. 13, from vv. 6–13 to ver. 14, and from ver. 14 to what follows; and finally the insertion of the testimony of John is accounted for in a way which most naturally and satisfactorily explains what seems, at first sight, so peculiar, and yet in a way which shows that it, in no proper sense, breaks the line of development of the ideas of light and revelation.

With reference to the individual words and phrases of the Prologue the following points may be briefly noticed: 1. The idea of the author in connection with several of the leading words is, undoubtedly, to be discovered from the main portion of the Gospel, rather than from the introductory passage alone. We may infer, however, from the statements of the Prologue itself, and from the origin of some of them, or their use elsewhere, what their significance as here employed is. This is true of λόγος, ἐν ἀρχῇ, ζωή, φῶς, σάρξ, etc. 2. That the word λόγος was derived from the Old Testament —a growth of the idea which is indicated even in the first chapter of Genesis, and which is developed gradually, as Godet shows, in the later times— is very widely admitted by the best scholars. That it was suggested to the writer, partly, if not wholly, by its use in the discussions of the time and region in which he wrote, seems altogether probable. In any case, the idea fundamental to it is that of God as revealing Himself. The Logos is the one through whom (or that by means of which), God is revealed. Introduced, as it is, as connected with the discussions alluded to and for the purpose of answering the question which was the central one in them, it is natural that its precise meaning should be left for the reader to determine from the propositions of which it is made the subject, and from the story of the one who is declared to be the Logos. Of these propositions, the first two which appear in ver. 1, affirm, in the first place, that the Logos was *in the beginning*—which, from the relation of the words to ver. 3, must, at least, mean that He existed before the creation, so that all things created have their origin through Him; and secondly, that He was *with God*—which expression is further explained by the words of ver. 18: *who is in the bosom of the Father*. They show that the revealing one existed antecedently to all revelation of God in or to the world, and that what He reveals comes from the inmost heart and being of God. But the third proposition goes beyond these, and declares that He was θεός. Of this word it may be said: (*a*) That it is not used elsewhere in this Gospel or in the other writings of this author, or indeed in any case in the New Testament, which can be compared with this, to indicate a being inferior to God; (*b*) That the absence of the article does not indicate any such inferiority, because, in the first place, as the writer desired to throw especial emphasis on this predicate by placing it at the beginning of the clause, it became necessary to omit it in order that the reader might not, by any means, misapprehend the meaning, and in the second place, because he evidently did not mean to say that the Logos was God in precisely the same sense in which that word is used in the phrase: *He was with God*. He was not the one with whom He was. He was θεός, but not, as the term is here used, ὁ θεός. If he desired to express what in theological language is set forth in such a sentence as: He was of the essence of God, but not the same person with the Father, and if he desired to do this by the use of the word θεός, there would seem to have been no more simple or better way of formulating his thought than by saying: He was πρὸς τὸν θεόν, and was θεός. But it is the declarations of Jesus Himself, and His miraculous signs which are given in the following chapters, which are intended by the writer to determine the full significance of both of these sentences. 3. It is worthy of notice that, while the word Logos disappears, so far as this special use of it is concerned, as soon as the Prologue reaches its end, the words ζωή and φῶς occur many times in the subsequent chapters. These words also draw closely together and intermingle with one another, as it were, in their idea. This fact, which at the first glance seems remarkable, is easy of explanation when the plan and purpose of the book are understood. To prove that Jesus is the *Logos*, in the mere sense that He answers to that which was a matter of philosophical inquiry to those around him, is a thing of little consequence to the writer. But that, as being the true Logos, He is the revealer and source of life and light, is the message which He has to give to the world, the εὐαγγέλιον of God. The satisfying of philosophical questioning is nothing to his view, we may say; the bringing of the human soul into union with God is everything. The close connection of the ideas of life and light is also very natural, for, as we learn from the author's first epistle, the life of God represents itself to him under the figure of light—that pure and perfect light which has no intermingling of darkness—and the ζωή or ζωὴ αἰώνιος of man is the participation in this same light-life. These words, accordingly, are not merely terms of philosophy and, as such, appropriate only to the Prologue, but living expressions of experience. The life is that of the soul illuminated by pure spiritual light. Its atmosphere in which it lives is light. The form of expression in the closing sentences of the Gospel (xx. 30, 31) is thus explained—where the term *Son of God* takes the place of Logos, but the term *life* remains. So also in the First Epistle i. 2, we have the words, "And the life was manifested . . . the eternal life which was with the Father." The word *life* in ver. 4, occurring as it does in the progressive development of thought from ver. 1 to ver. 5, probably has a more general meaning. But in its use afterwards it moves into the sphere of the spiritual, which is the only sphere in which the writer would have his own and his readers' minds abide. 4. That the verb κατέλαβεν of ver. 5 means *apprehended*, and not *overcame*, is rendered probable by the following considerations: (*a*) The former meaning lies nearer to the fundamental signification of the word *to lay hold of, seize upon*. The thought here moves in the spiritual region, and to lay hold of spiritually is to apprehend. (*b*) The other explanation of the word would indicate that the darkness is here looked upon as a hostile power contending with the light for the mastery. This is the sense perhaps in xii. 35, where darkness is viewed as seizing upon the man, as a power hostile to him. But such a conception does not seem to be in the writer's mind in this passage. The whole movement of thought is in the line of the revelation of God, which needs to become clearer because it had not before been laid hold of. The darkness is not a hostile force struggling with the light, but a blinding power for the human mind, preventing it from seeing the light. This verse corresponds, in this regard, with ver. 10, " the world knew him not." (*c*) The prevailing sense of σκοτία as used by John is that of darkness as preventing men from seeing the light, rather than that of a hostile power contending with the light; comp. the First Epistle i. 6, ii. 9, 11, Gosp. viii. 12. Indeed, the use of the word in xii. 35a seems only a sort of passing figure, for in xii. 35b the common meaning returns: " he that walketh in the darkness knoweth not whither he goeth." 5. The construction of ἐρχόμενον in ver. 9 is quite uncertain. The following considerations favor the connection of the word with πάντα ἄνθρωπον:—(*a*) The position which it has in the sentence points to its union as an adjective-word with this noun. (*b*) This connection gives to this verse its most natural meaning, as descriptive of the permanent work of the light in all ages—the following verses dividing this work with reference to the time before and the time after the incarnation. (*c*) The emphatic position of ἦν at the beginning of the sentence is better accounted for if it is an independent verb; John *was* not the light, yet the light *was*. (*d*) If the author's intention had been to connect the participle with ἦν, the form of the sentence would probably have been different. If his idea was *was coming* as equivalent to *came*, no satisfactory reason can be given for his not using the word *came*. If it was *was about to come*, some more clear expression of the idea and one less liable to misapprehension would have been chosen. In either case, the participle, as we may believe, would have been placed nearer to the verb. On the other hand, the principal objection to connecting the participle with ἄνθρωπον does not seem to be well-founded. This objection, which urges that the expression *every man coming into the world* is the same in meaning with *every man*, and therefore the participle is superfluous, might be of force as bearing against such a phrase in a book of the present day. But such modes of expression belong to the simple, primitive style of the narrative writers of the Bible and have a sort of emphasis peculiar to that style. Moreover, it is not necessary to regard the two expressions as equivalent to each other, for the participle may convey the idea: *as he was coming*, or, *on his coming*. 6. In ver. 14, the words *full of grace and truth* are to be connected with the subject of the main proposition, *the Logos*. The intervening words, *and we beheld his glory*, etc., are thus to be taken, as by R. V. and many commentators, including Godet, as a parenthesis. This is rendered probable not only by the fact that the adjective πλήρης is in the nominative case, but also by the evident immediate connection of the similar words in vv. 16,

17 with the Logos and Jesus Christ. The 15th verse, again, is with relation to the idea expressed by these words, a parenthetical passage, so that the thought moves directly on from ver. 14 to ver. 16. In relation to the matter of testimony, however, ver. 15 is parallel with ver. 6f., and has a similar emphasis and importance. 7. There is apparently somewhat of the same carefulness and accuracy of expression, within the limits of popular language, in the use of σάρξ, which we have noticed in the use of θεός as distinguished from ὁ θεός in ver. 1. The writer did not wish to say that the Logos became a man (ἄνθρωπος), which might be understood as indicating more than could be affirmed. The Logos did not lay aside the essence, but the μορφή, of God. He did not pass from the Divine state into that of a mere man. But He entered into human nature, taking upon Himself the μορφὴ δούλου. He did not, on the other hand, merely assume the σχῆμα ἀνθρώπου, but He became flesh, ἐγένετο σάρξ. Precisely what this involved is suggested by the peculiar expression used; but the fullness of the author's idea must, here again, be sought in the subsequent chapters. 8. Not improbably Godet's view of the words μονογενοῦς παρὰ πατρός: that they mean (as rendered in A. V. and R. V.) *the only begotten from the Father*, is correct. But his argument against Weiss, who understands the words as meaning *an only begotten from a father*, and as referring to the only son as inheriting the rank and fortune of his father,—namely, that this explanation would suppose that every father who has an only son has also a great fortune to give him, can hardly be regarded as having any considerable force. We do not measure our thought in such phrases by the lower cases, but by the higher. The glory belonging to our idea of an only son is not affected by the fact that there are many individual instances in which there is no glory for him. 9. The fact that ver. 18 is added at the end of the Prologue, and immediately after ver. 17 (which declares that the revelation of grace and truth, of which in ver. 14 the Logos was said to be full as He became flesh, was made through Jesus Christ), plainly connects the end with the beginning and shows that, in the view of the writer, Jesus is more than a man—that He is the one who is in the bosom of the Father, and who both was with God and was God. 10. It does not seem to the writer of this note that Godet's view of the plan and thought of the Prologue is the true one—that the three ideas are, The Logos, unbelief, faith, the first being presented in vv. 1–4, the second in vv. 5–11, and the third in vv. 12–18. On the other hand, the true view seems rather to be that which has been already suggested. The great doctrine of the book is, that Jesus is what is represented by the word Logos—the Divine revealer of God having entered into our humanity. The Prologue presents as its chief point the two propositions, vv. 1, 14, which contain the statements respecting the Logos, and ver. 17 which adds that concerning Jesus. From ver. 1 to ver. 14 there is a passage subordinate to the two main propositions, which shows the necessity of what is stated in ver. 14. The other two leading ideas of the book are testimony and believing, the former to the end of the latter (see xx. 30, 31)—and these two ideas are suggested in the Prologue, though only in a secondary way. They are

Additional Notes on John I / 523

both mentioned; but the former is made more prominent (ver. 6 f., ver. 15, ver. 14 *we beheld*, comp. 1 John i. 1 ff.), because testimony belongs rather to the beginning, and faith reaches its fullness of believing only at the end. Yet the testimony is always to the end of believing on the part of those who hear it—as truly in the case of John the Baptist at the first, as in that of John the evangelist at the last (comp. i. 7 with xx. 31).

7

The passage from i. 19 to ii. 11 is the Historical Introduction, as it may be called. The object which it has in view is to bring before the readers the personages who are to act the principal part in the story. The σημεῖα are done (ἐποίησεν) in the presence of the disciples (xx. 30). In this passage the disciples are introduced on the scene.

As to the disciples here mentioned, they were, not improbably, all of them disciples of John the Baptist. Of the first two who are mentioned this fact is distinctly recorded. Were these two persons present with John on the day preceding that on which they went to see Jesus? This question is not a vital one to our determination of the plan and object of this latter portion of the first chapter. But, if it is answered in the affirmative, it proves the connection between the testimonies of John to which reference has been made on page 497 above. That it should be thus answered is shown by the improbability that they would have taken the course they did if they had heard nothing more from John than the words of ver. 36. The additional unfolding of the idea here suggested, which was given on the preceding day, accounts for the impression produced by the mere pointing to Jesus when He appears again. But without this, there is a blank which needs to be filled. Moreover, as these disciples were temporarily absent from their homes for the purpose of hearing John the Baptist and following him, there is every reason to believe that they were present with him on each day of the time at their command. For this reason also, as well as because of the apparent close connection between the several testimonies of John, we may believe that these two persons had, in like manner, heard his conversation with the deputation of the Sanhedrim. Their going to Jesus, accordingly, is the first instance of πιστεύειν which answers to the μαρτυρία.

In the verses which contain the first two testimonies of John, 19–34, the following points may be noticed: 1. The record of John the Baptist here is quite different, and for quite a different purpose, from that of the other Gospels. The story of John's preaching as given by the Synoptics, is a representation of the character and substance of that preaching. This is true of the passing allusion to it in Mark, and also of the longer accounts in Matthew and Luke. But to this writer, John is of importance only as related to his testimony, and in the plan of this introductory passage this testimony only bears towards one result. We have not here, therefore, the general utterances of John, but only a few words which he said on three successive days. The circumstances of these occasions, however, called him to explain his peculiar mission and his relation to the Messiah. Hence it is not strange that he should have used some of the expressions which he used in addressing the people, and the presence here of the quotation from Isaiah, or the allusion to the baptism with water and to the mightier one who was to follow, cannot be urged as, in any measure, inconsistent with the other Gospels, which represent these words as used at a different time. These words must have been often on the Baptist's lips and have been spoken to various hearers. 2. In the second testimony (ver. 30), we find the words already mentioned in the Prologue (ver. 15) alluded to as having been spoken on a former occasion. This was not on the preceding day apparently, for no such words are introduced in the account of that day. We must conclude, therefore, that the hearers present on this occasion, and probably the two disciples, had been also present when John preached before the beginning of what is here narrated. These disciples had been, for a brief period at least, under the educating influence of the forerunner in a certain kind of preparation for belief in Jesus. 3. That the baptism of Jesus must be placed before ver. 19, is clear from the fact that it must have occurred at an earlier time than the day indicated in ver. 29, because of the allusion to it (vv. 33, 34) as already past. But if it preceded ver. 29, it must also have preceded ver. 19, because the forty days of the temptation followed the baptism and during this period Jesus could not have been accessible to others as he was here. Moreover, if He had been baptized on the day mentioned in ver. 19, that is, only a single day before ver. 29, it is scarcely possible that the words used by John the Baptist respecting the event should be only what we have here. 4. As to the meaning of the words *I knew him not* (vv. 31, 33), Godet holds that they declare that John did not know Jesus a man, for if he had known Him thus, he must have known Him also as the Messiah. Meyer, on the other hand, says that this expression leaves it quite uncertain whether he had any personal acquaintance with Jesus. Westcott regards the story in Luke as leaving it doubtful whether any such personal acquaintance existed. But, if the narrative in Luke is to be accepted, it seems almost impossible that John should not have had some such knowledge of Jesus as would prevent his saying so absolutely, I did not know him. The circumstances of Jesus' birth, and of John's own birth as related to that of Jesus, were so remarkable, that John could hardly have lost sight of Him altogether. Moreover, the words addressed to Jesus by John in Matt. iii. 14 are very difficult to be accounted for, if Jesus was altogether unknown personally to him. Weiss attempts to explain the difficulty by supposing that the $ᾔδειν$ does not refer to the time of the baptism, but to the time of the verb $ἦλθον$ which follows, that is to say, the time when John entered upon his public office. But this seems wholly improbable in the case of $ᾔδειν$ of ver. 33, which occurs in the midst of the account of what he saw at the baptism, and appears to be contrasted with the knowledge which he gained by seeing the fulfillment of the sign—he was without this knowledge even at the baptismal scene, until the moment when he saw the dove descending. It would seem, therefore, that the ex-

Additional Notes on John 1 / 525

planation must be sought for in connection with the idea of the Baptist's testimony, for which the whole matter is introduced. He did not know Jesus, in such a sense that he could go forth as the witness sent from God (ver. 6), and testify that Jesus was the Son of God, until the divinely promised proof had been given. However much the friends, or even the mother of Jesus herself, may have thought of a glorious mission as awaiting Him in life, they could not have felt sure that He was to hold the Messianic office, until they saw the evidences which came with His entrance upon His public career. But John—to be the great witness, giving the assurance of a Divine word—must certainly have waited for the sign, before he could feel that he knew as he ought to know. In this connection, also, it may be noticed that John's testimony seems to take hold, in some measure, upon the thoughts which the writer brings out in the Prologue (comp. ver. 30, *he was before me*, ver. 34, *the Son of God*), and surely, for the knowledge of these things, he needed a divine communication. He may have believed in Jesus' exaltation above himself (Matt. iii. 14) by reason of what he had heard of the story of His birth or the years that followed. He may, thus, have felt that he might rather be baptized by Jesus than baptize Him. He may even have had little doubt that He was the Messiah. But he could not *know* Him as such, until the word of God which had come to him was fulfilled.

8

In connection with the third testimony of John, *the result in believing* is given; the two disciples go to Jesus. With respect to the one of them who is not named, we may notice: 1. That he is, beyond any reasonable doubt, one of the apostolic company as afterwards constituted. This is proved by his connection with Andrew; by the fact that he is undoubtedly to be included among those disciples who went to Cana (ii. 2), and to Capernaum (ii. 12), and so, also, among those who are referred to as being present with Jesus at Jerusalem (ii. 17, 22); and by the fact that in the subsequent history the "disciples," who are made thus especially prominent, are clearly the apostles. 2. That he is particularly connected with Andrew and Peter. He must, therefore, have been one of the apostolic company who had this relation to those two brothers before their discipleship to Jesus began. It appears probable, also, that he is the same unnamed person who has similar intimacy with Peter after their entrance upon their apostolic office. 3. That the only persons whom the Synoptic Gospels present to us as thus united with Andrew and Peter are the two sons of Zebedee. 4. That there is, to say the least, a possible and not improbable allusion to his having a brother whom he introduced to Jesus. If so, the evidence that the two were James and John is strengthened, but this point is not essential to the proof. 5. That, if the companion of Andrew was either James or John, and if he is the one who is alluded to, but not named, in subsequent chapters, there can be no question as to which of the two he was. If he was the author, he could not be James, who was dead long before the book was written. Whether he was the author or not, James had died too early, as Godet has remarked, for any such report to spread abroad as that which is referred to in xxi. 23. Weiss, in his edition of Meyer's Commentary (as also Westcott and Hort), holds that πρῶτον, and not πρῶτος, is the true reading in ver. 41, and Weiss maintains, that, with either reading, the word does not suggest the finding of the brother of Andrew's companion, but that, on the other hand, it simply marks the finding of Peter as the first instance to which vv. 43, 45, answer as a second and third. Meyer, however, reads πρῶτος, and agrees with Godet, that there is here a reference to James. Westcott, also, who adopts πρῶτον as the text, agrees with these writers in the opinion that James is probably alluded to. It is observed that the indication of the verse is found not only in this word, but also in the emphatic ἴδιον, and in the fact that the verse follows and is apparently connected with ver. 40 (*one of the two*—he *first* findeth *his own*), and that the specifying of the finding of Peter as the *first* case of *finding* seems wholly unnecessary, and, considering the separation of the verses which give the account of the other findings from this one, antecedently improbable. Weiss also holds, that the finding of Peter took place on a different day from that of the visit of the two disciples to Jesus. But, while this is possible, it seems more probable that it occurred on the same day at evening, the days being reckoned by the daylight hours. In so carefully marked a narrative, we can hardly suppose a new day to be inserted with no designation of it. The result in *faith* of this first day was a conviction on the part of these disciples that they had found in Jesus the Messiah. Even this conviction could not, probably, in so short an interview, have reached its highest point. On the other hand, as related to the full belief of the later days with respect to all that Jesus was, this must have been only the earliest beginning of the development of years.

9

In connection with vv. 43–52 the following points may be noticed:—1. The impression produced upon the mind of Nathanael is occasioned (at least, so far as the record goes), by something beyond what occurred in the other cases. There is an exhibition of what seemed to him miraculous knowledge on Jesus' part. As to what this was precisely, there is a difference of opinion among commentators, as Godet states in his note. That Godet is right here, as against Meyer and others, is rendered probable by the very deep impression which evidently was made on Nathanael, and by the fact that the recording of what Jesus says of him, in ver. 47, can scarcely be explained unless we hold that these words, as well as those of ver. 48, affected his mind.—2. The answer of Nathanael, also, expresses more than what we find in the other cases. He says, indeed, what they say: Thou art the king of Israel (the Messiah). But he also says: Thou art the Son of God. We may believe that this second expression answers to the second element in the manifestation which Jesus made to him: namely, the miraculous insight into his character. Jesus awakened, by this means, a conviction in Nathanael's mind, that He had a peculiar relation

Additional Notes on John 2 / 527

to God; in some sense, at least, a divine side in His nature or character. The view that the title *Son of God* here is simply equivalent to *Messiah* is improbable, when we consider the peculiarities of this story, as compared with the others. But we cannot hold that Nathanael grasped at once the fullness of the significance of this term, as it is used in xx. 31.—3. The words of ver. 52 (51) are evidently spoken with reference, not only to Nathanael, but to all the disciples who were now with Jesus. It is quite probable that, in the plan of the book, they are inserted here as looking forward to all the σημεῖα which are to be recorded afterwards, and which, beginning with the one at Cana, proved to the disciples the union between Jesus and God.

4. That this gathering of disciples about Jesus is quite independent of any story in the Synoptics, and is antecedent to the call of which the account is given in Matt. iv. 18–22, Mk. i. 16–20 and Luke v. 1–11, is evident from the fact that the Synoptic narratives begin the history at a later date. Moreover, the readiness with which the four disciples (Andrew, Peter, James and John) left their business and their homes immediately upon the (Synoptic) call, is almost inexplicable unless there was some previous acquaintance and impression such as we discover here. Meyer affirms that John and the Synoptics are irreconcilable with each other in respect to this matter, because these five or six disciples are with Jesus in ii. 2 and remain with Him. Weiss, in his edition of Meyer, takes the opposite ground. He, however, maintains that we cannot assert that the μαθηταί, who are spoken in ii. 17–iv. 54, are the same with these five or six or that they include all of these. He even goes so far as to say that there is no indication in this chapter that Simon joined Jesus, and calls attention to the fact that in Luke v. 1 ff. the story of the call is centered upon Peter. Both of these writers have taken wrong positions; Meyer, in insisting that no place can be found for the call in John's narrative after the first chapter, and Weiss, in supposing that Peter may not have acted at this time as the others did, and that μαθηταί of ii. 17, etc., is not intended by the author to designate the same persons—or, at least, to give them a prominence—who are mentioned in ch. i. As Keil remarks, the statements with regard to the disciples in the second chapter, if we suppose them to be the same with those mentioned in ch. i., do not exclude the possibility of intervals of separation from Jesus, after their first meeting with Him, and of return to their former employments. It must be borne in mind that John's narrative is a selection of stories made for the purpose of setting forth *proofs* and the *growth of faith*, and not a complete or altogether continuous record of Jesus' life.

10

John 2

1. The first eleven verses of ch. ii. are evidently connected with the first chapter, because of the continuance of the designation of the days, because of the fact that in ver. 11 the miracle is connected with the faith

of the disciples mentioned, and because the story of the public life of Jesus and His first Messianic appearance evidently begins with ver. 13. The historical introduction, accordingly, closes with ii. 12. The explanation of the design of the miracle recorded in these verses is thus easily seen to be that which the writer indicates in ver. 11; it was to manifest the glory of Jesus before these disciples, to the end of confirming their belief in Him. Any other purpose, such as that of turning the minds of the disciples away from the severities of the old system to the free, joyful service of the new, must have been altogether subordinate and secondary. The book is written for testimony and its results, and the miracle was needed now for testimony. It was of the highest importance that these five or six men, who were to be apostles, should be established in their faith at this time. The character of the miracle was determined, as all the miracles of Jesus' life seem to have been, by the circumstances which presented themselves. So, in this case, it was a miracle at a wedding and a miracle of turning water into wine. That it taught or might teach other lessons was incidental; that it taught faith was the reason for performing it. It was a σημεῖον.

As to particular points in these verses, it may be remarked :—1. In the presentation of the story we may see that the writer is guided by the end which he has in view. The circumstances mentioned set forth the striking character of the miracle and its reality, and the narrative also makes prominent the words addressed by Jesus to His mother. The first two of these points have a direct bearing, evidently, on the manifestation of His glory (ver. 11). There can be little doubt that the same is true of the third. The words that are found in vv. 3–5 look towards a miraculous work as a possibility.—2. The answer of Jesus in ver. 4 can hardly be explained, if the request of Mary was only that He would, in some ordinary way, help the family out of their present embarrassment. This was so reasonable a suggestion on her part, it would seem, that He could not have replied to it either with such an element of severity in His words or with such a form of expression. Her meaning, therefore, must apparently have involved something beyond this. The instance most nearly resembling this, in which we find in this Gospel the words "*my* (or, *the*) *hour* (or *time*) *is not yet come*," is that in vii. 6, where the brethren of Jesus urge Him to make Himself known more publicly at Jerusalem. We may believe that, on the present occasion also, there was somewhat of the same thought in His mother's mind. She must have been looking for the time when He would come forward publicly; she must have expected it with increasing interest, and with even impatient desire perchance, as He moved forward in His manhood; she must have thought it near when He left her for John's baptism; she may even have known from Himself that it was near. He had now returned from the baptism with disciples—why should not this be the time? Whether we are to understand, therefore, that she was asking for an exhibition of miraculous power in the particular emergency of the hour or not, it seems impossible to doubt that there was in her mind some call for a display on His part of His

Messianic character and dignity which should go, in its publicity and effect, beyond the company then present, and become in itself the assumption as if before the world, of His office. The time for this had not yet come. The path which opened to His mind and that which opened to hers were different. He must go forward by slow steps, and begin by simply confirming the faith of the few disciples who were the foundations of His Church.

11

Beginning with ii. 13, the account of the first visit of Jesus to Jerusalem is given. There can be little doubt that the five or six disciples were with Him in this visit. Ver. 12 states that they went with Him from Cana to Capernaum, and that they (not He alone) remained there not many days. It is then said (ver. 13) that He went up to Jerusalem; and at the close of each story of what He did there (vv. 17, 22), the relation of His words or actions to the thoughts of the disciples is referred to. When we add to this the evident design of the writer to set forth the growing faith of the disciples in their association with Jesus, the probability in the case rises almost to certainty.

There are four points of special interest connected with these verses (13–25):—1. As the miracle at Cana had by reason of the supernatural power exhibited in it confirmed their faith, two means of a different order are now employed for the same end. The driving out of the dealers is an exhibition of His prophetic zeal. It was the power of the prophet that awed and overcame those who had desecrated the sacred place. The impression made on the disciples was immediate and profound (ver. 17). The testimony comes to them in a new line. As related to the scene at Cana, however, it comes in the right order of proof. The miracle is the first σημεῖον, the prophet's work is the second. The matter recorded in ver. 18 ff. is of another character. As we see by ver. 22, it was not fully understood at the time. The scene at Cana and the one with the dealers taught their lesson at once; the disciples believed (ver. 11), and they remembered and applied what was written (ver. 17). But this scene suggested a question which they could not answer. It was a question, however, to which their minds might naturally often turn, and it was one which would lead them to the thought of the wonderful element in His person and character. It worked as a proof by reason of the strangeness belonging to it. What could be the significance of those remarkable words? What a wonderful man must He be who could utter them of Himself! The different character of the signs, as the author brings them before us, may well arrest attention. 2. In respect to the last point (ver. 18 ff.), it is said that the disciples did not come to the right apprehension of the meaning of Jesus' words until after He rose from the dead. In the following verses, persons are spoken of who were led by the signs to believe, but not to believe in such a way that Jesus could trust Himself to them. These statements show clearly that the author is marking in the progress of his narrative the development of faith. These indications, also, are of such a nature that they point us to an author contemporary with the facts as the one who gives them. They are of the simple, artless sort, which men removed from the actual scenes do not think of. 3. The signs referred to in ver. 23 are not described or related in the chapter. The inference which must be drawn is, that the writer purposely selects those things only which affected the disciples, and those even which moved them in a different way from the miracle, properly so-called, which they had witnessed at Cana. 4. We may add that, at this point, ch. iii. opens with a testimony which lies wholly within the sphere of *words*.

As to the questions arising in connection with these verses, which relate to the difference between this Gospel and the Synoptics, it may be said, in the first place, that both of the two things mentioned seem better suited to the beginning of the public life of Jesus than to its end. The demand for a sign, with the particular answer here given, is more easily accounted for as made on His first appearance, than at the period when, after three years of ministry, He comes to Jerusalem for the last time and enters it with a sort of triumphal procession. It will be noticed, indeed, that in the Synoptical account these words about the temple are only mentioned as what the false witnesses reported that they had heard, and that Mark says, apparently with reference to this matter (comp. Mk. xiv. 59 with 58), that they did not agree with one another in their statements. This may most readily be explained, if the words of Jesus had been uttered two years before. As for the driving out of the traders, on the other hand, the act on the part of Jesus which is here related would seem to be just that which, in the first impulse of His mission, He would be not unlikely to do. It belongs in its character, as we might say, to first impulses, and not to the feelings of that later time when the deadly conflict with the Jewish authorities was at hand. It is, moreover, just such an act as—awakening astonishment by reason of its boldness and the prophetic impulse which characterized it—might naturally induce the leading Jews to ask the newly-appearing prophet what sign He had to show. The difficulty with respect to these points lies, therefore, not in the fact that this Gospel places the occurrences at the beginning of the history, but in the fact that the Synoptics (Matt. and Mk.) place them (or, rather, one of them) at the end. We may not be able to explain this difficulty, but the limitation of the Synoptic narratives may, in some way, have occasioned the representation which they give. Such questions belong, in large measure, with the comprehensive one, as to why the earliest writers confined themselves almost exclusively to the Galilean story.

12

John 3

The first twenty-one verses of the third chapter contain the account of the interview between Jesus and Nicodemus. This interview occurred during the visit to Jerusalem at the Passover, and, when viewed in its

Additional Notes on John 3 / 531

close connection with ii. 13–25, it cannot be reasonably doubted that the story is inserted here as a part of the testimony to Jesus. It is the first testimony of the *words*, which play so important a part in what follows, as the Cana miracle was the first of the *works*. On this passage the following suggestions may be offered:—1. It is evident that Nicodemus was one of those whose attention was aroused by the "signs" alluded to in ii. 23. His mind must, therefore, have been in a susceptible state, beyond most of those around him, and he came to Jesus honestly to inquire after the truth. The course taken by him on the occasion referred to in vii. 45–52 makes it probable that he was established in his belief in consequence of, and as following upon this interview. His action at the time of vii. 45 ff., was both honorable and courageous. So was that which is related of him in xix. 38–42. The latter action showed love to Jesus of a most tender order. And yet the mere statement of the author of this Gospel that he made his first visit to Jesus by night has been, as it were, the only thing borne in mind respecting him, and has determined the estimate of his character. The author, however, does not say that this first coming was by night because of unworthy fear, much less that Nicodemus was marked in his whole career by this characteristic. 2. That he visited Jesus with a mind open to conviction, and with an honest desire to hear what He had to say, is evident from the second verse as most naturally explained. There is no reason to believe that his first words were spoken in any other than a straightforward and sincere way. We must believe that some conversation on the part of both parties took place between ver. 2 and ver. 3. It is probable that Nicodemus came to inquire as to what Jesus had to say about the Messianic Kingdom, and that, after introducing the whole conversation by the words of ver. 2, he soon raised the question which he had in mind as to that subject. Otherwise, the words of Jesus in ver. 3 have an abruptness which is almost inexplicable. 3. The idea of Nicodemus with regard to the kingdom was, of course, the ordinary one of the time, according to which it was to be a temporal kingdom for the Jews. The entrance into it was through a Jewish birth, so far as the chosen nation was concerned. Jesus strikes at the very foundation of this idea, and makes the entrance to be only through a birth of another sort—a birth of the spirit. The difficulty which Nicodemus sets forth in the question of ver. 4 is connected with this marvelously new idea, and is to be interpreted accordingly, and not according to the literalism of its words. The state of Nicodemus' mind is that of ver. 9: "How can these things be?" —that is, the new doctrine is incomprehensible. He stood, in this regard, where the Jewish opponents of Paul stood, when he taught the doctrine of justification, not through possession of the law and the being a Jew outwardly, but through a new and living principle, even faith in Jesus Christ. 4. The meaning of the word ἄνωθεν—whether *from above* or *anew* —must be regarded as doubtful. The arguments in favor of the former meaning are: (*a*) The use of the word in the sense *from above* in the only other instances in John's Gospel which can be compared with this case. There are, however, only two such instances. In xix. 23 it is used of the tunic of Jesus, which is said to have been woven *from the top* throughout. (*b*) One of these two instances is in this present chapter (ver. 31). This fact—although the word occurs in the report of the expressions of John the Baptist on another occasion—would seem to indicate what the writer understood by it. (*c*) The Johannean idea of the spiritual birth is that of being born of God, of the Spirit, that is, *from above*, and not of a new or second birth. Born of the Spirit is an expression found in this very conversation. (*d*) For the idea of a second birth πάλιν or δεύτερον would have been more naturally selected. On the other hand, it is claimed (*a*) that the understanding of Nicodemus was that it was a second birth (see ver. 4); (*b*) that the word was so understood by the translators of the Peshito, Coptic, Old Latin and Vulgate versions; (*c*) that in the passage from Artemidorus, which is referred to by Godet—the only instance in the classics where ἄνωθεν γεννᾶσθαι is used, it has this meaning; so also the adverb in the two other passages cited by Godet in his note from Josephus and the *Acta Pauli;* (*d*) that the use in Gal. iv. 9 justifies this meaning; (*e*) that, if Jesus had here meant *from above*, He would have used the expression ἐκ θεοῦ, instead of this adverb. The tendency of the majority of commentators has been, on the whole, towards the latter view, or towards the position taken by R. V., which places *anew* in the text, and *from above* in the margin. If the second view is adopted, it must be observed—as is now generally admitted—that the word does not mean precisely *again* (πάλιν) or *a second time* (δεύτερον), but, as in Gal. iv. 9, *from the beginning*, as indicating the idea of *beginning over again*, and thus of a completely new birth. The writer of this note would merely express his own view that *from above* is somewhat more probably the correct rendering of the word, because this meaning seems more in accordance with the general Johannean idea of the spiritual life—that it comes, in every sense, from heaven—and also because this is evidently the meaning of ἄνωθεν in ver. 31. That Nicodemus spoke of a second birth does not seem to be the measure for the determination of Jesus' thought. In the bewilderment of his mind as to the words of Jesus, any idea of birth must have seemed to him to suggest a second birth of some sort, and especially as his idea of the kingdom was, that it was to belong to Jews by reason of their birth. Nicodemus was evidently unable to grasp the thought of Jesus with a clear apprehension of it. 5. With reference to ver. 5, the following brief suggestions are offered: (*a*) If we take the conversation as it stands recorded, we can hardly explain the words of this verse, unless they connect themselves with something which might easily have been before the mind of Nicodemus when the interview began. (*b*) This thing must have been outside of his old, Pharisaic ideas, for the whole exposition of the entrance-way and life of the kingdom is clearly intended to take him wholly away from those ideas—to awaken him, as it were, by a startling contradiction of what he had previously had in mind, to a new world of thought. (*c*) The only thing which can have suggested the words here used must, therefore, have been the teaching and work of John the Baptist. That this work and teaching had affected the mind of Nicodemus we may believe because of his coming to Jesus. His coming, in itself, showed that his attention had been easily turned to the great subject of the kingdom. A mind thus ready could not have overlooked the remarkable work of John, or have failed, if his attention was given to it, to consider the chief elements of John's doctrine. (d) One of the striking expressions of John, in setting forth his office and his relation to Jesus, was that respecting baptism with water and with the Spirit. If Nicodemus had known of John's preaching, it would seem that he must have had his attention drawn to this expression. (e) In explaining the matter of the entrance into the kingdom, therefore, it would not be unnatural for Jesus to turn the mind of Nicodemus away from his past ideas to the ideas belonging to the Christian system by *uniting* these two words *water* and *spirit*. The work for which the forerunner prepares the way, and which He himself introduces and sets on its course, is that by which men are drawn away from the outward and temporal view of the kingdom to individual spiritual life. (f) If there is in the words this uniting of His work with John's, we may easily understand why the word *water* falls away at once and the further development is wholly in the use of the word *spirit*. (g) The immediate and primary reference in ὕδατος is, accordingly, not to baptism as found in the Christian system, though, in the fullness of the idea of the sentence in the mind of Jesus, there may have been a secondary reference to it. But whatever may be said as to this point, there can be no doubt that the main thought of Jesus, which was intended to be conveyed to Nicodemus, was that of the spiritual birth as essential to membership in the kingdom. 6. The meaning of σάρξ, as used in ver. 6, is to be limited to the physical idea, and not to be regarded as including the moral. The object of this verse is to confirm, by the contrast here indicated, the necessity of the new birth. The natural birth, as into the Jewish people, can only result in what pertains to the physical or psychical sphere, but the kingdom of God is in a higher sphere. The aim of Jesus is, throughout, to show Nicodemus that his old views were utterly wrong. 7. The thought of ver. 8 is immediately connected with ver. 7. Nicodemus should not marvel at the idea of a new birth of the spirit, for the analogy of nature shows results coming from invisible sources. But it seems not improbable, also, that there is a suggestion here of the origin of membership in the kingdom as being widely different from what he had thought. It is an influence working in an unseen way, which may affect any one of any nation, and may leave any one unaffected—which neither moves along the lines of ordinary birth nor is connected with it. 8. The suggestions already made serve to explain the words of Jesus in the tenth verse. The object of what precedes having been to set forth the spiritual nature of the kingdom, the expression of astonishment follows, that one whose office it was, as teacher of Israel, to comprehend the Old Testament in its deepest meaning, should be so unable to grasp the spiritual idea.

13.

1. At ver. 11, Jesus makes a step in advance in the discourse, and now assumes in a more formal way the position of the teacher of this teacher. He declares to him, first of all, that He is qualified to make known to him the truth, because He has seen and knows; He has, what no human teacher has, the heavenly knowledge (vv. 11, 13). But Nicodemus, through dwelling in the psychical rather than the spiritual region, is not ready to receive and believe that which is to be communicated. 2. This want of belief on the part of Nicodemus does not seem to be referred by Jesus directly to sin or the sinful will, as in the case of the Jews afterwards, but to the fact that his thoughts are wholly in the outward and visible, as indicated by his questions respecting the new birth. The conversation apparently is designed to be an educating one to the end of faith, and so there is no sharp rebuke, but only the effort to bring him to see the need of entering into a higher sphere. 3. The *earthly things* must refer to the new birth, because this is the only matter which had been spoken of ($εἶπον$, ver. 12). The spiritual change, though having its origin and originating force in heaven ($ἄνωθεν, ἐκ τοῦ πνεύματος$), is yet accomplished on earth. It is, indeed, the earthly work of the new kingdom. The $ζωὴ αἰώνιος$ opens and begins here. This was the fundamental thing to be presented in answer to the question with which we may believe the conversation to have been commenced. If this could not be understood, what possibility could there be of understanding the things which were beyond this—the heavenly things? 4. The *heavenly things* must, undoubtedly, be indicated in the words of this conversation—otherwise there would be little significance in mentioning them. If, however, they are thus indicated, they must be found in what follows, and must, apparently, be centered in the mission and crucifixion of the Son of man to the end of the salvation of men. The fundamental fact and truth of the Gospel—the divine provision for bringing men to eternal life through believing on the only-begotten Son—cannot be understood by one who does not apprehend the necessity of the new birth, that is, by one who does not know that the kingdom of God is a kingdom in and over the soul, not to be entered by belonging to a particular nation. The necessity of the new birth may be realized on earth and the new birth is accomplished on earth, but the great divine plan, with its wide-reaching relations, which involves and is carried out by means of this spiritual regeneration, is a thing belonging to heaven, and one which must be revealed by the Son, who descends out of heaven and who is in heaven. Ver. 13 holds, in the thought as well as in its position, the intermediate place between ver. 12 and ver. 14: ver. 12, the heavenly things are mentioned; ver. 13, the Son is the only one who can reveal them; ver. 14, what they are.

14

The passage from ver. 16 to ver. 21 is supposed by Westcott, and by Milligan and Moulton, among the most recent writers on this Gospel, as

Additional Notes on John 3 / 535

well as by the writers whom Godet mentions, to contain reflections of the evangelist on the words of Jesus already spoken. On the other hand, Alford, Keil and others hold that these are the words of Jesus. The grounds on which the former view is maintained are the three referred to by Godet, and one or two others which may be closely united with them. As for these three, it must be admitted that they are deserving of serious consideration. The argument from the past tenses cannot be pressed, as it might be in some other writings, for the tendency towards the use of the aorist instead of the perfect is manifest in the New Testament, and, in this case, the reference in vv. 16, 17 is apparently to the act of love already accomplished, and besides, the ἦν of ver. 19 may be intended to cover a time before the appearance of the light, as well as the time of or after that appearance. The argument derived from μονογενής, to which other peculiar expressions are added by Westcott, such as *do the truth*, is the only one of weight. It would seem not improbable that John may have taken this word from Jesus, but the use of it by Jesus in this early conversation with Nicodemus is a thing hardly to have been expected. Was it not too soon after His first coming forward as a teacher, and was it not unlikely that He would have employed this peculiar term for the first time in a conversation with such a man? The argument derived from the fact that Nicodemus takes no longer any part in the conversation is of comparatively little force, because at ver. 14 Jesus passes from the earthly to the heavenly things, respecting which Nicodemus might naturally have been only a listener to what was told him. The connection of the 16th verse with what precedes by *for* is possible consistently with either view, but, considering the absence of any statement pointing to the writer as giving his own thought, it favors the assigning of the words to Jesus. The natural and easy progress of the discourse, if they are thus understood, and the appropriate close which they form to all that is said, together with the antecedent probability that the evangelist would not so abruptly join his own words to those of Jesus, are the arguments which bear most strongly against those already mentioned. The only instance in which it may be regarded as clear that the evangelist in any such way weaves his own matter into the narrative, is in the latter part of ch. xii., and there he only gives a kind of summary, at the close of Jesus' public work, of His teachings and their results. This, however, is quite a different thing from an immediate joining of his own words to those of Jesus as if they belonged to the same development of thought. It is claimed, indeed, that the writer connects his own reflections with the words of John the Baptist at the end of this chapter. But even if this is admitted, it will be observed (*a*) that ver. 31 is not so closely connected with ver. 30 as ver. 16 is with ver. 15 (ver. 16 opens with γάρ, while ver. 31 has an independent construction); (*b*) that it is less difficult to suppose that Jesus used the words of vv. 16–21, than that John the Baptist used those of ver. 31 ff.; and (*c*) that the writer may more easily be supposed to have been ready to supplement what John said with his own thoughts, than to add words of his own to what Jesus had said. It may be added (*d*) that by thus closely joining his own reflections to the discourse of Jesus, he must have known that he was not unlikely to mislead the reader, and to make him suppose that Jesus had uttered those central words of the Gospel (ver. 16), which He had not uttered. Is it probable that, in the first case where he presented Jesus' own testimony in words, he would have allowed himself to make such an impression?—While it cannot be said, therefore, that vv. 16–21 are certainly not the words of John, there are strong grounds to believe that they are not, and the probability of the case must be regarded as favoring the assigning them to Jesus.

In the verses of this discourse with Nicodemus we meet, for the first time in this Gospel, the words ζωὴ αἰώνιος. The careful examination of the use of this phrase by this author will make the following points manifest:—(a) The phrase ζωὴ αἰώνιος is used as substantially equivalent to ζωή. For example, when Jesus says v. 24: *He that believeth hath eternal life*, and in v. 40: *that ye may have life*, it cannot be doubted that the ζωή of the latter case is the ζωὴ αἰώνιος of the former.—(b) The ζωὴ αἰώνιος, according to John's idea, is possessed by the believer as soon as he believes; comp. iii. 36, v. 24, vi. 54. He that believeth *hath* eternal life; he that eateth my flesh *hath* eternal life. It is a thing of the present, therefore, and not merely of the future.—(c) That *eternal life* is thus *present*, is indicated by the explanation given by Jesus as to what it is, xvii. 3: *This is eternal life to know thee, the only true God and Jesus Christ whom thou hast sent*. The knowledge of God is eternal life, and this knowledge the believer has in this world (comp. 1 John ii. 13: because ye *know* the Father, v. 20: we *know* him that is true).—(d) The *eternal life* also belongs to the future; comp. vi. 27, the meat which abideth unto eternal life; xii. 25, he that hateth his life in this world shall keep it unto eternal life; iv. 36, gathereth fruit unto eternal life; v. 29, the resurrection of life.—(e) Eternal life, viewed with reference to the future, is connected in thought with expressions containing the phrase εἰς τὸν αἰῶνα; comp. vi. 51, If any man eat of this bread, he shall live forever and the bread is my flesh; vi. 54, he that eateth my flesh hath eternal life; vi. 58, not as the fathers did eat and died, he that eateth this bread shall live forever. The conclusion which we may draw from these facts is, that, to the view of this author, eternal life is rather a permanent possession of the soul than a future reward; that it begins with the new birth, and continues ever afterwards, as well in this world as in the world to come; that it moves onward uninterruptedly, so that there is no sight or taste of death, viii. 51–52. In this sense, the adjective is qualitative, rather than quantitative—eternal life is a peculiar kind of life. But when we ask why this particular qualitative word is used to describe the life, the suggestions of this Gospel lead us to believe that it is due to the fact that the life endures εἰς τὸν αἰῶνα—that it never has any experience of death—that it is endless. The qualitative word is thus also a quantitative one, and is used because it is quantitative. The endless life begins on earth.

The word *judgment*, in these verses, is possibly to be interpreted, with Meyer and others, in the sense of *condemnation* (κατάκρισις), and possibly, with Godet and others, in its own proper sense. It is not to be doubted that, though κρίσις means judgment, it sometimes has in the New Testament the idea of condemnatory judgment carried into it by the force of the context or of the subject under discussion. This is true of the word *judgment* in our language. That this is the meaning of κρίσις in these verses is indicated by the contrast with the word *save;* by the contrast between believers and unbelievers, so far as the general representation of the New Testament writers sets forth their fate; by the fact that ver. 19 naturally suggests the idea of condemnatory judgment; and by the references to the final judgment as including all men, which are found elsewhere. The other view is favored by the fact that neither here nor in ch. v. 24 ff., is the word κατάκρισις used. This word is, however, found only twice in the New Testament (2 Cor. iii. 9, vii. 3). Κατακρίνω does not occur in John's Gospel, except in the doubtful passage, viii. 1–11. It is to be observed, also, that the tendency of the Johannean thought is towards the inward sphere, rather than the outward; and as his conception of eternal life is not of the future reward or blessedness, so much as of the spiritual life in the soul, never seeing death, so it would seem natural that his idea of the relation of the believer to judgment should be that of having its issues already decided in the soul by the possession of faith, and thus of escaping judgment in its more outward form. While recognizing the force of the considerations in favor of giving to κρίσις the idea of judgment as distinguished from condemnation, the writer of this note believes that the other view is more probably the correct one. Viewed in relation to the decision as to destiny, the believer as truly as the unbeliever, it would seem, must be subject to this decision. In both cases alike, it is made, in the sense here intended, in the man himself. It is made already in each case, and no more in the one than in the other. But if the meaning is condemnation, it is true that the believer is not condemned, and that the unbeliever has been condemned already by and because of his unbelief. The 19th verse supports this meaning, for it represents the κρίσις as being that which is connected only with the rejection of the light, with the loving of darkness, and with the deeds which are evil and are to be reproved (ver. 20). But the κρίσις which relates to such works and the men who do them is a condemnatory judgment.

15

On verses 22–30 we may remark: 1. The object of the passage is, evidently, to introduce a final and impressive testimony of John the Baptist to Jesus. The insertion of this testimony indicates the importance which the writer gives, in his own mind, to John as a witness. It is most simply and easily explained, if we suppose that the writer was the unnamed disciple and had gained from John the first and strong impulse towards the life of faith. The emphasis laid upon this testimony and that in i. 19–35 will partly, if not wholly, account for the prominence given to John in the Prologue. We may well believe that these words of their old master or friend, being brought to their knowledge, strengthened greatly the belief of the five or six original disciples. 2. The statement of the 24th verse may be intended to correct a wrong impression, which readers of the Synoptics might derive from them as to the relation in time between the imprisonment of John and the beginning of Jesus' public ministry. But, whether this be so or not, this statement shows that the portion of Jesus' life which is recorded in these first chapters antedates the Synoptic account of His public work. 3. The words of ver. 27 are best taken as conveying a general truth, which in the present instance finds its application to both of the persons compared. That they have a reference to John himself is indicated by the close connection with ver. 28, where he denies and affirms only with respect to his own office, and with ver. 26, in which his disciples call upon him, as it were, to claim superiority to the new prophet, or at least equality with him. His answer to the complaint and implied demand of these disciples is, that he is content with the position and work assigned to him by God. He takes joyfully what God has given him, though it even involves a decreasing and passing away before the higher glory of Christ. But the words also refer, in his use of them, to Jesus, for it was the application to Him which was calculated especially to bring his disciples to a state of contentment with the present and prospective condition of things. He must increase, because He is the Christ. 4. These verses respecting John, though representing an incident in the country region of Judea after the close of the Passover feast, are so nearly connected with the first visit to Jerusalem, that they may be regarded as belonging, in the author's arrangement of testimony, with what occurred at that time. If we view the matter in this light, we find that the disciples had now received the σημεῖον consisting in a wonderful miracle, the σημεῖον in the strict sense, and, in addition to this, the proofs or σημεῖα given by the remarkable act of the prophet, by the great prophetic declaration respecting the temple, which offered food for thought even until His resurrection made its meaning clear, and by the words addressed to Nicodemus, which spoke to them both of the earthly and the heavenly things connected with the kingdom of God, the knowledge of which on His part showed that He had descended from heaven. Following upon all this, they had heard a last word from John, which answered, as it were, to the first suggestion which had pointed them to Jesus. He had said to them at the beginning, that he was not the Christ but only the forerunner, and had bidden them go and see the greater one for whom he was preparing the way. In the words addressed to his own followers, he now says to these former followers also, that his joy as the friend of the bridegroom is full, and that, while his work is closing, the one to whom they have joined themselves is to increase and to establish the kingdom. The presentation on the part of the author of this testimony in these different lines and the selection of these narratives which contain them are manifestly in accordance with an intelligent plan. But the plan is of just that character which attaches itself to, and finds its foundation in, the remembered experience and development of the inner life.

16

With respect to the question whether vv. 31–36 are a portion of the discourse of John the Baptist to his disciples, or whether, on the other hand, they are added by the evangelist, two suggestions may be offered: 1. In a certain sense, these verses form the conclusion of one section of the book. The testimonies which came to the disciples at the beginning of their course and in connection with the time of the first Passover, and which are apparently arranged with special care by the author, here come to their end. That at such a point the writer should allow himself to pass from the history into reflections of his own, would be less surprising than it would be elsewhere. The passage might be regarded in this respect, as having somewhat of the same position as the summary passage at the end of ch. xii. The case is different with vv. 16–21. 2. The difficulties in supposing John the Baptist to have used expressions such as we find in these verses are much greater than those which are alleged, in vv. 16 ff., as bearing against our understanding that the words there used were spoken by Jesus. It will not follow, therefore,—even if we hold that the evangelist gives his own thoughts and words in vv. 31–36,—that he does the same thing also in vv. 16–21.

The considerations which favor the view that vv. 31 ff. are the words of the evangelist are the following: (*a*) The greater appropriateness of the thoughts to the time of the evangelist's writing, than to that of the Baptist's speaking. The thoughts, it is claimed, are beyond what the Baptist could have had. (*b*) The phraseology is that of the writer of the Gospel, and not in accordance with what we know of John the Baptist. On the other hand, this view is opposed by the very close connection of these verses with those which precede, 27–30; and by the fact, as it is claimed, that there is a marked consecutiveness and coherence in the whole passage viewed as one discourse. Godet affirms that all the details of the discourse are in harmony with the character of John the Baptist. It can hardly be denied, however, that we seem to pass into a new form of expression, as we move from ver. 30 to ver. 31, and that in the latter verse we seem to be in the atmosphere of the evangelist's language. Moreover, ver. 32a is strikingly like ver. 11, and vv. 34–36 bear the stamp of expressions of Jesus which were used at a later time. The words of ver. 32b, on the other hand, are truer to the standpoint of John the Baptist, than to that of the writer near the end of the apostolic age. Perhaps the most correct view of the passage may be, that it is a report of what John the Baptist said, but that, under the influence of his own thoughts of Jesus' work and exaltation, and especially of what He had set forth in His conversation with Nicodemus in the earlier part of the chapter, he was led to express the Baptist's thought with an intermingling of his own language, or even with some intermingling of his own thought. The phenomena of the passage which point, in some measure, in the two opposite directions, would be satisfactorily met by such a supposition. But the entire separation of these verses from the historical occasion referred to in what precedes can scarcely be admitted, consistently with the probabilities of the case.

The words of ver. 32b, whether used by the Baptist or the evangelist, must be understood in a comparative, not in an absolute sense—this is proved even by ver. 33. There is no serious difficulty in any apparent opposition between this sentence and ver. 29 as compared with ver. 26. Indeed, the difficulty is much greater in case the words are supposed to be those of the evangelist, for the Gospel-message had had wide success before he wrote this book.

The word ἐσφράγισεν of ver. 33 seems to be used in connection with the general idea of the inner life which so peculiarly characterizes this chapter and this Gospel. The testimony of Christ to what He has seen and heard is the witness to the great spiritual truth—the plan of God for salvation and the life of faith (see ver. 16). The man who receives this witness, and thus believes, gives the answering confirmation of his inward life to the truth of God in this which is witnessed. He sets the seal of his own soul's belief to the words of Christ as the words of God, and the union of the soul with God is thus accomplished in the full sense of the word. He who does not receive the witness, in like manner, puts himself thereby apart from God and His life. Comp. 1 John v. 10 ff.: "He that believeth not God hath made him a liar; because he hath not believed in the witness that God hath borne concerning His Son. And the witness is this, that God gave unto us eternal life, and this life is in His Son. He that hath the Son hath the life; he that hath not the Son of God hath not the life."

The last clause of ver. 34, if the reading without ὁ θεός is adopted, is in a general form, and the precise application and meaning are somewhat uncertain. This form of the text is probably the correct one. We must observe, however, that the clause is introduced as a proof of the preceding, that is, a proof of the proposition that he whom God has sent speaks the words of God. The natural evidence of this would seem to be that the Spirit is given to Him without measure, rather than that the gift of the Spirit, when this great gift is made to the world or the souls of believers, is an unlimited one, or that the Son Himself gives the Spirit without limitation. The subject of the verb *gives* is, therefore, probably to be supplied from ὁ θεός of the preceding sentence, and not from the subject of λαλεῖ. For the same reason, the application of the general phrase is to the Son, although there is no αὐτῷ in the sentence. The connection with the following verse, also, serves to show that the thought is of the Father as giving to the Son.

17

If the words of vv. 31–36 are words of the evangelist himself, they are most naturally to be taken as his statement of the truth (as he saw it at the time of writing), which was involved in what John the Baptist had suggested by the comparison between himself and Jesus as the παρανύμφιος and the νύμφιος, and by the words, He must increase. They thus indicate what he himself thought, afterwards, that the testimony affirmed when fully apprehended in the wide reach of its meaning. If they are, on the other hand, the words of John the Baptist, that prophet must have been granted a vision of the exaltation and work of Christ which was beyond that of his time—a thing which, considering his peculiar office in relation to the Messiah, would not seem impossible. John was not only the greatest of the prophets of the older system, he was the last of the prophets. He was the one who handed over the truth of the Old Testament times, as it were, to the New Testament times; the one who pointed to Jesus the earliest disciples of the new system. Why may it not have been granted to him to see what Jesus was, to know that He possessed the Spirit without measure, and to understand that his own ministration of repentance was to be supplemented and perfected by the ministration of faith? If Abraham, with whom the covenant was originally made, rejoiced in the foreseeing of the day of Christ, and saw it with rejoicing, it would seem by no means strange that John the Baptist might have had a vision which opened to him more than others saw—and that he might have expressed what it brought to his mind, either in the precise words which we find here, or, if not this, in words which could be filled out in their significance by the evangelist while yet moving in the sphere of his thought.

However we may view the words, they suggest an inquiry of much interest—namely, how far may we believe that the faith of the disciples, of whom the author is particularly speaking, had advanced at this time? They had had before them manifestations of His power, His zeal, His outlook on the future, His claim to have descended from heaven, His insight into the nature of the kingdom of God, His view of eternal life as related to faith, and finally they had had a closing testimony of John the Baptist which was, apparently, more full and emphatic than any that he had given them at the beginning. They had thus seen all that they could hope to see, so far as the different kinds of evidence were concerned. But we cannot suppose that their belief as yet answered fully to the abundant measure of testimony which had been given them. What we are told in the Gospels of the slowness of their development in the new life, and in their comprehension of its teachings and mysteries, is altogether in accord with what we should expect from the circumstances in which they were. The strangeness of the doctrine of the spiritual kingdom and all that belonged to it, and the ever-deepening mystery in the character of Jesus, as He spoke to them of Himself and of the eternal life of the soul, must have made belief seem a hard thing oftentimes. They were opening in their life to a completely new world. Every day, every thought almost, brought them to new wonders. How could the inward life, long educated under the Jewish ideas, and with the controlling influence of the temporal and outward view of the kingdom, keep pace in its progress with the evidences which were set before them? The evidences might come rapidly—they might come fully; but for faith to grow to its fullness, they must be repeated again and again, they must work their way into the mind gradually, they must find themselves partially understood at one moment, but partially also only at a later, and perhaps a much later, moment. One manifestation of power or insight may have made them believe as soon as it was given; another may have only suggested questioning, or left them in bewilderment, until the great fact of the resurrection enlightened all the way which led onward to it.

When, however, the testimony was to be recorded, years after the history was ended, it was necessary that it should be given in the words in which it was uttered, and of course, as thus given, it would convey to the reader, who had entered into a deeper understanding of the Christian truth, a proportionally deeper and clearer meaning. To be appreciated as a part of the development of the apostles' belief, it must be viewed from the standpoint of the time in their progress when the words were uttered. When it is claimed that there is no advance of thought in this Gospel, that we reach the end immediately from the beginning, etc., those who make the criticism may be called upon to consider the author's plan and its necessary limitations. He does not propose to prove his doctrine —that is, the great truth that Jesus is the incarnate Logos—by a doctrinal course of argument, as if in a treatise. In such a work, he might have arranged his matter altogether at his own will. But he proves by a biography, and in accordance with a plan which involves two ideas: testimony and answering belief. He must select and arrange, accordingly, within the limits thus imposed. The advance indicated in a book of this character must be found largely in the growth of the *impression* of the testimony, rather than in that of the testimony itself. And even with regard to the impression, the necessities of the biographical element may prevent the presentation of a steady progress. Life, whether external or internal, does not move as the critical mind is disposed to demand that this Gospel should move.

Moreover, as to the presentation of ideas, Jesus had before Him, on the occasion mentioned in the beginning of this third chapter, one of the leading men of the Jewish nation, a man, no doubt, of intelligence and learning—"the teacher of Israel." This man came to test and judge Him as a professed prophet, and to ask Him with reference to the kingdom of God. How can we suppose, in such a conversation, that there would have been no utterance of the deeper truths of the new teaching. That the occasion was near the beginning of the public ministry is a matter of no importance here; the presence of the particular man was the determining point. The man's condition of mind and spirit called for the setting forth of the earthly and heavenly things, and we may believe that it was because they were thus brought forward, that he was gained as a disciple, as he might not have been by another kind of discourse. Another listener, or body of listeners, on another day, might have called for a more elementary or plainer method of instruction. But that other day might as easily have been a year later than this one, as a year earlier. The teaching was determined by the opportunity, not the opportunity by the teaching.

We may also look at the matter in another light. If we conceive of the discourse with Nicodemus as intended to bear, in the way of testimony, upon the minds of the disciples, or even upon them as being present and hearing it, we may well believe that Jesus thought it fit to give expression to thoughts which they could not yet fully comprehend, but which might find a lodgment in their minds and become seed-thoughts for future growths. Suggestive and always asking for explanation, such words as these must have been, first, a witness for them to some deep life and power in Him who uttered them; then, matter for reflection and further inquiry; then, as something of a similar character was uttered afterwards, a help towards further knowledge; and so continually a means of opening the mind to more light and of strengthening the heart in faith with every increase of knowledge.

In the case of these disciples, who were to be the intimate companions of His life and afterwards the source of instruction and authority in the Church, it was especially important that such seed-thoughts should be given for their future meditation, and this, too, at an early time in their discipleship. We see, in this Gospel, how much higher a place in the sphere of testimony is given by Jesus Himself to the *words* than to the *works*. It would seem that it must have been so, because the system itself was *truth*. These chief ministers of the truth must, therefore, above all others, have been educated by the *words;* and, we may believe, by words which, even from the first, called them to higher things than they were able at the moment to attain. What such a process of education made of the Apostle John, we can see in his writings, and surely, if it moved forward by the repetition of the same truths oftentimes, it was no education without progress. The progress, however, must be found in the testimony and the faith *as working together*.

18

John 4

With reference to the first eighteen verses of the fourth chapter, the following points may be noticed: 1. The statement of ver. 1, as related to the narrative, is introduced simply as accounting for the occurrence of the incident about to be mentioned. In relation to the plan of the book, however, it seems to belong with other passages in which the writer is at pains to show how carefully Jesus avoided all things which might hasten the final catastrophe before the appointed hour. He moved in all His life, so the writer would have his readers understand, with reference to that hour. 2. The words of ver. 2, which are a correction of the report which came to the Pharisees, can hardly have been added merely for this purpose. There must have been an intention on the evangelist's part to give his readers a fact of some consequence in itself with regard to the work of Jesus. The significance of the fact may possibly be found in the relation of Jesus to John. The baptism of water was the peculiarity of John's office, that of the Spirit the peculiarity of His own. In introducing the new system, however, it was natural that there should not be an abrupt and entire breaking off of the old. John was the one who opened the way, and the union of what followed with what preceded was through him. This union, in connection with the great symbolic act of baptism, was most naturally manifested by the continuance of what John had done; but the passing away of the old and the entering in of the new, was suggested by the fact that Jesus did not Himself baptize with water, but only with the Spirit.

3. The word οὕτως of ver. 6 is to be understood, with Godet, Meyer, R. V., and others, as equivalent to *as He was*, without ceremony. 4. The sixth hour almost certainly means noon here, the reckoning being from six in the morning, the beginning of the Jewish day. This method of reckoning is quite probably the uniform one in this Gospel, but it is not certainly so in every case. In the matter of counting the hours of the day, there is everywhere a tendency to vary, at different times, by reason of the fact that, whatever may be the starting-point of customary reckoning, the daylight hours are those which represent the period of activity and of events. It is to be remembered, also, that the author was living in another region from that in which the events recorded had taken place.

5. The conversation here opens very naturally, and there would seem to be no difficulty in supposing that Jesus may have directly answered the remark of the woman with the words of ver. 10. The difference, in this regard, between this case and that of Nicodemus (iii. 2, 3), is noticeable; in the latter, some intervening conversation must be supposed. 6. The living water of which Jesus speaks in ver. 10 is supposed by Godet to be *the eternal life*, and he refers to vv. 13, 14, as showing this to be the correct view. The words of those verses, however, speak of this water as being a well of water springing up into eternal life. We find also, in the sixth chapter, that the living bread and the bread of life are presented as that which is the means and support of life in the believer. It would seem more probable, therefore, that, in this expression, that which forms the basis and principle of the new life is referred to, than the new life itself. That which Jesus gives to the world—in one view, grace and truth, in another view, Himself as the source of life—may be understood as that to which He refers. 7. The word *eternal life*, in ver. 14, is placed in a parallelism with εἰς τὸν αἰῶνα, and, for this reason, it seems here to be carried forward in its meaning to the future. The thought in this place is of the future and final blessedness, as well as of the present inward life, and the former is thrown into prominence, as the contrast is intended to be between the passing away of the satisfaction coming from the earthly source and the never-ending blessing of the life in union with Him.

8. The turn in the conversation at ver. 16 is somewhat difficult to account for. It must be explained in connection with the progress of the story, and hence we may believe that it has reference to the end which Jesus had in view respecting the woman's spiritual life. In the case of Nicodemus, He met one of the leading men of the Jewish nation, who had

come to ask Him concerning the kingdom of God. Nicodemus' attention had been already aroused and his mind had moved in the domain of this great subject. In the case of this woman, on the other hand, attention was to be aroused, and, both for herself and the people of her city, the wonder of His personality and His knowledge must be brought before her mind. For this reason, partly if not wholly, it may be supposed that He left the words concerning the living water to make their impression, and turned at once to a new point which might even more excite her astonishment and stir her thought. This new point, also, would have a bearing upon her own personal life and awaken her moral sense. Godet thinks that Jesus did not wish to act upon a dependent person without the presence of the one to whom she was bound. The objection which Meyer presents is conclusive—"the husband was nothing more than a paramour." The reply which Godet makes, that the prophetic insight may not have been awakened in Jesus with regard to her antecedents until He heard her reply, "I have no husband," is, as Meyer remarks, "a quite gratuitous assumption," and, it may be added, one which contradicts all the probabilities of the case. The commentators have pursued this woman and her five husbands relentlessly, some of them even making all of the five, like the sixth, not her husbands, and some thinking of separation by divorce from some of them or that she had been unfaithful and forsaken them. But there is no foundation for suppositions of this character, as there is generally none for similar conjectures of one kind or another which, in other cases, a certain class of writers on the Old and New Testaments are disposed to make. Even Meyer, who holds that the five husbands had been lawfully married to her, says *such* a history had already seared her conscience, and appeals to ver. 29 as proof of this. He is obliged to add, however, "*how? is not stated.*" Ver. 29 says nothing about her conscience; it says only that she saw that Jesus knew the facts of her past history. It was His knowledge that impressed her.

19

The evident sincerity and earnestness of the woman in what follows may lead us to believe, that, in the words which are given in ver. 20, she did not intend merely to turn the conversation from an unpleasant subject. Whether she was yet awakened to desire instruction in righteousness from Jesus or not, she no doubt put the question with an honest purpose. The explanation given by Godet here is the more natural one, as compared with those of the writers who go to either extreme of interpretation which he mentions. In the reply of Jesus, the following points may be noticed:—1. The development of the thought here is, as it is in the interview with Nicodemus, determined by the state of mind of the person with whom Jesus was speaking, and by the circumstances of the conversation. At the same time, the conversation moves toward a final result which involves an important testimony, and in connection with this fact the story finds its place among these narratives which are selected by the author for purposes of proof, and as giving actual proofs which were brought before the minds of the disciples. The great truth of the spirituality of religion is brought out here, as it is in what was said to Nicodemus. But here it is suggested in connection with the matter of worship, instead of the entrance into the kingdom of God, because this was the question which occupied the mind of the one with whom Jesus was now speaking. If, however, God is a Spirit and true worship must therefore be spiritual, it naturally follows, for the mind that moves far enough to comprehend the truth, that the life in union with God must be entered by a new birth of the Spirit. But there is something further here: namely, a distinct declaration of the Messiahship of Jesus. This had not been stated in terms to Nicodemus, or in the scenes at the first Passover, or at the wedding-feast at Cana. In the matter of testimony it was an addition to all that preceded—the word from Jesus Himself saying: I am the Christ. He had said what might imply as much in His words to Nicodemus. He had suggested the thought by His reference to rebuilding the temple, and had given evidence of Messianic power in the first miracle. But now He declares it in a sentence which can have but one meaning. On His return, therefore, from Jerusalem towards Galilee after the first Passover, the last element in the testimony is presented to the disciples—through this chance conversation, as it seemed, in a Samaritan town—which may lead them to be confirmed in their belief that Jesus is the Christ, the Son of God.

The reason why this declaration was made to this Samaritan woman, and not publicly in Jerusalem, is explained, on the one hand, by the fact already alluded to—that the "hour" of Jesus was the directing-power of His life in relation to the entire matter of His manifestation of Himself, and, on the other, by the retirement and remoteness from the central life at Jerusalem of this town in Samaria. But for the inner life of the disciples it mattered little where the testimony was presented to their minds, while in the due order of impression its place was necessarily and properly after the testimonies mentioned in the earlier chapters. The declaration now given at the end would naturally throw its influence back, as they thought of it, upon all which had been heard or seen before, and would become a guiding and illuminating power in their reflections on what had occurred, and also on what they might find occurring in the future. We may see clearly, therefore, how the writer follows, in the insertion of this chapter, as truly as before, an intelligent plan.

20

With reference to particular points in vv. 21–26 the following suggestions may be offered:—1. In the words of ver. 21 we may see from the outset that Jesus' desire was to draw attention to the spirituality of worship, and it is not improbable that, as the account of the conversation was given to the disciples, it was His design to turn their thoughts also away from the ideas of place, which belonged to their former education,

Additional Notes on John 4 / 547

and to show them, at this early stage of their new life, the great difference between the new and the old.—2. The distinction made between the Jews and the Samaritans in ver. 22 is apparently to be determined as to its precise meaning by the last clause of the verse. It was because salvation was from the Jews, that it could be affirmed that they worshiped that which they knew and the Samaritans, that which they knew not. The latter did not stand on the same ground with the heathen nations. They were not entirely without the knowledge of the only true God. But they were not in the line of the Divine education under the Old Covenant, they did not receive the full revelation which had been made, and they were not the nation in the midst of whom appeared the Christ—to know whom, as well as the true God, is the eternal life. They were moving apart from the light, rather than in the light.—3. The true worship is evidently set in opposition to that of place, and thus to the ideas of both parties. But the added words show that Jesus in His thought goes beyond this mere opposition, and enters into the idea of spiritual worship as considered in itself. The foundation of it is the fact that God is a spirit. He therefore seeks as His worshipers those who worship in that sphere where He Himself dwells. The πνεῦμα is the part of man which is kindred in its nature to God, and which is capable of real fellowship and communion with God. It is that part of man into which the Divine Spirit enters by His influence and power. The only full communion with God, therefore, must be in the πνεῦμα. But as the πνεῦμα of man is in and with him wherever he may be, he must be, as a worshiper, independent of place, so soon as he understands the true sphere and nature of worship. The addition of the word ἀλήθεια must also be explained, it would seem, by the contrast with the idea of place. It cannot, for this reason, as well as for those given by Godet and Meyer (that the Jew or Samaritan could offer a sincere prayer, and that it follows so soon after ἀληθινοί), have the meaning *in sincerity*. Doubtless, it partakes of the signification of ἀληθινοί in this place, and means truth as answering to the true idea.—4. Godet supposes that John may have been present with Jesus and thus have heard this conversation. This is not impossible, though the impression of the narrative is that all the disciples had left Him for the time. That Jesus should have repeated the substance of the conversation to them soon afterwards, would seem very natural. It was an interview so remarkable in its results, indeed, that the disciples could hardly have failed to question Him particularly concerning it, and the truth which He had expressed was so adapted to the needs of their minds that He could not but have desired to bring it before them. There is, therefore, no difficulty in the fact that John is able to report the conversation, even if he was not an ear-witness of it.

21

The following points in vv. 27–38 may be noticed:—1. The impression produced upon the mind of the woman was that which came from the wonderful knowledge of Jesus respecting herself, that is, her past history. That upon Nicodemus, which led him to go to Jesus, came from the miracles. The influence which induced him to become a disciple, if indeed he became one in consequence of that first interview, was derived from the truth which he heard respecting the kingdom of God. The woman, though her past life differed from that of Nathanael, seems to have been affected by the same manifestation of unexpected knowledge or insight. That she should have personally met the Christ, seems almost impossible to her mind—that one who had exhibited such knowledge might perchance be the Christ, she could not but believe. This divided state of mind, as between the possibility and the impossibility, is expressed by the form of her question ($μήτι$) addressed to the people of her city.— 2. The words addressed by Jesus to the disciples in vv. 32, 34 do not seem to belong immediately to the testimony contained in this chapter, but they must have offered the disciples matter for reflection in respect to His mission. Vv. 35 ff., on the other hand, called their thought to their own mission as related to His. The interpretation of these last verses must take into account the fact that what is said is evidently suggested by the circumstances of the present scene, and, on the other hand, the fact of the general form of the statement. We may believe, therefore, that, just as the remark of the disciples about eating led Jesus to say what is recorded in ver. 34,—a word which teaches them of His relation to the Father,—so here, the sight of the people who were approaching gives Him a vision of the future and wide-extended work of the Gospel, as the disciples were to carry it forward. The general truth, in each case, is illustrated by what is taking place at the hour of their conversation. As related to the present scene, the disciples have returned in season to see the approaching people who are ready to believe, and perhaps to have part in receiving them as believers; but the work of sowing has been already done by Jesus. He has prepared for the result. And the ordering of the Divine plan in this way is, that they may share together in the rejoicing. This is a picture and representation of the future. So it will be in all their work; they will enter into the labors of others, and, at the end, both sowers and reapers will rejoice. So far as concerns the present scene, the sower is, undoubtedly, Jesus; but, as the words extend in their meaning and application over all the ministry of the disciples, the sowers may be all who have gone before them in the work of the kingdom of God. This twofold and enlarged application of the passage answers, apparently, all the demands of the several verses.—3. The word $ἤδη$ is probably to be connected with ver. 35, although there is no serious difficulty in joining it, as Godet does, with the following verse.—4. The phrase $ζωὴ\ αἰώνιος$ in ver. 36 seems to be clearly used in the sense which is common in other writings of the New Testament, but not so in John—that is, as referring wholly to the future life.

22

1. The repetition of the statement of ver. 29 in ver. 39 is confirmatory of the view given in the preceding note of the character and source of the impression produced on the woman's mind. The "many" alluded to in ver. 41 believed because of His word. We have, accordingly, in this whole section from iii. 1 to iv. 42, cases of persons who had their faith awakened by personal communication with Jesus and by listening to what He said. 2. The expression referring to the matter of belief which is peculiar to this case of the *many*, is that they said they knew this man to be *the Saviour of the world*. The testimony of Jesus, as thus indicated, was to the end of the universality of His work. Weiss, in his edition of Meyer's Commentary, holds that this expression is put into the mouth of these Samaritans by the evangelist, opposing thus the view of Meyer who agrees with Godet. But the natural pointing of the words of Jesus with respect to worship is towards the possibility of true worship in the case of any man, and independently of place, and this question of worship was the one which these people were most likely to have discussed with Jesus as the great question pertaining to their nation and the Jews. If in their communications with Him they become convinced of His wonderful character, and had even a glimpse of this independency of place belonging to the true worship, their thought must have gone out beyond national limitations to a universal worshiping of God. That they had a clear and full comprehension of this, as the writer had at the time of his writing, is not probable. Such a supposition is not required by their use of the words. But that they should have expressed the thought, which they must have derived as intimated above, by these words, is not to be regarded as unnatural. Jesus taught His disciples by the suggestion of great thoughts. They had but a feeble grasp of them at the first. At a later time, they entered into deeper knowledge. But the story, as told from the standpoint of the later period, must be interpreted, oftentimes, not from the time of the recording of it, but from that of the events. An illustrative example may be found in xvi. 30. How true to the life are the words of the disciples which are there recorded: "Now we know that thou knowest all things, and needest not that any one should ask thee." And yet, how evident it is that in relation to what His meaning was their minds had, at the most, only a glimmering of the light. Indeed, the very words of Jesus which follow seem to intimate this: "Do ye now believe? Behold the hour cometh, yea, is come, that ye shall be scattered every man to his own and shall leave me alone." The word which He spoke to Peter at the end with reference to His departure to the unseen world, might, in a certain sense, be applied to His life with His disciples in the region of the truth: "Thou canst not follow me now, but thou shalt follow me afterwards." So, in this case of the Samaritan believers, the words which were used were the expression of the first outgoing of their thought beyond the boundaries of their own nation and beyond the Jews. But the appreciation of what salvation for the world was—this could only be gained many

550 / Additional Notes on John 4

years afterwards. The story tells what they said, and they may well have said these words. The meaning of the words to their minds must be judged of, not by what we know, but by what they knew.

23

1. The explanation of ver. 44 which is given by Godet and Meyer, is in all probability the correct one: namely, that Jesus made His entrance upon His ministry in Galilee only after He had been at Jerusalem and had, as it were, assumed His office there—and after He had there gained the attention of the people in some degree—because of His knowledge of the general truth stated in this verse. Of the very recent writers on this Gospel, Keil, Westcott, Milligan and Moulton hold that the reference of the words *his own country*, so far as Jesus is concerned, is to Judea, and not to Galilee. He went away from Judea to Galilee, therefore, because He did not find honor in the former region. Westcott even thinks that it is impossible that John should speak of Galilee in this connection as Christ's own country. But let us observe: (*a*) that John does not anywhere state that Jesus had His home or birthplace in Judea; (*b*) that in vii. 41, 42, to which Westcott refers, the people question as to whether He can be the Christ because He comes from Galilee as they suppose; (*c*) that Philip speaks of Him to Nathanael in i. 45 as of Nazareth, and Nathanael, in i. 46, hesitates to believe because of this fact; (*d*) that He is called Jesus of Nazareth in all the Gospels; (*e*) that according to Matthew and Luke, who give the story of his birth at Bethlehem, His childhood's home was Nazareth; (*f*) that the proverb here used is referred by the earlier Gospels to Nazareth; (*g*) that the words: He came to his own, i. 11, which are sometimes referred to as favoring the idea that Judea is meant here, have no real force as bearing upon the question, *first*, because all the Jews were " His own " and not merely the Judean Jews, and *secondly*, because, if this be not so, there is evidently in those words no exclusive reference to His first visit to Jerusalem, but, on the other hand, a pointing to the whole attitude of the Jews, especially the leading Jews, towards Him. The relation of Jesus to Nazareth is presented in such a way in all the Gospels—this one as well as the earlier three—as to show that it was evidently looked upon as His home and that Galilee was His country, notwithstanding the fact that His birth had taken place at Bethlehem. 2. Ver. 43 takes up the narrative from vv. 1, 2 of this chapter and carries on the story of the return to Galilee, which had been interrupted by the account of the meeting with the woman of Samaria, etc. Those first verses intimate that Jesus had had very considerable success in Jerusalem and Judea—He was making and baptizing, it was said, more disciples than John. Ver. 45 indicates the same thing. The connection of the verses is, therefore, unfavorable to the view that the proverb is introduced here as referring to Judea. Weiss, on the other hand, holds that the connection here is with the matter of leaving Samaria, and he explains the 44th verse by saying that Jesus leaves Samaria, where He had already gained honor (ver. 42), to labor to the end

Additional Notes on John 4 / 551

of gaining it in Galilee—the disciples were to be left to reap the harvest in Samaria, while He was to go as a sower to a region where, according to the proverb, the foundation work was still to be done. But, in addition to what Godet says against this view, there is every reason to believe that the disciples accompanied Jesus into Galilee. The connection of this statement with the idea of sowing and reaping (vv. 35–38), is quite improbable. Those verses contain an incidental saying suggested by the circumstances of the visit to Sychar. But now the story moves on to an entirely new matter, and it is not to be believed that the writer would expect his readers to think of such a connection, without bringing it out more clearly in what he was writing.

24

With reference to vv. 46–54 it may be remarked: 1. The writer seems purposely to introduce the allusion to the former miracle at Cana. He is about to close that portion of his narrative which is, in any sense, united with the story of the first visit of Jesus to Jerusalem. The closing section of this part is a miracle wrought by Jesus, and in the same region where the story began. We may believe that this miracle set its seal upon the faith that had grown up in the minds of the disciples in connection with all the testimony which had now been received by them, as the former one had established the beginning of their belief, founded upon the first sight of Jesus. The careful arrangement of the author's plan, as related to the bringing out of the two ideas of testimony and belief, is seen again here, as it is both before this and afterwards. 2. That this story of the healing of the son of the royal officer is not to be identified with that in Matt. viii. 5 ff., Luke vii. 2 ff., is maintained by most of the recent commentators on this Gospel. The main points of difference, which are certainly very striking, and which bear upon all the elements of the story, are pointed out by Godet. In the case of two stories of common life, where the sick person was in one a son, in another a servant; where the disease was in one a paralysis, in the other a fever; where the person performing the cure was, in one, at one place, and in the other, at another; where all the words used on all sides were different; where, in one, the petitioner for the cure urges the physician to hasten to his house that he may cure the sick person before it is too late, and, in the other, tells him that it is unnecessary for him to go to the house at all; where in the one the petitioner finds the sick person healed on the same day on which he makes his request, and in the other only learns the fact on the next day; and where, to say the least, there is no evidence that the petitioner was the same person in the two cases, but, on the other hand, he is described by different words, and all his thoughts as related to the matter are different, it would be supposed that the two stories referred to different facts. But we are not expected by the exacting critics to deal with the New Testament narratives in this way. Weiss thinks that the oldest form of the Synoptic narrative is here found in Matthew and that he means by παῖς *son*, (not *servant*), that is to say, the υἱός of John, and that Luke misapprehended the meaning, and called the παῖς,

552 / Additional Notes on John 5

δοῦλος. May not Weiss himself possibly have misapprehended the meaning? Luke's advantages for determining this question would seem, on the whole, to be equally great with those of a scholar of this generation. But while Luke did not know that the sick person was a son, and not a servant, he is, according to Weiss, nearer the original source than Matthew, in saying simply that he was sick and near to death, instead of saying that he had paralysis. John, however, we may observe, moves off in another line, and thinks he had a fever. The reconstruction of the Gospel narratives must be admitted to be a pretty delicate task, when it has to make its winding way through the work of bringing two such stories into one. 3. The part of this passage which is most difficult to be explained is the 48th verse. The father who comes to Jesus seems to give no indication of any want of faith. On the contrary, his coming is, in itself, apparently an evidence of faith. Ver. 50 shows that he was ready to believe, even on the foundation of Jesus' assurance that his son lives, and without any movement on Jesus' part towards Capernaum. Immediately on his return home, and on seeing the fulfillment of the word of Jesus, he becomes His disciple. It is possible, indeed, that this word of Jesus in ver. 48 was the turning-point for the nobleman from a weak towards a stronger faith; but nothing in the narrative clearly indicates this. It is possible, on the other hand, that this call for miraculous aid turns the thought of Jesus to the general state of mind of the people, and that He has reference to this only in His words. But the words πρὸς αὐτόν, and the difficulty of supposing that He would address a man under such circumstances in this way, when the man's faith was not at all of the character described, are serious objections to this view. Probably we must explain the verse by combining both views, and at least find in the bearing of the words upon the man himself some designed educational influence as to the true nature of faith. 4. The miracle here wrought differs from the one recorded in ii. 1–11, in that it was wrought at a distance. It is in this respect that it gives a new testimony, and for this reason, as we may believe, it is introduced into the narrative. The other points in which its character varied from that of the one in Cana were less important for the writer's purpose.

25

John 5

The conclusion to which Godet comes with regard to the feast mentioned in the first verse—that it was the feast of Purim—is probably, though not certainly, correct. This feast will meet satisfactorily the fact of the absence of the article (which seems to be the original text), and the apparent demands of the narrative with respect to time. In a story which, notwithstanding the fact that it is evidently planned on the principle of selection, yet follows carefully the chronological sequence of events, it is scarcely possible that a whole year between this first verse (that is, what happened at the time of this feast) and vi. 4, would be altogether omitted. But this would be the fact, if this feast was a Passover. The same would be the case, substantially, if it was Pentecost. At the time of the other feasts of the year in which the first Passover occurred, Jesus had probably (according to the impression of the narrative) been absent from Jerusalem. The feast here referred to, must, therefore, have been either the Passover or Pentecost, if it was one of the more prominent feasts. The objections to the view that it was Purim do not appear to have special weight. As for the allusion to such a minor feast, it is to be observed that the narrative is not given for the occasion, but for what occurred. The miracle and the discourse belonged to the testimony. They must be recorded, of course, whenever they happened to occur. As for the presence of Jesus at this feast and His absence a month later at the Passover (vi. 4), His action, provided He was absent at the latter festival, may be accounted for in connection with the plan of His life and work. The appointed hour was not to be hastened. Keil is undoubtedly correct in saying that all which can be positively affirmed is, that the feast occurred between the Passover mentioned in ii. 13 and the one alluded to in vi. 4. But we may go beyond positive affirmations, and may look for probabilities. Looking at these, we find that the limits within which it may be placed are December and April (iv. 35 and vi. 4), and this fact points towards the feast of Purim.

With respect to the miracle and the man on whom it was wrought, the following points may be noticed: 1. The peculiarity of the miracle, as distinguishing it from the one mentioned in iv. 46 ff., is found in the long continuance of the illness. This miracle does not seem, however, to be recorded for its own sake, so much as with reference to the discourse to which it gave occasion. 2. It is held by many writers, that the words which Jesus addressed to the man, when he met him again after the healing: "Sin no more, lest a worse thing come upon thee," prove that the man's disease was occasioned by his sin. While this may be the fact, it is yet not certainly so. Jesus is evidently comparing the penalty of sin with the sickness. But it is not necessary, for this reason, to hold that the sin caused the sickness. Is He not rather urging him to become free from the spiritual malady in which he, like other men, is involved, as he had become free from his physical malady? The evidence that the bodily maladies referred to in the Gospel narratives were generally occasioned by special sins on the part of the individuals concerned, is very slight The opinion that such is the case is, substantially, founded wholly upon conjecture. 3. The fact mentioned in ver. 13, that the man was cured by Jesus without knowing who He was, is one which strikingly marks this story. It must have affected the minds of the disciples, as their thoughts, full of wonder, were turned more and more towards what Jesus was and what He was doing. 4. The opposition of the Jews is represented as excited by two things: first, by Jesus' violation of the Sabbath, and secondly, and in a still higher degree, by what His defense of Himself against their first charge seemed to them to involve. This last matter is evidently the starting-point for the discourse which follows, and thus it is in connection with this point that the whole substance of this chapter—both in its earlier and its later portion—is introduced. The idea which these Jews had of Jesus' claims is an important element in the chapter, as related to its thought.

26

There can be no reasonable doubt that what the Jews charged upon Jesus was, that He made Himself equal with God—ἴσον τῷ θεῷ. To this charge it is, that He addresses Himself; and the question of the chapter is, whether He accepts their understanding and defends His claim, or whether He explains Himself as not affirming what they allege, and thus escapes their charge by placing Himself in a position, not of equality with God, but of inferiority to Him. In connection with this subject, there are some points of special interest which may be noticed.

1. Viewing the book in the light of its plan, we may observe that, in the gradual development of the proof that Jesus is the Christ, the Son of God, the Divine Logos, the matter of His equality with God is the highest point. We should expect it to be brought forward as the latest rather than the earliest thing, and to be set forth by progressive testimony, rather than all at once. This would be a thing especially to be expected in a book in which testimony and proof were intended to move, in any measure, along with experience. The phenomena of the book are in accordance with what we should thus expect. The testimony of various sorts to various ends, which have been already referred to in these notes, have all been presented before this one is first introduced. The development of the testimony with reference to this point, on the other hand, is progressive. We do not find it, and cannot expect to find it, in its full presentation, in the present chapter.

2. The portion of the proof which is given here is suggested, as it naturally must have been, by the circumstances of the case. The work performed was that of healing, accompanied by a turning of the thought of the one who was healed to the new spiritual life. Jesus calls the thoughts of the Jewish adversaries, therefore, to the work which He has to do with relation to men and to the great question of judgment and salvation. These things pertain to His Messianic office in respect to which He is the messenger of the Father to the world, His commissioned agent for the carrying out of His plan. He presents Himself necessarily, therefore, with a certain element of subordination. But, with this element of subordination essentially connected with His office, there is set forth equality. The Son does what the Father does; even the greatest of all works, in the sphere of thought which is opened,—the gift of spiritual life and the final judgment are even wholly in the hands of the Son; the resurrection and the eternal destiny of all are in His power. And men are to honor the Son even as they honor the Father. What could have been the thoughts of His adversaries, as they heard these claims to equality in working and in honor, except that He actually assumed to Himself that equality which they had charged Him with assuming?

They could not have believed that He was explaining away the offensiveness to their minds of His words in ver. 17. They certainly did not believe this, as we see by the later chapters in the narrative.

3. They did not claim that He made Himself the same with the Father, but equal with Him. It must be observed that the evidences for His claims are such as, when taken in connection with their charge, were calculated to impress them with the conviction that He was supporting His assumption of the equality of which they spoke, and not putting Himself on a lower position. The miraculous works—even greater things than they had seen—and the Old Testament Scriptures were His witnesses. He even declared that He did not look to human testimony. The appeal to such evidences after such a charge, the declaration even that the Old Testament had its meaning and end in Him, could not have sounded in the ears of those hearers as a withdrawal of any claim to that which they had accused Him of claiming.

4. What must have been the thought of the five or six earliest disciples, as they added these words which rested upon this miracle to all that they had heard or seen before. Certainly their thought must have moved forward to higher ideas of Jesus, and what He now said must have made them wait eagerly and wonderingly for further revelations.

27

The discourse of Jesus is made by Godet to consist of three parts. Perhaps, it may better be divided into four. From ver. 19 to ver. 30, Jesus evidently gives His answer to their charge and explains His powers and office. From ver. 31 to ver. 40, He gives the evidences on which He rests in His declarations respecting Himself. From ver. 41 to ver. 44, He sets before them the reason why they will not accept Him for what He is—it is because they have not in their hearts the love of God. From ver. 45 to ver. 47, He points them to the final issue for themselves of their rejection of Him, and declares that it will be the author of the books containing their own law, who will be their accuser before God and whose writings will be their condemnation.

28

Vv. 19–29.—1. The reference in ver. 19 ff., to the union between the Son and the Father is to the complete union in working, which is founded upon love, and upon the immediate seeing of what the Father does which is connected with this love, and to that subordination in love, with respect to His earthly work, which necessarily appertains to Him as fulfilling the commission of the Father. No subordination beyond this is necessarily indicated by the words. 2. The answer which Jesus makes to the Jews is, therefore, not a denial of His equality with God, but an affirmation that, in His work alluded to, what He claims for Himself is only in harmony with God's plan and is in the union and subordination of love to

Him. 3. The thought is especially turned to the great work of the Son in reference to man. There seems to be no ground for doubting that the word ζωοποιεῖ, as used at the end of ver. 21, refers to spiritual life, and that it is this subject which is spoken of in vv. 24–27. The thought is thus connected with that in iii. 17 f., though the development of it is not the same, but is determined by the circumstances of the case. The words "and now is" of ver. 25, and the addition of the words "in the tombs," "come forth," and "resurrection of life," etc., in vv. 28, 29, which are not found in the earlier verses, can hardly be explained except as we hold that there is a turn of thought towards the future judgment at ver. 28, which has not been referred to until that point. 4. The use of the word *judgment* in this passage 24–27, as also vv. 28, 29, is kindred to that in iii. 17 ff. The same reasons, substantially, may be urged for giving the sense of condemnatory judgment to the word, as were presented in the note on the former passage. The manifest reference to the final judgment in vv. 28, 29, taken in connection with the general representation of the judgment in the New Testament, makes this distinction between favorable and unfavorable judgment altogether probable here.—5. The judgment alluded to in the earlier verses is, as it were, anticipatory of that mentioned in the later ones. This use of the word belongs in connection with the general idea presented in this Gospel, and brought out in this passage, that the eternal life begins in the soul when the man believes, and is not only a future possession to be hoped for, but a present one already realized. The judgment, in this sense, is a thing already accomplished, both on the favorable and unfavorable side. When the spiritually dead hear the voice of the Son of God, they pass out of death into life; when the physically dead hear His voice, they also pass into life,—but the latter passing into life is only the consummation of what is designated by the former. The decision is really made in the act of believing. The life moves forward from the moment of that act, and the last step in the process is only like all the others—a step in a progressive development. The same is true, on the other side, of the one who does not believe.—6. The words υἱὸς ἀνθρώπου, being without the article, are best taken as indicative of quality, rather than as equivalent to the same words with the article. At the same time, they do not exclude the Messianic idea. To the Son is given the authority to execute judgment because, as the Son of man, He is a son of man. This relationship which He has in nature to those who are to be judged is the ground on which, in the great plan of salvation, He is made the judge, and the question of life and death is made dependent on belief in Him. The qualitative character of the expression υἱὸς τοῦ ἀνθρ., including at the same time a certain reference to the title-character which belongs to the words when the article is added—this is, not improbably, the combined idea which is to be found in the two other cases in the New Testament, which are similar to this; comp. Rev. i. 13, xiv. 14. But in those passages, the influence of the words in Dan. vii. 13 may be more direct and manifest, and accordingly the explanation given here is less strongly indicated.—

7. Weiss holds, with respect to the last words of ver. 29, that the resurrection of those who have done evil is only for the purpose of the condemnatory judgment, and that thus, both here and elsewhere in the New Testament, no resurrection of the evil-doers, in the proper sense of the term, is spoken of—that the term as applied to them is to be understood only, as it were, κατ' ἀντίφρασιν. The doctrine of the resurrection of the unbelieving and evil portion of mankind is set forth, indeed, only in a few passages in the New Testament, and in these only in a general way. It seems, however, to be stated distinctly in Acts xxiv. 15, apparently also in this place, and possibly in 1 Cor. xv. 22. Passages such as Phil. iii. 11, Luke xx. 35 may be explained without involving an opposite doctrine. That the resurrection should be mainly referred to as connected with the righteous, is not strange, for it was for them the consummation of the blessedness of that life to which the New Testament writers would turn the thoughts and hopes of men.

29

Vv. 31–40.—1. The presentation of the testimony on which He rests His claims is opened by Jesus with the words of ver. 31. These words must be interpreted in connection with viii. 14, and must therefore be understood as conveying the idea, that, if the only witness which He has to offer is His own, He is content to be judged by the ordinary rule. Such, however, is not the fact. He is supported by the testimony of another, and that other even God Himself. Being thus able to appeal to this highest of all testimony, He is also able to say (viii. 14) that, though in a given case He actually bears witness of Himself, the witness is nevertheless true.—2. That the ἄλλος of ver. 32 is God, and not John the Baptist, is indicated by the reference to THE testimony in ver. 36, which clearly points back to this verse, and by the evident parenthetical and subordinate character of the reference to John. This reference to John, however, is quite significant, especially in connection with the prominence given to John's testimony in all the earlier part of this Gospel. The witness of John would have led these Jews to the truth, if they had suffered themselves to be influenced by it. It was a divinely-appointed testimony—preparatory and at the foundation. But it was not that on which Jesus rests and that which proves the truth. This latter is the testimony which comes from God only.

3. The testimony which comes from the Father is manifestly declared, in the first place, to be that of the miraculous works. Whether there are two other forms of testimony referred to, or only one, it is somewhat difficult to determine. That which is given in the Old Testament Scriptures is distinctly set forth; and this may, not improbably, be all that is intended by the words of vv. 37–40. It may be, however, that in ver. 37 there is a reference to something else—which, as it would seem, can be only the voice of God in the soul. The latter is favored by the fact that the direct mention of the Scriptures does not occur until ver. 39, and

even an indirect allusion to them is not apparent until ver. 38. The words, " Ye have neither heard his voice at any time, nor seen his form," may be regarded as pointing in the same direction. On the other hand, had this reference to the Divine voice in the human soul been intended, it would seem natural that it should have been brought out with greater fullness and clearness. On the whole, the reference to the testimony in the Scriptures may be regarded as covering all that is said in vv. 37 ff., and the words of ver. 37b may be taken in a semi-figurative sense, as implying that they had not really recognized God in His true teaching and the pointing of His revelation towards the Messiah and the Messianic kingdom, when they read and searched the Old Testament writings.—4. The verb ἐρευνᾶτε is, in all probability, an indicative. The development of the thought does not suggest a demand or exhortation, but a statement of their failure, through unwillingness, to appreciate the testimony of the book which they themselves were always looking into and the study of which they demanded.

5. The two testimonies which are here set forth—the works and the Scriptures—bear witness, the first as, in the strict sense, a σημεῖον which made known the power of God as possessed by Jesus; the second, as showing that the indications of the Old Testament all looked towards such a person and teaching and work as they now saw before them. To announce the coming of this Messianic era and the Messiah Himself, John the Baptist had appeared and given his witness to them. He had aroused their attention and interested their minds for the time. He had thus, as it were, opened the door for them to appreciate the new testimony presented in the works, and to understand fully the old testimony contained in the Scriptures. That they did not yield to the force of the testimony, either old or new, was indisputable proof that they had not the word of God abiding in them—that they had really never seen or known Him in His revelations—that their will was not to receive the witness which was given.

30

Vv. 41-44. The reason of their failure to accept the evidence presented to them is set forth, in these verses, in two forms. The first and fundamental reason is the absence of the true love of God in their hearts. The second reason, into which the first developed itself in its special manifestation, is the unwillingness to accept a Messiah who did not come in the line of earthly glory. The views of a temporal kingdom, as they held them, were connected with the selfish desire of exaltation. They were ready to receive one who came to them with no testimony but his own, and in his own name, if he only met these earthly views. But to the Divine testimony, whether in the sacred writings, or in the wonderful works, or in the words of the forerunner, they were unwilling to listen, because the one to whom all this witness was borne appeared among them simply as the messenger of God to tell the Divine truth, and by making known the true eternal life, to bring all who heard Him to personal righteousness and the possession of the kingdom of heaven within themselves through believing on the Son of God.

31

Vv. 45–47. 1. Meyer and Weiss hold that the last judgment is not referred to in these verses, because Christ is represented as the judge on that day, and therefore cannot be spoken of as an accuser in connection with it. Keil affirms the opposite, saying that, as the Jews did not acknowledge Jesus to be the Messiah or the judge, this consideration can have no weight in the decision of the question. The true view of this matter is, not improbably, to be found as we observe the peculiarity of the thought of this chapter and of other parts of this Gospel which are kindred to it. This writer does not leave out of view the final judgment, but his mind moves in the sphere of the present and permanent inward life, and the end is only the consummation. In a certain sense, therefore, judgment is present, though it is also in a certain sense future. The mind of the hearer or reader is left to pass from the one to the other, and thus to include both. 2. Moses is here spoken of as the foundation of the Jewish legal system and thus as, in a sense, the foundation or centre of the Old Testament. It may be that, according to this view of the matter, he and his writings are referred to as if including the whole idea of the Old Testament Scriptures; see ver. 39. If the reference is to the Pentateuch only, the allusion is doubtless to Deut. xviii. 15, and the other points which Godet mentions in his note.

That this first formal discourse of Jesus, which is recorded in this Gospel, is intended by the evangelist to serve as testimony to his readers cannot be questioned. That it is, in this respect, an advance upon what has preceded, is also clear. The relation of Jesus to the Father is here set forth —not indeed as fully as it is in later chapters, but in a part of the unfolding of its true idea, and as it is not in the conversation with Nicodemus. The occasion on which this discourse was given, it must be remembered, was a year, or nearly a year later than that conversation, and much must have been done and said by Jesus in the interval. That Jesus in the opening of the second year of His ministry should have advanced in His teaching as far as this discourse might indicate, cannot justly be regarded as improbable. It was, moreover, with the leading Jews that He carried on this discussion, not with the common people. If the deeper truths respecting His person and His relations to the Father were to be set forth in His earthly ministry at all—and how strange it would have been, if no such declaration had been made,—it would seem that, at this time, the beginnings of the full teachings might appear. The discourse of this chapter stands no less truly in its legitimate and natural historical position, as related to the teachings of the chapters which precede and follow, than it does in its proper place in the progress of the testimony, which the author brings before his readers in proof of the great doctrine of his book.

2

John 6:1-71

THE GREAT MESSIANIC TESTIMONY AND THE CRISIS OF FAITH IN GALILEE

THE war is now declared in Judea; the thread of the narrative is outwardly broken. John does not mention the return of Jesus to Galilee. But it is there that we find Him again at the beginning of chap. vi., and He remains there after this so long and with such persistency that He even astonished His relatives; as we read in chap. vii. This sojourn in Galilee includes the whole interval between the feast of Purim, in March (chap. v.), and the feast of Tabernacles, in October (chap. vii.), consequently seven consecutive months, in which it is natural to place the greater part of the events of the Galilean ministry described by the Synoptics.

This continued sojourn in Galilee and this long retirement in which Jesus keeps Himself away from Jerusalem, are the more striking since during this part of the year, two of the three great Israelitish feasts occurred at which the Jews were most anxious to be present, the Passover and Pentecost. The conduct of Jesus, therefore, needed explanation. This explanation appears from vii. 1: *"And Jesus sojourned in Galilee; for He would not sojourn in Judea, because the Jews sought to put Him to death."*—The sixth chapter is thus the continuation of the fifth, in the sense that the continued sojourn of Jesus in Galilee, the most striking event in which is related in chap. vi., was the result of the violent conflict which had brought about the removal of Jesus from Jerusalem after the miracle and the long discourse related in chap. v. Morally speaking, therefore, the thread of the story is not broken.

But why, among the whole multitude of facts which filled the ministry of Jesus in Galilee, did John select this one which is related in chap. vi., and this one only? *Reuss* thinks that the narrative which John gives of this scene so well described by the Synoptics is incompatible with the idea that he proposed to himself to complete them. There is an exception here, it is true, but it is explained without difficulty. For this purpose it is enough to go back to the idea which governs this whole part—that of the development of the national unbelief. The end of the sixth chapter will bring us to see that the point of time here described was that in which there was consummated in Galilee a crisis similar to that which occurred in Judea, with this difference, already indicated, that the unbelief in Judea is violent and aggressive, and can end only in murder, while in Galilee, where it proceeds from a simple feeling of being deceived after over-wrought expectation, it occasions only indifference: there is no killing, there is a going away and a going not to return (vv. 66, 67). As *Weiss* says: The Galilean half-way faith becomes unbelief. The revelation of Jesus' glory by means of the two miracles and of the discourses related in this chapter forms everywhere the basis of the narrative. But the special aim of this narrative is to describe the sad result in which such great favors issue in Galilee, as in Judea. In this very province, where faith for a moment seemed to have taken root (iv. 45), the Messianic work, as such, failed; and here also, the saying had to find its fulfillment: "*He came to His own, and His own received Him not.*" In the midst of this great disaster, however, the work of Jesus continued its peaceful and humble growth in a few; it even gained at this critical moment the most glorious tribute (vv. 68, 69).

Beyschlag has set forth the way in which the miracle of the multiplication of the loaves, by provoking the sudden explosion of the political hopes which were smouldering under the ashes among the Galilean people, brought to light the complete incompatibility which existed between the common Messianic idea and that of Jesus, and made evident the moral necessity of the rupture. John alone had apprehended the historic bearing of this decisive epoch in the ministry of Jesus; and this is the reason why he alone was able to present it in its true light. Here is what explains for us the exception which he has made in favor of this narrative, which he found already reproduced in the writings of those who preceded him, and the reason why he thought fit to concentrate in the representation of this event the summary of the entire Galilean ministry.

There are three parts in this chapter: 1. The two miracles: vv. 1–21; 2. The conversations and discourses which are connected with them: vv. 22–65; 3. The final crisis: vv. 66–71.

The Miracles: vv. 1–21

1. The Multiplication of the Loaves: vv. 1–13

Vv. 1, 2. "*After these things, Jesus withdrew to the other side of the Sea of Galilee, which is the Sea of Tiberias. 2. And*[1] *a great multitude followed him, because they saw*[2] *the miracles which he did*[3] *on*[4] *the sick.*"—If the facts related in chap. v. really occurred at the feast of Purim, those which are reported in chap. vi. took place only a few weeks afterwards (ver. 4), and the indefi-

---

[1] ℵ B D L some Mnn. It^{plerique} Cop. read δε instead of και.

[2] Instead of εωρων, εθεωρων is read in A and εθεωρουν in B D L.

[3] T. R. reads αυτου τα σημεια. ℵ A B D K L S Δ Π It. Syr. Vulg. Cop. reject αυτου.

[4] ℵ reads περι instead of επι.

nite connecting words μετὰ ταῦτα, *after these things*, are very suitable to this inconsiderable interval. *Meyer*, pressing the meaning of μετὰ ταῦτα, understands: "immediately after this sojourn in Judea." The ἀπῆλθεν, *went away*, would thus signify that He returned from Jerusalem to the country east of the Jordan; and *the multitude* mentioned in ver. 2 would be that which accompanied Jesus on His return from Judea. But, observes *Luthardt*, John could not have expressed himself in this way: Jerusalem was not in direct relation to the eastern shore of the Sea of Galilee. And how could these multitudes have accompanied Jesus to a remote distance from Judea at the very time of the Passover which called them to go to Judea. It is obvious that ver. 2 is the description of a general situation, on the basis of which the following scene is separately sketched (precisely as ii. 23–25 in relation to iii. 1–21, or iii. 22–24 to iii. 25–36, or iv. 43–45 to iv. 46–54). This is John's manner of narrating. This character of general picturing appears in the imperfect ἠκολούθει, *were following*, ἑώρων, *were seeing*, ἐποίει, *was doing*, in contrast with the aorist ἀνῆλθε, *went up* (ver. 3), which ushers in the account of the particular events which the author has in view. John omits therefore the express mention of the return to Galilee which is self-evident from vv. 43–45, and he means to say that Jesus began anew the Galilean work related by the Synoptics, which was marked by daily miracles, and in the course of which He was constantly accompanied by considerable multitudes. It was consequently from some point on the western side of the Sea of Galilee that He thought fit to retire to the opposite side πέραν (*beyond*). *Reuss*, placing himself at the opposite extreme to *Meyer*, says, "All this shows us that we do not here have a strictly chronological narrative, as has been very gratuitously supposed." The truth is that John, describing the historical development of Jewish unbelief, puts this scene in its true place, but without describing all the details of the events which preceded and followed.

John says nothing of the motives which led Jesus to this step, but the word ἀπῆλθεν *went away*, seems to indicate a seeking for solitude. And, indeed, according to Mark vi. 30, and Luke ix. 10, the apostles had just rejoined their Master, after having accomplished their first mission, and Jesus desired to give them some rest and to pass a short time alone with them. Moreover, according to Matt. xiv. 13, He had just heard of the murder of John the Baptist, and, under the shock of this news, which gave Him a presentiment of the nearness of His own end, He needed to collect His thoughts and to prepare His disciples for that other catastrophe. Thus our four naratives easily harmonize. Luke names Bethsaida as the place near which the multiplication of the loaves occurred. It has been claimed that he understood thereby Bethsaida in the neighborhood of Capernaum, and, consequently, that this event occurred, according to him, on the west shore. But Luke would, thus, put himself in contradiction, not only with the other evangelists, but with himself; for he says that Jesus withdrew with His disciples *into a desert place* belonging to a city called Bethsaida. Now this purpose of Jesus does not allow us to think of the city of Bethsaida, on the western shore, where He was in the centre of His activity and was always surrounded by crowds. Josephus (Antiqq. xviii. 2.1 and 4. 6) speaks of a city which had the name *Bethsaida Julias*, situated at the northeastern extremity of the sea of Tiberias; and the expression Bethsaida *of Galilee*, by which John xii. 21 designates the native city of Peter, Andrew and Philip (i. 45), has no significance unless there really existed a Bethsaida outside of Galilee. It is this one of which Luke means to speak. Bethsaida Julias was in Gaulonitis, in the tetrarchy of Philip, on the left bank of the Jordan, a little way above the place where it falls into the lake of Genesareth. It was there that Philip died and was magnificently interred. (*Furrer, Schenkel's Bibellex.*, I., p. 429.) If John had written in Galilee, and for Palestinian readers, he would have contented himself with the ordinary expression: *sea of Galilee*. But as he was writing outside of Palestine, and for Greeks, he adds the explanation: *of Tiberias*. The city of Tiberias, built by Herod Antipas, and thus named in honor of Tiberius, was well known in foreign countries. Thus the Greek geographer, Pausanias, calls the sea of Galilee: λίμνη Τιβερίς. Josephus uses indiscriminately the two designations here united by John. The imperfect ἑώρων, *they were seeing*, depicts the joy which this ever-renewed spectacle afforded them. The reading of the T. R. ἑώρων is supported by the *Sinaitic* MS. and even by the barbarism, ἐθεώρων, of the *Alexandrian*. *Weiss* observes that if the mission of the Twelve took place during the journey of Jesus to the feast of Purim (chap. v.), as *Gess* has supposed, the narrative of John accords very well with that of Mark, who places the multiplication of the loaves immediately the return of the Twelve.

Vv. 3, 4. "*And Jesus went up*[1] *into the mountain, and there he sat down*[2] *with his disciples.* 4. *Now the Passover, the feast of the Jews, was at hand.*" The expression, *the mountain*, denotes not a particular mountain, which was in the region (for the locality has not been designated), but the mountainous country, in contrast to the level of the shore. Jesus had sought a solitary place there, and was conversing in it with his disciples. John's expression has some resemblance to that of Matt. xv. 29, immediately after the second miracle of the loaves.

What is the purpose of the remark in ver. 4? Is it a chronological note? In that case, it would rather have been placed at the beginning of the narrative. It occurs here incidentally, after the manner of John, as an explanatory remark (comp. i. 24). But with what purpose? According to *Meyer*, to explain the great gathering which is spoken of in ver. 5. But this explanation forces him to distinguish this multitude from that of ver. 2, which is evidently inadmissible. *Weiss* acknowledges this, and sees in ver. 2, and ver. 5, the crowd of pilgrims who are about to go to Jerusalem for the Passover. But what had the caravans going up to this feast to do in this out of the way place? And is it not very clear, from ver. 2, that these numerous arrivals are no others than the multitudes who habitually accompanied Jesus in Galilee? The mention of the feast near at hand, must, therefore, serve to explain, not the presence of the

---

[1] ℵ D It^{aliq}; απηλθε (*went away*), for ανηλθε.   [2] ℵ D some Mnn.; εκαθεζετο for εκαθητο.

multitudes, but the conduct of Jesus towards them. Not being able to go to Jerusalem for the feast (vii. 1), Jesus, on seeing these multitudes hastening towards Him in the wilderness, recognizes in this unexpected circumstance a signal from the Father. He puts this concourse in comparison with the feast which is about to be celebrated in Jerusalem, and He says for Himself, for His disciples, for the multitude: "We also will have our Passover!" This is the thought which sets in its true light the following miracle, as the discourses which are connected with it prove. For Jesus represents Himself here as the one whose flesh and blood are designed to give life to believers, a point which undoubtedly calls to mind the sacrifice and eating of the Paschal lamb. By this fourth verse John gives us, therefore, the key of the whole narrative, as he had given us in iii. 1, by the words: *of the Pharisees*, that of the whole conversation with Nicodemus. The denials of *Weiss* and *Keil* seem to us to rest on no sufficient grounds. The term ἡ ἑορτή τ. Ἰουδ., *the feast of the Jews*, must, according to *Keil*, explain the word *Passover*, which was unknown to Greek readers, or, according to others, designate this feast as "the feast *par excellence* for the Jews;" but comp. ii. 13, and vii. 2. Perhaps John desires to make us understand the total separation which was more and more evident between Jesus and this people who were becoming foreign to Him. From the incident in Luke vi. 1–5, and the parallel passages, we discover in the Synoptics also a spring season passed in Galilee during the course of the ministry accomplished in that province.

Vv. 5–7. "*Jesus therefore, lifting up His eyes and seeing a great multitude coming to Him, says to Philip: Whence shall we buy*[1] *bread, that these may eat?* 6. *Now this he said to prove him; for,*[2] *as for Himself, He knew what He was going to do.* 7. *Philip answered*[3] *Him: Two hundred denarii-worth of bread is not sufficient for them,*[4] *that every one of them*[5] *may take a little.*" John does not say how long the confidential interview of Jesus with His disciples, which is mentioned in ver. 3, continued. The term ἐκάθητο, *he sat there*, ver. 3, which the *Sinaitic* MS. wrongly changes into ἐκαθέζετο proves that He remained for a certain time alone with them while the companies were successively coming up. For it is impossible to imagine five or six thousand persons arriving *all at once* in the locality into which Jesus had withdrawn (this in answer to *Weiss*). While Jesus and His disciples came directly by water from Capernaum or the environs, these crowds of people, who have observed from the western shore the point towards which the bark directed its course, made on foot (πεζῇ, Mark vi. 33; Matt. xiv. 13), the circuit of the northern shore of the lake, and thus arrived successively during the day at the scene of action. According to the Synoptics, Jesus went forth from the solitude (Matt. and Mark) and received them with kindness (Luke). Thus a part of the day was devoted

---

[1] K U V: αγορασομεν, instead of αγορασωμεν.

[2] ℵ: γαρ instead of δε; and afterwards δε instead of γαρ.

[3] ℵ D: αποκρινεται instead of απεκριθη; and

ℵ: ουν instead of αυτω.

[4] ℵ omits αυτοις.

[5] ℵ A B L Π and some Mnn. and Vss. omit αυτων (*of them*) which is read here by T. R. with 13 Mjj.

to teaching and healing. Then seeing the crowd which was so eager and was continually increasing (Mark vi. 33 : " *They ran thither afoot from all the cities* "), Jesus experiences that feeling of profound compassion which Matthew and Mark describe. But another feeling, of which John alone has caught the secret, is predominant in His heart : it is that of joy. No doubt, He had wished to be alone, and this arrival thwarted His purpose. But such earnestness, such perseverance are for Him an irresistible appeal. He enters with eagerness into the new situation which is opened to Him ; for He discerns here a thought of the Father and He prepares Himself to give to this body of people the feast for which the opportunity is thus granted Him. Indeed, in John, it is Jesus who takes the initiative ; He addresses Himself to Philip : "There are our guests ; we must give them supper. Have you already thought of it?" In the Synoptics, it is the disciples who are disturbed about the multitude, and urge Jesus to dismiss them. The need of food may have occupied the minds of Jesus and the disciples simultaneously as they saw the evening drawing on. But as for Jesus, He had already taken His resolution (ver. 6). The thought of what He was going to do had formed itself in His mind during the work of that day. The narrative of the Synoptics is written from the disciples' point of view, which must very naturally have prevailed in the stories emanating from the Twelve, particularly in those of Peter and Matthew, while John, who had read the heart of the Master, brings out the other point of departure—the inward impulse of the Lord. Thus, the disciples address themselves to Jesus and communicate their anxiety to Him. Jesus, having already formed His plan, says to them : " *Give ye them to eat*," and, in speaking thus, addresses Himself especially to Philip, as we have just seen. Why to him, rather than some other ? *Bengel* thinks that he was charged with the care of the *res alimentaria*. But it seems more probable from xiii. 29, that it was Judas who made the purchases. According to *Luthardt*, Jesus wished to bring an educating influence on Philip, who had a hesitating and over-careful character. This is possible. But the playful tone of Jesus' question : " *Whence shall we buy ?* " may lead us to suppose that *naiveté* was one of the traits of this disciple's character. This is the reason why Jesus addresses him this question, which was insoluble from the standpoint of natural resources ; and he, on his side, answers it with a good-natured simplicity. This slight touch gives an idea of the amenity which prevailed in the relations of Jesus to His disciples ; it appertained to the picture of the glory "*full of grace*" of the Word made flesh.

The expression : *to prove him*, does not have the solemn sense which this term ordinarily has. It signifies merely that Jesus desired to see whether, in this situation, he would know how to find the true answer of faith. Philip makes his calculation with prudence. It is good sense, not faith, which speaks through his mouth. The denarius was a Roman coin worth about fifteen cents ; two hundred denarii were, therefore, equivalent to thirty dollars of our money ; a large sum, which, however, was still far below the necessity of the case! Mark has also preserved this circumstance respecting the two hundred denarii; only, he puts this calculation in the mouth of *the disciples* in general. If the connection between the question of Jesus and Philip's answer were not so close in John, we might try to insert here between vv. 6 and 7 the brief conversation of Jesus with the disciples reported in Mark vi. 37. But it is much more probable that the reflection which Mark attributes to the disciples in general is nothing else than the reproduction of Philip's words, which are preserved by John in their most exact historical form.

Vv. 8, 9. "*One of his disciples, Andrew, Simon Peter's brother, says to him: 9. There is a*[1] *lad here, who*[2] *has five barley loaves and two fishes: but what are these for so many?*" John mentions, first, in an indefinite way, one disciple; then he makes a precise statement: "It was Andrew." We can believe that we hear him telling the story. And how can we fail to remember here, that Andrew was precisely the one, who, according to the tradition in the Muratorian Fragment, was present at the time of the composition of the Gospel? His character as *brother of Simon Peter* had already been pointed out in i. 41. Was not this sufficient? Certainly; but the person of Andrew cannot present itself to the mind of John, without his recalling to mind how nearly connected he was with Simon Peter, the principal one among the apostles. And yet it is claimed that one of the tendencies of the Johannean narrative is to disparage Peter! Andrew, thus, falls into the trap laid for his fellow-disciple, and it is, no doubt, with a sort of malicious humor that the evangelist is pleased to report *in extenso* their words, which form so strong a contrast to the magnificent display of power which is in preparation. The word ἕν, *one only*, which was restored by *Tischendorf* in 1859, is suppressed by him in his 8th ed., according to the Alexandrian authorities and *Origen;* but certainly wrongly. We can more easily understand how it may have been omitted than added. It brings out the scantiness of the resources which are at hand: "*One only who has anything, and he how little!*" It was some petty trader whom Andrew had just noticed in the crowd. Barley-bread was that used by the poorer classes.

Ver. 10. "*But*[3] *Jesus said: Make the people sit down. Now there was much grass*[4] *in the place. The men sat down, therefore, in number about*[5] *five thousand.*"[6] In these scanty provisions Jesus has found that which He needs, the material on which omnipotence can work. Now, in His view, the banquet is prepared, the table spread: "*Make the people sit down,*" He says to His apostles. The mountain-plateaus which rise behind the site of Bethsaida Julias displayed, at that time, their spring-time verdure. Mark, as well as John, draws the picture of this grassy carpet on which the multitudes took their places (ἐπὶ τῷ χλωρῷ χόρτῳ vi. 39). He describes, likewise, the cheerful spectacle which was presented by these regular ranks (συμπόσια συμπόσια, πρασιαὶ πρασιαί) of hundreds and fifties. Ἄνδρες de-

---

[1] Ἐν is omitted by ℵ B D L Π 15 Mnn. Italiq Orig.
[2] A B D G U Λ: ὅς instead of ὁ.
[3] ℵ B L Syr. Orig. omit δέ.
[4] ℵ reads τόπος πολύς (*much room*) instead of χόρτος πολύς.
[5] ℵ B D L: ὡς instead of ὡσεί.
[6] ℵ reads τρισχίλιοι (*three thousand*).

notes *the men* in the restricted meaning of the word; if they alone are indicated, it is not, as *Meyer* alleges, because the women and children were not seated, but because they kept themselves apart and the men only were *counted*. Women and children, in the East, always keep themselves at a respectful distance from the head of the family and his guests.

Ver. 11. " *Then*[1] *Jesus took the loaves, and having given thanks*[2] *he distributed*[3] *them to those who were seated; and likewise of the fishes, as much as they wished.*" This was the solemn moment. Jesus takes in the midst of this multitude the position of the father of a family, as in an ordinary supper, and particularly that of the Passover. He gives thanks, as the father surrounded by his family did for the blessings of God in nature and in the covenant. This moment seems to have been especially impressive to the spectators. It is made almost equally prominent in the four accounts; the multitude and the disciples themselves seem to have had the impression that it was this act of thanksgiving which caused omnipotence to act and which produced the miracle. Comp. ver. 23. After giving thanks, Jesus distributes the food, as the father did at the Paschal-supper. We have rejected from the text the words: *to the disciples and the disciples*, which are omitted by the Alexandrian authorities. It is more probable that there is an interpolation here, borrowed from Matthew. The little detail: *as much as they wished,* forms a contrast to the words of Andrew: " But what are these for so many " (ver. 9).

Vv. 12, 13. " *Then, when they were filled, he says to his disciples: Gather up the broken pieces which remain over, that nothing be lost.* 13. *So they gathered them up, and filled twelve baskets with broken pieces from the five barley loaves which remained over to those who had eaten.*"—In the Synoptics, the order given to the disciples is not mentioned. This order is the triumphant answer to the timid calculations of Philip and Andrew. We can understand, moreover, the close relation which exists in the feeling of Jesus between this word: *that nothing be lost,* and the act of thanksgiving which had produced this abundance. A blessing thus obtained must not be undervalued. Criticism has asked where the twelve baskets came from. The number leads us to suppose that they were the traveling-baskets of the apostles; for they had not set out suddenly, as the crowds had done; or they borrowed them from those standing by. The epithet τῶν κριθίνων, *of barley*, is designed to establish the identity of these fragments with the original source, the five loaves of the lad.

Not only is this miracle of the multiplication of the loaves found in all the four Gospels, but several characteristic details are common to the four accounts:—the crowds following Jesus into a desert place, the five loaves and the two fishes, the five thousand men, and the twelve baskets, and especially the solemn moment of the thanksgiving. Besides this, some features are common to three or two Gos-

---

[1] A B D L: ουν instead of δε.
[2] ℵ D It. Syr.: ευχαριστησεν και (*he gave thanks and*) instead of ευχαριστησας.
[3] ℵ D Γ: εδωκεν instead of διεδωκε; T. R. adds τοις μαθηταις οι δε μαθηται (*to the disciples, and the disciples*) with 12 Mjj. most of the Mnn. It[aliq]; words which are rejected by ℵ A B L Π some Mnn. It[plerique] Vulg. Syr. Cop. Orig.

pels, particularly to Mark and John (the fresh grass, the two hundred denarii). We see that at the foundation of the four accounts there is a fact, the principal features of which were ineffaceably imprinted on the memory of all the witnesses, but whose details had not been equally well observed and retained by all. John's account contains altogether peculiar features which attest the narrative of an eyewitness; thus the part of Philip, of Andrew and of the lad, and the character of the bread (*of barley*). But above all the narrative of John is the one which, as we have seen, makes us penetrate most deeply into the feeling of Jesus and the true spirit of this scene. Modern criticism claims that it was composed by means of materials furnished by the Synoptics, especially by Mark (so *Baur, Hilgenfeld*, and, in some degree, *Weizsäcker* himself, p. 290). But what! these so distinctly marked features, these most exact outlines of John's narrative are only charlatanism! Is it not clear that it is the narrative of the Synoptics which generalizes, in saying *the disciples* instead of Philip, Andrew, etc.,? and that we recognize here a narrative which traditional reproduction had robbed of its "sharp edges"?

According to *Paulus*, there is no need of seeing anything miraculous in this scene. Jesus and the disciples brought out their provisions, generously offering a share of them to their neighbors who followed their example, and, as each gave what he had, every one had enough. *Renan* seems to adopt this explanation of the fact, if not of the text: " Jesus withdrew into the desert. A large number of people followed Him. Thanks to an extreme frugality, the pious company had enough to eat; they believed, of course, that they saw in this a miracle." What, with all this, *Paulus* and *Renan* do not explain is, that so simple a fact could have carried the crowd to such a pitch of excitement that, on that same evening, they attempted to get possession of Jesus in order to proclaim Him King (vv. 14, 15)! *Olshausen* holds an acceleration of the natural process which multiplies the grain of wheat in the bosom of the earth; he thus furnishes matter for *Strauss*' ridicule, who asks whether the law of natural reproduction applies also to broiled fish? Lange supposes that it is not the matter itself of the provisions, which was multiplied, but the nutritive power of the molecules!—Either we place ourselves by faith in the region of the supernatural, which is created here on earth by the presence of Jesus, or we refuse to enter that higher sphere. In the latter case, the only part to take is to explain this story with Strauss as a mythical product. But what difficulties does not this hypothesis encounter in the perfectly simple, prosaic character of the four narratives, in the mass of small historical details in which they agree, in the authenticity of even one of the writings which contain the story, and finally in the fact that the narrative, before passing into our three Synoptics, had certainly formed a part of the apostolic tradition of which they are independent redactions (see the differences of detail). A fact which was necessarily accomplished with such notoriety could become the subject of a public narrative only on condition of having actually occurred.

2. Jesus walking on the water: vv. 14–21

Vv. 14, 15. "*The people therefore, having seen the miracle*[1] *which He did,*[2] *said: This is of a truth the prophet that should come into the world.* 15. *Jesus therefore, knowing that they were about to come and take Him by force to make*

---

[1] B Θs cop.: α . . . σημεια (*the signs which*) instead of ο . . . σημειον.

[2] א B D It^{plerique} Syr^{cur} omit ο Ιησους, which T. R. and 16 Mnn. read.

Him King,[1] *withdrew*[2] *again*[3] *into the mountain Himself alone."* Here is the beginning of the crisis of which we are to see the development even to the end of the chapter. A selection among the adherents of Jesus becomes necessary to purify His work from all political alloy. Jesus had received this multitude with open arms; He had made a feast for them. It was an emblem of that feast which He was procuring for them in a higher realm. By thus giving His bread, He had symbolized that gift *of Himself* which He had just made to mankind. But instead of rising to the hope and desire of such a spiritual banquet, the Galileans occupy their thoughts only with the material miracle, and in their exalted state see in it already the inauguration of a Messianic Kingdom such as they picture to themselves. This is what is expressed by the connection of the participle *having seen*, seen with their eyes, with the verb ἔλεγον, *they said*. This exalted state, altogether carnal it is true, is the indisputable proof of what was absolutely extraordinary in that which had just now occurred. The prophet, whom the multitude thought they recognized in Jesus, had been presented in i. 21, 25, as a personage distinct from the Messiah. But it seems from our vv. 14, 15, that many regarded Him as possibly being the Messiah Himself. They imagined probably that, after having been once proclaimed by the people, He would become the Messiah. The plot of which ver. 15 speaks implies the highest degree of enthusiasm on the part of the multitude. John does not tell us how Jesus became aware of it. The word γνούς, *knowing*, is explained, according to *Weiss*, by the conversations with these people; according to *Keim*, by certain indications in their mode of action. Certainly all this is possible. But an immediate perception, like that in v. 6, is not to be denied. The participle ὁ ἐρχόμενος, *he who comes*, is the present of idea; it is an allusion to the prophecy on which the expectation of such a personage rested, Deut. xviii. 18. The term ἁρπάζειν, *to seize*, does not allow us to doubt that the plan was to get possession of Jesus, even in spite of Himself, that they might go to Jerusalem and crown Him. The task of Jesus at this moment was a difficult one. If He went away again immediately with His disciples, the commotion instead of being quieted, would be in danger of extending widely in Galilee. If He remained there with His disciples, they might be infected by the contagion of this carnal enthusiasm which would find only too much sympathy in their hearts. It might even be asked whether some one among them, Judas for example, did not secretly direct the plot (vv. 70, 71). It was necessary, therefore, to take measures speedily: First of all, Jesus bestirs Himself to send back His disciples to the other side of the sea, in order to break all immediate connection between them and the multitude. Thus is the singular expression of Matthew (xiv. 22) and Mark (vi. 45) explained: "He straightway *constrained* His disciples to enter into the boat and to go before Him to the other side, till He should send the

---

[1] ℵ reads και αναδεικνυναι βασιλεα instead of ινα ποιησ. αυτ. βασ.

[2] ℵ It^allq Syr^cur read φευγει (*flees*) instead of ανεχωρησε.

[3] Παλιν, *again*, (after ανεχωρησε) is read in T. R. with ℵ A B D K L Δ It. Vulg. Syr^cur; omitted in 10 Mjj. Syr^sch Cop.

multitudes away." This term *constrain*, which is not suggested by anything in the Synoptical narrative, is explained only by the fact which John has just related (vv. 14, 15). Perhaps most of the apostles were ignorant of the true reason of this step which was so suddenly taken by Jesus. After this, Jesus calms and dismisses the multitude, which scatters itself through the neighboring region. Matthew and Mark also say : *"And having sent the multitudes away*, He withdrew to the mountain, apart, to pray." This moment in their narrative evidently coincides with the end of our ver. 15. After this only a part of the multitude—undoubtedly, the most excited part—remained on the spot (comp. ver. 22). The reading φεύγει, *flees*, of the Sinaitic MS., which is adopted by *Tischendorf*, is absurd, especially with πάλιν, *again*. This last word which is rejected by some Byzantine MSS. is to be retained. It contains an allusion to ἀνῆλθε, *he went up* (ver. 3), which was not understood by certain copyists. We must conclude from this that Jesus had approached the shore for the repast, which is in conformity with the Synoptics : *He went forth, He received them ;* and now He returns to the heights whither He had at first gone with His disciples. Αὐτὸς μόνος, *Himself alone*, is in exact contrast to the words of ver. 3 : *with His disciples. Weiss* also places the πάλιν, *again*, in connection with ver. 3, but without holding that Jesus had *descended* for the multiplication of the loaves. The meaning would thus be : " He went up to a still higher point." He supports his view by the : *they descended* (ver. 16), which, according to him, proves that the whole preceding scene had taken place on the height. This reason is of no value (see ver. 16), and *to go up again* is not equivalent *to go up higher.*

Vv. 16–18. *" When the evening was come, his disciples went down to the seashore ; 17 and having entered into the boat, they were crossing*[1] *the sea towards Capernaum ; and it was already dark*[2] *and Jesus had not*[3] *come to them. And the sea was agitated by a strong wind."* The word *went down* does not imply that they were still on the heights where they had spent the first part of the day with Jesus, but only (see the πάλιν of ver. 15) that the place where the miracle occurred was situated above the shore properly so called. What order had Jesus given His disciples before leaving them ? According to the Synoptics, that they should embark for the other side of the sea. This is likewise implied by the narrative of John ; for the supposition is inadmissible that they would have embarked, as is related in ver. 17, leaving Jesus alone on the eastern shore, if He had not made known to them His will in this regard. They even hesitate, as we see from vv. 16, 17, to execute this command ; they wait for this until the last light of the day. But how can we explain the end of ver. 17? These last words seem to say that they were expecting Jesus, as if He had had the intention of rejoining them (a view which is rendered more probable by the reading οὔπω, *not yet*, of the Alexandrian authorities). But this would be in contradiction to the order to depart which He must have given them. It has

---

[1] ℵ ερχονται instead of ηρχοντο.
[2] ℵ D 1 Mn.: κατελαβεν δε αυτους η σκοτια instead of κ. σκοτ. ηδη εγεγ.
[3] ℵ B D L 5 Mnn. It^plerique Cop. read ουπω instead of ουκ.

been held that the words: *He had not yet rejoined them*, were written only from the standpoint of that which really happened later, when Jesus came to them miraculously on the water;—but this sense seems quite unnatural. I think it is more simple to suppose that, inasmuch as the direction from Bethsaida Julias to Capernaum is nearly parallel with that of the northern shore of the lake, Jesus had appointed for them a meeting-place at some point on that side, at the mouth of the Jordan, for example, where he counted upon joining them again. If not, it only remains to hold with *Weiss* that the pluperfects (*the night had already come; Jesus had not rejoined them*) refer, not to the moment when the disciples were already on the sea, but to that when they embarked. But it is difficult to reconcile the imperfect ἤρχοντο, literally *they were coming*, with this meaning. It would be necessary in that case to suppose that in vv. 17, 18 John wished only to bring together the different grounds of anxiety which weighed upon the disciples; the night which prevented them from making their course on the water, the absence of Jesus and the violence of the tempest. Is not this rather an expedient than an explanation?

Vv. 19–21. " *When, therefore, they had gone about five and twenty or thirty furlongs, they see Jesus walking on the sea, and drawing near to the boat, and they were afraid. 20. But he says to them: It is I, be not afraid. 21. And as they were willing*[1] *to receive him into the boat, immediately the boat reached the point of the shore where they were going.*" There was no other means by which Jesus could rejoin His disciples, before their arrival at Capernaum, but the one which He employs, ver. 19. They were now in the middle of the sea. In its broadest part, the lake of Genesareth was, as Josephus, (*Bell. Jud.*, iii., 10, 7) says, forty stadia, nearly two leagues in width. If the expression of Matthew: "in the midst of the sea," is taken as an indication of distance (which appears to me doubtful), this detail accords with John's indication: twenty-five or thirty stadia. The present *they see* indicates the suddenness of the appearance of Jesus; the emotion of fear which the disciples experience, and which is more fully set forth in the Synoptics, does not allow the words ἐπὶ τῆς θαλάσσης *on the sea*, to be explained here in the sense in which they are used in xxi. 1: *on the sea-shore*. They think that they see a spectre approaching them. Jesus' words: *It is I, be not afraid*, must have made a very profound impression on the disciples, for it is reported in the same words identically in the four narratives. The imperfect ἤθελον (literally: *they wished*), ver. 21, appears to imply that Jesus did not enter into the boat: " They *were willing* to receive Him; but immediately they found themselves at the shore." There would thus be a contradiction of Mark and Matthew, according to whom Jesus really entered the boat, in Matthew after the episode of St. Peter. Chrysostom thinks himself obliged to infer from this difference that John was here relating another event than that spoken of by Matthew and Mark. But the close relation between this miracle and the multiplication of the loaves in the three Gospels, as well as the general

---

[1] ℵ: ηλθον (*they came*) instead of ηθελον.

similarity of the three accounts, do not permit us to accept this solution. J. D. Michaelis supposed that, instead of ἤθελον, ἦλθον must be read, which would solve the difficulty: *they came;* they drew near Him with the boat to receive Him. And, a singular circumstance, the *Sinaitic* MS. presents precisely the reading which was conjectured by this scholar. But it has too much the appearance of a correction to deserve confidence. Besides, Jesus moved so freely upon the waters that the boat had no need to come near to Him. *Beza* and many exegetes after him think that the verb *were willing*, here simply adds to the act of receiving, the notion *of eagerness*, comp. Luke xx. 46; Col. ii. 18. And *Tholuck* has given greater probability to this meaning by contrasting the words *were willing*, as thus understood, with ἐφοβήθησαν, *they were afraid*: they were afraid at the first moment, but now they received him *willingly*. There is one thing opposed to this explanation: it is that John has written the imperfect, *they were wishing*, which denotes in complete action, and not the aorist, *they wished*, which would indicate an action completed (i. 44). On the other hand, there is little probability that John could have meant to say, in contradiction to the Synoptics, that Jesus did not really enter the boat, as *Meyer* thinks. In that case, must he not have said, instead of καὶ εὐθέως, *and immediately*, ἀλλ' εὐθέως, *but* immediately? The meaning of John's narrative would be indeed that the sudden arrival at the shore prevented the execution of the disciples' purpose. As to ourselves, the relation between the two clauses of ver. 21, standing thus in juxtaposition, seems to us to be similar to that which we have already observed elsewhere in John (v. 17). It is a logical relation, which we express by means of a conjunction: "*At the moment when* they were eager to receive Him, the boat came to shore." The moment of the entrance of Jesus into the boat was thus that of the arrival. The thing took place so rapidly that the disciples themselves did not understand precisely the way in which it occurred. Ver. 33 of Matt. and ver. 51 of Mark must be placed at the moment of disembarking. One can scarcely imagine, indeed, that, after an act of power so magnificent and so kingly as Jesus' walking on the waters, He should have seated Himself in the boat, and the voyage should have been laboriously continued by the stroke of the oar? At the moment when Jesus set His foot on the boat, He communicated to it, as He had just done for Peter, the force victorious over gravity and space, which had just been so strikingly displayed in His own person. The words καὶ εὐθέως, *and immediately*, compared with the distance of ten or fifteen stadia (thirty to forty-five minutes) which yet separated them from the shore, allow no other explanation.

Such is the real sovereignty which Jesus opposes to the political royalty that fleshly-minded Israel designed to lay upon Him. He gives Himself to His own as the one who reigns over a vaster domain, over all the forces of nature, and who can, one day, free Himself and free them from the burden of this mortal body. If the multiplication of the loaves was the prelude of the offering which He would make of His flesh for the nourishment of the world,—if, in this terrible night of darkness, tempest and separation, they have experienced as it were the foretaste of an approaching more sorrowful separation, in this unexpected and triumphant return across the heaving waves, Jesus, as it were, prefigured His resurrection by means of which He will be restored to them and that triumphant ascension in which He will one day give the Church itself a share, when, raising it with Himself, through the breath of His Spirit, He will bring it even to the heavenly places.

When we bear in mind that every voluntary movement which is effected by our body, every impulse which we communicate to a body which we throw into the air, is—undoubtedly not an abolishing of the law of gravitation, but—a victory which we gain momentarily over that law through the intervention of a force superior to it, namely, that of the will, we can understand that matter, being itself the work of the Divine will, remains always open to this essentially supernatural power. There is nothing therefore to prevent the Divine breath from being able, in a given condition, to free the human body for a time from the power of gravity. Reuss finds that this miracle " places Jesus outside of and above humanity," and that, if it is real, it must no longer be said that the Lord divested Himself of His divine attributes. But to be raised above the law of gravity is less than to be wrested from death. Would the resurrection of Jesus, according to Reuss, prove that He was not a man? That of Lazarus, that he was not a man? The question of the κένωσις has absolutely nothing to do with this matter.

The Discourses: vv. 22–65

This section contains, first an historical introduction (vv. 22–24), then a series of conversations and discourses (vv. 25–65).

Vv. 22–24. "*On the morrow, the multitude who stood on the other side of the sea and who had seen* [1] *that there was no other boat there but one,* [2] *that into which the disciples had entered, and that Jesus entered not* [3] *with his disciples into this boat,* [4] *but that his disciples went away* [5] *alone—23 but* [6] *there came other boats* [7] *from Tiberias near to the place where they had eaten the bread* [8] *after the Lord had given thanks—24 when the multitude therefore saw* [9] *that Jesus was not there, neither his disciples, they themselves* [10] *got into the boats,* [11] *and came to Capernaum, seeking Jesus.*"—The carnal fanaticism of the multitude had constrained Jesus to separate His disciples from them and to

---

[1] T. R. reads ιδων with Γ Δ Λ and 9 other Mjj. most Mnn. Syr^cur; A B L It^plerique Syr^sch: ειδον, and ℵ D It^aliq; ειδεν.

[2] A B L It^plerique omit the words: εκεινο εις ο ενεβησαν οι μαθηται αυτου, which are read by ℵ D Γ Δ Λ and 9 other Mjj. Mnn. Syr. (but with many variants).

[3] Instead of συνεισηλθε, ℵ reads συνεληλυθει.

[4] Alex: πλοιον instead of πλοιαριον.

[5] ℵ omits απηλθον.

[6] B D L Θ⁸ omit δε.

[7] ℵ: επελθοντων ουν των πλοιων. D b Syr^cur: αλλων πλοιαριων ελθοντων.

[8] ℵ: εκ Τιβεριαδος εγγυς ουσης οπου και εφαγον αρτον (*from Tiberias which is near the place where they had eaten bread*).

[9] ℵ και ιδοντες instead of οτε ουν ειδεν.

[10] T. R. reads και αυτοι with U Γ some Mnn.; ℵ S It^plerique Syr. omit these two words; the 13 other Mjj. and the greater part of the Mnn. read αυτοι.

[11] ℵ: εις το πλοιον instead of the plural πλοια or πλοιαρια between which the other Mjj. are divided.—The following is the translation of the entire text of ℵ: "*On the next day, the multitude which stood on the other side of the sea saw that there was no other boat there than that into which the disciples of Jesus had entered, and that Jesus went not with them into*

separate Himself from the disciples very suddenly. He had now rejoined them, and the multitude set itself to seek after Him, still in the same spirit. The long and difficult sentence, vv. 22–24, has for its aim to bring out this idea: that the sole thought which occupied the minds of this company was that of Jesus (end of ver. 24: *seeking Jesus*). By examining attentively this complicated sentence, we can soon understand its true construction. Everything starts from the condition of the multitude on the following morning (*on the morrow the multitude who stood*, ver. 22), and looks to the resolution taken by them to set out for Capernaum (*they got into the boats*, ver. 24). The cause of this resolution is stated in the two determinative expressions: ἰδών, *seeing*, ver. 22, and ὅτε οὖν εἶδεν, *when therefore they saw* (ver. 24); then, indirectly, in the parenthesis, ver. 23, designed to explain the *possibility* of this resolution taken by the multitude. In this ver. 23 we find a form analogous to that which we met in i. 10 and ii. 9. It seems that the circumlocutions which characterize this passage are a symbol of the perplexity experienced by the crowd until the moment when the arrival of the boats inspired them with a sudden resolution. The first word: *on the morrow*, has already a bearing upon the last verb of the sentence: *they got into the boats* (ver. 24). The sense of the perfect participle ὁ ἑστηκώς, *who stood there*, is this: "who had remained since the previous evening and *who were still* on the shore at that moment." It seems to me that the article ὁ before the participle must serve to limit the idea of the substantive: "the part of the crowd who . . . " They were the most persistent ones. It is very evident that the entire multitude of the preceding day, the five thousand, did not cross the sea in these few boats. —The reading εἶδον or εἶδεν, adopted by *Tischendorf* (8th ed.), and by the latest commentators (*Weiss, Keil*), has in its favor the most ancient MSS. The reading ἰδών, *having seen*, is supported by fifteen of the later Mjj. (Γ Δ Λ etc.) and by the Curetonian Syriac; it is in my view the true reading. We must give to ἰδών the sense of the pluperfect which is rendered indispensable by the two ὅτι, *that*, which follow: "On the morrow, the multitude who *had seen* that there was only one boat there and that the disciples had gone away in this boat without Jesus."—The limiting expression: *who had seen*, as well as the adverb of time: *on the morrow*, are in logical relation to the final act: *they got into the boats* (ver. 24). The aorist εἶδεν or εἶδον cannot have the sense of the pluperfect because, as a finite verb, it is necessarily determined by τῇ ἐπαύριον, *on the morrow;* but the expression: "on the morrow the multitude saw (sing. or plur.)" affords no reasonable meaning; for it was not on the day after the miracle, but on the same evening, that the crowds saw that there was only one boat there and that the disciples had entered into it without Jesus. It would be necessary therefore to translate: *had seen*, which the limiting expression *on the morrow* renders impossible. This reading cannot therefore be sustained, unless we take ἦν, *was*, in the sense of *had been*, which is much more inadmissible than our

the boat, but the disciples only; the boats having then come from Tiberias, which was near the place where they had eaten the bread after the Lord had given thanks, having seen that Jesus was not there, nor His disciples, they entered into the boat and came . . . "

sense of ἰδών. The Alexandrian reading *saw* (sing. or plur.) was quite easily introduced by the mistaken idea that the ὅτε οὖν εἶδεν, *when* [the multitude] *saw*, of ver. 24 was the resumption of that of ver. 22, after the parenthesis ver. 23 (an error which is even at the present time found in *Keil*). This, then, is the meaning, The multitude who were standing there had on the preceding evening discovered two things: 1. That there was only one boat there; 2. That the disciples had departed in this boat, and that Jesus had not gone with His disciples (the two ὅτι of ver. 22). These two facts duly discovered held them back; for it seemed to follow from them that Jesus, whom they were seeking, must still be on that side of the lake. *Consequently* (οὖν, *therefore*, ver. 24)—that is to say, by reason of the departure of Jesus during the night—when, on the next morning, they saw neither Jesus nor His disciples (who might have come back to seek Him), they took the resolution of crossing the sea, availing themselves of the boats which had arrived in the interval, to endeavor to find Jesus again on the other side. The ὅτε οὖν εἶδεν, *when therefore they saw*, of ver. 24, is not, then, by any means a resumption of ἰδών, *having seen*, ver. 22.[1] It serves to complete it, by indicating a new and even opposite sight. According to ver. 22, indeed, it seemed that Jesus must still be there; according to ver. 24, they discovered that He was no longer there. Hence the resolution to go into the boats. As to the parenthesis (ver. 23), it explains how they were able to think of doing it. The arrival of these boats has occasioned difficulties. Did they come, perhaps, because it was known on the other side that this assemblage was formed in this desert place and needed boats for their return? *Westcott* makes a very probable supposition when he supposes that it was the tempest of the night which had forced them to take refuge under the eastern shore. The words, *that whereinto His disciples had entered*, may be a gloss; yet they have in their favor the *Sinaitic* MS., and are very suitable. The particular which is so expressly brought to notice: *after that the Lord had given thanks*, and which is not demanded by the context, recalls the vivid impression which that solemn moment had produced on the spectators and the decisive importance attached by them to that act.

The ἀλλά, ver. 24, does not signify *others;* it is the adversative particle *but;* at least provided the δέ of T. R. is not authentic, in which case this ἀλλά must rather be taken as an adjective (*others*). The particle καί, *also*, before αὐτοί would mean: "they, *as well as* the disciples and Jesus Himself." This word, however, is insufficiently supported by U Γ. The αὐτοί makes their persons prominent in contrast to those who had gone away before.[2] They decided at last to do themselves what all the rest had done. The verb so long expected ἐνέβησαν, *embarked*, well brings out the final act which ended this long indecision. Thus there are described with an astonishing precision, in this long sentence, all the impressions, fluctuations, various observations of this multitude, up to the point of the decision

---

[1] One might be tempted to connect ἰδών closely with ἑστηκώς: "*which remained there because they had seen that . . . and that thus* Jesus could not have departed."

[2] We have been obliged to render it by *also*.

which brings them to Capernaum, and gives occasion to the conversations of the next day. Let one imagine a Greek writer of Alexandria or of Rome, in the second century, narrating after this fashion! Nowhere, perhaps, does the defective and arbitrary character of the Sinaitic text betray itself as it does in this passage (comp. note 11, p. 574).

Although the idea which is predominant in the discourses, vv. 25–65, appears to be the same as that of chap. v., namely, that of *life*, there is a difference between the teachings contained in these two chapters, which corresponds to that of the two miracles, the application of which they contain. In the healing of the impotent man, it is Jesus who acts; the sick man is receptive. In the repast in chap. vi., the food is simply offered by Jesus; if nutrition is to be accomplished, man must act in order to assimilate it. This is the reason why, while in the discourse of chap. v. it is the *person of Jesus* that comes forward, in the conversations of chap. vi., it is rather the idea of *faith* which predominates. Without finding it necessary, as *Baur* does, to explain the composition of our Gospel by a systematic process, we may yet hold that John, in gathering up his recollections, was struck by the correlation between these two testimonies, which makes one the complement of the other, and that he designedly brought them together as presenting the complete description of the relation between divine and human agency in salvation.

Four phases can be distinguished in this conversation, determined in each instance by a manifestation of a portion of the hearers. The first (vv. 25–40) is brought on by a *question* of the Jews (εἶπον αὐτῷ, *they said to him*). The second (vv. 41–51) results from a serious *dissatisfaction* which manifests itself (ἐγόγγυζον, *they murmured*). The third (vv. 52–59) is marked by an *altercation* which arises among the hearers themselves (ἐμάχοντο, *they strove among themselves*). The last (vv. 60–65) is called forth by a *declaration* of the larger part of the earlier Galilean believers, who announce to Jesus their rupture with Him.—Did all these conversations take place in the synagogue? This has little probability. Ver. 25 would not lead us to suppose it. The remark of ver. 59 may be referred to the last phases only.

1. Vv. 25–40

This first phase is made up of four brief dialogues, each including a question of the Jews and an answer of Jesus. The last of these answers is more fully developed; Jesus expresses in it, with restrained emotion, the impressions with which the condition of His hearers filled His soul.

1. Vv. 25–27. The contrast between the food which perishes and that which abides.

Vv. 25, 26. "*And having found him on the other side of the sea, they said unto him: Rabbi, when camest thou*[1] *hither?* 26. *Jesus answered them and said: Verily, verily, I say unto you, You seek*[2] *me, not because you saw signs,*[3]

---

[1] Instead of γεγονας, ℵ reads ηλθες, D εληλυθας.
[2] ℵ omits ζητειτε με (*you seek me*).
[3] D It^{pliq} add και τερατα (derived from iv. 48).

but because you did eat of those loaves and were filled."—We have seen that the motive for the action of the multitude was the seeking for Jesus; this is recalled to mind by the first words of this passage: *"And having found him."* The question: *when* (not: how) *camest thou?* arises from the fact that they think it impossible that Jesus had made the journey on foot over the road which separates Bethsaida Julias from Capernaum (two to three leagues). The presence of Jesus produces on them the effect of an apparition. He replies, as on every occasion when He is questioned in the way of curiosity, not to the question of the interlocutor, but to the feeling which dictates it. Comp. ii. 4; iii. 3, etc. He unveils to these Jews what is false and fleshly in their way of seeking Him. As there is here a revelation of their inward feelings, of which they were themselves unconscious, He uses the emphatic affirmation, *amen, amen.* Jesus contrasts here with the false and vain seeking after His person, which aims only at the satisfaction of the earthly man (ver. 26), that salutary seeking which tends to fill the wants of the spiritual man (ver. 27). His miracles were the visible signs of the blessings of salvation which He brings to mankind. It will be necessary, therefore, not to rest in the material relief which they procure; it will be necessary to rise by their means to the desire of the superior gifts of which they are the pledge and the image; it will be necessary, before and above all, to believe on Him whom God points out to the world by giving to Him to do such works. We see how necessary it is to avoid translating the word σημεῖα, *signs*, here by *miracles* (*Ostervald, Arnaud, Rilliet*). It is precisely on the meaning *signs* that the whole force of this saying depends. The multitudes interpreted the multiplication of the loaves as the beginning of a series of wonders *of the same nature*, the inauguration of an era of miracles more and more brilliant and satisfying to the flesh. "Instead of seeing," as *Lange* says, "in the bread the sign, they had seen in the sign only the bread." This gross want of understanding is what gives to their search for Jesus a false, earthly, sensual, animal character. This tendency it is which Jesus points out to them from the very first word of the conversation, and particularly by the expression which betrays a sort of disgust: *and because you were filled.* What a difference between these people, who come with their gross aspirations, their earthly appetites, and the spiritual Israel which the Old Testament was intended to prepare and which cries out: "My soul thirsts after thee, oh living God!" This Israel would say to Him who multiplied the loaves: Give us more still! Do to-day for our hearts what thou didst yesterday for our bodies! The plural, *signs*, refers either to the two miracles related in the former part of the chapter, or rather to the miracles in general, which had been no better understood by the multitudes than the one of multiplying the loaves. We have rendered the article τῶν before ἄρτων by the demonstrative pronoun: "*those* loaves," because the word *the* contains an evident allusion to the loaves of the preceding day.

Ver. 27. *"Work to obtain, not the food*[1] *which perishes, but the food which*

---

[1] places μη after the first βρωσιν and with some Mjj. rejects the second βρωσιν.

endures to eternal life, that which the Son of man shall give[1] *unto you; for him hath the Father, God, sealed."*—Behold now the *true* way in which Jesus would be sought. It follows, indeed, from the contrast between ἐργάζεσθε, *work*, and ζητεῖτε, *you seek me* (ver. 26), that the work to which He exhorts His hearers is none other than the seeking for His person with a spiritual aim. The repast of the preceding evening had sustained them for that day. But, when the morning came, were they not obliged to eat again? That bread, miraculous as it was, had, thus, been only a temporary nourishment. What purpose would the renewal of a similar gift on this day have served? To this transient food Jesus opposes that which abides inherent in the human person as a permanent principle of life and action. The term ἐργάζεσθαι, *to work*, signifies here: *to obtain by one's labor* (see the examples drawn from classical Greek, in *Meyer*).—The words: *unto eternal life*, designate either the *effect* immediately produced (*Reuss*) or the final limit (*even to*); see at iv. 14. The future, *shall give*, is certainly the true reading; it is designed to raise the minds of the hearers to the nourishment of a higher nature which Jesus brings to the world, and of which the multiplied loaves were only the type and promise. This notion of *giving* seems at the first glance in contradiction to the order to *work* (ἐργάζεσθε). But the work by which man procures for himself this truly life-giving food does not consist in creating it, but in making himself fit to receive it, by believing on the divine messenger who brings it to him. The human *work* would remain useless, without the divine *gift*, as, also the divine gift remains inefficacious without the internal work by means of which the man appropriates it to himself. The name *Son of man* is also in connection with the thought developed afterwards, that Jesus is *Himself* this celestial food; for if it is placed within the reach of faith, it is by virtue of the incarnation (vv. 33, 38, 50, 58). The *for* relates to the word *will give*. Jesus is *sealed*, that is, personally pointed out to the world by His miracles in general, and more particularly by that of the preceding day, as the one who brings this life-giving bread to the earth and who gives it. This is the explanation, given by Jesus Himself, of the term *signs*. His miracles are the authentic *signs* of the salvation with which He is intrusted, in its different aspects. The word ὁ θεός, *God*, is placed at the end of the sentence to set forth distinctly the person of Him who, as possessor of supreme authority, has alone the power and the right to give such certifications.

The first dialogue has contrasted and characterized in an altogether general way the two kinds of good which may be sought from Jesus.

2. Vv. 28, 29. The brief dialogue which follows bears upon the true *means* of obtaining this really desirable good, the food which abides; it is the true mode of ἐργάζεσθαι (*working*).

Vv. 28, 29. *" They said therefore*[2] *to Him: What must we do,*[3] *to do the works of God? 29. Jesus answered and said to them: This is the work of God, that you believe*[4] *on Him whom He has sent."* As Jesus had said: " Labor

---

[1] ℵ D It^{aliq} read διδωσιν υμιν (*gives you*) instead of υμιν δωσει.

[2] A Syr. omit ουν (*therefore*).

[3] ζ, with some Mnn. only: ποιουμεν (*do*).

[4] ℵ A B L T: πιστευητε instead of πιστευσητε.

(literally, *work*)," the hearers, believing that they entered into His thought, ask Him: How work? In what do these works to be done for obtaining the food which Thou offerest consist? They call them the *works of God*, as being demanded by God as the condition of this gift. They start herein from the legal point of view, and see in these works to be done a work for which the miraculous food is the payment. It is impossible for me to see that there can be anything "grotesque" or improbable in this answer of the Jews (*Reuss*). It corresponds with many questions of the same kind in the Synoptics. (Matt. xix. 16; Luke x. 25, etc.) Jesus, in His turn, enters into this idea of works to be done; only He reduces them all to a single one: *the work*, in contrast to *the works* (ver. 28). This work is faith in Him; in other terms: the gift of God is to be, not deserved, but simply accepted. Faith in Him whom God sends to communicate it is the sole condition for receiving it. It is evident that, in this context, the genitive τοῦ θεοῦ, *of God*, designates, not the *author* of the work (*Augustine*), but the one with reference to whom it is done: the question is of the work which God *requires*. What is called Paulinism is implied in this answer, which may be called the point of union between Paul and James. *Faith* is really a work, *the* highest *work*, for by it man gives himself, and a free being cannot *do* anything greater than to give himself. It is in this sense that James opposes *work* to a faith which is only a dead intellectual belief; as it is in an analogous sense, that St. Paul opposes *faith* to works of mere observance. The living faith of Paul is, at the foundation, the living work of James, according to that sovereign formula of Jesus: "*This is the work of God, that ye believe.*" With the discussion of the true human work which leads to the possession of the heavenly gift is connected a new one on the *way* to the attaining of faith. The Jews think that in order to this end, there is need for them of new miracles. Jesus declares to them that the true sign is present; it is Himself.

3. Vv. 30–33. The way to reach faith.

Vv. 30, 31. "*Then they said to Him: What sign doest thou then, that we may see, and believe in thee? What work dost thou do? 31. Our fathers ate the manna in the wilderness, according as it is written: He gave them bread from heaven to eat.*" It is difficult to imagine these words on the lips of people who had been present the day before at the multiplying of the loaves. *B. Bauer* saw herein a proof of the non-authenticity of the narrative. *Schweizer* concluded from it that the whole preceding passage was interpolated. *Grotius* and others think that these interlocutors who speak thus had not been present at the scene of the preceding day. *De Wette* and *Weiss* suppose that this part of the conversation is located here out of its true place. *Lücke, Luthardt, Meyer* find here the proof of the psychological truth that the natural man is insatiable in respect to wonders. *Riggenbach*, and up to a certain point *Weiss*, recall the scarcely apparent way in which the multiplying of the loaves had been accomplished. The creative operation had not been seen. Others think that Jesus' hearers contrast this quite ordinary common bread which Jesus had given them with the manna, manifestly falling every morning *from heaven*, which Moses gave to their fathers, and that they find the first of these miracles far inferior to the second. But, however true these remarks may be, it must be confessed that they do not yet explain such questions as these: "What sign doest Thou? What workest Thou?" addressed to a man who had just done such a miracle and presented by people who had, the day before, wished to proclaim Him King. It is necessary, I think, to take account of a circumstance strongly brought out by *Weiss* and *Keil:* the dissatisfaction felt by this multitude in consequence of the absolute refusal of Jesus to consent to the great Messianic demonstration which they had planned. And, strange fact! while refusing to be proclaimed King and Messiah, He yet claimed to be recognized as the supreme messenger of God, as the object of faith, of a faith which dispensed with all the works prescribed by the law and even with every work; as the one who brought from heaven to men an imperishable life. Was the miracle wrought on the level with such pretensions? No, it did not even raise Jesus to the height of Moses, above whom He seemed nevertheless to place Himself by arrogating such a part to Himself! It is not therefore altogether without reason that they bring out the contrast between the scarcely apparent miracle of the day before and the magnificent display of power of which Moses had been the instrument before the people during forty years. *Redemptor prior descendere fecit pro iis manna; sic et Redemptor posterior descendere facietmanna,* said the Rabbis (see *Lightfoot* and *Wetstein*). This, at least, is what would have been expected of Him to justify pretensions such as His! The words quoted by the Jews are found in Ps. lxxviii. 24, 25. Comp. Exod. xvi. 4, 15. The verb *has given* has for its subject *God*. The expression *"from heaven"* denotes, in their mouth, only the miraculous *origin* of the divine gift, while Jesus, in His answer, thinks above all of its *essence:*

Vv. 32, 33. "*Jesus therefore said to them: Verily, verily, I say unto you: Moses did not give*[1] *you the bread from heaven; but my Father gives you the bread from heaven, the true bread; 33 for the bread of God is that which comes down from heaven, and gives life to the world.*" Until this point, the thought of the auditors seemed to move in accord with that of Jesus, but this was due to an ambiguity: Jesus made announcement of a bread of a higher nature, and the Jews accepted the offer willingly, but on the condition that this food should be not only miraculous in its origin, but also of a material nature, like the manna, an ambrosia falling from heaven. Jesus now gives an explanation which brings to light the opposition between His thought and theirs. The formula *amen, amen* foreshadows this contrast in the two points of view. The perfect δέδωκεν must be preferred to the aorist, which seems to have been introduced from ver. 31. The sense of the perfect is this: "The gift of the heavenly bread is not a thing which Moses accomplished for your fathers and yourselves." The predominant contrast is not that of the two objects (*Keil*), but that of the two

---

[1] Instead of δεδωκεν which is read by 15 Mjj. (among them ℵ) almost all the Mnn. and Orig., εδωκεν is read by B D L.

subjects. If they are in possession of the true bread from heaven, it is not by the act of Moses, it is by the gift of the Father who sends it to them at this very moment. This is what is indicated by the present δίδωσι, *gives*, which already affords a suggestion of what Jesus is about to say, namely, that it is God who makes this gift in His person. The word τὸν ἀληθινόν, *the true*, is added at the end of the sentence in order to place the spiritual, divine *essence* of this bread in contrast with such a gift as that of the manna, which, although miraculous in its origin, was material in its nature. The limiting words *from heaven* belong here and in the following verse, not to the verb *has given* (in opposition to Meyer)—but as in Ps. lxxviii. 24, to the substantive *bread*. The position of this limiting word in the Greek indicates this, and it is on the idea of *bread from heaven* that the discussion turns.

Ver. 33 applies this idea of true *bread from heaven*, to Jesus, but for the moment in obscure words. The difficulty of this verse is that the words *descending from heaven*, which are the paraphrase of the term *bread from heaven*, should be logically joined to the subject which is to be defined, and not to the attribute which contains the definition. It seems that it should be: "For the true *bread from heaven* is that which descends *from God*, from God Himself." I formerly tried to resolve this difficulty by applying the participle ὁ καταβαίνων, the *descending*, not to the bread, but to Jesus himself: "He who descends." *Meyer* and *Weiss* object that in that case ὁ καταβάς, "He who descended," would be necessary. Ver. 50 answers this objection. Nevertheless, I acknowledge that the ellipsis of ὁ ἄρτος (*the bread*) is more natural, although the idea of *descending* applies more easily to a person than to a thing (comp. ver. 38). *Weiss* himself has recourse to a very far-fetched explanation: it is to make ὁ ἄρτος τοῦ θεοῦ, *the bread of God*, the predicate of the two following participles: "The bread which descends from heaven and gives life to the world, is that which is the true bread of God." What seems more simple is to understand with *Keil:* "For the bread which God Himself gives (ver. 32) is the only bread which truly descends from heaven and can give life." Jesus thus opposes the true heaven, that is, the glorious life of God, to the local heaven from which, according to the opinion of His hearers, the manna descended. The expression τῷ κόσμῳ, *to the world*, is opposed to the theocratic particularism which boasted itself especially in the great national miracle —that of the manna. The greatness of the heavenly gift, as Jesus presents it here, no longer allows a national and particular destination. In proportion as Jesus sees the people refusing to follow Him in the spiritual sphere into which He wished to elevate them, He is led to turn his eyes towards mankind for whom He has come. The fourth part of the conversation (vv. 34–40) reveals completely the rupture which has just taken place between the thought of the people and that of Jesus.

4. Vv. 34–40. The two classes of hearers, the unbelievers and the believers.

Vv. 34, 35. "*They said therefore to Him: Lord, evermore give us this bread.*

35. *But*[1] *Jesus said to them: I am the bread of life; he that comes to me shall never hunger,*[2] *and he that believes on me shall never thirst."*[2] The Jews, still regarding the heavenly bread as a wonderful, but material food, declare themselves ready to follow Jesus always, if He will procure for them this food; and that daily. The *evermore* undoubtedly alludes to the gift of the manna which was renewed every morning. *This bread:* this food far higher than the manna itself. Here is the highest point of their carnal exaltation. But it is also the moment when Jesus breaks with them decidedly. Up to this moment, the questions and answers were directly connected with each other, and the particle οὖν, *therefore,* had indicated continuous progress. But the particle δέ of ver. 35, which seems to me to be the true reading, marks a sudden change in the course of the conversation; the ἀλλά, *but,* of ver. 36 will mark the complete rupture.

The words: "*I am* . . . ," are the categorical answer to the: *Give us,* of the Jews: "What you ask is accomplished: this bread is Myself. It only remains to feed on it; and the means for this end is simply to come to me with a soul which hungers and thirsts for salvation." Jesus finally explains His expression in ver. 27. *The food which endures* of which He there speaks is Himself; the work to be done in order to obtain it is faith in Him. The expression *bread of life* can signify: the bread which communicates life, but perhaps the relation between these two notions of bread and life is still closer. The true life, which is in God Himself, "*the eternal life which was in the beginning with the Father*" (1 John i. 2), was incarnated in this visible being; it became in Him capable of being laid hold of, touched, tasted. But in order that this food may give us life, there must be action on our part: *coming* and *believing.* These two terms are not exactly synonymous: the first denotes the act of approaching Christ with the seriousness of a heart with a sense of sin; the second, the confiding eagerness with which this famished heart takes possession of the heavenly food in Him. The force of the negative οὐ μή can be rendered by: *It is not to be feared that* ever . . . The οὐ πώποτε, *never,* is the answer to the πάντοτε, *evermore,* of ver. 34. The parallelism of the two clauses betrays a certain exaltation of feeling produced by the greatness of the fact declared. The figure of *drinking* does not properly suit the context: it is added to that of *eating,* perhaps because Jesus is thinking of the Passover supper. In the sequel of the discourse, we shall see that these two figurative expressions take each of them a meaning continually more distinct (vv. 53–57). And even here they are not absolutely identical. Hunger represents rather the feeling of weakness, of moral powerlessness; thirst, that of the sufferings of the conscience and the heart. Taken together, they express the deep uneasiness which drives the sinner to Jesus Christ. The appeasing of the thirst therefore refers rather to the peace; that of the hunger, to the new strength which the believer receives.

---

[1] Instead of δε which A Δ Λ and 11 Mjj. read, ουν is read in ℵ D Γ some Mnn. Sah.; B L T Ital\|q Syr. omit δε and ουν.

[2] The MSS. read πειναση or—σει, διψηση or —σει.

Coming, believing: these, then, are the conditions. But, adds Jesus with grief, it is precisely these conditions which are wanting in you.

Ver. 36. "*But I said unto you: you have seen me,*[1] *and yet you do not believe.*" They had asked to *see* in order to believe (ver. 30). But this condition was long since fulfilled: they have seen Him in all His greatness and goodness, as much as was necessary to believe, and yet the effect is not produced: *you do not believe.* Jesus has the right to draw this conclusion even from their request. No doubt they had faith enough to ask Him for the miraculous bread, but not to recognize Himself as the heavenly bread. This proves that they are still strangers to the spiritual needs which might lead them to Him, and to the work which He came to accomplish here on earth. This is what is signified to an ear as sensitive as that of Jesus by the prayer: "*Give us,*" while they already possess Him Himself. In this way they end by revealing their moral stupidity. Comp. two equally rapid and decisive judgments, the one at Jerusalem (ii. 19), the other at Nazareth (Luke iv. 23).

To what earlier saying does Jesus allude in the expression: "*I said unto you?*" The words in iv. 48 may be thought of, in which the relation between the two ideas of *seeing and believing* is altogether different. The declaration of v. 37, of which *de Wette, Lücke,* and *Reuss,* think, has also a very different meaning, and besides it was uttered in Judea. There is nothing here which troubles *Reuss.* On the contrary, in his view this only proves more evidently this fact: "That in the mind of the redactor all these discourses are addressed to one and the same public, the readers of the book." In order that this conclusion should be well founded, it would be necessary that no other more exact reference should present itself. Others suppose that Jesus cites a saying which John has not mentioned; but, in that case, to what purpose recall it expressly by the formula of quotation: *I said to you? Meyer* proposes to translate εἶπον ὑμῖν by: *dictum velim,* "regard it as said." This sense is unexampled in the New Testament. *Brückner* thinks that Jesus is calling to mind His whole teaching in general. But this expression indicates a positive citation. Jesus quotes Himself here, as He often quotes the Old Testament according to the spirit rather than according to the letter. On the arrival of the multitude, He had said to them: "*You have seen signs,* and yet you seek Me only for the renewal of material satisfaction and not because of Myself." It is this charge of ver. 26 which He repeats here in a little different form. "*You have seen Me,*" corresponds with: "*you have seen signs;*" and "*you do not believe,*" with "*you seek Me* only for the sake of the flesh and not that your soul may be satisfied." To say to Him: "*Give us,*" when one has Him as present—was not this to refuse to believe in Him as the true gift of God? The reading of the *Sinaitic* and *Alexandrian* MSS.: *you have seen* (without με, *me*), undoubtedly sets forth better the contrast between *seeing* and *believing.* The Alexandrian MS. itself, however, replaces the pronoun after πιστεύετε (μοι), and in the entire context it is the

---

[1] ℵ A Italiq Syrcur omit με.

person of Jesus which plays the chief part. The two καί . . . καί (*and . . . and*), are untranslatable: they forcibly bring out the moral contrast between the two facts which they so closely bring together.

Between this word of condemnation and the calm and solemn declaration of the following verses (37–40), there is a significant *asyndeton*. This omission of any connecting particle indicates a moment of silence and profound meditation. Jesus had received a signal from His Father; in the joy of His heart, He had given a feast to all this people; He had made for them a miraculous Passover. And these dull hearts have not understood it at all. They ask again for bread, the earth still and nothing but the earth, while He had desired, by means of this figurative repast, to offer them *life*, to open to them heaven! In the presence of this failure, which for Him is the prelude of the grand national catastrophe, the rejection of the Messiah, Jesus communes with Himself; then He continues: "It is in vain that you do not believe! My work remains, nevertheless, the Father's work; it will be accomplished without you since it must be; and in the fact of your exclusion nothing can be laid to my charge; for I limit myself to fulfilling in a docile way, at each moment, the instructions of my Father!" Thus the painful check which He has just experienced does not shake His faith, He rises to the contemplation of the assured success of His work in the hearts which His Father will give Him; and by protesting His perfect submissiveness to the plan of the Father, He lays upon the unbelievers themselves the blame of their rejection, and thus addresses to their consciences the last appeal.

Vv. 37, 38. "*All that which the Father gives me shall come unto me; and him who comes to me I will in no wise cast out;*[1] 38 *for I am come down from heaven*[2] *to do,*[3] *not my own will, but the will of him who sent me.*"[4] By the words: *All that which the Father gives me*, Jesus strongly contrasts the believers of all times with these men to whom He had just said: You do not believe! The neuter πᾶν ὅ, *all that which*, indicates a definite whole in which human unbelief will be unable to make any breach, a whole which will appear complete at the end of the work. The extent of this πᾶν, *all*, depends on an act of the Father designated here by the term *give*, and later by *teach* and *draw* (vv. 44, 45). The first of these three terms does not, any more than the other two, refer to the eternal decree of election; there would rather be, in that case, the perfect *has given*. Jesus speaks of a divine action exerted in the heart of the believers at the moment when they give themselves to Him. This action is opposed not to human freedom, but to a purely carnal attraction, to the gross Messianic aspirations, which had, on this very morning, drawn these crowds to Jesus (ver. 26). It is that hunger and thirst after righteousness (Matt. v. 6) which the preparatory action of the Father produces in sincere souls. Every time that Jesus sees such a soul coming to Him, He receives it as as a gift of God, and His success with it is certain. I do not think that it is neces-

---

[1] א D It^{aliq} Syr^{cur} omit εξω.

[2] A B L T some Mnn. read απο τ. ουρ., instead of εκ τ. ουρ.

[3] א D L: ποιησω, instead of ποιω.

[4] א C omit from του πεμψ. με ver. 38 to του πεμψ με ver. 39.

sary to translate ἥξει (*shall reach*), as if it were ἐλεύσεται (*shall come, advance towards*); for ἥκω signifies: "I am come and am here;" comp. viii. 42 and Apoc. iii. 3, xv. 4, where the substitution of ἔρχεσθαι (*to come*) for ἥκειν would certainly weaken the thought. Jesus means to say, not only that all those whom the Father gives Him will advance towards Him, will believe, but will reach the end. It will not happen to them, as to the present hearers of Jesus, to be shipwrecked on the way. The second part of the verse is *parallel* with the first. Commonly, an *advance* on the first is found here, by making the first words: *He that cometh to me*, the resumption of the last words of the preceding clause: *shall come to me*. (See *Meyer, Weiss*, etc.) But two things seem to me to exclude this interpretation: 1. The substitution in this second sentence of ἔρχεσθαι for ἥκειν, which would be a weakening, since the former says less than the latter; 2. The parallelism of the two present tenses (δίδωσι, *gives*, and τὸν ἐρχόμενον *him that comes*), and that of the two futures (ἥξει, *will reach*, and ἐκβάλω, *will cast out*). *He that comes to me* answers therefore to: *All that which the Father gives me*; they are the two sides, divine and human, of the inward preparation for salvation. Then: *shall come to me* answers to: *I will not cast out*; it is the accomplishment of the salvation itself in the positive and negative relation. Jesus seems to allude by this last term, *to cast out*, to the stern manner in which He had received this multitude which were so eager to come to Him, and had repelled them with a sort of harshness (vv. 26, 36). He received them thus only because He did not recognize in them gifts of the Father; for never will any heart burdened with spiritual wants and coming to Him under this divine impulse be rejected by Him. These words recall those of the Synoptics: "*Come unto me all ye that labor and are heavy laden, and I will give you rest*" (Matt. xi. 28). The second clause has, therefore, fundamentally the same sense as the first; but it completes it, first by individualizing the πᾶν, *all*, of the first clause (*he that*), then by substituting the negative form, which excludes every exception (*I will not cast out*) to the simple affirmation (*shall come*). The certainty of this welcome full of love promised to believers is justified in ver. 38 by the complete dependence in which Jesus placed Himself with relation to the Father, when coming here on earth. Having renounced every work of His own, He can only receive whoever draws near marked with the seal of the Father. The term καταβέβηκα, *I am come down*, contains the affirmation of His pre-existence. On the expression "*my own* will," see at ver. 30. If Jesus had wished to accomplish here below a work *for Himself*, distinct from that of the Father, His reception or His refusals would have been determined, at least in part, by personal sympathies or repugnances, and would not have altogether coincided with the preparation due to the work of God in the souls. But, as there is nothing of this, and as He has no will except to make that of His Father at each moment His own, it follows that whoever comes to Him as one commended by the Father, is sure to be welcomed by Him; comp. the same idea of voluntary dependence in the discourse of chap. v.

Ver. 39. "*Now this is the will of him who sent me,*[1] *that I should lose nothing of all that which he has given me, but that I should raise it*[2] *up at the last day.*"[3] The δέ is progressive: *now*. The will of the Father is not only that Jesus should receive, but also that He should *keep* those whom He gives to Him. And He has clothed Him, indeed, with the necessary powers to save His own, even to the end. He is charged of God with leading them to the glorious end of salvation and even with delivering them from death. Πᾶν, *all*, nominative absolute: put afterwards in its regular case in the pronoun αὐτοῦ. Was Jesus thinking perchance of the bread, also a gift of God, of which no fragment should be lost (ver. 12), and in comparison with which the gift of God of which He here speaks is infinitely more precious? —The object of the verb is a τι understood.—The perfect *has given* transports us to a more advanced time than ver. 37 (*gives*). The gift is now *realized* by the faith of the man, on the one side, and the welcome of Jesus on the other. But the end is not yet attained by this. It is necessary first to prevent the believer from falling back into the state of sin which would destroy him again, then to free him at the last day from physical death to the end of presenting him glorious before the face of the Father. We find here again the two-fold action which Jesus described in v. 21–29: the communication of the new spiritual life and thereby the gift of the resurrection of the body, which alone exhausts the meaning of the expression: *bread of life*. *Reuss* wished to apply the term *the last day* to the time of the death of each believer. But the passage v. 29 proves that Jesus is thinking, not of a particular phase of each individual existence, but of the solemn hour when all the dead, laid *in the tombs*, shall hear His voice and shall have a bodily resurrection. *Reuss* objects that "mystical theology has nothing to do with this notion." This only proves one thing: that "the mystical theology" which Reuss attributes to John is very different from that of the apostle. If this notion had so little importance to the author's mind, how is it that it reappears even four times in this passage and forms, as it were, its refrain (vv. 39, 40, 44, 54)? It is beyond all dispute that the bodily resurrection is presented in this passage, as well as in the discourse of chap. v., as the necessary crowning of the spiritual work accomplished by Christ in humanity. On this point, John is in accord with the Synoptics and with Paul (1 Cor. xv.). *Bengel* observes on these last words: *Hic finis est ultra quem periculum nullum*. On the inadmissibility of grace, see on x. 28–30. In closing this first part of the conversation, Jesus again insists on the human condition of faith which must correspond with His own work, for it was this which was wanting to His interlocutors.

Ver. 40. "*For*[4] *this is the will of my Father,*[5] *that whosoever beholds the Son*

---

[1] A B D L T 10 Mnn. It^{aliq} Syr. omit πατρος (*of the Father*).

[2] The MSS. are divided between αυτο (ℵ A B C etc.) and αυτον (E G H etc.).

[3] 12 Mjj. (B C etc.) reject εν.

[4] The MSS. are divided between γαρ *for*, (ℵ A B C D K L U Π 30 Mnn. It. Syr. Cop.) and δε which is read by T. R. with the 8 other Mjj.

[5] T. R. with 10 Mjj. (A E etc.): του πεμψαντος με (*of him who sent me*): ℵ B C D etc. του πατρος μου (*of my Father*); M Δ: του πεμψαντος με πατρος (*of the Father who sent me*).

588 / Unbelief Develops in Israel

and believes on him has eternal life, and I [1] *will raise him up at the last day."* [2] This verse reproduces, either by confirming it (*for,* according to the Alexandrian authorities and the ancient versions), or by completing it (*now,* according to the Byzantine authorities), the thought of ver. 39. The principal difference is that in ver. 40 Jesus sets forth by the side of the gift which the Father makes in the person of the Son, the subjective act of the man who beholds and believes. In this expression is the decisive point. The two present participles, θεωρῶν καὶ πιστεύων, *who beholds and believes,* indicate the rapid succession of the two acts: "He who gives himself up to the contemplation and in whom it is immediately changed into faith." This is the intentional antithesis of ver. 36: "*You have seen me, and you do not believe.*" The commission which the Father has given to Jesus is not to save all men indiscriminately. His work is to offer Himself to the sight of all, and, where the sight becomes contemplation and contemplation becomes faith, there to save. The Alexandrian reading: *of my Father,* is more in harmony with the term *Son.* On the other hand, the received reading: *of him that sent me,* accords better with the words: *he that beholds*: "He has sent me that I might offer myself for contemplation." The term θεωρεῖν, *to behold,* indicates a more reflective act than the simple ὁρᾶν, *to see,* of ver. 36. He only *beholds* who has been sufficiently struck by the mere sight to pause before the object with emotion. Jesus substitutes here the masculine πᾶς for the neuter πᾶν (ver. 39), of which He had made use, because faith is an individual act. The history of Jesus' ministry in the Synoptics is the commentary on this verse. Is it not by this sign, faith, that He recognizes those whom He can receive and save? Luke v. 20: "*Seeing their faith, he said, Man, thy sins are forgiven thee.*" He does not Himself know either the individuals or the number of persons of whom the whole *gift* (τὸ πᾶν) which the Father bestows upon Him will be composed; God, in sending Him, has given to Him only this watchword: *Whosoever believeth.* The two ἀναστήσω, in vv. 39, 40, may be made subjunctive aorists depending on ἵνα: "and that I may raise it up." It is certainly so, in my view, with that of ver. 39; but perhaps we must detach that of ver. 40 from the preceding and see in it a future indicative. "And this done, I charge myself with raising him at the last day, without any possibility that anything should be able to prevent the accomplishment of this last work." The pronoun με, *me,* especially placed as it is, seems to me to be better explained in this way.

In the presence of Jewish unbelief, Jesus has strengthened Himself anew by the assurance of the success of His work. He has explained the severity of His conduct towards the Jews: God has said: "He who sees and believes; and as for them, they have seen and have not believed." There was here a serious charge against his hearers. Far from accepting it, they endeavor to throw it back upon Him.

---

[1] A D some Mnn. omit εγω.

[2] ℵ A D K L S U II read εν which T R omits with 11 Mjj.

2. Vv. 41-51

A murmur which rises in the assembly (vv. 41, 42) forces Jesus to declare to the Jews distinctly their incompetency in this matter (vv. 43-46); after which, with an increasing solemnity, He again affirms Himself to be the bread of life (vv. 47-51); and this while adding in the last words (ver. 51 b) a striking, defining phrase, which becomes the occasion of a new phase of the conversation.

Vv. 41, 42. "*The Jews therefore murmured concerning him, because he said: I am the bread which came down from heaven. 42. And they said: Is not this Jesus, the son of Joseph, whose father and mother*[1] *we ourselves know? How then*[2] *does he say:*[3] *I came down from heaven?*" The term: *murmured*, must denote an unfavorable whispering which made itself heard in the circle of hearers. The objective words περὶ αὐτοῦ, *concerning Him*, are explained by the following words: The term Ἰουδαῖοι, *the Jews*, might refer to the emissaries of the Sanhedrim, who, according to the Synoptics, had come from Judea to watch the words and actions of Jesus in Galilee. But the following words: *we know*, are more easily explained in the mouths of the Galileans themselves. John applies to them here this title, which is customary in his Gospel (Introduction, p. 128), because of the community in unbelief which, from this time, unites them with the mass of the Jewish nation which persists in remaining Jewish and refuses to become believing. It is impossible for them to recognize a heavenly being, who has become incarnate, in Him with whose human filiation they are perfectly acquainted. The pronoun ἡμεῖς, *we*, does not necessarily indicate a personal acquaintance, from which it might be inferred that Joseph was still living. This expression may signify: "We know *the name* of his parents." Νῦν, *now*, may be read with some Alexandrian documents, instead of οὖν, *therefore*: it means: *in this state of things*. Criticism has asked how the people could be ignorant of the miraculous birth of Jesus, if this were a real fact, and why Jesus did not notice this point in His reply. But Jesus' birth had taken place in Judea; thirty years separated it from the period in which we now find ourselves. During the long obscurity which had enveloped the childhood and youth of Jesus, all had passed into oblivion, and that, probably, even in the places where the facts had occurred; how much more in Galilee, where the mass of the people had always been ignorant of them. Assuredly, neither the parents of Jesus, nor Jesus Himself could make allusion to them in public; this would have been to expose the most sacred mystery of family history to a profane, and, in addition to this, useless discussion. For the miraculous origin of Jesus is not a means of producing faith; it can be accepted only by the heart already believing. As *Weiss* says: "It is not really these scruples which are the cause of their unbelief. And this is the reason why Jesus does not stop to refute them." Instead, therefore, of descending

---

[1] ℵ adds καὶ before τὸν πατέρα and with b Syr^{cur} omits καὶ τὴν μητέρα.

[2] B C T Cop. read νῦν instead of οὖν.

[3] B C D L T a Cop. omit οὗτος.

590 / Unbelief Develops in Israel

to this ground, Jesus remains in the moral sphere, and discovers to the Galileans, as He had done to the inhabitants of Jerusalem, chap. v., the true cause of their unbelief.

Vv. 43, 44. "*Jesus therefore*[1] *answered and said to them: Murmur not among yourselves: 44. No one can come to me except the Father who sent me draw him; and I will raise him up at the last day.*"[2] In other words: "A truce to these murmurs; it is not my word that is absurd; it is you who are incapable of comprehending it, and all your "*hows*" will serve no purpose, so long as you remain in this moral condition." Jesus goes back again to the source of their discontent; the spiritual drawing which results from the inward teaching of God is wanting to them. This is what vv. 37–40 already made known to us. The word οὐδείς, *no one*, is the antithesis of πᾶν, *all*, ver. 37. There, Jesus said: all that which is given shall certainly come: here, nothing which is not drawn shall succeed in understanding and believing. This second declaration has a direct application to the hearers. The *drawing* of the Father designates the same fact as the *gift* (ver. 37), but this term serves to explain the mode of it; the gift is effected by means of an inward drawing which makes itself felt in the soul. We shall see at ver. 45 that this drawing is not a blind instinct, like the natural inclinations, but that it is luminous in its nature, like God Himself from whom it proceeds; it is a *teaching*. This teaching should have been accomplished by means of the *writings of Moses* taken seriously (v. 46, 47), by the *Word of God* inwardly received (v. 38). The law by making the Jew feel the insufficiency of his obedience and the opposition between his feelings and the Divine will, and prophecy, by exciting the expectation of Him who should remedy the evil, make Jesus a being known and desired, towards whom a profound attraction cannot fail to make itself felt as soon as He appears. *Weiss* sees in the drawing and teaching of the Father the divine testimony by means of miracles, v. 36, rendered efficacious in the heart by the Holy Spirit. This seems to me too external; and why then exclude the principal divine witness, that of the Word mentioned also in chap. v. ? We must observe the correlation between the subject *he that sent me* and the verb *draw;* the God who sends Jesus for souls, on the other hand, draws souls to Jesus. The two divine works, external and internal, answer to and complete each other. The happy moment in which they meet in the heart, and in which the will is thus gained, is that of the *gift* on God's part, of *faith* on man's part. Jesus adds that, as the initiative in salvation belongs to the Father, the *completion* of it is the task of the Son. The Father draws and gives; the Son receives and keeps, and this even to the glorious crowning of the work, the final resurrection. Between these two extremes is included the entire development of salvation. The sense of the last words is: And I will bring the whole to its end.

Vv. 45, 46. "*It is written in the prophets: And they shall be all taught of*

---

[1] Οὐν is omitted in B C K L T Π 10 Mnn. It^alia Syr. Cop.
[2] T. R. omits εν with ℵ Δ several Mnn.

God. Every one,[1] *who has heard*[2] *the Father, and has learned from Him, comes to me: 46 not that any one has seen the Father, except he who is from God,*[3] *he has seen the Father."* [4] This passage presents a remarkable example of the manner in which Jesus cites the Old Testament. It is not from this book that He derived the thought which He here developes; it arose in Him spontaneously, as is shown by the perfectly original form in which it has been previously expressed: the *gift,* the *drawing* of the Father. But, afterwards, He thinks fit to cite the Old Testament as the authority recognized by the people. If He was already in the synagogue (ver. 59), He might have in His hands the roll which contained the prophecies of Isaiah, and, as He said these words: " *It is written,*" He might read this very passage. Comp. Luke iv. 17 ff. This would explain the retaining of the copula, *and,* at the beginning of the quotation. These words are found in Is. liv. 13. Isaiah here declares that the whole Messianic community will be composed of persons *taught of God,* whence it follows that it is only men who are in the inward school of God who can truly give themselves to the Messiah. According to *Meyer,* the general expression, *in the prophets,* signifies: in the sacred volume containing the prophets. This meaning follows, indeed, from the terms *in* and *is written.* It is nevertheless true that Jesus is not thinking only of the passage of Isaiah, which He quotes textually, but that He sees all the prophets rising in chorus to testify to this same truth; otherwise, why not name Isaiah, as is done elsewhere? Comp. Jer. xxxi. 33, 34; Joel ii. 28 ff. The second part of the 45th verse is commonly understood in this sense: "Every man who, *after having heard* the teaching (ἀκούσας), consents to *receive* it internally (καὶ μαθών), comes to me." With this sense, the teaching would be given to all men, as objects of the pre-eminent grace of God, but it would be expressly distinguished from the free acceptance of this teaching, which is true of only a certain number of them. The πᾶς, *whoever,* would have, therefore, a much more restricted sense than the πάντες, *all,* of the first clause. But, convenient as this explanation would be to dispose of the doctrine of predestination, we believe that it is contrary to the true sense of the word *all* in the passage of Isaiah and in the mouth of Jesus. This word in the former designates only the members of the *Messianic* community, altogether like the word πᾶς in the mouth of the latter. The meaning is rather this: As Isaiah has declared, all my believers must be *taught* of the Father; but of these not one shall fail. The *whoever* merely individualizes the idea of *all.* Jesus does not place in opposition here the teaching given and the teaching received; for the question is of an inward teaching, working from the first in the heart. Hence it follows that if the Jews do not believe, it is because this divine teaching has not been effected in them. Hence their *inability* to believe (ver. 44); but this inability is

---

[1] Ουν *(therefore)* of the T. R., with 11 Mjj. Syr. etc., is omitted by ℵ B C D L S T, some Mnn. It^{plerique} Vulg. Cop.

[2] T. R. reads ακουσας with ℵ A B C K L T II the larger part of the Mnn. It^{aliq} Vulg. Syr.

Orig. Ακουων is read in 11 Mjj. 90 Mnn. It^{plerique}.

[3] ℵ : του πατρος *(of the Father),* instead of του θεου.

[4] ℵ D It^{aliq}: τον θεον *(God),* instead of τον πατερα.

wholly chargeable to them. Perhaps *Weiss* is right in insisting on the rejection of the word οὖν, *therefore*, which connects the two clauses of this verse. The second may be regarded as a reaffirmation of, as well as a conclusion from the first. We may hesitate between the readings ἀκούσας and ἀκούων, *who has heard* or *who hears*. On the one hand, the aorist may have been substituted for the present, because it was supposed that the first participle must be accommodated to the second. But, on the other hand, the present, which expresses the continuance of the hearing, is less suitable than the past, which indicates an act accomplished for the future at the moment when faith is produced. It is therefore through their previous want of docility with regard to the means prepared by God, that these hearers have brought themselves into an incapacity for believing. This saying implies in Jesus the infinitely exalted feeling of what His person and His work are. In order to come to Him, there is need of nothing less than a drawing of a divine order. "He feels Himself above everything which the natural man can love and understand" (*Gess*). The true sense of this passage does not imply the notion of predestination (in so far as it is exclusive of liberty), but, on the contrary, sets it aside. The inability of the Jews to believe arises from the fact that they come to Him, not as persons taught of God, but as slaves of the flesh. They possessed the means of doing better; hence their culpability.

Ver. 46. The phrase οὐχ ὅτι, *not that*, marks a restriction. This restriction can only refer to the term *teaching* (ver. 45). The notion of teaching seems to imply a direct contact between the disciple and the Master. Now no other but Jesus has possessed and possesses the privilege of immediate contact with God through sight. *All* can certainly *hear*, it is true, but He alone *has seen*. And this is the reason why the divine teaching of which He has just spoken is only preparatory; it is designed not to take the place of His own, but to lead to Him, the only one who has seen and consequently can reveal God perfectly, xvii. 3; comp. Matt. xi. 27. This saying is, certainly, one of those from which John has drawn the fundamental ideas of his Prologue (comp. i. 1, 14, 18). If the preposition παρά, *from*, were not connected with the words ὁ ὤν, *who is*, it might be applied solely to *the mission* of Jesus. But that participle obliges us to think of origin and essence; comp. vii. 29. This παρά is the counterpart of the πρός of i. 1; united, they sum up the entire relation of the Son to the Father. Everything in the Son is *from* (παρά) the Father and tends *to* (πρός) the Father.

Does the sight of the Father here ascribed to Jesus proceed from His divine state before the incarnation, as most interpreters and even *Weiss* think? This does not seem to me possible. It is the contents of the human consciousness which He has of God, which He sets forth to His brethren in human words. Comp. iii. 34, 35, where His knowledge of God is inferred from the communication of the Spirit without measure, which has been made to Him as man; the same in xiv. 10, where it is explained by the communion in which He lives here on earth with the Father. The perfect ἑώρακε, *has seen*, proves absolutely nothing for the contrary view; comp. viii. 38, and the analogous expressions, v. 19, 20, which evidently refer to His earthly existence. Only it must not be forgotten that the unique intimacy of this paternal and filial relation rests on the eternal relation of Jesus to the Father; comp. xvii. 24: "Thou didst love me before the foundation of the world." It is *because* this son of man is the eternal well-beloved of the Father, that God completely communicates Himself to Him. The readings of ℵ: "who comes *from the Father*," instead of "*from God*," and of ℵ D: "has seen *God*," instead of "*the Father*," arose undoubtedly from the desire to make our text more literally conformed to the parallel expressions of the Prologue; comp. for the first i. 14: παρὰ τοῦ πατρός, and for the second i. 18: Θεὸν ἑώρακε. By this saying Jesus gives it to be understood that after the divine teaching has led to the Son, it is He, the Son, who, in His turn, leads to the Father: "*I am the way, the truth and the life; no one comes to the Father but by me*" (xiv. 6). Through this idea Jesus comes back to the principal idea which had excited the murmuring of the Jews and He reaffirms it with still more of solemnity than before, in the words of vv. 47–51:

Vv. 47–51. "*Verily, verily, I say unto you: He who believes on me*[1] *has eternal life.* 48. *I am the bread of life.* 49. *Your fathers did eat the manna in the wilderness, and they are dead.* 50. *This is the bread that comes down from heaven, that a man may eat thereof and not die.* 51. *I am the living bread which came down from heaven; if any man eat of this bread,*[2] *he shall live*[3] *forever; and*[4] *this bread which I will give is my flesh which I will give for the life of the world.*"[5] The words *verily, verily,* are uttered with the sense of authority which Jesus derives from the unique position which He holds according to ver. 46, and in opposition to the objections of the Jews (vv. 41, 42). "It is thus, whatever you may say of it." Jesus' tone becomes gradually more elevated, and assumes more of energy and solemnity. The words εἰς ἐμέ, *on me*, omitted by four Alexandrian documents, are perfectly suited to the context, in which the principal idea is the person of Jesus.

Ver. 48. The affirmations follow each other in the way of *asyndeton*, like oracles. That of ver. 48 justifies that of ver. 47. By that of ver. 49 He gives back to His hearers their own word of ver. 31. The manna which their fathers ate was so far from the bread of life that it did not prevent them from dying. This word undoubtedly denotes physical death; but as being the effect of a divine condemnation.

Ver. 50. "Here is the bread which will truly accomplish the result that you desire." The ἵνα, *in order that*, might depend on ὁ καταβαίνων, *which comes down*, but it is better to make it depend on the principal idea: "It is here . . . *in order that* one may eat of it and not die," for: "in order that if one . . . he may not die." It is still the Hebrew paratactic con-

---

[1] ℵ B L T omit εις εμε (*on me*) in opposition to all the other Mss. Vss. and Fathers.

[2] ℵ It^aliq read εκ του εμου αρτου (*of my bread*), instead of εκ τουτου του αρτου.

[3] ℵ D L: ζησει, instead of ζησεται.

[4] ℵ omits και (*and*) and also, with D Γ, δε.

[5] The words ην εγω δωσω are omitted by B C D L T some Mnn. It^plerique Vulg. Syr^cur Orig. (twice) Tisch. ed. 1849. The T. R. is supported by 11 Mjj. the greater part of the Mnn. It^aliq Cop. Syr^sch Orig. (twice). ℵ reads ο αρτος ον εγω δωσω υπερ της του κοσμου ζωης η σαρξ μου εστιν (*the bread which I will give for the life of the world, is my flesh*).

struction. To perform the first of these acts is *ipso facto* to realize the second. Several commentators take the word *die*, in ver. 50, in the moral sense of *perdition*. But the preceding antithesis, the death of the Jews in the wilderness, does not allow this explanation. Jesus here and elsewhere, denies even physical death for the believer (comp. viii. 51); which He of course does not mean in the absolute sense in which it would become an absurdity (see *Keil* who makes the idea of the resurrection, ver. 40, an objection against me), but in the sense that what properly constitutes death in what we call by that name—the total failing of the physical and moral being, does not take place at the time when his brethren see him die. Morally and physically, Jesus remains his life, even at that moment, and, by His personal communion with him, takes away the death of death.

The affirmation of ver. 51a is the summing up of all that precedes, with the design of passing to a new idea (51b). The epithet ὁ ζῶν, *the living bread*, declares even more clearly than the expression *bread of life* (ver. 48), that Jesus is not only the bread which gives life, but that He is Himself the divine life realized in a human person; and it is for this end that He gives life to him who receives it within himself.

Ver. 51b. The second part of the verse is connected with the first by the two particles καί and δέ, which indicate an idea at once co-ordinated (καί, *and*) and progressive (δέ, *now*) with reference to all that precedes: " *And moreover;* " or : " And, finally, to tell you all." Jesus is now resolved to make them hear the paradox even to the end; for it is here indeed that, as *Weiss* says, the *hard saying* begins (ver. 60). At first Jesus had spoken in general of a higher food of which the miraculous bread of the day before was the image and pledge. Then He had declared that this bread was Himself, His entire person. And now He gives them to understand that He will be able to become the bread of life for the world only on condition of dying, of giving Himself to it as sacrificed. This is the reason why, instead of saying *me*, He from this time onward uses the expression, *my flesh*. How can His flesh be given as food to the world? Jesus explains this by this new determining phase: ἣν ἐγὼ δώσω, " (my flesh) *which I will give.*" These words are rejected, it is true, by the Alexandrian authorities, but no doubt because of the apparent tautology which they present with the words which precede: ὃν ἐγὼ δώσω, " (the bread) *which I will give.*" They should be retained in the text, as *Meyer* has acknowledged, notwithstanding his ordinary prepossession in favor of the Alexandrian readings, and whatever *Weiss, Keil, Westcott*, etc., may say. The limiting words *for the life of the world* cannot be directly connected with the words *my flesh;* what would the expression : " my flesh for the life of the world " mean? A participle like *given* or *broken* would be necessary. 1 Cor. xi. 24 is cited: "This is my body [broken] for you." But there, there is at least the article τό which serves as a basis for the limiting word. Weiss so clearly perceives the difference that he proposes to make the limiting phrase : *for the life of the world*, depend, not on the words *my flesh*, but on the verb ἐστίν, *is*, and to make *my flesh* an appositional phrase to *the bread:* "The bread which I will give, that is to say, my flesh, is for the life of the world." But even if it were possible to allow such an apposition and so harsh a use of the verb ἐστίν (the passage xi. 4 is too different to prove anything), would not the future δώσω, *I will give*, require that the verb *to be* should also be placed in the future: "The bread which I will give, my flesh, *shall be* for the life of the world?" His flesh will not be able to serve for the life of the world except after it shall have been given. The reading of the *Sinaitic MS.* is an unhappy attempt to restore the text after the omission of the words ἣν ἐγὼ δώσω had made it intolerable. The first *which I will give*, applied to the bread, is to be paraphrased thus: "which I will give *to be eaten;*" it sums up the preceding conversation. The second, applied to my flesh, signifies: "which I will give *to be sacrificed;*" it forms the transition to the following passage (*my flesh and my blood*). It is in view of this double relation and this double sense that the words: *which I will give*, had to be repeated. In fact, the flesh of Jesus cannot be eaten as *food* by each believer, until after it shall have been offered for the world as a *victim*. This expression: *my flesh*, especially in connection, as it is here, with the future *I will give*, which points to a fact yet to occur, can only refer to the sacrifice of the cross. The interpreters who, like *Clement* and *Origen, de Wette, Reuss, Keil*, etc., apply the term *give* to the voluntary consecration which Jesus makes of His person during His earthly life, take no account of the καὶ δέ, *and moreover*, which indicates a different idea from that which precedes, and of the future *I will give*, which permits us to think only of a gift yet to come. In this verse is betrayed more and more distinctly the preoccupation with the Paschal feast which filled the soul of Jesus from the beginning of this scene, which was one of the grandest in His life. The expression: "the life *of the world*" shows that the new Passover, of which Jesus is thinking, will have an altogether different extent from the old one: it is the entire human race which will be invited to it as soon as the victim shall have been offered and the feast of sacrifice can be celebrated.

3. Vv. 52-59

Ver. 52. "*The Jews therefore strove among themselves, saying: How can he give us his flesh*[1] *to eat?*" The term ἐμάχοντο, *strove*, goes beyond the ἐγόγγυζον, *murmured*, of ver. 41; it is now a violent debate following after a whispered murmuring. The words *among themselves* seem to contradict the appositional word *saying*, which apparently indicates that the saying was unanimous. But the same question might really be found on all lips, while yet there was no agreement among those who presented it. Some arrived at the conclusion: It is absurd. Others, under the impression of the miracle of the day before and of the sacred and mysterious character of Jesus' words, maintained, in spite of everything, that He was, indeed, the Messiah. At the sight of this altercation, Jesus not only persists in His affirmation, but strengthens it by using expressions which were more and more concrete. Not only does He speak of *eating His flesh* and *drinking His blood*, but He also makes of this mysterious act the

---

[1] B T It*plerique* add αυτου after την σαρκα.

596 / Unbelief Develops in Israel

condition of life (vv. 53-56); He speaks of eating *Himself* (ver. 57); and finally, sums up the whole conversation in the final declaration of ver. 58. The evangelist closes by indicating the place of the scene (ver. 59). The true text says: "*the* flesh," not: *His* flesh, although it is indeed the flesh of Jesus that is in question. That which is revolting to them is, that this is the flesh which must nourish them in eternal life.

Vv. 53-55. "*Jesus therefore said to them: Verily, verily, I say to you, that unless you eat the flesh of the Son of man and drink his blood, you will not have life in yourselves. 54. He who eats my flesh and drinks my blood has eternal life; and I will raise him up at the last day.*[1] 55. *For my flesh is truly food*[2] *and my blood is truly*[2] *drink.*"[3]—*Verily:* "It is so, whatever you may think of it!" The Lord attests this first in the negative form (ver. 53), then positively (ver. 54). The term *Son of man*, recalls the notion of the incarnation, by means of which the eternal life, realized in Him in a human life, is placed within reach of the faith of man. *Reuss* and *Keil* think that the terms *flesh* and *blood* may be understood here as in the passages where the expression *flesh and blood* denotes a living human person, for example, Gal. i. 16. But in these cases the blood is regarded as contained in the flesh which lives by means of it, while in our passage the two elements are considered as separated. The blood is shed since it is drunk; and the flesh is broken since the blood is shed. These expressions imply that Jesus has present to His thought the type of the Paschal lamb. It was the blood of this victim which, sprinkled on the lintels of the doors, had in Egypt secured the people from the stroke of the angel of death and which, in the ceremony of the sacrifice of the lamb in the temple, was poured out on the horns of the altar, taking the place in this case of the doors of the Israelite houses; its flesh it was which formed the principal food of the Paschal supper. The shed blood represents expiation; and *to drink* this blood is to appropriate to oneself by faith the expiation and find in it reconciliation with God, the basis of salvation. The flesh broken represents the holy life of Christ; and *to eat* it, is to appropriate to oneself that life of obedience and love; it is to receive it through the action of the Spirit who makes it our life. In these two inward facts salvation is summed up. If then Jesus does not directly answer the *How?* of the Jews, He nevertheless does give indirectly, as He had done with Nicodemus, the desired explanation. As in chap. iii. He had substituted for the expression "*born anew*" the more explicit words "*born of water and Spirit*," so He here completes the expression "*to eat His flesh*" by the expression "*to drink His blood*," which was suited to recall the type of the lamb and to give these Jews, who celebrated the Paschal feast every year, a glimpse of the truth declared in this paradoxical form. The ἐν ἑαυτοῖς, *in yourselves*, recalls the word addressed to the Samaritan woman iv. 14. Here again is the idea of the possession in Christ of a fountain of life springing up continually within the believer.

---

[1] The MSS. are divided between τη and εν τη.

[2] ℵ D E H M S U V Γ Δ Λ Mnn. It^{plerique} Vulg. Syr. Orig. (3 times): αληθως (*truly*); B C F* K L T Π 30 Mnn. Cop. Orig. (5 times); αληθης (*a true*).

[3] ℵ omits the words βρωσις ... εστι (confusion of the two εστι) and reads ποτον instead of ποσις.—D omits the words και ... ποσις.

Ver. 54. After having given this explanation in a negative form (without this eating and this drinking, impossibility of living), Jesus completes the expression of His thought by adding: By this eating and this drinking, assured possession of life. Then He raises the eye of the believer even to the glorious limit of this impartation of life—the resurrection of the body. The relation between these last words: "*And I will raise him up . . .* ," and the preceding ones is so close that it is difficult to avoid seeing an organic connection between the possession of the spiritual life and the final resurrection; comp. Rom. viii. 10, 11. However this may be, the bodily resurrection is by no means a useless superfetation relatively to the spiritual life, according to the thought which *Reuss* ascribes to John. Here is the fourth time that Jesus promises it in this discourse as the consummation of the salvation which He brings to mankind; comp. vv. 39, 40, 44. *Nature* restored and glorified is the end of the victory gained by the divine grace over sin.

The 55th verse justifies the preceding negation and affirmation. If to eat this flesh and to drink this blood are the condition of life, it is because this flesh and this blood are, *in all reality*, food and drink. A part of the critical authorities present the reading ἀληθῶς, " is *truly;*" the rest read ἀληθής: is *true* food . . . *true* drink. The former reading is more in conformity with the style of John. As *Lücke* observes, John ordinarily makes ἀληθής refer to moral veracity, in contrast to ψεῦδος (falsehood), but he also connects the adverb ἀληθῶς with a substantive (i. 48: ἀληθῶς Ἰσραηλίτης; perhaps viii. 31: ἀληθῶς μαθηταί). Moreover, the sense of the two readings is not sensibly different. The adverb or the adjective expresses the full reality of the vital communication effected by these elements, which are truly for the soul what food is for the body. Vv. 56, 57 explain how this communication of life is effected. By this food of the soul Christ *dwells* in us and we in Him (ver. 56), and this is *to live* (ver. 57).

Vv. 56, 57. "*He who eats my flesh and drinks my blood abides in me, and I in him. 57. As the living Father sent me, and I live by the Father, so he who eats me, he also shall live*[1] *by me.*" By drinking through faith at the fountain of the expiation obtained by the blood of Christ and by nourishing oneself through the Spirit on the life realized in His flesh, we contract a union with Him through which His person dwells in us and we in it. This *dwelling* of the believer in Jesus is for his moral being, as it were, a transplanting from the soil of his own life into the new soil which the perfect righteousness and the holy strength of Christ offer him: renunciation of all merit, all force, all wisdom derived from what belongs to himself, and absolute confidence in Christ, as in Him who possesses all that is needed in order to fill the void. The *abiding* of Christ, which corresponds to this abiding of the believer in Him, expresses the real effective communication which Christ makes of His own personality ("he who eats *me*" ver. 57). This mutual relation being formed, the believer *lives:* why? This is what ver. 57 explains.

---

[1] The MSS. vary between ζήσεται (ΓΔ etc.), ζήσει (ℵ B etc.), and ζῇ (C D).

Ver. 57. To be in communion with Jesus is to live, because Jesus has access Himself to the highest source of life, namely, God. "Life passes from the Son to the believer, as it passes from the Father to the Son," (*Weiss*). This second transmission is at once the model (καθώς, *as*) and the principle (καί, *also*) of the first. The principal clause does not begin, as Chrysostom thought, with the words κἀγὼ ζῶ, *I also live*, but with καὶ ὁ τρώγων, *also he who eats me*. There are two parallel declarations: the first, bearing on the relation between God and Jesus, the second, on the relation between Jesus and the believer; each one containing two clauses: the one relating to Him who gives; the other to him who receives. Jesus is a *messenger* of God, fulfilling a mission here on earth; He who has given it to Him is *the living Father*, ὁ ζῶν πατήρ, the author, the primordial and absolute source of life; it is in communion with this Father that Jesus, His Son and messenger, derives unceasingly, during His earthly existence, the life, light and strength which are necessary to fulfill His mission. "I live by the Father." The word ζῶ, *I live*, does not indicate merely the fact of existence; it is at once the physical and moral life, with all their different manifestations. Every time that He acts or speaks, Jesus seeks in God what is necessary for Him for this end and receives it. It is not exact to render διά (with the accusative) as we have been obliged to do, by the preposition *by* (*per patrem*). Jesus did not express Himself in this way (διά with the genitive) because He did not wish to say merely that God was the force *by means* of which He worked. But, on the other hand, it would be still more inexact to translate: *because of the Father* (*propter patrem;* Lange, Westcott), in the sense of: with a view to the service or the glory of the Father. For the preposition διά with the accusative signifies, not *with a view to* (the purpose), but *because of* (the cause). Jesus means to say that, as sent by the Father, He unceasingly has from God the moral cause of His activity. It is in the Father that He finds the source and norm of each one of His movements, from Him that He gets the vital principle of His being. The Father, in sending the Son, has secured to Him this unique relation, and the Son continues sedulously faithful to it (v. 17). Thus it happens that the life of the Father is perfectly reproduced on earth: Jesus is God lived in a human life. From this results the fact described in the second part of the verse. Grammatically speaking, this second part forms but one proposition. But, logically, the first member indicating the subject: "*He who eats me*," corresponds with the first proposition of the preceding declaration: "*As the Father sent me;*" and in the same way the predicate: "*He also shall live by me*," corresponds with the second member of the first proposition: "*And as I live by the Father.*" The relation which Jesus sustains to the Father has its reflection, as it were, in that which the believer sustains to Jesus, and is for the believer the secret of life. The first καί, *also*, corresponds with the καθώς, *as*, of the beginning of the verse: it is the sign of the principal proposition. It takes the place of a οὕτως, *so*, which was avoided because the analogy between the two relations was still not complete. For the first relation is more than the model: it is the principle, the moral reason of the second. The latter, while being analogous to the first, exists only in virtue of the other. The second καί before the pronoun makes the subject prominent: ἐκεῖνος, *he also*. The believer, by feeding on Jesus, finds in Him the same source and guaranty of life as that which Jesus Himself finds in His relation to the Father. Δι' ἐμέ, not strictly *by me* or *for me*, but *because of me*, the norm and source of his life. In each act which he performs, the believer seeks in Christ his model and his strength, as Christ does with relation to the Father; and it is thus that the life of Christ and consequently that of the Father Himself become his. A thought of unfathomable depth is contained in this saying: Jesus only has direct access to the Father, the supreme source. The life which He derives from Him, humanly elaborated and reproduced in His person, becomes thus accessible to men. As the infinite life of nature becomes capable of appropriation by man only so far as it is concentrated in a fruit or a piece of bread, so the divine life is only brought within our reach so far as it is incarnated in the Son of man. It is thus that He is for us *the bread of life*. Only, as we must take the piece of bread and assimilate it to ourselves in order to obtain physical life by its means, we must, also, in order to have the higher life, incorporate into ourselves the person of the Son of man by the inward act of faith, which is the mode of spiritual manducation. By eating Him, who lives by God, we possess the life of God. The living Father lives in One, but in this One He gives Himself to all. This is not metaphysics; it is the most practical morals, as every believer well knows. Jesus therefore reveals here at once the secret of His own life and of that of His followers. Here is the mystery of salvation, which St. Paul describes as "*the summing up of all things in one*" (Eph. i. 10). The Lord sought thus to make clear to the Jews what appeared to them incredible: that one man could be for all others the source of life. The formula here given by Christ is of course that of His earthly life; that of His divine life was given in ver. 26. It follows from these words that no other even miraculous food can give life.

Ver. 58. "*This is the bread which came down*[1] *from heaven: not as your fathers*[2] *did eat the manna*[3] *and are dead; he who eats this bread shall live*[4] *forever.*" The pronoun οὗτος does not mean: "*Such* is the bread" (Reuss, Keil); but "*This bread* (ver. 57) is that which came down,"—that which the manna was not in reality; *hence* the two opposite consequences pointed out in what follows. Here is the final appeal: to reject it, will be to die; to accept it, will be to live.

Appendix on vv. 51b–58

What does Jesus mean by the expressions: *to eat His flesh, to drink His blood?*

1. Many interpreters see here only a *metaphor*, designating the act by which faith morally unites itself with its object. According to some (*de Wette, Reuss*),

---

[1] ℵ omits ουτος and reads καταβαινων instead of καταβας.

[2] ℵ B C L T Cop. Orig. omit υμων after πατερες.

[3] The same, together with D, omit το μαννα (after υμων).

[4] Variants ζησει and ζησεται (ver. 57).

this object is the *historical person* of Jesus Christ as it appeared before the eyes of His hearers. The expression *My flesh* and *My blood* is to be taken in the same sense as *flesh and blood*, that is, "the human person." According to others, the object of faith is not only the living Christ (*the flesh*), but also the sacrificed Christ (*the blood*); and Jesus describes here at once the appropriation of His holy life and faith in His expiatory death. This interpretation, in one or the other of the two forms which we have just indicated, is easily connected with the beginning of the discourse; for spiritual assimilation by means of faith is certainly the idea from which the Lord starts: "*I am the bread of life, he that cometh to Me shall not hunger, and he that believeth on Me shall never thirst*" (ver. 35). Only we cannot understand, from this point of view, with what aim Jesus gives to this altogether spiritual conception an expression which is more and more paradoxical, material, and, consequently, unintelligible to His interlocutors. If this is all that He means to say, even in the last words of the interview, does He not seem to be playing with words and to lay Himself out needlessly to cause offense to the Jews?

2. This very real difficulty has impelled many commentators to apply these expressions to the scene of the Holy Supper, which Jesus had already had in mind at this time, and which was later to solve for His disciples the mystery of His words. But this explanation gives rise to a still greater difficulty than the preceding one. To what purpose this incomprehensible allusion to an institution which no one could foresee? Then, Jesus cannot have made the possession of eternal life depend on the accomplishment of an external act, like that of the Lord's Supper? In all His teaching, the sole condition of salvation is faith. The Tübingen School, which has attached itself to this interpretation, has derived from it an argument against the authenticity of the Gospel; and not without reason, if the explanation were well founded. But the pseudo-John, who should have wished, in the second century, to put an allusion to the Lord's Supper into the mouth of Jesus, would not have failed to employ the word σῶμα, *body*, used in the text of the institution of the Supper and in the Liturgical formulas, rather than σάρξ, *flesh*. A proof of this is found in the unauthentic addition which we read in the *Cambridge* MS. the *Amiatinus*, etc., at the end of ver. 56: "If a man receives *the body* of the Son of man as the bread of life, he will have life in Him." On the passages from *Justin* (Apol. I., 66) and *Ignatius* (*ad Smyrn.*, 7), see *Weiss*. These Fathers may have founded their expression on our passage itself.

To discern the true thought of our Lord, we must, as it appears to me, distinguish carefully, in the mysterious eating and drinking here described, the act of man and the divine gift, as Jesus does Himself in ver. 27. The human act is faith, faith alone; and inasmuch as the eating and drinking designate the believer's part in his union with Jesus Christ, these terms do not go beyond the meaning which the exclusively spiritual interpretation gives to them. To eat the flesh, is to contemplate with faith the Lord's holy life and to receive that life into oneself through the Holy Spirit to the end of reproducing it in one's own life; to drink the blood, is to contemplate with faith His violent death, to make it one's own ransom, to appropriate to oneself its atoning efficacy. But if the part of man in this mystical union is limited to faith, this does not yet determine anything as to the nature of the *divine gift* here assured to the believer. To taste pardon, to live again by the Spirit the life of Christ—is this all? We cannot think so. We have seen with what emphasis Jesus returns, at different times in the foregoing discourse, to the idea of the bodily resurrection; He does so again at ver. 54, and in the most significant way. The life which He communicates to the believer is not, therefore, only His moral nature; it is *His complete life*, physical as well as spiritual, His entire personality. As the grains which the ear contains are only the reappearing of the grain of seed mysteriously multiplied, so believers, sanctified and raised from the dead, are to be only the reproduction, in thousands of living examples, of the glorified Jesus. The principle of this reproduction is undoubtedly spiritual: it is the Spirit which causes Christ to live in us (ch. xiv.–xvi.); but the end of this work is physical: it is the glorious body of the believer, proceeding from His own (1 Cor. xv. 49). Jesus knew, Jesus profoundly felt that He belonged, body and soul, to humanity. It was with this feeling, and not that He might wantonly give offense to His hearers, that He used the terms which are surprising to us in this discourse. The expressions: to eat and drink, are figurative; but the corporeal side of communion with Him is real: "*We are of His body*," says the apostle who is least to be suspected of religious materialism (Eph. v. 30); and to show us clearly that there is no question here of a metaphor intelligible to the first chance scholar, he adds: "*This mystery is great, I speak in respect to Christ and the Church*" (ver. 32). This mystery of our complete union with His person, which in this discourse is expressed in *words*, is precisely that which Jesus desired to express by an *act*, when He instituted the rite of the Lord's Supper. We need not say, therefore, that this discourse alludes *to* the Lord's Supper, but we must say that the Lord's Supper *and* this discourse refer to one and the same divine fact, expressed here by a metaphor, there by an emblem. From this point of view, we understand why Jesus makes use here of the word *flesh* and in the institution of the Lord's Supper, of the word *body*. When He instituted the ceremony, He held *a loaf* in His hand and broke it; now, that which corresponds with this broken bread, was His *body* as an *organism* ($\sigma\tilde{\omega}\mu\alpha$) broken. In the discourse at Capernaum where the question is only of *nourishment*, according to the analogy of the multiplication of the loaves, Jesus was obliged rather to present His body as *substance* ($\sigma\acute{\alpha}\rho\xi$) than as an organism. This perfect propriety of the terms shows the originality and authenticity of the two forms.

There is one question remaining which, from the point of view where we have just taken our position, has only a secondary importance as related to exegesis;— namely, whether already at this period, Jesus thought of instituting the ceremony of the Lord's Supper.[1] He was aware of His approaching death; the news of the murder of John the Baptist had just reawakened in Him the presentiment of it (Matt. xiv. 13), He connected it in His thought with the sacrifice of the Paschal lamb, He knew that this death would be *for the life of the whole world* what the sacrifice of the lamb had been for the existence of the people of Israel. From these premises He might naturally enough be led to the thought of instituting Himself a feast commemorative of His death and of the new covenant, in order thus to replace the feast of the Paschal lamb, the sacrifice of which was the figure of His own. This thought might certainly have arisen on the day when, being deprived of the joy of celebrating the Passover at Jerusalem, and seeing the multitudes flocking towards Him from all sides, He improvised for them a Passover, instead of that which was about to be celebrated in the holy city. It was this feast, offered to His disciples as a *momentary* compensation, which Jesus afterwards transformed, in the Lord's Supper, into a *permanent* institution. And is

---

[1] On the silence of John with reference to this institution, see chap. xiii.

not this precisely the point of view at which St. John desired to place us, when he said at the beginning, ver. 4: "Now the Passover, the feast *of the Jews*, was near." This near approach was not altogether foreign to the thought of the other evangelists; it explains the expression, so similar to that of the institution of the Lord's Supper, with which they all begin the narrative of the multiplication of the loaves: "*He took the bread, and gave thanks.*"

Ver. 59. "*These things said Jesus, as he taught in the synagogue, at Capernaum.*" There was a regular meeting in the synagogue on the second, fifth and seventh days of the week (Monday, Thursday and Saturday). The day of the Passover must have fallen in the year 29, on Monday, April 18th (see Chavannes, *Revue de théol.*, third series, Vol. I., p. 209 ff.). If the multiplying of the loaves occurred on the evening before the Passover (ver. 4), the following day, the day on which Jesus pronounced this discourse, must consequently have been Monday, which was a day of meeting. But with what purpose does the evangelist insert this notice here? Does he mean merely to give an historical detail? It is difficult to believe this. *Tholuck* thinks that his design is to account for the numerous audience which the following narrative (*therefore*, ver. 60), implies. Is not this somewhat far-fetched? It seems to us, rather, that after having given the account of so solemn a discourse, the evangelist felt the need of fixing forever the locality of this memorable scene (comp. viii. 20). In order to be sensible of this intention we must, first, observe the absence of an article before συναγωγῇ, not: in *the* synagogue, but: in full synagogal assembly; then, we must connect the objective words *in an assembly* with *teaching*, and *in Capernaum* with *He said*, and paraphrase as follows: "He spoke thus, teaching in full synagogue, at Capernaum." The term διδάσκων, *teaching*, which denotes a teaching properly so called, recalls the manner in which Jesus had explained and discussed the Scriptural texts, vv. 31, 35; it is in accord with the solemnity of this scene.

The hearers had questioned, murmured, debated; now it is the better-disposed among them, and even some of the permanent disciples of Jesus, who make themselves the organs of the general discontent.

4. Vv. 60–65

Ver. 60. "*After having heard him speak thus, many of his disciples said. This saying is a hard one; who can listen to it?*" According to *de Wette* and *Meyer*, this exclamation relates to the idea of the bloody death of the Messiah, the great cause of stumbling to the Jews, which had been implied in the preceding declarations; according to *Weiss*, to the overthrow of all their Messianic hopes which resulted from all these discourses; according to *Tholuck* and *Hengstenberg*, to the apparent pride with which Jesus connected the salvation of the world with His own person, according to several of the older writers, *Lampe* and others, to the claim of Jesus to be a personage who had come down from heaven. Undoubtedly all these ideas are expressed in what precedes; but the most striking idea was evidently the obligation to eat His flesh and drink His blood in order to have life, and there was here indeed, also, the most paradoxical and most offensive idea. Grossly understood, it might indeed be revolting even to the disciples, and might force from them the cry: This is going too far; He talks irrationally! The term μαθηταί, *disciples*, here denotes persons who attached themselves to Jesus, who followed Him habitually, and who had even broken off from their ordinary occupations in order to accompany Him (ver. 66); it was from among them that Jesus had, a short time before, chosen the Twelve. Some of them were afterwards found undoubtedly among the five hundred of whom Paul speaks (1 Cor. xv. 6). Σκληρός (properly, *hard, tough*), does not here signify *obscure* (*Chrysostom, Grotius, Olshausen*), but *difficult to receive*. They think they understand it, but they cannot admit it.—Τίς δύναται, "*who has power to* . . . ?"—Ἀκούειν, "to listen calmly, without stopping the ears."

Vv. 61–63. "*But Jesus, knowing*[1] *in himself that his disciples murmured at this, said unto them: Does this word offend you?* 62. *And if you shall see the Son of man ascending where he was before?* 63. *It is the Spirit that gives life; the flesh profits nothing. The words which I speak*[2] *unto you are spirit and life.*" As *Lange* remarks, the words "*in himself*" do not exclude the perception of any external signs, but they signify that Jesus had no need of questioning any one of them in order to understand these symptoms. The word *offend*, is to be taken here in the gravest sense, as in Luke vii. 23: to cause to stumble *with respect to faith*.

The words ἐὰν οὖν (ver. 62), which we have translated by *and if*, do not depend upon any principal proposition. One must, therefore, be supplied. We may understand, "What will you then say?" But this question itself may and must be resolved into one of the two following ones: "Will not your offense cease then?" or, on the contrary: "Will you not then be still more offended?" This last question is the one which is understood by *de Wette*, *Meyer* and *Lücke*. According to *Weiss*, this second view is absolutely required by the οὖν, *therefore;* the first would have required *but:* "*But* will not your present offense cease?" True; nevertheless, this second form of the question, if one holds to it, cannot be any more satisfactory. What purpose indeed would it serve to refer them to a coming fact which would offend them still more? We must come to a third supposition which unites the two questions, by passing from the second so as to end with the first. "If therefore, one day, after you have heard this saying which is so intolerable to you, an event occurs which renders it altogether absurd, will you not then understand that you were mistaken as to its true meaning?" The apostle calls this event an ἀναβαίνειν, *ascending*. A whole class of interpreters find here the indication of the *death* of Jesus as the means of His exaltation to the Father (*Lücke, de Wette, Meyer, Reuss, Weiss*). "It is then indeed, Jesus would say, that your Messianic hopes will be reduced to nothing!" But are the ideas of

---

[1] Instead of ειδως δε, ℵ reads εγνω ουν and adds και before ειπεν.

[2] Instead of λαλω (*I speak*), which is read by ·ΔΓΛ and 7 Mjj. ℵ B C D K L T U 16 Mnn. It. Vulg. Orig. read λελαληκα (*I have spoken*).

604 / Unbelief Develops in Israel

suffering and disappearing identical, then, with that of ascending? When the idea of death on the cross is united with that of the heavenly exaltation of Jesus (iii. 15; xii. 34), the apostle uses the passive term, ὑψωθῆναι, *to be lifted up.* When he desires to present this death from the point of view of the disappearance which will follow it, he says ὑπάγειν, *to go away* (to the Father) but not ἀναβαίνειν. When John applies this last term to the exaltation of Jesus xx. 17, he does not mean to speak of His death; for it is after His resurrection. How could the term *ascend* designate the moment of His deepest humiliation? and that in speaking to Jews! Still more, according to all these interpreters, it is the death of Jesus with its consequences which is the *hard saying* at which the disciples are offended; —and yet the new offense, a still greater one, which should form the consummation of the first, is again the death! *Weiss* perceives this contradiction so clearly that, in order to escape it, he supposes that the mention of the death contained in ver. 53 was imported by the evangelist into the discourse of Jesus; the allusion to the great separation of death could have occurred only in this passage. This is to make over the discourse, not to explain it. The only natural and even possible interpretation is that which applies the term *ascend* to the ascension. It is objected that the fact of the ascension is not related by John and that the words: *if you shall see,* do not apply to this fact, since the apostles alone were witnesses of it. But the omission of the ascension in John is explained, like that of the baptism; his narrative ends before the first of these facts, as it begins after the second. Nevertheless John alludes to the one and the other (i. 32 and xx. 17). And as to the word *see,* it is not always applied to the sight of the eyes, but also to that of the understanding; comp. i. 52 "you shall see the angels ascending and descending;" iv. 19: "I see that Thou art a prophet;" but especially Matt. xxvi. 63: "Henceforth *you shall see* the Son of man seated at the right hand of power and coming on the clouds." This last passage is altogether analogous to ours. In the visible facts of Pentecost and the fall of Jerusalem, the Jews beheld, whether they would or no, the invisible ones, the sitting of Christ on the right hand of God and His return in judgment. As to believers, they have seen and still see through the eyes of the apostles. Jesus Himself, if He foretold these facts, must have clearly foreseen the ascension which is the condition of them. Various details confirm this meaning. In the first place, the present participle *ascending,* which forms a picture (see *Baümlein*); then, the opposition between this term and the term *descending from heaven* which, throughout this whole chapter, has designated the incarnation, as well as the words: *where he was before,* on which, as *Keil* observes, lies precisely the emphasis of the sentence; finally, the parallel in xx. 17. It is evident that this meaning is perfectly suited to the context: "You are offended at the necessity of eating and drinking the blood of a man who is here before you. This thought will seem to you much more unacceptable, when you shall see this same man ascend again into heaven from which He descended before, and His flesh and blood disappear from before your eyes. But at that time you also will be obliged to understand that the eating and drinking were of an altogether different nature from what you at first supposed." The following verse fully confirms this explanation.

Ver. 63. The first proposition is a general principle, from which they should have started and which would quite naturally exclude the mistake which they commit. *Chrysostom, Luther, Reuss* give to the word flesh here the sense of grossly *literal interpretation* and to the word spirit that of *figurative interpretation*. But the opposite of the spirit in this sense would be *the letter*, rather than *the flesh;* and the word flesh cannot be taken here all at once in a different sense from that which it has had throughout the whole preceding discourse. "The Spirit alone gives life," Jesus means to say; "as to the material substance, whether that of the manna, or that of my own body, it is powerless to communicate it." Does this saying exclude the substantial communication of the Lord's body, in the Lord's Supper? No, undoubtedly, since the Lord, as He communicates Himself to believers, through faith, in the sacrament, is *life-giving Spirit*, and the flesh and blood no longer belong to the substance of His glorified body (1 Cor. xv. 50).

From this general principle Jesus infers the true sense of His words. If He said simply: *My words are spirit*, one might understand these words with *Augustine* in the sense: My words are to be understood spiritually. But the second predicate: *and life*, does not allow this explanation. The meaning is therefore: "My words are the incarnation and communication of the Spirit; it is the Spirit who dwells in them and acts through them; and for this reason they communicate life" (according to the first clause of the verse). From this spiritual and life-giving *nature* of His words results the manner in which they are to be interpreted. The Alexandrian reading: "the words which *I have spoken*," is adopted as unquestionable by *Tischendorf, Westcott, Weiss, Keil*, etc., on the evidence of the most ancient Mjj. And one seems to be setting oneself obstinately against the evidence in preferring to it the received reading: "the words which *I speak* (in general)," which has in its favor only the St. Gall MS. and nine others of nearly the same time (9th century). My conviction is, nevertheless, that this is indeed the true reading. The first reading would restrict the application of these words to the sayings which Jesus has just uttered on this same day, while the pronoun ἐγώ, *I*, by making the nature of the *sayings* depend on the *character* of Him who utters them, gives to this affirmation a permanent application: "The words which a being such as *I* am, spiritual and living, utters, are necessarily spirit and life." *Weiss* does not appear to me to have succeeded in accounting for this pronoun ἐγώ, when he adopts the Alexandrian reading.

Vv. 64, 65. "*But there are among you some that believe not. For Jesus*[1] *knew from the beginning who they were that believed not, and who it was that should betray him; 65 and he said: For this cause have I said unto you, that no man can come unto me, except it be given him by my Father.*" To the exclamation: *This saying is a hard one*, Jesus had replied: "It is hard only

---

[1] Instead of Ἰησους, ℵ reads ο σωτηρ (*the Saviour*).

so far as you wrongly understand it." And now He unveils the cause of this want of understanding. Even among them, His disciples, apparently believers, there is a large number who are not true believers. The expression τινές does not so far limit the number of these false believers as the French [or English] word *some;* comp. Rom. iii. 3; xi. 17, and Heb. iii. 16, where this pronoun is applied to the whole mass of the disobedient and unbelieving Jewish nation. The word τινές designates any part whatever, whether great or small, of the whole. The evangelist by means of a fact gives the reason, in the second part of the verse, for the declaration pronounced in the first; this fact is that Jesus knows them even to the foundation, and this from the beginning. The word ἀπ' ἀρχῆς, *from the beginning*, applies undoubtedly, as *Lücke, Meyer, Westcott* think, to the earliest times of Jesus' ministry, when He set Himself to the work of grouping around Himself a circle of permanent disciples (xv. 27, xvi. 4; Acts i. 21, 22), or, what amounts nearly to the same thing, to the beginning of the relation of Jesus to each one of them (*Tholuck, Westcott, Keil*); He discerned immediately the nature of the aspirations which brought them to Him (ii. 22, 23). *Lange* and *Weiss* think that the term *beginning* designates the first appearance of the unbelief itself. *Chrysostom* and *Bengel* apply it to the moment when the hearers had begun to murmur on this very day. These last explanations are quite unnatural. Καί, *and:* and even, or: and in particular. The expression: *who it was who should*, is written, not from the standpoint of a fatalistic predestination, but simply from that of the accomplished fact (ver. 71). It follows undoubtedly from this word of John that Jesus did not choose Judas without understanding that, if there was to be a traitor among His disciples, it would be he; but not that He had chosen him in order that he should betray Him. He might hope to gain the victory over the egoistic and earthly aspirations which brought this man, like so many others, to Him. The privileged place which He accorded to him might be a means of gaining him, as also it might end in a deeper fall, if he trampled this grace under foot. As *Keil* says, "God constantly puts men in positions where their sin, if it is not overcome, must necessarily reach maturity. And God uses it then to serve the accomplishment of His plan." Still more, shall we not go so far as to say that the very fall in which this relation was to end might become the terrible means of finally breaking down the pride of this Titanic nature? The moment when Judas, receiving the fatal morsel from the hand of Jesus, must have felt all the greatness of his crime, might have become for him the moment of repentance and of salvation. "If," says *Riggenbach* (*Leben des Herrn Jesu*, p. 366), "in that night of prayer when the choice of the Twelve was prepared for (Luke vi. 12), the thoughts of the Lord Jesus were again and again brought back to this man, and if, while very clearly discerning his want of uprightness, He was obliged to recognize in this the signal from the Father, what shall we have to say? Literally the narrator says: "For He knew . . . *who they are* who do not believe and *who is* he who shall betray Him;" so far does he carry himself back with vividness to the moment when all this occurred.

John 6:66 / 607

The καὶ ἔλεγεν, *and he said,* leads us to suppose a moment of silence here, filled with the sorrowful reflection which the evangelist afterwards communicates to us. The διὰ τοῦτο, *for this cause,* refers to the expression: *some who do not believe.* "It is precisely to this that I wished to turn your attention when I said to you." A man may declare and believe himself His disciple without truly believing, because he joins himself to Him under the sway of motives which do not proceed from the teaching of the Father (ver. 45).

Without this divine and inward preparation, even in the most favorable position faith remains impossible. The quotation is not literal, any more than in the other cases where Jesus quotes Himself (vi. 36). In ver. 37, it was the coming believer who *was given* to Jesus; here it *is given* to him to come. *Westcott* observes correctly that the two elements, divine and human, appear here, the first in the word *is given,* the second in the word *come.* This saying of Jesus was a farewell; those to whom it was addressed understood it. Even after the day when the popular enthusiasm had reached its culminating point, the Galilean work of Jesus seemed as if destroyed; it presented the aspect of a rich harvest on which a hail-storm has beaten.

Ver. 66. "*From that moment*[1] *many of his disciples went back, and walked no more with him.*" In the picture which the Synoptics have drawn for us of the Galilean ministry,—particularly in that of St. Luke,—Jesus shows Himself often preoccupied with the necessity of making a selection among those crowds who followed Him without comprehending the serious character of the step. Comp. Luke viii. 9 ff.; ix. 23 ff.; xiv. 25 ff. Jesus preferred by far a little nucleus of men established in faith and resolved to accept the self-denials which it imposed, to those multitudes whose bond of union with His person was only an apparent one. But there was more than this: all His work would have been in danger if the spirit which was manifested on the preceding day had gained the ascendant among His adherents already so numerous. It was necessary to remove everything which, in this mass, was not decided to go with Him on the pathway of the crucifixion and towards a wholly spiritual kingdom. We can, from this point of view, explain the method pursued by Him in the foregoing scene. The words by which He had characterized the nature and privileges of faith were adapted to attach the true believers to Him more closely, but also to repel all those whom the instincts of a carnal Messianic hope brought to Him. The danger which His work had just incurred had revealed to Him the necessity of purifying His infant Church. Ver. 66 shows us this end attained, so far as concerned the group of disciples who most nearly surrounded the apostolic company. Ἐκ τούτου may be taken in a temporal sense: *from this moment* (*de Wette*), or in the logical sense: *for this reason* (*Meyer, Weiss,* etc.). For this second sense classical examples may be cited. The passage xix. 12 determines nothing. I would understand: *since this fact,* which includes both the time (from this

---

[1] ℵ D add here οὖν (*therefore*).

day) and its contents (that which had just occurred). The words ἀπῆλθον εἰς τὰ ὀπίσω, *went back,* include more than simple defection; they denote the return of these people to their ordinary occupations, which they had abandoned in order continuously to follow the Lord. The imperfect περιεπάτουν indicates a fact of a certain continuance; they no longer *took* part in His wandering kind of life (vii. 1). It was in consequence of this prolonged rupture that the following conversation took place. Jesus, far from being discouraged by this result, sees in it a salutary sifting process which He wished even to introduce into the midst of the circle of the Twelve; for here also He discerns the presence of impure elements.

Vv. 67–69. "*Jesus said therefore unto the Twelve: And you, you will not also go away?* 68. *Simon Peter answered*[1] *him: Lord, to whom shall we go? Thou hast words of eternal life; 69 and as for us, we have believed and have known that thou art the Holy One of God.*"[2] At the sight of this increasing desertion (οὖν), Jesus addresses Himself to the Twelve themselves. But who are these Twelve of whom John speaks as personages perfectly well known to the readers? He has, up to this point, only spoken of the calling of five disciples, in chap. i.; he has mentioned, besides, the existence of an indefinite and considerably numerous circle of adherents. In this example we lay our finger on the mistake of those who claim that John is ignorant of, or tacitly denies, all the facts which he does not himself relate. This expression: *the Twelve,* which is repeated in vv. 70, 71, implies and confirms the story of Luke vi. 12 ff.; Mark iii. 13 ff., which John has omitted as known; comp. the ἐξελεξάμην (ver. 70) with the ἐκλεξάμενος of Luke. Jesus' question expects a negative answer (μή). So *de Wette, Meyer, Weiss,* give to it this melancholy sense: "You would not also leave me?" Here, as it seems to me, and whatever *Weiss* and *Düsterdieck* may say, is an example of the errors into which grammatical pedantry may lead. Far from having the plaintive tone, this question breathes the most manly energy. Jesus has just seen the larger part of his earlier disciples leaving Him; it seems, therefore, that He must hold so much the more firmly to the Twelve, the last human supports of His work; and yet He Himself opens the door for them. Only, as he certainly does not wish to *induce* them to leave Him, and it is only a permission that He intends to give them, He cannot use the expression οὐχ ὑμεῖς θέλετε, *will you not,* which would be a positive invitation to depart. He limits Himself, therefore, to saying: *you surely will not . . . ?* a form which implies this idea: "But if you wish to go, you are free." It must not be forgotten, that, in the use of the particles, there are shades of feeling which prevent our subjecting their meaning to such strict rules as those which philology sometimes claims to establish. The καί before ὑμεῖς, *you also,* emphatically distinguishes the apostles from all the other disciples. At which one of them did Jesus aim, as He discharged this arrow? The close

---

[1] 9 Mjj. (א B C etc.), omit οὖν.

[2] The T. R. reads with 13 Mjj. (Γ Δ Λ Π etc.) It^plerique Syr.: ο χριστος ο υιος του θεου του ζωντος (*the Christ, the Son of the living God*); Syr^cur It^plerique omit του ζωντος. א B C D L: ο αγιος του θεου (*the Holy One of God*).

of the conversation will give us the answer. Peter hastens to take up the discourse, and, without troubling himself, perchance, enough to find out whether his feeling is shared by all his colleagues, he makes himself their mouthpiece; it is exactly the Peter of the Synoptics and the Acts, the bold confessor. His answer (ver. 68) expresses these two facts: the deep void which all other teaching has left in his soul, and the life-giving richness which he has found in that of Jesus. This confession of Peter is, as it were, an echo of the declaration of Jesus, ver. 63: "*My words are spirit and life;*" but it is not a mechanical imitation of it; it is the result of a personal experience already gained (ver. 69). By substituting "*the* words" for "*words*" our translations have transformed the ejaculation of immediate feeling into a dogmatic formula.

Ver. 69. The pronoun ἡμεῖς, *we*, sets the apostles in marked contrast with the disciples who had just deserted Jesus. The verbs in the perfect tense *have believed, known*, indicate things gained for the future and which are not necessary to be reconsidered. Jesus may declare in their presence the most surprising things; it matters not; the faith which they have in Him and the knowledge which they have of Him cause them in advance to accept all. There is a certain knowledge which precedes faith (1 John iv. 16); but there is also a knowledge which follows it and which has a more inward and profound character (Phil. iii. 10); it is of this latter that Peter here speaks. Under the power of an immediate impression they—John, Andrew and himself—had proclaimed Jesus as the Christ (i. 42, 50), and from that time they had, through a daily experience, recognized and established the truth of that first impression. The substance of Peter's profession is formulated somewhat differently in the Alexandrian and Byzantine readings. The expression: *Son of the living God*, in the second, is connected with the whole contents of the chapter; comp. ver. 57: "*The living Father.*" But what renders it suspicious is its resemblance to Peter's confession in Matt. xvi. 16. At the first glance, the designation: *the Holy One of God*, of the Alexandrian authorities is less easily justified in this context. But it is nevertheless connected with the idea expressed in ver. 27: *He whom the Father, God, has sealed*. The unexceptionable divine seal, by which the apostles had recognized Jesus as the Messiah was not especially His acts of power; it was His holiness. The term: *Holy One of God*, "set apart from the rest of men by His consecration," is not a Messianic designation either in the Old Testament or in the New Testament. It is the demons who used it the first time (Mark i. 24 and Luke iv. 34). They were led to it by the feeling of the contrast between Christ and themselves, impure spirits; Peter and the apostles, by that of sympathy. Comp. Luke i. 35; Acts iv. 27; Apoc. iii. 7.

Vv. 70, 71. "*Jesus answered them: Is it not I who have chosen you the Twelve?*[1] *And one of you is a devil! Now he spoke of Judas,*[2] *the son of*

---

[1] ℵ rejects τους and εις.
[2] B C G L read Ισκαριωτου (agreeing with Σιμωνος) instead of Ισκαριωτην which is read by T. R. with 11 Mjj. etc.—ℵ reads απο Καρυωτου, and 3 Mnn. απο Καριωτου.—D Itᵃˡⁱᑫ Σκαριωθ.—Syr.: *Iscariot*.

Simon, Iscariot, for he it was that should betray him, he, one [1] *of the Twelve."* Peter had spoken in the name of all; Jesus tears off the veil which this profession, apparently unanimous, threw over the secret unbelief of one of their number. Not only does He wish thereby to make Judas understand that He is not his dupe and prevent the offense which the thought that their Master had been wanting in discernment might cause to the other apostles. But He desires, especially, to awaken Judas' conscience and to induce him to break with the false position in which he seems to persist in continuing. Jesus addresses in His answer, not Peter alone, but all (αὐτοῖς, *them*). He brings strikingly together (καί) these two facts so shockingly contradictory: the mark of love which He has given to them all by their election and the ungrateful perfidy of one of them. The words ἐξ ὑμῶν have the emphasis: "From among you, chosen by myself." The word διάβολος, does not mean merely diabolical, or child of the devil (viii. 44); it denotes a second Satan, an incarnation of the spirit of Satan. The word of address: *Satan*, addressed to Peter in the scene at Cæsarea Philippi, makes him also an organ of Satan. But as for him, he was so only momentarily and through an ill-directed love. This Judas, to whom Jesus had just opened the door, nevertheless remains, covering himself with the mask of a hypocritical fidelity and accepting as his own Peter's profession. The term which Jesus had employed expressed already the deep indignation which was occasioned in Him by this persistency of Judas and the foreseeing of the hateful end to which this course of action must infallibly lead him.

Ver. 71. At the moment, no one of the disciples, unless perhaps John and Judas himself, understood to whom these words applied. The almost certain etymology of the word Ἰσκαριώτης is Ish-Kerioth, *man of Kerioth;* this was the name of a town in the tribe of Judah (Josh. xv. 25). According to all appearance, the apostle was the only one who was a native of Judea, that country hostile to Jesus. *Hengstenberg* prefers the etymology איש שקרים, *man of falsehoods*. John would thus anticipate the use of a name which could have been given him only after his crime; a supposition which is unnatural. The Alexandrian reading makes this surname an epithet of the father of Judas; the same is the case in xiii. 26. In xiv. 22, this word is without any variant and applies to Judas himself. It might be applied to the father and the son. The verb ἤμελλεν simply means, starting from the point of view of the accomplished fact: "He it was to whom it should happen . . . " The last words bring out the monstrous contrast between his position and his conduct.

From the beginning, a gnawing worm had been fastened to the root of the Galilean faith. John had characterized this evil by the words: πάντα ἑωρακότες . . . "*having seen all that he did*" (iv. 45). And Jesus, with the same feeling, had said (iv. 48): "*Unless ye see signs and wonders, ye will not believe.*" The sixth chapter brings before our eyes the premature falling of the fruit of this tree, which had for a time presented such fair appear-

---

[1] T. R. reads ων after εις with 13 Mjj. Mnn. It. Vulg. Cop. against B C D L Syr. which reject it.

ances. If one wishes to understand this crisis, it is enough for him to cast a glance at the Christianity of to-day. It declares and thinks itself Christian, but material instincts have, more and more, the preponderance over religious and moral needs. Soon the Gospel will not answer any longer to the aspirations of the masses. The words: "*You have seen me and believe not*," will have their application to them on a still vaster scale; and the time will come when the great defection of Christendom will, for a time, reproduce the Galilean catastrophe. Our epoch is the true commentary on the sixth chapter of the Gospel of St. John.

Objections have been made to the authenticity of these discourses. Critics have alleged their unintelligibility for the hearers (*Strauss, Leben Jesu*, vol. I., 2d part, pp. 680, 681) and the similarity of the dialogue to the one in chap. iv. (*Ibid.* p. 680). Comp. especially, ver. 34 with iv. 15; ver. 27 with iv. 13, 14. With reference to this second point we answer. 1. That the ever-renewed collision between the heavenly thought of Jesus and the carnal minds which it was trying to elevate even to itself must, at each time, introduce analogous phases; and 2. That it is not difficult to point out characteristic differences between chap. iv. and chap. vi. The chief one is this: While the Samaritan woman suffers herself to be transported to the celestial sphere whither Jesus would attract her, the Galileans, elevated for a moment, soon fall again to the earth, and break decisively with Him who declares that He has nothing to offer them for the satisfaction of their gross religious materialism.

As to the *first* point, we think that we have here an excellent opportunity to convince ourselves of the authenticity of the discourses of the fourth Gospel. If there is any one of them which can be accused of presenting the mystical character to which the name Johannean is often given, it is certainly this one. And yet, how without this discourse can we explain the great historical fact of the Galilean crisis which is connected with it in our narrative. This decisive event in the history of Jesus' ministry is not called in question by any one, and yet it is inseparable from the discourse which caused it! This discourse, moreover, is naturally connected with its starting point and has a clearly graduated progress. Jesus here declares to the Jews: 1. That they must seek after a higher food than the bread of the day before; 2. That this food is Himself; and 3. That, in order to appropriate it to oneself, one must go so far as to eat His flesh and drink His blood. This gradation is natural: it presents itself as historically necessary, the fact being given which served as its point of departure. Even the incomprehensibility of the last part for the mass of the hearers becomes one of the factors of the double result which Jesus desired to attain; the purification of the circle of His disciples and even of that of His apostles, and the radical rupture with the Messianic illusions on which the multitudes gathered around Him were still feeding.

As to the relation of the profession of the apostles, ch. vi., to that of Cæsarea Philippi (Matt. xvi. 13 ff.; Mark viii. 27 ff.; Luke ix. 18 ff.), it seems to me that it is difficult to imagine two questionings of Jesus, as

612 / Unbelief Develops in Israel

well as two responses of the disciples, so similar to one another nearly at the same time. There is nothing to prevent our placing between the scene at Capernaum and the confession of Peter in our chapter an interval of some weeks. The ἐκ τούτου, *from this time* (ver. 66), easily allows it. and we have thus the necessary time for locating the matter contained (in Matt. and Mark) between the multiplication of the loaves and this solemn conversation of Jesus with His disciples (Matt. xiv. 34–xvi. 12; Mark vi. 53–viii. 26). As for Luke, he is still more easily put in accord with John, since omitting all the intermediate passages, he directly connects the conversation of Jesus and Peter's profession with the multiplication of the loaves (ix. 17, 18). No doubt, the answer of Peter is somewhat differently expressed in Matthew ("*Thou art the Christ, the Son of the living God*") and in John ("*Thou art the Holy One of God*"); and Westcott finds in this difference a sufficient reason for distinguishing the two scenes. But in the Synoptics also the answer differs (Mark: "*Thou art the Christ;*" Luke: "*Thou art the Christ of God*"), a proof that we should not fasten our attention here on the terms, but on the sense: the Messianic dignity of Jesus (in opposition to the function of a simple prophet or a forerunner; comp. Matt. xvi. 14 ff.). For myself, I cannot comprehend how Jesus, after having obtained from the mouth of Peter either the profession reported by Matthew, or that of which John speaks, should almost at the same time have also asked a new one.

3

John 7:1-8:59

THE STRIFE AT ITS HIGHEST STAGE OF INTENSITY AT JERUSALEM

Seven months had elapsed without any appearance of Jesus at Jerusalem. The exasperation of the rulers, whose murderous character John had recognized from the beginning (v. 16, 18), had for a moment become calm; but the fire was ever smouldering under the ashes. At the first appearance of Jesus in the capital, the flame could not fail to burst forth anew, and with a redoubled violence.

We may divide this section into three parts:

1. Before the feast: vii. 1–13.
2. During the feast: vii. 14–36.
3. End and results of the feast: vii. 37–viii. 59.

Before the Feast: vii. 1–13

Ver. 1. "*And after this,*[1] *Jesus continued to sojourn in Galilee: for he would not sojourn in Judea, because the Jews were seeking to put Him to death.*" The situation described in this first verse is the continuation of that of

---

[1] Καὶ (*and*) is omitted by ℵ D It^plerique Sah. Syr.—9 Mjj. (ℵ B C etc.), place μετα ταυτα at the beginning of the verse, and not after Ιησους.

which the picture has been drawn in vi. 1, 2. Hence the καί, *and*, placed at the beginning; comp. vi. 1. If he does not any further mention the numerous body of attendants of which he had spoken at the beginning of chap. vi., it is perhaps owing to the general desertion which had temporarily followed the scene related in the sixth chapter. But he brings out more forcibly the persistence with which, during so long a period, Jesus limited His journeyings to Galilee. The term περιπατεῖν, *to go and come*, characterizes by a single word that ministry of itinerant evangelization which the Synoptics describe in detail. The imperfect tenses make prominent the continuance of this state of things. The sense of the words: *He sojourned in Galilee*, is rather negative than positive: "He did not go out of Galilee." The last words of the verse recall the state in which the preceding visit of Jesus had left the minds of men in Jerusalem (chap. v.), and thus prepare the way for the following narrative. In one sense, everything is fragmentary, in another, everything is intimately connected in the Johannean narration.

Let us here cast a glance at the contents of the Synoptic narrative up to the moment which we have reached in the narrative of John.

To our sixth chapter corresponds precisely the period contained in Matt. xiv. 13–xvi. 28, and in Mark vi. 30–viii. 38, including the multiplication of the loaves, the conversation with the Pharisees on washings and the cleanness of meats, the journey to the northwest as far as Phœnicia, (the Canaanitish woman), the return through Decapolis with the second multiplication of loaves, the return on the western shore of the lake, a new excursion on the opposite shore, together with the arrival at Bethsaida; finally, an excursion to the north of Palestine, with the conversation at Cæsarea Philippi. Thus we reach the moment parallel with the end of the sixth chapter and the beginning of the seventh chapter of John. It is October. Here are placed in the Synoptics the events which precede and accompany the return from Upper Galilee to Capernaum, the Transfiguration, the conversations on the approaching rejection of Jesus, the dispute among the disciples and the arrival at Capernaum (Matt. xvii. 1–xviii. end; Mark ix.). Then Mark (x. 1) and Matthew (xx. 1) relate the final departure from Galilee to Judea. This cannot be the journey to the feast of Tabernacles in John vii., as we shall show. This journey (in John) is omitted, like all the others, by the Synoptics; the final departure from Galilee indicated by them is certainly a fact *posterior* to the brief journey to Jerusalem described by John in chap. vii. Luke, as we have seen, connects the conversation at Cæsarea (ix. 17, 18) directly with the first multiplication of loaves. Then he recounts nearly the same facts as the two other Synoptical writers, the Transfiguration, the healing of the lunatic child, the conversation respecting the approaching sufferings and the return to Capernaum (ix. 18–50); finally he passes, like the other two, from this point to the final departure for Jerusalem (ix. 51.)

Ver. 2. "*But the feast of the Jews, called that of Tabernacles, was at hand.*" This feast was celebrated in October: six full months, therefore, according to John himself, separate this story from the one preceding, without his

614 / Unbelief Develops in Israel

mentioning a single one of the facts which we have just enumerated, and which filled this entire half-year. His intention, then, is certainly not to relate a complete history, and his silence with respect to any fact whatever cannot be interpreted as a proof of ignorance or as an implicit denial of it. The feast of Tabernacles, called in Maccabees and in Josephus, as here, σκηνοπηγία, was celebrated for eight days' reckoning from the fifteenth day of the seventh month (Tisri). During this time, the people dwelt in tents, made of leafy branches, on the roofs of the houses, in the streets and squares, and even on the sides of the roads around Jerusalem. The Jews thus renewed every year the remembrance of the forty years during which their fathers had lived in tents in the wilderness. The city and its environs resembled a camp of pilgrims. The principal ceremonies of the feast had reference to the miraculous blessings of which Israel had been the object during that long and painful pilgrimage of the desert. A libation which was made every morning in the temple, recalled to mind the waters which Moses had caused to spring forth from the rock. Two candelabra, lighted at evening in the court, represented the luminous cloud which had given light to the Israelites during the nights. To the seven days of the feast, properly so called, the law added an eighth, with which was perhaps connected, according to the ingenious supposition of *Lange*, the remembrance of the entrance into the promised land. Josephus calls this feast the most sacred and greatest of the Israelitish festivals. But, as it was also designed to celebrate the end of all the harvestings of the year, the people gave themselves up to rejoicings which easily degenerated into license, and which caused it to be compared by Plutarch to the feasts of Bacchus. It was the last of the great legal feasts of the year; as Jesus had not gone, this year, either to the Passover-feast or to that of Pentecost, it might be presumed that He would go to this feast. For it was assumed that every one would celebrate at least one of these three principal feasts at Jerusalem. Hence the *therefore* of the following verse.

Ver. 3–5. "*His brethren therefore said to him: Depart hence and go into Judea, that thy disciples also may behold*[1] *the works which thou doest; 4 for no man does*[2] *any work in secret, while seeking after*[3] *fame; if thou really doest such works, manifest thyself to the world. 5. For even his brethren did not believe*[4] *on him.*" We take the expression "*Jesus' brethren*," in the strict sense. Compare on this question pp. 357–361. At the head of these brethren was undoubtedly James, who was afterwards the first director of the flock at Jerusalem (Acts xii. 17; xv. 13; xxi. 18; Gal. i. 19; ii. 9). The exhortation which they address to Jesus is inspired neither by a too impatient zeal for the glory of their brother (*Hengstenberg, Lange*) nor by the malignant desire of seeing Him fall into the hands of His enemies (*Euthymius*). They are, beyond doubt, neither so good nor so bad. They are perplexed with regard to the claims of Jesus; on the one hand, they

---

[1] Instead of θεωρησωσι, B D L M Δ read θεωρησουσι; ℵ θεωρουσι.
[2] Instead of ποιει, ℵ b: ποιων.
[3] Instead of αυτος, B D d Cop. read αυτο.
[4] D L read επιστευσαν (*believed*).

cannot deny the extraordinary facts of which they are every day the witnesses; on the other, they cannot decide to regard as the Messiah this man whom they are accustomed to treat on terms of the most perfect familiarity. They desire, therefore, to see Him withdraw from the equivocal situation which He creates for Himself and in which He places them all by keeping Himself so persistently at a distance from Jerusalem. If He is truly the Messiah, why indeed should He fear to make His appearance before more competent judges than the ignorant Galileans. His place is at Jerusalem. Is not the capital the theatre on which the Messiah should play His part, and the place where the official recognition of His mission should be accomplished? The approaching feast, which seems to impose on Jesus an obligation to go to Jerusalem, appears to them the favorable moment for a decisive step. There is a certain analogy between this summons of the brethren and the request of Mary, chap. ii., as there will be also between the manner in which the Lord acts and His conduct at the wedding in Cana.

What do the brethren mean by the expression "*thy disciples*" (ver. 3)? It seems that they apply this name only to the adherents of Jesus in Judea. And this was indeed their thought, perhaps, in view of the fact that there only had Jesus properly founded a school similar to that of John the Baptist, by baptizing like him; comp. iv. 1: "*The Pharisees had heard that Jesus was making and baptizing more disciples than John the Baptist.*" All this had been told and repeated in Galilee; a great stir had been made respecting these numerous adherents of Jesus in Judea and at Jerusalem, at whose head might even be found members of the Sanhedrim. His brethren remind Him of these earlier successes in Judea, and this with the more timeliness because, since the scene of chap. vi., the larger part of His disciples in Galilee had abandoned Him, and He was now surrounded only by a fluctuating multitude. They mean, therefore: "These Messianic works which thou dost lavish upon these crowds, without any result,—go then, at length, and do them in the places where it is said that thou hast formed a school, and where thou wilt have witnesses more worthy of such a spectacle and more capable of drawing a serious conclusion from it." It is not necessary, therefore, to supply, with *Lücke* and others, ἐκεῖ: "thy disciples *there*," or to explain, as *Hengstenberg* and *Meyer* do: "thy disciples *in the entire nation*, who will come to the feast." John must certainly have added a word in order to indicate either the one or the other of these meanings. The term μαθηταί, *disciples*, is taken here by the brethren in a sense which is slightly emphatic and ironical.

Lücke has perfectly rendered the construction of ver. 4 by a Latin phrase: *Nemo enim clam sua agit idemque cupit celeber esse.* There exists no man who works in secret and at the same time aspires to make for himself a name. Αὐτός refers to this hypothetical subject of the verb ποιεῖ, *does*, whose real existence the word *no one* afterwards denies. The copula καί, *and*, strongly sets forth the internal contradiction between such a claim and such conduct (comp. the καί of vi. 36). Ἐν παρρησίᾳ is used here, whatever *Meyer* may say, in the same sense as in xi. 54 and Col. ii. 15: *in public*. From the idea of speaking *boldly* we easily pass to that of acting *openly* (*Keil*). The sense given by *Meyer:* "No one acts in secret and wishes at the same time to be a man of frankness," is inadmissible. By saying εἰ, *if*, the brethren do not precisely call in question the reality of the miracles of Jesus. This εἰ is logical; it signifies *if really*. Only they ask for judges more competent than themselves to decide on the value of these works. And for this end it is necessary that he should advance or retreat. Certainly, speaking absolutely, they were right: the Messianic question could not be decided in Galilee. The choice of the time remained; this was the point which Jesus reserved for Himself. By κόσμος, *the world*, the brethren evidently mean the great theatre of human existence, such as they knew it, Jerusalem. The style of ver. 4 has a peculiarly Hebraic stamp: these are the words of the brethren of Jesus taken as if from their lips. Comp. the analogous construction in 1 Sam. xx. 2.

Hengstenberg, Lange, Keil and *Westcott* endeavor to reconcile ver. 5 with the supposition that two or three of Jesus' brothers were apostles. Hengstenberg remarks first that these words may refer to Joses, the fourth brother of Jesus, and then to the husbands of His sisters. Perceiving indeed the improbability of this understanding of the matter, the others weaken as far as possible the force of the words: *They did not believe*. It is only a partial and momentary want of faith, or, according to Westcott, an effect of the insufficient influence exerted by their faith on their thought and their conduct. But this relative unbelief, as they call it, does not account for the absolute expression: *They did not believe on him;* especially when strengthened, as it is, by the word *neither*, by which John brings the brethren of Jesus into the category of all the other unbelieving Galileans. The reading of D L: *They did not believe* (aorist), is certainly a correction, intended to facilitate an interpretation of this sort. Moreover, what follows excludes this weakened meaning. How could Jesus address to His brothers, being *apostles*, those severe words: "*The world cannot hate you*" (ver. 7), while in xv. 19 He says to the apostles: "*If you were of the world, the world would love its own; but because you are not of the world . . ., therefore the world hates you.*" It certainly follows, therefore, from this remark, that even at this time, six months before the last Passover, Jesus' own brothers did not acknowledge Him as the Messiah. But, divided between the impression which His miracles produced upon them and the insuperable doubts of their carnal minds, they eagerly desired to reach at length a solution. This attitude is very natural; it accords with the role which is ascribed to them in the Synoptical narrative; comp. Mark iii. The perfect sincerity of John's story appears from the frankness with which he expresses himself respecting this fact which was so humbling to Jesus (see *Tholuck*). We may well remark also, with the same author, that these words of the brethren (vv. 3, 4) contain the complete indirect confirmation of the entire representation of the Galilean ministry which is traced by the Synoptics.

Vv. 6–8. "*Jesus therefore*[1] *says to them: My time is not yet*[2] *come; but your time is always ready.* 7. *The world cannot hate you; but it hates me, because I*[3] *bear testimony concerning it*[3] *that its works are evil.* 8. *Go ye up to the*[4] *feast, I go not*[5] *up to this feast, because my time is not yet fulfilled.*" The meaning of the demand of the brethren of Jesus was that He should present Himself at last at Jerusalem *as the Messiah*, and obtain there the recognition of that dignity, which could not be refused Him, if He was really what He claimed to be. Jesus could not explain to His brethren the reasons which prevented Him from deferring to their wish. If He had wished to answer altogether openly, He would have said to them: "What you ask of me would be the signal of my death; but it is not yet time for me to leave the earth." Of this explanation, into which Jesus does not wish to enter, He gives a hint. The words: *The world hates me*, sufficiently express the prudence which is required of Him. The term καιρός, *favorable moment*, must be understood in a manner sufficiently broad to make it possible to apply it both to Jesus (ver. 6a) and to His brethren (ver. 6b). It denotes therefore the moment of showing oneself publicly as one is: for the brethren, as faithful Jews, by going up to this feast; for Jesus, as Messiah, by manifesting Himself as such at one of the great feasts of His people, at Jerusalem.

The seventh verse explains this contrast between His position and theirs. There is a certain irony in the reason alleged by Jesus: "Your works and your words are not sufficiently out of harmony with those of the world to make it possible for you to provoke its hatred." It is otherwise in His case, who by His words and His life does not cease to unveil its deep depravity concealed under the outward show of Pharisaic righteousness (v. 42, 44, 47).

Ver. 8 draws the practical consequence of this contrast. The meaning of the reply of Jesus is naturally in accord with that of the question, and especially of the words: "Manifest thyself to the world." Jesus well knew that He must one day make the great Messianic demonstration which His brethren demanded, but He also knew that the time for it was not yet come. His earthly work was not accomplished. Moreover, it was not at the feast of Tabernacles, it was at that of the Passover that He must die. Hence, the special emphasis with which He says in the second clause, no longer as when speaking of His brethren: "Go up *to the feast*" (comp. the reading of B D, etc.), but "to *this* feast," or even "this particular feast." If the reply of Jesus is thus placed in close connection with the request of His brethren, it is no longer necessary, in order to justify it, to read with so many of the MSS.: "I go *not yet up*," instead of: "I go *not up*." The first reading is manifestly a correction by means of which an attempt was early made to remove the apparent contradiction between

---

[1] ℵ D omit ουν.
[2] ℵ: ου instead of ουπω.
[3] ℵ alone omits εγω and περι αυτου.
[4] B D K L T X Π 15 Mnn. It^plerique Cop. reject the first ταυτην (*this feast*) which is read by T. R. with 12 Mjj. (among which ℵ) Mnn. It^aliq Syr.
[5] T. R. reads ουπω (*not yet*) with B E F G H L S T U X Γ Δ Λ Mnn. It^aliq Syr^sch Ουκ (*not*) is read in ℵ D K M Π It^plerique Vulg. Cop. Syr^cur.

the reply of Jesus and His subsequent action (ver. 10). The reading, *not yet*, is not only suspicious for this reason; the meaning of it is altogether false. The antithesis which engages the thought of Jesus when He says: " I go not up to this feast," is not the contrast between this day and some days later; it is that between *this feast* and *another* subsequent *feast*. What proves this, is the reason which He alleges: *For my time is not yet fulfilled* (ver. 8). The condition of things had not changed when Jesus went up to Jerusalem a few days afterwards. This very solemn expression, therefore, could only apply to the period of time which still remained before the future feast of the Passover, the destined limit of His earthly life. The *not yet* which was well adapted to ver. 6, was wrongly introduced into our verse instead of *not;* comp. for this solemn sense of the word *to be fulfilled* Luke ix. 31, 51; Acts ii. 1, etc. As Jesus rejected at Cana a solicitation of His mother aiming substantially at the same result as the present summons of His brethren, and yet soon gave her satisfaction of her desire in a much more moderate way, so Jesus begins here by refusing to go up to Jerusalem in the sense in which He was urged to do so (that of manifesting Himself to the world), in order to go up afterwards in a wholly diffent sense. The conversion of His brethren, a few months afterwards, proves that the subsequent events were for them the satisfactory commentary on this saying, and that there did not remain in their minds the slightest doubt respecting the *veracity* and moral character of their brother. The following are the other explanations which have been given of this saying of Jesus. 1. That of *Chrysostom*, adopted by *Lücke*, *Olshausen, Tholuck, Stier:* "I go not *now*," deriving a νῦν (*now*), to be supplied, from the present ἀναβαίνω (*I go*). This ellipsis is not only needless, but false. Jesus, as we have seen, makes no allusion to a nearly approaching journey to Jerusalem, which perhaps was not yet even determined upon in His own mind. 2. *Meyer* holds that Jesus, in the interval between ver. 8 and ver. 10, formed a resolution which was altogether new; *Gess*, in like manner: God did not give Him the order until later (v. 19). *Reuss*, nearly the same: Jesus reserved to Himself the liberty of acting according to His own desire, without consulting any one. *Weiss:* In accordance with prudence, Jesus was obliged to say: I go not up; but as His father gave Him afterwards the order to go, a promise was given to protect Him; and this is what took place. All this is very well conceived. But if Jesus did not yet know the Divine will, should He have said so positively: *I go not up.* This was to declare Himself far too categorically. He should have answered more vaguely: "I know not yet whether I shall go up; do you go up; nothing prevents your doing so." 3. Others finally, as *Bengel* and *Luthardt*, explain in this way: "I go not up *with the caravan;* or, as *Cyril, Lange*, etc., "I go not up *to celebrate the feast*" (οὐχ οὕτως ἑορτάζων); which would not exclude the possibility that Jesus should go *to Jerusalem* during the feast. In fact, the full celebration of the feast, as the brethren of Jesus conceived of it, included certain indispensable rites, certain sacrifices of purification, which the pilgrims were obliged to offer before its beginning (xi. 55). And if it is objected that in ver. 10 John must have said, not: "He went up *to the feast*," but: "He went up *to Jerusalem*," this objection falls before the Alexandrian reading, which refers the words *to the feast*, not to: "And Jesus went up," but to the clause: "*When His brethren were gone up.*" This very ingenious interpretation is not wanting in probability; its only defect is its excess of ingenuity. That which I have given in the first place, and to which the context more directly leads, seems to me preferable. It removes from Jesus, not only the accusation of falsehood, but also that of inconsistency which the philosopher Porphyry in the fourth century brought against Him on this account. The meaning given by *Westcott*: "I cannot yet go up as Messiah; but this does not prevent my going up as a prophet," has a certain agreement with our explanation. Only it attributes to Jesus a reticence which is very much like mental reservation.

Vv. 9, 10. "*Having said this*[1] *to them*[2] *he remained in Galilee.* 10. *But when his brethren had gone up to the feast,*[3] *then he also went up himself, not openly, but as it were*[4] *in secret.*" The ninth verse signifies that He allowed His brethren to depart, and ver. 10 gives us to understand that, when He went up Himself afterwards, it was either entirely alone or with one or two only of His most intimate associates. Thus are the words: *as it were in secret*, most naturally explained. Ὡς, which is certainly authentic, softens the expression ἐν κρυπτῷ: Jesus was not *really* a man who concealed Himself, although He for the moment acted as such. But why go up, if this act might so soon bring the end of His activity? The answer is simple. Jesus was not able, even to the end, to withdraw from the obligation of giving testimony before the assembled people in Jerusalem. But He avoided going thither in company with the numerous caravans which were at that time proceeding on their way towards the capital. A new movement of enthusiasm might manifest itself, like that in ch. vi., and without the possibility on His part of restraining it. The state of men's minds, as it is described in vv. 11–13, proves that the danger was a very real one. It could not be prevented except by a course of action such as He adopts here. Besides, He thereby prevented the hostile measures which might have been taken against Him in advance by the authorities. What a sad gradation or rather degradation, since the first Passover in ch. ii.! There, He entered the temple as Messiah-King; in ch. v., He had arrived as a simple pilgrim; here He can no more even come publicly to Jerusalem in this character: He is reduced to the necessity of going thither *incognito*.

An hypothesis of *Wieseler* has found favor with some interpreters. According to this scholar, this journey is identical with that which is spoken of in Luke ix. 51 ff. This uniting of the two cannot be sustained. In Luke ix. Jesus gives to His departure from Galilee the character of the

---

[1] Δε is omitted by ℵ D K Π some Mnn. It^plerique Syr.

[2] ℵ D K L X Π some Mnn. It^plerique Cop. read αυτος (*he*) instead of αυτοις (*to them*).

[3] ℵ B K L T X Π place εις την εορτην (*to the feast*) before τοτε (*then*).

[4] ℵ D It^aliq Syr^cur omit ως before εν κρυπτω.

greatest publicity: He sends, two and two, His seventy disciples into all the cities and villages through which He is to pass (x. 1); He makes long stays (xiii. 22; xvii. 11); multitudes accompany Him (xiv. 25). And this, it is said, is to go to Jerusalem, *as it were, in secret!* It would be better to give up all harmony between John and the Synoptics, than to obtain it by thus violating the texts. Exegesis simply establishes the fact, as we have said above, that the journey of which John here speaks, as well as those of chaps. ii. and v., is omitted by the Synoptics. And, as *Gess* observes, the omission of the last two journeys (chaps. v. and vii.) is the less surprising, since Jesus seems to have gone to Jerusalem both times alone or almost alone. *Hengstenberg* thinks that this journey (together with the sojourn in Perea x. 40), corresponds to the departure mentioned in Matt. xix. 1; Mark x. 1. But the exegesis of the passage in Matthew by means of which this scholar tries to reach this result, is unnatural. See on ver. 1 and x. 22 for the relation between the journeys of John and those of the Synoptics, Luke ix. 51; Matt. xix. 1; Mark x. 1.

The following verses describe in an animated and dramatic way what occurred at Jerusalem before the arrival of Jesus, as soon as the fact of His absence was discovered.

Vv. 11–13. "*The Jews therefore sought him at the feast, and said, where is he?* 12. *And there was much murmuring concerning him among the multitudes.*[1] *Some said, He is a good man. Others said, No, but he leads the multitude astray. However, no one spoke openly of him for fear of the Jews.*" This narrative justifies the circumspect action of Jesus. This popular agitation proves the immense sensation which had been produced by His appearance and the impression which His last sojourn in Jerusalem had left (chap. v.). We find again in this representation, vv. 11–13, the contrast which appears continually in our Gospel between those whom the light attracts and those whom it repels. The term γογγυσμός, *murmuring*, denotes the *rumors* in both senses, friendly and hostile. The ὄχλοι are the groups of pilgrims. Ἀγαθός, *good man*, signifies here an *upright* man, in contrast with an impostor ("He leads the people astray"). Τὸν ὄχλον, *the multitude* (ver. 12), designates the common people who allowed themselves to be easily deluded by every demagogue. The words: *No one spoke openly*, must not be referred to those only who, though well disposed, did not dare to manifest aloud their sympathy. The rest also, those who said: "He is an impostor," did not speak freely, in the sense that through servility they went in their expressions beyond what they really thought. *Weiss* thinks, on the contrary, that they would have said yet more than was evil of Him, if they had not feared the change on the part of the leaders to a more favorable judgment. This explanation seems to me scarcely natural. However it may be, a pressure coming from above was exerted upon all, upon those who were well-disposed towards Jesus, as upon those who were ill-disposed.

---

[1] ℵ D It. Vulg. Syr. read τω οχλω instead of τοις οχλοις.

During the Feast: vii. 14–36

The first agitation had subsided; every one was quietly attending to the celebration of the feast, when all at once Jesus appears in the temple and sets Himself to the work of teaching. The authorities had not taken any measures against Him; and there was still time enough remaining for Him before the end of the feast to accomplish His work and to invite to faith the people who had come from all the regions of the world.

This passage includes three teachings of Jesus, interrupted and in part called forth by the remarks of His hearers. The first is an explanation respecting the origin of His *doctrine* and a justification of the miracle which was performed in chap. v. and which was made a means of attack upon His divine mission (vv. 14–24); the second is an energetic declaration of *His divine origin* called forth by an objection (vv. 25–30); the third contains, on occasion of a step taken by the rulers, the announcement of His approaching *end* and calls the attention of the Jews to the consequences which this departure will have for them (vv. 31–36). Following upon each of these discourses, John describes the different impressions which manifested themselves in the multitudes.

The difference of tone in these three testimonies is observable: in the first, defense, in the second, protestation, finally, in the third, warning.

The Origin of His Teaching and the Refutation of an Accusation: vv. 14–24

1. Vv. 14–18: His teaching.

Vv. 14, 15. "*Nevertheless, when the feast was already half finished, Jesus went up to the temple; and he taught there.* 15. *And* [1] *the Jews were astonished, saying, How does this man know the Scriptures, not being a man who has studied?*" The question of the Jews bears only upon the competency of Jesus (as *Tholuck* thinks, according to the Rabbinical customs of the later times); their astonishment, according to the text, arose from the boldness and skill with which He handled the Scriptural declarations. It is not necessary to understand an object with μεμαθηκώς, *having studied*, as our translators do ("not having studied *them*"). [The English translators, both in A. V. and R. V., translate without the objective word.] This word is absolute: not having passed through the school of the masters; "not being a learned man" (*Reuss*). Γράμματα, letters, denotes, undoubtedly, literature in general, and not only the sacred Scriptures (γραφαί, ἱερὰ γράμματα). Comp. Acts xxvi. 24. But as the sacred writings were among the Jews the essential object of literary studies, γράμματα certainly refers first of all to the Scriptures. This saying of the adversaries of Jesus proves, as *Meyer* justly observes, that it was a fact generally known that Jesus had not received any Rabbinical teaching.

---

[1] ℵ B D L T X: εθαυμαζον ουν, instead of και εθαυμαζον.

Vv. 16, 17. "*Jesus answered*[1] *them and said, My teaching is not mine, but his that sent me; 17 if any one wills to do his will, he shall know of the teaching whether it comes from God or whether I speak of myself.*" Jesus enters for form's sake into the thought of His hearers: in order to teach, it is surely necessary to have been the disciple of some one. But He shows that He satisfies this demand also: "I have not passed through the teachings of your Rabbis; but I nevertheless come forth from a school, and from a good school. He who gave me my mission, at the same time instructed me as to my message, for I do not derive what I say from my own resources. I limit myself to laying hold of and giving forth with docility His thought."

But how prove this assertion as to the origin of His teaching? Every man, even the most ignorant, is in a condition to do it. For the condition of this proof is a purely moral one. To aspire after doing what is good with earnestness is sufficient. The teaching of Jesus Christ, in its highest import, is in fact only a divine method of sanctification; whoever consequently seeks with earnestness to do the will of God, that is to say, to sanctify himself, will soon prove the efficaciousness of this method, and will infallibly render homage to the divine origin of the Gospel. Several interpreters, especially among the Fathers (*Augustine*) and the reformers (*Luther*), have understood by *the will of God* the commandment as to faith in Jesus Christ: "He who is willing to obey God *by believing in me*, will not be slow in convincing himself by his own experience that he is right in acting thus." The sense given by *Lampe* approaches this; he refers the will of God to the precepts of Christian morality: "He who is willing to practise what I command will soon convince himself of the divine character of what I teach." *Reuss*, in like manner: "Jesus declares (John vii. 17) that, in order to comprehend His discourses, one must begin by putting *them* in practice." The earnest practice of the Gospel law must lead in fact to faith in the Christian dogma. But, true as all these ideas may be in themselves, it is evident that Jesus can here use the words *will of God* only in a sense understood and admitted by His hearers, and that this term consequently in this context designates the contents of the divine revelation granted to the Israelites through the law and the prophets. The meaning of this saying amounts, therefore, to that of v. 46: "*If you* earnestly *believed Moses, you would believe in me,*" or to that of iii. 21: "*He who practices the truth, comes to the light.*" Powerless to realize the ideal which flees before it in proportion as it believes itself to be drawing near to it, the sincere soul feels itself forced to seek rest at first, and then strength, in the presence of the divine Saviour who offers Himself to it in the Gospel. Faith is, therefore, not the result of a logical operation; it is formed in the soul as the conclusion of a moral experience: the man believes because his heart finds in Jesus the only effectual means of satisfying the most legitimate of all its wants, that of holiness. Θέλῃ, *wills*, indicates simply aspiration, effort; the realization itself

---

[1] Most of the Mjj. add οὖν.

remains impossible, and this it is precisely which impels the soul to faith.[1] The intrinsic and communicative holiness of the Gospel answers exactly to the need of sanctification which impels the soul. See the normal experience of this fact in St. Paul: Rom. vii. 24, and viii. 2. *Suavis harmonia* (between θέλειν and θέλημα), says *Bengel*. There is a special feature in the teaching of Jesus which will not fail to strike him who is in the way of making the trial indicated in ver. 17. This feature will reveal to him in the most decisive way the divine origin of the teaching of Jesus:

Ver. 18. "*He that speaks from himself, seeks his own glory; but he that seeks the glory of him that sent him, this one is true, and there is no unrighteousness in him.*" The messenger who seeks only the glory of the master who sends him, and does not betray any personal interest in his communications, gives, in this very fact, proof of the fidelity with which he delivers his message; as certainly as he does not say anything with a view to himself, so certainly also he does not say anything as self-moved. The application to Jesus which is to be made of this evident and general truth is left to the mind of the hearers. The teaching of Jesus presents a characteristic which is particularly fitted to strike the man who is eager for holiness: it is that it tends altogether to glorify God, and God alone. From the *aim* one can infer the *origin;* since everything in the Gospel is with a view to God, everything in it must also proceed from God. Here is one of the experiences by means of which the moral syllogism is formed, through which the soul eagerly desirous of good discerns God as

---

[1] We may be permitted to quote here an incident in the history of missions which seems to us to furnish the most beautiful commentary on this saying of Jesus. It is taken from the account of the residence of MM. Hac and Gabet, Catholic missionaries in China, in 1846, at Lhassa, the capital of Thibet. "A physician, a native of the province of Yunnan, showed more generosity. This young man, after his arrival at Lhassa, led so strange a life that every one called him the *Chinese hermit*. He went out only to visit his patients, and ordinarily went only to the poor. The rich solicited him in vain; he disdained answering their invitations, unless he was forced by necessity to obtain some assistance; for he did not ever receive anything from the poor, to whose service he devoted himself. The time which was not absorbed in visiting the sick, he consecrated to study; he even passed the greater part of the night over his books. He slept little and took by day only one meal of barley meal, without ever using meat. It was only necessary, moreover, to see him in order to be convinced that he led a rude and painful life; his face was extremely pallid and thin, and, although he was at the most only about thirty years of age, his hair was almost entirely white. One day he came to see us while we were reciting the breviary in our little chapel; he stopped at the distance of a few paces from the door and listened gravely and in silence. A large colored image, representing the crucifixion, had doubtless fixed his attention; for as soon as we had ended our prayers, he asked us abruptly, and without stopping to show us the ordinary marks of politeness, to explain to him what this image signified. When we had satisfied his request, he crossed his arms on his breast, and, without saying a single word, he remained immovable, with his eyes fixed upon the image of the crucifixion; he kept this position during nearly half an hour; his eyes, at length, were moistened with tears; he extended his arms towards the Christ, then he fell on his knees, struck the ground three times with his forehead and rose, crying, 'There is the only Buddha whom men ought to worship!' Afterwards he turned towards us, and, after having made us a profound bow, he added: 'You are my masters, take me for your disciple.'" (*Voyage en Tartarie et en Thibet*, t. ii. p. 325–328.) Such is the profound affinity which exists between the soul which *is willing to do* what is good, as far as it has been revealed to the conscience, and Christ through whom alone it sees itself made capable of realizing it.

the author of the teaching of Christ. There is, at the same time, in this saying, a reply to the accusation of those who said: *He leads the people astray.* He who abuses others, certainly acts thus for himself, not with a view to God. In order thoroughly to understand this reasoning, it is sufficient to apply it to the Bible in general: He who is glorified in this book, from the first page to the last, to the exclusion of every man, is God; man is constantly judged and humbled in it. This book, therefore, is of God. This argument is the one which most directly affects the conscience.

The last words of ver. 18: *And there is no unrighteousness in him,* contain the transition from the teaching of Jesus (His λαλεῖν, vv. 17, 18) to His conduct (His ποιεῖν vv. 19–23), but this not in a general and commonplace way. If Jesus comes to speak here of His moral conduct, it is because there was thought to be discovered in it a certain subject of reproach which was alleged against the divinity of His teaching and His mission, and with reference to which He had it in mind, by this argument, to justify Himself.

Without the following verses, we might think that these last words: *And there is no unrighteousness in him,* apply only to the accusation stated in ver. 12: He is an impostor. But the argument contained in vv. 19–23 shows clearly, in spite of the denials of *Meyer, Weiss* and *Keil,* that Jesus is already thinking especially of the accusation which was still hanging over Him as violating the Sabbath, since His previous visit to Jerusalem (chap. v.). This was the the offense by which the summary judgment: *He deceives the people,* was justified in presence of the multitude. The term ἀδικία, *unrighteousness,* therefore, does not here signify, as some think: *falsehood:* but, as ordinarily: *unrighteousness,* moral disorder. Jesus passes to the accusation of which He was the object in chap. v., because He is anxious to take away with reference to this point every pretext for unbelief.

2. Vv. 19–24: His moral conduct.

Vv. 19–23. *"Has not Moses given* [1] *you the law? And yet no one of you keeps the law. Why do you seek to kill me?* 20. *The multitude answered and said: Thou art possessed by a demon; who is seeking to kill thee?* 21. *Jesus answered and said to them: I have done one work, and you are all in astonishment.* 22. *For this reason* [2] *Moses has given you circumcision (not that it is of Moses, but it comes from the fathers), and on the Sabbath you circumcise a man.* 23. *If a man receives circumcision on the Sabbath, that the law of Moses may not be broken, are you angry with me because I have healed a man altogether on a Sabbath?"* This passage is an example of the skill with which Jesus handled the law. But, to understand this argument, we must guard ourselves against generalizing, as most of the interpreters do, the idea of ver. 19: *No one of you fulfills the law.* Thus some, as *Meyer,* think that Jesus means: "How will you have the right to condemn me, you who yourselves

---

[1] B D H read εδωκεν, in opposition to the 15 other Mjj. which have δεδωκεν.

[2] ℵ omits δια τουτο (*on account of this*).

sin?" *Weiss,* nearly the same: "You who do not measure your conduct according to the rule of the law, how do you condemn me according to it?" But if Jesus had really violated the law, wherein would their violations justify His? Could He claim that there was no *imposture in Him?* Others (*Hengstenberg, Waitz, Stud. u. Krit.* 1881, p. 148) seek the explanation of this charge in the following question: *Why do you seek to kill me?* Their murderous hatred—in this is the transgression of the law with which He charges them. But the expression: *not to fulfill,* would be too feeble to designate a desire to murder. And with all this, no explanation is given of the meaning of the first question: *Has not Moses given you the law?* which appears to be absolutely idle. So we can scarcely be surprised that *Bertling* (*Stud. u. Krit.* 1880) has proposed, in spite of the authority of all the documents, to transpose the passage vii. 19–24 and place it before v. 17! All these difficulties vanish as soon as ver. 19 is referred to its true object, which clearly appears from vv. 22, 23. Jesus declares in the first place, in a purely abstract way, the fact at which He is aiming. "You yourselves, with all your respect for Moses your lawgiver, know well that occasionally you place yourselves above his law! And yet you desire to put me to death because I have thought that I could do as you do, and with much more right even than you." These words contain the fundamental thought of the following reasoning. And it is so true that Jesus, in speaking thus, is already thinking of the act of chap. v., that the expression: *wish to kill me,* reproduces the very terms of v. 16. This question is addressed to the multitude who surround Jesus only so far as He regards it as representing the entire nation with its spiritual directors.

Vv. 20, 21. Jesus was going to explain Himself, when the portion of this multitude which was not acquainted with the designs of the rulers, interrupts Him and charges Him with giving Himself up to gloomy ideas and suspicions without foundation. Despondency, melancholy, sombre thoughts were attributed to a diabolical possession (the κακοδαιμονᾷν of the Greeks). Jesus, without noticing this supposition, which must fall of itself, simply takes up again and continues His argument which had been already begun. He acknowledges having done *one work,* not a miracle in general, but an act in which one can see a work contrary to the Sabbatic ordinance: "And thereupon," He adds, "behold you are all crying out with offense and wishing for my death because of this work!" The word θαυμάζειν expresses here the horror which one feels at a monstrous act. Ἓν ἔργον, *one single work,* in contrast to all theirs of the same kind, which they, every one of them, do in the case which He is about to cite to them.

The first words of ver. 22: *Moses has given you circumcision,* reproduce the analogous words of ver. 19: *Has not Moses given you the law?* and complete them. The point in hand is to render this fact palpable to them: that *Moses* indeed, their own lawgiver, places himself on His side in the act which He is about to call to their minds. Indeed, this Moses who gave them the law of Sinai and established the Sabbath (ver. 19), is he who also prescribed to them circumcision (ver. 22). Now, by giving you this second ordinance, he has himself made all the Israelitish fathers of families transgressors of the first. For, as each one of them is bound to circumcise his child on the eighth day, it follows that every time that the eighth day falls upon a Sabbath, they themselves sacrifice the Sabbatic rest to the ordinance of circumcision. In the single word of Moses relative to circumcision (Lev. xii. 3), the inevitable collision of this rite with the Sabbatic ordinance was neither provided for nor regulated. It was the Israelite conscience which had spontaneously resolved the collision in favor of circumcision, rightly placing the well-being of the man above the Sabbatic obligation. In our first edition, we referred the διὰ τοῦτο, *for this cause*, with most modern interpreters (*Weiss, Keil,* etc.; *Waitz* does not decide), to the verb: *you are in astonishment,* of ver. 21. This reference is justified by the difficulty of making the *for this* bear upon the following idea: *Moses has given.* How, indeed, can we make Jesus say that Moses has given to the Jews the command to circumcise with a view to the conflict which would result from it with the Sabbatic command? We do not discuss the opinion of *Meyer* and *Luthardt*, who make the διὰ τοῦτο, *for this cause,* of ver. 22, refer to the clause οὐχ ὅτι, *not that . . .* , an interpretation which evidently does violence to the text. But is it not possible to justify the grammatical reference of the words: *for this,* to the totality of ver. 22? The following, in that case, is the sense: "It is precisely *for this,* that is to say, with the design of teaching you not to judge as you are doing—when you are scandalized (θαυμάζετε) at my Sabbath work—that Moses did not hesitate to impose the rite of circumcision upon you, while introducing into his law this conflict with the law of the Sabbath. Thereby, he has justified me in advance, by making all of you commit the transgression for which you are seeking to kill me." Thus understood, this *for this cause* contains the most piquant irony: "Moses has in advance pleaded my cause before you, by making you all jointly responsible for the crime with which you charge me, and by himself proving to you in this way that, when the good of man demands it, the rest of the Sabbath must be subordinated to a higher interest." If we accept this sense, we must make the *for this cause* refer also to the last clause of ver. 22: "*For this cause* indeed has Moses given you . . . and consequently you perform the rite of circumcision even on the Sabbath."

It is not easy to understand the purpose of the limitation: *Not that circumcision is of Moses, but of the fathers.* If it were intended, as a large number of interpreters will have it, to exalt the rite of circumcision by recalling to mind its high antiquity, it would weaken rather than strengthen the argument; for the more venerable the rite of circumcision is, the more natural is it that it should take precedence of the Sabbath, a point which diminishes the force of the argument. Besides, might it not have been answered: The Sabbath also is anterior to Moses, it is anterior even to Abraham, for it dates from the creation? *Hengstenberg* and many others think that, in inserting this remark, Jesus means to defend His Scriptural erudition, which was praised in ver. 15, from the charge of inaccuracy which the preceding declaration might bring upon Him. This explanation is puerile; if it were well founded, nothing would remain, as *Lücke* says, but to impute this parenthesis to the narrator. The true explanation is, perhaps, the following: "Although circumcision does not form a part of the totality of the Mosaic code, given by means of the angels and placed in the hands of the mediator (Gal. iii. 19; Heb. ii. 2), and although it was only the result of a patriarchal tradition, nevertheless Moses did not hesitate to assign to it, in the Israelitish life, a dignity before which he made the Sabbath itself give way; an evident proof that everything which is of importance to the salvation of man takes precedence of the Sabbath." This remark would serve to confirm the entire argument of the Lord. Or it might be necessary to explain the matter in this way: In general, the more recent regulation abolishes *ipso facto* the earlier one. It would seem, then, that the ordinance of circumcision must yield precedence to that of the Sabbath, which was more positive and *more recent*. And yet here there is nothing of the kind; it is the Sabbath that must give way. This circumstance would also rise in evidence against the absolute, exaggerated importance which was attributed by the Jews to the Sabbatic rest. *Renan* cites this passage as one of those which "bear the marks of erasures or corrections" (p. xxxii.). When properly understood, the passage becomes, on the contrary, from one end to the other, an example of the most concise logical argumentation.

The words of ver. 23: *that the law of Moses may not be broken*, have a special force: the Jews transgress the Sabbath (by circumcising on that day) precisely to the end that they may not disobey Moses!—In order thoroughly to understand the *a fortiori* of ver. 23, we must remember that there are in these two facts which are placed in a parallelism, circumcision and the cure wrought by Jesus, at once a physical and a moral side. In circumcision, the physical side consists in a local purification; and the moral side in the incorporation into the typical covenant of the circumcised child. In the miracle of Jesus, the physical fact was a complete restoration of the health of the impotent man, and the moral end, his salvation (v. 14 "*Thou hast been healed, sin no more*"). In these two respects, the superiority of the second of these acts to the first was beyond question; and consequently the infraction of the Sabbath was justified, in the point of view of its utility for the human being, in the second case still more than in the first. We must avoid the explanation of *Bengel* and *Stier*, who think that by the expression: *a whole man*, Jesus here means to designate the physical *and moral* man, in contrast to the purely physical man, the end in view in circumcision. Circumcision was not, in the eyes of the Jews, a merely medical affair.

What is remarkable in this defense is, in the first place, the fact that Jesus does not set forth the *miraculous* nature of the act which was made the subject of accusation; *one work*, He modestly says: it is nevertheless clear that the marvelous character of this work forms the imposing rear guard of the argument. In the next place, there is the difference between this mode of justification and that of chap. v.: Jesus here speaks to the multitudes; His demonstration is not dogmatic; He borrows it from a fact of practical life, of which every Jew was constantly a witness, if even he was not a participator in it: "What I have done, you all do, and for much less!" What could be more popular and more striking? We find again, at the foundation of this argument, the axiom which is formulated by Jesus in the Synoptics: "Man is not made for the Sabbath, but the Sabbath is made for man" (Mark ii. 27).

Ver. 24. "*Judge not according to the appearance; but pronounce the judgment*[1] *which is in accordance with righteousness.*" Ὄψις, *sight*, hence *appearance*, designates here the external and purely formal side of things. It was only from this defective point of view that the healing of the impotent man could be made the subject of accusation. There is no question here of the humble appearance of Jesus which had perverted the judgment of the Jews (*Waitz*). *Righteous judgment* is that which estimates the acts according to the *spirit* of the law. The article before the word κρίσιν, *judgment*, may denote either *the* judgment in this definite case, or, in general, *the* judgment in each case where there is occasion to pass judgment. In the first clause, which is negative, the present κρίνετε is very appropriate: for the question is of the judgment pronounced in this case on the act of Jesus. But in the second, the present is probably a correction in accordance with the first. The aorist, κρίνατε, is perfectly suitable: Judge righteously in every case (without reference to time).

2. *The True Origin of Jesus:* vv. 25–30

Vv. 25–27. "*Some of the inhabitants of Jerusalem said therefore, Is not this man here the one whom they seek to kill?* 26. *And behold, he speaks openly, and they say nothing to him. Can*[2] *the rulers*[3] *indeed*[4] *have recognized the fact that he is the Christ?* 27. *But as for this man, we know whence he is, while as for the Christ, when he shall come,*[5] *no one will know whence he is.*" So great freedom and eclat in the preaching of Jesus struck some of the dwellers in Jerusalem with surprise (οὖν, *therefore*). Knowing the intentions of the priestly authorities better than the multitude who had come from outside (ὁ ὄχλος, of ver. 20), they were on the point of drawing from this fact conclusions favorable to Jesus; but they feel themselves arrested by an opinion which was generally spread abroad at that time, and which seemed to them irreconcilable with the supposition of His Messianic dignity: that the origin of the Messiah was to be entirely unknown. We find an opinion which is nearly related to this expressed by *Justin*. About the middle of the second century, this Father puts into the mouth of the Jew Trypho these words: "The Christ, even after His birth, is to remain unknown and not to know Himself and to be without power, until Elijah comes and anoints Him and reveals Him to all." "Three things," say the Rabbis, "come unexpectedly: the Messiah, the God-send and the

---

[1] B D L T read κρινετε; T. R. with all the rest, κρινατε.

[2] ℵ D: μητι instead of μηποτε.

[3] ℵ αρχιερεις (*chief priests*) instead of αρχοντες.

[4] B D K L T X Π 25 Mnn. It^plerique Vulg. Cop. Syr^cur Orig. omit αληθως (*truly*), which T. R. reads with 11 Mjj.

[5] ℵ adds μη πλειονα σημεια ποιησει η before οταν ερχηται.

scorpion" (*Sanhedr.* 97a, see *Westcott*). This idea probably arose from the prophecies which announced the profound humiliation to which the family of David would be reduced at the time of the advent of the Christ (Is. xi. 1; liii. 2). It was true that it was not unknown, that the Messiah would be born at Bethlehem; but the words: *whence He is,* refer not to the locality, but to the parents and family of the Messiah. Those who speak thus imagine of course that they are acquainted with the origin of Jesus, in this second relation also. Comp. vi. 42. Thus they sacrifice the moral impression produced upon them by the person and word of the Lord to a mere critical objection: a bad method of reaching the truth!

Vv. 28, 29. "*Jesus cried therefore, teaching in the temple and saying: You both know me and you know whence I am: and yet I am not come of myself; but he who sent me is competent,*[1] *whom you know not.* 29. *As for me,*[2] *I know him; for I come from him*[3] *and he sent me.*" Jesus taking this objection as a starting-point (*therefore*), pronounces a new discourse which relates, no longer to the origin of His doctrine, but to that of His *mission* and of His *person* itself. The term ἔκραξεν, *he cried,* expresses a high elevation of the voice, which is in harmony with the solemnity of the following declaration. The words: *in the temple,* call to mind the fact that it was under the eyes and even in the hearing of the rulers that Jesus spoke in this way (comp. ver. 32). Jesus enters here, as in ver. 16, into the thought of His adversaries; He accepts the objection in order to turn it into a proof in His favor. In the first place, He repeats their assertion. The repetition of their own words, as well as the two καί which introduce the first two clauses, give to this affirmation an interrogative and slightly ironical turn: "You *both* know me, *and* you know . . . ?" This form of expression reveals an intention of setting forth a false claim on their part, for the purpose of afterwards confuting it. The third καί, *and,* forms an antithesis to the first two and begins the reply of Jesus. This is, with shades of difference, the sense given by most of the interpreters. *Meyer* and *Weiss* think that it is better to see in the first two clauses a concession: " Yes, no doubt you do know my person and my origin up to a certain point; but this is only one side of the truth; there is a higher side of it which you do not know and which is this." But it would have been difficult for His hearers to get this idea: " You know me; but you do not know me." Jesus rejects the very premises of their argument; and to the fact alleged by them He opposes a directly contrary one: " You think you know me, but you do not know me, either as to my mission or as to my origin (ver. 29)." And as they seem to suppose that He has given Himself His commission, He adds: "I have one sending me, and this one is the veritable sender, that is to say, He who alone has the power to give 'divine' missions." The adjective ἀληθινός has not here, any more than elsewhere, the sense of ἀληθής, *true,* as a large number of interpreters from *Chrysostom* to *Bäumlein* have thought. Jesus does not mean to say that the Being who

---

[1] ℵ: αληθης, instead of αληθινος.
[2] T. R. adds δε with ℵ D X some Mnn. It^aliq. Cop. Syr.
[3] ℵ: παρ' αυτω, instead of παρ' αυτου.

sends Him is morally true; no more does He mean that He is *real* (see my 2d ed.), that is, that He is not imaginary, and consequently that His mission is not fictitious and a matter purely of the imagination; this is not what ἀληθινός signifies. But the sense is: "The one sending me is the true sender." The last words: *whom you know not*, are very severe. How can Jesus charge Jews with not knowing Him of whom they make it their boast to be the only worshipers? But this strange ignorance is nevertheless the true reason why they cannot discern the divine origin of His mission. At the same time He shows them thereby, with much acuteness, that the very criterion by which they intend to deny Him, as Messiah, is precisely that which marks Him as such. In fact the postulate which is laid down by the Jews themselves, in ver. 27, is found thereby to be only too fully realized! It is an argument *ad hominem*, which Jesus allows Himself because He finds thus the means of presenting to this company of people the notion of the Messiah in its most exalted light, as He does in the following verses.

Ver. 29. To the ignorance of God with which He charges the Jews, Jesus opposes the intimate consciousness which He Himself has of God and of His true relation to Him. This relation is, first of all, a relation of essence (εἰμί, *I am*, I proceed *from Him*). In fact, this first clause cannot refer to the *mission* of Jesus which is expressly mentioned in the following one. Jesus affirms that He knows God, first by virtue of a *community of essence* which unites Him to Him. The second clause does not depend on the word *because*. It is an affirmation, which serves also to justify His claim to know God. The one sent has intimate communion with Him who sends Him, and consequently must know Him. Hence it follows that Jesus is the Messiah, and that in a sense much more exalted than that which the Jews attributed to this office.

Ver. 30. "*They sought therefore to take him; and yet no one laid hands on him, because his hour was not yet come.*" The result of this strong protestation (*therefore*) was to confirm His declared enemies in the design of arresting Him. It is clear that the ζητεῖν (*to seek*) was an affair of the rulers, as in v. 16, 18. They were strengthened in their resolution of accomplishing it and in the search for the means of arriving at the result. But the appointed hour had not yet struck. The expression: *his hour*, does not designate that of His arrest (xviii. 12), as *Hengstenberg* thinks, but that of His death as the result of His arrest (comp. vii. 8). The divine decree, to which the evangelist alludes thereby, does not exclude second causes; on the contrary, it implies them. Among these, the interpreters make especially prominent the veneration with which the multitudes at this time regarded Jesus. Yes, assuredly; comp. Luke xx. 19. But we may also think, with *Hengstenberg,* of the resistance which the conscience of His enemies was still opposing to the extreme measures to which their hatred was impelling them. When the hardening of their hearts was consummated and the Spirit of God ceased to restrain their hands, then the hour of Jesus struck. There is, therefore, no reason to assert, with *Reuss*, that "the historical interpretation of this verse creates a contradiction." The sequel is about to show us a first attempt in the sense indicated, but one which fails precisely because the moral ground was not yet sufficiently prepared. This verse is thus the transition to the following narrative, which relates the first judicial measure taken against Jesus.

3. *The Approaching Departure of Jesus:* vv. 31–36

Vv. 31, 32. *"But of the multitude[1] many believed on him, and they said, When the Christ shall come, will he do more miracles[2] than those which this man has done?[3] 32. The Pharisees heard[4] this talk which was circulating among the multitude concerning him, and the chief priests and the Pharisees[5] sent officers to take him."* While the adversaries of Jesus were becoming fixed in their hostile designs, a great part of the multitude were strengthened in faith. Ver. 31 marks a decided advance on ver. 12. The partisans of Jesus are more numerous, and their profession of faith is more explicit, notwithstanding the position of dependence in which they still were in relation to the rulers. If timidity had not arrested them, they would have gone forward to the point of proclaiming Jesus the Messiah. The reading ἐποίησεν, *has done*, is wrongly replaced in the Sinaitic MS. by ποιεῖ, *he does*. The question is of His earlier miracles in Galilee and in Judea itself: ii. 23; chap. v.; vi. 2.

This impression made on the multitude exasperates the rulers, especially those of the Pharisaic party. The place of the meetings of the Sanhedrim could not have been far from that where these scenes were passing (see on viii. 20). It is therefore possible that, in going thither, some of the rulers may have heard with their own ears this talk favorable to Jesus; or also spies may have brought it to them during their meeting; the term *heard* allows both meanings. This is the moment when the Sanhedrim suffers itself to be impelled to a step which may be regarded as the beginning of the judicial measures of which the crucifixion of Jesus was the end. It was certainly under the influence of the Pharisaic party, whose name appears twice in this verse. The second time, however, their name is preceded, according to the true reading, by that of the *chief priests;* the latter are mentioned separately, because they belonged at this epoch rather to the Sadducee party, and they are placed first because, if the impulse had been given by the Pharisees, the measures in the way of execution must have started from the chief priests, who, as members of the priestly families, formed the ruling part of the Sanhedrim. The officers who were sent undoubtedly did not have orders to seize Him immediately; otherwise they could not have failed to execute this commission. They were to mingle in the crowds and, taking advantage of a favorable moment when Jesus should give them some

---

[1] B K L T X Π place the words εκ του οχλου δε at the beginning of the verse; T. R. with 10 Mjj. places them after πολλοι δε, א D after επιστευσαν.

[2] 8 Mjj. (א B D etc.), omit τουτων after σημεια.

[3] א D It^{plerique} Vulg. Syr^{sch} ποιει (*does*) instead of εποιησεν (*did*).

[4] K M U Π add ουν, א D δε, after ηκουσαν.

[5] T. R. with 8 Mjj. (E H M S etc.) places οι φαρισαιοι before οι αρχιερεις; א B D etc. place οι αρχιερεις first.

handle against Him, and when the wind of popular opinion should happen to turn, to get possession of Him and bring Him before the Sanhedrim. There are in this story shadings and an exactness of details which show an eye-witness.

Vv. 33, 34. "*Jesus said*[1] *therefore : I am with you yet a little while, and then I go to him that sent me.* 34. *You shall seek me and shall not find me ;*[2] *and where I am you cannot come.*" Jesus was not ignorant of this hostile measure; and this is what awakened in Him the presentiment of His approaching death which is so solemnly expressed in the following words (*therefore*). In this discourse, He invites the Jews to take advantage of the time, soon to pass away, during which He is still to continue with them. There is a correspondence between the expressions : *I go away*, and : *He who sent me*. The idea of a *sending* involves that of a merely *temporary* sojourn here below. The practical conclusion of ver. 33, which is understood, " Hasten to believe ! " is made more pressing by ver. 34. Of the two clauses of this verse, the first refers to their national future; the second, to their individual fate. In the first, Jesus describes, in a striking way, the state of abandonment in which this people will soon find itself, provided it persists in rejecting Him who alone can lead it to the Father; a continual and ever disappointed expectation; the impotent attempt to find God, after having suffered the visitation of Him to pass by who alone could have united them to God. This sense is that in which Jesus cites this word in xiii. 33 (comp. xiv. 6). It is also that in which He will repeat it, soon afterwards, in a more emphatic form, viii. 21, 22. There cannot be any difficulty in applying the notion of the pronoun με, *me*, to the idea of the Messiah in general. To expect the Messiah is, indeed, on the part of the Jewish people, and without their being aware of it, to seek Jesus, the only Messiah who can be given to them. But there is something more terrible than this future of the nation—it is that of individuals. The expression : *where I am*, denotes symbolically the communion with the Father and the state of salvation which one enjoys in that communion. This is the blessed goal which they cannot reach after having rejected Him; for it is He alone who could have led them thither (xiv. 3). If then they allow this time to pass by, in which they can yet attach themselves to Him, all will be over for them. The present: *where I am*, signifies: "where I shall be at that moment ;" it can only be rendered in French by the future. This second part of the verse does not allow us to explain the term *: you shall seek me*, in the first part, either of a seeking inspired by hatred (*Origen*)—comp. xiii. 33—or of a sigh of repentance; such a feeling would not have failed to lead them to salvation.

Vv. 35, 36. " *Then the Jews said among themselves, Whither will he go then, that we*[3] *shall not find him ? Does he mean to go to those who are scattered among the Greeks and to teach the Greeks ?* 36. *What means this word which he*

---

[1] The αυτοις (*to them*) of the T. R. has in its favor only T and some Mnn.

[2] B T X read με after ευρησετε; the fifteen other Mjj. omit this pronoun.

[3] ℵ D omit ημεις which all the other Mjj. read.

has said: You shall seek me and shall not find me;[1] *and where I am you cannot come.*"[2] These words are, of course, ironical. Rejected by the only Jews who are truly worthy of the name, those who live in the Holy Land and speak the language of the fathers, will Jesus go and try to play His part as Christ among the Jews who are dispersed in the Greek world, and, through their agency, exercise His function as Messiah among the heathen? A fine Messiah, indeed, He who, rejected by the Jews, should become the teacher of the Gentiles! The expression διασπορὰ τῶν Ἑλλήνων, literally: *dispersion of the Greeks*, designates that portion of the Jewish people who lived outside of Palestine, dispersed through Greek countries. Τοὺς Ἕλληνας, *the Greeks*, refers to the Gentiles properly so called. The dispersed Jews will be for this Messiah the means of passing from the Jews to the Gentile peoples! They themselves, however, do not seriously regard this supposition as well founded; and they mechanically repeat the word of Jesus, as if not discovering any meaning in it. Meyer has asserted that this course of action would be impossible, if in ver. 33 Jesus really expressed Himself as the evangelist makes Him speak: "*I go to Him who sent me.*" These last words would have explained everything. They would have understood that a return to God was the thing in question. According to *Reuss* also, ver. 35 contains a too flagrant misapprehension to be conceivable. But either these words: *to Him who sent me* had left in their minds only a vague idea, or more probably, regarding Jesus as an impostor, they see in them only a vain boast designed to cover a plan of exile, as at viii. 22, a plan of suicide. We cannot form a sufficiently accurate idea of the gross materialism of the contemporaries of Jesus, so as to fix the limits of possibility in their misapprehensions. After having passed years with Jesus, the apostles still interpreted a bidding to beware of the leaven of the Pharisees as a reproof for having neglected to provide themselves with bread—it is they themselves who relate this misunderstanding in the Synoptical Gospels; how then should the Jews, to whom the idea of the departure of the Messiah was as strange as would be to us, at the present hour, that of His visible reign (comp. xii. 34), have immediately understood that, in the preceding words, Jesus was speaking to them of entering into the perfect communion with His Father?

The evangelist takes a kind of pleasure in reproducing *in extenso* this derisive supposition. Why? Because, like the saying of Caiaphas in chap. xii., it seemed at the time and in the regions in which John was writing and in which it was read, like an involuntary prophecy. Indeed, had not Jesus really become the Messiah of the Greeks? Was not John composing this Gospel in the country, and even in the language, of the Gentiles at the same time that the prophecy of Jesus contained in the preceding verses, and turned into ridicule by the Jews, was finding its accomplishment with respect to them in a striking and awful manner before the eyes of the whole world?

[1] B G T X read με after ευρησετε.
[2] After this word ελθειν, Cod. 225 continues with the words και επορευθη εκαστος and the story of the woman taken in adultery.

634 / Unbelief Develops in Israel

III.—*On and after the great day of the Feast:* vii. 37–viii. 59

The last and great day of the feast has arrived; Jesus lays aside the apologetic form which until now He has given to His teachings. His word assumes a solemnity proportioned to that of this holy day; He declares Himself to be the reality of all the great historic symbols which the feast recalls to mind. Such declarations only aggravate the unbelief of a part of those who surround Him, while they draw more closely the bond already formed between the believers and Himself.

Four Divisions: 1. The true source: vii. 37–52; 2. The true light: viii. 12–20; 3. The true Messiah: viii. 21–29; 4. The incurable nature of Jewish unbelief: viii. 30–59. The passage vii. 53–viii. 11, which contains the story of the woman taken in adultery, does not appear to us to belong to the genuine text of the Gospel.

1. *The True Source:* vii. 37–52

John reports the discourse of Jesus and gives the explanation of it (vv. 37–39); he describes the different impressions of the multitude (vv. 40–44); he gives an account of the meeting of the Sanhedrim, after the return of the officers (vv. 45–52).

Vv. 37–39. The discourse of Jesus.

Vv. 37, 38. " *On the last and great day of the feast, Jesus stood, and, speaking with a loud voice,*[1] *said: If any thirsts, let him come to me*[2] *and drink; 38. he that believeth on me, as the Scripture hath said, out of his belly shall flow rivers of living water.*" Almost all the interpreters at the present day acknowledge that the *last day* of the feast is not the seventh, which was distinguished in no respect from the others, but the eighth, which was marked by certain special ceremonies. No doubt, only seven feast days are mentioned in Deut. xvi. 13. The same is the case in Num. xxix. 12; but in this passage there is found, in ver. 35, this supplementary indication: "*And on the eighth day ye shall have a solemn assembly, and ye shall do no work;*" which agrees with Lev. xxiii. 36, and Neh. viii. 18: "*So they celebrated the solemn feast seven days, and on the eighth day was a solemn assembly, as it was ordained,*" as well as with Josephus (*Antiq.* iii. 10, 4, " *Celebrating the feast during eight days* "), 2 Macc. x. 7 and the statements of the Rabbis. The two modes of counting are easily explained: the life in tents continued seven days, and on the eighth day the people returned to their dwellings. Probably, in this return there was seen, according to the ingenious supposition of *Lange*, the symbol of the entrance and establishment of the people in the land of Canaan. Philo sees in this eighth day the solemn close of all the feasts of the year. Josephus also calls it: "the sacred closing of the year " (συμπέρασμα τοῦ ἐνιαυτοῦ ἁγιώτερον). This day was sanctified by a solemn assembly and the Sabbatic rest; the whole

---

[1] ℵ D It. Vulg. Cop.: εκραζεν (*he was crying*), instead of εκραξεν (*he cried*) which is read by all the rest.

[2] ℵ D It^{allq} omit προς με (*to me*).

people, abandoning their tents of leafy branches, went in a procession to the temple, and from thence every one returned to his house. The treatise *Succa* calls this day "the last and good day." The δέ indicates an advance: the narrative passes to something greater. The terms εἱστήκει (pluperfect, in the sense of the imperfect) and ἔκραξε, *cried*, designate a more solemn attitude and a more elevated tone of voice than ordinary. For the most part, Jesus taught sitting; this time, apparently, He stood up. He was about to apply to Himself one of the most striking Messianic symbols among all those which the national history contained. It is difficult to hold, with *Reuss*, that the figure of which He makes use at this solemn moment was not suggested to Him by some circumstance connected with the feast. Thus almost all the commentators think that He alludes to the libation which was made every morning during the sacred week. Led by a priest, the whole people, after the sacrifice, went down from the temple to the fountain of Siloam; the priest filled at this fountain, already celebrated by the prophets, a golden pitcher, and carried it through the streets amid joyful shouts of the multitude, and with the sound of cymbals and trumpets. The rejoicing was so great that the Rabbis were accustomed to say that he who had not been present at this ceremony and the other similar ones which distinguished this feast, did not know what joy is. On the return to the temple, the priest went up to the altar of burnt-offering; the people cried out to him: "Lift up thy hand!" and he made the libation, turning the golden pitcher to the West, and to the East a cup filled with wine from two silver vases pierced with holes. During the libation, the people sang, always to the sound of cymbals and trumpets, the words of Is. xii. 3: "*Ye shall draw water with joy out of the well of salvation,*" words to which the Rabbinical tradition quite specially attributed a Messianic significance. It may seem probable, therefore, that Jesus alludes to this rite. No doubt, objection is made that according to Rabbi Judah, this libation was not made on the eighth day. But even if it were so, *Lange* judiciously observes that it was precisely the void occasioned by the omission of this ceremony on this day that must have called forth this testimony which was designed to fill it. This method of acting was much better than that of creating a sort of competition with the sacred rite, at the very moment when it was being performed as on the preceding days in the midst of tumultuous joy. Nevertheless we have a more serious reason to allege against this reference of the word of Jesus to the ritual libation. Would it be worthy of Jesus to take for His starting-point in a testimony so important as that which He is about to give, a ceremony which is altogether human? What was this rite? An emblem contrived by the priests for recalling to mind one of the great theocratic miracles wrought in the desert, the pouring forth of the water from the rock. Now, why should not Jesus, instead of thinking of the humanly instituted emblem, have gone back even to the divine blessing itself, which this rite served to recall? The word which He utters stands in a much more direct relation to the miracle than to the ceremony. In the latter it was not the question of drinking, but only of drawing and pouring out the water, while, in the miracle in the wilderness, the people quenched their thirst from the stream of water coming forth from the rock. It is, then, not to this golden pitcher carried in the procession, but to the *rock* itself from which God had caused the living water to flow, that Jesus compares Himself. In chap. ii. He had presented Himself as the true temple, in chap. iii., as the true brazen serpent, in chap. vi., as the bread from heaven, the true manna; in chap. vii., He is the true rock; in chap. viii., He will be the true luminous cloud, and soon, until chap. xix. where He will finally realize the type of the Paschal lamb. Thus Jesus takes advantage of the particular circumstances of each feast, to show the Old Covenant realized in His person, so fully does He feel and know Himself as the essence of all the theocratic symbols. In view of all this we may estimate aright the opinion of those who make the fourth Gospel a writing foreign or even opposed to the Old Covenant (*Reuss, Hilgenfeld*, etc.)!

The solemn testimony of vv. 37, 38 therefore places us again face to face with the scene in the wilderness, which had been so vividly recalled, during the course of the feast, by the joyous ceremony of the libation. The first words: "*If any man thirsts,*" bring before our eyes the whole people consumed by thirst in the wilderness. To all those who resemble these thirsting Israelites, the invitation, which is about to follow, addresses itself. Thirst is the emblem of spiritual needs. Comp. Matt. v. 6: "Blessed are they that hunger and thirst after righteousness." These are the hearts which the Father has *taught* and *drawn* by means of a docile listening to Moses. The expression ἐάν τις, *if it happens that any one*, reminds us how sporadic these cases are; for the spiritual wants can be easily stifled. For every thirsty heart, Jesus will be what the rock from which the living water sprang forth was for the Israelites: "*Let him come unto me and drink.*" These two imperatives, thus united, signify: There is nothing else to do but to come; when once he has come, let him drink, as formerly the people did. *Reuss, Weiss* and *Keil* object to this interpretation of ver. 37, that in ver. 38 it is the believer who is represented as the refreshing stream. But ver. 38 can in no case serve to explain the idea of ver. 37. For there is between the two, not a relation of explanatory repetition, but a relation of distinctly marked advance. The believer, after having his own thirst quenched (ver. 37), becomes himself capable of quenching the thirst of other souls (ver. 38); this is the striking proof of the fullness with which his own spiritual wants have been satisfied. Now, if the idea changes from ver. 37 to ver. 38, the figure may also change. In ver. 37, the believer drinks of the water of the Rock; in ver. 38, he becomes himself a rock for others. How magnificently is the promise of ver. 37: *Let him drink*, confirmed by this experience! He will be so filled, that he will himself overflow in streams of living water. One of the greatest difficulties of this passage has always been to know what expression of the Old Testament Jesus alludes to, when He says in ver. 38: *as the Scripture has said;* for nowhere does the Old Testament promise to believers the privilege of becoming themselves fountains of living water. *Meyer, Weiss, Keil,*

Reuss, etc., cite passages such as Is. xliv. 3: "*I will pour water upon him that is thirsty . . . and my Spirit upon his seed*;" lv. 1: "*All ye who are thirsty, come to the waters;*" lviii. 11: "*Thou shalt be like a watered garden and as a fountain whose waters fail not.*" Comp. also Joel iii. 18; Zech. xiv. 8; Ezek. xlvii. 1 ff. etc. But, 1. In none of these passages is the idea expressed which forms the special feature of the promise of Jesus in ver. 38 —that of the power communicated to the believer of quenching the thirst of other souls. 2. Nothing in these passages can serve to explain the strange expression κοιλία, *his heart* (literally, *his belly*). *Hengstenberg*, always preoccupied with the desire to discover the Song of songs in the New Testament, cites Cant. iv. 12: "*My sister, my spouse, thou art a barred garden, a spring shut up, a fountain sealed,*" and ver. 15: "*Oh fountain of gardens, oh well of living waters, flowing streams from Lebanon!*" And as these citations strike against the same objection as the preceding, he tries to explain the figure of κοιλία by an allusion to Cant. vii. 2, where the navel of Sulamith is compared to a round goblet. What puerilities! According to *Bengel*, Jesus was thinking of the golden pitcher which served for the libation during the feast; according to *Gieseler*, of the subterranean cavern situated in the hill of the temple, from which escaped the waters which came forth by the fountain of Siloam. But these two explanations of the term κοιλία give no account of the formula of citation which refers us to the Old Testament itself (ἡ γραφή, *the Scripture*). By a desperate expedient, *Stier* and *Gess* desire to connect the words: *he that believeth on me*, with ver. 37, and to make them the subject of the imperative πινέτω: " Let him that believeth on me drink." One comes thus to the point of referring the pronoun αὐτοῦ, " of *his* heart," no longer to the believer, but to Christ. But where has the Scripture ever spoken of the κοιλία of the Messiah? And the construction is evidently forced. The pronoun αὐτοῦ cannot refer to the object ἐμέ *me*, but only to the subject of the sentence : "*he that cometh.*"[1] *Chrysostom* makes the Scriptural quotation bear upon the notion of *believing:* "He who believes on me *conformably to the Scriptures.*" But nothing in the idea of faith calls for a special appeal here to the Old Testament. *Semler, Bleek, Weizsäcker* think they see in this passage an allusion to an unknown apocryphal writing; *Ewald* to a lost passage of Proverbs. These would be singular exceptions in the teaching of Jesus. The true explanation seems to me to come from the event itself, of which we believe that Jesus was thinking in ver. 37. It is said in Exod. xvii. 6: " Behold, I will stand before thee there upon the rock in Horeb, and thou shalt smite the rock, and there shall come *from within it* (*mimmennou*) waters and the people shall drink;" and Num. xx. 11: "*And abundant*

---

[1] In his recent work, *Das Alte Testament bei Johannes* (1885), A. H. Franke favors the grammatical construction which I have just refuted, and starting from the application which Jesus makes, ii. 19-21, of the idea of the temple to His own body, he thinks that the Lord, in virtue of this typical relation, applies here to Himself the different passages of the prophets in which they promise that a stream shall come forth from the temple in the last times (Joel iv. 18; Zech. xiv. 8, and particularly Ezek. xlvii. 1, 2, etc.). Certainly, if this construction were adopted, this explanation of κοιλία αὐτοῦ (*his belly*) would be preferable to every other.

638 / Unbelief Develops in Israel

waters came forth," comp. also Deut. viii. 15; Ps. cxiv. 8. It seems to me probable that these passages had been read on the occasion of the feast, and, that, being present to all minds, they furnished the occasion for this citation: *as the Scripture hath said*. The expression of Jesus ποταμοὶ ὕδατος, *rivers of water*, reproduces that in the Mosaic narrative מים רבים (*abundant waters*). The expression κοιλία αὐτοῦ, *his belly*, is derived from the word *mimmennou, from within him*. This figure, borrowed from the interior cavity of the rock, from which the waters must have sprung forth, is applied first to Christ Himself, then to the man whose thirst Christ has quenched, and whom He fills with His presence and grace. The future ῥεύσουσιν, *shall flow*, recalls the similar form of the Old Testament: "*waters shall come forth.*" The word ὁ πιστεύων, *he that believeth*, is a nominative placed at the beginning as a nominative absolute, and one which finds its grammatical construction in the αὐτοῦ which follows: comp. vi. 39; xvii. 2, etc. If the change of idea and of figure from ver. 37 to ver. 38 appears abrupt, it must not be forgotten that, according to ver. 40, and from the nature of things, we have only a very brief summary of the discourse of Jesus.

Ver. 39. "*Now he said*[1] *this of the Spirit whom*[2] *they that believed on him*[3] *were to receive; indeed, the Spirit*[4] *was not yet,*[5] *because Jesus was not yet glorified.*"[6] *Lücke* and others criticise this explanation which John gives of the saying of Jesus. The future ῥεύσουσιν, *shall flow*, they say, is purely logical; it expresses the consequence which must result from the act of faith. Moreover, the living water is the eternal life which the believer draws from the words of Jesus, and by no means the Holy Spirit. *Reuss* finds here a proof of the way in which the evangelist misapprehends the meaning and import of certain sayings of the Lord. *Scholten* thinks he can reject this passage as an interpolation. Certainly, if ver. 38 only reproduced the idea of ver. 37, the promise of Jesus might refer to a fact which had already occurred at the time of His speaking: comp. v. 24, 25, vi. 68, 69 (the profession of Peter). But we have seen that the promise of ver. 38 passes far beyond that of ver. 37, and must refer to a more advanced and more remote state of believers. The facts prove that if, until the day of Pentecost, the apostles were themselves able to quench their thirst in the presence of Jesus, they could not before that event quench that of any one besides. The *rivers of living water*, those streams of new life which flowed forth from the heart of believers by means of the spiritual gifts (the different χαρίσματα, the gift of tongues, prophecy, teaching), all these signs of the dwelling of Christ in the Church by His Holy Spirit, appeared only after that day. Jesus distinctly marks this advance from the first state to the second in the passage xiv. 17, 18; and no one could

---

[1] א It^{alia}: ελεγεν (*he was saying*), instead of ειπεν (*he said*).

[2] The Mjj. are divided between ου (א D etc.) and ο (B E etc.).

[3] B L T read πιστευσαντες instead of πιστευοντες which is read by T. R. with 14 Mjj.

(among them א) Mnn. It. etc.

[4] We reject αγιον (*holy*) with א K T Cop. Orig. against the other Mjj. and Vss.

[5] B It^{plerique} Syr^{sch} add δεδομενον (*given*). D adds επ' αυτοις.

[6] א reads δεδοξαστο instead of εδοξασθη.

understand better than John the difference between these two states. Let us remember St. Peter, the Twelve, the one hundred and twenty, proclaiming the wonderful things of God at Jerusalem, and bringing on that day three thousand persons to the faith! Nothing like this had taken place before. John also does not, as *Lücke* supposes, confound the Divine Spirit with the spiritual life which He communicates. The figure of *living water*, of which Jesus makes use, unites these two ideas in one conception: the Spirit, as the principle, and life, as the effect. The term "*he said this of* . . .," is broad enough to include this double reference. The strange expression οὔπω ἦν, *was not yet*, occasioned the gloss δεδομένον, *given*, of the Vatican MS. and of some MSS. of the Itala, and ἐπ' αὐτοῖς, *upon them*, of the Cambridge MS. This expression is explained by the words of Jesus: "*If I go not away, the Paraclete will not come to you*" (xvi. 7), and by all the words of chaps. xiv. and xvi. which show that the coming of the Spirit is the spiritual presence of Jesus Himself in the heart; comp. especially xiv. 17, 18. Until the day of Pentecost, the Spirit had acted *on* men both in the Old Covenant and in the circle of the disciples; but He was not yet *in* them as a possession and personal life. This is the reason why John employs this very forcible expression: "*The Spirit was not,*" that is, as already having in men a permanent abode. *Weiss* supposes that the participle δεδομένον, *given*, might well be genuine, and that it may have been omitted because, according to 2 Cor. iii. 17, *Jesus* was made the subject of ἦν, *was*, in this sense: "Because Jesus was not yet spirit (pure spirit), since He was not yet glorified." But, in that case, why expressly repeat the subject Jesus in the following clause. And how unnatural is this comparison with the passage in Corinthians!

The relation which John establishes between the exaltation of Jesus and the gift of the Holy Spirit is explained in different ways. According to *Hengstenberg* and others, the ἐδοξάσθη designates the fact of the *death* of Jesus as the condition of the sending of the Spirit, because this gift implies the pardon of sins. The idea is a true one; but the term *to be glorified* is nowhere applied to the death of Jesus as such. In this sense, ὑψωθῆναι, *to be lifted up* (iii. 15; xii. 32, 34) would be necessary. According to *de Wette* and *Vinet*, in a fine passage from the latter which *Astié* quotes, the connection between the glorification of Jesus and Pentecost consists in the fact, that, if Jesus had remained *visibly* on the earth, the Church could not have walked by *faith* and consequently could not have lived by the Spirit. But in the word ἐδοξάσθη the emphasis is by no means on the putting aside of the flesh, but on the being clothed with glory. This remark seems to me also to set aside the explanation of *Lücke* and *Reuss:* "It was necessary that the veil of the flesh should fall, in order that the liberated spirit might freely manifest itself in the Church" (*Lücke*). It is neither the expiatory death nor the bodily disappearance which are laid down as the condition of Pentecost; it is the positive glorification of Jesus, His reinstatement, as man, in His glory as Logos. It is this supreme position which renders Him capable of disposing of the Spirit and of sending Him to His own. The truth expressed by John may also be presented in this other aspect. The work of the Spirit consists in making Christ Himself live in the heart of the believer. But it is evident that it is not a Christ who is not perfected, whom the Spirit is to glorify and to cause to live in humanity, but the God-man having reached His perfect stature. The epithet ἅγιον, *holy*, was probably added (see the variants) with the purpose of distinguishing the specifically Christian Spirit from the breath of God as it was already acting in the Old Covenant. By reading simply πνεῦμα one might take this word in the special sense in which it is so frequently used in the Epistles of St. Paul: the spiritual life as the fruit of the presence of the Holy Spirit in the Church, *the spirit born of the Spirit* (iii. 6); this would facilitate the explanation of *was not yet*. Nevertheless, we do not think it possible to defend this meaning.

2. Vv. 40–44. The impressions of the Multitude.

Vv. 40–44. "*Some among the multitude,*[1] *who had heard these words*[2] *said, This man is of a truth the prophet. Others*[3] *said, This is the Christ.* 41. *But others said, Does the Christ then come out of Galilee?* 42. *Has not the Scripture declared that the Christ comes of the seed of David and from the village of Bethlehem, where David was?* 43. *So there arose a division in the multitude because of him,* 44 *and some of them would*[4] *have taken him; but no one laid hands on him.*" These brief descriptions of the impressions of the people, which follow each of the discourses of Jesus serve to mark the two-fold development which is effected and thus prepare the way for the understanding of the final crisis. These pictures are history taken in the act; how could they proceed from the pen of a later narrator? John has given us only the *résumé* of the discourses delivered by Jesus on this occasion. This is what he gives us to understand by the plural τῶν λόγων, *these discourses*, which, according to the documents, is to be regarded as the true reading. We know already who this prophet was of whom a portion of the hearers are thinking. Comp. i. 12; vi. 14. The transition from this supposition to the following one: *This is the Messiah*, is easily understood from the second of these passages.

As there were two shades of opinion among the well-disposed hearers, so there were also two in the hostile party: some limited themselves to making objections (vv. 41, 42); this feature suffices to isolate them morally from those previously mentioned. Others (ver. 44) already wished to proceed to violent measures. *De Wette, Weiss, Keim* ask why John does not refute the objection advanced in ver. 42, which it would have been easy for him to do, if he had known or admitted the birth of Jesus at Bethlehem. From this silence they infer that he was ignorant of or denied the whole legend of the Davidic descent of Jesus and His

---

[1] Instead of πολλοι ουν εκ του οχλου ακουσαντες which is read by T. R. with 11 Mjj. Mnn. It^{aliq} Syr., in ℵ B D L T X It^{plerique} Vulg. Cop. Orig. εκ του οχλου ουν ακουσαντες is read.

[2] T. R. reads τον λογον (*this word*) with S X Δ Mnn. The 13 other Mjj. Mnn. It. Vulg. Syr^{sch} Cop. Orig. read των λογων (*these words*), and ℵ B D L T U add τουτων. ℵ D K Π add αυτου before or after λογων.

[3] B L T X : οι δε instead of αλλοι (ℵ D etc.) or αλλοι δε (T. R. with Mnn.).

[4] ℵ ελεγον (*said*) instead of ηθελον (*wished*).

birth at Bethlehem. But the evangelist relates his story objectively (*Weiss*), and it is precisely in the case of his believing the objection to be well founded that he would be obliged to try to resolve it. John often takes pleasure in reporting objections which, for his readers who are acquainted with the Gospel history, turn immediately into proofs.[1] At the same time he shows thereby how the critical spirit, to which the adversaries of Jesus had surrendered themselves had been a less sure guide than the moral instinct through which the disciples had attached themselves to Him. The γάρ, *for* (ver. 41), refers to an understood negative: "By no means, *for* . . . " The present ἔρχεται, *comes*, is that of the idea, the expression of what must be, according to the prophecy. Ὅπου ἦν "*where he was* (his home);" comp. 1 Sam. xvi. 44. The *some*, according to *Weiss*, formed a part of the officers sent to take Him. But, in that case, why not designate them, as in ver. 45? They were rather some violent persons in the crowd who were urging the officers to execute their commission. *To take Him*, in the sense of *causing* Him to be taken.

3. Vv. 45-52. The Meeting of the Sanhedrim.

Vv. 45-49. " *The officers therefore returned to the chief-priests and Pharisees. And they said to them, Why have you not brought him?* 46. *The officers answered, Never man spake like this man.*[2] 47. *The Pharisees answered them, Are you also led astray?* 48. *Has any one of the rulers or of the Pharisees believed*[3] *on him?* 49. *But this multitude, who know not the law, are accursed!*"[4] Although this was a holy day, the Sanhedrim or at least a part of this body held a meeting, no doubt awaiting the result of the mission of the officers (ver. 42). The union of the two substantives under the force of one and the same article indicates strongly community of action (comp. ver. 32). The pronoun ἐκεῖνοι, properly *those there*, is surprising, since it refers to the nearest persons. *Weiss* and *Westcott* try to explain it by saying that the priests and Pharisees were morally farther removed from the author than were the officers, as if the moral distance could take the place of grammatical remoteness. We find here again, more evidently than elsewhere, the pregnant sense of this pronoun in John; not: *those there* (in contrast to *these here*), but: those and not others; those, always the same, the eternal enemies of Jesus. By their frank reply (ver. 46) the officers, unintentionally, pay a strange compliment to these doctors whom they were accustomed every day to hear. *Tischendorf* has rightly restored, in his later editions, the last words of ver. 46; the omission of these words in the Alexandrian authorities arises from the confounding of the two ἄνθρωπος. By the *you also* (ver. 47), the rulers appeal to the vanity of their servants. John takes pleasure, in ver. 48, in again maliciously recalling one of these sayings of the adversaries of Jesus on which the contradiction made by facts impressed the stamp of ridicule (comp. the

---

[1] *Hilgenfeld* (*Einl.*, p. 719) distinctly acknowledges that the fact of the birth of Jesus in Bethlehem is implied in this passage as known by the author.

[2] B L T Cop. Orig. omit ως ουτος ο ανθρωπος, D It^{aliq} read ως ουτος λαλει. א ως ουτος λαλει ο ανθρωπος.

[3] א D : πιστευει instead of επιστευσεν.

[4] א B T 2 Mnn. Orig.: επαρατοι instead of επικαταρατοι.

conduct of Nicodemus in ver. 50). The commentators recall, on the suggestion of ver. 49, the contemptuous expressions contained in the Rabbinical writings with reference to those who are uneducated. "The ignorant man is not pious; the learned only will be raised from the dead." We must also recall the expressions: "people of the earth," "vermin," etc., applied by the learned Jews to the common people. By the words: *who know not the law,* the rulers insinuate that for themselves they have unanswerable reasons derived from the law for rejecting Jesus. Sacerdotal wrath willingly assumes an esoteric mien. The reading ἐπάρατοι belongs to the classical style; the LXX. and the New Testament (Gal. iii. 10–13) use the form ἐπικατάρατος.

But there is one present who calls them to order in the name of that very law which they claim alone to know:

Vv. 50–52. "*Nicodemus, who came to him before by night*[1] *and who was one of them, says to them,* 51. *Does our law then condemn a man before*[2] *hearing from him and taking knowledge of what he does?* 52. *They answered and said to him, Art thou, then, thyself also, a Galilean? Search and see that out of Galilee arises*[3] *no prophet.*" The part which Nicodemus plays on this occasion is the proof of the advance which has been made in him since his visit to Jesus. This is noticeably indicated by the apposition, "*who came to Jesus before.*" The omission of these words in the Sinaitic MS. is probably owing to a confounding of αὐτούς and αὐτόν. Νυκτός, *by night,* is omitted by the Alexandrian authorities; but we may hold that it has for its aim to bring out the contrast between his present boldness and his former caution. The πρῶτον or πρότερον, *before,* which the Alexandrian authorities read in place of νυκτός, likewise establishes the contrast between his present conduct and his previous course. The second apposition: *who was one of them,* ironically recalls their own question, ver. 48: "Has any one of the rulers . . ." ?

The term ὁ νόμος, *the law,* ver. 51, is at the beginning of the sentence; it contains a cutting allusion to the claim of the rulers that they alone have knowledge of the law (ver. 49). The subject of the verbs ἀκούσῃ and γνῷ is the law personified in the judge.

We see in ver. 52 how passion regards and judges impartiality. It discovers in it the indication of a secret sympathy, and in this it is not always mistaken. The Sanhedrim maliciously assume in their reply that one cannot be an adherent of Jesus without being, like Him, a Galilean: "It must be that thou art His fellow-countryman to give up thyself thus to His imposture." The last words which the narrative places in the mouth of Jesus' adversaries seem to contain an assertion which is contrary to the facts of the case; for, it is claimed, several prophets, Elijah, Nahum, Hosea, Jonah, were of Galilean origin. Hence the conclusion has

---

[1] T. R. reads ο ελθων νυκτος προς αυτον with E G H M S Γ Δ. It^{aliq} Vulg. Syr. In B L T Sah. ο ελθων προς αυτον προτερον is read; in D, ο ελθων προς αυτον νυκτος το πρωτον. ℵ omits the whole.

[2] ℵ B M K L T X Π Orig. read πρωτον instead of προτερον.

[3] Instead of εγηγερται, ℵ B D K T Γ Δ Π 30 Mnn. It^{plerique} Vulg. Syr. read εγειρεται.

been drawn (*Bretschneider, Baur*) that the members of the Sanhedrim, who must have known their own sacred history, could not have uttered these words, and that it is the evangelist who has wrongly attributed to them this error. If the perfect ἐγήγερται, *has arisen*, is read, we might with some writers understand the thought thus: "And see that a prophet has not (really) arisen in Galilee (in the person of this man)." There would thus be an allusion to the title *prophet of Galilee*, which was frequently given to Jesus. But this does not obviate the difficulty. For there still remains the phrase ἐρεύνησον καὶ ἴδε, *search and see that* . . . , which implies that the fact has not yet occurred. The more probable reading, the present ἐγείρεται, *does not arise*, also does not set aside the difficulty; for the proverb: "no prophet arises in Galilee" can only be an axiom resulting, according to them, from Scriptural experience ("search and thou shalt see"). The attempt at a complete justification of this appeal to history must be given up. Undoubtedly, the Galilean origin of three of the four prophets cited (Elijah, Nahum, Hosea) is either false or uncertain; see *Hengstenberg*. Elijah was of Gilead; Hosea, of Samaria, which cannot be identified with Galilee; Nahum, of El-Kosh, a place whose situation is uncertain. But Jonah remains. His case is an exception which passion might have caused the rulers to forget in a moment of rage and which, if it had been mentioned in the way of objection to the rulers, would have been set aside by them as an exception confirming the rule. Notwithstanding this isolated fact, Galilee was and still continued to be an outcast land in the theocracy. *Westcott:* "Galilee is not the land of prophets, still less of the Messiah." The gravest thing which they forget, is not Jonah, it is the prophecy Is. viii. 23–ix. 1, where the preaching of the Messiah in Galilee is foretold.

The story of the woman taken in adultery: vii. 53–viii. 11

Three questions arise with regard to this section: Does it really belong to the text of our Gospel? If not, how was it introduced into it? What is to be thought of the truth of the fact itself?

The most ancient testimony for the presence of this passage in the New Testament, is the use made of it in the *Apostolical Constitutions* (i. 2, 24) to justify the employment of gentle means in ecclesiastical discipline with reference to *penitents*. This apocryphal work seems to have received its definitive form about the end of the third century. If then this passage is not authentic in John, its interpolation must go back as far as the third or the second century. The Fathers of the fourth century, *Jerome, Ambrose, Augustine*, admit its authenticity and think that it was rejected in a part of the documents by men who were weak in faith and who were afraid that "their wives might draw from it immoral inferences" (Augustine). Certain MSS. of the *Itala* (*Veronensis, Colbertinus*, etc.), from the fourth century to the eleventh, the *Vulgate*, the *Jerusalem Syriac* translation of the fifth century, the MSS. D F G K H U Γ, from the sixth century to the ninth, and more than three hundred Mnn. (Tischendorf), read this passage, and do not mark it with any sign of doubtfulness. On the other hand, it is wanting in the *Peschito* and in two of the best MSS. of the *Itala*, the *Vercellensis*, of the fourth, and the *Brixianus*, of the

644 / Unbelief Develops in Israel

sixth century. *Tertullian, Cyprian, Origen, Chrysostom* do not speak of it. ℵ A B C L T X Δ, from the fourth century to the ninth, and fifty Mnn., omit it entirely (L and Δ leaving a vacant space); E M S Λ Π and forty-five Mnn. mark it with signs of doubtfulness. Finally, in some documents it is found transposed to another place: one Mn. (225) places it after vii. 36; ten others, at the end of the Gospel; finally, four (13, 69, etc.), in the Gospel of Luke, after chap. xxi. *Euthymius* regards it as a useful *addition;* Theophylact rejects it altogether.

From the point of view of external criticism, three facts prove interpolation:

1. It is impossible to regard the omission of this passage, in the numerous documents which we have just looked at, as purely accidental. If it were authentic, it must necessarily have been omitted of design, and with the motive which is supposed by some of the Fathers. But, at this rate, how many other omissions must have been made in the New Testament? And would such a liberty have been allowed with respect to a text decidedly recognized as apostolic?

2. Besides, there is an extraordinary variation in the text in the documents which present this passage; sixty variants are counted in these twelve verses. *Griesbach* has distinguished three altogether different texts: the ordinary text, that of D, and a third which results from a certain number of MSS. A true apostolic text could never have undergone such alterations.

3. How does it happen that this entire passage is found so differently located in the documents: after ver. 36, at the end of our Gospel, at the end of Luke xxi. finally between chaps. vii. and viii. of our Gospel, as in the T. R.? Such hesitation is likewise without example with respect to a genuine apostolic text.

From the point of view of internal criticism, three reasons confirm this result:

1. The style does not have the Johannean stamp; it has much more the characteristics of the Synoptical tradition. The οὖν, the most common form of transition in John, is altogether wanting; it is replaced by δέ (11 times). The expressions ὄρθρου (John says πρωΐ), πᾶς ὁ λαός, καθίσας ἐδίδασκεν, οἱ γραμματεῖς καὶ οἱ φαρισαῖοι, are without analogy in John, and remind us of the Synoptic forms of expression. Whence could this difference arise, if the passage were genuine?

2. The preamble vii. 53 presents no precise meaning, as we shall see. It is of a suspicious amphibological character.

3. Finally, there is a complete want of harmony between the spirit of this story and that of the entire Johannean narrative. The latter presents us in this part the testimony which Jesus bears to Himself and the position of faith and unbelief which His hearers assume on this occasion. From this point of view, the story of the woman taken in adultery can only be regarded as a digression. As *Reuss* very well says: "Anecdotes of this kind tending to a teaching essentially moral are foreign to the fourth Gospel." As soon as this passage is rejected, the connection between the testimony which precedes and that which follows, is obvious. It is expressly marked by the πάλιν, *again,* viii. 12, which joins the new declaration, viii. 12–20, to that of the great day of the feast, vii. 37 ff.

The authenticity of this passage is also no longer admitted, except by a small number of Protestant exegetes (*Lange, Ebrard, Wieseler*), by the Catholic interpreters (*Hug, Scholz, Maier*), and by some adversaries of the authenticity of the Gospel, who make a weapon of the internal improbabilities of the story (*Bretschneider, Strauss, B. Bauer, Hilgenfeld*). At the time of the Reformation it was judged to be unauthentic by *Erasmus, Calvin* and *Beza;* later, it was likewise expunged by *Grotius, Wetstein, Semler, Lücke, Tholuck, Olshausen, de Wette, Baur, Reuss, Luthardt, Ewald, Hengstenberg, Lachmann, Tischendorf, Meyer, Weiss, Keil.* According to *Hilgenfeld* (*Einleit. ins. N. T.*), this passage has in its favor preponderating testimonies; it places us in the very midst of the days which followed the great day of the feast; finally, it is required by the words of viii. 15. These arguments have no need to be refuted.

How was this passage introduced into our Gospel?

Hengstenberg attributes the composition of it to a believer who was an enemy of Judaism and who wished to represent, under the figure of this degraded woman, whom Jesus had yet restored, the Gentile world pardoned by grace. In order to give more credit to this fiction, the author inserted it in the text of our Gospel with a preamble, and it found its way into a certain number of copies. But the allegorical intention which is thus supposed does not appear from any of the details of the story; besides, it is not exactly true that the woman was pardoned by Jesus. We shall give attention to the objections raised by Hengstenberg against the internal truthfulness of the story.

It is more simple to find in this passage the redaction of some ancient tradition. Eusebius relates (*H. E.*, iii. 40) that the work of Papias contained "the history of a woman accused before the Lord of numerous sins, a history which was contained also in the Gospel of the Hebrews." *Meyer, Weiss* and *Keil* call in question the existence of any relation between this story of Papias and that with which we are occupied. But they have nothing to object against the identity of the two except the expression: *of numerous sins,* used by this Father, as if this very vague term could not be applied to the woman of whom our narrative speaks. The exhortation of Jesus: "*Go, and sin no more,*" undoubtedly does not refer to a single act of sin. For ourselves, it seems to us very difficult not to recognize in this story preserved by Papias that which is related in our pericope. A reader of Papias or of the Gospel of the Hebrews undoubtedly placed it as a note, either at the end of his collection of the Gospels, consequently at the end of John (hence its place in 10 Mnn.), or in a place which seemed to be suitable for it in the Gospel narrative, for example here, as an instance of the machinations of the rulers (vii. 45 ff.), or as an explanation of the words which are to follow viii. 15 ("*I judge no man*"), or indeed after Luke xxi. 38 (where it is found in 4 Mnn.), a passage which presents a striking analogy to our narrative (comp. especially viii. 1, 2 of John with this verse of Luke). It was made the close of that series of tests to which the Sanhedrim, and then the Pharisees and Sadducees had subjected Jesus on that memorable day of the last week of His life. If it was so, we may rank this story in the number of the truly historical, but extra-Scriptural narratives, which the oral tradition of the earliest times has preserved.

Hitzig and *Holtzmann* have supposed that this passage originally formed a part of the writing which, according to them, was the source of our three Synoptics (the alleged *primitive* Mark), and that it was found there between the 17th and 18th verses of chap. xii. of our canonical Mark. Our three Synoptics omitted it, because of the indulgence with which adultery seemed to be treated in it. On the other hand, it found entrance into the Gospel of the Hebrews and by this door entered into our Gospels, in different places. But no explanation is given as to how in so short a time the sentiment of the Church could have completely changed, so that to a unanimous rejection there shortly succeeded so general a

646 / Unbelief Develops in Israel

restoration. Our explanation appears to us at once more natural and less hypothetical. Moreover, Holtzmann himself now gives up the hypothesis of the Proto-Mark.

The question as to whether this story is the tradition of an actual fact or a valueless legend can only be solved by the detailed study of the passage. We will give the translation according to the T. R., indicating only the principal variations.

Vii. 53–viii. 11. 53. *"And every one went away* [1] *to his own house.* Viii. 1. *But Jesus went to the Mount of Olives.* 2. *And at the break of day, he came again* [2] *into the temple; and all the people* [3] *came to him;* [4] *and he sat down and taught them.* [5] 3. *Now the scribes and the Pharisees bring* [6] *to him a woman taken* [7] *in adultery;* [8] *and having set her in the midst of the company,* 4 *they say to him,*[9] *Master this woman has been taken in adultery, in the very act;* [10] 5 *now, in the law, Moses commanded* [11] *us to stone* [12] *such persons; as for thee therefore,*[13] *what dost thou say?* 6. *They said this to test him, that they might be able to accuse him;* [14] *but Jesus, stooping down, wrote with his finger on the ground.*[15] 7. *As they continued asking him, he lifted himself up* [16] *and said to them, He that is without sin among you, let him first* [17] *cast the stone at her.* 8. *Then he stooped down again and wrote on the ground.*[18] 9. *They having heard this* [19] *and being reproved by their conscience,*[20] *went out,*[21] *one by one,*[22] *beginning with the eldest even to the last;* [23] *and Jesus was left alone with the woman who was standing* [24] *in the midst of the company.* 10. *Then Jesus, lifting himself up* [25] *and no longer seeing any one but the woman,*[26] *said to her, Woman,*[27] *where are thine accusers?* [28] *Did no one condemn thee?* 11. *She said,*[29] *No one, Lord. Jesus said to her, Neither do I condemn* [30] *thee; go,*[31] *and sin no more."* [32]

Ver. 53. Does the expression: *every one went away* refer, as seems natural from the context, to the members of the Sanhedrim, who return to their homes after the meeting, vii. 45–52? In that case, the remark is an idle one. Or does it

---

[1] D M S Γ: επορευθησαν. U: απηλθεν. Δ: απηλθον.
[2] D: παραγινεται. U: ηλθεν. Mnn. παρηλθεν.
[3] G S U Mnn.: οχλος (*the multitude*).
[4] 5 Mjj. omit προς αυτον (*to him*).
[5] D 6 Mnn. omit the words και ... αυτους (from *and* to *teach*).
[6] Others: φερουσι, προσηνεγκαν.
[7] E G H K: καταληφθεισαν, D: ειλημμενην.
[8] D: επι αμαρτια (*in sin*).
[9] E G H K add πειραζοντες (*tempting him*). D: εκπειραζοντες αυτον οι ιερεις ινα εχωσιν κατηγοριαν αυτου.
[10] U: ταυτην ευρομεν επ' αυτοφωρω.
[11] D: εκελευσεν.
[12] D M S U Δ: λιθαζειν. Mnn.: λιθαζεσθαι.
[13] D συ δε νυν (*but thou now*).
[14] S U: κατηγοριαν κατ' αυτου. D M omit the words τουτο ... αυτου (from *they* to *accuse*).
[15] E G H K 90 Mnn. add μη προσποιουμενος (*without seeming* to have seen or heard); some Mnn. (in Matthaei): και προσποιουμενος (*and pretending* to write).
[16] D M S Vss.: ανεκυψεν και. U Δ: αναβλεψας (*having raised his eyes*).
[17] E G H πρωτον (*first*).
[18] U adds ενος εκαστου αυτων τας αμαρτιας (*the sins of each one of them*).
[19] D: εκαστος δε των Ιουδαιων (*each one of the Jews*).
[20] D M U Δ Mnn. Vss. omit the words και ... ελεγχομενοι (from *and* to *conscience*).
[21] L: εξηλθεν. M.: ανεχωρησαν.
[22] D omits εις καθ' εις (*one by one*).
[23] E G H K M Vss. omit εως των εσχατων (*even to the last*). D reads ωστε παντας εξελθειν (*so that all went out*).
[24] All the Mjj.: ουσα instead of εστωσα.
[25] Δ Mnn. αναβλεψας (*having raised his eyes*).
[26] D M S omit the words και ... γυναικος (from *and* to *the woman*). U Δ replace them by ειδεν αυτην και (*he saw her and*).
[27] D E F G H K Vss. omit η γυνη (*woman*): M S U Δ: γυναι.
[28] 8 Mnn. and Augustine omit the words που ... σου (from *where* to *accusers*); other variants.
[29] D: κακεινη ειπεν αυτω (*and she said to him*).
[30] E F G K Mnn.: κρινω (*judge*).
[31] D: υπαγε.
[32] D M U Vss. add απο του νυν before αμαρτανε (*from henceforth* before *sin no more*).

refer to the whole people who, when the feast was ended, returned from the temple to their dwellings. This meaning would in itself be more acceptable. It was perhaps the meaning of this verse in the context from which the story has been detached. But in the narrative of John nothing leads us to this meaning of the word *every one*. Herein is an indication of a foreign intercalation.

Viii. 1, 2. A striking analogy to the Synoptic narrative, both in the matter and the form; comp. Luke xxi. 38.

Vv. 3, 4. Γραμματεῖς, *the scribes*, is a ἅπαξ λεγόμενον in John; the Synoptic style. It is scarcely probable that already at that time these men, so proud of their knowledge, would have submitted to Him so grave a question and would have thus consented to concede to Him so great authority in the eyes of the whole people; comp. vii. 26.

Ver. 5. Stoning was ordained by Moses only for the case of an unfaithful *betrothed virgin* (Deut. xxii. 23, 24); for the adulterous *wife*, the kind of death was not determined (Lev. xx. 10). According to the Talmud, where the penalty is not specified, the law meant, not stoning, but strangling. And *Meyer* infers from this that this woman was an unfaithful betrothed virgin. This supposition is neither natural nor necessary. The declarations of the Talmud do not form a law for the time of Jesus. *Tholuck, Ewald* and *Keil*, as it seems to me, rightly hold, that where the law was silent, it was rather the punishment of stoning which was inflicted. This view is confirmed by vv. 2 and 27 of the chapter cited (Lev. xx.), where the penalty of death, not specified in ver. 10, is expressly designated as that by stoning. Comp. also Exod. xxxi. 4 and xxxv. 2, where the penalty of death is ordained for violators of the Sabbath, with Num. v. 32–34, where this punishment is inflicted, without any new determination having been given, under the form of stoning.

Ver. 6. In what did the snare consist? Some, *Augustine, Erasmus, Luther* and *Calvin* think that they desired to lead Jesus to pronounce a sentence whose severity would place it in contradiction to His ordinary compassion. Others, *Euthymius, Bengel, Tholuck, Hengstenberg, Weiss* and *Keil* suppose that the adversaries expected a decision in the line of clemency, which would have put Jesus in contradiction to the Mosaic statute. But, in both of these cases, there would have been no snare properly so called, no danger existing for Jesus except in case of an affirmative answer in the first explanation and of a negative answer in the second. *Hug* and *Meyer* suppose the snare more skillfully laid, that is to say, threatening Jesus on both sides. If He replies negatively, He contradicts Moses; if He replies in conformity with Moses, He enters into conflict with the Roman law which did not punish adultery with death. This appears to me to approach the truth. Only the Roman law has nothing to do here; for the Romans did not impose on the provinces their own legislation, and the conflict resultant from a simple contradiction between the two codes would have had nothing striking enough in the eyes of the people to seriously injure Jesus. The solution seems to me to be simple: If Jesus answered: Moses is right; stone her! they would have gone to Pilate and accused Jesus of infringing upon the rights of the Roman authority, which had reserved to itself the *jus gladii* here, as in all conquered countries. If He answered: Do not stone her! they would have decried Him before the people and would even have accused Him before the Sanhedrim as a false Messiah; for the Messiah must maintain or restore the sovereignty of the law. It is exactly the same combination as when the question was proposed to Him of paying tribute to Cæsar (Luke xx. and parallels). *Luthardt* and *Reuss* also adopt this explanation. *Weiss* objects, it is true, that they could not reasonably expect from Jesus that He would give the order to stone her; and that, in any case, He could still reserve the confirmation of the penalty for the Roman authority. But in the case of a sentence of condemnation it would have been in vain for Jesus to place all the limitations upon this answer that were possible—no account would have been taken of this before the Roman governor. He had been accused indeed of forbidding to pay tribute to Cæsar, though He had answered in precisely the opposite way.

The act of Jesus in the face of the question which is proposed to Him is not simply, as it is frequently understood from certain examples derived either from the Greek authors or from the Rabbis, a way of isolating Himself and expressing His indifference with regard to the subject proposed. In the first place, it could not be an indifferent question for Jesus in such a situation. Then, notwithstanding all that *Weiss* says, it seems to me that *Hengstenberg* is in the true line of thought when he sees in this act, thus understood, a sort of trick incompatible with the moral dignity of Jesus. If He gave Himself the appearance of doing a thing, it was because He was really doing it. He *wrote*, and that which He wrote must quite naturally, as it seems to me, be the words which He utters at this same moment (ver. 7). He writes the first part of it while He is stooping down the first time (ver. 6), and the second part when, after having raised Himself, He resumes the same attitude (ver. 8). Thereby Jesus takes the position of a divine judge both of the woman who is brought to Him and of the very persons themselves who present her to Him. A sentence is not only pronounced: it is written. This act has a meaning analogous to that of the saying of Jeremiah (xvii. 13): "Those who turn aside from Me shall be written in the earth."

Vv. 7, 8. The admirable, yet at the same time very simple, art of the answer of Jesus in ver. 7 consists in bringing back the question from the *judicial* domain, where His adversaries were placing it, to the *moral* ground, beyond which Jesus does not dream for a moment of extending His authority; comp. Luke xii. 14. A judge in his official function may certainly pass judgment and condemn, though being himself a sinner. But such is not, at this moment, the position of Jesus, who is not invested with the official function of a judge. It is also quite as little the position of those who submit the question to Him. In order to have the right to make themselves of their own motion the representatives and executors of the justice of God, it would be necessary therefore, that at least they should themselves have been exempt from every sin which was fitted to provoke a like judgment against themselves. Undoubtedly it might be objected that in former times the entire people was called to condemn such criminals by stoning them. But the time when God committed to the people the function of judges in the case of similar crimes had long since passed. Jesus takes the theocracy, not as being in its ideal form, but such as He finds it, providentially deprived of its ancient constitution and subjected to the foreign yoke. The interpreters who, like *Lücke, Meyer*, and so many others, restrict the application of the term *without sin* to adultery or, in general, to impurity, misconstrue the thought of Jesus. In His eyes "he who has offended in the matter of one commandment, is guilty of all" (James ii. 10). The skill of this answer consists in disarming the improvised judges of this woman, without however infringing in the least upon the ordinance of Moses. On one side, the words: *let him cast the stone*, sustain the code, but on the other, the words: *without sin*, disarm any one who would desire to apply it.

Ver. 9. If the Pharisees had been sincere in their indignation against the accused, it was the time to lead her to the presence of the officially constituted judge. But it was not the evil that they were set against: it was Jesus. Recognizing the fact that their design has failed, they take the only course which remains for them, that of withdrawing, and they make thus the tacit avowal of the odious intention which had brought them. Πρεσβύτεροι is not here an official name; it is the oldest who, as the most venerable representatives of public morality, had taken their place at the head of the company: ἔσχατοι, *the last*, does not mean the youngest or the last in respect to social position, but simply, as *Meyer* says, the last who left. The word *alone* implies only the departure of the accusers.

Vv. 10, 11. By the οὐδὲ ἐγώ, *neither do I*, Jesus gives the woman to understand that there was nevertheless one there who, without acting in contradiction to the rule of justice laid down in ver. 7, might really have the right of taking up the stone, if He thought it fit to do so; but this one even renounced it through charitable feeling and in order to leave her the opportunity of returning to virtue: " *Go, and sin no more.*" We must not see in the words of Jesus: *I do not condemn thee*, a declaration of pardon similar to that which He addresses to the penitent sinful woman in Luke vii. 48, 50. *Bengel* rightly remarks that Jesus does not say: " *Go in peace:* thy sins are forgiven thee." For the sinful woman who is in question here did not come to Jesus by reason of a movement of repentance and faith. By not condemning her, Jesus simply grants her the opportunity for repenting and believing. It is a promise of forbearance, not justification; comp. Rom. iii. 24, 25 (πάρεσις). And by saying to her: *Sin no more*, He indicates to her the path on which alone she can really lay hold upon salvation.

Thus vanish all the moral difficulties and all the historical improbabilities which *Hengstenberg* and others claim that they find in this story. As *Reuss* says: "The authenticity of the fact seems to be sufficiently established." This incident is in every point worthy of the wisdom, holiness and goodness of Him to whom it is attributed. Jesus clearly distinguished the judicial domain from the moral domain; He wakened in His adversaries the consciousness of their own sinfulness, and He made this woman understand how she must use the opportunity of grace which is accorded to her. Finally, in the words: *Where are the accusers?* we think we hear, as it were, the prelude of that triumphant exclamation of the Apostle Paul: "Who shall accuse? Who shall condemn?" (Rom. viii. 33, 34.)

The internal characteristics of this inimitable incident of the life of Jesus locate it chronologically in the same period with the other analogous facts related by the Synoptics, that is to say, immediately after the entrance into Jerusalem on Palm-day (Luke xx.; Matt. xxii., etc.). It is, moreover, at this moment only that so explicit a recognition of the authority of Jesus on the part of the members of the Sanhedrim can be understood.

2. *Jesus, the light of the world:* viii. 12–20

We find in this section: 1. A testimony (ver. 12); 2. An objection (ver. 13); 3. The answer of Jesus (vv. 14–19); 4. An historical notice (ver. 20).

Ver. 12. " *Jesus, taking up the discourse again, said to them: I am the light of the world; he who follows me shall not walk* [1] *in the darkness, but shall have* [2] *the light of life."*—The πάλιν, *again*, can the less be a simple transition to a new discourse since it is placed at the beginning with a certain emphasis and is accompanied by οὖν, *therefore*, which would, in that case, be a useless repetition (in answer to *Weiss*). It announces therefore a new testimony, analogous to that of vii. 37 ff., as if John meant to say: "Jesus, after having thus applied to Himself a first symbol, takes up the discourse again for the purpose of applying to Himself a second." Was this new discourse given on the same day as the preceding one? According to *Weiss*, ver. 20 proves the contrary, because it indicates a new situation. But was Jesus obliged to remain during the whole day as if fastened to one spot? The term ἐλάλησε, *He spoke*, indicates a less solemn attitude and tone than the expressions *He opened His mouth and cried*, in vii. 37. This is a continuation, a complement of the preceding discourse; this circumstance speaks in favor of the identity of the day. In any case, it must be said with *Luthardt*: "The historic thread which concerned the author was quite other than that of days and hours."

For what reason does Jesus designate Himself as the light of the world? *Hug* and others have thought that He alluded to the brightness which was shed forth by the two candelabras which were lighted at evening during the feast, in the court of the women, and the light of which, according to the Rabbis, shone over the whole of Jerusalem. This ceremony was very noisy; a sacred dance, in which grave men participated, took place around the candelabras; and it may be that Jesus made allusion to this solemn march in the following words: "He that followeth me shall not walk . . ." The singing and the music of instruments filled the temple; the festivity was prolonged even until daylight. The celebrated *Maimonides* affirms that this ceremony occurred on every evening of the feast, which would accord with the explanation of Hug. But the Talmud speaks of it only on occasion of the first evening. For this reason *Vitringa* and other commentators have thought that they must connect this saying rather with some prophetic passage which may have been read in the temple during that day; Is. xlii. 6: "*I will cause thee to be the covenant of the people, and the light of the nations.*" Comp. also Is. xlix. 6, 9. But it is not certain that there were regular readings from the Old Testament in the temple; even the existence of a synagogue in the sacred inclosure is doubtful (see *Lücke*). *Jarchi* speaks only of a synagogue " situated *near* the court, on the temple-mountain." And, above all, the saying of Jesus does not contain any sufficiently precise allusion to these prophetic passages. The commentators who hold that there is an allusion to the candelabras of the temple seem to me to commit the same mistake as in the explanation of the previous symbol (vii. 37 ff.). Thinking only of the ceremony which was celebrated in the time of Jesus, they forget what is much more important, the miraculous and beneficent

---

[1] Variation of πεμπατησει (T. R. with D E etc.) and περιπατηση (ℵ B Γ etc.).

[2] ℵ e read ἐχει (*has*) instead of ἐξει.

fact of which this ceremony was the memorial, and which was for Jesus certainly the essential point. The feast of Tabernacles, which at this time assembled the people together, was designed to recall to their minds the blessings of God during the sojourn in the wilderness. Hence, the tents of leafy branches under which they lived and which gave the name to the feast. Now among these blessings, the two greatest had been the water from the rock and the pillar of fire in the cloud. Jesus has just applied to Himself the first of these types. He now applies to Himself the other (hence the πάλιν, ver. 12). It is thus that Jesus celebrates the feast of Tabernacles, translating it, in some sort, into His own person. Only Israel is henceforth the whole world, the κόσμος, as in chap. vi. Jesus was the manna, not for the people only, but for humanity, and in vii. 37, the living water for *whosoever* is athirst. We have already explained in i. 4 and iii. 19 the term *light;* it is the perfect revelation of moral good, that is to say, of God, the living good. The expression: "*He that followeth me shall not walk . . . ,*" alludes, not to the torch-dance in the court, but to the pilgrimage of Israel in the desert. The people arose, advanced, stopped, encamped, at the signal which came from the luminous cloud; with such a guide, there was no more darkness for the travelers. Thus are the obscure things of existence, the night which the selfish will and passions spread over his life, dissipated for man from the moment when he receives Jesus into his heart. At every step, he begins by looking to Him, and he finds in Him the revelation of holiness, the only real truth. The *light of life* does not signify that which consists in life or which produces it, but that which springs from it (i. 4); a light which radiates from the life in communion with God and which directs the exercise of the understanding. The future περιπατήσει, in the Received Text, is probably a correction in accordance with the following ἕξει. The conjunctive aorist must be read οὐ μὴ περιπατήσῃ; comp. x. 5. The use of the form οὐ μή is founded upon the natural distrust of the heart: "It is *not to be feared*, whatever may be its own darkness, that it will be compelled still to walk in the night." Ἕξει: it will possess internally.

There is a profound connection between this testimony and that which precedes. In vii. 37, Jesus presented Himself as the life (ὕδωρ ζῶν); in viii. 12, He offers Himself as the light which emanates from the life. As to the response which man should make to these divine gifts, in the first passage it is the receptivity of faith (*shall drink*); in the second, the activity of practical obedience (*shall walk*).

Ver. 13. "*The Pharisees therefore said to him, thou bearest witness of thyself; thy witness is not true.*" Lücke and Weiss infer from the words *the Pharisees*, that the pilgrims had already departed from Jerusalem. But why could not the Pharisees have been among the multitude present at the feast? This last word: *is not true*, does not signify: "is false," but: "is not sufficiently guaranteed, not worthy of credit." There was a Rabbinical adage which said indeed: "No man bears witness of Himself." The objectors raise only a question of form; they are undoubtedly somewhat intimidated by the Lord's tone of authority. They might have quoted to Him

652 / Unbelief Develops in Israel

His own word of v. 31 : " If I bear witness of myself, my witness is not true." Jesus treats first the question of substance (ver. 14) ; then, that of form (vv. 15–18).

Ver. 14. *" Jesus answered and said to them ; Even if I bear witness of myself, my witness is true, because I know whence I came and whither I go ; but*[1] *you know not whence I come or*[2] *whither I go."* Jesus had accepted in chap. v. the position of an ordinary man ; this is the reason why he had cited in His favor the double testimony of the Father, through the miracles and through the Scriptures. Here, He asserts Himself and claims His true position, which He had voluntarily abandoned. This difference arises from the fact that the rupture between Him and His hearers is now further advanced. He asserts Himself more categorically. The inner light which He possesses with regard to His person places Him absolutely beyond the illusions of pride. And this is the reason why He is, at the same time, the light for others. The term οἶδα, *I know*, designates that unchangeably clear and transparent consciousness which Jesus has of Himself ; it bears at once on the place of His origin and of that to which He would return, on the beginning and the end of His existence. He who distinctly knows these two limits of His life comprehends it altogether. Jesus is distinctly conscious of Himself as of a being coming from on high and returning on high, and as one for whom, consequently, the earthly life is only a passing period with a mission to fulfill, a transition from heaven to heaven. The whole of Christianity rests upon this consciousness which Jesus had of His person. It is the heroism of faith to give oneself up to the extraordinary testimony which this being has borne to Himself. The words : *" you know not,"* are more than the announcement of a fact ; they contain a reproach. They also could know, if only they had their minds open to perceive. In the heavenly and holy character of the appearance of Jesus, every upright heart can discern the divinity of His origin as well as that of His destination. The disjunctive particle ἤ, *or*, in the second clause (see the critical note) is more forcible than the simple καί, *and*, in the first : Jesus adds knowledge *to* knowledge ; hence the *and* ; but as for them, when they are inquired of with reference to one point *or* another, they show always the same ignorance ; hence the *or*.

Vv. 15, 16. *" You judge according to the flesh ; I judge no one ; 16 and if I judge, my judgment is true,*[3] *because I am not alone, but I and the Father*[4] *that sent me."* The objection of the Pharisees, ver. 13, contained a judgment respecting Jesus. They treated Him as an ordinary man, as a sinner, like themselves. They accused Him of overrating Himself in the testimonies which He bore to Himself. It is to this that the charge refers : " *You judge according to the flesh."* We must not confound κατὰ τὴν σάρκα, " according to *the flesh,"* with κατὰ σάρκα, *in a fleshly way*. The flesh here is not

---

[1] F H K omit δε.
[2] We translate according to the reading η in B D K T U X Λ. Και is read in T. R. after ℵ E F G H L and many Mnn.

[3] T. R. reads αληθης with 12 Mjj. (ℵ Γ Δ etc.), and nearly all the Mnn., while B D L T X read αληθινη.
[4] ℵ D omit πατηρ after ο πεμψας με.

the veil extended before the eyes of the one who judges falsely (the carnal spirit or mind); it is rather, according to the article τήν, the appearance marked by weakness of the one who is the object of judgment, by reason of which, at first sight, he is not at all distinguished from other men. The first sense, however, is included in the second, for with a less carnal heart the Jews would have discerned in Jesus, under the covering of the flesh, a being of a higher nature and would have accorded to Him, in the midst of mankind, a place by Himself. This superficial estimate of which Jesus sees Himself to be the object on their part, awakens in Him the feeling of a contrast. While these blind persons allow themselves to make their estimate of Him, with a perfect confidence in their own light, He, the incarnate light, judges no one. Thus, those who are ignorant allow themselves to judge, while He who knows denies Himself this right. And yet, it cannot be denied, Jesus judges also; He Himself declares it in ver. 16. Writers have put themselves to great pains to explain this contradiction. The word *no one* has been paraphrased in this way: " No one, *according to* the outward appearances " (the flesh); so *Cyril.* Or, what amounts to nearly the same thing: " No one . . . *as you judge me* " (*Lücke*). Or again: " No one *now*, in contrast with the judgment to come " (*Augustine, Chrysostom* [1]). But according to these views, there is an addition of what is not said. Or, without an ellipsis and in the sense of iii. 17: "The *principal* aim of my coming, is to save; and if *in exceptional cases* I judge, it is only with reference to those who will not allow themselves to be saved " (*Calvin, Meyer, Astié, Luthardt, Weiss, Keil, Westcott,* with different shades of explanation). But the idea of these exceptional judgments is definitely excluded by the οὐδένα, *no one,* of ver. 15. *Reuss* makes iii. 18 apply here: " No one, because those who are judged have judged themselves." But how then are we to explain the words: *And if I judge?* To all these opinions I should prefer that of *Storr*, who translates ἐγώ, *I*, in the sense of *I alone.* Comp. ver. 26. What Jesus charges upon the Jews is that they think themselves competent to judge Him by themselves and according to their own light (ὑμεῖς, *you*). "As for me," Jesus means to say, " in so far as I am left to myself, reduced to my own human individuality, I do not allow myself anything of the kind; as such I judge no one." It is the same thought, in a negative form, as that of v. 30 in an affirmative form: *"As I hear,* I judge." The emphasis would thus be upon the pronoun ἐγώ, *I*, which its position in the sentence, indeed, makes prominent. And Jesus could thus add, without contradicting Himself, ver. 16: "And yet if I judge." For then, it is not really *He* who judges, since He does nothing but pronounce the sentences which He has heard from His Father. This is the sense which I formerly adopted. On weighing well the import of the word οὐδένα, *no one,* however, I ask myself whether Jesus did not mean that He judges no *individual,* in the

---

[1] *Hilgenfeld* (*Einleit.* p. 728) goes even so far as to infer from this verse that " the fourth Gospel rejects *all outward judgment*," and that according to it " the reign of the Spirit ends directly at the last day." These conclusions are arbitrary, and place the writer in contradiction to himself (v. 27-29).

sense that He pronounces on no one a final sentence; and if He judges the moral state *of the people* and the character of the acts of which He is a witness, these sentences which He pronounces are dictated to Him by His Father. We come back thus to the preceding sense, indeed, but by another path (the contrast of the individual with the people and with things). The received reading ἀληθής, *worthy of faith*, is more appropriate to this context then the variant of some Alexandrian and Greco-Latin authorities, ἀληθινή. Jesus does not intend to say that, in these cases, the sentence which He gives is a *real* sentence, but that it is a *true* sentence, to which one can trust. Thereby He returns to the idea from which He started, the truth of His testimony concerning Himself, and to the question of form which had been proposed to Him. He confirms the answer which He has just given by an article of the code:

Vv. 17, 18. " *And besides it is written* [1] *in your law that the testimony of two men is worthy of belief. 18. I bear witness of myself, and the Father who sent me bears witness of me.*" Jesus enters, at least in form, into the thought of His adversaries (as in vii. 16, 28). The Mosaic law required two witnesses, for testimony to be valid (Deut. xvii. 6; xix. 15). Jesus shows that in the judgments which He pronounces on the world (ver. 16), as well as in the testimonies which He bears to Himself (ver. 18), He satisfies this rule; for the Father joins His testimony to His own. Where the eye of the flesh can see only one witness, there are really two. This testimony of the Father is generally referred to the miracles, according to ver. 36. But the connection with ver. 16 leads us to a much more profound explanation. Jesus describes here a fact of His inner life, as in v. 30. The knowledge which He has of Himself and of His mission (ver. 12) differs essentially from the psychological phenomenon which is called in philosophy the fact of consciousness; it is in the light of God that He contemplates and knows Himself. Herein is the reason why His testimony bears, in the view of every one who has a sense for perceiving God, the stamp of this divine authority.[2] In the expression: *your law*, the adversaries of the authenticity have found a proof of the Gentile origin of the author (*Baur*). *Reuss* formerly explained it by the spirit of our Gospel, which has as its end in view nothing less than "a lowering and almost a degradation of the old dispensation." We have been able to judge from

---

[1] ℵ reads γεγραμμενον εστι instead of γεγραπται.

[2] An anecdote will perhaps explain this saying of Jesus better than any commentary. About 1660, Hedinger, chaplain of the Duke of Wurtemburg, took the liberty, at first privately and then publicly, to censure his sovereign for a grave fault. The latter enraged sent for him, resolved that he would punish him. Hedinger, strengthened by prayer, repaired to the presence of the prince, bearing on his face the expression of the peace of God and in his heart the sense of His presence. After having looked at him attentively, the prince said to him: "Hedinger, why did you not come alone, as I ordered you?" "I am alone, your Highness." "No, you are not alone." "Pardon me, your Highness; but I am alone." The Duke persisting with an increasing agitation, Hedinger said to him: "Certainly, your Highness, I came alone; but whether it has pleased my God to send an angel with me I cannot say." The Duke dismissed him without inflicting any injury upon him. The living communion of this servant of God with his God was a sensible fact even to the one whom passion exasperated.

the close of chap. v. as to what is the value of these assertions. *Weiss, Keil, Reuss* himself (now) see in this *your* an accommodation: "This law *on which you rest* at this moment for condemning me." I think rather, notwithstanding what *Weiss* and *Keil* say, that Jesus, in expressing Himself thus, is inspired by the feeling of the exceptional position which He is claiming in all this section. As He nowhere says, *our Father* (not even in the address of the Lord's Prayer), but: *your* Father, Matt. v. 16, 45, 48; vi. 8, 15, 32, etc.), or, when He wished to express the divine fatherhood at once with reference to Himself and to us: "*My* Father and *your* Father" (xx. 17), because God is not His Father in the sense in which He is ours, so no more can He say: *our* law, uniting under one and the same epithet His own relation and that of the Jews to the Mosaic institution. Who does not feel that He could not, without derogation, have said in vii. 19: "Has not Moses given *us* the law?" Jesus was conscious of being infinitely elevated above the entire Jewish system. His submission to the law was undoubtedly complete, but it was free; for His moral life was not dependent on the relation to an external ordinance. The word *men* is not found in the Hebrew text; this term, whatever *Weiss* may say, must have been added intentionally; it was suggested by the contrast between the human witnesses whom the law demanded, and the divine witness whom Jesus here introduces (*the Father who sent me*). In this judicial form Jesus expresses at the foundation the same thought as when He spoke in ver. 16 of the inner certainty of His own testimony. The idea of this entire passage is the following: "You demand a guaranty of that which I am saying of myself and of you; behold it: It is in God that I know myself and that I assert myself, as it is in Him that I know you and judge you." And it is in virtue of this divine light which shines within Him and by means of which He also knows others, that He is present as the *light of the world* (ver. 12). A fact so spiritual could hardly be understoood by every one; hence the following:

Ver. 19. "*They said to him therefore, Where is thy father? Jesus answered, You know neither me nor my Father; if you knew me, you would know my Father also.*" *Therefore:* "In consequence of this declaration." These discourses of Jesus are of so lofty import, that they sometimes produce upon us the effect of monologues, in which Jesus lays hold anew upon Himself and displays the treasures which He discovers in the centre of His being. The disciples themselves could only get glimpses of their meaning. John gathers them together as enigmas which the future would have to solve. But is not the same thing true at this hour, in the midst of the Christian Church, with reference to many of the words of the apostles? How many baptized persons comprehend what St. Paul said of the inner witness of the Spirit (Rom. viii. 16)? Thus the question of the hearers of Jesus has nothing inadmissible in it, as *Reuss* asserts. Jesus spoke of a second witness; but a witness must be seen and heard. Otherwise, what purpose does he serve? And how can we fail to suppose, in that case, that he who invokes such testimony is a dreamer or an impostor? *Luthardt:* "It is as if they wished to intimate that every liar can also appeal to God." The meaning of the question seems to me to be this : " If it is of God that thou art speaking, let Him make Himself heard ; if it is of some one else, let him show himself." The answer of Jesus means that it is impossible for Him to satisfy their demand. The living presence of God in a human being is a fact which cannot be perceived by the senses ; but if they possessed the spiritual organ necessary for understanding this Jesus who manifests Himself to them, they would soon discern in Him the God who is in intimate communion with Him ; and they would not ask : "Where is He ?" Comp. xiv. 10.

Ver. 20. "*Jesus spoke these words as he was teaching near the treasury, in the temple ;* [1] *and no one laid hands on him, because his hour was not yet come."* The position which the words ταῦτα τὰ ῥήματα, *these words,* occupy at the beginning of the sentence, gives them, notwithstanding the denial of *Weiss,* an emphatic sense : words of such gravity. Even the recollection of the locality in which they had been uttered had remained deeply engraved in the memory of the evangelist. The term γαζοφυλάκιον, *treasury*, probably designates, by reason of the preposition ἐν, *in,* the whole place where were deposited the sums collected for the maintenance of the temple and for other pious uses. It appears from Mark xii. 41, and Luke xxi. 1, that the *trunks* or chests of brass, thirteen in number, which were designed to receive the gifts of the faithful, were properly called by this name. They were in the court of the women, and bore, each of them, an inscription indicating the purpose to which the money which was deposited in it was consecrated. It was before the one which was designed for the poor that Jesus was sitting, when He saw the widow cast into it her mite. It is probable that the apartment called *treasury* was that in which were kept the sums coming from these trunks, and that it was near these trunks. This locality was almost contiguous to that in which was the famous hall called Gazith, where the Sanhedrim held its meetings, between the court of the women and the inner court (*Keil, Handb. der bibl. Archäol.* I., p. 146, note 13). This last circumstance explains the importance which the evangelist attaches to the indication of this locality (vii. 45–52). It was, in some sort under the eyes and in the hearing of the assembled Sanhedrim [2] (vii. 45–52), that Jesus was teaching when He uttered such words. The expression *in the temple* serves to make prominent the sacred character of the locality indicated : in the treasury, in the midst of the temple at Jerusalem ! The *and* which follows evidently takes, in this connection, the sense of : *and yet.* If there was a place where Jesus found Himself under the hands and at the mercy of His enemies, it was here ; but their arm was still paralyzed by their conscience and by the public favor which gathered around Jesus.

3. *"It is I."* viii. 21–29

Jesus had just applied to Himself the two principal symbols which the feast presented to Him. The following testimony completes the

---

[1] ℵ omits διδασκων εν τω ιρω.
[2] *Weiss* criticises with an exclamation point these expressions which he seems to take literally. It belongs to me to be astonished.

two which precede; it is a more general affirmation respecting His mission.

Vv. 21, 22. *"Jesus said therefore to them again,*[1] *I go away and you shall seek me and you shall die in your sin; whither I go, you cannot come. 22. The Jews therefore said, will he kill himself? for he said, whither I go, you cannot come."* The *therefore* seems to allude to the liberty which Jesus continued to enjoy (ver. 20), notwithstanding His preceding declarations. There is nothing to prevent our admitting that this new testimony also was given on the same day, the last and great day of the feast. It was the last time that Jesus found Himself in the midst of His whole people assembled together, before the feast at which he was to shed His blood for them. On the morrow, this multitude was about to disperse to all parts of the world. To this situation the grave and sorrowful tone of this discourse fully answers.

Ver. 21 admonishes the hearers of the importance of the present hour for the people and for each individual: Jesus, their only Saviour, is to be with them only for a little while longer. When once they have rejected Him, heaven, whither He is about to return, will be closed to them; there will remain for them nothing but perdition. This declaration is a more emphatic repetition of vii. 33, 34. As *Meyer* says, the *seeking* of the Jews will not be that of faith; it will be only the longing for external deliverance. The words ἐν τῇ ἁμαρτίᾳ ὑμῶν, *in your sin*, indicate the state of inward depravity, and consequently of condemnation, in which death will overtake them; Jesus alone could have delivered them therefrom. *Hengstenberg* and others translate: *by* your sin. This sense of ἐν is possible; but the former sense is better suited to the singular substantive. *Sin* is here the wandering of the heart, the estrangement from God, in general; in ver. 24, it will be the particular manifestations of this disposition. In xiii. 33, Jesus speaks to the apostles, in the same terms as here, of the impossibility of following Him; but for them the impossibility will be only temporary (ἄρτι, *at this hour*), for Jesus will return to seek for them (xiv. 3). For the Jews, on the contrary, there will be no longer a bridge between earth and heaven; the separation is made complete by the rejection of Him "without whom no one comes to the Father" (xiv. 6). In their turn, and as if by a sort of retaliation, the Jews go beyond the answer which they had made to His preceding declaration, vii. 35. "Certainly," they say, "if it is to Hades that thou meanest to descend, we have no intention of following Thee thither." This ridicule may be explained without the necessity of having recourse to the idea that a special punishment awaited in Hades those who took their own lives (Josephus, *Bell. Jud.*, iii. 8. 5). The following words are intended to explain to them the: *you cannot*, which irritates them:

Vv. 23–25. *"And he said*[2] *to them, you are from beneath, I am from above; you are of this world, I am not of this world. 24. Therefore I said to you, that you shall die in your sins; for, if you do not believe*[3] *that I am he, you*

---

[1] ℵ: ελεγεν ουν instead of ειπεν ουν παλιν.
[2] ℵ B D L T X : ελεγεν instead of ειπεν.
[3] ℵ D read μοι after πιστευσητε.

shall die in your sins. 25. *They said therefore to him, Who art thou? Jesus said*[1] *to them, Precisely that which I also declare to you.*" Jesus lets their jesting go unnoticed. He continues the warning which was begun in ver. 21. An abyss separates them from Him; this is the reason why He cannot serve them as a Saviour and raise them with Himself to heaven, His own country. The parallelism between the expressions: "*from beneath*" and "*of this world*" (ver. 23) does not permit us to include in the former the idea of Hades. We must rather see in the first antithesis: *from beneath* and *from above*, the opposition of *nature*, and in the second: *of this world* and *not of this world*, the contrast of disposition and moral activity. The *world* designates human life constituted independently of the divine will and consequently in opposition to it. One may be *from beneath* (by nature), without being *of the world* (by tendency), in case the soul attains to the desire of the higher good. The negative form: *I am not of this world*, expresses forcibly the repugnance inspired in Jesus by this whole course of human life, which is destitute of the divine inspiring breath.

Their perdition is consequently certain, if they refuse to attach themselves to Him, for He alone could have been for them the bridge between *beneath* and *above*. The brief clause by which Jesus formulates the contents of faith: " If you believe not *that I am . . .* " (literally), is remarkable because of the absence of a predicate. The whole attention is thus evidently directed to the subject, ἐγώ, *I:* "that *it is I* who am . . . and no other." It seems to me difficult to suppose that, in using this expression, Jesus is not thinking of that by which Jehovah often expresses what He is for Israel (e. g. Deut. xxxii. 39; Is. xliii. 10: *ki ani hou*, literally, *for I am He*). As has been said: in this word is summed up by God Himself the whole faith of the Old Testament: "I am your God, besides whom there is no other." In the same way, Jesus sums up in this word the whole faith of the new covenant: "I am the Saviour besides whom there is no other." It is remarkable that in the passage in Deuteronomy, the LXX. use, for the translation of these words, precisely the same Greek expression which we find here: ἴδετε ὅτι ἐγώ εἰμι; which leads us to think that Jesus used the same Hebrew expression as the Old Testament. The understood predicate was certainly *the Christ*. But Jesus carefully avoided this term, because of the political coloring which it had assumed in Israel. The hearers could understand paraphrases such as these: He whom you are expecting: He who alone can answer the true aspirations of your soul; He who can save you from sin and lead you to God. But this word *Christ* which He carefully avoids is precisely the one which His hearers desired to wrest from Him; this is the aim of their question: *who art thou then?* In other words: "Have at last the courage to speak out plainly!" His enemies might indeed use to their advantage as against His life an express declaration on His part on this decisive point.

The reply of Jesus is one of the most controverted passages in the

---

[1] ℵ D read ουν after ειπεν.

Gospel. There are two principal classes of interpretations, in accordance with the two chief meanings of ἀρχή: *beginning* (temporal) and *origin* (substantial or logical). In the first class must be reckoned that of *Cyril, Fritzsche, Hengstenberg:* "From eternity (ἀρχή, i. 1), I am that which I declare unto you." But why not, instead of the unusual phrase τὴν ἀρχήν, simply say ἀπ' ἀρχῆς, as in 1 John i. 1? Then, in this sense, would not the perfect λελάληκα have been more suitable than the present λαλῶ? Besides, the thought of Jesus would in any case have been altogether impenetrable for His hearers. The Latin Fathers, e. g., *Augustine*, translated as if it were the nominative: "who art thou? *The beginning* (the origin of things)." There would be but one way of justifying this sense grammatically; it would be to make the accusative τὴν ἀρχήν a case of attraction from the following ὅτι: "The beginning, that which I also say to you." But the construction, as well as the idea, remains none the less forced. *Tholuck*, abandoning this transcendental sense of ἀρχή, applies this word to the beginning of Jesus' ministry: "I am what I have unceasingly said to you ever since I began to speak to you." But why not simply say ἀπ' ἀρχῆς, as in xv. 27? And it must be admitted that the inversion of τὴν ἀρχήν cannot well be explained, any more than can the καί, *also*, before λαλῶ. There remains, in the temporal sense of ἀρχή, the explanation of *Meyer*. He holds that there is at once an interrogation and an ellipsis: "What I say to you concerning Myself from the beginning (is this what you ask me)?" The ellipsis is as forced as the thought is idle. And how can we explain the καί, the choice of the unusual term τὴν ἀρχήν, and the use of the present λαλῶ, instead of the perfect λελάληκα which would certainly be better suited to this meaning? The interpreters who give to ἀρχή a *logical* sense and make τὴν ἀρχήν an adverbial phrase: *before all, in general, absolutely*, are able to cite numerous examples drawn from the classic Greek. Thus *Luthardt* and *Reuss*: "*At first*, I am what I say to you"—which means: "This is the first and only answer that I have to give to you. If you wish to know who I am, you have only to weigh, *in the first place*, my testimonies respecting My own person." The sense is good; but to what subsequent way of explaining Himself would this *in the first place* allude (see, however, below)? And why not, in this sense, simply say πρῶτον (Rom. iii. 2)? *Chrysostom, Lücke, Weiss, Westcott* explain thus: "*In general*, why do I still speak with you?" Understand: "I do not myself know" (Lücke), or: "This is what you should ask me." I confess that I do not understand how it is possible to put into the mouth of Jesus anything so insignificant. Then, if we could overlook these ellipses, which are, however, quite unnatural, what are we to do with the ὅ τι? Are we to take it in the sense of τί or διατί, *why*, or *because of what?* *Weiss* acknowledges that the examples from the New Testament which are cited for one of these senses (e. g., Mark ix. 11), are not to be thus explained. The only analogous use of this word seems to me to be found in the LXX., 1 Chron. xvii. 6; comp. with 2 Sam. vii. 7. Is this sufficient to legitimate this use in our passage? Moreover, the very rare phrase τὴν ἀρχήν is not sufficiently justified on this interpretation. The only logical sense of this expression which seems to me probable is that which *Winer* has defended in his Grammar of the New Testament (§ 54, 1) and to which *de Wette, Brückner, Keil,* etc., have given their adhesion, and in the main *Reuss* also: "*Absolutely* what I also declare unto you," that is to say: "neither more nor less than what my word contains." Jesus appeals thus to His testimonies respecting His person as the adequate expression of His nature. "Fathom my *speech* and you will discern my *nature.*" This sense fully accounts for the minutest details of the text: 1. The striking position of the word τὴν ἀρχήν, *absolutely;* 2. The choice of the pronoun ὅ τι *all that which:* "whatever it may be that I may have said to you;" they have only to sum up His affirmations respecting Himself, the light of the world, the rock from which flows the living water, the bread which came down from heaven . . . , etc., and they will know what He is; 3. The particle καί, *also,* which brings out distinctly the identity between His nature and His speech; 4. The use of the verb λαλεῖν, *to declare,* instead of λέγειν, *to say, to teach.* As *Keil* well says in reply to *Weiss:* "His λαλεῖν does not designate what He has said of Himself on this or that occasion; it is His *discourse* in general, presented as an adequate expression of His nature;" finally, 5. The present tense of the verb, which gives us to understand that His testimonies are not yet at their end. It is objected, it is true, that τὴν ἀρχήν does not have this sense of *absolutely* except in negative propositions. But, in the first place, the sense of the proposition is essentially negative: "Absolutely *nothing else* than what I declare." And can we demand of the New Testament all the strictness of the classical forms? Besides, *Baümlein* cites the following example from Herodotus: ἀρχὴν γὰρ ἐγὼ μηχανήσομαι (i. 9, 1), an example whose value seems to be but little diminished by the fact that the phrase is followed by a negative proposition. This explanation seems to me indisputably preferable to all the others. I still ask myself, however, whether we cannot revert to the temporal sense of ἀρχή, *beginning,* and in that case explain: "*To begin,* that is to say, *for the moment,*" and find the *afterwards* or *at the end,* which should correspond to the beginning, in ver. 28 : "When you shall have lifted up the Son of man, *then* you shall know . . . " At present, Jesus reveals Himself only by His *speech*; but when the great facts of salvation shall have been accomplished, then they will receive a new revelation still more luminous. If this relation between ver. 25 and ver. 28 seems forced, we must, as I think, abide by the preceding explanation. We omit a multitude of explanations which are only varieties of the preceding meanings, or which are too entirely erroneous to make it possible to consider them.

The application of this answer of Jesus was that the thorough examination of the testimony which He bore continually to Himself was enough to lead to the discovery therein of His nature and of His mission as related to Israel and to the world. On this path, one will learn to know Him successively as the true temple (chap. ii.), as the living water (chap. iv.), as the true Son (chap. v.), as the bread from heaven (chap. vi.), etc. And in this way it is that His name *Christ* will be in a manner spelled out, letter after letter, in the heart of the believer, and will formulate itself there as a spontaneous discovery, which will be worth infinitely more than if he had learned it in the form of a lesson from an outward teaching. To be salutary indeed, this profession: "Thou art the Christ," must be, as in the case of Peter (vi. 66–69), the fruit of the experiences of faith. Comp. Matt. xvi. 17: "Flesh and blood have not revealed it unto thee, but my Father who is in heaven." Such was the way in which the homage of Palm-day arose. Jesus never either sought or accepted an adhesion arising from any other origin than that of moral conviction. This reply is one of the most marvelous touches of Jesus' wisdom. It perfectly explains why, in the Synoptics, He forbade the Twelve to say that He was the Christ.

Vv. 26, 27. "*I have many things to speak and to judge concerning you; but he who sent me is worthy of belief, and what I have heard from him,[1] that do I speak[2] to the world. 27. They understood not that he spoke to them of the Father.*"[3] Some interpreters, ancient and modern, have tried to connect this verse grammatically with the preceding, by making the last words of that verse: ὅτι καὶ λαλῶ ὑμῖν, a parenthetical clause, and the first words of ver. 26, πολλὰ ἔχω, the continuation of the clause which was begun with τὴν ἀρχήν (so *Bengel, Hofmann, Bäumlein*): "For the moment—since it is still the time when I am speaking with you—I have many things to say to you" (*Hofmann*); or: "Certainly I have—a thing which I am also doing —many things to say to you" (*Bäumlein*). But this sense of τὴν ἀρχήν is absolutely idle; and no less so that of the parenthetical clause. The attempt has also been made to connect ver. 26 logically with ver. 25. Thus *Luthardt* and *Reuss* introduce this antithesis: "It is of *yourselves* (not of myself) that I have to speak to you, and this will be for you a much more important thought to occupy your minds." But what was there of more serious importance for them than to know who Jesus was? *Weiss* finds a contrast between the idea: that it was not worth while to speak to them any longer (ver. 25), and the idea of the multitude of things which He had to say to them (ver. 26). This explanation falls together with the sense which *Weiss* gives to ver. 25. In my view, ver. 26 does not continue the thought of ver. 25. It is united with ver. 24. After having answered the question of the hearers in ver. 25, Jesus takes up again the course of His charges in vv. 21-24. In these verses he had uttered stern truths with reference to the moral state of the people; He simply continues in ver. 26: "Of these declarations and these judgments I have still *many*' (πολλά, at the beginning of the clause) to pronounce with regard to you." What is to follow in this same chapter, vv. 34, 37, 40, 41, 43, 44, 49, 55, gives us an idea of these many judgments which Jesus had in mind. "*But*," He adds, "painful as this mission may be for me, I cannot abstain from speaking to you as I do, for I only obey herein Him who dictates to me my message; now He is the truth itself, and my office here below can only be that of making the world hear what He reveals to me." From

---

[1] ℵ reads παρ' αυτω (*with him*) instead of παρ' αυτου.

[2] The MSS. are divided between λεγω (E F G etc.) and λαλω (ℵ B D etc.).

[3] ℵ D 3 Mnn. It^plerique Vulg. add του θεου at the end of the verse.

Chrysostom to *Meyer*, some explain the opposition expressed in the word *but* by this idea: "I have much to say to you; but *I refrain*, and this because you are unwilling to receive the truth." But with this sense, to what purpose make appeal to the divine truth which forces him to speak and *to say to the world* what He hears from above. And in what follows, does Jesus keep silence? Does He not, on the contrary, make the greatest number of charges and the most severe ones against His hearers that He has ever addressed to them? With reference to ἤκουσα, *I heard*, comp. v. 30. This past tense cannot, either in accordance with this parallel or with the context, refer to the pre-existent state. Jesus certainly cannot mean that He heard in heaven, before coming here below, the charges which He now addresses to the Jews.

Ver. 27. Criticism declares the want of understanding of the Jews which is mentioned in ver. 27 impossible. Can those of whom John speaks, then, be, as *Meyer* thinks, new hearers who had not been present at the previous discourses? Or must we understand with *Lücke:* They were not willing to acknowledge that it was the Father who really made Him speak in this way; or with *Weiss:* They did not understand that He had the mission to reveal the Father by declaring what He inwardly heard from Him. These are manifest tortures inflicted on the text. The ἔλεγεν cannot be taken here in the same sense as in vi. 71: *to speak of.* It must be observed that in this whole discourse from ver. 21, Jesus had spoken of *Him who sent Him*, without once pronouncing the name either of God or of the Father. Now among the multitude there might be found hearers who were unable to imagine so close a relation between a human creature and the infinite God as that of which Jesus was bearing witness, and who consequently asked themselves whether He did not mean to speak of some one of the persons who were to precede the Messiah and with whom Jesus sustained a secret relation, as the Messiah was to do with Elijah. Think of the strange misunderstandings attributed by the Synoptics to the apostles themselves! After eighteen centuries of Christianity, many things in the discourses of Jesus appear evident to us, which, through their novelty and the opposition which they encountered from inveterate prejudices, must have appeared strange in the extreme to the greater part of His hearers. No doubt, if the heart had been better disposed, the mind would have been more open.

To this want of intelligence in His present hearers, Jesus opposes the announcement of the day when the full light will come among them respecting His mission, after the great national crime which they are on the point of committing.

Vv. 28, 29. " *Jesus therefore said to them*,[1] *when you have lifted up the Son of man, then shall you know that I am he and that I do nothing of myself, but that I speak these things* [2] *to you according to the teachings of my* [3] *Father,* 29 *and that he that sent me is with me; the Father* [4] *has not left me alone, because*

---

[1] B L T omit αυτοις after ειπεν, and ℵ D add παλιν.

[2] ℵ: ουτως instead of ταυτα.

[3] Μου is omitted by ℵ D L T X It^{plerique}.

[4] ℵ B D L T X 5 Mnn. It^{plerique} Vulg. Cop. reject ο πατηρ after μονον.

I do always that which is pleasing to him." The lifting up of the Son of man refers especially to the death on the cross; this appears from the second person: *you have lifted up.* But Jesus could not hope that the cross would by itself cause the scales to fall from the eyes of the Jews and extort from them the confession: It is He! It could not produce this effect except by becoming for Him the stepping-stone to the throne and the passage to glory. The word *to lift up,* therefore, contains here the same amphibology as in iii. 14, and the second person of the plural assumes thus a marked tinge of irony: " When by killing me you shall have put me on the throne. . . ." The term *Son of man* designates that lowly appearance which is now the ground of His rejection. The recognition of Jesus here predicted took place in the conscience of all the Jews without exception when, after the sending of the Holy Spirit, the holy and divine nature of His person, of His work and of His teaching was manifested in Israel by the apostolic preaching, by the appearance of the Church, and then, finally, by the judgment which struck Jerusalem and all the people. At the sight of this, the want of understanding came to its end whether they would or not, and was transformed into faith in some, in others into voluntary hardening. This recognition never ceases to be effected in Israel by reason of the spectacle of the development of the Church; it will end in the final conversion of the nation, when they will cry out with one voice, as if on a new Palm-day: " *Blessed is He that cometh in the name of the Lord* " (Luke xiii. 35). What calm dignity, what serene majesty, in these words: *Then you shall know . . .*! They recall, as *Hengstenberg* remarks, those grave and menacing declarations of Jehovah: " Mine eye shall not pity thee . . . *and ye shall know that I am the Lord,*" Ezek. vii. 4. Comp. the same form of expression, Ezek. xi. 10; xii. 20; Exod. x. 2, etc. *Weiss* compares with this saying the word of Jesus respecting the sign of Jonah (Matt. xii. 39 ff.). A still more striking parallel in the Synoptics seems to me to be the word addressed to the Sanhedrim, Matt. xxvi. 64: " *You shall see the Son of man seated at the right hand of power and coming on the clouds of heaven.*" Some interpreters claim that John should have written οὕτως, *thus,* instead of ταῦτα, *these things.* But the thought is this: " and that I declare to you *these things* (ταῦτα) which you hear, *according to* (καθώς) the teaching which I have received from the Father." The expression is therefore correct. The whole of the end of the verse depends on γνώσεσθε, *you shall know.* Jesus here sums up all His preceding affirmations, while presenting them by anticipation as the *contents* of that future recognition which He announces: " *that I am he;*" comp. ver. 24: " *that I do and teach nothing of myself;*" comp. vii. 16, 17. This verse therefore means: " You yourselves will then say *amen* to all these declarations which you so lightly reject at this hour."

It appears to me natural to make the first clause of ver. 29 also depend on the verb, *You shall know;* it sums up the declarations of viii. 16–18. The following clause then reproduces very forcibly (by *asyndeton*) this last affirmation: *is with me.* In contrast with the present which escapes Him, Jesus with assured confidence lays hold of the future: " You may reject me if you will, yet the Father remains in inner communion with me, as I have said to you, and He will protect my work." One might be tempted to understand the words οὐκ ἀφῆκε in this sense. " In sending me, He has not *suffered me to come alone* here below; He has willed to accompany me Himself." This indeed would be the most simple sense of the aorist. But in this case, how are we to understand what follows : " *Because I do always that which is pleasing to Him ?*" Hengstenberg, who explains thus, has recourse to the divine foreknowledge: " He has not suffered me to come alone, since He well knows that I am faithful to Him in all things." This sense is evidently forced. We must therefore understand the aorist ἀφῆκε in the sense in which we find it in the passage, Acts xiv. 17 : " *God has not left Himself without witness.*" "God has, in no moment of my career, left me to walk alone, because at every moment He sees me doing that which pleases Him." An instant therefore, a single one, in which Jesus had acted or spoken of His own impulse would have brought a rupture between Him and God; God would have immediately withdrawn from Jesus Himself, and that in the measure in which this will of His own was fixed within Him. The voluntary and complete dependence of Christ was the constant condition of the co-operation of the Father; comp. the words of x. 17 and xv. 10, which express in the main the same thought. Certainly, if the evangelist had written his Gospel to set forth the theory of the Logos, he would never have put this saying into the mouth of Jesus. For it seems directly to contradict it. The communion of the Son and the Father is regarded here as resting upon a purely moral condition. But we see by this how real was the feeling which Jesus had of His truly human existence, and how John himself has taken for granted the humanity of his Master. Τὰ ἀρεστά, *that which is pleasing to Him*, designates the will of the Father, not from the point of view of the articles of a code, but in that which is most spiritual and inward in it. Indeed, this term does not express the contents only of the *doing* of Jesus, but its motive. He did not only *what* was pleasing to the Father, but He did it *because* it was pleasing to Him. It is proved by this saying that Jesus had the consciousness, not only of not having committed the least positive sin, but also of not having neglected the least good, and that in His feelings as well as in His outward conduct.

Here is one of the passages where we can make palpable the fact that the discourses of Jesus in the fourth Gospel are not compositions of the writer, but real discourses of Christ. 1. The communion with God which Jesus affirms can only be a real historical fact. It cannot have been invented by the author. If it were not in the experience, it would not be in the thought. 2. The allusion to the *Jewish law* (vv. 17, 18), in order to justify a fact of so inward a nature, contains a surprising accommodation, which necessarily implies the historical surroundings in which Jesus taught. 3. The locality indicated with so much precision in ver. 20 testifies of a perfectly accurate historical recollection; otherwise, there would be here a piece of charlatanism, which it would be impossible to reconcile with the seriousness of the whole narrative.

4. "*I and you*":   viii. 30–59.

Jesus, in His second discourse (vv. 12–20) attributed to Himself two modes of teaching: *testimony*, by which He reveals His origin, His mission, His work, and *judgment*, by which He unveils the moral state of His hearers. In this sense He had also said, ver. 26: "*I have yet many things to say and to judge concerning you.*" These more severe judgments which Jesus bore in His mind respecting the moral state of His people, we find expressed in the first section of the following discourse; it is *judgment* reaching its culminating point (vv. 30–50): you are not free; you are not children of Abraham; you are not children of God, but of the devil. Such are the severe judgments which are gradually introduced in the conversation between Jesus and even the least ill-disposed of His hearers. The second part is that of *testimony*. Jesus rises to His greatest height: He is the destroyer of death; He is before Abraham (vv. 51–59).

1. The judgment of Jesus respecting Israel: vv. 30–50.

And first its state of slavery: vv. 30–36.

Vv. 30–32. "*As Jesus spoke thus, many believed on him.* 31. *Jesus therefore said to those Jews who had become believers on him: If you abide in my word, you shall be really my disciples,* 32 *and you shall know the truth, and the truth shall make you free.*" The term "*believed*" designates here undoubtedly the disposition, openly expressed, to acknowledge Jesus as the Messiah. In this quite considerable number of believers, there were perhaps some members of the Sanhedrim; xii. 42: "*Many of the rulers believed on him.*" They perceived indeed that, in the words which Jesus had just uttered, there was something else than a vain boast. But Jesus is no more dazzled by this apparent success than he had been by the confession of Nicodemus (iii. 1, 2), and by the enthusiasm of the Galilean multitude (vi. 14, 15). Instead of treating these new believers as converts, He puts them immediately to the test by addressing to them a promise which, notwithstanding its greatness, presents a profoundly humiliating side. It is thus that Jesus often acts. At once, the one whose faith is only superficial stumbles at the holiness of the new word and falls; the one whose conscience has been laid hold of perseveres and penetrates farther into the essence of things. The particle *therefore* in ver. 31, sums up in a word the connection of ideas which we have just developed.

This new scene can scarcely have taken place on the same day with the preceding. Ver. 31 is explained in the most natural way by holding that those of the stranger pilgrims who had believed had departed on the day after the feast, and that, at this moment, Jesus was surrounded only by believing hearers who had until then belonged to the Jewish party. We are surprised, at the first glance, to meet in this gospel a connection of words such as *Jews who had become believers*. But this *contradictio in adjecto* is intentional on the part of the author; it is even the key of the following passage. These believers, at the foundation, belonged to the party of the adversaries; they were indeed still really Jews; they continued to share in the Messianic aspirations of the nation; only they were disposed to recognize in Jesus the man who had the mission to satisfy these aspirations. Theirs was nearly the condition of mind of the Galilean multitude, at the beginning of chap. vi. Undoubtedly, these Jewish believers were not all of the πολλοί, *many*, of the preceding verse, but only a group among them, as *Weiss* and *Westcott* think. In the view of the latter, the difference between the two limiting words, αὐτῷ, *him*, and εἰς αὐτόν, *on him*, ver. 30, is explained even by this fact. But the meaning seems to me rather: They believed on him (as the Messiah) because they for a moment put confidence in His word (*him*).

The nature of the promise made in vv. 31, 32, is admirably fitted to the end which Jesus proposes to Himself. He knows that emancipation from the Roman yoke is the great work which is expected of the Messiah; He therefore spiritualizes this hope, and presents it under this more elevated form to the heart of the believers. The pronoun ὑμεῖς, *you*, has as its aim to contrast these new disciples with the unbelieving multitude. According to *Weiss*, this word serves rather to place them in opposition to the *true* believers among the πολλοί; but this distinction was not sufficiently marked. We might also see here a contrast with the early disciples. The first sense is the most natural. The expression *to abide in* contains the idea of persevering docility. There will be for this rising faith obstacles to be overcome. The Word will find in their hearts inveterate prejudices; a relapse into unbelief is therefore for them, though believers, a serious danger. By this figure: *to abide in*, the revelation contained in the word of Jesus is compared to a fertile soil in which true faith must be rooted ever more deeply in order to thrive and bear fruit.

Ver. 32. Καί: and on this condition. They will really possess the quality of disciples; and on this path they will reach the complete illumination from which will result within them complete emancipation. The *truth* is the contents of the word of Jesus; it is the full revelation of the real essence of things, that is to say, of the moral character of God, of man, and of their relation. This new light will serve to break the yoke, not of the Roman power, but, what is more decisive for salvation, of the empire of sin. On what, indeed, does the power of sin in the human heart rest? On a fascination. Let the truth come to light, and the charm is broken. The will is disgusted with that which seduced it, and, according to the expression of the Psalmist, "the bird is escaped from the snare of the fowler." This is the true Messianic deliverance. If there is to be another more external one, it will be only the complement of this.

Vv. 33, 34. "*They answered him, We are Abraham's seed, and have never been slaves of any one; how sayest thou: you shall become free?* 34. *Jesus answered them, Verily, verily I say to you that whosoever commits sin is a slave* [*of sin*[1]]." According to some modern interpreters, those who thus answer Jesus cannot be the believing Jews of ver. 30, the more since Jesus charges them in ver. 37 with seeking to put Him to death, and, subsequently, calls them children of the devil. *Lücke* therefore

---

[1] D b omit της αμαρτιας (*of sin*.)

regards vv. 30–32 as a parenthesis, and connects ver. 33 with the preceding conversation (ver. 29). *Luthardt* thinks that in the midst of the group of well-disposed persons who surrounded Jesus, there were also adversaries, and that it was these latter who at this moment began to speak. Others give to the verb an indefinite subject: "They answered Him." But, on all these views, the narrative of John would be singularly incorrect. In reading ver. 33, we can only think of the believers of vv. 30–32. We shall see that the last words of ver. 37, also, do not allow any other application. It was not for no purpose that the evangelist had formed so marvelous a union of words in our Gospel as that of *believing Jews*. In these persons there were two men: the nascent believer—it was to him that Jesus addressed the promise vv. 31, 32—and the old Jew still living: it is the latter who feels himself offended, and who answers with pride (ver. 33). There was in fact a humiliating side in this word: *will make you free*. It was to say to them: you are not so. Making this step backward, they fell back into solidarity with their nation from which they had only superficially and temporarily separated themselves. The key of this entire passage is found already in these words, ii. 23, 24: "And many in Jerusalem believed on His name . . .; but Jesus did not *intrust Himself to them*." Under their faith He discerned the old Jewish foundation not yet shattered and transformed. In order that the promise of vv. 31, 32 should have been able to make a chord vibrate in their heart, they must have known experiences like those which St. Paul describes in Rom. vii.: the distress of an earnest, but impotent, struggle with sin. Jesus discerned this clearly, and for this reason He spoke to them, in ver. 31, of *abiding*, that is to say, of persevering in submission to His word. There is no confusion in John's narrative; we must rather admire its sacred delicacy.

The slavery which the hearers of Jesus deny cannot be of a *political* nature. Had not their fathers been slaves in the land of Egypt, in bondage, in the times of the Judges, to all kinds of nations, then subjected to the dominion of the Chaldeans and Persians? Were they not themselves under the yoke of the Romans? It is impossible to suppose them so far blinded by national pride as to forget facts which were so patent, as *de Wette, Meyer, Reuss*, etc., suppose; the last writer says: "They place themselves at the point of view, not of material facts, but of theory . . . There was submission to the Roman dominion . . . . , but under protest." But the words: *we were never*, do not allow this explanation. *Hengstenberg, Luthardt, Keil*, give to this expression a purely *spiritual* import; they apply it to the *religious* preponderance which the Jews claimed for themselves in comparison with all other nations. This is still more forced. The hearers of Jesus cannot express themselves in this way except from the view-point of the *civil* individual liberty, which they enjoyed as Jews. Hence the connection between the two assertions: "*We are Abraham's seed; we were never in bondage.*" With a single exception, which was specially foreseen, the law forbade the condition of bondage for all the members of the Israelitish community (Lev. xxv.). The dignity of a free man shone on the brow of every one who bore the name of child of Abraham, a fact which assuredly did not prevent the possibility that Jewish prisoners should be sold into slavery among the Gentiles (in answer to *Keil*). The question here is of inhabitants of Palestine such as those who were in conversation with Jesus. These Jews, when hearing that it was *the truth* taught by Jesus which should put an end to their bondage, could not have supposed that this declaration applied to emancipation from the Roman power. Now as, along with this national dependence, they knew no other servitude than civil or personal slavery, they protested, alleging that, while promising them liberty, Jesus made them slaves. They changed the most magnificent promise into an insult; "and," as Stier says, "thus they are already at the end of their faith." We can see whether Jesus was wrong in not trusting to this faith.

Ver. 34. The genitive τῆς ἁμαρτίας *of sin*, is omitted by the *Cambridge* MS., and an important document of *the Itala;* without this complement, the sense is: "*He is a slave*, truly a slave, while believing himself a free man;" a sense which is perfectly suitable. If, however, with all the other documents, the complement: *of sin* is sustained, it must be understood: "He is a slave, I mean a slave of sin." The sin to which the man at first freely surrenders himself becomes a master, then a tyrant. It ends by entirely confiscating his will. The passage Rom. vi. 16–18 presents an idea analogous to that of these words. The present participle ὁ ποιῶν, *who commits* (sin) unites the two notions of act and condition; the act proceeds from the condition, then it establishes it. It is a slavery for which the individual is responsible, because he has himself coöperated in creating it. The genitive *of sin* brings out the degrading character of this dependence; the following clause shows the terrible consequence of it:

Vv. 35, 36. "*The slave does not abide in the house for ever; the son abides for ever.*[1] 36. *If therefore the Son makes you free, you will be free indeed.*" If in ver. 34 the words τῆς ἁμαρτίας, *of sin*, are read, it is necessary to admit a change of meaning in the idea of slavery between ver. 34 and ver. 35. In ver. 34, the master is sin; in vv. 35, 36, the master is God, the owner of the house. This modification in the notion of moral slavery is undoubtedly to be explained by a thought which is also that of some passages in the Epistles of St. Paul: that the slave *of* sin, when he is a member of the theocracy, of the house of God, is made thereby a slave *with respect to God Himself.* In this moral condition, indeed, his position is servile; he renders to the master of the house only a forced obedience, because his will is governed by another master, sin. It cannot be denied, however, that the connection would be much more simple, if the words *of sin* were omitted in ver. 34. "He who commits sin is not a child, but a slave (with respect to God), ver. 34. Now, in such a moral state, the man possesses no permanent abode in the house of God (ver. 35). Separated spiritually from the Father of the family, he is not a real member

---

[1] ℵ X Γ omit the words ο υιος μενει εις τον αιωνα (*the son abides for ever*); no doubt, a confounding of the two εις τον αιωνα.

of the family." The meaning is thus perfectly simple.—Oὐ μένει: "He will remain in the house only as long as the master shall desire to make use of him" (*Luthardt*); he may be sold at any moment. What a threatening for those to whom Jesus was addressing Himself!—In contrast to this term *slave*, the term *son* must designate the *quality* of son; not the person of the Son. He who is truly a son through the community of spirit with the Master cannot be at all detached from that of which he has become an organic member. He can no more be separated from the kingdom of God than a child can be sold into slavery. But from ver. 36 the term Son is evidently applied to Jesus only. This is because in this house the filial dignity and the individual Son are mingled in one. There is here properly only *one* son, he who bears in himself the whole *gens;* all the rest become sons only by the act of *manumissio*, of liberation, on his part (ver. 32). Just as the passage Gal. iv. 21–31 seems to be only a development of ver. 35, so Rom. viii. 2: *"The law of the Spirit of life in Jesus Christ made me free* (ἠλευθέρωσέ με) *from the law of sin and death"* is the commentary on ver. 36. It is to the Son as the representative and heir of the paternal fortune that the right is committed by the Father of freeing the slaves. Ὄντως ἐλεύθεροι, *really,* that is to say, spiritually free in God, and consequently true members of His house and for ever.

Jesus has set aside the haughty assertion of ver. 33: *We were never in bondage.* He goes back now to the claim which was the point of support for that assertion: *We are Abraham's seed,* and He disposes of this also.

The moral sonship of Israel: vv. 37–47.

Vv. 37, 38. *" I know indeed that you are Abraham's seed; but you seek to kill me, because my word makes no progress in you.* 38. *As for me, I speak that which*[1] *I have seen with the Father;*[2] *and you do the things which*[3] *you have heard from your father."*[4] Jesus does not deny the genuineness of the civil registers in virtue of which His hearers affirm their character as children of Abraham. But He alleges a moral fact which destroys the value of this physical filiation in the spiritual and divine domain; it is their conduct towards Him and His word. Jesus here employs a method like that of John the Baptist, Matt. iii., and that of Paul, Rom. ix. By reason of the resistance which they oppose to His teaching, He addresses them as persons who have already returned to the solidarity of that Israelitish community which is desiring to make way with Him. Hence the charge which has been regarded as so strange (comp. vv. 31, 32): *" You seek to kill me."* But what more proper than the announcement of such a crime to make them feel the necessity of breaking finally the bond which

---

[1] ℵ B C D L X Orig. some Mnn. Cop. read *a* (*the things which*) instead of *o* (*that which*) which is read by T. R. with E F G H K M S T* U Γ Δ Λ Mnn. It. Syr.

[2] B D L T X Orig. reject μου, which is read by T. R. with the other MSS. and almost all the Vss.

[3] ℵ B C D K X (not L) read *a* (*the things which*) in the second clause. T. R. reads *o* (*that which*) with the others.

[4] B C K L X 15 Mnn. Cop. Orig. (frequently) read ηκουσατε παρα του πατρος (*the things which you have heard from the father*); T. R. with ℵ D E F G etc. It^{plerique} etc.: εωρακατε παρα τω πατρι (*the things which you have seen with your father*). B L T omit υμων after του πατρος.

still united them to a people so disposed. What justifies this severe assertion of Jesus is that He has just discovered, at this very moment, the impression of irritation produced in them by His word (ver. 33). The word χωρεῖν has two principal meanings: one, transitive, *to contain* (ii. 6)—this meaning is inapplicable here,—the other, intransitive: *to change place, to advance*. This verb is applied in this sense to water flowing, to a dart piercing, to a plant growing, to one body penetrating another, to invested money paying interest. Starting from this second meaning, some have explained: "has no place in you for developing itself," or: "has no *entrance, access* to you" (*Ostervald, Rilliet*). The former translation is not suitable for the word χωρεῖν; comp. 2 Cor. vi. 12; οὐ χωρεῖτε τὸν λόγον would have been necessary. With the second, these words would apply only to persons who have already manifested a beginning of faith. We must therefore explain, with *Meyer, Weiss, Keil: makes no progress in you.* The word of Christ struck in them, from the first uttered words, against national prejudices which they still shared with their fellow-countrymen, against the *Jewish heart* which they had not laid aside; like the seed which fell on the rocky ground, it had been blighted as soon as it had begun to germinate. This is the reason why Jesus had said at the beginning, "If you *abide*." Yet once more, there is no inaccuracy in the narrative. For him who goes to the foundation of things and who judges of the facts by placing himself at the point of view of Jesus and of John himself, everything is perfectly connected and well-founded.

In ver. 38, Jesus explains the resistance which His word encounters in them by a moral dependence in which they are and which is of a nature contrary to that in which He Himself lives. In speaking as He does, He obeys the principle which governs Him; they, in acting as they do, are the instruments of a wholly opposite power. In order to decide between the numerous various readings which are presented by the text of this verse, it is natural to start from this principle: that the copyists have sought to conform the two parallel clauses to one another, rather than to introduce differences between them. If we apply this rule, we shall arrive at the text which seems to us also to present the best sense intrinsically. It is that of the MS. K (with the exception, perhaps, of the pronoun μου which is read by this MS. in the first clause, and which may be rejected according to the principle suggested). This text of K is that which we have rendered in the translation.[1] The expression: *that which I have seen with my Father*, does not refer, as *Meyer, Weiss* and others think, to the state of the Lord's divine pre-existence; the parallel clause: *that which you have heard from your father*, excludes this explanation. For the two facts compared must be of a homogeneous nature. Weiss alleges the difference introduced intentionally by the change of the verbs (*see, hear*). But ver. 40 and v. 30 prove that no intention of this sort occasions this difference of expression. The question here is of a fact of incalculable importance in all human life. Behind the particular acts which are at

---

[1] Εγω ο εωρακα παρα τω πατρι λαλω· και υμεις ουν α ηκουσατε παρα τȜυ πατρος υμων ποιειτε.

the surface in the life of each man, there is concealed a permanent basis and, if I may venture to speak thus, a mysterious *anteriority*. All personal and free life has communication in its depths with an infinity of good or of evil, of light or darkness, which penetrates into our inner being and which, when once received, displays itself in our works (words or acts). This is what Jesus here represents under the figure of the paternal house whence we come forth and whence, as a son with his father, we derive our principles, our conduct, our habits: " From my *speaking* and from your *doing*, one may clearly see from what house we come forth, you and I." This is not all: at the foundation of each of these two infinites, good or evil, with which we are in ceaseless relation and of which we are the agents, Jesus discerns a *personal* being, a directing will, the *father* of a family who reigns over the whole house (*my Father, your father*). It is from him that the initiative on each side starts, that the impulses emanate. And as the moving power is personal, the dependence in which we are placed as related to it is also free, not inevitable. Jesus by His fidelity cultivates His communion with *the Father;* so He finds in this relation the initiative of all good (" that which I have seen ")—the perfect: "*that which I am having seen* with the Father." The Jews, through their spirit of pride and hypocrisy, maintain in themselves this relation to the opposite principle, to the other father; so they continually receive from him the impulsions to every species of perverse works (" that which you have heard ").

The *therefore* which unites the two parallel clauses has certainly a tinge of irony, as *Meyer* acknowledges: " You are consistent with the principle with which you are in communication, in doing evil, just as I am with mine in speaking what is good." The rejection of the pronoun μου after πατρί characterizes God as the sole Father in the true sense of the word. The singular pronoun ὅ, *that which*, in the first clause, answers to the thorough unity and the consistent direction of the will towards good. There is in it no vacillation, no contradiction. The plural pronoun ἅ, *the things which*, characterizes, on the contrary, the capricious inconsistency of the diabolical volitions. This contrast is connected with that of the perfect ἑώρακα and the aorist ἠκούσατε: the former designating a man who *is* what he is through the fact of having beheld; the latter, a variety of particular and momentary inspirations. The choice of the two terms *see* (Jesus) and *hear* (the Jews), to designate the two opposite kinds of moral dependence, is no less significant. *Sight* is the symbol of a clear intuition, such is only possible in the domain of the divine light and revelation. " In thy light we see light " (Ps. xxxvi. 10). The term: *to hear from* applies, on the contrary, to the secret suggestions which the perfidious mouth of an impostor whispers in the ear of his agents. Evil is the night in which one hears, but does not see. There is nothing even to the contrast of the two prepositions παρά (with the dative) *with*, and παρά (with the genitive), *from*, which does not contribute to the general effect of this inexhaustible saying: *with* is related to the idea of sight, as *from* is to that of hearing. If Jesus mentions on His own part *speaking* (λαλεῖν) and on the part of the Jews *doing*,

($\pi o \iota \epsilon \tilde{\iota} \nu$), it is because His activity consisted essentially, at this moment, in His testimonies and His judgments, while the Jews answered Him by hostile measures and projects of murder (ver. 37). If it were desired, with *Hengstenberg*, to give to ποιεῖτε, *you do*, the sense of the imperative *do*, it would not be necessary to see here a summons of the character of that in chap. xiii. 27; it would rather be necessary to refer the word *your father* to God, and to see in the word a serious exhortation. But all this is opposed to the connection with what follows.

Vv. 39–41a. "*They answered and said to him, Our father is Abraham. Jesus said to them, If you were*[1] *Abraham's children, you would do*[2] *the works of Abraham. 40. But now you seek to kill me, a man who has told you the truth which I have heard from God; Abraham did not do this. 41 a. You do the works of your father.*" The Jews feel themselves insulted by the insinuation of ver. 38; they affirm more energetically, and with a feeling of wounded dignity, their descent from Abraham. Jesus takes up again His answer in ver. 37 and develops it. In this domain, He says, there is no real paternal relationship where there is opposition in conduct. The Alexandrian reading: *If you are . . . you would do*, can be defended only by supposing a decided grammatical anomaly. John would at first lay down the fact as real (*you are*), to deny it afterwards in the second clause (*you would do*). In any case this explanation is preferable to that of *Origen* and *Augustine*, to which *Weiss* inclines, accepting the reading of B, "If you are . . . do then!" But Jesus is not exhorting, He is proving. This Alexandrian reading seems to be the result of an arbitrary correction. The verb of the principal clause ἐποιεῖτε ἄν, *you would do*, was first changed into the imperative ποιεῖτε, *do*, and after this it was necessary to transform the ἦτε (*if you were*) into ἐστε (*if you are*). Abraham was distinguished for an absolute docility to the divine truth (Gen. xii., xxii.), and by a respectful love for those who were the organs of it in his presence (Gen. xvi., xviii.); what a contrast to the conduct of his descendants according to the flesh! Observe the gradation (ver. 40): 1. To kill a *man*; 2. A man who is an organ of the *truth*; 3. Of the truth which comes *from God*. Their moral descent from Abraham being thus set aside, the result is this: "You have therefore another father, the one whose will you do and whose works you practice, as I do those of my Father."

Vv. 41b–43. "*They said therefore*[3] *to him: We are not children born*[4] *in fornication; we have only one father, God. 42. Jesus said*[5] *unto them, If God were your Father, you would love me; for I came forth and am come from God; for neither am I come of myself, but he sent me. 43. Why do you not recognize my speech? Because you cannot understand my word.*"

---

[1] Instead of ητε (*if you were*) which is read by T. R. with 14 Mjj. and nearly all the other authorities, Mnn. Vss. Orig. (3 times), εστε (*if you are*) is read in ℵ B D L T Orig. (10 times).

[2] All the MSS., even those which read εστε, have εποιειτε (*you would do*), except B which, with Orig. (10 times) reads ποιειτε (*do*); Vulg. Augustine: *facite*.—Αν is omitted by 11 Mjj 80 Mnn. Orig. (12 times).

[3] ℵ B L T It^plerique Syr. reject ουν.

[4] B D: ουκ εγεννηθημεν instead of ου γεγεννημεθα.

[5] The ουν of T. R. has in its favor only 7 Mjj. (ℵ D M etc.).

The Jews now accept the moral sense in which Jesus takes the notion of sonship and use it in their own behalf: " Let us not speak any more of Abraham, if thou wilt have it so; whatever it may be, in the spiritual domain, of which it seems that thou art thinking, it is God alone who is our Father. And we have been able to receive in His house only good examples and good principles." *We*, ἡμεῖς, at the beginning of the clause; persons such as we are! From the time of the return from the captivity (comp. the books of Nehemiah and Malachi), the union with a Gentile woman was regarded as impure, and the child born of such a marriage as illegitimate, as belonging through one of its parents to the family of Satan, the God of the heathen. It is probably in this sense that the Jews say: "We have only one Father, God." They were born in the most normal theocratic conditions; they have not a drop of idolatrous blood in their veins; they are *Hebrews, born of Hebrews* (Phil. iii. 5). Thus, even when rising with Jesus to the moral point of view, they cannot rid themselves altogether of their idea of physical sonship. *Meyer, Ewald* and *Weiss* think that they mean that their common mother, Sarah, was not a woman guilty of adultery. But how could a supposition like this come to their thought! *Lücke* and *de Wette* suppose rather that they assert the fact that their worship is free from any idolatrous element. But the question here is of origin, not of worship. It would be possible, according to the sense which we have given, that they were alluding to the Samaritans born of a mingling of Jewish and heathen populations.

But Jesus does not hesitate to deprive them even of this higher prerogative, which they think they can ascribe to themselves with so much of assurance. And He does this by the same method which He has just employed, in ver. 40, to deny their patriarchal filiation: He lays down a moral fact against which their claim is shattered. By virtue of His origin, of which He is distinctly conscious (ver. 14), Jesus knows that His appearing carries with it a divine seal. Every true child of God will be disposed to love Him. Their ill-will towards Him is, consequently, enough to annihilate their claim to the title of children of God. The true translation of the words : ἐκ τοῦ θεοῦ ἐξῆλθον καὶ ἥκω, is : " It is from God that I came forth and *am here*," (ἥκω, present formed from a perfect). Jesus presents Himself to the world with the consciousness that nothing in Him weakens the impression which the heavenly abode that He has just left must make upon accessible souls. Ἐξῆλθον, *I came forth*, refers to the divine fact of the incarnation; ἥκω, *I am here*, to the divine character of His appearing. And along with His origin and His presence, there is also *His mission* which He has from God: "For neither am I *come of myself*." This second point is fitted to confirm the impression produced by the first ones. He does not accomplish here below a work of His own choice; He continues in the service of that work which God gives to Him at each moment (*for . . . neither*). If they loved God, they would without difficulty recognize this character of His coming, His person and His work.

Ver. 43. Why then does all this escape them? How does it happen, in

674 / Unbelief Develops in Israel

particular, that they do not distinguish the tone, and, so to speak, the heavenly *timbre* of his *speech?* Λαλία, speech, differs from λόγος, *word*, as the form differs from the contents, the discourse from the doctrine. "You do not know my *speech;* you do not distinguish it from an ordinary human word. Why? Because you are unable to lay hold of and receive *my doctrine.*" There was wanting to them that internal organ by means of which the teaching of Christ would become in them a light perceived. Ἀκούειν, *to hear*, signifies here *to understand;* to listen with that calmness, that seriousness, that good will which enables one to apprehend. This inability was not a fact of creation; it results from their previous moral life; compare v. 44–47. Jesus now develops in full the idea of the first cause of their moral incapacity. This cause He had already declared in ver. 38. It is the dependence in which they are inwardly on an enemy of the truth, who fills their hearts with tumultuous and hateful passions, and thus renders them deaf to the voice of God which speaks to them through Jesus.

Ver. 44. *"You are born of the*[1] *father, the devil, and you wish to fulfil the desires of your father. He was a murderer from the beginning, and he is not in the truth, because there is no truth in him; when he speaks falsehood, he speaks of his own, for he is a liar and*[2] *the father of the liar.*" The light does not succeed in penetrating into this Jewish medium, because it is subjected to a principle of darkness. Ὑμεῖς, *you*, is strongly emphasized: "You who boast of having God as your Father." *Grotius* made τοῦ διαβόλου, *of the devil*, the object of πατρός, taking the former word in a collective sense: the father of the demons. *Hilgenfeld*, starting from the same grammatical construction, surprises the evangelist here in the very act of Gnosticism. This *father of the devil*, according to this critic, is the Demiurge of the Gnostics; in other words, the creator of this material world, the God of the Jews, who is designated here as the father of Satan, in accordance with the doctrine of the Ophites in Irenæus.[3] Jesus would thus say to the Jews, not: "You are the sons of the devil," but: "You are the sons of the father of the devil;" that is to say, the *brothers* of the latter. But where can we find in the Scriptures a word respecting the person of the devil's father? And how, on the supposition that this father of the devil was the God of the Jews, could Jesus have called this God of the Jews His own Father ("the house of *my Father*" ii. 16)? Finally, it is sufficient to compare 1 John iii. 10, in order to understand that He calls the Jews not the *brothers*, but the *sons* of the devil. The literal meaning is the following: You are sons of the *father* who is the *devil*, and not, as you think, of that other father who is God."

The lawless passions (ἐπιθυμίαι) by which this father is animated and which he communicates to them, are unfolded in the second part of the verse: they are, first, hatred of man, and then, abhorrence of truth; pre-

---

[1] T. R. omits, with some Mnn. only, τοῦ (*the*) before πατρός.

[2] Instead of καί, It^{aliq} and some Fathers read καθὼς και (*as also*).

[3] Hilgenfeld: "The Ophites regarded *Jaldabaoth* (the Creator of the world and the God of the Jews) as the *father of the serpent* (*Einl.*, p. 725).

cisely the tendencies with which Jesus had just reproached the Jews, ver. 40. The verb θέλετε, *you desire, you are eager for* (v. 35), is contrary to the fatalistic principle which *Hilgenfeld* attributes to John; it expresses the voluntary assent, the abounding sympathy with which they set themselves to the work of realizing the aspirations of their father. The first of these diabolical appetites is the thirst for human blood. Some interpreters ancient and modern (*Cyril, Nitzsch, Lücke, de Wette, Reuss*) explain the word ἀνθρωποκτόνος, *murderer,* by an allusion to the murder of Abel. Comp. 1 John iii. 12, 15: " *Not as Cain, who was of the evil one and slew his brother. . . . Whosoever hates his brother is a murderer.*" But the Scriptures do not ascribe to the demon a part in this crime, and the relation which Jesus establishes here between the murderous hatred of Satan and his character as a liar, leads us rather to refer the word *murderer* to the seduction in Paradise by which Satan caused man to fall under the yoke of sin and thereby of death. By thus separating him from God, through falsehood, he has devoted him to spiritual and physical ruin. The expression *from the beginning* may, on this view, be much more strictly explained. The sense of ἀρχή, *beginning,* does not differ from that of this word in i. 1, except that here the question is of the beginning of the human race, there of the beginning of creation. As to the quotation taken from 1 John, it proves nothing in favor of the allusion to the act of Cain; for that act is there cited as the first example of the hatred *of a man* to his brother. When Jesus said in ver. 40: " You seek to kill me, *a man,*" He already had in His mind the idea of that murderous hatred which is expressed by the word ἀνθρωποκτόνος. Whence did this hatred of Satan against man arise? Undoubtedly, from the fact that he had discerned in him the future organ of divine truth and the destroyer of his own lies. Thus the two features of his character are united: hatred of man and enmity to the truth. And we may understand how this double hatred must be concentrated in the highest degree upon Jesus, in whom at length was perfectly realized the idea of man and of man as the organ of divine truth. Some interpreters, ancient and modern, have applied the expression ἐν ἀληθείᾳ οὐχ ἕστηκεν to the fall of the devil. *Vulgate: in veritate non stetit; Arnaud: he did not abide in the truth; Ostervald: he did not persist in* . . . But the perfect ἕστηκα does not mean: *did not abide in;* its sense, in the sacred as in the classic Greek, is: "I have *placed* myself in a position and *I am there.*" Jesus therefore does not mean to say that the devil has abandoned the domain of truth, in which he was originally placed by God, but rather that he does not find himself there, or, more exactly, that he has not taken his place there, and consequently is not there.¹ The domain of *truth* is that of the real essence of things, clearly recognized and affirmed, holiness. And why does he not live in this domain? *Because,* Jesus adds, *there is no truth in him.* He is

---

¹ *Westcott* explains the form οὐκ instead of οὐχ before ἕστηκεν, in ℵ B D L X etc., by making this verb the imperfect of στήκω (ἕστηκεν); comp. Rom. xiv. 4 and elsewhere. He thinks that the context requires a past tense; I do not think so; the question is as to what the devil is and does now, and not of a revelation respecting his beginning.

wanting in inward *truth*, truth in the subjective sense, that uprightness of will which aspires after divine reality. We must observe, in this last clause, the absence of the article before the word ἀλήθεια, *truth:* Satan is cut off from *the truth*, because he is destitute *of truth*. One can abide *in the truth* (objectively speaking) in that which God reveals, only when one sincerely desires it. The ὅτι, *because*, is the counterpart of that in ver. 43. Like father, like son: each of the two lives and works in what is false, because he *is* false.

What Jesus has just set forth in a negative form, He reproduces in a positive form in the second part of the verse. Not desiring to derive anything from divine truth, Satan is compelled to draw everything that he says from his own resources, that is from the nothingness of his own subjectivity; for the creature, separated from God, is incapable of possessing and creating anything real. Lying is, in this condition, his natural language, as much as speaking the truth is the natural language of Jesus (ver. 38) in the communion with God in which He lives. Ἐκ τῶν ἰδίων, *from his own resources*, admirably characterizes the creative faculty of a being separated from God, who is capable no doubt of producing something, even sometimes great works, and of uttering great words, but whose creations, in proportion as he creates apart from God, are always only a vain phantasmagoria. The word ψεύστης, a liar, reproduces the idea: *He has no truth in him.* In the expression: "He is a liar and *also his father*," we must not make the word *his father* a second subject to *is*, as if the question were here also of the father of the devil (*Hilgenfeld*). The word: *and his father* is the predicate: "he is a liar and father of . . ." Otherwise ὅτι αὐτὸς ψεύστης ἐστὶ καὶ ὁ πατὴρ αὐτοῦ would have been necessary. Only it may be asked to what substantive it is necessary to refer the pronoun αὐτοῦ (*his*); to the word ψεύστης, *liar*, or the word ψευδοῦς, *falsehood*, in the preceding clause? I think, with *Lücke, Meyer* and others, that the context is decisive in favor of the first alternative. For the question here is, not of the origin of falsehood in general, but specially of the moral sonship of the individual *liars* whom Jesus has before Him (vv. 40, 44).[1] *Weiss* objects that in the expression: "he is a liar," the word *liar* is used in the generic sense. It is true; but we may certainly derive from it the notion of a concrete substantive. In both senses, there is a slight grammatical difficulty to be overcome. The theory of accommodation, by means of which it is often sought to weaken the force of the declarations of Jesus respecting the personal existence of Satan, may have some probability when it is applied to His conversations with the demoniacs. But here Jesus gives altogether

---

[1] The reading καθὼς καί (*as also his father*) in the Itala and in some Fathers, is a correction due to the Gnostics who desired, like Hilgenfeld, to find here the mention of the *father of the devil*. The Fathers, however, adopted this reading only on condition of reading before it ὃς ἄν (*he who*) instead of ὅταν (*when, each time when*); this is the translation which *Westcott* thinks may be given when following the ordinary reading, though at the same time acknowledging the harshness of the ellipsis of the subject of λαλῇ (any man whatsoever): "*Whoever* says what is false, speaks of his own; for he is a liar, *as also* his father, the devil." Respecting the explanation of Hilgenfeld, who finds here again the indication of the father of the devil, see Introd. p. 130 f.

spontaneously this teaching with respect to the person, the character and the part of this mysterious being.[1] After this Jesus comes back from the father to the children: they are enemies of the truth, just as the evil being is to whom they are subject:

Vv. 45–47. "*And because I say the truth to you, you believe me not. 46. Which of you can convict me of sin? And if*[2] *I say the truth, why do you not believe me?*[3] *47. He that is of God hears the words of God; for this cause you hear them not, because you are not of God.*" What, ordinarily, causes a man to be believed is the fact that he speaks the truth. Jesus has with the Jews the opposite experience. They are so swayed by falsehood, by which their father has blinded their hearts, that precisely because he speaks the truth, he does not find credence with them. Ἐγώ, at the beginning: *I*, the organ of the truth, in opposition to Satan, the organ of falsehood.

Ver. 46. To justify their distrust with respect to His *words*, it would be necessary that they should at least be able to accuse Him of some fault in His *actions*; for holiness and truth are sisters. Can they do this? Let them do it. This defiance which Jesus hurls at His adversaries shows that He feels Himself fully cleared, by His defense in chap. vii., of the crime of which He had been accused in chap. v. We must be careful, indeed, not to take ἁμαρτία, *sin*, in the sense of *error* (*Calvin, Melanchthon*) or of *falsehood* (*Fritzsche*). The thought is the same here as in vii. 18: Jesus affirms that there absolutely does not arise from His *moral conduct* any ground of suspicion against the truth of His teaching. We must imagine this question as followed by a pause sufficient to give opportunity to whoever should wish to accuse Him to be heard. . . . No one opens his mouth. The admission involved in this silence serves as a premise for the following argument: "Well, then, if (εἰ δέ, *now if*, or simply εἰ), as your silence proves, I teach the truth, why do you not believe?" Here

---

[1] If St. Augustine, and following his example the Catholic interpreters and some modern writers, have been wrong in seeing in the expression οὐχ ἕστηκεν the indication of the *fall* of the devil, Frommann and *Reuss* are no less in error in finding in our passage the idea of an *eternal* principle of evil. The term ἕστηκεν expresses, as *Meyer* says, *the actual fact:* "This passage declares the bad moral situation of the devil, *as it is*, without teaching anything as to the origin of this state . . . " "But," he adds, "the fall of the devil is necessarily implied by this saying." I think that it is even necessary to go a step farther. The perfect ἕστηκα, while designating *the present state* implies the notion of a *past act* to which this state is due; not in this case, if I mistake not, the idea of a fall *out of* truth already known, but that of a refusal to enter into revealed truth, to the end of becoming firmly established therein and of yielding submission to it. Every free being is called, at some moment in his existence, to sacrifice voluntarily his natural autonomy, and to subordinate his *ego* to the manifestation of good, to the *unveiled truth*, that is, to God who reveals himself. Herein is the decisive test for him, from which neither angel nor man escapes. The refusal of this voluntary annulling of oneself in the presence of the revelation of the good, of the perfect good, of God,—this is *evil* in its first form (simply negative). The exaggerated affirmation of the *ego*, positive evil, is its immediate result. This refusal to abdicate before the truth, to go out of oneself and to ingraft oneself in God—herein is the fall both of the devil and the man; it cannot be better formulated than in these terms: "not *to be* in the truth, because one has *not placed* himself there at the required moment, that of its revelation."

[2] T. R.: εἰ δε with 11 Mjj.; εἰ simply in ℵ B C L X Π 20 Mnn. It. Vulg. Syr. Cop.

[3] D omits the 46th verse (confounding of the two ου πιστευετε μοι).

678 / Unbelief Develops in Israel

again a pause; He had invited them to judge Him; in the face of His innocence which has just been established, He leaves them a moment now to pass judgment on their conduct towards Him. After this silence, He pronounces the sentence: "You are not of God: herein is the true reason of your unbelief towards me." The expression *to be of God* designates the state of a soul which has placed itself, and which now is, under the influence of divine action. It is the opposite of the οὐχ ἕστηκεν affirmed with regard to Satan. This state does not exclude, but implies, the free determination of the man. Otherwise, the tone of reproach which prevails in our verse would be unjust and even absurd. Ἀκούειν, properly, *to hear*, takes here, as often the French term does, the sense of *intelligent hearing* (hence the limiting word in the accusative). Comp. the manner in which the declaration of Jesus respecting the truth which gives freedom (ver. 32) had been received. The διὰ τοῦτο, *for this cause*, refers at once to the general principle laid down in the first part of the verse, and the following ὅτι: "It is for this cause . . . , that is to say, because . . ."

The *perfect* holiness of Christ is proved in this passage, not by the silence of the Jews, who might very well have ignored the sins of their interlocutor, but by the assurance with which Jesus lays this question before them. Without the immediate consciousness which Christ had of the perfect purity of His life, and on the supposition that He was only a more holy man than other men, a moral sense so delicate as that which such a state would imply, would not have suffered the least stain to pass unnoticed, either in His life, or in His heart; and what hypocrisy would there not have been in this case in addressing to others a question with the aim of causing them to give it a different answer from that which, in His inmost heart, He gave Himself! In other terms: to give a false proof whose want of soundness He hopes that no one will be able to prove.

Conclusion: vv. 48–50.

Vv. 48–50. "*The Jews therefore*[1] *answered and said to him, Say we not rightly that thou art a Samaritan and art possessed by a demon?* 49. *Jesus answered: I am not possessed by a demon, but I honor my Father, and you dishonor me.* 50. *But I seek not my own glory; there is one who seeks it and who judges.*" Some, as *Hengstenberg* and *Astié*, think that by calling Jesus a Samaritan, they wish to charge Him with *heresy*, as making Himself equal with God. But the term Samaritan can scarcely be regarded as a synonym of blasphemer. The Samaritans passed for national enemies of the Jews; now Jesus seemed to commit an act of hostility against His people by accusing all the Jews of being children of the devil. The madness of insanity, as it seemed to them, could alone give an explanation of such language; and this is what they express by the words: *Thou art possessed of a demon*, which are, as it were, the counterpart of the charge of Jesus. The meaning of this assault comes to this: Thou art as wicked as thou art foolish.

"*Who when he was reviled*," says St. Peter, "*reviled not again, but commit-*

---

[1] ℵ B C D L X omit οὖν.

ted himself to him who judges righteously " (1 Pet. ii. 23). These words seem to have been suggested to the apostle by the recollection of the following reply in our verses 49, 50. To the insult, Jesus opposes a simple denial. Ἐγώ, *I*, placed first, is pronounced with the profound feeling of the contrast between the character of His person and the manner in which He is treated. To the false explanation which the Jews give of His preceding discourse, Jesus substitutes the true one: "I do not speak of you as I do, under the impulse of hatred; but I speak thus to honor my Father. The testimony which I bear against you is a homage which I must pay to the divine holiness. But, instead of bowing the head to the voice of Him who tells you the truth from God, you insult Him—Him who glorifies the one whom you claim to be your Father." The conclusion is this: You cannot be children of God, since you insult me who speak to you only to honor God!

Nevertheless (ver. 50), Jesus declares that the affronts with which they loaded Him were to Him of little importance. It is God who looks to this; He commits to God the care of His glory; for He knows His solicitude for Him. He wishes to be honored only in the measure in which His Father Himself gives Him glory in the hearts of men. The two participles: *seeking* and *judging* give a presentiment of the divine acts by which the Father will glorify the Son and will chastise His calumniators: on one side, the sending of the Holy Spirit and the founding of the new Israel; on the other, the fall of Jerusalem and the final judgment. It is thus that "he commits himself to him who judges righteously." Besides, all do not dishonor Him; there are some who already honor Him by their faith:

2. The last testimonies of Jesus respecting His person: vv. 51–59.

Vv. 51–53. "*Verily, verily, I say unto you, If any one keep my word, he shall never see death. 52. The Jews therefore*[1] *said to him, Now we know that thou art possessed of a demon; Abraham is dead and the prophets also, and thou sayest, If any one keep my word, he shall never taste of death.*[2] *53. Art thou greater than our father Abraham, who is dead? And the prophets also are dead. Whom dost thou*[3] *pretend to be?*" The various relations of ideas which it has been sought to establish between ver. 50 and ver. 51 seem to me hardly natural. With the last word of ver. 50: *and who judges*, Jesus has come to an end with His present interlocutors. But He knows that among these numerous hearers who had believed in Him (ver. 30) and of whom many had immediately succumbed to the test (ver. 32), there are a certain number who have fulfilled the condition imposed by Him (ver. 31): *If you abide in my word;* it is to these, as it seems to me, as well as to His disciples in general, that He addresses the glorious promise of ver. 51. So *Calvin, de Wette*, etc., think. *Weiss* holds that the discourse simply continues: Jesus shows that His word will be the means through which God will glorify Him, by giving life to some and judging others by

---

[1] ℵ B C omit οὖν.

[2] B reads θανατον ου μη θεωρηση (as in ver. 51). T. R., γευσεται with E F H. All the rest γευσηται.

[3] Συ is rejected by 10 Mjj. (ℵ A B C, etc.), 50 Mnn. It. Vulg. Syr. Cop. Orig.

means of it,—which will show to all that He is the Messiah. The expression: *keep my word*, as well as the tone of the promise, carries us back to the exhortation of ver. 31 : *Abide in my word;* and the promise of never seeing death is the opposite of the threatening of ver. 35 : *The slave does not abide in the house for ever*. The term *death* is not taken in the exclusively spiritual sense, as if Jesus meant: *shall not be condemned.* Would there not be some charlatanism on Jesus' part in giving Himself the appearance of saying more than He really meant? It is indeed *death*, death itself, in the full sense of the word, which He denies for the believer. See at vi. 50 and xiv. 3. What an encouragement presented to those who persevered in His word : no longer to have to experience death in death !

The Jews do not altogether misapprehend therefore, as is claimed, when they conclude from these words that Jesus promises to believers a privilege which was enjoyed neither by Abraham nor by the prophets, and that He makes Himself greater than these; for it is manifest that He must Himself possess the prerogative which He promises to His own. The expression : *taste of death*, rests upon the comparison of death with a bitter cup which a man is condemned to drink. The word εἰς τὸν αἰῶνα, *for ever*, in vv. 51, 52, should not be explained in the sense : "He will die indeed, but not *for ever*." The sense is : "He shall never perform the act of dying." Comp. xiii. 8. The pronoun ὅστις, instead of the simple ὅς, signifies: "who, Abraham though he was." This objection forces Jesus to rise to the highest affirmation which He has uttered with reference to Himself, that of His divine pre-existence.

If Jesus is the conqueror of death for His own, it is because He Himself belongs to *the eternal order*. He comes from a sphere in which there is no transition from nothingness to existence, and consequently no more falling from existence into death, except in the case in which He Himself consented to give Himself up to its power.

Vv. 54–56. " *Jesus answered, If I glorify*[1] *myself, my glory is nothing; he who glorifies me is my Father, he of whom you say that he is your*[2] *God;* 55 *and yet you do not know him, but I know him; and if I say that I do not know him, I shall be like to you*[3] *a liar; but I know him and I keep his word.* 56. *Abraham, your father, rejoiced in the hope of seeing my day; and he saw it, and was glad.*" In one sense, Jesus glorifies Himself, indeed, whenever He gives testimony to Himself; but the emphasis is on ἐγώ, *I*, " I alone, without the Father, seeking and attributing to myself a position which has not been given to me." The word δοξάσω may be either the future indicative or the aorist subjunctive. Here is the answer to the question : *Whom dost thou claim to be ?* " Nothing except that which the Father has willed that I should be." And this will of the Father with regard to Him is continually manifested by striking signs which the Jews would

---

[1] Instead of δοξαζω, which is read by T. R. with 12 Mjj. and the Mnn., δοξασω is read in ℵ B C D It^{alia} Orig.

[2] Instead of υμων which is read by T. R with ℵ B D F X most of the Mnn. It^{plerique}, ημων (*our*) is read in the 12 other Mjj. 90 Mnn. Syr.

[3] Instead of υμιν which T. R. reads with A B D, the rest read υμων.

easily discern, if God were to them really what they claim that He is: *their* God. But they do not know Him; and therefore they do not understand the signs by which He whom they declare to be their God accredits Him before their eyes.

This ignorance of God which Jesus encounters in the Jews awakens in Him, by the law of contrast, the feeling of the real knowledge which He has of the Father, in whose name and honor He speaks: He affirms this prerogative with a triumphant energy, in ver. 55. It is, as it were, the paroxysm of faith which Jesus has in Himself, a faith founded on the certainty of that immediate consciousness which He has of God. If He did not assert Himself thus as knowing God, He would be also a liar like them, when they claim to know Him. And the proof that He does not lie is His obedience, which stands in contrast with their disobedience. Thus are the unheard of affirmations prepared for, which are to follow in vv. 56, 58. Οἶδα, *I know him*, designates direct, intuitive knowledge, in opposition to ἐγνώκατε (literally, *you have learned to know*), which relates to an acquired knowledge.

After having thus answered the reproach: *Thou glorifiest thyself*, Jesus comes to the question raised by them: *Art thou greater than our father Abraham?* and He does not hesitate to answer plainly: "Yes! I am, for after having been the object of his hope when he was on earth, my coming was that of his joy in Paradise where he now is!" There is a keen irony in this apposition: "Abraham, *your father*." Their spiritual patron rejoicing in the expectation of an appearance which excites only their spite! The word *rejoiced* designates the joy of hope, as is indicated by the ἵνα ἴδῃ, *to the end of seeing*. *To see* Him—this was the aim and object of the exultant joy of the patriarch. The question is evidently of what took place in Abraham's heart, when he received from the mouth of God the Messianic promises, such as Gen. xii. 3 and xxii. 18: "*In thy seed shall all the nations be blessed, because thou hast obeyed my voice.*" The expression *my day* can only designate the present time, that of Christ's appearance on earth (Luke xvii. 22). The explanations of *Chrysostom* (the day of the Passion) and *Bengel* (the day of the Parousia) are not at all justified here. *Hofmann* and *Luthardt* understand by it the *promised* birth of Isaac, a promise in which Abraham saw the pledge of that of the Messiah. But the expression: *my day*, can only refer to a fact concerning the person of Christ Himself.

The relation between the ἵνα ἴδῃ, *to see*, and the past εἶδε, *and he saw*, proves that this last term expresses the realization of the desire which had caused the patriarch to rejoice, the appearance of Jesus here below. The second aorist passive, ἐχάρη, well expresses the calm joy of the sight, in contrast with the exultant joy of the expectation (ἠγαλλιάσατο). Jesus therefore reveals here, as most of the interpreters acknowledge, a fact of the invisible world, of which He alone could have knowledge. As at the transfiguration we see Moses and Elijah acquainted with the circumstances of the earthly life of Jesus, so Jesus declares that Abraham, the father of believers, is not a stranger, in his abode of glory, to the fulfillment of the promises which had been made to Him,—that he beheld the coming of the Messiah on the earth. No doubt we know not in what form the events of this world can be rendered sensible to those who live in the bosom of God. Jesus simply affirms the fact. This interpretation is the only one which leaves to the words their natural meaning. The Fathers apply the εἶδε, *we saw*, to certain typical events in the course of the life of Abraham, such as the birth or the sacrifice of Isaac, in which the patriarch, by anticipation, beheld the fulfillment of the promises. These explanations are excluded by the marked opposition which the text establishes between the joy of the *expectation* and that of the *actual sight*. The same is true of that of *Hengstenberg* and *Keil*, who apply the last words of the verse to the visit of the angel of the Lord as Logos-Jesus (Gen. xviii.). The expression *my day* can receive, in all these applications, only a forced meaning. The Socinian explanation: "Abraham would have exulted, if he had seen my day," is no longer cited except as calling it to mind. What can be made of the second clause with this interpretation?

By bringing out this two-fold joy of Abraham, that of the promise and that of the fulfillment, Jesus puts the Jews to the blush at the contrast between their feelings and those of their alleged father.

Vv. 57, 58. "*Whereupon the Jews said to him, Thou art not yet fifty*[1] *years old, and thou hast seen Abraham!*[2] *58. Jesus said to them, Verily, verily I say unto you, Before Abraham came into being,*[3] *I am.*" From the fact that Abraham had seen Jesus, it seemed to follow that Jesus must have seen Abraham. The question of the Jews is the expression of indignant surprise. The number fifty is a round number; *fifty years* designates the close of the age of manhood. The meaning is: "Thou art not yet an old man." No inference is to be drawn from this as to the real age of Jesus, since ten or twenty years more, in this case, would be of no consequence. "I am not only his contemporary," Jesus replies, "but I existed even before him." The formula, *amen, amen*, announces the greatness of this revelation respecting His person. By the terms γενέσθαι, *became*, and εἰμί, *I am*, Jesus, as *Weiss* says, contrasts His eternal existence with the historical beginning of the existence of Abraham. *To become* is to pass from nothingness to existence; *I am* designates a mode of existence which is not due to such a transition. Jesus goes still further; He says, not *I was*, but *I am*. Thereby He attributes to Himself, not a simple priority as related to Abraham, which would still be compatible with the Arian view of the Person of Christ, but existence in the absolute, eternal, Divine order. This expression recalls that of Ps. xc. 2: "*Before the mountains were brought forth and thou hadst founded the earth, from eternity to eternity,* THOU ART, O *God!*" No doubt, eternity must not be considered as strictly *anterior* to time. This term πρίν, *before*, is a symbolic form, derived from the human consciousness of Jesus, to express the relation of *dependence* of time on

---

[1] Δ 3 Mnn. Chrys.: τεσσαρακοντα (*forty*).

[2] א: και Αβρ. εωρακὲν σε (*and Abraham hath seen thee*).

[3] D It^{aliq} omit γενεσθαι (*became*).

eternity in the only way in which the mind of man can conceive of it, that is, under the form of succession. There is no longer any thought, at the present day, of having recourse to the forced explanations which were formerly proposed by different commentators: that of *Socinus* and *Paulus:* "I am, as the *Messiah promised*, anterior to Abraham," or that of the Socinian catechism: Before Abraham could justify His name of Abraham (*father of a multitude*, by reason of the multitude of heathen who shall one day be converted) I am *your Messiah*, for you Jews. *Scholten* himself acknowledges (p. 97 f.) the insufficiency of these exegetical attempts. According to him, we must supply a predicate of εἰμί; this would be ὁ χριστός, *the Messiah*. But the antithesis of εἶναι and γίνεσθαι (*be* and *become*) does not allow us to give to the first of these terms another sense than that of existing. Besides, the point in hand is a reply to the question: "Hast thou then seen Abraham?" The reply, if understood as *Scholten* would have it, would be unsuitable to this question. The Socinian *Crell* and *de Wette* understand: "I exist in the divine intelligence or plan." *Beyschlag* goes a little farther still. According to him, Jesus means that there is realized in Himself here below an eternal, divine, but impersonal principle, the image of God. But as this impersonal image of God cannot exist except in the divine intelligence, this comes back in reality to the explanation of *de Wette*. This explanation of an impersonal ideal is opposed by three considerations: 1. The ἐγώ, *I*, which proves that this eternal being is personal; 2, the parallel with Abraham. An impersonal principle cannot be placed in parallelism with a person, especially when the question is of a relation of priority. Finally, 3. How could a Jesus conceived of as an impersonal principle have answered the objection of the Jews: *Thou hast then seen Abraham?* And yet if this word did not satisfy the demand of the Jews, it would be nothing more than a ridiculous boast.[1] This declaration has the character of the most elevated solemnity. It is certainly one of those from which John derived the fundamental idea of the first verses of the Prologue. It bears in itself the guaranty of its authenticity, first by its striking conciseness, and then by its very meaning. What historian would gratuitously ascribe to his hero a saying which was fitted to bring upon him the charge of being mad? It will be asked, no doubt, how Jesus can derive from His human consciousness an expression which so absolutely transcends it. This conception was derived by Him from the revelation of His Father, when He said to Him: "Thou art my beloved Son, in whom I am well pleased." There is a fact here which is analogous to that which is accomplished in the conscience of the believer when he through the Spirit receives the testimony that he is *a child of God* (Rom. viii. 16).

---

[1] *Beyschlag* himself has felt this; he now has recourse to another expedient, the one which *Weizsäcker* proposed: the distinction between the two theologies placed in juxtaposition in our Gospel; that of Jesus Himself and that of the evangelist (to which alone the idea of pre-existence belongs). But it is not easy to understand how from this point of view the authenticity of the Gospel can still be defended, as it is defended by Beyschlag (comp. on this question Introd., p. 123).

Vv. 59. "*Thereupon, they took up stones to stone him; but Jesus hid himself and went out of the temple.*"[1] In the face of this reply, there was indeed nothing left to the Jews except to worship—or to stone him. The word ἦραν, strictly : *they lifted up*, indicates a volition, a menace, still more, perhaps than a well-settled purpose. Comp. the stronger expression in x. 31. These stones were probably lying in the court, for the building of the temple, which was not yet finished. The word ἐκρύβη, *hid himself*, does not include, but rather excludes the idea of a miracle. Jesus was surrounded by a circle of disciples and friends who facilitated His escape. Whatever may be the authority of the documents and Versions which support the T. R. here (see the note), it is evident that the last words are a marginal gloss formed by means of the first words of the following chapter and of Luke iv. 30. Baur defends their authenticity, and tries to draw from them a proof of the Docetism of the author. But the normal expression, from the Docetic point of view, would have been, not ἐκρύβη (*he hid himself*), but ἄφαντος or ἀφανὴς ἐγένετο (*he vanished*).

Here is the end of the most violent conflict which Jesus had had to sustain in Judea. Chaps. vii. and viii. correspond in this regard with chap. vi. The general victory of unbelief is here decided for Judea, as it had been in chap. vi. for Galilee. So from this time Jesus gradually abandons the field of battle to His adversaries, until that other final ἐκρύβη, xii. 36, which will close His public ministry in Israel.

We have seen all the improbabilities, which criticism has found in such large numbers in this chapter and the preceding one, vanish before a calm and conscientious exegesis. The answers and objections of the Jews, which *Reuss* charges with being grotesque and absurd, have appeared to us, when placing ourselves at the point of view of those who make them, natural and logical. The argument of Jesus which, according to *Renan*, "is very weak when judged by the rules of Aristotelian logic," appears so only because it is forgotten that the question is of things which Jesus, counting on the moral consciousness of His adversaries, thought He might lay down as axioms. There is certainly, in the narrative of these two chapters, vii. and viii., not a single improbability which approaches that which there would be in supposing such conversations invented afterwards outside of the historical situation to which they so perfectly adapt themselves. There is no verbiage, no incongruity, no break of continuity. This reproduction of the conversations of Jesus is made with such delicacy, that one almost gives his assent to the hypothesis of a rationalist of the past century, *Bertholdt*, who supposed that the evangelist had taken notes of the discourses of Jesus at the very time when he heard them. Two features strike us especially in these two chapters : 1. The *dialogue* form, so full of reality, which could have engraved itself on the mind of a witness more easily than a consecutive discourse ; 2. The *summary* character of the testimonies of Jesus. There is always, at the beginning, a simple and grand affirmation without development, vii. 37, 38 ; viii. 12, 31, 32 ; then, in

---

[1] After ιερον, T. R. reads διελθων δια μεσου αυτων και παρηγεν ουτως (*passing through the midst of them, and so he departed*), with A C E F G H K L M S U X Δ Λ the Mnn. Syr. Cop.; these words are wanting in ℵ B D It^{plerique} Vulg. Sah. Orig. Chrys.

proportion as it becomes the subject of a discussion between Jesus and His hearers, the developments are given. These two features would be sufficient to prove the historical character of the narrative.

Second Cycle
John 9 and 10

The consequences of the first point of departure, the healing of the impotent man, chap. v., are exhausted. A new miracle produces a renewed breaking out of hatred among the Jews and calls forth a new phase of the conflict. Nevertheless, one feels that the worst of the conflict is past. The people of Judea, those even who had shown themselves for a moment disposed to believe, are offended, like the Galileans, at the absolute spirituality of the promises of Jesus. He begins from this time to abandon that lost community to its blindness; He labors especially to the end of gathering about Himself the small number of those who are to form the nucleus of the future community. So the incisive character of the preceding conversations gives place to the tone of resignation and of saddened love.

1. Chap. ix.: a new miracle opens the second cycle;

2. Chap. x. 1–21: with this miracle is connected a first discourse, and then the representation of its immediate effects;

3. Chap. x. 22–42: a second discourse, which, although given a little later and at another visit, is, in respect to its subject, only a continuation of the first; finally, a brief historical notice.

1

John 9:1-41

THE MIRACLE

1. The fact: vv. 1–12; 2. The investigation: vv. 13–34; 3. The moral result: vv. 35–41.

The fact: vv. 1–12

Vv. 1–5. "*And in passing, he saw a man blind from birth; 2 and his disciples asked him, saying, Master, who did sin, this man or his parents, that he should be born blind? 3. Jesus answered, Neither did he nor his parents sin; but that the works of God should be made manifest in him. 4. I must*[1] *work the works of him who sent*[2] *me, while it is day; the night comes, in which no one can work. 5. While I am in the world, I am the light of the world.*" These first five verses describe the situation in which the new miracle is wrought. If the last words of the preceding chapter in the T. R. are authentic, the first words of this would closely connect this scene with the preceding; comp. καὶ παράγων with παρῆγεν οὕτως. But there

---

[1] ℵ B D L Cop. Orig. read ημας (*we must do*) instead of εμε (*I must do*) which has in its favor the 12 other Mjj. the Mnn. It. Vulg. Syr.

[2] L. Cop.: ημας (*us*) instead of με.

would be in this case, as *de Wette* has clearly seen, an improbability in the story; for the question which the disciples address to Jesus in ver. 2 implies a more calm condition of mind than that in which they could have been on leaving the temple after the violent scene of chap. viii. Nothing in the authentic text forces us to connect one of these facts with the other. The formula καὶ παράγων, *and in passing*, only requires that there should not be placed between them a too considerable interval. If the scene in viii. 30–59 occurred in the morning, that which follows may have taken place in the evening of the same day. This time of the day suits well the figure which the Lord employs (vv. 4, 5). The blind man was sitting at one of the gates either of the temple, or rather of the city, to beg. The disciples learned from him or from others that he was blind from birth. The question which they address to Jesus seems to have been called forth by the marked attention with which he regarded this man (εἶδεν). From the point of view of Jewish monotheism, suffering, it seemed, could only be the consequence of sin. But, how apply this law to the present case? The only two alternatives which presented themselves to the mind were those which are indicated by the question of the disciples: but they seemed equally inadmissible. The dogma of the pre-existence of souls or that of metempsychosis might have given some probability to the first supposition; but these systems, although the second especially was not foreign to the Rabbinical teaching, were never popular in Israel. It would therefore have been necessary to hold that the misfortune of this man was an anticipatory chastisement of his future sins, or the punishment of some fault committed by him in the embryonic state (Gen. xxv. 22; Ps. li. 7). But these two explanations must have both appeared very improbable. The other supposition, that this man suffered for the sins of his parents, might be supported by Exod. xx. 5, but nevertheless it seemed contrary to the justice of God. The disciples, perceiving no reasonable solution, ask Jesus to decide the question. The ἵνα preserves always in some measure the idea of purpose: "*that he should have been* born thus, according to the divine plan." In His reply, Jesus does not deny the existence of sin in this man or his parents; but no more does He acknowledge the necessity of a moral connection between this individual or family sin and the blindness with which the unhappy man is smitten. He teaches the disciples that they should direct their attention, not to the mysterious cause of the suffering, but to the end for which God permits it and the salutary effects which we can derive from it. Individual suffering is not often connected, except in a *general* way, with the collective sin of humanity (see on v. 14), and does not give us the right to judge the one who suffers. But it always includes a call to fulfill a divine mission towards him by helping him temporally and spiritually. As evil has its work on earth, so God also has His, and it consists in making evil itself an occasion of good. All these acts by which we coöperate in the accomplishment of the divine intention, enter into what Jesus here calls *the works of God*. The sequel will show that this word comprehends in the thought of Jesus, together with the outward act which bears the stamp of the divine omnipotence (the miracle of healing vv. 6, 7), the spiritual effects which will result from it, the spiritual illumination and the salvation of the blind man (vv. 35–38). The summons to help and save this unhappy man made itself felt in the Lord's heart at the very moment when He had fixed His eyes upon him; hence the εἶδεν of ver. 1. The term φανερώθη, *be made manifest*, is explained by the fact that these works are originally hidden in the divine plan, before being executed. This point of view from which Jesus regards suffering is that which He seeks to make His disciples share from the end of ver. 3, and that which He develops in vv. 4, 5, by applying it to His own personal task during His sojourn here on earth.

When the master who has entrusted the task to the workman (ὁ πέμψας, *he who has sent*), gives the signal, the latter must act as long as the day of working continues. This signal Jesus has just discerned. Though it is a Sabbath, he cannot defer obeying until the morrow. Perhaps Jesus was at that moment beholding on the horizon the sun which was setting and was in a few moments going to disappear. This day which is about to end is for Him the emblem of His earthly life, which is near its termination (viii. 21). " When the night is come," He says, " the workmen cease their work. My work is to enlighten the world, like this sun; and for me, as for it, the task will be ended in a little while. I must not lose a moment, therefore, of the time which remains for me to fulfill it." The reading (" *we must work* ") which belongs to the most ancient Mjj., is defended by Meyer, Lange, Luthardt, Weiss, Westcott, Tischendorf, etc. In that case, it must be supposed that a substitution for it was made in the numerous documents which read ἐμέ, *I*, under the influence of the με which follows, as well as that of ver. 5. This is possible; but is it natural that Jesus should apply to all the disciples the duty which He is to fulfill? And is not the contrary supposition also possible? Was there not a desire to make of this altogether individual expression a moral maxim, and still more probably was there not a desire to avoid the application to the Lord of the following words which seemed incompatible with His state of heavenly glory: *The night comes, when no one can work.* It is impossible for me to harmonize the ἡμᾶς, *we*, with the με, *I*, which follows. For there is a close correlation between the two notions: *to be sent* and *do the work of*. I think therefore that ἡμᾶς has been wrongly substituted for ἐμέ, and that only two MSS. (א L) have been consistent throughout in logically adding to the change of ἐμέ to ἡμᾶς that of με to ἡμᾶς. The two others (B D), by neglecting to make this second change, have confessed and condemned the first. It is of importance to remark that the ancient Versions, the Itala and Peschito, support the received reading. The contrast of *day* and *night* cannot denote, in this context, that of opportunity and inopportunity, or that of the moment of grace and the hour when it can no longer be obtained; it can be here only the contrast between the time of *working* during the day, and that of *rest* when once the night is come. There is therefore nothing sinister in this figure: *the night.* But in what sense can the idea of *rest* be applied to the heavenly life of Jesus Christ? Does He not continue in heaven, through His Spirit, the work begun here on earth? True, but, in His heavenly existence, He in reality only reaps that which He sowed during His sojourn on earth (iv. 38). Consequently, a single divine call to do good neglected by Him here below, a single moment lost on earth, would have left an irreparable void in the work of salvation accomplished by the Holy Spirit after His departure. The whole material of the regenerating and sanctifying activity of the Spirit, even to the end of the present dispensation, is derived from the earthly work of Jesus.

The expression: *I am the light of the world*, ver. 5, has no relation to the figure of day and night, ver. 4; it is chosen with reference to the special work which the Lord must now accomplish in giving physical and spiritual light to the one born blind. We see from the conjunction ὅταν, *when*, which can only be rendered by *as long as*, how His sojourn in this world is to the view of Jesus a transitory and in some sort accidental thing. How should He not hasten to employ well a season which must end so soon?

Vv. 6, 7. "*Having said this, he spat on the ground and made clay of the spittle, and he anointed with this clay the eyes of the blind man,*[1] 7 *and he said to him; Go, wash in the pool of Siloam (a name which means, Sent).*[2] *He went away therefore and washed, and came seeing.*" By the words: *having said this*, the evangelist presents the following act as the immediate application of the principle which Jesus has just laid down. In Matt. xx. 34 (Mark x. 46), Jesus heals a blind man by a simple touch. In Mark vii. 33; viii. 23, He uses, as here, His saliva for effecting cures. He makes use of an external means, therefore, only in some cases. Hence it follows that He does not use it as a medical agency. Is this the vehicle or the conductor of His miraculous power, as some have thought? The same reason prevents us from deciding for this view. We must rather see in this manner of acting a pedagogic measure, not with the aim of putting the faith of the sick man to the test, as He is about to do with the blind man (*Calvin*), but to the end of entering into more direct and personal contact with him. When Jesus had to do with sick persons who possessed all their senses, He could act upon them with a look or with a word. But in cases like that of the deaf-mute (Mark vii. 33 ff.) and of the blind man (Mark viii. 23) we see Him making use of some material means to put them in relation to His person and to present to their faith its true object. It was necessary that they should know that their cure emanated from *His person*. This knowledge was the starting-point for their faith in Him as the author of their salvation. And if in the case with which we are occupied, Jesus does more than anoint the eyes of the blind man, if He covers them with a mass of clay, adding thus to the natural blindness an artificial blindness, and sends him to wash in Siloam, the aim of this course of action can hardly be that which *Meyer* and *Weiss* suppose,—to

---

[1] Instead of the reading of the T. R. καὶ επεχρ. τον π. επι τ. οφθ. του τυφλ. (*he anointed with clay the eyes of*) which is supported by 14 Mjj., most of the Mnn. It^{aliq.} Syr^{sch}, επεθηκε is read in B C, and in ℵ B L: αυτου τον π. επι τ. οφθ.; A the same, adding του τυφλου (*he applied his clay to the eyes of*).

[2] This parenthesis is wanting in Syr. and in a Persian translation.

give to the organ, which had never performed its functions before, time to be formed and to be made ready to act; for when once miraculous power is admitted, it cannot be limited in this way; it is more probable that in this point also the aim of Jesus was of a moral nature. The pool of Siloam had played an important part in the feast which had come to its end. In the solemn and daily libation (p. 75), this fountain had been presented to the people as the emblem of the theocratic favors and the pledge of all the Messianic blessings. This typical significance of Siloam rested upon the Old Testament which had established a contrast between this humble fountain, springing up noiselessly at the foot of the temple-mountain (*the waters of Shiloah which flow sweetly*), emblem of the divine salvation wrought by the Messiah (*Emmanuel*), and the *great waters* (of the Euphrates), the symbol of the brute force of the enemies of the theocracy (Is. viii. 7). What then does Jesus do by adding to the real blindness of this man, which He alone can cure, this artificial and symbolic blindness, which the water of Siloam is to remove? In the first place, He expressly gives to the sacred fountain a part in His work of healing, as He had not done in chap. v. with reference to the pool of Bethesda, and He thus places this work more evidently to the eyes of all under the protection of God Himself. God is thereby associated, as it were, in this new Sabbatic work (*Lange*). Then, He presents Himself as the real fountain of Siloam of which the prophet had spoken (Is. viii. 7) and thus declares to the people that this type of the grace of Jehovah is now fulfilled in Him.

It is undoubtedly this symbolic significance attributed to the water of Siloam, which explains the remark of the evangelist: *a name which signifies: Sent.* From the philological point of view, the correctness of the translation given by John is no longer disputed. It is acknowledged that the name *Siloam* is a verbal substantive or adjective from שלח, and derived from the passive participle Kal or rather Piel (with the solution of the daghesh forte in the ל into י). What was the origin of this title? The pool of Siloam, discovered by Robinson near the place where the three valleys of Tyropeon, Hinnom and Jehoshaphat meet together, is fed by a subterranean conduit recently discovered, which starts from the fountain of the Virgin in the valley of Jehoshaphat and crosses in a zigzag way the side of the rock of Ophel, the southern prolongation of the temple mountain. The name *sent* can therefore be explained in this sense: water *brought* from far. Or we may think, with *Ewald*, of the *jet* itself of the spring, that is of the intermittent fountain which feeds the reservoir (see more on p. 455). Or finally we may see herein the idea of a *gift* of Jehovah (*Hengstenberg*), springs being regarded in the East as gifts of God. In any case, this parenthesis has as its purpose to establish a relation between this spring celebrated by the prophet as the emblem of the Messianic salvation (the typical *sent*) and the *sent one* properly so-called who really brings this salvation.

As *Franke* remarks (p. 314), this case, being the only one in which Jesus rests upon the meaning of a name, must be explained by the circumstance that Isaiah had already brought the water of Siloam into connection with the salvation of which He recognized the accomplishment in Jesus.

Meyer and others explain this parenthesis by supposing that John saw prefigured in this name *sent* the *sending* of the blind man himself to Siloam. As if there were the least logical correspondence between this sending and the name of this reservoir; as if the name of *sent* were not above all the constant title of Jesus Himself in our Gospel. To get rid of this parenthesis which embarrassed him, *Lücke* had recourse, with hesitation, to the hypothesis of an interpolation. The *Peschito* actually omits these words. But this omission in a Syriac translation is very naturally explained, since the word translated belongs to that language.

According to the Alexandrian reading, we must translate in ver. 6: "He applied *His* clay to . . . " *Weiss*, to save this objectionable reading, proposes to refer the pronoun αὐτοῦ, not to Jesus, but to πτύσματος, *the saliva*: "He applied the clay of the saliva." The fact is that here, as frequently, one must know how to free one's self from the prejudice which attributes to the Alexandrian text a kind of infallibility. The preposition of motion, εἰς, *into*, is used with the verb νίψαι, *wash*, probably because the blind man was obliged to go down into the reservoir. *Meyer* explains the εἰς, by mentioning that in washing, the blind man would necessarily make the clay fall into the basin(!). It is a matter of course that the blind man found a guide among the persons present. How can *Reuss* make a charge against the narrative on the point of this omission? The evangelist says: *He returned seeing;* this signifies, no doubt, that the blind man returned to the place where he had left Jesus that he might render thanks to Him, and that, not finding Him there,—Jesus was only *passing* by (ver. 1),—he returned to his dwelling. This appears, indeed, from the following expression (ver. 8): *the neighbors*, as well as from vv. 35, 37. *Reuss*: "We are not told where the man went after having washed, why he did not return to his benefactor . . . " What is to be said of such criticism?

Vv. 8–12. "*His neighbors therefore, and those who before saw him begging,*[1] *said, Is not this he that sat and begged?* 9. *Some said, It is he; others, He is like* [2] *him. He said, I am he.* 10. *Thereupon they said to him, How were thine eyes opened?* 11. *He answered and said,*[3] *A man* [4] *called Jesus made clay and anointed my eyes, and said to me, Go to the pool of Siloam* [5] *and wash. Having gone thither and washed, I have recovered sight.* 12. *They said to him therefore, Where is this man? He says, I know not.*" These verses describe in the most natural and most dramatic way the effect produced by the

---

[1] T. R. reads τυφλες with 9 Mjj.; ℵ A B C D K L X 10 Mnn. It^{aliq} Vulg. Syr. Cop. read προσαιτης (*beggar*); It^{plerique}: τυφλος ην και προσαιτης.

[2] ℵ B C L X It^{aliq} Vulg. Syr. Cop.: ουχι αλλα ομοιος (*no, but he is like him*) instead of ομοιος (*he is like him*) which is read by T. R.

[3] Και ειπεν is omitted by ℵ B C D L It^{aliq}.

[4] ℵ B L some Mnn. read ο before ανθρωπος (*the man*).

[5] ℵ B D L X It^{aliq}. Syr^{sch}: εις τον Σιλωαμ instead of εις τον κολ. του Σ.

return of the blind man to his home. The evangelist distinguishes from the neighbors all those, in general, who were accustomed to see him (imperfect participle θεωροῦντες) asking alms. The question of ver. 8 is proposed by all; but two slightly different tendencies immediately manifest themselves in the solutions given in ver. 9. Some frankly recognize the fact: "Yes, it is he." Others seem to be already preparing for themselves a means of eluding it: "He is like him." In the Byzantine reading: *He is like him*, a resemblance is conceded which is calculated to establish identity. But according to the Alexandrian variant: "*No; but he is like him!*" there would be already a denial of identity; everything would be reduced to an accidental resemblance. In any case, it is evidently the latter class who, upon the declaration of the blind man, present to him the questions of ver. 10 and ver. 12. The expression *recover sight* (ver. 11) arises from the fact that blindness, even from birth, is a state contrary to nature.[1] The question of ver. 12 betrays the intention of provoking an inquiry; it is the transition to the following passage:

The Investigation: vv. 13-34

First appearance of the blind man: vv. 13-17. Confronting of the blind man with his parents: vv. 18-23. Second appearance of the blind man: vv. 24-34.

First appearance:

Vv. 13-17. "*They lead the man who was formerly blind to the Pharisees. 14. Now it was the Sabbath when[2] Jesus made the clay and opened the eyes of this man. 15. In their turn, the Pharisees also asked him how he had recovered his sight. He said to them, He put clay upon my eyes, and I washed, and I see. 16. Thereupon, some of the Pharisees said, This man is not from God, because he does not keep the Sabbath. Others said, How can a wicked man do such miracles? And they were divided among themselves. 17. Addressing the blind man again, they say to him, What dost thou say of him, in that he opened thine eyes? He answered, He is a prophet.*" Those who push for an investigation are the ill-disposed questioners of vv. 10, 12. The term *the Pharisees* cannot designate the entire Sanhedrim (comp. vii. 45). Had the Pharisaic party a certain organization perchance, and is the question here of its leaders? It is more natural to suppose that the question here is of the more violent ones. It was undoubtedly the day after the one on which the miracle had taken place.

Ver. 14. *Keil* remarks that the expression is not *for*, but *now* (δέ). There is therefore no indication here of the reason for which they brought him;

---

[1] With respect to the term ἀνέβλεψε (literally, *he saw again*), Meyer cites a passage from Pausanias (*Messen.*, iv. 12, 5. ed. Schubart) where that author also uses this term with reference to the cure of one born blind. To the mention of this fact, interesting in itself, we will add the following details: The question is of a Messenian diviner, named Ophioneus, who was blind from birth (τὸν ἐκ γενετῆς τυφλόν) and who, after a violent attack of headache, recovered his sight (ἀνέβλεψεν ἀπ' αὐτοῦ). Pausanias adds, however, that he lost it soon afterwards.

[2] Instead of οτε, ℵ B L X It^aliq read εν η ημερα.

it is an incidental remark, explanatory of what follows.—The words: *He made clay* are skillfully added in order to make prominent the anti-Sabbatic work in the miracle. *Renan* says of Jesus: "He openly violated the Sabbath." We have already seen that there is nothing of this (Comp. p. 461). In this case, as in that of chap. v., Jesus had trampled under foot, not the Mosaic Sabbath, but its Pharisaic caricature. The word πάλιν, *again*, alludes to ver. 10. This expression, as well as the repeated *and* in this ver. 15, indicates a certain impatience on the part of the blind man, whom these questions weary. He already penetrates their designs. Thus, also, is the somewhat abrupt brevity of his reply explained. The division which manifested itself in the public, is reproduced in this limited circle. Some, starting from the inviolability of the Sabbath ordinance, deny to Jesus, as a transgressor of this ordinance, any divine mission; from this results logically the denial of the miracle. Others, starting from the fact of the miracle, infer the holy character of Jesus, and thus implicitly deny the infraction of the Sabbath. Everything depends on the choice of the premise, and the choice depends here, as always, on moral freedom. It is at the point of departure that the friends of the light and those of darkness separate; the rest is only a matter of logic. We must not translate ἁμαρτωλός by *sinner*. The defenders of Jesus do not dream of affirming His perfect holiness; the termination ωλος expresses abundance, custom; thus: a man without principles, a violator of the Sabbath, a publican. The question addressed to the blind man in ver. 17, has as its aim to wrest from him a word which may furnish a pretext for suspecting his veracity. As for him, he recognizes in the miracle, according to the received opinion iii. 2, the sign of a divine mission, and he frankly declares it.

Confronting of the blind man with his parents:

Vv. 18–23. "*The Jews therefore did not believe concerning him, that he had been blind and had recovered his sight, until they had called the father and the mother of him who had recovered his sight; 19 and they asked them, saying, Is this your son, who you say was born blind? How then does he now see? 20. The parents answered them and said, We know that this is our son, and that he was born blind; 21 but how he now sees, we know not; or who has opened his eyes, we know not; he is of age, ask him;*[1] *he shall speak for himself. 22. The parents spoke thus, because they feared the Jews; for the Jews had already agreed that if any one should acknowledge him as the Christ, he should be put out of the synagogue. 23. Therefore said his parents, He is of age, ask him.*" By the term οἱ Ἰουδαῖοι, *the Jews*, John does not mean to designate a group of new individuals. They are still the same; only he designates them now, no longer from the point of view of their position in Israel, but from that of their disposition towards Jesus. The persons in question are the most hostile ones, those to whom ver. 16a refers. They suspect a collusion between Jesus and the blind man, and for this reason they wish to make inquiry of his parents. Of the three questions which ver. 19

---

[1] ℵ omits the words αυτον ερωτησατε (*ask him*). B D L X It^plerique place them before ηλικιαν εχει.

contains, the first two—those which relate to the blindness from birth of their son and the identity of the man who is cured with this son—are immediately answered by the parents affirmatively. There is something comical in the three αὐτός, *he*, by means of which they pass over from themselves to him the burden of answering the third. The term συνετέθεντο, *they had agreed*, ver. 22, denotes a decision formed, and not a mere project, as *Meyer* thinks; this follows from the word ἤδη, *already*, and from the knowledge which the parents have of this measure. The exclusion from the synagogue involved for the excommunicated person the breaking off of all social relations with those about him. The higher degree of excommunication would have had death as its result, if this penalty had been practicable under the Roman dominion. We find here a new landmark on the path of the hostile measures adopted with regard to Jesus; it is the transition between the sending of the officers (chap. vii.) and the decree of death in chap. xi. The cowardice of the parents is, as it were, the prelude of that of the whole people.

Second appearance:

Vv. 24–34. "*They called, for the second time, the man who had been blind, and they said to him, Give glory to God; we know that this man is a wicked person. 25. He answered*[1] *them, Whether he is a wicked person, I know not; one thing I know, that whereas I was blind, now I see. 26. They said to him again,*[2] *What did he to thee? How did he open thine eyes? 27. He answered them, I told you already, and you did not hear. Why would you hear it again? Do you also wish to become his disciples? 28. They reviled him and said to him, Thou art this man's disciple; we are disciples of Moses. 29. As to Moses, we know that God has spoken to him; but as for this man, we know not whence he is. 30. The man answered them and said, Herein*[3] *is the marvellous*[4] *thing, that you do not know whence he is; and yet, he has opened my eyes! 31. Now, we know that God does not hear the wicked; but if any one is his worshipper and does his will, him he hears. 32. Never has it been heard that any one has opened the eyes of one born blind. 33. If this man were not from God, he could do nothing like this. 34. They answered and said to him, Thou wert altogether born in sin, and thou teachest us! And they drove him out.*" After this confronting, a deliberation intervenes; it is determined to extort from the blind man the disavowal of the miracle in the name of the Sabbatic principle, in other terms, to annihilate the fact by dogma. The expression: *to give glory to God*, denotes the homage rendered to one of the divine perfections momentarily obscured by a word or an act which seems to be derogatory to it (Josh. vii. 19; 1 Sam. vi. 5). The blasphemy here was the declaration of the blind man: *He is a prophet*. It was in contempt of the holiness and truth of God to give this title to a violator of the Sabbath. This culpable assertion must be washed away by the opposite declaration: He is a wicked person. "*We know*" say the rulers

---

[1] The Alexandrian authorities reject και ειπεν, which T. R. adds.
[2] א B D It\ plerique Vulg. omit παλιν (*again*).
[3] T. R. with 11 Mjj.: εν γαρ τουτω; א B L: εν τουτω γαρ; D. Syr.: εν τουτω ουν; X Λ εν γαρ τουτο (*this one thing is*).
[4] א B L 3 Mnn. Chrys. read το before θαυμαστον.

694 / Unbelief Develops in Israel

(vv. 24, 29), setting themselves up as representatives of theological knowledge in Israel; in virtue of their knowledge, the miracle *cannot* be: therefore it *is* not. On his part, the blind man, while admitting his incompetency in theological questions, simply opposes fact to knowledge; his language becomes decidedly ironical; he is conscious of the bad faith of his adversaries. They feel the force of his position, and ask him again as to the circumstances of the fact (ver. 26), hoping to find in some detail of his account a means of assailing the fact itself. Not having succeeded in overthrowing the miracle by dogmatics, they wish to undermine it by criticism. This return to a phase of investigation already settled at once renders the blind man indignant and emboldens him; he triumphs in their impotence, and his reply borders upon irony: " You did not hear? You are deaf then!" They then cover their embarrassment by insult; between Jesus and the Sabbath, or, what amounts to the same thing, between Jesus and Moses, their choice is made. The blind man, seeing that there is a wish to argue with him, becomes more and more bold, and sets himself also to the work of arguing. If he has not studied dogmatics, he at least knows his catechism. Is there an Israelite who is ignorant of this theocratic axiom: that a miracle is an answer to prayer, and that the prayer of a wicked person is not answered. The construction of ver. 30 is doubtful. *Meyer, Luthardt* and *Weiss* explain: " In such a condition of things ($\dot{\epsilon}\nu$ τούτῳ), it is astonishing that you do not know whence he comes, and that he has opened my eyes." But, in this sense, the last words are useless. More than this, the idea : " and that he has opened my eyes " being the premise of the preceding conclusion: "whence he comes," should be placed before it. We must therefore make the $\dot{\epsilon}\nu$ τούτῳ, as is so frequently the case, refer to the following ὅτι: *in this that,* and give to the καί which follows the sense of *and yet* (as in so many other passages in John): "There is truly herein a marvel (without τό); or (with τό): "The real marvelous thing consists in this : that you do not know whence this man comes: and yet He has opened my eyes!" This last reading is evidently the true one. " There is here a miracle greater than even my cure itself; it is your unbelief." The γάρ (*for*), in Greek, often refers to an understood thought. Thus in this case: " You do not know this? *In fact,* there is something here which borders upon the marvelous!" *We know;* that is to say, we simple *Jews,* in general (ver. 31); in contrast to the proud *we know* of these *doctors,* in vv. 24, 29. The argument is compact; ver. 31 is the major premise, ver. 32 the minor, and ver. 33 draws the conclusion.

Defeated by his pitiless logic, whose point of support is simply the principle that *what is, is,* the adversaries of Jesus give way to rage. Saying to the blind man: *Thou wert altogether born in sin,* they allude to his blindness from birth, which they regard as a proof of the divine curse under which the man was born (vv. 2, 3); and they do not perceive that, by this very insult, they render homage to the reality of the miracle which they pretend to deny. Thus unbelief ends by giving the lie to itself. The expression: *they drove him out,* cannot designate an official excommunication; for this could not be pronounced except in a regular meeting. They expelled him violently from the hall, perhaps with the intention of having the excommunication pronounced afterwards by the Sanhedrim in pursuance of a formal deliberation.

It is asked what is the aim with which John related this fact with so much of detail. No striking testimony of Jesus respecting His person marks it as worthy of attention. It refers far more, as it seems, to the history and conduct of a secondary personage, than to the revelation of Jesus Himself. Evidently John accords to this fact this honorable place because it marks in his view a decisive step in the progress of Israelitish unbelief. For the first time, a believer is, for his faith, cast out of the theocratic community. It is the first act of the rupture between the Church and the Synagogue. We shall see in the following chapter that Jesus really regards this fact in this light.

The whole scene here described has an historical truthfulness which is obvious. It is so little ideal in its nature that it rests, from one end to the other, upon the brute reality of a *fact*. *Baur* himself acknowledges this. "The reality of the fact," he says, "is the point against which the contradiction of the adversaries is broken."[1] And yet this fact, according to him, is a pure invention! What sort of a man must an evangelist be who describes, with greatest detail, a whole series of scenes for the purpose of showing how dogmatic reasoning is shattered against a fact in the reality of which he does not himself believe? Does not criticism meet the same experience which here happens to the Pharisees in ver. 34? Does it not give the lie to itself? This whole chapter presents to modern criticism its own portrait. The defenders of the Sabbath ordinance reason thus: God *cannot* lend His power to a violator of the Sabbath; therefore the miracle ascribed to Jesus *does not exist*. *A non posse ad non esse valet consequentia*. The opponents of the miracles in the Gospel history reason in exactly the same way, only substituting for a religious ordinance a scientific axiom: The supernatural *cannot* be; therefore, however well attested the miracles of Jesus may be, they are not. The historical fact holds good against the ordinance, of whatsoever nature it may be, and it will end by forcing it to submit.

The moral result: vv. 35–41

Vv. 35–38 present the moral result of this miracle, and vv. 39–41 formulate that of the activity of Jesus in general.

Vv. 35–38. "*Jesus heard that they had driven him out; and having found him, he said to him: Dost thou believe on the Son of man?*[2] 36. *He answered and said, And*[3] *who is he, Lord, that I may believe on him?* 37. *Jesus said to him, Thou hast both seen him and he that speaks with thee is he.* 38. *He said, Lord, I believe. And he prostrated himself before him.*"[4] In order that the true aim which Jesus proposed to Himself might be attained (vv. 3, 4),

---

[1] *Theol. Jahrb.* iii., p. 119.
[2] Instead of του θεου (*of God*,), ℵ B⁻D Sah. read του ανθρωπου.
[3] Και (*and*) is omitted only in A L many Mnn. It. Vulg.
[4] ℵ omits ver. 38 and the first words of ver. 39 (as far as εις κριμα not inclusive).

the spiritual illumination and salvation of the blind man must result from his corporeal cure; and certainly his courageous fidelity in the face of the enemies of Jesus made him worthy to obtain this new favor. This connection of ideas is indicated by the first words of ver. 35: *Jesus heard . . . and . . .* In the question which He addresses to this man we formerly preferred the reading: *on the Son of God*, to that of the three ancient Mjj. which read: *on the Son of man*. It explains better the act of worship with which the scene ends (ver. 38). *Westcott* rightly observes, however, that the substitution of the technical and popular term *Son of God* for *Son of man* is much more probable than the reverse. And he cites the very striking example of vi. 69, where the term *Son of God* has evidently taken the place in the received text of *Holy One of God*. If we must read: *on the Son of man*, the meaning is: on the man who has an exceptional place among all His brethren and who is raised up in order to save them all. The question: *Dost thou believe?* does not signify: "Art thou disposed to believe?" (*Lücke*). It is one of those questions, such as were sometimes put by Jesus, whose import goes beyond the actual light of the one to whom it is addressed, but which is, even for this reason, fitted to call forth the desired explanation. "Thou who hast just conducted thyself with so much of courage, dost thou then believe?" Jesus ascribes to the conduct of the blind man an importance which it as yet only impliedly possesses. This man had recognized Him as a prophet and had courageously proclaimed Him as such; he had thus morally bound himself to receive the testimony of Jesus respecting Himself, whatever it might be. The blind man accepts without hesitation this consequence of his previous words. And this relation it is which is expressed with much vivacity by the particle καί, *and*, at the beginning of his question. This copula serves indeed to identify the light which he waits for with that for which the question of Jesus makes him hope; comp. Luke xviii. 26. Jesus might have answered: It is I, myself. He prefers to designate Himself by a periphrasis recalling to him who was previously blind the work which he has accomplished on his behalf: *Thou hast seen him*, and which gives a warranty to His present testimony: *It is he who speaks to thee*. The first καί in the reply of Jesus: *Thou hast both seen him*, connects this revelation with the promise of faith which the blind man has just made to Him. The successive καί set forth the ready, easy, natural linking together of all the moral facts which form the course of this story. In this rapid development, one step does not wait for another. Ver. 38 shows us the consummation of this gradual illumination. In these circumstances, in which there was neither pardon to ask for, nor supplication to present, the genuflexion could be only a homage of worship, or at least of profound religious respect. The term προσκύνειν, *to prostrate oneself*, is always applied in John to divine worship (iv. 20 ff. xii. 20).

In the presence of this man prostrate at His feet and inwardly illuminated, Jesus feels Himself called to proclaim a general result which His ministry will have throughout the whole world, and of which the event which has just occurred is, as it were, a first example.

Vv. 39–41. "*And Jesus said, I am come into this world to exercise this judgment, that those who see not may see, and that those who see may become blind. 40. And those of the Pharisees who were with him heard these words* [1] *and they said to him, And are we also blind? 41. Jesus said to them, If you were blind, you would not have sin; but now you say, We see; therefore,* [2] *your sin remains.*" [3] Here is a simple reflection to which Jesus gives utterance, and which is connected with the dignity of *light of the world* which He had attributed to Himself at the beginning of this scene (ver. 5). So the verb εἶπεν, *he said*, is left without a limiting personal object such as: to them. The coming of Jesus has for its end, strictly, to enlighten the world; but as this end cannot be attained in all, because all are not willing to allow themselves to be enlightened, it has another secondary end: that those who reject the light should be blinded by it. It is not necessary to see in the term κρίμα, *judgment*, the indication of a judicial act. Such a judgment had been denied in iii. 17. The question is of a moral result of the attitude taken by the men themselves with regard to Jesus, but a result which was necessary and willed from on high (ἦλθον εἰς). The term *in this world* recalls the expression: light *of this world* (ver. 5). The greater part of the interpreters (*Calvin, Lücke, Meyer*, etc.) give to the expression: *Those who see not*, a subjective meaning: "Those who feel and acknowledge that they do not see." This interpretation arbitrarily weakens the sense of the expression employed by Jesus and it does not suit the context, since the man whose cure occasions these words, did not feel his blindness more than other blind persons, and since, speaking spiritually, he did not simply feel himself more ignorant than others, but he was so in reality. *Those who do not see* are therefore men who are really sunk in spiritual ignorance. They are those whom the rulers themselves call in vii. 49: "*This multitude who know not the law*," the ignorant in Israel, those whom Jesus designates, Matt. xi. 25, Luke x. 21, as *the little children* (νήπιοι) contrasting them with the wise and intelligent. *Those who see* are, consequently, those who, throughout this whole chapter, have said, in speaking of themselves: *We know*, the experts in the law, those whom Jesus calls, in the passage cited, *the wise and intelligent* (σοφοὶ καὶ συνετοί). The former, not having any knowledge of their own to keep, yield themselves without difficulty to the revelation of the truth, while the others, not wishing to sacrifice their own knowledge, turn away from the new revelation, and, as we have just seen in this chapter, presume even to annihilate the divine facts by their theological axioms. Hence it results that the former are immediately enlightened by the rays of the sun which rises upon the world, while the imperfect light which the latter possess is transformed into complete darkness. We must notice the delicate contrast between μὴ βλέποντες (*those who see not*) in the first clause, which denotes a sight *not yet* developed, and τυφλοί, *blind*, in the second, which denotes the absolute blindness resulting from the

---

[1] ℵ D It^plerique Vulg. Cop. omit ταυτα.
[2] ℵ B D K L X some Mnn. It^plerique Vulg. Cop. omit ουν (*therefore*).
[3] D L X: αι αμαρτιαι .... μενουσιν (instead of the singular).

698 / Unbelief Develops in Israel

destruction of the organ. This passage expresses, therefore, the same thought as the words of Jesus in the Synoptics: "*I thank thee, Father, Lord of heaven and earth, that thou hast hid these things from the wise and intelligent, and hast revealed them unto babes*" (Matt. xi. 25; Luke x. 21). *Meyer* objects that in this sense the *seeing* or *not seeing* would relate to the law and the *becoming blind* to the Gospel, that there would thus be a twofold relation which is not to be accepted. But in the view of Jesus (comp. v. 45 ff.), the law, when thoroughly understood, and the Gospel are only one and the same increasing moral light. The knowledge of the law must lead, if it is earnestly applied, to the acknowledgment of the Gospel; if the latter had not come, the law itself would have covered the sight with an impenetrable veil (2 Cor. iii. 14, 15).

The Pharisees who were at this moment in the company of Jesus, ask Him ironically if He ranks them also, the doctors of Israel, in the number of the blind. I do not think that they make a strict distinction between the *non-seeing* and the *blind* of ver. 39. They keep to the general idea of *blindness* and ask if He applies it to them also.

The answer of Jesus to this sarcasm (ver. 41) is one of crushing severity. Instead of treating them as blind, as they no doubt expected, Jesus says to them, on the contrary: "It were a thing to be wished for, for your sakes, that you were so!" The expression: *Those who see not*, in this answer, designates those who have not the religious knowledge furnished by the profound study of the law. If those who interrogate Him at this moment had belonged to the ignorant portion of the nation, their unbelief might have been only a matter of surprise or of seduction, something like that *sin against the Son of man which can be forgiven in this age or even in the other*. But such is not their position. They are possessed of *the key of knowledge* (Luke xi. 52), they possess the knowledge of the law and the prophets. It is, then, with full knowledge that they reject the Messiah: *Behold the Son, this is the heir; come, let us kill him, and the inheritance shall be ours*. Here is the exact rendering of their feeling. Their unbelief is the rejection of the truth discerned; this is what renders it unpardonable: ἁμαρτία μένει, *their sin remains*. *Weiss* gives to this last word a slightly different sense: the sin of unbelief *remains* in them because the pride of their own knowledge prevents them from attaining to faith. But the expression *sin which remains* has certainly a more serious meaning (iii. 36); it has reference to the divine judgment. The meaning of this verse which we have just set forth (comp. *Luthardt, Weiss*, etc.) appears to me more natural than that given by *Calvin, Meyer* and most: "If *you felt* your ignorance, I could heal you; but you boast presumptuously of your knowledge; for this reason your malady is incurable." The expression: *You say (yourselves* say), proves nothing in favor of this meaning and against that given by us, as *Meyer* asserts. These words contain, indeed, an allusion to the ironical question of the Pharisees (ver. 40), by which they had denied their blindness. *Their own mouth* had thus testified that it was not light which had been wanting to them. "You yourselves acknowledge, by saying constantly, *We know*, that you are not of those who are ignorant of the preparatory revelations which God has granted to His people. You are therefore without excuse."

The relation here indicated between the ignorant and the learned in Israel is reproduced on a large scale in the relation between the heathen and the Jews, and with the same result. The sin of the heathen, who so long persecuted the Church, has been forgiven them, while the crime, consciously committed by Israel, of rejecting the Messiah, still rests upon that people. Jesus knew well that this judgment, in which His coming must issue, embraced the whole world; this is the reason why He said in ver. 39: "I am come *into this world,* in order that . . . " We shall find the same sentiment at the basis of the following section. Comp. x. 3, 4, 16.

2

John 10:1-21

THE FIRST DISCOURSE

The following discourse includes three parables: that of the *shepherd* (vv. 1-6), that of the *gate* (vv. 7-10), and that of the *good shepherd* (vv. 11-18); the section closes with an historical conclusion (vv. 19-21).

This discourse is not, like those of chaps. v. and vi., the development of a theme relating to the person of Christ, and suggested by the miracle which had preceded. Jesus does not explain here, on occasion of the healing of the man born blind, how He is the light of the world (ver. 4). But the discourse is, nevertheless, in close connection with the facts related in the preceding chapter; it is, properly speaking, only the reproduction of those facts in a parabolic form. The violent breaking in of the thieves into the sheepfold represents the tyrannical measures of the Pharisees in the theocracy, measures of which the ninth chapter has just presented a specimen; the attraction which the voice of the shepherd exercises upon the sheep and the fidelity with which they continue to follow his steps, recalls the simple and persevering faith of the blind man; finally, Jesus' action, full of tenderness towards this maltreated and insulted man, is found again in the picture of the good shepherd intervening on behalf of his sheep.

These three parables form three progressive pictures. On the occasion of the violent expulsion of the man born blind, Jesus sees the true Messianic flock separating itself from the ancient Israelitish community and grouping itself around Him; this is the first picture, vv. 1-6. Then, He describes the glorious prerogatives which, by His means, the flock once formed shall enjoy, in contrast to the cruel fate which is reserved for the ancient flock which remained under the egoistic and mischievous direction of its present leaders; this is the second picture, vv. 7-10. Finally, He places in a clear light the sentiment which is the soul of His Messianic ministry: disinterested love of the flock, in contrast to the mercenary spirit of the earlier shepherds; this is the third picture, vv. 11-18. We see that there is nothing vague or commonplace in these descriptions. They are the

700 / Unbelief Develops in Israel

faithful reflection of the state of things at the very moment when Jesus was speaking. Thus three ideas: 1. The way in which the Messiah forms His flock; 2. The way in which He feeds it; 3. The motive which urges Him to act thus; and in each case, as a contrast, the description of the ministry opposed to His own, as the theocracy at that time presented the example of it.

The Shepherd: vv. 1-6

Vv. 1-5. " *Verily, verily, I say unto you that he who does not enter by the door into the sheep-fold, but climbs up some other way, the same is a thief and a robber; 2 but he who enters in by the door is the shepherd of the sheep. 3. To him the porter opens; and the sheep hear his voice; and he calls* [1] *his own sheep by their name and leads them out. 4. And when he has put forth all his own sheep*,[2] *he goes before them, and the sheep follow him because they know his voice; 5 they will not follow* [3] *a stranger, but will flee from him, because they know not the voice of strangers.*" This picture deserves the name of allegory rather than that of parable. In the parable, there is a story which assumes a form independent up to a certain point of the moral application; in the allegory, the application makes itself felt immediately through every feature of the representation: the image does not take a form independent of the thought. The parable is a picture, the allegory a transparency. The Synoptics also present pictures of this sort; for example, that of the leaven and the grain of mustard-seed.

It has been supposed that the figures employed here by Jesus must have been borrowed from the spectacle which He had before His eyes at this very moment; that it was the hour when the shepherds brought back their flocks from the surrounding country into the city of Jerusalem;[4] and this supposition might be extended to the second picture by holding that Jesus was near the *sheep-gate* when He uttered the words of ver. 7 ff.[5] These suppositions have no impossibility. But as Jesus, in the preceding discourses, has applied to Himself several theocratic symbols, it is possible that He continues the same method. David invoked the Lord as his shepherd (Ps. xxiii.). Jehovah, in His highest manifestation, as Messiah, was represented by the prophets as the shepherd of Israel: Is. xl. 11; Ezek. xxxiv.; Zech. xi. The last passage in particular offers a quite remarkable analogy to the present situation. Like the shepherd of Zechariah, Jesus at this moment, after having vainly sought to gather Israel, renounces the hope of saving the nation; and leaving to the Pharisees (the foolish shepherd of whom Zechariah speaks) the direction of the main portion of the flock, He confines himself to bringing out of this fold which is about to be destroyed the few *poor sheep* who, like this blind man, look to Him.

---

[1] Instead of καλει, א A B D L X some Mnn. read φωνει.

[2] Instead of ιδια προβατα, B D L X some Mnn. It^{aliq} Cop. read ιδια παντα (*all*). א and some Vss. read simply τὰ ιδια.

[3] Some (A B D etc.): ακολουθησουσιν; T. R. with others (א K L etc.) ακολουθησωσιν.

[4] Neander, in his lectures.

[5] F. Bovet, *Voyage en Terre-Sainte*.

Lücke correctly observes that the formula *amen, amen*, never begins anything altogether new. It unites closely what follows with what precedes, either as a confirmation or as an antithesis. A sheep-fold in the East is not a covered building, like our stables: it is a simple inclosure, surrounded by a palisade or wall. The sheep are taken into it in the evening. Several flocks are ordinarily brought together in such an inclosure. The shepherds, after having committed them to the care of a common keeper, the porter, who, during the night, is charged with watching over their safety, return to their homes; in the morning, they return and knock at the door of the inclosure which is strongly fastened; the keeper opens it. They then separate each one his own sheep, by calling to them, and after having gathered their flock lead them to pasturage. As for robbers, it is by climbing the wall of the inclosure that they try to enter into the fold. To recall to mind these details which *Bochart* has described in his *Hierozoicon*, and which are confirmed by modern travelers, is almost to have explained our allegory. It is impossible for me to understand how *Weiss* can deny that the sheepfold denotes the theocracy, or more exactly the Kingdom of God in its preparatory form. According to him, this figure does not have in itself any value and is only a condition for the setting forth of two different ways of acting, that of the shepherd and that of the robbers, which are to be described. But ver. 16 says quite plainly that Israel is the αὐλή, the inclosure of the sheep. There is a shade of difference between the κλεπτής or *thief* and the λῃστής or *robber;* the second term suggests a more marked degree of violence and audacity than the first. The one steals, the other slaughters. Jesus means to describe thereby the audacity full of cunning with which the Pharisees had succeeded in establishing their authority in the inclosure of the people of God, beyond the limits of any charge instituted by God. Nothing in the law, indeed, justified the mission which this party had arrogated to itself in Israel, and the despotic power which it exercised. In opposition to this unauthorized ministry, the figure of *the door* quite naturally designates the legitimate entrance, consequently a *divinely instituted* function—in the context, especially the Messianic office announced and prefigured in the whole of the Old Testament. We need not allow ourselves to be turned aside from this altogether natural sense of the figure, as it results from the contrast between vv. 1 and 2, by the declaration of Jesus in ver. 7. That verse is not the explanation of the present parable; it is the beginning of a new parable in which different, although analogous, figures are freely employed in the service of an altogether different idea. Some interpreters, *Lücke, Meyer, Reuss, Luthardt,* etc., regard the *door* in this first parable as representing the person of the Lord Himself. Consequently they see in the shepherds who enter in by the door the true leaders of the sheep, who are introduced to them by Jesus. But with what fitness would Jesus proceed to speak here of the future pastors of His Church? Still if the disciples had played a part in the preceding narrative, this might help us to understand an anticipation which is so improbable! The door represents the Messianic office divinely instituted and forming the legitimate entrance into the theocracy prepared for its normal leader, the shepherd, that is to say, the Messiah. Undoubtedly, the word ποιμήν, *shepherd*, is in the Greek without an article, and consequently an adjective word. It designates the quality, not the individual : he who enters as *shepherd* (opposed to : as *robber*). But this form does not at all prevent the application of this figure to Jesus (ver. 12). He who comes in the character of shepherd has no need, like a robber, to scale the wall of the inclosure : the porter opens to him. Who is this *porter?* Quite naturally : he who is charged by God with introducing the Messiah into His divine office. Can it be, as *Bengel, Hengstenberg* and *Gess* think, the Father, who draws souls to the Son (vi. 44) ? But God, the owner of the flock, cannot be fitly represented as a servant of an inferior order, subordinate to the shepherd himself. According to *Stier* and *Lange,* He is the Holy Spirit : the same objection. Moreover, Jesus must designate by this figure an historical function, a ministry as positive as that of the Messiah Himself. According to *Chrysostom*, he is Moses, inasmuch as the law leads to Christ. This is very far fetched and refined. *Lampe* understood by the porter all those who were expecting Christ in Israel, and more especially John the Baptist. It seems to me that the nature of things and the beginning of our Gospel prove very clearly that Jesus, in expressing Himself in this way, thought of the forerunner and of the forerunner only. God had raised up John the Baptist expressly to point out the Messiah to the people and to introduce Him into their midst : " There appeared a man sent from God to bear testimony to the light, *to the end that all might believe through him* " (i. 6, 7). It was he whose testimony had brought to Jesus His first believing followers, and should have opened to Him the heart of the whole people. As to those who, like *Lücke, de Wette, Meyer, Luthardt, Weiss,* see in this point only an embellishment of the picture without application, there is no argument, properly so called, to oppose them. This is a matter of feeling. My impression is that every point in this picture answers to an historical reality.

It is not only the mode of entrance which distinguishes the shepherd from the robber ; it is also the manner in which, when he has once entered, he acts towards the flock. The robber lays hold of the sheep by violent measures ; the shepherd simply makes them hear his voice, and *his* sheep, immediately recognizing it, separate themselves from among those which belong to other shepherds and come to gather around him. The words : *the sheep hear his voice,* might refer to all the sheep contained in the inclosure, and the words which follow : *his own sheep,* apply solely to the sheep of the Messiah. But the expression : *hear his voice,* is used throughout all this passage in too internal a sense to apply to the purely outward hearing, as would be the case with the first sense. It appears to me, therefore, that it is better to apply the first words of ver. 3 already to the sheep of the Messiah in the theocracy, and that, if Jesus afterwards adds the epithet ἴδια (*his own*), it is, not to distinguish them from the preceding, but to emphasize the altogether new value which they acquire for His heart, when once, through the act of faith, they have really become His. These remarkable expressions rest upon the fact that between the voice of the Messiah and the heart of believers there exists a pre-established harmony, in virtue of which they recognize Him immediately when He shows Himself and speaks. This fact of which the experience of the first disciples (chap. i.), as well as that of the whole Church, bears witness, is explained by what has been said in the Prologue of the original pouring forth of life and light from the Logos into the human soul (i. 4, 10). It was from such words as those of our passage that John had derived that profound thought. The shepherd *pronounces* the particular name of each one of the sheep—this is the sense of the reading φωνεῖ—or he *summons* them to follow him by calling them by their name; this is what the reading καλεῖ signifies. In both cases, the question is of something more special than the general call to faith indicated by the words *his voice*. When they have once come to Him with faith, He gives them a sign of recognition and favor which is altogether personal. The name, in the Scriptures, is, as *Hengstenberg* says, the expression of the personality. This special designation which is given to each sheep is the proof of the most individual knowledge and the most intimate tenderness. Recall the name of *Peter* given to Simon (i. 43), and the apostrophe: *Mary* (xx. 16), in which Jesus sums up all that Mary is to Him and all that He is to her. Recall also the "Believest *thou?*" addressed to the blind man who was cured, ix. 35.

In the general picturing of the parable, the words: "*And he leads them out,*" designate the act of the shepherd leading his flock to pasturage. But the question is whether this feature refers only to the care which every shepherd gives daily to his flock, or whether it is not intended here to describe a definite historical situation: the going forth of the Messianic flock from the theocratic inclosure devoted to ruin. This sense only seems to me to correspond to the idea of the *entrance* of the Messiah into the sheepfold. In this is a historical fact to which that of the *going forth* of the shepherd and his sheep answers. *Reuss* resorts to ridicule, as usual: "If," he says, "the question were of making the believers go forth from the ancient theocracy, these same believers would be found two lines below entering it again" (alluding to ver. 9: *will go in and go out*). But this critic forgets that this last expression is borrowed from another parable, where the figures, as we shall see, take an altogether different meaning. Jesus has recognized the signal of the inevitable separation in the treatment to which the man who was born blind has been subjected, in his violent expulsion (ix. 34), as well as in the decree of excommunication which strikes Him Himself in the person of his adherents (ix. 22); in general, in the violent hostility of which He sees Himself to be the object (chaps. vii. and viii.). And it is the result of this condition of things which He describes in the term *to lead out,* as in the words: *he calls them,* He had described the historical formation of His flock.

Thus the shepherd has *called* and then has given a mark of tenderness to the sheep who have come to gather themselves about him; and now he *causes them to go forth* from the inclosure where they had been shut up. The term ἐκβάλλειν, *to drive, cast forth,* ver. 4, sets forth with emphasis the principal idea of the passage, as we have just pointed it out. This word designates an energetic and almost rough act by which the shepherd helps the sheep, which still hesitates, to break away from the other sheep of the fold and to give itself up to the chances of the new existence which the shepherd's call opens before it. The rest of the verse describes the life of the Messianic flock, thus formed, in the spiritual pastures into which its divine leader introduces it, then the persevering fidelity of the sheep, of which that of the blind man has just offered an example, and finally the intimate relation which exists henceforth between these sheep and their shepherd. There is great tenderness in the words: "When he has put them forth, he goes *before them.*" While they were still in the inclosure, he remained behind to put them forth, that there might not be a single one left (πάντα, *all,* according to the Alexandrian text). But when the departure is once accomplished, He places Himself at their head, in order that He may lead the flock. We see how accurate are the slightest features of the picture. Οἴδασι, *they know,* means more than ἀκούει, *they hear* (ver. 3); the latter term designated the acceptance of the first call; the other refers to the more advanced personal knowledge which results from daily intercourse. Hence it is, no doubt, that we have the plural οἴδασι following the singular forms which precede.

All along the way which the sheep follow, strange voices make themselves heard, on the right hand and the left, which seek to turn them aside from the steps of the shepherd; they are those of thieves who, not being able to play openly the part of robbers, use means of seduction or intimidation, as did the Pharisees in the preceding scene (ix. 14–40). But they succeed no better in breaking the bond which has been formed, than these had succeeded by violence in preventing its formation. The sheep is for the future made familiar with the voice of the shepherd, so that every voice which is not his produces upon it a strange and repellant effect [1]

We have already refuted the interpretation of those who apply this picture *to the pastors* of the new covenant. Their principal reason (ver. 7: *I am the door*) has no weight, the two pictures being different, as we shall see. The figure changes, in any case, from the second to the third parable; comp. ver. 7: "I am the door;" and ver. 11: "I am the good shepherd." Why not also from the first to the second? The application to Christian pastors wholly breaks the connection of the discourse, both with the preceding scene, and with the situation of the work of Christ at this moment, and finally with the representation of the development of the national unbelief which is the object of this whole part of the Gospel.

In this passage there comes out anew, in the clearest way, the idea of

---

[1] The incident is well known of the Scotch traveler who, having met under the walls of Jerusalem a shepherd leading home his flock, exchanged clothing with him, and, thus disguised, undertook to call the sheep to him. They remained immovable. The true shepherd then made his voice heard. All ran to him, notwithstanding his new dress.

the *organic unity* of the Old and New Covenant, an idea of which *Reuss* and the Tübingen school assert that no trace is to be found in the fourth Gospel.

Ver. 6. " *Jesus spoke this similitude to them; but they did not understand what that meant which he spoke to them.*" The word, παροιμία, *similitude*, properly designates a by-path, hence an enigmatical discourse. It is sometimes used in the translation of the LXX. to render *maschal;* it is taken in the sense of *proverb* in 2 Pet. ii. 22. The idea of a comparison is not so expressly brought out in this term as in the term παραβολή (see *Westcott*). The forcible expression τίνα ἦν, *what was*, for *what meant*, is derived from the fact that the true essence of a word is its meaning. They *did not understand;* because it was morally impossible for them to apply to the Pharisees the figure of thieves and robbers.

The door: vv. 7–10

Vv. 7–10. " *Jesus therefore spoke to them* [1] *again, saying, Verily, verily I say unto you, I am the door of the sheep.* 8. *All* [2] *those who came before me* [3] *are thieves and robbers; but the sheep did not listen to them.* 9. *I am the door: if any one enters in by me, he shall be saved; and he shall go in and go out, and shall find pasture.* 10. *The thief comes not but to steal and to kill and to destroy; I am come that they may have life,* [4] *and that they may have it abundantly.*" Jesus has described the simple and easy way in which the Messiah *forms* His flock, in contrast with the arbitrary and tyrannical measures by which the Pharisees had succeeded in getting possession of the theocracy; He now depicts, in a new allegory, which has only a remote relation in form to the preceding (comp. the two parables which follow each other in Mark; that of the sower and that of the ear of corn, iv. 3 ff., v. 26 ff.) what He will be to His flock when once formed and gathered, the abundance of the salvation which He will cause them to enjoy, as opposed to the advantage taken of the old flock by those intruders and the destruction to which they are leading them. The word πάλιν, *again* (ver. 7), was wrongly rejected by the Sinaitic MS.; the copyist thought that this picture was only a continuation of the preceding (because of the analogy of the figures). This is likewise held by some modern interpreters, but, as we shall see, is untenable. Πάλιν indicates therefore, as in Luke xiii. 20 (where it is placed between the parables of the grain of mustard seed and of the leaven; comp. Matt. xiii. 44, 45, 47), that Jesus adds still another parable to the preceding.

The picture vv. 1–5, which described the formation of the Messianic flock and its going forth from the theocratic inclosure, was borrowed from a morning scene; the second similitude, vv. 7–10, which describes the life full of sweetness of the flock when once formed and everything which it

---

[1] ℵ omits παλιν, and ℵ B αυτοις.
[2] Παντες is omitted by D b.
[3] Προ εμου is placed before ηλθον by T. R. with Mnn. only. A B D K L X Δ 60 Mnn.
[4] ℵ adds αιωνιον (*eternal*).

Cop. place these words after ηλθον. They are entirely omitted in the 9 other Mjj., 100 Mnn. It. Vg. Syr^sch.

706 / Unbelief Develops in Israel

enjoys through the intermediation of the Messiah, places us at mid-day. In the pasturage is an inclosure where the sheep enter and whence they go out at will. If they seek for shelter, they retire to it freely. If hunger impels them, they go forth—for the gate is constantly open for them—and they find themselves in full pasturage. They have thus at their pleasure security and food, the two blessings essential to the prosperity of the flock. In this new figure, the person of the shepherd entirely disappears. It is *the door* which plays the principal part. The inclosure here no longer represents the old covenant; it is the emblem of the perfectly safe shelter of salvation. *Lücke, Meyer, Luthardt, Weiss, Keil* explain the words: *I am the door of the sheep*, in this way: I am the door for coming to the sheep, the door by which the true shepherds enter into the midst of the flock. But in this sense the words refer either to the shepherds of the old covenant or to those of the new. In the former case, we must suppose that the ἐγώ, *I*, designates the *I* of the Logos as a spirit governing the theocracy. Who can admit a sense like this? In the second, it has no fitness of any kind. Moreover, this sense is very forced. The term: *door of the sheep*, naturally means; the door which the sheep use for their own going in and going out (ver. 9).

The privilege, represented by the use which the sheep make of the door, is that which Jesus gives the believing Israelites to enjoy, by furnishing them, like the one born blind, everything which can assure their rest and salvation. *Reuss* himself, abandoning the relation established by him (vv. 1, 2) between the two parables, says: " Yet once more Jesus calls Himself the door, but this time He is so for the flock itself" (thus: no longer for the shepherd, as in the first parable).

The persons designated in ver. 8 as *thieves* and *robbers* can only be the Pharisees (ver. 1). They are characterized here from the point of view, no longer of the manner in which they have established their power in the theocracy, but of the end in view of which they exercised it and of the result which they will obtain thereby. Not only had this audacious caste unlawfully taken possession, in the midst of the people of God, of the most despotic authority, but they were still using it only in a way to satisfy their egoism, their ambition and their cupidity. Hence follows the explanation of the expression, so variously interpreted: *All those who are come before me.* Whatever certain Gnostic writers may have said in former times or *Hilgenfeld* may even now say in his desire to make our Gospel a semi-Gnostic writing,[1] Jesus certainly could not thus speak of Moses and the prophets, and of any legitimate theocratic authority. The constant language of the evangelist protests against such an explanation (v. 39, 45-47; vi. 45; x. 34, 35, etc.). The verb εἰσί (*are*), in the present tense, shows clearly that He has in view persons who were now living. If He says ἦλθον, *came*, and πρὸ ἐμοῦ, *before me*, it is because He found them already at work when He began His own working in Israel. The

---

[1] "This *before me*, embraces *the whole Jewish past;* and the: *all those who* . . . , applies to *all* the preceding leaders of the flock of God."

term *come* indicates with relation to them, as with relation to Jesus, the appearance with the purpose of exercising the government of souls among the people of God. The parable of the vine-dressers in the Synoptics is the explanation of this saying of Jesus.

This interpretation of the first words of ver. 8 follows from the context and enables us to set aside, without any long discussion, the numerous, more or less divergent, interpretations which have been proposed; that of *Camerarius*, who took πρὸ ἐμοῦ in a local sense: "passing *before* and outside the door," that of *Wolf* and *Olshausen*, who gave to πρό the sense of χωρίς: "separating themselves from me, the true door;" those of *Lange* who understands πρό in the sense of ἀντί: "in my place," and *Calov*, who makes the expression *before me* signify: "before I had sent them;" that of *Gerlach*: "before the door was opened in my person;" as well as that of *Jerome, Augustine, Melanchthon, Luthardt*: "came of themselves, without having received a mission;" finally, that of *Chrysostom* and many others even to *Weizsäcker*: "came as false Messiahs." History does not mention any case of a false Messiah before the coming of Jesus. There is no need of renouncing, with *Tholuck* and *de Wette*, the possibility of any satisfactory solution, and declaring, with the latter, that this saying does not answer to the habitual gentleness and moderation of Jesus. As to the variant which rejects the words πρὸ ἐμοῦ, *before me* (א and others), it is only an attempt to do away with the difficulty.

The present εἰσί, *are*, indicates with sufficient clearness that we need not go far to find these persons. The last words: *The sheep did not hear*, remind us of the profound dissatisfaction which was left in the hearts of a multitude of Israelites by the Pharisaic teaching. John vi. 68: "*To whom shall we go?*" Matt. xi. 28–30: "*Come unto me, all ye who labor and are heavy laden, learn of me, for I am meek and lowly in heart; my yoke is easy, and my burden is light.*" The man who was born blind was a striking example of these souls whom the Pharisaic despotism roused to indignation in Israel.

In opposition to these pretended saviours who will be found to be in reality only murderers, Jesus renews in ver. 9 His affirmation: *I am the door;* then He develops it. *Meyer* and *Luthardt* maintain here their explanation of ver. 7, according to which Jesus is the door by which the true shepherd enters into the presence of the flock. They do not allow themselves to be held back either by the σωθήσεται, *shall be saved*, which they understand in the sense of 1 Tim. iv. 16: "Thou shalt both save thyself and them with thyself," nor by the νομὴν εὑρήσει, *shall find pasture*, which they apply to the discovery by the shepherd of good pasturage for the flock! *Weiss* and *Keil* acknowledge the impossibility of such interpretations and, resting upon the omission in ver. 9 of the complement τῶν προβάτων, *of the sheep* (comp. ver. 7), they adopt a modification in the meaning of the word θύρα, *door*, and think that it is now the door by which the sheep themselves can go in and go out. But the repetition of this declaration: *I am the door*, is simply introduced by the antithesis presented in ver. 8, absolutely as the second declaration: *I am the good shep-*

herd, ver. 14 (comp. ver. 11) will be by the antithesis presented in ver. 13. This is shown by the two ἐγώ at the beginning of vv. 9 and 14. There is here then no new idea. There is a more energetic reaffirmation of the same thought; and the omission of the complement *of the sheep* results quite naturally from the uselessness of such a repetition. By saying: *If any one enters in by me,* Jesus means to speak of the entrance into the state of reconciliation, of participation in the Messianic salvation by faith. *Reuss:* "Jesus is come to open to His own the door of refuge, by receiving them into His arms. The expression *go in and go out* does not mean that the sheep will go out of salvation to enter into it again. This is what Reuss would be obliged to hold, however, if he were consistent with the objection which he makes to the interpretation which we have given of ver. 3. These two verbs only develop the contents of the word σωθήσεται, *shall be saved.* To *go in and go out* is an expression frequently employed in the Scriptures to designate the free use of a house, into which one goes or from which one departs unceremoniously, because one belongs to the family of the house, because one is *at home* in it (Deut. xxviii. 6; Jer. xxxvii. 4; Acts i. 21). *To go in* expresses the free satisfaction of the need of rest, the possession of a safe retreat; *to go out*, the free satisfaction of the need of nourishment, the easy enjoyment of a rich pasturage (Ps. xxiii.). This is the reason why the word *shall go out* is immediately followed by the words which explain it: *and shall find pasture.*

Ver. 10. From the idea of pasture Jesus deduces that of *life;* He even adds to this that *of superabundance, of superfluity.* By this He certainly does not designate, as *Chrysostom* thought, something more excellent than life, glory, for example; but He means to say that the spiritual pasturage will contain still more nourishment than that which the sheep can take to itself; comp. vi. 12, 13, and the expressions: *fulness, grace upon grace,* i. 16. Such is the happy condition of the Messianic flock; Jesus puts it in contrast with the terrible fate reserved for the mass of the people which remains under the leadership of the Pharisees. After having served for the satisfaction of their pride, ambition and cupidity, they will perish morally, and at last even externally by the effect of this pernicious guidance. It seems that the three verbs express a gradation: κλέψῃ (*steal*), the monopoly of souls; θύσῃ (*kill*) the advantage taken of them and their moral murder; ἀπολέσῃ (*destroy*), the complete destruction which is to result from it—all this as an antithesis to the salvation through the Messiah (vv. 9, 10). To understand such severe expressions, we must recall to mind the measures of this haughty sect in Israel. The Pharisees disposed as masters of the Divine kingdom: they assumed the attitude of accredited intercessors, distributed the certificates of orthodoxy, and caused even the legitimate rulers to tremble (xii. 42; Matt. xxiii. 13, 14, and in general the whole chapter, and Luke xi. 39, 44).

The good shepherd: vv. 11-18.

Vv. 11-13. "*I am the good shepherd; the good shepherd gives*[1] *his life for his sheep.* 12. *But*[2] *the hireling, who is not a shepherd and to whom the sheep do not belong, sees the wolf coming and abandons the sheep*[3] *and flees; and the wolf snatches them and scatters the flock.* 13. *But the hireling flees*[4] *because he is a hireling and does not care for the sheep.*" The first picture was all resplendent with the fresh tints of the morning; the second depicted the life and activity of the flock during the course of the day; the third seems to place us at the moment when the shadows of the night are spreading, and when the sheep, brought back to the common inclosure by the shepherd, are suddenly exposed to the attack of the wolf which at evening lies in wait on their path. Jesus here appears again in His character as shepherd. But this third allegory is not confounded with the first. The governing element in the first was the contrast between the *shepherd* and the *thief;* in this one which we are about to study, it is the antithesis of the *good* shepherd and the *hireling* guardian. The salient feature is not, as in the first picture, the legitimacy of the Messianic mission, but the disinterested love which is the moving cause of it. It is this sentiment which makes Christ not only the shepherd, but the *good* shepherd.

The word καλός, *beautiful,* designates with the Greeks *goodness,* as the highest moral beauty. The sequel will show in what this beauty consists. This word καλός explains the article ὁ, *the:* He who perfectly realizes this sublime type. Then Jesus indicates the first trait of the character of this shepherd. It is love carried to the point of complete abnegation, even to the entire sacrifice of oneself. Some (*Meyer, Luthardt*) find in the expression ψυχὴν τιθέναι (literally: *to put his life*) the idea of a pledge given: Jesus pledges His life as a ransom for ours. But this idea of a ransom is foreign to the imagery of the shepherd and the sheep, and still more to that of the wolf under which the enemy is represented. This expression may be compared with that which we find in xiii. 4: ἱμάτια τιθέναι, *to lay aside his garments.* The idea is that of laying down His life. Comp. *Huther* on 1 John iii. 16. Keil, however, alleges against this second sense the words ὑπὲρ τῶν προβάτων, *on behalf of the sheep.* We must therefore give to τιθέναι the sense of: to place at the disposal of another, to surrender, to sacrifice; comp. xiii. 37. In ver. 12, we must not add the article and translate, as *Ostervald, Arnaud, Crampon* do: who is not *the* shepherd. Jesus means: who is not *a shepherd,* who has the place of a hireling. It is not the owner of the flock who acts thus, but a hired servant to whom the owner has intrusted it. Whom did Jesus mean to designate by this person? No one, say some interpreters in reply, particularly *Hengstenberg* and *Weiss:* there is here an imaginary figure intended to make prominent by means of the contrast, that of the good shepherd. But in

---

[1] ℵ D It^aliq Vulg. Aug. read διδωσιν instead of τιθησιν.
[2] B G L omit δε after μισθωτος.
[3] ℵ B L H some Mnn. omit τα προβατα.
[4] ℵ B D L omit the words of T. R.: δε μισθωτος φευγει (*but the hireling flees*).

that case it would be strange for it to be described throughout two entire verses as the counterpart of that of the good shepherd, and as quite as real as the latter. Most of the interpreters think that this person represents the Pharisees. But they would be presented here in too different a light from that in which they were depicted in the two preceding similitudes. A cowardly guardian is a different thing from a robber and an assailant. And, if the hireling represents the Pharisees, who will then be typified by *the wolf?* According to *Luthardt*, this person is the principle hostile to the kingdom of God, the devil, acting by means of all the adversaries of the Church. But Jesus, in chap. viii., has completely identified Pharisaism with the diabolic principle. He cannot therefore represent the first here as a mere hireling, a cowardly friend, the other as a declared enemy. *Lange*, in his *Life of Jesus*, understands by the wolf the Roman power. But it was not really under the blows of the Roman power that Jesus fell. *Meyer* had at first applied the figure of the wolf to all anti-Messianic power, Pharisaism included; but the result of this was that the hireling fleeing before the wolf was the Pharisees fleeing before the Pharisees! He has accordingly abandoned this explanation in the 5th edition. The wolf represents, according to him, the future hireling shepherds in the midst of the Christian Church. But what could have led Jesus to express at that moment an idea like this, and how could His present hearers have caught a glimpse of this meaning? It seems to me that the figure is explained if we recall to mind, on the one hand, the fact that a μισθωτός is a servant for wages, and, on the other, that there were in the theocracy no other accredited and paid functionaries except the priests and Levites. These were the ones to whom God had officially entrusted the instruction and moral guidance of His people. But, during the most recent times, the Pharisaic party had so far obtained the mastery over the minds of the people, by turning to their advantage the national pride, that whoever, even among the lawful rulers of the theocracy, did not submit to them, was immediately put under the ban and brought into discredit, as in our own days whoever in the Roman Church dares to cope with the spirit of Jesuitism. There were many, undoubtedly, in Israel who would have willingly maintained the truth of God. We have as a proof of this xii. 42, so far as relates to the rulers in general, and Acts vi. 7, so far as relates to the priests in particular. But, like so many intelligent and pious bishops in the present Catholicism, they in a cowardly manner kept silent. One man alone had the courage to face this formidable conflict with the dominant party, and to expose His life for the maintenance of the divine truth and for the salvation of the sheep. The: *Crucify! crucify!* was the answer of Pharisaism, cut to the heart by the "*Woe unto you, Scribes and Pharisees, hypocrites!*" The wolf represents therefore the principle positively hostile to the kingdom of God and to the Messiah, the Pharisees; and the hireling, the legitimate functionaries who by their station were called to fulfill the task which Jesus accomplished by voluntary self-devotion, the priests and Levites, accredited doctors of the law. The passage ix. 16, had already given us a glimpse within the Sanhedrim itself of a party well disposed towards Jesus, but which did not dare openly to oppose the violent threats of the Pharisees against Him. Jesus presents here only the historical factors which have co-operated in the accomplishment of the decree of His death. He has nothing to say of the profound and divine reasons which presided over the decree itself. The word ἁρπάζει, *snatches*, applies to the *individuals* whom the wolf assails (αὐτά), while the action of σκορπίζειν, *to scatter*, extends to the entire flock : τὰ πρόβατα, *the flock*, a word which we must be careful not to reject with the Alexandrian authorities.

Ver. 13. The Alexandrian authorities reject the first words : "*but the hireling flees.*" In that case, the *because* which follows, refers not to the last two propositions of ver. 12, but to the one which precedes them : *he flees.* After having thus described the cowardly guardians, Jesus returns to the description of the good shepherd and his conduct towards the flock, and expressly applies to Himself (ἐγώ, *I*, ver. 14) this figure.

Vv. 14-16. "*As for me, I am the good shepherd; and I know my sheep, and I am known by my sheep;* [1] *15 as the Father knows me and I know the Father; and I give* [2] *my life for the sheep. 16. And I have other sheep which are not of this fold; these also I must bring; and they shall hear* [3] *my voice; and there shall be one flock, one shepherd.*" The repetition of these words of ver. 11 : *I am the good shepherd*, is introduced through the contrast with the figure of the hireling (comp. ver. 9) ; and the epithet *good* is explained here by a new point, that of the relation full of tenderness which unites Jesus and His sheep. It is on this second point that the first—the self-devotion thus far described—rests. The word *to know* does not mean : I distinguish them from the rest of the Jews (*Weiss*). The import of this word is much more profound; and the meaning *distinguish* is not suitable in the three following sayings. Jesus penetrates with the eye of His loving knowledge the entire interior being of each one of the sheep, and perfectly discerns all which He possesses in them. For there is a close relation between this verb "*I know,*" and the possessive "*my* sheep." This knowledge is reciprocal. The believers also know what their shepherd is, all that He feels and all that He is willing to do for them. They thus live in the untroubled light of a perfect mutual knoweldge. From this intimate relation between Him and His sheep, Jesus goes back to that which is at once the model and source of it : His relation to the Father. The term καθώς, *as* (literally, *according as*) does not express a simple comparison, as ὥσπερ, *as*, would do. This word characterizes the knowledge which unites Jesus with his sheep as being *of the same nature* as that which unites Him to God. It is as if the luminous medium in which the heart of the Son and the heart of the Father meet each other, were enlarged so as to become that in which the heart of Jesus and that of His sheep meet each other. The καί signifies : "And consequently." It is in

---

[1] T. R. reads with 11 Mjj., all the Mnn. Syr. γινωσκομαι υπο των εμων. ℵ B D L It. Vulg. Cop.: γινωσκουσιν με τα εμα (*and my sheep know me*).

[2] ℵ D: διδωμι instead of τιθημι.

[3] The MSS. are divided between ακουσουσιν (B D etc.), and ακουσωσιν (ℵ A etc.).

virtue of this relation of such intimate knowledge that He consents to give Himself for them. The words: *I give my life for the sheep*, form a sort of refrain (comp. vv. 7, 11, 18), as we have found several similar refrains in our Gospel, in moments when the feeling is exalted (iii. 15, 16; iv. 23, 24; vi. 39, 40, 44, 54). In the context, the expression *for the sheep* must be applied to believers only; but yet this phrase does not contradict that according to which "*Jesus is the propitiation, not only for our sins, but for those of the whole world*" (1 John ii. 2). For the death of Jesus, in the divine intention, is *for* all, although in reality it profits only believers. Jesus knows full well that the ὑπέρ, *on behalf of*, will be realized only in these latter.

From these two points by which Jesus characterizes Himself as the perfect shepherd, springs the third, ver. 16. It would be impossible that the holiest and most devoted work of love should have for its object only these few believers, such as the disciples and the one born blind, who consented to separate themselves from the unbelieving people. The view of Jesus extends more widely (ver. 16), in proportion as He penetrates both the depth and the height (ver. 15). The death of a being like the Son must obtain an infinite reward. The *other sheep*, the possession of whom will compensate Him for the loss of those who to-day refuse to follow Him, are evidently the believing Gentiles. Jesus declares that He *has* them already (ἔχω, *I have*), and not merely that He *will have* them, for all that are of the truth, throughout the entire body of mankind, are His from before His coming. The question is not, I think, of a possession by reason of the divine predestination. We find here again rather one of the most profound and habitual thoughts of our Gospel, a thought which springs directly from the relation which the Prologue establishes between the Logos and the human soul (ver. 4 and ver. 10). The life and the light of the world, the Logos did not cease, even before His incarnation, to fill this office in the midst of the sinful world; and, among the heathen themselves, all those who surrender themselves and yield obedience to this inner light, must infallibly recognize in Jesus their ideal and give themselves to Him as His sheep as soon as He shall present Himself; comp. xi. 52 ("the children of God who are scattered abroad"); viii. 47 ("he that is of God hears the words of God"); xviii. 37 ("he that *is of the truth*"); iii. 21 ("he *that does the truth*, comes to the light"). The demonstrative adjective ταύτης, placed as it is after the substantive: "This fold," implies, according to *de Wette*, that Jesus regards the heathen nationalities also as a sort of folds, of preparatory groupings divinely instituted in order to prepare for the Gospel. But perhaps *Meyer, Weiss*, etc., are right in thinking that there is here a notion introduced into the text. However, it is incorrect to set xi. 52 in opposition to this idea, which verse by no means declares the contrary of this. The believing heathen may very well be *scattered* throughout their respective nationalities, as the believing Jews are in their own (answer to *Weiss*). *Meyer*, committing here again the error which he committed in the explanation of the first allegory—that of explaining the figures of one similitude by those of another—

understands the expression ἀγαγεῖν in the sense of *feed*, according to the figure of vv. 4, 9, and he is followed by *Luthardt* and *Weiss*. But the end of the verse (καί, " *and so* there shall be ") shows clearly that the Lord's idea is an altogether different one; it is that of *bringing* these sheep, to join them with the former ones. The Vulgate, therefore, rightly translates *adducere*. The parallel passage xi. 52: συναγαγεῖν εἰς ἕν, leads likewise to this explanation. When the *historical* application of the first similitude is missed, the meaning of the whole discourse is lost. The work of St. Paul, with the workings of the missionaries who have followed him even to our own days, is essentially what this term *bring* describes. This third similitude, announcing the call of the Gentiles, corresponds thus to the first, which described the going forth of the believers from the Synagogue. The words: *They will hear my voice,* recall the expression of the end of the Acts: " The salvation of God has been sent to the Gentiles and they will also hear it " (xxviii. 28). There is a solemnity in the last words simply placed in juxtaposition: *one flock, one shepherd.* They contain the thought which forms the text of the Epistle to the Ephesians: the breaking down of the old wall of separation between Jews and Gentiles by the death of Christ (Eph. ii. 14–17). This prophetic word is accomplished before our eyes by the work of missions in the heathen world. As to the final conversion of Israel, it is neither directly nor indirectly indicated.

These so new ideas of the death of the Messiah and of the call of new non-Jewish believers to participation in the Messianic salvation were fitted to raise many doubts in the minds of the hearers. Jesus clearly perceives it; this is the reason why He energetically affirms that the good pleasure of God rests upon this work and upon Him who executes it, and that it is the true aim of His mission to the world.

Vv. 17, 18. " *Therefore does my Father love me : because I give my life that I may take it again; 18 no one takes it away*[1] *from me, but I give it of myself; I have power to give, and I have power to take it again : this commandment I received of my Father.*" Διὰ τοῦτο, *for this reason,* refers ordinarily in John to a previously expressed idea, but one which is about to be taken up and developed in the following clause, beginning with ὅτι (*because*). The same is the case here. It is because of His voluntary devotion to this great work (vv. 15, 16) that His Father loves Him; that is to say, He adds, because He sacrifices His life to it, and this not in order absolutely to give it up, but with the express intention of recovering it, and thus of finishing the work of which He only makes a beginning here on the earth. No doubt, the Father eternally loves the Son; but, when once made man, the Son cannot be approved and loved by Him except on condition of perfectly realizing the new law of His existence, as Son of man. Now this law, which results for Him from the solidarity in which He is bound together with a fallen race, is that of saving it by the gift of His life; and the constant disposition of the Son to accept this obligation of love, is the object of the infinite satisfaction (of the ἀγαπᾷν) of the Father. It is in this sense that

---

[1] ℵ B read ηρεν (*took away*) instead of αιρει (*takes away*).

St. Paul calls the death of Jesus "an offering of a sweet smell" (Eph. v. 2). The last words serve to complete the preceding idea: "because I give my life, *and because I give it* that I may take it again." The self-devotion of the Son who consents to give His life is infinitely pleasing to the Father, but on one condition; that this gift be not the abandoning of humanity and of the work begun in it, which would be at the same time the forgetting of the glory of the Father. In other terms, the devotion to death would be of an evil sort if it had not for its end the return among men by means of the resurrection. As *Luthardt* with perfect correctness remarks: "Jesus must wish to resume His life again in order to continue, as glorified, His ministry of shepherd to the Church, especially to the Gentiles whom He has the mission to gather together (Eph. ii. 17)." The supreme end indicated in ver. 16 requires not only His death, but also His resurrection. It appears from the words: *that I may take it again*, that Jesus raises Himself from the dead. And this is true, for if it is in the Father that the power lies which gives Him life, it is Himself who by His free will and His prayer calls upon His person the display of this power. Ver. 18 is the emphatic reaffirmation of this character of freedom in the work of the Son, which alone makes it the object of the Father's satisfaction. Hence the *asyndeton*. It is not through powerlessness that the shepherd will succumb to the hostile power; there will come a moment when He will Himself consent to His defeat (xiv. 31). The word οὐδείς, *no one*, includes every creature; we may include in it God Himself, since if, in dying, the Son obeys the decree of the Father, He yet does it freely; God neither imposes on Him death nor resurrection. The words ἐξουσίαν ἔχω, *I have the power* (the competency, the authority), are repeated with a marked emphasis; Jesus had no obligation to die, not only because, not having sinned, He had the right to keep His holy life, but also because, even at the last moment, He could have asked for *twelve legions of angels*, who would have wrested Him from the hands of His enemies. In the same way, in giving up His life, it depended on Himself to demand it again or not to reclaim it. As *Luthardt* says: "In these two acts, the action of the Son comes before the action of the Father." The last words: *I have received this commandment*, are ordinarily referred to the commandment to die and rise again which had been given to Him by the Father. But would not such an idea tend to weaken all that Jesus had just developed? The true movement of the passage is the affirming of the full independence of the Lord. This is the reason why it seems to me that it is better to apply the term τὴν ἐντολήν, *this command*, to the commission with which Jesus has come to the earth and which gives Him the right to make free use of His own person, to die and to revive at will. The tenor of this commission, when the Father sent Him, was this: "Thou canst die or not die, rise again or not rise again, according to the free aspirations of thy love." Jesus calls it a *command* in order to cover with the veil of humility this incomparable prerogative.

Historical Conclusion: vv. 19–21

Vv. 19–21. "*There was therefore*[1] *again a division among the Jews because of these discoursings.* 20. *Many*[2] *of them said, He is possessed of a demon, and is mad; why do you listen to him?* 21. *Others said, These are not the discoursings of one possessed; can a demon open the eyes of the blind?*" Always the same result; a division, which forms the prelude to the final choice; comp. vii. 12, 30, 31, 40, 41; ix. 8, 9, 16. The word πάλιν, *again*, awakens the attention of the reader to the constant repetition of this result. The words: Why do you listen to Him? show with what uneasiness the decidedly hostile party observed the favorable impression produced by the discourses of Jesus on those who were better disposed. The answer of these latter (ver. 21) contains two arguments in juxtaposition. The first is the simple avowal of their impression: the discourse of Jesus does not appear to them to be that of a madman. But immediately they seem to be ashamed of this avowal and withdraw behind another argument which is less compromising: the patent fact of the cure of the blind man. The second argument might be connected with the first by an *And besides*.

Thus continually more and more do the sheep of Jesus in the vast inclosure of the theocracy separate themselves from the mass of the flock; and for the theme: *I and you*, which was that of chap. viii. is substituted more and more that theme which is to sum up the new situation: *I and mine*.

3

John 10:22-42

The Second Discourse

In chap. vii., vv. 19–24, we have seen Jesus return, in a discourse pronounced at the feast of Tabernacles, to the fact of the healing of the impotent man (chap. v.), and thus finish His justification of Himself which was begun at Jerusalem several months before (v. 17–47), at the preceding feast. The same is the case here. In the second part of chap. x. (22–42), He resumes the thread of the discourse pronounced after the cure of the man who was born blind, at the feast of Tabernacles, and thus completes the teaching begun in the previous visit. We have explained this mode of action (see on p. 450). The exasperation of His adversaries in the capital not permitting Him to treat the questions in full, He takes them up with a new beginning at a succeeding visit.

The feast of the Dedication (ver. 22) was celebrated about the middle of December. Two months must therefore have elapsed between the feast of Tabernacles and this feast. Where did Jesus pass all this time? As no change of place is indicated and as, in ver. 42, Jesus is plainly again *in Jerusalem*, Hengstenberg, Meyer, Weiss, and others infer from this that Jesus

---

[1] ℵ B L X It. reject ουν.   [2] ℵ D add ουν here.

716 / Unbelief Develops in Israel

remained during this whole period in the capital and its neighborhood; the last named, without hesitation, treat as a harmonistic expedient every opposite idea. But there is nothing less certain than the conclusion thus drawn from the silence of John. At the end of chap. v. the evangelist does not in any way mention the return of Jesus to Galilee, and yet it is there that the Lord is found again in the beginning of chap. vi. Still more; there is nothing more improbable than so prolonged a sojourn of Jesus in Jerusalem or in its neighborhood at this time. Let us recall all the precautions which Jesus had been obliged to take, in order to repair to that city at the feast of Tabernacles, that He might give to this visit the character of a surprise. Why? Because, as is said in vii. 1, "Jesus would not go into Judea, because the Jews sought to kill Him." And yet in such a state of things, He could have remained two whole months peaceably in Jerusalem in the presence of the hostile party, and after the conflict had been still further aggravated by the violent scenes related in chaps. vii.–x. 21! Such a sojourn could only have determined the catastrophe before the time (vii. 6). This impossible supposition is, moreover, positively incompatible with John's narrative. In the discourse in x. 25–30, Jesus reproduces in substance that which He had pronounced after the cure of the man who was born blind; He even expressly cites it (ver. 26: *as I said to you*). This fact implies that it was the first time that He found Himself face to face with the same hearers since the feast of Tabernacles, where He had used this allegory of the shepherd and the sheep. Finally, this supposition of a sojourn of two months in Judea between the feast of Tabernacles and that of the Dedication is certainly false, if the narrative of St. Luke is not a pure romance. Luke describes in the most circumstantial and dramatic way the departure of Jesus from Galilee, and His farewell to that province, in order to repair to Jerusalem (Luke ix. 51 ff.). He shows how Jesus gave to this act the most striking notoriety by the solemn threatenings addressed to the cities where He had accomplished His ministry, and by the sending out of the seventy disciples, who should prepare His way in southern Galilee, as far as Peræa, that is to say, in all the country through which He was about to go to Jerusalem for the last Passover. How could this departure accomplished with such great publicity be identified with the journey to the feast of Tabernacles mentioned by John in chap. vii., a journey which, according to ver. 10, was made *as it were in secret* and which brought Jesus *suddenly* to Jerusalem? It is to this, however, that the matter must resolve itself, if, after the journey in John vii., Jesus did not return to Galilee. Would it be true historic impartiality to condemn purely and simply one of the two narratives, when they can be so easily reconciled with each other! Jesus, after the feast of Tabernacles, returned to Galilee which He had left so suddenly, just as He had returned thither after the feast of Purim (end of chap. v.). He resumed His work there also for a certain time. Then (Luke ix. 51 ff.) He called upon His adherents to sever the last bonds, in order to follow Him to Jerusalem; He sent before Him the seventy disciples, to the end of preparing by this means the last appeal which He desired Himself to address to the cities and villages of southern Galilee which had not yet been visited, and it was then that He pronounced the condemnation of the cities on the borders of the lake of Gennesareth, the constant witnesses of His ministry. This prolonged pilgrimage, the account of which fills nine chapters of the Gospel of Luke (ix. 51–xviii. 18), must have been interrupted, according to this same Gospel—a strange circumstances—by a brief journey to Jerusalem; for the story in Luke x. 38–42 (Jesus in the house of Martha and Mary) which is placed, one knows not how, in the midst of this journey, transfers the reader all at once to Bethany, and the parable of the Good Samaritan, which immediately precedes, seems also to be connected with a visit to Judea. What means this excursion to Jerusalem implied in the narrative of Luke, perhaps without a knowledge of it on his part (for he does not mention Bethany)? How is it possible not to be struck with the remarkable coincidence between this journey and the journey to the feast of the Dedication related by John? After this rapid excursion to Jerusalem, Jesus proceeds to resume His slow journeying in the south of Galilee; then He crosses the Jordan to go into Peræa, as is distinctly stated by Matthew and Mark. This sojourn in Peræa, a little while before the Passion, is the point where the four Gospel narratives meet together. Compare indeed Matt. xix. 1; Mark x. 1, and Luke ix. 51; then Luke xviii. 15 ff., where the parallelism recommences between the narrative of this last writer and that of the other two Synoptics (the presentation of the young children, the coming up of the rich young man), and finally John x. 40–42. While following their own particular course, the four narratives are thus without difficulty harmonized.[1]

The following passage includes an historical introduction (vv. 22–24), a first address of Jesus, in which He shows the Jews the moral separation which exists between them and Himself (vv. 25–31), and a last teaching by means of which He seeks yet once more to remove what was for them the great stumbling-stone, the accusation of blasphemy (vv. 32–39). The passage closes with the description of the sojourn in Peræa (vv. 40–42).

Historical Introduction: vv. 22–24

Vv. 22–24. "*Now*[2] *they were celebrating the feast of the Dedication at Jerusalem;*[3] *it was winter.* 23. *And Jesus was walking about in the temple, in Solomon's porch.* 24. *The Jews therefore surrounded him; and they said to him, How long wilt thou hold our minds in suspense? If thou art the Christ, tell*[4] *us plainly.*" The feast of the Dedication (ἐγκαινία) was instituted by the Maccabees in remembrance of the purification of the temple after its profanation by Antiochus Epiphanes (1 Macc. iv.; Josephus, *Antiq.*, xii. 7. 6). It continued eight days, following the 25th of Cisleu, which, if it was

---

[1] It was in an analogous way that Tatian in the 2d century established the succession of the events, in the first known *Gospel Harmony*, the *Diatessaron*; comp. Zahn, *Tatians Diatessaron*, p. 259.

[2] B L substitute τότε (*then*) for δέ.

[3] ℵ B D G L X Π Itᵃˡⁱᵃ Cop. omit καί before χειμων ην, which is read by T. R. with all the rest.

[4] ℵ: ειπον, instead of ειπε.

718 / Unbelief Develops in Israel

then the year 29 of our era, fell in that year, according to the work of M. Chavannes cited on page 42, on the 19th or 20th of December. It was called τὰ φῶτα, *the lights*, because of the brilliant illumination with which it was celebrated, not only at Jerusalem, but in the whole country. Jesus took advantage of it to address once more, before the Passover, a last appeal to His people. We may conclude from what precedes that He probably made this rapid journey to Jerusalem while the seventy disciples were accomplishing in Galilee the mission which He had intrusted to them, and were there preparing the way from place to place for His last appeal. We have seen that He had probably accomplished the journey at the feast of Purim (John v.) while the Twelve were fulfilling a similar mission in Galilee (p. 453).

It was the unfavorable season of the year; and it was not possible to remain in the open air. Jesus, therefore, took his position in Solomon's porch, an ancient peristyle situated in the eastern part of the court, above the valley of Jehoshaphat. It was the last remnant of the ancient temple. This place which had been rendered dear to the heart of the evangelist by the remembrance of the circumstance which he is about to relate, seems to have been equally sacred to the Christians of the primitive church of Jerusalem (Acts iii. 11). The nature of the place facilitated (*therefore*, ver. 24) the kind of manœuvre which was executed at the moment by the Jews and which is described by the term ἐκύκλωσαν, *they surrounded him*. While Jesus was walking about in this peristyle, they took advantage of a favorable moment to place themselves between Him and His disciples and to force Him to speak. It appears to me that this must be the meaning of this strange expression: they surrounded Him in a circle. The scene of viii. 25 is renewed here in an intensified degree. They are weary of His answers which seem to them ambiguous. Some among them feel indeed that no man had ever so nearly approached the Messianic ideal. Let Him finally consent to play in earnest the part of the Messiah and to free the country from the Roman power, as formerly Judas Maccabæus purified the temple from the Syrian profanations, and they will willingly hail Him, and that at this very festival; if not, let Him frankly avow that He is not the Messiah, and not continue to excite the expectation of the people! We thus picture to ourselves the general sentiment. Some, more ill-disposed, wished perhaps—this is the idea of *Weiss*—to extort from Him the term *Christ*, in order that they might accuse Him. The expression τὴν ψυχὴν αἴρειν, properly, *to raise the mind*, is applied to all lively emotions; see in the Greek tragic poets. Here it expresses the expectation which an activity like that of Jesus excited, an activity which awakened all the national hopes without ever satisfying them. Philo uses the term μετεωρίζειν in exactly the same sense.

First address: vv. 25-31

Vv. 25, 26. "*Jesus answered them, I told you and you do not believe; the works which I do in my Father's name, these works bear witness of me.* 26.

But, as for you, you do not believe; for ¹ *you are not of my sheep, as I said to you.*" ² The position of Jesus with relation to the Jews had never been so critical. To answer yes, is not possible for Him; for the meaning which they give to the term *Christ* has, so to speak, nothing in common with that which He Himself attaches to it. To say no, is still less possible; for He is indeed the Christ promised of God, and, in this sense, the one whom they expect. His reply is admirable for its wisdom. He refers, as in viii. 25, to His testimonies in which He had applied to Himself the Messianic symbols of the old covenant and in some sort spelt out His title of Christ, so that if they *were willing* to believe, they had only to pronounce it themselves.³ Thus is His reply explained. The verb: *I said to you*, has no object; it is easy to supply the ellipsis: that which you ask me. To His own testimony, if it does not appear to them sufficient, there is added, moreover, that of the Father. His miracles were all *works of the Father;* for they were wrought with the invocation of His name; if Jesus were an impostor, would God have answered him thus? If these testimonies failed with them, it is the result of their unbelief (ver. 26). He is not the Messiah whom their heart demands: this is the reason why they affect not to understand what is so clear. The subject ὑμεῖς, *you*, placed at the beginning, signifies: It is not I, it is you, who are responsible for this result. And the following declaration: *You are not of my sheep*, shows them that the moral disposition is what is wanting to them that they may recognize in Him the divine Shepherd. The formula of quotation: *as I said to you*, is omitted by the Alexandrian MSS. But perhaps this omission arises from the fact that these words were not found textually in the preceding discourses. The authority of 12 Mjj., supported by that of the most ancient Vss., appears to us to guarantee their authenticity. In our first edition, we made them the preamble of ver. 27, especially because of the relation between the contents of this verse and that of vv. 3–5. The pronoun ὑμῖν, *you*, however ("as I said *to you*"), favors rather the connection of this formula of quotation with ver. 26. For Jesus has never applied to the unbelieving Jews the promises of ver. 27; while He has frequently addressed to them charges equivalent to that of ver. 26. The charge of *not being His sheep* really formed the basis of the parables, vv. 1–5 and vv. 7–10, in which Jesus had distinguished clearly from His sheep the mass of the people and their rulers, His interlocutors in general. *Reuss:* "Jesus had nowhere said this." Then again: "The allegory of the sheep," he says, "had been presented to an entirely different public." Finally, he maliciously adds: "It is only the readers of the Gospel who have not left

---

¹ ℵ B D L X 12 Mnn. It^{plerique} Vulg. Syr^{sch} Orig. read ὅτι οὐκ instead of οὐ γαρ.

² ℵ B K L M Π some Mnn. It^{aliq} Vulg. Cop. omit the words καθὼς εἶπον ὑμῖν which are supported by 12 Mjj., nearly all the Mnn. It^{plerique} Syr.; some Mnn. and Vss. repeat them: "*As I said to you* (ver. 26), *Did I not say to you?*" (ver. 27).

³ *Gess* (p. 99) rightly sets forth the complete agreement which is here manifest between John and the Synoptics. In these latter also Jesus, while accepting (in the conversation in Cæsarea) the title of Christ from His disciples, forbids them to pronounce this word before the people. As in John, He desires the fact of faith, and not the word (Matt. xvi. 20 and parallels).

the scene." We have shown that Jesus had said this, and it is not difficult to show that He had said it to the same hearers. For the discourse in x. 1–18 had not been addressed, as Reuss asserts, to pilgrim strangers who had come to the feast of Tabernacles and afterwards had departed, but to the inhabitants of Jerusalem, in response to *some of the Pharisees* (ix. 40) who had asked: "*And are we also blind?*" No doubt, we cannot hold that it was identically the same individuals who were found there again after two months; but it was the same population all whose members were alike in their dependence on the rulers and their general hostility to Jesus. The essential aim of the following words, in which Jesus describes the privileges of His sheep, is certainly that of making His hearers feel what an abyss separates them from such a condition. Nevertheless this description naturally becomes an invitation to come to Him, addressed to those who are the least ill-disposed.

Vv. 27, 28. "*My sheep hear*[1] *my voice, and I know them; and they follow me* 28 *and I give to them eternal life; and they shall never perish and no one shall snatch them out of my hand.*" Luthardt has divided the six clauses of these verses into two groups of three: on one side, the faith of the believer, his personal union with the Lord, and the fidelity with which he persists in this union (ver. 27); on the other, the gift of life which Jesus makes, the salvation which He assures to him, and the divine protection which He causes him to enjoy (ver. 28). But this division into two groups does not accord with the two κἀγώ, *and I*, at the beginning of the second and fourth clauses. These two pronouns indicate a *repeated* reciprocity between the conduct of the believer and that of Jesus, and thus speak in favor of the division of *Bengel*, who divides into three groups of two: 1st pair: faith of the believer in the word preached ("*hear my voice*") and personal testimony of Christ given to the believer ("*I know them*"). 2d pair: practical fidelity of the believer thus known and loved ("*they follow me*"), and, on Christ's part, communication of the highest good, eternal life ("*I give them . . .*"). The 3d pair states the indestructible character of the salvation which the believer thus possesses ("*they shall never perish*"), and the cause of this certainty, the fidelity of Jesus which will preserve them from every enemy ("*no one shall seize them . . .*"). The first pair refers rather, like the first similitude, vv. 1–6, to the *formation* of the bond; the second, like the second similitude, vv. 7–10, to the life *in* this position; the third, like the picture, vv. 11–18, to the *indestructible* nature of this relation. The *hand* is here less the emblem of power, than that of property: "They shall not cease to be *mine*."

Vv. 29, 30. "*My*[2] *Father who has given*[3] *them to me, is greater*[4] *than all; and no one is able to snatch them out of my*[5] *Father's hand;* 30 *I and the*

---

[1] א B L X Clem. Homil. ακουουσιν, instead of ακουει which is read by the T. R. with 14 Mjj., etc.

[2] א It^plerique omit μου.

[3] א B L It. Vulg. Cop. read ο δεδωκεν (*that which he has given me*), instead of ος δεδωκεν (*he who has given me*) which is read by T. R. with 14 Mjj. Syr. — D: ο δεδωκως.

[4] A B X It. Vulg. Cop.: μειζον, instead of μειζων which is read by T. R. with 15 Mjj.

[5] א B L Orig. reject μου.

Father are one." We might be tempted to find, with *Luthardt*, a strict syllogism in the thoughts expressed in vv. 29, 30. Major: My Father is greater than all (ver. 29). Minor: I and my Father are one (ver. 30). Conclusion: Therefore I shall victoriously defend them against all (ver. 29). But, in general, the reasoning of Jesus tends rather to extend in a spiral manner than to close in upon itself like a circle. This is the case here: the sentiment rises and enlarges. Jesus begins by indicating the absolutely certain guaranty of His right of property in the sheep: God who has given them to Him is more powerful than all the forces of the universe. That any one should be able to wrest them from Him, it is necessary that He should begin by wresting them from God. Then, from this point, His thought rises still higher, even to the idea of the relation in virtue of which *everything* is common between the Father and the Son. We see in this gradation the filial consciousness displaying itself even till it has reached its utmost depth (ver. 30).

There are four principal readings in ver. 29: 1. That of the T. R. and the eleven less ancient Mjj. (Γ Δ Π etc.): ὅς and μείζων: "The Father *who* has given them to me is *greater* than all." 2. That of B. It. ὅ and μεῖζον: "*That which* the Father has given me is *greater* than all." 3. That of A and X: ὅς and μεῖζον: "The Father *who* has given them to me is something *greater* (neuter) than all." 4. That of ℵ L, ὅ and μείζων, which has really no meaning unless we consent to give a masculine attribute (μείζων) to a neuter subject ὅ ("*what* the Father . . ."). It is the same with the third, in which the subject is masculine and the attribute neuter. How could God be represented as *a thing?* Finally, one must be singularly blinded by prejudice in favor of the text of B, to prefer, as *Tischendorf* and *Westcott* and *Hort* do, the second reading to the first. Not only do the ordinary documents of the Alexandrian text contradict one another; but the sense which is offered by the reading of the *Vatican* MS. has not the least internal probability. John would say, according to that reading, that *what the Father has given* to Jesus *is greater* than all or everything. It would thus be the flock of Jesus which is here called greater, in the sense of more precious, more excellent than all. But what a strange expression! Believers are of more value than the whole universe, perchance. But the Scriptures never express themselves in this way. They glorify God, not men, even the most faithful men. Moreover, the expressions: *no one shall snatch them* (ver. 28), *no one can snatch them* (ver. 29), show that the point in hand is a comparison of power, not between *the sheep* and their enemies, but between *God* Himself and these enemies. So *Luthardt, Weiss* and *Keil*, in this case, give up the reading against which we are contending. The following is the way in which these variants may have arisen. Offense may have been taken at seeing δέδωκε, *has given*, without an object, and, through a recalling of the expression in vi. 37, 39 (*that which the Father gives me, has given me*) and xvii. 3 (*that which thou hast given me*), the copyists may have changed ὅς (who) into ὅ (*that which*) and made ὁ πατήρ, the Father, the subject of *has given*. The transformation of μείζων into μεῖζον was the inevitable consequence of the first change. The other readings are mixtures resulting from the embarrassment in which the subsequent copyists found themselves.

The *hand*, when the Father is in question, represents power rather than possession. God has transmitted this to the Son; but *His* power remains the safeguard of the property of the Son which is common to Him with the Fathers. Can this guaranty insure believers against the consequences of their own unfaithfulness, as *Hengstenberg* asserts? The text says nothing like this. The question is of enemies from without, who seek to carry off the sheep, but not of unfaithfulness through which the sheep would themselves cease to be sheep.

According to *Weiss*, ver. 30 is intended to resolve the apparent contradiction between "guarded by my Father" and "guarded by me." I do not believe in this relation between ver. 30 and ver. 29, because in what precedes the idea of *guarding* has been in reality attributed only to God; the end of ver. 28 referred, as we have seen, to the right of property, not to the guarding of the sheep. Ver. 30 serves rather to explain why the Father inviolably guards that which belongs to the Son. It is because they have all things common, because they are *one*. If such is indeed the connection of ideas, ver. 30 cannot refer either to the unity of moral *will* (the Socinians), or of power (*Chrysostom* and many others, as *Lücke, de Wette*, etc.), or even solely to the community of action for the salvation of mankind (*Weiss*), as it has been described in vv. 19, 20, and in the sense in which Paul says, 1 Cor. iii. 9, of himself and Apollos: "He that planteth and he that watereth *are one* (ἓν εἰσί)," namely, as to the *end* which they propose to themselves in their work. Here the question is of the relation, not between two workmen, but between Christ as man and God. And if Jesus had only meant this, why did He not determine more clearly this notion of co-working, as Paul does in the following words (ver. 10), when he comes to speak of his relation to God: *We are God's fellow-workers?* Why above all give needlessly, and as it were wantonly, an offense to the Jews by employing an expression which appeared to say more than what He in reality meant to say? No, Jesus neither meant: "We *desire* one and the same thing," nor "We have the same *power*," nor, "We labor in the same *work*." In saying "We are *one*," He has affirmed a more profound unity, that which is the inner and hidden basis of all the preceding statements and which Jesus here allows to break forth, as in viii. 58 He had suffered the deepest foundation of His personal existence to show itself. *Reuss*, being altogether indifferent to the question, since he ascribes the discourses of John to the evangelist, recognizes without hesitation the true meaning of this verse: "The filial relation here, as throughout the whole book, is not only that of love or of the community of will and of action (the ethical relation), but also that of a community of nature and essence (the metaphysical relation)." The term *one* expresses the consciousness of union, not only moral but essential, with God Himself; the expression *we are* establishes the difference of persons. As to *we*, it would be in itself alone a blasphemy in the mouth of a creature; God and I, *we* (comp. xiv. 23)![1] It has been objected that the

---

[1] The minister of state, Thiers, who allowed himself one day to say: "The king and I,

expression: *to be one,* is elsewhere applied to the relation between Jesus and believers, which would prove that it has a purely moral sense. But the union of Jesus and believers is not a mere agreement of will; it is a consubstantial union. The incarnation has established between Jesus and ourselves a relation of nature, and this relation embraces henceforth our entire personality, physical and moral.

Ver. 31. "*The Jews therefore*[1] *brought stones again to stone him.*" Οὖν, *there-fore,* by reason of the blasphemy (ver. 30); comp. ver. 33. *Weiss* claims that, even understanding the words of ver. 30 in the sense which he gives to them, the Jews may have found therein a blasphemy. But, taken in the sense of a common action of God and Jesus, this thought certainly did not go beyond what in their view the Christ might legitimately say. But they had just asked Him whether He was the Christ. What was there in it, then, which could so violently offend them? Πάλιν, *again,* alludes to viii. 59. Only ἦραν, *they took up,* was used in the former case, while John now says ἐβάστασαν, *they brought.* Probably they did not have the stones at hand in the porch; it was necessary to go some distance to find them in the court. There was here, no longer a mere demonstration, as in chap. viii., but a serious attempt. The question was of accomplishing at length the act of stoning, which had several times been threatened. Shades of expression like this reveal the eye-witness, whose eyes followed anxiously this progress of hatred.

Second address: v. 32–39

The reply of Jesus treats of two subjects: 1. That of the *blasphemy* which is imputed to Him (vv. 32–36); 2. That of His *relation* to God which is contested (vv. 37–39).

Vv. 32–36: The accusation of blasphemy.

Vv. 32, 33. "*Jesus answered them: I have shown you many good works by the power of my*[2] *Father; for which of these works do you stone me?* 33. *The Jews answered him*[3] *it is not for a good work that we stone thee, but for blasphemy, and*[4] *because, being a man, thou makest thyself God.*" This time Jesus does not withdraw, as in viii. 59; He makes the stones fall from the hands of His adversaries by a question. Instead of *good works,* the translation should properly be *beautiful works* (*Rilliet*). The epithet καλά designates indeed not the beneficent character of the works, but their moral beauty, their perfection in holiness, in power, as well as in goodness. The term ἔδειξα, strictly, *I have shown,* characterizes these works as grand specimens of all those which the Father holds in reserve, and as the sensible and glorious proofs of the favor which the Son enjoys with Him. The Father shows Him these works in the ideal sphere (v. 19, 20), and He shows them to the world in the sphere of reality. The preposition ἐκ indicates that the will and power by which Jesus accomplishes these works pro-

---

we ..." provoked a smile in the whole Chamber; what would the creature deserve who should venture to include himself with God Himself in the pronoun *we?*

[1] Οὖν (*therefore*) is wanting in ℵ B L It^{aliq}.

[2] ℵ B D reject μου.

[3] T.R. adds λεγοντες (*saying*), with 9 Mjj. (D E G etc.) against 8 Mjj. (ℵ A B etc.) 20 Mnn. It. Vulg. Syr.

[4] ℵ omits και (*and*).

724 / Unbelief Develops in Israel

ceed from the Father (v. 36). The question of Jesus contains a keen irony, an expression of the deepest indignation. Undoubtedly, the ground on which the Jews intended to stone Him was not that which Jesus here ascribes to them; but in alleging another ground they imposed upon their consciences, and Jesus reveals to them the true condition of things by means of this question. Was it not on occasion of the healing of the impotent man that their murderous hatred had first manifested itself (chap. v.)? Had it not been increased in violence by the healing of the man born blind (chap. ix.)? And will it not be a third miracle, the resurrection of Lazarus (chap. xi.), which will bring it to its fatal limit? Jesus knew this full well: it was these great and beautiful works which, by marking Him as the Son, caused Him to be the object of their fury : *"This is the heir ; let us kill him!"* Apart from this hatred, they would not so readily have accused Him, who was by His whole life glorifying God, of being a blasphemer. This question in a sense paralyzes them; Jesus is able to speak to them again.

The Jews formulate the point in dispute, in ver. 33, as it presents itself to their perverted consciences. The term: *a blasphemer*, expresses the general idea, and the following clause: *and because...*, specifies the charge, by applying it to the present case.

Vv. 34–36. *"Jesus answered them, Is it not written in your*[1] *law*[2] *I said ye are gods?* 35. *If it called them gods to whom the word of God was addressed, —and the Scripture cannot be broken,—*36 *do you say of him whom the Father has sanctified and sent into the world, Thou blasphemest! because I said, I am the Son of God?"*[3] This argument has often been presented as an implicit retractation of the expressions in which Jesus seemed to have affirmed His divine nature. In this sense, He is supposed to say : " Mere creatures have been called gods, because they represent God in some one of His functions, that of judge, for example; this is the only sense in which I have ascribed divinity to myself." But Jesus would thereby, at the same time, retract all His earlier testimonies, the meaning of which we have established. Jesus is occupied solely, in this first part of His reply, vv. 34–36, with repelling the accusation of *blasphemy*. With this end in view, He reasons as follows: " The Scripture called mere human beings gods, as being invested with an office in which they were the representatives and organs of God on earth; were I then nothing more than a mere man, sent to accomplish a divine work, I should not deserve, according to the Scripture itself, to be treated as a blasphemer for having called myself Son of God." As an argument *ad hominem* the reasoning is irrefutable. Nevertheless, it still leaves room for this objection: Jesus called Himself God in an altogether different sense from that in which the Scripture gave this title to the Israelite judges. But a second point is to be observed here: it is the gradation in vv. 35, 36: " If the Scripture did not blaspheme in calling the persons gods *to whom the revelation was addressed,* how can I have spoken blasphemy in declaring myself God, I, whom God sends into the world as *His revelation itself?"* This alto-

---

[1] ℵ D It^{aliq} omit υμων.
[2] ℵ B D L X add οτι here.
[3] ℵ D E G : θεου instead of του θεου.

gether different position of Jesus as regards the divine revelation justifies the higher sense in which He attributes to Himself the title of God. The monotheism of the Bible differs absolutely from the cold and dead Deism which Jewish orthodoxy had extracted from the sacred books, and which separates the Creator by a gulf from man. This petrified monotheism is the connecting link between degenerate Judaism, Mahometanism and modern rationalism; but it is only a gross caricature of the Scriptural conception. Every theocratic function exercised in the name of Jehovah, who has conferred it, places its depositary in living connection with the Most High, makes him participate in His inspiration, and constitutes him His agent. Thereby the man, king, judge or prophet, becomes relatively a manifestation of God Himself. *"At that time, the house of David shall be as Elohim, as the angel of the Lord."* Zech. xii. 8. The Old Testament is, in its deepest tendency, in a constant advancing progress towards the incarnation, the crowning-point of the increasing approximation between God and man. This is the true basis of the reasoning of Jesus: If this entire course has nothing in it of blasphemy, the end in which it issues, the appearance of a man who declares Himself *one with God*, has in itself nothing in contempt of the majesty of God.

The quotation is derived from Ps. lxxxii. 6; and the term *law* denotes here, as in vii. 49, xii. 34, etc., the entire Old Testament, not as a denomination *a potiori parte*, but rather inasmuch as this whole book formed a law for the Israelitish thought and life. On the expression *your law*, see on viii. 17. Asaph, in this Psalm, addresses the theocratic judges. Ver. 1 describes their greatness, in virtue of their function as organs of the divine justice, which has been intrusted to them. God Himself sits in the midst of them; it is from Him that their judgments emanate. Then in vv. 2–5, Asaph contrasts the sad reality, the injustice of the actual judges, with the ideal greatness of their function. In ver. 6, he returns to the idea of the first verse, that of their official dignity. The words: *I said*, refer undoubtedly to the expression of Asaph himself in ver. 1: *" God is present in the congregation of God."* And thus he prepares for the transition to the warning of vv. 7, 8, in which he reminds them that they will themselves be one day judged, for an account will be demanded of them respecting this divine function with which they had been clothed. Jesus draws from the words of the Psalmist a conclusion *a minori ad majus*, precisely as in vii. 23. The basis of the reasoning is the admitted principle: that the Scriptures cannot blaspheme. By *those to whom the word of God is addressed*, Jesus evidently understands those judges, to whom the Holy Spirit addresses Himself, saying: *You are* . . . The parenthetical remark: *And the Scripture cannot be broken*, shows the unlimited respect which Jesus feels for the word of Scripture.

Let us suppose that it was the evangelist who invented all this argument; could he, the so-called author of the theory of the Logos, have resisted the temptation to put into the mouth of Jesus here this favorite title by which he had designated Him in the Prologue? This would be the altogether natural gradation: The law calls them judges to whom the

Word is addressed; how much less can I be accused of blasphemy, who am *the Word* itself, when I attribute to myself the title of God! John does not yield to this temptation; it is because it did not exist for him, since he limited himself to giving a faithful report of what his Master had said. Jesus designates Himself as *Him whom the Father has sanctified and sent.* The first expression might strictly refer to a fact in the earthly life of Jesus, such as that of the miraculous birth (*Luthardt*) or that of the baptism (*Weiss*). But in that case it would be necessary to refer the following expression: *sent into the world,* to an act later than the one or the other of these two events: according to *Weiss,* for example, to the command to begin His *public* ministry. Or it would be necessary to admit a retrograde order in the position of the two terms *sanctify* and *send,* which is quite as unnatural. The term *to send into the world* can of course only designate the mission which He received when He came from God to fulfill His work as Redeemer; and the term *to sanctify* must consequently designate the celestial act by which God specially set Him apart and consecrated Him for this mission. It was to this commandment, previous to the incarnation, that we were already referred by the expression *commandment,* ἐντολή, used in v. 18; comp. 1 Pet. i. 20. There was a consulting together between the Father and the Son before the coming of Jesus to the world, of which He Himself formulates the result when He says: "*I am come down from heaven, not to do my own will, but the will of him who sent me*" (vi. 38). How great is the superiority of such a being to all those to whom the divine revelation addresses itself here below! In reproducing the charge alleged against Him, Jesus passes to the direct discourse: *Thou blasphemest.* It is the lively repetition of the accusation, as it was still sounding in His ears. The following words: *because I said,* depend not on *thou blasphemest,* but on *you say.* The title *Son of God* evidently here reproduces the substance of the declaration of ver. 30: *I and my Father are one.* This example shows again how erroneous it is to see in the title *Son of God* the indication of a function, even of the highest theocratic function. Taken in this sense, this term does not involve absolutely any blasphemy at all. These Jews who had just addressed to Him the question: "If thou art the Christ, tell us plainly," evidently could not have found in this title of Christ a blasphemy. And, as for Jesus, He is here thinking, as ver. 30 shows, on something altogether different from His dignity as Messiah. That is only a corollary following from His altogether peculiar union with God. He is only endeavoring therefore to awaken in the hearts of His hearers the feeling of His close relation to God, being certain, not only that the conviction of His Messiahship will naturally result from it, but also that in this way only that idea will not be erroneously conceived. Hence what follows:

Vv. 37–39: The proof of the divinity of Jesus.

Vv. 37–38. "*If I do not the works of my Father, believe me not;* 38 *but if I do them, though you believe not me, believe*[1] *my works, to the end that you*

---

[1] Readings: πιστεύετε (א B D, etc.) and πιστεύσατε (T. R. with A E G, etc.).

may know and may understand[1] *that my Father is in me and I am in him.*"[2] There is much of gentleness in the manner in which Jesus here expresses Himself and reasons. He appeals with calmness from passion to sound reason. He consents that they should not believe on the ground of *the word*, although the testimony of a being like Himself ought to carry its proof in itself. But to His testimony there are united *the works* which the Father has accomplished through Him. If they have not ears, they have eyes; and what they do not infer from His words, they should, at least, infer from such works. The words: " If you do not believe *me*," mean : " If you do not accord belief to my personal affirmations." The reading of some Alexandrian authorities : ἵνα γνῶτε καὶ γινώσκητε, seems to me the best one: "To the end that you may learn to know (γνῶτε) and at last may understand (γινώσκητε)." These two terms taken together express the long and painful labor of that discovery which might have resulted from the first glance : *"Come and see"* (i. 47). The apparently pleonastic sense of this reading not having been understood by the copyists, they gave to the text the more common form which we find in the received reading : *to the end that you may understand and believe.* The words: *the Father in me, and I in the Father,* which indicate the contents of this obtained knowledge, recall the declaration of ver. 30 (*we are one*), but it does not follow from this, that, as *Weiss* will have it, it exhausts the sense of that declaration. It must not be forgotten that vv. 30 and 36 are the immediate expression of the contents of the consciousness of Jesus Himself, while ver. 38 formulates these contents only in the measure in which they can and should become the object of the moral apperception of believers. By beholding with the eye of faith, they will discover more and more clearly two things: the full communication which God makes of His riches to this human being, His organ on the earth (*the Father in me*); and the complete self-divesting by which Jesus, renouncing His own life, draws everything solely from the fullness of the Father and His gifts (*I in him*). This is the form in which faith can apprehend here below the unity of the Father and the Son. This relation is the *manifestation* of their essential unity, which Jesus had affirmed as the contents of His own consciousness.

Ver. 39. " *They sought therefore*[3] *again*[4] *to take him ; but he went forth out of their hands.*" Perhaps this softened form in which Jesus had just repeated the affirmation of His divinity had had the effect of calming somewhat the irritation of His hearers; they abandon the purpose of immediately stoning Him. But, while they are plotting that they may arrest Him and bring Him to judgment, He succeeds in breaking the circle which they had formed around Him, and, after having rejoined His disciples, in leaving the temple with them. Nothing in the story leads to the supposition of a miracle.

---

[1] T. R. reads with 13 Mjj. (A Γ etc.) πιστεύσητε (*that you may believe*); but B L X some Mnn. Cop. read γινωσκητε (*may understand*). ℵ: πιστεύητε. D It^plerique omit the second verb.

[2] ℵ B D L X read εν τω πατρι; T. R. with 12 Mjj.: εν αυτω.

[3] 9 Mjj. (B E G etc.) 40 Mnn. omit ουν.

[4] ℵ D 10 Mnn. It^plerique Vulg. Cop. omit πάλιν (*again*).

It is absolutely impossible to suppose that a later writer, the inventor of the theory of the Logos, should have imagined an argument such as this passage contains. How could such a man have thought of ascribing to Jesus an argument which, superficially understood, seems to contradict everything which he had made Him affirm hitherto with relation to His divinity? This mode of discussion evidently bears the character of immediate historical reality. It testifies, at the same time, of the most lively understanding of the Old Testament. Evidently this whole discourse can be attributed only to Jesus Himself.

Historical conclusion: vv. 40–42

Vv. 40–42. "*And he went away again beyond the Jordan, into the place*[1] *where John had baptized at the beginning;*[2] *and he abode there. 41. And many came to him, and they said: John did no miracle; but all that John said of this man was true. 42. And many believed on him there.*"[3] As we have already said, the Synoptics (Matt. xix. 1; Mark x. 1; and, because of the parallelism, Luke xviii. 15) also mention this sojourn in Peræa, a little before the last Passover. As Jesus certainly could not have remained a long time at Jerusalem without the result of bringing the conflict to its decisive issue, He abandoned the capital after the feast of Dedication, and went away to resume the pilgrimage which had been interrupted by this brief journey. It was thus that He arrived in Peræa, where we find Him in this passage of John. We feel, from the apostle's tone, that this sojourn was not without pleasure for Jesus and for His first disciples. There is a charm in finding oneself, on finishing one's career, in the places where it was begun. Jesus had, moreover, the joy of gathering a harvest here which had been prepared by the faithful labor of His forerunner. It would be difficult not to recognize in this description the personal recollection of the evangelist (see *Weiss*). The word *again* (ver. 40) does not by any means allude to a supposed sojourn in Peræa between vv. 21 and 22, as *Lange* thought, but certainly to that of which John had spoken in i. 28, when Jesus was at Bethany, near the Jordan, with His forerunner. The term τὸ πρῶτον (or, as the Sinaitic MS. reads, τὸ πρότερον) contrasts these first days with His later ministry, which was accomplished in altogether different localities (iii. 23). The meaning of the testimony which the believers of Peræa bear to Jesus is this: "If John did not himself do miracles, he did indeed at least predict everything which this one does, whose coming he announced." John thus grew greater to their view with all the greatness of Him who had followed him and to whom he had borne testimony. The word ἐκεῖ, *there*, should certainly be placed, according to the reading of the Alexandrian authorities, at the end of the verse; it is on this word that the emphasis rests. This faith which is so easily developed in Peræa forms a striking contrast with the persistent and increasing unbelief of the inhabitants of Judea, which has just been described in the preceding chapters. This

---

[1] א omits the words εις τον τοπον.
[2] א Δ: το προτερον instead of το πρωτον.
[3] 10 Mjj. (א A B D, etc.) make εκει the last word of the verse.

passage thus forms, by means of this contrast, as *Luthardt* remarks, the last point of the great act of accusation directed against *the Jews* in this part of the Gospel.

Third Cycle
John 11 and 12

Everything is henceforth ripe for the catastrophe; the development begun in chap. v. reaches its utmost limit. Yet one more *good work*, and the condemnation of Jesus will be finally pronounced. Chap. xi. places us in the presence of this denouement.

Of the sojourn in Peræa the Synoptics relate to us some particular incidents which John omits: the conversation with the Pharisees respecting divorce, the presentation of the little children, the scene of the rich young man, the ambitious request of James and John. The fourth evangelist mentions only the fact which brings this sojourn to a close—the visit to Bethany.

It is evident that the point of view of the development of Jewish unbelief governed this selection; comp. the story of the session of the Sanhedrim, as the consequence of the miracle (vv. 47–53), the relation established between this miracle and the entrance into Jerusalem on Palm-day (xii. 17–18), and, finally, the relation between the latter and the final catastrophe (xii. 19).

The entire cycle is divided into three sections:

1. Chap. xi.: The resurrection of Lazarus, with its immediate result, the sentence of condemnation pronounced upon Jesus;

2. Chap. xii. 1–36: Three events which form the transition from the active ministry of Jesus to His passion;

3. Chap. xii. 37–50: A retrospective glance cast by the evangelist at the great fact of Jewish unbelief which has been described since chap. v.

1
John 11:1-57
THE RESURRECTION OF LAZARUS

No scene in this gospel is presented in so detailed and dramatic a manner. There is none from which appears more distinctly the character of Jesus as at once perfectly divine and perfectly human, and none which more fully justifies the central declaration of the Prologue: "The Word was made flesh."

Three phases: 1. The preparation: vv. 1–16; 2. The event: vv. 17–44; 3. The consequence: vv. 45–57.

The preparation: vv. 1–16

John first describes the general situation, vv. 1, 2; then, the conduct of Jesus towards the two sisters, vv. 3–6; finally, His conversations with the disciples before departing, vv. 7–16.

730 / Unbelief Develops in Israel

Vv. 1, 2: *"Now a certain man was sick, Lazarus, of Bethany, of the village of Mary and Martha, her sister. 2. Mary was she who anointed the Lord with ointment and wiped his feet with her hair; and it was her brother, Lazarus, who was sick."* As it is the sickness of Lazarus which is the occasion of all that follows, the word ἀσθενῶν, *sick*, is placed at the beginning. The particle δέ is the *now* of transition (v. 5). The name of the place where Lazarus lived is carefully noticed, because it is the situation of this village (in Judea) which occasions the following conversation between Jesus and His disciples. But how can the author designate Bethany as the village *of Mary and Martha*, two persons whose names have not yet been mentioned in this gospel. He evidently supposes that the two sisters are known to the readers through the evangelical tradition, especially through the fact related in Luke x. 38–42. *Bethany*, at the present day, *El-Azirieh* (from *El-Azir*, the Arabian name of *Lazarus*) is a poor village situated on the eastern slope of the Mount of Olives, three-quarters of a league from Jerusalem, which is inhabited in our day by about forty Mussulman families. The supposed house of Lazarus, and also his sepulchre, have been pointed out since the fourth century, as they are still pointed out. The two prepositions, ἀπό and ἐκ, used here as parallel to each other, are not absolutely synonymous, as *Meyer* and *Weiss* think. The passage i. 45 does not prove anything in favor of this assertion. It seems to me that the first clause refers rather to the residence, the second to the origin: Lazarus lived at Bethany, *whence* he was. The name of Mary is placed first, as more conspicuous because of the fact mentioned in ver. 2. But it seems to follow from vv. 5, 19, that Martha was the eldest and from Luke x. 38 ff., that she was the principal personage in the house. The narratives in Matt. xxvi. 6 ff., and Mark xiv. 3 ff., prove that the oral tradition did not in general mention the name of Mary in the story of the anointing; for the expression there is simply *a woman*. And perhaps this omission may explain the form of the narrative of John in ver. 2: "This Mary, of whom I am here speaking to you, is the woman of whom it is related that she anointed . . . and wiped . . ." Through the closing part of the verse John returns from this episode to the fact which forms the subject of the narrative, by connecting the information to be given respecting Lazarus with the name of Mary as the last one mentioned: "*She it was whose brother, Lazarus, was sick.*"

Hengstenberg devotes twenty-six pages to the work of proving that (according to the idea which was generally prevalent before the Reformation) Mary, the sister of Lazarus, is the same person with Mary Magdalene (Luke viii. 2) and with the woman of sinful life who anointed the feet of Jesus (Luke vii. 36 ff.). He composes a little romance on this theme, according to which Galilee was the scene of Mary's dissolute life; Martha, her sister, in the course of a feast-journey, formed the acquaintance of the rich Pharisee Simon, a resident at Bethany, and married him; afterwards, she received into her house her sister Mary, who had abandoned her erroneous ways, and also her brother Lazarus, who had fallen into poverty. Thus we have an explanation of the entrance of Mary into the banqueting-room (Luke vii.); she was there, as it were, at home, and the attack of

Simon was the malicious bantering of a brother-in-law. There is nothing, even to the parable of the poor Lazarus and the wicked rich man, which may not in this way find its explanation, etc., etc. This dissertation proves only one thing; the facility with which a sagacious and learned man proves everything which he *wishes* to prove. The only argument which has any value is a certain resemblance in the expressions between John xi. 2 and Luke vii. 37, 38. But the scene is so different; on one side, Galilee; on the other, Judea; there, the first period of Jesus' ministry; here, one of the days which precede His Passion; there, a discussion as to the pardon of sins; here, a conversation on the sum expended; and the repetition of such homage is, according to the customs of the East, so natural, that we cannot accord the least probability to the double identity of persons which Hengstenberg seeks to establish.

Vv. 3, 4. "*The sisters therefore sent to Jesus to say to him, Lord, behold, he whom thou lovest is sick. 4. Jesus, having heard this, said: This sickness is not unto death; but it is for the glory of God, that*[1] *the Son of God may be glorified thereby.*" The message of the sisters is full of delicacy; this is the reason why the evangelist reproduces it as it came from their lips (λέγουσαι, *saying*). The address, *Lord,* alludes to the miraculous power of Jesus; the term ἰδε, *behold,* to the impression which this unexpected announcement will not fail to produce upon Him; finally, the expression ὃν φιλεῖς, *he whom thou lovest,* to the tender affection which binds Jesus to Lazarus and makes it their duty not to leave Him in ignorance of the danger to which His friend is exposed. On the other hand, they do not insist; how could they press Him to come, knowing as they did the perils which await Him in Judea? They lay the case before Him: "Judge for thyself as to what must be done."

The words of Jesus (ver. 4) are not given as a reply to this message; the statement is: *he said,* not: *he answered.* They are a declaration which was directed as much to the disciples who were present, as to the absent sisters. The ever original and very often paradoxical character of the sayings of the Lord must be very imperfectly understood, if one imagines that He meant seriously to say that Lazarus would not die of this sickness, and that only afterwards, in consequence of a second message, which is assumed by the narrative, He recognized His mistake (ver. 14). No doubt, as *Lücke* observes, the glory of Jesus here on earth did not imply omniscience; but His moral purity excluded the affirmation of that of which He was ignorant. *Reuss* very fitly says: "Here is no medical statement." The expression which Jesus makes use of is amphibological; whether it contained an announcement of recovery, or a promise of resurrection, it signified to the disciples that the *final* result of the sickness would not be death (οὐ πρὸς θάνατον). *The glory of God* is the resplendence which is shed abroad in the hearts of men by the manifestation of His perfections, especially of His power acting in the service of His holiness or of His love. And what act could be more fitted to produce such an effect than the triumph of life over death? Comp. Rom. vi. 4. In ver.

---

[1] ℵ repeats αλλα before ινα.

40, Jesus reminds Martha of the saying which He here utters, in the words: "*Did I not say unto thee, that, if thou believedst, thou shouldst see the glory of God?*" We may and should infer from this expression, that, at the moment when Jesus was speaking in this way, the death of Lazarus and his resurrection were already present events to His view. For the very grave terms: *for the glory of God, to the end that* . . ., indicate more than a mere miracle of healing (see *Keil*). We must therefore go back to this very moment in order to locate rightly the hearing of the prayer for which He gives thanks in ver. 42. This manifestation of divine power must also have shed its brightness over Him who was its agent. How can God be glorified in the person of His Son, without a participation on the part of the latter in His glory? Ἵνα, *in order that*, does not therefore indicate a second purpose in juxtaposition with the one which had been previously indicated (ὑπέρ); it is the explanation of the means by which the latter will be attained. We see in this passage how far the meaning of the name *Son of God* passes, in the mouth of Jesus, beyond that of the title *Messiah:* it designates here, as in ver. 30, *the one who is so united with the Father* that the glory of the one is the glory of the other. The pronoun δι' αὐτῆς, *by means of it*, may be referred to *the glory;* but it is more natural to refer it to *the sickness*. This saying recalls that of ix. 3; but it passes beyond it in greatness, in the same degree in which the resurrection of Lazarus surpasses in glory the healing of the one who was born blind.

Vv. 5-7. "*Now Jesus loved Martha and her sister and Lazarus. 6. When therefore he heard that he was sick, he remained yet two days in the place where he was; 7 then, when this time had passed, he says to the disciples,[1] Let us go into Judea again.*"[2] It might be supposed that the remark introduced parenthetically into the narrative, in ver. 5, has as its purpose to prevent the idea that the delay of two days mentioned in ver. 6 arose from indifference. But the οὖν, *therefore*, of ver. 6, is opposed to this explanation. In order fully to understand the design of this remark, account must be taken of the μέν of ver. 6, which supposes a δέ understood in ver. 7: "Jesus loved Martha and Mary . . . and Lazarus. . . . When therefore He heard of it, He remained, *it is true* (μέν); *but*, afterwards He said: Let us go . . . " We perceive thus that the remark of ver. 5: *He loved*, refers not to the: *He remained*, of ver. 6, but to the order *to set out* given in ver. 7. This quite simple explanation does away with several forced suppositions, for example, that Jesus meant: *Although* Jesus loved, or this other: *Because* He loved, He remained, to the end of testing longer the faith of the two sisters. Jesus uses here the term of dignity, ἀγαπᾶν, instead of that of tenderness φιλεῖν (ver. 3), either, as the interpreters think, because the question is of the affection of Jesus for the two sisters— but would not the Lord's disciple be raised above such prepossessions?— or rather because the nobler term is better suited to the pen of the evangelist, while the expression of tenderness was more appropriate in the

---

[1] A D K Γ Δ Λ Π 20 Mnn. add αυτου after μαθηταις.

[2] ℵ omits παλιν. A reads πολιν (*to the Jewish city*).

John 11:5-7 / 733

mouth of the sisters. Martha occupies here, as in ver. 19, the first place (see on ver. 1). *Bretschneider, Strauss* and *Baur* explain the two days' delay mentioned in ver. 6 by a personal motive on Jesus' part. He purposely desired to allow Lazarus to die, in order that He might have the opportunity, not only of healing him, but of raising him to life; these writers find here a proof of the non-authenticity of the narrative. But there is no allusion in the text to such an intention of Jesus; and even ver. 15: "*I rejoice for your sakes that I was not there,*" positively excludes it; for Jesus may well rejoice in a divine dispensation, but not in a thing which He had voluntarily and purposely caused. Moreover, it will appear from the sequel of the story that, at the moment when Jesus received the message of the sisters, Lazarus had already breathed his last. If indeed, counting backwards, we reckon the four days mentioned in vv. 17 and 39, which elapsed from the burial of Lazarus to the arrival of Jesus at Bethany, these days can only be as follows: the fourth and last is that in which Jesus makes the journey from Peræa to Bethany. From Bethany to Jericho is a journey of about six hours, and from Jericho to the Jordan of an hour and a half. It was therefore, in all, a journey of seven and a half or eight leagues from the Jordan, near the place where Jesus was, to Bethany; it might easily be made in one day. The second and third days are the two which Jesus passed in Peræa after having received the message of the sisters. Finally, the first is that in which the messenger arrived in Peræa to inform Jesus. It was therefore in the course of this day, a little while after the departure of the messenger, that Lazarus died, and also in the course of the same day that he was buried, according to the Jewish custom. Thus towards evening, when Jesus received the tidings of His friend's sickness, He was already in the tomb. We see clearly how erroneous is the reckoning of *Keim* who says (i., p. 495): "Three days were needed for Jesus to *go* from that region of Peræa to Bethany." *Meyer* is no less in error when he takes as the starting point of the *four* days which had elapsed since the burial of Lazarus (ver. 17) the day which *followed* the two days of waiting in Peræa. How could Jesus have taken three whole days for reaching Bethany from the Jordan? As to the reason which prevented Jesus from setting out on the journey immediately, it may be supposed, no doubt, with *Lücke* and *Neander*, that it was the work of His ministry in Peræa. But is it not better to say, with *Meyer*, that it was the waiting for the signal from the Father, by which Jesus always regulated His action? God might certainly act as Jesus, as a *man*, would not have done, and prolong the time of waiting with the design of making the miracle more manifest and more striking, with a view to the glory of His Son and His own glory.

Ver. 7. The δέ which should answer to the μέν of ver. 6 is omitted, as often in Greek, because the opposition which the μέν had in view gives place to the simple historical succession; see *Weiss*. The expression ἔπειτα μετὰ τοῦτο, literally: *afterwards, after that*, ver. 7, is not a pleonasm; it tells how long this waiting appeared both to the sisters and to Jesus Himself. It must be noticed that Jesus did not say: "Let us go to

Bethany," but "Let us go *into Judea.*" It is an allusion to the peril which threatens Him in that country; by it He calls forth on the part of His disciples the expression of the feeling of apprehension which He knows to be in the depths of their hearts and which He wishes to overcome before starting on the journey. It is with the same purpose that He adds the word πάλιν, *again,* which reminds them of the dangers which He had just incurred during His last sojourn in Jerusalem. *Meyer* protests in vain against this intention; it appears clearly from the narrative.

Vv. 8–10. "*The disciples say to him; Master, the Jews were but now seeking to stone thee, and dost thou return thither? 9. Jesus answered, Are there not twelve hours in the day? If any one walk during the day, he does not stumble, because he sees the light of this world; 10 but if any one walk in the night, he stumbles, because the light is not in him.*" At the word Judea, as Jesus expected, the disciples uttered a protest. He took advantage of their objection to give them an excellent teaching with respect to their future ministry. The answer of Jesus (vv. 9, 10) has naturally a double meaning. The first meaning is clear: He who accomplishes the journey to which he is called during the twelve hours of the day, does not stumble; the light of the sun enlightens him and makes him discern the obstacles in his path; while he who wishes to continue his journey even after the night has come, is in danger of perishing. In the application, some give to the idea of *day* a purely moral sense. According to *Chrysostom, de Wette, Brückner* the day designates a virtuous life, a life passed in communion with God, and the sense is: On the line of duty marked out, one has no serious danger to fear; but as soon as one turns aside from it, he exposes himself to the danger of perishing. The sense is good; but the figure of the *twelve hours* is not explained. This last expression leads naturally to the *temporal* application of the idea of *day*. *Bengel, Meyer, Hengstenberg, Weiss* and *Reuss* have felt this. They understand by the *twelve hours of day* the divinely measured time *of the earthly life:* "The time which was granted me has not yet elapsed; so long as it continues, no one can injure me; but when it shall have elapsed, I shall fall into the hands of my enemies." So already *Apollinaris,* "The Lord declares that before the time of His Passion, the Jews could do nothing to Him: the day is the time until the Passion; the night, the time after the Passion." This sense seems to me incompatible with ver. 10, in which the term προσκόπτειν, *to stumble,* cannot designate a purely passive state, like that of Jesus falling into the hands of the Jews, and in which the expression: *There is no light in him,* cannot apply to Jesus. *Meyer* answers: "This is a point which pertains to the figure and which has no significance." But ver. 10, which forms half of the picture, cannot be treated in this way. I think (partly) with *Tholuck, Lange* and *Luthardt,* that the day here designates at once the *time* of life and the *task* assigned for this time; it is the day of the workman's labor, as in ix. 4. Only here the figure is borrowed from the situation in which Jesus finds Himself with His disciples. It is the morning; the sun rises; they have before them a good day's journey, twelve hours of daylight. During all this time, they will journey without danger. Before it is night, they will have reached the end of the journey, Bethany. In the moral sense this means: "I can go without fear to Judea, whither duty calls me. The twelve hours which are granted me for the accomplishment of my task will remain intact. The sun of the divine will, in assigning me my task, enlightens my path; I shall not stumble. The danger of stumbling and falling would begin for me only at the moment when, fleeing in a cowardly way from a foreseen danger, I should wish arbitrarily to prolong the time of my life, and to add a thirteenth hour of walking to the twelve which legitimately belong to me. From that moment I could only stumble, sin, perish. For the hour of life which God had not given me, would be an hour without duty or mission; the sun of the divine will would no more enlighten my course." In other terms: "The Jews cannot take away from me one moment of the time which is accorded me, so long as I am in the accomplishment of my task; a real danger will assail me only if, as you would have me do, I seek arbitrarily to prolong my career, by refusing to go whither duty calls me." This word applies to the believer who, in the time of persecution, would prolong his life by denying his faith, to the physician who would flee from the approach of a contagious malady, etc. The man, after being placed in such a situation, can only sin and perish. *Meyer* objects to this sense, that the disciples asked Jesus only not to shorten His life, and did not ask Him to prolong it. But this amounts to precisely the same thing. To desert duty for fear of shortening one's life, is not this to strive to prolong it beyond due measure? The expression: *the light is not in him*, signifies that the divine will, no longer presiding over that life, cannot serve to direct it; such a man lives only on a venture, because he ought not to live any longer. The parallel 1 John ii. 10, 11, confirms this meaning. The analogy of the expressions and ideas between the two passages is remarkable. John there applies to the believer who loves or does not love his brother what Jesus here says of the man who is obedient or not obedient to the will of God. This saying is, both in matter and form, the counterpart of that in which Jesus gave the reason, ix. 4, of the act of healing the man who was born blind. Only, according to the fine remark of *Lange*, there it was evening; He saw the sun descending to the horizon: "I must not *lose* a moment of the time which remains for me to enlighten the world." Here it is morning: "The time which is assigned me is sufficient for accomplishing my whole task; I must not through cowardice seek to *add* an hour to the day of work which is divinely assured to me." In these two words: to lose nothing, to add nothing, is certainly summed up the duty of man in relation to the time of his earthly work.

Vv. 11–13. "*He spoke thus, and after this he says to them, Lazarus, our friend, sleeps; but I go to awaken him. 12. Whereupon they said to him;*[1] *Lord, if he sleeps, he will recover. 13. But Jesus had spoken of his death, and*

---

[1] T. R. reads ειπον ουν οι μαθ. αυτου with 10 Mjj. the Mnn. It^{plerique} Vulg. ℵ B C D K X read αυτω either before or after οι μαθ., and reject αυτου. A and 1 Mn., which Tischendorf follows, reject οι μαθ. αυτου and read αυτω.

736 / Unbelief Develops in Israel

they thought that he was speaking of the rest of sleep." The words ταῦτα εἶπε, *he spoke thus, and* . . . , are not superfluous. They signify that this general maxim which He had just stated was applied by Him on the spot to the present case. *Weiss* wrongly asserts that this application is not found in what follows. It is in the words: *I go to awaken him*. The epithet: *our friend*, appeals to their affection for Lazarus, just as the expression: *he whom thou lovest*, in ver. 3, had made an appeal to His own friendship for him. Some interpreters have thought that it was at this moment that, either through a new message (*Neander*); or through His prophetic consciousness (*Weiss*), Jesus Himself learned of the death of Lazarus. But the promise of ver. 4 has proved to us that He had known this circumstance in a supernatural way, from the moment when the message of the two sisters had drawn his attention to the condition of His friend. Jesus likes to present death under the figure of sleep, a figure which makes it a phase of life.

Strauss found the misunderstanding of the disciples in ver. 12 inconceivable. *Reuss* calls it "a misapprehension which has precisely the import of that of Nicodemus." He adds: "Men do not ordinarily sleep several days in succession." But after having heard the words of ver. 4, it was natural that the disciples should not have believed in the possibility of the sick man's death. They might therefore think that this sleep of which Jesus was speaking was the crisis of convalescence, and that He wished to bring the sick man out of it healed by awaking him. It is very evident that, in their extreme desire not to go into Judea, they seek for a pretext, good or bad, for deterring Jesus from departing thitherward. In this situation, what improbability is there in this reply? The word σωθήσεται signifies here: will be healed of himself, without participation on thy part. The general term κοίμησις (*sleep*, ver. 13) is derived from κεκοίμηται (ver. 11), and must be determined here by a special complement (τοῦ ὕπνου).

Vv. 14–16. "*Then Jesus therefore said to them openly, Lazarus is dead; 15 and I rejoice for your sakes that I was not there, to the end that you may believe; but let us go to him. 16. Whereupon Thomas, who is called Didymus, said to his fellow-disciples, Let us also go, that we may die with him.*" After having set aside (vv. 9, 10), the motive alleged by the disciples against this journey, and indicated the reason (vv. 11, 12) which obliges Him to undertake it, Jesus concludes by explaining Himself and gives the order for departing. Παρρησίᾳ, as in xvi. 25: in strict terms, without figure. There would have been, as we have already seen, a manifest falseness in our Lord's expressing Himself, as He does in ver. 15, if this death had been the intentional effect of His own mode of action. The words: *to the end that you may believe* are the commentary on the limiting words: *for your sakes*. Undoubtedly the disciples were already believers; but, as *Hengstenberg* says, by growing, faith comes into being. At each new stage which it reaches, the preceding stage seems to it in itself nothing more than unbelief. Jesus knows how the increase of faith which is about to be produced in them around this tomb will be necessary for them, in a little time, when they shall find themselves before that of their Master. There is something abrupt in the last words: *But let us go to him.* It is a matter of constraining them and of overcoming in them the last remnant of resistance. They yield, but not without making manifest the unbelief hidden in the depths of the hearts of some of them.

The words of Thomas to the other disciples betrays indeed more of love for the person of Jesus than of faith in the wisdom of His course of action. Their meaning is this: "If He actually desires to have Himself killed, let us go and perish with Him." The Thomas who speaks thus is indeed the same whom we shall meet again in xiv. 5, xx. 25; much of frankness and resolution, but little of disposition to subordinate the visible to the invisible. This quite undesigned consistency in the role of the secondary personages, is, as has been admirably brought out by *Luthardt*, one of the striking features of John's narrative and one of the best proofs of the historical truth of this work. The name *Thomas* (in the Aramaic האמא, Hebrew האם) signifies *twin*. The name *Didymus*, which has in Greek the same meaning, was undoubtedly that by which this apostle was most commonly designated in the churches of Asia Minor, in the midst of which John wrote. Thus is the repetition of this translation in xx. 24 and xxi. 2 explained. *Hengstenberg, Luthardt,* and *Keil* see in this name of twin an allusion to the fact that Thomas carried in himself two men, a believer and an unbeliever, a Jacob and an Esau! He was a δίψυχος man (*Keil*)!

What wisdom and what love in the manner in which Jesus prepares His disciples for this journey which was so repugnant to their feeling! What elevation in the thoughts which He suggests to their hearts on this occasion! What grace and appropriateness in the images by which He endeavors to make these thoughts intelligible to them!

The Miracle: vv. 17–44

1. Jesus and Martha: vv. 17–27.

Vv. 17–19. "*Jesus on his arrival found that he had been in the tomb four days already.* 18. *Now Bethany was near to Jerusalem, at the distance of about fifteen furlongs;* 19 *and*[1] *many of the Jews had come to*[2] *Martha and Mary to console them concerning their brother's*[3] *death.*"—For the four days, see on ver. 6.—Ἡμέρας is objective, rather than circumstantial. See on v. 6. The expression: *He found*, marks the situation as it was according to the information given Him on His arrival. John sets forth the nearness of Bethany to Jerusalem, in order to explain the presence of such a large number of Jews (ver. 19). Fifteen stadia make a distance of about forty minutes. This distance is reckoned from Jerusalem as the starting-point, ἐγγὺς τῶν Ἱεροσολύμων; in this way the following preposition

---

[1] א A B C D L X: πολλοι δε instead of και πολλοι.

[2] T. R. reads προς τας περι Μαρθαν κ. Μ. with 12 Mjj. (A. Γ, etc.), and nearly all the Mnn., while א B C D L X 4 Mnn. read προς (or προς την) Μαρθαν κ. Μ.

[3] א B D L omit αυτων.

738 / Unbelief Develops in Israel

ἀπό is explained. The imperfect *was* refers to the part played by Bethany in this event which was already remote in time at the moment of John's writing. It is unnecessary to suppose that John is thinking of the destruction of this village in the Roman war. The turn of expression which is so common among the Greeks, αἱ περὶ Μάρθαν (ver. 19), is removed by the Alexandrian reading, but wrongly, even according to *Meyer* and *Tischendorf*. It occurs again twice in the New Testament (Acts xiii. 13, xxi. 8). That it was introduced here by the copyists seems to me very questionable. This form of expression points to Martha and Mary as surrounded by the servants of their household; it implies that the two sisters were in easy circumstances. It is commonly inferred from 1 Sam. xxxi. 13 and 1 Chron. x. 12, that the ceremonies of condolence continued for eight days; but the question in those passages is of royal personages. The passages cited by *Lightfoot* (pp. 1070 ff.) also seem to me insufficient to prove this usage. The sequel proves that the term *Jews* which is here used preserves the unfavorable sense which it has throughout this entire Gospel. Notwithstanding the fact that Martha and Mary were closely connected with these persons, they yet mostly belonged to the party hostile to Jesus. This point is mentioned in order to make prominent the change of feeling which was produced in a certain number of them (vv. 36–45).

Vv. 20–24. "*When Martha heard that Jesus was coming, she went out to meet him; but Mary still sat in the house.* 21. *Martha therefore said to Jesus: Lord,*[1] *if thou hadst been here, my brother would not have died;*[2] 22 *And*[3] *even now, I know that whatsoever thou shalt ask of God, God will give it thee.* 23. *Jesus says to her, Thy brother shall rise again.* 24. *Martha says to him, I know that he shall rise again in the resurrection, at the last day.*" Martha, no doubt occupied with her household affairs, was the first to receive the news of the Lord's arrival, and, in her eagerness, she ran to meet Him, without the thought of telling her sister, whose grief was keeping her in the inner apartment. Such as the two sisters are represented to us in Luke x. 38 ff., such precisely we find them again here. The narrative of John seems even to allude to that of his predecessor. On the opposite supposition, the harmony in the characters is only the more striking. The words of Martha (ver. 21) are not a reproach. How could she be ignorant that her brother was dead even before Jesus had received the news of his sickness? How, especially, could she allow herself to complain of His mode of acting, at the very moment when she is about to ask of Him the greatest of gifts? She simply expresses her regret that Jesus had not been there at the time of the sickness, and this regret serves only to prepare the way for the request which she has to make. She says, according to the T. R. and the Byzantine authorities: οὐκ ἐτεθνήκει, " would not be at this moment sunk in death," instead of ἀπέθανεν, " would not have gone through the act of dying," which is read by the Alexandrian authorities (see on ver. 32).

---

[1] B omits κυριε (*Lord*).

[2] Instead of ετεθνηκει which is read by A E F G H M S U Γ Δ Λ nearly all the Mnn., απεθανεν is read in ℵ B C D K L X Π.

[3] ℵ B C X reject the αλλα (*but*) of the T. R. before και νυν.

The T. R. adds, with several Mjj., ἀλλά before καὶ νῦν: "*but* even now." This *but* is unnecessary: "I know that even now in his death my brother can experience the virtue of Thy prayer." The indefinite expression *whatsoever* leaves that to be understood which is too great to be expressed. There is an evident reserve of delicacy in this indirect request. It is no doubt the greatness of the work expected which is expressed in the repetition of the word θεός, *God*, at the end of the two clauses of ver. 22: "Thou art the well-beloved of *God*, *God* will give Thee the life of my brother." This confidence is inspired in Martha not only by the general knowledge which she has of Jesus and by the resurrections which had been effected in Galilee, but more especially by the message of ver. 4, and by this sudden arrival, which involved in itself also a promise.

There is in Martha's faith more of vivacity than of light. She believes in the miracle of power; but she is not yet initiated into the spiritual sphere within which alone such an act will assume its true meaning and value. Before satisfying her request, Jesus endeavors to put her into a condition to receive it. He proceeds, with this end in view, as He did in chaps. v. and vi., by giving to His promise at first the most general form: *Thy brother shall rise again*. *Hengstenberg* even supposes that He makes no allusion in these words to the approaching resurrection of Lazarus, which, according to him, does not deserve the name of a resurrection. For the return to this wretched earthly existence cannot be called by this fair name. But is it not doing violence to the text, to refuse to see in these words the promise of the event which is to follow? The belief in the resurrection of the pious Israelites, as the opening act of the Messianic kingdom, had been already announced in Dan. xii. 2 and 2 Macc. vii. 9, 14, etc.; it was generally spread abroad in Israel, and that especially "in the circles in which the Pharisaic teaching prevailed."[1]

There is not by any means, in the answer of Martha, an indication, as has been supposed, of a fall from the height of faith to which her heart had been raised. Only, in speaking thus, she wishes to assure herself of the meaning which Jesus Himself attaches to His promise. If she speaks only of the *final* resurrection which is to her mind certain, it is that she may give to Jesus the opportunity to explain Himself, and to declare expressly what she scarcely dares to hope for in the present case. There is as it were an indirect question here. Everything in Martha breathes a masculine faith, full of energy and activity. But this faith is not as spiritual as it is strong; it has not yet in a sufficient degree the person of the Lord as its object. Jesus, on His part, endeavors, in His reply, to develop it in this direction.

Vv. 25, 26. "*Jesus said to her, I am the resurrection and the life; he that believes on me, even though he were dead, yet shall he live; 26 and whosoever lives and believes on me shall never die; believest thou this?*" Martha has just spoken of the resurrection as of a future *event*; Jesus sets in opposition to

---

[1] Schürer, *Neutest. Zeitgesch.*, p. 395 ff. The differences which existed in the matter of this general expectation of the resurrection are completely set forth by this author.

this event *His person* (ἐγώ, *I;* εἰμί, *I am*), as being in reality the resurrection. Victory over death is not a physical fact; it is a moral work, a personal act; it is *the doing* of Jesus Himself (v. 28, 29: vi. 39, 40, 44); and consequently He can accomplish it when he pleases, to-day even, if He wishes, as well as after the passing of ages. Jesus thus brings back the thought of Martha to Himself and gives to her faith its true object. He substitutes for adherence to dogmatic truth confidence in His person. This is what He had also done in chaps. iv. and vi., where, after some moments of conversation, He had substituted Himself for the abstract notions of living water and bread from heaven. After having declared Himself to be the resurrection, Jesus proclaims Himself as *the life*. It might be supposed that He means to speak of the glorious and perfect life which follows the resurrection. But according to the explanation which follows (vv. 25, 26), it is better to hold, with *Luthardt*, that Jesus passes from the outward resurrection to the more profound fact which is its spiritual *condition*. If He is the principle of the physical resurrection, it is because He is that of *life* in the most exalted sense of that word (v. 26, vi. 51). The spiritual life which He communicates to His own is for them, if they are dead, the pledge of a return to corporeal life; and, on the other hand, while still living, they are raised by it above the passing accident of physical death. The first declaration applies to Lazarus and to the other believers who were already dead. In virtue of the new life which they have received by faith, they continue living, and consequently they may, at the moment when Jesus wills, be recalled to corporeal existence. The second declaration (ver. 26) applies to the two sisters and to all the believers who were still living; they remain sheltered from death; for to die in full light, in the serene brightness of the life which is in Jesus, and to continue to live in Him (ver. 25) is no more the fact which human language has designated by the name of death (see on vi. 50, viii. 51). Jesus means therefore: In me the dead lives, and the living does not die. The terms *to die*, in the first clause, and *to live*, in the second, are to be taken in the strict sense.

This saying, by carrying the thought of Martha from the momentary and corporeal fact of the resurrection to its spiritual and permanent principle, gives to the person of Christ its true place in the miracle, and to the miracle its true religious significance. The resurrection of her brother becomes for her as if an emanation of the life of Jesus Himself, a ray of His glory, and thus the means of uniting the soul of Martha to Him, the source of life. *Reuss* sees in this answer of Jesus a means of setting aside the popular idea of the corporeal resurrection, or at least of divesting it of all theological value. One must be singularly preoccupied by his own theory to draw from this reply a conclusion which is so foreign to the context and so contrary to the perfectly free and clear affirmation of v. 28, 29. Jesus thus returned to the subject from which Martha had turned aside, the resurrection of Lazarus. Before acting, He asks her further: " *Believest thou this?* "

Ver. 27. " *She says to him, Yes, Lord, I believe that thou art the Christ, the Son of God, who was to come into the world.*" To see in this confession of

Martha, as some have done, only a simple avowal of a want of understanding with reference to the preceding words of Jesus: " I do not comprehend all these profound things of which thou art speaking to me, but I hold thee to be the Messiah," is strangely to depreciate its significance. This meaning would give to this scene which is of so grave import a character almost ridiculous. By her answer: *Yes, Lord,* Martha certainly appropriates to herself all that which Jesus has just affirmed respecting His person. Only, she does not feel herself in a condition to formulate spontaneously her faith in the things which are so new for her, and she makes use of terms which are familiar to her in order to express the thought that Jesus is to her all that which is greatest, and that, whatever He may affirm respecting His person, He will never say too much for the faith of her who speaks to Him. *The Christ:* the end of the theocratic revelations and dispensations; *the Son of God:* evidently something else than *the Christ*, unless there is an idle tautology here: the personage in whom God manifests Himself as in no other, and who is in an intimate and mysterious relation with God. The expression: *who comes into the world*, is not a third title, but an apposition explanatory of the two others. The present participle ἐρχόμενος, *who comes*, is the present of idea: the one who, according to the divine promise, should come, and in fact comes. *The world:* the foreseen theatre of his Messianic activity. There is a great psychological truth in this reply of Martha: by designating Him thus, she implicitly acknowledges that He is indeed all that which He has said: *the resurrection and the life.*—'Εγώ: *I* whom thou art questioning; πεπίστευκα (perfect): this is a conviction which I have gained.

2. Jesus and Mary: vv. 28–37.

Vv. 28–30. "*And having said this,[1] she went away and called Mary, her sister, secretly, saying, The Master is here and calls thee. 29. She, as soon as she heard this, rises[2] directly and comes[3] to him. 30. Now, Jesus was not yet come into the village, but was still[4] in the place where Martha had met him.*" The words: *He calls thee*, are sufficient to prove that Jesus had indeed given this commission to Martha. He must have desired to prepare Mary, as He had prepared her sister; the miracle could not be really beneficial to the one or the other except on this condition. Very probably, though *Weiss* does not admit this idea, the precaution which Martha takes in discharging His message (λάθρα, *secretly*) had been recommended to her by Jesus; He had heard how Mary was surrounded; and, if He did not flee from danger, no more did He seek it (see on ver. 30).

The liveliness of Mary's emotion on hearing this message is pictured in the verbs in the present tense: ἐγείρεται, *she rises*, and ἔρχεται, *she comes*. This reading, indeed, is preferable to the Alexandrian readings ἠγέρθη and ἤρχετο, *she rose* and *she came*, as in this case *Tischendorf* and *Weiss* acknowl-

---

[1] ℵ B C L X: τουτο instead of ταυτα, which is read in the 14 other Mjj. nearly all the Mnn. It. Vulg. Syr.

[2] ℵ B C D L X It. Sch.: ηγερθη (*rose*) instead of εγειρεται.

[3] The same (except D): ηρχετο (*came*) instead of ερχεται.

[4] ℵ B C X It. Vulg. Cop.: ην ετι (*was still*) instead of ην (*was*).

edge, who think that the aorist and imperfect were substituted for the present under the influence of the preceding ἤκουσεν, *she heard*. The Alexandrian reading appears to me to have been formed under the influence of iv. 30; but there are not the same reasons for presenting in the picturesque form the arrival of Mary here, as that of the Samaritans in chap. iv. In these cases it is painful to see how the position taken by *Westcott* and *Hort* deadens their critical tact. Jesus had not entered into Bethany. This was not only because the tomb must necessarily have been outside of the village (*Luthardt*). There must have been some important reason which detained Him; otherwise He would have gone directly where His heart summoned Him, to the house of mourning. His purpose was undoubtedly to avoid everything which could attract attention; and the intention of the following verse is precisely to show how this design failed by reason of a will superior to His own, which had resolved to give to this miracle the greatest possible splendor. Jesus had done what He ought; God did what He wished. There happened here something like what is related in Matt. ix. 31; Mk. vii. 24, 36.

Vv. 31, 32. "*The Jews therefore who were with her in the house and were comforting her, when they saw that she rose up suddenly and went out, followed her, supposing*[1] *that she was going*[2] *to the tomb to weep there.* 32. *When therefore Mary had come to the place where Jesus was, and saw him, she fell at*[3] *his feet, saying to him, Lord, if thou hadst been here, my brother*[4] *would not have died.*" One and the same thought had filled the soul of the two sisters and perhaps that of the dying man in his last hours: If Jesus were here! But on this common foundation of grief and regret some significant differences between the two sisters appear. We have remarked the masculine character of Martha's faith. Mary, on the contrary, seemed to be altogether overwhelmed by her grief: hers was a nature wholly feminine. And, like persons of vivid impressions, she makes no energetic effort to overcome the dejection which got the mastery of her. She lets herself fall at Jesus' feet, which Martha had not done; it is, moreover, the place which she loves (Luke x. 39; John xii. 3). She does not add to the expression of her grief, as does her sister, a word of faith and hope. There are, finally, in the exclamation which is common to her and Martha, two shades of differences which are not accidental. Instead of ἐτεθνήκει, *he is dead* (the actual state), which the Byzantine authorities place in the mouth of Martha, ver. 21, she says: ἀπέθανε: he has done *the act* of dying; it is as if she were still at the cruel moment in which the separation was accomplished. This shade of difference in the received reading (ver. 27) speaks in favor of its authenticity. Then the pronoun μου, *of me*, is placed in the mouth of Mary *before* ὁ ἀδελφός, *the brother*, and even, according to the Alexandrian reading, before ἀπέθανε: a part of *herself*, as it were, is gone. Thus, in Martha, a nature practical and full of elasticity, capable of energetically reacting against a depressing feeling; in Mary, a

---

[1] Instead of λεγοντες (*saying*) which T. R. reads with 13 Mjj. It. etc., ℵ B C D L X 7 Mnn. Syr^sch Cop. read δοξαντες (*thinking*).

[2] ℵ : οτι Ιησους υπαγει (*Jesus goes!*)

[3] ℵ B C D L X : προς instead of εις.

[4] ℵ B C L Δ place μου before απεθανεν.

sensibility given up, without the least trace of reaction, to the feeling which absorbs her. What truth in every feature of this picture!

Jesus knows the human heart too well to attempt to apply to Mary the method which He has just employed with Martha. With a grief like hers, there is no need of teaching and speaking; there is need of sympathizing and acting.

Vv. 33, 34. " *When therefore Jesus saw Mary weeping and the Jews who were with her weeping, he shuddered in his spirit and was troubled,*[1] *34 and he said, Where have you laid him. They say unto him, Lord, come and see.*" The particle *therefore* establishes a relation of causality between the grief of Mary and those with her and the extraordinary emotion by which Jesus is seized at this moment. This relation is likewise indicated by the words: *when He said*, and by the repetition of the participle *weeping*, which, like a refrain, ends the two clauses. It is now generally acknowledged that the term ἐμβριμᾶσθαι (from βριμάζειν, *to neigh, to roar*) can only designate a shudder of indignation. See the thorough demonstration in the essay of *Gumlich*, *Stud. u. Krit.*, 1862, pp. 260–269. This sense is applicable even to passages such as Matt. ix. 30, Mark i. 43, in which this word marks the stern tone of menace. We must set aside therefore, first of all, the meaning: *to be seized with grief* (*Lücke*), and *to groan deeply* (*Ewald*). But what can be the object of Jesus' indignation? According to *Chrysostom*, *Cyril*, and other Greek interpreters, this is the same emotion which He experiences on hearing the sobs and which He endeavors in vain to master. According to *Chrysostom*, τῷ πνεύματι, *His spirit*, designates the *object* of His indignation (He is indignant against His own spirit, that is to say, against the inward weakness which He feels), while *Cyril* sees in the Spirit the divine nature of Jesus reacting against His human nature; the same nearly, even at the present day, *Hilgenfeld*. The meaning given by *Chrysostom*, having very little naturalness in itself, would in any case require the use of ψυχή, *the soul*, instead of πνεῦμα, *the spirit*. For the soul is the seat of the *natural* emotions; comp. xii. 27; πνεῦμα, *the spirit*, designates the domain of the higher impressions appertaining to the relation of the soul to the divine. And if Jesus really struggled against a sympathetic emotion, how was it that He surrendered Himself to it the very next moment with perfect simplicity (ver. 35)? The explanation of *Cyril* tends to make the divine being and the human in Jesus two distinct personalities. *Meyer* and *Weiss* think that Jesus was indignant at the hypocritical tears of the Jews, which form a shocking contrast to the sincere grief of Mary. *Reuss* also inclines to this idea: Jesus revolts at the ostentation of this insincere grief. But the two participles *weeping* are in a relation of agreement, not of contrast. Others apply this movement of indignation to the want of faith which Jesus discerned at once in Mary and in the Jews (*Keim, Strauss*). But in the word *weeping*, twice repeated, the notion of grief is expressed, rather than that of unbelief; and a moment later, Jesus also weeps Himself! Some interpreters (*Calvin, Olshausen, Luthardt, Hengstenberg, Keil*) think

---

[1] D some Mnn. Sah.: εταραχθη τω πνευματι ως εμβριμωμενος.

that the indignation of Jesus is directed against the power of death and against Satan, the invisible enemy who wields this terrible weapon against men (viii. 44). It would be necessary to admit, with this explanation, that, while the indignation felt by Jesus (ver. 33), is directed towards the murderer, the tears which He sheds in ver. 35 are the expression of the pity with which the victims inspire Him. But how does it happen that nothing of a like nature manifests itself in Jesus in the other resurrections which He has effected? There must be in this case a peculiar circumstance which produces this altogether exceptional emotion. An analogous emotion is mentioned only in xiii. 21, at the moment when Jesus sees the treason of Judas in preparation: " *He was troubled in his spirit.*" The *spirit* is the seat of the religious emotions, as the *soul* is that of the natural affections. Thus in xii. 27, Jesus says: *My soul is troubled*, because the foreseeing of His sufferings makes His nature shudder, while here and in chap. xiii. it is in His *spirit* that He is agitated, because in both cases He sees Himself in immediate contact with evil in its blackest form, and because with a holy horror he feels the nearness of the invisible being who has taken possession of the heart of Judas, and (in our passage) of that of His declared enemies. This parallel throws light on the groaning of Jesus in ver. 33. On one side, the sobs which He hears around Him urge Him to accomplish the raising of His friend to life; but, on the other hand, He knows that to yield to this solicitation, and to cause the glory of the Father to break forth conspicuously at this moment, is to sign the sentence of His own death. For it is to drive to extremes His enemies and him who leads them to act. From the most glorious of His miracles they will draw a ground of condemnation against Him. A portion of these very persons whose sighs were pressing Him to act, will be among those who will cause Him to pay with His life for the crime of having vanquished death. Horror seizes Him at this thought; there is a diabolical perversity here which agitates His pure soul even to its lowest depths. We may recall the words of Jesus: "I have done many good works; for which do you stone me?" This is what is most directly referred to in these words. This agitation extended so far as to produce in Jesus an outward commotion, a physical trembling, expressed by the words: *He was troubled*. But the expression is chosen by the evangelist in such a way as to remove any idea of an unreasonable or merely passive agitation: the question therefore is not of a simple reaction of the moral on the physical with the purpose of restraining within Himself the impression produced upon Him (*Weiss*), or with that of preparing Himself by an energetic resolution for the conflict which He was about to engage in with the devil and with death (*Augustine, Calvin, Hengstenberg, Keil*). The Greek term can scarcely express such ideas. It seems to me that the physical agitation indicated by these words: *He was troubled*, is the mark of an energetic reaction by which Jesus, in some sort, threw off the emotion which had for a moment overpowered Him and recovered the full control of His being. This internal revolution terminated in this sudden and brief question: *Where have you laid him?* The two καί, *and*, bring out the intimate connection between these different emotions which succeed each other so rapidly within Him.

Vv. 35–37. *"Jesus wept.*¹ 36. *The Jews therefore said, Behold how he loved him. 37. But some of them said, could not he who opened the eyes of the blind, have caused that this man also should not have died?"* The storm has passed; on approaching the tomb Jesus feels only a tender sympathy for the grief which had filled the heart of His friend at the moment of separation and for that which the two sisters had experienced at the same hour. The term δακρύειν, *to weep*, does not indicate, like κλαίειν (ver. 33), sighs, but tears; it is the expression of a calm and gentle grief. *Baur* does not allow that one can weep over a friend whom one is to see again. This feature, according to him, proves the unauthenticity of the narrative. Assuredly, if this Gospel were, as he believes it to be, the product of speculative thought, this thirty-fifth verse would not be found in it; Jesus would raise His friend to life with the look of triumph and a buoyant heart, as the true Logos who had nothing human but the appearance of man. But the evangelist has said from the first: "The Word was made *flesh*," and he maintains the proposition with perfect consistency. "One does not raise the dead with a heart of stone," says *Hengstenberg*. Heb. ii. 17 teaches us that he who wishes to assist an unfortunate one, should, first of all, sink deeply into the feeling of the suffering from which he is about to save him. It is a strange fact that it is precisely the Gospel in which the divinity of Jesus is most strikingly affirmed, that leads us also best to know the profoundly human side of His life. The very criticism of the German savant proves how little such a Jesus is the child of speculation. The solemn brevity of the clauses in these verses, 34, 35, must be observed.

Even at the side of this tomb we find the inevitable division which takes place about the person of Jesus at each of His manifestations in acts or words. Among the Jews themselves there are a certain number whose hearts are moved at the sight of these tears; sympathy for misfortune is neutral ground, the purely human domain, on which all souls meet which are not completely hardened. But some among them find in these tears of Jesus a reason for suspecting His character. One of two things: either He did not have the friendship for Lazarus which he now affects to feel, or He did not really possess the miraculous power of which He claimed to have given the proof in the healing of the man born blind; in any case, there is something suspicious in His conduct. Some interpreters give a favorable meaning to this question of the Jews, ver. 37 (*Lücke, Tholuck, de Wette, Gumlich* and also, up to a certain point, *Keil*). But the evangelist identifies, by the very form of the expression (*some among them*), these Jews of ver. 37 with those of ver. 46. And with this sense it is not easy to understand the relation which can have existed between this question of the Jews and the new emotion of Jesus, ver. 38. *Strauss* finds it strange that these Jews do not appeal here to resurrec-

---

¹ ℵ D some Mnn. read και (*and*) before εδακρυσεν.

tions of the dead which Jesus had accomplished in Galilee, rather than to the healing of the man born blind. But it is precisely an evangelist of the second century who would not have failed to put into the mouth of the Jews an allusion to these resurrections, which were at that time well-known throughout all the Church by the reading of the Synoptics. The historical fidelity of the narrative of John appears precisely from the fact that the inhabitants of Jerusalem appeal to the last striking miracle accomplished by Jesus in this very city and before their eyes. This healing had occasioned so many discussions and so many different judgments that it naturally presents itself to their thought.

3. Jesus and Lazarus: vv. 38–44.

Vv. 38, 39. "*Jesus therefore, shuddering in himself again, comes to the sepulchre; it was a cave and a stone was placed before it. 39. Jesus says, Take away the stone. The sister of the dead man*[1] *Martha, says to him, Lord, by this time he stinketh; for he has been dead four days.*" The new inward disturbance which Jesus feels is evidently called forth by the malevolent remark of the Jews (ver. 37); John himself gives us to understand this by the *therefore* (ver. 38). But this agitation seems to have been less profound than the first, and more readily overcome. This very natural detail is a new proof of the fidelity of the narrative.

The sepulchre was a cave dug in the rock, either horizontally or vertically. The verb ἐπέκειτο signifies, in the first case, that the stone was placed *before* the entrance of the cave; in the second, that it was placed *on* its opening. Numerous tombs are seen around Jerusalem both of the one form and the other. If the tomb which is shown at the present day as that of Lazarus, was really such, it was of the second sort. It is a cave hollowed out in the rock into which one descends by a narrow staircase of twenty-six steps. *Robinson* has proved the non-authenticity of the tradition on this point, as on many others. The stones by which these caves were closed might easily be removed; they were designed only to keep off wild beasts. There is between the second movement of indignation in Jesus and the decisive command: *Take away the stone*, a relation analogous to that which we have noticed between the first emotion of this kind and the question: *Where have you laid him?* We can easily imagine the state of expectation into which this question threw the whole company.

Did the remark of Martha (ver. 39), proceed, as some interpreters think, from a feeling of incredulity. But could she who hoped for the return of her brother to life before the promise of Jesus (vv. 22, 23), have doubted after such a declaration? This is impossible. By this remark she does not by any means wish to prevent the opening of the sepulchre; she simply expresses the anxiety which is caused in her mind by the painful sensation about to be experienced by Jesus and the spectators because of one who was so near and dear to her. As the dead man's *sister*, she feels

---

[1] The MSS. are divided between τεθνηκοτος (T. R. with the Byzantines) and τετελευτηκοτος (א A B C D K L II).

a kind of embarrassment and confusion. We must recall to mind how closely the idea of defilement was connected, among the Jews, with that of death and corruption. Here, therefore, is an exclamation dictated by a feeling of respect for Him to whom she is speaking: *"Lord,"* and by a sort of delicacy for the person of him who is in question: *the sister of the dead man.* It has been thought (*Weiss, Keil*) that the affirmation of Martha: *by this time he stinketh*, was on her part only a supposition, since she justifies it logically by adding: *For he is there four days already.* But we must rather see in these words the declaration of a fact which she has herself ascertained by visiting the sepulchre; comp. ver. 31. The words: *For he is there . . . already*, indicate the cause, not the proof, of the fact which the care of the two sisters had not been able to prevent. This reflection, far from proving, as *Weiss* thinks, that Lazarus had not been embalmed, implies, on the contrary, that he had been, with all possible care, but only after the manner of the Jews. Among the Egyptians the entrails and everything which readily decays were removed, while among the Jews the embalming was limited to wrapping the body in perfumes, which could not long arrest corruption. The expectation of Jesus' arrival had certainly not prevented them, as some have supposed, from performing this ceremony. Does not ver. 44 show that Lazarus had his limbs enveloped with bandages like other dead persons (comp. xix. 40)? But even if Martha's remark did not arise from a feeling of incredulity, the fact indicated might nevertheless occasion in her a failing of faith at this decisive moment; so Jesus exhorts her to raise her faith to the whole height of the promise which He has made to her.

Vv. 40–42. *" Jesus says to her, Did I not say to thee, that if thou believest thou shalt see*[1] *the glory of God?* 41. *They took away the stone*[2] *therefore. And Jesus lifted up his eyes and said, Father, I thank thee that thou hast heard me.* 42. *As for myself, I knew indeed that thou dost always hear me ; but I said it because of the multitude who surround me, that they may believe that thou didst send me."* Some interpreters refer the words: *Did I not say . . . ?* to the conversation in vv. 23–27. And it is certainly, indeed, to the expressions: *He who believes on me* (vv. 27 and 26), and *Believest thou this?* (ver. 27) that our thoughts are turned by the words of Jesus: *If thou believest . . .* But the characteristic expression of our verse: *the glory of God,* is wanting in these declarations, while it constitutes the salient feature of the promise of ver. 4. It is therefore this last promise that Jesus especially recalls to Martha. He well knew that it had been reported to the two sisters by the messenger; it had formed the starting-point of the conversation of vv. 23–27, which was only its confirmation and development. The *glory of God* is here, exactly as in Rom. vi. 4, the splendid triumph of the omnipotence of God, in the service of His love, over death and corruption (ver. 39). This is the magnificent spectacle

---

[1] Instead of οψει which is read by T. R. with K U Γ II, 15 Mjj. read οψη.

[2] ℵ B C D L X: τον λιθον (*the stone*) simply. T. R. adds, with 9 Mjj. Byz. (E G H etc.), the words ου ην ο τεθνηκως κειμενος (*where the dead was laid*); A K II more briefly: ου ην (*where he was*).

which Jesus promises to Martha, and which He sets in opposition to the painful impressions which she apprehends for the bystanders and herself, when once the stone shall have been taken away. There is no reproach in the words: Did I not say . . .? as if Martha were wanting in faith in speaking as she did. In the presence of the manifest signs of dissolution already commenced, Jesus exhorts her to a supreme act of faith, by giving her His promise as a support. She has already climbed the arduous slopes of the mountain; only one last summit to reach, and the spectacle of the glory of God, of life triumphant over death, will display itself to her eyes. Man would always see in order to believe; Martha is called to give an example of the opposite course: to believe in order to see. These words of Jesus do not imply that He makes the fulfillment of His promise depend, as *Meyer*, *Weiss* and others think, on Martha's faith. He is now decidedly pledged and cannot withdraw. What He subordinates to the supreme act of faith which He demands of her, is not the miracle, it is the joy which she will have from it ("*see* the glory"). The bodily eye beholds only the external wonder; but the divine love putting itself at the service of man to triumph over death—this is a spectacle which one beholds only with the eyes of the soul. It was the inner sense for beholding it which Jesus had endeavored to form in Martha in the conversation which He had just had with her; He must not lose, at the decisive moment, the fruit of this effort. The received reading: *the stone from the place where the dead was laid*, seems to be a paraphrase. The Alexandrian text reads briefly: *the stone;* see our translation. This reading, however, does not easily explain the origin of the other two. May not that of A K Π: *the stone from the place where he was*, be the primitive text? Its brevity (οὗ ἦν) explains, on one side, the Byzantine gloss, and, on the other, the omission, in the Alexandrian documents, of this explanatory clause. Jesus *lifts his eyes:* the visible heaven is for man the most eloquent witness of the invisible wealth and power of God. By penetrating with His look its infinite depths, Jesus seeks inwardly the face of the Father; what more human! it is indeed in reality the Word made flesh (comp. xvii. 1). The miracle is already accomplished to the view of Jesus; this is the reason why He renders thanks as if for a thing which is done: *Thou hadst heard me.* He thus confirms the view pronounced by Martha with relation to His miracles (ver. 22); they are so many prayers heard. But what distinguishes His position from that of other divine messengers, who have accomplished similar works by the same means, is the perfect assurance of being heard, with which He addresses God. He draws freely, as Son, from the divine treasure. *Besser* admirably says: "No doubt, He performed all His miracles through faith, but through faith *which was peculiar to Him*, that of being the Son of God manifested in the flesh."

If Jesus expresses His gratitude aloud, as He does here, it is not, as He Himself adds, because there is anything extraordinary in the conduct of the Father towards Him on this occasion. This act of thanksgiving is anything but an exclamation wrested from Him by surprise at an exceptional hearing of prayer; constantly heard by the Father, He thanks Him continually. That which, at this solemn moment, impels Him to give thanks to His Father aloud, is the sight of the people who surround Him. He has prepared His disciples and the two sisters, in the special conversations with them, to behold and understand the work which He is about to do. He desires also to dispose the people whom His Father has unexpectedly gathered around this tomb, to behold *the glory of God*, that is to say, to see in the miracle, not only a wonder, but a sign. Otherwise the astonishment which they experience would be barren; it could not result in faith. Here is the reason why Jesus expresses aloud, at this moment, the sentiment of filial thankfulness which incessantly fills His heart. Criticism has called this prayer "a prayer of ostentation" (*Strauss, Weisse, Baur*), and has found in this circumstance a ground for suspecting the authenticity of the narrative. It has not grasped the meaning of the act. Jesus does not render thanks because of the people, but He *expresses aloud* His act of thanksgiving because of the people. The Jews had said of the healing of the man born blind: As an infraction of the Sabbath, this cannot be a divine work. By rendering thanks to God on this day in presence of all the people, even before performing the miracle, Jesus positively calls upon God to grant or to refuse Him His coöperation. In the face of such a prayer God must be recognized either as the guarantor of His mission or as the accomplice in His imposture. Comp. the test of Carmel in the life of Elijah, and the quite similar expression of Jesus Himself in Luke v. 22–24. If Lazarus rises and comes forth at the call of Jesus, it will be God who has displayed His arm; Jesus will be recognized as sent by Him. If not, truly let all His other miracles be attributed to Beelzebub, and let Him be declared an impostor! Such is the situation as Jesus' act of thanksgiving establishes it. It is interesting to compare this expression: *Thou hast heard me*, with the assertion of *Reville*, following *Scholten* and saying: "The fourth Gospel has no knowledge of Jesus praying as a man." (*Revue de théol.*, 1865, iii., p. 316.)

Vv. 43, 44. "*And after having spoken thus, he cried with a loud voice, Lazarus, come forth. 44. And*[1] *the dead man came forth, his feet and hands bound with bandages; and his face was wrapped in a napkin. Jesus says to them, Loose him and let him*[2] *go.*" The loud voice is the expression of a determined will which has the feeling of its own sovereignty. As one awakens a man from sleep by calling him by his name, so Jesus brings back Lazarus from death which is only a more profound sleep (vv. 11, 12) by loudly calling him. "Undoubtedly these external signs are only, as *Hengstenberg* says, for the persons present; the power of raising to life resides, not in the voice, but in the will which expresses itself through it;" we will rather say: in the power of God of which Jesus disposes by virtue of the hearing of His prayer. In speaking to the daughter of Jairus and to the young man of Nain, He simply said: *Arise*, or: *Awake*, because they were lying on the bed or the bier; here

---

[1] Και is wanting in B C L Sah. It is found in all the other Mjj. (including ℵ) and Vss.

[2] B C L read αυτον after αφετε.

He says: *Come forth,* because Lazarus is shut within the sepulchre. The simplicity and brevity of these two words: δεῦρο ἔξω (literally, *Here without!*) form a magnificent contrast with their efficacy. How can *Weiss* assert that the voice of Jesus does nothing but recall *to the light* Lazarus whom God had raised to life? Do not the words of vv. 19, 20 show us the power of God really acting through Jesus, and Jesus Himself raising the dead to life by this power of which He is the organ?

The act of *coming forth,* ver. 44, presents no difficulty, either because the bandages by which the shroud was fastened were sufficiently loose to allow movements, or because each limb was wrapped separately, as was the practice among the Egyptians. The detail: *His face was wrapped about with a napkin,* is the pencil-stroke of an eye-witness and recalls the ineffaceable impression produced on the bystanders by this spectacle of a living man in the costume of the dead. While they remained motionless with astonishment, Jesus, with perfect composure and as if nothing extraordinary had occurred, invites them to participate in the work: Each to his office; I have raised to life; it is for you to loose him. The command: *Let him go,* recalls that which Jesus gave to Jairus and his wife after having raised their child to life. Nothing disturbs His calmness after these unparalleled works which He has just accomplished. The term ὑπάγειν, *go away,* has something victorious in it, altogether like the command of Jesus to the impotent man who was healed: *Take up thy bed, and walk!*

The resurrection of Lazarus is the miracle of friendship, as the wonder of Cana is that of filial piety; and this, not only because the affection of Jesus for the family of Bethany was the cause of it, but especially because Jesus performed it with a distinct consciousness that, in raising His friend, He was rendering more certain and hastening His own death (comp. vv. 8–16 and vv. 33–38). The self-devotion of friendship rises here to the point of heroism. John had understood this. This thought is the soul of his narrative; it appears clearly from the following passage.

The effect produced by the miracle: vv. 45–47

1. And first, the immediate effect on the spectators:

Vv. 45, 46. "*Many therefore*[1] *of the Jews, those who had come*[2] *to Mary and had seen that which*[3] *he had done, believed on him.* 46. *But some of them went away to the Pharisees and told them that which*[3] *Jesus had done.*" Again a division among the spectators, and a still more profound one than on any of the previous occasions. For it penetrated even into the midst of the Jewish party. It is impossible, indeed, to include the *some* of whom ver. 46 speaks in the class of the πολλοί, *many,* of ver. 45, and to ascribe to them, as a consequence, a benevolent intention in the step which they take before the enemies of Jesus, as *Origen* thought. There is an antithesis between the two subjects: *many* and *some,* as between the two verbs:

---

[1] ℵ: δε instead of ουν.
[2] D: των ελθοντων instead of οι ελθοντες.
[3] Instead of α, ο is read in B C D in ver. 45, and in C D M in ver. 46.

believed (ver. 45) and *went away* (ver. 46). Only it must be carefully noticed that the first (the πολλοί, of ver. 45) are not merely a part of the visitors of Martha and Mary, but include them all; this is indicated by the participles in the nominative with the article οἱ: *Those who had come and who had seen.* In the opposite case, the participles ought to be in the genitive: many *of those* who came and saw. The *some* of ver. 46 are therefore other Jews (ἐξ αὐτῶν refers to the word Ἰουδαίων alone), *who saw* without having *come*, either inhabitants of Bethany, or visitors who were not with Mary when she had run to the tomb and who had not been present at the scene. This explains the difficult expression: "who came *to Mary*." Why to Mary only? Is she named here as the one best known (*Weiss*) or as the most afflicted (*Luthardt, Keil*)? Both of these explanations are very unnatural. She is named because it was *near her* that the Jews who came found themselves when they went to the sepulchre and *with her* that they had been witnesses of the miracle (comp. vv. 31, 33).

2. The more remote effect of the resurrection of Lazarus: vv. 47–53.

Vv. 47–50. " *The chief priests and Pharisees therefore gathered an assembly, and they said, What shall we do? For this man does many miracles.* 48. *If we let him alone, all will believe on him, and the Romans will come and they will destroy both*[1] *our place and nation.* 49. *But one of them, Caiaphas, who was high-priest of that year, said to them: You know nothing at all,* 50 *and you do not consider*[2] *that it is better for us*[3] *that one man should die for the people, and that the whole nation should not perish.*" The resurrection of Lazarus was not the cause of Jesus' death; but it occasioned and hastened the decree of His condemnation. The cup was full; this made it overflow. The Pharisees are specially named because they were the instigators of this hostile meeting (ver. 46; ix. 45); but it was the chief priests who officially convoked it. The absence of the article before συνέδριον might be explained by supposing that John is here using this word as a proper name. It is more natural, however, to take the term in the general meaning of *assembly* or *council*, which it has also in the profane Greek. The present ποιοῦμεν, "what *do* we " takes the place of a future; it makes prominent the imminence of the danger. " It is absolutely necessary to do something, but what?" Ὅτι: *because of the fact that*. "His doing must decide ours." The fear expressed in ver. 48 was not without foundation. The least commotion might serve the Romans as a pretext for depriving the people of Israel of the remnant of independence which they still enjoyed, and in that case what would become of the power of the Sanhedrim? The disquietude of the rulers has reference especially to the destruction of *their* power. This is emphatically expressed by the position of the pronoun ἡμῶν (*of us, our*) before the two substantives. Jesus reproduced this thought of the rulers in the words of the laborers in the vineyard, Matt. xxi. 38: " *Let us kill him and secure the inheritance.*" Jerusalem, Israel, belong to them. " *Our place* " natur-

---

[1] D K Π 10 Vss. omit και before τον τοπον.
[2] ℵ B D L some Mnn. Orig. read λογιζεσθε instead of διαλογιζεσθε.
[3] The MSS. are divided between ημιν (*us*) (T. R. with A E G etc.), and υμιν (*you*) (B D L M X T). ℵ omits both.

752 / Unbelief Develops in Israel

ally designates the capital, as the seat of their government, rather than the temple (*Lücke, de Wette*, etc.), or the whole of Judea (*Bengel*). In the first sense, this term is also more naturally connected with the following expression: *our nation;* that which we govern from this place. As they speak from a political point of view, contrasting nation with nation, they employ the term ἔθνος, and not λαός, which is the name of honor for the people of Israel.

The expression: *one of them,* hardly allows us to suppose that Caiaphas was presiding over the assembly. Although, indeed, it seems now to be proved that the high-priest was at the same time president of the Sanhedrim (*Schürer, Lehrb. der N. T. Zeitgesch.*, p. 411), we must not forget that this was not a regular meeting (ver. 47). In the midst of a company of irresolute spirits, who are wavering between conscience and interest, an energetic man, who boldly denies the rights of conscience and unscrupulously puts forward reasons of state, has always the chance of carrying his point. If this had occurred in the best days of the theocracy, the expression: *High-priest of that year*, would be incomprehensible; for, according to the law, the pontificate was for life. But, since the Roman dominion, the masters of the country fearing the power which a permanent office gives, had adopted the custom of frequently replacing one high-priest by another. According to Josephus (*Antiq.*, xviii. 2. 2), the Roman governor Valerius Gratus "took away the high-priestly office from Ananus and conferred it on Ishmael; then, having deposed the latter a little while afterwards, he established as high-priest Eleazar, the son of Ananus: after a year had elapsed, he deposed this last person and nominated Simon in his place; he held the office only one year, and Joseph, surnamed Caiaphas, was made his successor." Caiaphas remained in office from the year 25 to the year 36 of our era; consequently, the entire ministry of Jesus was passed under his pontificate. These frequent changes justify the expression of the evangelist, and deprive criticism of the right to assert that the author of our Gospel was ignorant of the fact that the high-priesthood, from its foundation, was a life-office. But if Caiaphas had been high-priest for eleven official years, how could St. John use three times (vv. 49–51; xviii. 13) the expression: "High-priest *of that year?*" We find the pronoun ἐκεῖνος used here in the particularly emphatic sense which it has so frequently in this Gospel; not, that more remote year, in opposition to some other nearer one, but, that *unique*, decisive year, in which the Messiah was put to death and the priesthood, with the theocracy, came to its end. The apostrophe of Caiaphas to his colleagues has a certain character of rudeness. This feature, as *Hengstenberg* observes, agrees with the behavior of the Sadducean sect to which Caiaphas belonged; comp. Acts iv. 6 and v. 17, and Josephus, *Antiq.*, xx. 9. 1. In *Bell. Jud.*, ii. 8, 14, this historian says: "The Pharisees are friendly to each other, and cultivate harmony among themselves with a view to the common benefit; but the manners of the Sadducees are much more rude both towards each other and towards their equals, whom they treat as strangers." *Hengstenberg* takes διαλογίζεσθε in an intransitive sense and the following ὅτι in the sense of *because: You do not consider, seeing that it is more advantageous that . . .* " But it is more natural to make the clause which begins with ὅτι the content of διαλογίζεσθε : " You know nothing and *you do not consider that . . .*" The reading διαλογίζεσθε: "You do not know how to clear up by reasoning . . . " is preferable to the simple λογίζεσθε which results from negligence or from a mistaken correction. The reading ἡμῖν, *for us,* has fundamentally the same sense as the variant ὑμῖν, *for you;* but it somewhat better disguises the egoistic and personal character of the opinion expressed (comp. the ἡμῶν of ver. 48). The use of the terms λαός and ἔθνος in ver. 50 is not arbitrary. The first (corresponding to the Hebrew *am*) designates the multitude of individuals forming the theocratic nation, in opposition to the single individual who is to perish, while the second, answering to *goi,* designates Israel as a political body in contrast with the foreign nationality, that of the Romans.

Vv. 51, 52. *" Now he did not say this of himself; but being high-priest of that year, he prophesied that Jesus should die for the nation, 52 and not for the nation only, but also that he might gather in one body the children of God who are scattered abroad."* This opinion of the high-priest was made especially remarkable by the contrast between the divine truth which it expressed and the diabolical design which inspired it. The evangelist calls attention to this. Some interpreters (*Luthardt, Brückner*) deny that John ascribes the gift of prophecy here to the high-priest as such. It was not as high-priest, but as high-priest *of that year,* that Caiaphas uttered this prophetic declaration. But the relation between the present participle ὤν, *being,* and the aorist, προεφήτευσεν, *he prophesied,* leads us naturally to the idea that the evangelist attaches to the office of Caiaphas the prophetic character of the words which he uttered at this moment. This must be acknowledged even if we are to find here only a Jewish superstition. In the Old Testament, the normal centre of the theocratic people is, not the royal office, but the priesthood. In all the decisive moments for the life of the people, it is the high-priest who is the organ of God for passing over to the people the decision with which its salvation is connected (Exod. xxviii. 30; Num. xxvii. 21; 1 Sam. xxx. 7 ff.). It is true that this prerogative came not from a prophetic gift, but from the possession of a mysterious power, the Urim and Thummim. It is also true that from the time of the captivity, and even from the reign of Solomon, there is no longer any question of this power (see Keil, *Bibl. Archæol.*, p. 191). But the high-priest nevertheless remained by reason of his very office the head of the theocratic body, and this in spite of the moral contrast which might exist between the spirit of his office and his personal character. If the heart of the high-priest was in harmony with his office, his heart became the normal organ of the divine decision. But if there was opposition in this personage between the disposition of his heart and the holiness of his office, it must be expected that, as in the present case, the divine oracle would be seen coming from this consecrated mouth in the form of the most diabolical maxim. What, indeed, more worthy of the Divine Spirit than to condemn His degenerate organ thus to utter the truth of God at the very moment when he was speaking as the organ of his own particular interest! Without attributing to Caiaphas a permanent prophetic gift, John means to say that, at this supreme moment for the theocracy and for humanity, it was not without the participation of the Divine activity that the most profound mystery of the plan of God was proclaimed by him in the form of the most detestable maxim. John has already more than once remarked how the adversaries of Jesus, when speaking derisively, were prophesying in spite of themselves: "*No one knows whence he is*" (vii. 27). "*Will he go and teach the Greeks*" (vii. 35)? If the devil often travesties the words of God, it pleases God sometimes to parody those of the devil, by giving to them an unexpected truth. This "divine irony" manifested itself in the highest degree on this occasion, which was the prelude to the accomplishment of the most divine mystery under the form of the most monstrous act.

According to some interpreters, the ὅτι is not a direct complement of the verb *he prophesied*. *Meyer:* " he prophesied *as to the fact that* . . . " *Luthardt, Weiss, Keil:* " he prophesied, seeing that *really* Jesus was to . . . " Ver. 52 is what has led them to these explanations, because this verse goes in fact beyond the import of the saying of Caiaphas. But it is quite unnatural to take this word: *he prophesied*, in an absolute sense: John certainly did not mean to insist so especially on this idea of prophecy. The meaning is simply: " he declared prophetically *that* to . . . " As to ver. 52, it is an explanatory appendix, which John adds in order to indicate that in the divine thought the force of the expression: *one for all*, had a far wider application than that which Caiaphas himself gave it. John never forgets his Greek readers, and he loses no occasion of recalling to them their part in the accomplishment of the divine promises. If we take into consideration the parallelism between this ver. 52 and the saying of x. 16, we shall have no hesitation in applying the term *children of God* to heathen predisposed to faith through the revelation of the Logos (i. 4, 10); the sense is the same as that in which John uses the expressions: *to be of God* (viii. 47), *to be of the truth* (xix. 37). The term *children of God* naturally involves an anticipation; it designates the actual condition of these future believers from the point of view of its result which was to come. *Meyer, Luthardt* and others prefer to explain this term from the standpoint of the divine predestination. But we should be obliged to infer from this that all the rest of the heathen are the objects of an opposite predestination.

Ver. 53. "*From this day forth, therefore, they took counsel together* [1] *to the end that they might put him to death.*" The *therefore* intimates that the proposition of Caiaphas was accepted (*Luthardt*), probably in silence and without the intervention of an official vote. From this day forward, a permanent conspiracy was organized against the life of Jesus. The daily conferences of His adversaries became, according to the expression of *Lange,* " meetings of Messianic murder." There was no more hesitation

---

[1] Instead of συνεβουλευσαντο, ℵ B D 4 Mnn. Orig. (once) read εβουλευσαντο.

as to the end; the indecision was henceforth only with reference to the time and the means. Such was the importance of this meeting and consequently, in an indirect way, that of the resurrection of Lazarus.

3. The sojourn at Ephraim: vv. 54–57.

Jesus is forced to withdraw to a retired place. On their part, the rulers take a new step in the path on which they have now entered.

Vv. 54–57. "*Jesus therefore abode no more openly among the Jews; but he departed thence and went into the country near to the wilderness, into a city called Ephraim;* [1] *and he remained* [2] *there with his* [3] *disciples. 55. Now the Passover of the Jews was at hand; and many went up to Jerusalem out of the country before the Passover, to purify themselves. 56. They sought for Jesus therefore and said among themselves, as they stood in the temple, What think you? Do you think that he will not come to the feast? 57. Now the chief priests and the Pharisees had also* [4] *given commandment* [5] *that, if any one knew where he was, he should declare it, in order that they might take him.*" Ephraim is mentioned sometimes with Bethel (2 Chron. xiii. 19; Joseph. *Bell. Jud.* iv. 9. 9). This city was therefore a few leagues northward of Jerusalem; according to Eusebius, eight miles, according to Jerome, twenty miles to the northeast of that capital. This locality, by reason of its retired situation and its proximity to the desert, was favorable to the design of Jesus. He might in the solitude prepare His disciples for His approaching end and, if He was pursued, He might retire into the desert. This desert is, as *Lange* says, the northern extremity of the barren strip of country by which the plateau of the mountains of Judah and Benjamin is separated throughout its whole length from the valley of the Jordan and the Dead Sea. From this place Jesus could, at will, on the approach of the Passover, either join the pilgrims from Galilee who went directly to Jerusalem through Samaria, or go down to Jericho, in the plain of the Jordan, to put Himself at the head of the caravan which came from Peræa. We know from the Synoptics that He took the latter course. Μετά (ver. 54) is not synonymous with σύν; the meaning is: "He confined Himself there to the society of His disciples;" and not only: He was there with them.

Ἐκ τῆς χώρας (ver. 55) does not refer to the *country* of Ephraim in particular (*Grotius, Olshausen*) but to the *country region* in general, in opposition to the capital (ver. 54): "They went up from different parts of the country." The law did not prescribe special purifications before the Passover; but, in several passages of the Old Testament, it was ordained that the people should purify themselves on the eve of any important occasion (Gen. xxxv. 2; Exod. xix. 10, 11, etc.). This principle had naturally been applied to the Passover feast (2 Chron. xxx. 16–20).

Ver. 56 vividly depicts the restless curiosity of these country people who, assembled in groups in the temple, were discussing with reference

---

[1] ℵ L It. Vulg. Iren. read Εφρεμ instead of Εφραιμ.

[2] ℵ R L Orig. read εμεινεν instead of διετριβεν.

[3] B D I L Γ Δ omit αυτου.

[4] 11 Mjj. (ℵ A B etc.) 35 Mnn. It. Vulg. Syr. Cop. Orig. omit καί, which is read by T. R. with D EG H I S Γ Mnn.

[5] ℵ B I M 3 Mnn. Orig. read εντολας instead of εντολην.

to the approaching arrival of Jesus; comp. vii. 12.—'Εστηκότες, *standing*, in the attitude of expectation.—Ὅτι does not depend on δοκεῖ; it is more natural to separate the two clauses and to make two distinct questions. The aorist ἔλθῃ may perfectly well refer to an act which is to be accomplished in the immediate future.

To the other grounds which rendered the coming of Jesus improbable, ver. 57 adds a new one, which is more special. It would not have been very difficult for the authorities to discover the place of Jesus' retreat. The edict which is here spoken of was therefore rather a means of intimidating Him and His followers, and of accustoming the people to regard Him as a dangerous and criminal person. It is a new link in the series of hostile measures so well described by St. John from chap. v. onward; comp. v. 16, 18; vii. 32; ix. 22; xi. 53; and this is indicated by the καί, *also*, in the T. R.; perhaps the word was omitted in the Alexandrian text, as not being understood. The chief priests were the authority from which the decree officially emanated; the evangelist adds the *Pharisees*, because this party was the real author of it. Comp. vii. 45. In the Babylonian Gemara (edited from ancient traditions about 550) the following passage is found: "Tradition reports that on the evening of the Passover Jesus was crucified (hanged), and that this took place after an officer had during forty days publicly proclaimed: This man who by his deception has seduced the people ought to be crucified. Whosoever can allege anything in his defense, let him come forward and speak. But no one found anything to say in his defense. He was hanged therefore on the evening of the Passover" (Lightfoot, *Hor. Hebr. et. Talm.*, p. 490). This remarkable passage may be compared with this of John. In both, we discover, a few weeks before the Passover, a public proclamation on the part of the Sanhedrim, relative to the approaching condemnation of Jesus. On the other hand, the difference between the two accounts is so marked that one of them cannot have arisen from the other.

On the resurrection of Lazarus

"This narrative," says *Deutinger*,[1] "is distinguished among all the narrations of the fourth Gospel by its peculiar vivacity and its dramatic movement. The characters are drawn by a hand at once firm and delicate. Nowhere is the relation of Christ to His disciples set forth in so life-like a manner; we are initiated by this narrative into that intimate intercourse, that affectionate interchange of feelings and thoughts, which existed between the Master and His own followers; the disciples are described in the most attractive way; we see them in their simple frankness and noble devotion. The Jews themselves, of whom we know scarcely anything in our gospel except their obstinate resistance to the efforts of Jesus, show themselves here in a less unfavorable aspect, as friends of the two afflicted sisters; the man is discovered in the Jew. But above all, how distinct and delicate is the sketching of the character of the two women; with what nicety and what psychological depth is the difference in their conduct described!" In these

---

[1] *Das Reich Gottes nach dem Apostel Johannes*, 1862, vol. ii., p. 62.

characteristics of the narrative which are so well summed up by the German writer, we find the first proof of its intrinsic truthfulness: "invented stories are not of this sort." And especially, it was not thus that invented stories were formed in the second century; we have the proof of this in the Apocryphal narratives.

The reality of the event here related appears also from its connection with the whole course of the previous and subsequent history of Jesus. The evangelist is fully conscious of the consequences of the event which he describes; he distinctly marks them in the course of his narrative: ver. 47 (*therefore*) and ver. 53 (*from that day forth*). Comp. xii. 9–11, 17–19. *Renan* calls the resurrection of Lazarus "a necessary link in the story of the final catastrophe." The former, therefore, is not a fictitious event, if the latter is not. Finally, this narrative contains with exactness a mass of details which would be in manifest contradiction to the aim of the narrative, provided the latter were composed artificially with the purpose of teaching and illustrating the speculation of the Logos; thus the tears of Jesus, the moral and even physical agitation which is attributed to Him, His prayer for the securing of the miracle, and His thanksgiving for the hearing of the prayer. Nothing can be more truly human than all these features of the story, which are altogether the opposite of the metaphysics of Philo.

Objection is made, 1. That such a miracle is absolutely inconceivable, especially if we explain the words: *by this time he stinketh*, in the sense of dissolution already begun. Herein perhaps lies what has led some interpreters, who are defenders of the reality of the miracle (*Weiss, Keil*) to find in these words only a logical supposition on Martha's part. "The bond between the soul and the body," says *Weiss*, "was not yet finally broken so as to allow the beginning of dissolution." *Reuss* does not admit this method of cheapening the miracle. "The odor of the decaying body" seems to him to be an essential feature of the narrative which was designed to illustrate the declaration: "I am the resurrection and the life." And he is the one who is right. When we shall know thoroughly what life is and what death is, we shall be able to decide what is suited to this domain and what is not. While waiting for this, we must say: He who has created the organic cell within the inorganic matter is not incapable of re-establishing life within the inanimate substance.

Objectors allege, 2. The omission of this miracle in the Synoptics. But in the Synoptics themselves are there not many differences of the same kind? Has not each one of them preserved elements of the highest interest which are omitted in the others? They are collections of particular anecdotes, of isolated or orally transmitted events. The formation of these collections was affected by accidental circumstances of which we are ignorant. Thus Luke alone has preserved for us the account of the resurrection of the young man of Nain. It is to be observed, moreover, that the three Synoptical narratives are divided into two great cycles: the events of the prophetic ministry of Jesus in Galilee, and those of the week of the Passion in Jerusalem; they only glance at the intermediate sojourn in Peræa. Now the resurrection of Lazarus belongs to this epoch of transition and for this reason it may easily have lost its place in the general tradition. Luke himself, says *Hase*, "has only his fragmentary story respecting the two sisters (x. 38 ff.), the prelude of this one, while ignorant of what belongs to their persons and their abode" (p. 512). Finally, the fact which can more particularly explain the omission of this incident in the Apostolic tradition, from which, for the most part, our Synoptic narratives came, is the hesitation which might have been felt either to open to the view of the public an interior life so sacred as that of the family beloved by Jesus, or of exposing the members of that family themselves to the vengeance of the rulers, who at the time of the first preaching of the Gospel were still the masters of the country. Comp. xii. 10, where they deliberate as to putting Lazarus to death at the same time with Jesus. The case stood thus until the destruction of Jerusalem and the fall of the Sanhedrim. This is the reason why John, when these events were once consummated, could feel free to draw forth this scene from the silence into which it had fallen since the day of Pentecost. *Meyer*, *Weiss* and others object that the Synoptical authors, writing probably at a time when the members of the Bethany family were already dead, would not have allowed themselves to be stopped by this consideration. But they forget that the omission was occasioned in the oral tradition from the earliest times of the Church, and that it had passed quite naturally into the written redaction of the primitive proclamation of the Gospel story, that is to say, into our Synoptic Gospels.

Moreover, the explanations which have been attempted in order to eliminate this miracle from the circle of the authentic facts of the life of Jesus, present, none of them, any degree of probability whatever.

1. The so-called natural explanation of *Paulus, Gabler* and *A. Schweizer.* In consequence of the message of ver. 3, Jesus judged the malady to be by no means dangerous; then, after having received notice again (*Paulus* reckons as many as four messages), He comes to see that the matter is a mere lethargy. Having reached the sepulchre, He observed in the supposed deceased person some signs of life; whereupon He gave thanks (vv. 41, 42) and called Lazarus forth. The latter revived by the coolness of the sepulchre, by the odor of the perfumes, and at the moment of the opening of the tomb, by the warmth of the external air, rose up in full life. Thus *Paulus* and *Gabler*. According to *A. Schweizer*, the confidence of Jesus in the cure of His friend was founded only on His faith in the divine aid promised in a general way to His cause; and the pretended miracle was only the happy coincidence of this religious confidence with the circumstance that Lazarus was not really dead. This explanation has not been judged more severely by any one than by *Strauss*[1] and *Baur*.[2] The former has shown, in opposition to Paulus and Gabler, that the expressions by which Jesus announces the resurrection of Lazarus are too positive to be only conjectures founded upon uncertain symptoms, and that the meaning of the entire narrative, in the thought of the narrator, is and can be only that which every reader finds in it: the resurrection of Lazarus, who was dead, by the miraculous power of Jesus. As to the manner in which Schweizer treats our Gospel in general and this passage in particular, the following is Baur's judgment: "Destitute of all feeling for the unity of the whole, he tears our Gospel to shreds, that he may eliminate as superstitious interpolations all things of which he does not succeed in giving a shallow rationalistic explanation, and may leave all which he allows to remain to the marvellous action of chance." These last words are especially applicable to the opinion of Schweizer respecting this miracle.

But what explanations do these two critics oppose to this of their predecessors?

2. The *mythical* explanation of *Strauss.* The Old Testament related resurrections of dead persons effected by mere prophets; the Christian legend could do

---

[1] *Vie de Jésus*, t. ii., pp. 154–165.   [2] *Theol. Jahrb.*, vol. iii., 1844.

no less than ascribe to the Messiah miracles of the same kind. But is it really to be admitted that the legend succeeded in producing a narrative so admirably shaded and in creating personages so finely drawn? "One cannot understand," says *Renan* justly, "how a popular creation should have come to take its place in a framework of recollections which are so personal as those which are connected with the relations of Jesus to the family of Bethany." Moreover, legend idealizes; how could it ever have invented a Christ moved even to the inmost depths of His being and shedding tears before the tomb of the friend whom He was going to raise to life? Then is not *Baur* right as against Strauss, when he says: "If a mythical tradition of this sort had really been spread abroad in the Church, it would not have failed to enter, with so many other similar ones, into the Synoptic narrative. It is contrary to all probability that so important a miracle, to which was attributed a decisive influence on the final catastrophe, should have remained a local legend restricted to a very limited circle." Notwithstanding these difficulties, *Réville* "feels no embarrassment" in explaining the history of Lazarus by the mythical process. The legend meant to represent by Lazarus the Jewish proletariat (comp. Luke xvi. 20), which Jesus rescues from its spiritual death by loving it and weeping over it. "He bent over this tomb (Israelitish pauperism!) crying out to Lazarus: Come forth, and come to me! and Lazarus came forth pale . . . tottering."[1] We may not discuss such fancies. *Renan* judges them no less severely than ourselves: "Expedients of theologians at their wits' end," he says, "saving themselves by allegory, myth, symbol" (p. 508). There is, above all, one circumstance which ought to prevent any serious critic from attributing to this narrative a legendary origin. Myths of this sort are fictions isolated from one another; but we have seen how the story of the resurrection of Lazarus belongs thoroughly within the organism of the fourth Gospel. The work of John is evidently of one cast. With regard to such an evangelist, criticism is irresistibly driven to this dilemma: historian or artist? It is the merit of Baur to have understood this situation, and, since by reason of his dogmatic premises he could not admit the first alternative, to have frankly declared himself in favor of the second.

3. The *speculative* explanation of Baur, according to which our narrative is a fictitious representation designed to give a body to the metaphysical thesis formulated in ver. 25: "*I am the resurrection and the life.*" This explanation suits the idea which Baur forms of our Gospel, which, according to him, is altogether only a composition of an ideal character. But is it compatible with the simplicity, the candor, the prosaic character, and if we may be allowed the expression, the common-place of the whole narrative? From the one end to the other, the situations are described for their own sake and without the least tendency to idealize (comp. for example, the end of the chapter: the sojourn at Ephraim, the proclamation of the Sanhedrim, the conversations of the pilgrims to Jerusalem). Still more, the narrative offers features which are completely anti-rational and anti-speculative. We have shown this: this Jesus who groans and weeps is the opposite of a metaphysical creation. The very offense which these features of the narrative cause to Baur's mind, prove this. The products of the intellect are transparent to the intellect. The more mysterious and unexpected these features are, the more is it manifest that they were drawn from reality. The feeling is impressed on every reader

---

[1] *Revue germanique*, Dec. 1st, 1863, p. 613.

that the author himself seriously believes in the reality of the fact which he relates, and that he does not think of inventing. When Plato comes to clothe his elevated doctrines with the brilliant veil of myths, we feel that he himself hovers above his creation, that his mind has freely chosen this form of teaching and plays with it. Here, on the contrary, the author is himself under the sway of the fact related; his heart is penetrated by it, his entire personality is laid hold of. If he created, he must be regarded as the first dupe of his own fiction.

4. The more recent critics turn in general towards another mode of explanation. *Weisse* had already expressed the idea that our narrative might be merely a parable related by Jesus and that tradition had transformed it into a real fact. The idea reappears at the present day in *Keim, Schenkel, Holtzmann*, etc. It is the parable of the beggar Lazarus (Luke xvi.), which has given occasion to our narrative; the author of our Gospel drew from it the theme of his representation. *Renan* imagines a similar comparison. He explained originally the resurrection of Lazarus by a pious fraud, to which Jesus Himself was not a stranger. "The friends of Jesus desired a great miracle which should make a strong impression upon the unbelief of Jerusalem. . . . Lazarus, yet pale from his sickness, had himself wrapped with bandages like a dead person and shut up in his family tomb. . . Jesus desired once more to see him whom He had loved. . . " The rest is easily understood. Renan excuses Jesus: "In that impure city of Jerusalem, He was no longer Himself. . . . In despair, driven to extremity. . . He yielded to the torrent. He submitted to the miracles which public opinion demanded of Him, rather than performed them." "No enemy of the Son of man," says *Hase* rightly, "has ever declared anything worse against Jesus, than that which this romantic well-wisher has here said." At present, Renan, yielding the general feeling of reprobation which this explanation aroused, thinks that in a conversation of Mary and Martha with Jesus, they told Him how the resurrection of a dead person would be necessary to bring the triumph of His cause and that Jesus answered them: "If Lazarus himself were to come back to life, they would not believe it." This saying became afterwards the subject of singular mistakes. . . . The supposition in fact was changed . . . ; tradition attributed to Mary and Martha a sick brother whom Jesus had caused to go forth from the tomb. In a word, the misapprehension from which our narrative springs resembles one of those cock-and-bull stories which are so frequent in the little towns of the East (13th ed., pp. 372–374). For a complete refutation, we will only call attention to the point that the narrative is of a fact which is just the opposite of the idea expressed by the saying which is said to have furnished the text for it. The idea of *Weisse* is wrecked against difficulties which are no less serious. There is nothing in common between the parable of Luke xvi. and our narrative except the name of Lazarus, "very common among the Jews" (*Hase*). The entire parable has as its starting-point the poverty and complete destitution of Lazarus. In the story of John, on the contrary, the brother of Martha and Mary is surrounded by friends, cared for, in the enjoyment of consideration and competence. There, Abraham refuses to allow Lazarus to leave Hades and reappear here on earth. Here, Lazarus returns to the earth and is restored to his sisters and friends. The result of this return to life is that many Jews, until now unbelieving, "believe on Jesus," a point which is directly contradictory to the last words of Jesus in the parable. So *Reuss* concludes the discussion by saying: "It must be acknowledged that all the attempts to set aside the miracle are arbitrary. No

explanation of all those which have been proposed bears in itself a character of probability and simplicity such that one is tempted to substitute it for the traditional form of the narrative."

We add further one general observation: In its first phase, the apostolic preaching confined itself to proclaiming this great fact: Jesus is risen. This was the foundation on which the apostles built up the Church. The detailed scenes of Jesus' ministry might indeed play a part in the particular conversations, but the great official proclamation did not place anything beside the death and resurrection of the Messiah, the facts on which rested the salvation of the world. Any particular miracle was a fact too accidental and secondary compared with these, to have the importance attached to it which we, from our historical and critical point of view, are tempted to give to the mention or the omission of it. We have one of the most striking examples of this in the silence of the three Synoptics and of John himself respecting one of the most important and most undeniable facts of the evangelical history: that of the appearance of Jesus to the five hundred brethren, mentioned by Paul in 1 Cor. xv. 6. After this let one argue, if he will, from the silence of one, two, or even three evangelical writings against the reality of a fact of the evangelical history! *Spinoza*, according to the testimony of Bayle, is said to have declared to his friends, "that if he could have persuaded himself of the resurrection of Lazarus, he would have dashed in pieces his own system and embraced without repugnance the common faith of Christians." Let the reader take up anew the narrative of John and read it again without any preconceived opinion ... the conviction to which the pantheistic philosopher could not come will form itself spontaneously within him; and on the testimony of this narrative, every feature of which bears the stamp of truth, he will simply accept a fact which criticism endeavors in vain to do away by means of a series of attempts of which every one is the denial of the one that preceded it.

2

John 12:1-36

THE LAST DAYS OF THE MINISTRY OF JESUS

This section includes three parts: 1. The supper of Jesus at Bethany: vv. 1–11. 2. His entry into Jerusalem: vv. 12–19. 3. The last scene of His ministry in the temple: vv. 20–36.

These three facts are selected by the evangelist as forming the transition from the public ministry of Jesus to His Passion. This appears, in the first part, from the discontent of Judas, the prelude of His treason, and from the response of Jesus announcing His approaching death; in the second, from ver. 19, which shows the necessity in which the rulers found themselves, after Palm-day, of rendering homage to Jesus or of ridding themselves of Him. Finally, in the third, from the entire discourse of Jesus in answer to the step taken by the Greeks, and from His final farewell to the Jewish nation, ver. 36. In the first two divisions, the evangelist at the same time sets forth the influence which the resurrection of Lazarus had upon the course of things as he describes it: vv. 2, 9–11,

17–19. Thus all things in this narrative, though apparently fragmentary, are in reality closely linked together. *Luthardt* rightly says: "This chapter is at once a closing and a preparation."

1. *The Supper at Bethany:* vv. 1–11

In the presence of the great struggle of whose approach every one has a presentiment, the devotion of the friends of Jesus becomes loftier; by way of counter-stroke, the national hostility, which has its representative even among the Twelve, breaks out in this inmost circle; Jesus announces to the traitor with perfect gentleness the approaching result of his enmity towards Him.

Ver. 1. "*Six days before the Passover, Jesus came therefore to Bethany where Lazarus*[1] *was whom he had raised from the dead.*" It would seem from the Synoptics that Jesus came directly to Jerusalem from Peræa, passing through Jericho. In order to bring them into agreement with John, it is enough to suppose that Jesus descended from Ephraim into the valley of the Jordan and rejoined before Jericho the great caravan of pilgrims who came from Galilee through Peræa. He thus took, in the reverse way, the same road which Epiphanius afterwards traversed—who relates to us "that he went up from Jericho to the plateau with a man who accompanied him across the desert, from Bethel to Ephraim." In truth, I do not understand why this so simple hypothesis should shock the impartiality of *Meyer*. He presents as an objection the statement in xi. 54; but the time of silence was now past for Jesus. We know from Luke that already before entering into Jericho Jesus was surrounded by a considerable multitude (xviii. 36), that he passed the night at the house of Zacchæus (xix. 1 ff.), and that the expectation of all was excited in the highest degree (xix. 11; Matt. xx. 20 ff.). The distance from Jericho to Bethany might be passed over in five or six hours. The main part of the caravan continued its journey even to Jerusalem on the same day, while Jesus and His disciples stopped at Bethany. This halt is not mentioned by the Synoptics; there is no reason for calling it in question. Very often one or two of the Synoptics present before us similar vacancies, which can only be filled by the aid of the third. Twice, a case of this kind is presented in the narrative of the following days: Mark xi. 11–15 informs us that one night elapsed between the entry on Palm-day and the expulsion of the traders; we should not suppose this interval when reading the accounts of Matthew and Luke. According to Mark. xi. 12, 20, a day and a night passed between the cursing of the fig-tree and the conversation of Jesus with His disciples on the subject, while in reading Matthew one would suppose that this conversation followed the miracle immediately. These apparent contradictions arise from the fact that, in the traditional teaching, the moral and religious importance of the facts by far outweighs their chronological interest. If such is the relation of the Synoptical nar-

---

[1] The words ο τεθνηκως (*the dead man*) which is read here by T. R., with 14 Mjj. the Mnn. It^{plerique} Cop. etc., are omitted by ℵ B L X It^{aliq} Syr. Tisch. (8th ed.).

ratives to each other, in spite of their general parallelism, it is not surprising that this phenomenon reappears, on a still greater scale, in the relation between the Synoptics and the fourth Gospel, which is absolutely independent of the tradition.

The οὖν, therefore, is connected with xi. 55: "*The Passover of the Jews was near.*" The turn of expression πρὸ ἓξ ἡμ. τ. π., *six days before* . . . , may be explained by a Latinism (*ante diem sextum calendas*) in which the preposition is transposed (*Bäumlein*); or perhaps the most natural explanation of this form of expression is the same as that of the construction xi. 18 (where it is applied to local distance). The determination of time (six days) is added, in the genitive, to the word which indicates the starting-point of the reckoning (the Passover); comp. Amos i. 1, LXX: πρὸ δύο ἐτῶν τοῦ σεισμοῦ, *two years before the earthquake* (Winer, § 61, 5). Jesus knew that He would have need of all this time to make a last and striking impression on the minds of the people of the capital. On what day, according to this expression, are we to place the arrival of Jesus at Bethany? The answers are very different in consequence of the uncertainty in which writers find themselves respecting the following points: 1. Are we, or not, to include either the day of the arrival at Bethany or the first day of the Passover in the *six days* mentioned? 2. Must the first day of the Passover be fixed, in the language of John, on the 15th, as the first great Sabbatic day of the Paschal week, or already on the 14th, as the day of preparation on which the lamb was sacrificed? Finally, 3. Must Friday (which is certainly the day of the week on which Jesus was put to death) be regarded as the 15th of Nisan of that year (according to the meaning ordinarily attributed to the Synoptics), or as the 14th, the day of the preparation (according to the meaning which most give—rightly, as it appears to me—to the narrative of John)? It is impossible to pursue in detail the manifold solutions to which these different possibilities give occasion. The summary result is the following: Some (*Tholuck, Lange, Wieseler, Hengstenberg, Luthardt, Lichtenstein, Keil*) place the arrival of Jesus at Bethany on Friday, a week before the Friday on which Jesus died; others (*Meyer, Ewald, Weiss*) on Saturday, the Sabbath which preceded the Passion; others (*de Wette, Hase, Andreæ*, etc.) on Sunday, the next day; finally, *Hilgenfeld, Bauer, Scholten, Bäumlein*, on Monday. Among these possible different suppositions, that which appears to me, at this time, the most probable, is that set forth by *Andreæ*, in the excellent essay entitled: *Der Todestag Jesu* (in the *Beweis des Glaubens*, July and Sept., 1870). The sixth of the days mentioned in ver. 1 is Friday, the day of Jesus' death, that is, according to the very clear meaning of the chronology of John (see the detailed treatment of this whole question at the end of chap. xix.), the 14th of Nisan, or the day of the preparation of the Passover of that year. It would follow from this that the day of the arrival at Bethany was Sunday, the 9th of Nisan, at evening. Jesus, after having passed Saturday (Sabbath) at Jericho at the house of Zacchæus, went up on the next day, Sunday, with the caravan from Jericho to Bethany, where he stopped, leaving the others to continue their journey to Jerusalem, and it was on the evening of the same day that the banquet was offered to Him which is about to be related. The next day, Monday, the solemn entrance into Jerusalem took place.

In my first edition, I left out the 14th (Friday, the day of Jesus' death) from the *six days*, as already included in the Passover feast. In fact, this day plays the principal part in the story of the institution of the Passover in Exodus (chap. xii.), and Josephus (*Antiq.* xii., 15, 1) counts eight feast days, which shows that he includes the 14th. But, on the other hand, we must recognize that there is a difference between the feast of *unleavened bread* and the feast of *the Passover* properly so called: if the former necessarily included the 14th, on which the leaven was removed from the Israelitish houses, the latter did not properly begin until the 15th, to end on the 21st, these two days having the Sabbatical character and forming the beginning and ending of the Paschal week. Then another difficulty in this way of counting is, that in starting, in the count of six days, from Thursday the 13th, and in going back from that day, we come to Saturday as the day of the journey from Jericho to Bethany. Now, it cannot be admitted that Jesus made so long a journey on the Sabbath. *Meyer*, to escape this consequence, holds that Jesus had passed the night in a place quite near to Bethany, in order that He might be able to reach there the next day without violating the Sabbath ordinance, according to which one could not make a journey on that day of more than twenty minutes. But why, in that case, did He not arrange so as to reach Bethany also on that evening? And, besides, there was no place where one could stop between Jericho and Bethany. I had proposed a somewhat different solution, which seems to me now to be that of *Weiss:* Jesus had made most of the journey from Jericho to Bethany on Friday, but He arrived only at the earliest hour on Saturday (from six to seven o'clock in the evening); and thus this Saturday was indeed the *first* of the *six days before the feast*. The feast was not offered Him until the next day at evening, towards the end of this Sabbath; the next day but one, Sunday, He made His entry into Jerusalem. This combination, however, is far less simple than that which has been proposed by *Andreæ;* and how could the rest of the caravan which was going to Jerusalem have still made their journey from Bethany to Jerusalem without violating the Sabbatic prescription?

According to *Hilgenfeld, Baur,* etc., who take the 15th as the starting-point for the calculation, and include that day in the six, the arrival at Bethany took place on Monday, the 10th of Nisan. According to some of these interpreters, the evangelist sought by this date to establish a typical relation between the arrival of Jesus and the Jewish custom of setting apart the Paschal lamb on the 10th of Nisan. Such an intention would evidently compromise the historical character of our narrative. But this alleged relation between the arrival of Jesus and the setting apart of the lamb, is not in any way indicated in the narrative; and the idea of this comparison could not have entered the minds of the Greek Christians for whom the author designed his work.

Vv. 2, 3. "*Therefore they made him a feast there, and Martha served; but*

Lazarus was one of those[1] *who were at table with him.*[2] *3. Mary therefore, having taken a pound of ointment of pure nard, which was of great price, anointed the feet of Jesus with it and wiped his feet with her hair; and the whole house was filled with the odor of the ointment.*" When did this supper take place? Of course, according to our hypothesis, on Sunday evening, the day of Jesus' arrival. The subject of ἐποίησαν, *they made,* is indefinite; this form answers in Greek to the French *on.* Hence it already follows that this subject cannot be, as is ordinarily represented: the members of the family of Lazarus. Moreover, this appears from the express mention of the presence of Lazarus and of the activity of service on Martha's part, all of them circumstances which would be self-evident if the supper had taken place in their own house. As the undetermined subject of the verb can only be the persons named afterwards, it follows that they are, much rather, the people of the place. A part of the inhabitants of Bethany feel the desire of testifying their thankfulness to Him who by a glorious miracle had honored their obscure village. It is this connection of ideas which seems to be expressed by the *therefore* at the beginning of ver. 2, and, immediately afterwards, by this detail: "*Lazarus, whom he had raised from the dead.*" That which, no doubt, very specially impelled them to render to Jesus, at this moment, this public homage, was the hatred to which they saw Him exposed on the part of the rulers. This feast was a courageous response to the edict of the Sanhedrim (xi. 57); it was the proscribed one whom they honored.

The text does not tell us in what house the supper took place. Lazarus being there as a guest, not as host (ver. 2), it follows that the scene occurred in another house than his own. Thus is the harmony very naturally established with the narrative of Matthew and Mark, who state positively that the supper took place in the house of Simon the leper, a sick man, no doubt, whom Jesus had healed and who has claimed the privilege of receiving him in the name of all. It is inconceivable that this very simple reconciliation should appear to *Meyer* a mere process of false harmonistics. *Weiss* himself says: "The form of expression used excludes the idea that Lazarus was the one who gave the supper." Every one could not receive Jesus: but every one had desired to contribute, according to his means, to the homage which was rendered to Him: the people of Bethany, by the banquet offered in their name; Martha, by giving her personal service, even in the house of another person; Lazarus, by his presence, which in itself alone glorified the Master more than all that the others could do; finally, Mary, by a royal prodigality, which was alone capable of expressing the sentiment which inspired her.

The general custom among the ancient nations was to anoint with perfume the heads of guests on feast-days. "*Thou preparedst the table before me; thou anointest my head with oil; my cup overflows,*" says David to Jehovah, when describing under the figure of a feast which his

---

[1] ℵ B L It. Vulg. read εκ before των ανακειμενων. Mnn. only. All the Mjj.: ανακειμενων συν αυτω.

[2] T. R.; συνανακειμενων αυτω with some

God gives to him the delights of communion with Him (Ps. xxiii. 5). The forgetting of this ceremony is noticed by Jesus (Luke vii. 46), as an offensive omission. At Bethany such a mistake was not committed; it was Mary who charged herself with this office, reserving to herself the accomplishment of it in her own way. Μύρον is the generic term which comprehends all the liquid perfumes, and νάρδος, *nard*, the name of the most precious kind. This word, of Sanskrit origin (in Persian *nard*, in Sanskrit *nalada*), denotes a plant which grows in India, and of which some less celebrated varieties are found in Syria. The juice was enclosed in flasks of alabaster (*nardi ampullae*), and it was used not only to anoint the body, but also to perfume wine. (See Riehm, *Handwörterb.*) We have translated πιστικός by *pure*. This word, which is unknown in classic Greek, is not again found in the entire New Testament, except in the corresponding passage in Mark. Among the later Greeks, it serves to designate a person *worthy of confidence*; thus the one to whom the care of a vessel or a flock is committed. It signifies, therefore, nard on which one can rely, not adulterated. This meaning is the more suitable, since nard was subjected to all sorts of adulterations. Pliny enumerates nine plants by means of which it could be counterfeited, and Tibullus uses the expression *nardus pura*, which almost gives to our πιστικῆς, in Mark and John, the character of a technical epithet. The meaning *drinkable* (from πίνω, πιπίσκω) is much less probable, not only because the natural form would be πιστός, or ποτιμός, but especially because the notion of potableness has no relation to the context. The attempt has also been made to derive this word from the name of a Persian city, *Pisteira*, a name which was sometimes abridged to *Pista* (comp. *Meyer* on Mark xiv. 2). This is a worthless expedient (comp. *Hengstenberg* and especially *Lücke* and *Wichelhaus*). The epithet, πολυτίμον, *very costly*, can only refer to the first of the two substantives (in opposition to *Luthardt, Weiss*, etc.); for it was not the plant which had been purchased (νάρδον), but the perfume (μύρον). Λίτρα, *a pound*, answers to the Latin *libra*, and denotes a weight of twelve ounces; it was an enormous quantity for a perfume of this price. But nothing must be wanting to the homage of Mary, neither the quality nor the quantity.

These flasks of nard hermetically sealed were probably received from the East; to use the contents of them, the neck must be broken; this is what Mary did, according to Mark (xiv. 3). This act having a somewhat striking character, she must have performed it in the sight of all the guests, consequently over the head of Jesus already seated at the table. His head thus received the first fruits of the perfume (comp. Matt. and Mark: "she poured it *on his head*"). Only after this, as no ordinary guest was here in question, and as Mary wished to give to her guest not merely a testimony of love and respect, but a mark of adoration, she joined with the ordinary anointing of the head (which was self evident; comp. Ps. xxiii. 5; Luke vii. 46) an altogether exceptional homage. As if this precious liquid were only common water, she pours it over His feet, and in such abundance that it was as if she were bathing them with it; so she is obliged to wipe them. For this purpose she uses her own hair. This last fact carries the homage to a climax. It was among the Jews, according to *Lightfoot* (II., p. 633), "a disgrace for a woman to loosen the fillets which bound up her hair and to appear with disheveled hair."[1] Mary bears witness, therefore, by this means that, as no sacrifice is too costly for her purse, so no service is too mean for her person. All that she *is* belongs to Him, as well as all that she *has*. We may understand thus the ground of the repetition, certainly not accidental, of the words τοὺς ποδὰς αὐτοῦ, *his feet*. To this, the least noble part of His body it is, that she renders this extraordinary homage. Every detail in this narrative breathes adoration, the soul of the act. Perhaps the report of the homage rendered to Jesus by the sinful woman of Galilee had reached Mary. She was unwilling that the friends of Jesus should do less for Him than a stranger.

The identity of this event with that which is related in Matt. xxvi. 6–13, and Mark xiv. 3–9, is indisputable. It is said, no doubt, in the latter passages, that the perfume was poured on *the head*, in John, on *the feet;* but, as we have just seen, this slight difference is easily explained. After the anointing in the ordinary form (that of the head), this *bathing of the feet* with perfume began, which here takes the place of the ordinary bathing of the feet (Luke vii. 44). John alone has preserved the recollection of this fact which gives to the scene its unique character. It cannot be supposed that Mary poured on the head of Jesus a whole pound of liquid. As to the place which this story occupies in the two narratives, it constitutes no more serious objection against the identity of the event. For in the Synoptics the place is evidently determined by the *moral* relation of this act to the fact related immediately afterwards, the treachery of Judas (Matt. vv. 14–16; Mark vv. 10, 11). This association of ideas had determined the uniting of the two facts in the oral tradition, and from this it had passed into the written redaction. John has restored the fact to its own place. The relation of the anointing of Jesus at Bethany with the event related in Luke vii. is entirely different. We have already mentioned the points which do not allow us to identify the two narratives (p. 171). *Keim* declares that a homage of this kind cannot have occurred twice. But the anointing belonged necessarily, as well as the bathing of the feet, to every meal to which there was an invitation (Luke vii. 44). The details in which the two scenes resemble each other are purely accidental. *Simon the leper* of Bethany, of whom Matthew and Mark speak, has nothing in common with *Simon the Pharisee*, of whom Luke speaks, except the name. Now, among the small number of persons with whom we are acquainted in the Gospel history taken alone, we can count twelve or thirteen Simons; and can there not have been two men, bearing this so common name, in whose houses these two similar scenes may have taken place? The one lived in Judea, the other in Galilee; the one receives Jesus into his house in the course of His Galilean ministry; the other, a few days before the Passion. The discussion in Galilee has reference to

---

[1] *Sotah*, fol. 5, i. "The priest unties the hair of the suspected woman. . . . as a mark of disgrace." *Vajicra Rabba*, fol. 188. 2. "Kamith, who had had seven sons high-priests, answered those who asked her to what she owed such an honor: 'To the fact that the beams of my chamber have never seen the hairs of my head.'"

768 / Unbelief Develops in Israel

the pardon of sins; in Judea, to the prodigality of Mary. And if the two women wiped the feet of Jesus with their hair, in the case of the one, it is the tears which she gathers up, in that of the other, it is a perfume with which she has embalmed her Master. This difference sufficiently marks the two women and the two scenes. Christian feeling, moreover, will always protest against the identification of Mary of Bethany with a woman of bad morals.

Vv. 4–6. " Then [1] one of his disciples, Judas, the son of Simon, the Iscariot,[2] he who was soon to betray him, says: 5. Why was not this ointment sold for three hundred denarii and the price given to the poor ? 6. Now this he said, not that he cared for the poor, but because he was a thief, and kept [3] the purse and took what was put therein." This outbreak of indignation on the part of Judas is occasioned by the mean passion with which the evangelist charges him; but, like his treachery, it has a deeper source than avarice. For a long time (vi. 70) there had been in this heart a gloomy discontent with respect to the course followed by Jesus (vi. 70, 71; comp. with ver. 15), and this feeling only waited for a pretext to manifest itself. In the Synoptics, it is *the disciples* (Matthew), *some* (Mark), who protest. It seems that on this occasion, as on others, Judas played among his fellow-disciples the part of the leaven which leavens the whole mass. Westcott says: " He expressed what the others thought." There is no doubt more than this: he excited among them a movement of discontent which would not have been awakened without him. We find here again a relation between John and the Synoptics which we have already pointed out in other stories. In the latter, the outlines are effaced: the former alone reproduces the characteristic features, as we might expect from a witness. Judas knows the exact price of the commodity in question, as if he were a tradesman. For the value of the denarius, see on vi. 7. The sum indicated was nearly equivalent, in the time of the emperors, to two hundred and sixty francs. It is found as identically the same sum in Mark. We have already remarked several similar coincidences between the two evangelists (ver. 3; vi. 7, 10). Even independently of the subsequent fact of the treachery of Judas, attested by the four evangelists, it would be very rash to ascribe the accusation here formulated by John against Judas to a feeling of personal hatred, as modern criticism has allowed itself to do. The word γλωσσόκομον (properly γλωσσοκομεῖον) denotes literally the *case* in which musicians kept the mouth-pieces of flutes; whence: box. This purse was probably a small portable cash-box. The property of Jesus and His disciples was mingled with that of the poor (xiii. 29). This fund was supplied by voluntary gifts (ver. 5; Luke viii. 1–3). We may see in xx. 15 how in the word βαστάζειν, the sense of *bearing*, the only one used, in general, in the New Testament, is easily changed into that of *taking away, purloining* (*de Wette, Meyer*). The simple meaning *to bear* is not impos-

---

[1] ℵ B read δε instead of ουν.
[2] Many variants in the designation of Judas. ℵ B L: Ιουδας ο Ισκαριωτης; T. R. with 10 Mjj. (A I K etc.): Ιουδ. Σιμωνος Ισκαριωτης;
D: Ιουδ. απο Καρυωτου, etc.
[3] Instead of ειχεν και (*he had and*), ℵ B L Q: εχων (*having*).

sible, however, if, with the Alexandrian authorities, we read ἔχων, *having*, instead of καί . . . εἶχε., *and he had . . . and.* . . . For by this means all tautology as between this clause and the following disappears. But it is absurd, in any case, to claim that the sense of *taking away* is excluded because of the article τά before βαλλόμενα, as if this article must signify that he took away *everything* which was placed in the box! It has been asked why Jesus, if He knew Judas, intrusted to him this office so perilous to his morality. We will not say, with *Hengstenberg*, that Jesus saw fit thus to call forth the manifestation of his sin, as the only means of accomplishing a cure. By such a course of action, Jesus would have put Himself, as it seems to us, in the place of God more completely than was accordant with the reality of His humanity. But is there clear proof that Jesus intervened directly in the choice of Judas as the treasurer of the company? Might not this have been an arrangement which the disciples had made among themselves and in which Jesus had not desired to mingle. *Weiss* thinks that Jesus had chosen Judas at first because he had a special gift in the financial sphere, and that afterwards He did not wish to interfere with a relation in which He recognized a divine dispensation.

Vv. 7, 8. " *Jesus therefore said to him : Let her alone ; she has kept it for the day of my burial.*[1] 8. *For the poor you have always with you; but me you have not always.*"[2] We translate according to the reading of the T. R. which alone seems to us admissible. The imperative ἄφες is absolute: " *Let her alone* (in peace); cease to disturb her by thy observations." The reason is given afterwards. With the Alexandrian variant, ἄφες has for its object the following clause, either in the sense given by the *Vulgate, Meyer, Bäumlein*, etc. " Let her keep *this* (αὐτό, the remainder of the ointment of which she had poured out only a part) to embalm me on the day of my death,"—or in that given by *Bengel, Lange, Luthardt, Weiss, Keil:* " Allow her to *have reserved* this ointment for this day, which, by the act which she has done with respect to me, becomes, as it were, that of an anticipated burial." This last sense is grammatically inadmissible. The expression ἀφιέναι ἵνα, *to allow*, necessarily refers to the future, not to the past. With that meaning, why not say quite simply : ἄφες αὐτὴν τετηρηκέναι? How are we to understand that *Weiss* justifies so forced an explanation by asserting that there was no other way of expressing this idea? The meaning given by *Meyer* is still more impossible. By what right can we suppose that only a part of the ointment had been poured out; that there was a remainder, and that it is this remainder which is designated by αὐτό? Moreover, when thus understood, the words of Jesus no longer form an answer to the objection of Judas. The latter had not disputed Mary's right to keep the whole or a part of this ointment for the purpose of using it in the future on a more suitable occasion; quite the contrary; that which he charged against her was that she had wasted and not kept it. We must acknowledge therefore with *Lücke* and *Hengstenberg*, that,

---

[1] T. R. reads with 12 Mjj. (A I Γ etc.), the Mnn. Syr[sch] : αφες αυτην. εις την ημεραν τ. ενταφ. μου τετηρηκεν αυτο. ℵ B D K L Q X Π 4 Mnn It[plerique] Vulg. Cop. : αφες αυτην ινα εις την ημ. τ. ενταφ. μου τηρηση αυτο.

[2] D omits ver. 8.

however this reading is interpreted, it offers no tolerable meaning. It is an unhappy correction from the hands of critics who thought that the embalming of a man did not take place before his death. The received reading, on the contrary, offers a simple and delicate sense. Jesus ascribes to the act of Mary precisely that which was wanting to the view of Judas, a purpose, a practical utility. "It is not for nothing, as thou chargest her, that she has poured out this ointment. She has to-day anticipated my embalming;" comp. Mark xiv. 8: "She has been beforehand in embalming my body for my burial;" in other terms: She has made this day the day of my funeral rites of which thou wilt soon give the signal. Ἐνταφιασμός: the embalming and, in general, the preparations for burial. The word τετήρηκεν, *she has kept*, is full of delicacy. It is as if there had been here on Mary's part a contrived plan and one in harmony with the utilitarianism on which the reproach of Judas rested.

Can ver. 8, which is wanting in D, have been introduced here by the copyists from the text of the two Synoptics, and can this manuscript alone be right as against all the other documents? It is more probable that it is one of those faulty omissions which are so frequent in D. The sense is: "If the poor are really the object of your solicitude, there will always be opportunity to exercise your liberality towards them; but my person will soon be taken away from the assiduous care of your love." The first clause seems to contain an allusion to Deut. xv. 11. The present ἔχετε, *you have*, in the first clause, is owing to the πάντοτε, *always*, and the following present is introduced by the first.

Beyschlag correctly observes respecting this passage: "It is asserted that the fourth evangelist likes to depreciate the Twelve; but why then does he, and he alone, place all to the account of Judas?" It is further said: He has a special hatred to Judas. This is to affirm beyond question the authenticity of the Gospel; for what writer of the second century could have cherished a personal hatred against Judas? Let us also remark that the slight modifications which John introduces into the Synoptic narrative are perfectly insignificant from the standpoint of the *idea* of the Logos. They can only be explained by the more distinct knowledge which he has of the fact and by the more thoroughly historical character of the whole representation. We see, finally, how false is the idea of *dependence* with relation to the narrative of Mark, which *Weizsäcker* attributes to the fourth evangelist, by reason of the three hundred denarii which are common to the two accounts and the coincidences in expressions (*Untersuch*, p. 290). The superiority of the narrative of John shows its independence.

Vv. 9–11. "*A great multitude therefore of the Jews learned that he was there; and they came, not because of Jesus only, but that they might see Lazarus also whom he had raised from the dead.* 10. *But the chief priests took counsel that they might put Lazarus also to death,* 11 *because many of the Jews went away and believed on Jesus.*" The pilgrims who came from Jericho with Jesus, on arriving at Jerusalem, had spread abroad the report of His approach. And all those inhabitants of the country region of Judea, of whom mention has been made in xi. 55, 56, and who made Jesus, already many days before His arrival, the subject of their conversation, on learning that He is sojourning so near them, could not restrain their impatience to see Him, as well as Lazarus, the living monument of His power. The term *Jews* preserves here the sense which it has throughout the whole Gospel: the representatives of the old order of things. This was precisely the poignant thing for the rulers; the very people on whom they had always counted to make head against the people of Galilee, the inhabitants of Judea and even those of Jerusalem, began to fall away. Ὑπάγειν, *to go away,* but without noise. In this new attitude and particularly in these visits to Bethany some precautions were taken. Thus is the way prepared for the solemn entrance of Jesus into Jerusalem. The people are altogether disposed to an ovation. It only needs that Jesus should give a signal and give loose rein to the enthusiasm of the multitude, that the hour of the royal manifestation may strike, which had been so long desired by His mother (ii. 4) and demanded by His brethren (vii. 4), but had been until now refused by Him.

The entrance into Jerusalem: vv. 12–19

Jesus had striven on every occasion to repress the popular manifestations in His favor (vi. 15; Luke xiv. 25–33; xix. 11 ff., etc.). Now He allows free play to the feelings of the multitude and surrenders Himself to the public homage which is prepared for Him. What precautions had He still to take? Ought He not once at least in His life to be acknowledged and saluted in His character of King of Israel? In any case, the hour of His death was near; that of His royal advent had therefore sounded.

The tradition of the Christian Church fixes the entrance of Jesus into Jerusalem on the Sunday which preceded the Passion. The most probable explanation of ver. 1 has not confirmed this view; it was probably Monday. Three of the evangelists do not speak of the time of day when this event occurred. Why then may we not connect our view with the one who positively indicates it? This one is Mark. He says, xi. 11: "*And Jesus entered into Jerusalem and into the temple; and, having looked round about upon all things, as it was already late, he went away to Bethany with the Twelve.*" These words imply that, after having entered into Jerusalem, Jesus did nothing further of importance on that day, because the hour was already too late. Hence it follows that the entrance took place during the second half of the day. How is it possible to call this a harmonistic conclusion, as *Weiss* does? Does John say anything contrary to this narrative of Mark?

Vv. 12, 13. "*The next day, a great multitude of persons who had come*[1] *to the feast, having heard that Jesus was coming to Jerusalem took branches of palm-trees* 13 *and went forth to meet him,*[2] *and they cried,*[3] *Hosanna! Blessed*

---

[1] ℵ Δ omit ο before ελθων.
[2] A K U II 50 Mnn. read απαντησιν instead of υπαντησιν (11 Mjj.). D G L X: συναντησιν.
[3] ℵ D L Q: εκραυγαζον instead of εκραζον. ℵ A D K Q X II add λεγοντες.

be he that cometh in the name of the Lord, the king of Israel!" This multitude is much more considerable than that of which mention was made in vv. 9–11; it included most of the pilgrims of all countries who *had come to the feast*. They had heard from those who had gone to Bethany on the preceding evening, that Jesus was really there and that He was Himself preparing to come to Jerusalem. They went forth, therefore, in large numbers to meet Him, and to form a body of attendants on His entrance into the city. Those who started earliest went even to Bethany; the rest must have successively met Him on the road. Thus, in proportion as He advanced, already surrounded by many disciples and friends, He found from place to place joyous groups on the way. Hence an easy explanation is given of the ovation of this day, which, in the Synoptic narrative, has a somewhat abrupt character and remains in a certain degree inexplicable. Not having mentioned the stay of Jesus at Bethany, the other gospels naturally represent Him as entering into the city with the caravan of pilgrims who come with Him from Jericho.

All at once an inspiration of celestial joy passes over this multitude. Their rejoicing and their hopes break forth in songs and significant symbols. Luke, in particular, admirably describes this moment: "*And as he drew near from the descent of the Mount of Olives, the whole multitude of the disciples began to rejoice and praise God for all the miracles which they had seen*" (xix. 37). John gives us to understand what was the one among all these miracles which played the greatest part in the enthusiasm of the multitude and which had produced this very general effect both on those who accompanied and on those who met the Lord: namely, the resurrection of Lazarus.—The palm, by reason of the permanent beauty of its magnificent crown of leaves, is the emblem not only of strength, beauty and joy, but also of salvation (see *Keil*). In 1 Macc. xiii. 51, Simon returns to Jerusalem *with songs and branches of palm-trees, to the sound of the harp and of cymbals, because the enemy was driven out of Israel*. In Lev. xxiii. 40, in the institution of the feast of Tabernacles, it is said: "*Ye shall take . . . branches of palm-trees . . . , and ye shall rejoice seven days before the Lord.*" On each day during this last feast a procession, in which branches of palm-trees were carried, was made around the altar of burnt-offering; comp. Apoc. vii. 9. On this day all was done spontaneously. An allusion has been found in the articles τά and τῶν before βαία and φοινίκων (*the* branches of *the* palm-trees) to the branches which were well-known by tradition and which gave the name to the day; it is more simple to understand by them: "The branches of the palm-trees which were found on the road," as if John had said: Having stripped *the* palm-trees of *their* branches. The term βαίον already in itself means *branch of the palm-tree*. But the complement τῶν φοινίκων is added by John for the readers who were not acquainted with the technical term.

The cries of the multitude, as well as the terms: *son of David* (*Matt.*), *King of Israel* (*John*), leave no doubt as to the meaning of this manifestation; it was certainly the Messiah whom the people intended to salute in the person of Jesus. The acclamations reported by John (ver. 13), the equivalent of which is found in the Synoptics, are taken from the 118th Psalm, particularly from vv. 25, 26. It was probably a chant composed for the inauguration of the second temple, and the quoted words refer to the procession received by the priests on its arrival at the temple. Numerous Rabbinical citations prove that this Psalm was regarded as Messianic. Every Israelite knew these words by heart: they were sung at the feast of Tabernacles, in the procession which was made around the altar, and at the Passover in the chant of the great Hallel (Ps. cxiii.–cxviii.) during the Paschal supper. *Hosanna* (from נא הושיעה, *save, I pray thee*) is a prayer addressed to God by the theocratic people on behalf of His Messiah-King; it is, if we may venture to use the expression, the Israelitish *God save the King*. It seems to us more natural to refer the words *in the name of the Lord* to the verb *comes*, than to the participle *blessed*. The expression: *He that comes in the name of the Lord*, designates in a general way, and still quite vaguely, the divine messenger *par excellence*, on whose person and work Israel implores the benedictions of heaven; then there comes after this the great word whose import every one understands, the by no means equivocal term *King of Israel*. Of course, all in this multitude did not cry out exactly in the same way; this explains the differences in the popular acclamations reported by the evangelists. As in vi. 5, Jesus had seen in the arrival of the multitudes in the desert the call of His Father to give a feast to His people, so in the impetuosity of the multitude who hasten towards Him with these triumphal acclamations, He recognizes a divine signal; He understands that, in accordance with the words of the very Psalm from which the people borrow their songs, this is "*the day which the Lord has made, and we must rejoice in it*" (Ps. cxviii. 24); and he responds to the salutation of the people by a true Messianic sign.

Vv. 14, 15. "*Jesus, having found a young ass, sat thereon, according as it is written,* 15. *Fear not, daughter*[1] *of Zion; behold, thy king cometh seated on an ass's colt.*" The conduct of Jesus is ordered by the nature of things. Since He wishes to-day to accept this homage, He cannot remain mingled with the multitude. On the one hand, He must in some sort put Himself on the scene; but, on the other, He wishes to do it only in the most humble way and in the way most appropriate to the spiritual nature of His royalty. In the ancient times, the ass does not seem to have been in Israel a despised animal; comp. Judg. v. 9, 10; x. 4; 2 Sam. xvii. 23. Later, the horse and the mule were preferred to it; comp. Sirach, xxxiii. (xxxvi.) 25 (24). The prophet Zechariah himself indicates the meaning which he here attaches to this symbol, when he says (ix. 9): "*Behold thy king cometh unto thee just, having salvation and humble.*" The young ass represents for him the humility of the Messiah and consequently the peaceful nature of His kingdom: "*I will cut off the chariots of war . . . and the king shall speak peace unto the nations*" (Zech. ix 10). The two ideas of humility and of peace are closely connected, as, on the other hand, are those of wealth and military power. The expression εὑρών, *having found*,

---

[1] T. R. with 8 Mjj. (א E G etc.): θυγατερ; 9 Mjj. (A B D etc): θυγατηρ.

seems at the first glance incompatible with the narrative of the Synoptics, according to which Jesus sends two of His disciples with the express order to bring Him the young ass. But εὑρών does not signify : having found *without seeking ;* witness the εὕρηκα of Archimedes ! This word may be translated by : *having procured for Himself,* as in the expressions εὑρίσκων δόξαν, κέρδος, βίον, to procure glory, gain, subsistence for oneself (see Passow). Nothing, therefore, can be inferred from this term as to the *how* of this finding, and it is natural to suppose that John, in this summary expression, sums up the narrative of the Synoptics, which was sufficiently well-known in the Church. He also abridges the quotation of Zechariah ; for it concerns him only to establish the general relation between the prophecy and its accomplishment. The expression *daughter of Zion* designates the population of the city personified. John substitutes : *Fear not,* for the *Rejoice* of the prophecy ; it is the same sentiment, but somewhat less strongly expressed : "Fear not ; a king who comes thus cannot be a tyrant." If Jesus had never entered into Jerusalem in this way, this prophecy would nevertheless have been realized. His entire ministry in Israel was the fulfillment of it. But, by realizing *to the very letter* the figure employed by the prophet, Jesus desired to render more sensible the spiritual and true accomplishment of the prophecy. Everything, however, occurred so simply, so naturally, that, at the moment, the disciples did not think of the prophecy and did not grasp its relation to that which had just taken place.

Ver. 16. "*Now the disciples did not understand these things at the moment ; but when Jesus had been glorified, then they remembered that these things were written of him and that they had done these things to him.*" It was only afterwards, when after the ascension, and when enlightened by the Holy Spirit, they retraced the earthly life of their Master, that they discerned the meaning of this event and recognized in it the fulfillment of a prophecy. In the light of the heavenly elevation of Jesus, they understood this fact which had prefigured it (*these things*). There is, therefore, no reason to turn aside from the natural sense of ἐδοξάσθη, *was glorified,* and to refer this term, as *Reuss* does, to the death of Jesus, as the transition to His exaltation. What a charlatan the pseudo-John of *Baur,* who, by means of this want of understanding invented by him, would give himself the appearance of having himself been one of these disciples whom the ascension had enlightened ! We are surprised at the expression "*that they had done these things to him*" ; for, in the scene related by John, the apostles had done nothing to Jesus. So many take ἐποίησαν in the sense in which it is found in ver. 2 : "*They* (indefinite) *had done to him,*" and assign as subject to this verb *the multitude* (vv. 12, 13). But the subject of *they had done* cannot be different from that of *they understood* and *they remembered.* John wished to set forth precisely the fact that the disciples understood afterwards what they had done *themselves* in the fulfillment of a prophecy of which no one of them dreamed. The co-operation of the disciples, indicated by John, is described in detail in Luke xix. 29–36 and the parallels. We find here a new proof of the abridged character of his narrative and his thoroughly conscious relation to the narrative of the Synoptics. We see from the words: *they had done these things to him*, how arbitrary is the idea of *Keim*, according to which John's narrative tends to make the disciples and Jesus passive in this scene, and this because the author wished to give utterance to his repugnance to the idea of the Jewish Messiah!

Vv. 17, 18. " *The multitude therefore who were with him when* [1] *he called Lazarus out of the tomb and raised him from the dead bore witness to him;* 18 *and it was for this cause also* [2] *that the multitude went to meet him, because they had heard that he had done this miracle.*" John does not have it as his aim to present the complete picture of the entrance of Jesus, but rather to show the double relation of this event to the resurrection of Lazarus (its cause), on the one hand, and to the condemnation of Jesus (its effect), on the other. It is this connection which he brings out in vv. 17–19. If ὅτι, *that*, is read in ver. 17 with five Mjj. and the most ancient translations, the meaning is: that by coming forward the multitude *bore testimony* that He had caused the resurrection of Lazarus. There is nothing in this case to prevent the multitude of ver. 18 from being the same as that of ver. 17. John would simply say that the miracle which they were celebrating by accompanying Jesus (ver. 17) was the same one which had induced them to come to meet him (ver. 18). But the reflection of ver. 18 is, with this meaning, an idle one. It is self-evident that the event which they celebrated is also that which made them hasten to Him. If ὅτε (*when*) is read, with the most ancient Mjj., it is quite otherwise. John relates that the multitude which had been with Jesus at the tomb of Lazarus, and which had been present at his resurrection, by accompanying Jesus bore testimony to this great miracle of which they had themselves been witnesses. And here are the true authors of the ovation of Palm-day. They were there relating to the numerous pilgrims who were strangers what they had themselves heard and seen. We thus understand better this dramatic amplification, which in the former reading makes the effect quite prolix: *When he called Lazarus out of the tomb and raised him from the dead.* The mere mention of the fact, with the ὅτι, would have been sufficient. If ὅτε (*when*) is read, the participle ὁ ὤν is an imperfect: " *who was with him when* . . . " xi. 42.

In the 18th verse, John speaks of the second multitude—the one which came to meet Jesus on the road to Bethany. The διὰ τοῦτο, *for this cause*, refers to the following ὅτι, *because*. And it was *for this* that the multitude came to meet Him, to wit, *because*. Not only did this miracle form the principal subject of the conversations of those who came; but it was *also* (καί) this same miracle, which, having come to the knowledge of the whole multitude of pilgrims, impelled them to go and meet Him. The comparison of the words of Luke (xix. 37) which we have already cited, shows that which we have so often established: how frequently the outlines of

---

[1] Ὅτε (*when*) is the reading of the T. R. (ςᵉ) with ℵ A B C H M Q S U Γ Δ Λ 100 Mnn., while D E K L It^plerique Syr. and ς read ὅτι (*that*).

[2] B E H Δ Λ omit καί.

the Synoptic picture are vague and undecided as compared with the so distinctly marked features of the Johannean narrative.

Ver. 19. "*Whereupon the Pharisees said among themselves, You see that you prevail nothing; behold, the world is gone after him.*" Vv. 17, 18 bring out the influence of the resurrection of Lazarus on the scene of Palm-day; ver. 19 indicates that of this scene on the final catastrophe. Πρὸς ἑαυτούς, instead of πρὸς ἀλλήλους, because, belonging to the same body, it is as if they were speaking *to themselves.* ᾽Ιδε, *behold,* alludes to the unexpected spectacle of which they had just been witnesses. There is something of distress in the term ὁ κόσμος, *the world,* "all this people, native and foreign," and in the aorist ἀπῆλθεν, *is gone:* "It is an accomplished thing; we are alone!"—θεωρεῖτε may be explained as an imperative; but it is better to take it as an indicative present. These persons mutually summon each other, with a kind of bitterness, to notice the inefficacy of their half-measures. It is a way of encouraging each other to use without delay the extreme measures advised by Caiaphas. It is these last words especially which serve to place this whole passage in connection with the general design of this part of the Gospel.

The more closely the narrative of John is studied, the less is it possible to see in it the accidental product of tradition or of legend. Instead of the juxtaposition of anecdotes which forms the character of the Synoptics, we meet at every step the traces of a profound connection which governs the narrative even in its minutest details. The dilemma is therefore, as *Baur* has clearly seen, real history profoundly apprehended and reproduced, or a romance very skillfully conceived and executed.

The last scene in the temple: vv. 20–36

Of all the events which occurred between Palm-day and Thursday evening, the evening before the Passion, John mentions but one, which is omitted by the Synoptics: the attempt of a few Greek proselytes to approach Jesus and the discourse in which He expressed the feelings to which this unexpected circumstance gave rise in Him.

If John so specially sets forth this event, it is not in order to relate an event omitted by his predecessors; it is because it has according to him a peculiar importance, and is in direct connection with the purpose of his whole narrative. He had beheld in it, beyond the closing of the public activity of Jesus, the prelude to the agonies of the Passion. It is therefore an essential landmark in his narrative. He does not say at what moment this event must be placed. According to the words of Mark (xi. 11), it cannot have taken place on Palm-day. It issued, moreover, in the final rupture of Jesus with the people; and we know that, during the days which followed Palm-day, Jesus resided in the temple, as if in His palace, and exercised there a sort of Messianic sovereignty. The next day after His entrance into Jerusalem, Tuesday, Jesus purified the temple by the expulsion of the traders. The following day, Wednesday, He coped with the official authorities, who demanded an explanation as to the origin of the power which He arrogated to Himself; then, successively, with the Pharisees, the Sadducees, the Scribes, who approached him with captious questions; and in His turn He presented to them, from Psalm cx., the great question of the divinity of the Messiah, which was to be the subject of His judicial sentence; then, after having pronounced the malediction upon the rulers of the people, He withdrew, towards evening, to the mount of Olives, where He displayed before the eyes of four of His disciples (Mark) the picture of the judgment of Jerusalem, of the Church, and of mankind. The last words of our narrative (ver. 36): "*Jesus said these things; then, departing he hid himself from them,*" may therefore lead us to suppose that the scene related by John occurred on this same Wednesday evening, at the moment when Jesus was leaving the temple to go to Bethany (comp. the solemn farewell, Matt. xxiii. 37-39). In this case, it must be supposed that Jesus did not return to Jerusalem on Thursday morning, at the time when all the people were expecting Him in the temple, and that He passed the whole of Thursday in retirement at Bethany. This might very well be indicated by the expression: *he hid himself from them.* But perhaps in this way Wednesday will be too full. It is possible also that Jesus returned again to Jerusalem for a few moments on Thursday morning; it would then be at that time that the scene here related by John took place. Nevertheless, the expression: *he hid himself from them,* is more easily justified on the first supposition.

Vv. 20-22. "*There were certain Greeks among those who went up to Jerusalem to worship at the feast,* 21 *who came to Philip, who was of Bethsaida in Galilee, and made this request of him: Sir, we desire to see Jesus.* 22. *Philip goes and finds Andrew and tells him; and Andrew and Philip tell it again*[1] *to Jesus.*" The Greeks belonged to the number of those heathen who, like the Ethiopian eunuch (Acts viii.), had in their own country embraced the Jewish religion and who had come to celebrate the great feasts in Jerusalem. They were not, as some have thought, Jews speaking Greek and dwelling among the heathen (ἑλληνισταί). The spacious court of the Gentiles was designed for these proselytes, according to the words of Solomon, 1 Kings viii. 41-43. If these strangers had been witnesses of the entrance of Jesus into Jerusalem and had been present at the driving out of the traders—that act by which Jesus had restored to its true use the only portion of the sanctuary which was open to them,—we may the more easily understand their desire to enter into a more intimate relation with such a man. Certainly, they did not desire merely, like Zacchæus (Luke xix. 3) to see Jesus with the bodily eye; which would limit the intervention of Philip to *showing* Him to them (*Brückner, Weiss*). The request, thus understood, would not give a ground for such a step with relation to Philip, nor for Philip's action as related to Andrew, and that of the two as related to Jesus, nor for the solemn reflections of the latter. What these Greeks desired was certainly to have a private conversation with Him on religious

---

[1] T. R. reads και παλιν Ανδρεας και Φιλιππος λεγουσιν with 12 Mjj. A B L: ερχεται Ανδρ. κ. Φιλ. και λεγουσιν. ℵ: και παλιν ερχεται Ανδρ. κ. Φ. και λεγουσιν. The Vss. also vary very much.

subjects. Who can tell even, whether, as witnesses of the opposition which Jesus encountered from the rulers of His nation, they may not have desired to invite Him to turn to the heathen, who could better appreciate than these narrow Jews did, a sage and teacher like Him. Ecclesiastical history (Euseb., i. 13) has preserved the memory of an embassy sent to Jesus by the King of Edessa, in Syria, to invite Him to come and fix His abode with him and to promise Him a royal welcome, which would compensate Him for the obstinacy of the Jews in rejecting Him. In the circumstance which occupies our attention we must recognize, with the disciples and with Jesus Himself (see what follows), one of the first manifestations of sympathy for the Gospel on the part of the heathen world, the first sign of the attractive power which His moral beauty was soon to exert upon the whole human race. Jesus, at the moment when this request was conveyed to Him, was undoubtedly in the court of the women, which was entered after having crossed that of the Gentiles. He often taught in this place (p. 656). The article τῶν and the present participle ἀναβαινόντων indicate a permanent and well-known category of persons, the class of proselytes, not only among the Greeks (it is not necessary to supply Ἑλλήνων) but of every nation, who were ordinarily seen arriving at the time of the feasts. The προσῆλθον, *they came to*, has in it something grave and solemn. The word of address: *Sir*, shows what respect they feel for the disciple of such a master. The imperfect ἠρώτων, *they asked*, expresses an action already begun which waits its completion from the answer of Philip. By the term ἰδεῖν, *to see*, these strangers present their desire in the most modest form. The appositional phrase: *from Bethsaida in Galilee*, serves undoubtedly to explain the reason why these Greeks addressed themselves to Philip. They were perhaps from a region in the neighborhood of Galilee, from Decapolis, for example, on the other side of the sea of Galilee, where there were cities which were entirely Greek. It is remarkable that Philip and Andrew, the two disciples who served as intermediaries for these proselytes, are the only ones among the apostles who have a name of Greek origin. The Greek name went, no doubt, hand in hand with Greek culture (*Hengstenberg*).

We discover here again the circumspect nature of Philip: he feels the gravity of the step which is asked of him. Jesus had always limited His activity to the Jewish people, according to the principle which He had laid down for Himself for the whole period of His earthly ministry (Matt. xv. 24): "*I was not sent except to the lost sheep of the house of Israel.*" He does venture alone to take the initiative in a request which would lead Jesus to turn aside from His ordinary course of action, and he takes the matter into consideration with Andrew, the one of the four disciples, who are placed first in rank in the apostolic catalogues, who is always put nearest to Philip. We have already seen him twice mentioned with Philip, in chaps. i. and iv.; and we are reminded here also that these two apostles, so particularly named by John, seem, according to the tradition, not to have been altogether strangers to the composition of our Gospel. The two together decide to present the request of the Greeks to Jesus.

Andrew, more active and decided than Philip, was probably the one who charged himself with making the request; for this reason it is that his name is placed first. Of the three readings, that of א is evidently a mingling together of the two others. That of A B L is the most concise and most probable one (see *Meyer*). The question is one of no consequence.

This request produces upon Jesus a very profound impression. Why is this? In the first place, it awakens in Him the feeling of His relation to the heathen world, which until now has been in the background in His thoughts. He sees Himself destined to extend His work also over this immense domain. But this spiritual royalty, as He is well aware, can only be realized so far as He shall Himself have been freed from His Jewish environment and raised to a new form of existence; and this transformation implies His death. Thus the path to Calvary reveals itself to His view as the only one which can lead to the establishment of the new order of things. This is the reason why the request of these heathen agitates Him even to the depths of His soul (ver. 27). The heathen knock at the gate . . . all the bearing of the present hour both on His work and His person, both on the world and on Israel itself, is in this fact. It is a decisive hour, it is the great revolution of the universe which makes itself known. So, rather than reply by a yes or no to the request which is addressed to Him, He becomes absorbed in the reflections which are called forth within Him by this step. Did He receive these heathen? Did He refuse to have an interview with them? The story does not tell us. The following is the inference which *Reuss* draws from this fact: "The author limits himself to introducing them, then he leaves them there without giving any further attention to them. From this we may again judge of the degree of historical reality in these conversations which are contained in our Gospel." A number of jests directed against the commentators who "flounder in the difficulties of a blindly literal interpretation, and who cannot understand that such discourses are addressed not to the interlocutors, not even to the disciples, but only to the readers of the book." To this lofty mode of discussion we will oppose the words of *Renan:* "Here are verses which have an unquestionable historical stamp." And without going as far as *Westcott* does, who thinks that "the Greeks were immediately admitted, and that it was in their presence that Jesus pronounced the following words," we regard it as probable that in crossing the court of the Gentiles, on going out of the temple, Jesus would have given to these Greeks a testimony of sympathy which He never refused to any one of those who sought Him. John is silent respecting this point, as he is respecting the return of Nicodemus to his home, because the importance of these scenes is not, for him, in the facts of a material order. As *Luthardt* says, it is not the external, which concerns him in the history, but the moral substance of the facts. This substance is the impression produced on the soul of Jesus, and the discourse which reveals it.

Ver. 23. "*Jesus answered*[1] *them, The hour is come when the Son of man is*

---

[1] א B L X: αποκρινεται, instead of απεκρινατο which is read by T. R. with 13 Mjj. It. Syr.

to be glorified." The Alexandrian authorities read the present: *answers.* The T. R., with 13 Mjj. and the ancient Vss., reads the aorist middle ἀπεκρίνατο, *answered.* These two forms are very rare in our Gospel (two or three times, each of them). The aorist middle is more suitable than the aorist passive (the common form). It indicates a meditation to which Jesus gives himself, rather than a direct response.

The words: *The hour is come,* contain in the germ the whole following discourse, which is intended to reveal the importance of the present hour. And this, first, for Jesus Himself (vv. 29, 30); then, for the world (31-33); finally, for Israel in particular (34-36).

For Jesus it is the hour of His elevation and His personal transformation by the painful passage of death. That which has just happened has made Him feel the imminence of the crisis. The term δοξασθῆναι, *to be glorified,* applies here first of all, as in ver. 16 and vii. 39, to the heavenly exaltation of His person. His recognition as Messiah and the extension of His kingdom among the heathen (*Lücke, Reuss*) do not explain this term; these facts will be only the consequences of the change accomplished in His person (xvii. 1, 2, 5). The term *Son of man* is here suggested to Jesus by the feeling of His indissoluble connection with humanity, of which He will soon be the glorified representative. It is at that time that He will be able to do what is denied Him at this moment, to communicate without restraint with the Greeks and the whole world. In the 24th verse, Jesus expresses by means of a figure and in ver. 25 in plain terms, the *painful* condition which is imposed with reference to this glorification:

Ver. 24. *"Verily, verily, I say to you, Unless the grain of wheat dies after having fallen into the ground, it abides alone; but if it dies, it bears much fruit."* Before He can answer to the need of salvation for the heathen world, the first symptom of which has just reached Him, something of serious moment must happen in Himself. So long as the grain of wheat remains in the granary, it is preserved, but without acquiring the power of reproducing itself; it is necessary that it should be cast into the earth, that its covering should be decomposed, that it should perish as a seed, in order that it may live again with a new existence, and may have a new birth in a multitude of beings like itself. We know the considerable part which is played by the grain of wheat in the Greek mysteries. The emphatic affirmation, *amen, amen,* refers to the contrast which Jesus knows to exist between this painful necessity of His death and His disciples' dreams of glory.

Ver. 25. Application of the figure: *"He who loves his life, loses[1] it; and he who hates his life in this world, shall preserve it unto life eternal."* The relation between this sentence and the two preceding verses does not allow us to doubt that Jesus here applies it to Himself. To this fundamental law of human life, which He has so often declared with reference

---

[1] ℵ B L: απολλυει (*loses* it) instead of απολεσει (*shall lose* it), which is read by T. R. with the other Mjj.

to His disciples (Matt. x. 39, xvi. 25; Mark viii. 35; Luke ix. 24; xvii. 33), He here declares that He is Himself subjected, like themselves. By the expression, *his life*, ψυχή, Jesus designates the breath of the natural life, with all the faculties with which this life is endowed in the case of man. This physical and psychical life is good, as the *starting-point* of the human existence; Jesus also possesses it. But the destiny of the natural life is not to sustain and perpetuate itself as such; it must be transformed, by a superior force, into a spiritual, eternal life; but, in order to do this, it must be voluntarily surrendered, sacrificed, immolated in the form of self-renunciation. Otherwise, after having flourished for a time, and more or less satisfied itself, it decays and withers for ever. This law applies even to a pure being and to his lawful tastes. One may be called to sacrifice an honorable desire in order to respond to a higher duty; to refuse this call is to keep one's life, but in order to lose it. Everything which is not surrendered to God by a free act of sacrifice, contains a germ of death. Jesus, seeking his own safety, His personal life, might now, if He wished, escape from death, become the Socrates of the Greeks, the Cæsar of the Romans, the Solomon of the Jews; but this way of *preserving* His life would be to lose it. Not having surrendered it to God, He could not receive it from Him transformed and glorified (ver. 23); and, thus preserved, it would remain devoted to unfruitfulness and to earthly frailty. In order to become a Christ, He must renounce being a sage; He must not wish to ascend the throne of a Solomon, if He desires to take His place on that of God. *Lange* has profoundly remarked that this saying contains in particular the judgment of Hellenism. What was Greek civilization? The effort to realize an ideal of human life consisting in enjoyment and escaping the law of sacrifice. It is probable that the true reading is the present *loses* (ἀπολλύει) which was replaced by the future *shall lose* (ἀπολέσει), under the influence of the verb of the following clause. The idea of *losing* goes beyond that of *abiding alone* (ver. 14). The term μισεῖν, *to hate*, expresses the feeling of a generous contempt, arising from the view of what one would lose by devoting himself to the keeping of this natural life. The expression: *unto life eternal*, placed in opposition, as it is here, to *in this world*, refers not only to the more elevated nature of this life (*Reuss*), but also to the future epoch in which it will break forth in its perfection. This saying, which means that man gives himself to find himself again, is that which Jesus has most frequently uttered (see above); it expresses the most profound law of human life. How should not this moral axiom, which governed the life of the Master, be applicable also to that of the disciples? It is evidently with a view to these latter also, that Jesus expresses it for a last time in this so solemn moment.

Ver. 26. "*If any one serves me, let him follow me; and where I am, there shall also my servant be; if*[1] *any one serves me, him will my Father honor.*" *To follow*, here: on the pathway of sacrifice, which alone leads to the glorious metamorphosis. The Greek term: *where I am*, is a present of antici-

---

[1] ℵ B D L X It. Syr. reject καὶ (*and*) before ἐάν τις.

pation; it refers to the state of the celestial glory of Jesus, as the promise: *shall be there also*, refers to the participation of the faithful disciple in that state (xvii. 24). Τιμήσει, *shall honor*, recalls the *shall be glorified*, δοξασθῇ, of ver. 23. The Father will honor the faithful servant who has consented to bear the shame of His Son in renouncing all glory of his own; he will make him participate in the glorification of this Son. Herein is for both the *keeping* of the life which they have given up. Perhaps Andrew and Philip had seen with a somewhat carnal satisfaction the conduct of these strangers desirous to render homage to their Master. Jesus, accustomed to silence continually within Himself even the most lawful aspirations of the natural life, in view of His divine mission, suppresses by a word these ambitious thoughts on the part of His disciples. Then, immediately after having thus declared the law which obliges Him to die, He feels in His whole being the reaction of this formidable thought.

Vv. 27, 28a. " *Now is my soul troubled, and what shall I say? Father, save me from this hour? But for this cause came I unto this hour.* 28a. *Father, glorify thy name.*" The soul, ψυχή, is the seat of the natural emotions, as *the spirit*, πνεῦμα, is that of the religious emotions. *Weiss* disputes this distinction by appealing to the altogether similar emotion described in xi. 33. But it is precisely this expression, especially when compared with xiii. 21, which confirms it. In these two passages the question is of a shuddering of a religious and moral nature at the evil which is approaching Him in the most hateful form. Here, on the contrary, it is the prospect of personal griefs and of death which so violently agitates Him. The term ψυχή, *soul*, is therefore perfectly in its place. I do not understand the import of the explanation of *Weiss*, which is intended to identify ψυχή and πνεῦμα: "The spirit becomes the soul in man" (see *Keil*). The perfect τετάρακται, *is troubled*, indicates a *state* in which the Lord feels Himself entirely overwhelmed. And this extraordinary trouble reveals itself especially to His consciousness by the hesitation which He feels, at the moment when He is seeking to pour out His emotion in prayer. Ordinarily, He has a distinct view of that which He should ask of His Father; now, this clearness fails Him. Like the believer in the state which St. Paul describes in Rom. viii. 26, He knows not how He should pray. He is obliged to lay before Himself for a moment the question: *What shall I say?* This question He does not address, properly speaking, to God, nor to man, but to Himself. The sacrifice of His own life is in itself a free act; He could still, if He saw fit, ask of God to release Him from it. And the Father would hear him, as always, even should it be necessary to send Him *twelve legions of angels*. But would not this prayer, while delivering Him, destroy mankind? Jesus does not feel Himself free to pray thus. He is already too far advanced on the path on which He is to realize the salvation of the world, to stop so near the end. The word *now*, which begins the sentence, characterizes this distress as an anticipation of that which awaits Him in the presence of the cross: *already now*, although the terrible hour has not yet struck. After the question: *What shall I say?* how are we to understand the words: *Father, save me from this hour?* Is this the real prayer wherein this moment of uncertainty through which He has just passed, terminates? This is what is supposed by *Lücke, Meyer, Hengstenberg, Ebrard, Luthardt, Westcott*. What would be its meaning? "Release me from the necessity of dying," as when He offers the prayer in Gethsemane: "*Let this cup pass from me*"? This is held by the first three. But there he adds: *if it is possible,* and by the πλήν which follows, He commits it immediately to the Father's will (Matt. xxvi. 39). And how can we explain the sudden change of impression in the following clause? After having uttered seriously and without restriction the petition: "Save me from this hour!" could He add, as it were in a single breath: "But for this hour am I come"? *Luthardt, Ebrard,* and *Westcott* perceive this clearly. So they propose to understand the σῶσόν με, *save me*, not in the sense: "Deliver me from death," but in the sense: "Bring me victoriously out of this present inward struggle," either by shortening it or by giving it a happy issue. But how are we to explain the following adversative particle ἀλλά, *but?* Here *Westcott* proposes an absolute *tour de force*. "But to what purpose say this? The favorable issue is not doubtful." This sense of *but* is altogether forced; and there is no more opposition between: to come forth from the struggle, and: to have come for it. However we may turn this phrase, we are always brought back to see in it a hypothetical prayer. It is the voice of nature which at first makes itself heard in answer to the question: *What shall I say?* Then, in the following words Jesus represses this voice. To address this petition to God would be to deny all that He has done and endured until now. And finally, giving vent to the voice of the spirit, He definitely stays Himself in the prayer which alone remains, when once this moment of trouble is past: *Glorify thy name!* that is to say: "Derive from me Thy glory, by doing with me what Thou wilt. Nothing for me, everything for Thee!" What more instructive than this conflict between these two factors which solicit the will of Jesus? It allows us to penetrate into the inmost recess of His heart. What do we there discover? Precisely the opposite of that impassive Jesus whom our critics assert the Christ of John to be.

The expressions: *for this cause,* and: *for this hour,* seem to constitute a pleonasm. We might make this clause a question: "Is it then for this that I am come to this hour?" that is, to try to put it off indefinitely? Or we may make the words *for this hour* an explanatory apposition to *for this:* "It is for this that I am come, that is, for this hour." These two meanings are forced, the first, because of the two questions which already precede; the second, because the εἰς is not the natural resuming of the διά, but rather the direct objective word to ἦλθον and the antithesis of σῶσον ἐκ. *Hengstenberg* explains: "It is that my soul may be troubled that I am come . . . ," which is still more forced. *Lücke* and *Meyer* make the words *for this* bear upon the idea of the following prayer (ver. 28): *Father, glorify thy name.* This is to do violence to the sentence beyond measure. Is it not quite simple to see in the neuter *this* the expression, in a slight degree mysterious, of that *something* which has just brought trouble upon His soul, and which He is tempted to seek to remove by

His prayer, the dark and unutterable contents of the hour which is approaching? "It is because of this death which I am to undergo, that I have persevered in this path until this hour." All that he has done and suffered in view of the cross does not permit Him to give way at the moment when the hour of this terrible punishment is about to strike. Comp. iii. 14.—The pronoun *thy* (ver. 28), by reason of the place which it occupies, is emphasized. It is opposed, as *Weiss* says, to the personal character of the preceding prayer which Jesus has set aside.

Colani, in his criticism of the *Vie de Jésus* by *Renan*, by a strange inadvertence makes Jesus say: "Father, glorify *my* name," an expression which, he says, "has no meaning except from the standpoint of the Logos-doctrine."[1] The more involuntary this alteration is, the better is it fitted to make us see the difference between the profoundly human Jesus of John and the fantastic Christ whom criticism ascribes to the evangelist. That, after this, Colani sees in this scene only "an emblematic, almost simulated, agony" is easy to understand; to whom does the fault belong? *Reuss*, who claims that the silence of John respecting the scene of Gethsemane arises from the fact that "even a passing weakness would have been a feature incompatible with the portrait of the Johannean Christ," finds himself greatly embarrassed by the narrative which occupies us. The following is the way in which he escapes from the difficulty. "The emotion of Jesus is not that of a momentary and touching weakness . . . , it is that of a great soul, of a divine heroism . . . whose resolution is rather strengthened than shaken in the presence of the supreme catastrophe." We leave the reader to judge whether this exegesis reproduces or contradicts the true tone of the text to be explained, particularly of these words: "Now is my soul troubled." What we admire in this passage, is the perfectly human character of the struggle which, at the thought of His approaching death, takes place in the heart of Jesus between nature and spirit. And then it is the sincerity, the candor, shall we say, with which He expresses His inmost feelings, *His weakness* (Heb. v. 2), before all this company of people, not hesitating to make them acquainted with the perplexity into which the prospect of His approaching sufferings plunges Him. This scene is, as has always been acknowledged, the prelude to the one in Gethsemane. Only in the latter, Jesus, at the highest point of His distress, really utters the cry: *Save me from this hour!* while at the moment which we have now reached, He only asks whether He shall pray thus. This delicate shade is suited to the difference of the two situations and proves the strictly historical character of each of them. The opinion that John suppressed the scene of Gethsemane as incompatible with the divine character of the Logos, falls of itself before this passage. Finally, let us establish the remarkable gradation in the three analogous scenes, Luke xii. 49, 50, John xii. 27 and the one in Gethsemane. This comparison makes us understand the increasing emotion with which Jesus was slowly approaching the cross. These three features borrowed from the four narratives easily unite in one single picture. How can *Réville* express himself as follows, in the *Revue de théologie*, 1865, III., p. 316, "The fourth Gospel makes Jesus an exalted being, as to His moral life, above temptation and internal conflict, and it removes from its narrative all the traditional statements which might suggest a contrary idea." *Renan*, on the contrary,

[1] *Revue de théologie*, 3d series, I., p. 382.

observes with reference to this passage: "Here are verses which have an indubitable historical stamp. They are the obscure and isolated episode of the Greeks who address themselves to Philip."

Vv. 28b, 29. "*Whereupon there came a voice from heaven, I have both glorified it and I will glorify it again. 29. The multitude therefore that stood by and heard it, said that it thundered; others said, An angel has spoken to him.*" Each time that the Son performs a great act of self-humiliation and personal consecration, the Father answers by a sensible manifestation of approval. What had happened at the baptism and the transfiguration is now renewed. At this hour which is the closing of Jesus' ministry, and in which He devoted Himself to death, is the time—or never—for the Father publicly to set the seal of His satisfaction upon His person and His work.

Lücke, de Wette, Hengstenberg, Weiss, regard this voice from heaven as a simple thunder-clap. By reason of the coincidence of this external phenomenon with His prayer, Jesus, in their view, interpreted it freely in the sense indicated by the evangelist. Is not thunder often called in the Old Testament, *the voice of the Lord?* The Rabbis gave a name to these prophetic voices, these mysterious inspirations which a word accidentally heard calls up in the hearts of believers, namely, *Bath-Kol* (*daughter of the voice*). But the text does not favor this interpretation of the phenomenon here related. According to John, it is not a clap of thunder taken to be a voice from heaven; it is, on the contrary, a voice from heaven which a part of the multitude regard as a clap of thunder; comp. *Meyer.* How could Jesus say: *this voice* (ver. 30)? How could this voice be translated by Him or by John into a definite expression in words? Whence would arise in these words the contrast between the past (*I have glorified*) and the future (*I will glorify*), a contrast which has no connection with anything in the prayer of Jesus? How, finally, could one part of the multitude itself discern in this sound an articulate language which they attribute to an angel? The text permits us to think only of a divine phenomenon. As to the Rabbinical superstition called *Bath-Kol,* it cannot be cited here, since one would infer from such signs only a human voice. The past *I have glorified* refers to the ministry of the Lord in Israel, which is close upon its end; the future *I will glorify,* to the approaching action of Jesus on the whole world, when from the midst of His glory He will enlighten the heathen. Between these two great works which the Father accomplishes through the Son, is placed precisely the hour of suffering and death which is the necessary transition from the one to the other. There is no ground therefore to draw back before this hour. It is, moreover, well surrounded. Before,—the name of God glorified in Israel; after,—the name of God glorified in the whole world. Here indeed is the most consoling response for the filial heart of Jesus (xvii. 1, 2, 4, 5). The two καί, *and, and,* bring out the close connection between the work done and the work to be done: "I who have accomplished the one, will also accomplish the other."

The whole multitude hear a sound; but the meaning of the voice is perceived by each one only in proportion to his spiritual intelligence. Thus, in human speech the wild beast perceives only a *sound*, the trained animal discovers in it a *meaning*, a command, for example, which it immediately obeys; man only discerns in it a *thought*. Ὄχλος: the greater number; ἄλλοι: others in smaller numbers; comp. Acts ix. 7 with xxii. 9; xxvi. 13, 14, where an analogous phenomenon occurs at the time of the appearance of Jesus to Paul. In order to understand a vision, there must be an internal organ and this organ may be more or less favorably disposed. At Pentecost, where some see only the effects of drunkenness, others discern a revelation of the glorious things of God (Acts ii. 11–13). The perfect λελάληκεν, instead of the aorist, signifies that to their view Jesus is for the future a person *in possession* of this heavenly sign.

Vv. 30–32. "*Jesus answered and said: Not for my sake has this voice*[1] *made itself heard, but for your sakes.* 31. *Now is the judgment of this world;*[2] *now shall the prince of this world be cast out.* 32. *And I, when I shall have been lifted up from the earth, will draw all*[3] *men unto me.*" In declaring that this voice does not make itself heard for His sake, Jesus does not mean to say that He has no need to be strengthened; but only that He had not needed to be strengthened in this way, that is, by a sensible manifestation. What the procedure of the Greeks has been for Him, in awakening vividly within Him the feeling of the gravity of the present hour, this heavenly phenomenon should be for them, by revealing to them the decisive importance of the crisis which is accomplished in this moment. And first, as to the world, this hour is that of the most radical revolution (vv. 31, 32). It is that of its judgment (ver. 31a), of the expulsion of its former master (ver. 31b), and of the advent of its new monarch (ver. 32). The word νῦν, *now*, at the beginning of the first two clauses, sets forth expressly this decisive character of the present moment for humanity.

To judge is to declare the moral state, not only as evil but also as good. I cannot accept, therefore, the meaning which *Weiss* gives here to the word κρίσις, *judgment*, in applying it only to the condemnation of the world as the consequence of the rejection and the death of Christ. No doubt, the cross is the basis of the condemnation of the world, as it reveals completely the moral state of natural humanity. This throne, erected for Jesus by man, shows the depth of hostility to God which is in his heart. But this is not the only side of the judgment of the world by the work of Christ; comp. iii. 21 following iii. 18–20. Passing before the cross, one part of mankind find in it their salvation through faith, while the other part through unbelief complete their condemnation. Here is the judgment of the world which is the consequence of Holy Friday. It will begin inwardly on this very day. Its first great outward manifestation will be Pentecost; the second will be the fall of Jerusalem. The final universal judgment will be the solemn ratification of it (ver. 48).

---

[1] T. R. with 11 Mjj. (E F G); αυτη η φωνη, instead of η φωνη αυτη, in 7 Mjj (ℵ A B etc.).

[2] ℵ omits the words νυν ο αρχων τ. κ. τουτου substituting for them και (a confusion of the two του κοσμου τουτου).

[3] Instead of παντας, ℵ D It. Vulg. read παντα (*every man* or *all things*).

But, at the same time that the cross will manifest the moral state of the world, it will exhaust the measure of toleration accorded to its prince. The crucifixion of the Son of God is the most odious, the most unpardonable crime of Satan: this crime puts an end to the long-suffering of God towards him, and, consequently, to his dominion over mankind. The Rabbis habitually designate Satan as the *prince of the world* (*Sar haholam*). But they place the Jews outside of his empire, which includes only the Gentiles. Jesus, on the contrary, counts this rebellious people as belonging to it (chap. viii.), which He even especially calls *the world* (xv. 18). *Out* signifies not only; out of his office and power, but above all: out of his former domain, the world, mankind in the natural state. This meaning appears from the relation of these words to those which precede. "With the consummation of the redemptive work," says *Weiss*, "the expulsion of the devil begins." One soul after another is taken away from him, and the progress goes on advancing even to the final day. Thus this saying does not contradict those which still ascribe to Satan an activity in the world.

To the deposition of the former ruler answers the advent of the new sovereign. Jesus expressly designates Himself as the one who is called to fill this office: κἀγώ, *and I*. But, a strange fact, as He substitutes Himself for Satan, it is not on the earth, from which Satan is driven out, that He establishes His kingdom. The Jews imagined that the Messiah would become *here on earth* the successor of His adversary, that He would be another prince *of this world*. But no, He will leave the world, as does also His rival; He will be obliged to leave it that He may be elevated above it, and it is from this higher sphere that He will draw His subjects to Him, and will realize His kingdom. However little familiar we may be with the language of Jesus, we may understand that the expression *be lifted up* must be taken here in the same amphibological sense as in iii. 14 and viii. 28. His suspension on the cross is identified with the elevation to the throne to which it is for Him the way. *Meyer* objects against this double sense of the word *be lifted up* the limiting phrase ἐκ τῆς γῆς, *out of the earth*, which proves, according to him, that Jesus is thinking not of His death, but of the ascension. It is no doubt very evident that the expression *out of the earth* does not refer only to the small distance of two or three cubits between the ground and the feet of the crucified one. But it is this very expression: *out of the earth*, which forces us to see in the word *be lifted up*, an allusion to the punishment of the cross. If Jesus had thought only of the ascension, the natural limiting phrase would have been *into heaven* or *to the Father*. By saying *from the earth*, He indicates the violent manner in which He will be expelled from this domain over which He is to reign. There will be made for a time an abyss between the earth and Himself. This will render necessary for a time the heavenly and invisible form of His kingdom. Now it is to the cross that this temporary separation between the earth and Him will be due; comp. Gal. vi. 14.

The cross and the ascension taken together therefore freed Jesus from all earthly bonds and especially from all His national obligations towards Israel. They thus put Him in a position to extend His activity over the whole world, to become *the Lord of all* (Rom. x. 12). This is what enables Him to say "*I will draw them all unto me;*" *all*, not only the Jews, but all men, and consequently the Greeks. From this word *all* and from this future *I will draw*, His response to the request which had called forth this discourse clearly appears. The hour of the call of the Greeks draws near; but, before it strikes, another hour is to strike! Some limit the *all* to the elect; others give it this sense: men of every nation; *Meyer* seems to find in it the idea of final universal salvation. But ἑλκύειν, *to draw*, does not necessarily denote an effectual drawing. This word may refer only to the preaching of the cross throughout the whole world and the action of the Holy Spirit which accompanies it. This heavenly drawing is not irresistible. The last word: *to me*, literally, *to myself*, makes prominent the personal position of Jesus as the supra-terrestrial centre of the kingdom of God. Once exalted to heaven, He becomes at the same time the author and the end of the divine drawing, and gathers around Himself His new people, heavenly like Himself.

These two verses sum up the whole history of the Church; both from a negative and polemical point of view: the gradual destruction of the kingdom of Satan, and from a positive point of view: the progressive establishment of the kingdom of God.

Ver. 33. "*Now this he said, signifying by what death he should die.*" This explanation of John is declared to be false by some modern interpreters (*Meyer, Reuss*, etc.), Jesus having spoken, according to them, of the Ascension, not of the cross. But we have seen that the idea of the cross was necessarily implied in the preceding words, and it must, indeed, be remarked that the apostle does not say δηλῶν, *declaring*, plainly, but only σημαίνων, *indicating, giving to understand*. John means simply to say that in giving this form to His thought, Jesus gives an anticipatory hint of the kind of death which He must undergo. *Reuss* would indeed draw from this false explanation of the Evangelist a proof in favor of the authenticity of the words of ver. 32. We think we have better reasons for holding the authenticity. This striking passage in which Jesus, after having shuddered in view of the cross, strengthened Himself by tracing in broad outlines the picture of the immense revolution which it will effect, may be compared with that of St. Paul, Col. ii. 14, 15, where that apostle represents Jesus as making a spectacle of the infernal powers, despoiling them of their power and triumphing over them on the cross. Comp. also the passage, 2 Cor. v. 14—17, according to which the death of Christ is virtually a principle of death for the whole human race, but thereby the means of universal renewal. According to the Jewish programme, the Messianic kingdom was to be the glorification of the earth, and the Messiah the visible sovereign of this new Eden; how could the Messianic character of Jesus, therefore, accord with the idea of leaving the earth? Hence the following question of the Jews, ver. 34.

Ver. 34. "*The multitude answered*[1] *him, We have heard from the law that the*

---

[1] ℵ B L X add ουν to απεκριθη.

Christ abides for ever; how sayest thou then, The Son of man must be lifted up? Who is this Son of man?" Ver. 34. "How sayest thou, *thou?"* This *thou* is opposed to *we*, ἡμεῖς: we who are acquainted with the law and those among us who explain it. The passages to which the Jews allude are those in which the Messiah is represented as founding on the ruins of the heathen empires an eternal kingdom : Is. ix. 6; Ps. cx. 2–4; Dan. vii. 14, etc. On the term *the law*, see p. 725. In order to resolve the difficulty, the objectors themselves make a supposition respecting which they ask to be enlightened. Jesus has the habit of designating Himself as the Son of man; might this name perhaps designate in His mouth a personage different from the Christ? This question is not without analogy to that which John the Baptist addressed to Jesus from the centre of his prison : " Art thou he that should come or are we to look for another? " (comp., p. 323 f.). The Jews certainly do not mean : Is this Son of man thyself or some other ? He has just applied to Himself this title, ver. 23. As Jesus has always refused to take openly before them the title of Christ, they ask themselves rather if the term Son of man does not designate a different personage from the Messiah, one of the numerous forerunners who were looked for. *Meyer* and *Weiss* explain differently : " What a strange Messiah is he who wishes to go away, instead of transforming everything ! " But the terms of the question do not express this idea. The expression must have been : What sort of Christ is this ! and not : *Who is this Son of man?* These words of the people appear to me to prove that the title *Son of man* was not generally used in Israel to designate the Messiah; and, as we have already seen, it was precisely for this reason that Jesus had chosen it to designate Himself habitually (comp., p. 338 f.). We find ourselves in accord on this point with Colani.[1] The question proposed by His hearers leads Jesus to explain to them the vital importance of the present hour for Israel in particular.

Vv. 35, 36. " *Jesus therefore said to them, The light is with you* [2] *only a little while longer; walk while* [3] *you have the light, lest the darkness overtake you; and he that walks in the darkness knows not whither he goes.* 36. *While* [4] *you have the light, believe on the light, that you may become children of light. Jesus said this to them; then, departing, he hid himself from them."* Jesus does not reply to them directly. It was no longer the time to teach and discuss. He addresses to their hearts a last warning, a final appeal, by making them feel the decisive importance of the present hour for themselves and for their whole people. This is the reason why John says εἶπεν *he said, declared*, not ἀπεκρίθη, *he answered*. The day of salvation is at its end; the sun which still enlightens Israel is going to disappear in a few moments. When the sun sets, those who have a journey to make must hasten before

---

[1] *Jesus-Christ et les croyances messianiques de son temps*, p. 75 ff. But how can this author say : In order to find in the mouth of Jesus this title of Son of man, we must go back " at least four months earlier (viii. 28)." He forgets ver. 23 which immediately precedes.

[2] T. R. with A E F G H S U∆∆ Mnn. Syr: μεθ' υμων *(with you)*; ℵ B D K M X Π 20 Mnn. It. Vulg. Cop. : εν υμιν *(among you)*.

[3] A B D K L X Π 4 Mnn. : ως *(as)*, instead of εως *(so long as)* which T. R. reads with 11 Mjj.

[4] ℵ A B D L Π: ως instead of εως.

the night comes on. By this journey, Jesus means the act of believing, for all those who are still far removed from Him. When once the heavenly revealer shall be no longer present, the unbelieving people will be like a traveler lost in the night, who wanders at a venture without seeing either pathway or end. If vv. 31, 32 sum up the whole history of the Church, it may be well said that ver. 35 contains that of Israel from the day on which Jesus was speaking to the present hour. The apostolic preaching was no doubt still granted to this people, but how, when once launched on the declivity of unbelief, could Israel, *as a people*, have changed its course. And when the preaching of the apostles, that last gift of grace, had rescued a certain number of individuals from the ruin, it was soon withdrawn from the nation. Since then, Israel wanders in the wilderness of this world, as a caravan without a goal and without a guide. The two readings: *with you* and *among you* differ only in the figure. It is not altogether so with the readings ἕως, *while* (T. R.) and ὡς, *as* or *according as*. Meyer, Weiss, Luthardt, Keil, adopting the second, give to ὡς its ordinary logical sense: *as, conformably to the fact that*: "Walk according as you have the light," that is to say: "Because of the fact that you still have the light, come to it, believe!" It is with reason, as it seems to me, that *Bäumlein* declares this explanation of ὡς impossible. The words: *yet a little time*, force us to give it the temporal sense. We must, therefore, either understand it in the sense of *when* which the French *comme* so often has (comp. for this use of ὡς in the New Testament, Luke xii. 58: "*As* thou goest," for: "*While* thou goest)," or read ἕως, *while*, notwithstanding the Alexandrian authorities. The initial ε of this word was undoubtedly confounded with the final ε of the preceding word περιπατεῖτε. I should not be surprised, however, if it were otherwise in ver. 36, and if the true reading here were ὡς. The idea of *because of the fact that* is much more admissible in this sentence, "*Because of the fact that* you have the light, believe in the light;" comp. Gal. vi. 10, where the ὡς may be explained in the same way. This is precisely the reading of the *Sinaitic* MS. It is the more easily explained, in this case, how in ver. 35 the ὡς may have been substituted for ἕως. In two sentences so near together and so similar, the copyists may have made either the first conform to the second, or the reverse. An equal solemnity reigns in these two appeals of vv. 35 and 36; only in the former the tone of pity prevails; in the latter, that of tenderness. The last word of the Saviour to His people was to be an invitation, not a menace: "Since you still possess in me the living revelation of God (φῶς, *the light*), acknowledge it, believe on it, to the end that you *may become* (γένησθε) *children of light*." Through faith in Christ man is so penetrated by light that he himself becomes luminous.

Such was the farewell of Jesus to Israel. The words: *He said these things*, signify that He gave them no other response. Thereupon He withdraws; and on the following day He does not reappear. The people waited for Him in the temple as usual (Luke xxi. 38); but in vain. It was at this time no longer a mere cloud which veiled the sun; the sun had set, the night was come.

3

John 12:37-50

RETROSPECTIVE GLANCE AT THE MYSTERIOUS FACT OF JEWISH UNBELIEF

This passage forms the close of the second part of the Gospel (v. 1–xii. 36). The evangelist interrupts his narrative that he may give himself up to a meditation on the fact which he has just set forth. What is this fact? Is it, as some interpreters suppose (*Reuss, Westcott*, for example) the public ministry of Jesus? The entire part—chaps. v.–xii.—is the representation of the public activity of the Lord, while chaps. xiii.–xvii. describe His *private activity*. This view appears to us very superficial. Between these two parts, there exists a much more profound contrast than that of a more or less limited circle of activity; it is that of unbelief and faith, of unbelief in the people and of faith in the disciples. Is it not obvious that the real subject of the following epilogue, that which preoccupies the mind of John and becomes for a moment the subject of his meditation, is not the public ministry of Jesus, but the unbelief of the Jewish people. The question to which John replies is this: How explain the failure of the work of the Messiah in Israel? It is indeed one of the most obscure problems of history. It rose in all its greatness, after the preceding part of the Gospel, before the eyes of the historian and his readers. In the first passage, vv. 37–43, Jesus explains the *causes* of this mysterious fact; in the second, vv. 44–50, he shows the gravity of it by summing up its tragical *consequences*.

The causes of Jewish unbelief: vv. 37–43

If the Jews are the chosen people, prepared of God to the end of receiving the Messiah and of carrying salvation to other nations, ought they not to have been the first to open their arms to Jesus? Or, if they did not, must it not be inferred from this fact that Jesus was not really the Messiah? Chaps. ix.–xi. of the Epistle to the Romans are designed to examine into this great paradox of the religious history of mankind; it was the great apologetic question of the time of the apostles. Thus it is that the following passage in John contains many of the thoughts which likewise form the basis of St. Paul's dissertation.

Vv. 37, 38. "*Now, although he had done so many miracles in their presence, they did not believe on him, 38 that the word which Isaiah the prophet had spoken might be fulfilled: Lord, who has believed our preaching and to whom has the arm of the Lord been revealed?*" However irrational is the fact with which John is about to occupy himself, it must be accomplished, for it was foreseen and *foretold*. How many motives to believe were there for the Jews in the appearance of Jesus, particularly in His miracles which were the testimony of God, the seal with which He marked His Son, *signs* the meaning of which it was easy to apprehend, especially for Jews (1 Cor. i. 22)! The word τοσαῦτα, *so many*, in our gospels, refers always to number, not to

792 / Unbelief Develops in Israel

greatness; comp. vi. 9, xxi. 11; it is also sometimes its meaning in the classics; comp. the expression τοσαῦτα τε καὶ τοιαῦτα. These words imply that Jesus had done a much larger number of miracles than the six related in this book; comp. vii. 3, xx. 30. John did not wish therefore to relate everything that he knew. The term σημεῖα, *signs*, calls to mind the divine purpose in these works, and the words ἔμπροσθεν αὐτῶν, *in their presence*, their complete publicity. The imperfect, *they did not believe*, sets forth the continuance, the obstinate persistency of the Israelitish unbelief, notwithstanding the signs which were renewed every day before their eyes.

Scarcely any one seeks any longer to weaken the sense of ἵνα, *in order that*, by making it a ὥστε, *so that*. The passage quoted is Is. liii. 1. The prophet, at the moment of describing the humiliation, the death and the exaltation of the Messiah, asks himself whether there will be any one in Israel who is disposed to welcome with faith a *message* such as this, so contrary to the carnal aspirations of the people. Now the Messiah to whom the prophecy refers cannot hope for a better welcome than the message itself. These two things, the message and the Messiah who is its subject, are so completely one and the same thing to the view of the prophet that in the second clause, parallel to the first, there is no more any question except of the Messiah (*the arm of the Lord recognized*). The reply to the question *Who has believed?* is, in the thought of the prophet, either no one, or a small number of persons; they can be counted. According to some, the expression ἀκοὴ ἡμῶν, *our hearing*, signifies: *that which we hear* from the mouth of Jehovah, either we prophets (*Hengstenberg*), or we Jews who have attained to faith, the prophet being included (*Hofmann, Delitzsch, Keil*). But it is much more natural to explain: "*That which we cause to be heard* (we prophets)." It is certainly not the people hearing; it is the prophets preaching who can raise such a question. The first expression: *that which we preach*, refers to the suffering Messiah described in the following picture; the second: *the arm of the Lord,* to the *acts* of divine power of which He will be the agent, especially at His resurrection and at His exaltation, which are the crowning points of this picture (Is. liii. 10–12). The prophecy had thus declared that a Messiah, such as God should send, would not find faith in Israel; His humiliation would to such a degree shock this people, who would not even have eyes to discern the manifestations of the divine power in His appearance. But the fact might be *foretold* without being *desired* by God. Well, it was at once desired and announced, so far that God Himself coöperated in its execution. Such is the advance from ver. 38 to ver. 39. Yes, in this blindness there is something supernatural!

Vv. 39, 40. "*And indeed they could not believe, because Isaiah said again,* 40 *He has blinded their eyes and hardened* [1] *their hearts, that they should not see with their eyes and understand* [2] *with their heart, and be converted,* [3]

---

[1] The Byz. (Γ Δ etc.) read πεπωρωκεν; the Alex. (A B K L X): επωρωσεν; ℵ Π επηρωσεν.

[2] Instead of νοησωσιν, K Π Chrys. συνωσιν.

[3] ℵ B D: στραφωσιν, instead of επιστραφωσιν (T. R. with 10 Mjj.); 5 Mjj. (K L etc.): επιστρεψωσιν.

and I should heal[1] *them."* The omnipotence of God itself worked to the end of realizing that which His omniscience had foretold, and to make Israel do the impossible thing. Not only they *did not believe* (ver. 37); but they *could not believe* (ver. 39). The word πάλιν (*again*) reminds us that there is here a *second* idea, serving to explain the fact by completing the first. This logical relation answers to the meaning of the two expressions of Isaiah quoted by John. The διὰ τοῦτο, *for this cause*, refers, as ordinarily in John (v. 18, x. 17, etc.), to the following ὅτι, *because* : " And *this is the reason why* they could not believe : *it is because* Isaiah in another passage (πάλιν) said." It is in vain that *Weiss* tries to make the διὰ τοῦτο, *for this cause*, also refer to the preceding idea, namely, that of the fact; it refers to the following ὅτι and consequently to the *cause* of the fact (see *Keil*). These words are taken from Is. vi. 9, 10. The word of address, *Lord*, added by the LXX., passed thence to John. The quotation differs both from the Hebrew text and from that of the LXX., in that according to the former, it is Isaiah who is said to blind and harden the people by his ministry : " *Make the heart of this people fat ;* " according to the latter, this hardening is a simple fact laid to the charge of Israel : " *The heart of this people is hardened ;* " in John, on the contrary, the understood subject of the two verbs (*he has blinded, he has hardened*) can only be God. This third form is evidently a deliberate correction of the latter, in order to go back to the meaning of the former. For this fact accomplished by Isaiah, being the execution of the command of God, is rightly attributed by John to God Himself. This passage proves that the evangelist, while attaching himself to the Greek translation, was not dependent on it and was acquainted with the Hebrew text(comp., p. 197 f.). Τυφλοῦν, *to make blind*, designates the depriving of intellectual light, of the sense of the true and even of the useful, of simple good sense ; πωροῦν, *to harden the skin*, the depriving of moral sensibility, the sense of the good. From the paralysis of these two organs unbelief must necessarily result; the people may see miracle after miracle, may hear testimony after testimony, yet they will not discern in the one whom God thus points out, and who gives all these testimonies to Himself, their Messiah. The subject of the two verbs is undoubtedly God (*Meyer, Reuss*), but God in the person of that Adonai who (according to Is. vi. 1) gives the command to the prophet. The reading of nearly all the Mjj. is ἰάσομαι, *and I shall heal them*. This future might signify : " And I shall end by bringing them to myself through the means of their very hardening." The two καί *and* . . . *and,* however, are too closely related to each other for such a contrast between the last verb and those which precede it to be admissible. The force of the formidable ἵνα μή, *in order that I* . . . , evidently extends as far as the end of the sentence. The construction of the indicative with this conjunction has nothing unusual in it (1 Cor. xiii. 3 ; 1 Pet. iii. 1 ; Apoc. xxii. 14); it is frequent also in the classic Greek with ὅπως. We might undoubtedly explain in this way : " lest they should be converted, in which case I will

---

[1] All the Mjj., except L Γ, read ιασομαι, instead of ιασωμαι.

heal them" (for: I would heal them). But the other sense remains the more natural one: God does not desire to heal them; it is not in accordance with His actual intentions towards them. This is precisely the reason why He does not desire that they should believe—a thing which would force Him to pardon and heal them.

If such is the meaning of the words of the prophet and of those of the evangelist, how can it be justified? These declarations would be inexplicable and revolting if, at the moment when God addresses them to Israel and treats Israel in this way, this people were in the normal state, and God regarded them still as *His* people. But it was by no means so; when sending Isaiah, God said to him: "*Go and tell* THIS *people*" (Is. vi. 9). And we know what a father means, when speaking of his son, he says: *this* child, instead of *my* child: the paternal and filial relation is momentarily broken. An abnormal state has begun, which obliges God to use means of an extraordinary character. This divine dispensation towards Israel enters therefore into the category of *chastisements*. The creature who has long abused the divine favors falls under the most terrible of punishments; from an *end* it becomes for the time a *means*. In fact man can, by virtue of his liberty, refuse to glorify God by his obedience and salvation; but even in this case he cannot prevent God from glorifying Himself in him by a chastisement capable of making the odious character of his sin shine forth conspicuously. "God," says *Hengstenberg,*"has so constituted man, that, when he does not resist the first beginnings of sin, he loses the right of disposing of himself and forcibly obeys even to the end the power to which he has surrendered himself." God does not merely *permit* this development of evil; He *wills* it and *concurs* in it. But how, it will be said, will the holiness of God, as thus understood, be reconciled with His love? This is that which St. Paul explains to the Jews by the example of their ancient oppressor, Pharaoh, Rom. ix. 17: In the first place, this king refuses to hearken to God and to be saved; he has the prerogative to do so. But after this he is passively used for the salvation of others. God paralyses in him both the sense of the true and the sense of the good; he becomes deaf to the appeals of conscience and even to the calculations of self-interest properly understood; he is given up to the inspirations of his own foolish pride, in order that, through the conspicuous example of the ruin into which he precipitates himself, the world may learn what it costs wickedly to resist the first appeals of God. Thereby he at least serves the salvation of the world. The history of Pharaoh is reproduced in that of the Jews in the time of Jesus Christ. Already at the epoch of Isaiah the mass of the people were so carnal that their future unbelief in the Messiah, the man of sorrows, appears to the prophet an inevitable moral fact (Is. liii.). We must even go further and say, with Paul and John, that, things being thus, this unbelief must have been *willed* of God. What would have become of the kingdom of God, indeed, if an Israel like this had outwardly and without a change of heart received Jesus as its Messiah and had become with such dispositions the nucleus of the Church? This purely intellectual adherence of Israel, instead of advancing the divine work in the heathen world, would have served only to hinder it. We have the proof of this in the injurious part which was played in the Apostolic Church by the Pharisaic minority who accepted the faith. Suppose that the Jewish people *en masse* had acted thus and had governed the Church, the work of St. Paul would not have been possible; the Jewish monopoly would have taken possession of the gospel; there would have been an end of the universalism which is the essential characteristic of the new covenant. The rejection of the Jews thus disposed was therefore a measure necessary to the salvation of the world. It is in this sense that St. Paul says in Rom. xi. 12: "that the fall of Israel has become the riches of the world," and ver. 15: "that its rejection has been the reconciliation of the world." How, indeed, could the Gentiles have welcomed a salvation connected with circumcision and the Mosaic observances? God was therefore obliged to make Israel blind, that the miracles of Jesus might be as nothing in their eyes and as not having taken place, and to harden them, that His preachings might remain for them as empty sounds (Is. vi.). Thus Israel proud, legal, carnal, rejected and could be rejected *freely*. This decided position did not in reality make Israel's lot worse; but it had for the salvation of the Gentiles the excellent results which St. Paul develops in Rom. xi. Far more than this, by this very chastisement, Israel became what it had refused to be by its salvation, the apostle of the world; and, like Judas its type, it fulfilled, willingly or unwillingly, its irrevocable commission; comp. Rom. xi. 7–10. Moreover, it is clear that, in the midst of this national judgment, every *individual* remained free to turn to God by repentance and to escape the general hardening. Ver. 13 of Isaiah and ver. 42 of John are the proof of this.

As to the relation of the Jewish unbelief to the divine *prevision* (vv. 37, 38), John does not indicate the metaphysical theory by means of which he succeeds in reconciling the foreknowledge of God with the responsibility of man; he simply accepts these two data, the one of the religious sentiment, the other of the moral consciousness. But if we reflect that God is above time, that, properly speaking, He does not *foresee* an event which is for us yet to come, but that He *sees* it, absolutely as we behold a present event; that, consequently, when He declares it at any moment whatsoever, He does not *foretell* it, but *describes* it as a spectator and witness, the apparent contradiction between these two seemingly contradictory elements vanishes. Once foretold, the event undoubtedly cannot fail to happen, because the eye of God cannot have presented to Him as *existing* that which will not be. But the event does not exist because God has seen it; God, on the contrary, has seen it because it *will be*, or rather because to His view it already *is*. Thus the real cause of Jewish unbelief, foretold by God, is not the divine foreseeing. This cause is, in the last analysis, the moral state of the people themselves. This state it is which, when once established by the earlier unfaithfulnesses of Israel, necessarily implies the punishment of unbelief which must strike the people at the decisive moment, the judgment of hardening.

Ver. 41. "*This did Isaiah say, when*[1] *he saw his glory and spoke of him.*" John justifies in this verse the application which he has just made to Jesus Christ of the vision of Is. vi. The Adonai whom Isaiah beheld at that moment was the divine being who is incarnated in Jesus. Herein also John and Paul meet together; comp. 1 Cor. x. 4, where Paul calls the one who guided Israel from the midst of the cloud *Christ*. Some interpreters have tried to refer the pronoun αὐτοῦ, *of him,* not to Christ, but to God. But the last words: *and spoke of him,* would be useless in this sense and

---

[1] ℵ A B L M X some Mnn. Cop. Sah. read ὅτι (*because*) instead of ὅτε (*when*) which is read by 12 Mjj. (D Γ Δ, etc.), the Mnn. It. Syr. Chrys.

this remark would be aimless in the context. The Alexandrian reading, "*because he saw,*" instead of "*when he saw,*" is adopted by *Tischendorf, Weiss, Keil,* etc. But it does not appear to me acceptable. Its only reasonable sense would be: "because he really saw his glory and spoke of Him so long beforehand (a thing which seems impossible)." But this reflection would be very coldly apologetic and quite useless for readers who were accustomed to hear the prophecies quoted. It is much more easy to understand how the conjunction ὅτε, which is quite rarely used, may have been replaced by ὅτι, which appears in every line, than how the reverse could have taken place. The ancient Latin and Syriac versions are agreed in supporting the received text. The sense of the latter is simple and perfectly suitable. "It was of Christ, who manifested Himself to him as Adonai, that Isaiah spoke *when* he uttered such words." John proves that he has the right to apply this passage here.

It might be inferred from vv. 37–41 that no Jew had either believed or been able to believe; vv. 42, 43, while completing this historical *résumé*, remove this misapprehension, but, at the same time, explain the want of significance of these few exceptions with reference to the general course of the history.

Vv. 42, 43. "*It is true, nevertheless, that, even among the rulers, many believed on him; but because of the Pharisees they did not confess their faith, lest they should be put out of the synagogue; 43 for they loved the glory which comes from men more than*[1] *the glory which comes from God.*" This exception confirms the rule, since it proves that, even where faith had been awakened, the fear of men suppressed the profession and development of it. We see from this remarkable expression how heavy was the yoke which Pharisaism made to rest as a burden upon Israel (see the parables of chap. x.). The moral cause of the hardening and blinding of the people (ver. 40) was precisely this power of Pharisaic fanaticism, which was incompatible with the spirit of the Gospel. Respecting ὅμως, *nevertheless,* comp. Gal. iii. 15; 1 Cor. xiv. 7. The words: *lest they should be put out of the synagogue,* confirm what was said in ix. 22. The word δόξα, in ver. 43, is taken nearly in its etymological sense: *opinion,* whence: *approbation.* The difference of reading (ὑπέρ and ἤπερ) is probably due to *itacism* (the pronouncing of η and υ as ι). If ὑπέρ is read, there are two forms of comparison combined here, as if for the purpose of better setting forth the odiousness of such a preference. Those who are commonly ranked in the class of these cowardly persons, are men like Nicodemus and Joseph of Arimathea. I cannot adopt this application (xix. 38–42). Those rather are in question who remained outwardly attached to the Jewish system, such as Gamaliel and many others, the Erasmuses of that time. On the necessity of profession for salvation, comp. Rom. x. 10.

The consequences of faith and unbelief: vv. 44–50

Israel was not only blinded with reference to the signs; it was deaf as regarded the testimonies which accompanied them, and this is what

---

[1] ℵ L X 5 Mnn. read υπερ instead of ηπερ.

finally renders its unbelief unpardonable. Such is the meaning and spirit of this passage; it is not a summary of the teaching of Jesus in general. It is a *résumé* made from the special standpoint of Jewish unbelief. The first part sets forth the privilege connected with faith (vv. 44–46); the second, the condemnation which will strike unbelief (vv. 47, 48); the third, the reason of the gravity of these two moral facts which was so decisive (vv. 49, 50). Criticism rightly disputes the view that Jesus ever delivered the following discourse; it alleges, with good grounds, the absence of all indication relative to the occasion and locality in connection with which this discourse was given, as well as the want of any new idea (see *Keim*, for example). But it falls into error in concluding from this that there is an artificial composition here which the evangelist places in the mouth of Jesus (*de Wette*), and in extending this conclusion to the discourses of Jesus, in general, in the fourth Gospel, discourses which are only the expression of the author's own thoughts (*Baur, Reuss, Hilgenfeld*).

Is it admissible that the evangelist himself would have ever dreamed, at this point of his narrative, of presenting to us a discourse of Jesus as really uttered by him? This is, indeed, what those suppose who make Him speak thus on going out from the temple (*Lampe, Bengel*), or at the time when he re-entered it again after the departure mentioned in ver. 36 (*Chrysostom, Hengstenberg*), or in a private conversation in presence of His disciples (*Besser, Luthardt*, 1st ed.). Of these three suppositions, the first two clash with ver. 36, which evidently indicates the closing of the public ministry of Jesus. The third, withdrawn by *Luthardt* himself (2d ed.), has against it the term ἔκραξε (*he cried* aloud.) What, in addition, excludes the idea of a discourse really delivered by Jesus at this time, is that the passage contains only a series of reminiscences of all the previous teachings, and that it is the only one which is destitute of any indication of occasion, time and place. The evangelist has with ver. 36 ended his part as *narrator* as to this portion of the history. In ver. 37 he contemplates the mysterious fact which he has just described and *meditates* on its causes and consequences. There is then here a discourse composed by John, indeed; but he does not attribute it as such to Jesus; he gives it as the summary of all the testimonies of Jesus which the Jews ought to have believed, but which they rejected. Here precisely is the reason why this passage contains no new idea, and bears no indication of time or place. The aorists (ἔκραξε, εἶπεν), recall all the particular cases in which Jesus had pronounced such affirmations respecting Himself; they must be rendered thus: "And yet He had sufficiently said . . . , He had sufficiently cried aloud . . . " Or as *Bäumlein* expresses it: "Jesus hatte aber laut erklärt." This interpretation forces itself more and more upon modern exegesis. Hence it follows that each one of the following declarations will rest upon a certain number of passages included in the preceding discourses. To the rejection of the miracles of Jesus which were the testimony of *God*, (vv. 37–43), Jewish unbelief has added the rejection of the testimony of *Jesus* respecting Himself.

Vv. 44–46. "*Now Jesus cried, saying, He that believes on me, believes not on* me, but on him that sent me; 45 and he that beholds me, beholds him that sent me; 46 I am come as a light into the world, that whosoever believes on me, may not abide in the darkness." How many times had not Jesus borne witness to His full communion with the Father, that relation in which nothing obscured the manifestation in His person of this invisible Father of whom He was the organ! To believe on Him, is therefore to penetrate by the act of faith through the human person of Jesus even to the infinite source of every good which appears in Him (v. 19, 20; vi. 57; viii. 16, 29, 38; x. 30, 38).

The negation: He believes not on me, has its complete truth in this sense —that the believer does not believe on the man Jesus as if He were come or had acted in His own name (ver. 43); in Jesus, it is really God, and God only, who is the object of faith, since God alone appears in Him. It is not, therefore, necessary, to give to not the sense of not only. The sight, which is in question in ver. 45, is that which is developed along with faith itself, the intuition of the inmost being of the person who is beheld. As to the correlation of the two acts so intimately connected, believing and beholding, see vi. 40, 69. Jesus, the living revelation of God, becomes, by means of this spiritual sight, the light of the soul (iii. 19; viii. 12; ix. 5, 39). Thus he who believes in Jesus possesses God and by his faith attests the truth of God to the view of others (iii. 33). What importance there is for a human being in the acceptance of such a manifestation! To the importance of faith corresponds that of the refusal to believe.

Vv. 47, 48. "And if any one hear my sayings and keep[1] them not, I judge him not; for I came not to judge the world, but to save the world. 48. He that rejects me and receives not my sayings has already his judge; the word which I have spoken, this it is which will judge him at the last day." Woe to him who does not believe on Jesus and His word in which He manifests Himself and bears testimony of Himself! As His presence is the pure manifestation of God, His word is the perfect revelation of the thought of God. This will be the one touchstone of the judgment. The declaration of ver. 47 does not exclude the personal role of Jesus in this great act. It merely says that the sentence which He will pronounce at that time will be simply that which will follow from the position which the man has taken with regard to His word; it is the idea of iii. 18 ($\mathring{\eta}\delta\eta$ $\kappa\acute{\epsilon}\kappa\rho\iota\tau\alpha\iota$), v. 24; viii. 15. The reading $\phi\nu\lambda\acute{\alpha}\xi\eta$, keep, is to be preferred to the received reading $\pi\iota\sigma\tau\epsilon\acute{\nu}\sigma\eta$ (and believe not); for the former term is less common than the latter; it applies not to the keeping in the conduct— with this meaning, Jesus employs the word $\tau\eta\rho\epsilon\hat{\iota}\nu$—but to inward appropriation and possession. The last words of ver. 47 reproduce the idea of iii. 17; comp. ix. 39, 41.

In ver. 48, where the rejection of Jesus is identified with that of His words, the express mention of the last day is very remarkable. As Gess observes, "the moral judgment of humanity through the word is incessantly effected even now, according to the entire Gospel. And yet the notion of the last judgment is so indispensable in the thought of the

---

[1] ℵ A B K L X some Mnn. It^{aliq}, Syr^{sch}, read $\phi\nu\lambda\alpha\xi\eta$ (keeps) instead of $\pi\iota\sigma\tau\epsilon\nu\sigma\eta$ (believes).

evangelist, that he expresses it here as the limit without which the purely moral judgment would fail of its consummation" (II. p. 452). How is it that *Reuss, Scholten, Hilgenfeld* affirm that the final judgment is denied in our Gospel! And what is striking is that the evangelist mentions, in speaking thus, a fact which is not indicated in the saying of Jesus on which this is founded (iii. 17). The last two verses explain the reason why the position taken by man with regard to Jesus and His word has so decisive an importance. It is because He has nothing of His own mingled in His teaching, and that He has transmitted it, as to substance and form, exactly as He received it from the Father.

Vv. 49, 50. "*For I have not spoken from myself; but the Father who sent me has himself given me commandment*[1] *what I should say and how I should say it;* 50 *and I know that his commandment is life eternal; what I say therefore I say even as my Father has said to me.*" If the word of Jesus is the standard of judgment, it is because it is that of God Himself, both as to substance (τί εἴπω) and as to form (τί λαλήσω). The ἐντολή, *the commandment*, of which Jesus here speaks is not a mandate received once for all before leaving heaven. This idea is incompatible with iii. 34, v. 19, 20, 30, viii. 16 (see *Gess*, pp. 542, 543). Jesus receives for each case the commission which He has to fulfill; He hears before speaking, and He hears because He listens. This constant docility arises in Him (ver. 50) from the certainty which he has of the vivifying and regenerating force of that word which the Father intrusts to Him. Whatever may be the objections which it excites, or the doubts which are set in opposition to it, He is conscious of its virtue by means of which it produces in souls *eternal life*. For this reason (*even as*, ver. 50*b*), He gives it to men just as He receives it, without allowing Himself to make any change in it. Comp. v. 30; vii. 16, 17; viii. 28; then vi. 63, 68.

John formulates very exactly in these few propositions the absolute value which Jesus had constantly attributed to His person and His word. This summary cannot be that of a discourse which the evangelist had the consciousness of having himself composed. It is not possible that he would have drawn up this formidable charge against the unbelief of Israel in the name of discourses which Jesus had never given; still more impossible that he could have founded his indictment, in ver. 37, on miracles which were only inventions of his own. To attribute to him such a mode of proceeding would be to make him a shameless impostor or a madman. And what is to be thought of the writer who should put into the mouth of Jesus these words: "*I have said nothing from myself; my Father has commanded me what I should say, and how I should say it,*" and who should make Him say this, while having the consciousness of having himself made Him speak all along and of making Him still do so at this time? Are there not enough impossibilities here? Let us remark also how this retrospective glance, interrupting the narrative, fails of appropriateness if we suppose it to have been composed in the second century, at a time when the question of the rejection by the Jews was no longer an actuality; on the contrary, how natural it is on the part of a man who was himself an eye-witness of this abnormal and unexpected fact of Jewish unbelief.

---

[1] ℵ A B M X 30 Mnn. read δεδωκεν instead of εδωκεν.

Before leaving this second part of the gospel story, let us cast a glance backward over the course of the narrative. We have seen in process of accomplishment before our eyes, through all the vicissitudes so dramatically described, the development of the national unbelief and the progressive separation between a people almost wholly fanaticized by its rulers and a feeble minority of believers. Well! Let us for an instant, by a thought, suppress this entire picture, all these journeys of Jesus to Jerusalem, all these conflicts in the very centre of the theocracy—as must be done as soon as we reject the credibility of our Gospel—behold, we are in presence of the final catastrophe attested by the Synoptics no less than by St. John: How are we to explain this sudden and tragic denouement? Only by the collisions which took place in a retired province of the Holy Land on occasion of a few Sabbath cures? No: the serious historian, even when accounting for the entrance on Palm-day, can never dispense with this whole series of conflicts in Jerusalem at which we have just been present.

THIRD PART

THE DEVELOPMENT OF FAITH IN THE DISCIPLES

John 13:1-17:26

THE third part of the Gospel describes the last moments which Jesus passed with His disciples; while making us acquainted with the supreme manifestations of His love towards them, it initiates us into the full development of *faith* in their hearts. John thus contrasts with the gloomy picture of Israelitish unbelief the luminous picture of the formation of faith in the future founders of the Church. Christ accomplishes this work in the hearts of His followers: 1. By two *acts*, the washing of their feet and the removal of Judas, through which He purifies the apostolic circle from the last remains of carnal Messianism; 2. By a series of *discourses*, in which He prepares His disciples for the approaching separation, gives them the necessary instructions with a view to their future ministry and elevates their faith in His person to the highest point which it can reach at this moment; 3. By a *prayer* of thanksgiving, by which he affixes the seal to His work now finished. Under the sway of these last manifestations, the faith of the disciples reaches its relative perfection, as fruits reach their maturity in the warm rays of the autumn sun. This faith is subjected to a double test, that of humiliation, through the deep humility of Jesus in the act of washing the feet, and that of self-sacrifice, through the prospect of a violent conflict to be met from the side of the world and a victory to be gained only through the spiritual force of Christ. With such prospects, what becomes of the earthly hopes which they still entertained in their hearts? But the faith of the apostles comes forth from this test triumphant and purified. It has laid hold of the divine person of Christ: "We believe that thou camest forth from God" (xvi. 30). This is enough; Jesus answers: *"At last you believe"* (xvi. 31). And He blesses His Father with an outpouring of thanks (chap. xvii.) for having given Him these eleven who believe in Him and who will bring the world to faith.

Thus therefore there are three sections:

1. Chap. xiii. 1–30: The purification of the apostles' faith by two decisive facts.

2. Chap. xiii. 31–xvi. 33: The strengthening and development of this faith by the last teachings of Jesus, which contain the final revelation of His person.

3. Chap. xvii.: The thanksgiving for this earthly ministry now ended.

1

John 13:1-30

THE FACTS

1. The washing of the disciples' feet: vv. 1–20.
2. The removal of Judas: vv. 21–30.

The washing of the disciples' feet: vv. 1–20.

This section includes a preamble (vv. 1–3), the fact (vv. 4–11), finally, the explanation of the fact (vv. 12–20).

1. Vv. 1–3: Preamble.

We have already discovered at the beginning of several narratives short introductions describing the situation, at once external and moral, in which the fact about to be related is accomplished; thus ii. 23–25; iii. 22–24; iv. 1, 2, 43–45. Each of these preambles is, with relation to the narrative which is to follow, what the Prologue i. 1–18 is for the whole Gospel, a general glance fitted to give the reader acquaintance with the subject in advance. Such is the design of the preamble in vv. 1–3. And as the substance of the general Prologue is borrowed from the teaching of Jesus in the sequel of our Gospel, so in the same way, as we easily discover, this particular preamble is entirely derived from the facts and discourses which will follow.

Ver. 1. "*Before the feast of the Passover, Jesus, knowing that his hour was come,*[1] *when he should leave this world to go to the Father, after having loved his own*[2] *who were in the world, he perfectly testified to them all his love.*" The words *before the feast of the Passover* are connected with the preceding determination of time: *six days before the Passover* (xii. 1), but with a difference of expression which cannot be accidental. There it was said: "Before *the Passover*," a word which designates, as ordinarily, the Paschal supper on the evening which ended the 14th of Nisan (Exod. xii.; Lev. xxiii. 5; Num. xxviii. 16). Here John says: "Before *the feast* of the Passover;" this wider term undoubtedly includes the entire day of the 14th of Nisan on which the leaven was removed from all the Israelite dwellings, and which was already counted for this reason among the days appertaining to *the feast*. This appears from Num. xxxiii. 3 (comp. also Josh. v. 11), where the day of the 15th Nisan is designated as the morrow after the Passover (LXX.: τῇ ἐπαύριον τοῦ πάσχα). To prove that the 14th could not be included in the feast, *Keil* cites Lev. xxiii. 6; Num. xxviii. 17; but it must not be forgotten that in these last passages the complement of the word *the feast* is not *of the Passover*, but *of unleavened bread* (τῶν ἀζύμων); the eating of the unleavened bread began indeed only with the Paschal supper, on the evening of the 14th–15th, to continue seven days until the 21st. This was the week of unleavened bread. If, then, we include the

---

[1] T. R. with the Byz. (E F G H etc.) reads ελληλυθεν; the Alex. (א B K L etc.): ηλθεν.

[2] א: Ιουδαιους (*the Jews*) instead of ιδιους !

day of the 14th in the expression *the feast of the Passover* in xiii. 1, the expression *before the feast of the Passover* places us, at the latest, on the evening of the 13th. But if, on the contrary, we identify, as some interpreters do (*Hengstenberg, Lange, Hofmann, Luthardt, Keil,* etc.), the beginning of the feast with the very moment of the Paschal supper, then this expression places us on the evening of the 14th, a few moments before the opening of this sacred supper. We shall see later the importance of this difference of explanation. This chronological determination refers naturally to the principal verb: ἠγάπησεν, *he loved*. As this verb expresses a feeling existing habitually in the heart of Jesus, and not an historical act, some interpreters have denied this reference. Some have made this determination of time: *before the feast*, refer to the verb ἐγείρεται, *rises*, ver. 4 (*Bleek, de Wette*); but what, in this case, can we do with the verb ἠγάπησεν, *he loved?* There is not the least indication of a parenthesis. Others endeavor to make this determination of time refer to the participle εἰδώς, *knowing,* (*Luthardt*, 1st ed., *Riggenbach*), or to ἀγαπήσας, *having loved*, (*Wieseler, Tholuck*). But, placed as it is, at the beginning of this whole section, this chronological indication can refer only to the principal action, the indication of which governs it altogether: ἠγάπησε, *he loved*. And this relation, which is the most simple, is also that which offers the best sense. How could John say that Jesus had been conscious of His approaching departure (εἰδώς) or had loved (ἠγαπήσας) His own *before the feast?* The verb ἀγαπᾶν, *to love,* must designate here, as appears from the aorist, not the feeling only, but also its external manifestations (especially those the story of which is to follow). John means that it was on the evening before the first day of the feast, when He was going to leave His followers, that Jesus manifested all His love for them and in some sort surpassed Himself in the testimonies which He gave them of this feeling.

To this first determination of a chronological nature, a second of a moral nature is attached: " *Jesus, knowing that . . .* " It was while having the perfectly distinct consciousness of His impending departure that Jesus acted and spoke as John is about to relate to us. This thought presided over these last manifestations of His love. *Hengstenberg* and others connect this participle with the principal verb through the idea of a contrast: "*Although He knew* indeed . . . , nevertheless He loved and humbled Himself thus," as if the prospect of His future exaltation could have been for Jesus a hindrance in the way of acting as He does! John had no need to deny a supposition so absurd. He means, on the contrary, that *because* He saw the hour of separation approaching, He redoubled His tenderness towards those whom He had until then so faithfully loved. Who does not know how the foreseeing of an imminent separation renders affection more demonstrative! Thus most,—*His own:* those whom He had gained by His love. There is a deliberate antithesis between the terms: *the Father,* with whom all is rest, and *the world,* where all is conflict and peril. Then, a third determination, serving to connect the act of ἠγάπησε, *he loved,* with an entire past of the same character which this last evening was going to complete. The expression: *His hour was come,* forms a contrast with that which we have so often met: "*His hour was not yet come.*"

The phrase εἰς τέλος, *for the end,* does not have in classical Greek the sense *until the end;* at least, *Passow* does not cite a single example of it; to express this idea of duration, the classical writers said rather διὰ τέλους. In the New Testament we can scarcely fail to find the meaning *until the end* in the εἰς τέλος of Matt. x. 22 and the parallels (though the idea of duration is found rather in the verb *shall persevere*). But the phrases ordinarily employed in this sense are either ἕως τέλους, or μέχρι or ἄχρι τέλους; 1 Cor. i. 8; 2 Cor. i. 13 (ἕως); Heb. vi. 14 (μέχρι); and Apoc. ii. 26 (ἄχρι). But what prevents us from accepting this meaning here which is adopted by our versions, is that it would be useless. Was it then necessary to affirm that Jesus *did not cease* to love his own up to the moment when He died for them? The true meaning of εἰς τέλος in the New Testament, as in the classics, is *for the end,* that is to say, sometimes: *at the end,* at the last moment; sometimes, *to the utmost, to make an end of it.* The first of these two meanings is certainly that which must be adopted in Luke xviii. 5: "lest she come *at the end* even to wearying me"; the second is found in 1 Thess. ii. 6: "the wrath is come upon them *to the utmost,*" that is to say, to make an end of it with them, in manifesting itself completely. Comp. the εἰς τέλος in the LXX., Josh. x. 20 (even to an entire destruction); 2 Chron. xii. 12, xxx. 1, and a multitude of other examples in the Psalms of Solomon and the Testaments of the Twelve Patriarchs (*Hilgenfeld, Einl.,* p. 243). In our passage, this meaning seems to me the only possible one. But the question is of love, and not of wrath. This phrase signifies therefore: the manifestation of His love even to its complete outpouring, in a way to exhaust it, in some sort. As an analogy to the sense of ἠγάπησε, *he loved,* including the feeling and its manifestations, *Odyss.* ψ, 214, may be cited, where Penelope says to Ulysses: "Pardon me that I did not immediately on first seeing you love you as much as (ὣδ' ἠγάπησα) I now do when I press you in my arms."

This first verse must be regarded as forming the preamble, not of this chapter only, but of this whole part of the Gospel, chaps. xiii.–xvii. We shall see, indeed, that it is in the discourses of chaps. xiv.–xvi., and in the prayer of chap. xvii., much more than in chap. xiii., that the thoughts of Jesus which are summed up by John in the *knowing that* of ver. 1 come to light; comp. xiv. 12: "*I go to my ather,*" xv. 18: "*If the world hate you, you know that it hated me before you,*" xvi. 28: "*I leave the world and go to my Father,*" xvi. 33: "*You shall have tribulation in the world,*" xvii. 11: "*I am no more in the world, but they are in the world, and I come to thee.*" Comp. also xiii. 34; xv. 9, 11, 14; xvii. 23, 24, 26, etc. But—and this it is which it seems to me has not been sufficiently marked—with the second verse, there begins a second more particular preamble, relating only to the scene described in the following narrative (chap. xiii.). This second preamble, like the first, contains three determinations; one of *time;* a supper having taken place; the second, relating to the *present condition* of things: "the devil having already put into the heart . . ."; the third, of a *moral* nature: "Jesus, knowing that . . . " We easily discover the correspondence of these three determinations with the facts and conversations of the following narrative. They serve to place in a clear light the thought of Jesus during the scenes which are immediately to follow, those of the washing of the disciples' feet and of the dismissal of Judas.

Vv. 2, 3. "*And a supper having taken place,*[1] *when the devil had already put into the heart of Judas Iscariot, the son of Simon, to betray him,*[2] 3 *Jesus*[3] *knowing that the Father had given*[4] *all things into his hands, and that he came from God and went to God.*" And first, the temporal determination: *a supper having taken place.* The Alexandrian reading γινομένου, *taking place*, seems to me inadmissible. This expression could scarcely refer to anything but the Paschal supper: "While this supper took place Jesus rises." But for this it would be necessary that the article τοῦ, *the*, should be wanting, that is to say, that the substantive should have been sufficiently determined by what precedes, which is not the case since the first words of ver. 1: "*before the feast of the Passover*" are rather suited to set aside the idea of the Paschal feast than to give rise to it. The present or imperfect, *taking place*, appears to me to be an adaptation, by the copyists, of this participle to the present ἐγείρεται, *he rises*, of ver. 4. It was not understood that the descriptive present *rises* might perfectly accord with the past tense of the participle: "(a) supper having taken place, Jesus rises." It does not appear to me possible that this supper can be the Israelite Paschal supper. The word δεῖπνον, designating that solemn supper, must necessarily have been marked by the article. The second determination is expressed in the two Alexandrian and Byzantine texts in two quite different forms; the Byzantine: "*the devil having already put into the heart of Judas that he should betray him.*" The Alexandrian: "*the devil having already put into the heart that Judas Iscariot, son of Simon, should betray him.*" Into whose heart? That of the devil, Meyer and Reuss answer. They take the Greek phrase: *to put into the heart*, in the sense of: to conceive the design of. But this sense is not tolerable. And where in Scripture is the devil's heart spoken of? Then, one does not put a thought into one's own heart. And why not say ἑαυτοῦ (*of himself*)? Finally, since when does the devil dispose of men in such a way that it is enough for him to decide to make one of them a traitor, in order that this one should indeed become a traitor. It must therefore be explained: put into the heart of *Judas* (*Bäumlein, Luthardt, Weiss*); but this term: *into the heart*, could not be thus used absolutely and without any complement fitted to define it. This reading is therefore inadmissible. It is probably due to a correction resting on the false idea that the fact expressed by the received reading

---

[1] Γινομενου (*taking place*) is read in ℵ (γεινομ.), B L X Orig. (4 times), instead of γενομενου (*having taken place*) which T. R. reads with all the other Mjj. all the Mnn. and Vss. Orig. (once).

[2] ℵ B L M X It^aliq, Vulg. Orig. (7 times) read του διαβ. ηδη βεβληκ. εις τ. καρδ. ινα παραδω αυτον Ιουδας Σ. Ισκαριωτης. But T. R. with 11 Mjj., the Mnn., It^plerique, Syr., Orig. (3 times), reads του διαβ. ηδη βεβληκ. εις τ. καρδ. Ιουδα Σ. Ισκαριωτου ινα αυτον παραδω. ℵ B D; παραδοι instead of παραδω.

[3] ℵ B D L X do not repeat ο Ιησους here.

[4] ℵ B D K L Orig.: εδωκεν instead of δεδωκεν.

806 / The Development of Faith

would constitute an anticipation of that which is to be related afterwards in ver. 27; but wrongly; for at the moment when the supper took place, the treachery was really consummated in the heart of Judas; still more, according to the Synoptics, everything was already agreed upon between him and the Sanhedrim. The Byzantine reading simply says: *the devil having already put into the heart of Judas . . . that he should betray him.* The design of this indication is not to set forth the long-suffering and benevolence of Jesus (*Chrysostom, Calvin, Luthardt*), or the perfect clearness of mind with which He goes to meet His fate (*Meyer*); nor again to indicate that time was pressing (*Lücke*). John wishes to give grounds for the different allusions which Jesus is about to make to the presence of the traitor throughout the whole course of the following scene (comp. vv. 10, 18, 21, 26) and especially to explain the conduct and the severe word of Jesus in ver. 27. The Alexandrian reading παραδοῖ, instead of παραδῶ (T. R.), is explained in two ways by the grammarians: either as a contraction of the optative παραδοίη (see in *Kühner, Ausführl, Gramm.* a multitude of examples taken from Plato and other authors), or as a contraction of the subjunctive δόῃ, from δόω (for δίδωμι); so *Bäumlein*, after Buttmann. As the first determination: *a feast having taken place,* answers to the first of ver. 1 (*before the feast*), so the reflection (*the devil having put . . .*) answers to that of ver. 1: *having loved his own.* The blackest hatred forms the counterpart to the most tender love.

The picture of the external and moral situation is completed by a third indication which helps us to penetrate into the inner feeling of Jesus and unveils to us the true meaning of the act of humiliation which is about to follow: "*Jesus knowing that . . .*" This *knowing* is by no means the resumption of that of ver. 1; for it has a quite different content. It is not the sorrowful feeling of the approaching separation: it is the consciousness of His greatness which inspires in Him the act of humiliation which He is going to accomplish. Here, more frequently even than in ver. 1, the commentators interpret in the sense of: "*Although* knowing; although feeling Himself so great, He humbled Himself." This is, according to our view, to misconceive, even more seriously than in ver. 1, the evangelist's thought, as well as that of Jesus Himself. It is not *in spite of* His divine greatness, it is *because of* this very greatness, that Jesus humbles Himself, as He is going to do. Feeling Himself the greatest, He understands that it belongs to Him to give the model of real greatness, by humbling Himself to the lowest part; for greatness in the Messianic kingdom which He comes to inaugurate on the earth, consists in voluntary humiliation. This kind of greatness, still unknown here on earth, *His own* must at this moment behold in Him, to the end that His Church may never recognize any other. It is therefore *inasmuch as* He is Lord, and not *although* He is Lord, that He is going to discharge the office of a slave. Moreover, it is Jesus Himself who expresses this idea (vv. 13, 14): "*You call me Master and Lord . . . If then,*" and it is from these words that it is derived. Hence we understand the accumulation of clauses which recall to mind the features of the supreme greatness of Jesus: 1.

His sovereign *position:* everything is put into His hands; 2. His divine *origin:* He comes from God; 3. His divine destiny: He returns to God (the repetition of the word *God* is to be remarked). It is in the consciousness of what He is, that He does what no other has ever done. The example becomes thus for His own decisive, irresistible: the servant cannot remain with proud bearing when the Master humbles Himself before him.

2. Vv. 4–11: The fact.

Vv. 4, 5. "[Jesus] *rises from the supper and lays aside his garments; and, taking a towel, he girds himself. 5. Then he pours water into the basin; and he began to wash the feet of his disciples and to wipe them with the towel wherewith he was girded.*" Ver. 3 has initiated us in advance into the meaning of this act. If need were, this would suffice to explain the reason of it. So *Ewald* and *Meyer* do not seek to find any outward motive. Jesus, however, does not act, in general, by a mere impulse from within; He yields to a given occasion in which He discerns the signal from the Father. St. Luke relates to us, xxii. 24–27, that there arose at the supper a dispute among the disciples on the question to whom the first place among them belonged. Whereupon Jesus said: "The first among you must take the place of the last." Then, giving Himself as an example: "Who is greater, he that sits at meat or he that serves? But I am among you as he that serves." This answer of Jesus might be applied to His way of acting, in general, in the midst of His own; and it is thus, perhaps, that it was understood by Luke to whom this saying of the Lord had been handed down as separated from the story with which we are now occupied. But for ourselves, knowing the act which Jesus performed at this supper, it is impossible not to connect it with the saying and explain the latter by the former. The washing of the feet was undoubtedly occasioned by the dispute of which Luke speaks. Jesus wished to eradicate from the hearts of His disciples the last remnant of the old leaven of pride and Messianic ambition which still infected their faith and manifested itself in so offensive a manner in the discussion of which Luke has preserved the remembrance. But why give this form to the lesson which He desired to leave with His followers at this final meeting? Luke places the dispute at the very end of the supper, and, if necessary, it might be supposed that, being pained by the fact that no one of them at the beginning of the meal had offered to discharge this humble office, and that, in consequence, the washing of the feet had not taken place, Jesus had at first kept His feeling to Himself, but afterwards, an opportunity presenting itself, He expressed it precisely as He did in the case mentioned in Luke vii. 44. The washing thus was performed, as a mere example, at the end of the supper. The natural place, however, for such a ceremony is at the beginning of the meal, and it may be easily supposed that Luke placed as a supplementary detail in the account of the meal a fact which he knew belonged to it, but the exact moment of which he did not know. Indeed, he simply says: "*There was also a dispute.*" Jesus was already seated at table (ver. 4); the apostles took their places (vv. 6, 12). It was perhaps on this occasion that the dispute broke out, each claiming to have the right to be seated next to the Saviour. At this moment Jesus rises and, by charging Himself with the humble office which each one of them should have spontaneously hastened to perform, He gives them to understand who is really the greatest in His kingdom. The matter in hand here is not indeed to give His disciples a lesson of kindness, of condescension, of mutual serviceableness. Comp. vv. 13–15, and especially ver. 10 which, from this point of view, is no longer intelligible. Jesus wishes to teach them that the condition for *entering* and *advancing* in a kingdom like His own, is the reverse of what takes place on earth, to know how to humble oneself, to efface oneself; and that, the more each one shall outstrip the other in this divine art, the more he will become like Him, at first in spirit, and then in glory.

Each feature of the following picture betrays the recollection of an eyewitness; John describes this scene as if beholding it at this very moment. Jesus assumes the garb of a slave. *His garments:* here, the upper garment. Jesus keeps only the tunic, the garment of the slave. He girds Himself with a towel, because He must carry the basin with both hands. Νιπτῆρα, with the article: *the* basin, the one which was there for this purpose and which belonged to the furniture of the dining-hall. *Nihil ministerii omittit,* says *Grotius.*

Vv. 6–11. " *He comes therefore to Simon Peter, and he*[1] *says to him, Lord,*[1] *Dost thou wash my feet?* 7. *Jesus answered and said to him, What*[2] *I do, thou knowest not now, but thou shalt know hereafter.* 8. *Peter says to him, No, thou shalt never wash my feet. Jesus answered him, If I wash thee not, thou hast no part with me.* 9. *Simon Peter says to him, Lord,*[3] *not only my feet, but also my hands and my head.* 10. *Jesus says to him, He that is bathed has need of nothing except to wash his feet,*[4] *but he is altogether clean; and you are clean, but not all.* 11. *For he knew him that should betray him; therefore said he,*[5] *You are not all clean.*" It must be observed, indeed, that this conversation with St. Peter comes upon this scene as an unexpected episode. Οὖν, *therefore* (ver. 6): when going from one to another according to the order in which they were seated. The natural conclusion to be drawn from this *therefore* is that Peter was not the first whose feet Jesus washed; he was not seated therefore beside Him (comp. ver. 24). The feeling of reverence which called forth this resistance on Peter's part expresses itself in the antithesis of the pronouns σύ, *thou,* and μού, *me,* and in the title *Lord.* Here, as in Matt. xvi. 22, it is respect which produces in this apostle the want of respect. The antithesis of ἐγώ and σύ (*I—thou*) in ver. 7, answers to that of σύ and μού (*thou—me*) in ver. 6. The expression μετὰ ταῦτα, *hereafter,* signifies according to *Chrysostom, Grotius, Tholuck, Reuss*: by the light which the experiences of thy future ministry will give. But the relation between γνώσῃ, *thou shalt know,* and γινώσκετε, *know ye* (ver. 14),

---

[1] ℵ B omit: εκεινος; ℵ omits κυριε (*Lord*).
[2] ℵ reads α εγω instead of ο εγω.
[3] ℵ rejects κυριε (*Lord*).
[4] T. R. with A E G M S U Γ Δ Λ: η τους ποδας νιψασθαι (*than to wash his feet*); B C K L: ει μη τους ποδας νιψασθαι (*if not to wash his feet*); ℵ c νιψασθαι (has no need *to wash, but*).
[5] B C L add οτι.

shows that Jesus is thinking rather of the explanation which He is about to give at the very moment, after having finished the act which was begun.

The gentleness of Jesus emboldens Peter; he had only questioned (ver. 6); now he positively refuses, and even for ever. If this refusal of Peter springs from modesty, it is nevertheless true that, as *Weiss* says, this modesty is not destitute of self-will and pride. Jesus answers him in the same categorical tone, and there is certainly an echo of Peter's *for ever* in the *no part with me* of Jesus. This relation it is which prevents us from holding, with *Weiss* and *Reuss*, that these words mean: " Thou dost not at this moment share in my feelings," or " Thou art not in communion with me " (present, ἔχεις, *thou hast*). The ἔχεις may perfectly well be a present of anticipation and may refer to the blessedness to come. The phrase μέρος ἔχειν μετά, *to have part with*, indicates the participation of the inferior in the booty, the riches, the glory of his leader (Josh. xxii. 24; 2 Sam. xx. 1; 1 Kings xii. 16). The refusal of Peter to accept the humiliating service which Jesus desires to render him, is equivalent to a rejection of the spirit of His work, to the resolution to persevere in the love of the carnal grandeur from which precisely Jesus desires by this act to purify His disciples. In rejecting the humiliation which his Master imposes upon Himself for his sake, Peter rejects in principle that which he was one day to impose upon himself for the sake of his brethren. The reply of Jesus is in harmony with this meaning; it reproduces with a natural force the warning which He addressed to all the disciples, on occasion of a quite similar dispute among them: " *Except you are converted and become as little children*, not only will no one of you be the greatest in the kingdom of heaven, but *you will not enter into it at all* " (Matt. xviii. 1–4).

Ver. 9 presents to us, in the case of Peter, one of those sudden changes of impression which we frequently observe in him, in the Synoptic narrative. Here is the same Peter who rushes upon the water and a moment afterward cries " I perish! " who strikes with the sword and who takes to flight, who enters into the house of the high-priest and yet denies his Master. The perfect accordance between these scattered features, and the image full of life which results from them, admirably prove in this case as in all the others, as *Luthardt* has so well set forth, the complete reality of the Gospel history. The whole meaning of the act of Jesus was in the fact of washing *the feet*. The nature of the act changed absolutely as soon as it concerned the head, for in that case it was no longer an act of humiliation. Jesus follows Peter on this new ground and this is what introduces the different meaning given to the act in His answer. At the foundation, what Peter asked for, without being conscious of it, was, instead of the removal of a stain, a complete renovation and, as it were, a second baptism; he implicitly denied the work already done in him (xv. 3). This is what gives the key to the answer of Jesus. This answer has of course a double meaning. Jesus rises immediately, as in the conversation with the Samaritan woman, from the material to the spiritual domain. As after having bathed in the morning, a man regards himself as clean for the whole day and contents himself with washing his feet when he returns from without, that he may remove the accidental soiling which they have contracted in walking, so he who, by earnestly attaching himself to Christ, has broken with sin once for all, has no need at each particular defilement to begin anew this general consecration; he has only to cleanse himself from this stain by confession and recourse to Christ. We must recall here what Jesus says to His disciples, xv. 3: "You are already clean through the word which I have declared to you." In receiving His word, they had received in principle the perfect holiness of which it is the standard in the life in Him. There is nothing more except to change the law into act by ever placing oneself anew on the foundation which has been laid. *Weiss* thinks that all notion of *pardon* in the symbol of washing is foreign to this context. But the fundamental rupture with sin which Jesus compares to the *complete bath*, implies a general pardon and reconciliation with God, and each act of destroying a particular sin, represented by the *washing of the feet*, implies the particular pardon of that sin. *Reuss* objects that the answer of Jesus, thus explained, would turn aside the symbol from its primitive sense. We have seen that the sense of the symbol was altogether different from that of the disposition towards kindness to one's neighbor; that Jesus desired to eradicate a bad propensity from the hearts of the disciples. This is what gives occasion to the new turn which the explanation of the symbol takes in consequence of the demand of Peter. I believe with *Reuss*, that, whatever *Weiss* may say, Jesus is here thinking of the baptism of water, the symbol of general purification, and means that it is no more necessary to renew this act (that which Peter asked) than that of faith itself whose symbol it is. The reading εἰ μή, *if it is not*, in a few Alexandrian documents, is a correction of the ἤ, in the T. R., which is slightly irregular; ἤ, *than*, for οὐδενὸς ἄλλου ἤ, *nothing else than*. The rejection of the words ἢ τοὺς πόδας, in the *Sinaitic* MS., completely changes the meaning: "He who is bathed has no need to wash himself; but he is all clean." This reading is a correction occasioned by the difficulty of distinguishing between the total bath and the partial washing. The last words: "*but he is clean altogether*," are to be explained thus: "*But*, far from having to bathe entirely a second time, as thou dost demand, his body is in general clean. It is enough to cleanse the local defilement which the feet have contracted."

But is this state of reconciliation and consecration indeed the state of all? No; there is a disciple who has broken the bond connecting him with Jesus or in whose heart this bond has never existed. He it is who would really have need of the inward act of which Peter had just asked for the symbol. Here is the first revelation of the treachery of Judas, in the course of the supper. By expressing in this way the grief which the thought of this crime causes Him to feel, Jesus makes a last effort to bring Judas to repentance. And if He does not succeed, He will, at least, have shown to His disciples that He was not the dupe of his hypocrisy (ver. 19).

3. Vv. 12–20: The explanation.

Vv. 12–17. "*When therefore he had washed their [1] feet and [2] taken his garments again, having resumed his seat at table,[3] he said to them, Know you what I have done to you?* 13. *You call me Master and Lord,[4] and you say well, for so I am.* 14. *If I then, the Lord and the Master, have washed your feet, you also [5] ought to wash one another's feet.* 15. *For I have given [6] you an example, that, as I have done to you, you also may do.* 16. *Verily, verily, I say unto you that the servant is not greater than his lord, nor he that is sent greater than he that sent him.* 17. *If you know these things, happy are you, if you do them.*" Jesus feared nothing for His Church so much as hierarchical pretensions. The disciples knew that their Master was establishing a kingdom. This single word was fitted to awaken in them ideas of dominion in the earthly sense; for this reason He shows them that, in this kingdom, the means of mounting higher is to descend, and the way to the first place is to put oneself without hesitation in the last. In ver. 13, *ye call me* properly means: You designate me thus when you address to me the word: *thee, Master.* Hence the two substantives in the nominative. The title of *Master* refers to teaching; that of *Lord,* to dominion over the entire life. It is the reproducing of the titles *Rabbi* and *Mar* which Jewish pupils gave to their masters. The most exalted title, that of *Lord,* is placed second, agreeably to the natural gradation. The T. R. accords here with the Alexandrian authorities. It is from the words: *For so I am,* that John has properly derived the εἰδώς, *knowing,* of ver. 3. Since the fourth century, the Church has discovered in vv. 14, 15, the institution of a rite; and it is well known what this ceremony has become where it is still practised in a literal sense.[7] But neither the term ὑπόδειγμα, *example,* nor the plural, *these things* (ver. 17), suits the idea of an institution; and, in ver. 15, Jesus would have been obliged to say ὅ, *that which,* instead of καθώς, *as.* To humble oneself in order to serve, and to serve in order to save: such is the moral essence of this act, its permanent element. The form was accidental and, as we have seen, borrowed from the given situation, consequently a passing thing. The washing of the feet which is mentioned in 1 Tim. v. 10 is a duty of hospitality and is only in a moral relation with what is prescribed in vv. 14, 15. The meaning of the sentence in ver. 16, which is also found in the Synoptics, but with a different application (Luke vi. 40; Matt. x. 24, 25; comp. John xv. 20) is here, as in Matt. x., that the subordinate should not consider unworthy of him that which his superior has consented to do. But the Lord knows that it is

---

[1] ℵ reads αυτου (*his*) instead of αυτων (*their*).

[2] ℵ A L It^{plerique} Syr. omit και before ελαβεν.

[3] Instead of αναπεσων, ℵ B C Syr. read και ανεπεσεν and A L It^{plerique} και αναπεσων.

[4] 6 Mjj. (Byz.) read ο κυρ. και ο διδασκ.; T. R. with all the rest (12 Mjj.); ο διδ. και ο κυρ (*the Master and the Lord*).

[5] D It^{plerique} Syr. read ποσω μαλλον (*how much more*) before και υμεις.

[6] ℵ A K M Π: δεδωκα instead of εδωκα (13 Mjj.).

[7] See in *Westcott* the summary history of this rite, declared obligatory by a council held in Toledo (694), celebrated in the churches of Spain and Gaul, performed on Holy Thursday by the Pope as the representative of Christ, received also in the Greek Church, where it is maintained in the convents, combated by the reformers; adopted in England from Wolsey (1530) to the reign of James II.; also by the Mennonites in Holland and by the Moravian Church in which it has fallen into disuse.

easier to approve and admire humility than to practise it; for this reason He adds the words of ver. 17. Εἰ, *if*, "if truly;" as is really the case; it is the general supposition; ἐάν, *in case that;* it is the more particular condition. The happiness of which Jesus speaks is not merely that of *knowing* the duty of voluntary humility (*Westcott*), nor the inward delight which the disciple enjoys in performing it (*Weiss*); it is an actual superiority of position before God henceforth and in the future economy. A man is so much greater in the view of Jesus and so much nearer to Him in proportion as he consents to humble himself the more, as He did, in order to serve his brethren (Matt. xviii. 4).

Vv. 18, 19. "*I do not say this of you all ; I[1] know those whom[2] I have chosen ; but that the Scripture may be fulfilled, He who eats bread with me [3] has lifted up [4] his heel against me.* 19. *From henceforth I tell you before it comes to pass, that when it is come to pass, you may believe that I am he.*" The idea of the happiness of the disciples, who walk in the path of humility, calls forth in the heart of Jesus the feeling of a contrast; there is present a person who, indomitable in his pride, deprives himself of this happiness, and draws upon himself the opposite of the μακαριότης (ver. 17). Ἐξελεξάμην, *I have chosen*, is referred by *Reuss* to the election to salvation; in this sense the term would not be applicable to Judas. This would be a new proof of the predestinationism of John. But nothing more, on the contrary, appears in all these narratives than human responsibility and culpability. Am I mistaken in surmising that the reading τίνας (*whom*) relating to the character has, in the Alexandrian authorities, been substituted for the οὕς (*those whom*) of the T. R. under the influence of this false interpretation? The election of which Jesus speaks refers to that of the Twelve, inclusive of Judas; comp. vi. 70. And *to know* signifies *to discern*, not, to approve, to love. The words: *I know*, serve to justify the preceding declaration: *I do not say this of you all.* If the *for* of 4 Mjj. is a gloss, it is a proper gloss. The *in order that* might be made to depend on the following verb *has lifted:* "In order that the Scripture might be fulfilled, he who eats has lifted." Jesus would thus insert the Scripture citation in His own discourse. But it is more natural to suppose an ellipsis, by explaining, with *Meyer*: "I have nevertheless chosen him in order that," or, what seems more simple, by supplying "*This has happened*, in order that," comp. xix. 36; 1 John ii. 19; Matt. xxvi. 56. This last ellipsis more expressly carries back the responsibility of the choice of Judas to God, whom Jesus has obeyed, see on vi. 64. Ps. xli., from the tenth verse of which the quoted passage is borrowed, is only indirectly Messianic; its immediate subject is the afflicted righteous person; but this idea is perfectly realized only in the suffering Messiah. Among the afflictions by which the righteous person is smitten, the Psalmist (David, according to the title; according to *Hitzig*, Jeremiah) puts in the first place the treachery of an intimate

---

[1] א A K Π 30 Mnn. It^{alia} Cop. Syr. read γαρ after εγω.

[2] א B C L M Orig. read τινας (*whom*), instead of ους (*those whom*).

[3] B C L: μου (*my bread*), instead of μετ' εμου (*bread with me*).

[4] א A U Π: επηρκεν, instead of επηρεν.

friend. In the mouth of David, this feature has reference to Ahithophel. "This last stroke," Jesus means to say, "cannot fail to reach me also, in whom all the trials of the suffering righteous are united." Such, in this context, is the sense of the formula: *in order that it might be fulfilled.* Weiss claims that John wishes to put these words of the Psalm into the mouth of the Messiah Himself. Not a word in John's text justifies this assertion. If we compare xviii. 9 with xvii. 12 it will suffice to make us see how contrary it is is to the evangelist's thought thus to press the idea of: *in order that it might be fulfilled.* Instead of the singular ἄρτον, *bread*, in conformity with the Hebrew, the LXX. have the plural ἄρτους, and, for all the rest of the passage, the translation of John is equally independent of that of the LXX.[1] *To lift up the heel*, in order to strike, is the emblem of brutal hatred, and not, as some have thought, of cunning. This expression is applied indeed to the present state of Judas, who has already prepared his treachery and is on the point of carrying it into execution. One may hesitate between the perfect ἐπῆρκεν and the aorist ἐπῆρεν. It is also difficult to decide between the two readings ἐμοῦ, *of me* and μετ' ἐμοῦ, *with me;* the first may have been derived from the LXX.; the second, from the parallel passages, Mark xiv. 18; Luke xxii. 21 (*Weiss*). Thus foreseen and foretold by Jesus, this treachery, which otherwise might have been a cause of stumbling to His disciples, will afterwards be transformed into a support for their faith. This is what Jesus desires to bring out in ver. 19, and not, as *Weiss* thinks, to set forth the proof of His Messiahship which will result from the fulfillment of the prophecy; comp. the words: *before it comes to pass*, which, in this case, would lose their force. The ἀπ' ἄρτι is opposed, not to the similar declarations which are still to follow respecting Judas (*Weiss*), but to the subsequent realization of the fact predicted.

Ver. 20. "*Verily, verily, I say unto you: He that receives him whom I shall send, receives me, and he that receives me, receives him that sent me.*" The relation between this saying and those which precede is so far from clear that *Kuinoel* and *Lücke* proposed to consider this verse as a gloss derived from Matt. x. 40. *Meyer* and *Hengstenberg* think that, in the presence of the treachery of Judas, Jesus wished to encourage His apostles by reminding them of the greatness of their mission. *Bäumlein* says: "A fragment from a larger whole, to which perhaps the institution of the Holy Supper belonged." *Luthardt* and *Keil* place this saying in connection with the washing of the feet; the disciples must learn from Jesus to render the same service to those whom He shall send to them. But, as we have seen, the meaning of the act of washing was altogether different, and this saying is too far separated from that act. Vv. 18, 19, are a simple digression occasioned by the contrast between the fate of Judas and the happiness of the faithful disciples (ver. 17). Ver. 20 is immediately connected with the idea of this happiness declared in vv. 16, 17. The one sent by Jesus, humble and faithful, who serves like Him, bears with him his Master, and, in His Master, God Himself. Jesus had just said: "*The*

---

[1] The LXX.: εμεγαλυνε επ' εμε πτερνισμον.

servant is not greater than the Master;" He now seems to say: " And he *is not less great* than He." To receive him is, consequently, to receive in him Jesus, and in Jesus God Himself; comp. Matt. xviii. 4, 5, and the parallels. In Luke xxii. 29, 30, Jesus, after having said: " Behold, I am among you as he that serves," adds: " *I give you the kingdom as my Father has given it to me.*" To give the kingdom, in its true spiritual form—is it not to bear God in oneself and communicate Him to the one who receives you? This saying, therefore, accords perfectly, as to its meaning, with our ver. 20.

Bretschneider and *Strauss* regarded this story of the washing of the feet as a legendary creation which emanated from the consciousness of the Church. But, as Baur observed with respect to the resurrection of Lazarus, if such a fictitious story had been the product of the Christian consciousness and had been circulated in the Church, it could not have failed to appear also in the Synoptics. *Baur* therefore regards this incident as consciously invented by the evangelist to serve the moral idea. But it is difficult to explain in this way the production of so simple and life-like a scene, and especially the composition of the inimitable conversation between Jesus and Peter. Even *Schweizer* has admirably brought out the stamp of historical truthfulness impressed upon this whole story. *Keim* thinks that Jesus would not on this evening have come so directly into collision with the feeling of the disciples. But it was a matter of inculcating upon them ineffaceably the spirit of His work and of their future mission; and this was the last moment for doing this. The omission of this incident in the Synoptics is made an objection. Probably the institution of the Lord's Supper, that fact of capital importance for the Church, eclipsed this one in the oral tradition relative to this last meal. *Hilgenfeld* surmises that the evangelist meant to substitute this narrative, imagined by him, for that of the institution of the Lord's Supper which he designedly omitted (*Einl.*, p. 711), as too distinctly recalling the Jewish Paschal supper. But what result could be attained by this means in the second century, when the Lord's Supper was celebrated throughout the whole Church, unless that of rendering his Gospel liable to suspicion? The discourse directed against false greatness, which is added by Luke to the narrative of the supper, naturally implies a fact of this kind. There was nothing to prevent the author from placing the two stories in juxtaposition. The better known story would have confirmed the one which was less known. It is very evident that John desired to rescue from oblivion what the tradition had neglected, and that he omitted what was sufficiently well known and what had no *particular* connection with the principal aim of his work.

The dismissal of Judas: vv. 21–30

Here also is a work of Jesus' love towards His own. As long as Judas was present, His heart was under restraint, and could not give vent to all the feelings of which He was full. Ver. 31 expresses in a life-like way the feeling of deliverance which Jesus Himself experiences on seeing the traitor withdraw; and it is at this moment that that rich outpouring begins which fills chaps. xiv.–xvii. These final moments of intimate association were indispensable to the Lord's work.

Judas had represented, in the circle of the Twelve, the spirit of carnal Messianism, directly opposed to that which Jesus had just vindicated by the act of washing the feet; comp. vi. 64, 70. If he was unwilling to renounce this spirit and humble himself, he must depart; it was the spirit of the false Messiah, of the Jewish Messiah, of the Antichrist that departed with him.

Vv. 21, 22. "*After having said this, Jesus was troubled in his spirit and testified and said, Verily, verily, I say unto you that one of you shall betray me. 22. The disciples therefore*[1] *looked upon one another, not being able to understand of whom he was speaking.*" Jesus' emotion does not spring from any personal impression, like the fear of death, the grief of wounded affection or pity for the traitor; there would, in that case, be the word ψυχή, *soul*, as in xii. 27. The limiting word τῷ πνεύματι, *in his spirit*, shows that this emotion has its seat in a higher region than that of the natural sensibility, even though the noblest. It is, as in xi. 33, 38, a shock of a religious nature, a kind of horror which His pure heart feels at the contact with the instrument of this Satanic crime and the approach of its invisible author. On this difference between ψυχή, *the soul*, and πνεῦμα, *the spirit*, see on xii. 27. The words: *having said this*, connect this emotion closely with the preceding words, in which Jesus had twice alluded to the treachery of Judas; the term: *he testified* contrasts the positive declaration which is to follow with the vague indications of vv. 10, 18. The *amen, amen*, marks the divine certainty of the declaration in face of the difficulty in receiving it, which must have existed for the apostles. But the apostles (ver. 22) doubt rather respecting themselves and their own hearts, than respecting the Master's word. "*Is it I?*" they, each of them ask, with a humble docility. The Synoptics say the same thing. According to Matt. xxvi. 25, Judas himself also addresses this question to Jesus. This fact has been thought incredible. But to be the only one to keep silence, when all ask such a question, would not this have been to betray oneself? As to the reply of Jesus: "*Thou hast said*," in Matt. xxvi. 25, it is in reality only the summary of the following scene in the narrative of John; it is by the act related here, ver. 26, that Jesus made this reply to him.

Vv. 23, 24. *Now*[2] *one of the*[3] *disciples, he whom Jesus loved, was reclining on his bosom ; 24 Simon Peter beckoned to him to ask who this one might be.*"[4] Among the ancients, persons reclined rather than sat at table, each guest having the left arm supported on a cushion, so as to support the head, and the right arm free, for eating; the feet were extended behind. Each guest thus had his head near the breast of the one whose place was at his left hand; this was John's place as related to Jesus, at this last meal. The unanimous tradition of the primitive Church designates John as the dis-

---

[1] B C omit ουν.

[2] B C L omit δε.

[3] 11 Mjj. (א A B C etc.) add εκ before των μαθητων.

[4] Instead of πυθεσθαι τις αν ειη (to inquire who it was) which is read by T. R. with 14 Mjj. (A D Γ Δ Λ Π etc.) most of the Mnn. Syr. Cop., και λεγει αυτω ειπε τις εστιν (*and he says to him: tell us who it is*) is read in B C I L X It^{plerique} Vulg. Orig. א unites the two readings: πυθεσθαι τις αν ειη περι ου ελεγεν και λεγει αυτω ειπε τις εστιν (*to inquire who was the one of whom he spoke, and he says to him: tell who it is*).

ciple to whom ver. 23 applies. Our Gospel itself allows no doubt of this; as we have shown in the Introduction (Comp., p. 32 f.). This appears from xxi. 2, compared with vv. 7 and 20–23 of the same chapter. Among the seven disciples who are named in ver. 2, Peter, Thomas, and Nathanael are of course excluded, since the disciple whom Jesus loved is nowhere designated by his name in the Gospel, while these three are thus designated several times. The last two disciples, who are not named, do not seem to have belonged to the circle of the apostles; there remain, therefore, only the two sons of Zebedee. As James is excluded by the fact of his early death (comp. what is said of the disciple whom Jesus loved, ver. 22: " *If I will that he tarry till I come, what is it to thee?* "), John only remains. The Synoptic narrative leads to the same result: The disciple whom Jesus loved being necessarily one of the three privileged apostles, and Peter and James being excluded for the reasons indicated, John alone remains. If he designates himself by this periphrase, it is certainly not through vanity as has been asserted—it is precisely from humility that he avoids declaring his name, but with the feeling of the infinite condescension of Him who had deigned to treat him, during His earthly existence, as *His friend*. The reading of the T. R., agreeing with 14 MSS., among which are the *Alexandrian* and *Cambridge* MSS., and with the *Peschito*, is very simple: " Simon Peter beckons to him to ask who it is of whom he speaks." But the Alexandrian authorities, the *Vatican* and *Ephrem* MSS., etc., and the *Itala* read: " Simon Peter beckons to him and says to him: Tell who it is of whom he speaks." The *Sinaitic* MS. unites the two readings and puts them in juxtaposition, a fact which, in any case, proves the high antiquity of both. Against the first is alleged its great clearness and simplicity; this can be a reason for rejecting it only if the second presents a really admissible meaning. Otherwise the latter must be regarded as the result of an accidental error or of a faulty correction. The attempt has been made to give it two meanings. *Ewald:* " He makes a sign and says: Tell (to Jesus) who is the one of whom he speaks." But, in this case, either: of whom *thou speakest*, or: *ask him*, instead of *tell* would be necessary. The majority (*Weiss, Keil, Luthardt*) think that Peter, supposing that John already knows from Jesus who is the traitor, simply says *to John:* " Tell me who it is of whom he (Jesus) speaks." But the: *he beckons*, implies that Peter and John were not seated near one another, while the: *he says to him*, would imply proximity. To solve this contradiction, these last words must, in this case, be explained: " he says to him *by a sign* " (νεύων λέγει). Is this use of λέγειν natural? But, above all, how could Peter have supposed so positively and mistakenly (ver. 25) that John already knew this secret? For myself, I persist in believing that in this case, as in so many others, it is an error to bind oneself to the Alexandrian text. The reading of this text seems to me to result from a gloss, sometimes *added to* (*Sinait.*), sometimes *substituted for* (*Vatican*), the primitive text which has been preserved in the other documents. It follows from ver. 24 that Peter was not seated at Jesus' side; otherwise he might have himself put the question to Him.

Vv. 25–27a. "*He*[1] *therefore*[2] *leaning back*[3] *on Jesus' breast, says to him, Lord, who is it?* 26. *Jesus answers him: He it is to whom I shall give a piece of bread when it is dipped.*[4] *And having dipped*[5] *the piece,*[6] *he gave it to Judas Iscariot, son of Simon.*[7] 27a. *And, after he had taken the piece, then*[8] *Satan entered into him.*" The received reading ἐπιπεσών (which is found in the *Sinaitic,* and *Alexandrian* MSS., etc.), *leaning,* strictly *throwing himself,* indicates a sudden movement, in harmony with the liveliness of the feeling which produces it. It is perfectly suitable, provided we do not add οὕτως, *thus,* as *Tischendorf* and *Meyer* do, which is wholly without meaning. The οὕτως can only be maintained with the reading ἀναπεσών: "seated at table *as he was;*" it would be an allusion to ver. 23: *on the breast of Jesus,* so *Bäumlein.* But the reading ἀναπεσών may easily have arisen from xxi. 20 and the adverb οὕτως may have been added to complete this participle, which could only be a repetition of ver. 23. In the course of the Paschal meal, the father of the family offered to the guests pieces of bread or meat which he dipped in a broth composed of fruits boiled in wine; these fruits represented the blessings of the Promised Land. And even outside of this special meal it is customary in the East, it seems, for the host to offer the guest whom he wishes to honor a piece of meat (see *Westcott*). Jesus, connecting Himself with this custom, answers John in this form which was naturally intelligible only to him. As a sign of communion, it was a last appeal to the conscience of Judas. If, in receiving it, his heart had broken, He could still have obtained pardon. This moment was therefore decisive; and it is this that John makes manifest by the τότε, *then* (ver. 27), a word of tragic weight. The Alexandrian reading adds, after the words: "*having dipped the morsel,*" the following: *he takes it and,* which could only mean: "he takes it *from the dish;*" a very idle meaning. "Until this time," says *Hengstenberg,* "Judas had stifled in himself, in the interest of his passion, the conviction of the divinity of Jesus. Now the ray of divine omniscience[9] which had, in the preceding warnings (vv. 10, 18) only grazed the surface, penetrates him. Jesus says to him plainly by this sign and by the words which accompany it (Matt. xxvi. 25, "*Thou hast said*"): Thou art the one who eats my bread and yet betrays me! But He also gives him to understand that he is still of the number of His own. He might therefore return backward. But he would not; and the violent effort which he was obliged to make in order to close

---

[1] K S U Γ Λ read ουτος instead of εκεινος.

[2] ℵ D L M`X Δ some Mnn. It^plerique Vulg. read ουν instead of δε, which T. R. reads with 7 Mjj. Mnn. It^aliq. B. C. omit the particle altogether.

[3] B C K L X Π 20 Mnn. Orig. read αναπεσων instead of επιπεσων. 10 Mjj. read ουτως (*thus*) after επι- (or ανα-) πεσων; this word is omitted in the T. R. with ℵ A D Π.

[4] B`C L: βαψω το ψωμ. και δωσω. T. R. with the rest: βαψας το ψωμ. επιδωσω.

[5] ℵ B C L X Orig.: βαψας ουν. T. R., with the rest: και εμβαψας.

[6] B C L M Orig. add λαμβανει και after ψωμιον (*he takes it and*).

[7] The Alex. (ℵ B C etc.): Ισκαριωτου. T. R. with the rest (A Γ Δ etc.). Ισκαριωτη.

[8] ℵ D L It^plerique omit τοτε (*then*).

[9] I have not intended, in quoting this fine passage, to make all its expressions my own, as *Weiss* supposes; there is in it what passes beyond my way of understanding the supernatural knowledge of Jesus (see on iv. 17 ff.). I do not even think that there was occasion here to speak of faith in the divinity of Jesus.

his heart against the heavenly powers opened its doors to the diabolical powers. It is even from these last that he must seek the strength to accomplish this final act of resistance. As it is said of David: "*He strengthened himself in God,* so Judas strengthened himself in Satan." The dwelling of Satan in a soul has its degrees, as well as that of the Holy Spirit. Luke (xxii. 3) has united the phases which John distinguishes (comp. ver. 2). The present moment is that in which the will of Judas was finally confiscated by the power to which he had gradually surrendered himself. Until then he had acted freely and as if by way of experiment; he had played with the enemy. From this moment it will be impossible for him to draw back; it will be the enemy who will play with him. It has been asserted that John ascribes this result to a magical action of the morsel of bread, and that there was here, according to him, a miracle by means of which Jesus "*demonized* the soul of the disciple."[1] If John had wished to express such an idea he would have written, not μετὰ τὸ ψωμίον, *after the morsel*, but μετὰ τοῦ ψωμίου, *with the morsel*. It is also asked: Who then saw Satan enter into Judas?[2] Perhaps, John himself, we will answer. The terrible conflict which was carried on within him at this moment could not remain unnoticed by the eyes of him who anxiously observed the traitor, and something infernal in the expression of his features bore testimony of the decisive victory which the devil had just gained in his heart. *Weiss* and *Keil* are willing to admit here only a pure "psychological assurance." But such an assurance has as its basis either some perception or a revelation. Would these interpreters then adopt this second alternative? *Keim* has judged the conduct of Jesus at this moment with severity, in case John has exactly described it; it would even, up to a certain point, excuse Judas.[3] But Jesus carefully spared the traitor, in making him known to no one but John only.

Vv. 27b-30. "*Jesus therefore said to him: What thou doest, do quickly. 28. But no one of those who were at table knew why he said this to him. 29. For some thought that, as Judas had the bag, Jesus meant to say to him, Buy the things which we have need of for the feast, or that he bade him give something to the poor. 30. He therefore, having taken the morsel, went out immediately. Now it was night.*" The words of Jesus to Judas are not a permission (*Grotius*); they are a command. But, it is said, Jesus pushed Judas into the abyss by speaking to him thus. Jesus had no longer any ground to spare him, since from this decisive moment no return was possible for Judas. The evening was already far advanced (ver. 30), and Jesus had need of the little time which remained to Him to finish His work with His own. Judas in his pride imagined that he held the person of his Master in his hands. Jesus makes him understand that he, as well as the new master whom he obeys, is only an instrument. The word τάχιον signifies: *more quickly;* the meaning is therefore: "*hasten* thy begun work." John says: *no one of those who were at table* (ver. 28). Perhaps he

---

[1] *Revue de théol.*, 3d series., I., p. 255.
[2] *Ibid.*
[3] "*Freilich wenn Jesus ihn so prostituirte, wie bei Johannes, war Judas einigermassen entschuldigt.*" iii., p. 262.

tacitly excepts himself. *Weiss* thinks not. He believes also that John did not understand the import of the injunction of Jesus. From the words: *for the feast,* some infer that this evening could not be that on which the people celebrated the Paschal supper. For how could purchases be made on a Sabbatical day, such as that was? And if the Paschal supper, the essential act of the feast, was already finished, there were no more purchases to be made *for the feast.* But, on the other side, it may be said that if this evening had been that of the 13th–14th of Nisan, the entire day of the 14th would still remain for making purchases. And how could the disciples have supposed that Jesus sent Judas out for this purpose in the darkness of the night (*Luthardt, Keil*)? This passage, therefore, does not seem to us fitted to solve the difficult question which is in hand. Nevertheless it appears to me that the *for the feast* is more naturally understood if it was yet on the evening which preceded the day of the 14th, the first of the feast of the Passover (see on ver. 1). We are amazed at the skill with which Judas had been able to disguise his character and his plans. Even at this last moment, his fellow-disciples were entirely blinded with regard to him. On His part, Jesus could not without danger unmask him more openly than He does here; with the impetuosity of a Peter, what might have occurred between him and the traitor? This whole scene, described in vv. 27–29, was an affair of a moment. For this reason the words: *having taken the morsel,* ver. 30, are directly connected by οὖν with ver. 27: *and after having taken the morsel.* It is between the participle *having taken* and the verb *he went out,* that *Hengstenberg* wishes to place the institution of the Lord's Supper. But the εὐθέως, *immediately,* too closely connects the second of these two acts with the first. The last words: *it was night,* make us think of Jesus' words in Luke xxii. 53: "This is your hour and the power of darkness." They complete the picture of a situation which had left on the heart of John ineffaceable recollections. The Johannean narrative is studded throughout with similar incidents, which are explicable only by the vividness of personal recollection. Comp. i. 40, vi. 59, viii. 20, x. 23, etc. *Augustine* (see *Westcott*) adds to these words: *Erat autem nox,* this gloss: *Et ipse qui exivit erat nox.*

At what time in the meal is the institution of the Lord's Supper to be placed? We adopt the view, as we propose this question, that this meal is in fact the one in which, according to the Synoptics, Jesus instituted this ceremony. *Bengel, Wichelhaus* and others, it is true, have tried to distinguish two suppers: the first, that of John xiii., took place at Bethany; xiv. 31 indicates the moment when Jesus departed from that place to repair to Jerusalem; the second, that of the Synoptics, took place on the next day at evening, at the time of the Israelite Paschal supper. But the prediction of the denial of Peter, with the words: *Even this night,* in both passages, renders this supposition inadmissible. We hold, moreover, that, if the author of the fourth Gospel does not mention the institution of the Lord's Supper, it is not because he is ignorant of it or that he would deny it, but because this fact was sufficiently well known in the Church, and because there was nothing to lead him specially to recall it to mind in his narrative (see on ver. 20).

If the case stands thus, where is the institution of the Lord's Supper to be inserted in our narrative? According to *Kern*, after xiv. 31, as the foundation of the discourse in xv. 1 ff.: "*I am the true vine,*" etc. But, at this time, Jesus rises and gives the order to depart: is this a suitable situation for such a ceremony? According to *Olshausen, Luthardt,* after xiii. 38 (prediction of Peter's denial) and before the words: *Let not your heart be troubled.* This opinion would be admissible, if the Synoptics did not agree in placing the prediction of the denial *after* the institution, and even (two of them) on the way to Gethsemane. *Lücke, Lange, Maier* and others: in the interval between ver. 33 and ver. 34, because of the connection between the idea of the *new commandment* and that of the *new covenant* in the institution of the Supper. But the direct connection between the question of Peter: *Lord, whither goest thou?* (ver. 36) and the words of Jesus: *Whither I go, ye cannot come* (ver. 33), make it difficult to insert so considerable a ceremony between these two verses. *Neander, Ebrard:* in the interval between ver. 32 and ver. 33. There is, indeed, between vv. 31, 32 and vv. 33, 34 a certain break of continuity. The idea of the glory of Jesus (vv. 31, 32) may have *preceded* the institution of the Supper, and the latter have been followed no less naturally by the idea of the approaching departure of Jesus (vv. 33, 34). In itself, there is nothing to oppose this solution. *Paulus, Kahnis* and others decide for the interval between ver. 30 and ver. 31, immediately after the departure of Judas. The words: *When therefore he was gone out, Jesus said* (see at ver. 31) are not favorable to this opinion, and the words of vv. 31 and 32 have the character of an exclamation called forth by the departure of Judas. *Meyer, Weiss, Keil* (the last two, because of the first two Synoptics, who place the institution of the Supper immediately after the revelation concerning the traitor) content themselves with saying: after ver. 30, without attempting to make a more precise statement. But what, in this case, are we to do with the narrative of Luke who, on the contrary, places the revelation of the traitor immediately after the institution of the Supper. If he works on the foundation of Mark's narrative, how does he modify it in so perceptible and arbitrary a manner? And if he has a source which is peculiar to himself, why should it not have its own value by the side of that of the two other Synoptics? His account of the institution of the Supper is fully confirmed by Paul. The opinion of these critics is, therefore, precarious. The idea of *Hengstenberg* (at the moment of ver. 30 and before the departure of Judas) is not compatible with the expression: *he went out immediately. Stier* has decided for the interval between ver. 22 and ver. 23; but the question of Peter in ver. 24 is so closely connected with that of the disciples in ver. 22! *Bäumlein* suggests the interval between ver. 19 and ver. 21, where the quite isolated words of ver. 20 are placed. The idea of receiving Jesus in the person of His messengers, and of receiving in Him God Himself, is indeed in harmony with that of the dwelling of the Lord in His own; thus with that of the Supper.

In my first edition, the authority of Luke's narrative and certain indications in that of John led me to place the washing of the feet quite at the end of the meal. The institution of the Lord's Supper must consequently have preceded it, and thus I went back, with *Seiffert*,[1] even to the beginning of the meal, vv. 1–3, for the locating of the Supper, while seeking an allusion to this last pledge of the divine love in the expression: *He ended by testifying to them all his love.* I have abandoned

---

[1] *Ueber den Ursprung des ersten canonischen Evangeliums.*

this idea altogether: 1. Because there is an improbability in placing the washing of the feet at the end of the meal; 2. Because ver. 26 (the morsel given to Judas) proves that they were still in the midst of the meal, after that act; 3. Because the indication, Luke xxiii. 24, is very vague: "*There was also a dispute among the disciples.*" It is impossible to draw from this a conclusion with relation to the moment when the dispute occurred.

Beyschlag has brought out an important circumstance; it is that according to the Synoptics the institution of the Supper did not take place at one single time, but that it was divided into two very distinct acts; the one *during*, the other *after* the meal (Luke xxii. 20 and 1 Cor. xi. 25). The first may, therefore, be placed before ver. 18, and the second after ver. 30. *Westcott* arrives at nearly the same result. He places the act relating to the bread between 19 and 20 and that relating to the cup between 32 and 33. If we study the Synoptic narratives, we find in all the three these three elements: 1. The farewell word (*I will no more drink of this fruit of the vine*); 2. The institution of the Supper; 3. The revelation of the traitor. In the three accounts, the second is placed in the middle; but the first is placed as the third in Luke, at the beginning in the other two, from which it follows that the question of the participation of Judas in the Supper is not so simple as it appears to be at the first glance, and may be resolved at once affirmatively (with relation to the bread) and negatively (with relation to the cup). A second observation which goes to support the preceding is that, according to John, Jesus spoke of Judas not once, but three times, at different moments in the repast. The Synoptics have concentrated these three revelations in a single one, which they have placed, either before, or after, the institution of the Supper. It is very possible, therefore, that the two forms of the Synoptic story respecting this point are not exclusive of each other, and that we may be led to represent the matter to ourselves in this way: First, the word of farewell: This is my last meal (Luke); then, a word relating to the betrayal (Matthew and Mark); then, the institution of the Supper, so far as the bread was concerned (the three); a new word relating to Judas (Luke); finally, his going out and the institution of the cup.

With reference to the conduct of Judas, I will add some considerations to those which were presented at the end of chap. vi. This man had attached himself to Jesus, not for the satisfaction of his moral needs, as one *drawn, taught* and *given* by God (vi. 39, 44, 45), but by political ambition and gross cupidity. For he hoped for a brilliant career in following Him whom so many miracles proved to be the Christ. But when he perceived that the path followed by Jesus was the opposite of that which he had hoped, he was continually more and more irritated and embittered from day to day. He saw himself at once deceived on the side of Jesus and compromised by his character as a disciple before the rulers of the hierarchy. His treachery was therefore the result at once of his resentment against Jesus, by whom he believed himself to be deceived, and of his desire to restore himself to favor with the great men of the nation. As soon as he realized that this last purpose failed, despair took possession of him. Judas is the example of a faith and repentance which do not have as their origin moral needs.

It is important to notice finally *the relation between the narrative of John and that of the Synoptics* to the subject of this whole scene. What strikes us is that in the Synoptics the relation between Jesus and Judas in this meal is presented as a particular story, forming in itself a whole, while in John the setting forth of the matter is gradual, varied and in a manner blended with the narrative of the whole of the repast in a life-like way. How can we fail to understand the historical superiority of this second form? Does not *Beyschlag* rightly say : " By the dramatic clearness of John's narrative the obscurities of the Synoptic story are scattered"?

2

John 13:31-16:33

THE DISCOURSES

Jesus has just taken leave of Judas, an eternal leavetaking: *Do what thou hast to do!* He turns now towards His own, and the farewell which He addresses to them is an: until we meet again (*Gess*).[1] The departure of Judas has restored to His restrained feeling all its freedom. He can henceforth, during the short time which remains to Him, pour forth His feelings, partly in conversations called out by their questions, partly in teachings which come spontaneously from His heart and which end by revealing to His disciples what He is for them. Softened as they are by the love of which He has just borne witness, humbled as they have never been, even by His humility, the apostles are now well prepared to receive and to appropriate to themselves His last revelations.

A series of short dialogues (comp. the questions of Peter, Thomas, Philip and Judas) opens these communications of an entirely familiar character. The subject of these conversations is naturally the approaching separation, with regard to which Jesus seeks to reassure them (chap. xiv). Ver. 31 of this chapter, by the external fact which is indicated in it, separates these conversations from the following discourses. In the latter, Jesus transports Himself in thought to the period when His disciples will have to continue His work and to labor in His name for the salvation of the world, and He promises them His aid in view of this task. It is the idea of His spiritual union with them which forms the basis of these teachings (xv. 1–xvi. 15). Finally, the thought returns to its starting-point, the impending separation. The dialogue-form reappears and Jesus then finds the decisive words which inspire them with the strength of which they have need at this sorrowful moment: xvi. 16–33. Thus a dying father, after having gathered his family about him, begins by speaking to them of his end ; then, their future career opens itself before his eyes: he shows them what they will have to do here on earth and what the earth will be to them. After which, returning to the present situation, he draws from the depths of his paternal heart a last word which alleviates the final farewell.

This progress is so natural that we are obliged to say that, if this situation existed and if Jesus spoke at this moment, He must have spoken in this way. The discourse is constantly elevated, simple, tender, on the level of the situation ; there reigns in it a deep but repressed emotion. The logical connection is not for an instant broken, but it is never made

---

[1] See his excellent work ; *Bibelstunden über Ev. Johannis*, C. XIII.-XVII. 2te Aufl., 1873.

conspicuous. Distinctness of intuition is united with inwardness of feeling, and we yield ourselves easily to the gentle undulation of the thought which results from the movement of the heart. We know of only two passages in our sacred books which offer any analogy to this one, and both of them owe their origin to analogous situations. They are the last discourses of Moses, in Deuteronomy, where the legislator takes leave of his people, and the second part of Isaiah, where the prophet, transporting himself in spirit beyond the future ruin and rising again of Israel, describes its work in the midst of the world.—*Hilgenfeld* establishes an opposition between these discourses and the last teachings, of an eschatological character, which the Synoptics have handed down to us (Matt. xxiv., Mark xiii.). The evangelist with his lofty spiritualism substituted, according to his view, for the visible return at the Parousia the spiritual coming of Jesus. But the notion of the coming and work of the Spirit is by no means wanting in the Synoptics; it is at the foundation of the parables of the talents and the pounds, in Matthew and Luke; of that of the virgins, in Matthew; comp. also the promises Matt. xxviii. 18-20 ; Luke xxiv. 48, 49, etc. And, on the other hand, the idea of the outward and visible consummation is not wanting in John, as we have seen (v. 28, 29, vi. 39, 40, 44, 54, xii. 48; comp. 1 Ep. ii. 28). The kingdom of the Spirit and the selection which results from it, to the view of John, only prepare for the kingdom of Christ and the final judgment.

The separation ; its necessity : xiii. 31-xiv. 31

After some words uttered by Jesus under the immediate impression of the departure of Judas (vv. 31-35), Jesus replies to different questions relative to His approaching removal which He has just announced to them ; that of Peter (ver. 36-xiv. 4), that of Thomas (vv. 5-7), that of Philip (vv. 8-21), and that of Judas (vv. 22-24); He closes with some reflections with which the present situation inspires Him (vv. 25-31).

1. Vv. 31-35

Vv. 31, 32. " *When therefore*[1] *he was gone out, Jesus says, Now has the Son of man been glorified ; and God has been glorified in him.* 32. *If God has been glorified in him,*[2] *God will also glorify him in himself,*[3] *and will straightway glorify him.*"—These two verses are as if a cry of relief which escapes from the heart of Jesus at the sight of the withdrawing traitor. Some documents reject οὖν, *therefore*, which would allow us, with many commentators, to connect the words ὅτε ἐξῆλθεν with the preceding clause : " It was night when he went out." But this useless appendage would weaken the solemn gravity of the brief clause : " *Now it was night.*" And the verb λέγει, *he says*, would also come in too abruptly. Ὅτε οὖν must therefore be read:

---

[1] T. R. reads οτε ουν with ℵ B C D L X some Mnn. It. Vulg. Cop. Orig., while ς rejects ουν with the other Mjj. 90 Mnn. Syr.

[2] ℵ B C D L X II 12 Mnn. It[plerique] omit the words ει ο θεος εδοξασθη εν αυτω, which are read in T. R. with 12 Mjj. (A Γ Δ etc.) Mnn. It[aliq] Vulg. Cop. Syr. Orig.

[3] ℵ B H Δ read εν αυτω instead of εν εαυτω.

824 / The Development of Faith

"*When therefore he was gone out, Jesus says.*"—The νῦν, *now*, which begins the following words, puts them quite naturally in connection with the fact which has just taken place, the departure of Judas. *Hengstenberg, Weiss* and *Keil* do not believe in such a connection. This *now*, according to them, refers to the impending end of His earthly activity, the result of which Jesus contemplates with joy. This, as it seems to me, is to fail to recognize the connection of ideas which John himself wished to set forth by saying so expressly : "*When he was gone out, He says.*"—The past tense ἐδοξάσθη, *is glorified*, sums up all the past life of Jesus, up to the scene which has just occurred, and which, in certain respects, is the crowning point of it. Empty human glory, which He had always rejected, has just been expressly declared to be excluded from His work and that of His apostles. The washing of their feet has condemned it ; it has just gone out with Judas, who was the stubborn representative of it among the disciples. The true glory, that which comes from God, that which consists in humility and charity, has been realized to the utmost in the person of Jesus; it has just triumphed over the false glory. Some interpreters have referred this term *is glorified* to the *future glory* of Jesus, either through His death (*Meyer*), or through His exaltation to the right hand of God (*Luthardt, Gess*). But, in ver. 32, Jesus sets in opposition to this verb in the past tense the future δοξάσει, *will glorify*, to designate His glorification which is to come. Comp. also xvii. 10, where He declares Himself *already now* glorified (δεδόξασμαι) in the hearts of the apostles.

We understand from this why He designates Himself as the *Son of man*. It is indeed by the humiliation with which He has placed Himself on the level with His brethren and made Himself their servant, that He has obtained this glory.—A glory which consists even in humility does not, like human glory, make him who possesses it a usurper of the glory of God. For this reason He is able to speak of it without scruple as He does here. Its essence is to give all glory to God, as He immediately adds : "*And God is glorified in him.*" In this glory of Jesus that of God Himself has shone forth. The perfection of the paternal character of God has been manifested fully in the person and work of the Son of man, ver. 32. But God cannot abandon him who has made himself the instrument of His glory. "He honors him who serves Him" (xii. 26).—The first words of ver. 32 : *If God is glorified in him*, are rejected by the Alexandrian authorities. But even Tischendorf condemns this omission. *Weiss* also : "One cannot set aside the suspicion that the omission of these words in the most ancient Codd. is the result of the confounding of the two ἐν αὐτῷ." *Westcott* and *Hort* retain them in spite of everything. The examples of such omissions in the Alexandrian text, however, are numerous, especially in the *Sinaitic* MS.—The clause : *If God is glorified in him*, fully explains the transition from the past tense *is glorified* to the future *will glorify*, ver. 32. The instrument of the glory of God on the earth, Jesus will be glorified by God in heaven. Could God do less than that which the Son of man has done for Him ? This correlation is expressed by the word καί, *also*, which is placed for this reason at the beginning of the clause ; comp. xvii. 4, 5. Whether we read ἐν αὐτῷ with B. etc., or ἐν ἑαυτῷ with the T. R. and all the Mjj. except four, the meaning is still : *in God*. The two limiting phrases : *in him* (Jesus), and *in him* or *in himself* (God), answer to each other. When God has been glorified in a person, He draws him to His bosom and envelops him *in* His glory. It is thus that the future of Jesus is illuminated to His view in the brightness of His past. And this future is near. The departure of Judas has just revealed to Him the fact of its imminence by announcing that of His death. *Soon*, says Jesus, alluding to His exaltation through the resurrection and ascension. The second καί is explanatory : "*and that soon.*"—After having thus, under the influence of what has just occurred, given vent to His personal impressions, Jesus turns to His disciples and makes them the subject of His whole thought.

Vv. 33–35. "*My little children, yet a little while*[1] *I am with you ; you will seek me, and, as I said to the Jews : Whither I go, you cannot come, so now I say to you.* 34. *I give you a new commandment, that you love one another ; as I have loved you, that you also love one another.* 35. *By this shall all men know that you are my disciples, if you have love one to another.*" [2]—The term of tenderness, τεκνία, *my little children*, is found nowhere else in our Gospels ; it is the *soon* of ver. 32, implying the near separation, which suggests it to Him. The disciples appear to Him as children whom He is about to leave as orphans on the earth. What a void in their life is that which will result from the disappearance of Jesus ! He Himself feels, in all its vividness, what they will experience. "*You will seek me ;* you will wish to rejoin me." And for Himself, how desirous He must be to carry them away immediately with Himself into the divine world which He is about to enter again ! But what He had declared to the Jews six months before (vii. 34, viii. 21) is still for the moment applicable to the disciples : they are not ready to follow Him. Only there is this difference between them and the Jews, that for them this impossibility is merely temporary : comp. xiv. 3 : "*I will take you to myself, that where I am, there you may be also,*" while Jesus said to the Jews : "You shall die in your sins." For the Jews the obstacle of the natural condemnation, which faith alone could have removed, will continue for ever by reason of their unbelief. As to the disciples, while waiting till they shall rejoin Him, He leaves to them a duty which will be at the same time their consolation ; the one which results from their new situation and which is indicated in ver. 34 : the duty of loving one another. It is by loving each other that they will supply the outward absence of Him who has loved them so tenderly.

The expression ἐντολὴ καινή, *new commandment*, has embarrassed the interpreters, because the Old Testament already commanded that one should love one's neighbor *as oneself* (Levit. xix. 18) and because it does not seem possible to love more than this. Or must we say, with *Knapp*, in his celebrated dissertation on this subject, and, as it seems, also with *Reuss* and *Weiss*, that Jesus, by His example and His word, teaches us to love our neighbor *more than ourselves ?* This thought is more specious than just. Or must we

---

[1] ℵ L X It^{aliq} add χρονον after μικρον.   [2] ℵ reads μετ' αλληλων instead of εν αλληλοις.

give to the word καινή here an extraordinary meaning, such as *illustrious* (*Wolf*), *ever new* (*Olshausen*), *renewed* (*Calvin*), *renewing the man* (*Augustine*), *unexpected* (*Semler*), *the last* (*Heumann*)? Nothing of all this is necessary. The entirely new character of Christian love results, in the first place, in an outward way from the *circle* in which it is exercised : *one another ;* this love applies not to all the human family in general, like the law of affection written on the conscience, nor, more specially, to members of the Israelite nation, like the commandment in Leviticus ; it embraces all those whom the common faith in Jesus and the love of which they are the object on His part unite. But the term *new* goes yet far deeper than this : it is a love new in its very *nature:* it starts from an altogether new centre of life and affection. The love of the Jew for the Jew arose from the fact that Jehovah was the God of both and had chosen them both in Abraham ; every Israelite became for every other, through this common blessing, like a second self. Jesus brought into the world and testified to His own a love specifically different from any love which had appeared until then, that which attaches itself to the human personality in order to save it. From this new hearth there springs forth the flame of an affection essentially different from any that the world knew under this name before. *In Christ :* this is the explanation of the word *new*. It is a family affection, and the family is born at this hour ; comp. 1 John ii. 8.—It is impossible for me to regard the words : *as I have loved you*, as *Meyer, Luthardt, Weiss* and *Keil* do, as depending on this first clause : *that you love one another*. The repetition of these last words at the end of the verse thus becomes useless. Jesus begins by saying : *that you love one another ;* then, taking up this command with a new emphasis, He adds to it, at this time, the characteristic definition : " I mean : that, *as I have loved you*, you should also love one another." Comp. in xvii. 21 the same construction exactly. Καθώς, *as*, indicates more than a simple comparison (ὥσπερ); it designates a conformity. The love which unites believers among themselves is *of the same nature* as that which Jesus testifies to the believer (x. 15); each one, so to speak, loves his brother with the love with which Jesus loves both him and this brother.

To the obligation resulting from the words : *as I have loved you*, Jesus adds the loftiest motive, that of His glory. For him who has felt himself beloved by Him, there can be no motive more pressing.—Ἐμοί has perhaps more force as a dative than as a nominative plural : disciples belonging *to me*, the new Master. The history of the primitive Church realized this promise of Jesus : " They loved one another, even before knowing one another," said Minutius Felix of the Christians ; and the scoffing Lucian said : " Their Master has made them believe that they are all brethren."— Here begins a series of questions which were all raised in the hearts of the disciples by the thought of the threatened separation. The first is quite naturally this : Is there no means of avoiding this separation, even though temporary ? It is Peter, the boldest of all, who makes himself the organ of this desire, which is incompatible with the words of Jesus (ver. 33).

John 13:36-14:4

Vv. 36–38. "*Simon Peter says to him, Lord, whither goest thou? Jesus answered him,*[1] *Whither I*[2] *go, thou canst not follow me now, but thou shalt follow me afterwards.* 37. *Peter says to him, Lord,*[3] *why cannot I follow thee now?*[4] *I will lay down my life for thee.* 38. *Jesus answered him,*[5] *Wilt thou lay down thy life for me? Verily, verily, I say unto thee, The cock shall not crow, till thou hast denied*[6] *me thrice.*"—What especially impressed St. Peter in the preceding words is the thought of ver. 33 : "*Whither I go, you cannot come.*" Jesus is going to glory; Peter does not doubt this (ver. 32); why then, after having walked with Him on the waters and having ascended with Him the Mount of Transfiguration, can he not follow Him to glory, to return with Him soon to the earth, when he will establish His kingdom ? Peter had merely said : *Whither goest thou?* but evidently, as a child who, when asking his father : Whither art thou going ? means : Cannot I go with thee ? Jesus understood the purpose of his question, and He replies to it by saying : *Thou canst not.* The temporary separation is inevitable ; does Jesus think of the task which Peter will have still to accomplish here on earth by his apostolic ministry (*Weiss*) ? Or must this word *can* be understood in a purely moral sense : "Thou art not yet capable of making the sacrifice necessary for following me" (*Tholuck*)? The words of xiv. 2, 3 cause us rather to think of reasons of another nature, at once objective and subjective. On the one hand, the redemption is not yet effected, and consequently the place of Peter is not yet prepared in heaven ; on the other, Peter himself is not yet prepared for the place ; the Holy Spirit has not yet made of him a new man. Peter, however, imagines that Jesus speaks thus only because He believes him incapable of facing death ; and in the ardor of his zeal, exaggerating the measure of his moral strength, he declares himself ready to undergo martyrdom (ver. 37). Jesus, who knows him better than he knows himself, then declares to him that, even in this respect, he is still incapable of accompanying Him (ver. 38).—The cock-crowing of which Jesus speaks is that which properly bore this name ; the second, that which precedes the break of day, about three o'clock in the morning (Mark xiii. 35). In the prediction of the denial in Mark (xiv. 30) allusion is also made to the first, the one at midnight.—The prediction of his denial seems to have produced on the apostle a very profound impression ; he is, as it were, thunder-struck by it, and from this moment he does not speak any more until the end of these discourses.

xiv. 1, 2. "*Let not your heart be troubled. Believe in God ; believe also in me.* 2. *In my Father's house there are many mansions ; if it were not so, I would have told you;*[7] *I go to prepare a place for you.*"—The division of the chap-

---

[1] B C It^{plerique} Vulg. Cop. reject αυτω after απεκριθη.
[2] ℵ D U add εγω before υπαγω.
[3] ℵ some Mnn. Vulg. Cop. omit κυριε (*Lord*).
[4] C D L X read νυν instead of αρτι.
[5] ℵ A B C L X : αποκρινεται, instead of απεκριθη αυτω.
[6] B D L X : αρνηση, instead of απαρνηση.
[7] ℵ A B C E K L Π 20 Mnn. It^{aliq} Vulg. Syr. Cop. read οτι (*that* or *because*) before πορευομαι (*I go to prepare for you*).

ters here is very faulty ; for the following words are in close relation with the preceding conversation, and particularly with the words of Jesus : *Thou shalt follow me afterwards.* Extending this same promise to all the disciples (comp. ver. 33), Jesus explains to them in what way they will be able to rejoin Him. He is going away for the moment to prepare for them their place in heaven (ver. 2); then He will return to seek them in order to transport them thither (ver. 3). We must place ourselves at this particular point of view in order to thoroughly understand the exhortation to *confidence,* which ver. 1 contains. Very far from bringing trouble to their hearts, His departure should fill them with the sweetest hope. They should have confidence *in God,* who directs this work and does not leave their Master to perish through weakness, and *in Jesus* Himself, who executes the work on His part, and who, far from being separated from it by death, is going to continue and complete it above. I think, with most, that the two πιστεύετε, *believe,* are more in harmony with the imperative ταρασσέσθω, *let it not be troubled,* if they are both taken as imperatives. Others take them both (*Luther*) as indicatives (*you believe*), or only the first (*Erasmus, Calvin, Grotius*), or only the second (*Olshausen*). Jesus would, in order to dispel their trouble, remind them of the faith which they already have in Him or in God or in both. This would be quite useless. In the second member, the limiting word *in me* is placed before the verb ; this is in order better to set forth the antithesis of the two limiting phrases *in God* and *in me* : " Have confidence in God ; in me also have confidence."

A first motive for confidence is given in ver. 2 ; it refers rather to confidence in God. Jesus points out to them that the house of the Father, to which He returns, is wide enough to receive them all and many others with them. The image is derived from those immense oriental palaces in which there is an apartment, not only for the sovereign and for the heir to the throne, but for all the king's sons, however numerous they may be. The term πολλαί, *many,* does not by any means refer to a *diversity* among these mansions (as if Jesus would allude to the different degrees of heavenly felicity), but only to their *number :* there are as many as there are believers ; each one will possess his own in this vast edifice.—This heavenly dwelling is above all the emblem of a spiritual state : that of communion with the Father, the filial position which is accorded to Christ in the divine glory, and in which He will give believers a share. But this state will be realized in a definite place, the place where God most illustriously manifests His presence and His glory—heaven. *Lange* thinks that when uttering these words Jesus pointed His disciples to the starry heaven ; but xiv. 31 proves that they were still in the room.—According to the Alexandrian reading, ὅτι, *that* or *because,* must be read after the words *I would have told you:* "I would have told you *that* I go away," or " *because* I go away." The first of these meanings is incompatible with ver. 3, where Jesus says precisely that He is going away and for the purpose of preparing. The Fathers who, in general, adopt this meaning, have not been successful in getting rid of the contradiction to that which follows, which it implies. *Weiss* and *Keil,* with their systematic preference for the Alexandrian authorities, try the second meaning, *because ;* the former, by making this conjunction bear on the verb *I would have told,* but without being able to derive from it an intelligible thought ;[1] Keil, by referring the *because* to : *there are many mansions,* which forces us to make a parenthesis of the intermediate words : " There are many mansions... —if not... I would have told you—because I am going to prepare a place for you there." But wherein is the stated proof : *I go to prepare,* more certain than the fact affirmed : *there is room?* And this parenthesis, which is not indicated by anything, is unnatural. In this case again it must be acknowledged that the reading of the Alexandrian authorities is indefensible ; the ὅτι is an addition arising from the fact that it was desired to make the following words the contents of the verb *I would have said.* Some, whether rejecting or preserving the ὅτι, take the preceding words in the interrogative sense : " *Would I have said to you* (that I am going to prepare a place for you) ?" But He had nowhere said anything of this kind. Others translate : " *Would I say it to you* (at this moment)?" But, in this case, the imperfect (ἔλεγον ἄν) would be necessary. We must, therefore, return to the simplest interpretation : "If it were not so, I would have told you." That is to say : "If our separation were to be eternal, I would have forewarned you ; I would not have waited until this last moment to declare it to you ;" or, as *Grotius* says, *Ademissem vobis spem inanem.*

Their faith in God must make them understand that the Father's house is spacious. But it is also needful that the *access* to it should be opened to them, and that they should have their dwelling there assured. Here it is that faith in Jesus intervenes, as the complement of faith in the Father. He is their πρόδρομος, their forerunner, to heaven (Heb. vi. 20). Under this image He causes them to view both His death, which, through reconciliation, will open for them the entrance to heaven, and His exaltation, by means of which there will be created in His person a glorious state in which He will afterwards give them a share. And the following is the way in which He will *prepare* it.

Ver. 3. "*And if I shall have gone and*[2] *prepared*[3] *a place for you, I will come again and take you to myself, that where I am, there you may be also.*"— The place being once assured and prepared for them, they must be brought to reach it. It is He who will also charge Himself with this office. The rejection of καί, *and,* before ἑτοιμάσω in some MSS. ("and when I shall have gone, I will prepare") would introduce an unnatural and even absurd *asyndeton* between the idea of *preparing* and that of *returning* which follows, and would at the same time lead to a complete tautology with the preceding sentence. The reading ἑτοιμάσαι, *to prepare,* is a further correction which was rendered almost indispensable by the rejection of the καί.— To the two verbs : "*when I shall have gone* and *shall have prepared,*" corre-

---

[1] Because He who goes away to prepare for them a place must know better than any one whether there are mansions there to be prepared. What a proof ! To prove His word by His knowledge and His knowledge by His word !

[2] Καί (*and*) is omitted by A E G K Γ Δ Λ 40 Mnn.

[3] D M 60 Mnn. Syr. : ετοιμασαι (*to prepare for you*), instead of και ετοιμασω.

spond the two verbs of the principal clause : *I will come again* (literally, *I come again*) and *I will take you to myself*. The present *I come again* indicates imminence. Notwithstanding this, *Origen* and other Fathers, *Calvin, Lampe,* and, among the moderns, *Hofmann, Luthardt, Meyer, Weiss,* and *Keil,* refer this term to the *final* and glorious *coming* of the Lord. Undoubtedly this promise is addressed to believers in general, but it has in view, nevertheless, first of all, the disciples personally, whom Jesus wishes to strengthen in their present disheartenment ; and He consoles them, it is said, by means of an event which no one of them has seen and which is still future at this hour ! In thus explaining the word *I come,* it is forgotten that Jesus never affirmed the nearness of His Parousia, and that, indeed, He rather gave an indication of the opposite : "*As the bridegroom delays his coming*" (Matt. xxv. 5) ; "*If the master comes in the second watch, or if he comes in the third*" (Luke xii. 38) ; "*At evening or at midnight or at the cock-crowing or in the morning*" (Mark xiii. 35) ; comp. also the parables of the leaven and the grain of mustard seed. Moreover, we have the authentic explanation of this word *come* in ver. 18, where, as *Weiss* acknowledges, it cannot be applied to the Parousia. *Ebrard* thinks that the point in question is the *resurrection* of Jesus. But the true reunion, after the separation caused by the death of Jesus, did not yet take place at the resurrection. The appearances of the Lord were transient ; their design was simply, through faith in the resurrection, to prepare for the coming of the Spirit. *Grotius, Reuss, Lange, Hengstenberg,* and *Keil* refer the word *come* to the return of Jesus at the *death* of each believer ; comp. the vision of Stephen. But in ver. 18 this sense is altogether impossible, and no example can be cited, not even xxi. 23, where it would lead to an intolerable tautology. This coming refers, therefore, as has been recognized by *Lücke, Olshausen, Neander,* to the return of Jesus through the Holy Spirit, to the close and indissoluble union formed thereby between the disciple and the glorified person of Jesus ; comp. all that follows in vv. 17, 19–21, 23 ; especially ver. 18, which is the explanation of our : *I come again.* *Weiss* alleges against our view that the question here is of a *personal* return. We defer this to ver. 18.—The following verb : *I will take you to myself,* indicates another fact, which will be the result of this spiritual preparation. This is the introduction of the believer into the Father's house, at the end of his earthly career, either at the moment of his death, or at that of the Parousia, if he lives until that time. Καί, *and,* has the sense of *and consequently,* or of, *and afterwards,* as is indicated by the contrast between the present (*I come*) and the future (*I will take*). This will be the entrance of the believer, prepared by spiritual communion with Jesus, into the abode secured for him by the mediation of this same Jesus. Πρὸς ἐμαυτόν, *to myself* (xii. 32) ; He presses him to His heart, so to speak, while bearing him away. There is an infinite tenderness in these last words. It is for Himself that He seems to rejoice in and look to this moment which will put an end to all separation : " *That where I am, there you may be also ;*" comp. xvii. 24. The community of *place* ("*there where*") implies that of *state.* Otherwise the return of Jesus in spirit would not be necessary in order to prepare in each particular case this reunion. What touching simplicity and what dramatic vivacity in the expression of these ideas, so profound and so new ! *The Father's house, the preparation* of the dwelling-place, the coming to *find*, finally the *taking to Himself*, this familiar and almost childlike language resembles sweet music by which Jesus seeks to alleviate the agony of separation in the minds of the apostles. Thus ends the first conversation, called forth by the question of Peter : "Why cannot I follow thee ?" Answer : "Even thy martyrdom would not be sufficient to this end ; my return in the Spirit into thy heart : this is the condition of thy entrance into my heavenly glory." Comp. iii. 5.

But Jesus observes that many questions were still rising in their minds, that their hearts were a prey to many doubts, and, in order to incite them to ask Him, He throws out to their ignorance a sort of challenge, by saying to them :

Ver. 4. "*And whither I go you know, and the way you know.*"[1]—We translate according to the received reading, which has in its favor 14 Mjj., the *Peschito* and most of the manuscripts of the *Itala*. According to it, Jesus attributes to the disciples the knowledge both of the *end* and of the *way*. According to the Alexandrian reading : "And whither I go, you know the way," He attributes to them only the knowledge of the *way*. The difference is not great. For if, according to the second reading, the knowledge of the end is not declared, it is certainly implied, and this by reason of ver. 2, where the end (*the Father's house*) had been clearly pointed out. But did the apostles know the way to reach it ? Yes and no ; yes, since this way was Jesus and Jesus was what they knew better than anything else. No, in the sense that they did not know Him as the way. This is the reason why, if Jesus can say to them with truth : *You know the way*, Thomas can answer him with no less truth : *We know it not*. Preoccupied until then with another end, the earthly kingdom of the Messiah, their imagination had not transferred their hopes from the world to God, from the earth to heaven ; they were thinking, in fact, like the Jews (xii. 34) : "*We have heard that the Christ abides forever* (on the earth, which is glorified by Him) ; *how then dost thou say, The Son of man must be lifted up ?*" Comp. Acts i. 6. And this false end to a certain extent veiled the truth from them. It is Thomas, the disciple who was particularly positive in his spirit, who becomes here, as at other times, the organ of doubting thoughts and discouraged feelings which exist more or less in them all ; comp. xi. 16, xx. 25.

3. Vv. 5–7

Vv. 5, 6. "*Thomas says to him, Lord, we know not whither thou goest, and*[2] *how do we know the way?*[3] *6. Jesus says to him, I am the way and the truth and the life; no one comes to the Father but by me.*"—Peter desired to follow

---

[1] Instead of the words οιδατε και την οδον οιδατε, ℵ B C L Q X, read οιδατε την οδον.

[2] B C L It^{aliq} omit και before πως.

[3] B C D It^{aliq} : οιδαμεν την οδον (*do we know the way ?*) instead of δυνάμεθα την οδον ειδεναι (*can we know the way ?*) in T. R. with 15 Mjj. Syr. It^{aliq}.

832 / The Development of Faith

Jesus immediately; this request having been rejected, Thomas wishes at least to understand clearly what is to take place, whither Jesus is going and by what way, and the more because the disciples are one day to follow Him. Thus far, the departure of Jesus leaves him nothing but obscurity. End and way, everything is lost for him in vacancy. Jesus, in His reply, lays hold especially upon the idea of *the way* while recalling to mind clearly the end in the second part of the verse. From the connection of these words with the question of Thomas it follows that the dominant idea of the three following terms is that of *way*, and that the other two must serve to explain it. From the second part of the verse it is also clear that the way which is in question is that which leads to the Father and His house, and not the way by which one can come *to* the truth and the life, as *Reuss* formerly supposed. The figurative expression *way* is therefore explained without a figure by the two terms : *truth* and *life*. Truth is God *revealed* in His essence, that is to say, in His holiness and love (ver. 9). Life is God *communicated* to the soul and bringing to it a holy strength and perfect beatitude (ver. 23). And as it is in Jesus that this revelation and communication of God to the soul are effected, so it is through Jesus also that the soul comes to the Father and obtains through Him the entrance into the Father's house. The three terms, *way, truth* and *life*, are not, therefore, co-ordinated (*Luther, Calvin :* beginning, middle, end); no more do they express a single notion : *vera via vitæ* (*Augustine*). Jesus means to say : I am the means of coming *to the Father* (the way), *in that* I am the truth and the life.—Reuss justly observes with reference to the word *I am*, that this expression excludes every other means parallel to this. *Gess :* " A man can at the most *show* to others the right way ; he cannot *be* either the way or the truth or the life."—In the following clause, the words : *to the Father*, set forth a nearer end than the figurative expression of ver. 2. The question here is of communion with the Father here on earth, which is the condition of communion with Him in heaven (*His house*).

Ver. 7. " *If you had known*[1] *me, you would have known*[2] *my Father also ; and*[3] *from henceforth you know him and have seen him.*"—This verse reproduces the idea of the last clause of the preceding verse, that of coming to the Father through Jesus. If Jesus is really the manifestation of God (ver. 6), to have well known Him Himself would be enough for the arriving through Him at the knowledge of God (pluperfect ἐγνώκειτε). This is the sense of the received reading which is perfectly suitable ; it is also that of the reading of some Alexandrian authorities which read ᾔδειτε for the second ἐγνώκειτε. It seems that Jesus hereby denies to them this twofold knowledge ; and in fact it is only after having received the Spirit that they will possess it fully (ver. 20). Yet He afterwards partially concedes it to them, because they possess the beginning of it already. *Meyer* takes the term *from henceforth* literally : "since my preceding declaration" (that of ver. 6). This sense is too restricted and even insignificant. *Chrysostom* and

---

[1] ℵ D : εγνωκατε (*have known*), instead of εγνωκειτε (*had known*).

[2] ℵ D : γνωσεσθε (*you will know*) ; T. R. with A N Γ, etc. : εγνωκειτε αν (*you would have known*) ; B C L Q X : αν ηδειτε.

[3] B C L Q X omit και.

Lücke find here an anticipatory indication of the approaching illumination at Pentecost; but how can the *from henceforth* and the pluperfects allow this sense ? Jesus alludes to all that has just occurred in the course of this last evening. The washing of the feet and the dismissal of Judas, with all that He had said to them since then, were well fitted to bring to light the true character of God and the spiritual nature of His kingdom. The germ of the true knowledge of God had from henceforth been deposited in them. By showing Himself to them, as He had just done, even the inmost depths of His heart, Jesus had revealed to them forever the essence of God. The reading of ℵ D, adopted by *Tischendorf* (8th ed.) : "If you *have known me*, you *will know* my Father also," comes doubtless from the scruple which the copyists felt at making Jesus say that His disciples had not known Him up to that moment (see *Luthardt*).— *Weiss*, accepting the reading of some Alexandrian authorities which omit the καί (*and*) before ἀπ' ἄρτι, *from henceforth*, makes γινώσκετε an imperative, in this sense : "Know Him from henceforth as He is revealed to you in me, and thereby you will have seen Him ; you will be in possession of the life." But this imperative scarcely suits the adverb : *from henceforth ;* and we do not say : Know God, as we say : "Believe in God " (ver. 1).

This last word : *you have seen Him*, seems intended, as already ver. 4, to call forth the expression of some opposite thought. It is, as it were, a new challenge offered to this inward trouble which Jesus perceives in them. To have become *beholders* of God (perfect, ἑωράκατε)—was it not the greatest thing which the apostles could desire ? This privilege had, to a certain degree, been granted to Moses and to Elijah, under the old covenant. Certainly, if Jesus could cause them to enjoy it, their faith would for the future be immovable. Isaiah had positively made this promise for the Messianic times : " *The glory of the Lord shall be manifested, and all flesh shall see it* " (Is. xl. 5). Thus is the demand of Philip naturally explained : "Thou sayest ; *you have seen ;* we answer : show us!"

4. Vv. 8–21

Vv. 8, 9. " *Philip says to him, Lord, show us the Father, and it suffices us. 9. Jesus says to him, So long a time*[1] *am I with you, and thou hast not known me! Philip, he who has seen me, has seen the Father ; and* [2] *how sayest thou, Show us the Father ?*"—On occasion of these interruptions which the disciples allow themselves to make, *Gess* observes how fully at ease they feel with the Lord, and how fully this sort of relation justifies the words : " *I have called you my friends,*" xv. 15.—Peter had asked to follow Jesus. Thomas had desired at least to know whither He was going, and by what way. Since they can neither *follow* nor *understand* clearly, Philip would at least have a pledge of the glorious future which is reserved for them ; and what pledge more sure than an appearance of God Himself ! Is not the desire for the immediate sight of God an aspiration which dwells in the deepest recess of the

---

[1] ℵ D L Q : τοσουτω χρονω, instead of τοσουτον χρονον.

[2] ℵ B Q It^{pleriq} Vulg. Cop. πως instead of και πως.

heart of man? Comp. the request of Moses, Exod. xxxiii. 18. It was the same point of view as that of the Jews when they asked of Jesus a sign from heaven. This desire would be well founded if the essence of God consisted in power; the true theophany might in that case consist in a resplendent manifestation. But God is holiness and love; the real manifestation of these moral perfections can only consist in a moral life such that in it, in its acts and words, the moral perfection of the divine character shall shine forth. Now this unique spectacle, this perfect theophany, the visible resplendence of God, the disciples have had before their eyes for more than two years; how is it that they have not better appreciated the privilege which has been accorded to them? What majesty in this reply! The foundation of the human consciousness of Jesus is so thoroughly the feeling of His divinity, that He scarcely understands that the knowledge of His true nature has not formed itself in the hearts of His disciples.—The word of address: *Philip*, serves to recall this disciple to himself as he forgets himself at the point of making such a demand. We may, like *Luthardt*, write this vocative with the preceding sentence which is addressed to the disciple individually, or connect it with the following, which, as a general maxim, serves to bring back the apostle to the truth. The perfect tenses, ἔγνωκας, ἑωρακώς, ἑώρακε, *hast known, has seen*, contrast the permanent state with the sudden and isolated act expressed by the aorist δεῖξον, *show us*.—The idea of the simple moral union of Jesus with God cannot exhaust the meaning of these words. A Christian, even a perfected one, would not say, "He who has seen me has seen the Christ." How much less could a man, even a perfect man, say, "He who has seen me, has seen the Father." This expression is understood only as the Son continues here below, under the form of the human life, the revealing function which He possesses, as the Word, in His condition of divine life.

Vv. 10, 11. "*Believest thou not that I am in the Father, and that the Father is in me? The words that I speak[1] unto you, I speak not of myself; and the Father, who dwells in me, he does the works.[2] 11. Believe me when I say to you that I am in the Father, and that the Father is in me; and, if not, believe me[3] because of the works.*"—Jesus indicates to Philip two signs by which he ought to have recognized and may even at this moment recognize in Him the true appearance of God. He does not say that the Father and Himself are one and the same person. He constantly prays to the Father, saying: *Thou*. But it is a union by which they live *the one in the other* (comp. *Gess*), and this relation has as its background the life of the Logos. The words *Believest thou not?* show Philip that his prayer must be regarded as inconsistent with his faith.—There are in the union of Jesus with the Father two aspects: *I in the Father*: Jesus emptying Himself in order to transfer Himself to God; and *the Father in me*: God communicating to Jesus all His wealth of strength and wisdom. On one side, Jesus making a void in Himself; on the other, God filling this void.—After this, Jesus characterizes

---

[1] B L N X Cop. read λεγω instead of λαλω.
[2] ℵ B D read αυτου after εργα (*his works*) and reject αυτος. L X add αυτος (*himself*) after ποιει τα εργα.
[3] The μοι (*me*) is omitted by ℵ B L It^{aliq} Vulg. Syr.

each of the two sides of this relation by that one of the manifestations of His life which is most fitted to bring it to light : the first by *His words;* the second, by *His works.* Not one of His words that He derives from Himself and does not receive from God ! Not one of His works that is not wrought through Him by God Himself ! Of His own wisdom, *nothing !* By the strength of God, *everything.* The negative clause is better suited to wisdom ; the active form, to power. The following verse explains why the words are placed here before the works : comp. the reverse order in viii. 28, where Jesus is speaking to the unbelieving Jews. The first sign of the community of life and action between Jesus and God, for prepared hearts, is His teachings ; for those less disposed, it is His works. We may hesitate between the readings λαλῶ and λέγω, in the first clause. In the second, the term λαλῶ, in any case, is perfectly suitable. Jesus is only the organ of the Father : God *speaks ; Jesus announces.*

In ver. 11, Jesus demands from His disciples faith in His union with the Father on the authority of the testimony which He has borne to Himself. In the second clause, the imperative *believe* is without an object according to the reading of ℵ B L : " Believe," speaking absolutely, which seems logical. Nevertheless, the reading *me* in the other authorities may also be defended : " Believe me, if not on the ground of my word, at least because of my works ; " comp. x. 38. Jesus evidently means by these His supernatural works, His miracles. The miracles are a proof for him who does not believe in the words, because this divine testimony, not passing through the mouth of Jesus Himself, has an objective character. By these words, Jesus assigns to miracles their true place in apologetics.—In the first editions of this work, I regarded the following passage as designed to add to the objective revelation of God, accomplished in the person of Jesus (vv. 8–11), the subjective, internal theophany, the work of the Spirit, which is about to be described in vv. 12–24. It seems to me now that another connection must be adopted (see on ver. 12).

Vv. 12–14. " *Verily, verily, I say unto you ; He that believes on me, he also shall do the works which I do, and he shall do still greater things than these, because I go to the Father,*[1] 13. *and whatsoever you shall ask the Father in my name, I will do it, that the Father may be glorified in the Son.* 14. *If you*[2] *ask anything in my name, I*[3] *will do it.*"—The question of Thomas respecting the *way* had brought Jesus to speak of the work by which He leads His own to communion with the Father ; that of Philip had brought Him back to what He had already been here on earth, as the perfect revelation of the Father. He had thus been turned aside from the essential object of the conversation : the encouragement to be given to the disciples, in view of the separation which was distressing them (ver. 1). He now resumes this subject, and adds to the promise of a future reunion in the Father's house that of a much nearer meeting, that in which He will return to dwell in them

---

[1] ℵ A B D L Q X It. reject μου after πατερα (*the Father*).

[2] ℵ B E H U Γ Δ 30 Mnn. It^{aliq} Vulg. Syr. read με (*me*) after αιτησητε (*shall ask*) ; omitted by T. R. with 9 Mjj.

[3] A B L It^{aliq} Vulg. Cop. read τουτο (*this*), instead of εγω (*I*).

through the Holy Spirit and will continue through them here on earth the work which He has Himself begun here. Such is the thought of the whole following passage, vv. 12–24. The question of Judas does not introduce a new subject ; it affords Jesus the occasion of finishing the preceding development. —According to *Keil*, ver. 12 has as its purpose to reassure the disciples with regard to their future apostolic activity, respecting which they were anxious. According to *Weiss*, Jesus desires to show them how their own works will take the place of His, which are about to fail them and by reason of which, nevertheless, they are attached to Him. But there is no longer a question of these ideas in what follows. The question is now of the spiritual reunion which will follow the impending separation, and which will prepare the way for the final reunion promised in vv. 1–3. Ver. 12 forms the transition to this new promise. Jesus begins by setting forth the *effect* (the works which they will do), in order to go back to the *cause* (His power acting in them). The expression : *shall do the works which I do*, refers to miracles similar to those of Jesus, which were wrought by the apostles, and the following expression : *he shall do even greater things*, refers, not to more extraordinary outward works—the greatness of miracles is not thus measured (*Weiss*)—but to works of a superior *nature* even to corporeal healings. What St. Peter did at Pentecost, and St. Paul did throughout the world,—what a simple preacher, a simple believer effects in causing the Spirit to descend into a heart—Jesus could not do during His sojourn on earth. For, in order that such things should be realized, it was necessary " that the wall of separation between God and men should have been destroyed and the Holy Spirit have been given to mankind" (*Gess*) ; in other words, that, as the end of the verse says, the glorification of Jesus should have been accomplished : "*because I go to the Father ;*" comp. vii. 39. The branch, united to the vine, can bear fruits which the vine itself cannot bear. *Greater* does not, therefore, mean here : more stupendous, but more excellent ; and this term does not refer merely to the *extension* of the apostolic ministry beyond the limits of the theocracy, as *Lücke, Tholuck, Olshausen, de Wette* understand it—this difference is here only secondary—but to the *nature* of the works accomplished.

This superiority of spiritual productiveness promised to the disciples will be founded upon the exaltation of Christ's own position : "*Because I go to the Father.*" We see clearly here that the expression : *to go to the Father*, denotes not death only, but death and the ascension together.— Jesus says, according to the Alexandrian authorities : *to the Father*, not : *to my Father*. Indeed, God shows Himself, in thus acting, as the Father of the disciples no less than of Jesus Himself.—We must not close the explanation which the *because* leads us to look for with ver. 12, by making ver. 13, as *Westcott* would still have it, a principal clause. Ver. 13 necessarily belongs to this explanation. It is not sufficient that Jesus should be exalted ; it is necessary that He should still act from the midst of His glory : *because I go . . . and . . . I will do it.* Καί : *and thus. Whatsoever you shall ask* indicates the disciple's part in these works ; it must not be passed over in silence ; otherwise Jesus could not say *they will do them* (ver. 12). This part will be simply prayer. The believer asks, and the all-powerful Christ works from the midst of His glory. But the question here is not of prayer in general. It is to prayer of a special kind that Jesus attributes this efficacious co-operation with Him, *to prayer in His name*. To ask in the name of any one is, in ordinary life, to ask in place of a person, as if on his part, and applying to oneself, in virtue of His recommendation, all his titles to the favor demanded. If we had only this passage in which the expression : to pray *in the name of Jesus*, were used, we should accordingly think that to pray thus is to ask something in the assured consciousness of our reconciliation with God and our adoption in Christ, to pray to God as if we were the representatives, and, in some sort, the mouth of Jesus. But is this explanation, in itself very natural and the one which I adopted in the preceding editions, applicable to the passage xiv. 26 : "The Holy Spirit whom my Father will send *in my name*"? It does not seem to me so. The other explanations do not appear to satisfy this requirement any more fully ; thus those of *Chrysostom*, "pleading my name ;" of *Calov*, " on the foundation of my merits ;" of *Lücke, Meyer, Gess*, etc., "praying in communion with me, from the midst of the spiritual element of my own life ;" of *de Wette*, " in view of my cause ;" or of *Weiss*, "in so far as it is a matter of works done for the accomplishment of the mission which I give you." All these explanations are true, certainly, but they touch only one side of the idea, not the centre. I think, therefore, that we must rather abide by that of *Hengstenberg, Keil* and *Westcott* (with differing shades) : to ask a thing of God as Father *on the foundation of the revelation* which Jesus has given us of Himself and of His work, or, as *Keil* says, "plunging by faith into the knowledge which we have received of Him as Son of God humbled and glorified." By acting thus we necessarily address to God a prayer which has all the characteristics set forth in the preceding explanations. This sense answers also to that of the term *the name* in the Scriptures. For the *name* sums up the knowledge which we possess of a being ; it is his reflection in our thought. This sense applies very satisfactorily to the formula of ver 26.—*I will do it*, says Jesus ; He thus sets forth the greatness of His future position as the organ of omnipotence acting in the service of the fatherly love of God. Had He not said in ver. 1 : "Believe in God, and believe also *in me*."—And all this will take place, Jesus adds, *for the glory of the Father* in the person of the Son, for the Son does not dream of founding a kingdom here on earth which shall belong to Him alone.

Ver. 14 is a reaffirmation of that astonishing promise ; this is indicated already by the asyndeton : "Yes, it will indeed be so !"—By the words : ὅτι ἄν, *whatsoever*, Jesus opens an immeasurable field to the Christian ambition of His disciples. The received reading ἐγὼ ποιήσω, "*I* will do it," is certainly the true reading. Some Alexandrian authorities have mechanically reproduced verbatim the expression of ver. 13. But Jesus purposely modifies it, by substituting ἐγώ for τοῦτο : "*I*, who have never deceived you, and who am to be clothed with omnipotence with my Father, I pledge myself to do it." Thus, while His disciple shall pray in His name on the earth, He will act from heaven, on God's part, to execute the work, so intimate will be the

838 / The Development of Faith

union effected in Him between heaven and earth.— It seems to me absolutely impossible to keep in the text the με, *me*, which the Alexandrian authorities give as the object of αἰτήσητε : "Whatsoever you shall ask *me* in my name." It is inadmissible that one should ask anything of a person in his own name, except in the sense : for his own cause, which cannot be that of this phrase. *Tischendorf*, *Weiss* and *Westcott* endeavor vainly to defend this reading. Comp. besides, xv. 16, xvi. 23, 24. — To weigh the words which are constantly found at the beginning of all the epistles of St. Paul : "I cease not to make mention of you in my prayers," is, as *Stier* has said, sufficient to give us an understanding that it is by prayer in the name of Jesus that the apostles gave existence to the Church. — From the means by which they will perform these works superior to His own—prayer in His name,—Jesus now passes to the divine source which shall give birth to such prayer in their hearts—the Holy Spirit.

Vv. 15–17. "*If you love me, keep*[1] *my commandments.* 16. *And I will pray the Father, and he shall give you another support, that he may abide*[2] *with you eternally,* 17. *the Spirit of truth, whom the world cannot receive, because it sees him not neither knows him ;*[3] *but*[4] *you know him, because he abides with you ; and he shall be*[5] *in you.*"—Here is the supreme gift, because it is the source of all the rest, through the prayers which it inspires in the believer. And first, ver. 15, the moral condition necessary to the end that this gift should be granted to man. A preparation is needed : "Love me ! *Fulfil my will !*" Ver. 17 will justify this moral condition. The commandments of which Jesus speaks are the charges which He has given them while He has been with them, and particularly the instructions which He has given them on this last evening (xiii. 14, 15, 34, xiv. 1). The T. R., with almost all the Mjj., the *Itala* and the *Peschito*, reads the imperative τηρήσατε, *keep*, while B L read τηρήσετε, *you will keep*. The first is a direct summons to obedience in the name of the love which they have for Him. The second contains a reflection on the necessary relation between the two things. It seems to me that there is no reason to hesitate between these two readings. The second probably arises from the following future : *and I will pray*.— To the moral condition Jesus adds the objective condition, or the efficient cause of the divine gift, His own intercession. This intercession will have for its object the gift of the Holy Spirit. The words of xvi. 26, where it is said : "*I say not unto you that I will pray the Father for you,*" refers to the time which follows after this gift.—The term παράκλητος, literally, *called towards*, was taken by *Origen* and *Chrysostom* in the active sense : *comforter* παρακλήτωρ (Job xvi. 2 in the LXX). It was under the influence of the Vulgate that this false sense passed into our French versions. It is acknowledged at the present day that the word παράκλητος, of the passive form, must have a passive sense : he who *is called* as a sustaining help, as a support ; it is precisely the meaning of the Latin term *advocatus*, and of

---

[1] Instead of τηρησατε (*keep*), B L Cop. : τηρησετε (*you will keep*) ; ℵ : τηρησητε.

[2] ℵ B L Q X It^{plerique} Cop. Syr.: η (*may be*) instead of μενη (*may abide*).

[3] ℵ B *a* omit the second αυτο.

[4] ℵ B Q omit δε after υμεις.

[5] B D 5 Mnn. It. Syr.: εστιν (*is*), instead of εσται (*will be*) in all the other Mjj.

our word *advocate:* the defender of the accused before the tribunal. Perhaps the term used by Jesus was *Goël*, champion, defender. The Greek term has this meaning also in profane Greek, as in Demosthenes, Diogenes Laertius, Philo. John himself gives it this meaning in his first Epistle ii. 1, "*We have a paraclete (advocate) with the Father, Jesus Christ, the righteous.*" The meaning *teacher* (*Theodore of Mopsuestia, Ernesti, Hofmann, Luthardt*) has no foundation philologically, and the expression *the Spirit of truth* (ver. 17) is not sufficient to justify it. What Jesus will ask of the Father on their behalf is, therefore, another supporter, ever within their reach, ever ready to come to their aid, at the first call, in their conflict with the world. From this fundamental signification the following applications easily proceed: support in moments of weakness; counsellor in the difficulties of life; consoler in suffering. Thereby He will do for them what the beloved Master, who was now leaving them, had done during these last years. By saying *another*, Jesus implicitly gives *Himself* the title of Paraclete ; it is an error, therefore, to find here a difference of idea from that in the first Epistle (ii. 1). This gift which the Father will make to them, will come not only at the request of Jesus, but, as He says in xv. 26, through His mediation : "*The Paraclete whom I will send to you from my Father.*" As it is He who asks for Him on our part, so also it is He who sends on God's part. And He will not come, soon to withdraw Himself, as Jesus does ; but His dwelling in them will be eternal. *Meyer* understands εἰς τὸν αἰῶνα : "*even to the coming age.*" But the word αἰών, in the N. T. as in the classics (ἐξ αἰῶνος, δι' αἰῶνος, εἰς αἰῶνα) denotes an indefinite duration, and, with the article, eternity.—The Holy Spirit, a divine being, sent from the Father, to take the place of a mere man—supposing that Jesus were only this—is this conceivable ?

The appositional words, *the Spirit of truth* (ver. 17), serve to explain the term *Paraclete*, which was still obscure to the disciples. This expression can neither signify who *is* the truth—it is Jesus who is the truth, nor who *possesses* the truth,—this would be useless. The teaching of the Spirit is here contrasted with that of the word, as in xvi. 25. The teaching by means of the word can never give anything more than a confused idea of divine things ; however skilfully this means may be used, it can only produce in the soul of the hearer an image of the truth ; so Jesus compares it to a parable (xvi. 25). The teaching of the Spirit, on the contrary, causes the divine truth to enter into the soul ; it gives to it a full reality within us by making us have experience of it ; it alone makes the word a truth for us.—But, as Jesus has already intimated in ver. 15, in order to be fitted to receive this divine teacher, a moral preparation is necessary. The soul in which He comes to dwell must be already withdrawn from the profane sphere. This is the reason why Jesus says : *Keep my instructions;* and the reason why He here adds : *whom the world cannot receive.* It was not owing to any arbitrary action that, on the morning of the day of Pentecost, the Spirit descended on one hundred and twenty persons only, and not on all the inhabitants of Jerusalem : the former only had undergone the indispensable preparation. Jesus explains wherein this preparation which is wanting in the world consists : it is necessary to have *seen* and *known* the Spirit, in order to receive Him. The Spirit identifies Himself too intimately with our personal life to allow the possibility of His being imposed upon us ; that He may come to us, He must be desired and called, and for this end we must already have, in some manner, formed acquaintance with Him. But how can this be, if one has not yet received him ? The example of the disciples teaches us. During the years which they had passed in the society of Jesus, His word, His acts, constant emanations of the Spirit, had furnished them the means of *beholding* this divine agent in His most perfect manifestation and of *knowing* what was most holy and exalted in Him, and their hearts had rendered homage to the perfection of this inspiration from above which constantly animated their Master. This had not been done by *the world*, the Jews, who, on hearing Jesus speak, said : "He has a demon," and who, on seeing His miracles, ascribed them to Beelzebub. They thus remained strangers to the action of the Spirit, they even became hostile to it ; this is the reason why they were not in a condition to *receive* Him. It is impossible for me to understand what meaning *Weiss* can give to the two verbs : *to see* and *to know*, outside of this explanation and without falling into the *petitio principii :* in order to receive the Spirit, it is necessary to see Him ; and in order to see Him, it is necessary to have Him. If a reply is made by saying that these two present tenses : to see and to know, are presents of anticipation, which refer to the time when the disciples *will have received* the Spirit, the fact is forgotten that the question here is of the moral conditions *for* receiving Him.—The preparatory action of the Spirit on the disciples is expressed by the words : *He dwells with you ;* and the more intimate relation which He will form with them from the day of Pentecost by the words: "He shall be *in you*." We must not, therefore, read either, in the first clause, μενεῖ (in the future), *shall dwell*, with the *Vulgate*, nor, in the second, ἐστί, *is*, with the *Vatican* and *Cambridge MSS.* The whole meaning of the sentence lies precisely in the antithesis between the present *dwells* (comp. μένων, ver. 25) and the future *shall be*. This contrast of time is completed by that of the two limiting words : *with you* (comp. παρ' ὑμῖν of ver. 25) and *in you*.—To make the last clause : *And he shall be in you*, depend on the ὅτι, *because*, which precedes, leads to no reasonable meaning : You know Him now because He will be in you ! This last phrase expresses, on the contrary, a new fact, an advance of the highest importance : "*And thus*, in virtue of the knowledge which you have gained of Him by beholding Him in my person, He will be able to come *into you*." This distinction between the preparatory action of the Spirit *on* man (by means of His historical manifestations in Christ, and then in the Church) and His real dwelling *in* the individual, is, as it were, at the present day effaced in the consciousness of Christianity, and the confounding of two such different positions involves incalculable consequences.—"Until now Jesus, living *with* them, had been their support ; now they will have the support *in their own hearts*" (*Gess*) *;* and this support will be the Holy Spirit, that is to say again, Jesus Himself in another form ; it is this last idea so delightful to the hearts of the disciples which the following words, vv. 18–23, develop.

Vv. 18, 19. "*I will not leave you orphans : I come again to you.* 19. *Yet a little while, and the world shall see me no more ; but you shall see me ; because I live, you shall live also.*"—The term *orphans* is in harmony with the address *my little children* (xiii. 33) ; it is the language of the dying father. The *asyndeton* between ver. 18 and the preceding verse is sufficient to prove the essential identity of thought between these words and those of vv. 16, 17. This form, as we have seen, indicates in general a more emphatic affirmation of the thought already expressed. This observation consequently sets aside every other explanation of the words : *I come again to you*, than that which refers them to the return of Jesus through the Holy Spirit (vv. 16, 17). This is the explanation of almost all the modern writers (even of *Meyer* and *Luthardt*, 2d ed.). Moreover, this explanation is the only possible one, because of the entire following passage, vv. 19–23, which can only be the development of the 18th verse (see especially vv. 21, 23). Nevertheless, some refer this promise to the appearances of the risen Jesus (*Chrysostom, Erasmus, Grotius, Hilgenfeld*). Even *Weiss* joins them, abandoning thus his own explanation of ἔρχομαι, *I come*, in ver. 3. But these appearances had a momentary character and were not a true return of Jesus ; comp. the remarkable expression, Luke xxiv. 44 : "while *I was* yet with you." The purpose of these appearances was only to establish the faith of the disciples in the resurrection of Jesus, and thereby to prepare for His return in spirit into their hearts, but not to accomplish it. How could these appearances be His return, since His ὑπάγειν, His departure, includes at once His death and His ascension (ver. 28, xiii. 1) ? The return must be, therefore, posterior to the latter.—The application of ver. 18 to the Parousia (*Augustine, Hofmann, Luthardt,* 1st ed.) is also impossible ; comp. vv. 19, 23 : in ver. 19, the *seeing* of Jesus *again* coincides with His disappearance for the world ; and according to ver. 23, the return to believers is described as purely inward, while of the final coming it is said : "*And every eye shall see him.*" All that can and must be granted is, that the appearances of the Risen One served to *prepare for* and render possible His return through the Holy Spirit, and that this spiritual coming of Christ will have its consummation in the coming of the glorified Saviour.—The Spirit is, no doubt, *another* support in that His action differs from that of Jesus as visible ; but His coming is, nevertheless, the return of Jesus Himself. The Spirit is not the substitute for Jesus, as *Weiss* asserts ; otherwise the promise of the Paraclete would answer only imperfectly to the need of the disciples, whose hearts demanded the return of the Master Himself. If then *Weiss* alleges that the word *I come* can only denote a personal coming, we say in reply that it is indeed Christ in person whom the Holy Spirit gives to us. As to xvi. 22, which *Weiss* also alleges, see on that passage. *Tholuck* has concluded from the expression *I come*, that the Holy Spirit is only the person of Jesus Himself spiritualized, and *Reuss* affirms that "although the literal exegesis argues for the distinction of persons (between Christ and the Spirit), practical logic refuses to admit it." He "even hazards the opinion that in the discourses of Jesus the abstract notion of the Word is replaced by the more concrete notion of the Spirit." John is innocent of such serious confusion. As no writer of the old covenant would have used the terms Spirit of God and Angel of the Lord one for the other, so the confounding of the Word with the Spirit is inadmissible in a writer of the new covenant. No doubt, St. Paul says : " *The Lord is the Spirit* " (2 Cor. iii. 17). But he does not for this reason confound the person of the glorified Lord with the Holy Spirit. This is a region in which it is of importance to take account of shades of thought. According to xvi. 14, the Spirit is, not the Lord, but the power which *glorifies* Him, which makes Him appear, live and grow within us, and that by taking what is His and communicating it to us. The parts of each are perfectly distinct. They are as distinct in the work of Pentecost as in that of the incarnation. In begetting Jesus in the womb of Mary, the Holy Spirit did not become the Christ. After the same manner, the Holy Spirit, by glorifying Jesus and making Him live in us, does not for this reason become Jesus. The Word is the principle of the outward revelation, the Spirit that of the inward revelation. Jesus is the object to be assimilated ; the Spirit is the power by which the assimilation is accomplished. Without the objective revelation given in Jesus, the Spirit would have nothing to fertilize in us ; without the Spirit, the revelation granted in Jesus remains outside of us and is like a parable which is not understood. Hence it follows that the Spirit who comes is, in a sense, Jesus who comes again ; from one without us, Jesus becomes one within us. The consummated work of the Spirit is *Christ formed* in the believer, or, what expresses the same idea, it is the believer having reached *the perfect stature of Christ* (Gal. iv. 19, Eph. iv. 13). How can *Weiss* say that this idea is Pauline, not Johannean ? Jesus' *being in* the believer is of the same nature as God's *being in* the person of Christ, according to xvii. 22, 23. This idea includes that which we have just developed. It is contained in the expression ἐν χριστῷ, which has no other meaning in Paul than it has in John.

The words : *Yet a little while* (ver. 19), are in accordance with the present *I come*. They reduce to nothing, so to speak, the duration of the separation. —The *asyndeton* leads us to see in what follows a development of the promise of ver. 18.—The sight of which Jesus speaks is to be permanent, as is indicated by the present θεωρεῖτε, *you see me ;* it is that constant inward contemplation which St. Paul describes in the words which are so similar to the ones before us, 2 Cor. iii. 18 : " *We who behold the glory of the Lord with unveiled face.*" While the world, which has only known Jesus after the flesh, sees Him no more after He has physically disappeared, He becomes, from that moment, visible to His own in the spiritual sphere into which they are transported by the Spirit and in which they meet Him. The difference in the application of the word θεωρεῖν, *see*, in the two clauses proves nothing against this meaning ; it is precisely on this intentional difference that the meaning of the phrase rests ; comp. vv. 22, 23. This intimate intercourse is the source of all the strength of the Christian in his conflict with himself and with the world. This is the reason why, in what follows, the idea of *living* is, without any transition, substituted for that of seeing.

In the following phrase, the two clauses may be made dependent on ὅτι :
"You see me because I live and *because* you also shall live." This is what is
done by *Meyer, Luthardt, Weiss*, either in that they apply the whole to the
new life produced by the Holy Spirit (Christ and the believers seeing each
other again inasmuch as they are transported into the same sphere of life) ; or,
as *Weiss*, by referring the seeing again to the appearances of the Risen One :
"You see me again because you and I then live again." But the contrast
between the present *I live* and the future *you shall live* is not sufficiently explained in these two interpretations. And in that of *Weiss* how are we to
explain the word : *You shall live?* The appearances of the Risen One did not
make the disciples *live* (ζῆν) ; they renewed their courage. Life, throughout
our entire gospel, is communicated by the Holy Spirit (vii. 39). A second
construction consists in making the first clause alone depend on ὅτι, and
explaining : "*You see me* (then), *because I live;* and (as a consequence of
this sight of me living) *you also shall live.*" Our spiritual *sight* of Jesus results
from His heavenly *life*, and this sight produces life in us. But the strongly
accentuated opposition between the ἐγώ, *I*, and the καὶ ὑμεῖς, *and you* or *you
also*, causes us to prefer a third construction : that which makes the ὅτι
depend on the following verb ζήσεσθε, *you shall live : But you see me* (in
opposition to *the world sees me no more) ; because I live, you shall live also.*"
They see Him ; and, as He whom they thus behold is living, this beholding
communicates life to them.—By the present *I live*, Jesus transfers Himself,
as in vv. 3 and 18, to the approaching moment when death shall be finally
vanquished for Him and when He will live the perfect, indestructible life ;
and by the future, *you shall live*, to the still more remote time when His
glorified life will become theirs. Thus is the relation between *I live* and
you shall live naturally explained ; comp. the similar relation between *I
come* and *I will take*, in ver. 3. The present designates the principle laid
down once for all, the future the daily, gradual, eternal consequences.

Vv. 20, 21. "*In that day you shall know that I am in my Father and you in
me and I in you.* 21. *He who has my commandments and keeps them, he it is
who loves me; and he who loves me shall be loved by my Father, and I will love
him and will manifest myself to him.*"—The absence of a particle between
these words and the preceding and following ones betrays the emotion with
which Jesus contemplates and foretells the decisive day of Pentecost. It
is, in a new form, the reaffirmation of the same promise.

The expression *that day* indicates a precise moment, not a period, as
Reuss thinks. And as the great circumstances of Jesus' ministry connect
themselves naturally with the Jewish feasts, and as the feast of the Passover,
which was about to be the time of His death, was to be followed soon by
that of Pentecost, there is nothing to prevent us from thinking, whatever *Lücke, de Wette, Weiss*, etc., may say, that the day of which He is here
speaking was already in their view the day of Pentecost ; comp. the ἔτι
μικρόν, *in a little while*, ver. 19. However this may be, Jesus contrasts this
day of the coming of the Spirit, whatever it is, with the present moment,
when the disciples have so much difficulty in forming an idea of the relation of their Master to the Father (vv. 9, 10). Ὑμεῖς, *you* : "from your own

experience, and not only, as to-day, from my words." Comp. xvi. 25. The object of this spiritual illumination of believers will be, first, the relation of Jesus to the Father ; they will have a consciousness of Jesus as of a being who lives and acts in God, and in whom God lives and acts as in another self. This immediate consciousness of the relations between Jesus and God will spring from the living consciousness which they will receive of their own relation to Jesus ; they will feel Him living in them and will feel themselves living in Him ; and in the experience of this relation to Him (*they* transported *into Him* and *He* transported *into them*), they will understand that which He had said to them, without succeeding in making Himself understood, of what God is to Him and what He is to God. Then, finally, the transcendent fact of the communion between Jesus and God will become for them the object of a distinct perception through the immediate experience of their own communion with Jesus. These are the μεγαλεῖα τοῦ θεοῦ, *the wonderful things of God*, which Peter and the disciples celebrate in new tongues on the day of Pentecost.

Ver. 21 states with preciseness the manner of this illumination. Jesus had said summarily, ver. 15 : "*Keep my commandments, and I will pray the Father.*" Here he enumerates in detail all the links of the chain of graces which will be connected with this practical fidelity of His followers : It is necessary to *hold* inwardly (ἔχειν) His word, and to *observe* it practically (τηρεῖν) ; this is not done by the world, which has heard it, but rejected it ; for this reason it is not fitted to receive these higher graces. By means of this moral fidelity, 1. Such an individual (ἐκεῖνος, that exceptional man) assumes the character of a being who truly loves Jesus (ὁ ἀγαπῶν με). 2. Hence he becomes *the beloved of the Father*, who, loving the Son, also loves whoever makes Him the object of his love. This love of the Father is not that which is spoken of in iii. 16 : "*God so loved the world.*" These two loves differ as the compassion of a man for his guilty and wretched neighbor and the tender affection of a father for his child, or a husband for his wife, differ. 3. The Son, seeing the eye of the Father turning with tenderness towards the disciple who loves Him, feels Himself united with the latter by a new bond ("*and I will love him*") ; He loves him still more tenderly in proportion as He sees the love of the Father enveloping him. 4. Finally, from all this follows the supreme miracle of the love of the Father and the Son : the perfect revelation which Jesus gives to the disciple of Himself : *I will manifest myself to him.* This is the condition of the *you shall know*, ver. 20. This altogether extraordinary term ἐμφανίζειν refers to the inward manifestation of the Messiah. It will not by any means suit the external and passing appearances of the Risen One, to which even *Weiss* gives up referring it ; but to substitute what ? Certain manifestations of the nearness of Jesus granted to His disciples in the course of their life, like that of the Lord to Moses (Exod. xxxiii. 13, 18) ; "but in any case not by means of the Spirit," adds this interpreter. And yet the *asyndeta* after ver. 17 prove, by themselves alone, that Jesus is here developing the promise of the gift of the Spirit ; and ver. 23 shows clearly enough what Jesus means to speak of in ver. 21. It is precisely this wholly inward character of the manifestation described in ver. 21 which calls forth the question of Judas in ver. 22.—In the face of these interruptions of the disciples, *Gess* compares Jesus to a skilful pilot who does not suffer himself to be turned aside by the rushing waves, but by a prompt stroke of the helm gives each time to the ship the desired direction.

5. Vv. 22–24

Ver. 22. "*Judas, not Iscariot, says to him, Lord, and* [1] *what is come to pass, that thou art to show thyself to us, and not to the world?*"—The mode of the revelation of which Jesus had just spoken entirely perplexed the minds of the disciples, which were ever directed towards the outward manifestation, visible for all, of the Messiah-King and His glorious kingdom. It was especially in the lower group of the apostolic company, influenced by the carnal spirit of Iscariot, that such thoughts persistently continued. The Judas or Jude here mentioned bears this name only in Luke (Gosp. vi. 16, Acts i. 13). In the catalogues of Matthew (x. 3) and Mark (iii. 18) he is designated by the names (surnames) *Lebbeus* and *Thaddæus:* the bold or the cherished one. He occupies one of the lowest places among the apostles. The explanation : *not Iscariot*, is intended to remove the supposition of a return of Judas after his going out, xiii. 30.—By saying : *What is come to pass?* Judas asks for the indication of a new fact causing the change of the Messianic programme, the proof of which he thinks he observes in the words of Jesus in ver. 21. The καί, *and*, before τί γέγονεν, is the expression of surprise ; it was omitted in some MSS., as superfluous.—*To us* signifies here : "To us *only.*"

Vv. 23, 24. "*Jesus answered and said to him, If any one loves me, he will keep my word ; and my Father will love him and we will come to him, and make our abode* [2] *with him. 24. He who does not love me, does not keep my words ; and the word which you hear is not mine, but the Father's who sent me.*"—Jesus continues His discourse, as if He had not heard the question of Judas ; for the first part of ver. 23 is only the reproduction of ver. 21 developed and stated with greater precision. And yet He answers the question proposed, by more energetically reaffirming the promise, as well as the moral condition which had called forth the objection ; comp. the same mode of replying in Luke xii. 41 ff. To love Jesus, to keep His word, to be loved by the Father,—these are the conditions on which the promised revelation will be made (ver. 23) ; now the world does not fulfil them ; it is animated by dispositions of an opposite character (ver. 24).—As to the conditions and nature of this revelation, Jesus develops them grandly. The revelation of Himself which He will give to the believer will be nothing less than His own dwelling in his soul, and this will be one with the dwelling of God Himself within him. How can we think here only of the appearances of the Risen One, or even of temporary aid granted to the disciples by the glorified Lord in the work of their ministry ? It is incomprehensible how *Weiss* can persist in such an interpretation to the very end.—Here, as in x. 30, Jesus says

---

[1] A B D E L X It^{plerique} (not ℵ) reject καί (*and*) before τι.   [2] Instead of ποιησομεν, ℵ B L X : ποιησομεθα.

we in speaking of *God* and *Himself;* this expression, if it is not blasphemous or absurd, implies the consciousness of His essential union with God.— The conception of the kingdom of God which we find here is not foreign to the Synoptics; comp. Luke xvii. 20 : " *The kingdom of God comes not with observation ; it is within you*" (ἐντὸς ὑμῶν) ; and Matt. xxviii. 18–20. A very similar figure is found in Apoc. iii. 20 : " *If any one opens the door, I will enter in to him, and will sup with him, and he with me."*—Ver. 2 proves that the term μονή, *dwelling*, can designate not only an inn, but the permanent domicile (see Passow). This expression perhaps places the idea of this verse in connection with that of ver. 2. Here on earth, it is God who makes His abode with the believer ; in heaven, it will be the believer who will make his abode with God. The first of these facts (ver. 23) prepares for the second (ver. 3).—*Weiss* rests upon the παρ' αὐτῷ, properly *near him,* to support the view that the question is not of an inward dwelling. The *unio mystica* between Christ and the believer, must have been designated, according to him, by ἐν αὐτῷ, *in him.* But the preposition παρά, *with,* is necessarily introduced by reason of the figure of a dwelling (μονὴν ποιεῖν) and cannot in any way serve to determine the mode of this union. And it follows from the terms ἐμφανίζειν and πρὸς αὐτόν, as from the parallel Apoc. iii. 20, that this mode is internal and spiritual.

Ver. 23 justified the *to us* in the question of Judas ; ver. 24 answers to : *and not to the world.* Between the two clauses of ver. 24, this idea must be understood : "It is not a small thing to reject my teaching ; and indeed (καί) it is the teaching of God Himself" (xii. 49, etc.). Conclusion understood : "How, with such a disposition, hostile to the word both of the Son and the Father, could one be fit to become their abode !" Comp. what was said of the *world* in vv. 15, 17.—Thus have the reasons for encouragement presented by the Lord been gradually raised one upon another : "You shall have a place secured for you with me in the Father's house. . . . Through me, the way, you cannot fail to reach the end. . . . Already here on earth, you have seen the Father. . . . You shall be able to continue my work on the earth. . . . Another divine support will give you strength for it. . . . In this inward support, it is I myself who will join you again. . . . The Father Himself will with me come to dwell with you. . . ." Is there not here what may justify the : *Let not your heart be troubled* (xiv. 1) ? The following passage, which closes this first outpouring, returns to its starting-point, in that it even makes the *Be not troubled,* a *Rejoice.*

6. Vv. 25–31

Vv. 25, 26. "*I have spoken these things to you while I am yet with you.* 26. *But the support, the Holy Spirit, whom my Father will send in my name, will teach you all things, and will bring all things to your remembrance which I have said to you.*" We might endeavor to connect these words with the preceding; for it is through the gift of the Holy Spirit, who is about to be spoken of again, that the great promise of vv. 22–24 will be accomplished. But the perfect λελάληκα, *I have spoken to you,* rather indicates a conclusion; the conversation reaches its end and returns now to its starting-point. Ver. 25 therefore is not to be connected with ver. 24 ; it recalls the contents of the entire discourse. What Jesus has just said to the disciples of the future reunion, above (vv. 1–3), and here below (vv. 12–24), is all that He can reveal to them on this subject for the moment. If this future is still enveloped in obscurity for them, the teaching of another master will dissipate the mists, and will explain to them all His promises by realizing them. Ταῦτα, *these things*, at the beginning, in contrast with πάντα, *all things* (ver. 26) : " This is what I am able to tell you now; another will afterwards tell you *the whole.*"—The epithet *holy* given to the Spirit, ver. 26, recalls the deep line of separation which Jesus had just drawn, in vv. 17, 24, between the profane world and the disciples already sanctified by their attachment to Jesus. As holy, the Spirit can only come to dwell in these last.—The expression : *in my name*, is to be explained, as in ver. 14, with this difference, that it refers here to an act of God (*shall send*), and no longer to the human act of prayer (*shall ask*). On the side of God, it is *sending* in virtue of the perfect revelation which He has given of the person and work of His Son; while on man's side, it is asking in virtue of the more or less imperfect possession which he has gained of this revelation. *Weiss*, in despair of finding any satisfactory sense in the words *in my name*, if they are made to refer to the act of sending, applies them to the *object* of the mission: God will send the Holy Spirit to be *in the place of* Christ, as His substitute with believers. But the Spirit is not the substitute for Christ; Christ Himself comes again in Him; then, the grammatical relation of the limiting words *in my name* to the verb *send*, does not authorize this sense.—The pronoun ἐκεῖνος, *he*, he alone, brings into strong relief the person of this new teacher who will tell everything, in contrast with the earthly person of Jesus who is going to be taken away from them (ver. 25). The Spirit will do two things: *teach everything ; bring to remembrance everything* which Jesus has taught. These two functions are closely connected; He will teach the new by recalling the old, and will recall the old by teaching the new. The words of Jesus, the remembrance of which the Spirit will awaken in them, will be the matter from which He will derive the teaching of the complete truth, the germ which He will fertilize in their hearts, as, in return, this internal activity of the Spirit will unceasingly recall to their memory some former word of Jesus, so that in proportion as He shall illuminate them, they will cry out : Now, I understand this word of the Master ! And this vivid clearness will cause other words long forgotten to come forth from forgetfulness. Such is, even at this day, the relation between the teaching of the written Word and that of the Spirit.—Καί: and specially.—Naturally the first πάντα, *all things*, embraces only the things of the new creation accomplished in Jesus Christ, the plan and work of salvation. The first creation, nature, is not the subject of the revelation of the Holy Spirit; it is that of scientific study.

Vv. 27–29. " *Peace I leave with you ; my peace I give to you ; not as the world gives, do I give it to you ; let not your heart be troubled, neither let it be afraid.* 28. *You have heard how I said to you, I go away, and come to you. If you loved me, you would have rejoiced because I*[1] *go to the Father ; for my*[2] *Father is greater than I.* 29. *And now I have told you these things before they come to pass, that when they have come to pass, you may believe.*"—The promise of vv. 25, 26 had as its aim to tranquillize the disciples in relation to the *obscurities* which still hovered over their Master's future and their own. Vv. 27–29 tend to reassure them with reference to the dangers to which they see themselves exposed in this future which is opening before them. Jesus evidently alludes to the Israelite salutation: *Peace be unto thee (Schalom leka)!* Meyer and *Reuss* take the word εἰρήνη in an objective sense : *salvation* (שלום, full prosperity). But the adjective "*my* peace " and the end of the verse where the question is of causing *trouble* to cease, should have prevented this false interpretation. On leaving them, Jesus would make them enjoy a perfect inward quietness, such as that which they behold in Himself. This peace arises in Him, in the presence of death, from His absolute confidence in the love of the Father. This confidence it is which He wishes to inspire in them, and by means of which His peace will become theirs. This is the legacy which He gives them (ἀφίημι, *I leave*), and this legacy He draws from His own treasury : *my* peace. The verb δίδωμι, *I give*, is in connection with τὴν ἐμήν (*mine*) : one *gives* of *his own*. In Luke x. 5, 6, Jesus confers on His disciples the power which He exercises here Himself : that of imparting *their* peace.—The contrast between the peace of Jesus and that of the world is ordinarily referred to the *nature* of the two : the peace of the world consisting in the enjoyment of blessings which are only such in appearance ; that of Jesus in the possession of real and imperishable blessings. *Luthardt* and *Keil* find here another contrast : that between true and false peace. But it follows from the omission of the object : *peace*, in the second clause ("*I do not give as the world gives*"), and from the conjunction καθώς (*according as*), that the contrast relates rather to the act of *giving* than to the object of the gift : " When I give, it is really giving, it is giving with efficacy, while, when the world says farewell to you in the ordinary form : Peace be unto you ! it gives you only empty words, a powerless wish." I cannot understand wherein this sense is below the seriousness of the situation, as Meyer claims. This peace, which He communicates to them by this very word, should banish from their hearts the *trouble* which Jesus observes there still (μὴ ταρασσέσθω), and preserve them, even by this means, from the danger of *being afraid* (δειλιᾶν), which would result from this troubled state.

But it is not enough for Jesus to see them reassured, strengthened ; He would even see them *joyous* (ver. 28). And they would really be so, if they well understood the meaning of this departure which is approaching. The ἠκούσατε, *you have heard*, refers to vv. 2, 12, 18 ; the quotation, as so often, is made freely.—Jesus adds : *and I come*, because without this He could not ask them to find in His departure a subject of joy. The words : "*If you loved me,*" signify here : If you loved Me in an entirely disinterested way, loving Me for Myself, and not for yourselves. These words are of an

---

[1] א A B D K L X Π 10 Mnn. It. Vulg. Syr. Cop. Orig. omit ειπον between οτι and πορευομαι (*because I go away*), instead of : (*because I said, I go away*).

[2] A B D L X 8 Mnn. It plerique Vulg. reject μου after πατηρ.

exquisite delicacy. Jesus thereby finds the means of making joy on their part a duty of affection. He turns their attention to the approaching exaltation of His position (comp. xiii. 3, 31, 32) ; and what true friend would not rejoice to see his friend raised to a state more worthy of him ? Jesus does not here give expression to the idea of the more powerful activity of which this exaltation will be for Him the means (xvii. 12). He appeals only to their friendly hearts.—We must reject, with the Alexandrian authorities, the word εἶπον (the second) and read : *because I go away*, and not : " because *I said to you*, I go away."—The reason why they should rejoice for Him on account of this change is that *His Father is greater than He*. In returning to God, therefore, He is going to find again a form of existence more free, more exalted, more blessed. Jesus felt the burden of the earthly existence, while patiently bearing it. Did He not say : " How long shall I be with you ? How long shall I bear with you ?" (Luke ix. 41.) His surrendering of divine existence, His acceptance of human existence was for Him an ordeal which was to cease through His exaltation to the presence of God ; comp. the πρὸς τὸν θεόν, i. 1, 18. The explanation of *Lücke, de Wette*, etc., " God will be a better protector for you than I could be by my visible presence," ignores the natural meaning of the words and what there is of the personal element in this appeal to their affection : *if you loved me*.—Since the second century of the Church exegesis has understood in two different ways the explanation which follows respecting the relation between the Father and the Son (see *Westcott's* excellent dissertation). Some have understood : "greater than the Logos as such," inasmuch as the Father is very naturally superior to the Son, while others have referred this superiority of the Father merely to the human nature of Jesus. This second explanation does not seem to me possible, in the first place because, if the *state* of the Son can change, His person, His *ego*, remains ever identical with itself ; the subject who is speaking at this moment cannot, therefore, be any other than the one who speaks in passages such as viii. 58, xvii. 5, 24. Then, applied merely to the human nature of Jesus, as apart from His divine nature, these words become almost blasphemous, or at least ridiculous. As *Weiss* says, " such a comparison between God and a created being would be a folly bordering upon blasphemy." We have already recognized the fact, in studying the Prologue (i. 1), that the Logos, as such, is subordinate to God. As *Marius Victorinus* said (365) : " As *having* everything from the Father, He is inferior to Him, although, as having *everything* from Him, He is His equal." *Reuss* has wrongly seen a disagreement between these words and the divinity of Christ, as it is taught in the Prologue (i. 1). For even in the Prologue we find the notion of subordination expressly declared as it is here, and, on the other hand, our passage breathes, in Him who thus speaks, the most lively feeling of His participation in divinity. God alone can compare Himself with God, and the Arians, in seeking for a support in this text, have at least been guilty of unskilfulness. Here is certainly one of the passages by which the apostle was inspired in formulating his Prologue.

Ver. 29. This disappearance of Jesus, so contrary to their thoughts, might in itself shake their faith ; but Jesus applies to this trial what He had said of the treachery of Judas : through the fact that He has foretold it to them, it will, on the contrary, turn to the strengthening of their faith. And now, finally, the summons to depart :

Vv. 30, 31. "*I will no more speak much with you ; for the prince of this world*[1] *is coming, and he has nothing in me.* 31. *But that the world may know that I love my Father and*[2] *that I act according as the Father has commanded me,*[3] *arise, let us go hence.*"—Jesus feels the approach of His invisible enemy. There is here not merely the presentiment of the near arrival of Judas, but also of the conflict which He will have to undergo with Satan in Gethsemane.

Two quite different explanations of these verses may be given, the result of which, however, is fundamentally the same. Either the *and*, καί, before ἐν ἐμοί, is understood in a concessive sense : "*He comes, and* [in truth] *he has nothing in me* which can be a reason for his power over me ;" then Jesus adds : "*but* (ἀλλά) in order that the world may know the love which I have for my Father, I yield myself to him freely. *Arise !*" Or this καί, *and*, may be taken in the adversative sense, as so frequently in John : "He is coming ; *but* he has no hold upon me ; *nevertheless* (ἀλλά), in order that the world may know, . . . *arise and let us go hence,* and that I may be delivered to this enemy !" This second meaning seems to me to present a clearer thought ; καί is frequently adversative in John, and we have explained the reason of it ; comp. e.g. vi. 36 and xv. 24.—"*No more speak much*" does not exclude the few discoursings which are still to follow.—*The prince of this world*, see xii. 31.—*Nothing in me :* nothing which appertains to his domain and which gives him a right and power over me, the object of his hatred. These words imply in Him who utters them the consciousness of the most perfect innocence. The *in order that* has often been made dependent on ποιῶ, *I do;* "In order that the world may know . . . my love for my Father, . . . I am going to do according to what He has commanded me." But the καί, before καθώς, does not allow this construction. Or the ἵνα has been made to depend on a verb understood : "*This happens thus* in order that the world may know that I love my Father, *and that* I do what he has commanded me ;" so *Tischendorf ;* and this would be better. But how much more lively is a third construction, which makes the *in order that* depend on the two following imperatives : "In order that the world may know, . . . arise, let us go hence !" This way of speaking is absolutely the same with that triumphant apostrophe of Jesus, which is preserved by the three Synoptics (Matt. ix. 6 and parallels) : "*That you may know* . . . arise and walk !"—To *arise* in order to go to Gethsemane was indeed to yield Himself voluntarily to the perfidy of Judas, who was to seek Him in that place well known by him, and to the power of Satan, who was preparing there for Jesus a last decisive conflict, the complement of that in the desert. Jesus knew well that they would not come to seize Him in the midst of the city, in the room where He was at this moment.

---

[1] Τουτου, in T. R., is founded only on some Mnn. It.

[2] A E It^aliq omit και.

[3] Instead of ενετειλατο, B L X It. Vulg. read εντολην εδωκεν.

The imperatives : *arise, let us go*, may not have been immediately followed by a result ; this is what *Meyer, Luthardt, Weiss, Keil* and *Reuss* think, who suppose that Jesus still remained in the room until after the sacerdotal prayer. They rest upon the *He went out* in xviii. 1, and on the solemn prayer of ch. xvii., which cannot have been made outside. We shall see that these reasons are not decisive. On the other hand, we do not understand why John should have mentioned so expressly the order to depart, if it had not been followed by a result ; or at least why did he not, in this case, indicate the delay by a word of explanation, as in xi. 6 ? *Gess* says rightly : "Since Jesus, by the order of ver. 31, gave the signal for departing, we must represent to ourselves the following discourses, chs. xv., xvi., as uttered on the way to Gethsemane."

On the conversations in chap. xiv

The subject on which this chapter turns is indeed that which the situation calls for : the approaching separation. Jesus calms His disciples, who are profoundly troubled by this prospect, by promising them a twofold meeting again, the one more remote in the Father's house, at the end of their earthly career, the other altogether inward and spiritual, but very near. The historical fitness of these two great thoughts is perfect.—As to the questions of Thomas, Philip and Judas, *Reuss* finds that they proceed from such strange misunderstandings and such gross mistakes that it is impossible to accord to them any historical truthfulness. But exegesis has ascertained, on the contrary, that they are completely appropriate to the apostles' point of view at that moment. So long as Jesus was with them, notwithstanding their attachment to His person, they still shared in the ideas which were generally received. It was the death of their Master, His ascension, and finally Pentecost, which radically transformed their idea of the kingdom of God. There is, accordingly, nothing surprising in the fact that Thomas, like the Jews in ch. xii., should complain of understanding nothing about a Christ who leaves the earth ; or that Philip, like the Jews who demanded a sign from heaven, should, in place of His visible presence, ask for a sensible theophany ; or, finally, that Judas should ask anxiously what a Messianic coming could be of which the world should not be a witness. Two conceptions, that of the disciples and that of Jesus, do not cease to come into collision in these dialogues, and in order to have reproduced them so naturally and dramatically, at a period already advanced, when light had come on all these problems which at that moment occupied the disciples' minds, one must certainly have been present at these conversations, and have himself taken a lively part in them. This appears, moreover, from the manner in which the evangelist initiates us in this story into the intimate and familiar relations of Jesus with the disciples and the character of the personages who form the apostolic circle. Either all this—these proper names, these questions attributed to each one, these personal addresses of Jesus—is a play unworthy of a serious man, or it is the narrative of a witness who himself participated in the emotions of this last evening.

The position of the Disciples in the world after the outpouring of the Spirit
John 15:1-16:15

Jesus had just promised to His own, in ch. xiv., the twofold reunion, heavenly and earthly, in which the separation should issue, the thought of which was now so greatly troubling them. In ch. xv. He transports Himself in thought to the epoch when the earthly and purely internal reunion shall be consummated through His spiritual return. The glorified Christ has returned and lives in His own. They are united to Him, and, through Him, among themselves. Under His impulse they work all together, like the members of one and the same body, in the Father's work. Such is the new position with a view to which He now gives them the necessary directions, warnings and encouragements. They are like the branches which crown a fruitful vine and offer to the world its savory fruits. But the world, instead of blessing them, will take the axe to destroy this noble plant of heaven. Its hatred, however, will have no other effect than to display the divine force which will sustain them and by means of which they will overcome the world. Thus there are three principal ideas : 1. The new condition of the disciples after the return of Jesus through the Holy Spirit : xv. 1–17 ; 2. The hostility of the world to this new society : xv. 18–xvi. 4 ; 3. The spiritual victory which the Holy Spirit will gain over the world by their means : xvi. 5–15. The three personages of this coming drama : the disciples, the world, the Holy Spirit. Each one of them is successively predominant in one of the three parts of the following discourse.

1. xv. 1–17

After the words : "Let us go hence," Jesus and the disciples left the room which had just been to them, as it were, the vestibule of the Father's house. Whither do they go ? According to *Westcott :* to the temple, which was open during the nights of the Passover feast. There was suspended the well-known golden vine which suggests to Jesus to represent Himself in the figure developed at the beginning of the following discourse. There is nothing less probable, as it seems to me, than this hypothesis. Why should not John have indicated this locality as he has always done, and how in a place like this could Jesus have found a sufficiently solitary spot for His last conversations and His last prayer ? We imagine Jesus and the apostles rather as silently traversing the streets of Jerusalem, and soon finding on the slope which descends into the valley of Cedron a retired spot where they stop. Surrounded by this little circle of disciples, in view of Jerusalem and the Jewish people now assembled in that city, Jesus contemplates the immense task which awaits His disciples as those who are to continue His work. Transporting Himself in thought to the moment when His spiritual return will be consummated, He endeavors first of all to make them comprehend the nature of this situation which is so new for them, and the obligations which will spring from it. And first, the *position*, vv. 1–3 (*in me*) ; then the *duty* of this position, ver. 4 (*to abide* in me) ;

finally, the consequences of this duty fulfilled or not fulfilled, vv. 5-8 (*to bear fruit* or *to burn*).

Vv. 1-3. "*I am the true vine, and my Father is the vine-dresser.* 2. *Every branch in me which bears not fruit, he takes away ; and every branch which bears fruit he prunes, that it may bear more fruit.* 3. *As for you, you are already clean because of the word which I have spoken to you.*"—The pronoun ἐγώ, *I*, placed at the beginning, and the epithet ἡ ἀληθινή, the *real* vine, lead us naturally to suppose that Jesus wishes to establish a contrast here between His person and any vine whatsoever which is not in His view the true vine. What outward circumstance leads Jesus to express Himself in this way? Those who hold that Jesus has not yet gone out of the room, or give up the attempt to resolve the question (*de Wette*), either have recourse to the use of the vine in the institution of the Holy Supper (*Grotius, Meyer*), or suppose that Jesus pointed the disciples to the shoots of a vine which projected into the room (*Knapp, Tholuck*), or even that He was thinking of the golden vine which adorned one of the gates of the temple (*Jerome, Lampe;* see *Westcott*). *Hengstenberg, Weiss* and *Keil* think that Jesus wishes to contrast His Church with Israel, which is so often represented under the figure of a vine, in the Old Testament (Is. v. 1 ff., Ps. lxxx. 9 ff.). But the continuation of the figure (*branches, fruits, pruning, burning,* etc.) shows that it is not a symbolic vine which occupies His thought. If we hold that when uttering the words of xiv. 31, Jesus has really gone out from the room and the city, the explanation becomes very simple. On the way to Gethsemane, Jesus stops before a vine covered with branches ; He looks upon His disciples grouped about Him, and finds in this plant the emblem of His relation to them. What significance has the objection of *Weiss* that any other plant might have served Him as a symbol? It was this plant which was there ; and it offered Him points of agreement which no other presented to Him. Among all the plants, the vine has certainly a special dignity resulting from the nobleness of its sap and the excellence of its fruits ; this is what explains the use which the Old Testament makes of it as a figure of Israel, the noblest of the nations.

The word *vine* includes here the stock and the branches, as the term ὁ χριστός, 1 Cor. xii. 12, designates Christ and the Church. The point of comparison between Christ and the vine is the organic union by which the life of the trunk becomes that of the branches. As the sap which resides in the branches is that which they derive from the vine, the life in the disciples will be that which they will draw from Jesus as glorified. God is compared to the *vine-dresser* because it is He who, by the sending of Jesus, has founded the Church, who possesses it and cultivates it, without by His dispensations, within by His Spirit. Jesus means thereby to make them appreciate the value of this plant which God Himself has planted, and for which He, in such a personal way, has a care. What is said here does not preclude the fact that God accomplishes this work by the intermediate agency of Jesus as glorified. Only the figure does not allow this aspect of the truth to be noticed ; for Jesus is here compared to the vine itself, and it is in the relation of His *unity* with His own that He appears in this

854 / The Development of Faith

parable. In the remarkable words of Eph. i. 22, Paul has found the means of uniting this twofold relation : Jesus one with the Church ; Jesus protecting and governing the Church.—The culture of the vine includes two principal operations : the purification of the *vine* and the purification of the *branches*. The first is that by which every *sterile branch* is cut off (the αἴρειν) ; the second, that by which the fruitful branches are pruned, that is to say, are freed from *useless shoots*, in order that the sap may be concentrated in the cluster which is forming (the καθαίρειν). As the question in this passage is only of the relation of Jesus to the members of His community, apparent or real, the first of these images cannot be applied, as *Hengstenberg* has applied them, to the rejection of unbelieving Israel. If an example is presented to the view of Jesus, it can only be that of Judas and of those disciples who, in ch. vi., had broken the bond which united them to Him. In any case, He is thinking of the future of His Church ; He sees beforehand those professors of the Gospel, who, while being outwardly united to Him, will nevertheless live inwardly separated from Him, whether in consequence of a decree which will prevent them from being truly converted, or as the effect of their neglecting to sacrifice even to the uttermost their own life and to renew daily their union with Him.—Ἐν ἐμοί, *in me*, may refer to the word *branch : every branch in me*, united with me by the profession of faith ; or to the participle φέρον : *which does not bear fruit in me*. By *fruit* Jesus designates the production and development of the *spiritual* life, with all its normal manifestations, either in ourselves or in others, through the strength of Christ living in us (Rom. i. 13). It may happen that the believer, after a time of fervor, may allow his own life to regain the ascendancy over that which he derives from the Lord, and that the latter may be about to perish. Then the pruning-knife of the vine-dresser intervenes. After having for a time tolerated this dead member in the Church, God, by a temptation to which He subjects him, or by an outward dispensation which separates him from the surroundings in which he was, or by the stroke of death, severs him externally from the community of believers with which only an apparent bond connected him.

The second operation, the purification of the *branches*, has in view the true believers who really live in Christ through the Holy Spirit. It is intended to cut off all the shoots of their own life which may manifest themselves in them, and which would paralyze the power of the Spirit. Ver. 3 will show that it is the divine word which properly has the mission of pruning these shoots ; but if this means is not employed or is not sufficient, God makes use of other more grievous instruments, which, like a well-sharpened pruning knife, cut to the quick the natural affections and the carnal will (1 Cor. xi. 30–32). In this way the whole being of the disciple is finally devoted to the production of the divine fruit.

In ver. 3 Jesus declares to the disciples that He ranks them in the second class of branches, and no longer in the first. The work of *pruning* alone concerns them, and even, in principle, it is already accomplished in them. By receiving Christ and the word which He has declared to them, " they have given the death-blow to the old man " (*Gess*), even though he has yet to die. By the moral education which they have received from Jesus, the principle of perfect purity has been deposited in them. For the word of Christ is the instrument of a daily judgment, of a constant and austere discipline which God exercises on the soul which remains attached to Him. On this part attributed to the word of Jesus, comp. v. 24, viii. 31, 32, xii. 48.—Διά (with the accusative) not *by*, but *because of*.—Ὑμεῖς : *you*, in opposition to all those who are not yet in this privileged position.—From the nature of this position (*in me*) Jesus infers the *duty* of the position : *to abide* in Him.

Ver. 4. " *Abide in me, and I in you ; as the branch cannot bear fruit of itself, unless it abides*[1] *in the vine, no more can you, unless you abide*[2] *in me.*— To continue in the vine is for a branch the condition of life, and consequently its only law. All the conditions of fruitfulness are included in this. The imperative proves that one abides in this relation, as one enters it, *freely*, by the faithful use of the divinely offered methods. Ver. 7 will show that the fundamental means is the word of Jesus.—Ἐν ἐμοὶ μένειν, *to abide in me*, expresses the continual act by which the Christian sets aside everything which he might derive from his own wisdom, strength, merit, to draw all from Christ, in these different relations, through the deep longings of faith. This condition is so completely the only one laid down for the action of the force of Christ in him, that in the following clause Jesus omits the verb—although it would properly be necessary for another person and at another time (*I will abide*)—as if to make them feel that this act on His part is an immediate and necessary consequence of the act demanded of the believer ; where the latter is accomplished, the former cannot fail to be realized. In this way, the action of Christ, no less than our own, is boldly placed under the control of our freedom. It is naturally on this second fact (*I in you*), of which the first : *You in me*, is only the condition, that the fruitfulness of the branch directly depends.

Hence the end of ver. 4 ; the duty imposed on the believer results from the immediate unfruitfulness with which his separation from the vine would affect him as a branch. Here, as in ver. 19, ἐὰν μή is an explanation of ἀφ' ἑαυτοῦ, and not a limitation applied to the whole preceding idea : " by himself, *that is to say*, if he does not abide. . . . "—The theme here formulated is not that of the moral powerlessness of the natural man for any good ; it is that of the unfruitfulness of the believer left to his own strength, when the question is of producing or advancing the spiritual life, the life of God, in himself or in others.

After having described the new position and the law which it imposes, Jesus sets forth in the following verses, 5–8, the *sanction* of this law of life and death which He has just declared. And first, in ver. 5, the glorious results which the fruitful branch will obtain and the opposite result of unfaithfulness.

Ver. 5. " *I am the vine, you are the branches ; he who abides in me and I in him, this one bears much fruit ; for apart from me, you can do nothing.*"—

---

[1] ℵ B L : μενῃ instead of μεινῃ (T. R. with 14 Mjj).

[2] ℵ A B L : μενητε instead of μεινητε which T. R. reads with 13 Mjj.

Jesus begins by summarily reaffirming the nature of the relation. While contemplating the natural vine which He has before His eyes, He recognizes in it the image of the complete dependence on Him in which His disciples are : " Yes, here indeed is what I am to you and what you are to me : I, the vine ; you, the branches ! Do not therefore allow yourselves ever to fall into the temptation of making yourselves the vine, by desiring to derive anything from yourselves." The meaning is, therefore : "In me, rich fruitfulness ; apart from me, barrenness." If this second idea is given as a proof of the first ($\H{o}\tau\iota$, *because*), it appears at the first glance scarcely logical. But if Christ is so completely *everything* that the believer can do nothing without Him, does it not follow that the latter can do *much*, so long as he shall remain united with Him ?—Then, in ver. 6, the fate of the branch which has become unfruitful, and in vv. 7, 8, the fate of the branch united with Christ and fruitful in Him.

Ver. 6. *" If any one abides[1] not in me, he is cast forth as the branch, and is withered ; then they gather these branches,[2] they throw them into the fire, and they burn."*—It was in Palestine precisely the season of the vine-dressing ; perhaps, as *Lange* observes, Jesus had before His eyes at this very moment the fires which were consuming the branches recently cut off.—The threatening of ver. 6 cannot be referred to the Jewish nation and its destruction by the Romans, as *Hengstenberg* has asserted. Jesus is thinking of the unfaithful believer ; it is a warning which the disciples should recall to mind after they had received the gifts of Pentecost.—The aorists $\epsilon\beta\lambda\acute{\eta}\theta\eta$, *has been cast forth* (out of the vine), $\epsilon\xi\eta\rho\acute{a}\nu\theta\eta$, *has been withered*, are explained, according to *Bäumlein*, as in the numerous cases where this tense serves to designate a truth of daily experience. *Meyer* thinks rather that Jesus transports Himself in thought to the time when the judgment shall have been already pronounced. Is it not more simple to suppose that the punishment is so regarded as forming only one thing with the fault (not abiding), that it seems already accomplished in it ?— As subject of $\sigma\upsilon\nu\acute{a}\gamma\upsilon\upsilon\sigma\iota$, *they gather*, we must understand the servants of the vine-dresser ; in the application, the angels (Luke xii. 20, Matt. xiii. 41). —The *fire*, emblem of the judgment ; comp. another image in Luke xiv. 34, 35.—$\mathrm{K}a\acute{\iota}\epsilon\tau a\iota$, *they burn*, the present of duration takes here its full force. The thought remains suspended in view of this fire which burns, and burns always.—It appears clearly from Ezek. xv. 5 that the wood of the vine, when once cut, was regarded as no longer able to serve any use except for burning. Hence the expression of *Augustine : aut vitis, aut ignis.*—Vv. 7, 8 describe the glorious results of the perseverance of the believer in the communion with Christ.

Vv. 7, 8. *" If you abide in me and my words abide in you, ask[3] what you will, and it shall be done for you. 8. Herein is my Father glorified, that you bear much fruit, and so you shall become[4] my disciples."*—The parallelism

[1] ℵ A B D : $\mu\epsilon\nu\eta$, instead of $\mu\epsilon\iota\nu\eta$.
[2] D L X Δ Π 20 Mnn. It^{aliq} Syr. : $a\upsilon\tau o$ (*it*) instead of $a\upsilon\tau a$ (*them*).
[3] A B D L M X Γ 50 Mnn. It^{aliq} : $a\iota\tau\eta\sigma a\sigma\theta\epsilon$ (*ask*), instead of $a\iota\tau\eta\sigma\epsilon\sigma\theta\epsilon$ (*you shall ask*), which T. R. reads with ℵ and 11 other Mjj., etc.
[4] B D L M N Δ : $\gamma\epsilon\nu\eta\sigma\theta\epsilon$ (*that you become*), instead of $\gamma\epsilon\nu\eta\sigma\epsilon\sigma\theta\epsilon$ (*you shall become*), which T. R. reads with ℵ A and 9 Mjj.

between the two conditions indicated, ver. 7, would lead us to expect as the form of the second the words : "And *I* abide in you" rather than : "And *my words* abide in you." Jesus wishes to make known to His own by this change of expression, that it is the constant remembrance of and habitual meditation upon His words, which is the condition on which He will be able continually to make His strength dwell in them and act through them. In this relation, the disciple will not begin by acting, but simply by *asking*. For he knows that it is the divine strength thus obtained which must do everything. The words of Jesus, meditatively considered, become in the believer the food for holy thoughts and pious purposes, heavenly aspirations, and thereby the source of true prayers. While meditating on them, he comprehends the work of God ; he measures its depth and height, its length and breadth, and fervently asks for the advancement of that work in the definite form which answers to the present needs. A prayer thus formed is the child of heaven ; it is the promise of God (the word of Jesus) transformed into supplication ; in this condition the hearing of it is certain and the promise which is so absolute: *It shall be done for you*, has no longer anything that surprises us.—The Alexandrian authorities read the imperative *ask*, the others the future *you shall ask*. The first has more liveliness.

The result of this fruitfulness of the disciples will be the glorification of the Father (ver. 8). What is there that honors the vine-dresser more than the extraordinary productiveness of the vine to which he has with partiality given his care ? Now, the vine-dresser is the Father (ver. 1). The ἐν τούτῳ, *herein*, refers evidently to the ἵνα, *in order that* or *that*, which follows ; this conjunction here takes the place of ὅτι, because the idea of bearing fruit presents itself to the mind as an *end* to be attained.—The aorist ἐδοξάσθη, properly *has been glorified*, characterizes this result as immediately gained at the moment when the condition, the production of fruit, is realized. *Winer* and others prefer to see in this aorist an anticipation of the final result.— While contemplating with filial satisfaction the glory of His Father, which will result from time to time from the activity of the disciples, Jesus seems to press to His heart these precious beings with a redoubled affection. They will thus continue the work of their Master, who has only thought of glorifying the Father, and will deserve more and more the title of *His disciples*. Καί : *and thus*. Instead of the future *and you shall become*, the Alexandrian authorities read the subjunctive: *and that you may become* (γένησθε, dependent on ἵνα). *Tischendorf* himself rejects this reading, which is only a correction after φέρητε.—The dative ἐμοί is more pressing and more tender than the genitive ἐμοῦ would be : "You will belong to me more closely as my disciples." One must always *become* a disciple ; one *is* not such once for all.— As the vine does not itself bear any cluster, and offers its fruits to the world only through the medium of the branches, so Jesus will diffuse spiritual life here on earth only through the instrumentality of those who shall have received it from Him. In forming a Church, He creates for Himself a body for the pouring forth of His life and for the glorification of God on the earth. The vine keeps itself in the background in this great work, that it may only allow the branches to appear ; it is for them, in their turn, to put themselves in the background, that they may render homage to the vine for all which they effect. The epistles to the Ephesians and the Colossians set forth, in a completely original form, this same relation between Christ and believers. The figures of the *head* and *body* correspond absolutely, in these letters, to those of the vine and the branch in this passage. When Paul says of the glorified Christ "*that all the fulness of the Deity dwells bodily in him,*" and "*that we have all fulness in him,*" he only formulates the meaning of the parable of the vine and the branch, as it has just presented itself to us. And this also explains why the propagation of the spiritual life advances so slowly in humanity. The vine effects nothing except through the branches ; and these too often paralyze the action of the vine, instead of propagating it !

The condition for abiding in Christ is to remain under the action of His word (ver. 7) in the enjoyment of His love, and this latter depends on obedience to His commandments, and especially to that of brotherly love: vv. 9–17.

Vv. 9–11. "*As the Father has loved me, I also have loved you; abide in my love.* 10. *If you keep my commandments, you shall abide in my love,*[1] *as I have*[2] *kept my Father's commandments and abide in His love.* 11. *I have spoken this to you that my joy may be*[3] *in you and that your joy may be fulfilled.*"—It is the love of Jesus which has formed the bond between Him and ourselves. In this love has the stream of the divine love burst forth on the earth ; first, the love of the Father for Jesus, of which He gave Him the assurance at the baptism, and which is that with which He loved Him before His incarnation (xvii. 24); then, the love of Jesus for His own, which is of the same nature as that of God for Him (καθώς, not ὥσπερ). The initiative in these two cases comes from the more exalted being. What then is the condition to the end that the relation may be maintained and strengthened ? It is simply necessary that the inferior being should accept this love and respond to it. He has not to awaken it ; he has only to abide under its beams. But in order to this, he must not force it to turn away from him ; and this is what he will do by unfaithfulness and disobedience. Jesus calls attention to the fact that He does not here impose on the believer with reference to Himself any other condition than that to which He has Himself submitted with reference to the Father. His life was an act of permanent submission to the divine injunctions ; without this submission, he would have ceased instantly to be the object of the satisfied love of the Father (viii. 29, x. 17). Such is also the position of the believer with regard to the love of Christ. The expression *my love* can designate here only the love of Jesus for His own ; comp. the words : *As I have loved you,* and the whole development in vv. 13–16. The Lord uses with reference to Himself the verbs in the past because He has reached the end of His earthly life. The second clause of ver. 9 : *and I have loved you,* does not depend on καθώς, *as* : "As my Father has

---

[1] ℵ omits the words εαν . . . εν τη αγαπη μου (confusion with ver. 29).

[2] ℵ D It.: εγω instead of καγω.

[3] A B D It. Vulg. read η (*may be*) instead of μεινη (*may abide*).

loved me *and as* I have loved you." For the principal verb, which would, in that case, be : *abide*, is not in any logical relation to the first clause of ver. 9 : *as my Father has loved me*. The meaning is : "And I also, I have loved you ; continue therefore the objects of this love."—And how so ? By faithfulness to His injunctions like to that which He Himself testifies with reference to the will of the Father (ver. 10).—In demanding this of them Jesus is assured by His own experience that He is not imposing on them a burden, but rather is revealing to them the secret of perfect joy (ver. 11). It is this constant rejoicing in the love of the Father in the path of obedience which has constituted His own joy here on earth ; and this joy will be reproduced in His disciples in the same path. It is then, indeed, *His joy* into which He initiates them and to the possession of which He invites them in these words : "*I have said this to you* in order that . . ." *My* joy cannot therefore here signify : the joy which I will produce in you (*Calvin*); or the joy which I feel on your account (*Augustine*); or the joy which you feel on my account (*Euthymius*). The question is of the joy with which He Himself rejoices in feeling Himself to be the object of the Father's love. Comp. the analogous expression *my peace*, xiv. 27.—Thus through obedience their joy will increase even to fulness. For every act of fidelity will draw closer the bond between Jesus and themselves, as every moment in the life of Jesus drew closer the bond between Him and His Father. And to feel oneself included with the Son in the Father's love—is not this *perfect joy?* The reading $\mathring{\eta}$ seems preferable to $μείνῃ$. The notion of *being* is sufficient ; that of *abiding* would be superfluous ; comp. xvii. 26.

Ver. 12. "*This is my commandment, that you love one another as I have loved you.*"—Comp. xiii. 34. This is the normal relation of the branches to one another, which has as its condition the normal relation of each one to the vine. So *Hengstenberg* finds in vv. 1-11 the *résumé* of the first part of the summary of the law, and in vv. 12-17, that of the second.—In vv. 13-16, Jesus raises the mutual love of His own to its full height by giving as a model for it that which He has had for them. These four verses are the commentary on the word *as* in the words : "*As I have loved you.*" And first, ver. 13 : the point to which His love has carried devotion—death ; then, vv. 14, 15 : the character of full intimacy which He has given to this relation of love ; it was the confidence of the friend rather than the authority of the master ; finally, ver. 16 : the free initiative with which He has Himself laid the foundation of this relation. The meaning of this whole development is this : "When therefore you ask yourselves what limits are to be set to your mutual love, begin by asking yourselves, what limits, in these various points, that love which I have had for you has set for itself !" Or : "And when you would know what it is to love, look at me !" (*Gess*).

Ver. 13. "*No one has greater love than this, that a man*[1] *lay down his life for his friends.*"—In the relation to *friends*, there is no greater proof of love than the sacrifice of one's life on their behalf. There is undoubtedly a greater proof of love, *absolutely speaking*,—it is to sacrifice it for enemies,

---

[1] ℵ D It. omit τις after ἵνα.

Rom. v. 6–8. Ἵνα keeps the idea of aim : "the highest point to which love, in this relation of friends, can *aspire* to raise itself."

Vv. 14, 15. "*You are my friends, if you do whatsoever*[1] *I command you.* 15. *I call you no longer servants, because the servant knows not what his master does ; but I have named you friends, because I have made known to you all things which I have heard from my Father.*"—In ver. 14, the emphasis is, not on the condition : *If you do,* . . . but on the affirmation : *You are my friends ;* Jesus means : "It is not without reason that I have just said : *for his friends* (ver. 13), for this is indeed the relation which I have formed with you and which will be maintained if you show yourselves obedient and faithful." What more touching than a master who, finding a servant really faithful, gives him in the house the rank and title of friend !

Ver. 15 serves to prove the *reality* of this position of friends which He has given them. He has shown an unbounded confidence in them by initiating them unreservedly into the communications which His Father made to Him with relation to the great work in which He had called them to labor with Him. The master employs his slave without explaining to him what he intends to do. Jesus has communicated to them the whole thought of God with regard to the salvation in which they are to co-operate. No doubt there remain yet many things to teach them (xvi. 12). But, if He has not yet revealed these to them, it is not from a want of confidence and love ; it is in order to spare their weakness and because only another can discharge this task. It has been objected to this οὐκέτι ("*I no longer* call you"), that the address *my friends* is found in Luke xii. 4, much earlier than the present moment ; as if the tendency to make them His friends had not existed in Him from the beginning, and must not have manifested itself already on certain occasions ! It has also been objected that the apostles continue to call themselves *servants of Jesus Christ ;* as if, although it pleases the master to make the servant his friend, the latter were not so much the more bound to remind himself and others of his natural condition !

Ver. 16. "*You have not chosen me ; but I have chosen you and appointed you, that you should go and bear fruit, and that your fruit should remain ; that, whatsoever you may ask the Father in my name, he may give*[2] *it you.*"—The very origin of the relation thus formed between them depends only on Him. Jesus has the consciousness of the greatness of the proof of love which He has given them by associating them of *His own impulse* in that work which constitutes the highest activity of which man can be judged worthy. By the term : *I have chosen you*, He alludes, as in vi. 70 and xiii. 18, to the solemn act of their election to the apostleship, related in Luke vi. 12 ff. The word ἔθηκα, *have appointed*, designates their gradual installation into this office, as well as their spiritual education, for which He had labored with so much perseverance.—The expression ὑπάγητε, *that you should go*, refers to their apostolic mission in the world, and sets forth the relative independence which they will

---

[1] The MSS. read either ο (B It^{aliq}) or α (א D L X It^{aliq} Vulg. Cop), or with T. R. οσα (13 Mjj. Mnn. Syr).

[2] Instead of ινα ο τι αν and δω (or δωη), א reads οτι αν and δωσει

enjoy as they take His place in this task.—The *fruit* designates here, more specially than in ver. 2, the communication to other men of the spiritual life which they themselves possess. This fruit does not perish, as that of earthly labor does : *it remains.*—The second ἵνα, *in order that,* cannot be dependent on the first, as *Hengstenberg, Luthardt* and *Keil* would have it, as if Jesus meant that they would go and bear fruit in order that, being thus in communion with the Father, they might be heard by Him. This thought is unnatural. The second *in order that* is simply co-ordinate with the preceding, as in xiii. 34 ; comp. as to the substance and form, the two clauses dependent on ὅτι, xiv. 12, 13. Jesus reminds them that the very efficacy of their labor will be due to the revelation which He has given them of His person and the prayer which will result from it, the prayer in His name. Thus, through their dependence on the verb : *I have appointed you,* these words mean : "And you are now, through my name which you know, in the glorious position of gaining for yourselves directly from the Father whatsoever you will have to ask from Him." All this as the fruit of the free initiative of His love towards them.

Ver. 17. "*I give you these precepts, that you may love one another.*"—The pronoun ταῦτα cannot refer to the ἵνα which follows : "I command you *this, that* you love one another." For the plural proves that this expression includes all the preceding instructions and suggestions since xv. 1, particularly the words of vv. 12–16. The ἵνα must therefore be translated by *in order that;* it indicates, in conformity with the idea of ver. 12, the purpose of these injunctions.—This work is all love ; love in its first origin, the love of the Father ; love in its great manifestation, the love of Christ ; finally, love in its end, the full flowering of mutual love among believers. Love is its root, its trunk and its fruit. This is the essential characteristic of the new kingdom, whose power and conquests are due only to the contagion of love. This is the reason why Jesus leaves no other law than that of love to those who, through faith, have become members of His body.

Luthardt observes that in the first seventeen verses of this chapter, there is found only one particle of connection. This long *asyndeton* has an especial solemnity. Here is the last wish of Jesus speaking to His own (see xvii. 24).—Such a style could not belong to a Greek author ; these words came forth from Hebrew thought.

2. xv. 18–xvi. 4

Opposite to this spiritual body whose inward life and outward activity He has just described, Jesus sees a hostile society arise, which has also its principle of unity, hatred of Christ and of God : *the world,* natural humanity, which will declare war against the Church, and which is represented at this moment by the Jewish people. Jesus draws a first picture of its hatred to believers, vv. 18–25. Then, after having pointed out in passing, as if to reassure the disciples, the succor which will be given them, He reproduces with still more living colors the description of the hostility of the world, ver. 26–xvi. 4.

Vv. 18–20. "*If the world hates you, know that I have been the object of its hatred before you.*[1] 19. *If you were of the world, the world would love what belongs to it; but because you are not of the world and I have drawn you out of the world, therefore the world hates you.* 20. *Remember the word which I have said to you:*[2] *the servant is not greater than his master; if they have persecuted me, they will also persecute you; if they have kept my word, they will keep yours also.*"—Jesus does not wish merely to announce to His disciples the hatred of which they are going to be the object on the part of the world; He wishes to fortify them against it; and He does so by saying to them, first: it will hate you *as me* (vv. 18–20); then: it will hate you *because of me* (vv. 21–25). Nothing makes us more ready to suffer as Christians than the thought that there happens to us only what happened to Christ, and that it happens to us *for* Him. Γινώσκετε may be taken as an imperative, like μνημονεύετε (*remember*), ver. 20 : "Consider what has happened with regard to me, and you will understand that everything which happens to you is in the natural order." The indicative sense, however, is more simple : "If a similar experience befalls you, *you know* the explanation of it already : you know indeed that. . . ."—By their union with Christ, the disciples represent henceforth on earth a principle foreign to humanity which lives apart from God, *to the world.* This manifestation therefore appears strange to the world; it is offended by it; it will seek to get rid of it.—'Εξελεξάμην, *I have chosen,* indicates here the call to faith, not to the apostleship; by this word *to choose* Jesus would designate the act by which He has drawn them to Himself and detached them from the world; the thought of divine predestination is not found here, any more than in ver. 16. The close relation formed by this act of Jesus between Himself and the disciples is formulated in ver. 20 by the expressions *master* and *servant.* The quoted axiom has the same sense as in Matt. x. 24, but a different sense from John xiii. 16. In ch. xiii. it is an encouragement to humility; here it is an encouragement to patience.—It is natural to regard the two cases set forth by Jesus in ver. 20 as both real. The *mass* of the people will no more be converted by the preaching of the apostles than by that of Jesus. But as Jesus has had the satisfaction of rescuing isolated *individuals* from ruin, this joy will also be granted to the disciples. This meaning seems to me preferable to that of *Grotius*, who gives to the second clause an ironical sense, or to that of *Bengel*, who takes τηρεῖν, *to keep*, in the sense of maliciously watching, or, finally, to the interpretation of *Lücke, Meyer, de Wette, Hengstenberg, Weiss*, who see in the two sides of the alternative proposed only two abstract propositions between which the apostles can easily decide which one will be realized for them; as if Jesus and themselves had not also gained some of the members of the κόσμος.

Vv. 21–25. "*But they will do all this to you*[3] *for my name's sake, because they know not him who sent me.* 22. *If I had not come and spoken to them, they would not have had sin; but now they have no excuse for their sin.* 23. *He who hates me, hates my Father also.* 24. *If I had not done among them works*

---

[1] ℵ D It^(plerique) omit υμων (*you*).
[2] Instead of του λογου ου εγω ειπον, ℵ reads του λογον ον, D: τους λογους ους ελαλησα.
[3] B D L It^(alia) Syr.: εις υμας instead of υμιν. ℵ omits this word.

such as no other has done,[1] *they would not have had sin ; but now they have seen, and nevertheless have hated both me and my Father.* 25. *But this is so, that the word may be fulfilled, which is written in their law : They hated me without a cause.*"—The apostles should not be disturbed because of this so general hatred, imagining that they have themselves provoked it, and believing that they see in it the proof that they are on a wrong path : "*But* (ἀλλά) take courage ; it is because of me.*"*—"*Because of my name,*" says Jesus ; that is, because of the revelation of my person which you have received, and which you will declare to them.—The reason why this revelation, which should make Israel rejoice, will exasperate that people, is that they *do not* truly *know God.* The idea of God has been perverted in the heart of this people. This is the reason why they are offended at the appearance of Jesus, and will be offended at the preaching of His apostles. The book of the Gospels is the setting forth of the first of these facts, and the book of the Acts that of the second. In consequence of their blindness, Israel will rather see in the holiest man an impostor than the one sent from God.

Ver. 22. This blindness which has prevailed in their entire history (see the discourse of Stephen, Acts vii.) might have still been forgiven them, if, at this decisive moment, they had finally yielded. But the rejection of this supreme divine manifestation characterizes their state as an invincible antipathy, as *the hatred* of God, a sentiment which constitutes the unpardonable sin. Some (*Bengel, Luthardt, Lange, Hengstenberg, Keil*) think that the sin which would not have been imputed to them is their very *unbelief* with reference to Jesus. But this sin, if Jesus had not come, would not have been even possible (*Weiss*). It would be necessary, therefore, to understand the first words in this sense : "If I had not come in such or such a way, for example, with the holiness which I have displayed, and had not borne witness for myself in so convincing a manner." But Jesus simply says : If I had not *come*—that is, as Messiah. The meaning, therefore, is this : "The former sin of Israel, its long resistance to God, would have been forgiven it, if it had not now crowned all by the rejection of Jesus as He *came* as Saviour, and bore testimony to Himself as such." This last sin destroys all the excuses which Israel could have alleged for its conduct in general ; it proves incontestably that this people is animated by an ill-will towards God ; that it does not sin through ignorance. The idea is not altogether the same as in ix. 41.

Ver. 23. In the rejection of Jesus there is hatred towards Him, and in this hatred towards Him, the Jewish malignity reveals itself clearly as *hatred of God :* it is distinguished thereby from a mere ignorance, like that of the heathen. More than this :

Ver. 24. If the testimony which Jesus bore to Himself did not succeed in enlightening them, His works ought at least to have procured credence for His testimony. The one who did not have a consciousness sufficiently developed to apprehend the divine character of His teachings, had at least eyes to behold His miracles.—For the first two καί, see vi. 36 : they have caused

---

[1] The MSS. are divided between πεποιηκεν (T. R. with E G H etc.) and εποιησεν (ℵ A B D etc.).

things which seemed incompatible to move together : *seeing and hating ;* and this at once (the two following καί) with reference to me and my Father : these last two καί are additive, not adversative.

Ver. 25. 'Αλλά : "*But* there is nothing astonishing in this." The righteous man of the old covenant had already complained by the mouth of David (Ps. xxxv. 19, lxix. 5) of being the object of the *gratuitous* hatred of the enemies of God. If their hatred was wholly laid to their own charge, notwithstanding the faults of the imperfectly righteous man, with how much stronger reason can the perfectly righteous One appropriate to Himself this complaint, which is, at the same time, His consolation and that of those who suffer like Him and for Him !—*Weiss* asserts here, as with reference to the other quotations of this kind, that the evangelist puts in the mouth of even the Messiah these words of the Old Testament. The evangelist would then imagine the Messiah as also uttering these words of ver. 6 from Ps. lxix : O God, Thou knowest my foolishness, and my sins are not hid from Thee ; or he could never have read them ! As for Ps. xxxv., it is impossible to find in it a line which could have led any reader whatever of the Old Testament to the Messianic application.—*In order that* depends on a "This has happened," or "This must have happened," understood, as in so many other cases (ix. 3, xiii. 18, 1 John ii. 19, Mark xiv. 49, etc.). On the term "*their law*," see on viii. 17. De Wette finds irony in these words : "They practise faithfully their law." This meaning seems far-fetched.

Vv. 26, 27. "*But*[1] *when the support shall have come, whom I will send you from the Father, the Spirit of truth who proceeds from the Father, he shall testify of me ;* 27. *and you also shall testify, because you are with me from the beginning."*—*Weiss* sees in this intervention of the Spirit's testimony a fact which Jesus alleges in order to demonstrate the truth of the word *without cause*, ver 25. But this connection is unnatural ; it would have required a γάρ in ver. 26. It is more simple to suppose that, in speaking of the hatred of the world, Jesus interrupts Himself for a moment in order to show immediately to the disciples the power which will sustain them in this terrible conflict. He only indicates this help for a moment in passing. The idea will be completely developed in the following passage, xvi. 5–15, when the picture of Jewish hostility will be finished.—In saying : *whom I will send*, Jesus is necessarily thinking of His approaching reinstatement in the divine condition ; and in adding : *from the Father*, He acknowledges His subordination to the Father, even when He shall have recovered that condition.—Jesus here designates the Spirit as *Spirit of truth*, in order to place Him in opposition to the falsehood of the world, to its voluntary ignorance. The Spirit will dissipate the darkness in which it tries to envelop itself.—Most of the modern interpreters, *Meyer, Luthardt, Weiss, Keil,* refer the words : *who proceeds from the Father*, to the same fact as the preceding words : *whom I will send you from the Father*,—to the sending of the Holy Spirit to the disciples. The attempt is made to escape the charge of tautology by saying that the first clause indicates the relation of

---

[1] א B Δ omit δε after οταν.

the Spirit to Christ, and the second His relation to God (*Keil*) ; as if in this latter were not already contained the *from God*, which, repeated in the second clause, would form the most idle pleonasm. It must be observed that the second verb differs entirely from the first ; ἐκπορεύεσθαι, *to proceed from*, as a river from its source, is altogether different from *to be sent :* the ἐκ, *out from*, which is added here to παρά, *from the presence of*, also marks a difference. But especially does the change of tense indicate the difference of idea : whom *I will send* and *who proceeds from*. He whom Jesus will send (historically, at a given moment) is a divine being, who emanates (essentially, eternally) from the Father. An impartial exegesis cannot, as it seems to me, deny this sense. It is that the historical facts of salvation, to the view of Jesus, rest upon eternal relations, as well with reference to Himself, the Son, as to the Spirit. They are, as it were, the reflections of the Trinitarian relations. As the incarnation of the Son rests upon His eternal generation, so the *mission* of the Holy Spirit is related to His eternal *procession* from the very centre of the divine being. The context is not in the least contradictory to this sense, as *Weiss* thinks ; on the contrary, it demands it. What Jesus sends testifies truly for Him only so far as it comes forth from God.—The Latin church is not wrong, therefore, in affirming the *Filioque*, starting from the words : *I will send*, and the Greek church is no more wrong in maintaining the *per Filium* and subordination, starting from the words : *from the Father*. In order to bring these two views into accord, we must place ourselves at the Christological point of view of the Gospel of John, according to which the homoousia and the subordination are simultaneously true.—The pronoun ἐκεῖνος, "*he*, that being, and he alone," sums up all the characteristics which have just been attributed to the Holy Spirit, and makes prominent the unique authority of this divine witness.—Does this testimony given to the person of Jesus consist only in the *presence* of the Spirit on the earth, as proof *de facto* of His glorification ? This sense would not suit either the name *support* nor that of Spirit *of truth*, and would not account for the pronoun *you*, in the promise : "I will send to you." The question here is rather of the testimony given before the world, in answer to its hostile attitude, by the intermediate agency of the apostles ; for example, by the mouth of Peter and the one hundred and twenty on the day of Pentecost.—But if it is so, we ask ourselves how can Jesus afterwards distinguish this testimony from that of the apostles themselves, in ver. 27 : *And you also shall bear witness for me ;* and the more, since the particle καὶ δέ indicates a marked gradation (comp. vi. 51); καί, *and also ;* δέ, *and besides*. To understand the distinction, we must begin with ver. 27, which is the simplest one. The apostles possess a treasure which is peculiar to them, and which the Spirit could not communicate to them—the *historical* knowledge of the ministry of Jesus from its beginning to its end. The Spirit does not teach the facts of history ; He reveals their meaning. But this historical testimony of the apostles would, without the Spirit, be only a frigid narrative incapable of creating life. It is the Spirit which brings the vivifying breath to the testimony. By making the light of the divine thought fall upon the facts, He makes them a **power** which lays hold upon souls. Without the facts, the Spirit would be only an empty exaltation devoid of contents, of substance; without the Spirit the narrative of the facts would remain dead and unfruitful. The apostolic testimony and the testimony of the Spirit unite, therefore, in one and the same act, but they do so while bringing to it, each of them, a necessary element, the one, the historical narration, the other, the inward evidence. This relation is still reproduced at the present day in every living sermon drawn from the Scriptures. Peter, in like manner, distinguishes these two testimonies in Acts v. 32 : *"And we are witnesses of these things, as well as the Holy Spirit whom God has given to those who obey him."* We understand, after this, why, when the apostles wished to fill the place of Judas, they chose two men who had accompanied Jesus from the baptism of John even to His resurrection (Acts i. 21, 22).—The καὶ ὑμεῖς signifies therefore : "And you also, you will have your special part in this testimony."—The present μαρτυρεῖτε, *you bear witness*, which we have translated by the future, does not by any means refer, as *Weiss* and *Keil* think, to the present moment, when the disciples are already bearing witness. Besides the circumstance that the fact was at that time true only in a very limited sense, why should it be mentioned here, since the question is of the future and the testimony of the Spirit? This present transports the disciples to the time when the Spirit shall speak : "*And then*, on this foundation you bear witness also."

xvi. 1–4. "*I have spoken these things to you, that you may not be offended.* 2. *They shall put you out of their synagogues; yea, the hour is coming that whoever kills you will think that he is doing service to God.* 3. *And they will do these things to you,*[1] *because they have not known the Father nor me. But I have told them to you in order that, when the hour shall have come, you may remember*[2] *that I told you of them. I did not say them to you at the beginning, because I was with you.*"—After this interruption, designed to encourage the apostles, Jesus comes to the more serious things which He has to announce to them on the subject which occupies His thought. The preceding picture makes especially prominent the culpability of the persecutors; the following words describe rather the sufferings of the persecuted. The faith of the apostles might have been shaken in view of the impenitence and hostility of their people.—Ἀλλά, as often, a term of gradation (2 Cor. vii. 11) : "Not only this; but you must expect what is worse." Ἵνα designates the contents of the hour, as *willed* of God. The fanatical zeal of Paul, at the time of Stephen's martyrdom, is in certain respects an example of the spiritual state described in ver. 2 (Acts xxvi. 9), although in him ignorance surpassed hatred, and hatred of Jesus was not in his heart hatred of God, as in the case indicated in xv. 23 ; comp. 1 Tim. i. 13. Ver. 3 describes the climax of moral *blindness :* to imagine oneself to be serving God by the very act which is the expression of the most intense hatred against Him !

---

[1] T. R. reads υμιν after ποιησουσιν with ℵ D L some Mnn. It^{plerique} Cop.; 12 Mjj. Mnn. It^{aliq} Syr. reject it.

[2] A B Π Syr. read αυτων twice, after ωρα (*the hour of these things*) and after μνημονευητε. L Mnn. It. Vulg. read it after ωρα only ; ℵ Y Τ Δ Λ and 7 Mjj. Cop. after μνημονευητε only. D omits it both times.

Such a mode of action can proceed only from the fact that one has reached the point of absolutely failing to know God and Christ. Ver. 4 returns, after the digression, to the thought of ver. 1, and closes it by uniting itself with vv. 2, 3. The ἀλλά, *but*, has been explained in various ways. It seems to me to form an antithesis to the understood idea : "I understand the horror which the prospects that I open before you must inspire within you ; *but* I have thought it more useful to reveal them to you freely at last, a thing which I should not have been willing to do until the present moment."—These events, which in themselves would have been for them a cause of stumbling, will, when once foretold, be changed by the words which He utters at this hour, into a support for their faith ; comp. xiii. 19 and xiv. 29.—As long as Jesus was with them, it was upon Him that the hatred fell ; He sheltered them, so to speak, with His body. Now that they are about to find themselves unprotected, they must be forewarned ; comp. Luke xxii. 36, 37, words which, in another form, contain an analogous thought, and which must have been pronounced nearly at the same moment with these of John. It seems to us impossible to reconcile with these words : "*I did not say these things to you from the beginning,*" the place which is occupied in the discourse of Matt. x. by the positive prediction of the persecutions of which the Church will be the object. It cannot be said, with *Chrysostom* and *Euthymius*, that the sufferings here predicted are much *more terrible* than those of which Matt. x. 17, 21, 28 speaks ; nor, with *Bengel* and *Tholuck*, that the present description is *more detailed* than that ; nor again, with *Hofmann* and *Luthardt*, that Jesus makes this prediction of the persecutions the *more exclusive* object of the discoursing at this farewell moment. All these distinctions are too subtle. It is in vain that *Westcott* rests for support upon the expression ἐξ ἀρχῆς, which would indicate a continuity, and not merely, like ἀπ' ἀρχῆς, a point of departure. It is better to recognize the fact that Matthew unites in the great discourse of ch. x. all the instructions given at different times to the Twelve respecting the future persecutions of which they will be the object, as in chs. v.–vii. he unites all the elements of the new Christian law, and in chs. xxiv., xxv. all the eschatological prophecies; and this because, in the composition of the *Logia*, he did not take account of the *chronological* order, but only of the subjects treated. This characteristic finds its explanation as soon as the mode of composition of the first Gospel is understood (see my *Etudes bibliques*, ii. pp. 18, 19, 3d ed.).

3. xvi. 5–15

Jesus now describes *the victory* which the disciples will gain over the world which has risen up against Him. He first connects with His departure the coming of the divine *agent* (already announced in xv. 26, 27), who will gain the victory through them, vv. 5–7 ; He then describes the *manner* of this victory, vv. 8–11 ; finally, He speaks to the disciples of the interior operation of the Spirit, which is the *condition* of it, vv. 12–15.

Vv. 5–7. "*But now I go away to him who sent me ; and no one of you asks me, Whither goest thou?* 6. *But, because I have said these things to you, sorrow has filled your heart.* 7. *But I tell you the truth: it is expedient for you that I go away; for, if I*[1] *go not away, the support will not come to you; but when I shall have gone away, I will send him to you.*"—The idea of the departure in vv. 5, 6 is naturally connected with the last words of ver. 4 : "because *I was* with you." It forms the transition to the promise of the Paraclete in ver. 7, since the departure of Jesus is the condition of the sending of the Holy Spirit. *De Wette* and *Lücke* have needlessly proposed to place ver. 6 between the two clauses of ver. 5.—The connection is clear ; from the great conflict Jesus passes to the great promise. Jesus is grieved at seeing His disciples preoccupied only with the separation which is approaching, and not at all with the glorious goal to which this departure will lead Him. Love should impel them to ask Him respecting that new state into which He is about to enter (xiv. 28). Instead of this, He sees them preoccupied only with the desolate condition in which His departure is to leave them, and plunged thereby into a gloomy dejection. *Weiss* thinks that Jesus means : "You do not ask me further because now you understand." But the light does not come into their minds until later (vv. 29, 30). There is evidently in the words : "No one of you asks me," a friendly reproach. As *Hengstenberg* says : "Jesus would have been glad to find in them at this moment the joyous enthusiasm of hearts which open themselves to the prospects of a new epoch, and which do not unceasingly continue to put presumptuous questions respecting what it promised them." The questions of Peter, Thomas and Philip did not bear upon this luminous side of His near departure, and besides, at the moment when Jesus was speaking, they were already quite at a distant point of the conversation.

The words : *Because I have said these things to you* (ver. 6), signify, as following upon ver. 5 : **Because I have spoken to you of separation, of conflict, of sufferings.** In ver. 7 Jesus makes appeal first, as in xiv. 2, to the conviction which they have of His veracity. The ἐγώ, *I*, at the beginning, emphasizes in opposition to their ignorance the knowledge which He Himself possesses of the true state of things. Then He announces to them spontaneously a part of these joyful things which they were not eager to ask of Him. This departure is His re-establishment in the divine state, and the latter is the condition of the sending of the Spirit which He will secure for them. We find here again the idea of vii. 39 : "*The Spirit was not yet, because Jesus had not yet been glorified.*" That He may on their behalf dispose of this supreme agent, it is necessary that He should be Himself restored to the divine state. This mission implies, therefore, the complete glorification of His humanity.—He does not, in this passage, make any mention of the sacrifice of the cross and of the reconciliation of the world, that first condition of the gift of the Spirit. This silence is explained by the declaration of ver. 12 : "*I have yet many things to say to you; but you cannot bear them.*" John explains himself very distinctly on this point in his Epistle (ii. 1, 2, v. 6, 8) ; which proves, indeed, that he has not allowed

---

[1] T. R. with ℵ B D L Y It^alia omits εγω, which is found in 10 Mjj., 120 Mnn. It^plerique Syr.

himself to make Jesus speak here after his own fancy. Besides, *Reuss* is himself obliged, indeed, to acknowledge that this part of the discourse is addressed expressly to the Eleven, and not, as he always affirms, to the readers of the evangelist, and he tries in vain to escape the consequence which follows from this fact in favor of the *historical* truth of these discourses.

Vv. 8–11. "*And when he shall have come, he will convince the world of sin, of righteousness and of judgment; 9, of sin, because they believe not[1] on me; 10, of righteousness, because I go to my[2] Father and you will see me no more; 11, of judgment, because the prince of this world is judged.*" Here is the description of the victory which, through the agency of the disciples, the Holy Spirit will gain over the world. The discourse of St. Peter at Pentecost and its results are the best commentary on this promise. It will be a victory of a moral nature, the mode of which is expressed by the term $\dot{\epsilon}\lambda\dot{\epsilon}\gamma\chi\epsilon\iota\nu$, *to convince of wrong* or *of error;* here both the one and the other.—This word does not also designate a definitive condemnation, as the Fathers, and then *de Wette* and *Brückner*, thought, as if the Holy Spirit were to demonstrate to lost humanity the justice of its condemnation. Ver. 11 proves that the prince of the world alone is already *judged*. If, then, the world can profit by the reproof of the Holy Spirit, it is still capable of salvation. This is proved by the effect of the apostles' preaching, in the Acts, in the case of a portion of the hearers. The reproof given by the Spirit may lead either to conversion or to hardening ; comp. 2 Cor. ii. 15, 16. The apostles are not named as instruments of this internal operation of the Spirit. Their persons disappear in the glory of the divine being who works by their means. But it is certainly through their intervention that it takes place, as the $\pi\rho\grave{o}\varsigma\ \acute{v}\mu\tilde{a}\varsigma$ of ver. 7 proves ; comp. also vv. 13–15.

The error of the world on the one side, and the divine truth on the other, will be demonstrated with regard to three points. The absence of the article before the substantives, *sin, righteousness, judgment,* leaves to these three notions the most indefinite meaning. Jesus will give precision to the application of them by the three ὅτι, *in that* or *because*, which follow. If this explanation of Jesus Himself failed us, we should undoubtedly regard the idea of righteousness as the intermediate one between the two others : *righteousness* applying itself to *sin* to produce *judgment*. But the explanation of Jesus places us on an altogether different path. Only it concerns us to know whether we must translate the three ὅτι by *in that* or *because*. In the first case, the fact mentioned afterwards is that in which the sin, righteousness, judgment, consist, and the conjunction ὅτι may be regarded as dependent on each of the three substantives ; in the second, the conjunction in each instance depends on the verb *convince*, and announces a fact which will establish the truth of God and the error of the world on these three points. The first interpretation, as it appears to me, cannot be applied to the second of these points.

The *world*, here the Jewish world, was in error respecting sin, seeking to

---

[1] Some Mnn. It^{plerique} Vulg. read ουκ επιστευσαν (*did not believe*).

[2] ℵ B D L some Mnn. It^{plerique} Vulg. Cop. omit μου after πατερα.

find it only in the shameful excesses of tax-gatherers and the gross infractions of the Levitical law. Israel condemned and rejected Jesus as a malefactor because of His violations of the Sabbath and His alleged blasphemies. The Spirit will reveal to it its own state of sin by means of a crime of which it does not dream, unbelief towards its Messiah, the messenger of God ; comp. the discourse of Peter, on the day of Pentecost, Acts ii. 22, 23, 36 ; and iii. 14, 15. Sincere Jews recognized immediately the truth of this reproof (Acts ii. 37). And this office of the Spirit continues always. Jesus is the good ; to reject Him is to prefer the evil to the good and to wish to persevere in it ; comp. iii. 19, 20. This is what the Spirit without cessation makes the unbelieving world feel by His agents here on earth.—Thus $\pi\varepsilon\rho\iota$ $\dot{\alpha}\mu\alpha\rho\tau\iota\alpha\varsigma$ $\ddot{o}\tau\iota$ does not mean : He will convince the world of sin *which consists* in unbelief ; but He will convince it of its state *of sin* in general, and this by rendering it palpable to it by means of a decisive fact, its unbelief with regard to the Messiah. It goes without saying that this work of the Spirit is not to be confounded with the *usus elenchticus* of the law.

The Jewish world is also in error as to the way in which it has understood *righteousness*. Exalting itself with pride in its meritorious works, Israel has taken its position in opposition to Jesus as the representative of righteousness, and has rejected Him from its midst as an unworthy member. The Holy Spirit will fulfil with reference to this judgment the function of a court of appeal. Holy Friday seemed to have ascribed sin to Jesus, and righteousness to His judges ; but Pentecost will reverse this sentence ; it will assign righteousness to the condemned One of Golgotha and sin to His judges. This meaning results first from the contrast between the two terms *sin* and *righteousness*, then from the following explanatory clause, according to which the righteousness which is here in question is that which glorification will confer upon Jesus in the invisible world, and which the sending of the Spirit by Him to His own will proclaim here below. This righteousness cannot therefore be, as *Augustine, Melanchthon, Calvin, Luther, Lampe, Hengstenberg*, etc., think, the justification which the *believer* finds in Christ, or, as *Lange* supposes, the righteousness of God, who deprives the Jews, as a punishment for their unbelief, of the visible presence of the Messiah and of His earthly kingdom ("*you shall see me no more*"). In the words : *because I go to my Father*, Jesus presents His ascension, the end in which His death issues, as intended to afford the demonstration of His righteousness ; and He adds what follows : *and you will see me no more*, to complete this proof : "You will feel me to be present and active, even when you shall see me no more." The body of Jesus will have disappeared ; but His divine activity in this state of invisibility will prove His exaltation to the Father, and consequently His perfect righteousness (Acts ii. 24, 26).

The *judgment*, of which the Holy Spirit will furnish to the world the demonstration, will not be that great judgment of the Gentiles which the Jews were expecting, nor even that of the Jewish world convinced of sin. For the final sentence of the one party and the other is not yet pronounced. The *prince of this world* alone has from henceforth filled up the measure of his perversity, and can consequently be finally judged. Until Holy Friday.

Satan had not displayed his murderous hate, except with reference to the guilty. On that day, he assailed the life of the perfectly righteous One. In vain had Jesus said : *He has nothing in me.* Satan exhausted on Him his murderous rage (viii. 44 and 40). This murder without excuse called forth an immediate and irrevocable sentence against him. He is judged and deprived of power. And it is the Holy Spirit who proclaims this sentence here on earth, by calling the world to render homage to a new Master. This summons reveals the profound revolution which has just been wrought in the spiritual domain. Every sinner rescued from Satan and regenerated by the Spirit is the monument of the condemnation of him who formerly called himself the prince of this world.

Thus by the testimony of the Spirit the world, righteous in its own eyes, will be declared sinful ; the condemned malefactor will be proved righteous ; and the true author of this crime will receive his irrevocable sentence : such are the three ideas contained in this passage, whose powerful originality it is impossible not to recognize. It does not differ except as to form from xii. 31, 32 ; the three actors mentioned—the world, Satan and Jesus—are the same, as well as the parts which are attributed to them. Our passage only adds this idea : that it is the Holy Spirit who will reveal to men the true nature of the invisible drama consummated on the cross. The result of this reproof of the Spirit is that some remain in the *sin* of unbelief and participate thus in the *judgment* of the prince of this world, while others range themselves on the side of the *righteousness* of Christ, and are withdrawn from the judgment pronounced upon Satan.— But if this victory of the Spirit is to be gained by means of the apostles, it must be that previously the work of the Spirit has been consummated *in them.* This is the reason why Jesus passes from the action of the Spirit on the world *through* believers to His action *in* believers themselves (vv. 12–15).

Vv. 12, 13. "*I have yet many things to say to you ; but you have not now*[1] *the strength to bear them.* 13. *When he, the Spirit of truth, shall have come, he will lead you into all the truth ;*[2] *for he shall not speak of himself ; but whatsoever*[3] *he shall have heard,*[4] *he shall speak, and he shall announce to you the things to come.*"—Jesus begins by assigning a place to the teaching of the Spirit following upon His own. At this very moment He had just told His disciples so many things which they could only half understand ! From the standpoint of confidence, He had concealed nothing from them (xv. 15) ; but with a view to their spiritual incapacity, He had kept to Himself many revelations which were reserved for a later teaching. This subsequent revelation will, in the first place, bear upon the very contents of the teaching of Jesus, which it will cause to be better understood (xiv. 25, 26) ; then, on various points which Jesus had not even touched ; for example, redemp-

---

[1] ℵ omits αρτι (*now*).
[2] T. R. with 11 Mjj. Mnn.: εις πασαν την αληθειαν. A B Y Orig.: εις τ. αλ. πασαν. D L It^{pl erique} : εν τη αληθεια παση. ℵ : εν τη αληθεια.
[3] Αν is omitted by ℵ B D L 4 Mnn.
[4] T. R. with 10 Mjj.: ακουση. B D E H Y. Orig.: ακουσει (*shall hear*). ℵ L: ακουει (*hears*).

tion through the death of the Messiah, the relation of grace to the law, the conversion of the Gentiles without any legal condition, the final conversion of the Jews at present unbelieving, the destiny of the Church even to its consummation—in a word, the contents of the Epistles and the Apocalypse, so far as they pass beyond those of the teaching of Jesus.

The Spirit is presented in ver. 13 by the term ὁδηγεῖν, *to show the way*, under the figure of a guide who introduces a traveller into an unknown country. This country is *the truth*, the essential truth of which Jesus has spoken —that of salvation—and this truth is Himself (xiv. 6). This domain of the new creation, which Jesus can only show them from without, in the objective form, the Spirit will reveal to them by making them themselves enter into it through a personal experience.—The two readings εἰς and ἐν harmonize with the verb ὁδηγεῖν; according to the second, the disciples are considered as being already within the domain where the Spirit leads them and causes them to move forward.—The word *all* brings out the contrast with the incomplete teaching of Jesus.

The infallibility of this guide arises from the same cause as that of Jesus Himself (vii. 17, 18): the absence of all self-originated and consequently unsound productivity. All the revelations of the Spirit will be drawn from the divine plan realized in Jesus. Satan is a liar precisely because he speaks according to an altogether different method, deriving what he says *from his own resources* (viii. 44). The term ὅσα ἄν, *all the things which*, leads us to think of a series of momentary acts. On every occasion when the apostle shall have need of wisdom, the Spirit will communicate to him whatever of the objective truth will be appropriate to the given moment.—Whether we read the future with the *Vatican*, or the present with the *Sinaitic* MS., or the aorist subjunctive with the T. R., the verb *shall hear* must in any case be completed by the idea: from God respecting Christ (xv. 26). The question is evidently of the teaching of things *not yet heard* on the earth (ver. 12), consequently of the special revelation granted to the apostles, distinct from that which every Christian receives by means of theirs. That revelation has a *primordial* character, while this latter one is a mere internal reproduction of the light contained in the apostolic teaching, first oral, then written. It is therefore only indirectly included in this promise. The expression "*all the truth*" contains the thought that during the present economy no new teaching respecting Christ will come to be added to that of the apostles. —To this teaching of the Spirit belongs, as a peculiarly important element, the revelation of the destiny of the Church, of *the things to come*. Καί, *and even*. As Jesus is not only the Christ *come*, but also the Christ *coming* (ὁ ἐρχόμενος, Apoc. i. 4), these *things to come* (ἐρχόμενα) are also contained in His person. The words of xiv. 26 contained the formula of the inspiration of our Gospels; ver. 13 gives that of the Epistles and the Apocalypse.

Vv. 14, 15. "*He shall glorify me, for He shall take of what is mine and shall announce it to you.* 15. *All that the Father has is mine; therefore I said that he takes*[1] *of mine and shall announce it to you.*"—The asyndeton

---

[1] T. R. with A K Π, a part of the Mnn. It^(plerique) Vulg. Cop. reads λήψεται (*shall take*).

between vv. 13 and 14 proves that Jesus only reproduces under a new and more emphatic form in ver. 14 the thought of vv. 12, 13. The work of the Spirit introducing the apostles into the truth will be only the increasing glorification of Jesus in their hearts. After the Father shall have exalted Christ personally to glory, the Holy Spirit will cause His celestial image to beam forth from on high into the hearts of the disciples, and, through them, into the hearts of all believers. There is a mysterious exchange here and, as it were, a rivalry of divine humility. The Son labors only to glorify the Father, and the Spirit desires only to glorify the Son. Christ, His word and His work—herein is the sole text on which the Spirit will comment in the souls of the disciples. He will, by one and the same act, cause the disciples to grow in the truth and Jesus to grow greater in them. For the understanding of this word *glorify*, comp. the experience admirably described by St. Paul in 2 Cor. iii. 17, 18 and iv. 6.

In designating the source from which the Spirit will draw as *that which is mine*, Jesus seems to contradict what He has said in ver. 13 ; at least, if "from the Father" is understood after *shall hear*. Jesus gives the explanation of this apparent contradiction in ver. 15, by means of the words : "*All that the Father has is mine.*" The Father's treasure is common to Him with the Son. This word reveals, as does no other, the consciousness which Christ had of the greatness of His manifestation. The *Christian* fact is the measure of the *divine* for humanity. There is nothing essentially Christian which is not divine ; there is nothing divine which does not concentrate and realize itself in the Christian fact.—"*Therefore I said*" means here : "Therefore I have been able to say."—The present *takes* is better attested by documentary evidence (ver. 15) than the future *shall take*, and it is more in accordance with the present tenses, *has*, *is ;* the future is a correction in accordance with ver. 14, *He takes :* it is the present of the idea, designating the permanent function. After the present *takes*, the future *will declare* signifies : " and, after having taken, He will announce in each particular case." *Westcott* calls attention to the three : *and He will announce to you* (vv. 13, 14, 15), which form, as it were, a consoling refrain. Thus there is not a real breath of the Spirit which is not at the service of the person of the historic Christ. So St. Paul makes the cry of adoration : "*Jesus Lord!*" the criterion of every true operation of the divine Spirit (1 Cor. xii. 3) ; comp. also 1 John iv. 3. If we recall to mind how the glorifying of the creature constitutes in the Scriptures the capital crime, we shall understand what such words imply with relation to the person of Christ.

All these discourses, and in particular this masculine ἐκεῖνος, *he*, ver. 14, rest on the idea of the *personality* of the Holy Spirit. As *Weiss* says on account of xv. 26 : " The Spirit is conceived as a personal manifestation like to that of Christ Himself."

But B D E G L M S U Y Δ Λ Syr. most of the Mnn. read λαμβανει (*takes*). ℵ omits the whole 15th verse (a confounding of the two αναγγελει υμιν).

874 / The Development of Faith

The last Farewell: John 16:16-33

From these distant prospects which He has just opened to the disciples with respect to their future work (xv. 1–xvi. 15), Jesus returns to the great matter which occupies the thought of the present moment, that of His impending departure. This is natural ; thus He should close. At the same time, the conversational form reappears, which is no less in the natural course of things.

Vv. 16–18. " *Yet a little while, and you see me no more ;*[1] *again, a little while, and you shall see me, because I go to the Father.*[2] 17. *Therefore some of his disciples said among themselves : What does this mean, which he says to us : Yet a little while and you do not see me ;*[3] *again, a little while and you will see me ? And that other word : Because I*[4] *go to the Father.* 18. *They said therefore : What does he mean by this word :*[5] *A little while ? We do not understand what He says.*"—The promise of Jesus' return, in order to be consoling, must not be at too long a remove. Jesus affirms its very near realization. Two brief periods of time and it will take place ! *Weiss*, with *Lange*, *Hengstenberg*, etc., refers this return to the appearances of Jesus after His resurrection. The sequel (see especially vv. 25, 26) will show the impossibility of this explanation. But from this point the *asyndeton* between vv. 15, 16 leads us to suppose a much more profound connection of thought between these two sayings than could be the case with this meaning. If, in conformity with what precedes, the passage in ver. 16 ff. is referred to the spiritual seeing again through the coming of the promised Paraclete, as in xiv. 17–23, everything in what follows is simply explained. Filled with the idea of His glorification by the Spirit in the hearts of the disciples (vv. 13–16), Jesus calls this return a mutual *seeing again* (vv. 16, 22). It is in this living reappearance in the soul of His own that the approaching separation will end without delay.—The first μικρόν, *a little while*, refers to the short space of time which separates the present moment from that of His death ; the second, to the interval between His death and the day of Pentecost. Four Alexandrian authorities reject the words which close the verse : *Because I go to my Father ;* they would, in this case, have been introduced here in the other documents from ver. 17. But it seems to me rather that the expression : *You will see me because I go away*, appeared absurd and contradictory, and that these last words were omitted here. If they were allowed to remain in ver. 17, it was because there the ὅτι might be regarded as depending on ὃ λέγει, in the sense of *that*, and not on *you will see* in the sense of *because*. But it was not considered that, by preserving them in ver. 17, their omission in ver. 16 was condemned, since ver. 17 is the repetition of ver. 16. A glance at *Tischendorf's* note shows that *Origen* is probably the author of this omission, as of so many other errors in the Alexandrian text. This

---

[1] Instead of ου (*not*), ℵ B D L Λ read ουκετι (*no more*).

[2] ℵ B D L It^{aliq} Cop. omit the words οτι .... πατερα, which are read in 13 Mjj. most of the Mnn. It^{aliq} Syr. etc.

[3] ℵ omits the words μικρον και .... παλιν

(confusion of the two μικρον και).

[4] Εγω is omitted by ℵ A B L M Δ Π, 11 Mnn. It^{plerique}.

[5] Instead of τουτο τι ε. ο λεγει, B L Y It. Orig. read τι ε. τουτο ο λ., and ℵ D τι ε. τουτο.

because, which embarrassed Origen, is clear as one refers this seeing again to Pentecost. It is *because* Jesus returns to the Father that He can again be seen by believers through the Holy Spirit (vii. 39, xvi. 7).—Nevertheless, in expressing Himself as He does, Jesus proposed a problem to His disciples ; He is not unaware of it. These two brief delays (*a little while*), which were to have opposite results, and the apparently contradictory idea : " *You will see me because I go away*," must have been for them enigmas. We find here again the educational process which we have already observed in xiv. 4, 7. By these paradoxical expressions, Jesus designedly calls forth the revelation of their last doubts, to the end of having the power entirely to remove them.

The kind of *aside* which took place among some of the apostles (ver. 17) would not be easily explained, if they were still surrounding Jesus, as had been the fact at the time when He uttered the words of xv. 1 ff. It is probable, therefore, that, when uttering the 16th verse, Jesus puts Himself again on His course of march, the disciples following Him at some distance. This explains how they can be conversing with each other, as is related in vv. 17, 18. The words : *I go away to my Father*, were perhaps the signal for starting.—The objections of the disciples are natural, from their point of view. Where for us all is clear, for them all was mysterious. If Jesus wishes to found the Messianic kingdom, why go away ? If He does not wish it, why return ? Then, how can they imagine these contrary phases which are to be accomplished one after another ? Finally : *I come, because I go away !* Is there not reason for their crying out : *We do not understand what He says* (ver. 18) ? All this clearly proves the truth of the narrative ; could a later writer have thus placed himself in the very quick of this situation ? Καὶ ὅτι : "*and this, because.*" This word increases for them the difficulty of understanding. There is, as it were, a kind of impatience in their manner of expression in ver. 18.

Vv. 19, 20. " *Now*[1] *Jesus knew that they desired*[2] *to ask him, and he said to them : Do you inquire among yourselves concerning this that I said : In a little while you will not see me, and again in a little while you will see me.* 20. *Verily, verily, I say to you that you will weep and lament, but the world will rejoice ; you*[3] *will be sorrowful, but your sorrow will be turned into joy.*"—Jesus anticipates their question, and gives them a last proof of His higher knowledge, not only by showing them that He knew of Himself the questions which occupy their thoughts, but also by solving, as far as possible at this moment, all these enigmas. Only, instead of explaining to them the supreme facts which are about to succeed each other so rapidly—an explanation which they could not understand—He limits Himself to describing to them the opposite feelings through which they will themselves suddenly pass, and which will be the consequences of these facts : the greatest joy will suddenly succeed to the greatest grief ; and all this will be brief, like the hour of childbirth for a woman ; there would only be needed for Jesus time for

---

[1] ℵ B D L omit ουν after εγνω.
[2] ℵ : ημελλον instead of ηθελον.
[3] ℵ A D A It^plerique Syr.^sch Cop. omit δέ (*but*).

going to His Father and returning. It is a terrible hour for them to pass through ; but He cannot give them escàpe from it ; and after this, their joy will be unmingled and their power without limits. Such are the contents of vv. 20-24.—The tears and lamentations of ver. 20 find their explanation in ch. xx., in the tears of Mary Magdalene and in the entire condition of the disciples after the death of Jesus. The appearances of the Risen One only half healed this wound ; the perfect and enduring joy was only given on the day of Pentecost (ver. 22). The words : *But the world shall rejoice*, as far as : *sorrowful*, are not the real antithesis of the first clause. They form only a secondary contrast. The real antithesis of the first clause is in the last words of the verse : *But your sorrow shall be turned into joy.* The ἀλλά, *but*, expresses this opposition strongly, while marking the contrast with the clause which immediately precedes.

Vv. 21, 22. "*A woman, when she is in travail, has sorrow, because her hour is come ; but when she has brought forth the child, she remembers no more her anguish for the joy she has that a[1] man is born into the world.* 22. *And you also now have sorrow ;[2] but I will see you again, and your heart shall rejoice ; and your joy no one shall take[3] from you.*"—The point of comparison is the sudden passage from extreme sorrow to extreme joy. It must be limited to this. The idea of the bringing forth of a new world, which is to result from this hour of anguish, does not seem to be in the thought of Jesus.—The expression *her hour* perhaps alludes to the sorrowful hour through which Jesus Himself is to pass (*my* hour). The word *a man* sets forth the greatness of the event accomplished, and gives the ground of the mother's joy.

Ver. 22 makes the application of the comparison. The term : *I will see you*, cannot be synonymous with : *you shall see me* (vv. 16, 17, 19). The fact of the spiritual seeing again is presented here from the point of view of Jesus, not of the disciples. The death of Jesus not only separated the disciples from Him, but also *Him* from the disciples. He Himself, when transporting Himself to this moment, said in ver. 4 : "When *I was* with you ;" and after His resurrection, in Luke xxiv. 44 : "When I was *yet* with you." It is for this reason that, not being able at that time to keep them Himself, He prays the Father to keep them in His stead (xvii. 12, 13). There is no longer between Him and them the bond of sensible communion, and there is not yet that of spiritual communion. For this reason, when He shall return to them spiritually, it will be a seeing again for Him as well as for them. After this interval, in which He no longer Himself held the reins of their life, will come the day of Pentecost, when He will again have the flock under His own hand, and will sovereignly govern them from the midst of His divine state. The resurrection in itself alone could not yet form this new bond. Weiss has therefore no good foundation for finding in this expression : *I will see you again*, a proof in favor of his explanation (comp. ver. 25). The last words : *and no one*, are to be explained according to him in the sense that, even when the Risen One had once departed, the joy of the resurrection never-

---

[1] ℵ reads ο before ανθρωπος.
[2] A D L 12 Mnn. It^{aliq} Cop.: εξετε instead of εχετε.
[3] B D Γ It^{aliq}: αρει (*shall take*), instead of αιρει (*takes*).

theless continued in the hearts of the disciples ; but see on ver. 24.—The present αἴρει, *takes away*, is the true reading. Jesus transports Himself in thought to that day.

Vv. 23, 24. "*At that day you shall not question me as to anything : verily, verily, I say to you, that all that which*[1] *you shall ask the Father,*[2] *he will give it to you in my name.* 24. *Hitherto you have asked nothing in my name ; ask,*[3] *and you shall receive, that your joy may be fulfilled.*"—Jesus here describes the privileges connected with this spiritual seeing again, the source for them of the joy promised in ver. 22. They will be : a full *knowledge* (ver. 23a) and a full *power* (ver. 23b). In the first clause the emphasis is on ἐμέ, *me* (the accentuated form); they will have no need to ask *Him*, as visibly present, concerning what shall appear to them obscure and mysterious, as they had the intention to do at this moment (ver. 19). Having the Paraclete within them, they will be able to ask all freely and directly from the Father (comp. xiv. 12–14). The reading of A : ὅ, τι ἄν, *whatsoever*, may well be the true one. After having changed this ὅ, τι into ὅτι, *because*, one of the pronouns ὅ or ὅσα was necessarily added as an object ; then the ὅτι was omitted as useless (*Meyer*). *Weiss* prefers, with *Tischendorf*, the ἄν τι of the *Vatican* MS., which was altered in consequence of the introduction of the recitative ὅτι. In any case, the sense is the same. It is very evident that so considerable a change in their relation to God and Christ as that which is here promised to the apostles could not have resulted from the appearances of the Risen One. *Weiss* endeavors in vain to maintain this application. Acts i. 6 proves clearly that after the resurrection the disciples did not cease to ask questions of Jesus personally when they saw Him again. So *Weiss* gives to ἐρωτᾷν here, not its ordinary meaning *to ask a question*, but the meaning *to ask for* a thing, a meaning which it sometimes has certainly (iv. 31, 40, 47, xiv. 16, etc. : to ask whether one will give). But why in this case use two different verbs (ἐρωτᾷν and αἰτεῖν) to say the same thing ? And, above all, the relation to ver. 19 and ver. 30 absolutely excludes this meaning. The word ἐρωτᾷν has certainly the meaning to inquire (to ask light), and αἰτεῖν the more general sense of praying, to ask a gift or help. Jesus therefore means : "You will no longer address your questions to me, as when I was visibly with you ; and in general I declare to you that as to what you may have need of, you will be able, because[1] of the communion established henceforth through the Holy Spirit between yourselves and Him (your Father), to address yourselves directly to Him."—The limiting phrase *in my name* would refer, according to the T. R., which has in its favor some Mjj. and the ancient versions, to the word *ask ;* to this ver. 24 also points ; nevertheless, this reading may come from the parallel passages in xiv. 13 and 26, and from the following verse. These words should be placed with the *Vatican* and *Sinaitic* MSS., etc., at the end of the verse, in connection with the verb *to give*.

---

[1] Instead of οτι οσα αν which the T. R. reads with 10 Mjj. Mnn., A reads οτι (probably ο τι) αν, B C D L Y It. Orig. αν τι, ℵ οτι ο αν, X some Mnn. οτι ο εαν.

[2] ℵ B C L X Y Δ Sah. Orig. place εν τ. ονομ.

μου (*in my name*) after δωσει υμιν (*will give you*), while T. R. with A D Γ Λ Π It. Syr. place these words after τον πατερα (*the Father*).

[3] ℵ some Mnn. read αιτησασθε instead of αιτειτε.

878 / The Development of Faith

It is on the basis of the divine revelation which God has given of Jesus to believers and of the knowledge which they have received from Him, that He will give to them the gifts and helps thus promised.—But as this full revelation of Jesus is made in their hearts only by the Spirit (xiv. 17–23), it follows that until the day of Pentecost the disciples could not have really prayed *in the name of Jesus*. There is therefore no reproach in the words: "Hitherto you have not prayed in my name," as if Jesus meant that they had been wanting in faith or zeal ; it is simply the true indication of their moral state up to the time of the inward revelation which the Spirit will effect within them. From that moment, united in heart with Him, they will be able to pray as if they were Himself. By the present imperative : *ask* (αἰτεῖτε), Jesus transports Himself to this great day which is foretold. Perfect and enduring joy will then take the place of the extreme grief of a moment.—Jesus, however, perceives how all this must remain obscure to them. He acknowledges this, and refers them to that very day itself which He has just promised them, when everything will be finally made clear for them.

Vv. 25–27.—"*I have spoken these things to you in similitudes ; but*[1] *the hour is coming when*[2] *I shall no more speak to you in similitudes, but when I shall speak*[3] *to you openly of the Father.* 26. *In that day ye will need only to ask in my name ; and I say not to you that I will pray the Father for you ;* 27, *for the Father himself loves you, because you have loved me and have believed that I came forth from God.*"[4]—It is not necessary to understand by the *similitudes* of which Jesus speaks the figures of the vine and the branches or the woman in childbirth, which He has just used, still less of the parables which have been preserved for us by the Synoptics. He means to characterize in general the manner of speaking of divine things in figurative language; comp. the terms *Father's house, way, to come, to see again, to manifest oneself, to make one's abode,* etc. It belongs only to the Spirit to speak the language which is really adequate to the divine truth. All teaching in words is but a figure, so long as the Spirit Himself does not explain. Παρρησία here: *in appropriate terms*, which do not compromise the idea by exposing it to a false interpretation; comp. xi. 14. On the word παροιμία, see x. 6.—We may hesitate between the two verbs ἀπαγγέλλειν which signifies rather *to announce* (Alex.) and ἀναγγέλλειν, *to declare* (Byz.).—From the words περὶ τοῦ πατρός, *concerning the Father*, Weiss concludes that this promise can bear only upon the contents of vv. 23, 24, and that the expression to speak *in figures* refers only to the symbolic term *Father* by which Jesus has just designated God. But how can we in a natural way explain in this sense the plurals ταῦτα and παροιμίαι ? Then *Keil* asks with good reason if the name of Father was for Jesus a simple figure. Is it not evident that the question here is of the teaching of the Holy Spirit, which will be a revelation of the Father, of His character, His will, His plans with relation to

---

[1] ℵ B C D Γ X Y It^{plerique} Orig. omit αλλα (*but*):

[2] ℵ reads οπου instead of οτε.

[3] The MSS. are divided between απαγγελω (ℵ A B etc.) and αναγγελω (E G H etc.).

[4] Instead of θεου (*God*), B C D L X 2 Mnn. Syr^{sch} Cop. Sah. read πατρος (*the Father*).

humanity ? Besides, *Weiss* finds himself obliged, from ver. 25 onward, to acknowledge that there can be no longer a question as to the appearances of the Risen One, since the language in which Jesus spoke with His disciples after His resurrection did not differ at all from the ordinary human language which He had made use of previously. But how is it that he does not see that in acknowledging that the state described from ver. 25 onward is that which will follow the day of Pentecost, he retracts by this very fact his whole previous interpretation from ch. xiv. onward ? For ver. 26 evidently does not describe a different state from that in vv. 23, 24 ; the-*day* of which ver. 26 speaks and that of which vv. 23 and 25 speak cannot be any other than that of xiv. 20-23. Why should not the *speaking openly of the Father* be the inward fact described in xiv. 23: "The Father and I, we will come and make our abode with him." And if the expression : *I will openly announce* in our ver. 25 refers to the day of Pentecost, as *Weiss* concedes, why should it not be the parallel of the : *I will come again* of xiv. 18 ?

The declaration of ver. 26 seems, at the first glance, to contradict that of xiv. 16. But in this latter passage, Jesus is still speaking of the time which will precede the day of Pentecost ; He says that He will pray for the disciples, *in order that* He may be able to send the Spirit to them ; here, on the contrary, the Paraclete is supposed to be already present and acting in them; this is the reason why they pray themselves to the Father in the name of Jesus, because they are in direct communication with Him. Consequently, as long as they abide in this state of union with God, the intercession of Jesus (Rom. viii. 34, Heb. vii. 25) is not necessary for them. But as soon as they sin, they have need of *the advocate with the Father, Jesus Christ the righteous* (1 John ii 1, 2). The expression : *I say not that I will pray,* is very admirably adapted to this state. He does not say that He will pray ; for so long as they shall be in the normal state of fidelity, they will have no need of this ; He prays then *through* them, not *for* them. Nevertheless, He does not say that He will not pray; for it may be that they will still have need of His intercession, if any separation intervenes between them and the Father. We see how completely *Grotius* and others have mistaken the idea in understanding the words : "I say not to you that . . ." in the sense : "*not to say that* I also will pray for you." This is to make Jesus say just the contrary of His thought, as is clearly shown by ver. 27.

On the words : *The Father loves you because you have loved me,* comp. xiv. 21, 23. The perfect tenses indicate a condition already gained : "Because you *are become* those who love me and believe. . . ." In general Jesus does not place faith after love; but here He speaks of a special faith, of the belief in His divine origin. They were heartily attached to His person for a long time before comprehending all His greatness, as they were beginning to comprehend it now.—Jesus comes back in these words from the future, the day of Pentecost, to the work now accomplished in them, because this is the condition and basis of that future (xiv. 17). And in fact the supreme moment is approaching : it is time to affix the seal to this faith now already formed. To this end, Jesus formulates the essential contents of it in a definite proposition : "you have believed *that I came forth from God.*" *Tischendorf* himself rejects the reading of the *Sinaitic* MS. and the other thirteen Mjj. which read : *from the Father*, instead of : *from God*. It is the *divine* origin and mission of Jesus, and not His *filial* relation with God, which must be emphasized at this moment as the essential object of the apostles' faith. The case is wholly different in ver. 28. The preposition παρά, *from*, and the verb ἐξῆλθον, *I came forth*, express more than the simple mission, which would be designated by ἀπό and ἐλήλυθα ; these terms characterize the divine sphere, in general, from which Jesus derives His origin. They well bring out the heroism of the apostles' faith. In this being of flesh and bones, this weak, despised man, they have been able to recognize a being who came to them from the divine abode.

Ver. 28. "*I came forth from*[1] *the Father, and am come into the world; and again I leave the world and go to the Father.*"—What the disciples had the most difficulty in understanding was that Jesus should leave the world where, in their thought, the Messianic kingdom was to be realized. They had, moreover, no clear idea of the place to which He was going. Jesus starts from what is more clear, in order to explain to them what is less so. They have believed and understood that His *origin* is divine, that He has not, like the rest of men, behind His earthly existence, nothingness, but the bosom of the Father (ver. 27). Hence it follows that this world is for Him only a place of passage, that He has *come* to it, and come only to do a work in it, not to establish Himself here. What more natural, then, than that, when once this work is accomplished, He should leave the world, in which He found Himself only for a special purpose, and should *return* to God His true home ? The ascension is the natural counterpart of the incarnation, and the divine future derives its light from the divine past. The symmetry of the four clauses of this verse throws an unexpected light on the history of Jesus and on each of the four great phases in which it is summed up : self-renunciation, incarnation, death, ascension. The expression *come forth from God* indicates the renouncing of the divine state, the divesting Himself of the μορφὴ θεοῦ (*the form of God*) according to the language of Paul (Phil. ii. 6) ; the : *come into the world*, the entrance into the human state and into the earthly existence, the : *being made flesh* (i. 14), or the : *taking the form of a servant* (Phil. ii. 7). The *leaving the world* does not indicate the abandoning of the human nature, but the rupture of the *earthly* form of human existence. For Stephen also beholds Jesus glorified in the form of the Son of man (Acts vii. 56), and it is as Son of man that Jesus reigns and comes again (Matt. xxvi. 64, Luke xviii. 8).—Finally, the *going to the Father* designates the exaltation of Jesus, in His human nature, to the divine state which He enjoyed as Logos before the incarnation.—The Alexandrian reading ἐκ, *out of*, has, as *Lücke* himself has remarked, a dogmatic savor which is of too pronounced a character to be the true one (comp. i. 18). Παρά, *from*, in the Sinaitic MS. and the other Mjj. includes, as in ver. 27, the two ideas of the *origin* and the *mission*.—Jesus here says *the Father*, in-

---

[1] Instead of παρα (*from*), B C L X 2 Mnn. Cop. Orig. read εκ (*out of*).

stead of *God* (ver. 27). The question is no longer, indeed, of the contents of the apostolic faith, as in ver. 27. All the tenderness of His filial relation to the Father, which He has renounced, pictures itself to His thought. The term πάλιν, *again*, which might be translated by : *in return*, indicates the correlation between the coming and the departure ; it is as it were a : consequently ; for the one justifies the other. The apostles understand that if He *goes away*, it is because He has *come;* and that if He goes *to God*, it is because He has come *from God*.

Vv. 29, 30. " *His disciples say to him*,[1] *Lo, now thou speakest plainly, and dost use no similitude ;* 30, *now we know that thou knowest all things and hast no need that any one should ask thee ; for this we believe that thou camest forth from God.*"—On hearing this simple and precise recapitulation of all the mysteries of His past, present and future existence, the disciples are, as it were, surrounded by an unexpected brightness ; a unanimous and spontaneous confession comes from their lips; the doubts which were tormenting them from the beginning of their conversations are scattered ; it seems to them that they have nothing more to desire in the matter of illumination, and that they have already arrived at the day of that perfect knowledge which Jesus has just promised to them. Not that they have the folly to mean to affirm, contrary to the word of Him whose omniscience they are proclaiming at this very moment, that the time is already come which has just been promised them as yet to come ; but the light is so clear that they know not how to conceive of a more brilliant one. By answering so directly the thoughts which were agitating them in the centre of their hearts, Jesus has given them the measure of the truth of His words in general and of the certainty of all His promises. They have just had, like Nathanael at the beginning, experience of His omniscience, and, like him, they infer from it His divine character.—The relation of the words : *Thou hast no need that any one should ask thee*, to those of ver. 19 : *Jesus knew that they wished to ask him*, is beyond dispute ; only this relation must be understood in a broad sense and one worthy of this solemn scene (in answer to *Meyer*).—In the confession of the disciples, as in the expression *Son of God*, i. 50, the two ideas of divine mission (ἀπό) and origin (ἐξῆλθες) are mingled.

Vv. 31–33. " *Jesus answered them : Now you believe.* 32. *Behold, the hour is coming, and is now*[2] *come, when you shall be scattered every one to his own home, and when you shall leave me alone; but I am not alone, because the Father is with me.* 33. *I have said these things to you, that in me you may have peace ; in the world you shall have*[3] *tribulation ; but be of good courage, I have overcome the world.*"—Here is for Jesus a moment of unutterable sweetness ; He is recognized and understood—He Jesus—by these eleven Galileans. This is for Him enough ; His work is for the moment ended ; the Holy Spirit will finish it by glorifying Him in them, and through them in mankind. There remains nothing further for Him but to close the conversation and give thanks. John alone understood the greatness

[1] ℵ B C D A Π 2 Mnn. It^{aliq} reject αυτω.
[2] ℵ A B C D L X Cop. omit νυν before εληλυθεν.
[3] Instead of εξετε (*you shall have*) which T. R. reads with D some Mnn. It^{plerique}, εχετε (*you have*) is read in the other documents.

of this moment, and has preserved for us the remembrance of it. The words : *Now you believe*, must not therefore be understood in an interrogative, and in some sort ironical sense, as if Jesus would call in question the reality of their faith. I do not think even that ἄρτι, *now*, forms a contrast with the very near want of fidelity to which Jesus is about to allude, as if He would say : "True, you believe now ; but in a short time, how will you be acting !" Could Jesus, in ch. xvii., give thanks to His Father with such outpouring of heart for a faith which He had just characterized in such a way ? Comp. especially xvii. 8 : "*They have known truly* (ἀληθῶς) *that I came out from thee, and they have believed that thou didst send me*," words in which Jesus certainly alludes to our ver. 30. The word *now*, therefore, seems to me rather to mean here : "Now at last you have reached the point to which I have been laboring to lead you : you have recognized me for what I am, and have received me as such."—The connection in ver. 32 is not a *but ;* it is a simple *no doubt ;* in ver. 33 will be found the final *but* answering to this *no doubt*. This scarcely formed faith is about to be subjected, it is true, to a severe test ; the bond will be broken, at least externally. But the spiritual bond will remain firm and will triumph over this trial and all others.—The νῦν, *now*, which we have rendered by *already*, is omitted by the Alexandrian authorities ; it may have been rejected because it seemed that the moment indicated was not yet present.— The first aorist passive σκορπισθῆτε, *you shall be scattered*, is more suited to extenuate than to aggravate the fault of the disciples ; it is, as it were, a violent blow which will strike and stun them. These words recall the quotation from Zechariah in the Synoptics : "*I will smite the shepherd, and the sheep shall be scattered*" (Matt. xxvii. 31). It is in the following words : "*you will leave me alone*," that the idea of culpable desertion is expressed, but in the tone of sadness rather than of reproach.— Ἔκαστος εἰς ἴδια, *each one to his own ;* each to his respective abode. Weiss finds in this expression the idea of the breaking off of the communion between them, as a sign of the shaking of their faith in the Messiah. It indicates rather the seeking of a secure shelter, far from the danger which touches their Master.—Καί, evidently in the adversative sense : *and yet*.

Ver. 32 reassures the disciples as to the person of their Master ; ver. 33 tranquillizes them for themselves. Everything that Jesus has said to them on this last evening should breathe into them a complete quietness, resting upon the foundation of the faith which they have in Him (xiv. 1). No doubt, He could not conceal from them that they would have to sustain a struggle with the world (xv. 18–xvi. 4). But in the presence of the tribulations which this struggle will bring, it is necessary that their peace should take the character of *assurance* and become courage, θάρσος.—There is an opposition between the two limiting terms : *in me* and *in the world ;* the first designates the sphere from which peace is drawn ; the other, the domain whence anguish arises. Ἐγώ, *I*, brings out with force the unique personality of Him who, having already overcome for Himself, makes His victory that of His followers. — The *victory* which Jesus has already gained is, above all, internal ; He has resisted the attractions of the world and surmounted its terrors. But there is more : this moral victory is about to be realized externally in the consummation of the redemptive work, on the cross accepted in advance, which will be henceforth the cause and the monument of the world's defeat. This victory will be continued by means of the Eleven, who will be the bearers of it here on earth.

3

John 17:1-26

THE PRAYER

The shout of victory with which Jesus closed His conversations with the disciples was an anticipation of faith. To transform the victory which was announced into a present reality, nothing less was needed than the action of the omnipotence of God. It is to Him that Jesus turns.

This prayer is ordinarily divided into three parts : 1. The prayer for His own person, vv. 1-5 ; 2. The prayer for His apostles, vv. 6-19; and 3. The prayer for the Church, vv. 20-26. And this is indeed the course of the prayer. But the thought is one : when Jesus prays for Himself, it is not His own person that He has in view, it is *the work of God* (see on vv. 1, 2); when He prays for His apostles, He commends them to God as agents and continuers of this work ; and when He extends His regard to all believers present or future, it is as if to the *objects* of this work, in other terms because these souls are the theatre where the glory of His Father is to shine forth ; for His work and the glory of the Father are for Him one and the same thing. The framework of the prayer is accordingly that which is indicated by the generally adopted division, but the single thought is that of the work of Christ, or *the glory of the Father*. This prayer is thus throughout an inspiration of the filial heart of Jesus.

This prayer is more than a simple meditation. Jesus had *acted* (ch. xiii.) and *spoken* (chs. xiv.-xvi.); now He uses the form of language which is, at the same time, word and act : He *prays*. But He does not only pray, He prays aloud ; and this proves that, while speaking to God, He speaks also for those who surround Him; not to show them how He prays, but to associate them in the intimate communion which He maintains with His Father, and to induce them *to pray with Him*. It is an anticipated realization of that communion in glory which He asks for them in ver. 24 : "*That they may behold the glory which thou hast given me ; that where I am, they also may be with me.*" He lifts them to the divine sphere where He Himself lives.

This prayer has been called *sacerdotal*. This is, indeed, the act of the High-Priest of mankind, who begins His sacrifice by offering Himself to God with all His people present and future.

Vv. 1-5 : Jesus asks again His divine glory.

Vv. 1, 2. "*These things spoke*[1] *Jesus ; then he lifted up*[2] *his eyes to heaven*

---

[1] ℵ : λελαληκεν instead of ελαλησεν.
[2] ℵ B C D L X 7 Mnn. It^aliq Vulg. Cop. : επαρας ... ειπεν (*having lifted up ... he said*),
instead of επηρε ... και ειπεν, which T. R reads with A and 12 Mjj. It^aliq Syr.

and said : Father, the hour is come; glorify thy Son, that thy Son[1] also[2] may glorify thee; 2, as thou hast given[3] him power over all flesh, that to all those whom thou hast given him he should give[4] eternal life."—If Jesus had uttered the preceding words on the way from Jerusalem to Gethsemane, He must now have been on the point of crossing the brook Cedron. At this decisive moment, He collects Himself and prays. — The words : *He spoke these things*, clearly distinguish the preceding discourses from the solemn act of prayer. This also is indicated by the lifting the eyes towards heaven. Until this point, Jesus had looked upon the disciples while speaking to them. To raise the eyes towards heaven is a natural effort of the soul to the end of escaping from the earthly prison, an aspiration after beholding the living God, whose glory is, above all, resplendent in the pure serenity of the heavens. No doubt this act can have taken place in a room (Acts vii. 55) ; but it is much more easily intelligible in the open air ; comp. xi. 41, Mark vii. 34. The words : *And he said*, mark the moment when, beyond the visible heaven, His heart met the face of God, and when in the God of the universe He beholds His Father. The Alexandrian reading : "*having lifted up his eyes, he said,*" is more flowing and more in the Greek style ; the received reading : "*he lifted up his eyes and said,*" is more simple and Hebraistic ; could this be a proof in favor of the first ? — The name *Father* expresses the spirit of the whole prayer which is to follow. Jesus certainly employed the Aramaic term *Abba;* comp. Mark xiv. 36. This term, in which He was accustomed to concentrate the holiest emotions of His filial heart, became sacred to the Christians, and passed as such into the language of the New Testament, as the expression of the sentiment of divine adoption and filial adoration (Rom. viii. 15, Gal. iv. 6). — The *hour* is that of which John and Jesus Himself had said many times, in the course of this Gospel, that *it was not yet come:* it is that of His exaltation through death. But in order that it may result in the glorification of the Son, the intervention of the Father will be necessary ; this is what Jesus asks for by the word : *Glorify!* Some explain this glorification of Jesus by the *moral perfection* which, with the divine aid, He will cause to shine forth in His sufferings, and by the *attractive power* which He will thus exercise over the hearts of men. These explanations are, as *Reuss* acknowledges, incompatible with ver. 5, where we see beyond question that Jesus is thinking of His *personal* reinstatement in the divine state which He had had before His incarnation. Only it is not necessary to restrict this glory which Jesus asks again—as the orthodox interpreters in general suppose—to the enjoyment of divine blessedness and glory. For the aim of this request of Jesus is not His own satisfaction, but the continuation and finishing of His work, as is shown by the following words : *that thy Son may glorify thee.* What He desires is new means of action. He asks consequently for the restoration to His complete divine state, the possession of the divine omnipresence, omniscience and

[1] ℵ B C It^{aliq} omit σου after υιος (*the son*, instead of *thy son*).
[2] ℵ A B C D 3 Mnn. It^{plerique} Vulg. Syr. Cop. Orig. omit και (*also*) after ινα.
[3] Alex.: δεδωκας instead of εδωκας (this variant is almost constantly repeated throughout this passage).
[4] Instead of δωση αυτοις (T. R. with 7 Mjj), 9 Mjj (B E H etc.): δωσει αυτοις ; ℵ : δωσω αυτω.

omnipotence of which He had divested Himself in order to appropriate to Himself a true human state. He cannot continue to glorify God and to develop the work of salvation, the foundation of which is now laid, except on this condition. His personal state must be transformed quite as much as it was transformed when Jesus passed from the divine state to the human existence. He speaks of Himself in the third person : *thy Son*. This is what we always do when we wish to draw the attention of the one to whom we address ourselves to what we are *for him*. There is nothing suspicious, therefore, in this manner of speaking which John attributes to Jesus. It is, moreover, in conformity with the ordinary manner in which He speaks of Himself in the Synoptics, where He habitually designates Himself by the title : the Son of man. What would be more justly open to suspicion, would be the form presented by the Alexandrian reading, which is adopted by *Tischendorf* and defended by *Weiss* and *Westcott:* "that *the Son may glorify thee.*" Instead of expressing the filial feeling of Jesus, as the received text "*thy* Son " does, this reading has a purely dogmatic tinge, precisely as in the analogous passages i. 18 and xvi. 28. — The particle καί after ἵνα, "that *also*," is omitted by the Alexandrian authorities and is rejected by *Tischendorf*, etc. But this little word may easily have been omitted. It brings out well the relation between the glorification of the Father by the Son and that of the Son by the Father, and consequently the filial spirit which animates this petition : Jesus wishes to be glorified by His Father only that He may be able *in His turn* to glorify Him.

Ver. 2 is an explanatory annex to ver. 1. Jesus reminds the Father of that which gives Him the right to say to Him : *Glorify me!* In praying thus, He acts only in conformity with the decree of God Himself : *As thou hast given him power*. This gift consists in the decree by which God conferred the sovereignty over the whole human race (*all flesh*) upon the Son, when He sent Him to fulfil here on earth His mission of Saviour (x. 36) ; comp. Eph. i. 10. — The work of salvation which He has to fulfil in the midst of mankind has indeed as its condition the position of Lord ; comp. Matt. xxviii. 18 : " All power has been given to me," a passage in which the sovereignty which has been gained serves as a basis for the command to teach and baptize all the nations—that is to say, to take possession of them. — The second clause : *that he may give life,* is parallel to the second clause of ver. 1 : *that he may glorify thee*. The true means of glorifying God is to communicate eternal life—that is to say, to associate men with the life of God. In presenting the aim of His petition under this new aspect, Jesus therefore gives the ground for it in a different way. His petition is equivalent to saying : "Grant me the Ascension, that I may be able to bring to pass the Pentecost." For it is through the gift of the Holy Spirit that Jesus communicates life to believers (vii. 37-39). *Weiss* does not recognize this relation, which is so simple, between the life and the Spirit, and wishes to see here only the *extension* of the action of Jesus to the whole world.— Πᾶν, all, designates the future body of believers, that unity, that ἕν (of which ver. 33, xi. 52, Eph. ii. 14, speak) which God has eternally completed and given to the Son (Rom. viii. 28). The word πᾶν is a nominative absolute :

comp. vi. 39. Afterwards, the same idea is taken up again and placed in its regular case in the limiting word αὐτοῖς, *to them*. This plural pronoun individualizes the contents of the totality, which is the object of the gift. For if the gift made by God to Christ is a collective act including every one who believes, the communication of life by Christ to believers is an individual fact.—The term : *that which thou hast given him*, recalls the expressions of ch. vi : "those whom the Father *teaches, draws, gives* to the Son" (vv. 37, 44, 45, 65) ; they are those whom the influence of the law and prophecy lead with eagerness for salvation to the feet of Jesus.—The form δώσῃ is not Greek ; it recurs, however, in Apoc. viii. 3 and xiii. 16 in some MSS. We must see in it either a future subjunctive, a later form of which some examples, it is thought, are found in the New Testament (*Bäumlein* cites ὄψησθε, Luke xiii. 28 ; καυθήσωμαι, 1 Cor. xiii. 3 ; κερδηθήσωνται, 1 Pet. iii. 1 ; εὑρήσῃς, Apoc. xviii. 14) ; or may it be the subjunctive of an incorrect aorist ἔδωσα, instead of ἔδωκα ? It would indeed have been difficult to say δώκῃ. But the true reading is perhaps δώσει (*Vatic.*), of which it was thought a subjunctive must be made because of the ἵνα (comp. the reading γινώσκωσι in ver. 3). The reading δώσω in the *Sinaitic* MS. is incompatible with the third person used throughout the whole passage. The reading αὐτῷ, *to it* (the πᾶν), in the same MS., is also an evident correction.—The meaning of the expression : *all that which thou hast given him*, is less extensive than that of the term *all flesh ;* it refers only to believers. If Jesus has received power over *every man* living, it is with reference to *believers* whom it is His mission to save. Comp. Eph. i. 22 : "He has given Him *to the Church as head over all things*," that is to say, as *its* head, who, at the same time, is on its behalf established over all things.

Ver. 3 establishes the connection between the idea of *glorifying God* (ver. 1) and that of *giving eternal life* (ver. 2) : to live is to know God ; to glorify God is, accordingly, to give life by giving the knowledge of Him.

Ver. 3. "*Now this is eternal life, that they should know thee, the only true God, and him whom thou has sent, Jesus Christ.*"—Jesus contemplates that eternal life in which He is to make mankind participate ; He fathoms the essence of it ; it is the *knowledge* of God. Such a knowledge is certainly not, in His thought, a purely rational fact. The Scriptures always take the word *know* in a more profound sense. When the question is of the relation between two persons, this word designates the perfect intuition which each has of the moral being of the other, their intimate meeting together in the same luminous medium. Jesus has described in xiv. 21–23 the revealing act from which there will result for His own this only real knowledge of God. It is the work of the Spirit, making Jesus, and with Him God, dwell in us.—The epithet *only* neither refers, as *Luthardt* says, to the word *true*, nor to the word *God*, but to the entire phrase *true God*. The term ἀληθινός, *true*, declares that this God is the only one who answers perfectly to the idea expressed by the word God. How is it possible not to find here, with *Meyer*, the contrast to manifold divinities and divinities unworthy of this name which appertained to the reigning polytheism ? I do not see how *Weiss* can refuse to admit this tacit antithesis. It suits precisely the idea of the extension of Christ's action beyond the limits of Israel, which is, according to him, the idea of ver. 2. Does not the word *all flesh* call up the image of all these peoples foreign to Israel, which compose the idolatrous portion of mankind ?—But *Meyer* is certainly mistaken in making the words : *the only true God*, the attribute of σέ, *thee* : "recognize thee *as* the only. . . ." In this construction the word *know* takes a meaning too intellectual and one contrary to the part here ascribed to the knowledge as being one with the life itself. The expression : the only true God, is appositional with σέ : "*to know thee, thyself, the only true God.*" Thus the word *to know* preserves the profound and living sense which it should have. This does not at all exclude the contrast with polytheism indicated above.

If Jesus had prayed only with a view to Himself, He would have limited Himself to these words : "*That they should know thee, the only true God.*" But He prays aloud, and consequently associating in His prayer those who surround Him. This is the reason why He adds : "*and him whom thou hast sent, Jesus Christ.*" While rendering homage to God, as the first source of eternal life, He has the consciousness of being Himself the sole intermediate agent through whom those who listen to Him can have access to this source ; for it is in Him that God manifests and gives Himself (xiv. 6). The possession of eternal life is identified therefore in His view, for all that is called man, with the knowledge of Himself, Jesus, as well as with that of God. Since *Augustine,* some interpreters (*Lampe,* etc.) have made the words "(*him*) *whom thou hast sent,*" etc., a second apposition to σέ, *thee*. The aim of this impossible construction is evidently to save the divinity of Christ ; but this is exposed to no danger with the natural construction. The words : "*Him whom thou hast sent,*" are certainly the object of the verb *that they should know*. No more need we make the word *Christ* the attribute of *Jesus :* "that they should know Jesus whom thou hast sent as the Christ ;" this construction would bring us back to the intellectual sense of the word *know*. The words *Jesus Christ* are in apposition with the object, *him whom thou hast sent*. But we need not unite them in one single proper name, in conformity with the later use of this phrase, as *Weiss, Reuss* and some others do, who see in such an expression, which could not, as they say, be placed in the mouth of Jesus Himself, a proof of the freedom with which the evangelist has reproduced this prayer. *Tholuck* also finds here a coming in of the later ecclesiastical language ; even *Westcott* regards these words, as well as the preceding ones : *the only true God,* as glosses due to the evangelist who is explaining the Master's prayer—an explanation which is indeed certainly superfluous. *Bretschneider* is the one who has most severely criticised this form ; he sees in it a gross historical impropriety from which he derives a proof against the authenticity of the Gospel. We think that this objection, on the contrary, springs from the fact that one does not place himself, in a sufficiently living way, in the historical situation in which this prayer was uttered. Until now, Jesus had always avoided assuming before the people the title of *Christ*. Rather than use this term, subject to so many misapprehensions, when the ordinary designation *Son of man* was not sufficient, He had had recourse to more strange circumlocutions (viii. 24, x. 25 ff.). He had acted in the same way in the circle of His disciples (xiii. 13, 19). Once only, and by way of exception, in Samaria, on non-Jewish ground, He had openly assumed the title of Messiah (iv. 26). In the Synoptics, He conducts Himself in the same way. Matt. xvi. 20, while accepting Peter's confession, He takes occasion to forbid the disciples to designate Him publicly as the Christ. This reticence must not continue to the end. And since the moment was come when the new word of command for mankind, *Jesus Messiah*, was to be proclaimed throughout the whole earth by the apostles, it was necessary that once at least they should hear it coming expressly from the lips of their Master Himself. And under what more favorable circumstances and in what more solemn form could this watchword of the new religion be proclaimed than in this last conversation with His Father, which was setting the seal upon His whole work ? This is what Jesus does in this solemn formula : *Jeschouah hammaschiach* (*Jesus Messiah*). John has not therefore committed an inadvertence here. He has faithfully reproduced this inexpressibly serious and thrilling moment, when he heard Jesus Himself, by this declaration, explicitly sanction at last the faith which had not ceased to develop itself within him since the day when he for the first time drew near to Jesus (i. 42)—that faith which he and his colleagues had henceforth the mission of preaching to the world. Would to God that all the confessions of faith, throughout the Church, had always been, like this, acts of adoration !—It has been objected that the word $\chi\rho\iota\sigma\tau\acute{o}\nu$, without the article, can only be regarded as a proper name. But comp. ix. 22, where John says, " If any one confessed him as the Christ," without using the article. As to i. 17, we have there the technical form indeed, but as a reproduction by the pen of the evangelist of the more living form which is found in our prayer.—This second clause of the verse separates the new religion from Judaism, as the first does from Paganism.—The Arians and Socinians have combated the divinity of Jesus Christ by means of this verse in which Jesus is placed beside and apart from the only true God. But John takes the same course in speaking of the Logos, i. 1. No one is more express in his statements of subordination than John. And yet, at the same time, no one teaches more distinctly the participation of Jesus, as the Word, in the Divine nature. In this very verse Jesus is presented as the *object*, and not only as the *intermediate agent*, of the knowledge which *is* eternal life. How could the knowledge of a creature be the life of the human soul ?—The conjunction $\mathit{\tilde{\iota}\nu\alpha}$, *that*, is used here rather than $\mathit{\tilde{o}\tau\iota}$, because this knowledge is presented as an *end* to be reached, the supreme good to be obtained.—After this outpouring, Jesus returns to the prayer of ver. 1 ; He presents to God in a new form the same ground to justify the petition : *Glorify me!* He insists on all that He, Jesus, has already done, to establish on the earth this twofold knowledge which is eternal life, and on the actual necessity of a change in His position in order to finish this divine work (vv. 4, 5).

Vv. 4, 5. "*I have glorified thee on the earth; I have accomplished[1] the work which thou hast given me to do. 5. And now, Father, glorify thou me, with thyself, with the glory which I had with thee before the world was.*"—After having thus described the life which He desires to communicate to the world, Jesus returns to His request: *Glorify me*, in ver. 1. He has founded this request on what He is to do in the future; He now justifies it by what He has already done hitherto. As far as He has been able to do it here below, in His earthly condition, He has *glorified* God, He has caused His holy and good character to shine in the hearts of men. But to do more than this, He must have a new position, with new means of activity. It is thus that in ver. 4 the way is prepared for the repetition of His petition in ver. 5.—The Alexandrian reading τελειώσας, *having accomplished*, seems to me much more after the Greek than the Hebrew style,—in other terms, much more Alexandrian than apostolic. The juxtaposition of the two verbs in the T. R. is therefore, in my view, preferable to their syntactic fitting to each other in the other text.—The words: "*I have accomplished the work*," express with a sublime candor the feeling of a perfectly pure conscience. He does not perceive in His life, at this supreme moment, either any evil committed or even any good omitted. The duty of every hour has been perfectly fulfilled. There has been in this human life which He has now behind Him, not only no spot, but no deficiency with reference to the task of making the divine perfection shine forth resplendently.

Ver. 5. The most potent means of action of which He has need in order to continue this task, He can only obtain by recovering His state anterior to the incarnation. And this is the purpose for which He asks it again. There cannot be any temerity on His part in doing this, since this state of divine glory appertains to His nature, and He has voluntarily renounced it in order to serve God here on earth.—By the words: *with thyself*, Jesus opposes the divine sphere to that in which He is at present living (*on the earth*, ver. 4.), xiii. 32.—The expression: *the glory which I had*, is opposed to His present humiliation. No doubt, in His human state He has also a glory, even a glory "as that of the only begotten Son having come from the Father" (i. 14). But it differs from His heavenly glory as the dependent form of the human existence differs from the autonomous form of the divine existence. This filial position in relation to God, which He has as man, is only a reflection of the filial position which He has had as God. *Reuss* thinks that this verse does not imply absolute pre-existence, eternity, but only a certain priority with relation to the world. But from the biblical point of view, the *world* embraces all that appertains to the sphere of *becoming*, and beyond this sphere there is only *being*, eternity. Comp. the opposition between γίνεσθαι and εἶναι, i. 1, 3, viii. 58, and Ps. xc. 2.—Παρὰ σοί, *with thee*, cannot have the purely *ideal* sense which the Socinians give to it, and which now again *Beyschlag*[2] and *Sabatier* endeavor to maintain in somewhat different forms. This theory does violence to John's terms no

---

[1] ℵ A B C L Π 5 Mnn. It^aliq Syr. Cop.: τελειωσας (*having accomplished*) instead of ετελειωσα.

[2] Beyschlag at present appears to me to modify his point of view and to adopt two contradictory theories in our Gospel.

less than to those of Paul (Phil. ii. 6–11). He who says, *I had . . . with thee*, emphasizes *His* own personality previous to the incarnation, no less than that of God (ver. 24). The *I* who asks for the glory is the one who has had it. It is equally impossible to find here the least trace of the idea which Sabatier finds in the passage of Paul (Phil.),—that of a progress from the glory of Christ before His earthly life to His glory afterwards. The only difference between these two conditions is that this latter glory is possessed by Him even in His humanity, elevated to the sphere of the divine existence (Acts vii. 55, Matt. xxvi. 64, where the term *Son of man* is still applied to the glorified Christ). See on viii. 58.—From the fact that Jesus says : *before the world was*, and not "*before I came* into the world," Schelling[1] concluded that the humiliation of the Logos began from the time of the creation, and not only with the incarnation. This conclusion is not well founded exegetically. For Jesus only means here to oppose this glory to a glory which may have had some sort of beginning in time.

Vv. 6–19 : Jesus asks for the support of His apostles in faith and their full consecration to the divine work.

It seems to me that it is altogether wrong for *Weiss*, with *Lücke, de Wette*, etc., to connect the passage, vv. 6–8, with what precedes, as developing the work of Christ on the earth, and as still intended to give a ground for the first petition : *glorify me*. The question henceforth is rather of what the disciples have become through the work of Christ, to the end of giving a ground for the prayer on their behalf (ver. 9). As it is with a view to the work of God that He asks His own glory again, it is also in view of this work that He commends to His Father the instruments whom He has chosen and prepared for the purpose of continuing it. This prayer has first an altogether general character : *I pray for them*, ver. 9 ; then it is given, with precision and in form, in two distinct petitions : τήρησον, *keep them* (ver. 11), and ἁγίασον, *sanctify them* (ver. 17), which are the counterpart of the δόξασόν με, *glorify me*, for Jesus Himself. Vv. 6–8 prepare the way for the first general petition, for which vv. 9, 10 will finally give the grounds.

Vv. 6–8. "*I have manifested thy name to the men whom thou hast given*[2] *me out of the world ; thine they were, and thou hast given them to me ; and they have kept*[3] *thy word.* 7. *Now they have known*[4] *that all that thou hast given me is from thee.* 8. *For the words which thou hast given me I have given them ; and they have received them, and they have known*[5] *truly that I came forth from thee, and they have believed that thou didst send me.*"—The general idea expressed in these words is that of the *worth* which the apostles have acquired by the ministry of Jesus among them and by the success of this work. Thus is the way prepared for the prayer by which Jesus is about to commend them to the care of the Father. And first, what Jesus has done for them. The aorist ἐφανέρωσα, *I have manifested*, is connected with the similar aorists in ver. 4. The most important portion of the work which Jesus felicitates Himself in

---

[1] In his oral courses.
[2] Here, as elsewhere, the Alexandrian authorities read εδωκας instead of δεδωκας.
[3] א : ετηρησαν, instead of τετηρηκασι (B D L: τετηρηκαν).
[4] א : εγνων, instead of εγνωκαν.
[5] Και εγνωσαν is omitted by א A D It^{aliq}.

having accomplished (ver. 4) was precisely the preparation and education of these eleven persons.—The *name of God*, which He has revealed to them, designates the divine character fully manifested to the consciousness of Jesus Himself, and through Him to the disciples in proportion as the consciousness of their Master has become their own (Matt. xi. 25, 26). It is by revealing Himself as Son, that Jesus has revealed God to them as the Father. This is the reason why He must necessarily testify of Himself, as He does in the Fourth Gospel ; it was an essential element of His teaching respecting God.—After having recalled His labor on their behalf, Jesus recalls to the Father what He has Himself done for them. The apostles were *His*, and He has given them to Jesus. The question here is not of what they were as men and as Jews, but of the relation which they sustained to God through their inward disposition, as faithful Jews ; comp. the expressions : *to be of God* (vii. 17, viii. 47), *to be of the truth* (xviii. 37), *to do the truth* (iii. 21). These expressions designate the moral state of the Israelites or heathen who adhere to the light of the law or of conscience. These beings who belong to God, God has led to Jesus by the inward drawing or teaching of which He has spoken in vi. 37, 44, 45, 65. And He possesses them now as gifts of the Father.—Then, to what God and Jesus have done for the disciples, Jesus adds what the disciples have themselves done. This gift of themselves, once accomplished, they have faithfully maintained. Notwithstanding all the temptations to unfaithfulness which have assailed them during these years (Luke xxii. 28), they have kept in their heart the teaching of Jesus. They have preserved intact and pure from all alloy this *name* of God imprinted by Him upon their consciousness. The words "*thy* word," instead of "*my* word," are explained in ver. 7 : the word of Jesus has been only a reproduction of that of the Father. Finally, Jesus sets before the Father all that which the disciples have become through this communication which He has made to them of His Word. They have discerned its divine origin, and they have received it in this character. There is at the first glance a tautology in the two expressions: *which thou hast given me*, and : *is thine*. But the first is derived from the consciousness of Jesus ; the second is borrowed from that of the apostles : "They have recognized that all which I gave them from thee came really from thee." It is, that in fact (ver. 8.) Jesus never added anything to it from His own resources. Then, from the recognition of the absolutely divine character of His word, they are raised finally to the faith in the divine origin of His person (*I came forth*) and His mission (*thou hast sent me*). In these words there breathes also the feeling of inward joy and lively recognition which Jesus has just experienced a few moments before : for it is very recently that this result for which He blesses the Father at this moment has been obtained (xvi. 29–31). The harvest seems scanty, no doubt : eleven Galilean artisans after three years of labor ! But this is enough for Jesus : for in these eleven He beholds the pledge of the continuance of the divine work on the earth.—There is an advance in the three verbs of these two verses : "*They have known :*" on the authority of their consciousness ; "*they have received :*" by submission to this testimony ; "*they have believed :*" by the surrender of their whole being to Him who thus manifested to them His divine character. The forms ἐγνωκαν, τετήρηκαν, are Alexandrian, and the question to be determined is, as in so many other similar cases, whether the apostles themselves used them or whether they were introduced by the Alexandrian copyists.—After having thus prepared the way for His petition, Jesus utters it, and ends by giving the ground of it :

Vv. 9, 10. "*I pray for them ; I pray not for the world, but for those whom thou hast given me, because they are thine.* 10. *And all that which is mine is thine, and that which is thine is mine,*[1] *and I am glorified in them.*"—From the infinite value which these antecedents give to the person of the disciples, Jesus draws this conclusion : "*I pray for them.*" Ἐγώ, *I*, at the beginning : "*I*, who have labored so much to bring them to this point and to whom they now belong." Then, immediately afterwards, and before the verb, the limiting words περὶ αὐτῶν, *for them :* "*For them*, this fruit of my labors, this present which thou hast made to me." This general prayer is equivalent to an : "I commend them to thee." Thus is the antithesis explained : *I pray not for the world.* Jesus has not the same grounds for commending the world to God ; if He wished to pray here for the world, He would formulate His petitions on its behalf quite differently. Luther rightly says : "What must be asked for the world is that it should be converted, not that it should be *kept* or *sanctified.*" Assuredly the refusal of Jesus to pray for the world is not absolute. He Himself says on the cross : "*Father, forgive them !*" Is not this to pray for the world ? Only He does not, as here, allege this ground : *They have known* (ver. 8) ; He says, on the contrary, "*For they know not what they do.*" He cannot make an appeal to God for the world, as for a precious being which belongs to Him, as He does here for His disciples. All that He can do on the cross is to make an appeal to His compassion towards a being who is guilty and is lost. Moreover, the words of ver. 21 : "*That the world may know that thou hast sent me,*" contain also an implicit prayer on behalf of the world. Comp. iii. 16. The refusal of Jesus to pray for the world becomes absolute only when its moral character of opposition to God is irrevocably fixed, and when it has become the society "of those who not only are enemies of God, but who desire to *remain* such" (*Gess*).—Before expressing the more special petitions included in this general prayer, Jesus presents again the two principal claims which the disciples have to the divine interest : 1. God has Himself given them to Jesus, and He must keep this gift for Him. Still more, by thus becoming the property of Jesus, they have not ceased to be that of God. For all property is common between them, and this bond connecting them with Jesus strengthens forever that which bound them to God. Would a mere creature express himself in this way ? Luther says : "Every man can say, What I have is thine ; but the Son alone can say, What is thine is mine." The present, "*are* thine," is purposely substituted for the imperfect, "*were* thine," ver. 6, in order to express the idea that the gift made to Jesus has only served to confirm their *belonging to God*. 2.

---

[1] Instead of και τα εμα . . . σα εμα, ℵ reads και εμοι αυτους εδωκας.

The second ground which commends them henceforth to the Father's interest is, that they are become the depositaries of the glory of the Son (perfect, δεδόξασμαι). We must not make this clause depend on the ὅτι of ver. 9, which would render the sentence dragging, and would force us to make a parenthesis of the first part of ver. 10.—The expression : *I am glorified in them*, has been understood in different ways. There is no reason to depart from the constant sense of the term : *to be glorified*. Notwithstanding His form of servant, Jesus has been manifested to them inwardly in His divine character ; even before having been restored to His glory, He has regained it within them by the fact that they have recognized Him as the Son of God. This is the testimony which Jesus has borne to them, vv. 7, 8.—With this general commendation there are connected two more precise petitions. The first : *keep them*, is prepared for by ver. 11a, expressly stated ver. 11b, and supported by reasons vv. 12–15.

Ver. 11. "*And I am no more in the world ; but they*[1] *are in the world; and I come to thee. Holy Father, keep them in thy name, them whom*[2] *thou hast given me, that they may be one, as*[3] *we are.*"—At the moment of asking God more specially for His protection for His disciples, the thought of Jesus naturally turns towards the dangers to which they will be exposed in the state of desertion in which His departure is about to leave them : "Keep them, these precious vessels (vv. 6–10), which are from this moment *so exposed* (vv. 11–15)." Jesus is no longer with them, in the world, to keep them, and He is not yet with God so as to be able to protect them from the midst of His heavenly glory. There is a sorrowful interval, during which His Father must charge Himself with this care. This reason would be absolutely incomprehensible, if the Fourth Gospel really taught, as *Reuss* thinks, that the Logos is susceptible neither of humiliation nor of exaltation, or, as *Baur* affirms, that death is for Him only the divesting of bodily appearances. Ver. 5 has proved that, when once His divine state is abandoned, there remains for Him, as a mode of existence, only His earthly presence with His own, and vv. 11, 12 prove that, when this presence comes to an end, there is nothing else to do for them except to lay them in the arms of the Father. *Weiss* thinks that even in His state of exaltation He will do nothing except through asking it of the Father. The passages which he alleges do not seem to me to prove this (xiv. 13, 16) ; and this idea is in direct contradiction to Matt. xxviii. 20.

The title : *Holy Father*, must be used in connection with the petition presented. Holiness, in man, is the consecration of his whole being to the task which the divine will assigns to him. Holiness, in God, is the free, deliberate, calm, immutable affirmation of Himself who is the good, or of the good which is Himself. The holiness of God, therefore, as soon as we are associated therewith, draws a deep line of demarcation between us and the men who live under the sway of their natural instincts, and whom the

---

[1] ℵ B read αυτοι instead of ουτοι.
[2] T. R. with Mnn. only It^aliq Vulg. Cop. reads ους (*those whom*) ; ℵ A B C E G H K L M S Y Γ Δ Λ Π some Mnn. : ω (*which*) ; D U X

11 Mnn. Syr.: ο (*which*) It^plerique omits all from ω (ους) to ημεις.
[3] B M S U Y 12 Mnn. read και after καθως.

Scriptures call *the world*. The term: *Holy Father*, here characterizes God as the one who has drawn this line of separation between the disciples and the world. And the petition: *keep them*, has in view the maintenance of this separation. Jesus supplicates His Father to keep the disciples in this sphere of consecration, which is foreign to the life of the world, and of which God is Himself the centre and the author. The words: *in thy name*, make the relation of the divine character which is granted to the apostles as it were the inclosing wall of this sacred domain in which they are to be kept.—The reading which nearly all the Mjj. present would signify: "in thy name *which* thou hast given me." But where in the Scriptures is the name of God spoken of as given to the Son? The expression: "*My name is in him*" (Exod. xxiii. 21), is very different. I do not accept this reading even though it is so strongly supported; comp. ver. 12, where it is even far more improbable. Since the received reading: *those whom* (οὕς) thou hast given me, has in its favor only Mnn., I think that the reading ὃ δέδωκας, "*that which* thou hast given me," must be preferred, which is preserved in the *Cambridge* MS., but that we must make these words the explanatory apposition of αὐτούς, *them*, which precedes; it is the reverse construction of that in ver. 2, where the plural αὐτοῖς is the explanatory apposition of the singular πᾶν. Comp. also ver. 24 (in case the reading ὃ for οὕς must be adopted in that verse): "Keep them in my name, them, *that which* thou hast given me." This reading gives the same sense as that of the T. R. (οὕς); and it easily explains the origin of the Alexandrian reading (ᾧ substituted for ὃ which was referred to ὀνόματι). The conjunction *that* may depend either on δέδωκας, or, what is the only possible meaning with the reading which we prefer, on *keep them:* "Keep them in the sphere of thy knowledge (those whom thou hast given to me to introduce into it), that they may remain one as we are, and that no one of them may be lost in isolation by means of the rupture of the bundle which my care had formed." What indeed would have become of Thomas if, after the resurrection, he had persisted in keeping himself separated from his brethren?—The words *as we are* signify that, as it is by the common *possession* of the divine nature that the Father and the Son are one, it is by the common *knowledge* of this nature (*the name*), that the disciples may remain closely united among themselves and may each one of them be individually kept.

Vv. 12, 13. "*When I was with them*,[1] *I kept them in thy name; those whom*[2] *thou hast given me, I have watched over; and none of them is lost, except the son of perdition, that the Scripture might be fulfilled.* 13. *But now, I come to thee; and I say these things while I am in the world, that they may have my joy fulfilled in themselves.*"—Vv. 12–15 justify the petition: *Keep them*, by developing the ground of it, as it had been briefly indicated in ver. 11a: They have *need* of thy protection.—"*When I was with them*," resumes

---

[1] T. R. reads here, with 14 Mjj. (A X Y etc.) εν τω κοσμω (*in the world*), which B C D L It. Cop. omit.

[2] Instead of ους (*those whom*) which T. R. reads, with 15 Mjj. (ℵ A D etc.), It. Syr. B C L read ω (*which*). They add και before εφυλαξα. ℵ reads και εφυλασσον instead of ους δεδωκας ... εφυλαξα.

the idea of : *I am no more* . . . (ver. 11). The words of the T. R. : *in the world*, are probably a gloss.—The ἐγώ, *I*, contrasts Him who has kept them hitherto with Him who is to do it for the future. The ἐτήρουν, *I kept them*, indicates the result obtained (*conservabam*) ; the ἐφύλαξα, *I have guarded*, relates to the action put forth for this end (*custodivi*).—The reading ᾧ is still more inadmissible in this verse than in the preceding. It has only three Mjj. in its favor, instead of sixteen in ver. 11. The reading ὅ is also abandoned by the three Mjj. which supported it, and has here in its favor only the Egyptian Versions. It only remains to read οὕς (*those whom*), with the T. R. and the majority of the Mjj., which suits the meaning of ver. 11.—By the word *son of perdition* and the citation of the prophecy, Jesus discharges Himself from responsibility, without lessening that of Judas. As to the latter, he has freely yielded himself to play the part traced out beforehand by the prophecy. We may compare here what is foretold concerning Antichrist. We know through prophecy that this person will exist, and yet this fact will not prevent the man who shall accept this part from freely doing so. Comp. p. 795, the remarks on the relation between the divine foreknowledge and human freedom. In the Hebraistic phrase *son of* the abstract complement indicates the moral principle which determines the tendency of the individual thus designated. The passage of which Jesus is thinking is Ps. xli. 10, cited in xiii. 18. Must we conclude from the expression εἰ μή, *if it is not*, that Jesus counted Judas also in the number of those *whom the Father had* previously *given Him ?* I do not think that this form of expression obliges us to draw this conclusion ; comp. Matt. xii. 4, Luke iv. 26, 27, etc.

This remark was a parenthesis intended to justify, with regard to the loss of Judas, the watchfulness of the Lord. After this Jesus returns (ver. 13) to the idea of His approaching departure ; this is the fact which gives the ground for His petition. And He adds that, if He *utters aloud* (this is the meaning of λαλῶ) these words in presence of His disciples, before leaving them, it is that He may associate them in the joy which He Himself enjoys. This joy is that which is inspired in Him by the certainty of the protection with which the Father shelters Him at all times, a certainty which is also to become theirs.—The need which they have of being kept is set forth in the following words in a still more pressing way than before. They are not only going to remain *alone* in the world, but as objects of its *hatred*.

Vv. 14, 15. "*I have given them thy word; and the world has hated them, because they are not of the world, as I am not of the world.* 15. *I ask not that thou shouldest take them out of the world, but that thou shouldest keep them from the evil.*"—The word of Jesus, which they have faithfully received, has made them strangers in the world, as Jesus Himself was. They are become thereby, like Him, beings antipathetic to purely earthly humanity. Jesus might therefore easily allow Himself to ask of God to withdraw them from the world with Himself. But no; for He has separated them from the world for the precise purpose of preparing them to fulfil a mission to the world. It is necessary that they should remain here to fulfil this task; only it must not be that the line of demarcation which He has succeeded in drawing between the world and them, by placing His word in them, should be effaced. While remaining in the world, they must be *kept from the evil* which reigns therein. Jesus thus closes this passage by presenting again the petition which was its text. The limiting word τοῦ πονηροῦ, it seems to me, must be taken here in the neuter sense : *from the evil*, and not : *from the evil one ;* for the preposition ἐκ, *out of*, refers rather to a *domain*, from the midst of which one is taken, than to a person from whose power one escapes. It is otherwise in the Lord's Prayer, where the preposition ἀπό and the verb ῥύεσθαι are used, two expressions which rather refer to a *personal* enemy (Matt. vi. 13). It is wrong, therefore, for *Reuss, Weiss*, etc., to explain here: "*from the power of* the devil." *Hengstenberg* observes that the form τηρεῖν ἐκ does not appear again except in the Apoc. (iii. 10).— From the prayer : *Keep them*, which has rather a negative aim (to prevent their return to the world), and which especially refers to their own salvation, Jesus passes to the second petition, which has a positive end in view, and which refers rather to their mission : *Sanctify them*. It is prepared for in ver. 16, stated in ver. 17, then justified and developed in vv. 18, 19.

Vv. 16, 17. "*They are not of the world, as I am not of the world.* 17. *Sanctify them by thy truth ;* [1] *thy word is truth.*" [2]—Ver. 16 is the transition from the first petition to the second. Jesus has introduced them into the sphere of holiness in which He Himself lives; but it is not only necessary that they should abide there (*keep them*); they must also penetrate farther therein, that they may be strengthened ; for they have the mission to introduce the world into it.—Ἁγίασον, *sanctify :* this word does not merely designate their own moral perfection (*Lücke, de Wette*), but also the consecration of their whole life to the service of God's work (ver. 18). According to x. 36, a consecration preceded the sending of Jesus to the earth: "me whom the Father has *sanctified* and sent into the world." He was marked with a seal of holiness that He might establish here on earth the kingdom of holiness. The same thing is to be repeated for His disciples. The word ἁγιάζειν, *to sanctify*, is not synonymous with καθαρίζειν, *to purify*. *Holy* is not the opposite of *impure*, but simply of *natural* or profane (without the idea of defilement). To sanctify is to consecrate to a religious use what hitherto had appertained to the common life, without the idea of sin. Comp. Exod. xl. 13, Levit. xxii. 2, 3, and Matt. xxiii. 17 : "Which is greater, the gold or the temple which sanctifies the gold ?" But from the Old Testament point of view, the consecration was an external, ritual act; in the new covenant, where all is spiritual, the seat of consecration is above all the heart, the will of the consecrated person. Jesus, therefore, in saying *Sanctify them*, asks for them a will entirely devoted to the good— that is, to God and to His service, and consequently to the task which God gives them to discharge in the world. All their forces, all their talents, all their life, are to be marked with the seal of consecration to this great work, the salvation of men; a thing which implies the renouncing of all

---

[1] Σου, which T. R. reads with 12 Mjj., nearly all the Mnn. Syr. Cop. is omitted by ℵ A B C D L It^{pl erique} Vulg.; ℵ omits the words σου ...

αληθεια (confusion of the two αληθεια).
[2] B reads η (*the*) before αληθεια.

self-gratification, however lawful it may be, the absence of all interested aims, of all self-seeking. This is the sublime idea of Christian *holiness*, but regarded here, where the question is of the apostles, as about to be realized under the special form of the Christian *ministry*, in the same way as each believer is to realize it under the form of the special task which is providentially assigned to him. We have given to ἐν, in the translation, the instrumental sense *by*, as in i. 31, 33. The divine truth is thus designated as the *agent* of the consecration. *Meyer*, *Weiss* and others translate *in*: " *In this sphere* of truth, where I have placed them, complete the work of sanctifying them." But to what purpose, in this case, the addition of the words: "Thy word is truth"? Must they not serve to present *the truth* as the *means* by which alone this consecration can be effected? *Weiss* tries in vain to give another sense.—The T. R. reads σοῦ (*of thee*) with the words *the truth* in the first clause; this pronoun is wanting in the Alexandrian authorities, and was probably added from the following clause (*thy word*).—The *truth* is the adequate expression of the character of God and of His relation to us. This truth is found only in the word of God addressed to the world by the mouth of Jesus. The second ἀλήθεια does not have the article: This word is truth, nothing but truth.—In support of this prayer, Jesus alleges two reasons, one drawn from what they will have to do for the world (ver. 18), the other from the work which He accomplishes upon Himself on their behalf (ver. 19). Their mission is His, and His holiness will be theirs.

Vv. 18, 19. "*According as thou hast sent me into the world, I also have sent them into the world.* 19. *And for their sakes I*[1] *sanctify myself, that they also may be sanctified in truth.*"—If Jesus asks for them the spirit of their charge (ver. 17), it is because He has confided to them *the charge* itself. The term ἀπέστειλα, *I have sent*, alludes to the title of *apostles* which He has given them. But how does Jesus say that He has sent them into the world, when they are already in it? It is because He has drawn them to Himself and raised them into a higher sphere than the life of the world (ver. 16), and it is from thence that He now sends them to the world, as really as He was Himself sent from heaven. And the mission which He gives them is only the continuation of that which the Father has given Him (καθώς, *according as*); herein is the first reason which He presses in support of His petition: *Sanctify them*.

The second is set forth in ver. 19. The force of καί, *and*, at the beginning of this verse, is this: "And to obtain for them this consecration which I ask for, I begin by consummating my own." Jesus asks nothing of the Father except after having done, or when doing Himself what depends on Himself to the end of making possible the realization of His prayer; comp. vv. 1, 6, 8, 12, 14. It is on what He does for His own sanctification that theirs will be founded. The words ὑπὲρ αὐτῶν, *for them*, are at the beginning because they set forth the aim of His work with reference to Himself. The word *sanctify* does not by any means imply, as we have seen, the removal

---

[1] ℵ-A omit ἐγώ.

of defilement ; for it is not synonymous with *purify* (καθαρίζειν); it is therefore a wrong course in some interpreters to find in this word a proof of the existence of sin in Jesus. The majority of interpreters (*Chrysostom*, *Meyer*, *Reuss*, *Weiss*, etc.) apply this word to the consecration which Jesus makes of His person at this moment in view of His expiatory death. *Weiss* sustains this meaning by the ordinary use of the word *hiquedisch* in the Old Testament to designate the idea of sacrificing. But this last reason proves nothing ; for this term, as well as the Greek word, designates all consecration, even that which does not issue in death ; comp. Matt. xxiii. 17, which we have just cited. And this sense is not admissible here, because it is inapplicable in the following clause, unless we see, with *Chrysostom*, in the sanctification of the apostles their acceptance of martyrdom, or refer it, as *Meyer* and *Reuss* do, to the gift of the Holy Spirit as the result of the expiatory death, or give up, as *Weiss* does, assigning the same meaning to the verb ἁγιάζειν in the two clauses, and find therein a special nicety of expression ; all which interpretations are quite improbable, the first, because the greater part of the apostles do not seem to have been martyrs ; the second, because the relation between the two acts of consecration would be much too indirect ; the third, because the ἵνα, *that*, as well as the καί, *them also*, implies two consecrations of a homogeneous character. We must, therefore, with *Calvin*, abide by the natural meaning of ἁγιάζειν : to take a thing away from a profane use in order to consecrate it to the service of God. Jesus possessed a human nature, such as ours, endowed with inclinations and repugnances like ours, but yet perfectly lawful. Of this nature He continually made a holy offering ; negatively, by sacrificing it where it was in contradiction to His mission (the culture of the arts and sciences, for example, or the family life) ; positively, in consecrating to the task assigned Him of God all His powers, all His natural and spiritual talents. It is thus "*that He offered Himself to God without spot, through the eternal Spirit*" (Heb. ix. 14). When the question was of sacrificing a gratification, as in the desert, or of submitting to a sorrow, as in Gethsemane, He incessantly subjected His nature to the work to which the will of the Father called Him. And this was not effected once for all. His human life received the seal of consecration increasingly even till the entire and final sacrifice of death, when "by the things which He suffered" He finished the "learning obedience" (Heb. v. 8).—The pronouns *I* and *myself* set forth the energetic action which Jesus was obliged to exercise upon Himself in order to attain this result.—Thereby Jesus realized in His own person the perfect consecration of the *human life*, and He thus laid the foundations of the consecration of this life in all His followers. This is what is expressed by the following clause: *That they also may be sanctified*, which develops the meaning of the first words : *for them.* According to *Weiss*, Jesus speaks here of a purely negative fact : the removal through the expiatory sacrifice of Christ of the guilt resulting from the defilements contracted by the believer, a guilt which would prevent his consecration to God. This is to fail to recognize the difference in meaning between the two terms *sanctify* and *purify*, and arbitrarily to change the meaning which the word *sanctify* had in the preceding clause. The meaning is indeed as follows : The sanctification of every believer is nothing else than the communication which Jesus makes to him of His own sanctified person. This is what He had already intimated in vi. 53–57 and 63, and what St. Paul develops in Rom. viii. 1–3, where he shows that Christ began by *condemning* sin in the flesh (condemned to non-existence), in order that the (moral) righteousness, required by the law, might be realized in us. Jesus created a holy humanity in His person, and the Spirit has the task and the power to reproduce in us this new humanity : " *The law of the Spirit of life which is in Jesus Christ has made me free from the law of sin and death.*" In this point, as in all others, the part of the Spirit consists in taking *what belongs to Jesus* (this perfectly holy human life), to give it to us. If this holy life had not been realized in Christ, the Spirit would have nothing to communicate to us in this regard, and the sanctification of humanity would have remained a barren aspiration. It is difficult to understand how *Weiss* can say that, with this interpretation, everything is reduced to the imitation of the example of Christ.—Let us remark finally that by reason of ver. 17, the question here is of the apostles, not only as Christians, but especially as *ministers* (ver. 18). Jesus Himself, while sanctifying Himself as *man* and for the purpose of realizing in Himself the ideal of human holiness, sanctified Himself at the same time as *Saviour* and for the purpose of giving life to mankind. In the same way, the task of the apostles will not only be to realize the consecration in that general form under which all believers are called to it ; by freeing them from every earthly vocation and sending them into the world as His ambassadors, Jesus desired that their personal sanctification might be effected under the particular form of the apostleship. This form is not more holy, but it has, more than any earthly vocation, the character of a special consecration to the work of God. Ἐν ἀληθείᾳ, *in truth*, must have here, because of the want of the article, the adverbial sense : *in a true way*, in opposition both to the false Pharisaic consecration and to the ritual consecration of the Levitical priesthood. Thus from the general petition : *I pray for them*, there have been evolved these two clearly progressive petitions : " *Keep them* in holiness ! *Consecrate them* by an increasing holiness, to the end that they may become, after me and like me, the agents of the sanctification of the world." It is natural that Jesus should pass from this to a prayer on behalf of the world itself, at least as to the future believing portion of it, vv. 20–26. Jesus prays for *the believers* and asks for them two things : vv. 20, 21, spiritual unity ; vv. 22–24, participation in His glory ; finally, He justifies these petitions in vv. 25, 26.

Vv. 20–26. Jesus prays for the union of believers with Himself and among themselves.

Vv. 20, 21. " *And it is not for these only that I pray, but for all those who believe*[1] *on me through their word,* 21, *that they all may be one ; that, as thou, Father, art in me and I in thee, they also may be*[2] *in us, that the world may*

---

[1] T. R. with D² some Mnn. It^plerique Vulg. Sah.: πιστευσοντων (*who shall believe*). The 19 Mjj. all the other Mnn. Syr. Cop.: πιστενοντων (*who believe*).

[2] Ἐν before ωσιν is rejected by B C D It^aliq Sah.

believe[1] *that thou hast sent me.*"—Jesus has commended to God the *author* and the *instruments* of the work of salvation; He now prays on behalf of the *object* of this work, the body of believers. The Church appears here elevated by faith into unity with God, and rendered capable thereby of beholding and sharing the glory of the Son. It is the realization of the supreme destiny of humanity which He contemplates and asks for, the contents of that "*hidden wisdom which God had foreordained before the ages for our glory*" (1 Cor. ii. 7). The question therefore is not only, as is often supposed, of the union of Christians among themselves, but above all of the union which is the basis of this, that of the body of believers with Christ and, through Him, with God Himself. This sublime unity it is which Jesus, in what follows, contrasts with that of the world. The true reading is certainly the present participle πιστευόντων, *the believers*, and not, as the T. R. reads, almost without any authorities, the future πιστευσόντων, *those who shall believe*. These believers are undoubtedly not the believers at the moment when Jesus is praying, since they had believed through His word and not through that of the apostles. But He pictures to Himself all believers, speaking absolutely. He sees them in spirit, these believers of all times and places, and by His prayer He unites them in one body and transports them, in some sense, to glory. This present cannot be rendered, in French, in an altogether exact way. In *Reuss's* view, this present participle proves that it is the evangelist and not Jesus who is speaking. This is to ascribe great unskilfulness to so able a composer.—The last words assign to the apostolic teaching a capital part in the life of the Church. Jesus recognizes, in the future, no faith capable of uniting man to God and preparing him for glory except that which is produced and nourished by the word of the Eleven. The term *word* (λόγος) does not, as the term *testimony* (μαρτυρία) might do, designate merely the narration of the evangelical *facts;* it contains also the revelation of the religious and moral meaning of the facts. It is the contents of the Epistles, as well as that of the Gospels. Men cannot really come to faith in Christ (εἰς ἐμέ, *on me*), at any time, except through this intermediate agency. How can *Reuss* infer from this passage that the apostles have no other privilege relatively to other believers but that of *priority ?* This saying assigns to them a unique place in the life of the Church. No teaching capable of producing faith can be other than a reproduction of theirs.—The following verses present the object of the petition under the form of an *end* to be attained by this very prayer (ἵνα, *in order that*); ver. 21 designates this end in itself; ver. 22 states what Jesus has done already to the end of the possibility of its realization; ver. 23 shows it perfectly attained.—It seems to me that the first clause of ver. 21 is formed only of the words: *that all may be one*, which indicate the general idea; then, that the clause: *as thou, Father, . . .* depends on the following *that*, by an inversion similar to that of xiii. 34. There is, therefore, here an explanatory resumption : "That they may be one ; that, *I say*, *as* thou, Father, . . . they also may be in us." This construction does not

---

[1] ℵ B C : πιστευη, instead of πιστευσῃ.

have the dragging character of that which makes the *as* depend on the first *that*. After having asked for the general unity of believers (*all*), Jesus describes it as a unity of the most elevated order; it partakes of the *nature* (καθώς) of that of the Father and the Son. As the Father lives in the Son and the Son in the Father, so the Son lives in the believers and, by living in them, He unites them closely one with another. Instead of : "that they may be *one* in us," some Mjj. read: "that they may be in us." It may be said that the context requires the idea of the *unity* of believers, and that the small word ἐν was easily lost in the ἐν ἡμῖν which precedes. The idea, however, does not imperatively require this word. It is by being *in* Christ and through Him *in* God (*in us*), that believers find themselves living in each other. That which separates them is what they have of self in their views and will; that which unites them is what they have of Christ, and thereby of the divine, in them. It is clear that this dwelling of Christ and consequently of God in them is the work of the Spirit, who alone has the power to cast down the barrier between personalities, without confounding them.—Such an organism, exercising its functions on the earth, is a manifestation so new that the sight of it must be a powerful means of bringing the world to *faith* in Him from whom it proceeds. Here is the content of the third *that*, which is subordinate to the two preceding ones, and indicates the final purpose of them. The word *believe* is never taken in the New Testament otherwise than in a favorable sense (except in James ii. 19, which relates to an altogether peculiar case). It cannot therefore designate a forced conviction, such as that which may be found in Phil. ii. 10 f. No doubt, Jesus does not mean to say that the whole world will believe; this would be contradictory to what He said of the world in xv. 20, 22, 24. We must recall to mind the fact that the question is of an *end* which cannot be accomplished for all. In any case, Jesus declares that in the world estranged from God there are yet elements capable of being gained for faith. And what the sight of a local and passing phenomenon, like that of the primitive Church in Jerusalem, produced among the Jewish people (Acts ii. 44–47),—will not the same spectacle, when magnified, produce this also on a grander scale, one day, throughout the entire world ? Perhaps even Jesus is thinking more especially of the conversion of the Jews at the end of time, when they shall see the Church realized in all its beauty among the Gentiles. In xv. 18, 20, the word *world* designates, above all, the Jewish people. This supposition is confirmed by the words : *that it is thou who hast sent me*, that is to say : "that I, this Jesus of Nazareth, whom they have rejected, am really the promised Sent one whom they were expecting." Rom. xi. 25, 31. Comp. 1 John i. 3; Eph. iv. 13.—After having presented to God this end worthy of His love, Jesus recalls in ver. 22, as in vv. 4, 6, 14, 18, how He has Himself prepared the work of which He asks the completion, and in ver. 23 He describes its glorious consummation.

Vv. 22, 23. *"And the glory which thou hast given me, I have given them, that they may be one, as we are one,*[1] *23, I in them and thou in me ; that their*

---

[1] B C D L reject ἐσμεν, and ℵ ἐν ἐσμεν.

unity may be perfect, that[1] *the world may know that thou hast sent me and that thou hast loved*[2] *them as thou hast loved me."*—In this whole prayer, Jesus rests His petitions on the fact that He has already begun that of which He asks the completion. Hence the ἐγώ, *1*, placed at the beginning. —What is the glory of which Jesus has already made a gift to His own, and by means of which He has laid the foundation of the unity which He asks for ? *Chrysostom* and, at the present day, *Weiss* understand by it the glorious power of sustaining their apostolic ministry by miracles. But this outward sign has nothing in common with the inward sphere in which the thought of Jesus is here moving. How could a result like this, which is expressed by the following ἵνα, *that*, proceed from a miraculous power, an external, passing and individual phenomenon ? *Hengstenberg* refers this term *glory* to the participation of believers in the *unity* of the Father and the Son ; but this explanation leads to a tautology with the following clause. *De Wette, Reuss, Meyer*, apply this term *glory* to the kingdom which is to come, and the word *give* to a property only *by right ;* but this is to anticipate the meaning of ver. 24. Jesus starts, on the contrary, in ver. 22 from a fact already accomplished, in order to make it the point of departure for a coming good (ver. 23) which will precede the final glory (ver. 24). We read, ver. 24, that the glory of Jesus consists in being the eternal object of the Father's love ; the glory which He has communicated to believers is, therefore, the becoming by faith what He is essentially, the objects of this same divine love ; comp. ver. 23 (*that thou hast loved them as thou hast loved me*) and ver. 26. This glory, which is that of adoption, Jesus has communicated to His own by bringing things to this point,—that God can, without obscuring His holiness, convey to them the love which He has for Jesus Himself. By this means we understand the following clause : *that they may be one, as we* [*are*] *one.* This love of the Father, of which they are all the objects in common, unites them closely among themselves and makes them all one family of which Jesus is the elder Brother (Rom. viii. 29, Eph. i. 10).

The first words of ver. 23, in a clause which is simply placed in juxtaposition with the preceding : "that they may be one as we are," remind us of the *mode* of this unity : God living in Christ, Christ living in each believer, and this to the end that the limit of a perfect unity may be attained, and that the organism of humanity consummated in God may appear.—The aim of this admirable unity is that the world *may know.* This word is undoubtedly not the synonym of *believe*, ver. 21. The term *know* includes with the *faith* of believers (ver. 21) the forced *conviction* of rebels. For how could the word κόσμος, *the world*, designate only the believers ? The question is of the universal homage, voluntary or involuntary, rendered to Christ—such as is described in Phil. ii. 10, Rom. xiv. 10-12. The whole universe renders homage to the divine messenger who, by transforming believers into His own image, has succeeded in making them loved as He is Himself loved.—Thus is the way prepared for the pointing out of the final

---

[1] ℵ B C D L X It^{aliq} Cop. Orig. reject καί (*and*) before ινα γινωσκη.

[2] D 7 Mnn. It^{aliq} Cop.: ηγαπησα (*that I have loved them*), instead of ηγαπησας.

end of the ways of God towards the Church of Christ, its participation in the *glory* of the Son of God :

Ver. 24. *"Father, my will is that those whom thou hast given me*[1] *be with me where I am, that they may behold my glory which thou hast given me, for thou lovedst me before the foundation of the world."*—Perfect unity is the last step before the goal of perfect glory. The repetition of the invocation *Father,* vv. 24, 25, indicates the increasing urgency with which Jesus prays, as He draws nearer the end. The reading ὃ δέδωκας, *"that which thou hast given me,"* is probably the true one ; it brings out the unity of the believers, that perfect ἕν which the body of the elect will form (ver. 23). —Θέλω : Jesus no longer says, *I pray,* but *I will!* This expression is found nowhere else on His lips ; it is ordinarily explained by saying that the Son expresses Himself thus, because He feels Himself fully in accord on this point with the Father. But was not this the case in general in all His prayers ! This unique expression must be in harmony with the unique character of the situation. And the unique point in this latter is that it is a question of Jesus as dying. It is His testament which Jesus here places in the hands of His Father, and, as the expression is, His *last will.*—All that which Jesus has just asked for them had for its aim to render them fit for the immediate beholding of His glory, from the very moment of their death (xiv. 3). There is no question here of the Parousia, as *Weiss* thinks. The sphere of this divine manifestation is at once inward and heavenly.— *Meyer* thinks that the glory, of which Jesus says that the Father *has given* it to Him, cannot be His divine glory before the incarnation, and must designate His glory after His exaltation, and He sees in the following words : *for thou lovedst me before,* . . . the *ground* on which God thus glorifies Jesus. But the ground of the exaltation of Jesus is quite differently described, not only by Paul (Phil. ii. 9–11), but also by John himself, x. 17, xiii. 32, xv. 10 : it is His perfect obedience even to death and even to the death of the cross. The ὅτι therefore means : *in that,* and serves to explain *wherein* this glory of the Son *consists :* it is in having been the eternal object of the Father's love. Is there any glory to be compared with this ? The word *given* may be incompatible with a certain conception of the divine Trinity ; it is not so with that of John, which includes as a necessary element the relation of subordination between the Son and the Father ; comp. i. 1 *(with God)* ; i. 18 *(in the bosom of the Father)* ; v. 26 ("it has been *given* him to have life in himself"), etc. The words : *before the foundation of the world,* imply eternity, for the world includes all that which has come into existence. This saying of Jesus is that which leads us farthest into the divine depths. It shows Christian speculation on what path it must seek the solution of the relations of the Trinity ; love is the key of this mystery. And as this love is eternal, and consequently has no more an end than it has had a beginning, it may one day become for believers the permanent object of an immediate contemplation, through which they will find themselves initiated into the mystery of the essence of the

---

[1] Instead of οὕς *(those whom),* ℵ B D Cop. ὅ *(that which).*

Son and of His eternal generation. Far more ; as, by the complete community which the Son has succeeded in establishing between them and Him, they are the objects of a similar love to that of which the Son is the object, they will find themselves thus introduced into the eternal movement of the divine life itself. This appears from the word *behold.* One does not behold a fact of this order without being in some manner associated with it. Here is the height to which Jesus elevates the Church. After having drawn His spouse from the midst of a world sunk in evil, He introduces her into the sphere of the divine life.

Vv. 25, 26 have as their aim to justify this last will of Jesus, not only from the standpoint of grace, but even from that of *righteousness,* precisely that one of the divine perfections which might seem opposed to the petition of Jesus in behalf of His own.

Vv. 25, 26. "*Righteous Father, the world, it is true, has not known thee; but as for me, I have known thee; and these have known that thou hast sent me.* 26. *And I have made known to them thy name, and will make it known, that the love wherewith thou hast loved me*¹ *may be in them, and that I may be in them."* —Jesus does not say, as He did in ver. 11 : "*Holy Father."* And He certainly has His reasons for substituting here for the title *holy* the title *righteous.* What follows does not permit us to doubt that He takes this word in the sense of *justice* strictly so-called, retributive justice. *Hengstenberg, Meyer, Weiss, Keil, Westcott,* etc., have clearly seen this. In fact, Jesus opposes to the world, which has refused to know God and has thus rendered itself unworthy to be admitted to the contemplation of His glory, His own (οὗτοι, *these*), who have consented to know God and have thus become worthy of the privilege which He asks for them (ver. 24). Hence, as it appears to me, it follows that in the first words of ver. 25 the καί before οὗτοι and the καί before ὁ κόσμος are two καί of contrast, such as we have seen so many times in John (i. 10, vi. 36, xv. 24), serving to bring together, by reason of their very opposition, the two contrary facts. But what has prevented interpreters from apprehending this relation is the fact that John intercalates between the two terms of the principal contrast a third term intended to introduce the second : "But as for *me,* I have known thee." If the believers have arrived at the knowledge of God, it is not of themselves, but only by means of the knowledge which their Master had of God and which He has communicated to them. The δέ, *but,* indicates a first antithesis with reference to the καί, which precedes, relatively to the world,—a fact which makes the second καί, before οὗτοι, appear no longer other than the completing of the antithesis expressed by this δέ which accompanies the ἐγώ. We may compare xvi. 20, as an example of an antithesis in some sort broken by a secondary antithesis intercalated between the two members of the principal contrast. This explanation draws near to that of *Bäumlein,* and is in the main accepted by *Keil. Meyer* also explains the first καί as indicating an opposition, but an opposition to the idea of righteousness expressed in the invocation *Righteous Father !* "*And yet* (although thou

---

¹ ℵ reads αὐτούς (*them*) instead of με.

art righteous) the world has not known thee as such." This non-recognition is, according to this view, that of which Paul speaks in Rom. i. 19, which consisted in the blindness of men with reference to the revelation of God in the works of nature. But this idea has not the least connection with the context. Jesus has Himself said (in xv. 22, 24) that all the sins previous to His coming would not have been imputed to the world, if it had not put the crowning point upon them by the rejection of Him. The terms *to know* and *not to know* God can refer here only to the acceptance or rejection of the revelation of the character of God in the appearance of Jesus.— *Weiss* sees in the first καί, not an opposition to the second, but a particle which connects this verse with that which precedes. But what logical connection is it possible to establish between the admission of believers to the spectacle of the glory of Christ (ver. 24) and the refusal of the world to know God! This, then, is the meaning of this prayer: "The world, it is true, is the just object of Thy rejection by reason of its refusal to know Thee; but these, in receiving me, who have brought to them the knowledge of Thee, are become worthy of the privilege which I now ask of Thee for them."

Ver. 26. No doubt the light which has dawned in the hearts of the disciples through the revelation of God in Christ as yet only begins to appear. But Jesus pledges Himself to communicate to them for the future the fulness of the knowledge of the Father which He Himself possesses.— The future: *I will make known*, does not refer to the death of Jesus, as *Weiss* supposes, but, according to the preceding chapters (xiv. 21, 26, xvi. 25), to the sending of the Holy Spirit and the entire work of Jesus in the Church after the day of Pentecost. *Reuss* well renders the admirable thought contained in the words: *And that the love wherewith thou hast loved me may be in them:* "The love of God which, before the creation of the physical world, had its adequate object in the person of the Son (ver. 24), finds it, since the creation of the new spiritual world, in all those who are united with the Son." What God desired in sending His Son here on earth was precisely that He might form for Himself in the midst of humanity a family of children like Him, of which He should be the elder Brother (Rom. viii. 29). —Jesus adds: *And that I myself may be in them*. Connected as it is with the preceding words, this expression must mean: "And in loving them thus, it will still be myself in them whom thou wilt love, and thus thy love will not attach itself to anything that is defiled." Its object, indeed, will be Jesus living in them, His holy image reproduced in their person.

What simplicity, what calmness, what transparent depth in this whole prayer! "It is indeed," as *Gess* says, "the only Son who here speaks to His Father. Everything in these beautiful words is *supernatural*, because He who speaks is the only Son who has come from heaven; but at the same time everything in them is *natural*, for He speaks as a son speaks to his father." The feeling which is the soul of this prayer, the ardent zeal for the glory of God, is that which inspired Jesus throughout His whole life. His three petitions—that for His personal glorification, that for the consecration of His apostles and that for the glorification of the Church, are indeed the sentiments which must have filled His soul in view of the blow which was about to put an end to His earthly activity. In the details not a word has been met whose appropriateness and fitness to the given situation has not been proved by exegesis. Can it be possible to hold, with *Baur*, that, at the distance of more than a century, a Christian should have succeeded in reproducing thus the impressions of Jesus? This would be to say that there existed then another Jesus than Jesus Himself.

Weiss and *Reuss* hold, as we do, that this is the composition of an immediate witness. But they find in certain passages—in ver. 3 for example—the proof that the disciple has reproduced the thoughts of the Master after his own fashion. The second asks whether John had, then, in his hands tablets and pencil to take down word for word the prayer of Jesus.—But, if John truly regarded Jesus as the Logos, we ask once again how could the respect which he must have had for His words have permitted him to make Him speak, and especially pray, according to his own fancy? He undoubtedly did not have his pencil in hand ; but the memory is proportionate to the attention and the attention to the interest ; now must not that of John have been excited to the highest degree? On the other hand, the words of Jesus, simple, grave, earnest, were of a nature to impress themselves more deeply and distinctly on the heart of John than any other words. Moreover, it is not impossible that, at an inconsiderable remove of time from that evening, John should have felt the need of committing to writing what he recalled to mind of these last conversations and this prayer. Or again, the unceasingly renewed meditation upon these words engraved upon the tablets of his heart and ever refreshed by the action of the Spirit, may have supplied the place of any external means. This inward miracle, if one will call it so, is far less improbable than the artificial composition of such a prayer.

But is the profound calmness which reigns in this scene compatible with the agony in Gethsemane which immediately follows it in the other Gospels? *Keim* asserts that John by this narrative *annihilates the Synoptical tradition.*— The conflict in Gethsemane has the character of a sudden crisis, of a violent shock, in some sort of an explosion, after which calmness was re-established in the soul of Jesus as quickly as it had been troubled. This passing crisis has a double cause : the one natural, the singular impressibility of the soul of Jesus, of which we have seen so many proofs in our Gospel, particularly in ch. xi. and xii. 27. By virtue of the very purity of His nature, Jesus was accessible, as was no other man, to every lawful emotion. His soul resembled a magnetic needle, whose mobility is only equalled by the perseverance with which, in every oscillation, it tends to recover its normal direction. Gethsemane must have been for Jesus, not punishment, but the struggle with a view to the *acceptance* of punishment ; and thus the anticipatory suffering of the cross. Such an anticipation is sometimes more painful than the reality itself. The supernatural cause is pointed out by Jesus Himself, xiv. 30 : " *The prince of this world is coming.*" Comp. Luke xxii. 53 : " *This is your hour and the power of darkness.*" The extraordinary character of this agony betrays itself in its suddenness and even its violence. St. Luke had closed his narrative of the temptation in the desert with the words : " *The devil withdrew from him,* ἄχρι καιροῦ, until another favorable moment." The hour of Gethsemane was that moment which Satan judged favorable to subject Jesus to the new test which he was reserving for Him. There is nothing here which is not in perfect accord with the normal development of Jesus' life.

The sacerdotal prayer is, as it were, the amen added by Jesus to His work accomplished here on earth ; it forms thus the climax of this part, which is intended to trace out the *development of faith* in the disciples (chs. xiii.–xvi.), and corresponds, notwithstanding the difference of forms, with the passage in xii. 37–50, in which John gave his reflections on the history of Jewish unbelief (chs. v.–xii.).

FOURTH PART

THE PASSION

John 18:1-19:42

The intention of the evangelist, in the following narrative, is certainly not to give a narration as complete as possible of the Passion, as if no narrative of this event existed side by side with his own. The most pronounced adversaries of the authenticity of our Gospel, *Baur* and *Strauss*, are at the present day in accord with the orthodox interpreters, *Lange* and *Hengstenberg*, on the point that the narrative of the fourth evangelist stands in constant relation to those of his three predecessors. The difference is only on the question of the end which the author proposes to himself in composing this fourth narrative. According to *Baur* and *Strauss*, the pseudo-John borrows from the Synoptics the materials which are indispensable to the end of giving some probability to his romance of Jesus–Logos. According to the commentators of the opposite side, John endeavors simply to fill up the vacancies in the earlier narrations, or to present the facts, already previously related, in their true light.

We are convinced that, as the latter writers think, the choice of materials is frequently determined by the intention of completing the accounts already current in the church. Thus, when John relates the examination of Jesus in the house of Annas, which the Synoptics omit, and omits the appearance before the Sanhedrim, which the first Gospels relate with detail, this intention seems evident. It will appear also from a multitude of other examples. But, on the other hand, the narrative of John has presented, up to this point, a too serious meditative character and too profound elaboration to allow the possibility of holding that, in the part which is to follow, it is not governed by any higher thought, and is obedient only to chance, as would be the case in a narrative which confined itself to relating that which others had not related.

In the narrative of the Passion in John, we shall find, as throughout his whole work, the triple point of view indicated in the introduction (Vol. I., p. 228 f.). Jesus causes *His glory* to shine forth through the vail of ignominy by which it was covered, and this especially through the freedom with which He surrenders Himself to the fate which awaits Him ; this is here, as always, the luminous foundation of the whole narrative. On this foundation there stands out in relief, as a dark figure, the *Jewish unbelief* unmasking its moral perversity by a series of odious acts and disloyal words, and, after having thus pronounced its own condemnation, reaching its consummation in the murder of the Messiah. Finally, in contrast with it, we discern *the faith* which is hidden in the person of the disciples gathering up the scattered rays of the glory of Jesus, and growing in silence, as plants during a storm. The second of these three features is that which prevails in the following narrative.

Three principal scenes :
1. The arrest of Jesus : xviii. 1–11.
2. His double trial, ecclesiastical and civil : xviii. 12–xix. 16.
3. His punishment : xix. 17–42.

1

John 18:1-11

THE ARREST OF JESUS

John omits here the account of the agony of Jesus in Gethsemane ; but he clearly assigns to this fact its place by these words of ver. 1 : *where there was a garden into which he entered.* In reading these words, no Christian, in possession of the first three Gospels, could fail to think of that narrative. The reason of this omission, as well as of the omission of the accounts of the transfiguration, the institution of the Holy Supper, and so many others, is that John knew that this scene was sufficiently well known in the church, and that it had no special relation to the end which he set before himself. There cannot be a dogmatic design in this omission ; this is proved by the story in xii. 24–27, which belongs exclusively to John, and in which he has preserved for us the moral essence of the scene in Gethsemane.

Strauss exclaims : " Every attempt to insert in John's narrative, between chs. xvii. and xviii., the agony of Gethsemane is an attack upon the moral elevation and even the manly character of Jesus."[1] According to this, John would have been the first to commit an outrage of this kind (xii. 27). Strauss concludes from this that the Synoptic narrative is "a more naïve poetic fiction " than that of John, which presents to us " a more well-considered and carefully contrived poetic fiction." Thus those who relate, lie in relating ; he who omits, lies in omitting ! This is the point at which criticism arrives by pursuing its course even to the end. It destroys itself.

Vv. 1–3. The arrival of the band. "*After having said these things, Jesus went out with his disciples beyond the brook Cedron,[2] where there was a garden, into which he entered as well as his disciples. 2. Now Judas, who betrayed him, also knew this place, because Jesus had often met[3] there with his disciples. 3. Judas, then, having taken the cohort, with officers sent by the chief priests and Pharisees, comes thither with lanterns, torches and weapons.*"—The verb ἐξῆλθε,

---

[1] *Das Leben Jesu*, 1864, p. 553.
[2] A S Δ It^{aliq} Vulg. and some other Vss. read του κεδρων (*of Cedron*), א D It^{aliq} Cop. Sah. : του κεδρου (*of the cedar*), T. R. with B C E G H K L M U X Y Γ Δ Π most of the Mnn. Orig. and Tisch.: των κεδρων (*of the cedars*).
[3] 9 Mjj. (E G M etc.) read και after συνηχθη.

910 / The Passion

he went out, is ordinarily referred to the departure from the supper room. See on xiv. 31. In our view, this verb, being directly connected, as it is, with the limiting phrase πέραν τοῦ χειμάρρου, *beyond the brook*, designates a time farther removed, and signifies rather : " He went out *from the city* to pass across the brook." This is acknowledged by *de Wette*, even though he holds, with so many others, that the discourses of chs. xiii.-xvii. were pronounced in the supper room.—The received reading, which is that of the *Vatican* MS. and of most of the Mjj. and Mnn., and of Origen, is τῶν Κέδρων, and would signify " the brook of *the cedars ;*" there would be evidently an error of John here, for the name Cedron comes from קדרון (*Kidron*), *black* (black water). In Josephus also the name Κέδρων is a nominative singular (for example, χείμαρρος Κεδρῶνος, *Antiq.* viii. 1, 5). The reading of the *Sinaitic* and *Cambridge* MSS. is τοῦ Κέδρου, *of the cedar*. It is evident that these two readings are the work of copyists, some of whom conformed the substantive to the article (by substituting Κέδρου for Κέδρων), others the article to the substantive (substituting τῶν for τοῦ), and that the true reading—apparently very improbable—is that of the *Alexandrian* MS. and of the *Sangallensis*, τοῦ Κέδρων, which alone easily explains the two others. *Westcott*, in honor of the *Vatican*, maintains the reading τῶν Κέδρων, by appealing to a legend of the Jerusalem Talmud, according to which there were some cedars on the Mount of Olives ; *Tischendorf*, out of regard for the *Sinaitic* MS., reads τοῦ Κέδρου. Behold what prepossession can effect ! The same variety of readings is found again in several MSS. of the Old Testament (LXX) ; see 2 Sam. xv. 23 and 1 Kings xv. 13.—The brook Cedron has its source half a league to the north of Jerusalem, and falls into the Dead Sea at the southward after a course of six or seven leagues. It is ordinarily dry during nine months of the year ; for more than twenty years, as we were told in Jerusalem, not a sign of water had been seen in it. Its bed is at the bottom of the valley of Jehoshaphat, between the temple hill and the Mount of Olives. After having passed the little bridge by which this dried-up bed is crossed, one finds on the right a plot of ground planted with ancient olive trees, which is asserted to be the garden of Gethsemane. There is no valid reason, whatever *Keim* may say, against the truth of this tradition. The word πολλάκις, *often*, in ver. 2, might apply only to the preceding days ; but it is more probable that it refers also to the earlier sojourns of Jesus in Jerusalem. This garden undoubtedly belonged to friends of Jesus. It ordinarily served as a place of meeting for the Lord and His disciples (συνήχθη, the aorist : *he met with*), when they returned from Jerusalem to the Mount of Olives and to Bethany, and wished to avoid passing all together through the streets of the city. Comp. Luke xxi. 37, xxii. 39. —The term σπεῖρα always designates, in the New Testament (Matt. xxvii. 27, Acts xxi. 31), and in Josephus, the Roman legion or a part of the legion which occupied the citadel of Antonia, at the north-eastern angle of the temple. A detachment of Roman soldiers had seemed necessary to support the servants of the Sanhedrim. For Mark xiv. 2 proves that a rising in favor of Jesus was feared ; and for this reason it had been necessary to ask for orders from the governor. This detachment was commanded by the tribune himself, the *chiliarch*, mentioned in ver. 12. The article ἡ, "*the* cohort,*" designates the well-known cohort ; and, if it seems to indicate the presence of this entire body of soldiers (600 men), we must find here either a popular expression or a manner of speaking which is justified by the presence of the commander-in-chief. The Synoptics do not speak of this escort. The message of Pilate's wife, however, which is related by Matthew, proves that, since the preceding evening, the governor had been occupied with this matter ; and this circumstance confirms the fact of the participation of the Roman soldiery in the arrest. *Keim* turns this narrative into ridicule, by speaking ironically of "*half an army ;* " this wretched piece of pleasantry is quite gratuitous. *Bäumlein* and others have contended against the application of the term σπεῖρα to the Roman garrison, and have thought that the question was only of the guard of the temple. But the constant meaning of this word does not allow this explanation.—The ὑπηρέται, *officers*, are, as in vii. 32, 45, the sergeants of the temple. They were the persons who had properly the task of arresting Jesus. The Roman cohort was only to give them aid in case of resistance. Ver. 10 shows that servants belonging to the houses of the chief priests had also joined the band.—The meaning of the words φανοί and λαμπάδες is questionable. The first seems to us rather to designate lanterns ; the second, resin torches. All this apparatus : "Lanterns and torches and weapons " (the two καί, *and*, are to be noticed), by its very uselessness casts a kind of ridicule upon this scene. It is feared that Jesus may hide Himself, and yet He surrenders Himself voluntarily (ver. 4), or that He may defend Himself ; . . . but what purpose would these weapons have served, if He had wished to make use of His power (ver. 6) ?

Vv. 4–9. The meeting of Jesus with the band. "*Jesus therefore,*[1] *knowing all that which was to come upon him, went forth and says to them :*[2] *Whom are you seeking for ? 5. They answered him, Jesus of Nazareth. Jesus says to them, I am he. Now Judas, who betrayed him, was also standing among them. 6. When therefore Jesus said to them, I am he, they went backward and fell to the ground. 7. Jesus asked them a second time, Whom are you seeking for ? They said, Jesus of Nazareth. 8. Jesus answered, I have told you that I am he ; if therefore you are seeking me, let these go their way ; 9, that the word might be fulfilled which he had spoken : I have lost none of those whom thou hast given me.*"—In coming forward spontaneously and as the first to meet the band, Jesus has a purpose which the sequel will explain. He desires, by giving Himself up, to provide for the safety of His disciples. The word *He went forth* might mean: from the remote part of the garden or from the midst of His disciples ; but it is more natural to understand : from the garden itself. He comes forward boldly even before the gate, while His disciples remain grouped behind Him in the garden ; thus are the words of ver. 26 easily explained.—The kiss of Judas, in the Synoptics, which is said to be incompatible with John's account, is naturally placed at the moment

---

[1] ℵ D L X It^{plerique} Syr. Cop.: δε instead of ουν.

[2] B C D It^{plerique} Vulg.: εξηλθεν και λεγει, instead of εξελθων ειπεν (*having gone forth, he said*).

when Jesus, coming forth from the garden, meets the band, and thus immediately before the question : *Whom are you seeking?* John alone does not mention this incident, and yet he is accused of personal animosity against Judas !—Jesus, after having experienced this last perfidy from His disciple, turns towards the band, addressing to them the question relative to their commission : He desires to have this distinctly stated, in order to shelter those who are not the object of it—that is, His disciples. The insertion of the remark relating to Judas, at the end of ver. 5, has been explained in different ways. *Luthardt* rightly says: "These words are placed between the declaration *I am he* and the effect produced by it, because they are designed to explain this effect." The impression of fear produced on the witnesses by the words *I am he*, which were pronounced with majesty and seemed to fall as a threatening from heaven—this impression could have been felt by no one of those present so vividly as by the faithless disciple, who had so often heard this same word as the affirmation of the unique dignity of Jesus ; and it was no doubt from him that the emotion was communicated to those who surrounded and followed him.—The same moral ascendency to which the traders and money-changers in the temple had yielded, and which had many times arrested the multitude at the moment of stoning Him (comp. also Luke iv. 30), causes the band suddenly to fall back, and this unexpected movement on the part of those who were foremost occasions the falling down of a certain number of those who are following them. There is no direct act of God's omnipotence here overthrowing these persons, but it would be quite as much an error to see herein only an accidental effect. This result was desired on the part of Him who produced it. By thus making them feel His power, Jesus meant to show them that it would be dangerous for them to go beyond their commission, and thereby to secure the retreat of His disciples. We see how mistaken *Weiss* is in seeing in such a miracle only a miracle of display.— Then, in a milder tone, which leads the officers to approach Him again, Jesus interrogates them a second time ; and after He has again caused them distinctly to declare that it is He, and He alone, whom they have the commission to arrest, He surrenders Himself while stipulating for the liberty of all His disciples. Then it was that the beautiful image was fulfilled which Jesus had used, x. 12 :. The shepherd sees the wolf coming, and he does not flee, because he cares for the sheep. The question was not only of the preservation, but even of the *salvation* of the disciples. John felt this indeed, and this is what gives the explanation of the remark in ver. 9. The example of Peter, the most courageous one among them, shows that an arrest would have been, at that moment, for some of the apostles the signal for a deep fall, perhaps for an irreparable denial. And Jesus, who had said to the Father : "*I have watched over those whom thou hast given me, and none of them is lost*" (xvii. 12), must fulfil to the end this serious task. All this causes *Reuss* to smile compassionately. He sees in the application which the author here makes of these words only a proof of his disposition to "indulge in double sense;" he even asks whether Jesus, in rendering an account to God of the care which He had had of His disciples, " would have hinted that He took care not to let them spend the following night in the guard-house." For our own part, this quotation seems to us instructive. No one can suppose that John was ignorant of the spiritual sense of the words of Jesus in xvii. 12 : "I have kept those whom thou hast given me, and no one of them is lost ; " and yet he applies it here to a material fact, which undoubtedly pertained, though only indirectly, to the salvation of the disciples. Here is an example fitted to make us see the broad way in which we should treat the Scriptural quotations in general.

Vv. 10, 11. Peter's attempt at defence. "*Then Simon Peter, having a sword, drew it and struck the high-priest's servant and cut off his right ear.*[1] *The servant was named Malchus.* 11. *Jesus therefore said to Peter, Put up the sword*[2] *into the sheath ; shall I not drink the cup which my Father has given me to drink ?*"—Does not John allude to Peter's natural character by designating him by his name Simon ? Comp. xxi. 15-17.—Luke xxii. 38 proves that the apostles had, in fact, brought arms with them.—This fact had been already related by the Synoptics ; why does John mention it ? He wishes, no doubt, to restore to it the precision which it had lost in the oral narration : the name of Peter had been omitted, and, very probably, intentionally ; that of Malchus had been forgotten.

The intention of depreciating Peter is again imputed to the author ; but wherein ? His action is certainly wanting neither in courage nor in faith nor in love.—And Malchus ? How can there be discovered in this name the least trace of a speculative, ideal or religious intention ? Nevertheless, *Keim* asks : "If these names were known, how should Mark and Luke omit them ?" As if what Luke and Mark were ignorant of might not have been known by another who was better informed ! How can any one persuade himself that a serious Christian of the second century, writing at a distance from Palestine, at Alexandria, in Asia Minor, or at Rome, would have set up the claim of knowing the name of a servant of the high-priest's house, and, besides, the part played by a relative of this servant (ver. 26)! Is such pitiable charlatanism compatible with the character of the author of the Fourth Gospel ? The trifling detail : "the *right* ear," is also found in Luke (xxii. 50) : this is, according to *Strauss*, a legendary amplification. To what a degree of puerility is not the evangelical narrative thus brought down !—The act of Peter, while testifying of a powerful faith and of the sincerity of his declaration in xiii. 37, was nevertheless compromising to his Master's cause. Peter, by this act, had almost taken away from Jesus the right of saying to Pilate (ver. 36) : "*If my kingdom were of this world, my servants would have fought for me.*" The reply of Jesus has traced for the Church its line of conduct in times of persecution. It is that of passive resistance, which the Apocalypse calls (xiii. 10) "*the patience of the saints.*"— The image of the cup to designate the lot to be submitted to recalls the similar expression in Jesus' prayer in Gethsemane, in the Synoptics.—Luke alone mentions the miraculous healing of Malchus. This fact explains why Peter was not indicted for the crime of rebellion.

[1] ℵ B C L X It. Vulg. : ωταριον instead of ωτιον.

[2] Σου which T. R. reads is found only in some Mnn. Vulg^{plerique}.

2

John 18:12-19:16

THE TRIAL OF JESUS

1. The ecclesiastical trial: xviii. 12–27; 2. The civil trial: xviii. 28–xix. 16.

The Trial before the Sanhedrim: xviii. 12–27

The following section contains the account of an appearance of Jesus in the house of Annas, the ex-high-priest, an account with which that of the denial of St. Peter is, as it were, interlaced. But this appearance is not mentioned in the Synoptics. On the other hand, they relate how Jesus was led from Gethsemane to the house of Caiaphas, where He appeared before the Sanhedrim and was condemned to death; and this solemn and decisive meeting is not mentioned by John.

Some think that there was in reality but one meeting, that of which the Synoptics give an account and which they place in the house of Caiaphas; whether, as *Baur, Scholten, Keim,* etc., they declare that the meeting in the house of Annas, related in our Gospel, is only an invention of its author, or, as some ancient writers, *Calvin, Lücke, de Wette, Tholuck, Langen,*[1] *Lutteroth,*[2] they think that there was only a momentary stay in the house of Annas, after which they went immediately (in ver. 15) to the house of Caiaphas, in which the appearance took place which is related by John vv. 19–23, an appearance which, in any case, must be regarded as identical with the scene of Jesus' condemnation in the Synoptics. Neither the one nor the other of these opinions is admissible. In what interest would the author of the Fourth Gospel have invented this appearance in the house of Annas? It is answered: In order to present the Jews in a more odious light by making Jesus to be condemned by two of their high-priests in succession. But by relating the story in this way, the pseudo-John would not even make Jesus to be condemned by *one* high-priest, since the session in the house of Annas is a simple inquiry without a judgment, and the session of the Synoptics, where the judgment was really pronounced, is omitted! The second opinion comes into collision with ver. 24, which proves that it was only after the inquiry in the house of Annas that Jesus was sent to the house of Caiaphas (see on that verse). If the locality of the two scenes is different, their contents are none the less so; the first is a mere preliminary investigation, the second a judicial act in all due forms, the official pronouncing of the judgment. Besides, what purpose would this stay at the house of Annas have served, and why should John have mentioned it so expressly if nothing occurred there? *Lutteroth* supposes that it was regarded as suitable to inform Annas, in passing, of the success of the arrest. But would it have

---

[1] *Die letzten Lebenstage Jesu,* 1864.   *de l' évangile de saint Matthieu,* 1876.
[2] *Essai d' interprétation des dernières parties*

been worth while to mention such a detail ?— As it was not possible to arrive at a satisfactory conclusion, either by denying the examination in the house of Annas or by confounding it with the session in the house of Caiaphas, *Beyschlag* has tried the opposite method; he thinks that the meeting in the house of Annas took place as John relates it, but that after this there was no other during the night, like that which is related by Matthew and Mark; that the latter is nothing else than that which, according to Luke, took place on the following morning (xxii. 66–71); the first two Synoptics placed it in the course of the night, because they confounded it with the examination in the house of Annas, of which they do not speak. The reason alleged for this hypothesis is that, if the judgment had been given during the night, there would have been no need of a session on the following morning, such as that of which Luke gives an account. We shall discover the error of *Beyschlag* as to this last point. But what renders this view more suspicious is the gross error which is thus imputed to Mark and Matthew.

It does not seem to us that any question is to be raised as to the fact of two perfectly distinct night sessions, one of which took place in the house of Annas (John) and the other in that of Caiaphas (Matthew and Mark); this is acknowledged by most at the present day—*Neander, Meyer, Weiss, Luthardt, Keil, Reuss*, etc. The Synoptics omitted the first, either because they were ignorant of it, or because it did not occasion any important result. John, on his part, was not ignorant of the second, for he clearly alludes to it in the *first* of ver. 13, which implies as *secondly* the appearance before Caiaphas (see on this word); then, in ver. 24, which expressly mentions as a *subsequent* fact the sending of Jesus to Caiaphas by Annas himself; finally, in ver. 28, where Jesus is led to Pilate, not from Annas' house, but from *that of Caiaphas*. Thus John, if he does not give an account of the session in the house of Caiaphas, very exactly indicates its place, as he had done in ver. 1 with reference to the scene of Gethsemane. Moreover, what completes the proof that John cannot either have been ignorant of or have denied the judgment-scene in the house of Caiaphas, is the whole of the sequel in his own narrative. He represents to us the Sanhedrim as going to ask of Pilate the confirmation and execution of the *death-sentence* which they had pronounced (ver. 31, xix. 7, 11, 16). Now in the session in Annas' house, of which John has given the description, no condemnation was pronounced. John's narrative itself therefore implies a meeting of the Sanhedrim in the proper sense of the word, exercising its functions as a high-court of justice for the judgment of the accused, and consequently the entire meeting in the house of Caiaphas as Matthew and Mark describe it. It will be asked what, in this case, was the purpose of the appearance in the house of Annas. It was, above all, to serve the purpose of drawing from the mouth of Jesus some compromising expression suited to furnish a reason for His condemnation; for there was embarrassment on this subject, as the summoning of the false witnesses in the Synoptics proves. Besides, the judicial customs required this formality. A capital sentence could be pronounced by the Sanhedrim only on the day which followed that on which the accused had appeared in court.¹ In this case it was impossible to observe this rule fully, since the decision had been made to hasten the time; comp. Mark xiv. 2. But they must at least try to save appearances as far as possible, and to offer the semblance of a first preliminary meeting, before that at which the sentence should be pronounced. The Synoptics, as was in harmony with the nature of the oral tradition, preserved only the remembrance of that which was historically conspicuous; John, in comformity with his ordinary course of action, omits the solemn session which was sufficiently well known through the Synoptic narrative, and restored the part of the facts which was omitted by them—no doubt, not for the purpose of materially completing them, but that he might not suffer the radiance of the glory of Jesus to be lost, which had shone forth in the meeting held in the house of Annas. *Luthardt* and *Weiss* think that, if John has related the scene in the house of Annas, it is only with a view to Peter's denial, which is connected with it, and which he wished to relate in order to show the fulfilment of the words of Jesus in xiii. 38. But if the story of this appearance had had this purpose only, it would have been sufficient to indicate it, without describing the scene in all its details.

Hilgenfeld explains the omission in John of the scene of the condemnation of Jesus by the Sanhedrim, by reason of the fact that the *Jewish Messiahship* of Jesus had been very strongly emphasized there, a thing which was displeasing to the pseudo-John. But with the freedom which the author used in respect to the history (according to this school), there was nothing easier for him than to modify the account of this scene, for example, by making the sentence of Jesus bear only upon the affirmation of His dignity as *Son of God*, which was perfectly in accordance with the spirit of his work. Besides, if the idea of the Messianic office was so repugnant to him, why should he have called it to mind from the first and even in the last words of his Gospel (i. 42-46 and xx. 31)? *Keim*, however, gets excited, and says: "Who is so blind . . . as to seek for truth in a narrative which—after having introduced the examination in the house of Annas as a fact of a decisive character—sets aside (*ignorirt*) in the most unpardonable way that which took place in the house of Caiaphas" (pp. 322, 323)! But what decisive result, then, did the meeting in Annas' house have? The result, according to John himself, was nothing, to the great annoyance of the enemies who counted on discovering some complaint against Him for the great judicial session which was about to follow. As to the session in the house of Caiaphas, it is by no means set aside (*ignorirt*), as we have just seen, since John very correctly and repeatedly assigns to it its place (ver. 24).—*Reuss*, in his *Histoire évangélique* (p. 663), expresses himself thus: "John says nothing, and we will add, without falling into an error, knows nothing of the official examination and of the trial before the court, because all this takes place with closed doors." We have proved, on the contrary, that John knows perfectly well the facts which he omits. How should he not have been aware of the judgment of Jesus by the Sanhedrim, if it were only through the oral tradition which passed into the Synoptics and through the Synoptics themselves, with which John was acquainted, as even *Reuss* himself now confesses. If, then, he

---

¹ *Schürer*, pp. 416, 417, according to *Sanhedrin*, iv. 1, v. 5.

did not relate this scene, it is because he did not wish to do so, and we know the reason why he did not. Though this fact may be contrary to the system of Reuss respecting the Fourth Gospel, it is nevertheless indisputable. As to *Renan*, with much more impartiality than the theologians, he is unsparing in his admiration of John's narrative. "Our author alone," he says, "represents Jesus as brought to the house of Annas, the father-in-law of Caiaphas. Josephus confirms the correctness of this account. . . . This circumstance, of which the first two Gospels give no hint, is a beam of light. How should a sectary, writing in Egypt or in Asia Minor, have known this? . . . It is a strong proof of the historical value of our Gospel" (pp. 522 and 407). In fact, the relationship of Annas and Caiaphas, which, as we shall see, is an important element in the explanation of the narrative, is a matter of information which John must have received at first hand, for Josephus himself does not mention this fact, although it is perfectly in accordance with his narrative.

1. Jesus before Annas

Vv. 12–14. "*The cohort and the tribune and the officers of the Jews seized Jesus, therefore, and bound him,* 13, *and they led[1] him first to Annas; for he was father-in-law of Caiaphas, who was high-priest of that year.[2]* 14. *Caiaphas was he who had given this counsel to the Jews: that it was expedient that one man should die[3] for the people.*"—The word πρῶτον, *first*, contains a tacit correction of the Synoptics, according to which Jesus was led *directly* to the house of Caiaphas; comp. an altogether similar remark in iii. 24.—It has been supposed that this *in the first place*, or *first*, alludes to the subsequent sending of Jesus to Pilate; but see on vv. 24, 28. According to these verses, the understood *secondly* is certainly the sending to Caiaphas.—Annas had himself been high-priest during the years 6–15 of our era, thus about fifteen years before this time. We see in Josephus that he was the influential man of the period. John, however, gives us to understand that the true reason why Jesus was led at this moment to his house was rather his relationship to Caiaphas, the high-priest. By virtue of this relationship, the two personages constituted, as it were, but a single one. Comp. the expression in Luke iii. 2.—On vv. 13, 14, comp. xi. 50, 51. By establishing the identity of this personage with the one mentioned in ch. xi., John would give us to understand what kind of justice Jesus had to expect on the part of a judge who had already expressed himself in this way.

2. The first denial

Vv. 15–18. "*Now Simon Peter followed Jesus, as well as another[4] disciple, and that disciple was known to the high-priest, and he entered in with Jesus into the court of the high-priest.* 16. *And Peter was standing without at the door;*

---

[1] ℵ B D 6 Mnn.: ηγαγον instead of απηγαγον. — ℵ B C D X Δ It^{aliq} omit αυτον.

[2] Cod. 225 adds after πρωτον: απεστειλεν ουν αυτον ο Αννας δεδεμενον προς Καιαφαν τον αρχιερεα (*Annas sent him therefore bound to Caiaphas the high-priest*). Syr^p adds the same words in the margin. Cyril reads after εκεινου: απεστειλαν δε αυτον δεδεμενον προς Καιαφαν τον αρχιερεα (comp. ver. 24).

[3] ℵ B C L X 13 Mnn. some Vss.: αποθανειν instead of απολεσθαι.

[4] ℵ A B 5 Mnn. and probably It. Vulg. Syr. Cop. Sah. omit ο (*the*) before αλλος (*an*-other disciple).

the other disciple, who was known to the high-priest,[1] *went out therefore and spoke to her who kept the door, and brought in*[2] *Peter.* 17. *The maid that kept the door, therefore, says to Peter, Art not thou also of this man's disciples? Peter answers, I am not.* 18. *Now the servants and the officers were standing there, having made a fire of charcoal, because it was cold ; and Peter*[3] *was standing among them and warming himself.*"—While the Synoptics relate in a consecutive way the three denials of Peter, probably because in the oral preaching the narrative of this event formed an altogether peculiar little story, an ἀπομνημόνευμα, John separates the three acts of denial in the course of his narration, passing alternately from Peter to Jesus and from Jesus to Peter. This better articulated narrative certainly reproduces the true course of things, and nothing more clearly reveals in the author of our Gospel the witness of the facts, who through his own recollections exercised power over the received tradition. "The same superiority," says *Renan*, rightly, "in the account of Peter's denials. All is more circumstantial, better explained." —With the article ὁ, *the*, the term *the other disciple* could only be referred to the disciple whom Jesus loved, whose particular connection with Peter we have already ascertained in xiii. 21, 24. But this article is wanting in the Alexandrian documents and in the ancient Versions. Nothing, moreover, in the context justifies the use of the definite article. If we read, as we should, "*an*other disciple," it may be John himself ; this is the more common supposition. The periphrasis, however, of which he makes use in order to preserve his anonymous character is rather this : "the disciple *whom Jesus loved*" (xiii. 23, xix. 26). I formerly attempted to justify this change of expression by saying that "it was not the occasion for using a term of tenderness when the disciples had just abandoned their Master ;" but this explanation is somewhat subtle. Did not John designate by this phrase some other disciple, his brother James, for example, whom he does not mention by *name* anywhere in his whole Gospel, any more than he does himself or his mother ?—We do not know the relations which Zebedee and his sons may have had with the household of the high-priest. Perhaps the very profession of Zebedee had furnished the occasion for it. Thanks to these relations, this disciple had been able to enter within the priestly palace with the company, and soon he was able to gain admission for Peter, who had undoubtedly asked of him this service.

But of what high-priest does John mean to speak when he says in ver. 15 : *into the court of the high-priest* (αὐλή, more probably here the interior court than the palace itself) ? On the one hand, if the relation of ἠκολούθει, *followed*, ver. 15, to ἀπήγαγον, *led him away*, ver. 13, is considered, it seems that there can be no question except of the palace of Annas. On the other hand, according to vv. 13, 14, how can we suppose that there can be a question of another high-priest than Caiaphas, who has just now expressly received the title? Undoubtedly, Annas is also called ἀρχιερεύς (Acts iv. 6). *Schürer* has even shown that this title might be applied to all the members of the

---

[1] Instead of ος ην γνωστος τω αρχ., B C L read ο γν. του αρχ.

[2] ℵ : εισηνεγκε instead of εισηγαγεν

[3] ℵ B C L X some Mnn. It^{pleriq} Vulg. Syr. Cop. read και before ο Πετρος (and Peter *also*).

privileged families from which the high-priests were ordinarily taken. Nevertheless, this title has nowhere in our Gospel this broad sense, and it would be difficult indeed to believe that after having contrasted, as he has done in ver. 13, Caiaphas as "*the high-priest* of that year," with Annas, his *father-in-law*, John would designate this latter person, a few lines farther on, simply by the title of *high-priest*. How could the readers, who had never heard of Annas, have supposed that he also bore this title ? It is, therefore, clearly the house of Caiaphas of which John means to speak, if he has not written in an unintelligible way. But, in that case, it is asked how the relations which the disciple sustained to the high-priest Caiaphas and the members of his household could open to him the entrance into the abode of Annas, to whom Jesus was first led. There is but one solution to this question, which the narrative of John itself suggests, setting aside that of the Synoptics ; it is that these two personages lived in the same palace. The bond of close relationship which united them explains this circumstance, and it is for this reason, undoubtedly, that John has so expressly noticed this particular. *Meyer* is wrong, therefore, in saying that the text does not offer the least indication in favor of this opinion. John's account leads directly to it.

The Hebrews very commonly had female doorkeepers (Josephus, *Antiq.* vii. 2, 1; Acts xii. 13; 2 Sam. iv. 6, according to the text of the LXX).— The καί, *also* ("Art not thou *also*"), shows that this woman already knew the unnamed disciple as one of the adherents of Jesus.—The three denials of Peter, as *Luthardt* observes, have three distinct historical starting-points, which are more or less distributed among the four evangelists : 1. The introduction of Peter into the court by a friend, who was himself known as a disciple of Jesus; 2. The recollection which had been retained of Peter by those who had seen him at the time of the arrest of Jesus ; 3. His Galilean dialect. To these external circumstances, which called forth his trial, was added an internal one which facilitated his fall : the recollection of the blow which he had struck, and which exposed him, more than all the rest, to the danger of being involved in the judgment of his Master. Fear therefore combined with presumption ; and thus was the warning which Jesus had given him verified : "*The spirit is willing, but the flesh is weak.*"

The δοῦλοι, *servants*, ver. 18, designate the domestic servants attached to the priestly house; the ὑπηρέται, *officers*, are the official servants of the Sanhedrim, charged with the police duties of the temple.—The last words of ver. 18 : *Peter was standing with them and warming himself*, are repeated literally in ver. 25. They are placed here, as a stepping-stone with a view to the approaching resumption of the story relating to Peter, after the appearance of Jesus in the house of Annas. Hence it follows : 1. That there is an absolute impossibility in the way of placing the last two denials in another locality than the first ; and 2. That these last two denials took place, not *after*, but *during* the examination of Jesus.—The verbs in the imperfect tense are picturesque, and signify that the situation described continues during the whole examination which is about to be related, so that, according to the narrative, the scene of vv. 25, 26 (Peter) took place simultaneously with that of vv. 19–23 (Jesus).

3. Appearance in the house of Annas

Vv. 19–21. *"The high-priest therefore asked Jesus concerning his disciples and his doctrine. 20. Jesus answered him : I have spoken[1] openly to the world; I have always taught in open synagogue[2] and in the temple, where all[3] the Jews come together, and I have said nothing in secret. 21. Why askest thou me?[4] Ask[4] those who have heard me what I have said to them: behold, these know what I have said."*—It is generally held that, as the examination took place in the house of Annas, it was he who directed the investigation. But this would imply that the high-priest of vv. 13–16 was Annas, which we have seen to be contrary to the natural meaning of John's narrative. This session was a purely private one; it had its necessary place, as we have seen, in the course of the trial; the presence of the officer in ver. 22 implies the official character of the scene. The duty of presiding over it fell, therefore, to the high-priest officially. It has been supposed that Annas was exercising functions here in the character of *Ab-beth-din* (chief of the court of justice). But this dignity appertained to the high-priest himself (*Schürer*, p. 413). *Keim* rightly says (certainly not to support the narrative of John): "If Caiaphas was truly the acting high-priest and, at the same time, the soul of the sudden onset which was proposed against Jesus, it belonged to him, and not to his father-in-law, to acquaint himself with the matter and to make a report to the Sanhedrim" (iii. p. 322). If it was otherwise, according to John, what purpose would the characterizing of Caiaphas, in ver. 13, have served ? When, in ver. 22, the officer says to Jesus : *Answerest thou the high-priest so?* it is unnatural to think of another personage than the actual high-priest, the one who has just been expressly designated as such in vv. 13, 14. *Reuss* brings forward in opposition to our view ver. 24, in which the high-priest must necessarily be *another* personage than the one who is called thus in ver. 19. At the first glance, this observation appears just. But if Jesus was led away *to the house of Annas*, it was quite naturally Annas who gave the order to conduct Him to the house of Caiaphas, while yet it would not follow from this fact that it was Annas himself who presided over the preliminary session.

The question proposed to Jesus had as its design to draw from Him an answer suited to give a ground for His condemnation. For there was embarrassment felt respecting the course to be pursued in this matter, as the recourse to the false witnesses proves.—What is asked of Jesus is not the names of His disciples, as if the question were of a list of accomplices ; it is information as to the number of His partisans and the principles which serve them as a standard.—Jesus, understanding that they were only

---

[1] ℵ A B C L X Y Δ: λελαληκα, instead of ελαλησα.

[2] T. R. reads τη before συναγωγη (*the* synagogue) with A and some Mnn. only.

[3] T. R. with some Mnn. only : παντοθεν (*from all quarters*) ς with 10 Mjj. (Y Γ Δ Λ etc.) : παντοτε (*always*); ℵ A B C L X Π : παντες (*all*).

[4] T. R. with Byz. : επερωτας and επερωτησον ; Alex.: ερωτας and ερωτησον.

seeking to wrest from Him an expression which might be turned to account against Him, simply appeals to the publicity of His teaching. He is not the head of a secret society, nor the propagator of principles which fear the light of day.—Συναγωγῇ, without an article (according to the true reading): *in synagogal assembly;* the word ἱερόν, *temple,* has the article, because this edifice is unique. When Jesus instructed His disciples in private, it was not for the purpose of telling them something different from what He declared in public.—The testimony of the ancient Versions decides in favor of the Alexandrian reading : "*all* the Jews ; " not, the Jews *from all parts* or *continually.*

Vv. 22, 23. " *When he had said this, one of the officers, who was at his side, struck him with a rod, saying, Answerest thou the high-priest so ? 23. Jesus answered him, If I have spoken evil, bear witness of the evil; but if I have spoken well, why dost thou smite me?* "—The answer of Jesus certainly contained a tacit rebuke intended for the one who thus interrogated Him. An officer who wished to court the favor of his chief takes occasion to remind Jesus of the respect due to the ruler of Israel. The word ῥάπισμα properly means : a blow with a rod. Undoubtedly in Matt. v. 39 the verb ῥαπίζειν is taken in the sense of striking in the face. The proper sense, however, is here the more natural one; comp. the term δέρειν, *to flay,* ver. 23. Μαρτυρεῖν : to prove by a regular giving of testimony.—Jesus does not literally fulfil here His own precept, Matt. v. 39; but by this reply, full of dignity and gentleness, He endeavors to bring the man to himself, which is precisely the moral fulfilment of that precept.

Ver. 24. " *Annas therefore*[1] *sent him bound to Caiaphas, the high-priest.*"— This verse has always perplexed those who have held that at ver. 15 Jesus was led to the house of Caiaphas, and that the session which John has just described is the great session of the Sanhedrim, which is related by the Synoptics. This twofold error is what has occasioned the transposition of this verse in some documents to a place after ver. 13 (see the critical note on that verse). It is this likewise which has led some interpreters, such as *Calvin, Lücke, Tholuck, de Wette, Langen,* to take ἀπέστειλαν in the sense of the pluperfect, *had sent.* But when the aorist has the sense of the pluperfect, the context clearly indicates it. Precisely the contrary is here the case. Besides, the particle οὖν, *therefore,* if it is authentic, excludes this explanation, and it is even probable that this is precisely the reason which has made some reject it and others change it into δέ, *now:* "*Now,* Annas had sent. . . . " By inserting this notice here, the evangelist simply wished, as by the πρῶτον, *first,* of ver. 13, to reserve a place expressly for the session in the house of Caiaphas, which was indeed otherwise important, and of which he does not give an account. Comp. ver. 1 (for the scene in Gethsemane) and ver. 5 (for the kiss of Judas). *Lutteroth* gives to this verse a sentimental cast. There is, according to him, a picture here; John means to say: Behold! This Jesus, thus struck by the officer, was standing there with His hands bound, in the condition in which *Annas had* [previ-

---

[1] T. R. (ςe) with B C L X It^alia some Mnn., reads οὖν (*therefore*); ℵ Syr^sch some Mnn. : δε (*now*) ; ⸆ with 13 Mjj. (A etc.) omits the particle altogether.

ously] *sent Him to Caiaphas!* But this sense has nothing in common with the simplicity and sobriety of the apostolic narrative; it implies, moreover, the pluperfect sense as here given to the aorist.—Jesus had undoubtedly been unbound during the examination; after this scene, Annas causes Him to be bound again, in order to send Him to the house of Caiaphas. Probably He was unbound a second time during the session of the Sanhedrim. This explains why in Matt. xxvii. 2 and Mark xv. 1, He is bound anew at the time of leading Him away to Pilate.—*To Caiaphas :* in the part of the palace where Caiaphas lived, and where were the official apartments and the hall for the meetings of the Sanhedrim. This body had been called together in the interval; for all the members were in Jerusalem for the feast. The title of high-priest reminds us of the wholly official character of the session which was in preparation, as well as that of the place where it occurred.

4. Second and third denial

Vv. 25–27. "*And Simon Peter was standing and warming himself. They said therefore to him, Art not thou also one of his disciples? He denied and said, I am not.* 26. *One of the servants of the high-priest, a kinsman of him whose ear Peter cut off, says to him, Did I not see thee in the garden with him?* 27. *Peter denied again; and immediately the cock crew.*"—As far as ver. 18, according to John, all has happened in the house of Annas; and as ver. 25 expressly places us again in the situation of ver. 18, it is evident that the following facts also occur at his house; it is the same court, the same fire, the same persons; so that those who, like *Weiss*, are unwilling to admit that Caiaphas and Annas lived in two different apartments of the same priestly palace, are obliged to hold that Matthew and Mark have made a mistake in placing the denial of Peter in the house of Caiaphas. As for ourselves, we have already stated the reasons which seem to us to support the contrary opinion.—The sending of Jesus to Caiaphas, mentioned already in ver. 24, in reality followed the last denial (ver. 27). For the facts of vv. 25–27 took place simultaneously with vv. 19–23. This circumstance explains the incident, related by Luke, of the look which Jesus cast upon Peter (xxii. 61). Jesus crossed the court to go from the apartments of Annas to those of Caiaphas (ver. 24). He heard at this moment the cock-crowing (ver. 27); and then it was that His eye met that of Peter. The epithet δεδεμένον, *bound*, makes us understand more fully the impression produced on the unfaithful disciple by the sight of his Master in this condition.

The subject of εἶπον, *they said* (ver. 25), is indefinite. According to Matthew, it is a maid-servant who sees Peter approaching the gate to go forth from the court to the front of the house. According to Mark, it is the same maid-servant who had already troubled him in the first instance and who denounces him to the servants who were gathered about the fire. In Luke, it is indefinitely ἕτερος, *another* person. It is probable that the portress spoke of Peter to one of her companions, who denounced him to the assembled servants. From this group came forth instantly the question addressed to Peter.—After the second denial, Peter seems to have played the bold part, and to have set himself to speak more freely with the persons present. But his Galilean accent was soon noticed, and attracted the more particular attention of a kinsman of Malchus, a fact which occasioned the third denial.—John does not mention the imprecations which Matthew puts into Peter's mouth. If, then, any one was animated by hostile feelings towards this disciple, it was the first evangelist, and not the author of our narrative. Though he does not speak of Peter's repentance, the narrative of the scene in xxi. 15 ff. evidently implies it.—The story of the denial of Peter is, besides those of the multiplication of the loaves and of the entrance of Jesus into Jerusalem, the only one which is related at once by John and the Synoptics. There is no discourse here to be accounted for, as in ch. vi., and no series of events to be explained, as in ch. xii. John's purpose, therefore, could only have been to reproduce in all their grievous reality the two simultaneous scenes of the appearance of the Master before the authorities and the disciple's denial, which had formed the prelude of the Passion. In any case, we may discover here how the oral tradition related the facts with less of life and flexibility than is done by the pen of an eye-witness. The latter alone has reproduced the minutest articulations of the history; and it is not without reason that *Renan* speaks of "its varied and sharply defined points."

The Trial before Pilate: xviii. 28–xix. 16

Had the Romans, in making Judea a province of the empire, taken away from the Jews the right of capital punishment? Our narrative affirms this positively by putting in the mouths of the latter the words (ver. 31): "*It is not permitted us to put any one to death.*" To this have been objected the execution of Stephen, Acts vii. 57 ff., and the permission which Titus had granted the Jews to put foreigners, even Romans, to death who had invaded the inclosure of the temple court (Josephus, *Antiq.* vi. 2, 4). But the first event was an extra-legal act of popular fury, and the permission given by Titus is quite an exceptional case. According to the Talmud, as according to John, the right of inflicting capital punishment belonged no longer to the Sanhedrim. And it was precisely at the time of the judgment of Jesus that this change took place, "forty years before the destruction of the temple."[1] Probably, in the time which followed the annexation, the governors desired to use moderation towards the conquered people. But the despotic Pilate had reduced the Jews to the common law of the provinces. This was the reason which obliged the rulers to bring Jesus before this governor in order to obtain from him the confirmation and execution of the sentence which they had just pronounced.—Pilate was from the year 26 procurator of Judea, under the order of the proconsul of Syria. He was deposed in 36 by Vitellius and sent to Rome, to be judged there for all the wrongs which he had committed. According to "Greek historians" (Euseb. ii. 7), he was put to death under Caligula.—Such were the reasons

---

[1] *Sanhedr.* fol. 24, 2: *Quadraginta annis capitalia ab Israele ante vastatum templum ablata sunt judicia*

which made the Jews hold a third session—that *of the morning*, which took place very early, no longer in the high-priest's house, but in the vicinity of the temple, either in the famous hall paved with mosaic (*lischkath haggazith*), situated in the interior court at the south of the temple, or in the synagogue *Beth midrasch*, between the court of the women and the outer court (see *Keim*, III. p. 351). This is confirmed by Matthew (xxvii. 1), Mark (xvi. 1), and especially Luke (xxii. 66 ff.)[1] The last mentioned has preserved for us the most complete account of this session, perhaps mingling in it some particulars borrowed from the great session in the night, which he passes over in silence. In any case, the examination and the judgment of Jesus must have been repeated a second time, though summarily, and confirmed in this morning session, which was the only legal and plenary one (πάντες, *all*, Matt.). We must observe the expression of Matthew, ὥστε θανατῶσαι αὐτόν, *to put him to death*, which indicates the seeking for *ways and means* to succeed in obtaining from Pilate the execution of the sentence, as well as the expression of Luke : "*They led him into their assembly*," ver. 66, which can only refer to the passage from the house of Caiaphas (ver. 54) to one of the two meeting-halls near the temple, of which we have just spoken.

The Jews ask Pilate to confirm their sentence *without an examination* (ver. 30). The latter refuses ; this is the first phase of the negotiations : vv. 28–32. Then they set forth a *political* accusation : He made Himself a king. Pilate judges this accusation unfounded ; then he makes two ineffectual attempts to deliver Jesus with the support of the people ; this is the second phase : ver. 33–xix. 6. The Jews then bring forward a *religious* charge : He made Himself Son of God. On hearing this accusation Pilate endeavors still more to deliver Jesus ; this is the third phase : xix. 7–12a. At this moment, the Jews, seeing their prey ready to escape them, put aside all shame, and employ the odious expedient of *personal* intimidation to make the judge's conscience yield. On this path they suffer themselves to be carried away even to the point of the denial of their dearest hope—that of the Messiah ; they declare themselves vassals of Cæsar ; this is the fourth phase : xix. 12b–16.

Ver. 28. "*They lead Jesus therefore from Caiaphas to the Prætorium. Now it was early. And they did not themselves enter into the Prætorium, that they might not be defiled, but that*[2] *they might eat the Passover.*"—The *Prætorium* was at Rome the place where the prætor sat when he administered justice. This name had been applied to the palaces of the Roman governors in the provinces. Most interpreters hold that this term designates here the palace of Herod, which was in the western part of the upper city. In proof of this the passage of Josephus, *Bell. Jud.* ii. 14, 8, is cited, where it is said that "Florus lived *at that time* (τότε) in the royal palace ;" but this passage proves precisely that the Roman governor did not ordinarily live there. It is more probable that Pilate occupied a palace

---

[1] *Lightfoot*, *Hor. Hebr.* in Matt. xxvii. 1. *Keim:* "The day meeting was required to complete, in point of legality, that of the night. For the meetings of the Sanhedrim, especially in the case of a capital judgment, were required to be held in the day-time and in the morning, *before man has eaten or drunk.*"

[2] ℵ A B C Δ reject the second ἵνα.

contiguous to the citadel Antonia, where the Roman garrison was stationed, at the north-west corner of the temple. It is there, at all events, that tradition places the starting-point of the *Via Dolorosa*.—Πρωί (T. R. πρωία), *in the early morning*, includes the time from three to six o'clock (Mark xiii. 35). The Roman courts opened their sessions at any hour after sunrise (*Westcott*). Pilate, as we have seen, was forewarned, since the previous evening, of what was taking place, and he had no doubt consented to receive the Jews at this early hour.

The scruple which prevents the Jews from entering into the governor's house places us again face to face with the contradiction which seems to exist between the narrative of John and that of the Synoptics. If, as these latter seem to say, the Jews had already *on the previous evening* celebrated the Paschal meal, how can we explain the fact that, through defiling themselves by contact with the leaven which would necessarily be found in a Gentile house, they fear that they may be unable to celebrate this meal on this same evening? The only way of escaping this contradiction, it seems, would be to give a wider sense to the expression *to eat the Passover*, by referring it, not to the Paschal meal properly so called, but to the food of the feast in general, such as the unleavened bread and the flesh of the peace-offerings which were celebrated during the seven days of the feast. Some passages are thought to have been found in the Old Testament where the word *Passover* is taken in this more general sense; thus Deut. xvi. 2, 3: "*Thou shalt sacrifice the Passover to the Lord, of the flock and of the herd, and with it* (these meats) *thou shalt eat unleavened bread seven days.*" Comp. the analogous expression 2 Chron. xxx. 22 (literally): "*And they ate the feast* (the feast-sacrifices) *seven days, offering sacrifices of peace offerings and praising the Lord;*" 2 Chron. xxxv. 7-9: "*And Josiah gave to those of the people who were there lambs and kids, to the number of thirty thousand, all of them for Passover offerings, and three thousand bullocks, of the king's substance.*" To confirm this conclusion it is alleged that, according to the Talmud, the defilement which the Jews would have contracted by entering the Prætorium would have continued in any case only until the end of the day, and consequently would not have prevented them from eating the Paschal meal in the evening.—But the passages cited do not prove what they would need to prove. As to the first (Deut. xvi. 2, 3), the term *Passover* is applied exclusively, in vv. 5, 6, which immediately follow, to the Paschal lamb; hence it follows that in ver. 2 the expression *of the herd and of the flock* is not an explanatory apposition of the word *pesach* (Passover), but a supplementary addition by which all the secondary sacrifices which complete the Paschal supper during the course of the week are designated. At all events, if the term *Passover* really included here, *together with* the Paschal lamb, all the other sacrifices of the feast, it would not follow therefrom that it could designate, as would be the case in our passage, these last *apart from the first*. As to the *with it*, it refers to all the sacrificial meats which were to be accompanied by unleavened bread during the entire week.—In 2 Chron. ch. xxx. the name *Passover* is applied in vv. 15, 17, 18 *exclusively* to the Paschal lamb. Why, then, should the chronicler in ver. 22

substitute for the proper term : to eat the Passover, the more general expression *to eat the feast*, if it was not because he wished now to speak of the sacrifices of the feast, *exclusive of* the eating of the Paschal lamb ? Besides, the reading : *and they ate (vajokelou) the feast*, is very doubtful. The LXX certainly read : *vajekallou, and they finished the feast;* for they translate : καὶ συνετέλεσαν.—In the third passage (2 Chron. xxxv. 7–9) the distinction between the lambs or kids which were intended to serve for the Paschal meal (*pesachim*) and the bullocks which were consecrated to the other sacrifices and feasts is obvious.—But even supposing that in some passages of the Old Testament the term *Passover* had received from the context a wider meaning than ordinary, would it follow from this that a phrase so common in the New Testament, in Josephus and in the Talmud, as that of *eating the Passover*, could be applied, without any explanatory indication, to entirely different meals from the Paschal supper, and this even to the exclusion of the latter ?

As to the objection derived from the duration of the defilement which the Jews would have contracted : 1. It is impossible to form any certain conclusion, with reference to the time of Jesus, from a passage of the Rabbi Maimonides written about the year 1200. 2. This passage refers to a defilement arising from contact with dead animals, etc., and not to the defilement arising from leaven, and with special relation to the Paschal feast. The same is the case with the examples borrowed from other kinds of defilement (Lev. xv. 5 ff., 19 ff.). After the analogy of Num. ix. 6 ff., the Jews would simply have been obliged to put off the celebration of the Passover until the 14th of the following month. 3. If the question were only of the feast-meals in general, the members of the Sanhedrim might have abstained altogether from taking part in them ; for these meals were voluntary ; the Paschal supper alone did not allow of abstention.[1] 4. The defilement thus contracted would, in any case, have forced the priests, who were members of the Sanhedrim, to abstain from participating *in the sacrifice* of the lamb in the afternoon, an abstention which was incompatible with their official duty.

For all these reasons it is impossible for me to adopt the opinion of many and learned interpreters who refer the expression *to eat the Passover* in our verse to the peace-offering (the *Chagigah*), which the Jews offered on the 16th of Nisan at mid-day ; we will mention among the modern writers only *Tholuck, Olshausen, Hengstenberg, Wieseler, Hofmann, Lange, Riggenbach, Bäumlein, Langen, Luthardt, Kirchner* and *Keil*.

The pronoun αὐτοί, *themselves*, contrasts the Jews, with their Levitical purity, to Jesus, whom nothing could any longer defile, so defiled was He already in their eyes. He was immediately delivered over to the governor, and introduced into the Prætorium. From this time, therefore, Pilate will go from the Prætorium to the Jews (vv. 29, 38, xix. 4–12) and from the Jews to the Prætorium (ver. 33, xix. 1, 9). *Keim* judges this situation to be historically impossible, and jests about this ambulant judge, this *peripa-*

---

[1] See the Article of *Andreæ* already cited (xiii. 1) in the *Beweis des Glaubens*, 1870.

tetic negotiator, whom the narrative of John presents to us. But the apostle clearly perceived that this situation had an exceptional character, and he has precisely explained it by this ver. 28. Pilate does not feel himself free in his position with regard to the Jews ; the sequel shows this only too clearly. This is the reason why he bears with their scruples.—The *first position* taken by the Jews :

Vv. 29-32. "*Pilate therefore went out[1] to them and said,[2] What accusation do you bring against[3] this man?* 30. *They answered him, saying, If he were not an evil doer,[4] we should not have delivered him to thee.* 31. *Pilate therefore[5] said to them, Take him yourselves, and judge him according to your law.* Whereupon the Jews answered him, It is not permitted us to put any one to death; 32, *that the word might be fulfilled which Jesus had spoken,[6] signifying by what death he should die.*"—The ordinary residence of the governor was Cæsarea ; but he went to Jerusalem at the time of the feasts. Pilate was fond of displaying before the eyes of the people on these occasions the pomp of Roman majesty. Philo (*Leg. ad Caium*) represents him as a proud, obstinate, intractable man. Nevertheless, it is probable that the fanaticism of the Jews was also an important element in the contentions which they continually had with him. "All the acts of Pilate which are known to us," says *Renan*, "show him to have been a good administrator." This portrait is somewhat flattering ; but it is partially confirmed by the picture which Josephus himself has drawn of his government, *Antiq.* xviii. 2-4.— Οὖν, *therefore:* in consequence of the fact that the Jews were unwilling to enter into his palace.

The answer of the Jews to Pilate (ver. 30) is skilful ; it is dictated by two reasons : on the one hand, they endeavor to keep the largest possible share of their ancient autonomy, by continuing in the main the judges, and leaving to Pilate the part of executioner ; and, on the other hand, they undoubtedly are also apprehensive of not succeeding before him with their political and religious grievances. The manœuvre was well contrived. But Pilate understands them ; he refuses the position which they wish to give him. He plays cautiously with them. Entering apparently into their thought, delighted at finding a means of relieving himself of the affair, he replies without hesitation : "Very good ! Since you wish to be sole judges of the case, be so! Take the accused and punish Him yourselves (ὑμεῖς, ver. 31), of course within the limits of your competency." The Sanhedrim had, in fact, certain disciplinary rights, like that of excommunicating, scourging, etc. There was no need of Pilate in order to inflict these punishments ; only this was not death. Some interpreters have thought that Pilate really authorized them to put Jesus to death, but with this understood reservation : "If you can and dare " (*Hengstenberg*). But this is to make Pilate say yes and no at the same time. XIX. 6 proves nothing in favor of this meaning, as we shall see.

---

[1] ℵ adds εξω after Πιλατος, B C L X Syr. before προς αυτους ; others after these words.
[2] ℵ B C L X : φησιν instead of ειπεν.
[3] ℵ B omit κατα.
[4] ℵ reads κακον ποιησας, B L κακον ποιων, instead of κακοποιος.
[5] B C omit ουν ; A K U Π read δε.
[6] ℵ omits ον ειπεν.

This answer did not suit the Jews; for they wished that, at any cost, Jesus might be put to death. It forced them, therefore, to make confession of their dependence, at least in this regard (ver. 31). And this circumstance seems to the evangelist significant (ver. 32); for, if they had been their own masters, or had allowed themselves to be carried away, as afterwards in the murder of Stephen, to act as if they still were so, Jesus would have undergone the Jewish, and not the Roman punishment; He would have been stoned; this was the punishment of the false prophets, according to the Talmud (see *Westcott*). But He would not have been lifted up upon the cross, from which, by His calmness, His submission, His patience, His pardon, His love, He incessantly draws all men to Himself as He had announced beforehand (iii. 14, viii. 28, xii. 32); what a difference from the tumultuous punishment of stoning! Comp. also xix. 36, 37.

The *second position* taken by the Jews:

Vv. 33–35. "*Pilate entered again therefore into the Prætorium, and he called Jesus and said to him, Art thou the king of the Jews?* 34. *Jesus answered him:*[1] *Sayest thou*[2] *this of thyself,*[3] *or did others tell it thee of me?* 35. *Pilate answered: Am I a Jew? Thine own nation and the chief priests*[4] *have delivered thee to me; what hast thou done?*"—John's narrative evidently presents a gap here. There is nothing in what precedes to give a reason for the question of Pilate to Jesus: *Art thou the king of the Jews?* Such an inquiry implies, therefore, an expression on the part of the accusers which gives occasion for it. This supposition is changed into certainty when we compare the narrative of the Synoptics, particularly that of Luke. "*We found him,*" say the Jews on approaching Pilate, "*troubling the nation, forbidding to pay tribute to Cæsar, saying that he is the Christ, the King*" (xxiii. 2). Luke, as well as Mark and Matthew, has omitted the whole first phase of the accusation, which has just been related by John. The Synoptics begin their narrative at the moment when the Jews come down again to their more humble part as accusers, and concede to Pilate his position as judge. Hence it follows that John, after having supplied in what precedes that which the Synoptics had omitted, now implies as known to his readers the political accusation mentioned by them. We see how intimate and constant is the relation between his narrative and theirs. *Keil* concludes from the words *he called Jesus*, that up to this moment Jesus had remained outside. But see above. He called Him *aside* in the Prætorium itself, to a place where he could speak with Him alone. To his question, Pilate certainly expected a frank negative answer. But the position was not as simple as he imagined. There was a distinction to be made here, not to the thought of Pilate, but to that of Jesus. In the political sense of the term *king of the Jews*, the only one known to Pilate, Jesus might reject this title; but in the religious sense which every believing Jew gave to it and in which it was equivalent to Messiah, Jesus must accept it, whatever the consequences of this avowal might be. Jesus must know, then, whether this title, with regard to which Pilate was interrogating Him, was

---

[1] 9 Mjj. (A B C etc.) omit αυτω.
[2] א : ειπας instead of λεγεις.
[3] B C L : απο σεαυτου instead of αφ' εαυτου.
[4] א be : ο αρχιερευς (*the high-priest*).

put forward by Pilate himself, or whether it had been put forward by the Jews in the conversation which he had just had with them. The objections of *Meyer* and *Weiss* (in his *Commentary*) against this explanation do not seem to me sufficient to shake it. According to *Meyer*, Jesus asks of Pilate simply an explanation which He had *the right* to ask. But He nevertheless did it with some *purpose*. According to *Weiss*, Jesus wished to know whether He must now give an explanation respecting the Messianic idea! Finally, according to *Tholuck, Luthardt, Keil*, etc., He thereby called Pilate's attention to the suspicious source of this accusation (*others, the Jews*). It would, in that case, have been more simple to answer by a *No* only; but, after this, the really affirmative answer of Jesus in vv. 36, 37 would become an absurdity. These two verses are compatible with the question of Jesus only on our explanation, which is that of *Olshausen, Neander, Ewald*, and at present, it seems to me, of *Weiss* himself (*Life of Jesus*, II. p. 563). We must conclude from these words that Jesus had not Himself heard the accusation of the rulers, and consequently that He was already, as we have stated, ver. 28, in the Prætorium at the time when it was brought forward by them.

Pilate, not understanding clearly what is the aim of this distinction, answers abruptly: "What have I to do with your Jewish subtleties?" There is profound contempt in the antithesis: ἐγώ . . . Ἰουδαῖος (*I . . . a Jew?*). Then, abandoning the Jewish jargon which he had allowed his accusers to impose on him for the moment, he interrogates Him as a frank and simple Roman: "Now then, to the point! By what fault hast thou brought upon thyself all that which is taking place at this moment?"

Vv. 36, 37. "*Jesus answered, My kingdom is not of this world. If my kingdom were of this world, my servants would have fought that I might not be delivered to the Jews. But now is my kingdom not from hence. 37. Thereupon Pilate said to him, Art thou a king, then? Jesus answered him, Thou sayest it; I*[1] *am a king; I*[1] *was born and am come into the world to bear witness to the truth.*[2] *Whoever is of the truth hears my voice.*"—Jesus does not answer directly; but the answer appears from what He is about to say. He certainly possesses a kingship; this kingship, however, is not of a nature to disturb Pilate.—The expression ἐκ τοῦ κόσμου, *of this world*, is not synonymous with ἐν τῷ κόσμῳ, *in this world*. For the kingdom of Jesus is certainly realized and developed here on earth; but it does not have its *origin* from earth, from the human will and earthly force. Jesus gives as a proof of this the manner in which He has surrendered Himself to the Jews. His *servants* are that multitude of adherents who had surrounded Him on Palm-day, and not merely, as *Lücke* and *Luthardt* suppose, hypothetical beings: "the servants whom I should have in that case." The meaning given by *Bengel* and *Stier: the angels*, could not have been even dimly seen by Pilate.—The attempt has been made to give to νῦν, *now*, a temporal sense: "My kingdom is not now of this world, but it will be otherwise hereafter." But, at the coming of the Lord, His kingdom will be no more *of* this world than it is to-day. *Now* must be taken, as often, in the logical sense: it contrasts the

---

[1] B L Y 10 Mnn. It^{aliq} omit one of the two εγω which are read here by T. R., one after ειμι, the other before εις τουτο.

[2] ℵ: περι της αληθειας instead of τη αληθεια.

ever-present reality of the truth with the non-existence of error.—Pilate certainly expected a simple denial. His answer expresses surprise. The meaning of the particle ουκουν, if it were accented ούκουν, would be : *certainly not*. Pilate would say : " Thou art certainly not a king," with or without an interrogation point. But the reply of Jesus : " Thou sayest it," by which He appropriates to Himself the contents of Pilate's words while reaffirming them for Himself, favors the accentuation ούκοῦν, *not . . . then*. " It is, then, not false, the claim that is imputed to thee ?"—The affirmative formula employed by Jesus : *Thou sayest it*, is foreign to the classic Greek and even to the Old Testament, but it is very common with the Rabbis. Its meaning cannot be that which *Reuss* would give to it (*Hist. év.*, p. 676): " It is *thou* who sayest that I am a king ; *as for me*, I am come into the world to bear testimony, . . . " which would mean simply : I am not a *king*, but a preacher of the truth, a *prophet*. In this sense, a σύ, *thou*, in contrast with an ἐγώ, *I*, would have been absolutely necessary ; and then, a *but*, to contrast the saying of Jesus with that of Pilate. Besides, the meaning of the formula : *thou sayest it*, is well known ; comp. Matt. xxvi. 64.—Ὅτι might signify : *seeing that:* "Thou sayest it rightly, *seeing that* I really am such." It is more natural, however, to explain this conjunction in the sense of *that:* "Thou sayest (it) well, *that* I am a king." The importance of the idea makes Jesus feel the need of again formulating it expressly.—*Hengstenberg* separates altogether from this declaration the following words, which he applies simply to the *prophetic* office of Jesus Christ. But it is very evident that Jesus means to explain by what follows the sense in which He is a *king*. He comes to conquer the world, and for this end His only weapon is to bear witness to the truth ; His people are recruited from all men who open themselves to the truth. The first of the two consecutive ἐγώ, *I*, which are read in the T. R., must be rejected. Jesus certainly did not say : " I am a king, *I*." The two εἰς τοῦτο, *for this*, refer to the following ἵνα (*that*), contrary to the translation of *Ostervald* and *Arnaud:* "I was born for this (to be a king) and . . . "—" *I was born* " refers to the fact of birth which is common to Him with all men, while the words : "I am come into the world " set forth the special *mission* with a view to which He has appeared here on earth. It is His work as prophet which is the foundation of His kingly office. The truth, the revelation of God—this is the sceptre with which He bears sway over the earth. This mode of conquest which Jesus here unveils to Pilate is the opposite of that by which the Roman power was formed, and *Lange* brings out with much reason that, as xii. 25 contained the judgment of the Greek genius, this declaration of Jesus to Pilate contains the judgment of the Roman genius by the Gospel.—The expression *to be of the truth* recalls to mind iii. 21, vii. 17, viii. 47, x. 16, etc. It denotes the moral disposition to receive the truth and to put oneself under its holy power when it presents itself in living form in the person of Jesus Christ. By the word *whoever*, Jesus addressed no longer merely the conscience of the judge, but also that of the man, in Pilate (*Hengstenberg*).

Ver. 38. " *Pilate says to him, What is truth ? And after he had said this, he went out again to the Jews and says to them, As for me, I find no crime in him."*—Pilate's exclamation is neither the expression of a soul eager for the truth (the Fathers), nor that of a heart in despair, which has long sought it in vain (*Olshausen*). It is the profession of a frivolous scepticism, such as is often met with in the man of the world, and particularly in statesmen, who are quite indifferent in general to this class of questions ; witness the manner in which Napoleon was accustomed to speak of ideologists ! If Pilate had seriously sought for the truth, it would have been the moment to find it and lay hold of it. In any case, what he is now convinced of is that the person whom he has before him, whether He is a dreamer or a sage, is not a rival of Cæsar. Thus with "that broad sentiment of justice and civil government which," as *Renan* says, "the most ordinary Roman carried with him everywhere," he declares to the Jews his conviction of the innocence of Jesus as to the political accusation raised against Him.

After this, what was his duty ? To discharge Jesus purely and simply. But, fearing to displease the Jews, who had well-founded reasons to accuse him to his superiors, he wishes to avoid taking a step which would make them his sworn enemies, and he has recourse to a series of expedients. The first is not related by John ; it is the remitting of the affair to Herod, on account of the mention which had been made of the Galilean origin of Jesus in the accusation of the rulers (Luke xxiii. 5) ; this scene is described by Luke xxiii. 6–12 ; it is omitted by John as well known and not having led to any result. It was the appearance before Pilate which John was especially anxious to reproduce. In the declaration which, in John, closes ver. 38, are united the two expressions of Pilate related by Luke xxiii. 4, 14, which preceded and followed the sending of Jesus to Herod.—The second expedient is that of which John gives an account very summarily in vv. 39, 40, and which is related in detail by the Synoptics.

Vv. 39, 40. *" But you have a custom that I should release unto you a prisoner at the Passover feast. Will you therefore that I release unto you the king of the Jews?* 40. *They all*[1] *cried out therefore again,*[2] *saying, Not this man, but Barabbas! Now Barabbas was a robber."*—In the very brief narrative of John with relation to this episode, it is Pilate who seems to take the initiative in the proposal made to the people, while, in the dramatic picture of Mark, it is the people who rush forward with loud cries and demand the liberation of a prisoner. Evidently there is a vacancy here in John like that which we have noticed between ver. 32 and ver. 33. It is easy to establish the harmony with Mark. The people take advantage of a favorable moment—perhaps of that when Jesus had been sent to Herod—to ask for what was always granted them. And on Jesus' return, Pilate tries to give Him the benefit of this circumstance.—The origin of the custom to which this scene refers is unknown. It has been supposed that, since this custom was connected with the Passover feast, it involved an allusion to the deliverance of the Jews from the captivity in Egypt. This is possible. In any case, it is proper to hold that it was something which remained from an

---

[1] א B L X 15 Mnn. omit παντες (*all*).   παλιν (*again*).
[2] G K U Π 50 Mnn. It^(plerique) Syr. Cop. omit

ancient prerogative, which the people themselves exercised at the time of their national independence (see *Hase*). The words ἐν τῷ πάσχα, *at the Passover*, do not by any means contain, as *Lange, Hengstenberg*, etc., allege, the proof that the Paschal supper had been already celebrated. The 14th of Nisan already formed a part of the feast (see on xiii. 1). It is even more probable that the deliverance of the prisoner took place on the 14th than the 15th, in order that he might take part in the Paschal supper with the whole people. In making this proposal to the Jews, Pilate certainly counted on the sympathy of the people for Jesus, as it had manifested itself so strikingly on Palm-day. For Pilate knew perfectly that it was *for envy* that the rulers desired the death of Jesus (Matt. xxvii. 18), and that the feeling of a portion of the people was opposite to theirs.—In the designation *king of the Jews* irony prevails, as in ver. 14. Only the sarcasm is not addressed to Jesus, for whom Pilate from the beginning feels a sentiment of increasing respect, but to the Jews. Their king : this, then, is the only rival whom they will ever have to oppose to Cæsar ! But it is said in Mark xv. 11, "*the chief priests stirred up the people, that he should release Barabbas unto them.*" The friends of Jesus remained silent, or their feeble voices were drowned by those of the rulers and their creatures. Some resolute agitators imposed their will on the multitude. Thus is the πάντες, *all*, of John explained, which answers to the παμπληθεί of Luke, and which is no doubt wrongly omitted in the Alexandrian documents. For why should it have been added ?—Until this point in John's narrative the Jews had not uttered any exclamations, and it surprises us to read the words, "*All cried out again.*" But it is otherwise in the narratives of Mark (xv. 8 : ἀναβοήσας ὁ ὄχλος) and Luke (xxiii. 5, 10 : "*They were urgent saying . . . they vehemently accused him*"). Here also the narrative of John fits perfectly into that of his predecessors.—The word λῃστής does not always mean *robber*, but sometimes *a violent man* in general. According to Mark and Luke, Barabbas had taken part in an insurrection in which a murder had been committed. *Westcott* justly observes that in these troublous times acts of violence were frequently committed under the mask of patriotism.—The gravity of the choice made by the people is indicated by one of those brief clauses by which John characterizes an especially solemn moment. Comp. xi. 35, xiii. 30.—The name of the person who was proposed with Jesus for the choice of the people admits of two etymologies : *Bar-abba, son of the father*, or *Bar-rabban, son of the Rabbin*. In the first case, it should be written with only one *r ;* in the second with two *r's*. The first mode of writing the word is found in almost all the MSS. ; it is also that of the Talmud, where this name occurs very frequently (*Lightfoot*, p. 489). But the term "son of the father" may mean two very different things ; either : son of the father, God ; or : son of the father, the Rabbin. This second meaning is more applicable to an ordinary name. That this incident should have been occasioned or skilfully taken advantage of by Pilate, to deliver Jesus in this way, was, in any case, so far as concerned him, a denial of justice. For after the declaration of ver. 38, he should have released Him as innocent, and not as a malefactor liberated by way of grace. This first weakness was soon followed by another more serious one. We come to the third expedient which was tried by Pilate : the scourging of Jesus.

XIX. 1-3. *" Then Pilate therefore took Jesus and scourged* [1] *him ; 2, and the soldiers, having plaited a crown of thorns, placed it upon his head and arrayed him in a purple robe ;*[2] *and they said, Hail, king of the Jews! And they struck him with rods."*—Pilate had ascended his tribunal to pronounce the liberation of Barabbas. It was at this time that he received the message from his wife (Matt. xxvii. 19). *Hengstenberg* thinks that his washing his hands must also be placed at this time. But this act must have accompanied the pronouncing of the condemnation, which did not take place until later (vv. 13-16). After the two ineffectual efforts which have been described, Pilate has recourse to a third and last expedient. According to the Roman criminal code, scourging must necessarily precede the punishment of crucifixion. This is proved by a multitude of passages from Josephus and the ancient historians.[3] Comp. Matt. xx. 19, Luke xviii. 33, where Jesus, when predicting His Passion, does not separate scourging from crucifixion ; Matt. xxvii. 26 and Mark xv. 15 imply the same thing. But on this occasion a strange thing occurs. Pilate orders the punishment by scourging, without yet pronouncing the decision as to the penalty of crucifixion ; he does not expressly make the first of these two punishments the preliminary step to the second. He evidently hopes, by giving this satisfaction to the enemies of Jesus, to awaken the pity of the more moderate ones among them, as well as the compassion of the multitude and the zeal of His friends, and thus to succeed in averting the extreme punishment. Scourging, as it was practised among the Romans, was a punishment so cruel that the condemned person very often succumbed to it. The scourge was made of rods or thongs armed at the extremity with pieces of bone or lead. The condemned person received the blows while fastened to a small post so as to have the back bent and the skin stretched. With the first blows, the back became raw and the blood spurted out. Sometimes death followed immediately.[4] —The maltreatment described in vv. 2, 3 is only the act of the soldiers ; Pilate allows it with the design of turning to account that which takes place.—The crown of thorns, the purple robe, the salutation—this whole masquerade is a parody on Jewish royalty.—The thorny plant is probably the *Lycium spinosum*, which grows abundantly about Jerusalem, and the flexible stalk of which, armed with strong thorns, can be easily plaited. The red mantle was a common soldier's mantle, representing the purple robe worn by kings. This mockery was addressed far less to Jesus personally, whom the soldiers did not know, than to the whole nation, despised and detested by the Romans. It is the Jewish Messianic expectations that the soldiers ridicule in the person of Him who passes for having desired to realize them.

---

[1] ℵ L X Cop. Sah.: λαβων . . . εμαστιγωσε.
[2] ℵ B L U X A II 20 Mnn. It^{plerique} Mg. Cop. Sah. add here και ηρχοντο προς αυτον (*and they came to him*).
[3] Thus *Justin* says (21, 4) : " The body lacerated by the rods is nailed to the cross."
[4] *Cicero*, in the orations against *Verres*, uses the expressions : " to be scourged to death ;" " thou shalt die by the rods ;" " he was carried away as dead, and died soon afterwards " (see Keim).

—This maltreatment and this scourging are evidently the same as those which are spoken of in Matt. xxvii. 27 and Mark xv. 16 ; only these evangelists place them after the condemnation was pronounced, the reason of which fact we shall see. If the accomplishment of the scourging which was ordered by Pilate in these passages of the two Synoptics is not mentioned afterwards in them, it is perhaps because it had already taken place at an earlier moment (John).

Pilate, having allowed things to take their course, pursues his purpose :

Vv. 4–6. *" Pilate went out[1] again and says to them, Behold, I bring him out to you, that you may know that I find no crime in him.[2] 5. Jesus therefore went out, wearing the crown of thorns and the purple robe. And he says to them, Behold[3] the man ! 6. When therefore the chief priests and the officers saw him, they cried out :[4] Crucify, crucify[5] ! Pilate says to them, Take him yourselves and crucify him ; for, as for me, I find no crime in him."*—The scourging had taken place in the court of the Prætorium (Mark xv. 15, 16), as had also the maltreatment which had followed. As soon as this scene is ended, Pilate goes out with Jesus. This spectacle, as he thought, could not fail to call forth a favorable interference of the people and furnish him the means of resisting the hatred of the priests. A strange way, however, of proving that he finds no fault in Jesus—to inflict on Him such a punishment ! In ver. 4, Pilate means to say : "Well, you must understand ; there is enough of it now. I have consented to this in the way of compliance with your requests ; I will go no farther !" The term $\phi o \rho \epsilon \tilde{\iota} \nu$ is more grave than the simple $\phi \acute{\epsilon} \rho \epsilon \iota \nu$; comp. Rom. xiii. 4. In the expression : *Behold the man !* there is a mingling of respect and pity for Jesus and a bitter sarcasm with reference to the absurd part which the Jews impute to Him : "There is the wretched being against whom you are enraged !" But once again Pilate is baffled ; no voice rises from the multitude on behalf of the victim, and he finds himself face to face with the will of the rulers, who persist in pushing matters to extremity, without being satisfied with this halfway punishment. The previous concessions have only emboldened them. Full of indignation and vexation, Pilate then said to them : Take Him yourselves, and crucify Him !—words which, in this context, can only mean : "Do it yourselves, if you will ! I leave you free ; for myself, it is impossible for me to take part in such a murder !" This emotion was noble ; but it was nevertheless fated to remain barren ; for three times already Pilate had abandoned the ground of strict right, on which alone he could have resisted the violent pressure which was exerted upon him.

Of course, the Jews could not think of using the impunity which Pilate offered them. How could they have themselves provided for the execution ? When once the people were delivered from the fear which the Roman power inspired, the rulers clearly perceived that they could not themselves success-

---

[1] ℵ D Γ It^{plerique} : εξηλθεν simply ; T. R. with 9 Mjj. (E G H etc) : εξηλθεν ουν ; 6 Mjj. (A B K etc.) : και εξηλθεν.

[2] ℵ : οτι αιτιαν ουχ ευρισκω.

[3] ℵ B L X Y : ιδου instead of ιδε.

[4] ℵ : εκραξαν.

[5] T. R., with B L some Mnn. Vulg^{plerique}, omits αυτον (*him*), which is read by 15 Mjj. It^{aliq} Syr. etc

fully conduct this great affair. By a sudden reaction, the partisans of Jesus might turn violently against them and, drawing on the common mass of the people, might wreck everything. Measuring the dangers of this offer, therefore, they have recourse to a *third* expedient :

Vv. 7–9. " *The Jews answered him*,[1] *We have a law, and according to our*[2] *law, he ought to die; for he made himself Son of God.* 8. *When therefore Pilate heard this saying, he was the more afraid.* 9. *And he entered into the Prætorium again,*[3] *and says to Jesus, Whence art thou? But Jesus gave him no answer.*"—The Romans generally allowed the conquered nations the enjoyment of their laws and their national institutions, exactly as at present the French do with relation to the Mussulmen of Algiers, says *Renan.* The Jews, placing themselves at this point of view, appeal to the article of *their law* (Levit. xxiv. 16), which condemns blasphemers to death, and they imperiously demand of Pilate the application of this article. We may here lay our finger upon the difference, which is so often misapprehended, between the title *Son of God* and that of Messiah, or king of the Jews. The inquiry as to the Messianic or royal claim of Jesus is ended : they pass now to an *entirely new complaint.* And how happened it that the Jews came so late to base the accusation of blasphemy on a title with regard to which there had been a dispute so long from a wholly different point of view ? In vain does *Weiss* try to escape this result by alleging that the question is not of a new complaint, but that the Jews are simply seeking to clear themselves of the matter of asking for the death of an innocent man. The sequel clearly shows that the examination begins altogether anew.—The words of the Jews produced on Pilate an effect which they did not expect. They confirmed a dreadful presentiment which was more and more forming itself within him. He had heard of the miracles of Jesus, of His elevated and mysterious character, of His teachings and His conduct ; he had just received from his wife a strange message ; Jesus Himself was producing on him an impression such as he had never received from any man ; he asks himself if all this is not explained by this title of Son of God ! What if this extraordinary man were really a divine being who had appeared on the earth ? The truth presents itself to his mind naturally under the form of heathen superstitions and mythological recollections. We know, indeed, how sudden is the passing from scepticism to the most superstitious fears. *Reuss* is not willing to admit that this was the ground of the increase of fear which John indicates in Pilate. He explains this fact by the authority of *the law*, which was opposed to his own, and which threw him into an ever-increasing embarrassment. But, in what follows, everything turns upon the dignity of the Son of God. It is this idea which, as we shall see, preoccupies the mind of Pilate, and becomes the subject of his new conversation with Jesus. Here, therefore, is the foundation of his fear. Pilate, having heard the word : Son of God, brings Jesus back to the Prætorium, that he may converse with Him respecting it privately. The question : *Whence art thou?* cannot refer to the *earthly* origin of Jesus ;

---

[1] ℵ It^{plerique} omit αυτω (*him*). (*our*).
[2] 10 Mjj. (ℵ B etc.) It^{plerique} Orig. omit ημων   [3] ℵ omits παλιν.

Pilate knows full well that He is from Galilee. The meaning certainly is: "Art thou from the earth or from heaven?" It is in vain, therefore, that *Reuss* claims that it should be applied simply to the *mission*, and not to the *origin* of His person, supporting his view by ix. 29. In the Sanhedrim one might, indeed, propose the question as to the mission of Jesus: whether He was a true or a false prophet. But this distinction had no meaning for a man like Pilate.—We are surprised at the refusal of Jesus to answer. According to some, He kept silence because He feared that, by answering in accordance with the truth, He would keep alive a pagan superstition in the mind of His judge. According to others, He refused to answer a question which is for Pilate a mere matter of curiosity. *Lampe, Luthardt, Keil,* think that He does not wish, through revealing His divine greatness to Pilate, to prevent the plan of God from being carried out even to the end. The true answer appears to me to follow from all that precedes: Pilate knew enough about the matter with regard to Jesus to set Him free; he had himself declared Him innocent. This should have sufficed for him. What he would know beyond this "did not appertain to his province" (*Ebrard*). If he did not deliver Jesus as an innocent man, he deserved the responsibility of crucifying Him, the Son of God. His crime became His punishment.— Moreover, *Hengstenberg* justly remarks that this silence is an answer. If the claim which the Jews had accused Jesus of making had not been well founded, He could not have failed to deny it.

Vv. 10, 11. "*Pilate says*[1] *to him: Speakest thou not to me? Knowest thou not that I have power to release thee and power to crucify thee?*[2] 11. *Jesus answered,*[3] *Thou wouldest have*[4] *no power at all against me, except it were given thee from above; therefore, he that delivered*[5] *me unto thee is guilty of a greater sin.*"—Pilate feels that there is a reproach in this silence. He reassumes all his haughtiness as judge and Roman governor. Hence the ἐμοί, *to me*, at the beginning of the clause ("*to me*, if not to others"), and the repetition of the words, *I have power.*—The T. R. places the *to crucify thee* before the *to release thee*. Undoubtedly the idea of the impending punishment is that which prevails in the conversation; but the expression becomes still more weighty if it closes with the terrible word *to crucify thee*. Pilate thinks that he has the disposal of Jesus; he speaks only of his power, without thinking of his dependence and his responsibility. Jesus reminds him that in reality he has not the disposal of anything; for his power is given him. —The word *given* is opposed to the twofold *I have* of Pilate. The reading ἔχεις, *thou hast*, of ℵ A, etc., is evidently an error.—This time Jesus speaks; He also assumes His dignity; He takes the position of judge of His judge, or rather of all His judges; and as if He were already Himself seated on His tribunal, He weighs in His infallible scales both Pilate and the Sanhe-

---

[1] ℵ A some Mnn. Syr. Cop. omit ουν.

[2] A B E Syr. place απολυσαι σε (*to release thee*) before σταυρωσαι σε (*to crucify thee*). T. R. with D L X and 10 other Mjj. read in the reverse order.

[3] ℵ B L It^{aliq} Syr. add αυτω.

[4] ℵ A L X Y Δ Π 10 Mnn. Cop.: εχεις (*thou hast not*) instead of ειχες (*thou wouldst not have*).

[5] ℵ B E Δ Λ It. Vulg.: παραδους (*he who delivered me*), instead of παραδιδους (*he who delivers me*) in the T. R. with A and 12 other Mjj.

drim. The διὰ τοῦτο, *because of this*, refers to the word *given*. "Because this position, in virtue of which thou hast power over me, is given thee—this is the reason why thou art less guilty than the one who delivers me to thee in virtue of a power which he has arrogated to himself." In fact, God, by subjecting His people to the Roman power, had made it subject to the imperial jurisdiction which was at that moment delegated to Pilate. But the Sanhedrim, by taking possession of the person of their King, notwithstandstanding all the proofs which He had given of His divine mission, and by delivering Him to the pagan authority, arrogated to itself a right which God had not assigned to it, and committed an act of theocratic felony.—*He who delivered me to thee*, therefore, is neither Judas,—Jesus could not, with this meaning, have said : *to thee*,—nor Caiaphas, who only acts in the name of the body which he represents, and who is not named in this whole scene. It is the Sanhedrim, the official representative of the Jewish people, in whose name this body acted.—The explanation of this saying of Jesus which we have just given approaches that of *Calvin:* "He who delivers me to thee is the more guilty of the two, because he makes a *criminal* use of thy *legitimate* power." Some interpreters think that Jesus means to distinguish between the function of judging, which is official, and that of accusing, which is voluntary. But the Jews did not merely accuse, they had judged. The other explanations do not account for *because of this*. Thus the following ones : Pilate is less guilty "because he sins through weakness rather than through wickedness" (*Euthymius*) ;—"because he has less knowledge than the Jews" (*Grotius*).—Far from being irritated by this answer, Pilate is profoundly impressed by the majesty which breathes in it. Hence the fourth phase of the trial : it is the last effort of Pilate to deliver Jesus, but one which fails before a *fourth* and last expedient held in reserve by the Sanhedrim. As *Hengstenberg* observes, "it is a bad policy to gain the world,—that of beginning by granting it the half of what it asks."

Ver. 12. "*From this time Pilate sought to release him ; but the Jews cried out,*[1] *saying, If thou releasest this man, thou art not Cæsar's friend ; for whoever makes himself a king, opposes Cæsar.*"—Ἐκ τούτου : *from and by reason of* this word uttered by Jesus ; comp. vi. 66.—John seems to say that all the efforts which had been previously made by Pilate with the aim of releasing Jesus had been nothing in comparison with those which he made from now on, under the impression of this last saying which he had just heard. *Weiss* rejects this meaning, and sees in the *he sought* only this idea : he was proposing to end the matter by releasing Him, when the words of the Jews prevented him from doing so. But the imperfect : *he was seeking*, implies a series of efforts and of new attempts with the Jews.—Only the latter had prepared a weapon which they had resolved not to use except in the last extremity ; so ignoble was it in their view both for him who was its object and for those who employed it. It was that of personal intimidation. The reigning emperor, Tiberius, was the most suspicious of despots. The accusation of high treason was always well received by this tyrant. *Qui atroc-*

---

[1] T. R. with 9 Mjj. (E H K etc.) : εκραζον ; Mnn.: εκραυγασαν. ℵ : ελεγον. A I L M Y Π 24 Mnn. Orig.: εκραυγαζον ; B 13

issime exercebat leges majestatis, says Suetonius. The most unpardonable offence was that of having suffered his authority to be imperilled. Such is the danger which the Jews call up before the dismayed view of Pilate. This equivocal term *King of the Jews,* with the political coloring which it could not fail to have in the eyes of Tiberius, would infallibly make Pilate appear as an unfaithful administrator, who had attempted to screen from punishment an enemy of the imperial authority ; and his trial would be a short matter ; this Pilate knew well. It is true that the trial of this last expedient was, on the part of the Jews, a renouncing of their great national hope, the very idea of the Messiah, and a making themselves vassals of the empire. Such a victory was a suicide. In this regard also it is easy to understand how, in their plan of battle, they should have reserved this manœuvre for the last ; it was the stroke of desperation. The effect of it was immediate :

Vv. 13–16a. *"Having therefore heard these words,*[1] *Pilate brought Jesus out and sat down on the judgment seat, in the place called the Pavement, and in Hebrew, Gabbatha.* 14. *Now it was the Preparation of the Passover, and*[2] *about*[3] *the sixth*[4] *hour. And he says to the Jews, Behold your King!* 15. *They cried out,*[5] *Away with him, away with him, crucify him! Pilate says to him, Shall I crucify your King? The chief priests answered, We have no King but Cæsar.* 16a. *Then he delivered him to them to be crucified."*—The plural τῶν λόγων τούτων, *these words,* in the Alexandrian documents and others, shows that ver. 12 only summarizes the words of the Jews. Before the threat which it implied, the judge, who was already so long renouncing his own proper part, bows his head and submits. Without saying a word more, he brings Jesus forth from the Prætorium ; for the sentence must be pronounced in the presence of the accused ; and he ascends his tribunal a second time.— The name λιθόστρωτον signifies : *place paved with stones.* Before the Prætorium there was one of the pavements of mosaic on which the Roman magistrates had the custom of placing their judgment-seats. The Aramæan name *Gabbatha* is not the translation of the preceding ; it is borrowed from the character of the place. It signifies : *eminence, hill.*

John inserts here the indication of *the day* and *the hour* when the sentence was pronounced. With what purpose ? Is it because of the solemnity and importance of this decisive moment for the destiny of mankind ? Or does he desire by this means to explain the impatience of the Jews, which manifests itself in ver. 15, to see this long trial come to its close at last and the punishment consummated before the end of this day ?—*It was the Preparation of the Passover,* says John. The interpreters who think that the Paschal supper had been celebrated on the preceding evening give to παρασκευή, *preparation,* the technical signification which it sometimes has in the Patristic language, that of *Friday,* this day being the one on which the food for

---

[1] T. R. reads with K U Λ Π a part of the Mnn. Syr. τουτον τον λογον (*this word*) ; all the rest τουτων των λογων (*these words*).

[2] T. R. reads with E H I S Y Γ Λ : ωρα δε ; 9 Mjj. (א A B etc.) : ωρα ην ; K : ωρα δε ην.

[3] The MSS. are divided between ως and ωσει

(T. R. with 4 Mjj.).

[4] Instead of εκτη (*sixth*) L X Δ 3 Mnn. read τριτη (*third*).

[5] Instead of οι δε εκραυγασαν K Y Π : οι δε εκραυγαζον ; B L X : εκραυγασαν ουν εκεινοι ; א : οι δε ελεγον.

the Sabbath was prepared : "*the Preparation of the Sabbath.*" Comp. Matt. xxvii. 62, Luke xxiii. 54, and especially Mark xv. 42 : "*the Preparation, which is the day before the Sabbath.*" The complement τοῦ πάσχα, *of the Passover*, must necessarily in this case recall *the Passover week*, to which this Friday belonged. But from the fact that παρασκευή in itself took this technical meaning of *Friday*, it does not follow that, when this word is followed by a complement like τοῦ πάσχα, *of the Passover*, it does not preserve its natural sense of *preparation :* "the preparation *of the Passover.*" This complement has as its precise purpose to distinguish this preparation of the Passover from the simple ordinary preparation for the Sabbath. If the question were only that of indicating the day of the week, why add the complement here: *of the Passover*, which gives the reader absolutely no information, since after xiii. 1, xviii. 28, etc., no one would be ignorant that it was the Passover week at this time. Every Greek reader, when hearing this phrase, would necessarily think of the 14th of Nisan, known as the day on which the Passover supper was prepared. This date agrees with those of xiii. 1, 29, xviii. 28, and leads us, as do all these passages, to the idea that the Passover supper was not yet celebrated, but was to take place on the evening of this day.

According to John, the sentence of Jesus was pronounced *about the sixth hour*—that is, about noon, at least if we do not adopt the method of reckoning according to which John would make the day begin at midnight, in accordance with the custom of the Roman courts. It is certainly difficult to bring this hour of noon into harmony with the account of Matthew, according to which at that hour Jesus had been already for some time suspended on the cross, and still more difficult to reconcile it with Mark xv. 25, where it is said that it was at the *third hour*—that is, at nine o'clock, that Christ *was crucified*. But is the difficulty really any less if, with *Rettig, Tholuck, Wieseler, Keil, Westcott*, etc., we hold that John reckons from midnight, and that the hour indicated is consequently *six o'clock* in the morning ? Was not this, according to the Synoptics, the hour when, following upon the session of the morning, the Sanhedrim brought Jesus to Pilate ? *Keil* makes the reckoning thus : At five o'clock, the last session of the Sanhedrim until six or half past six ; then the negotiations with Pilate, and the pronouncing of the sentence a little later. But is it possible to confine within so brief a space 1. The first appearance before Pilate ; 2. The sending to Herod ; comp. the words ἐν λόγοις ἱκανοῖς (Luke xxiii. 9) ; 3. The discussion relative to the release of Barabbas ; 4. The scourging, with the scene of the *Ecce homo ;* 5. The renewal of the examination after this scene, and finally the pronouncing of the condemnation ? No ; the greater part of the morning is not too much for so many things. The reading τρίτη, *third* (nine o'clock), in some MSS. of John, would therefore be in itself very suspicious, even if it were not so evidently a correction intended to reconcile the two narratives. *Eusebius* supposed that some ancient copyist made of the gamma (Γ = 3) a stigma (ς = 6). This supposition in itself has little probability. Let us rather call to mind, the fact that the day as a whole was divided, like the night, into four portions of three hours each. This fact explains why in the whole New Testament mention is scarcely ever made of any hours except the *third, sixth* and *ninth* (comp. Matt. xx. 1-5), and also why, as *Hengstenberg* remarks, the expressions *nearly, about,* are so frequent in it (Matt. xxii. 46, Luke xxiii. 44, John iv. 6, Acts x. 3, 9). This word *about* is also added by John in our passage. It is certainly allowable, therefore, to take the middle course, either in Mark or in John, especially if we recall the fact that, as *Lange* says, the apostles did not have watch in hand. As the third hour of Mark, properly nine o'clock, may include all the time from eight to ten, so the sixth hour in John certainly includes from eleven to twelve. The difference, therefore, is no longer so very great. But especially, 2, account must be taken of an important circumstance, noticed by *Lange:* it is that Matthew and Mark, having given to the scourging of Jesus the meaning which it ordinarily had in such a case, made it the *beginning* of the punishment. We see this clearly from the manner in which they both speak of it, connecting it closely with the pronouncing of the condemnation, Matt. xxvii. 26 : *"He gave Jesus up to them after having scourged Him."* Comp. Mark xv. 15. They have therefore united in one the two judicial acts so clearly distinguished by John, that of the *scourging* and that of the final *condemnation,* and they have thus quite naturally dated the second at the same moment as the first. How can *Weiss* call this solution an affirmation without proof ? It clearly follows from the comparison of the narratives. *Hofmann* has proposed the following solution : a mark of punctuation must be placed after the word παρασκευή, and we must translate : "It was Friday, and the sixth hour of the Passover" (omitting the δέ after ὥρα with the principal Mjj.).—But the hours of the *day,* not those of the *feast,* are reckoned.

There is a bitter irony in the words of Pilate : *Behold your King!* But it is directed towards the Jews, not towards Jesus. Towards the latter, Pilate constantly shows himself full of a respectful interest, which, near the end, amounts even to fear. In this sarcasm there is at the same time a serious side. Pilate understands that, if there is a man through whom the Jewish people are to fulfil a mission in the world, it is this man.—The rage of the rulers increases on hearing this declaration. The three aorist imperatives express the impatience and haste to have the matter ended. Pilate henceforth consents to yield ; but first he wishes to give himself the pleasure of yet once more striking the dagger into the wound : *Shall I crucify your king?* He avenges himself thus for the act of baseness to which they compel him. The Jews are driven thereby to the memorable declaration by which they themselves pronounced the abolition of the theocracy and the absorption of Israel into the world of the Gentiles. They who cherished only one thought—the overthrow of the throne of the Cæsars by the Messiah—suffer themselves to be carried away by hatred of Jesus so far as to cry out before the representative of the emperor : *"We have no other king but Cæsar."* *"Jesum negant,"* says *Bengel, "usque eo ut omnino Christum negent."*

After this, all is said. By denying the expectation of the Messiah, Israel has just denied itself ; at such a price does it secure the end that Jesus should be surrendered to it. 'Αυτοῖς, *to them*, says John, and not to the Roman executioners. For the latter will be only the blind instruments of the judicial murder which is about to be committed.

Modern criticism (*Baur, Strauss, Keim*) regards this entire representation of Pilate's conduct as fictitious. The thought of the author is to personify in Pilate the sympathy of the pagan world for the Gospel, and to throw upon Israel almost the whole responsibility of the crime. But 1. The fact is not presented otherwise in the Synoptics, in the Acts and in the Epistles. In Matthew, *the governor marvelled* (ver. 14) ; he knows that it is *for envy* that the rulers deliver Jesus to him (ver. 18) ; he endeavors by means of the people to effect His release, rather than that of Barabbas (vv. 17, 22). He asks indignantly : " *What evil, then, has he done ?*" (ver. 23). He sees *that he prevails nothing,* and ends by yielding, while he declares himself, by a solemn act, *innocent of the blood of this righteous man* (ver. 24). Such is the description of the condemnation of Jesus by Pilate in the Gospel which is called Jewish-Christian. Does it really differ from John's description ? Mark brings out still more clearly than Matthew the eagerness with which Pilate takes advantage of the spontaneous request of the multitude that a prisoner should be released to them, and the support which he counts upon finding in the popular sympathy for the saving of Jesus (vv. 8–10). Luke adds to the other attempts of Pilate that of the sending of Jesus to Herod, and the twice repeated proposal to release Him at the cost of a simple scourging (vv. 16, 22). " *Having the desire to release Jesus*" is expressly said in ver. 20. Then in ver. 22 : " And he said to them *the third time,* Why, what evil has he done ?" In the Acts, the conciliatory tendency of which book towards Judaism is made prominent at the present time, Peter, as well as John, charges the Jews with the whole responsibility for the murder : " *You* have crucified him *by the hands* of wicked men," ii. 23 ; comp. iii. 15. Even James, when addressing the rich men of his nation, says to them : " *You have condemned and put to death the Righteous One*" (v. 6). Finally, the Apocalypse—that book which is represented as the most pronounced manifestation of Jewish-Christianity—designates Jerusalem as " the Sodom and spiritual Egypt where our Lord was crucified," xi. 8. The notion of place (*where*) in this passage very evidently includes those of causality and responsibility.—2. Moreover, the second century, in which it is claimed that the composition of the Fourth Gospel must be placed, was, from Trajan to Marcus Aurelius, a time of bloody persecution on the part of the pagan world against the Church, and it would be very strange that at that epoch an author should have attributed to the Roman governor an imaginary character with the purpose of personifying in him *the sympathy* of the pagan world for the Gospel !—3. Finally, the scene described by John is its own defence. It is impossible to portray more to the life, the astuteness, the perseverance and the impudent suppleness of the accuser, determined to succeed, at any cost, on the one side, and, on the other, the obstinate struggle, in the heart of the judge, between the consciousness of his duty and the care for his own interests, between the fear of sacrificing an innocent man, perhaps more formidable than He appeared to be outwardly, and that of driving to extremity a people already exasperated by crying acts of injustice, and of finding himself accused before a suspicious emperor, *one stroke of whose pen* (*Reuss*) might precipitate him into destruction ; finally, between cold scepticism and the transient impressions of natural religiousness and even pagan superstition. *Reuss* acknowledges that it is " the Fourth Gospel which gives the true key of the problem" of Pilate's inconceivable conduct : " Jesus was sacrificed by him to an exigency of his position" (p. 675). Excepting the natural vacancies resulting from " the fact that no witness saw the whole from one end to the other," the Gospel narrative (that of John included) " bears, according to this author, the seal of entire authenticity" (*ibid*). These two figures, in fact—one of a cold and diabolical perversity (Caiaphas, as the representative of the Sanhedrim), the other of a cowardice and pitiable vacillation—both contrasting with the calm dignity and holy majesty of the Christ, form a picture which we do not hesitate to call the masterpiece of the Gospel of John, and which, by itself alone, might, if necessary, serve as a certification of authenticity for this entire work.—Whence did he derive such complete information ? Perhaps he saw everything himself. The judicial sessions among the Romans were public, and he was not prevented from entering the court of the Prætorium by the same scruples as the Jews. For he did not have to eat the Passover supper in the evening.

3

John 19:16b-42

THE EXECUTION OF JESUS

1. The crucifixion : vv. 16b–18 ; 2. The inscription : vv. 19–22 ; 3. The parting of the garments : vv. 23, 24 ; 4. The filial legacy : vv. 25–27 ; 5. The death : vv. 28–30 ; 6. The breaking of the legs and the spear-thrust : vv. 31–37 ; 7. The burial : vv. 38–42.

John does not desire to present a complete picture of the crucifixion of Jesus. He brings out some circumstances omitted by his predecessors, and at the same time completes and gives precision to their narratives.

The crucifixion :

Vv. 16b–18. "*Now*[1] *they took Jesus ;*[2] *and, bearing his cross,*[3] *he went out of the city [going] to the place called the place of the skull, in Hebrew Golgotha,* 18, *where they crucified him, and with him two others, on either side one, and Jesus in the midst.*"—These two verses sum up very briefly the Synoptic narrative. The subject of *they took* is : the Jews (ver. 16a) ; it was they who executed the sentence by the hands of the soldiers. It would be otherwise if the following words : *and they led Him away*, in the T. R., were authentic. For the subject would then be : the soldiers.—According to ancient testimonies, condemned persons were obliged to bear their own cross, at least the horizontal piece of wood. This is implied, moreover, in the figurative expression used by Jesus in the Synoptics : "*If any man will come after me*, . . . *let him take up his cross* " (Matt. xvi. 24 and parallels). John alone mentions this particular in the sufferings of Jesus. And in this he does not

---

[1] The MSS. are divided between δε (T. R. with 14 Mjj.) and ουν (B L X).

[2] After τον Ιησουν, T. R. reads with A M U Γ: και απηγαγον (*and led him away*) ; 9 Mjj. 130 Mnn. : και ηγαγον ; B L X some Mnn. It^pleriq

Cop. reject these words ; א : οι δε λαβοντες τον I. απηγαγον αυτον.

[3] T. R. with 11 Mjj. : αυτου (εαυτου) ; B X : αυτω ; א L Π : εαυτω.

contradict the Synoptics, who relate that Simon of Cyrene was compelled to perform this office. For the participle βαστάζων, *bearing*, is closely connected with the verb ἐξῆλθεν, *he went forth bearing*. At the moment of setting out, Jesus was subjected to the common rule. Afterwards it was feared, no doubt, that He might succumb, and advantage was taken of the meeting with Simon to free Him from the burden.—Moses had prohibited capital executions in the enclosure of the camp (Levit. xxiv. 14, Num. xv. 35), and the people remained faithful to the spirit of this law, by putting criminals to death outside of the walls of cities (1 Kings xxi. 13, Acts vii. 58). It is on this custom that the exhortation in Heb. xiii. 12, 13 is founded. Ἐξῆλθεν accordingly means : *He went forth from the city*. The Holy Sepulchre is now quite a distance within the interior of Jerusalem ; but the city wall may have been displaced. The bare rock in this place seems to prove, even now, that this part of the city was formerly not inhabited. Moreover, there exists no certain tradition respecting the place of the crucifixion and that of the burial of Jesus.—The name *place of the skull* does not come from the executions which took place on this spot ; the plural would then be necessary : place of *skulls ;* and among the Jews such remains would not have been left uncovered. The origin of the name was undoubtedly the rounded form and the bare aspect of the hill. *Golgotha* : גלגלת, in Aramaic גלגלתא, *skull*, from גלל, *to roll*. The word ἑβραιστί, which is found four times in our Gospel, is found again twice in the Apocalypse, but nowhere else in the whole New Testament.

The cross had the form of a T. It was not very high (see ver. 29). Sometimes it was laid on the ground, the condemned person was nailed to it, then it was raised up. But most frequently it was made firm in the ground ; the condemned person was raised to the proper height by means of cords (*in crucem tollere*) ; then the hands were nailed to the transverse piece of wood. That they might not be torn by the weight of the body, the latter rested on a block of wood fastened to the shaft of the cross, on which the condemned sat as on horseback. There has been a long discussion, in modern times, on the question whether the feet were also nailed. The passages from ancient writers cited by *Meyer* (see on Matt. xxvii. 35) and *Keim* are decisive ; they prove that, as a rule, the feet were nailed. Luke xxiv. 39 leads us to think that this was the case with Jesus. The condemned commonly lived on the cross twelve hours, sometimes even to the third day.

This kind of death united in the highest degree the pains and infamy of all other punishments. *Cradelissimum teterrimumque supplicium*, says Cicero (*in Verrem*). The increasing inflammation of the wounds, the unnatural position, the forced immobility and the rigidity of the limbs which resulted from it, the local congestions, especially in the head, the inexpressible anguish resulting from the disturbance of the circulation, a burning fever and thirst tortured the condemned without killing him.—Was it the Jews who had demanded the execution of the other two condemned persons, in order to render the shame of Jesus more complete ? Or must we find here an insult on Pilate's part to the Jewish people represented by these two companions in punishment of their King ? It is difficult to say.

The inscription :

Vv. 19-22. "*Pilate also caused an inscription to be made and to be put[1] upon the cross ; there was written : Jesus of Nazareth, the King of the Jews. 20. Many of the Jews therefore read this inscription, because the place where Jesus was crucified was near the city ; and it was written in Hebrew, in Greek, and in Latin.[2] 21. The chief priests of the Jews said therefore to Pilate : Write not, The King of the Jews,[3] but that he said, I am King of the Jews. 22. Pilate answered, What I have written, I have written.*"—John here completes the very brief account of the Synoptics. According to the Roman custom, the *cruciarius* carried himself, or there was carried before him, on the road to the crucifixion, an inscription (*titulus*, τίτλος, ἐπιγραφή, σανίς, αἰτία) which contained the indication of his crime, and which was afterwards fastened to the cross. Pilate took advantage of this custom to stigmatize the Jews by proclaiming even for the last time this malefactor to be their King.—*Tholuck* and *de Wette* have thought that ἔγραψε must be explained in the sense of *had written ;* Meyer and Weiss hold that Pilate had the inscription written during the crucifixion, and placed on the cross after it. But the δὲ καί, *now also*, is a connection sufficiently loose to allow us to place these acts at the very time of the crucifixion, which is more natural. The mention of the three languages in which this inscription was written is found also in Luke, according to the ordinary reading ; but this reading is uncertain. Hebrew was the national language, Greek the language universally understood, and Latin that of the conquering nation. Pilate wished thus to give the inscription the greatest publicity possible. Jesus, therefore, at the lowest point of His humiliation, was proclaimed Messiah-King in the languages of the three principal peoples of the world.—The expression : *the chief priests of the Jews*, ver. 21, is remarkable. It is found nowhere else. Hengstenberg explains it by an intentional contrast with the term *King of the Jews*. The struggle, indeed, was between these two theocratic powers. This explanation, however, is far-fetched ; the expression means, more simply, that they were acting here as defenders of the cause of the theocratic people.—The imperfect *they said* characterizes the attempt which fails. The present *write not* is the present of the idea. Pilate answers with the twice repeated perfect : *I have written ;* it is the tense of the accomplished fact. We find Pilate here again as Philo describes him : *inflexible in character* (Hengstenberg).

The parting of the garments :

Vv. 23, 24. "*The soldiers therefore, when they had crucified[4] Jesus, took his garments and made four parts, one for every soldier, and then the tunic ;[5] now the tunic was without seam, woven from the top throughout. 24. They said therefore one to another :[6] Let us not rend it, but let us cast lots for it whose it shall be. That the Scripture might be fulfilled which says :[7] They parted my*

---

[1] A K 12 Mnn.: επεθηκεν for εθηκεν.

[2] Instead of εβρ., ελλην., ρωμ., B L X 8 Mnn. Cop. Sah. read εβρ., ρωμ., ελλην.

[3] ℵ omits vv. 20 and 21 as far as αλλ' οτι not included.

[4] Instead of οτε εσταυρωσαν, ℵ has οι σταυρωσαντες.

[5] ℵ It^{aliq} Syr^{sch} omit the words και τον χιτωνα (*and the tunic*).

[6] ℵ : αυτους instead of αλληλους.

[7] ℵ B It^{plerique} omit η λεγουσα (*which says*).

garments among them, and upon my vesture they cast lots. These things therefore the soldiers did."—Here, also, John completes his predecessors, so far as the description of the tunic and the accomplishment of the prophecy are concerned. The Roman law *De bonis damnatorum* adjudged to the executioners the garments of the condemned. It is generally held that the entire detachment was composed of four men.[1] Keim thinks that each cross had its particular detachment.[2] The soldiers performed two operations. They divided among themselves either the different pieces of clothing, such as the caps, girdles, under-garments, sandals and tunics of the two malefactors, or the garments of Jesus alone (αὐτοῦ, *of him*, ver. 23), if the question is only of the particular detachment which had to do with Him. Then, as the tunic of Jesus could not be divided, and was too precious to be placed in one of the parts, they cast lots for it. This tunic was undoubtedly a gift of the women who ministered to Jesus (Luke viii. 2, 3, Matt. xxvii. 55). It was woven throughout its whole length, as, according to Josephus, the garment of the priests was. Hence the use of the lot (*therefore,* ver. 24). Thus was realized to the very letter the description of the Psalmist, as he drew the picture of the King of Israel at the height of His sufferings. Criticism claims, it is true, that the two members of the verse quoted by the evangelist (Ps. xxii. 19) are entirely synonymous, and that John is the sport of his own imagination in wishing to distinguish either between the verbs *to divide* and *to cast lots*, or between the substantives ἱμάτια, *garments*, and ἱματισμός, *robe* (LXX). But a more profound study of the parallelism in Hebrew poetry shows that the second member always adds a shade or a new idea to the idea of the first. Otherwise the second would be merely an idle tautology. It is not repetition, but progression. Thus, in this verse, the gradation from the plural בְּגָדִים, *garments*, to the singular לְבוּשׁ, *tunic*, is manifest. The first term designates the different pieces making up the outer clothing and the second the vestment, properly so called, after the removal of which one is entirely naked, the tunic. The passage in Job xxiv. 7–10 confirms this natural distinction. The advance from one verb to the other is no less perceptible. It is already a great humiliation to the condemned person to see his garments *divided*. After this he must say to himself that there is nothing left for him except to die. But what greater humiliation than to see lots drawn for his garments, and thus see them treated like a worthless plaything! David meant to describe the two degrees, and John calls to the reader's notice the fact that in the crucifixion of Jesus they are, both of them, literally reproduced ; not that the fulfilment of the prophecy was dependent on this detail, but it appeared more distinctly by reason of this coincidence ; and this the more because everything was carried out by the instrumentality of rude and blind agents, the Roman soldiers ; comp. the remarks on xii. 15, 16.—It is on this last idea that John wishes to lay stress when he concludes the narrative of this scene with the words : *These things therefore the soldiers did.* The Roman governor had proclaimed Jesus *the King of the Jews ;* the Roman soldiers,

---

[1] Philo, *in Flaccum.*
[2] Comp. Acts xii. 4, where we find four detachments, each of four men ; undoubtedly one for each of the four watches.

without meaning it, pointed Him out as the true David promised in Psalm xxii.

Strauss thinks (new *Vie de Jésus*, p. 569 ff.) that, when the Messianic pretensions of Jesus had been proved false by the cross, the Church sought in the Old Testament the idea of the suffering Messiah, and found it there, especially in Ps. xxii. and lxix. Thenceforward there was imagined in this programme a whole fictitious picture of the Passion. Thus the facts, in the first place, created the exegesis ; then the exegesis created the facts. But 1. The idea of the suffering Messiah existed in Jewish theology before and independently of the cross (see on pp. 311 f. 324). 2. It will always be difficult to prove that *some* righteous person, *whoever* he may have been, under the Old Covenant could have hoped, as the author of Ps. xxii. does, that the effect of his deliverance would be the conversion of the Gentile nations and the establishment of the kingdom of God even to the ends of the earth (vv. 26–32).

The filial legacy :

Vv. 25–27. *"Now there stood near the cross of Jesus his mother and his mother's sister, Mary*[1] *the wife of Clopas, and Mary Magdalene. 26. Jesus, therefore, seeing his mother and beside her the disciple whom he loved, says to his mother,*[2] *Woman, behold thy son. 27. Then he says to the disciple, Behold thy mother. And from that hour*[3] *that disciple took her to his home."*—This incident has been preserved for us by John alone. Matthew and Mark say, indeed, that a certain number of Galilean women were present, but *"beholding from afar."* It follows from John's narrative either that some of them, particularly the mother of Jesus, were standing nearer the cross—this detail may easily have been omitted in the Synoptic tradition—or that, at the moment of Jesus' death, they had withdrawn out of the way, in order to observe what was about to take place ; for it is then only that the presence of these women is mentioned in the Synoptics.—Παρά does not mean *at the foot*, but *beside ;* the cross was not very high (ver. 29).—We have already stated, in the *Introduction* (see on pp. 29, 30), that *Wieseler*, holding to the reading of the *Peshito* (see critical note 1), finds in this verse the mention, not of *three* women, but of *four*. He thus escapes the difficulty that two sisters should bear the same name, Mary—the mother of Jesus and the wife of Clopas. The sister of Mary, the mother of Jesus, according to him, is not named ; and she is consequently no other than Salome, the mother of John, indicated by Matt. xxvii. 56 and Mark xv. 40 as also present at the crucifixion. *Wieseler's* opinion has been adopted by *Meyer, Luthardt, Weiss, Westcott*, etc. The incident here related becomes, it is said, much more intelligible ; for if the mother of the apostle John was the sister of Mary, and this apostle the first cousin of Jesus, we can explain more easily how Jesus could entrust His mother to him, notwithstanding the presence of her sons. This interpretation seems to me inadmissible. By omitting a καί, *and*, before the words : *Mary, the wife of Clopas* (at least, if the text of *all* our

---

[1] Syr^{sch} and the Persian and Ethiopian Vss. read και before Μαρια η τ, K. (*and* Mary, the wife of Clopas).

[2] ℵ B L X It^{aliq} omit αυτου.

[3] A E 40 Mnn. Sah. : ημερας (*day*) instead of ωρας.

MSS. without exception is correct), the evangelist would have expressed himself in a quite equivocal way. And if this so close relationship between Jesus and the sons of Zebedee had existed, how should there not have been the slightest trace of it in the entire Gospel history ? Is it not more simple to hold that John abstained from mentioning his mother, as he does in the rest of the Gospel ? Undoubtedly it is scarcely possible that two sisters should bear the same name. But the Greek term γαλόως, which means *sister-in-law*, was so little used that John might prefer to avail himself of the simpler term ἀδελφή (*sister*) to express this idea. These words of Jesus, thus understood, contain nothing unkindly either to His own brothers, who did not even yet believe on Him, or to the mother of John himself, who was by no means separated thereby from her son. Hegesippus declares positively that Joseph's brother, whom he also calls the uncle of Jesus (or of James), was named Clopas (see on p. 358 f.). This name must in this case be regarded as the Greek form of the Aramaic חלפי, *Alphæus*. *Reuss* sees herein "one of the grossest mistakes of modern exegesis," and thinks that Clopas is a Jewish corruption of the Greek name *Kleopatros*. But in speaking thus *Reuss* himself confounds Clopas with *Cleopas*, a name which is also known in the New Testament (Luke xxiv. 18).—Respecting Mary, the wife of Clopas, see note on p. 358 f.—The Synoptics do not mention the presence of Jesus' mother, perhaps because she left the cross immediately after the fact reported by John, and because they do not speak of the presence of the friends of Jesus and of the women except at the end of the whole story.

Stripped of everything, Jesus seemed to have nothing more to give. Nevertheless, from the midst of this deep poverty, He had already made precious gifts ; to His executioners He had bequeathed the pardon of God, to His companion in punishment, Paradise. Could He find nothing to leave to His mother and His friend ? These two beloved persons, who had been His most precious treasures on earth, He bequeathed to one another, giving thus at once a son to His mother, and a mother to His friend. This word full of tenderness must have completely broken Mary's heart. Not being able to endure this sight, she undoubtedly at this moment left the sorrowful spot.—The word *to his home* does not imply that John possessed a house in Jerusalem, but simply that he had a lodging there ; comp. the same εἰς τὰ ἴδια applied to all the apostles, xvi. 32. From this time, Mary lived with Salome and John, first at Jerusalem and then in Galilee (*Introduction*, note on p. 35). According to the historian Nicephorus Kallistus (died in 1350), she lived eleven years with John at Jerusalem, and died there at the age of fifty-nine. Her tomb is shown in a grotto a few paces from the garden of Gethsemane. According to others, she accompanied John to Asia Minor and died at Ephesus.—On the word : *Woman*, which has nothing but respect in it, see on ii. 4.

Keim, after the example of *Baur*, regards this incident as an invention of pseudo-John, intended to exalt the apostle whose name he assumes, and to make him the head of the Church, superior even to James and Peter. *Renan* attributes this same fiction to the school of John, which yielded to the desire of making its patron the vicar of Christ. For every one who has the sense of truth, this scene and these words do not admit of an explanation of this kind. Besides, is it not Peter whom our evangelist presents as the great and bold confessor of Jesus (vi. 68, 69)? Is it not to the same apostle that the direction of the Church is ascribed in ch. xxi. and this by a grand thrice repeated promise (vv. 15-17)? Finally, this supposition would imply that the mother of Jesus is here the type of the Church, a thing of which there is no trace either in this text or in the whole Gospel.

The death :

Vv. 28–30. "*After this, Jesus, knowing*[1] *that all was now finished, that the Scripture might be fulfilled,*[2] *says, I thirst.* 29. *There was*[3] *a vessel there full of vinegar ; and the soldiers, having filled a sponge with vinegar and having put it on the end of a hyssop stalk,*[4] *brought it to his mouth.* 30. *When Jesus therefore had taken the vinegar, he said, It is finished. Then, having bowed his head, he gave up his spirit.*"—John completes by means of some important details the narrative already known respecting the last moments of Jesus.— Μετὰ τοῦτο, *after this,* must be taken in a broad sense, as throughout our whole Gospel. It is between the preceding incident and this one that the unspeakable anguish of heart is to be placed from the depth of which Jesus cried out : "My God, my God, why hast thou forsaken me ?"—The expression : *All is finished,* refers to His task as Redeemer, so far as He was able to accomplish it during His earthly existence, and, at the same time, to the prophetic picture in which this task had been traced beforehand. There remained, however, a point in the prophecy which was not yet accomplished. Many interpreters (*Bengel, Tholuck, Meyer, Luthardt, Bäumlein, Keil*) make ἵνα, *that,* depend on τετέλεσται : "Knowing that all was accomplished *to this end, that* the Scripture might be fulfilled." This sense does not seem to me admissible. The fulfilment of the Scriptures cannot be regarded as the *end* of the accomplishment of the work of Jesus. Moreover, it follows precisely from vv. 28, 29 that, if the redemptive work was consummated, there was, nevertheless, a point still wanting to the fulfilment of the prophetic representation of the sufferings of the Messiah, and that Jesus does not wish to leave this point unfulfilled. The *that* depends therefore on the following verb λέγει : *Jesus says.* So *Chrysostom, Lücke, de Wette, Weiss,* etc. Only we must not, with *Weiss,* attribute the purpose to God ; it is that of Jesus Himself, as the εἰδώς, *knowing that,* shows. By saying *I thirst,* Jesus really meant to occasion the literal fulfilment of this last point of the sufferings of the Messiah : "*They gave me vinegar to drink*" (Ps. lxix. 22). Jesus had been for a long time tormented by thirst—it was one of the most cruel tortures of this punishment—and He could have restrain-

---

[1] E G H K S Y Γ 70 Mnn. Cop.: ιδων (*seeing*), instead of ειδως.

[2] Instead of τελειωθη, א D^suppl some Mnn.: πληρωθη.

[3] A B L X It^aliq omit the ουν (*therefore*), which T. R. reads with the other Mjj., with the exception of א, which reads δε (*now*).

[4] א B L X some Mnn. It^aliq Sah. read σπογγον ουν μεστον οξους υσσωπω περιθεντες (*having put on a hyssop stalk a sponge full of vinegar*), instead of οι δε πλησαντες σπογγον οξους και υσσωπω περιθεντες which T. R. reads with 13 Mjj. Syr. (*they having filled a sponge with vinegar and having put it on a hyssop stalk*).

ed even to the end, as He had done up to this moment, the expression of this painful sensation. If He did not do it, it was because He knew that this last point must still be fulfilled, and because He desired that it should be fulfilled without delay. John says τελειωθῇ, and not πληρωθῇ (which is wrongly substituted by some documents). The question, indeed, is not of the *fulfilment* of this special prophecy, but of the *completing* of the fulfilment of the Scripture prophecies *in general.* *Keil* thinks that this momentary refreshment was necessary for Him, in order that He might be able Himself to give up His soul to God.—The drink offered to Jesus is not the stupefying potion which He had refused at the moment of the crucifixion, and which was a deadening wine mixed with myrrh (Mark) or wormwood (Matthew). Jesus had refused it, because He wished to preserve the perfect clearness of His mind until the end. The potion which the soldier offers Him now is no longer the soldiers' wine, as it was ordinarily called ; for, in that case, the sponge and the stalk of hyssop would have been to no purpose. It was vinegar prepared for *the condemned* themselves.—In the first two Gospels, the cry of Jesus : "Eli, Eli ! . . . My God ! my God ! . . ." had called forth from a soldier a similar act, but three hours had elapsed since then.—Hyssop is a plant which is only a foot and a half high. Since a stalk of this length was sufficient to reach the lips of the condemned person, it follows from this that the cross was not so high as it is ordinarily represented.—*Ostervald* and *Martin* translate altogether wrongly : "They put hyssop *around* [the sponge] ;" or "*surrounding it* with hyssop." A Dutch critic, *de Koe* (*Conjecturaal Critik en het Evangelie naar Johannes*, 1883), has proposed to substitute for ὑσσώπῳ (*hyssop*) ὑσσῷ, *a lance.* The conjecture is ingenious, but not sufficiently well founded.

"*I thirst*" was the fifth expression of the Saviour, and "*all is finished*" the sixth. The first three of His seven expressions on the cross had reference to His personal relations : they were the prayer for His executioners (Luke), the promise made to the thief, His companion in punishment (Luke), the legacy made to His mother and His friend (John). The following three referred to His work of salvation : the cry "My God . . ." (Matthew and Mark), to the moral sufferings of the expiatory sacrifice ; the groan : "*I thirst*" (John), to His physical sufferings ; the triumphant expression : "*It is finished,*" to the consummation of both. Finally, the seventh and last, which is expressly mentioned only by Luke : "*Father, into thy hands I commend my spirit,*" is implied in John in the word παρέδωκε, *he gave up ;* it refers to Himself, to the finishing of His earthly existence. This Greek term is not exactly rendered by our phrase *to give up the ghost.* It expresses a spontaneous act. "*No one takes my life,*" Jesus had said ; "*I have power to lay it down and I have power to take it again*" (x. 18) ; it would be necessary to translate by the word *hand over* (commit). Such was also the meaning of the *loud cry* with which, according to Matthew and Mark, Jesus expired.—The word κλίνας, "*having bowed* His head," indicates that until then He had held His head erect.

The breaking of the legs : vv. 31-37.

Ver. 31. "*The Jews therefore, that the bodies might not remain on the cross during the Sabbath, because it was the preparation*[1] (*for the day of that Sabbath*[2] *was a high day*), *asked Pilate that the legs of the crucified might be broken, and that they might be taken away.*"—John describes here a series of Providential facts, omitted by his predecessors, which occurred in quick succession, and which united in impressing on the person of Jesus, in His condition of deepest humiliation, the Messianic seal. The Romans commonly left the bodies of the condemned on the cross; they became the prey of wild beasts or of dissolution. But the Jewish law required that the bodies of executed criminals should be put out of the way before sunset, that the Holy Land might not, on the following day, be polluted by the curse attached to the lifeless body, a monument of a divine condemnation (Deut. xxi. 23, Josh. viii. 29, x. 26, Josephus, *Bell. Jud.* iv. 5, 2). Ordinarily, no doubt, the Romans did not trouble themselves about this law. But, in this particular case, the Jews would have been absolutely unable to bear the violation of it, because, as John observes, the following day was neither an ordinary day nor even an ordinary Sabbath; it was a Sabbath of an altogether exceptional solemnity. Those who think that, according to John himself, the Jewish people had already celebrated the Passover on the preceding evening, and that at this time the great Sabbatic day of the 15th Nisan was ending, give to the word παρασκευή, *preparation*, the technical sense of *Friday*, and explain the special solemnity of the Saturday which was to follow by the fact that this Sabbath belonged to the *Passover* week. They call to mind also the fact that on the 16th of Nisan the offering of the sacred sheaf was celebrated, a well-known act of worship by which the harvest was annually opened. But neither the one nor the other of these reasons can explain the extraordinary solemnity which John ascribes to the Sabbath of the next day. The 16th of Nisan was in itself so little of a Sabbath that, in order to cut the ears on the evening of the 15–16th, which were intended to form the sacred sheaf, the messengers of the Sanhedrim were obliged to wait until the people cried out to them: "The sun is set;" then only did the 16th begin, and then only could they take the sickle. Thus in Levit. xxiii. 11–14 the 16th is called "the day *after the Sabbath.*" How could the weekly Sabbath derive its superior sanctity from its coincidence with this purely working day? As to the technical sense of *Friday*, given to παρασκευή, it is set aside here by the absence of the article. Finally, the γάρ, *for*, clearly puts the idea of *preparation* in a logical relation to that of the extraordinary sanctity of the Sabbath which was to begin at six o'clock in the evening, and thus obliges us to keep for this word its natural sense of *preparation*. Hence it follows that the time of Jesus' death was the afternoon of the 14th, and not that of the 15th, since the Sabbatic day was on the point of beginning, not of ending. The words: "*For it was the preparation,*" signify at once preparation for the Sabbath (as Friday) and

---

[1] The words επει παρασκευη ην (*because it was the preparation*), are placed by ℵ B L X V 10 Mnn. It^plerique Vulg. Syr. Cop. Sah. immediately after οι ουν Ιουδαιοι (*the Jews therefore*), and not after εν τω σαββατω (T. R. with 12 Mjj.).

[2] Instead of εκεινη which T. R. reads with some Mnn. It^aliq Vulg. (*that day of the Sabbath*), εκεινου is read in all the other documents (*the day of that Sabbath*).

preparation for the great Paschal day (as the day before the 15th of Nisan). There was, therefore, on this day a double preparation, because there was an accumulation of Sabbath rest on the following day, which was at once the weekly Sabbath and the great Sabbath, the first day of the feast. By the words : "it was the preparation," the evangelist reminds us indirectly that the essential act of the preparation, the slaying of the lamb, took place in the temple at that very moment, and that the Paschal supper was about to follow in a few hours. This was the reason why it was a matter of absolute necessity, from the Jewish point of view, that the bodies should be put out of the way without delay, before the following day should begin (at six o'clock in the evening).—Pilate, respecting this scruple, consented to the thing which was asked of him. The breaking of the legs did not occasion death immediately, but it was intended to make it certain, and thus to allow of the removal of the bodies. For it rendered any return to life impossible, because mortification necessarily and immediately resulted from it. The existence of this custom (σκελοκοπία, crurifragium), among the Romans, in certain exceptional cases, is fully established (see the numerous passages cited by *Keim*). Thus *Renan* says : "The Jewish archæology and the Roman archæology of ver. 31 are exact." If *Keim* himself has, notwithstanding this, raised difficulties, asking why the Synoptics do not mention this fact if it is historical, it is easy to answer him : Because Jesus Himself was not affected by it. But His person alone was of importance to them, not those of the two malefactors. Neither would John have mentioned this detail except for its relation to the fulfilment of a prophecy, which had so forcibly struck him.—Is it necessary to understand ἀρθῶσι, *might be taken away*, simply of removal *from the cross*. I think not. What concerned the Jews who made the request was not that the bodies should be unfastened, but that they should be put out of sight. The law Deut. xxi. 23, which required of them this request, had no reference to the punishment of the cross, which was unknown to Israel.

Vv. 32–34. "*The soldiers therefore came and broke the legs of the first, then of the other who was crucified with him.* 33. *But, when they came to Jesus, seeing that he was already dead,*[1] *they did not break his legs ;* 34, *but one of the soldiers pierced his side with his spear, and immediately there came thereout blood and water.*"—The word : *they came*, is more naturally explained if we hold with *Storr, Olshausen* and *Weiss* that they were different soldiers from those who had accomplished the work of crucifixion. They had been sent especially for this purpose with the necessary instruments.—If the purpose for which the limbs of the condemned were broken was that of which we have spoken, this treatment was made useless with respect to Jesus by the fact of His death. The spear-thrust of the soldier was, therefore, as it were, only a compensation for the operation which was omitted ; it signified: If thou art not dead already, here is what will finish thee. It would be absurd to demand examples for such an act, which had in it nothing judicial.—The verb νύσσειν indicates a more or less deep thrust,

---

[1] ℵ : ευρον αυτον ηδη τεθνηκοτα και ου, instead of ως . . . τεθνηκοτα, ου

in contrast to a cut. This term is sometimes used in Homer to designate mortal wounds.—Is the fact of the outflowing of the blood and water to be regarded as a natural phenomenon ? In general, undoubtedly, when a dead body is pierced, no liquid comes forth from it ; nevertheless, if one of the large vessels is reached, it may happen that there will flow from the wound a blackish blood covered with a coating of serum. Can this be what John calls *blood and water ?* This is improbable. *Ebrard* accordingly supposes that the lance reached the deposits of extravasated blood. *Gruner (Commentatio de morte Jesu Christi vera,* Halle, 1805) also has this opinion. He thinks that the lance pierced the aqueous deposits which, during this long-continued torture, had been formed around the heart, and then the heart itself. *William Stroud* (London, 1847) alleges phenomena observed in cases of sudden death in consequence of cramp of the heart. These explanations are all of them quite improbable. The expression : *blood and water,* naturally denotes two substances flowing simultaneously, but to the eyes of the spectators distinct, a thing which has no place in any of these suppositions. *Baur, Strauss,* etc., conclude from this that there is a necessity for a symbolic interpretation, and find here again the purely ideal character of the narrative. The author meant to express by this fact of his own invention the abundance of spiritual life which will, from this moment, flow forth from the person of Christ *(Baur)* ; the water more especially represents the Holy Spirit, the blood the Holy Supper, with an allusion to the custom of mixing the wine of this sacrament with water *(Strauss,* in his new *Life of Jesus).* But what idea must we form of the morality of a man who should solemnly affirm that *he had seen* (ver. 35) that which he had the consciousness of having beheld only *in idea.* In favor of this allegorical explanation an appeal has been made to the words in 1 John v. 6 : "*He came not by water only, but by water and blood.*" But these words do not have the least connection with the fact with which we are occupied. The *water* of which John speaks in his epistle denotes, as iii. 5, baptism : Jesus did not come, like the forerunner, only with the baptism of water, the symbol of purification, but with the *blood* which brings the expiation itself. In our view there remains but one explanation : it is that which admits that this mysterious fact took place outside of the laws of common physiology, and that it is connected with the exceptional nature of a body which sin had never tainted and which moved forward to the resurrection without having to pass through dissolution. At the instant of death, the process of dissolution, in general, begins. The body of Jesus must have taken at that moment a different path from that of death : it entered upon that of glorification. He who was the *Holy One of God,* in the *absolute* sense of the word, was also *absolutely* exempt from *corruption* (Ps. xvi. 10). This is the meaning which the evangelist seems to me to have ascribed to this unprecedented phenomenon, of which he was a witness. Thus is explained the affirmation, having somewhat the character of an oath, by which, in the following verse, he certifies its reality; not that the affirmation of ver. 35 refers only to this fact ; for it certainly has reference to the totality of the facts mentioned vv. 33, 34 (see below). *Weiss* holds that there is a natural phenomenon here which cannot be certainly explained ; but he thinks that John saw in the blood the means of our redemption and in the water the symbol of its purifying force. In this case, a grossly superstitious idea must be imputed to the apostle : by what right ? The text says not a word of such a symbolic sense. According to *Reuss*, also, the blood designates the redemptive death, and the water baptism, and we have here a mystical explanation of a fact which struck the author. All this has no better foundation than the opinion of those who think that the evangelist wished to combat the idea that Jesus was not really dead (*Lücke, Neander*), or the idea that He had only an apparent body (*Olshausen*). The first of these ideas is entirely modern ; the second ascribes to the author an argument which has no force, since the Docetæ did not in the least deny the sensible *appearances* in the earthly life of Jesus.—The absence of all corruption in the *Holy One of God* implied the beginning of the restoration of life from the very moment when, at death, in the case of every sinner the work of dissolution which is to destroy the body commences.

Vv. 35–37. "*And he who saw it has borne witness, and his testimony is true,*[1] *and he knows that he says true, that you also*[2] *may believe.*[3] *36. For these things came to pass that the Scripture might be fulfilled : No one of his bones*[4] *shall be broken. 37. And another word also says : They shall look on him whom they pierced.*"—Some (*Weisse, Schweizer, Hilgenfeld, Weizsäcker, Keim, Bäumlein, Reuss, Sabatier*) claim that in these words of ver. 35 the author of the Gospel expressly distinguishes himself from the apostle, and that he professes to be only the reporter of the oral testimony of the latter. He declares to the readers of the Gospel that John the apostle saw this, that he bore witness of it, and that he had the inward consciousness of saying a true thing in relating this fact. Thus these words, which have always been regarded as one of the strongest proofs of the Johannean composition of our Gospel, are transformed into a formal denial of its apostolic origin. We have already examined this question in the *Introduction*, read pp. 193–197. We will also present here the following observations :

1. As to the school of *Baur*, which asserts that the author all along wishes to pass himself off as the apostle, it should evidently have been on its guard against accepting this explanation. It has not been able, however, to refrain from catching at the bait ; but it has clearly perceived the contradiction into which it is brought thereby ; see the embarrassment of *Hilgenfeld* with respect to this question, *Einl.*, p. 731. In fact, if the author wishes throughout his entire work to pass himself off as the apostle John, how should he here openly declare the contrary ? The reply of *Hilgenfeld* is this : "He forgets (falls out of) his part " (p. 732). A singular inadvertence, surely, in the case of a *falsarius* of such consummate skill as the one to whom these critics ascribe the composition of our Gospel !—Other critics, such as *Reuss*, find themselves no less embarrassed by the apparent advantage

---

[1] ℵ : αληθης, instead of αληθινη.
[2] 15 Mjj. (ℵ A B etc.) 25 Mnn. It. Vulg. Syr. read και before υμεις ("that you *also* may believe") ; T. R. omits this word with 7 Mjj. (E G etc.) and the other Mnn.
[3] ℵ B : πιστευητε instead of πιστευσητε.
[4] 60 Mnn. It[plerique]: απ' αυτου instead of αυτου (according to Exod. xii. 46, in the LXX).

which they yet try to derive from these words. In fact, there exists in ch. xxi. 24 an analogous passage in which the depositaries of our Gospel—those who received the commission to publish it—expressly attest the identity of the *redactor* of this work with the apostle-witness of the facts, with *the disciple whom Jesus loved*. How can we explain such a declaration on the part of the depositaries of the work, if the author had in our passage himself attested his non-identity with the apostle, the eye-witness? Do they knowingly falsify? *Reuss* does not dare to affirm this. Are they mistaken? It would be necessary to conclude from this that those who published the book had themselves never read the work to which they give the attestation in opposition to his. Still more, if they received from the author his book to be published, they must have known him personally; moreover, it is from the personal knowledge which they have of him and his character that they come forward as vouchers for his veracity. How, then, could they be deceived with respect to him?—2. And on what reasons are suppositions so impossible made to rest? Above all, the pronoun ἐκεῖνος is alleged, by which the author designates the apostle, distinguishing him from himself. But throughout the whole course of our Gospel we have seen this pronoun employed, not to oppose a nearer subject to a more remote subject, but in an exclusive or strongly affirmative sense, with the design of emphasizing somewhat the subject to which it refers; comp. i. 18, v. 39, vii. 20, ix. 51, xix. 31, etc., and very particularly ix. 37, where we see that when the one who speaks does so by presenting himself objectively and speaking of himself in the third person, he can very properly use this pronoun.[1] Being forced to speak of himself in this case, John uses this pronoun, because he had *alone* been witness of the special fact which he relates.—3. *Keim* no longer insists on this philological question; he makes appeal to "rational logic," which does not allow us to hold that a writer describes himself objectively at such length. But comp. St. Paul, 2 Cor. xii. 3! And it is precisely "rational logic" which does not allow us to ascribe to another writer, different from John, the affirmation: *And his testimony is true*. A disciple of John declaring to the Church that the apostle, his master, did not falsify or was not the dupe of an illusion! The first of these attestations would be an insult to his master himself; the second, an absurdity; for has he the right of affirming anything respecting a fact which he has not seen and which he knows only by the testimony of John himself?—4. *Reuss* rests upon the perfect μεμαρτύρηκε, *has borne witness*. The narrative of the witness, according to this, is presented as a fact which was long since past. But comp. i. 34, where the: *I have borne witness*, applies to the declaration which John the Baptist has just uttered at the very moment. The same is the case here; this verb applies to the declaration which the author has just made in the preceding lines respecting the fact related: "It is said; the testimony is given and it continues henceforth;" such is the sense of the perfect.—5. It seems to me that we must, above all, take account of the expression: "*He knows that he says true.*" Here is the meaning which we are forced

---

[1] See on the use of the pronoun ἐκεῖνος in the Fourth Gospel, *Steitz, Stud. und Krit.*, 1859, pp. 497–606, and *Buttmann, ibid.*, 1860, pp. 505–536.

to give to these words : "The witness from whom I have the fact knows that he says true." But by what right can the writer bear testimony of the consciousness which this witness has of the truth of what he says ? One testifies as to one's own consciousness, not that of another.—6. *Hilgenfeld, Keim, Bäumlein, Reuss, Sabatier*, cite as analogous xxi. 24. "*This is the disciple* (the beloved disciple) *who testifies these things and wrote these things; and we know that his testimony is true.*" But the very similarity in the expressions makes us perceive so much more clearly the difference between them. The attestants say, not as in our passage : "*he knows* (οἶδε) that he says true," but : "*we know* (οἴδαμεν) that he says true ;" they do what the evangelist should have done in our passage, if he had, like them, wished to distinguish himself from the apostle ; they use the first person : *we know*.

The adjective ἀληθινή does not here, any more than elsewhere, mean *true* (ἀληθής); the meaning is : a real testimony, which truly deserves the name, as announcing a fact truly seen. Καὶ ὑμεῖς, *you also:* "you who read, as well as I who have seen and testified." The question is not of belief in the fact reported, but of *faith* in the absolute sense of the word, of their faith *in Christ*, which is to derive its confirmation from this fact and from those which are mentioned afterwards, as it was these facts which had already confirmed the faith of the author himself. It is not only from the fact of the outflowing of the blood and water that this result is expected. The *for* of ver. 36 proves that the question is of the way in which the two prophecies recalled to mind in vv. 36,37 were fulfilled by the three facts related in vv. 33,34.—The first prophecy is taken from Exod. xii. 46 and Num. ix. 12 ; not from Ps. xxxiv. 21, as *Bäumlein* and *Weiss* think ; for this last passage refers to the preservation of the *life* of the righteous one, not to that of the integrity of His body. The application which the evangelist makes of the words implies as admitted the typical significance of the Paschal lamb ; comp. xiii. 18, a similar typical application.—The Paschal lamb belonged to God and was the figure of the Lamb of God. This is the reason why the law so expressly protected it against all violent and brutal treatment. It is also the reason why the remains of its flesh were to be burned immediately after the supper.

As the prophecy was fulfilled by what did not take place with reference to Jesus (the breaking of the legs), it was also fulfilled at the same time by what *did* take place in relation to Him (the thrust of the lance), ver. 37. Zechariah (xii. 10) had represented Jehovah as *pierced* by His people, in the person of the Messiah. The action of the Jews in delivering Jesus up to the punishment of the cross had fully realized this prophecy. But this fulfilment must take a still more literal character (see on xii. 15, xviii. 9, xix. 24). The meaning of the Hebrew term דקרו, *they have pierced*, was considerably weakened by the LXX, who undoubtedly deemed this expression too strong as applied to Jehovah, and rendered it by κατωρχήσαντο, *they insulted*, outraged God by idolatry. The evangelist goes back to the Hebrew text ; comp. also Apoc. i. 7. The term *they shall look on*, ὄψονται, refers to that which will take place at the time of the conversion of the Jews, when in this Jesus, rejected by them, they shall recognize their Messiah. The look

956 / The Passion

in question is that of repentance, of supplication, of faith, which they will then cast upon Him (εἰς ὅν) ; a striking scene magnificently described in the same prophetic picture, Zech. xii. 8–14.

In order to understand clearly what John felt at the moment which he here describes, let us imagine a believing Jew, thoroughly acquainted with the Old Testament, seeing the soldiers approaching who were to break the legs of the three condemned persons. What is to take place with regard to the body of the Messiah, more sacred even than that of the Paschal lamb ? And lo, by a series of unexpected circumstances, he sees this body rescued from any brutal operation ! The same spear-thrust which spares it the treatment with which it was threatened realizes to the letter that which the prophet had foretold ! Were not such signs fitted to strengthen his faith and that of the Church ? This is what John had experienced as an eye-witness and what he meant to say in this passage, vv. 31–37.

The entombment of Jesus : vv. 38–42.

Here, as in the preceding passage, John completes the narrative of his predecessors. He makes prominent the part which was taken by Nicodemus in the funeral honors paid to Jesus, and sets forth clearly the relation between the advanced *hour* of the day and the *place* of the sepulchre where the body was laid. He thus accounts for facts whose relation the Synoptics do not indicate.

Vv. 38–40. *"After this[1] Joseph of Arimathea, who was a disciple of Jesus, but secretly for fear of the Jews, went and asked Pilate that they might take away the body of Jesus ; and Pilate gave him leave. He came[2] therefore, and took away[2] the body of Jesus.[3] 39. Nicodemus, who at the first came to Jesus by night, came also, bringing[4] a mixture[4] of myrrh and aloes, about a hundred pound weight. 40. They took therefore the body of Jesus and wrapped it in[5] linen cloths with the spices, according as the Jews are accustomed to bury."*—The request of the Jews, ver. 31, refers to the three condemned persons ; but, as John has observed, the order of Pilate had only been executed with reference to two of them. Joseph then presents himself before him with an entirely new request, which applies to Jesus only. *Bäumlein :* "Sometimes, especially on occasion of a feast, the bodies of those crucified were given up to relatives. Philo *in Flacc.*, §10." Mark relates that Pilate, on hearing this request, was astonished that Jesus was already dead—a fact which, according to *Strauss*, contradicts the permission which he had just given for the breaking of the legs. But this operation did not cause death immediately, as *Strauss* himself acknowledges ; it served only to make it sure. Pilate therefore might be astonished that the death of Jesus was so speedily accomplished. Perhaps also his surprise was caused by the fact which was reported to him, that Jesus was dead even before the performing of this operation. For, as is also attested by Mark xv. 44, he caused a detailed account of the way in which the things

---

[1] Δε is omitted by 7 Mjj. (א A B etc.) It.
[2] Instead of ηλθεν and ηρεν, א It^{aliq} read ηλθον and ηραν (they *came* and they *took away*).
[3] Instead of το σωμα του I., B L X Λ read το σωμα αυτου ; א ; αυτον ; It^{plerique} ; αυτο.
[4] א reads εχων (*having*), instead of φερων. א B : ελιγμα (*a roll*) instead of μιγμα.
[5] א B K L X Y Π It^{aliq} Vulg. omit εν before οθονιοις.

had taken place to be given him by the centurion who had taken charge of the crucifixion.—*Arimathea* probably denotes, not the city of *Rama*, two leagues north of Jerusalem, or the other Ràma, now *Ramleh*, ten leagues north-west of the *capital*, near to Lydda, but *Ramathaim* (the noun, with the article represented by the syllable *ar*), in Ephraim, the birthplace of Samuel (1 Sam. i. 1). In any case, Joseph was now settled at Jerusalem with his family, since he possessed here a burial-place, but only recently, because the sepulchre had not yet been used.—By mentioning Joseph and Nicodemus, John brings out, in the case of both, the contrast between their present boldness and the cautiousness of their previous conduct. That which, as it seemed, must completely dishearten them—the ignominious death of Jesus—causes the faith of these members of the Jewish aristocracy to break forth conspicuously, and delivers them from all human fear. No doubt, on seeing the Lord suspended on the cross, Nicodemus recalls to mind the type of the brazen serpent which Jesus had set before him at first (iii. 14).—Τὸ πρῶτον designates here, as in x. 40, the beginning of Jesus' *ministry*. If Nicodemus had been for John, as *Reuss* seems to affirm, merely a fictitious type, how could he make him appear again here as a real and acting person, and this while expressly recalling the scene of ch. iii.?— Myrrh is an odoriferous gum ; aloes, a sweet-scented wood. After they had been pounded, there was made of them a mixture which was spread over the whole shroud in which the body was wrapped. Probably this cloth was cut into bandages to wrap the limbs separately. The words : "As *the Jews* are accustomed," contrast this mode of embalming with that of the Egpytians, who removed the intestines and, by much longer and more complicated processes, secured the preservation of the corporeal covering.—The hundred pounds recall to mind the profusion with which Mary had poured the spikenard over the feet of Jesus, ch. xii. ; it is a truly royal homage. The Synoptics tell us that the holy women had the intention also, on their part, to complete this provisional embalming, but only *after the Sabbath*.

Vv. 41, 42. "*Now there was in the place where he was crucified a garden, and in the garden a new sepulchre wherein no one had ever yet been laid.*[1] 42. *It was there that they laid Jesus, because of the Preparation of the Jews ; for the sepulchre was near.*"—According to Matthew, the sepulchre belonged to Joseph himself, and this was the reason of the use which was made of it. According to John, this sepulchre was chosen because of its proximity to Golgotha, since the Sabbath was about to begin. These two reasons, far from contradicting, complete each other. What purpose would the proximity of the sepulchre have served, if it had not belonged to one of the Lord's friends ? And it was certainly the circumstance that Joseph owned this sepulchre near the place of crucifixion, which suggested to him the idea of asking for the body of Jesus.—John and Luke (xxiii. 53) remark that the sepulchre was new. Comp. Luke xix. 30 : "*You shall find a colt tied whereon yet never man sat.*" These are providential facts, which belong to the royal glory of Jesus. When a king is received, objects which have not

---

[1] ℵ B : ην τεθειμενος, instead of ετεθη.

yet been used are consecrated to his service.—The expression . *the Preparation of the Jews*, signifies, according to those who hold that the death of Jesus took place, not on the 14th, but on the 15th : *the Friday of the Jews*. But what would be the object of so singular an expression ? It was designed, answers *Rotermund*,[1] to give us to understand how it happened that the day following a Sabbatic day (the 15th) was again a Sabbath (Saturday). By this means the first Sabbath became, as it were, *the preparation* for the second. But if the first of the two days was Sabbatic, like the following one, the carrying away of the body, which they did not wish to do on the next day, could not any more have been done on this day. The quite simple meaning is that it was the hour when *the Jews* (thus is the complement *the Jews* explained) prepared their great national and religious feast by sacrificing the lamb. They were obliged to hasten because, with the setting of the sun, this day of preparation, the 14th, a non Sabbatic day, came to its close, and because the following day, the 15th, was in that year a doubly Sabbatic day (ver. 31); comp. Luke xxiii. 56.

On the Day of Jesus' Death

Respecting the day of the *week* on which the death of Jesus took place, the agreement of the four evangelists is manifest ; it was a Friday (Matt. xxvii. 62, Mark xv. 42, Luke xxiii. 54, John xix. 31). But they appear to differ as to the question whether this Friday was the 14th or the 15th of the month Nisan— an apparently insignificant difference, but yet one which implies a more considerable one. For on this depends the question whether Jesus had celebrated on the preceding evening the Paschal supper with all the rest of the Jewish people,—in that case Jesus would have died on the 15th,—or whether the people were to celebrate this supper later, on the evening of the day of His death,—in this case the day of His death was the 14th. For the Paschal supper was celebrated on the evening which formed the transition from the 14th to the 15th.

The View of John

According to John xiii. 1, Jesus celebrated His last supper *before the feast of the Passover*. *Rotermund* (in the article which is cited above) affirms, no doubt, with *Langen*, that the Passover feast began only on the 15th, and that, as a consequence, this supper, which took place *before the feast*, must be placed on the evening of the 14th, and must therefore be identified with the Paschal supper. But see on xiii. 1. John would not have designated this supper simply by the words : "*A* supper," or even, if one will have it so, "*the* supper." For the benefit of his Greek readers, he could not have refrained from designating this supper as that *of the Passover*.—The passage xviii. 28, notwithstanding all the efforts of some scholars (comp. also *Kirchner, Die jüdische Passahfeier*, 1870), plainly declares that the Jewish Paschal supper was not yet celebrated on the morning when Jesus was condemned, and consequently that Jesus was put to death on the 14th, and not on the 15th.—The passages xix. 14, 31, 42 lead to the same result. Neither *Kirchner* nor *Rotermund* has succeeded in proving that expressions such as these : *the Passover Friday, the*

---

[1] *Von Ephraim nach Golgotha, Stud. und Kritik.*, 1876, I.

Friday of the Jews, are natural. That it was a Friday is certain ; that the word παρασκευή *(preparation)* may designate Friday, as the preparation for the Sabbath, is unquestionable. But that in John's context this term *paraskeué, preparation*, can have the technical sense of Friday, is inadmissible.—After the observations of *Kirchner* and *Luthardt*, I give up alleging xiii. 19 as decisive, although one still asks oneself how a purchase could have been made during the Passover night, all families, whether rich or poor, being at that time gathered around the Paschal table, and all the shops being consequently closed.

The Apparent View of the Synoptics

This view seems to follow evidently from the three parallels, Matt. xxvi. 17 : " The first day of unleavened bread (the 14th of Nisan), the disciples of Jesus came to him saying, Where wilt thou that we prepare for thee the Passover supper?" Mark xiv. 12 : "And on the first day of unleavened bread, when they sacrificed the Passover, the disciples said to him ;" Luke xxii. 7 : "The day of unleavened bread came, when the Passover must be sacrificed, and he sent Peter and John." It seems altogether natural to place this question of the disciples, or (according to Luke) this commission which Jesus gives to two of them, on the morning of the 14th, when the preparations of the Paschal supper were made for the evening. And from this fact precisely it is that the apparent contradiction to the narrative of John arises ; for, if Jesus gave this order on the 14th in the morning, the supper which the disciples were to prepare for the evening could only be the Paschal supper, from which it would follow that His last supper coincided with the Paschal supper of that year. Now, according to John, as we have just proved, the Jewish Paschal supper must have taken place only on the evening which *followed* that of the last supper of Jesus, on the evening of the day of His death.

Here is one of the greatest differences between the Synoptics and John. Since the earliest times it has attracted the notice of all those who have closely studied the Scriptures. And already in the second century, as we shall see, we encounter numerous traces of the discussions which it has raised.

The Attempts at Solution

From the time of St. Jerome, the view of the Synoptic narrative became prevalent in the Church ; it continued so even until the Reformation : Jesus had celebrated the Passover with the whole people before He died. But at that epoch the revival of Biblical studies caused the need to be felt of giving a more exact account of the Gospel narratives ; their apparent disagreement was obvious, and the attempt was made to resolve it. *Calvin* and *Theodore Beza*, then *Scaliger* and *Casaubon*, brought out the idea, already expressed by *Eusebius* and *Chrysostom* (see *Tholuck*, p. 41), that the Jews, in order that they might not have to celebrate two successive Sabbatic days (Friday, the 15th of Nisan, as the first day of the feast, and the next day, the 16th, which fell in this year on Saturday), had exceptionally delayed by one day the great day of the feast, while Jesus had, for Himself, kept the legal day. Thus would the fact be explained that He, at this time, celebrated the Passover a day sooner than the rest of the people. It appears that, at the present day also, when the 15th of Nisan falls on a Friday, the Jews transfer the feast from this day to Saturday. This solution is very simple and natural. Only we do not find either in the

New Testament, or in Josephus, or in the Talmud, any trace of such a transposition, which would constitute a grave derogation from the law.

Other reasons have been sought which might lead Jesus in this circumstance to deviate from the generally-received usage. *Stier* has thought that He attached Himself to the mode of action of some sects, like that of the Karaites, who had the custom of celebrating the Paschal supper, not on the evening of the 14th-15th, but on that of the 13th-14th.—*Ebrard* has supposed that because of the great number of lambs to be slain in the temple (sometimes more than 250,000, according to Josephus) from three to six o'clock in the afternoon, the Galileans had been authorized to sacrifice and eat the lamb on the 13th instead of the 14th.—*Serno* applies the same supposition to all the Jews of the dispersion. But these hypotheses have no historical basis, and are, in any case, much less probable than that of the Reformers.—*Rauch* has affirmed that the Israelites in general celebrated the Paschal supper, legally and habitually, on the evening of the 13th-14th, and not that of the 14th-15th. But this opinion, which, even if adopted, would yet not resolve the difficulty, strikes against all the known Biblical and historical data.

Lutteroth, in his pamphlet, *Le jour de la préparation*, 1855, and in his *Essai d' interprétation de l' Evangile de saint Matthieu*, 1876, places the day of the conversation of Jesus with His disciples much earlier, on the 10th of Nisan, when the Jews set apart the lamb which was to be sacrificed on the 14th. It was, according to him, on the same 10th day that Jesus was crucified ; He remained in the tomb on the 11th, 12th, and 13th ; the 14th was the day of His resurrection. This entirely new chronology is shattered by the first word of the conversation. How is it possible that the 10th of Nisan should be called by the evangelists *the first day of unleavened bread*, especially when this determination of the time is made still more precise, as it is in Mark, by the words : "*when the Passover is sacrificed.*" It is true that *Lutteroth* tries to make this *when* refer only to the idea of unleavened bread : " the unleavened bread which is to be *eaten when* the Passover is sacrificed " (!). The words of Luke xxii. 7 : " The day of unleavened bread came, when the Passover must be sacrificed," are still more rudely handled : it is not an historical fact which Luke relates, it is a moral reflection by means of which the evangelist announces at the beginning that the Passion will have an end (!) (*Essai*, pp. 410, 411 [1]).—After all these fruitless attempts, one can understand how a large number of critics limit themselves at the present day to establishing the disagreement and declaring it insoluble ; this is what is done by *Lücke, Neander, Bleek, de Wette, Steitz, J. Müller, Weiss, de Pressensé*,[2] etc.

The Truth of John's Narrative

But if the contradiction exists, it remains to determine which of the two narratives deserves the preference. Then it must be explained how so grave a difference can have arisen in the Gospel narrative.

---

[1] We desire to say that, notwithstanding these eccentricities, the works of *Lutteroth* are nevertheless monuments of solid learning and persevering investigation. Pages 60, 76, 77 of the pamphlet on the Passover prove interesting points of contact in Patristic literature with the particular views of the author respecting this question.

[2] " We regard thus far the contradiction," says this author (viith ed.), " as insoluble, while entirely justifying the narrative of John " (p. 603, note).

The critics of the Tübingen school—*Baur, Hilgenfeld, Keim*—are not embarrassed : it is the Synoptics that have preserved the true historical tradition. As to John's narrative, it is a deliberate alteration of the real history, intended, on the one hand, to make the death of Jesus, as the true Paschal lamb, coincide with the time of the sacrificing of the lamb in the temple, and, on the other hand, to throw into the shade the Jewish Paschal supper by making the last supper of Jesus a simple farewell meal. But neither the one nor the other of these ends required a means so compromising as that which is thus ascribed to pseudo-John. Such a disagreement with the first three Gospels, which were already received throughout the whole Church, and with the apostolic tradition, of which these writings were known to be the depositaries, exposed the work of the fourth evangelist to the danger of being greatly suspected, and that in a very useless way for him. For to present Jesus as the true Paschal lamb, there was no need of such a desperate expedient as that of misplacing the well-known day of His death ; it was enough that this event should be placed in the Paschal week ; there was, therefore, nothing to be changed in the tradition of the Church ; comp. the words of Paul in 1 Cor. v. 7 : " Christ, our Passover, has been sacrificed for us ;" those of Peter, 1 Ep. i. 19, and all the passages of the Apocalypse where Christ is called *the Lamb*. As to the Jewish Passover, there was no need in the second century to depreciate it ; it was already replaced everywhere, both in the Church and in the sects, by the Christian supper (*Schürer*, pp. 29–34).

A second class of critics, as we have seen, try to interpret the texts of John so as to put them in accord with what they think to be the meaning of the Synoptic narrative. They are, for example, *Lightfoot, Tholuck, Olshausen, Hengstenberg, Wieseler, Luthardt, Wichelhaus, Hofmann, Lichtenstein, Lange, Riggenbach, Ebrard, Bäumlein, Langen, Keil*. But all their efforts have been unsuccessful in bringing out from John's text a sense contrary to that which is obvious on reading it.

As to the third class, which concedes a real difference between our Gospel narratives, the greater part give the preference to that of John ; thus, among the moderns, *Weiss, Pressensé* (see note on p. 960), *Reuss* himself (*Théol. joh.* pp. 59, 60). And, in fact, if the conflict is real, the choice cannot be doubtful. The witnesses in favor of the historical exactness of John's narrative are the following :

1. *The Synoptics* themselves.—These writings contain a series of facts, and a certain number of words, which are in complete accord with John's narrative and in no less evident disagreement with the view which is attributed to them. If there was an hour sacred to the Jewish conscience, it was that of the Paschal supper ; and yet it was at this hour that a multitude of officers and servants of the chief priests and elders had left their houses and their families, assembled around the Passover table, to go and arrest Jesus in Gethsemane ! Still more, we know that everything which was reprehensible on the Sabbath, as, e.g., to climb a tree, to ride on horseback, to hold a session of a court, was also prohibited on the festival day (*Traité Beza*, v. 2) ; and yet there were held, on that Sabbatic night of the 14th–15th, at least two sessions of the court, in one of which the sentence of death for Jesus was pronounced ; and then all those long negotiations with Pilate, as well as the sending to Herod, took place ; all this, notwithstanding the festival and Sabbatic character of the 15th of Nisan ! It is answered that a session of the court was permitted on the festival day,

provided that the sentence was not put *in writing*, and that, in general, the rule of the *festival* days was less rigorous than that of the *Sabbaths* properly so called. But, at the foundation, all the difference between these two kinds of days is limited to the authorization to prepare the necessary articles of food on the festival day, if even we are allowed to draw a general conclusion from Exod. xii. 16. Now would so slight a difference be sufficient to justify the use of such a day which is here implied?—That Simon of Cyrene, *who is returning from the fields* (Matt. xxvii. 32) ; that Joseph of Arimathea, who is going to *purchase* a linen cloth (Mark xv. 46) ; those women who give up embalming the body, because *the Sabbath is drawing near* (Luke xxiii. 56)—is all this explicable on the supposition that the day when these things happened was itself a Sabbatic day, the 15th of Nisan? No doubt it is answered that Simon was returning from a simple walk in the country, or that he was a countryman who was going to the city ; then, that purchases might be made on a festival day, provided they were not *paid for on the same day*. It is nevertheless true that the impression made by the narrative of the Synoptics is that the day of Jesus' death was a *working* day, entirely different from the Sabbatic day which was to follow ; that it was, consequently, the 14th, and not the 15th of Nisan.

This is what appears also from a certain number of expressions scattered throughout the Synoptic narrative. Thus Matt. xxvi. 18 : "My time is at hand ; let me keep the Passover at thy house with my disciples." What is the logical connection which unites the two propositions of this message? The only satisfactory relation to be established between them is this : "It is necessary for me to hasten ; for to-morrow it will be too late ; I shall be no longer here ; act, then, so that I may be able to eat the Passover at thy house immediately with my disciples ($\pi o \iota \tilde{\omega}$, the present)."—Matt. xxvii. 62 : The evangelist calls the Saturday during which the body of Jesus reposed in the tomb : "*the morrow which is after the preparation*." In this phrase it is impossible that the word *preparation* should have the sense of *Friday*, as if Matthew had meant to say that the Sabbath during which Jesus was in the tomb was *the next day after a Friday!* We do not designate the more solemn day by that which is less so, but the reverse. If the day of the 15th is designated here from its relation to the less solemn day of *the preparation* which had preceded it, it is because this day of preparation had become much more important, as the day of Jesus' death. From this singular phrase, therefore, it follows that Jesus was crucified on the 14th.—The same conclusion must be drawn from Mark xv. 42 : "Seeing it was *the Preparation, that is, the day before the Sabbath.*" It is of the day of Jesus' death that Mark thus speaks. Now, it is impossible that Mark, a Jew by birth, should have characterized a day like the 15th of Nisan as a simple Friday, preceding the Sabbath (Saturday), this 15th day being itself a Sabbath of the first rank. And if the expression : *preparation, that is, the day before the Sabbath*, can in the ordinary usage designate a Friday, this technical sense is inapplicable in a context where the reason is explained why a work was allowed which could not be done on the following day. The term *preparation* has here its general sense according to which it is applied to any day of the week preceding a Sabbath. Mark explains thereby the act of Joseph of Arimathea in burying Jesus, after having bought a linen cloth. "All this was possible," he says, "because it was the preparation, the day before the Sabbath and *not the Sabbath*. This is what the expression in Luke

xxiii. 54 also signifies : "That day was the preparation, and the Sabbath was about to dawn."

All these facts and words, no doubt, do not imply that the redactors of the Synoptic narratives fully understood the conclusion to be drawn from them as to the day of Jesus' death. But they are indications, which are so much the more significant since they seem to be unconscious, of the real tradition relative to the day of this death and of the complete conformity of this tradition with the narrative of John.

2. *The Talmud.*—Some passages of this monument of the Jewish memorials and usages declare expressly that Jesus *was suspended on the cross on the evening of the Passover* (beérev happésach), that is to say, in the Jewish language, the *evening before* the Passover. The erroneous details which are sometimes mingled in these passages with this fundamental statement do not at all diminish the value of the latter, because it is reproduced several times and identically—a fact which indicates an established tradition. If it is objected that the Jewish scholars derived this statement, not from their own tradition, but from our Gospels, this is to acknowledge that they understood the latter as we ourselves understand them.

3. *St. Paul.*—*Keim* cites this apostle as a convincing witness in favor of the Synoptic view. We recognize, he says, in the institution of the Holy Supper (1 Cor. xi.), all the forms of the Jewish Paschal supper—a fact which can be explained only if this last supper of Jesus coincided with the Passover, and if it consequently took place on the evening of the 14th–15th, and not on the evening of the 13th–14th. But Jesus may very well have used the forms of the Paschal supper on an evening before that on which that supper was celebrated ; for, as He says Himself, "his time was at hand," and He was forced to anticipate. From the expression of Paul in 1 Cor. xi. 23 : " The Lord Jesus *in the night in which he was betrayed,*" it follows rather that that night was not the night of the Paschal supper ; otherwise Paul would have characterized it in another way than by the betrayal of Judas.

All the witnesses whom we are able to consult, even the Synoptics, who are set in opposition to John, do homage, therefore, to the accuracy of his narrative.

The real Meaning of the Synoptic Narrative

But, I would ask, is it indeed certain that the Synoptics really say what they are made to say? They say expressly that " the first day of unleavened bread" (Matt., Mark, Luke), "when the Passover was sacrificed " (Mark), " came" (Luke), and that " the disciples asked Jesus" (Matt., Mark), or that Jesus Himself, taking the initiative, sent John and Peter from Bethany to Jerusalem (Luke), with a view to seeking a place for celebrating the Passover. This conversation is unhesitatingly placed on the morning of the 14th of Nisan for the very simple reason that the days are reckoned, as we ourselves reckon them, making the official day coincide with the natural day. But, in calculating thus, it is forgotten that among the Jews the official day began at six o'clock in the evening, and that thus, when it is said : " The day of unleavened bread came," this indication, properly understood, places us, not in the morning of the 14th, but in the evening of the 13th–14th. Taking the Synoptics literally, we are obliged to hold that the conversation between Jesus and the disciples of which they tell us took place, not on the 14th in the morning, but late in the afternoon of the 13th, *between the two evenings*, according to the customary expression[1]—that is, between the moment when the sun sinks to the horizon and that when it disappears, a moment which is the transition point between the civil day and the day following.

Rotermund asserts, no doubt, that, notwithstanding this official way of reckoning the days, it was always the beginning and the end of the *natural* day which determined the popular language. But the contrary follows from Luke xxiii. 54, which designates the last moment of Friday evening by the words : " It was the preparation, and the *Sabbath* was about to dawn," as well as from the phrase which was customary among the Jews, according to which *erev haschabbath, evening of the Sabbath,* denotes the evening, not of Saturday, but of Friday. Moreover, we can cite a telling fact taken from Jewish life at the time of Jesus. On the 16th of Nisan, in the morning, the sacred sheaf was offered as the firstfruits of the entire harvest of the year. This sheaf was cut in a field near to Jerusalem, on the preceding day at evening, or, as we should say, on the 15th at evening. The messengers of the Sanhedrim arrived in the field followed by the people : " Has the sun set ?" they asked.—" It has," answered the people. —" Am I to cut ?"—" Yes, cut."—" With this sickle ?"—" Yes."—" Into this basket ?"—" Yes."—And why all these formalities ? Because the 15th was a Sabbatic day, and because manual labor, like that of the reaper, must not be done until after it was established that the 15th was ended, and until the 16th, a working day, had begun. We see from this how deeply the way of reckoning days, which we attribute here to the Synoptics (from evening to evening, and not from morning to morning), had penetrated into the Jewish social life. There is also a circumstance which comes to the support of what we are here saying. It was already alleged by *Clement of Alexandria*, and its importance has been acknowledged by *Strauss*. The crowd of pilgrims was so great in Jerusalem at the Passover feast, that no one waited until the morning of the 14th to secure for himself the place where he might celebrate the Paschal supper with his family in the evening. It was on the 13th that this search for a place was attended to. So Clement of Alexandria calls the 13th the $\pi\rho o\varepsilon\tau o\iota\mu\alpha\sigma\acute{\iota}\alpha$, the *pro-preparation ;*[2] for the preparation itself was the day of the 14th. It was certainly, therefore, on the day of the 13th, and not that of the 14th, that the disciples spoke to the Lord, or He to them, with the purpose of procuring the place which they needed for the next day at evening.[3] The conversation reported by the Synoptics must have taken place, therefore, at the latest, about five or six o'clock in the afternoon of the 13th, according to our mode of reckoning the days. Jesus, at that time, sent to Jerusalem the two disciples in whom He felt most confidence, charging them to secure a room. In the thought of all the disciples, it was for the next day at evening ; but Jesus gives His two messengers to understand that it was for that same evening. This is what the terms of the message imply which He intrusted to them for the host whom He had in view : "*My time is at hand :* I must hasten." And why this course of

---

[1] Exod. xii. 6 : " The whole assembly of the children of Israel shall kill the lamb *between the two evenings*"—that is, late in the afternoon of the 14th.

[2] *Clement* expresses himself thus : " On the 13th He taught His disciples the mystery of the type of the lamb, when they asked Him, saying : Where wilt thou that we prepare for thee the Passover ? For this day was the pro-preparation of the Passover."

[3] *Strauss* himself says (*Leben Jesu für das Volk*, p. 533) : " It was naturally difficult, if not impossible, in view of the crowd of foreign pilgrims, to procure on the morning of the first day of the feast a place in the city for the evening."

action, which was full of mystery? The reason for it is simple. Judas must not know in advance the house where Jesus would spend this last evening with His disciples.—From six to eight or nine o'clock, the disciples would have time enough for preparing the supper, even for killing and preparing the lamb, which was already set apart since the 10th of Nisan. Undoubtedly they did not sacrifice it in the temple. But could they have done this, even on the official day and at the official hour—they who must have been excommunicated as adherents of Jesus (ix. 22)? However this may be, according to the primitive institution of the Passover (Exod. xii. 6, 7), it belonged to every Israelite to sacrifice his lamb in his own house; the sacrificing in the temple was a matter of human tradition. And at that time, when the Israelitish Passover was about to come to an end, to be replaced by the sacramental supper of the new covenant, it was altogether natural to return to the simplicity of the starting-point. The priestly sacrificing was useless when the typical lamb had no longer any other part to fill than that of serving as the inauguration of the new supper which was to replace the old. It has been objected (*Keim, Luthardt*) that Jesus did not have the right to change the legal day of the Passover. But if He was *the Lord of the Sabbath*, the corner-stone of the whole ceremonial law (Mark ii. 28), He was certainly the same also with respect to the Passover. The legal Paschal supper was no longer for Him, at that moment, anything but the calyx, withered henceforth, from the bosom of which the commemorative supper of the perfect Redemption was about to blossom.

Let us also observe an interesting coincidence between the well-known Jewish usages and the narrative of the Synoptics, as we have just explained it. On the evening of the 13th, about six o'clock, the lamps were lighted in order to search the most obscure corners of the houses and to remove every particle of leaven. Then, before the stars appeared, a man went from every house to draw the pure water with which the unleavened bread must be kneaded. Does not this usage very naturally explain the sign given to Peter and John when Jesus said to them: " On entering the city, you will meet a man bearing a pitcher of water; follow him into the house where he shall enter'' (Luke xxii. 10)?

The solution which we here present is not new; it is at the foundation the same which was already set forth in the second century by the two writers who were especially occupied with this question at the time when it seems to have deeply engaged the attention of the Church, *Apollinaris*[1] of Hierapolis and *Clement* of Alexandria.[2] The first expresses himself thus: " The day of the 14th is the true Passover of the Lord, the great sacrifice, in which the Son of God, put in the place of the lamb, was delivered up to be crucified." The second says, with still more precision: " In the preceding years, Jesus had celebrated the feast by eating the Paschal lamb according as [on the day when] the Jews sacrificed it. But on the 13th, the day on which the disciples interrogated Him, He taught them the mystery [of the type of the lamb]. . . . It was on this day (the 13th) that the consecration of the unleavened bread and the pro-preparation of the Passover took place; . . . and our Saviour suffered on the day following (the 14th): for He was Himself the true Passover. . . . And this is

---

[1] We write the name thus according to the ordinary usage (instead of *Apolinarius*).

[2] In the fragments of different works preserved in the *Chronicon Paschale*, a compilation of extracts from ancient authors, made from the fourth to the seventh century, and discovered in Sicily in the sixteenth century (*Le jour de la préparation*, by Lutteroth, p. 59).

the reason why the chief priests and scribes, when leading Him to Pilate, did not enter into the Prætorium, that they might not be defiled and might eat the Passover in the evening without any hindrance." In reality, therefore, we have only reproduced Clement's solution in the most violent of the Paschal disputes of the second century, of which we shall soon speak. *Weiss*, who rejects every solution, yet acknowledges that, strictly speaking, Mark xiv. 12 is the only passage which is opposed to what we have just set forth. What seems to him incompatible with it is the remark: "The first day of unleavened bread, *when the Passover was sacrificed.*" But why could not these last words be applied to the evening of the 13th, if this evening, according to the Jewish manner of reckoning, belonged already to the 14th, on the afternoon of which the lamb was sacrificed? *Weiss* cannot himself refrain from adding that, in any case, the question of the disciples, if placed in the morning of the 14th, is improbable, for the people did not ever expect to occupy themselves at that time with the place of the supper. *De Pressensé* has nothing else to object except the words of Matt. xxvi. 20 : " And when the evening was come, he reclined at table with the Twelve," which implies, he says, that the preparations for the supper were made, not a few moments earlier in the evening, but during the course of the day. This remark would perhaps be well founded if the evangelist had had in view, in writing these lines, the question which occupies us. But Matthew does not seem, any more than the other two Synoptics, to have accounted for the problem which is raised by the traditional account ; he simply meant to say that this last supper of Jesus took place, not in the daytime, but in the evening.

It is probable that two circumstances contributed to the want of clearness which prevails in the Synoptical narration : first, the very easy confounding of the civil and natural day, and then the fact that the institution of the Holy Supper had impressed on this last supper a character very similar to that of the Paschal feast.

Finally, let us recall to memory the lights which exegesis has asked from astronomy with respect to this question. The question being to determine whether, in the year of Jesus' death, the great Sabbatic day of the 15th of Nisan fell on Friday, as the Synoptic narrative, or on Saturday, as the narrative of John implies, the calculation of the lunar phases might serve, it was thought, to decide the question. Two astronomers set themselves to the work, *Wurm*, of Göttingen (*Bengel's Archiv.*, 1816, II.), and *Oudemann*, Professor at Utrecht (*Revue de théologie*, 1863, p. 221). But it is necessary to begin by determining the year of Jesus' death, and scholars still differ on this point. *Ideler* and *Zumpt* place it in 29 ; *Winer, Wieseler, Lichtenstein, Caspari, Pressensé*, etc., in 30 ; *Ewald, Renan*, in 33 ; *Keim*, in 35 ; *Hitzig*, in 36. In this state of things, the two astronomers have extended their calculation to the whole series of years 29-36 of our era. The result, as to the year 30, which we think, with most of the critics, to be the year of the death, is the following : In this year, the 15th of Nisan fell on a Friday. This result would condemn our explanation ; but *Caspari*, taking up anew the calculation of *Wurm*, starting from the same data as this astronomer, has arrived at the opposite result. According to him, in the year 30 the 15th of Nisan was Saturday, as it must be according to our explanation. The fact is, that we find ourselves here face to face with the incalculable uncertainties and subtleties of the Jewish calendar. *Wurm* himself declares that one can speak here only of *probabilities*, that there will ever remain an uncertainty *of one or two days*. Now, everything depends on a single day (*Keim*, III., p. 490–500). It is safer to work upon positive texts than upon such unsettled foundations. And as for ourselves, everything being carefully weighed, we think that the most probable date of Jesus' death may be stated thus : *Friday, the 14th of Nisan (7th of April), in the year* 30.

We are happy to agree, on the question of the relation between John and the Synoptics, with some modern scholars : *Krümmel, Darmstadt-Litteraturblatt,* Feb., 1858 ; *Baggesen, Der Apostel Johannes,* 1869 ; *Andreæ,* in the *Beweis des Glaubens,* Der Todestag Jesu, July to September, 1870.—On the consequences of the historical superiority of John's narrative, with reference to the authenticity of the Fourth Gospel, see Introd., pp. 77–79.

Glance at the History of the Paschal Controversies

The fact which lies at the foundation of that long disagreement between the primitive churches is the following : The churches of Asia Minor celebrated the Paschal feast by fasting during the whole of the 14th of Nisan and by communicating on the evening of this day, at the time when the Jews were eating the lamb. The other churches of Christendom, Rome at their head, fasted, on the contrary, during the days which preceded the Passover Sunday, which was always the Sunday that followed the 14th ; then they received the sacrament in the morning of this Passover Sunday.—In both cases the communion terminated the fast.

First phase of the discussion. About 155,[1] Polycarp, in a visit which he makes to Rome, has a conversation on this subject with Anicetus, the bishop of Rome. Each defends the rite of his own church in the name of an *apostolic tradition* of which it claimed to be the depositary (originating at Ephesus from John and Philip, at Rome from Paul and Peter). There is no proof that on this occasion they entered within the exegetical and dogmatic domain of the question. The ecclesiastical peace remained undisturbed. " The diversity in the rite served rather," as *Irenæus* says, " to establish agreement in faith."[2]

Second phase. Fifteen years later, in 170, there breaks out, in the midst even of the churches of Asia, at Laodicea, a disagreement on the subject of the Passover. There are persons there—who are they ? we shall have to examine this point—who, like the Asiatics, celebrate the 14th in the evening, but resting upon this fact : that it was on the 14th in the evening that Jesus instituted the Supper, in conformity with the time prescribed by the law for the Paschal supper, and they rest upon the narrative of Matthew, according to which the Lord was crucified on the 15th.[3] We see that from the domain of tradition the question is carried to that of exegesis. *Melito* is the first who writes on this subject, with what view we do not know. Then, *on occasion* (ἐξ αἰτίας) of his book—not against him, as *Schürer* still claims—*Apollinaris*[3] and *Clement of Alexandria* also take up the pen. Both, according to the fragments quoted in the *Chronicon Paschale,* prove that Jesus celebrated His last supper on the

---

[1] Recent discoveries, due especially to Waddington, seem to prove that the martyrdom of Polycarp occurred in 155 or 156, and not later, as was supposed.

[2] *Letter to Victor* (Euseb. *H. E.*, v. 24).

[3] The following are the words which Hippolytus, in the *Philosophumena*, puts into the mouth of these persons : " The Lord kept the Passover and suffered on that day ; *this is the reason why I should do as He did.*" Comp. also the answer which Apollinaris gives to them, that " in that case the Gospels would contradict each other" (p. 143).

13th, and that He died on the 14th. They specially allege John's narrative in favor of this view.

But who are the Laodicean adversaries whom these two writers oppose? *Baur, Hilgenfeld, Schürer, Luthardt,* answer : They are the churches of Asia themselves, with their celebration of the 14th. Apollinaris was even in Asia the adversary of the Asiatic rite. It is difficult to believe this. For, 1. Eusebius presents the churches of Asia before us as unanimous : " The churches *of the whole of Asia* thought, according to an ancient tradition, that they must observe the 14th by the celebration of the Holy Supper." If this consensus of all the churches of Asia had been broken by so considerable a bishop and doctor as Apollinaris of Hierapolis, Eusebius, the pronounced adversary of the Asiatic rite, would not have failed to notice it. Baur alleges that a little later *Polycrates,* when enumerating in his letter to Victor, a bishop of Rome, all the illustrious personages who practised the Asiatic rite, does not mention Apollinaris. But he names only the dead. Apollinaris might also be found among the numerous bishops of whom Polycrates speaks without naming them, who surrounded him at the time when he was writing his letter, and who gave their assent to it. 2. If Apollinaris had made a division as related to his colleagues in Asia, the dispute would, no doubt, have broken out in his home, at Hierapolis, rather than at Laodicea. 3. The polemic of Apollinaris by no means implies opposition to the Asiatic rite and adhesion to the occidental rite. The adversaries justified their observance of the 14th by resting upon the fact that this was the evening on which Jesus had *instituted the Supper.* Apollinaris remarks that this view puts the first three Gospels in contradiction to that of John. But this does not prevent him from celebrating the 14th also—only for another reason. In any case, it is impossible to understand how this view of Apollinaris, according to which Jesus died on the 14th, not the 15th, could have favored the Roman observance, according to which the Holy Passover Supper was celebrated on the following Sunday. 4. Schürer is embarrassed here by a manifest contradiction : According to him, the Asiatic rite did not rest on any fact of the Gospel history, neither on the time of the institution of the Supper nor on the day of Jesus' death. It arose only from the fact that the 14th was the day of the Jewish Paschal supper, which had been simply transformed, in Asia, into the Christian Supper. But, on the other hand, in the presence of the polemics of Apollinaris, he is forced to acknowledge that his adversaries fixed the Supper on the 14th, in remembrance of the day of *the institution of the Supper.* These two grounds of the same observance not coinciding, he ought not to maintain that the Laodiceans combated by Apollinaris are no others than the churches of Asia in general.

It is with reason, therefore, that *Weitzel* and *Steitz,* with whom are associated *Ritschl, Meyer, Réville,* etc., have been led to see in the Laodiceans, contended against by Apollinaris, a Judaizing party which arose in the Church of Asia, and which had as its aim to preserve for the Holy Supper the character of a *complete Jewish Passover supper,* as they imagined that the Lord also had celebrated that supper before He died. Then the polemic of *Apollinaris* and *Clement* takes effect. These people said : " We wish to do *as the Lord did* [celebrate the Paschal supper on the 14th], and this by eating the Paschal lamb as He did." The two Fathers answer : " The Lord did not do this. He *carried back* the Paschal supper of the 14th to the 13th in the evening, and this by instituting the Supper." This opinion evidently did not prevent Apollinaris from remaining faithful to the rite of his Church, since, as Schürer himself acknowledges, if the churches of Asia celebrated the 14th, as did the Laodiceans, it was not as having been the day of the *institution of the Supper*.

I would differ in opinion from *Weitzel* and *Steitz* only on two points : 1. The Laodicean adversaries, against whom Apollinaris contends, do not seem to me to have been an Ebionite sect properly so called, but only a branch of the Church of Asia, with a more pronounced Judaizing tendency. 2. The rite of the churches of Asia did not arise, probably, as these scholars think, from the fact that, in their view, Jesus died on the 14th, but quite simply from the fact that in these churches the day of the Israelitish Paschal supper was maintained. This is what results from the following words of Eusebius : " The churches of Asia thought they must celebrate the 14th, *the day on which the Jews were commanded to sacrifice the lamb;*" then more clearly still from those of Polycrates : " And all my relatives (bishops before me) celebrated the day when *the people removed the leaven.*" The Asiatic rite is expressly placed in connection with the *day* of Christ's death only in two passages of the fourth and fifth centuries—one in *Epiphanius*, the other in *Theodoret* (see Schürer, pp. 57, 58)—a fact which shows clearly that this point of view was not the prevailing one at the beginning of the discussion.

Third phase. Between 180 and 190 a certain Blastus (comp. the *Adv. Hær.* of the pseudo-Tertullian, c. 22) attempted to transplant the Asiatic rite to Rome. It was probably this circumstance which reawakened the dispute between the Churches of Rome and Asia, represented at this epoch, the one by Victor, the other by Polycrates. The latter, in his letter to Victor, no longer defends his cause by the traditional arguments, as Polycarp had done thirty years before. " He went through *all the Holy Scriptures* before writing (πᾶσαν ἁγίαν γραφὴν διεληλυθώς)." And he declares that " his predecessors also observed the 14th *according to the Gospel* (κατὰ τὸ εὐαγγέλιον)." These words give rise to reflection. It has been sought to get rid of them by means of subtleties (see the embarrassment of *Schürer*, p. 35). They evidently prove, as do those which precede, that Polycrates and the bishops of Asia had succeeded in establishing an agreement *between the Gospels*, by means of which these writings not only did not contradict one another (τὸ εὐαγγέλιον, the *one* Gospel in the four), but also were in accord with the law itself (*all the Scriptures*). Such expressions imply that Polycrates and his bishops had found the Asiatic rite confirmed first by the law (the question is of the Paschal institution, Exod. xii., fixing the Paschal supper on the 14th), then by the unanimity of the canonical Gospels, which has no meaning unless Polycrates harmonized the Synoptics with John by interpreting them as we ourselves have done. There is, therefore, a perfect equivalency between these words of Polycrates and that which Apollinaris had maintained against the Laodiceans, when he said : " Not only is their opinion contrary to the law, which requires that the lamb should be sacrificed on the 14th (and consequently that Christ also should die on the 14th), but also there would be [according to the opinion which they defend] disagreement between the Gospels [since, according to them, Matthew fixed the death of Christ on the 15th, while John places it on the 14th]." This dispute was quieted by the efforts of Irenæus and many others, who interposed with Victor and arrested him as he was proceeding to violent measures.

Fourth phase. It is marked by the decision of the Council of Nice, in 325, which enjoined upon the Orientals to fall in with the Occidental rite, which was now generally adopted. "At the end of the matter," says Eusebius (in his περὶ τῆς τοῦ πάσχα ἑορτῆς, *Schürer*, p. 40), "the Orientals yielded ;" "and thus," adds the same historian, "they broke finally with the murderers of the Lord, and united with their co-religionists (ὁμοδόξοις)." In fact, the practical consequence of the Asiatic rite was that the Christians of Asia found themselves to be celebrating the Holy Paschal Supper at the same time as the Jews were celebrating their Passover supper, thus separating themselves from all the other Christians who celebrated the Supper on the following Sunday. This rite became in the view of the other Churches, as it were, the sign of a secret sympathy for the unbelieving Jews. This was what determined its defeat. There were, nevertheless, Christians who, like the Judaizers of Laodicea, persisted in the observance of the 14th for the reason that Jesus had instituted the Supper on that day at evening. They figure under the names of *Audians, Quarto-decimans*, in the lists of later heresies. Athanasius frankly confesses that they are not easily to be refuted when they allege these words of the Synoptics : "*On the first day of unleavened bread, the disciples came to Jesus*" (*Schürer*, p. 45).[1] We here come upon the first symptom of the preponderance which the Synoptical narrative finally gained in the Church over that of John, and which it maintained through the middle ages and even to modern times. The Synoptics, more popular than John and apparently more clear, forming besides a group of three against one, and especially no longer encountering in the way of counterpoise the fear of a mingling of the Christian Supper and the Jewish Passover, carried the day in the general feeling. Jerome is the one of the Fathers who contributed most to this victory.

But how are we to explain *the origin of the two observances—the Asiatic and the Roman*—in the second century?[2]—Paul had no fear of bringing into the Church the celebration of the Jewish Passover feast (Acts xx. 6 ; comp. 1 Cor. v. 7, 8 with xvi. 8). He transformed and spiritualized its rites—this is beyond doubt ; the Holy Supper was substituted for the Paschal supper of the lamb and unleavened bread ; but the time of the celebration was the same ; this seems to follow from Acts xx. 6. John certainly did not do otherwise ; it was thus that the celebration of the Holy Supper on the evening of the 14th of Nisan was quite naturally introduced into Asia. But the churches of the West, more estranged from Judaism, felt a certain repugnance to this unity in point of *time* which was established between the Jewish and the Christian feast, and to the kind of dependence in which the simultaneousness placed the second with relation to the first. They therefore threw off the yoke ; and, instead of celebrating the Holy Passover Supper on the 14th at evening, as they already had the institution of the weekly Sunday, distinct from that of the Jewish Sabbath, they fixed this ceremony for the morning of the Sunday which in each year followed the 14th of Nisan, or, to speak more properly, the full moon of March.[3] Thus, no doubt, the occidental

---

[1] It is to one of these obstinate and henceforth schismatic Quarto-decimans that we must apply the words of Eusebius, in the work cited above (*Schürer*, p. 40): "But if any one says that it is written : *On the first day of unleavened bread*."—It is obvious that this objection embarrasses Eusebius as well as Athanasius.

[2] *Schürer* seems to us to have thrown real light on this important and difficult point, pp. 61 ff.

[3] This is the way in which it happens, observes Schürer rightly, that the name Easter is applied at the present time to the day of the resurrection rather than to that of the death.

observance grew up, which finally carried the day over the primitive observance. The Church is free in these matters.

The result of this long and complicated history, so far as relates to the subject which occupies our attention, seems to us to be this : From the time when the Church occupied itself with the exegetical side of the question, it attached itself to the Johannean narrative. It made use of it, on the one hand, to refute by the pen of Apollinaris the exegetical basis on which the Laodicean party rested the observance of the 14th (by making that day, according to Matthew, the day of the *institution of the Supper*) ; on the other hand, to defend against Rome, by the pen of Polycrates, the Asiatic celebration of the 14th, by presenting the Supper as the Jewish Passover spiritualized—that is to say, as the feast of the Christian redemption, the counterpart of the deliverance from Egypt. The matter in question, therefore, for the Church of Asia, was not that of celebrating the 14th of Nisan as the day of the *institution* of the Supper, nor even, properly speaking, as the day of Jesus' *death* (against *Steitz*). It simply *Christianized* the Jewish Passover. The Asiatic observance, therefore, does not furnish, as *Baur* has claimed, an argument against the Johannean origin of the Fourth Gospel ; quite the contrary, the polemic of Apollinaris against the Laodiceans, and that of Polycrates against Victor, are a striking testimony given to the narrative of the Fourth Gospel.

To sum up, the difference between John and the Synoptics may be stated and explained as follows :

In drawing up the oral tradition, the Synoptical writers contented themselves, as he did, with placing the last supper of Christ on the 14th of Nisan, the first day of unleavened bread, without *expressly* distinguishing between the first and the second *evening* of that day. Now, as Jesus had given to this last supper, celebrated on the evening of the 13th–14th, the forms of the Paschal supper, which took place on the evening of the 14th–15th, in order to substitute the Holy Supper for the Paschal feast for the future, a misunderstanding might easily arise ; it might be imagined that this supper was itself the Paschal feast of the 14th, which necessarily had the effect of carrying over the day of the death of Jesus to the 15th. John (as he had done so many times in his work) desired to dissipate the sort of obscurity which prevailed in the Synoptics, and to rectify the misunderstanding to which their narrative might easily lead. He therefore intentionally and clearly re-established the real course of things to which, moreover, the Synoptic narrative bore testimony at all points.

FIFTH PART

THE RESURRECTION

John 20:1-29

The fourth part of the Gospel has shown us the Jewish people carrying *unbelief* with reference to Jesus even to complete apostasy, and consummating this spiritual crime by the crucifixion of the Messiah. In the fifth we see the fidelity of the disciples raised to complete *faith* by the supreme earthly manifestation of the glory of Jesus—His resurrection.

The narrative of John pursues its independent path through the somewhat divergent narratives of the Synoptics, and, without any effort, gives us a glimpse of their harmony. In a first section (vv. 1-18), the evangelist relates how, in consequence of the report of Mary Magdalene, the two principal apostles attained to faith in the resurrection, and describes the first appearance of Jesus. The second section, vv. 19-23, relates His appearance in the midst of the Twelve, by means of which He established faith in the apostolic company. The third (vv. 24-29) describes the finishing of this work, which remained unfinished after the preceding appearance.

Mary, Peter and John at the sepulchre; Appearance to Mary: vv. 1-18

1. Vv. 1-10

The entire first part of this section tends towards the words of ver. 8: "*And he saw and believed.*" After this, the appearance of Jesus to Mary Magdalene makes the latter the messenger who should prepare all the disciples for faith, as she had brought the first two to the sepulchre.

Vv. 1-3. "*On the first day of the week, Mary Magdalene goes to the sepulchre early, while it was yet dark, and she sees that the stone is taken away*[1] *from the sepulchre; 2, she runs therefore and comes to Simon Peter and to the disciple whom Jesus loved, and says to them, They have taken away the Lord from the sepulchre, and we know not where they have laid him. 3. Peter therefore went forth, and the other disciple, and they came to the sepulchre.*"—In the expression μία τῶν σαββάτων, we may give to the word σάββατα the meaning Sabbath: "the first day (μία) starting from the Sabbath." But Luke xviii. 12 proves that σάββατον or σάββατα signifies also the entire *week*, as forming

---

[1] ℵ some Mnn. It^{aliq} Cop. Sah. add απο της (*from the door of the sepulchre*). θυρας before εκ του μνημειου (ℵ) or του μνημειου.

the interval between two Sabbaths. It is better therefore to explain μία : the first [of the days] of the week. The name Μαγδαληνή (*Magdalene*) is derived from that of village of *Magdala*, probably *El Megdjil*, two leagues northward of Tiberias, on the borders of the lake of Gennesareth. The greater the deliverance which Mary Magdalene owed to Jesus (Luke viii. 2, Mark xvi. 9), the more ardent was her gratitude, the more lively her attachment to His person. John does not speak of the purpose which brought her to the sepulchre, but it is indicated by the Synoptics : it was to embalm the Lord's body. Did she come alone ? This is in itself scarcely probable, at so early an hour in the morning. The Synoptics inform us that she had companions who came with the same intention as herself. They were Mary, the mother of James, Salome, Joanna and some others who had come with Jesus from Galilee (Matt. xxviii. 1, Mark xvi. 1, Luke xxiv. 10). There is in John's narrative itself a word which gives us to understand that she did not come alone. It is the plural οἴδαμεν, *we know ;* for, whatever *Meyer* may say, it is impossible to understand by this *we:* I, Mary, and you, the disciples (!). If Mary alone is mentioned, it is because of the part which she plays in the following scene. *Meyer* makes the οὐκ οἶδα, *I do not know*, of ver. 13 an objection. But this contrast is precisely what disproves it. There she is alone with the angels, and naturally she speaks only in her own name, as she also says : *My Lord*, and no longer : *the Lord* (ver. 2).—These women or some of them came together. But, as soon as from a distance they saw the tomb open, Mary Magdalene, carried away by her vividness of impression, hastens to go and tell the disciples, while her companions come even to the sepulchre. There is a slight chronological difference between John, Matthew and Luke, who say : "*As it was dark*," or "*at the dawn of day*," and Mark, who says : " *The sun having risen*." Perhaps there were several groups of women in succession whom each evangelist unites in a single one. Hence this slight difference as to the time of arriving. It was during the absence of Mary that her companions received the message of the angel, related by the three Synoptics.—Matthew xxviii. 9, 10 relates that, on their return from the sepulchre, there was an appearance of Jesus to these women. But the narrative in Mark xvi. 8 and especially the words of the two disciples from Emmaus, Luke xxiv. 22, 23 : "They had a vision of angels, saying that he was alive," are incompatible with this fact. This appearance to the *women* is, therefore, no other than the appearance to Mary Magdalene (which is to follow in John) generalized. All the details of the appearance coincide. The First Gospel applies to the entire group what happened to one of its members. As Mary Magdalene saw the Lord only after the other women had returned to the city, we may understand how the two disciples from Emmaus were able to depart from Jerusalem without having heard of any appearance of Jesus (Luke xxiv. 24). There had been, therefore, in fact, no other appearances in the morning of this day, except that of the angels to the women and then to Mary Magdalene, and finally that of Jesus to the latter. There is no reason here for making the loud outcry against our narratives which is uttered by criticism (*Keim*, III., p. 530).

974 / The Resurrection

The repetition of the preposition πρός, *to*, in ver. 2, leads us to think that the two disciples had different homes, which is natural if John lived with his mother and with Mary, the mother of Jesus.—The term ἐφίλει, *loved*, has something of familiarity in it beyond ἠγάπα ; it is undoubtedly used here because the matter in question is a simple indication of a fact, without any particular emphasis, Jesus Himself being absent.—The imperfect ἤρχοντο, *they were coming, repairing*, is pictorial ; comp. iv. 30. This imperfect of continuance reflects the feeling of inexpressible expectation which caused the hearts of the disciples to beat during the running to the sepulchre.

Vv. 4–7. "*And they ran both together; and the other disciple*[1] *ran more quickly than Peter, and he came first to the sepulchre ; 5, and, stooping down, he sees the linen cloths*[2] *lying on the ground ;*[3] *yet he did not enter in 6. Simon Peter, following him, comes, and he entered into the sepulchre ; and he beholds the linen cloths lying on the ground,*[2] *7, and the napkin, which had been placed upon his head, not lying with the other linen cloths, but rolled up and lying in a place by itself.*"—John, being younger and more agile, arrives first. But his emotion is so strong that he timidly stops at the entrance to the sepulchre, after having looked in. Peter, of a more masculine and practical character, resolutely enters. These details are so natural, and so harmonious with the personality of the two disciples, that they bear in themselves the seal of their authenticity. They recall those of ch. i.—The present *he sees* (ver. 5) is contrasted with the aorist *came* (ver. 4) ; the same contrast occurs again between the verbs *he entered* and *he beholds* (ver. 6). This difference springs from the contrast between the moment of arrival or of entrance and the continuance of the examination which follows or precedes. The word θεωρεῖ, *beholds*, unites in one the observation of the fact and the reflection on the fact. These linen cloths spread out did not suggest a removal ; for the body would not have been carried away completely naked. The napkin, especially, rolled up and laid aside carefully, attested, not a precipitate removal, but a calm awakening. Here was what might suggest reflection to the two disciples.

Vv. 8–10. " *Then entered in also the other disciple who had first come to the sepulchre ; and he saw and believed. 9. For they did not yet*[4] *understand the Scripture which says that he should rise from the dead. 10. Then the disciples returned to their own homes.* "—The singular verbs *he saw* and *he believed* are remarkable. Until this point two disciples had been spoken of, and in the following verse the story joins them again : *They did not understand*. These two verbs in the singular, which separate the plural verbs, cannot have been placed here unintentionally : the author evidently wishes to speak of an experience which is peculiar to himself. He cannot testify for the other disciple ; but he can do so for himself. This must, indeed, have been one of the most ineffaceable moments of his life. He initiates us into

---

[1] ℵ omits και ο αλλος μαθητης (*and the other disciple*).

[2] A X Syr. Cop. Sah. place οθονια before κειμενα.

[3] ℵ omits the end of ver. 5 after ου and the whole of ver. 6 (a confounding of the two τ. o. κειμενα).

[4] ℵ It^aliq : ουκ ηδει (*he did not understand*).

an incomparable personal reminiscence, into the way by which he reached the belief in the resurrection, in the first place, and then, through this, the perfect faith in Christ as Messiah and Son of God. The idea of *believing*, indeed, does not refer, as some have thought, to the contents of the report of Mary Magdalene: "they have taken Him away." This fact was the object of sight, not of faith. By examining the condition of the tomb and the position of the linen cloths, the disciple comes to the conviction that it is Jesus Himself who has done this ; consequently, that He is alive. We should have expected that he would make mention at this time of a special appearance of the Lord to His beloved disciple : He did appear, indeed, to Peter and James. But no ; everything in the narrative is sober : *he saw and believed*. There was no need of anything more. Nevertheless, we must not find here an eulogy which John would bestow upon himself and which would resemble a boast. The following verse sufficiently shows the spirit of humility which prevails in this narrative. These words must be paraphrased in this sense : "He saw and believed *at length*." John is himself astonished at the state of ignorance in which he, as well as Peter, had remained until this moment with regard to the scriptural prophecies foretelling the resurrection of the Messiah. He says ᾔδεισαν, which is an imperfect in sense : "*They were not understanding.*" Even then they did not yet grasp the meaning of the prophecies announcing the death and resurrection of the Messiah. Only after the resurrection did they open their eyes to these prophetic revelations (Ps. xvi. 10, Is. liii. 10, etc. ; comp. Luke xxiv. 25–27 and 45).—As to Peter, we do not know whether the view of the condition of the sepulchre brought him also to faith. John does not say this ; for the question here is of an inward personal fact. Perhaps there was needed, in order that this result might be fully secured in the case of Peter, the appearance of the Lord which was granted to this disciple on this same day (Luke xxiv. 34, 1 Cor. xv. 5).—The parallel, Luke xxiv. 12, is very probably only a gloss drawn up by means of John's narrative.—This whole passage, relating to the disciple whom Jesus loved and to Peter, presents one of the most striking features of the autobiographical character of our Gospel.

The Tübingen school, followed by *Strauss* and *Renan*, think that this narrative is a fiction designed to raise John to the level of Peter. The author, a disciple of John, systematically endeavored to make his master the equal of Peter. What ! By ascribing to him more agile limbs, yet also, on the other hand, less energy and courage ! Or by ascribing to him faith of a more spiritual character, in opposition to the carnal character of the Christianity of Peter, and consequently of the Twelve ? But John accuses himself also of a carnal want of understanding with regard to the prophecies. All this Machiavellism attributed to the evangelist vanishes away at the simple and unprejudiced reading of this story, which is so simple and so dramatic.

Colani sees in these words of ver. 9 : "*They did not yet understand the Scripture,*" a contradiction as related to the predictions of the resurrection which are placed in the mouth of Jesus by the Synoptics. If these predictions were real, the evangelist ought rather to have said : "They did not yet understand *the predictions of Jesus.*"[1] But if there was needed only the sight of the linen cloths and the napkin to determine the faith in the heart of the disciple, this was certainly due to the promises of Jesus ; they had not sufficed to make him believe in the resurrection of the *body* of Jesus, because he applied them undoubtedly to His glorious return from heaven ; but it was they which made this external circumstance sufficient to bring John to faith. John was not obliged to mention this fact, since of the prophecies of Jesus respecting His resurrection he had quoted only the enigmatical saying in ii. 19.

2. Vv. 11–18

Mary Magdalene has just been for the two chief disciples the messenger announcing the empty sepulchre ; she receives the first manifestation of the Lord, and becomes for all the messenger of the resurrection.

Vv. 11–13. "*But Mary was standing near the sepulchre,*[2] *weeping at the entrance ;* 12, *and, as she wept, she stooped down to look into the sepulchre ; and she sees two angels,*[3] *clothed in white, sitting, one at the head and the other at the feet, in the place where the body of Jesus had lain ;* 13, *and they say to her, Woman, why weepest thou ? She says to them, Because they have taken away my Lord, and I know not where they have laid him.*"—Peter and John withdraw, one of them at least already believing ; Mary remains and weeps, and as one does when vainly seeking for a precious object, she looks ever anew at the place where it seems to her that He should be. There is nothing to prevent our taking the present participle καθεζομένους, *sitting*, in its strictly grammatical sense. She perceives the two angels at the moment of their appearance. This fact does not contradict the earlier appearance of an angel to the women who had first visited the tomb. The angels are not immovable and visible after the manner of stone statues.—Mary answers the question of the celestial visitors as simply as if she had been conversing with human beings, so completely is she preoccupied with a single idea : to recover her Master. Who could have invented this feature of the story ? *Weiss*, without any reason, sees here a reminiscence of the appearance of the angel to the women, which has slipped into the wrong place.

Vv. 14–16. "*After having spoken thus, she turned herself back ; and she sees Jesus standing there, but without knowing that it was Jesus.* 15. *Jesus says to her, Woman, why weepest thou ? Whom seekest thou ? She, supposing that he was the gardener, says to him : Sir, if thou hast borne*[4] *him hence, tell me where thou hast laid him, and I will take him away.* 16. *Jesus says to her, Mary ! She, turning herself, says to him, in Hebrew,*[5] *Rabboni, which means, Master.*—Mary, after having stooped down into the sepulchre, raises herself and turns about, as if to seek for Him whom she is asking for. Perhaps she heard some noise behind her. The supposition of Mary has been

---

[1] *Jésus-Christ et les croyances messianiques de son temps*, p. 112.

[2] Instead of προς το μνημειον, A B E G H L M Δ Λ 60 Mnn. read προς τω μνημειω, א εν τω μνημειω (rejecting εξω with A It^{plerique} Syr.).

[3] א omits δυο (*two*) before αγγελους.

[4] א : ει συ ει ο βαστασας.

[5] א B D L O X Δ Π 7 Mnn. It^{plerique} Syr. Cop. read after αυτω, εβραιστι (*in Hebrew*), which T. R. omits with 9 Mjj.

explained by the garment which Jesus wore. But she might easily suppose that the one who was there at that early morning hour and who thus interrogated her was the gardener. And as to garments, workmen were not often clothed except with a girdle (xxi. 7).—The difficulty of recognizing Jesus arose from two causes ; notwithstanding the identity of the body of Jesus, there was wrought a change in His whole person by His passing into a new life ; He appeared ἐν ἑτέρᾳ μορφῇ, says Mark (xvi. 12). His disciples, in seeing Him again, experienced something like what occurs in us when we meet a friend after a long separation ; we need more or less length of time in order to recognize him ; then, all at once, the simplest manifestation is enough to make the bandage fall from our eyes. But there was also an internal cause. Mary's want of faith in the promises of Jesus caused the idea of His return to life to be absolutely foreign to her present thought.—Jesus, as always, adapts His action to the needs of the soul which suffers and loves. What is most personal in human manifestations is the sound of the voice ; it is by this means that Jesus makes Himself known to her. The tone which this name of Mary takes in His mouth expresses all that which she is for Him, all that which He is for her.—It follows from the word στραφεῖσα, *having turned about*, that she had turned again towards the tomb. For she was agitated, and was searching on one side, then on the other. And now, at the sound of this well-known voice, trembling even to the depths of her soul, she in turn puts all her being into the cry : *Master!* and throws herself at His feet, seeking to clasp them, as is shown by ver. 17.—*Rabbouni*, which is found only here and Mark x. 51, is a form of the word *Rabban*. The ʼ is either the ʼ paragogic or the suffix *my*. In the second case, it may gradually have lost its signification, which explains why the evangelist does not translate it. The word ἑβραϊστί, *in Hebrew*, which is read in the most ancient Mjj., is suspicious ; it may be defended, however, by recalling to mind how the word *rabbouni* was strange to the ears of the Greek readers of the Gospel.

Vv. 17, 18. "*Jesus says to her: Touch me not, for I am not yet ascended to my Father;*[1] *but go to my brethren*[1] *and say to them,*[2] *I ascend to my Father and your Father, to my God and your God. 18. Mary Magdalene comes to the disciples and tells*[3] *them that she has seen the Lord and that he has said these words to her.*"—As Mary extends her arms towards Him, Jesus seems to put Himself on His guard ; what is His thought ? Could He fear this touch, which might have something painful in it for Him, either because of His wounds, which were scarcely cicatrized (*Paulus*), or by reason of the delicate nature of His body, in a sense freshly born (*Schleiermacher, Olshausen*) ? As *Reuss* says, one cites such explanations only as a remembrance. Or might this touching seem contrary to the dignity of His body henceforth made divine (*Chrysostom, Erasmus*) ? This explanation is incompatible with the invitation which He gives to Thomas to touch Him ; comp. also Luke xxiv. 39.—*Lücke* thought of the use of the verb ἅπτεσθαι in the phrase *to*

---

[1] א B D It^aliq reject μου after πατερα, and א D reject it after αδελφους.

[2] א adds ιδου (*behold*) before αναβαινω (*I ascend*).

[3] א A B I X : αγγελλουσα for απαγγελλουσα.

touch the knees, for *to worship, to supplicate*, in Homer. The attempt has even been made to unite these words, in this sense, to what follows : "I am not yet glorified ; it is not yet, therefore, the time to worship me." But ἅπτεσθαι alone never has this meaning, and Jesus accepts a few days afterwards the adoration of Thomas.—It has been supposed (*Meyer, Bäumlein*) that Jesus wishes to remove a feeling of anxiety from the heart of Mary, who is trying to assure herself of the reality of what she sees. But in that case ψηλαφᾶν would rather be the proper word than ἅπτεσθαι. Or the meaning *to hold back* has been given to the word *to touch*. "Do not stop to hold me as if I were ready to escape thee, but go to my brethren" (*Neander*). But with this meaning, it would have been κρατεῖν (*to lay hold of*). This reason excludes also the explanation of *Baur:* "Do not hold me : for it is necessary that I ascend to my Father, to whom I have not yet returned."— The ἅπτεσθαι, the *touching*, which Jesus forbids is not that of anxiety, but that of joy (2 Cor. vi. 17, Col. ii. 21) : "Clasp not my feet ; I have not come to renew the old earthly relations. The true *seeing again* which I have promised you is not this. To return in a real and permanent way, it must be that I shall have first ascended. That time has not yet come." Or, as *Steinmeyer* says, "it is, indeed, rather for leave-taking that I have come." The disciples imagined that the death of Jesus was the *return to the Father* of which He had spoken to them, and His reappearance (xiii. 1) seemed to them the beginning of His permanent abiding with them. They confounded His death with the ascension, and the promised return with the Parousia. But Jesus declares to them by this message of Mary that *He is not yet ascended*, and that it is only now that *He is going to ascend*. Instead of enjoying this moment of possession, therefore, as if Jesus were really restored to her, Mary must rise and go to tell the disciples what is taking place. Jesus does not say ἀνέβην (the aorist), but ἀναβέβηκα (the perfect) ; He denies that He is already in the state of one who has done the act of ascending and who can contract with His own the higher relation in which they will possess Him again.—"*But go*" is opposed to the act of staying to enjoy. The message with which Jesus charges her for His disciples consequently signifies : "I am not yet in my state of glory ; but as soon as I shall be in it, I will give you a share in it, and then nothing shall any longer interpose between you and me." Hence the expressions : "*my brethren*" and "*my Father and your Father.*" There is here a foretaste, as it were, of the future communion. These terms set forth the indissoluble solidarity which will unite them to Him in the glorious state into which He now enters. He had not until now called them *His brethren ;* the same expression is found again in Matt. xxviii. 10. It contains more than *Weiss* thinks, when he sees in it only the idea that His exaltation will not alter His fraternal relation to them. No more do I think that Jesus wishes to bring out thereby the community *of action* which will unite them (*Steinmeyer, Keil*). He calls them His *brethren* as sharing in the divine adoption which He has acquired for them ; they will enjoy with Him filial communion with God Himself. The words : "*my Father and your Father,*" are the explanation of it. On this expression : *my brethren*, comp. Rom. viii. 29.—In the name of *Father* there is filial intimacy ; in that of *God*, complete dependence, and this for the disciples as for Jesus Himself.—But within this equality so glorious for the believers, there remains an ineffaceable difference. Jesus does not and cannot say *our Father, our God*, because God is not their Father, their God, in the same sense in which He is His Father and His God.—The present ἀναβαίνω, *I ascend*, has been variously explained : either as designating the certain and near fact, like the presents : *I go to the Father* (ὑπάγω, πορεύομαι) in the previous discourses, or as going so far as even to identify the day of the resurrection with that of the ascension (*Baur, Keim*) ; whence a contradiction between John and the Synoptics. The first sense is impossible ; for the opposition : "I am not yet ascended, . . . but I ascend," forces us to give to the present its strict meaning. The second is not any more admissible, since this appearance has no characteristic which distinguishes it from the following ones, which would necessarily be the case if the ascension, the complete glorification, separated them. The : *I ascend*, must designate thus a present elevation of position which is not yet the ascension. We cannot, whatever *Weiss* may say, escape the idea of a progressive exaltation during the days which separated the resurrection from the ascension—an exaltation to which the gradual transformation of the body of Jesus, which appears clearly from everything that follows, corresponds. On the one hand, *He is no longer with the disciples*, living with them the earthly existence (Luke xxiv. 44) ; on the other, He is also not yet in the state of glorification with the Father. It is a state of bodily and spiritual transition exactly denoted by the word *I ascend*.

By this message Jesus desires to raise the eyes of Mary and of His disciples from the imperfect joy of this momentary seeing Him again, which is only a means, to the expectation of the permanent spiritual communion, which is the end, but which must be preceded by His return to the Father (xiv. 12, 19, xvi. 7, 16). This warning applies to all the visits which shall follow, and is designed to comfort His followers for the sudden disappearances which shall put an end to them.—The present, *she comes* (ver. 18), expresses in all its vividness the surprise produced in the disciples by this arrival and this message.

We have said that the appearance to the women related by Matthew (xxviii. 9, 10) seems to us to be identical with that which John has just described with more detail. And indeed it is enough to convince us of this, if we compare the words : "Touch me not," and, "Go, and say to my brethren," with these : " *They held him by the feet,*" and : " *Go, and say to my brethren.*" Some modern critics, also identifying the two scenes, have supposed that John's narrative is rather a poetic amplification of the short story of Matthew, formed by means of those of Mark and Luke.[1] But how is it not seen that the story of Matthew is a vague traditional summary, while John's description reproduces the real scene in all its primitive freshness and distinctness ?

---

[1] *Keim*, for example (III. p. 558) : "The evangelist of Christian mysticism borrows from Matthew the visit of Mary Magdalene to the sepulchre and the message to the disciples."

980 / The Resurrection

The First Appearance to the Disciples : vv. 19-23

The risen Lord advances by degrees in His manifestation of Himself. The appearance of Jesus to Mary Magdalene, prepared for by that of the angels, prepares in its turn, by the message entrusted to Mary for the disciples, for His appearance in the midst of them. Two particular manifestations of the Risen One took place before this one in the course of that day—the appearance to the two disciples of Emmaus and that which was granted to Peter (Luke xxiv. 13-32, 34, Mark xvi. 12, 13). That in the evening to all the disciples, which is described in what follows, is evidently identical with that which Luke (xxiv. 36 ff.) and Mark (xvi. 14) relate. This appearance had as its essential aim to establish in them faith in the resurrection, and thereby to strengthen their faith in Him ; it was to serve also as a preparation for their apostolic mission.

Vv. 19, 20. *" The evening having come, therefore, on this same first day of the week, the doors of the place where the disciples were*[1] *being shut because of the fear which they had of the Jews, Jesus came and stood in the midst of them and says to them, Peace be to you ! 20. And, after he had said this, he showed them his hands and his side.*[2] *The disciples therefore rejoiced when they saw the Lord."*—The plural θυρῶν (*the doors*) denotes a two-leaved door. The words : *"because of the fear,"* refer to the fact of the closing which is mentioned again in ver. 26, but without the explanation here given.—It has been thought that this external fact was designed only to characterize the moral state of the disciples (*Lücke*), and that, on the arrival of Jesus, the gates were quite naturally opened (*Schleiermacher*). *Strauss*, on the other hand, is so indignant at this explanation, that he goes even so far as to declare that a real hardening of mind against the meaning of the gospel text is necessary in order to maintain it. *Calvin* and *de Pressensé* suppose that the doors opened miraculously of themselves (comp. Acts xii. 10). But the term ἔστη, *he stood*, indicates less an entrance than a sudden appearance, and in ver. 26, where the fact of the doors being closed is mentioned again, it is put in connection, not with the fear of the apostles, but with the mode of the appearance itself. I think, therefore, with *Weiss, Keil*, etc., that the *sudden* presence of Jesus in the midst of the disciples cannot be explained except by the fact that the body of Jesus was already subjected to the power of the spirit. In truth, this body was still that which had served Him as an organ during His life (ver. 20); but, as already before His death this body obeyed the force of the will (vi. 16-21), so now, through the transformation of the resurrection, it had approached still nearer to the condition of the glorified and spiritual body (1 Cor. xv. 44). The expression ἔστη is found again in the narrative of Luke (xxiv. 37); there it is in evident connection with the feeling of terror which the disciples at first experience and with the supposition that it is a *spirit;* for He was present when no one had seen Him

---

[1] T. R. adds συνηγμενοι (*assembled*) which is omitted in ℵ A B D I Λ 6 Mnn. It^{aliq} Syr.

[2] T. R. with 12 Mjj. (E G H etc.) Syr.: εδ. αυτοις τας χειρας και την πλευραν αυτου. ℵ D I : εδ. τας χειρας και την πλευραν αυτοις. A B : εδ και τας χειρας και την πλευραν αυτοις.

enter. With this manner of appearing His sudden disappearances correspond (Luke xxiv. 31 : ἄφαντος ἐγένετο).

The salutation of Jesus is the same in Luke and in John : *Peace be to you!* Weiss sees here only the ordinary Jewish salutation ; but why, in that case, repeat it twice (ver. 21)? Evidently Jesus makes this formula the vehicle of a new and more elevated thought. He invites His disciples to open their heart to the peace of reconciliation which He brings to them in rising from the dead. "*Having come*," says Paul (Eph. ii. 17), "*he preached peace.*"—Ver. 20. The words : *And having said this*, establish a relation between the wish of ver. 19 and the act related in ver. 20. To convince them of the reality of His appearance was to give them the proof of the divine good-will which restored to them their Master, to change their terror into peace and even into joy.—The fact that He does not show them His feet cannot prove anything in favor of the opinion that on the cross the feet had not been nailed. The pierced hands and side were enough to prove His identity. Besides, it follows from Luke xxiv. 40 that this detail has merely been omitted by John.

Vv. 21-23. "*Jesus*[1] *therefore said to them again, Peace be to you! As the Father has sent me, even so I send*[2] *you.* 22. *And, having said this, he breathed on them and says to them, Receive [the] Holy Spirit.* 23. *Whosoever*[3] *sins you remit, they are remitted*[4] *to them ; whosoever sins you retain, they are retained.*"—It is no longer only as to believers that Jesus desires to give them peace ; it is in view of their future vocation. Peace is the foundation of the apostleship ; hence the repetition of the prayer : *Peace be to you!* This message of reconciliation, which Jesus brings to them, they will have the task of preaching to the world (2 Cor. v. 20). Jesus first confers on them the office (ver. 21 b); then He communicates to them the *gift*, in the measure in which He can do so in His present position (ver. 22); finally, He reveals to them the wonderful greatness of this task (ver. 23).

There is properly only *one* mission from heaven to earth : it is that of Jesus. He is *the apostle* (Heb. iii. 1). That of the disciples is included in His, and will finally realize it for the world. Hence it comes to pass that Jesus, when speaking of Himself, employs the more official term ἀπέσταλκε : it is an *embassy ;* while, in passing to them, He uses the more simple term πέμπω : it is a *sending*.

Ver. 22. The *endowment* in view of this sending.—As there is properly only one mission, there is also only one *force* for fulfilling it—that of Jesus, which He communicates through His Spirit.—The words : *Having said this*, serve, like ver. 20, to connect the following act with the preceding words. There are two extreme opinions as to the value of the act described in this verse. According to *Baur, Hilgenfeld* and *Keim*, the evangelist transfers to this day Pentecost as well as the ascension (ver. 17). But the : *I ascend* of

---

[1] T. R. reads Ιησους, before παλιν, with 13 Mjj. (A B I etc.) ; this word is omitted by ℵ D L O X It^plerique Vulg. Cop.

[2] Instead of πεμπω, ℵ : πεμψω (*I will send*) ; D L O : αποστελλω.

[3] Instead of τινων, B It^aliq : τινος.

[4] T. R. reads αφιενται with 11 Mjj. (E G I etc.) ; A D L O X : αφεωνται ; ℵ Syr.: αφεθησεται (*shall be remitted*).

ver. 17 could not have been accomplished in the course of this day; for ver. 20 proves that Jesus did not yet have His glorified body. But it is from the Father that He is to send the Spirit (vii. 39, xvi. 7). Moreover, the absence of the article before πνεῦμα ἅγιον, *Holy Spirit*, shows that the question here is not yet of the sending of the Paraclete promised in chs. xiv.-xvi. Hence others—*Chrysostom, Grotius, Tholuck*—have concluded that there was a purely symbolic act here, a sensible pledge of the future sending of the Spirit. But this sense is incompatible with the imperative λάβετε, *receive! You shall receive* would be necessary. This expression implies a present communication. The question here is neither of a simple promise nor of the full outpouring of the Spirit. Raised Himself to a stage of higher life, Jesus raises them, as far as He can do so, to His new position. He associates them in His state as raised from the dead, just as later, through Pentecost, He will make them participate in His state as one glorified. He communicates to them the peace of adoption and the understanding of the Scriptures (Luke xxiv. 45); He puts their will in unison with His own, that they may be prepared for the common work (ver. 21). Some commentators—*Reuss*, for example—see here an allusion to Gen. ii. 7 : " *The Lord breathed into the nostrils* (of man) *a breath of life.*" But the thought of Jesus seems to me to refer rather to the future than to the past. This preparatory communication will necessarily make them understand, when the wind of the Spirit shall blow, that this wind is nothing else than the personal breath of their invisible Master.

Ver. 23. The new work which is intrusted to them is here displayed in all its *greatness;* the matter in question is nothing less than giving or refusing salvation to every human being ; to open and close heaven—this is their task. The old covenant had a provisional pardon and a revocable rejection. With the coming of the Holy Spirit, the world enters into the domain of unchangeable realities. This power of pardoning sins (Matt. ix. 6) or of retaining them (John ix. 41, xv. 22, 24), which the Son of man had exercised, will be theirs for the future by virtue of His Spirit who will accompany them.—The expressions which Jesus employs indicate more than an *offer* of pardon or a *threatening* of condemnation, more even than a *declaration* of salvation or of perdition by means of the preaching of the Gospel. Jesus speaks of a word which is accompanied by efficacy, either for taking away the guilt from the guilty or for binding it eternally to his person. He who is truly the organ of the Spirit (ver. 21) does not merely say : " Thou art saved "—he saves by his word—or " Thou art condemned "—he really condemns, and this because, at the moment when he pronounces these words by means of the Spirit, God ratifies them. The present ἀφίενται (literally, *are pardoned*) indicates a present effect ; God pardons these sins at the very moment. The perfect ἀφέωνται, which some Mjj. read, would signify : "are and remain pardoned." This perfect was probably introduced for the sake of the symmetry of the clause with the following (κεκράτηνται). The copyists did not understand that in the first there is a question of a present momentary *fact*, the passage from the state of condemnation to the state of grace, while the second relates to a *state* which continues, the condemnation established forever.

The order of the two propositions indicates that the first of the two results is the true aim of the mission, and that the second does not come to its realization except in the cases where the first has failed.—It does not seem to me that anything gives us the right to see here a special power conferred on the apostles as such. The question is not of right, but of force. It is the πνεῦμα which is its principle. I do not see any reason, therefore, to apply this prerogative to the apostles alone, as *Keil* would have it. *The disciples* of vv. 18, 19 are certainly all believers taken together ; the two from Emmaus were present, and many others, not apostles, with them, according to Luke xxiv. 33. And why should the gift of the Spirit be restricted to the apostles ? They certainly have a special *authority*. But the forces of the Spirit are common to all believers. *Weiss* supposes that the prerogative here conferred by Jesus is no other than that of distinguishing between venial sins and mortal sins (1 John v. 16). But this application is much too special and foreign to the context. Besides, the similar promise made to Peter, Matt. xvi. 19, had already been extended, in a certain measure, to the whole Church, Matt. xviii. 18.

The Second Appearance to the Disciples (Thomas): vv. 24–29

A last principle of unbelief still remained in the circle of the Twelve. It is extirpated, and the development of faith reaches its limit in all the future witnesses for Christ.

Vv. 24, 25. *"But Thomas, one of the Twelve, he who was called Didymus, was not with them when Jesus came. 25. The other disciples therefore*[1] *said to him, We have seen the Lord ; but he said to them : Unless I see in his hands the print of the nails, and put my finger into the print*[2] *of the nails, and put my hand into his side, I will not believe."*—On δίδυμος, *twin*, see xi. 16. We have learned to know Thomas through xi. 16 and xiv. 5 ; the impression produced on him by the death of his Master must have been that of the most profound discouragement : "I told Him so ;" this is what he, no doubt, repeated to himself. His absence on the first day could not be without relation to this bitter feeling. This is confirmed by the manner in which he receives the testimony of his brethren. There is tenacity even in the form of his words, and especially in the repetition of the same terms. Here is what makes us doubt about the reading τόπον, *the place*, instead of the second τύπον, *the print*. This reading, adopted by *Tischendorf, Weiss, Keil*, etc., is not only feebly supported,. but it takes away from the denial of the disciple this marked character of obstinacy. On the other hand, it must be acknowledged that the second τύπος may easily have been substituted for τόπος under the influence of the preceding one. If Thomas does not speak of Jesus' feet, it is ridiculous to conclude from this fact, with some interpreters, that the feet had not been nailed.

Vv. 26, 27. *"Eight days afterwards, his disciples were assembled again in*

---

[1] ℵ adds ουν after οτε and rejects it in ver. 25 after ελεγον (*when therefore Jesus came, they said to him*).

[2] A I It^plerique Vulg. Orig. read τοπον (*the place*) instead of τυπον, and ℵ εις την χειραν (sic) αυτου, instead of εις τον τοπον των ηλων (*unless I put my finger into his hand and put my hand into his side*).

the room; and Thomas was with them. Jesus comes, the doors being shut, and he stood in the midst of them, and said: Peace be to you! 27. Then he says to Thomas, Reach hither thy finger, and see my hands, and reach hither thy hand, and put it into my side, and become not unbelieving, but believing."—Jesus had bidden the disciples, through the women, to return to Galilee (Matt. xxviii. 7, Mark xvi. 7). How does it happen that they were still in Judea eight days after the resurrection? Are we not allowed to suppose that what detained them was the fear of abandoning Thomas and of losing him, if they left him behind in the condition of mind in which he was?—In His salutation Jesus includes this disciple also; it is even to him that He specially addresses it; for he is the only one who does not yet enjoy the peace which faith gives.—The almost literal reproduction of the rash words of Thomas is designed to make him blush at the grossness of such a demand. It may be supposed, with *Weiss*, that the term βάλλειν εἰς, *to put into*, means simply to stretch out the hand under the garment of Jesus, in order to touch the scar.—By the expression: *Become not*, Jesus makes him feel in what a critical position he actually is, at this point where the two routes separate: that of decided unbelief and that of perfect faith. A single point of truth, a single fact of the history of salvation, which one obstinately refuses to accept, may become the starting-point for complete unbelief, as also the victory gained over unbelief, with regard to this single point, may lead to perfect faith.

Vv. 28, 29. *" Thomas answered*[1] *and said to him, My Lord and my God! 29. Jesus says to him,*[2] *Because thou hast seen me,*[3] *thou hast believed. Blessed are they who, without having seen, have believed."*—What produces so profound an impression upon Thomas is not only the reality of the resurrection, which he touches with his hands, it is also the omniscience of the Lord, which the latter proves by repeating to him, just as they were, the words which he thought he had uttered in His absence. This scene recalls that of Nathanael (ch. i.). Just as in the case of the latter, the light shines suddenly, with an irresistible brightness, even into the depths of the soul of Thomas; and by one of those frequent reactions in the moral life, he rises by a single bound from the lowest degree of faith to the highest, and proclaims the divinity of his Master in a more categorical expression than all those which had ever come forth from the lips of any of his fellow-apostles. The last becomes in a moment the first, and the faith of the apostles attains at length, in the person of Thomas, to the whole height of the divine reality formulated in the first words of the Prologue. It is in vain that *Theodore of Mopsuestia*, the Socinians and others have wished to apply to God, not to Jesus, Thomas' cry of adoration, by making it either an expression of praise, or an exclamation in honor of God. It should not be, in that case, εἶπεν αὐτῷ, "He said *to Him;*" besides, the term *my Lord* can only refer to Jesus. The monotheism of Thomas is made an objection. But it is precisely because this disciple understands

---

[1] 7 Mjj. (א B C D G etc.) It^pleriq. reject καὶ (*and*) before απεκριθη (*answered*).

[2] Instead of λεγει, א : ειπεν δε.

[3] All the Mjj. 150 Mnn. It. Syr., after εωρακας με, reject Θωμα (*Thomas*), which T. R. reads with some Mnn.—א reads καί (*also*) after με.

that he bears towards Jesus henceforth a feeling which passes beyond what can be accorded to a creature, that he is forced, even by his monotheism, to place this being in the heart of Deity.—The repetition of the article and that of the pronoun μου give to these words a peculiar solemnity (*Weiss*).

Ver. 29. In itself, this address of the disciple would not have a decisive value. It might be an exaggeration of feeling. But what gives it an absolute importance is the manner in which Jesus receives it. The Lord does not check this outbreak of feeling, like the angel of the Apocalypse, who says to John : "*Worship God!*" He answers, on the contrary : "*Thou hast believed,*" and thus accepts the expression by which Thomas has proclaimed His divinity. In an article by *Lien* (May, 1869), it is objected that this approving answer of Jesus may refer not to the expression : *My God*, but to the belief of Thomas in the fact of the resurrection. But if Jesus had approved of the exclamation of the disciple only in part, He would have found the means of removing the alloy, while preserving the pure gold.— The perfect πεπίστευκας, *thou hast believed*, signifies : "Thou art henceforth in *possession* of faith." This verb might also be taken in an interrogative sense. For *Meyer* observes, not without reason, that there is in the words : *because thou hast seen*, a shade of reproach which accords well with this sense. —In the last words Jesus points out the entirely new character of the era which is beginning, that of a faith which should be contented with testimony, without claiming to be founded on sight, as that of Thomas had done.—This saying closes the history of the development of faith in the apostles, and gives a glimpse of the new phase which is about to begin— that of the faith of the Church resting upon the apostolic testimony. *Baur* thinks that Jesus here opposes to faith in *external facts* that which has its contents only in itself, in *the idea* of which the believer is henceforth fully conscious. But vv. 30 and 31 express a thought directly opposite to this. So *Baur* has declared them to be interpolated, without the least proof. The contrast which Jesus points out is altogether different : it is that of a carnal faith, which in order to accept a miracle wishes absolutely to *see* it, and a faith of a moral nature, which accepts the divine fact on the foundation of a *testimony* which is worthy of confidence. It was granted to Thomas to be saved on the former path ; but from this time forward it will be necessary to content oneself with the second. Otherwise faith would be no longer possible in the world except on condition of miracles renewed unceasingly and celestial appearances repeating themselves for every individual. This is not to be the course of the divine work on earth.—The aorist participle ἰδόντες, properly : *who shall have seen*, indicates an anterior act with relation to faith, and the aorist participle πιστεύσαντες, *who have believed*, is spoken from the standpoint of the development of the Church regarded as consummated.

This answer of Jesus to Thomas is the normal close of the fourth Gospel. It indicates the limit of development of the apostolic faith, and the starting-point of the new era which is to succeed it on the earth. The apostolic faith, as it has just risen to the full height of its object, will be able henceforth to re-echo throughout the world by means of the testimony of the chosen messengers, so as incessantly to reproduce itself.

ON THE RESURRECTION OF JESUS CHRIST

Strauss has said, in speaking of the resurrection of Jesus :[1] "Here is the decisive point, where the naturalistic view must retract all its previous assertions or succeed in explaining the belief in the resurrection without bringing in a miraculous fact." And Strauss is right. The question here is of a miracle *sui generis*, of the miracle properly so called. The usual expedients for explaining the miracles of Jesus, "the hidden forces of spontaneity," the mysterious influence exerted upon the nerves "by the contact of an exquisite person"—all this has no longer any application here ; for no other human being co-operated in the resurrection of Jesus, if it took place. If Jesus really came forth alive from the tomb after His crucifixion, there is nothing left but to say with St. Peter : GOD *has raised up Jesus.*

It is said : Such a fact would overthrow the laws of nature. But what if it were, on the contrary, the law of nature, when thoroughly understood, which required this fact ? Death is the wages of sin. If Jesus lived here below as innocent and pure, if He lived in God and *of God*, as He Himself says in John vi. 57, life must be the crown of this unique conqueror. No doubt He may have given Himself up voluntarily to death to fulfil the law which condemns sinful humanity ; but might not this stroke of death, affecting a nature perfectly sound, morally and physically, meet in it exceptional forces capable of reacting victoriously against all the powers of dissolution ? As necessarily as a life of sin ends in death, so necessarily does perfect holiness end in life, and consequently, if there has been death, in the resurrection. Natural law, therefore, far from being contrary to this fact, is the thing which requires it.

But if this fact is rational, when once the perfect holiness of Jesus is admitted, is it possible ? To deny that it is, would be to affirm an irreducible dualism between *being* and *virtue*. It would be to deny monotheism. The divine will is the basis of being, and the essence of this will is to move towards the good. In creating being it has therefore reserved to itself the means of realizing the good in all the forms of existence and of causing the absolute sovereignty of holiness to be triumphant in the being. This is all that we can determine *a priori* from the theistic standpoint. "Every historian," says Strauss, "should possess philosophy enough to be able to deny the miracle here as well as elsewhere." Every true historian, we will answer, should have philosophy enough, above all, to let the word yield to the facts, here as elsewhere.

Let us, in the first place, study the four, or rather the five, narratives of the appearances of the Risen One.

The Narratives

John mentions three appearances of Jesus (to Mary Magdalene, the Twelve, Thomas), all three in Judea and in the week which followed the resurrection. —Is this to say that the author did not know of a larger number ? The twenty-first chapter, which proceeds from him directly or indirectly, proves the contrary. For this chapter mentions a new one which took place in Galilee. That to Thomas closes the Gospel properly so called, for the reasons which belong to the plan and aim of the work (see on xx. 28, 29).

Matthew relates two appearances : that to the women in Judea, which seems

---

[1] *Das Leben Jesu*, 1864, p. 288.

to be only a generalized double of the appearance to Mary Magdalene (in John), and that to the Eleven on the mountain where He had appointed for them a meeting-place. It was in the latter that Christ made known to the apostles His elevation to the Messianic royalty, to the sovereignty over all things. This is the reason why it closes the first Gospel, which is designed to demonstrate the Messianic dignity of Jesus, and in the view of the author serves to sum up all the others. This took place in Galilee, like that of the twenty-first chapter of John.

If we set aside the unauthentic end of *Mark*, we find in this Gospel only the *promise* of an appearance to the believers in Galilee. We are ignorant of what the true conclusion of this work must have contained. What we now possess, composed from John and Luke, mentions the appearance to Mary Magdalene (John) and those to the two from Emmaus and to the disciples on the evening of the day of the resurrection (Luke).

Luke mentions three appearances: that on the road to Emmaus, that to Peter, that to the disciples on the evening of the first day; all three in Judea and on the very day of the resurrection. It would be difficult to believe that he did not know of others, since he had labored for the evangelization of the Gentile world with St. Paul, who, as we are about to see, mentions several others. Luke himself, in Acts i. 3, speaks of *forty days* during which Jesus showed Himself alive to the apostles. He simply desired, therefore, to report the first appearances which served to establish in the hearts of the apostles the belief in the fact of the resurrection.

As for *Paul*, he enumerates in 1 Cor. xv. 3 ff., as facts appertaining to the apostolic tradition which he has himself received, first the appearances to Peter and to the Twelve which immediately followed the resurrection; then a later appearance to more than five hundred brethren, some of whom he himself knew personally; moreover, two appearances, one to James, the other to all the apostles. Finally, to these five he adds that which was granted to himself on the road to Damascus.—We are already acquainted with the first two, one from Luke, the other from Luke and John. The third surprises us, since it is not related in any of the four gospels. But it is probably identical with that of which Matthew speaks, which took place on the mountain of Galilee, whither Jesus had summoned all His followers from before His death (Matt. xxvi. 32, Mark xiv. 28), though in Matthew He addresses only the Eleven in order to call them to their mission to the whole world. The fourth (James), mentioned by Paul alone, is confirmed by the conversion of the four brothers of Jesus (Acts i. 14). The fifth (all the apostles) is evidently that of the ascension, the word *all* alluding not to James, as has been thought, but rather to Thomas, who had been absent at the time of the first appearance to the Eleven. If mention is not made of the first two appearances in John and Luke, those to Mary Magdalene and the two from Emmaus, it is because they have a private character, Mary and the two disciples not belonging to the circle of the official witnesses chosen by Jesus to declare publicly what concerned Him.

Notwithstanding the diversity of these accounts, it is not difficult to reconstruct by their means the whole course of things. There are ten appearances known:

1. That to Mary, in the morning, at the sepulchre (John and Matthew);
2. That to the two from Emmaus, in the afternoon of the first day (Luke and Mark);

3. That to Peter, a little later, but on the same day (Luke and Paul);
4. That to the Eleven (without Thomas), in the evening of this first day (John, Luke, Mark);
5. That to Thomas, eight days afterwards (John);
6. That to the seven disciples, on the shore of the sea of Galilee (John xxi);
7. That to the five hundred believers, on the mountain of Galilee (Matthew, Paul);
8. That to James (Paul);
9. That of the ascension (Luke, Paul).

Finally, to complete the whole : 10. That to Paul, some years afterwards, on the road to Damascus.

Evidently no one had kept an exact protocol of what occurred in the days which followed the resurrection. Each evangelist has drawn from the treasure of the common recollections what was within his reach, and reproduced what best answered the purpose of his writing. They did not dream of the future critics; simplicity is the daughter of good faith. But what is striking in this apparent disorder is the remarkable moral gradation in the succession of these appearances. In the first ones, Jesus consoles; He is in the presence of broken hearts (Mary, the two from Emmaus, Peter). In the following ones (the Twelve, Thomas), He labors, above all, to establish faith in the great fact which has just been accomplished. In the last ones, He more particularly directs the eyes of His followers towards the future by preparing them for the great work of their mission. It is thus, indeed, that He must have spoken and acted, if He really acted and spoke as risen from the dead.

The Fact

What *really occurred*, which gave occasion to the narratives which we have just studied?

According to the contemporary Jews, whose assertion was reproduced in the second century by Celsus and in the eighteenth by the author of the Wolfenbüttel Fragments, the answer is : nothing at all. This whole history of the resurrection of Jesus is only a fable, the fruit of a premeditated deception on the part of the apostles. They had themselves put the body of Jesus out of the way, and then proclaimed His resurrection.—To this explanation we cannot reply better than by saying, with *Strauss:* " Without the faith of the apostles in the resurrection of Jesus, the Church would never have been born." After the death of their Master the apostles were too much disheartened to invent such a fiction, and it was from the conviction of His resurrection that they drew the triumphant faith which was the soul of their ministry. The existence of the Church which has religiously renewed the world is explained with yet greater difficulty by a falsehood than by a miracle.

Others, *Strauss* at their head, answer : Something occurred, but something purely internal and subjective. The apostles were, not impostors, but dupes of their own imagination. They sincerely believed that they saw the appearances which they have related. On the day of Jesus' death, or the next day, they fled to Galilee; and, on finding themselves again in the places where they had lived with Him, they imagined that they saw and heard Him again; these hallucinations were continued during some weeks, and here is what gave rise to the narratives of the appearances.—But, 1. From this point of view, the first scenes of the appearances of Jesus must be placed in Galilee, not in Jerusalem, as is the case in all the narratives, even in that which may be called the most decidedly Galilean—that of Matthew (xxviii. 1-10).—2. According to all the accounts, and even according to the calumny against the disciples invented by the Jews, the body of Jesus, after the descent from the cross, was left in the hands of the Lord's friends. Now, in the presence of the dead body, all the hallucinations must have vanished. We shall thus be brought back to the first explanation, which makes the disciples impostors—an explanation which Strauss himself declares impossible. If it is said : The Jews got possession of the body and carried it off,—they worked in this case against themselves and for the success of the falsehood which they ascribed to the apostles. And why not bring into broad daylight this point tending to prove criminality instead of confining themselves to accusing the disciples of having put Him out of the way ?—3. The hallucinations which are supposed are incompatible with the state of mind of the disciples at this time. The believers so little expected the resurrection of Jesus that it was for the purpose of embalming His body that the women repaired to the sepulchre. If they still had a hope, by reason of the promises which the Lord had made to them before His death, it was that of His return from heaven, whither they believed that He had gone. "Remember me when thou shalt come into thy kingdom," said the thief on the cross. And this, indeed, was undoubtedly what the disciples from Emmaus meant when they said, Luke xxiv. 21 : "Already it is the third day since these things came to pass." The restoration to life of His body broken on the cross was not dreamed of by any one. What those hoped for who hoped for anything was a Parousia, not a resurrection properly so called. And this also is what they think that they behold at the first moment, when Jesus appears to them ; they take Him for a *pure spirit* returning from heaven. How in such a condition of mind could they have been themselves the creators of the appearances of the Risen One ?—4. And what if these appearances consisted only in a luminous figure, an ethereal form floating in the distance, seen between heaven and earth, and soon vanishing in the sky ? But it is a person who approaches, who asks them to touch him, who converses with them, who blames them for seeing in him only a spirit, who speaks in a definite way and joins acts with his words (" He breathed on them, saying : Receive ye the Holy Spirit"), who gives positive orders (to assemble on a mountain, to baptize the nations, to tarry in Jerusalem), who has friendly conversations with some of them (the two from Emmaus, Thomas, Peter) ; hallucination does not comport with such features. We must always come back to the supposition of fiction and falsehood. As to a legendary formation, it cannot be thought of here, since Paul, even during the lifetime of the witnesses, alludes to all these accounts.—5. That a nervous person has hallucinations is a fact often noticed ; but that a second person shares these illusions is a thing unexampled. Now this phenomenon takes place simultaneously not in two, but in eleven, and soon even in five hundred persons (1 Cor. xv. 6). The hallucinated Camisards of Cevennes are cited, it is true. But the noises which they heard in the air, the rolling of drums, the singing of psalms, do not in any respect resemble the definite communications which the Lord had with those to whom He appeared and the distinct sight of His person and His features. And if all this were only visions beheld simultaneously by so large a number of persons, it would be necessary to imagine the whole company of the believers raised to such a strange and morbid degree of exaltation that it would become absolutely incompatible with the calm self-possession, the admirable clearness of mind, the practical energy of will, which every one is forced to admire in the founders of the Church.—6. But the most insoluble difficulty for the partisans of this hypothesis is that which *Keim* has better set forth than any one else—I mean the sudden ending of the appearances. At the end of a few weeks, after eight or nine visions so precise that Paul counts them, as it were, on his fingers—on a certain marked day, that of the ascension, all is over. The visions cease as suddenly as they came ; the five hundred who were exalted have returned, as if by enchantment, to cold blood. The Lord, ever living to their faith, has disappeared from their imagination. Although far inferior in intensity, the Montanist exaltation endured for a full half century. Here, at the end of six weeks, the cessation is complete, absolutely ended. In the presence of this fact, it becomes evident that an external cause presided over these extraordinary manifestations, and that, when the cause ceased to act, the phenomenon came to its end. We are thus brought to seek for the historical fact which forms the basis of the narratives that we are studying.

I. Some modern writers (*Paulus, Schleiermacher,* and others) think that the death of Jesus was only apparent, and that after a long swoon He came to Himself again under the influence of the aromatics and the cool air of the sepulchre. Some Essenic friends also perhaps aided Him with their care. He appeared again, accordingly, among His followers like one risen from the dead ; such is the foundation of the accounts of the appearances which we read in our gospels.—*Strauss* has refuted this hypothesis better than any one else. How, after so cruel a punishment as that of the cross, could Jesus, having been restored by purely natural means, move with perfect ease, go on foot to a distance of some leagues from Jerusalem, and also return to that city the same afternoon ; how could He be present without any one seeing His entrance ; and disappear without any one noticing His departure ? How, above all, could a person who was half dead, who was with difficulty dragged out of his tomb, whose feeble vital breath could not, in any case, have been preserved except by means of care and considerate measures, have produced on the apostles the triumphant impression of a conqueror of death, of the prince of life, and by the sight of Himself have transformed their sadness into enthusiasm, their disheartenment into adoration ? And then, finally, in the interval between these visits, what became of this moribund person ? Where did He conceal Himself ? And how did He bring to an end this strange kind of life in which He was obliged to conceal Himself even from His friends ? The critics would persuade us that He died in a Phœnician inn, sparing His disciples the knowledge of this sad ending ; . . . it must also be added : leaving them to believe in His triumph over death, and boldly to preach His resurrection ! This is imposture transferred from the disciples to the Master Himself. Does it become thereby more admissible ?

II. The opinion which, without denying the miracle, approaches most nearly to the preceding, is that of *Reuss* and *de Pressensé.* There was in the case of Jesus a real return to life, but in exactly the same body which had previously served Him as an organ. In fact, this body still bears the prints of the nails and of the spear-thrust. De Pressensé adds, in proof of this explanation, that Jesus, after the walk to Emmaus, did not reach Jerusalem till a certain time after His two travelling companions, since He did not go to the company of the disciples in the upper chamber until after the arrival of the latter. He will allow us to attach no great importance to this argument. Why could there not have been an interval between the time of His return and that of His appearance in the chamber where the disciples were assembled? Is it not clear that the Lord's body, although identical in some respects with His previous body, underwent by means of the miraculous fact of the resurrection a profound transformation of nature, and that from that time it lived and acted in entirely new conditions? It appears and disappears in a sudden manner, it obeys the will so far as to become visible in an apartment the doors of which had not opened, it is not recognized by those in whose midst Jesus had passed His life. All this does not allow us to believe that the resurrection consisted for Jesus, as it did for the dead whom He had Himself raised to life, only in a return to the life in His former body. They had returned into their former sphere of infirmity and death ; Jesus entered within the higher sphere of incorruptibility.

III. *Weiss* puts forth an entirely opposite opinion. According to him, the resurrection was the complete glorification of the Lord's body, which from this time became *the spiritual body* of which St. Paul speaks, 1 Cor. xv. 44–49. But how are we to explain in that case the sensible appearances of Jesus? For there is no relation between such a body and our earthly senses. It only remains to hold, with *Weiss*, an act of condescension by which the Risen One appropriated to Himself, at certain moments, a sensible form, which He afterwards laid aside. But this material form was not an envelopment of some sort ; it bore the traces of the wounds which had been inflicted upon it on the cross. Was there only an appearance here, a sort of disguise ? This is impossible. Or, if these visible prints were real, how could they belong to the spiritual body? Moreover, if we take into account the words of the Lord to Mary : "I am not yet ascended, but I ascend to my Father and your Father," it is impossible to mistake the difference between the resurrection and the complete glorification of the Lord. We see from this declaration that the resurrection is indeed the entrance into a higher state, but that this state is not yet perfect. There remains a place for a last divine act, the ascension, which will introduce Him into His state of final glory.

IV. There is only a shade of difference between the theory of *Weiss* and *Sabatier* (set forth in the *Christianisme au XIXe siècle*, April, 1880). According to the latter there was no return to life for the body put to death on the cross ; the real fact was the reappearance of the Lord with an entirely new body, the *spiritual* body of which St. Paul speaks. The material elements of the body in which Jesus had lived here on earth are returned to the earth.—At the foundation, what Sabatier thus teaches is nothing else than what the disciples expected, a Parousia, Jesus glorified returning from the other life, but not a resurrection. And yet it is a fact that the reality did not correspond to the expectation of the disciples, but that it went completely beyond it. They went to embalm ; they tried to find where the body had been laid ; and it was this body which was alive !—Then how can we explain otherwise than by a resurrection the tomb found empty ? We have seen that the two suppositions of a removal by the disciples or by the Jews are equally impossible. The return of the material elements to the earth must have been effected by the hands of some agent. Could Jesus have been the digger of His own grave ?— Besides, how could Jesus, with a purely spiritual body, have said to the disciples : "Touch me," show them His wounds, ask them for food, and this to the end of convincing them of the material reality of the body which He had? Sabatier answers that these details are found only in Luke and John, who present to us the appearances under a form materialized by legend, while the normal tradition is still found in Matthew and Mark, and besides in Paul (1 Cor. xv.). In Matthew? But he relates that the women laid hold of *the feet* of Jesus ; the feet of a spiritual body? In Mark? But we do not have the conclusion of Mark's narrative. In Paul? But he enumerates five appearances, some of which are identical with those of Luke, and he thus confirms the accounts of the latter. Is it probable, moreover, that Luke, St. Paul's companion in preaching, had on this fundamental point of the resurrection of the Lord a different view from the apostle? And what does Paul himself desire to prove in the fifteenth chapter of First Corinthians? That we shall receive a new body without any organic relation to our present body? On the contrary, he emphasizes in every way the close bond of union between these two successive organs of our personality. It is *this mortal* which will put on immortality, *this corruptible* which will put on incorruption. Only the corruptible elements of flesh and blood will be excluded from this transformation, which, according to Phil. iii. 21, will make of the body of our humiliation a body of glory like the present body of the Lord. For a resurrection Sabatier substitutes a creation. By breaking every bond between the present body and the future body, he does away with the victory of the Lord over death, and consequently over sin and condemnation, and thus, while thinking only to treat of a secondary point, does violence to the essence of the Christian redemption.

V. The strangest means of escaping from the notion of a corporeal resurrection and yet attributing some objectivity to the appearances of the Lord was imagined by *Weisse*, and then adopted and developed by *Keim*. The appearances of Jesus risen from the dead were *spiritual* manifestations of Jesus glorified to the minds of His disciples. Their reality belonged only to the inner world ; they were nevertheless positive historical facts. But the disappearance of the body of Jesus remains still unexplained, as in most of the preceding hypotheses. And what a strange way of acting is that of a being, *pure spirit*, who, appearing to the mind of His followers, should take so much pains to prove to them that He is indeed flesh and bones, and not pure spirit! And how should the apostles, who were so little expecting a bodily resurrection, have come to substitute for purely spiritual revelations gross material facts?

After having exhausted all these so different explanations, we return to the thought which naturally comes forth from the words of the Lord : "*I am not yet ascended, but I ascend.*" The interval between the resurrection and the ascension of the Lord was a period of transition. He had indeed recovered His former body, but, through the change which was made in His personal position, this body was subjected to new conditions of existence. It was not yet the spiritual body, but the spirit disposed of it more freely ; it was already the docile organ of the will. Thus are the opposite phenomena explained which characterize the manifestations of the Lord in this period of His existence ; in particular, the sudden appearances and disappearances. Objection is made because of this fact : that the Lord ate. There would be reason in this objection if He ate for hunger, but this act was not the result of a need. He wished to show that He *could* eat—that is to say, that His body was real, that

He was not a pure spirit or a phantom. The ascension consummated what the resurrection had begun.

There are three miracles in the development of nature : 1. The appearance of matter ; 2. The appearance of life in matter ; 3. The appearance of the conscious and free will in the domain of life. There are three decisive miracles in the history of the Lord : 1. His coming in the flesh, or His entrance into material existence ; 2. The realization of life, of holy communion with God in this corporeal existence ; 3. The elevation of this life to the liberty of the divine life by the resurrection and ascension.

CONCLUSION

John 20:30,31

In concluding his narrative, the evangelist gives an account of the *manner* in which he has proceeded (ver. 30) and of the end which he proposed to himself (ver. 31) in composing it.

How are we to explain this so sudden ending, after the conversation of Jesus and Thomas ? The narrative contained in the appendix, ch. xxi., shows clearly that the author was not at the end of the materials which he possessed. It is not to be doubted, therefore, that this ending is in close and essential connection with the design which has governed the whole narrative, with the *idea* itself of the *book*. If the author wished to trace out *the development of the faith of the disciples and of his own*, the *birth* of this faith must be the starting-point of the narrative—this is indeed the case ; comp. i. 19 ff.—and the consummation of this faith must be the end of it. This consummation we find in the exclamation of Thomas.

We need not be astonished, therefore, at not finding in such a gospel the account of the *ascension*, any more than we have found in it that of the *baptism* of Jesus. Both the one and the other of these events are situated outside of the limits which the author had drawn for himself. And we see how destitute of foundation are the consequences which an ill-advised criticism has drawn from this silence, to contest both the faith of the author in these events, and the reality of these facts themselves.[1] If John believes in the reality of the bodily resurrection of Jesus—and the preceding chapter leaves no doubt in this regard—and if he cannot have thought that the body of the Risen One was subjected again to death, there remains but one possibility : it is that he attributed to Him, as the mode of departure, the ascension, as the apostolic Church in general accepted it. This is proved, moreover, by the words which he puts into the mouth of Jesus, vi. 62 and xx. 17. It would be proved, if need were, by his very silence, which excludes every other supposition.

Vv. 30, 31. "*Jesus therefore did many miracles, other than these, in the presence of His*[2] *disciples, which are not written in this book.* 31. *But these are written that you may believe*[3] *that Jesus is the Christ, the Son of God, and that, believing, you may have life*[4] *in his name.*"—The $\mu\acute{\epsilon}\nu$ prepares the way for the following contrast. The apostle desires to set forth clearly the fact that his thought was not to trace out the complete picture of all that he has seen

---

[1] *Keim*, III. p. 616 : " John knows nothing of a visible ascension, although Jesus speaks of it once in one saying" (vi. 62).

[2] Αυτου is omitted by A B E K S Δ 13 Mnn.

[3] א B : πιστευητε instead of πιστευσητε.

[4] א omits και (*and*) before ινα (*in order that*), and, with C D L T^d 12 Mnn. It^{aliq}. adds αιωνιον to ζωην (life *eternal*).

and heard, for the contrary supposition would end in rendering suspicious the facts related in other writings and not mentioned by him, which is far from his thought. He has made, among the multitude of facts included in the history of Jesus, a choice appropriate to the end which he proposed to himself. In the face of this declaration of the author, how can serious critics reason thus : John omits, therefore he denies or is ignorant of, for example, the story of the miraculous birth, the temptation, the healings of lepers or demoniacs, the transfiguration, the institution of the Lord's Supper, Gethsemane, the ascension, etc. !—According to some interpreters, from *Chrysostom* to *Baur*, the words : *the signs which Jesus did*, designate only the appearances related in this chapter, as *signs* or proofs of the resurrection ; from which it would follow that these verses, 30 and 31, are the conclusion, not of the gospel, but only of the narrative of the resurrection. This opinion is incompatible : 1, with the term ποιεῖν, *to do :* one does not *do* appearances ; 2, with the two expressions *many* and *others :* the appearances were neither so numerous nor so different ; 3, the expression *in this book* shows that the question is of the entire work, and not only of one of its parts.— The *signs* of which John means to speak are essentially the miracles, but not as separate from the teachings, " which are almost always the commentary on them " (*Weiss*).—By the terms : *in the presence of His disciples*, John makes prominent the part appointed for the Twelve in the foundation of the Church. They were the *accredited witnesses* of the works of Jesus, chosen to accompany Him, not only for the development of their personal faith, but also with a view to the establishment of faith in the whole world ; comp. xv. 27 and Acts i. 21, 22. Whatever *Luthardt, Weiss* and *Keil* may say, it seems to me difficult not to see in the position of the pronoun τούτῳ, *after* the substantive βιβλίῳ : " this book," a tacit contrast to other writings containing the things omitted in this. This expression, thus understood, accords with all the proofs which we have met of the knowledge which John already had of the Synoptics. The apostle therefore confirms by these words the contents of these gospels, which were earlier than his own, and tells us that he has labored to complete them.

And what *end* did he propose to himself in writing a history of Jesus under these conditions ? Ver. 31 answers this question. He wished to bring his readers to the same faith by which he was himself filled. He consequently selected from the life of his Master the facts and testimonies which had the most effectually contributed to form and strengthen his own faith. From this selection it is that the Gospel of John originated.—In saying *you*, the apostle addresses himself to certain definite Christians, but persons who, as *Luthardt* says, represent for him the whole Church. They *believe* already, no doubt ; but faith must ever advance, and at every step, as we have seen, the previous faith appears as not yet deserving the name of faith (see ii. 11 and elsewhere).—John characterizes Jesus, the object of faith, in such a way as to indicate the two phases which had constituted the development of his own faith : first, *the Christ ;* then, *the Son of God*. The first of these terms recalls to mind the accomplishment of the prophecies and of the theocratic hope. It was in this character that the faith of the disciples had at first welcomed

Him (i. 42, 46). The solemnity with which this notion of *Messiah* is called to mind in this verse, the summary of faith, absolutely sets aside the idea of a tendency opposed to Judaism in the author of the fourth Gospel. But the recognition of the Messiah in Jesus had been only the first step in the apostolic faith. From this point John and his associates were soon raised to a higher conception of the dignity of Him in whom they had believed. In this Messiah they had recognized *the Son of God*. The first title referred to His office ; this one refers to His *person* itself. It is especially since the fifth chapter of our Gospel that this new light finds its way into the souls of the disciples, under the sway of the declarations of Jesus. It has reached its perfection in the words of Thomas : *My Lord and my God*, which have just closed the Gospel.—If these two terms had the same meaning, the second would here be only a mere tautology. The first refers to the relation of Jesus to Israel and to men, the second to His personal relation to God.—If John proposed to make his readers sharers in his faith, it is because he has learned by his own experience that this faith produces life : *that, believing, you may have life*. To receive Jesus as the Son of God is to open one's heart to the fulness of the divine life with which he is himself filled ; human existence is thus filled with blessedness and strength in communion with God. The words *in His name* depend, not on *believing*, but on the expression *have life*. This name is the perfect revelation which Jesus has given of Himself, by manifesting Himself as Christ and as Son of God.

Either, therefore, the author who speaks thus of the design of his book deceives us, or he did not write in the interest of speculation. He aims, not at knowledge, but at faith, and through faith at life. He is not a philosopher, but a witness ; his work as a historian forms a part of his apostolic ministry. In all times, those who *have not seen* will be able through his testimony to reach the same faith and the same life as himself. We are thus enlightened as to the method and the spirit of his book.

APPENDIX

John 21:1-25

After the conclusion xx. 30, 31, this section is a surprise to the reader. It contains two scenes : one of a general interest for the whole circle of the disciples (vv. 1–14) ; the other of a more special interest, having reference to the two principal apostles (vv. 15–23). It ends with a new conclusion, the appendix, vv. 24, 25.—The composition of this section must be later than that of the gospel ; this appears, 1, from the formula of conclusion at the end of the preceding chapter ; and, 2, from the connection which we have proved between the conversation of Jesus with Thomas and the general plan of the book. Some—*Hengstenberg, Lange, Hoeleman, Hilgenfeld*, etc.—have sought to efface the final point, set by the author himself in the passage xx. 30, 31. *Lange* seeks to make us regard ch. xxi. as an epilogue serving as a counterpart to the prologue i. 1–18. "In the same way," he says (*Life of Jesus,* iv. p. 752), "as the evangelist has represented in ch. i. the ante-historic reign of Christ, . . . in the same way he now draws the picture of His post-historic reign, even to the end of the world." But this comparison is more ingenious than real. It is the apostles who are on the stage in the following narrative, much more than the Lord Himself ; and it is their future destiny which is here foretold, rather than the reign of the glorified Lord which is described. The counterpart of the prologue, from the point of view indicated by Lange, is not ch. xxi. ; it is the Apocalypse. *Weitzel* has made a remark which seems to me to have scarcely any better foundation.[1] "Each of the other three Gospels," he says, "closes with a section relative to the future activity of the apostles ; comp. Matt. xxviii. 19, 20, Mark xvi. 20, Luke xxiv. 53. Chapter xxi. has the same part in our Gospel." It is evident that Jesus, after having risen from the dead, speaks to the apostles in each Gospel respecting their coming work. But such words differ too widely from ch. xxi. of John for any one to be able to draw a conclusion from this fact.—This appendix was certainly composed after the Gospel ; but it must have been composed soon enough to have made it possible to add it to the principal work before the latter was put in circulation in the Church. Otherwise there would undoubtedly have been formed, as for the Gospel of Mark, two classes of copies, one not having the appendix, the other drawing its material from the manuscript in which it had been originally inserted. It is, therefore, between the time of the composition of the Gospel and that of its

---

[1] *Das Selbstzeugniss des vierten Evangelisten über seine Person*, in the *Stud. u. Kritik.*, 1849, p. 578 ff.

publication that we must place the redaction and addition of this chapter. *Renan* gives nearly the same judgment : "I close the first redaction," he says, " at the end of ch. xx. Chapter xxi. is a nearly contemporaneous addition, either of the author himself or of his disciples " (p. 534). This date is confirmed by the passage which contains the words relative to the future of John (vv. 21-23). We have seen this (Introduction on pp. 166, 167) ; it is at the time when the death of John, quite recent or foreseen as imminent, seemed to contradict the well-known promise of Jesus, that the correction contained in this passage must have appeared necessary. This fact fixes the date of our chapter. Only we need not infer from this, with *Weiss, Reuss* and others, that this correction was the sole purpose of the redaction and of the addition of the entire chapter. Two reasons oppose this : 1. The preamble, vv. 1-20, which would be too considerable ; 2. The 14th verse, which too distinctly separates the two parts of the narrative. On the *author* of this appendix, see at ver. 25.

In the appearance, xx. 19-23, Jesus had conferred on the disciples their mission. In the first scene of ch. xxi.—that which concerns the seven disciples, vv. 1-14—He gives them a forever ineffaceable sign of the magnificent success assured to this mission, so far as they shall work in it under His direction.

Jesus and the Disciples : vv. 1-14

This first scene includes two pictures : that of the *fishing* and that of the *repast*.

The fishing : vv. 1-8.

The theatre of this story is remarkable : it is the shores of the sea of Tiberias, in Galilee. By it the Johannean tradition, from which in any case this story emanates, establishes the connection between the narrative of Matthew, which (with the exception of the appearance to the women at Jerusalem) relates only one Galilean appearance, and that of Luke, which contains only appearances in Judea (comp., however, *the forty days* of which Luke speaks, Acts i. 3). Our story furnishes the positive reconciliation between these two forms of narrative, by proving that there had really been appearances on these two theatres. The disciples therefore returned to Galilee after the feast, and temporarily resumed there their previous manner of life. Then, towards the end of the forty days, no doubt at the bidding of Jesus, they repaired to Jerusalem, where they were to begin the work of public preaching ; and it is during this new sojourn in Jerusalem that the command must be placed, which the Lord gave to the apostles on the day of the ascension, not to leave that city until the coming of the Holy Spirit (Luke xxiv. 49, comp. with Acts i. 3, 4). Harmonistic expedients, cries *Meyer ;* anti-harmonistic prejudice, we will answer.

According to Matthew xxvi. 31, 32 and xxviii. 7-10, all the believers (*the flock*), even the women,—*you* is addressed also to them,—were to assemble again in Galilee after Jesus' death, and there to see Him again. The appearances in Judea, while gathering the apostles together, were only the beginning of this complete reunion of the flock. Through the obstinacy of Thomas, an entire week elapsed before this preliminary end could be reached. It was after having recovered this sheep who went astray, that the apostles were able to return to Galilee, where Jesus appeared to them at first on the shore of the sea, then on the mountain designated by Him (comp. Matt. xxviii. 16). Although Matthew, in the account of this appearance, the most important of all by reason of the revelations which it contains respecting Christ and the foundation of His Messianic Kingdom, mentions only the leaders of the flock, the Eleven, as responsible agents of this work, we understand, from 1 Cor. xv. 6, that this was the great meeting of all the Galilean believers, to the number of more than *five hundred* persons, which Jesus had had in view from before His death, and in which he took leave of His Church.

Vv. 1, 2. "*After this, Jesus manifested himself once more to the disciples,*[1] *on the shore of the sea of Tiberias ; and this is the way in which he manifested himself. 2 Simon Peter and Thomas, called Didymus, and Nathanael, of Cana in Galilee, and the sons of Zebedee*[2] *and two others of his disciples, were together.*"—The transition μετὰ ταῦτα, *after these things*, is familiar to John (v. 1, vi. 1, vii. 1, etc.). It serves to join the appendix to the Gospel, and especially to the narrative of the last appearance, xx. 29. The expression ἐφανέρωσεν ἑαυτόν is also in conformity with John's style (vii. 4, φανέρωσον σεαυτόν ; xi. 33, ἐτάραξεν ἑαυτόν) ; this form makes prominent the conscious and free will with which Jesus comes forth from the sphere of invisibility to manifest Himself. Until now, being visible, He had manifested His glory ; now he manifests His person.—The term *sea of Tiberias* is in the New Testament a purely Johannean designation (vi. 1). The Synoptics say *sea of Galilee* (Matt. iv. 18) or *lake of Gennesaret* (Luke v. 1). The Old Testament knows neither the one nor the other of these expressions. Josephus employs them both.—The clause : *And this is the way in which*, is not useless ; it gives an indication beforehand of the solemnity of the scene which is to follow.—Of the seven persons indicated in ver. 2, the first five only are apostles ; the last two belong to the number of *the disciples*, in the broad sense which is so frequently the sense of this word in our Gospel (vi. 60, 66, vii. 3, viii. 31, etc.). If it were otherwise, why should they not be designated by name, as well as those who precede ? *Hengstenberg* affirms that "every one must understand that they were Andrew and Philip " (!).—The *sons of Zebedee* occupy, therefore, the last place among the apostles properly so called. This fact is significant ; for in all the apostolic lists they are constantly joined with Peter, and placed with him in the first rank. The only reason which explains this circumstance is that the author of this narrative, in its oral or written form, was himself one of the two sons of Zebedee. It has been objected that John never names either himself or his brother. But no more does he do this here ; he only designates himself, because he was obliged to indicate his presence in view of the following scene, ver. 7, and especially ver. 22.—Respecting Thomas Didymus, see on xi. 16.—The explanation : *of Cana in Galilee*, had not been given in chap. i. The author makes up for this omission here.—May not the two *disciples* who are not

---

[1] D H M U X Γ 40 Mnn. It^{pleriq} Syr. Cop. add αυτου to μαθηταις.   [2] ℵ D E read οι υιοι, instead of οι.

named be that Aristion and that presbyter John of whom Papias speaks as old *disciples of the Lord* (μαθηταὶ τοῦ Κυρίου), who lived at Ephesus at the time when John wrote, and who had there almost the rank of apostles ?[1]

Vv. 3, 4. "*Simon Peter says to them, I go a fishing. They say to him, We also go with thee. They went forth[2] and entered[3] immediately[4] into the boat; and they took nothing that night. 4. But when the morning was already[5] come,[6] Jesus stood on[7] the beach; the disciples, however, knew[8] not that it was Jesus.*"
—Between their first call and the beginning of the active ministry of their Master (see at ii. 12), the disciples had returned to their ordinary profession. They seem to have acted in the same way when once they had returned to Galilee after the resurrection. As ordinarily, the initiative comes from Peter. —The word πιάζειν, *to take*, which is used in vv. 3 and 10, is found again six times in our Gospel, nowhere in the Synoptics (*Hengstenberg*). On the other hand, the word πρωία does not occur again in John. *Bäumlein* rightly observes that the *asyndeta* λέγει, λέγουσιν, ἐξῆλθον, etc., are in John's style.— This long night of toil without result had, no doubt, recalled to the apostles that which had preceded their calling to the office of preachers of the Gospel (Luke v.).

Vv. 5, 6. "*Jesus says to them, Children, have you anything[9] to eat? They answered him, No. 6. He said to them, Cast the net on the right side of the boat, and you shall find. They cast it therefore;[10] and they were not able[11] to draw it because of the multitude of the fishes.*"—The term παιδία, *young people, boys*, is not foreign to the language of John (1 Ep. ii. 13,18). If the more tender term τεκνία, *little children*, is not used, as in xiii. 33, it is because Jesus could not have expressed Himself thus without making Himself known. He uses the expression of a master speaking to his workmen. The negative sense of the interrogative form μή τι may, as in vi. 67, be rendered thus : *You have nothing then* . . . ? The sequel will explain this question. Jesus does not look merely at a catching of fish, as in Luke v., but at a *meal*. It is not necessary, therefore, to suppose, with *Chrysostom, Tholuck* and others, that Jesus wished to present Himself to them as a trader who was desirous of purchasing fish.—The word προσφάγιον is not found again in John ; it denotes literally what is added to bread at a meal ; in this case, the *fish*.—The apostles suppose that this stranger understands fishing, and that he has noticed some indication fitted to give occasion for his advice. It has been thought that the opposition between the left side of the boat, where they had cast the net during the night to

---

[1] One more little specimen of *Reuss'* style : On occasion of this supposition, which we expressly have stated as such, he says : "As to the two disciples, we must apply to the commentators who know everything."

[2] A P It^{aliq} add και (*and*) before, and ℵ G L X ουν (*therefore*) after, εξηλθον (*they went forth*).

[3] T. R. with Δ Λ: ανεβησαν (*went up*); almost all the Mjj. : ενεβησαν.

[4] ℵ B C D L X Δ some Mnn. It. Vulg. Syr. Cop. omit ευθυς (*immediately*).

[5] ℵ some Mnn. It^{plerique} Vulg. Syr^{sch} omit ηδη (*already*) here.

[6] A B C E L 10 Mnn : γινομενης (*coming*), instead of γενομενης.

[7] ℵ A D L M U X read επι, instead of εις (τον αιγιαλον).

[8] ℵ L X : εγνωσαν (*knew*), instead of ηδεισαν.

[9] ℵ omits τι.

[10] ℵ D Cop.: οι δε εβαλον instead of εβαλον ουν.

[11] ℵ B C D L Δ Π 10 Mnn. It^{plerique} Vulg.: ισχυον instead of ισχυσαν.

no purpose, and the right side, where they were about to make their magnificent draught, typified the contrast between the failure of the work of evangelization in Israel and its infinitely rich fruits in the Gentile world. But, besides the fact that this seems contrary to what is related in Acts ii.-v. and xxi. 20 (μυριάδες), it is necessary to hold to the general idea of the immense success which will be gained in the world by the preaching of the Gospel, at every time when the apostles shall suffer themselves to be directed by the Lord, and shall work with Him. This meaning could not escape them, provided they remembered the terms of the original call : "*I will make you fishers of living men.*" They could understand it, however, only after having recognized Jesus.

Vv. 7, 8. "*Then that disciple whom Jesus loved says to Peter, It is the Lord! Simon Peter, when he heard that it was the Lord, put on his garment and girded himself (for he was naked); and he cast himself into the sea. 8 But the other disciples came with the boat*[1] (*for they were not far from the land but about the distance of two hundred cubits*), *dragging the net with the fishes.*"— How characteristic of the two apostles are the features which appear in these two simple incidents ! John contemplates and divines; Peter acts and springs forward. "It will not fail to be noticed," says *Reuss,* " that Peter has need to be instructed by John ;" which means that by this detail the author seeks to elevate John above Peter. But in all that follows (vv. 7, 11, 15-17, 19) everything tends, on the contrary, to give Peter the first rank. What results from this is simply that the story tends to characterize the two principal apostles by their different gifts, as they afterwards showed themselves throughout their whole career : Peter, the man of missionary activity ; John, of contemplative knowledge.—The garment called ἐπενδύτης is an intermediate one between the χιτών, the under garment, the shirt, and the ἱμάτιον, the outer garment, the mantle ; it is the *blouse* of the workman. After having taken it off, Peter was really *naked,* except for the *subligaculum,* the *apron,* required for decency. But we may also hold, with *Meyer,* that he had kept on an undergarment ; the Greek usage of the word γυμνός, *naked,* authorizes this sense. The word διεζώσατο, literally, *he girded himself,* includes the two ideas of *putting on* the garment and *fastening* it.—While Peter springs into the water and swims to the Lord, John remains with the other disciples in the boat. Πλοιαρίῳ, a local dative (*Meyer*), or, better perhaps, instrumental : by means of the boat (in contrast with Peter, who had thrown himself into the water to *swim*). They simply drew the net. The *for* explains how they could have recourse to this means : *They were not far distant from the shore.* Two hundred cubits make nearly a hundred metres (somewhat more than a hundred yards). Ἀπό is not used for measuring distance except in our Gospel (xi. 18) and in the Apocalypse (xiv. 20), as *Hengstenberg* remarks. The same author observes that the terms πλοῖον and πλοιάριον are used alternately in this section, as in vi. 17 ff.

It has been supposed that this story of a miraculous fishing refers to the same event as the similar story in Luke v. 4 ff.; some (*Strauss, Weisse,* etc.)

---

[1] ℵ reads αλλω before πλοιαριω (with *the other* boat !).

seeing in John's story a free reproduction of Luke's ; others, as *Weiss*, finding rather in Luke's story an anticipatory reminiscence of the event related in John xxi. The transposition of a fact in the evangelic history would undoubtedly not be an impossibility. But how can we believe that Peter throwing himself into the water to go to Jesus standing on the shore is only a variation of Peter prostrate on his knees before Him in the boat and saying to Him : "Depart from me, for I am a sinner !" etc., etc. ? I think rather that, when Jesus wished to reinstate Peter and place him again at the head of his brethren in the work of the apostolic office, He did so through recalling to his mind, by this magnificent draught of fishes, the circumstances of his first call, and, through encouraging him, by the renewal of this symbol of the unprecedented successes which would crown his work, to give himself anew entirely to this task.

The meal : vv. 9–14.

Vv. 9–11. "*When therefore they were come to land,*[1] *they see a fire of coals there, and a fish laid thereon and bread.* 10. *Jesus says to them, Bring of the fish which you have just taken.* 11. *Simon Peter went up*[2] *on the boat and drew the net to land,*[3] *full of great fishes, a hundred and fifty-three; and although there were so many, the net was not broken.*"—If this draught of fishes is for the disciples the symbol and pledge of the success of their preaching, the meal is undoubtedly the emblem of the spiritual and temporal assistance on which they may count on the part of their glorified Lord, as long as this work shall continue. *Grotius*, *Olshausen* and others have thought that in contrast with the sea which represents the field of labor, the land and the meal represent heaven, from whence Jesus aids the believers, and where He receives them after death. We are more naturally led to the first sense by the preceding question : "You have, then, nothing to eat ?"—The word ἀνθρακία, *coal-fire*, is found only here and in the story of the denial of St. Peter, and this in John only (xviii. 18; Mark and Luke have πῦρ and φῶς).—The singular ὀψάριον, *roasted fish*, is taken by *Luthardt*, *Meyer*, *Weiss*, in the collective sense : *fish*, as if there were several. They rest upon ver. 13. But in that place there is the article, which may have the generic sense. If there were several, why should Jesus request them to bring *of their own ?* Ver. 10 and vi. 9, where the plural is used, speak rather in favor of the singular sense of ὀψάριον. Only the narrative does not lay stress upon this ; for in that case ἓν would have been necessary.—Whence came this bread and fish ? *Luthardt* thinks of the ministry of angels ; *Bäumlein* and *Weiss* attribute the whole to the action of Peter. This disciple may, indeed, have kindled the fire ; but whence could he have procured the bread and the fish ? *Lampe* thinks that Jesus had procured these articles of food from some fishermen of the neighborhood ; at all events, He did not create them ; this procedure would be contrary to all the antecedents (ii. 7, vi. 9 ; compare these pp. 349, 350 , also on p.567). The words : *it is the Lord*, relieve us, undoubtedly, from the necessity of

---

[1] ℵ H : ανεβησαν, Λ : επεβησαν, instead of απεβησαν.

[2] ℵ L : ενεβη instead of ανεβη.

[3] ℵ A B C L P X Δ Π : εις την γην instead of επι της γης.

disturbing ourselves with this question (Luke xix. 31).—The articles of food offered by Jesus must be made complete by the product of their own fishing. This detail would be absolutely incomprehensible, unless this whole scene had a symbolic sense. Jesus wishes to tell them that He will occupy Himself with their wants, but that their faithful labor must co-operate with His benediction and His aid; comp. Ps. cxxviii. 2: *"The fruit of thy labor thou shalt eat."*—*He drew:* of course, with the aid of his companions; but Peter was the one who directed.—The number *one hundred and fifty-three* has been made the text of the strangest commentaries. *Cyril of Alexandria* sees herein the emblem of God and the Church (100 representing the Gentiles, 50 the Jews, 3 the Trinity). *Augustine* gives himself to unheard-of subtleties (see *Westcott*, who enumerates a large number of other strange explanations, of *Gregory the Great*, *Rupert of Deutz*, etc.). *Hengstenberg* sees in this number an allusion to the 153,600 Canaanitish proselytes who were received into the theocracy in the time of Solomon (2 Chron. ii. 17). According to an expression which is somewhat common at the present day among our critics, this number came from the idea accepted at that time among naturalists, that the total number of kinds of fishes is 153. *Koestlin* has, indeed, cited a passage from Jerome, which seems to prove the existence of this idea among the learned men of the period by a saying of a Cilician poet, named Oppian, a contemporary of Marcus Aurelius: "Those who have written on the species of animals, . . . and among them the very learned Oppian, the Cilician, say that there are 153 kinds of fish, which were all taken by the apostles, and of which none remained uncaught."[1] This number would, therefore, be the symbol of the totality of the Gentile nations. *Hilgenfeld*, to complete this interpretation, holds that the fish and the bread which Jesus had previously prepared represent the Jewish people. But *Strauss* observes (*Leben Jesu*, 1864, p. 414) that Oppian does not himself indicate the total 153, but that he gives only a not very clear enumeration, the sum of which may as easily be a larger or smaller number as this number itself. Then the work of Oppian is later than that of John, and we are led by the sentence of Jerome himself to conclude that John's number has been taken advantage of for the purpose of this scientific fable. As to the idea of *Hilgenfeld* (*Einl.*, p. 718), how can we suppose that a reasonable writer should have been willing to represent the Jewish people under the figure of a roasted fish and bread?[2]

The mention of this number is no more surprising than that of the number of men who were fed and of baskets which were filled, after the multipli-

---

[1] *Jerome* on Ezek. xlvii. 9: "Aiunt qui de animantium scripsere naturis et proprietate, qui ἁλιευτικά tam latino quam græco didicere sermone, de quibus Oppianus Cilix est poeta doctissimus: cliii. esse genera piscium, quæ omnia capta sunt ab apostolis et nihil remansit inceptum."

[2] We shall only indicate in passing the still more fantastic explanations of some modern writers, who find the key of this number in the calculation of the letters in the name of Peter; thus Egli, according to the Hebrew form: *Schimeon Jonah* (Simon, son of Jona); Volkmar (*Himmelf. Mose*, p. 62), according to the form *Schimeon* (71) *bar* (22) Jonah (31) Kepha (29); total 153; and finally Keim himself, in this other form: *Schimeon* (71) Jochanna (53) Kepha (29), in his *Gesch. Jesu*, iii. p. 564. But the name of Peter does not have the least importance in this part of the narrative.

cation of the loaves, in ch. vi. It is the simple fact recalled to mind to prove two things : 1. The richness of the draught of fishes ; 2. The lively interest with which the apostles counted the fishes that were taken.—The fact that the net was unbroken is mentioned, perhaps, as a symbol of the special protection of the Lord given to the Church, and to all those whom it contains.

Vv. 12-14. *" Jesus says to them, Come, and breakfast. But[1] none of the disciples dared to ask him, Who art thou ? knowing that it was the Lord. 13. Jesus comes near[2] and takes the bread and gives it to them, and the fish likewise. 14. This was[3] now the third time that Jesus manifested himself to his[4] disciples after he had risen from the dead."*—Jesus takes the part of host. He was standing at a little distance, but now He comes forward. A feeling of respectful fear prevents the disciples from approaching this mysterious person. Jesus invites them to eat ; but even then they do not dare to address Him. It is no longer the familiar relation of former days. Nothing is more natural than the apparent contradiction between *know* (to surmise) and not dare to interrogate. The terms τολμᾶν and ἐξετάζειν are not used elsewhere in John.

The indication given at ver. 14 divides the narrative into two parts. The beginning of ver. 15, however : *When therefore they had breakfasted*, connects the following conversation with the scene of the meal, ver. 13. The author desired to separate what in this appearance had an ordinary character and was related to the work of evangelization represented by the disciples in general who were present, from that which specially concerned the part and the destiny in the future of the two principal apostles, Peter and John.—The expression τοῦτο ἤδη τρίτον, *this was already the third time*, contains one of those niceties which we have noticed in several instances in the course of this Gospel. It recalls the forms already explained in ii. 11 : ταύτην ἐποίησε τὴν ἀρχήν, and iv. 54 : τοῦτο πάλιν δεύτερον σημεῖον ἐποίησεν. Like these, it has as its aim to correct tacitly the Synoptic narrative. According to Matthew (and Mark ?) the first appearance of Jesus to the disciples seemed to have taken place in Galilee, not in Judea. By no means, says our author : when He appeared to them in Galilee, *it was already the third time* that He showed Himself to them as having risen from the dead. The two preceding appearances to which he alludes are evidently the last two of ch. xx. : vv. 19 ff., vv. 26 ff. He does not count the one to Mary Magdalene, because, as he expressly says, it is of appearances *to the disciples* that he wishes to speak. *Reuss* objects that the disciples present were only seven in number. What matter ? It was a considerable group of them, and it was led by Peter. In the appearance xx. 19 ff. they were not, any more than here, all together.—As to the appearances to the two from Emmaus and to Peter (Luke, Paul), they belong to another category; they are appearances to certain individuals, not *to the disciples*. The word

---

[1] B C omit δε.
[2] ℵ B C D L X omit ουν (*therefore*).
[3] ℵ G L X omit δε after τουτο.
[4] A B C L some Mnn. omit αυτου after μαθηταις.

already allows us to suppose other *subsequent* appearances; they are those of Matt. xxviii., and of 1 Cor. xv. 7, and Acts i.

Peter and John: vv. 15–23

Peter: vv. 15–19a.

The following conversation completes the preceding scene by the express reinstallation of St. Peter not only in the apostolic office, but in the direction of the apostolic company and work. No doubt Jesus had announced to him the pardon of his sin in the special appearance which He had granted to him (Luke xxiv. 34, 1 Cor. xv. 5). In the appearance to the disciples in general, xx. 21–23, He had already treated him as an apostle. But He had not yet restored to him the whole of his old position, of which his denial had deprived him—that of chief of the apostles. This is what He does in the first part of the following conversation (vv. 15–17).

Ver. 15. "*When therefore they had breakfasted, Jesus says to Simon Peter, Simon, son of Jona,*[1] *lovest thou me more than these do? He says to him, Yes, Lord, thou knowest that I love thee. He says to him, Feed my lambs.*"[2] As there is a relation, which is perhaps not accidental, between the outward situation in which Peter had been called the first time to the ministry and that which has just been described, there is also a relation between the situation in which he had lost this office by his denial and the fire of coals near which he recovered it.—The title *Simon, son of Jona,* or, according to the reading of some Alexandrian authorities, *Simon, son of John,* is not unintentionally opposed to that of *Simon Peter,* of which the evangelist makes use in this same verse. It reminds Peter of his natural origin, and consequently of the state of sin from which the call of Jesus had drawn him, but into which he had sunk again by his fall. The allusion to the threefold denial of the apostle in the three following questions is not doubtful, whatever *Hengstenberg* may think. The threefold profession of his love for Jesus is to efface, in some sort, the threefold stain which he has brought upon himself. Jesus Himself is anxious to furnish him the occasion for it. By adding: *more than these do,* He certainly reminds Peter of the presumptuous superiority which he had attributed to himself when he said, Matt. xxvi. 33, Mark xiv. 29: "*Even if all the rest shall be offended in thee, I will not be offended.*" No doubt, John has not mentioned this saying; but his narrative is in constant relation to that of the Synoptics. One cites only as a remembered curiosity the interpretation which makes the word *these* the object of *lovest thou,* and which refers it to the fishing implements or to the fish: "Lovest thou me more than thou lovest thine old profession?" Peter, with a humility enjoined by the remembrance of his fall, at first in his answer rejects these last words: *more than these;* then he substitutes for the term ἀγαπᾶν, *to love* in the higher and spiritual sense of the word, love with the love of reverence, the term φιλεῖν, *to cherish,* love in the sense of personal attachment. He thinks that he can without presumption ascribe

---

[1] B C D L It^plerique read Ιωαννου (*John*) instead of Ιωνα. ℵ omits this word.

[2] C D: πρόβατα (*sheep*) instead of αρνια (*lambs*).

to himself this latter feeling ; and yet he does not do it without expressing a certain distrust of himself and without seeking the guaranty of the testimony of his heart, to which he does not dare to trust any longer, in the infallible knowledge of the hearts of men, which he now attributes to his Master. The question here is not of omniscience in the absolute sense of the word. Comp. ii. 24, 25. This appeal softens, as *Luthardt* says, the too decided character which a simple *yes* would have had.

Upon this answer, Jesus gives back to him the care of the flock. "He confides those whom He loves to the one who loves Him," says *Luthardt*. The expression : *the lambs*, designates, according to some, a particular class of the members of the Church, the children and beginners ; but the whole flock, at the point where things then were, was composed only of those who were beginning and weak. This saying reminds us of that which Jesus had addressed to Peter before his fall : " When thou shalt be restored, strengthen thy brethren " (Luke xxii. 32). The lambs are thus the whole flock of the faithful, apostles and simple believers. The term *feed*, βόσκειν, *cause to feed*, denotes the care of a flock from the point of view of nourishment. This function, in the spiritual sense, implies an inward sympathy which can only spring from love.

Vv. 16, 17. "*Jesus says to him again the second time,*[1] *Simon, son of Jona,*[2] *lovest thou me? He says to him, Yes,*[3] *Lord, thou knowest that I love thee. He says to him, Lead my sheep.*[4] 17. *He says to him the third time, Simon, son of Jona,*[5] *lovest thou me? Peter was grieved because he had said to him the third time, Lovest thou me? And he said to him,*[6] *Lord, thou knowest all things, thou knowest that I love thee. Jesus says to him, Feed my sheep.*"[7]— Jesus renews His question, "in order," as *Weiss* says, "to press Peter to a more severe examination of himself."—As the : *more than these*, had attained its end, Jesus now pardons the apostle ; but he persists in the use of the more elevated term to designate the love, ἀγαπᾶν. Peter, on his side, does not have the boldness to apply such a term to himself ; but he so much the more emphatically affirms his love in the more modest sense of the word φιλεῖν, and by appealing anew to the scrutinizing glance of the Lord. On this condition, Jesus again confides to him His flock, but with two characteristic differences. For the word βόσκειν, *feed*, which refers especially to the collective or private teaching by the word, He substitutes the term ποιμαίνειν, *to lead*, a term which denotes rather the government of the Church as a whole. According to the *Vatican* and *Ephrem* MSS., He uses here the term προβάτια, properly speaking *little sheep*, beloved sheep, instead of πρόβατα, *sheep*. And this reading may be the true one ; for, while expressing a shade of feebleness, like the word *lambs*, this word yet denotes a more advanced state, and forms the transition to the term *sheep*, πρόβατα, in the third phase of the conversation.

---

[1] ℵ omits δευτερον (*the second time*).
[2] Here also B C D It^{plerique}, this time with ℵ, read Ιωαννου (*John*) instead of Ιωνα.
[3] ℵ omits ναι (*yes*).
[4] B C read προβατια (*young sheep*) instead of προβατα, which all the rest read.
[5] ℵ B D It^{plerique} : Ιωαννου instead of Ιωνα.
[6] ℵ A D X : λεγει instead of ειπεν.
[7] A B C : προβατια (*young sheep*), instead of προβατα.

Finally, the third question leaves no longer any doubt for Peter respecting the humiliating fact which the Lord wishes to recall to him, and this recollection affects him the more painfully as Jesus this time substitutes for the term ἀγαπᾶν, as Peter had himself done from the beginning, the term φιλεῖν, whereby He seems to call in question even the attachment of an inferior order which the apostle had modestly claimed for himself. Peter feels the point of the sword penetrating to the quick. This time he suppresses the *yes*, the expression of his personal consciousness, and limits himself to making an appeal even more humbly to the penetrating glance of the Lord : " *Thou knowest all things !*" It is under this glance of omniscience that he places himself, as if to say : " See for Thyself if I do not love Thee !" This appeal to the higher knowledge of Jesus springs from the painful feeling of the great illusions which he had indulged respecting himself (*Weiss*). Three ancient manuscripts read here (as two of them do above) προβάτια ; but is it not probable that the copyists, not apprehending the shades of meaning, wrongly repeated this diminutive, and that Jesus said this time πρόβατα, my *sheep*, which denotes again the whole flock, but considered as in the normal condition ? Jesus resumes the term *feed*, whereby He gives Peter to understand that the general government of the Church is not to prevent the shepherd from occupying himself with the individual and collective instruction of the members of his flock. Acts xx. 31 shows clearly that it was thus that the apostles understood their holy commission. The passage 1 Peter v. 1–4 seems to be an echo of these words of Jesus addressed to the author of that epistle. *Westcott* rightly sets forth with emphasis the thrice repeated pronoun μου (*my*). The Lord does not give up His right of property in those whom He confides to His servants. " *Oves meas pasce*," says Augustine, " *sicut meas, non sicut tuas.*"

After having restored to Peter his former governing position, Jesus announces to him, vv. 18, 19a, what will be the *end* of his ministry. The connection between this new idea and the preceding dialogue is easy to be apprehended. Peter learns in what way it will be given to him to testify to his Master the love of which he has just made profession, and thus completely to efface his denial.

Vv. 18, 19a. " *Verily, verily, I say to thee, When thou wert younger, thou girdedst thyself, and walkedst whither thou wouldest ; but, when thou shalt have become old, thou shalt stretch forth thy hands, and another shall gird*[1] *thee and lead thee whither*[2] *thou wouldest not.* 19a. *In speaking thus, he signified by what death he should glorify God.*"—The form ἀμὴν, ἀμήν, *verily, verily*, belongs exclusively to John. It is necessary indeed to notice, in the following verse, the correspondence between the three members of the two propositions. To the : *thou wert younger*, answers the : *when thou shalt have become old*. Peter must, therefore, have been at that time in the intermediate period between youth and old age. This accords with the fact that he was already married some time before this (Luke iv. 38). He is placed between the spontaneous movements of the young man (*thou wert*) and the grave passiv-

---

[1] ℵ D Π : αλλοι ζωσουσιν (*others shall gird thee*).

[2] ℵ : ποιησουσι σοι οσα (*shall do to thee all that which*), instead of οισει οπου.

ity of the old man (*thou shalt be*). Only the latter will receive from the circumstances a still more serious character than is ordinarily the case.—To the words: *thou girdedst thyself*, the words : *thou shalt stretch forth thy hands and another shall gird thee*, correspond. It is impossible to apply these words, as so many interpreters (several Fathers, *Tholuck, de Wette, Bäumlein*, etc.) have done, to the act of extending the arms upon the cross for crucifixion. How should this point precede the following ones, which represent the apostle as led to the place of punishment ? It is rather, as *Reuss* says, the gesture of passivity face to face with violence. This girding will be the chain of the malefactor ; comp. Acts xxi. 11. In this word the annihilation of self-will, the dominant trait in the natural character of Peter, has been found. But the divesting of self began for him long before the period of old age.—Finally, to the words : *And thou walkedst whither thou wouldest*, the last point is set in opposition : "*And he shall lead thee whither thou wouldest not.*" This term *would* refers here to the repugnance of the natural heart to suffering. According to *Bleek*, the word *another* designates Jesus Himself. But this explanation is connected with the purely moral sense, falsely ascribed to the preceding words : φέρειν, *to carry*, more emphatic than ἄγειν, *to lead* (Mark. xv. 22).—The term : *by what death*, refers to death by martyrdom in general, and not specially, as *Reuss* thinks, to the punishment of crucifixion ; it excludes the idea of a natural death. The author speaks of the death of Peter as of a fact known by the readers. This had taken place, according to most authorities, in July, 64 ; according to others, one or two years later. The expression *to glorify God*, used to designate martyrdom, entered into the later ecclesiastical terminology ; we find it here in its original freshness. The phrase τοῦτο δὲ εἶπεν σημαίνων is especially Johannean, as well as the ποίῳ θανάτῳ which follows ; comp. xii. 33.

John : vv. 19b–21.

This conversation relates to the future of John, as the preceding to the future of Peter.

Vv. 19b–21. "*When he had spoken thus, he says to him, Follow me.* 20. *And Peter, turning about, sees the disciple whom Jesus loved following*[1] (*he who leaned on Jesus' breast at the supper and said,*[2] *Lord,*[3] *who is he that betrays thee?*). 21. *Peter, seeing him,*[4] *says to Jesus, Lord, and this man, what shall befall him?*"—Very diverse meanings have been given to the command : *Follow me. Paulus* understood it in the most literal sense : "Follow me to the place whither I am going to lead thee, that I may converse with thee alone." And this is indeed also the most natural sense, as *Tholuck, Weiss* (up to a certain point) and *Westcott* acknowledge. *Chrysostom* and *Bäumlein* understand : "Follow me in the active work of the apostolic ministry." *Meyer :* "Follow me in the way of martyrdom, where my example leads thee." *Luthardt :* "Follow me into that invisible world into which I have already entered, and to which martyrdom will lead thee." But the following words :

---

[1] א omits ακολουθουντα ος.
[2] א : λεγει instead of ειπεν. א C D add αυτω.
[3] א C omit κυριε.
[4] א B C D It^{plerique} Vulg. Cop. Orig. add ουν after τουτον.

"*Peter, turning about,*" prove that the question is really of a departure of Peter with Jesus—a departure which has begun to take place—and they consequently speak in favor of the literal sense of the word *follow*. This sense is, moreover, that of this same word (ἀκολουθοῦντα) in the following verse. After having announced to Peter his martyrdom, Jesus begins to walk away, bidding Peter follow Him. John, seeing this, follows them, without having been expressly invited; he feels himself authorized to do so by his intimate relations with Jesus. *Keil* objects that Jesus disappears miraculously, and does not go away thus on His feet. But if He had a conversation to carry on privately with Peter, why could He not have withdrawn for a moment with him? It does not follow from this, however, that the meaning of the command: *Follow me*, is purely outward. It is clear that, by this first step, Peter enters on that path of obedience to Jesus which will lead him to the tragic end of his apostleship. It is thus that the higher sense naturally connects itself with the lower, as in i. 44. This symbolism forms the basis of the entire Gospel of John.—What could be the object of the private conversation which Jesus desired to have with Peter? It is possible that He proposed to give him the instructions necessary for the convoking of those few hundreds of Galilean believers to whom He wished to manifest Himself personally before entirely withdrawing His visible presence from the earth (1 Cor. xv. 6). Matthew expresses himself thus, xxviii. 16, in speaking of this so considerable assemblage: "*on the mountain which Jesus had appointed for them.*" There was, then, a definite command, a meeting-place assigned with a designated hour. All this implies a communication; and if Peter received it at this moment, this was his re-installation *de facto* in that function of leader of the flock which had just been restored to him *de jure*. The word *turning about* reminds us of xx. 14, 16; it is a form altogether Johannean.—John followed Jesus and Peter; by what right? This is doubtless what the two descriptive phrases by which he is characterized are intended to explain: *The one whom Jesus loved*, and: *The one who reclined on the breast of Jesus and said to Him.* . . . He who had enjoyed such a degree of intimacy with the Master well knew that nothing could occur between Jesus and Peter which must remain a secret to him. This phrase is not, therefore, an unfounded panegyric of John, which contradicts the Johannean origin of the narrative. The καί after ὅς, "*who also*," brings out the relation between this exceptional intimacy and his character of beloved disciple.

The motive of Peter's question, ver. 21, was, not only according to the Tübingen school, but also according to men like *Olshausen, Lücke, Meyer, Bäumlein*, a feeling of jealousy with respect to John. Is it possible to ascribe to a man to whom Jesus has just confided His sheep a character having so little nobility? "If I am to undergo martyrdom, I hope that he also will not escape it!" Peter and John were, on the contrary, closely united, and truly loved each other (ver. 7). The first, with his manly nature, felt for the second, who was more timid and sensitive, what an elder brother feels for his tender and delicate younger brother. It is sympathy which inspires the question: *And this one, what shall befall him?* It is natural that the emotion awakened in the soul of Peter by the announcement of his own tragic end should express itself in his heart in this thought : "This one—must he, then, also pass through this experience ?"

Vv. 22, 23. "*Jesus says to him, If I will that he tarry till I come, what is it to thee? Follow thou me!*.[1] 23. *The report spread abroad, therefore, among the brethren that this disciple should not die; but Jesus did not say* [2] *to him that he should not die, but, If I will that he tarry till I come.*" [3]—This question of Peter, although springing from an affectionate feeling, had something indiscreet in it ; this the Lord makes him feel by the words : *What is it to thee?*—The *coming of the Lord*, in the fourth Gospel (ch. xiv.-xvi.), denotes His coming *in the Spirit*, from the day of Pentecost. This meaning is not applicable here, since Peter, as well as John, was present at that event. In the passage xiv. 3, the expression "the coming" of Jesus includes, in addition to His return in the Spirit, the *death* of the apostles. This application has been attempted here, in the sense that Jesus would predict for John a gentle and natural death at the end of a long apostolic career, in contrast with the martyrdom of Peter. This, or nearly this, is the view of *Grotius, Olshausen, Weitzel* and *Ewald*. But could the Lord mean to say that He returns only for those of His followers who die by a natural death, and not for those who perish by a violent death ? This would be a strange, even an absurd idea, and one which is contradicted by the story of the death of Stephen. As the coming of the Lord denotes in the Synoptics and with John himself (1 Ep. ii. 28, iii. 2) the glorious return of Jesus at the end of the present economy, *Meyer, Reuss, Weiss* and others apply this sense here : "If I will that he tarry *till my Parousia*." It was thus that the contemporaries of John interpreted this saying, until the time of his death ; for it is only thus that we can understand the inference, which they drew from it, that he would not die—that is, that he would belong to that company of believers who, being alive at the moment of the Parousia, will not be raised, but translated (1 Cor. xv. 51). This explanation was so much the more natural at that period, since there was a belief in the nearness of the Parousia. It continued even after the death of John, in the form of the popular legend, according to which John was said to have laid himself down in his grave and to be sleeping there until the return of Christ, or in that of the Greek legend, according to which John was said to have been raised immediately after his death, and was to reappear with the two witnesses of the Apocalypse in order to sustain the Church in its last struggle against Antichrist. But, setting aside these legends, if this view is accepted, it must be resolutely maintained, with *Weiss*, that Jesus shared the error of His contemporaries in relation to the nearness of His return, which would absolutely contradict the Synoptic documents (see my Commentary on the Gospel of Luke, Vol. I. pp. 325, 336), or fall back, with *Meyer*, upon the hypothetical form of Jesus'

---

[1] ℵ A B C D It^(plerique) Vulg. Orig. place μοι before ακολουθει.

[2] ℵ B C Orig. : ουκ ειπεν δε, instead of και ουκ ειπεν.

[3] We reject here the words τι προς σε (*what is it to thee?*) which are omitted by ℵ some Mnn. It^(aliq).

words : *If I will*, which is no less inadmissible, for Jesus could not have presented as possible (on the condition of His good pleasure) a thing which was impossible.—He promised, according to others (*Lange, Luthardt*, etc.), the preservation of John's life until the great judgment in the fall of Jerusalem, which may indeed be called the first act of the Coming of Christ ; comp. Matt. x. 23 : "I say to you that you shall not have gone over the cities of Israel, till the Son of man be come ; " and xxvi. 64 : "*Henceforth* you shall see the Son of man seated at the right hand of power *and coming on the clouds of heaven.*" Peter did not see this great manifestation of the glorified Christ, but John survived it. Yes, objects *Weiss*, but far too long for this explanation. But the length of time that John still lived after this event is of little consequence. For the *until* has nothing exclusive in it. Of all these proposed views, this would seem to us the least improbable. The attempt has also been made to apply this saying to the Apocalyptic vision, which Jesus here promised to John (*Bengel, Hengstenberg*) ; or a proof has been sought in it in favor of the necessity of the apostleship even till the end of time (*Thiersch*) ; *Schelling* (comp. *Bonnet*) saw in it the promise of the Johannean period, which, succeeding that of Peter (the middle ages) and that of Paul (the Reformation), would close the earthly development of the Church.—I have already before this observed that, as the primitive epoch of humanity had its Enoch and the theocratic epoch its Elijah, the Christian epoch might well have also its leader freed from death. And I have asked whether John might not in a mysterious way accompany the progress of the Church on earth, as in the scene of the draught of fishes he accompanied to the shore the boat which was suddenly abandoned by Peter. One raises such a question evidently only when one is not completely satisfied with any of the solutions which more naturally present themselves.[1]

From this point is discovered to us the unity of ch. xxi. The foundation of the whole scene is the miraculous draught of fishes, which typifies the future of the Christian ministry, in general. On this foundation the two special narratives stand forth, having relation to the part and destiny of the two principal apostles—Peter, who will leave the boat of the Church suddenly by the violent death of martyrdom, and John, who will accompany it even to the shore.

After this saying relative to John, Jesus again invites Peter to follow Him in order to receive His orders, and to resume, from that moment, the active service of the ministry and of the direction of the apostolate, which had been temporarily interrupted. The σύ, *thou*, which Jesus makes prominent here (comp. the difference in ver. 19), contrasts Peter with John : "*Thou*—do thou think of what I command *thee*, and leave to God His own secrets." The Alexandrian authorities place the μοι, *me*, before the verb,

---

[1] The idea expressed by *Holtzmann* (art. *Johannes*, in Schenkel's *Bibellexicon*), that this saying of Jesus is only a personal application to John of the promise in Matt. xvi. 28, Mark ix. 1, Luke ix. 27, is ingenious, but does not suit either the situation so precisely described in which the Synoptics place this promise, or that no less precisely described one in which our Gospel places the saying which is occupying our attention.

which would give it a special emphasis : "Occupy thyself with *me* and with no other !" This seems to me forced. The author, without indicating in ver. 23 the meaning of the saying of Jesus, which perhaps he does not himself know, contents himself with correcting the misapprehension which was connected with it.—The last words : *what is it to thee?* are not indispensable, and it is possible that the reading of the *Sinaitic* MS., which omits them, is the true one. The present οὐκ ἀποθνήσκει, *he does not die*, is that of the idea. We feel that the author reproduces this λόγος, this *saying*, just as it was repeated in the Church at the very moment when he was writing.

To whom are we to ascribe the redaction of this supplement? The stamp of the Johannean style and manner is so impressed upon it from one end to the other, that there are only two alternatives : either a man living in habitual association with the apostle drew up this narrative, after having often heard it from his lips, or John himself drew it up. Between these two suppositions, the choice is of little consequence. In favor of the second may be alleged : 1. The last place assigned to the two sons of Zebedee among the apostles named in ver. 1 ; 2. The very delicate way in which the finest shades of the conversation between Jesus and Peter are given. For the former may be urged : 1. The use of some terms which are not found again in the writings of John ; 2. The relation between ver. 23 and ver. 24, which easily leads us to regard him who wrote ver. 23 as one of those who say : *We know*, in ver. 24 ; perhaps, also, as the one who speaks in the first person singular in ver. 25.

Baur and a part of his school have seen in the redaction and addition of this appendix a manœuvre designed to exalt John, the apostle of Asia Minor, above Peter, the patron of the Church of Rome. But it is precisely Peter who is made prominent in this story (comp. vv. 1, 11, 15–17, 19, 22). So *Koestlin* and *Volkmar* have made a complete turn, and claimed that, contrary to the intention of the whole Gospel, this chapter is a Roman addition designed to make Peter prominent, whom the author of the fourth Gospel had constantly tried to depreciate. *Reuss* expresses himself more circumspectly : the author desired to re-establish the consideration for Peter, compromised by his denial.—The first two suppositions counterbalance each other. The third would suit rather the end which Jesus proposed to Himself in the scene itself, than the design which presided over its redaction.

Conclusion of the Appendix : vv. 24, 25

Vv. 24, 25. "*This is the disciple who testifies of these things and who wrote them;*[1] *and we know that his*[2] *testimony is true.* 25. *There are also many other things which*[3] *Jesus did ; and if they were written in detail, I do not think that the world itself could contain*[4] *the books*[5] *which would be written.*"—This postscript attests two things : 1. The composition of the Gospel by the apostle

---

[1] Instead of και γραψας, B D Cop. read και ο γραψας.

[2] B C D place αυτου before η μαρτυρια.

[3] Instead of οσα, which T. R. reads (with 13 Mjj. A D, etc.), א B C X read α.

[4] א B C Cop. : χωρησειν instead of χωρησαι.

[5] א A B C D some Mnn. It^{plerique} Vulg. Syr. Cop. Sah. Orig. omit αμην after βιβλια. This whole verse 25 is wanting in א (not in Cod. 63, as was erroneously stated after the time of Mill, Wetstein, Griesbach ; see Tischendorf, 8th ed.).

John (ver. 24) ; 2. The infinite richness of the evangelic history, which would not let itself be confined in any written word, whatever might be its extent (ver. 25).

There are three very different opinions respecting the origin of these two verses. Some (*Hengstenberg, Weitzel, Hoelemann, Hilgenfeld*, etc.) ascribe them both to the author of ch. xxi., who is at the same time the author of the entire book, either the apostle John (the first three) or a pseudo-John (Hilgenfeld). So *Lange* and *Schaff*, who ascribe only the words : "*And we know that his testimony is true*," to another hand. *Meyer, Tischendorf*, etc., ascribe ver. 24 to the author of the whole, but they see in ver. 25 a later interpolation. The third party (*Tholuck, Luthardt, Keil*) regard vv. 24, 25 as both added by another hand than that of John, the author of the whole of ch. xxi. *De Wette, Lücke, Weiss* ascribe them also to the author of the appendix, but without admitting that he is the apostle.

The pronoun οὗτος, *he*, can only refer to the disciple whom Jesus loved (ver. 23), and the pronouns τούτων and ταῦτα, *these things*, only to the contents of the entire book. For the appendix alone (vv. 1–23) would not have importance enough to occasion such a declaration. It may even be asked whether ch. xxi. is itself included in the expression : *these things*—in this case we should also have in ver. 24 the attestation of the Johannean origin of this chapter—or whether it is not rather the author himself of this ch. xxi., who concludes the appendix by bearing witness to the Johannean origin of the Gospel properly so called. This second view seems to me more probable ; for, as we have seen, the connection of vv. 23 and 24 is so close that it is difficult not to ascribe them to the same pen.

As the conclusion xx. 30, 31 ended the Gospel, so this new conclusion, an imitation of the previous one, closes the entire work, completed by the appendix. The author of this postscript says of the beloved disciple, that it is he *who testifies* (ὁ μαρτυρῶν) of the facts related and *who wrote them* (ὁ γράψας). If we do not hold that there is a pure and simple imposture here, we must acknowledge that "this declaration, which is so precise, excludes all possibility of a merely *indirect* composition by the apostle John." Thus *Weiss* expresses himself in answer to *Weizsäcker* and *Hase ;* we add : and to *Reuss*. The latter thinks that the redactors of this supplement (those who say : "*we* know") may have acted in good faith in erroneously ascribing the redaction of the Gospel to the apostle John. At a certain distance they may have mistaken the distinction which the author had himself expressly made between his person and that of the apostle—witness in the passage xix. 35 (*Théol. joh.*, p. 105). But *Reuss* surrenders himself here to an amiable illusion. By affirming the Johannean redaction of the Gospel, these men give themselves out as persons who are acquainted with the state of things, who even know the apostle personally (see below) ; an involuntary error is therefore impossible. They say : who *testifies* and who *wrote*. The present *testifies* refers, according to most (*Weiss, Keil*, etc.), to the permanence of the testimony in this writing composed by John. But in this case the epithet ὁ μαρτυρῶν, *who testifies*, should have been placed after ὁ γράψας : "*who wrote*, and who thus testifies in the Church in a lasting way." But the priority of the words *who testifies* and the contrast between this *present* participle and the *past* participle which follows do not allow any other meaning than : "who testifies at present, still at this hour" (*Meyer, Luthardt*, etc.). This postscript was added, therefore, during the lifetime of the apostle, "*Johanne adhuc in corpore constituto*," as a manuscript of the Vatican says, citing Papias (Tischendorf : *Wann wurden uns. Ev. verf.*, p. 119) ; which agrees with the design of the appendix. Who, more than John, should have been anxious that the meaning of the saying which the Lord had uttered with respect to him should be set right ?—The verb οἴδαμεν, *we know*, cannot have as its subject John himself, either alone, as *Chrysostom* would have it, reading οἶδα μέν, *I know undoubtedly*, or in company with the persons who surround him (*Weitzel*), or even the readers (*Meyer*). It can only be a plurality of individuals outside of which John himself is found. Who then ? The Fragment of Muratori places on the scene the apostle Andrew and other apostles (Philip perhaps) who lived in Asia at that time, and then the bishops of Ephesus.[1] If the question is of apostles, the *we know* signifies : that, knowing of themselves the facts related, they can testify to their accuracy ; "recognoscentibus cunctis," says the same Fragment. But if this *we* designates the Christians who surrounded John at Ephesus, this "we know" means that, having lived personally with John, they know his sincerity and declare him incapable of relating anything false. There is nothing to prevent us from uniting in the *we* these two classes of persons, in whose number may also be found Aristion and the presbyter John, of whom Papias speaks.[2] The persons who speak thus were in any case the depositaries in whose hands the apostle had placed his work and who had received from him the charge to publish it at a suitable time. It was in the discharge of this commission that they added, no doubt, the appendix of ch. xxi., and then they affixed to it the attestation of ver. 24. Perhaps it was rendered necessary in their view by the striking differences which existed between the history of John and the Synoptic narratives which were already spread abroad in the Church.

Does ver. 25 come from the same plurality of witnesses ? Three indications prevent us from thinking so : 1. The grammatical and syntactic form is more complicated than that of ver. 24 ; 2. The singular οἶμαι, *I think*, forms a contrast with the plural οἴδαμεν, *we know*. Finally, 3. The exaggeration, not without emphasis, which characterizes this verse is in contrast with the simple gravity of ver. 24. On the other hand, we have no right to conclude from this that this verse was interpolated at a time posterior to the publication, as *Meyer* and *Tischendorf* think. True, the *Sinaitic* MS. omits it, but this MS. is alone in this case, and we know how it abounds in omissions and inaccuracies. We may suppose, moreover, an intentional omission occasioned by the strange hyberbole which distinguishes this verse. As it is wanting nowhere else, it is probable that, as in

---

[1] "John, the disciple, being exhorted by his fellow-disciples and his bishops, said . . . ; in this same night it was revealed to Andrew, one of the apostles . . . " The expression *his bishops* (*episcopis suis*) does not allow us to think of any other country than Asia Minor. There only John had had a diocese for himself, whose bishops, installed by him, might have been called *his*.

[2] *Introd.*, p. 43.

ver. 24, it was added to the Gospel at the time of its publication. It is probably a personal addition proceeding from that one of the friends of John, who, in company with all his associates, had drawn up the 24th verse. He afterwards added, of his own impulse, ver. 25. Hence the change from the first person plural to the first person singular, a thing which proves his good faith. Hence also may come, perhaps, the difference of style between these two verses. The tone of the latter is not without some resemblance to that of the emphatic descriptions of Papias, in his picture of the millennial reign, or in his story of the death of Judas, and one might be tempted to find in the aged bishop of Hierapolis the subject of the verb : *I think*. Herein may be the truth pertaining to that strange note in the manuscript of the Vatican which we quoted just now, according to which Papias was the secretary of John in the redaction of his Gospel.[1] In any case, the author of this verse means to say that, if this Gospel is all of it the truth (ver. 24), it is not the *whole* truth. And in speaking thus, the object of his enthusiasm is evidently not the apostle and his writing, but the Master and His work. A complete evangelic narrative is, in his view, a task which cannot be realized by reason of the boundlessness of its subject. He expresses this just and profound sentiment by means of a somewhat strange Oriental hyperbole, such as we find constantly in the letters of Ignatius, but taking care to weaken it by the words : *I think*. It is, indeed, that the infinite inevitably goes beyond the finite, and that the category of the *spirit* is always absolutely superior to that of *space*. Let writings be added to writings to describe " the glory of the only begotten Son of God, full of grace and truth," one of two things must follow : either this series of writings will not exhaust the subject, or, if they exhaust it, they will not be contained in the world !

From this study of the twenty-first chapter we conclude : 1. That the story, vv. 1-23, comes, if not from the hand, at least from the oral narration of the author of the Gospel ; 2. That ver. 24 is an attestation emanating from the friends who surrounded him and who, after having called forth the composition of his work, had received it from him in trust to publish it at the fitting time ; 3. That ver. 25 proceeds from the hand of the one among them who had drawn up the postscript, ver. 24, in the name of all ; 4. That the addition of this solemn attestation (vv. 24, 25) was made, also, during the lifetime of the apostle.—After this, it only remains to hold : either that John is the author and the redactor of our Gospel, as those who publish it testify, or that the anonymous author who composed it in the second century (after having presented himself to the world in this narrative with all the characteristics of the apostle) has carried his shamelessness so far as to cause to be given out by an accomplice of his fraud, or rather—for to such a man nothing is impossible—has himself given out, as if in the name of one or several of John's friends, a certificate of his identity with the apostle. If any one is willing to accept such a story, let him accept it. In our view, it contains its own refutation.

---

[1] Tischendorf : *Wann wurden unsere Evangelien verfasst*, p. 119.

1016 / Appendix

The work, the study of which we are closing, traces out the realization of an ideal which, as we have more than once observed, in order to be described must have been beheld, and in order to have been beheld, must have been lived. It is not an abstract description, like a character of La Bruyère ; it is a concrete picture, detailed, abounding in positive and precise facts, as well as in sayings original and full of appropriateness—a true human life which is like the transparency through which the divine life shines even upon us.—Every sincere heart will always feel itself as incapable of denying this ideal as it is powerless to create it.

ADDITIONAL NOTES BY THE AMERICAN EDITOR

1

John 6

1. IF the feast referred to in v. 1 was the feast of Purim (see Godet's note on that verse, part of p. 452 f., and note of Am. Ed., on p. 552 f.), the Passover alluded to in ver. 4 was the second one in the course of the public ministry of Jesus; comp. ii. 13 and xiii. i. The insertion of this reference to the feast is no doubt partly, if not wholly, for the purpose of marking the time. Although the chronological arrangement of the narrative is evidently not the primary object of the writer of this Gospel, there is a constant reference to the progress of time in the presentation of what Jesus says and does. If there be anything more here than the mere designation of the date, it may be questioned whether the explanation of Godet, or those of Luthardt, Keil, etc., which connect it with the thought and development of the following discourse, can be insisted upon. There seems, on the one hand, to be no sufficient reason for rejecting the view of Weiss, that the statement is added in connection with the gathering of the crowds; yet, on the other hand, the character of the discourse seems to bring it into a certain relation to the Passover. Godet's explanation has, perhaps, too much of refinement and elaboration.—2. The question why Jesus addressed Philip rather than some other member of the apostolic company is an idle one, and one which cannot be answered. The attempt of Luthardt to find here an indication that "deliberateness was the ruling feature of Philip's nature," can hardly be considered successful. As Weiss remarks, the fact that the author speaks of Philip as the one questioned points to a personal recollection of the scene on his part. But this is all that we can say with confidence. A later writer, composing the history according to his own will and for a doctrinal purpose, would not have inserted such a detail as this, or that which follows respecting Andrew, in the story which he derived from the Synoptics.—3. The details of the story, so far as the multiplying of the loaves, the arrangement and number of the people, and the gathering up of the fragments are concerned, are the same with those in the earlier Gospels. The differences in minor points may be explained either on the supposition of the presence of this writer at the time and the absence of the others (Mark, Luke), or of an intention on their part to relate the matter with less particularity.—4. Ver. 14 shows that John intended to present before his readers something more than the Synoptic writers had in mind. They give the facts of the story and add nothing further, but he records the miracle as a σημεῖον and the impression which, as such, it produced upon the minds of the people who saw it. The apostles were evidently present at this time. They saw the miracle, and we cannot doubt that it was also a

σημεῖον to their minds. Indeed, the declaration of Peter on behalf of them all, which we find at the end of this chapter, is no doubt to be connected, in some special sense, with the impression received from this miracle and the one which immediately followed, vv. 16-21. The two miracles were, accordingly, a part of the progressive proof which confirmed and strengthened the faith of the disciples.—5. The character of the miracle of the loaves corresponds with that of changing the water into wine, in the fact that superabundant provision was made for all, and that creative power was exhibited in both—here in multiplying the loaves, and there in making a new material. There was a difference, however, in the two cases : in the first place, the immense number whose wants were supplied gave a certain greatness to the work which increased the impression of it, and, secondly, the relation of it to those who were filled and who came again to Jesus on the following morning, suggested thoughts which belonged in the central region of the Christian truth. That this miracle, like the one in ch. v., is recorded mainly for the purpose of the discourse which was connected with it, cannot be doubted. In this respect, it went beyond the one at Cana. That miracle had apparently brought to the minds of the disciples the knowledge of the power of Jesus, but had given them little, if indeed any, teaching as to His truth. At that time, indeed, they needed especially the evidence which His power, in itself alone, could give. But now they had been with Him for a year, and the miracles were wrought especially for the teaching. —As bearing upon the truth which He taught, however, and as thus related to the miracle of ch. v., the story and discourse of this chapter are in the true order of progress. The discourse of ch. v. set before them the relation of Jesus to the Father, and thus the divinity of His nature ; that of ch. vi. brings to their minds the relation of this divine Son, who had come into the world as the messenger of the Father, to the life of their souls ; the necessity to the eternal life of feeding upon Him. The thought of this sixth chapter is one which could not have been fully comprehended at the moment ; but it was one which, once finding its way into their minds, must become a seed thought for all their future course, and one which would be, in its suggestions, an ever-growing testimony to the fact that Jesus was the Son of God. We see, therefore, that, so far from mere repetition, there is intentional and natural progress here, as there has been up to this point. The writer does not reach the end at the beginning, as has been claimed, but moves forward with a definite and progressive plan of proof, which bore its fruits in a growing life in the hearts of those who received into themselves its legitimate influence.

2

Vv. 16-21 contain the account of the second miracle mentioned in this chapter. This miracle is inserted between the first miracle and the discourse which followed on the next day. If the narrative is viewed simply in the light of biography, the reason why the event is placed here is obvious ; it is placed where it belongs in the order of time. But if we look at the plan of the book as related to the purpose stated in xx. 30, 31, it is worthy

Additional Notes on John 6 / 1019

of notice that this chapter presents two developments of faith. The multitude, who were impressed by the miracle of the loaves, declared their conviction that Jesus was the Messiah. They accordingly believed; but the course which they pursued the next day, and the effect upon their minds of His presentation of the necessity of living in and upon Him (see vv. 60, 66), prove that their faith was like that of those who are mentioned in ii. 23–25. The apostles, on the other hand, are not only described as having a faith of a higher order than that of these half-way disciples, but are represented as giving utterance to a more confident and established belief than they had expressed at any previous moment (vv. 68, 69). Is it not probable that the second miracle, following upon the first—a miracle which was so peculiarly fitted to produce a deep impression, both in itself and in the circumstances attendant upon it—was an essential element in this new development of the apostles' faith? May we not account for the upward movement of their belief, as contrasted with the downward movement in that of the many who went back, as connected partly with this second wonderful fact? Certainly the fact that it followed so immediately after the miracle of the loaves was calculated to make them ready and able to say, not only: We have believed, but: We have believed and *know* that Thou art the Holy One of God. The insertion of this miracle, therefore, as well as the other, falls most naturally within the line of the writer's great purpose. The reader who will place himself in thought in the circumstances in which the apostles were at the time, and will open his mind, as they did, to the reception of the evidences, cannot fail to see how their faith grew stronger, or to feel that his own faith is growing stronger under the same influence. The signs which were given in the presence of the disciples, says the author, are written in his book that the reader may, by following the record of them, be led forward in the same progress of faith.

In the account of this second miracle which is given by Matthew, xiv. 33, the apostles in the boat are represented as saying, as they witnessed it, "Of a truth Thou art the Son of God." If this is the record of what they actually said at this moment, it may suggest, in connection with John ver. 14, the likeness and also the difference between the belief of the multitude and that of the Twelve. If, on the other hand, as may not improbably be the fact, Matthew, in his more brief narrative of the whole occasion, places at this point what, in the succession of the events, was really said by Peter in the name of the apostles at the time indicated by John in ver. 69, we have a suggestion in Matthew's narrative of that which is represented by John as the result of the miracles and the discourse taken together.

May not the words of Mark (vi. 51, 52), who says that the apostles were exceedingly amazed when Jesus entered the boat and the wind ceased, but that they did not understand concerning the loaves, suggest that the full conviction indicated in Matt. xiv. 33 came only after the discourse, as indicated in John ver. 69?

The difficulty connected with the words ἤθελον and εὐθέως is to be recognized. In the story as given by Mark and Matthew, Jesus seems to be represented as entering the boat (in Matthew, with Peter, who had gone to meet Him on the sea), and the boat seems to have moved gradually towards the shore, only over calm waters. In John's account, on the other hand, the impression which the reader would naturally get from the verb ἤθελον is that Jesus did not enter the boat, and εὐθέως would imply that the boat reached the shore immediately. The explanation given by Godet is a possible one, but can hardly be considered altogether satisfactory. It is to be observed, however, that in brief stories such as we find in the Gospels, which are told by all the writers for a purpose which is beyond the mere details considered in themselves, differences of this sort are not unnatural—differences which may not be altogether explicable at a distance of centuries from the date of writing, but with reference to which, even now, we may see possibilities capable of removing them. The New Testament narratives, in this regard, may fairly claim to be treated by opposing critics with as calm a consideration of all these possibilities as should be given in the case of other histories. The harmonists and the critics alike have sometimes been disposed to demand too much of the Gospel writers in this regard.

3

Vv. 22–24. The main idea of these verses is sufficiently clear, but there is an irregularity in the sentence which it is, perhaps, impossible to explain with entire success. The simplest construction seems to be that which Godet, R. V., etc., give, and which makes ver. 23 a parenthesis. But this construction does not fully clear away the difficulties, for, if the reading εἶδον or εἶδεν is adopted in ver. 22, that verse states a fact to which nothing is added by a regular construction which may answer to it and complete the statement; or if, on the other hand, ἰδών is taken as the text, it would seem that the sentence ought to read, When the multitude (ver. 24), who had seen that there was only one boat there, etc. (ver. 22), saw that Jesus was not there (ver. 24), they got into the boats which had come from Tiberias since the preceding evening, and crossed over (ver. 24). The reason for the peculiar arrangement of the sentence may, not improbably, be this—that the writer desired to picture the state of mind of the multitude just as it changed, from the beginning of the scene to the end. They first noticed the facts which would naturally lead them to conclude that Jesus was still on the eastern side of the lake; then, that boats had come from the other side in the late evening or early morning; then they thought that, as the disciples had not returned and Jesus was nowhere to be seen, it might be that He had followed them to the western side; then, that, by availing themselves of the newly-arrived boats, they might find Him again and thus successfully accomplish what they desired. The broken sentence gives thus a picture, not other than life-like, of the succession of thoughts or suggestions under such circumstances. It is, at the most, a sacrifice of grammatical regularity for the higher end of vivid description. It is, also, that sort of vivid description which points to a living knowledge of the facts on the part of the writer.

4

Vv. 25–40. 1. The abruptness in the turn of thought from the question of the people to the answer of Jesus may indicate an omission of some intermediate words in the report of the conversation. These words, however, must have revealed to the mind of Jesus that their thoughts were moving in the sphere of earthly curiosity and earthly desire, and so, as everywhere in this Gospel (and to some extent the same thing is noticeable in the earlier gospels), He turns them away at once from the earthly to the spiritual things.—2. Ver. 26 does not seem to intimate that they came to Jesus now for the purpose of having food provided for them again, as it had been on the day before, but that, in view of the fact that they had had such provision for temporal wants in one line, they hoped to find in Jesus one who would, as the great prophet, bring them the blessings which might belong to a temporal and earthly kingdom. They saw the miracle of the preceding day and were impressed by it. They said, Of a truth this is the prophet. But they did not see in it a true $\sigma\eta\mu\varepsilon\tilde{\iota}ov$, in the sense in which Jesus intended it. They did not have the faith which took hold of the inner life. Hence they asked (ver. 30) for a sign, when He called for this faith, as if no sign had been already given.—3. Faith is presented in this passage as an $\xi\rho\gamma ov$, and as the one comprehensive $\xi\rho\gamma ov$. But this seems to be rather incidental to the form of the sentence than indicative of a doctrine of faith as a work. As they called on Him to tell them what they must do in working for the meat which abides to eternal life, He tells them that the sum of what they have to do is gathered up into believing in Him. But this believing is set forth in the following discourse as involving the closest union with Jesus, the feeding upon him, and thus it is represented as a working and transforming power renewing the whole life of the soul.—4. In the demand which they make for a new sign it is probable that the miracle wrought on the preceding day may have led them to refer to the manna, rather than any other wonderful manifestation in the Old Testament history. Not a mere provision for a day, like that which He had just given, but something great and continuous, such as had come through Moses, might reasonably, as they thought, be asked for, before they should accept Him as one on whom eternal life for themselves should so wholly depend.—5. The progress of thought from ver. 32 to ver. 35 is as follows : Jesus first denies that the bread which answers to the true idea of bread which He now has in mind ($\dot{a}\lambda\eta\theta\iota\nu\dot{o}\nu$) was given by Moses, and affirms that it is given by God (ver. 32) ; secondly, He gives the proof of the affirmative statement—it is God who gives the true bread, because the bread of God is that which descends and gives life to the world, and that which thus gives life can alone be the $\dot{a}\lambda\eta\theta\iota\nu\dot{o}\varsigma$ $\check{a}\rho\tau o\varsigma$ (ver. 33) ; thirdly, He declares that He is Himself this bread (ver. 35). The construction of ver. 33 is in accordance with the order of the words, $\check{a}\rho\tau o\varsigma$ being the subject and $\dot{o}$ $\kappa a\tau a\beta.$ $\kappa.\tau.\lambda.$ the predicate. The fact that God's bread is that which gives life is the proof that not Moses, but God, gives the ideal bread. The emphasis of the last clause of ver. 33 is especially on the words $\zeta\omega\grave{\eta}\nu$ $\delta\iota\delta o\grave{\upsilon}\varsigma$

τῷ κόσμῳ. The ideal bread must be the life-giving bread. The close connection between ver. 35 and ver. 33 seems to show that the genitive ζωῆς is to be explained as equivalent to διδοὺς ζωήν.—6. The reference in the word εἶπον of ver. 36 is supposed by Weiss, Keil, Milligan and Moulton, among the most recent commentators, to be to the words of ver. 26. Westcott says : "The thought is contained in ver. 26, and the reference may be to those words ; but more probably the reference is to other words like them, spoken at some earlier time." The general character and plan of John's Gospel makes it probable that in such cases there is an allusion to something which he has himself recorded, and, if this be the fact in this case, the reference to ver. 26 is somewhat more probable than that to v. 37 ff.— 7. The emphasis in ver. 37 ff. is on the word πᾶν. It is, therefore, the universality of the blessing with reference to those who believe, rather than the question of Divine election as limiting it only to them, which is here in mind.—8. Vv. 37–40 are closely connected in thought with ver. 35. As Christ is the life-giving bread, the one who comes to Him and believes on Him will never hunger or thirst (ver. 35), because every such person is a gift to Christ according to the will of the Father, and this will is that the gift, when once made, should never be lost. Four points may be noticed here :—(*a*) The emphasis which is laid on the absolute security of the continuous and ever-enduring blessing. (*b*) The foundation of this security in the fact that Christ's mission to earth is to do the Father's will—there can be no selfish or arbitrary action on His part, therefore, with reference to those who come to Him by the Father's gift. (*c*) The gift of the Father is immediately united with the existence of faith in the one who comes to Christ (comp. vv. 39, 40 in their parallelism, and the relation of the latter to the former through the particle γάρ) ; the Father draws (ver. 44), and the susceptible soul comes with faith by reason of the drawing influence. (*d*) The experience of those who thus come is set forth from the beginning to the end—first, they are none of them rejected when they come ; secondly, they are none of them lost afterwards, but are all kept safely ; thirdly, they have eternal life from the moment of believing, and it is in this life that they are kept ; fourthly, the consummation at the end is the resurrection. The whole is a development of life, in the carrying out of the Divine will by Christ, which naturally and necessarily moves forward to its completeness.—9. The connection of ἔχῃ ζωὴν αἰώνιον (ver. 40) with μὴ ἀπολέσω (ver. 39) points to the idea of duration in αἰώνιον (the quantitative idea) ; the contrast of the ἔχῃ and ἀναστήσω, on the other hand, points to the present possession of the life, and thus to the qualitative idea. The two elements are united in the Johannean thought.

5

Vv. 41–51a. 1. The Jews mentioned in ver. 41 were probably persons who were present during the conversation with the ὄχλος, and in this sense a part of it ; but we may infer from the technical use of this expression that they formed only a part of the company, and were of a similar character to that of the leading adversaries of Jesus in Jerusalem, who are ordinarily designated by this title in the Fourth Gospel.—2. The opinion of Meyer seems to be correct, that ver. 42 conveys, rather than otherwise, the impression that Joseph, as well as Mary, were still alive at this time. As the design of the sentence, however, is found, not in itself, but in the words which follow in the closing part of the verse, no conclusion can be confidently drawn from it.—3. The general thought of this passage is similar to that of the verses which immediately precede—the non-receptivity of the unsusceptible soul, and the life which the susceptible soul receives through Christ. The following points, however, may be especially noticed : (*a*) The *giving* of the Father is here explained as a *drawing*—it is a Divine influence working upon the soul. (*b*) The soul, in connection with this drawing influence, hears the Father's voice and learns from Him. (*c*) As thus learning, the soul is ready to find in Christ the full revelation of the Father and of the life (the light-life in which there is no darkness), and thus to believe on Him. (*d*) Believing on Him and finding eternal life in Him, the soul recognizes in Him the bread which gives life and the bread which has life in itself (ὁ ἄρτος τῆς ζωῆς—ὁ ἄρτος ὁ ζῶν, vv. 48, 51), and, feeding upon this bread, it will find its life not ending in death, as was the case with those who ate the manna, but continuing forever.—4. The whole development of thought in this discourse, which bears upon the inner life of the soul, seems to show clearly that, in such verses as 44 and 37, the question is not of God's electing purpose, but of the inward susceptibility to Divine influence. And the same is true of other similar passages in this Gospel.

6

Vv. 51b–59. 1. In ver. 51b a new thought is presented—that the bread of which the discourse is speaking is the flesh of Christ. That the reference in these words is to the participation by faith in Christ as dying for the world's salvation, and not to the Lord's Supper, is proved, first, by the fact that union with Christ by faith is the main thought of the whole discourse ; secondly, by the fact that the life of the believer through Christ is placed in correspondence with that of Christ through the Father ; thirdly, by the entire subordination of the idea of the blood to that of the bread—the former comes in, apparently, only in an incidental way, and the thought returns to the bread alone in ver. 58. The blood has, therefore, no such relation to the bread here as the cup has to the bread in the Supper ; fourthly, because no similar representation of the participation in the Supper as related to the life of the soul is given elsewhere ; fifthly, because no allusion to the Supper is made in the Gospels, in any other place, until it was instituted, and its institution seems to have had such reference to the closing hours of Christ's life and to the future of the disciples after His death as to make an allusion to it beforehand improbable, and especially at this time and in the presence of an audience of this character. So far as we can judge, the apostles had no such understanding of its meaning and import, when it was instituted, as must have been the case, it would seem, if, as they heard this discourse or thought of it afterwards, they supposed it to refer to a physical eating or to any special rite. The purpose of the Lord's Supper is given by Paul in connection with the words of the institution of it, in 1 Cor. xi. 25, "This do in remembrance of me ;" it would be strange, indeed, if such a more complete unfolding of the idea should have been presented to a company of murmuring and unbelieving Galilean Jews. Weiss ed. Mey. says : "It cannot even be said that at least the same idea out of which the Lord's Supper sprang is here expressed (Olshausen, Kling, Tholuck, etc.; comp. Kahnis, Keim, Hengstenberg, Ewald, Godet), or that the appropriation of Christ's life, brought about by faith in His death, which is here demanded as absolutely necessary, forms also the sacred fundamental idea of the institution of the Supper and the condition of its blessedness, from which the application of the passage to the Lord's Supper (but also at the same time to baptism and the efficacy of the word) necessarily arises (Meyer, with a reference to Harless, p. 130 ff.), but, at the most, that a like symbolism to that which is here used lies at the basis of the institution of the Supper." This statement is to be regarded as containing (as Weiss remarks) the most that can properly be said.—The difficulty which is suggested by Godet on page 40, that Jesus, instead of explaining His spiritual conception (if the view above given is adopted), only adds "an expression which is more and more paradoxical, material, and, consequently, unintelligible to His interlocutors," seems to the writer of this note to have no real foundation. It was not the design of Jesus, in these spiritual discourses with His adversaries, to make explanations on the low level of their thought, but rather by repeating His ideas in their boldest and loftiest form to challenge their minds to wrestle with them. He wished to force them to see how far removed they were from the life of which He was speaking, by the very difficulty they found in comprehending the terms in which it was described. He would compel disciples and enemies alike to think, and would give them words and truths which might become seeds for future growth, for the very reason that they were, at the beginning, hard to be understood.

7

Vv. 60–65. The very difficulty in the way of understanding, which has just been referred to, caused the division between the temporary and permanent disciples—the true and the false ones—which needed to be made. The temporary and false ones went back because of the hard saying. The principal question connected with these verses is that of ver. 62. With reference to this question the following points may be noticed : (*a*) If λόγος of ver. 60 refers, as the connection would seem to show that it does, to what had been said about eating His flesh, etc., the point now in mind must be the same : If you are offended by this which I have said, how will it be if, etc.—(*b*) The words "ascending where I was before" are most naturally contrasted with His present condition, and thus refer to the time of and after His ascension.—(*c*) The 63d verse shows that the purpose of Jesus was to bring the minds of these professed disciples to interpret His words spiritually, and to see that His teaching and the life of which He spoke were wholly in the spiritual sphere.—(*d*) Vv. 64, 65 present again the absence of faith and of the divine drawing as the foundation of their whole difficulty.—In view of these considerations two conclusions may be drawn : (*x*) that the thought of ver. 62 is of a greater difficulty in the matter of comprehension, when He should have passed away from earth to heaven, rather than a less one ; and (*y*) that the cause of this greater difficulty would be the entire removal of the earthly and physical element. Like the discourse which precedes, therefore, these verses are intended to be a demand upon these hearers to rise into a higher sphere of thought, and place themselves face to face with the Divine truth.

8

Vv. 66–71. 1. The design of the discourse of this sixth chapter, so far as the apostles were concerned, was undoubtedly to strengthen their faith by calling their thoughts to the mystery of the union of the soul with Christ. We have in this chapter the two kinds of evidence, that of the works and that of the words. The dependence of the latter on the former, and the higher character of the latter, are strikingly exhibited here. In this regard the chapter is a central one of this Gospel.—2. The evangelist gives in vv. 68, 69 a new declaration of the apostles' faith. Peter and his associates did not fully understand the words of Jesus, but, in connection with the growth of their love and faith in the progress of their life with Him until now, they found in them no "hard saying," as the others did, but only a new utterance of truth which was to be received and studied in the time to come. They believed that He was the Holy One of God, and that He had the words of eternal life, and so, in the presence of these profound thoughts and sayings, they were ready to listen and wait for greater light. It cannot be supposed that, at the time of the first miracle at Cana, their minds could have opened at all to such sayings. There had been a steady and continuous development since then.—3. As related to the evidence for the truth that Jesus is the Christ, the Son of God (xx. 31), this chapter carries the reader's thought into the region of His life-giving power—the inward union of His life with that of the believer as essential to the eternal life of the soul—more fully than the chapters which precede. There is no mere repetition of what goes before, but a suggestion of a new thought, and of a thought which belongs here in the natural order of the growth of the apostles' own inner life and of the proof of the truth for other minds. The Holy One of God as the source of eternal life—the words of Peter's confession—contain the thought of the discourse and the belief of the Twelve as it was now moving forward.—4. The explanation of the difficulties connected with the choice of Judas is to be found in the fact that Jesus acted in accordance with the providential plan of the world's life. We carry back the difficulty thus to the region of the Divine counsels, and there it is only to be placed with the mysteries of other human lives. The case of Judas was a remarkable one, because of the conspicuous position

1026 / Additional Notes

which his betrayal of Jesus gave him. But the wonder of all living, as related to moral discipline, losses and victories, is beyond the limit of our earthly vision.

9

John 7

Vv. 1–13. 1. The history now moves forward over a period of six months to the Feast of Tabernacles in October. Nothing can be more manifest than the combination in this Gospel of the two elements, as we may call them, of biographical order and the selection of material for another than a biographical end. A full recognition of this fact is necessary in order to a candid and judicial examination of many of the difficulties in this Gospel, which are suggested by those who doubt its apostolic authorship or its truthfulness.—2. The true explanation of the demand of the brethren seems to be this: that they wished Him to go to Jerusalem, as the proper place for the assuming publicly of His Messianic office. If He was unwilling to do this, it must be that He was conscious of the weakness of His claims. By this demand they would test Him, and they thought He was failing to meet it. The attitude of the brethren does not seem to have been like that of the leading Jews, one of bitter hostility. The fact that they came to believe so soon after the resurrection of Jesus (Acts i. 14) seems to show that they were less "slow of heart to believe." In Mark iii. 21 they appear to be desirous of protecting Him from harm, as one carried away by enthusiasm under a delusion, rather than ready to deliver Him to the hands of His enemies. But they were not prepared to believe, even at this time, when His public ministry was within six months of its ending. Perhaps the very fact of His delay in making Himself known in the manifest and prominent way of which they had thought in their picturing of the Messiah's advent, was a main ground of their doubt and hesitation. They were impatient to have this doubt removed, if it could be. They were not ready to believe, until it was removed.—3. The word καιρός, vv. 6, 8, may be regarded as kindred in its use to ὥρα, and thus as referring here, when used of Jesus, to the time of His great manifestation of Himself as the Messiah. This view, which is substantially that of Godet, gives the simplest explanation of these verses. What they desired was not merely that He should go to Jerusalem, as an ordinary Jew would go, for the celebration of the feast, but that He should go for the purpose of this public manifestation. That this is the correct view is shown (a) by the ἵνα clause of ver. 3; (b) by the expressions *openly*, as opposed to *in secret*, and *manifest thyself to the world* (ver. 4), comp. *not openly* (ver. 10); (c) by the fact that the hatred of the world is given as the reason why the time must be delayed (ver. 7); (d) by the satisfactory explanation which it gives of the *I go not up* (οὐκ) of ver. 8 (which is more probably the correct text), as connected with the *he went up* of ver. 10; (e) by the accordance of this passage, if thus explained, with the plan and character of John's Gospel. It thus becomes not a mere biographical item of little importance for any further purpose, but a part of the great progress towards the end which this writer carefully follows in his work.—4. Vv. 12, 13 present strikingly the position both of the people and the leaders at this time. It is evident from this Gospel that the Jewish rulers and leading enemies of Jesus moved slowly in the development of their plans against Him. As yet, they had not made public the course which they intended finally to take. Even their own partisans among the people were, apparently, uncertain whether they might not suddenly change to a more favorable attitude. The position of the rulers was, throughout the whole course of the history, a difficult one. They could not, with safety, move too slowly, for the impression made by Jesus on the minds of the people was becoming more and more favorable, and might, at any moment, cause a dangerous excitement or uprising. They could not move too rapidly, for they must have some foundation for severe measures, which should be in some degree satisfactory to the public judgment. The result was, that, for a considerable period after their own feelings were settled in hostility, and probably after their plans were formed with somewhat of definiteness, they still kept the announcement of their purpose from the people. The life-like way in which the course of the rulers is described in this Gospel, from the beginning to the end, is one of the strong indications that the author was himself acquainted with the characters of those of whom he wrote. As he looked back over the remembered experience, from the standpoint of his later life, when he had come to understand all the events from the side of the Divine plan, he felt, and accordingly he declares, that the rulers' failure to carry out their purpose was because *Jesus' hour* had not yet come. But it is evident that he knew equally well, and that he would have his readers know, that the reason of their delay was the feeling in their own minds that *their hour* had not yet arrived. They were waiting for that hour, and even at the end they moved forward to the final act, not because the time seemed fully ripe, but because it seemed impossible to delay any longer.—The verses now before us belong to the time of deliberation and waiting. They were seeking for grounds of decisive action. They were ready to seize upon every occasion for violent dispute. They were sometimes carried away by indignation, and almost prepared to lay hands upon Him (comp. e.g. ver. 30). But this was the sudden outbreak of passion ; when reason resumed control, they restrained themselves and waited for a more favorable moment.

10

Vv. 14–24. 1. There is, apparently, an abrupt turn in the narrative at ver. 14, if we look only at the outward form of the story. But, when the following verses are closely studied, it seems almost certain that there is a connection with ch. v. and the opposition excited by His work of healing on the Sabbath, which is there mentioned. May it not be, therefore, that the question of ver. 15 is, not merely one of wonder at the character of His teaching, but one expressing their sense of the impropriety of His setting Himself up to be a teacher, and in His teachings even to override the Mosaic law, as shown by His willingness to violate the Sabbatic ordinance ? If this view is taken, the movement of the thought towards ver. 19 ff. is more easily explained.—2. In the answer of Jesus, ver. 16 ff., the following points are worthy of notice : (*a*) The origin of His teaching, though not found in their schools, is such as may well give Him the knowledge which surprises them. He has learned directly from God. (*b*) The evidence of this is found in the fact that the moral teacher who speaks from himself will manifest a self-seeking spirit. As He, on the other hand, is only seeking the glory of the one who sends Him forth as a teacher, it must be that He is not an impostor or merely self-moved. (*c*) The question as to whether this one who sends Him is God, and whether the teaching is God's teaching, is one which any man can decide by placing himself in the right attitude towards God. The way to the light in the sphere of religion is through the will—the willingness to do the will of God.—3. The words ἀληθής and ἀδικία, united by καί in ver. 18, suggest the connection between this passage concerning the teaching and the following verses, which carry back the thought to ch. v. We may thus explain what seems to be a sudden change of subject at the beginning of ver. 19.—4. The central point of vv. 19–23 is apparently in ver. 21 : ἓν ἔργον κ.τ.λ. This *one work* evidently means the miracle of ch. v., and it is with reference to this that the allusion to the law of Moses is introduced.—5. Ver. 20 (comp. viii. 48, x. 20) brings before us the only kind of reference which John makes in his Gospel to demoniacal possession, if indeed this can be properly called such. The absence of instances of such cases of possession in this Gospel has been made an argument against their reality. But such an argument cannot be insisted upon, because John writes so manifestly on a plan of selection that his omissions or insertions may be owing to reasons which we cannot now fully understand, and also because his allusions to miracles are connected with the growth of faith in the disciples, and, especially, with the inner life of the soul.—6. If we could omit διὰ τοῦτο, with Tisch., 8th ed., on the authority of the Sinaitic MS., we should escape a difficulty. But the external evidence appears to be so strong in favor of the insertion of the words that they must be received. If regarded as belonging to the text, they are probably to be connected with θαυμάζετε of ver. 21. Westcott says the usage of John is decisive against this, but it must be noticed that there is no case in John's writings which is parallel with this one, and that there are weighty reasons on the other side, such as the strong and appropriate emphasis secured by this connection of the words and the difficulties which are involved in uniting them with ver. 22. The explanation of Godet, which is similar to that of Westcott, and of Milligan and Moulton, is perhaps the best which can be offered, if the latter connection is assumed. But—apart from any improbability that Moses would be represented as introducing the provision alluded to for the purpose of teaching them to judge rightly on the matter now in question—if Jesus had intended to make such a representation, the sentence, it would seem, would have been arranged differently. As the verses stand, the argument proceeds simply and naturally from ver. 22 to ver. 23, if these words are unconnected with ver. 22. The argument is : Moses' law, through one of its provisions, involves a violation of the Sabbath ordinance ; if this is so, why be angry with me for a similar violation ? The union of διὰ τοῦτο with ver. 22 complicates and obscures the thought. Tregelles, R. V. marg. and A. R. V. connect these words with ver. 21 ; Westcott and Hort and R. V. text with ver. 22. —7. Ver 24, if διὰ τοῦτο belongs with ver. 22 and is explained as Godet proposes, brings out a thought which is already foreshadowed by those words. If, on the other hand, the phrase is attached to ver. 21, ver. 24 is an added exhortation, naturally suggested but not previously indicated. This verse will have no bearing on the question of the connection of διὰ τοῦτο, for it can be explained satisfactorily on either view respecting that question.

11

Vv. 25-36. 1. The Ἱεροσολυμεῖται are evidently a different class from the ὄχλος, and are more fully acquainted with the desires of the rulers ; but even they are left in some doubt and perplexity. That the supposed designs are not carried out is a matter of surprise to them, so that they even ask doubtingly whether it can be that the rulers, after all, recognize that Jesus is the Christ. This accurate description of the state of mind of all parties is what a later writer, of the introvertive character of this author, would have been little disposed to think of or to give. It comes into the narrative, from time to time, incidentally, and testifies of the eye and ear witness.—2. In ver. 28 Jesus acknowledges what they claim as to their knowledge of His origin, but affirms that He has a different origin which they do not understand. He thus, in reality, meets the difficulty in their minds, and shows that He can be the Christ whose origin is unknown, notwithstanding the fact that they know whence He is. This explanation, notwithstanding what Godet says in opposition to it, seems to be the most simple one and meets the demands of the passage.—3. The words *I am from Him*, of ver. 29, may, not improbably, imply a *community of essence* between Jesus and God, as Godet holds ; but whether it can be positively affirmed that it must have this meaning, and cannot be in a parallelism of meaning with *He has sent me*, may be questioned. Meyer holds, with Godet, that the clause *He has sent me* is not dependent on ὅτι. Weiss ed. Mey. holds the same view. There seems to be no difficulty in adopting either construction, but, if the latter clause is independent, the argument for Godet's view of the meaning of the former clause becomes stronger.—4. The reference in ver. 34, *You shall seek me and not find me*, etc., must, it would seem, be to a seeking for the Messiah as connected with the securing of the life and blessedness of the Messianic kingdom. This verse can hardly be unconnected in thought with viii. 21, where *dying in their sins* takes the place of the words *not find me*, of this verse. The thought is apparently, therefore, that, after rejecting Him and after His death, they would, in their continual seeking after the Messiah— which He truly was—continually fail, and so they would die in their sins and be separated from Him and His kingdom. The reference to the Divine judgments in the destruction of Jerusalem, which Meyer gives, is not suggested by the passage, and is too limited for the general character of the expression. Weiss is correct, also, in denying the position taken by Meyer, that the explanation given above is inconsistent with the distinct personal reference, and "empties the words of their tragic nerve and force." The force, says Weiss, properly, "lies in the fact that in their seeking after a Messiah they will, without being themselves conscious of it, be seeking after Him who is the only true Messiah, but is then forever separated from them."

12

Vv. 37–52. 1. The explanation given by Godet of the reference to the living water in ver. 37 and the light in viii. 12 as connected with the two great Divine gifts to the Israelites in their life in the wilderness, which was commemorated in this feast, seems to the writer of this note to be the best one which has been offered. At the end of the feast, and when all minds were naturally turned toward the experiences in the desert, it was natural that Jesus should represent Himself and the new life under these figures, as He had done under the figure of the water of the well, at Sychar, and of the bread, in the sixth chapter.—2. The remark of the evangelist in ver. 39, though not having precisely the same form as those in ii. 21, 22, etc., may not improbably be regarded as, like them, indicating an understanding of the meaning of Jesus' words which was obtained only after His ascension. The last clause of the verse declares simply what was the fact with regard to the coming of the Spirit. It does not affirm any absolute necessity in the case. If the Divine plan, however, was to reveal the truth at first by the incarnation of the Logos in the person of a man, with the necessary limitations of a single human life, we can easily understand how the wider and greater spiritual influence should have been introduced only after the glorification of Jesus.— 3. The interruption on the part of the people breaks off this discourse, and hence we are unable to determine as confidently as might otherwise be the case what the precise meaning of ver. 38 is. But there is evidently an advance here beyond the thought of iv. 14. In that passage, it is the internal life of the believer which is referred to, but here the outgoing of this internal life in its blessing influence for others is set forth. This working of the interior life outward was, of course, dependent for its fulness on the greater outpouring of the Spirit which began with the Day of Pentecost. It was to be one means by which that glorification of Jesus on earth was to be accomplished, which is alluded to in xii. 23 and xvii. 1, and which was to be connected with and follow upon His glorification in heaven.—4. With reference to vv. 41, 42 two points may be noticed : (*a*) that the supposition on the part of the people here spoken of, that Jesus came from Galilee, may easily be explained in connection with the fact that His life had been passed there almost from its very beginning, and (*b*) that John does not state his own view, but theirs. The conclusion that he did not know of the birth of Jesus at Bethlehem is simply an inference drawn from the fact that he does not insert here a correction of this error. But his object in the narrative is clearly to give the accurate statement of the condition and progress of opinion in the minds of the people and their rulers, and not to show how far that opinion was correct or incorrect. The critics everywhere demand that the evangelist should follow a plan in accordance with their own preconceived ideas, but he was writing from a different standpoint and with a different purpose.—5. The conduct of Nicodemus here is certainly far from that moral cowardice which has been so generally charged upon him because he came to Jesus at first by night. It is worthy of remark that the oldest and best authorities mostly omit the word νυκτός here. The author makes no reference in this passage, therefore, to his coming by night. But, whether he alludes to this fact or not, he does not give any indication of any disapproval of his course.—6. The last clause of ver. 52 may be best explained by supposing that the persons opposing Nicodemus were not speaking of ordinary prophets, but of a great prophet, like ὁ προφήτης of ver. 40, or the Christ. Galilee was not the region, they thought, from which such a prophet could be expected to come. If this was their meaning, the difficulty supposed to arise from the case of Jonah is removed.

13

Vii. 53—viii. 11. In addition to the remarks of Godet in his full and able discussion of this passage, the writer of these notes would say only a few words. The recent English commentator, J. B. McClellan (The New Testament, a new translation, etc., etc., Vol. I. The Gospels, London, 1875), takes very strong ground in favor of the genuineness of the passage, and, as one of the latest presentations of that side of the question, the reader may be referred to his work. The external argument here will depend largely for its force on the weight which is given to the oldest manuscripts. The comparatively small school among critics to which McClellan and Dean Burgon belong depreciate the value of ℵ and B, and, in this case, the former dismisses them with the remark : "We are entitled—nay, we are *bound* entirely to throw out ℵ B, as already discredited and worthless witnesses in a matter of this kind, in consequence of their ignorant or criminal omission of Mark xvi. 9-20." If these and the other oldest MSS. are to be allowed a place worthy of respect in the matter of testimony, there can be but little doubt that the external evidence is decidedly against the genuineness of the passage as a part of John's Gospel. As for the internal argument, the following remarks, it is believed, are justified : (*a*) The progress of thought from vii. 37 to viii. 12 is so natural, especially if Godet's explanation of the rivers of living water and the light is correct, that the connection of the two verses in the same discourse is antecedently probable. The passage in question seems to break the unity.—(*b*) It can scarcely be questioned that there is a Synoptical, rather than a Johannean, character in this story, its language and style. No similar phenomenon of so remarkable a character is found in this Gospel.—(*c*) The peculiarities of expression, and particularly the use of δέ instead of οὖν, are points not easily reconciled with the Johannean authorship. McClellan says, indeed, with regard to δέ, that John uses it nearly as often as οὖν (the former about 204 times and the latter 206 times). He also calls attention to the fact that in chs. i., iii. 1-24, xiv., etc. the particle οὖν is not used at all. The question in such cases is not to be determined by mere numbers, but by careful examination of the several instances which are alleged. The absence of the particle in chs. i., xiv., etc., is connected with the paratactic construction which is so characteristic of

John in passages like these, and hence such passages have no bearing on the question now under consideration. As to the other point, the exclusive use of δέ in this passage, as contrasted with that of οὖν, or οὖν and δέ together, in the preceding and following context, is a matter which cannot fail to be noticed by the careful student. Nowhere else in the Gospel is such a use of δέ in a long passage to be found. If δέ is found at all, it is found in connection with οὖν, as in vii. 37–52.—When the great number of variants is considered, in connection with these peculiarities of expression, the internal evidence must be regarded, like the external, as pointing somewhat strongly towards the view that the verses are an interpolation. It must be added, that the story does not seem to fall, as naturally as do the other narratives of this Gospel in general, into the line of testimony and of the development of belief in the minds of the disciples. This point, however, which is also hinted at by Godet, cannot be insisted upon as by any means decisive. R. V. places this passage in brackets and separates it from the preceding and following verses, with an indication in the margin as to the facts in the case so far as the external evidence is concerned.

14

John 8

Vv. 12–20. 1. If the passage containing the story of the woman taken in adultery is omitted, ver. 12 follows soon after vii. 37, and contains what we may believe to have been the second point of the discourse, which would have been developed in both of its parts more fully, had it not been for the interruptions from the multitude and the Pharisees. The question by which Jesus is interrupted in these verses turns the discourse into a new line, and leads Him to speak of the testimony on which He rests. As to the consistency of what He says in ver. 14 with what is said in ver. 31, see Note 29 found on page 557. This fourteenth verse declares that, in the present case, although He testifies of Himself, His testimony is true, because He is the only man who has the knowledge on which reliable testimony can be founded. In connection with this statement, we must explain vv. 17, 18. In one sense, it seems evident that Jesus does not comply here with the demand of the Mosaic law to which He appeals. There is but one witness besides Himself. But the case is one which allows no more. The only two who can bear testimony are the two who know—and these two, by the necessity of the case, are the one sending and the one sent, for "no man has seen God at any time," i. 18. The only-begotten Son, therefore, having come in the flesh, must not only be the revealer of God, but He must also be the human witness for Himself. Indeed, the witness of God on His behalf must, in some measure, come through Him. While there is not, therefore, a fulfilment of the Mosaic requirement, in the letter of it, there is a full satisfaction of its spirit.—2. The expression, *You judge according to the flesh*, ver. 15, seems to be immediately connected with the words of ver. 14. As they are wholly unqualified for judging, through want of knowledge, they judge according to the fleshly standard. They look upon Him as a mere man like themselves. They judge apart from any connection with God. He, on the other hand, in case He passes judgment, does so in union with the Father, and hence His judgment answers to the true condition of things and the true idea. The peculiar form of the sentence : "I judge no one, and if I judge . . . I and the one who sent me," favors the view that there is a reference to a final and decisive judgment which is not made independently of God. In view of this fact, Jesus does not make it His work here on earth to judge any one, and if, on any occasion and in any subordinate sense, He does so, He still does it in accordance with the Father's mind. It seems evident that the last clause of ver. 15 and ver. 16 are parenthetical in their character, and that the thought moves on from vv. 14, 15a, as above explained, to ver. 17 f.—3. The question of the Pharisees in ver. 19 is a challenge to produce the evidence of the Father, of whom He speaks. We can scarcely suppose that, after all which Jesus had said in Jerusalem, these Jewish leaders could have doubted whom He meant by His Father, or could have intended to imply a doubt. But they demanded the production of the evidence from the Father in some conspicuous way which might answer the demands of the law. They said, in substance, You cannot give us the proof from God. The second witness thus fails you. Where is your Father ? This seems to be the force of the interrogative particle ποῦ. They did not say τίς, for this was not the question which was in their minds.—4. In His answer, Jesus presents before them the incapacity which they have, in their present moral state, to appreciate the testimony of God, which comes with its full force only to the soul which has susceptibility to the truth. To know God, they must know Him who reveals Him. Thus we have a new declaration and testimony to the truth for which the Gospel was written.

15

Vv. 21–29. 1. Meyer holds that the words of ver. 21 f. were spoken on a different day from those of the preceding verses. Godet and others hold that it was the same day. Weiss (comp. Keil) regards the question as one which does not admit of a decisive answer. The position of Weiss is probably the correct one, but there seems to be no serious difficulty in supposing that all which is recorded in this chapter took place on one and the same day, the place only being changed at ver. 21.—2. In the words of Jesus contained in ver. 21 (comp. ver. 24) we find, in addition to what is said in the similar sentence in vii. 34. the words, *You will die in your sin* (*your sins*, ver. 24). As remarked in Note XI., 4, above, this clause seems to show that the seeking referred to is a seeking for the Messiah as connected with the securing of the life and blessings of the Messianic kingdom. With respect to these words two points may be noticed : (*a*) That the words are addressed by Jesus to those to whom He had already presented Himself as the Messiah, and in ver. 24 the result mentioned is connected with not believing that He is what He thus claims to be. (*b*) That dying in sin is apparently presented as a finality—a limit beyond which the hope of entrance into the kingdom is excluded. This passage must be regarded as one of the most impressive ones in the New Testament, as indicating the termination of the period of probation at the end of this life. With regard to the question whether it can be properly understood as indicating this only in the case of those who have the knowledge of Christ given them before death, it should be observed, in the first place, that everything which Jesus said was, of course, said to those who heard Him and thus knew of His claims ; secondly, that His general manner of teaching was that of addressing personally those who heard Him, and declaring to them the blessing or evil which awaited them, and not of giving doctrinal statements as appertaining to a theological system. The particular declarations of such a teacher are, in general, to be extended more widely from the individual example to mankind, than in the case of one who teaches in the other way. (c) Death is evidently referred to, in these words, as if it were the great deciding-point in human history as related to the matter of escape from the consequences of sin. (d) Jesus does not intimate anywhere else that the other (Gentile) nations will, unlike the Jews, have an opportunity of entering the Messianic kingdom after death. The indications of any such view on the part of the apostolic writers are also, to say the most that can be said, very few and very uncertain. (e) The knowledge of Jesus as the Messiah and of the Christian system which the Jewish hearers of Jesus, generally speaking, can be said to have had—when the contradiction of all their preconceived notions is considered : His refusal to assume earthly power, His obscure origin, His new idea of righteousness, His view of the Messianic kingdom, almost incomprehensible to their earthly mindedness, educated as they were under the influence of the Pharisaic teachers—was, in reality, so little developed, that it is difficult to say how far allowances may not properly have been made for their ignorance, after a similar manner with those which it is thought must be made for the heathen.—It is an assumption, which requires proof, that, when Christ and the apostles carried the Christian message to the men whom they chanced to meet, they placed them in an entirely new position, so far as the limiting of the probation is concerned. The proof needed is, to say the least, neither abundant nor decisive.—3. The words of ver. 23 seem to give the real ground of their continuance in sin and dying in it at the end. It was because they are from the things below and from this world. This was the reason why, when Jesus was presented before them as the Messiah, and as the way, the truth and the life, they did not believe in Him. The antecedent thing lying back of their unbelief was the state of their hearts and will. The refusal to believe, when He came to them, was only the outcome of this. It would seem, therefore, that the true view of the declaration of Jesus here is to be reached by taking the verses together. The man who is in the state of heart and will in which these Jews were, whoever or wherever he may be, will, if he remains in it, die in his sins, and dying thus will not be able to go to the place where Jesus is—that is to say, will not have the blessedness of the eternal life in heaven.—4. Weiss agrees with Godet in making ἐκ τῶν κάτω—ἄνω refer to the opposition of nature—i.e., origin, and ἐκ τοῦ κόσμου κ.τ.λ. to the contrast of disposition and moral activity ; and this, though

Additional Notes on John 8 / 1035

not necessarily, is yet not improbably the correct view.—5. The two explanations of the difficult phrase τὴν ἀρχήν κ.τ.λ. (ver. 25) which are found in the text of R. V. and in the margin of A. R. V. are the most satisfactory which have been offered : "*Even that which I have also spoken unto you from the beginning,*" and "*Altogether that which I also speak unto you.*" The use of τὴν ἀρχήν in each of these two senses is justified by examples. In the former case, He declares that He is what He has been telling them even from the beginning of His public discoursing—that is, the Messiah, the one sent from God, the one who has seen God and come forth from God to bring the full revelation of Him to the world. In the other case, the meaning may perhaps be the same, except that the idea of *from the beginning* is not contained in the words ; or it may more probably be this : that the answer to the question will be found in the *words* of Jesus : "Fathom my *speech* and you will discern my *nature*" (see Godet's note).—6. The connection of ver. 26 is rather with ver. 25 than ver. 24. The prominent thought of this verse is in the last part of it. The verb λαλῶ, which occurs in vv. 25, 26, 28, seems to show a close connection in thought throughout these verses, and to favor the idea that in the discoursings of Jesus was to be found the truth with regard to Himself. It will be noticed that the λαλῶ of vv. 26, 28 refers to a speaking forth of what was given to Him by the Father to proclaim. This indicates that the λαλῶ of ver. 25 also has a similar reference—at least, that it represents Jesus, in answer to their question, as the one sent from God as a messenger and revealer. The whole context, therefore, is rather favorable than otherwise to the view given in A. R. V. marg.—that the meaning of ver. 25 is, *Altogether that which I also speak unto you.* The bearing of all this upon the meaning of ἐγώ εἰμι, of ver. 24, is towards the conclusion that the predicate of εἰμι is *he*—i.e., the one sent or the one from above, the Messiah—and that these words are not to be understood as meaning *I am*, in the sense of Deut. xxxii. 39.—7. In regard to ver. 27, the explanation given by Weiss, with whom Keil essentially agrees, or that given by Godet, may be adopted. That the hearers of Jesus must have generally, or oftentimes, connected the words which He spoke with God, cannot be questioned. But, considering the fact that His declarations and teachings were so widely removed from the preconceived ideas of the people, it is not surprising that at times they should have failed to understand His meaning, or that they should even have misunderstood, at one time, statements which were apparently no less clear than those which they partially comprehended at another. The representations of John as to these understandings and misunderstandings are seen to be life-like, so soon as we place ourselves in the real condition and circumstances of the time.—8. Ver. 28 refers to the time which follows the crucifixion and ascension. The declaration of this verse, *you will know,* etc., doubtless has its explanation in connection with the outpouring of the Spirit and the wider proclamation and triumph of the Gospel ; but the probability is that it indicates the beginning of what will be realized in its fulness only as time passes onward. But even now, in the present and intermediate period, before the realization of this future, the Father, He adds, is still with Him ; and whatever His enemies may do in rejecting Him, He is strong and victorious in the truth which He proclaims.—9. There is an evident unity of thought in this whole passage, and the closing words of ver. 29 present the opposite character of His state of mind and life to theirs, which will finally result in the fact that the place where He is to be will be closed to them.

16

Vv. 30–50. 1. Whether the words of Jesus contained in these verses were spoken on the same day as those which precede (Meyer) or on the following day (Godet)—Weiss says correctly that this point cannot be determined —there is apparently a close connection between the two passages. Many believed in consequence of what He had just said. Of these some were of the leading Jewish party, the Ἰουδαῖοι, but these latter were believers only in a sense corresponding with that indicated in ii. 23 ff. Jesus, therefore, takes up the thought of the preceding verses, and tells them that, in order to their being His disciples in the real sense of the word and their having a real knowledge of the truth, they must abide in His word—i.e., they must believe that He is the one sent from above, and must inwardly live in the sphere of those teachings which, having heard from God, He speaks to the world.—2. The peculiar additional idea, beyond the preceding, which characterizes these verses, is that of freedom. This idea becomes the starting-point of the conversation and discourse which follow. Whether it was designedly introduced as a test of the reality of their faith, or was incidental to the development of His thought respecting the truth which He revealed, cannot be determined. Possibly it was intended to connect His thought with the idea of freedom from the Roman dominion, which so greatly occupied the minds of the Jews at the time ; but all that can be confidently affirmed is, that the Jews here referred to understood it at first in the political sense.—3. The connection of the verses points strongly towards *the Jews who believed Him* as the subject of the verb *answered* in ver. 33. If this is the correct understanding of the writer's meaning, it must be inferred that their belief was of the most superficial character, and this case shows that the author uses the verb πιστεύειν even of the lowest degree of belief in Jesus. The different stages of development indicated by this word, in this Gospel, are very noticeable, and, when carefully observed, they throw light upon the author's plan.—4. The explanation of the words *We have never been in bondage to any one*, which is given by Godet, is favored by Weiss, and is perhaps the best one which can be given.—5. In ver. 37 Jesus addresses these persons as if they were seeking to kill Him. There is a difficulty in supposing that the believing Jews were now desiring to kill Him, but the Jewish party to which they belonged were undoubtedly forming their plans with this end in view. It is possible that He classes them with their party, not because He saw a feeling of this kind in their hearts at the moment, but because this was the feeling of those with whom they had acted, and He saw that they would return to a union with them when their superficial and temporary faith failed.—6. The contrast between

Additional Notes on John 8 / 1037

the readiness to receive and abide in the truth and the state of mind in which the Jews are is continued throughout this entire passage. They would not believe that He was the one sent from above to speak the words of God (ver. 24). They would not abide in the word which, as such a Divine messenger, He spoke (ver. 31). They were even seeking to kill Him because He thus spoke the truth (ver. 40). They showed thus that they were slaves of sin and children of the devil, and, as they were resolved to continue as they now were, they would die in their sins (ver. 21). There is, thus, a manifest unity in the discourse, and the allusions to bondage and fatherhood are only for the purpose of more clearly and emphatically bringing out the ideas suggested in ver. 21 ff. This unity favors, but does not absolutely prove, that vv. 30-50 are to be placed on the same day with vv. 21-29. 7. There is evidently a turn of thought in ver. 41 ff., both on the part of the Jews and of Jesus—from their relation to Abraham to their relation to God. The transition is through the words ἡμεῖς ἐκ πορνείας οὐ γεγεννήμεθα. These words, it will be observed, are contrasted with ἕνα πατέρα ἔχομεν τὸν θεόν, and are also evidently connected with the denial on Jesus' part that Abraham was their father. The true understanding of the passage therefore must, as it would seem, be found in connection with this twofold reference. As He denies their sonship to Abraham, they think that He may refer to sonship in another than the natural sense. But they did not conceive of their sonship in this other sense, except through their descent from Abraham. Hence they say, We are not other than real and legitimate children of Abraham, and therefore we are in the true and most direct sense children of God.—8. The words ἐκ τοῦ θεοῦ ἐξῆλθον indicate pre-existence, and, like the other expressions which Jesus uses of Himself in this discourse, as coming from and revealing the Father, they carry us back in thought to i. 18. These expressions move forward, as we may say, towards ver. 58, where the pre-existence is most distinctly declared.—9. The tendency of opinion among the most recent commentators is very strongly towards referring the phrase "*He was a murderer from the beginning*" to the introduction of death into the world through sin (Rom. v. 12). The argument for this view is derived from ἀπ' ἀρχῆς; from the fact that the discourse in general has reference to the truth and the moral sphere and relationships; from the fact that the ψευστής of ver. 44 points most naturally to Satan's deception of our first parents; and from the somewhat similar passage, 1 John iii. 18. The reference to the murder of Abel by Cain (de Wette, Lücke, and others) is favored by 1 John iii. 12; by the fact that this reference of the words makes what is said of Satan exactly correspond with what is charged upon the Jews—opposition to the truth and the desire of actual murder; and by the fact that the murder of Abel was the first one in history.—10. The last clause of ver. 44 is most simply explained by making αὐτοῦ refer to ψεῦδος. Westcott proposes, as a more probable translation, "Whenever a man speaketh a lie, he speaketh of his own, for his father also is a liar"—"that is, a man by lying reveals his parentage, and acts conformably with it." This, however, involves an altogether improbable, not to say violent, change of subject from that of the immediately preceding sentence.—11. In closing this part of His discourse, Jesus appeals again to His own truthfulness and freedom from sin and self-seeking, as proving His claim that He is from God (vv. 45–49).

17

Vv. 51–59. 1. In ver. 51 Jesus turns the discourse to the more positive side, and brings out one of the great thoughts presented in this Gospel, namely, that the eternal life, which begins in the soul at the moment of believing, has no experience of death forever. Physical death is a mere incidental event in the continuous progress of that life ; death as the contrast to the life of the Messianic Kingdom (that is, in the spiritual sense), and thus the death of the future, is altogether excluded.—2. It is the misunderstanding and opposition of the Jews which leads Jesus away from the direct development of the thought of ver. 51, and brings Him again to set forth and defend His claims, and to carry forward His expressions to greater distinctness. The two special points of consideration in the verses which follow are those in ver. 56 and ver. 58.—3. The statement of ver. 56 is to be explained in view of the contrast between $ἠγαλλ.$ $ἵνα$ $ἴδῃ$ and $εἶδεν$. No satisfactory account can be given of this contrast, except on the supposition of a vision given to Abraham during his earthly life, and the realization of the vision as he saw the fact from his heavenly abode. This verse is Jesus' answer to the question of the Jews in ver. 53, "*Art thou greater than our father Abraham?*"—4. Ver. 58 may be said to be, in a certain sense, His answer to their question, "*Whom makest thou thyself?*" That ver. 58 declares His pre-existence is placed beyond doubt, (*a*) by the contrast between $εἰμί$ and $γενέσθαι$; (*b*) by the fact that, as distinguished from the other places in this Gospel where the phrase $ἐγώ$ $εἰμί$ is found, no predicate is here suggested by the context, and that thus $εἰμί$ must have the meaning *to exist;* (*c*) by the reference to time in the words of the Jews in ver. 57 ; (*d*) by the fact that the whole thought of the context is that of His superiority to Abraham, as connected with having seen him and with freedom from death.— 5. If we take into consideration the various points in this chapter :—The uniting of Himself with the Father as the only two witnesses who can bear witness as to the one sent from heaven ; the declaration that, if they knew Him, they would know God, and that their true relation to God was dependent on their true relation to Him ; the claim that His words are the truth of God, and that He derives what He says from what He has seen with His Father ; the making death in sins and exclusion from the Messianic Kingdom, on the one hand, and freedom from all real sight and experience of death, on the other, to rest upon the acceptance or rejection of Him ; the affirmation of pre-existence, of a coming out from God, of a being from Him, of being all that is contained in His discoursing with respect to Himself from first to last ;—if we take all this into consideration, we may clearly perceive how closely related this chapter is to ch. v., and how, here, as there, He "makes Himself equal with God"—only there He calls the thoughts of His hearers to His life-giving power and the final judgment and resurrection as the proofs of this equality, while here He refers them to His pre-existence and His intimate knowledge of God and union with Him. In the natural order of presentation, as well as of impressiveness in the way of proof for the minds of the disciples, the thoughts of the fifth chapter belong before those of the eighth. Ch. v. sets forth the fact of His life-giving power for the soul ; ch. vi. explains this power as like that of food in the physical life ; ch. vii. 37, viii. 14, present it as the quickening and enlivening spiritual force and the light of the soul ; ch. viii. exhibits it as the Divine truth known by Jesus from His intimate union with the Father and revealed to the world by Him as sent from the Father.—6. The action of the Jews in ver. 59 is similar to that in ver. 18—they were moved by the claims which they understood Him to make, to attempt to kill Him. When the progress and connection of the thought in the chapters are observed, this action on their part may be regarded as indicating that they still thought Him, in the eighth chapter, to be claiming for Himself equality with God. In this connection it is also noticeable that, while Jesus had in ch. v. presented God only as the witness for His claims, in this chapter He places Himself with God, and demands recognition in view of the testimony of the two as fulfilling the requirement of the Mosaic law.—7. The discourses of chs. v., vii., viii. were given to the Jews of Jerusalem, that of ch. vi. to a company of people in Galilee ; but the condition of heart and will was alike in both. Though addressed to different audiences, the thoughts fall into a natural order, and they are presented by the author, according to his principle of selection, in the succession both of time and proof.

18

John 9

Vv. 1–41. 1. The miracle recorded in this chapter occurred probably on the same day with the discourses of the closing part of ch. viii., and not improbably (if vii. 53–viii. 11 be rejected) on the day mentioned in vii. 37. —2. The question of the disciples in ver. 2 is one of much difficulty. The exact correspondence in the form of the question respecting the man himself and of that which refers to the parents would seem to indicate the same possibility, to their view, of *his* sinning, which was manifest in the matter of *their* sinning. This fact bears somewhat strongly against the interpretation which makes this double question simply a means of indicating that they saw no possibility of explaining the blindness. On the other hand, there is not sufficient evidence to make it very probable that the disciples supposed that a man could sin before birth. There are some indications, however, of a belief, more or less extended, in the pre-existence or transmigration of souls, and in the existence of sin in the embryo condition of the child ;—and in their desire to obtain from Jesus His explanation of this calamity the disciples might, in their perplexity as to its connection with sin, have asked not only whether it was due to the sins of the man's parents (a thing which they themselves could allow) or to his own sins (a cause which, though not admitted by themselves, would be by some other persons).—3. The close sequence of vv. 3, 5 may indicate that, to the thought of Jesus, the works of God in this case were to be in the line of light for this man. The physical illumination which is effected by restoring his sight is thus made emblematic of the illumination of the soul, and the miracle is, in this way, brought into immediate connection with the conversation and discourse which precede it in the eighth chapter. The miracle in this case follows the discourse as illustrating and confirming its truth, if this view is correct, instead of suggesting the thoughts of the discourse, as is generally the case in this Gospel. But, here as elsewhere, it takes its place in the development of the proof, in connection with the teaching :—the works and the words.—4. The relation of the external means, which are sometimes used by Jesus when performing miracles, and sometimes not, to the end in view, can only be conjectured. Their use may, not improbably, have been determined by something in the man himself on whom the miracle was wrought, or in the spectators, which made such an element in the work essential to the spiritual impression which Jesus desired to produce.—5. The life-like character of this story of the blind man is more striking than that of any other, perhaps, in the whole circle of the Gospel narrative—the question of the neighbors, etc., and the different answers which they received (vv. 8, 9) ; the simplicity of the man's answer when interrogated by them as to his cure (vv. 11, 12) ; the attitude of the Pharisees with regard to the matter—first, trying to make the man believe that Jesus was not a Divinely-sent helper, because He healed on the Sabbath ; then, refusing to believe that he had been blind and that Jesus had healed him ; then, summoning his parents, in the hope that they would deny it ; then, calling the man again and attempting to overbear him by the charge that Jesus was a sinner, and by referring to Moses ; and, finally, when they found themselves unsuccessful, saying, "Thou wert altogether born in sins, and dost thou teach us," and thereupon driving him out ; again, the progress in the man's answers—first, The man called Jesus told me to go, and I went and gained the blessing, but I know not where He now is ; then, I think He is a prophet ; then, Whether He is a sinner or not, I do not know, but one thing I do know : whereas I was blind, I now see ; then, I have told you the whole story once, why tell it again ; then, It is surely a marvellous thing that you do not know whence such a man is, a man who has done such a wonderful miracle ; if He were not from God He could not have done it ; and lastly, when Jesus appears again and tells him that He is the Son of man, he says, Lord, I believe. Everything in the words and actions of all the participants in the scene has that inimitable naturalness which, in the case of a writer of the peculiar order of mind and character which belonged to the author of this Gospel, could not have been exhibited in his story had he not been personally acquainted with the scene. Whatever the author may have been, he had not the gifts which belong to the writer of fiction who pictures what is unknown with all the reality of life.—6. Two striking facts are noticeable in this chapter : (*a*) The miracle has a peculiar character, and is the most remarkable one recorded in this Gospel, with the exception of the raising of Lazarus. It is the giving of sight to one who was born blind. The miracle at Bethesda, where the man who was healed had been thirty-eight years in his illness, leads to the opening of the discourse of ch. v., which sets forth the equality of Jesus with God ; this miracle of healing the man who had never seen closes the further development of that thought in ch. viii. Certainly there is no mere repetition, but progress in the miraculous works which are recorded. They are selected from the "many signs which Jesus did" as connected with the development of the author's plan from its beginning to its end. (*b*) As in the case of the story of the Samaritan woman, Jesus here declares Himself distinctly to this man as the Son of man. The effect of this declaration, as it came to the knowledge of the disciples at the end of this succession of discourses, chs. v.–viii., and after the miracles, chs. v., ix., as well as the one in ch. vi., must have been greatly to strengthen their belief that "Jesus was the Christ," and that life would come through faith in Him.—Westcott says, with regard to vv. 35–41: "The ejection of the blind man who had been healed from the council of the Pharisees furnished the occasion for the beginning of a new society distinct from the dominant Judaism." And in connection with this fact he thinks it is, that Jesus offers Himself here as *the Son of man*. But it seems very doubtful whether this can be affirmed. There is certainly no indication of the formation of a new society at this time, or as following upon this event.—7. In ver. 35 Tregelles, Alford, Meyer, Keil, read υἱὸς τοῦ θεοῦ ; Westcott and Hort agree with Tischendorf, 8th ed., and Godet in reading υἱὸς τοῦ ἀνθρώπου ; Weiss also seems to prefer this reading. R. V. reads *Son of God* in the text, *Son of man* in the margin. McClellan calls the latter reading "another glaring blunder of only ℵ B D and Theb !"—8. The words of ver. 39 seem to have followed immediately after those which passed between the man and Jesus, but to have been addressed to the company of persons who surrounded Jesus, or, at least, to have been spoken in their presence. The κρῖμα, as Meyer remarks, "is an *end*, but not the *ultimate end* of the appearance of Jesus." The expression *You would not have sin* may, perhaps, be explained as referring to an absolute want of all knowledge of right and duty, like this man's blindness to the things of sight, or it may refer to the matter of unbelief. If the former is the true meaning, the negative part of the sentence will hold good in all cases in proportion as the want of knowledge is complete or partial.

19

John 10

Vv. 1–21. 1. Meyer says that the new chapter should begin with ix. 35. This is correct, at least so far as the close connection of the early verses of this chapter with ix. 35 ff. is concerned. This connection is manifest from the opening words of the chapter, there being no words of transition or indication of any other day or place. The figure which is employed is one which might easily be suggested by the circumstances, and needs no special explanation. The blind man's case illustrates that of the sheep which hears the voice of its own shepherd, while the action of the Pharisees is that of the thieves and robbers. This connection shows that, not only in ver. 1, but also in ver. 8, the persons referred to are those who, like the Pharisees, professed to be the religious guides and teachers of the people, but who were not in the prophetic line which ended in the coming of the true Messiah.— 2. Godet holds that there are three parables in this passage—that of the shepherd, that of the door, and that of the Good Shepherd. Perhaps it is more correct to say that there is one formal parable (comp. ver. 6), and that, while lingering within the sphere of this, Jesus presents Himself in two aspects which are easily suggested by it. The true explanation of ver. 8 is, again, indicated by this immediate connection of ideas. The thieves and robbers of ver. 8 are such as are not in union with Him and not in that Divine line in which He comes.—3. The parable, vv. 1–5, presents the two ideas of the door and the shepherd, as related to the matter of access to the sheep and their listening to the voice of the one who enters. Jesus afterwards declares that He is the door, and also that He is the shepherd (the Good Shepherd). The true view of the passage seems, therefore, to be this: that the matter is presented in a more general way at first, and then the more specific application is made afterwards. This blind man who had now been healed listens to Jesus and rejects the Pharisees, as the sheep listen to the voice of their own shepherd and flee from a stranger. He and all who have susceptibility to the truth recognize the teacher who brings it and refuse the one who does not. They are of the truth, and therefore they know it when they hear it. In the parable, accordingly, we may believe that the words *door*, etc., are to be regarded as belonging to the figurative representation only, the whole being designed to bring out the thought just mentioned. Only after ver. 6 are we to look for the individual and personal application of the particular words. The question which has been raised by some writers, therefore, as to a personal reference in $\theta\nu\rho\omega\rho\delta\varsigma$ of ver. 3 (whether to Moses, John the Baptist, the Holy Spirit, or some other), is at once set aside, no such reference being intended. This word does not occur in the part of the passage which follows ver. 6. This view of the passage, also, explains the last part of the sixth verse most satisfactorily. The Pharisees who were with Jesus, ix. 35 ff., did not understand as yet, because the parable was as yet presented in a general way. What follows is of the nature of an explanation, such as is added to the parables in some other cases. The word $\pi\alpha\rho o\iota\mu\iota\alpha$ does not seem to correspond exactly with $\pi\alpha\rho\alpha\beta o\lambda\eta$, which is used by the Synoptics, and in the present instance the preceding verses, to which it refers, contain an allegory rather than an ordinary parable of the narrative order.—4. The expression "I am the door of the sheep" (ver. 7) may mean the door of entrance to the sheep, or the door for the sheep. The correspondence of $\epsilon i\sigma\epsilon\lambda\theta\eta$ with $\epsilon i\sigma\epsilon\rho\chi\delta\mu\epsilon\nu o\varsigma$ of ver. 2 favors the former view, but the words *shall be saved, shall find pasture*, and *that they may have life* point very strongly towards the other explanation. In a passage where there is such a manifest freedom in changing the thought from verse to verse (comp. vv. 9, 11), it cannot be regarded as necessary to limit our interpretation of these expressions by those of ver. 2. If such limitation is not forced upon us, the argument derived from the other elements in the case leads to the conclusion that Jesus is speaking of the door by which the sheep may go in and go out. The opening of this door gives free access to the sources of life, which the sheep may find quietly and peacefully. But the thieves and robbers, who cannot open the door, but climb over the wall of the inclosure, come only to destroy.—5. The thought now turns to a comparison of Christ with the shepherd. The transition is apparently suggested, or is, at least, easily made through the words of the last clause of ver. 10. He is not only the shepherd, but the Good Shepherd, who lays down His life for the sheep. From the necessity of the case, this change from the figure of the door to that of the shepherd is accompanied by a change from the thief to the hireling, as representing the Pharisaic leaders. The sphere of thought now is that of dangers to the flock from enemies—the shepherd protects them at the risk of life, the hireling flees. The repetition of the phrase *lays down his life*, in vv. 15, 17, 18, however, and the presentation of the same idea in other places in this Gospel, seem to indicate something more than this primary idea which belongs to the passage—namely, a reference to the death which He was about to suffer for the redemption of His people. The reaching out of the thought to this greater idea is seen especially in the following verses, 14 ff., where the relation of the shepherd and the sheep is more fully brought out—with reference to the intimate knowledge which each has of the other, and the gift which the former makes for the latter.—6. It is in connection with this wider reach of the thought that the reference to the ingathering of the Gentiles is introduced in ver. 16. The παροιμία thus widens at the end into an application to the consummated kingdom of God in the world. Beginning with the comparison of Jesus Himself with the Pharisaic teachers, which was suggested by the case of this man who had been healed and then had believed, it terminates with a vision of the future which was to follow after Jesus' death and resurrection. —7. Vv. 17, 18 now add the thoughts which fundamentally belong to this matter of His sacrifice of Himself for the sheep—that He lays down His life with the purpose of taking it again ; that He does this voluntarily, and not by the greater force of another ; that this power to lay it down and resume it He has as a prerogative belonging to Himself ; that He does the whole work in accordance with the commission and command of His Father. The addition of these thoughts, which are naturally suggested as following upon what had been said in the development and explanation of the παροιμία, served to bring the minds of the hearers and the disciples back to what was set forth in ch. viii. of the relation of Jesus to the Father and His Divine origin, and in this way to complete the whole extended discourse from vii. 37 to this point. To the minds of the disciples, as they reflected upon this parable and what followed it—especially as, in their subsequent remembrance of the words, they understood the mystery of Jesus' death and resurrection and of the opening of the Gospel to the Gentiles, and as they came to know more fully in their own experience the union of soul between themselves and the Good Shepherd—the words here recorded must have become, in a peculiar sense, an added proof that Jesus was the Son of God, the source of life. It cannot be thought strange, by any candid person, that the story of this blind man should have made an ineffaceable impression on the mind of John, and that the details of it and of the remarkable words which followed it should have been inserted by him among the signs which Jesus did in the presence of His disciples.

20

Vv. 22–32. 1. The argument presented by Godet, as against Meyer, Weiss and others, seems satisfactory as showing that Jesus probably left Jerusalem and its neighborhood during the two months which intervened between the Feast of Tabernacles and that of the Dedication. That He did not remain in Jerusalem is certainly rendered probable by the fact that, in vv. 26, 27, He refers to the discourse of vv. 1–18 as if this were the last one which had been given to the hearers. That He remained neither in the city nor its vicinity is probable, because of the danger connected with the increasing excitement against Him. In a narrative prepared, like John's, on the principle of selection, and with separations of months between successive parts, the want of indication of a removal to a more distant region previous to ver. 40 can hardly be pressed as conclusive against an earlier removal.—2. Meyer calls attention to the designation of the particular part of the temple as indicating that the writer was an eye-witness. He also says that the verb ἐκύκλωσαν " graphically sets forth the urgency and obtrusiveness of the Jews," but, apparently with correctness, he rejects the view which Godet holds, that they pressed in between Jesus and His disciples, and thus enclosed Him in their midst. There seems, at least, to be no sufficient reason for this view.—3. In the words of ver. 24 the Jews evidently call upon Jesus to declare Himself distinctly as to whether He is the Christ. It is proper to bear this demand in mind when considering the answer which He gives in the subsequent verses. This answer begins with the statement that He has already told them what He is. If there is a definite reference to a particular occasion here, it is, no doubt, to the discourses and conversations of chs. viii.—x. 18, in the closing part of which the allusion to the sheep (vv. 26, 27) is found. Such a definite reference is probably to be admitted. After this He appeals to the testimony of His works, and then calls their attention to the same cause of their unbelief which He had given in the former discourse—they had not the susceptibility to the truth, they were not of His sheep. Following upon this, He declares that those who are His sheep have eternal life as His gift, and cannot be wrested from Him so as to lose it. It is in this way that He comes to the more complete statement of His Divine position than has been made at any previous time. The sheep, He says, cannot be taken from Him, because they are given Him by the Father, from whom, as being greater than all, they cannot be taken away ; and then He adds, that He and the Father are one. This oneness is either oneness of being or of power—the latter idea is that of the immediate context, and seems to the writer of this note to be the one intended in this expression. But power is the central element of being, when the natural attributes are considered, and thus unity of power, when connected with the close relations between Jesus and the Father already indicated throughout the preceding part of the Gospel, implies unity of being. The Jews evidently understood this to be the meaning, as they did in v. 18, for they plainly affirm it, and prepare to stone Him for blasphemy (vv. 31, 33) ; and, on His part, He proceeds, as He did in ch. v., to give a renewed statement of His claims and the evidence for them which they had themselves seen. He is in the Father, and the Father in Him, and this as connected with their oneness of power. He is thus the Son of God and is of the Divine nature. That in these latter statements there was no softening of His previous affirmations, or explaining away of His claims, is proved by the renewed act of hostility on the part of the Jews in ver. 39. To their demand, therefore, "If thou art the Christ, tell us plainly," His final answer is, not merely, "I am the Christ," but "I am one with the Father—He is in me and I am in Him." As the evangelist says in His concluding words, xx. 31, and in his Prologue, Jesus is not only the Christ, but the Son of God, the incarnate Logos.—4. Weiss objects to the explanation of ἓν ἐσμεν as referring to unity of power, on the ground that this is the thing intended to be proved. But this does not seem to be the correct view—the thing to be proved is that, if no one can snatch the sheep out of the Father's hand, it follows that no one can seize them out of Jesus' hand, and the proof of this is the oneness of power. Westcott, on the other hand, agrees substantially with what has been said above on this point, and says : "The thought springs from the equality of power (*my hand, my Father's hand*) ; but infinite power is an essential attribute of God ; and it is impossible to suppose that two beings distinct in essence could be equal in power."

21

Vv. 33–42. 1. There can be no doubt that the Jews understood Jesus as claiming to be God. Ver. 33 clearly proves this. The words of the following verses are to be explained, accordingly, in view of this fact.—2. There are two parts in the answer of Jesus : vv. 34–36, and vv. 37, 38. For the appreciation of the meaning, it must be borne in mind that Jesus enters upon an argument, and does not merely make a new assertion. It is natural, therefore, that what He says should have a progressive character, and should present the claim which He makes through the evidences for it. The claim is that of ver. 30, with what it suggests—which they had interpreted in the sense of ver. 33b. In such a progressive argument we might easily expect Him to begin, as He does, with a sort of *argumentum ad hominem*, founded upon the Old Testament, which they could not reject, and to say, If the O. T. addresses magistrates as gods, in their capacity as God's ministers in the world, surely there is no blasphemy in the appropriation of this title by one who, in a far more exalted sense, is God's ambassador—the one whom He has sent into the world to reveal Himself. His position is therefore, He says, exalted enough, even from the point of view of the Divine messenger and teacher revealing the truth—in which capacity they might easily recognize Him—to justify the title. But now He moves forward to the more positive side. What His real position is, they may know by the evidence of the works. If they will not be convinced by His words, let these latter teach them. These will show that there is something more in Him than the highest Divine messenger, that He is even the one who is consecrated and sent into the world to make known the truth—that there is a vital and essential union between Him and the Father (*the Father in me and I in the Father*), that union which is implied in, and the necessary condition of, unity of power (I and the Father are one, ver. 30).—3. In ver. 40 Jesus is represented as going again into the region where He is first brought before the reader, in i. 28. The public ministry of Jesus, in a certain sense, closes at this point, and, in accordance with the carefully-arranged plan of the book, it seems not unnatural that the writer should thus bring the narrative again to its starting-point. The introduction of John the Baptist again, at the close, is characteristic of the author. The testimony which John had given before his death produces its fruit when Jesus is drawing near to the time of His own death, and that which had led the writer himself to Jesus, at the beginning, is now represented as bringing many others to a like faith. They believed, as he had done, because of the confirmation which the sight and hearing of Jesus gave to what John had told them. The placing of this testimony and its results at the end of these most striking declarations of Jesus respecting Himself is worthy of notice, as connected with the development of the proof of the truth which the author desires to establish. The insertion of these three verses can hardly be explained, except as they are regarded as having relation to such a plan of the Gospel as has been indicated in these notes—the plan of setting forth progressive testimony and a growing faith which moves along with it ; and their presence here, accordingly, gives a new evidence that the author wrote his Gospel under the guiding influence of this plan.—4. The statement here made respecting John corresponds with the declaration of the Prologue with reference to him and with his statements respecting himself in chs. i. and iii. The σημεῖα of this Gospel are, all of them, σημεῖα in the sense of xx. 30, 31. John was not the light, but his mission was to bear testimony to the light. The object of his mission and testimony was "that all might believe through him." This object was realized in the case of the persons here mentioned. The prominence given to John's testimony in this Gospel is thus easily explained.

22

John 11

Vv. 1-16. 1. The writer turns at the beginning of this chapter to the narrative of those things which were more immediately connected with the death of Jesus ; the eleventh and twelfth chapters set forth what was more public and what brought the hostility of the enemies to its highest point, and the following chapters (xiii.-xvii.) what belonged within the circle of

His immediate friendship with His disciples.—2. The raising of Lazarus is the greatest of the miracles recorded in the Gospel history, but it was not the cause of Jesus' death. It was, at the most, one of the special causes of the hastening of the determination on the part of the Jewish leaders to take more decisive measures. The careful reader of the history will see that the rulers were steadily, though slowly, moving towards this end from an early period. They were determined to set aside and destroy His influence and power, but they were afraid to move too rapidly. They hesitated, therefore, and for a considerable period kept their counsels to themselves. But events moved faster than they thought, and the influence of Jesus was constantly increasing. They were in the condition, accordingly, of men who are impelled by circumstances which they cannot control to act more precipitately than prudence or fear would dictate. This miracle thus hastened their action and brought on the final resolution. In view of it, they became convinced that they could not wait as they had done, that the hour was at hand, and that, in the deadly conflict, either He or themselves must perish. But, if the raising of Lazarus had not occurred, the result would not have been changed. It is doubtful whether it would even have been delayed beyond the feast which was then approaching. The progress of things was such, at this time, that the crisis must come.—3. In the consideration of the question as to the omission of this miracle from the narrative of the Synoptics, the exact position and bearing of it on the result is an all-important element. Its relation to the end was not such as to make the account of it necessary to their narrative, or to render its omission, together with all that which immediately preceded the last week in Jerusalem, a matter of special difficulty. To John's plan and purpose, however, the recording of it might well have been regarded as in a high degree important, if not essential, for it was the last and greatest of the σημεῖα. To have omitted this miracle from his narrative would have been to leave the proof *from the works*, as presented to his readers, without that which would give it its greatest emphasis and its most convincing force. The very apprehension of the Jewish rulers respecting the influence of this miracle may give us some measure of its value to the mind of one who, as an eye and ear witness of the history, was familiar with all the facts, as he was presenting the proofs of the truth to the minds of others. With the record of it, his argument from the "works" reaches its climax.—4. As to particular words and phrases in vv. 1–16, the following points may be noticed :—(a) The prepositions ἀπό and ἐκ seem to be used in ver. 1, as in i. 45, as substantially equivalent to each other. The same thing seems to be true, in this case, of the verbs φιλεῖν and ἀγαπᾶν (vv. 3, 5).—(b) The words οὐ πρὸς θάνατον (ver. 4) must refer to the final result, since the resurrection of Lazarus was in the thought of Jesus, though it could not, at this moment, have been in that of His disciples.—(c) If ver. 5 is to be regarded, with Meyer, as having a parenthetical character, in so far as the οὖν of ver. 6 is connected with ver. 4, the force of this οὖν and of vv. 6, 7 is best explained as showing how the action of Jesus was guided by the thought of promoting the glory of God in this case. If, on the other hand, as would seem, more probably, to be the correct view, the οὖν refers back to ver. 5, the explanation given by Westcott may be regarded as the best one. He says: "The delay and the return were alike consequences of the same Divine affection and of the same Divine knowledge. Because the Lord loved the family, He went at the exact moment when His visit would be most fruitful, and not just when He was invited."—(*d*) The thought of ver. 9 is most simply taken as indicating that the danger suggested by the disciples was not to be apprehended—the appointed time for His work was not yet ended ; and ver. 10 serves to strengthen this thought by intimating that it is only after the appointed time is over that the danger comes. Godet's explanation of ver. 10 as meaning, "If I were to seek to prolong my career by refusing to go where duty calls, a real danger would attend my course," and thus as referring to the desire of the disciples that He should remain where He was, though ingenious, appears to be somewhat artificial and improbable.—(*e*) The words of ver. 12 can hardly be explained unless we hold that the disciples were thinking of Jesus as knowing or having heard of the condition of Lazarus, and as intending to go to Bethany for the purpose of miraculously curing his disease. In their eagerness to keep him from the dangers of that region, they seize upon this favorable indication, and press it upon Jesus, without fully understanding or reflecting upon the circumstances in all their bearings. The very difficulty which lies in the way of an altogether satisfactory explanation of their words may even be regarded as showing the reality of the story. Their minds were working, not reflectively and with calmness, but under the influence of anxiety for their Master and with an eagerness for any escape from threatened danger.—(*f*) Ver. 15 answers in its thought to ver. 4, and shows the design of the miracle as related to faith. It will be noticed, also, that the faith is that of the disciples. The last miracle, like the first, has its individual reference to them. But the faith here was far beyond the faith which followed the miracle at Cana ; it was an addition to all the growth from that time to the present. —(*g*) The words of Thomas in ver. 16 point to the apostolic authorship of the book, for a later writer would have felt little interest in recording such a saying, and certainly would have been unlikely to invent it for the purpose of inserting it here.

23

Vv. 17–27. 1. The opinion of Godet is probably correct, that the death of Lazarus occurred on the day when the messenger came to Jesus from the sisters, after he had started from Bethany.—2. The persons referred to in ver. 19 must be regarded as belonging to the party of the rulers, because of the usual sense of the term *the Jews* in this Gospel. They were evidently friends of the two sisters, and had come to them for the purpose of consolation. Their minds would seem, therefore, to have been occupied at this time, as far as possible, with other feelings than those of hostility to Jesus.— 3. Ver. 22 seems to show that Martha had a hope—probably in view of the other cases which had occurred—that Jesus might now, by the exercise of miraculous power, raise her brother to life ; and she understands His words in reply as not fulfilling this hope. Jesus then turns her thought to Himself.—4. The words, *I am the resurrection and the life*, find their explanation in what follows. The life into which faith introduces the soul is one which abides ; the believer lives, even though physical death comes ; he lives so truly and permanently that he never has any real experience of death in its deepest meaning ; he lives, even in that he has, so to speak, the principle of the resurrection within himself. Christ is thus the source and animating principle of his inner life and the power which secures the resurrection. The resurrection is, as it were, the development of the life. He calls upon Martha to grasp this truth, and she answers the call with the declaration of her belief that He is the Christ, the Son of God. We have here, certainly, a very near approach to the words of xx. 31 : " But these are written that you may believe that Jesus is the Christ, the Son of God, and that believing you may have life in His name."

24

Vv. 28–44. 1. There seems to be no sufficient reason to suppose, as many commentators do, that Jesus had bidden Martha to call her sister secretly. She acted probably on her own impulse—possibly because she feared a meeting of Jesus with the Jews, but more probably because of the natural desire that her sister, like herself, might meet the Master more privately. Mary rose as quickly on hearing of His arrival as Martha had moved before, and she said to Him the same words. The differences in the character of the two sisters, which have been often insisted upon, and much to Martha's disadvantage, rest on rather weak foundations, so far as this passage, or even the one in Luke x. 40–42, is concerned.—2. The word ἐνεβριμήσατο has troubled all the writers on this Gospel. That the use of the word, outside of the New Testament, is confined to the feeling of anger or indignation, must, apparently, be admitted. It is to be observed, however, that the instances in which it occurs are not very numerous, and that words of this character, expressive of emotion, are those which may, perhaps, more easily than other words, pass into a somewhat wider or looser sense in the progress of a language from age to age. In the present case it is exceedingly difficult to find any satisfactory explanation of the word as meaning anger or indignation. The scene was one of sorrow—the sisters were weeping, Jesus Himself wept, even the Jews were weeping. Anger would seem inconsistent with the occasion. The idea that the tears of the Jews were crocodile tears, which Meyer suggests, is entirely without foundation in the text, and contrary to the whole impression of the apostle's language. The suggestion that His indignation was excited against Satan, as having brought death into the world, is improbable, considering that there is no distinct reference to Satan in the sentence or in the context. This suggestion has all the characteristics of a device made to meet a difficulty. That He was indignant at Himself, or that His divine nature was indignant at His human nature, because He could not restrain His tears, is a supposition scarcely worthy of mention. That His indignation was aroused by the want or weakness of faith in the sisters is opposed by everything in the story ; their faith was not weak as compared with that of His nearest disciples, and they were full of love to Him. Godet's suggestion, that the sobs of those around Him, pressing Him to raise His friend to life, turned His thought to His own death, and that He was indignant at the diabolical perversity of His enemies, some of whom were present, which would make the act of raising Lazarus a means of bringing about His crucifixion, is, to say the least, remote from any statement made in the verses, and has in it a certain artificiality. How can the author have been supposed to suggest all this to the reader's mind, when he says nothing about it, except in this one quite indefinite word, and when everything points to sorrow and not to indignation ? In view of all the circumstances of the case, it may be seriously questioned whether the change of the word to a slightly different sense—the violent emotion of grief, rather than anger—is not to be supposed, in this passage, as belonging to the later language or the individual writer.—3. Meyer, in accordance with his theory of "crocodile tears," regards the words of ver. 37 as indicating that the τινές there spoken of were "maliciously and wickedly disposed to treat Jesus' tears as a welcome proof of His inability" to heal Lazarus. Weiss has a similar view. Godet also. Godet argues for this view from the fact that the expression, *But some of them*, is found in ver. 46 as designating the evil-disposed party, and from the difficulty of discovering otherwise any relation between these words and the new emotion (ἐμβριμώμενος) in ver. 38. But the expression τινὲς δέ is one which might be found in any case where there happened to be two divisions, and can prove nothing ; and the emotion of anger (as Godet supposes it to be) has as loose a connection with what precedes in ver. 33, as it would have in ver. 38 if ver. 37 were taken in the favorable sense. The natural sense of ver. 37, as the expression of weeping and sympathizing friends of the sisters, is the favorable one, and there is no indication to the contrary.—4. Meyer finds the "mobile, practical tendency" of Martha, as contrasted with Mary, exhibited here in her words (ver. 39), which indicate a shuddering at the exposure of her brother's body to the gaze of those present. But the most that can be affirmed is, that it was she, and not Mary, who spoke. The reason of her speaking may have been something else than a greater "mobile, practical tendency." The recording of Martha's words here is, no doubt, connected with the author's desire to present the miracle in its greatness ; the glory of God was to be displayed in the most wonderful manner.—5. The simplest explanation of the closing words of ver. 41 is that the requests of Jesus and the answers from the Father are so coincident that the answer anticipates the possibility of utterance in words, and so the utterance becomes a thanksgiving that the prayer is already heard. The relation of the whole action in the case to the production of faith is prominently set forth in this prayer, as well as in the words addressed to Martha in ver. 40.

25

Vv. 45–53. 1. The result of the miracle was the production of the desired faith, not only in the sisters and the disciples, but also in many of the Jews who had come to express their sympathy with Mary. The strict rules of construction make οἱ ἐλθόντες the same with πολλοί, while Ἰουδαίων refers to the whole body usually called the Jews in this Gospel. There is no serious objection to this view of the sentence. If it be adopted, the αὐτῶν may refer to the ἐλθόντες (Meyer), or it may refer to the Ἰουδαίων (Godet). If, on the other hand, οἱ ἐλθόντες, by an irregularity, takes the place of τῶν ἐλθόντων, the statement would seem to correspond better with what we might antecedently expect as more probable. The declaration, in that case, is: Many of those Jews who have already been spoken of as coming to Mary believed, but some of them (those who did not believe) went and told the Pharisees. This explanation gives so simple and natural a meaning that it commends itself, if the substitution of the nominative participle can be supposed.—2. The difficulty which has been found by some writers in the fact that Caiaphas is spoken of in ver. 49 as high-priest of that year has no real foundation. The statement is not introduced with reference to Caiaphas, but to Jesus. The man who was high-priest in that remarkable year when Jesus died uttered the prophecy respecting His death.—3. The utterance of Caiaphas is spoken of as a prophecy. This is apparently a kind of figurative expression, by which the author would intimate, not that Caiaphas was inspired of God, but that, in the providential plan respecting Christ, it came to pass that an utterance was made which proved to be prophetic of the immediate future, and was made by the head of the Jewish system.—4. The precise condition of the minds of the Sanhedrim at this time is strikingly exhibited in these verses. They were awakened to see that the policy of inaction or delay would be no longer safe. The influence of Jesus, rapidly becoming greater, was likely to be much increased by this remarkable miracle, and action was necessary on their part, or it might be too late. It was natural that the party favoring more vigorous measures should now succeed in leading the body to commit itself and to begin more seriously and resolutely to work towards effecting the murder of Jesus.—5. The understanding of this prophetic utterance was made known to the author and his fellow-apostles, no doubt, by the events which followed, and the words took their place in the line of testimony— the testimony unconsciously given, in this case, by an enemy—to Christ and His future work.—6. It is noticeable that, while the raising of Lazarus is represented in this chapter as inciting the Jewish authorities to more active and decisive measures, it is not referred to afterwards as constituting an element in the accusation made against Him at His trial. This fact, which has been urged as bearing against the reality of the event and the truthfulness of the story, seems to indicate, on the other hand, the exact relation which the event had to the end. It excited the enemies to action, but it was not the cause of Jesus' death. It was not a matter to be brought forward in the trial, but it was one important circumstance which led to the hastening of the trial. Moreover, the trial before Pilate was, as Meyer remarks, connected rather with an accusation of a political character; while that before the Sanhedrim, it may be added, turned more towards a charge of blasphemy.

26
John 12

Vv. 1–11. 1. The question as to the day on which Jesus came to Bethany, and, in connection with this, the day of His entrance into Jerusalem, is a complicated and difficult one, because of the uncertainty respecting the day of the week on which the Jewish Passover took place in this year, and also the uncertainty as to whether the counting of days here is in accordance with the Jewish or the Roman method. According to the most natural impression derived from John's narrative, the Passover occurred on Friday, the day of Jesus' death. According to the Jewish method of reckoning, six days before this would be Sunday. But if xiii. 1 refers to the first day before the Passover, and this was Thursday, the Roman method is adopted by the author, and the sixth day was Saturday. The latter supposition seems more probable. If this be the case, the arrival must have taken place very early in the morning, and from a place in the immediate neighborhood, because it was the Sabbath; and the supper in Simon's house was given in the evening, after the Sabbath hours had passed. The entrance into Jerusalem, accordingly, was made on Sunday. This is the more common view, and the traditional one of the Church, with respect to the time of the triumphal entry. Godet held this view in his first edition, but in his second and third editions he places the arrival on Sunday and the entrance on Monday.[1]—2. Godet insists that the feast mentioned in ver. 2 was not in the house of the sisters and Lazarus, and Weiss says that the form of expression used respecting the latter shows that he was not the master of the house and giver of the feast. The story of Matthew and Mark represents the feast as having taken place in the house of Simon the leper, and there is nothing in John's narrative, certainly, which is inconsistent with this representation. But it can scarcely be affirmed, with correctness, that the expressions used by John prove that the supper was not given by the sisters and Lazarus. The context in the preceding chapter has presented them as the prominent persons; no one else is named here; the verb ἐποίησαν is used without an expressed subject, and the subject to be supplied is naturally suggested by the names of these persons. As all the persons are participants in the scene, it was certainly not unnatural (as it might have been, under other circumstances) to say, They made a feast for him, and one of them had one part connected with it, another another, etc.—3. The little detail (ver. 3), *and the house was filled with the odor of*

---

[1] The translator in several places in Vol. I., though not in all, has used the designation *Palm Sunday* for this day, instead of *Palm-day*. The former expression accords with usage, but not with the view of Godet, who places the entrance into Jerusalem on Monday. This word of explanation seems to be required, and is accordingly offered here.

the ointment, is one of the incidental indications in this Gospel that the author knew the facts because he lived with Jesus. A later writer, evolving a speculative theory from his own musings, would not have thought of inserting such a statement.—4. The word ἐβάσταζεν is taken by R. V. text, Meyer, and many commentators in the sense of *took away, purloined.* This view is supported by the literal meaning of κλέπτης, and by the alleged tautology if the sense of *bore* or *carried* is given to the verb. The tautology, however, is not inconsistent with the simple measured style of the Gospels, and the word κλέπτης may easily have a certain loose or semi-figurative sense, as pointing to avariciousness displaying itself under such circumstances. That Judas was a thief, on the other hand, in the sense that he actually stole money from the small sum belonging to the company of disciples—often or generally not exceeding about thirty or forty dollars, it would seem, comp. vi. 7 with ver. 5 of the present passage —is a thing nowhere else intimated in the Gospel history, and very difficult to believe. How could he have been tolerated in the company if he was known to be a thief of this low and base order ? R. V. marg., A. V., de Wette, Lücke, Ewald, Luthardt and others give the verb the meaning *carried* or *bore.*—5. If the reading ἵνα . . . τηρήσῃ is adopted in ver. 7, the simplest explanation, perhaps, is connected with the supposition that Jesus views the use made of the ointment as, not literally indeed, but in a certain true and deep sense, a keeping it for the embalming of His body. From this twelfth chapter onward to the end of the seventeenth Jesus evidently anticipates His death as if already present, or even as having occurred.— 6. The statements of vv. 9–11 show that the place of the story of Lazarus in the narrative is that which has been already indicated. It had a great influence in the way of producing faith, and, on the other hand, in urging forward the chief-priests and Pharisees in their murderous designs. This was all. The rulers did not form their plan in consequence of this event ; they had formed it long before. They did not carry it out because of this event ; they would have carried it out had there been no such miracle. The results of the miracle—even in the turning away of many of their own party towards faith in Jesus—alarmed them, and made them yield to the bold suggestions of men like Caiaphas.—7. In the development of the narrative as related to the matter of faith, it is interesting to notice that, at the end, the writer brings out so emphatically its presence, even among those who belonged to the bitterly hostile party. The story shows progress in its plan, everywhere and in every line.

27

Vv. 12–19. 1. The story of the entrance of Jesus into Jerusalem is given by John with a different purpose from that of the Synoptic writers. The latter relate the story simply as an occurrence in Jesus' life, having indeed the remarkable character which belongs to it, but yet only one among the incidents of the closing part of the history. In John's Gospel it stands, as Godet remarks, between the resurrection of Lazarus (its cause) and the condemnation of Jesus (its effect), as a kind of connecting link to unite the two. We may add : it is also introduced with reference to the matter of faith—this being another instance where the author represents the limitation of the understanding of the disciples before the time when Jesus was glorified. That the account should, in some respects, differ—in the insertion or omission of details—from that which is given by the Synoptics, may afford no occasion for surprise when these considerations are borne in mind. The reference to the entrance as from Bethany is not strange, as the author's desire is to connect the matter with the miracle and the feast which had taken place. Matthew has no such special occasion for alluding to Bethany, but has occasion to speak of Jericho. We may easily believe, as Godet says, that "while the body of the caravan continued its journey to Jerusalem, Jesus and His disciples stopped at Bethany."—2. The relation of the raising of Lazarus to the great movement of this day is, undoubtedly, set forth with much distinctness and emphasis in this passage ; but, so far as the influence on the final catastrophe is concerned, the point made prominent is, again, the alarm occasioned in the minds of the Pharisees. The very careful and exact manner in which this story is told, as related to all its different bearings, is clearly indicative of an intelligent and deliberate plan on the author's part.

28

Vv. 20–36. 1. The persons called Ἕλληνες were undoubtedly Gentiles by birth, but yet Gentiles who had become proselyted Jews, because they went up to celebrate the feast. Whether their request to see Jesus was allowed or not, the narrative does not say. If we may judge from the ordinary readiness of Jesus to meet those who honestly desired to meet Him, we may believe that these representatives of the Gentiles were admitted to His presence. It would seem hardly probable that, after such expressions of His feeling and thought in view of their appearance, He would have refused to speak with them. But the author's plan moves away from this point. He is looking towards testimony and proof, not towards the history or experience of these few men. Hence he turns the reader to what Jesus said, and leaves him with the impression which comes from His words.—2. The glorification of the Son of man which is spoken of in ver. 23 is evidently that which comes through the extending of His kingdom over the world. This is indicated, (*a*) by the fact that the expression is suggested by the approach of these representatives of the Gentile nations ; (*b*) by the words of the 24th verse ; (*c*) by the reference of vv. 31, 32 to the overthrow of Satan and the drawing of all men to Himself. This coming glory is suggested to Him, as if in vision, by the approach of these Greeks, and the future appears as if already realized. The future centred itself in the hour of His death for the world, and this hour is so near that it seems to have already come.—3. The words of vv. 27, 28 correspond somewhat closely with those which were uttered in the garden of Gethsemane. As to the sudden change of feeling indicated by these words as compared with those of vv. 23 ff., the following suggestions may be offered :—(*a*) The whole passage evidently shows that Jesus

Additional Notes on John 12 / 1055

was thinking of His death as close at hand. With this in view, it was natural that two sets of feelings should have risen in His mind—now, of the triumph of His work, which even as a prophet or reformer, far more as the Son of God, He must have had before His thought as He looked forward, in His confidence in the Divine truth, into the future ; and again, of the trial and suffering which were just coming upon Him in the hour of His crucifixion. It would have been strange, indeed, if it had been otherwise. —(*b*) As the Divine messenger to the world, who was to suffer death for its sins, and, through this suffering, was to accomplish the work of redemption, the existence of these two feelings in His mind is yet more fully explained. And to such a Divine messenger they would come in quick succession and in almost immediate connection with each other, as the end drew near. A similar succession of feeling, though not in such nearness of time, is seen in the discourse on the last things, where the coming of the Son of man in power and great glory is declared, and in the scene in the garden.—4. The omission in this Gospel of the words spoken in Gethsemane, which resemble those recorded here, may be accounted for from the fact that the author's plan made it desirable to bring in this whole matter of Jesus' victorious and sorrowful feeling at the close of that portion of his book which related to His public ministry. Having once presented the matter here, he had no occasion to repeat it afterwards ; and, so far as was related to his plan of proof, etc., the words in Gethsemane were only of the nature of a repetition of what was uttered at this time.—5. The question whether the words *Save me from this hour* are to be taken interrogatively or affirmatively, is one which cannot be decisively answered. If they are understood in the latter way, they correspond more nearly with the words in Gethsemane, *If it be possible, let this cup pass from me ; nevertheless*, etc. For this reason, they seem to the writer of this note to have this construction and meaning. Weiss and Keil take them interrogatively, and the latter writer says that the absence here of the *if it is possible*, and the change from *nevertheless*, etc., in Matthew, to *but for this cause*, etc., here, shows that this cannot be an actual prayer, but must be understood as a question. Milligan and Moulton and Alford give the affirmative sense, as also does Meyer.—6. The words of Meyer respecting the voice from heaven seem conclusive as showing that it was an objective occurrence : " John himself, who was an ear-witness, describes it as such ; he repeats its express words ; to take the first half of these words referring to the past as the product of a merely subjective perception is without any support in the prayer of Jesus ; Jesus Himself in ver. 30 gives His confirmation to the occurrence of an actual voice ; finally, the ἄλλοι also, ver. 29, must have heard a *speech*." Weiss, on the other hand, claims that a voice, the understanding of which depends on spiritual conditions, cannot be a voice of articulate sound. The comparison which Godet makes of the understanding of the human voice by animals and men may, perhaps, be helpful in the way of illustrating this matter ; and the condition of mind in different hearers in many ordinary cases has some influence on what they gain from the voice heard—it may even determine whether they think it to be a voice or a mere sound.—7. In vv. 30, 31 Jesus rises again to the contemplation of the success and triumph of the future. The judgment of the world and the casting of its prince out of his power and dominion seem to His mind to be accomplished, since His death, now at hand, makes it certain that these things will come to pass ; and He looks forward to the ingathering of all men into His kingdom. The reference here is probably to the last times, when the Gospel shall be triumphant everywhere, when Jews and Gentiles alike shall be saved (Rom. xi. 25, 26). Towards this consummation the movement would be constant from the day of Christ's death and resurrection and of the outpouring of the Spirit.—8. The writer explains the words *be lifted up* as referring to the manner of Jesus' death—thus, to His crucifixion. It was the hour of His death which was ever before Jesus' mind at this time. But in the idea of His death we may believe that all was in cluded which belonged with it as essential to His great work—namely, His resurrection and ascension and the descent of the Holy Spirit.—9. In His answer to the people in ver. 35 f. Jesus once more calls their minds to Himself as the light, and seems to say that, by putting themselves in connection with the light while it still lingers with them in His personal presence, and thus becoming sons of light, they will discover for themselves, after His removal, how He can be lifted up, and yet can be the Christ who abides forever.

29

Vv. 37–50. 1. The writer closes this first great division of his work with a declaration of the failure and success of the miracles of Jesus, so far as the matter of faith in the case of the hostile party was concerned—as, at the end of the book, he sets forth his purpose and hope with reference to the recording of them for all his readers. The σημεῖα had been abundant, but this party would not believe.—2. This unbelief is connected in two ways with the prophetic words uttered by Isaiah—first, as a fulfilment of what he said, and, secondly, as finding its foundation or cause in another statement of his. The two prophetic statements are those declared to have been made in view of the time of Christ. The first and third of these points (ver. 38 and ver. 41) may be explained in connection with the general view which the New Testament writers had of the Old Testament. They found its whole meaning in Christ, and they thus carried Him, as it were, into every part or sentence of it which corresponded with His experience or work. Their view, in the truest and deepest sense, perchance, was the right one. But the special difficulty here lies in connection with the second point (vv. 39, 40). The explanation of this point must, apparently, involve two things—first, the responsibility of the individual, which limits the inability to what is moral, and, secondly, the Divine activity, which must be of the nature of a judicial hardening. The literal interpretation of the words, when pressed to its utmost extreme, is contradicted by the general representations of the New Testament respecting the sinfulness of men.— 3. The exception mentioned in ver. 42 is apparently presented as showing the success which Jesus had gained, notwithstanding the failure just described, and in connection with all that has been said in these later chapters respecting the rulers. The persons here alluded to do not seem to be such as Nicodemus or Joseph of Arimathea, nor such as Gamaliel. The two former were, probably, not actuated by the motive indicated in ver. 43. The last, as Meyer remarks, "did not get as far as faith."—The word δόξα of ver. 43 means the glory *which comes* from men or from God. —4. As to the passage vv. 44-50, it is generally held by the recent commentators to be a sort of summary of the teachings of Jesus as given in the foregoing chapters, just as the preceding verses have presented a kind of summation of the results of His work. This is quite probably, though not indeed certainly, the correct view. The verses are introduced as if they might be a new discourse, and yet no occasion or mark of time is given. The thoughts and expressions are, to say the least, more strikingly similar to what has been said before than is the case with any other discourse, and no new idea is presented. The position of the verses also—following the summing up of results—favors the view that they are a *résumé* of the teachings, rather than a new discourse ; and, on the whole, this view of them is to be adopted.—5. The thoughts of this passage follow each other in the natural order :—Faith in Jesus brings the soul into union with God ; the object of the coming of Jesus into the world is to bring the light of God, that the soul of the believer may dwell in the light-life which has no darkness, the life like God's life ; as Jesus thus comes to save the world, and not to judge it, He gives forth His teachings, which have been committed to Him by the Father, and they determine the judgment ; these teachings which are given to Him as His Divine commission are eternal life, in that, being received by faith, they become the source of eternal life to the soul ; in the proclamation of these teachings Jesus speaks in exact accordance with the Father's communication of His will and of His truth.— The thoughts contained in these verses, in the completeness of their setting forth of His message, as well as in the fact that the passage gathers into itself only what has been said in different places before, seem to be the summary of what He gave to the world in this earlier portion of this Gospel. —6. It is worthy of notice that at this point the σημεῖα, so far as they are found in the sphere of *miraculous works*, cease to be recorded. What remains of the book contains only the σημεῖα which pertain to the region of the *words* of Jesus. The works are the primary and lower proofs, to the view of this writer ; the words are of the higher order. The former are designed to arrest the attention of the world and to bear upon the earlier development of faith. The latter are adapted to the thoughtful and growing disciples, whose minds open more and more widely to the truth. Just in accordance with this character and purpose of the two kinds of evidence, we find that, when the conflict with the world and the public ministry of Jesus come to their end, and the disciples have been growing in the fulness of their belief even to the last days, the outward miracles are no longer mentioned, and the discourses of intimate friendship and love, as between Christ and His Father and the followers of Christ, begin. How can it be fitly said that this Gospel has no progress, or that it ends at its beginning ?

30

John 13

Whatever view may be taken of the details of the plan of this Gospel, there can be no doubt that there is a new and marked turn in the narrative at the beginning of this chapter—the events of the last evening and the last day of Jesus' life being now considered. At the opening of this new division of the work we find a designation of time, πρὸ τῆς ἑορτῆς τοῦ πάσχα, and the record of what occurred at a supper in which the Lord and His disciples participated. The position of these words would, in itself, seem to indicate that the author's design was to mark by means of them the date of the occasion which he is about to describe. The same thing seems to be clearly indicated by the prominence given to the words in the verse to which they belong, and the relation of this verse to those which immediately follow. That verse 1 is a complete sentence, of which ἠγάπησεν is the principal verb, is beyond question ; that vv. 2–5 form another sentence, which is closely connected (καί) with ver. 1, is equally clear. The nature of the first sentence (a declaration as to the feeling of the heart : *loved*), as related to that of the second (the setting forth of an act manifesting this feeling), proves this connection. Such a general proposition respecting love, independently of any relation to the act of love, would be uncalled for and unnatural in this place. We may say, therefore, with much confidence, that the progress of the discourse here shows the connection of the words "before the feast of the Passover" to be with the verb *loved*, and, through that verb, with the leading verbs of vv. 2–5. The thought of the verses, when taken together, is accordingly this : Before the feast of the Passover Jesus showed that He loved His disciples, by performing the act described.

That this is the true view of the connection of πρὸ κ.τ.λ., as related to the first verse considered by itself, is rendered altogether probable by the following considerations : 1. That the emphasis given to these words by their position in the sentence is most easily accounted for if they qualify the leading verb ; indeed, it can hardly be satisfactorily explained otherwise.—2. That there are serious, or even insuperable objections in the way of connecting them with either of the participial words. These words are εἰδώς and ἀγαπήσας. The connection with the latter is not to be admitted, because the placing of the words before εἰδώς would lead the reader to unite them with that participle, if with either of the two ; and that with the former must be rejected, because no satisfactory reason can be given for calling attention, in this subordinate clause, to the circumstance that Jesus knew the fact mentioned before the feast, while every reason which the nature of the case allows makes such a designation of time as related to the leading verb appropriate.

The act which is described, therefore, and thus the supper at which the act was performed, took place at the time marked by the expression πρὸ τῆς ἑορτῆς τοῦ πάσχα. That this supper is the one in connection with which

Additional Notes on John 13 / 1059

the Lord's Supper was instituted is indicated by the fact that it was evidently on the same evening (the evening before Jesus' death), and by the fact that the words respecting the betrayal by Judas and the denials by Peter, which in the Synoptics are placed in close connection with the time of instituting the Lord's Supper, are connected with this occasion. The Lord's Supper is, accordingly, declared here to have taken place before the feast of the Passover.

The phrase which marks the date is somewhat doubtful in its meaning. Meyer, Weiss and others, who hold that the Supper was on the 13th, admit that this verse does not determine the question. Our passage, says Meyer, does not state *how long* before the feast. It is noticeable, indeed, that there is no indication that the event occurred *one* day before the Passover, as in the case of ch. xii. 1 *six* days. When we consider, however, 1, that John's dates are usually given with reference to a distance of one time from another, unless the identity of time is distinctly stated ; 2, that this is the case in xii. 1, where the first of the designations of time connected with the closing days of Jesus' life is found ; 3, that the supper, if occurring on the evening of the 14th, was so closely connected with and conceived of as the Passover supper, that a dividing of the time so as to make prominent the part which preceded the actual eating of the lamb, etc., would seem improbable ; 4, that if the feast, as Godet thinks, included the whole of the 14th, the words before the feast must, strictly interpreted, carry us back to the evening of the 13th,—we may admit that the probability of the case lies, at least in some degree, on the side of giving to πρό the sense of *a day before*. If, therefore, the later passages of this Gospel which bear upon this question are found to point more probably towards the 13th than the 14th as the evening of the Supper, this verse may be regarded as strengthening, rather than otherwise, the evidence which they give.

The expression εἰς τέλος, which is taken by Meyer as meaning *at the end* or *at last*, by Godet as meaning *completely, in the highest degree, to the uttermost*, and by Weiss as possibly having either of these significations, but probably the latter, is understood by R. V. text, as by de W., Alf., Winer and others, in the sense of *to the end*. The possibility of this last sense is admitted by Godet, and is proved by Matt. x. 22 and the parallels. The objection urged against it by Godet in this place—that it was unnecessary to say that Jesus did not cease to love His own until the moment when He died for them—seems not to be well founded. We should know, indeed, that Jesus loved His disciples, because of His actions, even if the evangelists had nowhere stated the fact. But this does not make such a statement on their part idle or unnatural. In the present case, the writer of the Fourth Gospel had reached a point where he was to leave behind him the story of the public ministry of Jesus, and turn to the description of His last hours and His parting interview with His disciples. What could be more natural, and more expressive of the feeling which John had in the remembrance of that final meeting, than to say that, having loved His own who were in the world all through His life with them, He now showed that His love for them continued to the end, by an act which love alone could have dictated. The tendency of the most recent writers seems to be towards a rejection of this view (so Westcott, Moulton, Keil, Grimm). The meaning *at the end*, however, is, so far as the New Testament is concerned, doubtful, to say the least. Luke xviii. 5, if the rendering of A. V. and R. V. is correct in that passage, as Godet himself allows in his Com. on Luke that it may be, is not an instance in proof of this meaning, but rather of *to the end;* and 1 Thess. ii. 16, to which Meyer makes reference, is to be interpreted as signifying *to the uttermost.* This last signification is objected to by Meyer in the present verse, and with some reason, it would seem, notwithstanding that Weiss denies it, on the ground that it involves " an inappropriate gradation, as though Jesus had now exercised His love to the utmost." It is doubtful whether we can properly say that this was the utmost exhibition of love which He ever made before His death. Moreover, the contrast of ἀγαπήσας and ἠγάπησεν, together with the time element in the sentence, seems to point towards a continuance of the love, which had covered the whole of the past life, even to the end. The interpretation of R. V. text, therefore, appears to be the simplest and best. R. V. marg. reads *to the uttermost.*

The act of washing the disciples' feet appears, from the explanatory suggestions of ver. 12 ff., to have been intended, so far as its lesson of instruction was concerned, to teach humility. We learn from Luke xxii. 24 ff. that at the supper there was a contention among the apostles as to which of them was to be accounted the greatest. This fact might seem to give a very natural occasion for an action on Jesus' part of the character here described by John. If the supper alluded to in the two Gospels was the same —and the evidence for this is satisfactory—we can hardly separate the two things. But if they are not to be separated, the contention spoken of by Luke must have preceded the act of Jesus, not only because it would so easily have suggested the act, but especially because, after the performance of such an act by Jesus, it is almost impossible to suppose that the apostles could have engaged in such a contention.—This action of Jesus thus had a twofold significance : it taught the lesson of humility and the serving character of Christian love, and it revealed, in a very striking way, the love which Jesus had for these chosen friends. In accordance with his constant thought of the inward life and of what Jesus was for the soul, John centres his words upon the latter point alone. He makes the testimony of love, wonderful as it was in this last day of Jesus' life, a testimony to what Jesus was as the Christ, the Son of God, and the source of eternal life to the believer.

31

With reference to the individual words and phrases of vv. 1–11 the following suggestions may be offered : 1. The *hour*, which has been spoken of in the earlier part of the Gospel as not yet come, is here, as in xii. 23, referred to as already present. In connection with this fact, it may be noticed that, in the discourses of this last evening, Jesus seems often to speak as if the final moment were already past, and He was at the hour which immediately followed His death.—2. The fact of the absence of the article before δεῖπνον does not prove that the supper in question was not the Passover supper, but it is to be admitted that this fact is more easily accounted for if it was a supper on another evening. The word "necessarily," which Godet uses, seems hardly to be justified.—3. Godet holds that εἰδώς of ver. 3 is not to be understood, with Meyer, Weiss and others, as meaning *although* He knew, but *because* He knew. It seems to the writer of this note that the view of Meyer, etc., is more probably correct. The greatness of the love manifested in this condescending act is shown in the fact that it was done when, on the one side, Jesus was conscious that Judas, who was one of the company, was resolved to betray Him, and, on the other, when He was assured that all things had been given to Him by the Father. Notwithstanding the presence of the traitor—may we not also say: the contention among the apostles, which showed their earthly-mindedness—and notwithstanding His knowledge that His work and His time of humiliation were ended and His glorification was at hand, He did this service of love. It was in this way that He taught most impressively and effectively the lesson of humility.—4. Westcott presses the distinction between ἐξῆλθεν ἀπὸ θεοῦ which is found here, and ἐξῆλθον ἐκ τοῦ θεοῦ in viii. 42—the former marking *separation*, and the latter *source*. In his note on viii. 42 he calls attention to the same point, and also to the use of the verb with παρά as emphasizing the idea of the personal fellowship of the Father and the Son (xvi. 27). The use of the three prepositions is, certainly, worthy of special notice, and the distinction in their meaning, as connected with the many indications of the union between the Son and the Father, points strongly towards, if indeed it does not prove, the correctness of Westcott's view of ἐξῆλθον ἐκ, as setting forth the true divinity of the Son. In the present verse the idea is rather of the mission of the Son than of His nature or origin—He came from God, and is now going to Him, and, in connection with His accomplished work, the Father gives all things into His hands.—5. The position of Peter at the table and the question whether Jesus came to him first cannot be determined from ver. 6. Ver. 24 would seem to show that he did not sit next to John, and also that he did not sit next to Jesus on the other side, but that he was at some other part of the table, where the indication by signs would be easier and more natural. If any inference can be drawn from the word ἔρχεται, it will be rather against than in favor of the idea that Jesus began with Peter.—6. The explanation which is given in the following verses shows that the words of Jesus addressed to Peter have a bearing upon the Christian life, and do not refer to a mere agreement in feeling at the moment. The act of Jesus, while teaching humility, also taught the need of cleansing the life from the remaining tendencies to evil ; and the refusal to accept the act (as would be understood in the light of the higher knowledge, which would come with the spiritual revelation) was, in reality, the putting oneself outside of the true idea of that life. The words of ver. 10 suggest the thought of the passage in this view of it.—7. The turn of the thought in ver. 10 from the individual to the company is easily explained in connection with the deep impression of the approaching act of Judas, which all the Gospels show to have been resting on the mind of Jesus at this time. This turn of thought would scarcely have entered the mind of a later writer—it belongs to the life of the remembered scene. The explanatory words of ver. 11 also point to an apostolic author, for, as Westcott remarks, these words are natural if the recollection of the writer "carries him back to the time when" they "arrested the attention before they were fully intelligible;" but "no one who had always been familiar with the whole history would have added them."

32

Vv. 12-20. 1. The explanation of the act performed by Jesus which is here given evidently points towards humility, and thus is easily connected with the dispute among the disciples, recorded by Luke, as to which of them was the greatest. But ver. 10 shows that this humility in the matter of service was to be manifested in the way of mutual help in purifying and perfecting the Christian life of all.—2. The example of Jesus, alluded to in ver. 15, must accordingly be taken in this fulness of meaning ; the act was primarily one of humility, but secondarily one of cleansing, and the former had its purpose and end in the latter.—3. At ver. 18 there is again a turn to the case of Judas. The word ἐξελεξάμην refers apparently to the choice of Judas as one of the apostolic company. The ἵνα clause points to this choice as connected with the Divine plan, and thus indicates the explanation of it which was suggested in the notes on the sixth chapter. Jesus adds here, for the first time, what is repeated afterwards, that a part of His design in this last conversation with the disciples was to prepare them for the great surprises and trials which were about to come upon them in the immediate future, and to make these things become thereby a means, not of shaking or destroying their faith, but, on the other hand, of strengthening it.—4. The connection and meaning of this verse are most simply explained if it is made to follow directly upon the last clause which precedes it. They were to go forward in their mission, after His departure from them, in the power and with the message of faith in Him. This faith in Him was to unite every one who had it with God Himself. Their mission, therefore, was to be carried out, with the sustaining power of the assurance that the one who, in receiving them, received Him, would also receive God in and through Him. All this was to be involved in their belief (ὅτι ἐγώ εἰμι) that Jesus was in reality what He had proclaimed Himself to be.

33

Vv. 21-30. 1. The words at the beginning of ver. 20, ἐταράχθη τῷ πνεύματι, show how the mind of Jesus was, at this time, filled with the thought of the betrayal, and thus how natural it was for Him to allude to Judas in the earlier verses.—2. The external evidence seems, on the whole, to be favorable to the reading εἰπὲ τίς ἐστιν in ver. 24. If this text is adopted, it may imply a supposition on Peter's part that John had been already informed as to the one whom Jesus referred to, or it may be understood as meaning that he should inquire of Jesus, and then make it known. It would seem

Additional Notes on John 13 / 1063

probable that, if they all asked the question indicated in Matthew xxvi. 22, it must have been just before what is recorded in ver. 24 of John's account.—3. The entering of Satan into Judas, which is here mentioned, must mean something more than the words "having put it into the heart," which are found in ver. 2. The receiving of the ψωμίον was, it may be believed, the deciding-point in the history of Judas' betrayal. After this act he was completely under the power of the evil spirit. By accepting this offering of friendship, and then going forth to carry out the designs of the enemies, he really at this moment betrayed the Son of man with a kiss.— 4. Whether John includes himself when he says "No one knew," ver. 28, is uncertain ; but, as the purpose of Jesus appears to have been to speak only obscurely, it seems not improbable that he does. The form of expression in these verses would appear to indicate that a part of the company had no explanation at all to suggest with respect to the words spoken by Jesus to Judas, while a part thought of two possible explanations.—5. The bearing of ver. 29 on the question of the evening of the supper is not decisive. The sacred character of the Passover supper and of the evening on which it was celebrated renders it improbable that any one would leave, or be expected to leave the company before the feast, or that purchases would be made on that night. Moreover, we know that some preparations for this supper with the disciples were made two days before the Passover, and it would seem as if others of the kind indicated here would not have been left until the last moment. On the other hand, it is claimed that, if this was the evening of the 13th, there was a whole day before the Passover meal, and consequently there was no need for haste. Weiss urges, in answer to this, that the disciples may not have thought of Judas as about to go out immediately, but the story apparently indicates that their thought was connected with his hasty departure.—The expression *for the feast* favors the view that the Paschal supper had not yet come, and yet not decisively, for the word may be used to designate that which followed the first evening.—On the whole, this verse, like ver. 1, is reconcilable with either view, but the argument in both cases turns slightly towards the 13th as the date of this supper of Jesus and His disciples.—6. The Lord's Supper is probably to be placed after the departure of Judas. This accords with the order of the narrative as given in Matthew and Mark ; it is most easily reconciled with the progress of John's narrative as compared with the others ; and Luke, in this case as in some others, can easily be understood as not making the exact order of time a matter of special importance. Luke places the dispute as to who should be regarded as the greatest immediately after the institution of the Supper—a thing which seems to be almost impossible. It would appear antecedently probable, also, that as Jesus knew that Judas would leave the company, He would wait until he had gone before He instituted the memorial feast and began the discourse of intimate friendship. If the institution of the Supper follows ver. 30, it may be best placed between this verse and ver. 31, or before ver. 33.

34

Vv. 31–38. 1. The departure of Judas, leaving Jesus alone with His faithful disciples, turns His thoughts again to the glory and triumph awaiting Him, comp. xii. 23, but now both to the earthly (ver. 31) and the heavenly glory (ver. 32). A participation in this heavenly glory will be given to His followers also, but it cannot be now. In the intermediate period, while they were to be still on earth and in the midst of the unbelieving world, they would need some new uniting power to take the place, as it were, of His own personal presence. This power was to be in their love to one another. At this moment, and by the giving of the new commandment, Jesus seems, in a certain sense, to have formed the disciples into the Christian Church, as it was to exist on earth after His death.—2. The explanation of the new commandment is to be discovered in connection with this fact. The command consists, it may be said, of two elements—*love* and *one another*. The newness of it cannot lie in *love*, for this command had belonged to the earlier teaching of Christ, and even of the Old Testament. It must, therefore, lie in the words *one another*. But these words, both because of the circumstances in which they were spoken and of the fact that, as related to men in general, they were not new, must have reference to the Christian company. The love enjoined is, accordingly, that which belongs to the membership of this company. Every member is to love every other member because of the common love of Christ to both. The measure of this love is indicated in the words *as I have loved you*, but this measure cannot be that of the absolute greatness of the love, for the capacities of Christ in this regard are beyond those of the disciples. The love to be exercised, we may also say, cannot be explained as the same in degree in all cases, for Christ did not love all the eleven disciples in equal degree. But He loved according to the possibilities of His nature, as affected by the circumstances of each case, and the disciples are, in like manner, to love one another according to the possibilities of their nature as affected by similar circumstances. This love, which was founded upon the common bond to the common Lord, was to be a power also upon the world, leading the world to know that they were His disciples, and thus turning the thoughts of the world to Him.—3. The conversation respecting Peter's denials is represented here, quite evidently, as having taken place in the supper-room, for we cannot at all suppose that they went out from the room before xiv. 31, if, indeed, they did before xviii. 1. Luke xxii. 31 ff. also places the conversation before the departure from the room. On the other hand, Matthew and Mark place it after the departure and when they were on the way to the Mount of Olives. Meyer thinks that the conversation may have been twice repeated, in whole or in part, but such a repetition within the space of two or three hours seems quite improbable. It is more probable that the earlier Gospels have disregarded the exact order of time here.

35

John 14

Vv. 1–11. 1. The discourse which occupies the fourteenth chapter is apparently suggested by the thought expressed in xiii. 36 : "Thou canst not follow me now, but thou shalt follow me afterwards." The announcement of His approaching death, which Jesus had given to His disciples, and all things that had come before their minds in the recent days, had filled them with surprise and grief. They were bewildered, as well as sorrowful. The thought of His death and separation came upon them with terrible suddenness, for they had not comprehended His meaning when He had spoken to them previously of the fate which He was to meet. The words addressed to Peter were really addressed to them all, and they needed strength and support in view of the coming separation. To this end Jesus now speaks, and He presents to their minds, in this chapter, three grounds of consolation and encouragement :—first, the promise of a future reunion with Him in Heaven (vv. 1–11) ; secondly, the assurance of great success in their work for Him after His departure (vv. 12–14) ; thirdly, the promise of the Holy Spirit as a Helper (vv. 15–24). The last two points relate to what would be experienced by them in their future earthly life ; the first, to what would come after its ending. But this which refers to the remoter future is placed at the beginning, because it was the first thing which they needed for their comfort as they heard the words, You cannot follow me now ; you must wait until a future time. That their hearts might not be troubled, they must have the certainty of that future.

2. The two verbs πιστεύετε are probably imperatives : "Believe in God and believe in me." This confidence in God and in Jesus Himself was that which would raise their hearts above trouble. The positive demand thus stands in contrast with the negative. For the understanding of this chapter and those which immediately follow, the standpoint which Jesus takes should be carefully noticed. He seems clearly to assume the position of one who has come from His own home to a foreign land for a temporary sojourn and work there. While there, in the midst of this work, He has formed intimate and tender friendships with certain friends. The time has now come for Him to return to His home. They have still to remain where they are, continuing the work which He has begun, but His part of it, as Himself personally present among them, is ended. After a time their work also will be finished, and then they may follow Him. Now, as such a friend, at such a moment, He says to them : I am going back to my Father's house and to leave you alone ; but do not let your hearts be distressed by this ; on the other hand, have confidence in my Father and in me, that in the end all will be well.

3. The assurance given with regard to the future reunion contains three elements :—the declaration that there is room enough for all in the Father's house, the statement that He is going thither to prepare a place for the disciples, and the promise that He will come again and take them to Himself.

1066 / Additional Notes

Two points of special interest may be noticed in vv. 2, 3, which present this assurance :—(a) The evidence which is incidentally involved in the words, "If it were not so, I would have told you," that the book is written from the remembered personal experience of the author as one of the apostolic company. On this point see note on pp. 508, 509. (b) The word ἔρχομαι of ver. 3. To what does this refer ? Four answers have been given to this question. In the first place, the verb has been supposed to refer to the Parousia. In this sense it is possibly or probably used in xxi. 23. The objection to this view is that which Godet suggests—namely, that the event was too remote to offer the consolation which they needed. It would have been like the thought of the final resurrection to the mind of Martha, when she desired to have her brother presently restored to her. The disciples did not live to see the Parousia ; and that event is even yet in the future.—In the second place, it has been referred to the return of Jesus to the disciples at His resurrection. But He did not take them to heaven then, nor receive them to any permanent reunion with Him.—Thirdly, it has been understood in the sense of ἔρχομαι of ver. 18, and as referring to the coming of Christ to His followers in and through the Holy Spirit. But evidently, according to the statement of ver. 23, the coming there referred to is a spiritual coming of Christ to be with the believer where the latter is—that is, on earth, and not a coming to take the believer to be with Christ where He is—that is, in heaven.—A fourth reference has been given by some writers—namely, a return of Christ at the death of each believer, to receive him to Himself. The objection to this view is founded upon the fact that this sense of ἔρχομαι is not found elsewhere, either in this Gospel or in the rest of the New Testament writings. The writer of this note would suggest, however, the possibility of explaining the matter in connection with the position taken by Jesus in these discourses (see 2 above). May not the return, the coming again, be used here, not in its ordinary or technical sense, but in connection with the *figurative representation*, as it may be called, of the whole discourse ? As the departing friend goes back to the house of his father and prepares a place for those whom he leaves behind, in order that they may have a home there when the time appointed shall arrive, and as he then returns to take them with him to his home, so Jesus here says that, at the end of the work of each one of His disciples, He will come, as the friend comes, and receive them to Himself. The coming thus belongs to the figure, and may be properly used in this sense because of the figure. In this way the reference may be to the death of each believer, without assuming a new *technical* sense of the words *to come again*.

4. The word ὁδόν of ver. 4, if interpreted by the preceding context, will naturally mean the way of *death* by which Jesus went to His Father's house. If interpreted by the following context, it will mean Jesus Himself or faith in Him. The more probable interpretation would seem to the writer of this note to be the former. The following words of Jesus turn the mind of Thomas to the way for *him* to reach the Father—thus directing the inquirer away from the point on which he was curious to inquire to a spiritual suggestion or teaching for himself which lay near to his question. We see

Additional Notes on John 14 / 1067

many examples of this kind in John's Gospel.—5. In ver. 6 Jesus says, "I am the way"—that is, He is the one through whom (δι' ἐμοῦ, at the end of the verse) the soul comes to the Father. He then adds, "and the truth and the life." These words set forth, what has been declared in substance in earlier chapters of the Gospel, that in Jesus is the full revelation of the Divine truth and of the eternal life. In the sense in which the words are here used, and according to the thought now before the mind, Jesus is the way because in Him is the truth and the life.—6. Philip asks for some special manifestation of God beyond what had been given them—perhaps he did not himself have a definite idea as to what it should be. In answer to his request, Jesus points to the two great proofs of His being Himself the manifestation of God, which have been presented throughout the Gospel—the *words* and the *works*—and places them again in their right order, the *words* first, and, if these fail to convince, then the *works*. That the expression "believe me that I am in the Father and the Father in me" refers to the *words* as evidence, can hardly be questioned.—7. Vv. 7-11 have somewhat of a transition character, as leading the way from vv. 4-6 to ver. 12 ff. But the connection of their general thought with that of ver. 6 gives them a more special relation to the preceding context, and, in dividing the chapter into its sections, they may properly be assigned to the first section, which thus extends from ver. 1 to ver 11.

36

Vv. 12-14. 1. The word μείζονα is not improbably to be taken as an independent neuter adjective ; but, whether thus taken or as agreeing with an ἔργα to be supplied, it must be understood as having a more extended meaning than the ἔργα of the previous clause. The miracles wrought by the apostles were not greater than those which Christ performed. The reference here is to the success which they would have in their work as preachers of the Gospel in the extending of the Divine kingdom.—2. The verb ποιήσω of ver. 13 is probably to be joined immediately with πορεύομαι of ver. 12, and made, like the latter verb, dependent on ὅτι. The grounds of assurance of their success are: that He is going to the Father (His exaltation to heaven), and that, in connection with and as resulting from this, their prayers will be answered. Whether this is the true construction of the passage or not, however, the close union of the sentences shows that the answer to prayers here referred to is that which is connected with the labors of the apostles in the carrying forward of the Messianic work. With regard to these prayers two points must be noticed :—first, that they are in the name of Christ, and, secondly, that they are in the line of spiritual things. The idea that every prayer of every individual believer will certainly be answered by a granting of the particular request which is made, is one which is not set forth in the New Testament, and one which would make the mind of the petitioner determine the order of events. The Christian idea of prayer cannot be inconsistent with the submission of all requests to the will of God ; infinite, not finite wisdom must govern the world.

37

Vv. 15–24. 1. The meaning of the word παράκλητος has been much discussed. It is evidently founded upon the verb παρακαλεῖν as a verbal adjective, and the fundamental sense of the word is *called to one's side*, or *aid*. That it has, in the classical usage, the special sense of *advocate*—that is, of a person called to one's aid in this particular line—is to be admitted. This is also the meaning of the word in 1 John ii. 1. But there is nothing in the word itself which necessarily limits it to this signification. Certainly, the offices of the Spirit as they are set forth in these chapters must be considered in determining the idea of Jesus as He used the word. Bishop Lightfoot, in his essay on the Revision of the English Version of the New Testament, claims that the word *advocate* answers to these offices. It seems to the writer of this note, on the other hand, that this is the one idea which is not presented in these chapters. Jesus is set forth by John in the first Epistle (ii. 1) as the advocate, acting for the believer. But while the relation of the Spirit as a helper, a teacher, even a comforter, is brought out by the different statements of these chapters, that of advocate does not seem to be set forth. The designation, Spirit of *truth*, xiv. 16, the words "He shall *teach* you all things," xiv. 26, the statement that He is to *bear witness* of Christ, xv. 26, are descriptive of a teacher, not of a legal advocate. The declaration that He shall convince or convict the world, xvi. 7, is not of such convincing as specially belongs to an advocate, but the figure is rather of one who is carrying on a discussion with another, and who in the discussion convinces the other of the error of his view and the correctness of his own. Lightfoot claims that Paul has the same idea in Rom. viii. 16, 26; but it would seem that, when the Spirit bears witness with our spirits that we are children of God, He is fulfilling another function than that of an advocate; and even when He is spoken of as helping us in our infirmities by making intercession for us with groanings which cannot be uttered, it is questionable whether the idea of advocate includes all that is meant. The Spirit, Jesus says, would teach them, would lead them into the knowledge of the truth, would declare to them things which were to come, would take of the things of Christ and make them known to the disciples, would aid them in their work of bearing witness to the truth, would so take the place which He had Himself filled as to manifest to them His love and the Father's love, and, in this way, keep them from a state of orphanage, would give them an abiding joy. But all this is the work of a teacher, or a comforter and strengthener. The word Helper belongs to the fundamental meaning of the word, and includes the different ideas which are suggested in the several verses of chs. xiv.–xvi. It may be observed, also, that the discourse which Jesus is here giving is one of consolation with reference to His approaching departure from them. The Spirit is to fill for them the place which He had been filling. He was to be ἄλλος παράκλητος. But the place which Jesus had specially filled thus far was that of helping, teaching, comforting, strengthening, rather than that of the advocate.

2. The word ἔρχομαι, in ver. 18, from its immediate connection with

Additional Notes on John 14 / 1069

what is said of the Spirit, as well as from the following context, must be regarded as referring to the coming of Christ to the disciples *in and through the coming of the Spirit*. There can be but little doubt that this passage, and the verses of the sixteenth chapter, which follow the statements respecting the Spirit (xvi. 16 ff.), have the same reference, and are to be explained in connection with each other. These passages are inconsistent with the idea of the return for the period of the forty days following the resurrection of Jesus, because of the permanency of His abiding with the disciples which they suggest. They are also inconsistent with the idea of the second coming, because the indications both of ch. xiv. and ch. xvi. are that Christ is not to be personally with the disciples during the period here alluded to. This latter reason also bears against the reference to the forty days.—The sense of the verb ἔρχομαι in this verse is thus peculiar, differing from any use of the verb which we find elsewhere. As it is contrasted with the idea of orphanage or bereavement, the suggestion of the word seems to be connected with the figure of the departing friend which has been spoken of as lying at the basis of the entire discourse. In this view of the matter, the peculiar use of ἔρχομαι in this verse may serve to show that the explanation suggested with regard to its meaning in ver. 3 may be the correct one.

3. The evidence that the μικρόν of ver. 19 and the corresponding passage in ch. xvi. refer forward to the time of the coming of the Spirit is as follows :—(*a*) that it is described as a time when the world will not see Christ, and when the disciples alone will behold Him, and they apparently with a spiritual sight, not with the bodily eye (vv. 19b, 20) ; (*b*) that the manifestation made to the disciples will be a manifestation of love and an abiding of God and Christ with the disciples, not of the disciples with God and Christ (vv. 21-24) ; (*c*) that the new sight is connected with the fact of Jesus' departure to the Father (xvi. 17) ; (*d*) that it is to be a state of permanent joy, as contrasted with what was temporary, like the forty days (xvi. 20-22) ; (*e*) that it is apparently described as a period of communion with the Divine Being through prayer, as distinguished from personal intercourse with Jesus ; (*f*) these evidences are to be considered in connection with the fact that, in both chapters, the whole passage immediately follows the promise of the coming of the Spirit.

38

Vv. 25-31. 1. The phrase ταῦτα λελάληκα is repeated several times in these chapters, and evidently refers, in each case, to the entire section which precedes. Here, the reference is to the whole discourse of this chapter. After presenting the three grounds of consolation and encouragement, Jesus closes with a few parting words—a kind of benediction of friendship. —2. The promise given here with regard to the Paraclete is, that He will teach them all things and bring to their remembrance all things which Christ had spoken to them. How far this latter phrase may indicate an exact verbal recalling of Christ's words and teachings may be open to question ; but there can be no doubt that a special influence of the Spirit upon the memory is promised, which should guard the apostles against error in their calling to mind and setting forth to others the doctrine which Jesus had taught them.—3. The words of ver. 27 are the parting salutation, evidently founded upon the common "Peace be with you" of the hour of separation. Meyer quotes from Luther the comment : "These are last words, as of one who is about to go away, and says good-night, or gives his blessing." We cannot doubt, in view of this closing passage of the chapter, that the position which Jesus takes is that of the friend who is leaving his intimate associates behind him in a foreign land and returning to his home.—4. Ver. 28 is also to be explained in connection with this idea ; and the thought of the Father as greater than Himself is probably introduced here as indicating the joy and blessedness which would come to Him when He should return to heaven. They should rejoice in the joy of the friend who was leaving them, instead of simply sorrowing over their own loss and bereavement.—5. The simplest and most natural explanation of ver. 30 is that the last clause, "he has nothing in me," means there is nothing common to him and me—the sphere in which he moves is that of hostility; he is the ruler of the world, which is at enmity with me and my truth—and hence there is no time now for further conversation in this sphere of intimate and loving friendship. But now is the time to go forth and, by meeting that which is to come, to show to the world that Jesus loves the Father and obeys His command.—6. The construction of ἐγείρεσθε, ἄγωμεν ἐντεῦθεν—whether it is to be taken as an independent sentence or as connected by ἀλλά with what precedes, so as to be the leading verb of this part of the contrast—is uncertain. To the writer of this note it seems probable that the latter construction is the one intended by the author, and that the ἄγωμεν ἐντεῦθεν is contrasted by ἀλλά with λαλήσω.— 7. The question whether Jesus actually went out from the room with His disciples at this time is probably to be answered in the negative. This appears from the following considerations :—(a) that there is no distinct statement that they went out until xviii. 1 ; (b) that the other Gospels represent the going out which followed the Supper as being a departure for the Mount of Olives, etc., which corresponds with what John says at the beginning of ch. xviii. ; (c) that as He certainly did not leave the city before xviii. 1, it follows that if He left the room at the end of ch. xiv., the discourses of chs. xv. and xvi., and the prayer of ch. xvii., must have been uttered in the city streets—but this seems quite inconsistent with such utterances.

39

John 15

Vv. 1–11. 1. The fifteenth and sixteenth chapters evidently belong together and form one continuous discourse. This discourse consists of four parts :—first, the relation of the disciples to Jesus (vv. 1–11) ; secondly, their relation to one another (vv. 12–17) ; thirdly, their relation to the world (ver. 18–xvi. 4); fourthly, the coming and work of the Spirit (xvi. 5–24). The closing verses of ch. xvi. (25–33) are of the nature of a conclusion, though closely connected in thought, at the beginning, with the verses which precede.—2. The main thought of the first part is that of the abiding of the disciple in Jesus. To set this forth, the figure of the vine and the branches is introduced.—3. On the words of these verses a few suggestions may be made:—(a) The adjective ἀληθινή, here as elsewhere in this Gospel, has the meaning: *which answers to the true idea.*—(b) The cleansing of the fruitful branches is accomplished by the word which Christ has spoken. This word has already effected its result in the hearts of the eleven faithful disciples, and the final exhortation which Jesus gives to them is to continue in the union with Him which is already begun.—(c) The words *without me you can do nothing* (ver. 5) are to be interpreted in connection with the idea of fruit-bearing, which is the idea of the verse. The fruit-bearing power depends wholly on the abiding in the vine. In a similar way the words of ver. 6 are to be explained as belonging to the figure, and the spiritual application of them is not to be carried into the individual expressions, but connected with the entire expression as a whole.—(d) It will be observed that the reference to the answers to prayer in ver. 7 is to such answers as are connected with results in the spiritual life.—(e) The words *my love* (ver. 9), like *my peace* (xiv. 27) and *my joy* (ver. 11), are to be explained of love going forth from Jesus, and not love to Him. They were to continue in such a state that His love could abide with them as His friends.—(f) The end in view of the whole presentation of the relation of the disciples to Christ is declared, in ver. 11, to be that their joy may be made complete by having the joy which He Himself has, as abiding in the Father's love, dwelling in their souls.

40

Vv. 12–17. 1. The statement of ver. 13 is, of course, to be interpreted in view of the subject which is occupying the thought of Jesus. The love of enemies is not under contemplation.—2. The proof which Jesus gives, that He regards them as friends (ver. 15), is that He has made known to them all things which He has heard from God. This is not to be understood as inconsistent with what is said in xvi. 12, but only as declaring that He had treated them with all openness and friendliness, concealing nothing for the purpose of concealment.—3. The word ἐξελεξάμην of ver. 16, from its connection with φίλους, seems to refer to the choice of the eleven as friends. In the relation of the thought to the bearing of fruit, the idea of the apostleship is no doubt before the mind, and not improbably the turn to this idea is to be found in the verb ἔθηκα.—4. The second ἵνα clause of ver. 16 is to be understood, with Meyer, Weiss, Godet and others, as co-ordinate with the first. This co-ordination, and the placing of the second ἵνα clause where it is, serve to show, once more, how completely the thought of answers to prayer is limited, in these chapters, to the matters of spiritual life and fruit-bearing.

41

Vv. 18—xvi. 4. 1. The word γινώσκετε, which Godet prefers to take as an indicative, is better taken as an imperative. Jesus is giving them comfort and strength in view of the hatred of the world, and bids them bear in mind the fact that they would only be meeting what He had met before. He then reminds them, as a second thought, that it was the fact that He had chosen them, and that thus they did not belong to the world, which was the reason of the hatred. The hatred would therefore be an evidence that they were really His followers. Ἐξελεξάμην evidently means here a choice, not to the apostleship, but to discipleship as contrasted with the world.—2. Meyer regards the conditional clauses of ver. 20 as abstract cases supposed, the minds of the apostles being left to decide which would be realized. Godet, on the other hand, thinks both suppositions are intended to represent real cases. The mass of the people will not receive their message, but some will. The fact that the entire context refers to the opposition of the world seems to make the view of Meyer the more correct one.—3. The statement that they would not have had sin, vv. 22, 24, is to be explained in connection with the accompanying statement : "But now they have no excuse for their sin." It is sin with no possible ground of excuse for it of which Jesus is speaking.—4. We see in vv. 22, 24 the two evidences, which are presented throughout this Gospel, brought forward once more—the words and the works—and the parallelism and partial repetition in these two verses are to be accounted for as connected with the desire to set them forth.

5. In vv. 26, 27 Jesus makes a new reference to the Spirit, by way of encouragement and support in view of the opposition of the world. As this was His purpose, it was natural that He should set forth here the testimony which the Spirit should give, and which should help the disciples in their conflict with the world. In xiv. 16 Jesus says that He will ask the Father, and the Father will give the Spirit ; here, He says that He will send the Spirit from the Father ; in xvi. 7 He says that He will Himself send the Spirit. The same indication of close union between Himself and the Father is given here, which we find in many places in this Gospel. Godet presses the distinction of the prepositions ἐκ and παρά, and the difference in the tense of πέμψω and ἐκπορεύεται, as showing that in the latter verb there is a reference to an emanating (essentially and eternally) from the Father. That this may be the correct view may be allowed, but as the verb ἐκπορεύεται is itself used with the preposition παρά, and as it does not, in itself, necessarily mean come forth out of the being or nature of God, it must be regarded as doubtful whether this interpretation can be insisted upon.—6. The present tense in μαρτυρεῖτε is doubtless used because the testimony of the disciples had already begun. The allusion to the disciples is secondary to the allusion to the Spirit, but it calls to mind the fact that they were, and were to be, a power in the world for the truth.

John 16

Vv. 1–4. After the words of encouragement, the passage is closed with the sentence ταῦτα λελάληκα κ.τ.λ., expressing the purpose of this part of the discourse, and a repetition, with somewhat more of definiteness, of the statement of the persecutions which they must expect from the world. In this more definite statement two points are made prominent—that they would be put out of the synagogue, and that they would be exposed to death by violence. The former refers probably to a temporary exclusion from the synagogue, with its consequence, exclusion from social intercourse, and thus to one of the first results of determined hostility ; the latter, to the extreme of all evil which could be inflicted by adversaries. Thus the ἀλλά of ver. 2 contrasts the greater with the less ; not only the one, but, what is even far more, the other.—In ver. 4—evidently in consequence of the repetition just alluded to—the ταῦτα λελάληκα is repeated ; and the clause beginning with ἵνα in ver. 4 corresponds with the similar clause in ver. 1. By remembering, when these things should come upon them in the future, that Jesus had already forewarned them, they would be secured from the danger indicated by the verb σκανδαλισθῆτε.—The difficulty which has been found in connection with the last part of ver. 4, by reason of the fact that in Matt. x. and elsewhere, Jesus had given forewarnings of persecution, etc., is most simply explained by observing the whole preceding passage. Jesus had not given them this full statement with relation to the time of their separation from Him, as He does here, and He did not need to do so, because He was still with them. But now the time of His departure had come, and the future might be full of dangers to their faith if they were not forewarned.

Vv. 5–15. 1. Vv. 5, 6 form a transition passage, having a connection both with ver. 4 and ver. 7, the new section finding its proper beginning with the latter verse. The thought of vv. 5, 6 is kindred to that of xiv. 28—instead of rejoicing in the thought of what was to come to Him, of the place to which He was going, they were filled with sorrow of heart in view of their own loss. This failure to think of His happiness is here indicated by the words, "And no one of you asks me, Whither art thou going ?" This statement is not inconsistent with the implied question on this subject in xiv. 5, for the words of Thomas there involve, at the most, only a request for information, while here Jesus is speaking of the interest of a friend in the joy which is to be bestowed upon one whom he deeply loves. The connection with ver. 4 is seen in the contrast of νῦν to ἐξ ἀρχῆς ; but instead of going on to say, as we might have expected from the preceding, "Now I am going away, and I give you the needed prediction of what is to come," He turns to the condition of mind of the disciples, and makes their sorrow at His separation from them an introduction to a renewed promise respecting the Spirit. "It is expedient for you that I go away, because upon my going away the coming of the new Helper, who will lead you in all the truth and give you permanent joy, is dependent."

2. The work of the Spirit is set forth in this passage both in its relation to the world and to the disciples. The relation to the former is given in vv. 8–11. It will be noticed that the work which the Spirit will do is described by the verb ἐλέγξει, and has reference to three points: *sin, righteousness* and *judgment*. The verb presents the Spirit apparently as engaged in an argument or controversy with the world, and as convincing the world of the truth of His view of the matters in question and of the error of its view. This convincing is also, perhaps, to be regarded as a convicting and putting to shame. The three nouns which are connected with the verb are without the article or any defining word. This fact seems to indicate clearly that they are to be taken in the most general sense. This is true of all of them alike. The ὅτι clauses in vv. 9, 10, 11 give the ground on which the convincing or conviction is founded, and by means of which it is effected. The Spirit takes hold of the facts suggested in these ὅτι clauses, and uses them as proofs of His view with regard to sin, righteousness and judgment. The true interpretation of these sentences seems, accordingly, to be this : He shall convince the world with respect to sin— the truth of His view of it—by laying hold of and pressing the fact that they do not believe on Christ. This unbelief in Christ is the central sin, and all sin is that state of the heart which leads a man to refuse, when Christ is offered, to believe on Him. The world does not hold this view of sin, but the Spirit, by His testimony and His reasoning, convinces it that this is the true view. So of righteousness ; the Spirit, while laying hold upon and pressing the fact that Christ goes away to the Father, so that He is seen no more—that is, the great consummation of His work in the ascension to heaven—will convince the world of His idea of righteousness: that righteousness consists in the union of the heart with God, the entrance to which is through faith. The world's idea of righteousness is of something outward and perfunctory. His idea is of something inward : the conformity of the man in the inmost recesses of the soul to what he ought to be. And again of judgment ; the Spirit convinces the world of the truth of His view with respect to this also. The word *judgment* here is to be taken as condemnatory judgment, because this is the judgment pronounced on the ruler of the world. The Spirit accomplishes His end here, as in the former cases, by laying hold upon and pressing the fact which is set forth in the ὅτι clause: namely, the fact that the ruler of the world is already condemned. He is condemned in the sense that Christ's finished work has condemned his spirit and secured the final condemnation of himself and also his exclusion from his kingdom. That the work of Christ does this the Spirit impresses upon the world, and, by doing so, He shows the world that there is a condemnatory judgment awaiting its spirit and itself.

3. The work of the Spirit for the disciples is now set forth again, in contrast with that which He does for the world. The work for the world is that of convincing or convicting. The Spirit testifies and reasons and persuades. But in His work for the disciples, He only passes beyond the limitations which were necessarily imposed upon Jesus in His communications with them, by reason of the fact that they were as yet at the beginning and

were comparatively unenlightened. He leads them in the whole sphere of the truth and announces to them the coming things. Godet says that xiv. 26 contains the formula of inspiration of our Gospels, ver. 13 that of the Epistles and the Apocalypse. Whether this distinction can be properly made, and the statement of Godet pressed to the strictness of its letter, may be questioned. The "coming things" may, not improbably, include more than what are ordinarily spoken of as eschatological.

4. In doing this work for the disciples the Spirit will glorify Christ, for the announcements which He makes, whether of the general truth or of the things to come, will all be of what appertains to Christ—His system of teaching and His kingdom. This will and must be so, because all things which the Father has, and from which communications can be made to men, belong to Christ. The reference is, of course, to those things which fall within the sphere in which the whole thought is moving. Ver. 14, says Alford, "is decisive against all additions and pretended revelations subsequent to and besides Christ, it being the work of the Spirit to testify to and declare the things of Christ, not anything new and beyond Him." Alford also declares that ver. 15 " contains the plainest proof by inference of the orthodox doctrine of the Holy Trinity."

43

Vv. 16-24. 1. The connection of the $\mu\iota\kappa\rho\acute{o}\nu$ with what precedes and the similarity in the expression to that in xiv. 19 show that the two passages refer to the same thing. For the evidence that the reference is to the time of and after the coming of the Spirit, see Note number 37, 3, above. It has been claimed that as $\theta\epsilon\omega\rho\epsilon\hat{\iota}\tau\epsilon$ of ver. 16 is used of the bodily sight, so $\check{o}\psi\epsilon\sigma\theta\epsilon$ must have the same meaning. But the possibility of a change to a spiritual sense can hardly be denied, when we study the sayings of Jesus which are recorded in this Gospel ; and whether such a change is made in this case is to be determined by the indications of the following context. These, as we have already seen, make the change evident.—2. The words $\check{o}\tau\iota\ \dot{v}\pi\acute{a}\gamma\omega$ $\kappa.\tau.\lambda.$, which are found in the T. R. at the end of the 16th verse, are omitted by Tischendorf, 8th ed., Westcott and Hort, Meyer, Alford, Weiss, and others. The external evidence is very strong against the genuineness of the words. The explanation of their use in the 17th verse is less difficult, if they are read in ver. 16 ; but it is, no doubt, possible to account for them in ver. 17 as derived from ver. 10. In the latter case Weiss is right, as against Meyer, in supposing that the words are introduced by the disciples as making the difficulty of understanding the meaning still greater, rather than with the feeling that the explanation of the latter words might serve for the clearing up of the former.—3. The answer which Jesus gives to their question and difficulty begins in ver. 20. But He reaches the explanation in an indirect way, by calling to their minds, first, the sorrow which they would feel, and the triumphant joy of the world, in consequence of His removal by death. This sorrow, however, would be only of brief duration, for, secondly, in consequence of His seeing them again, they would

1076 / Additional Notes

have a permanent joy. The coming joy, thirdly, would be connected with the fact that they would have intercourse with the Father through prayer in the name of Jesus, the answers to which would make their rejoicing complete. This third point in the answer shows the meaning of the ὄψεσθε and ὄψομαι :—it is that seeing which belongs to the period of prayer (αἰτεῖν) addressed to the Father in the name of Jesus, and not of questions (ἐρωτᾶν) addressed to Jesus Himself—that is to say, the period when Jesus was not physically, but spiritually present with the disciples.—4. Weiss claims that the emphatic ἐμέ shows that Jesus is speaking of a time when He is personally (physically) present with the disciples, because, when He was not thus present, there could be no thought of such questioning of Him. But the real force of this emphatic ἐμέ is this : that their permanent joy was to be connected with a new intercourse with the Divine Being, not that of questions presented to *Him*, but of prayers offered to *God the Father* in His name. The emphasis on ἐμέ is thus completely accounted for, while the general reference is to the time which was to follow the coming of the Spirit.— 5. That ἐρωτᾶν *must* mean *ask* in the way of *question*, cannot be affirmed ; in ver. 26 it probably means *ask* in the way of *petition*. But the contrast of the 23d verse renders it almost certain that such is the meaning of the verb ἐρωτήσετε in this case. It is hardly possible that, when Jesus was present with them so that they could speak with Him, they should not have asked Him questions.

44

Vv. 25–33. 1. That the time referred to in ver. 25 ff. is the same with that described in vv. 20–24 is indicated by the fact that the same great characteristic of the period mentioned is here set forth as in the previous verses :—the communication with the Father in the name of Christ. It is also indicated by the fact that after the ταῦτα λελάληκα of ver. 25 there is no distinct suggestion of a new subject, such as we find in xv. 12, 18.—2. The force of the words καὶ οὐ λέγω κ.τ.λ. of ver. 26 is undoubtedly this : that the presentation of a request from Himself would not be necessary, because the Father would have an independent personal love for them on the ground of their acceptance of Him and love towards Him. The words "I do not say," instead of an expression such as "I deny that I will, or say that I will not," as well as the very nature of the relation between Jesus and the disciples—we may add, the indications elsewhere given of Jesus as an intercessor—show that He does not mean to deny that He will thus ask the Father for them. He did not need, indeed, to assure them of this, for they could not doubt that it would be so. But the one thought here is, that they might have confidence, when approaching the Father in prayer, that He had a personal love for them, and, by reason of this, would be ready to answer their petitions—and this would be a vital element in their future permanent joy.—3. The words of the disciples in vv. 29, 30, which have a special reference to ver. 28, in its connection with what precedes, are a new declaration and measure of their belief. Coming, as this declaration does, at the close of the discourses and conversations of Jesus in chs. xiii.–xvi., it must be regarded as their profession of faith in view of this latest and most remarkable σημεῖον, in the sphere, not of works, but of words ; and, by its position and its contents taken together, it shows an increase in their belief beyond any former utterance.—4. In vv. 31, 32 Jesus acknowledges their faith (ἄρτι πιστεύετε is an affirmation, not a question), and, at the same time, reminds them that it is not yet perfected. It will show its remaining weakness as the approaching evils and dangers come. Therefore He has spoken to them all the words of this discourse (the ταῦτα λελάληκα of ver. 33 points back to the whole of chs. xv., xvi.), that they may have peace and good courage in the midst of tribulation, being assured that He has overcome the world.

45

John 17

Vv. 1-5. 1. The prayer of Jesus has three parts : the first, a prayer for Himself, vv. 1-5 ; the second, a prayer for His disciples, vv. 9-19 ; and the third, a prayer for all subsequent believers, vv. 20-24. Vv. 6-8 form a transition passage between the first petition and the second, and vv. 25, 26 are a kind of conclusion.—2. The petition for Himself is that He may be glorified. The meaning of δόξασον in ver. 1 is to be understood of that glory which is connected with the return of Jesus to His Father, and which is more particularly set forth in ver. 5. It was by means of this glorification that He would be enabled, in connection with the sending of the Spirit and the greater power which would be exerted for the advancement of His kingdom upon the earth, to accomplish the purpose indicated in the ἵνα clause—the glorification of the Father upon the earth, in accordance with the measure of the Divine gift of power over all flesh which was bestowed upon Him. To realize the fulfilment of all that was involved in this gift, so that eternal life should be given absolutely to all whom the Father had given to Him, it was necessary that He should pass away from the limitations of His earthly condition to the heavenly state. The hour for this departure from earth to heaven having now come, He prays for the realization of the heavenly glory.—3. In vv. 4, 5 this glory is spoken of as that which Jesus had with the Father before the existence of the world. He prays to be restored to His former glory. The end in view is that mentioned above; but what the glory referred to is, is now more definitely stated. The ground, also, is presented on which it is asked for : because, through the accomplishment of His work, Jesus has already glorified the Father on earth. He has finished the task assigned Him, and now, when the appointed hour arrives, He asks for the reward.—4. Ver. 3 gives a definition or explanation of the meaning of eternal life. This life is the knowledge of God and Jesus on the part of the soul of man—which is, in one aspect of it, the idea that is everywhere set forth in this Gospel as belonging to these words. There can be no doubt that John views eternal life as a peculiar kind of life—it is the life which consists in the knowledge of God, the light-life, the life which resembles God's own life, and which is entered by faith. But the adjective *eternal* does not seem to be applied to it for the reason that it is the light-life, etc., but because, when it is once possessed by the soul, it never ends.—The definition is introduced here in connection with the words of the preceding verses. To give eternal life, it is necessary to give the knowledge of God and of Christ. To give this knowledge to the "all" spoken of in ver. 2, without exception and in its fulness, it is necessary that Jesus should be glorified.—5. The fifth verse distinctly declares the pre-existent state of Christ and His glory in union with the Father in that state. No other legitimate interpretation and explanation of the words can be given.—6. The prayer of Jesus for Himself is evidently not made for the purpose of securing simply a reward or blessedness for Himself, but with a view to the glorifying of God in the accomplishment of the great mission which had been assigned to Him. The work of the Messianic kingdom was not yet completed. It was only the work of His earthly life that was done; and He prays for what is beyond this life, to the end that the glory of the Father, which has already been partially secured, may be completely secured—that is, that the kingdom may be fully established.

46

Vv. 6–19. 1. Vv. 6–8 are connected both with the preceding and with the following context. In relation to the preceding verses, they indicate, by the presentation of the case of those in whom the work had been accomplished in the highest degree, and through whom, as the human instruments, it was to be carried forward in the time to come, the proof of what is stated in ver. 4. On the other hand, these verses evidently prepare the way for the petition of ver. 9, giving a reason why these persons, and not the world, are commended to the care of the Father. In these verses there is, in reality, a summing up of what has been presented in the entire record of this Gospel as connected with the reception of the Divine life :— (*a*) The persons in question are those who have the susceptibility to the truth, *Thine they were and Thou gavest them to me;* (*b*) Jesus has made known to them the Father's name—the name, here as elsewhere, standing as the representative of all that is involved in the revelation of God through Christ; (*c*) This revelation comes through the word which Jesus has spoken to them; and they have kept it in their heart and life; (*d*) In receiving and keeping the word, they have recognized fully the great truth which it involved—namely, that the origin of Christ's teachings and mission is from the Father. The work which had been given Him to do is thus fulfilled in their case.

2. Vv. 9–13. The prayer is for the disciples, and not for the world. The explanation of the exclusion of the world here is, not that those who belong to the world are excluded from the prayers of Christ, but that this prayer is, like the discourses of the preceding chapters, a prayer of the departing one who is leaving his friends behind him. At such an hour, the prayer for enemies does not have its proper place. The petition is for the friends only, with reference to the state of separation from Jesus which was

just before them.—3. The particle ὅτι of ver. 9 is to be connected with σοί εἰσιν and δεδόξασμαι, the words from the first καί to the second ἐμά of ver. 10 being parenthetical in their character. The ground of the prayer which is here presented is thus, in substance, what has been already mentioned—that they belong to the Father, and that Jesus has been glorified in them. In ver. 11 the additional reason, relating to the future, is given—that they were to remain in the world bereft of His care.—4. The petition for the disciples is set forth in two forms : first, in the more general way in ver. 11, *keep them in thy name*, and, secondly, more particularly in vv. 15, 17—in ver. 15 on the negative side, *keep them from the evil*, and in ver. 17 on the positive side, *sanctify them in the truth.*—5. The explanation of ver. 13 given by Meyer seems to be the correct one : "*But now I come to thee*, and since I can no longer guard them personally as hitherto, *I speak this* (this prayer for thy protection, ver. 11) *in the world* ('jam ante discessum meum,' Bengel), *that they*, as witnesses and objects of this my intercession, knowing themselves assured of thy protection, *may bear my joy* (as in xv. 11, not xiv. 27) *fulfilled in themselves.*"

6. Vv. 14–19. Ver. 14 is to be regarded as introductory to ver. 15, as ver. 16 is to ver. 17. In both cases, the fact that the disciples are not of the world, as Jesus Himself is not of the world—and thus (ver. 14) that they are objects of the hatred and enmity of the world—is made the ground of the special petition. The turn of thought, therefore, from the more general to the more particular request is made, not at ver. 15, but at ver. 14.—7. The words τοῦ πονηροῦ of ver. 15 may be neuter, or they may be masculine. This is the only instance in which the expression is found in this Gospel, but in the First Epistle of John there are five cases which may be compared with the one in this verse. In 1 John ii. 13, 14 the masculine form is beyond doubt, *you have overcome the evil one*, τὸν πονηρόν. In 1 John iii. 12—Cain was ἐκ τοῦ πονηροῦ—the connection of the verse with those which precede, in which the devil is spoken of, makes it substantially certain that the words are masculine and refer to the evil one. In 1 John v. 18 the reference to the evil one is certain, for the words are ὁ πονηρός, and in 1 John v. 19, where the dative ἐν τῷ πονηρῷ is used, the contrast of the two closely united sentences is such as to give an overwhelming probability in favor of the same reference. So far, therefore, as the usage of the writer can be determined from these passages, the argument derived from it is altogether in favor of the same explanation of the phrase in the verse before us. The same explanation is favored by the fact that John's Gospel seems distinctly to present the idea of two spheres or kingdoms, each presided over by a ruler. The use of τηρεῖν ἐκ in Rev. iii. 10 may be regarded as justifying the use here, if τ. πον. is taken as masculine. Godet, who holds that this genitive with ἀπό and ῥύεσθαι in Matt. vi. 13 refers to the evil one, thinks that the preposition ἐκ is more naturally referred to a domain, from which one is taken, than to a personal enemy. Of the most recent commentators on this Gospel, Weiss, Keil, Westcott, Milligan and Moulton, like R. V., regard the words as masculine.—8. Ver. 17 gives the positive form of the request : *Sanctify them in the truth.* The word ἁγίασον

refers, as we may believe because of its connection with the idea of τηρήσης κ.τ.λ., and also with the words of ver. 18, to that consecration of the disciples with reference to their future work, which would be accomplished for them by their being made holy in the sphere of the Divine truth. "The prayer," says Westcott, "is that the consecration which is represented by admission into the Christian society may be completely realized in fact; that every faculty, offered once for all, may in due course be effectually rendered to God (Rom. xii. 1)."—9. The last sentence of ver. 17, *Thy word is truth*, is best understood, with Godet, DeWette and others, as denoting the means by which the sanctifying process is to be accomplished, or rather (since the ἐν of the first part of the verse is not the instrumental preposition, as Godet takes it, but means *in the sphere of*) as giving a more definite statement of what is referred to in the words *the truth*. Thy word is truth, hence when I pray for these disciples, says Jesus, I pray for their consecration in the sphere of the truth.—10. Ver. 18 gives the special reason for making the prayer a prayer for their consecration—namely, that they have a mission like to His own, and ver. 19 adds the declaration that to this end He also consecrates Himself in offering Himself to death. This fact: that He thus devotes and consecrates Himself, is also, like the words of ver. 18, a reason for urging His petition (ver. 17).

47

Vv. 20–26. 1. Vv. 20–24. The prayer now turns to the great company of believers in all coming time. These will become believers through the word, spoken or written, of the apostles. The prayer for them is, that they may be one. This was presented in ver. 11 with reference to the apostles themselves, as the end for which Jesus asked that the Father would keep them. The unity here referred to is set forth more fully in the following words and verses. It is evidently such a unity as would, by its natural influence, lead the world to believe in the divine mission of Christ (ver. 21); it was one which was in correspondence, in some sense, with that which exists between the Father and the Son (vv. 20b, 22); it was one which was founded upon an indwelling of Christ in them, answering, in some sense, to the indwelling of the Father in Christ (ver. 23a); it was a perfected unity, which should, by its very existence, prove that the Father loved them after a similar manner to that in which He loved Christ (ver. 23b). These points, taken together, show that the unity is something more than the unity of love mentioned in xiii. 34, 35. In addition to the principle of love to one another which makes the company of believers one, there is here a common life-principle which they gain from the revelation and teaching, and also from the spirit of Christ. The spirit of Christ dwells in them and makes their spirits life (Rom. viii. 10). As Christ lives on account of and in the Father, so they live on account of and in Christ.—2. In ver. 24 there is a further request for these believers, which reaches out into their future life in heaven. There is no determination in this verse as to the time when this future union will begin, but, if xiv. 3 can be interpreted as in Note no. 35$_b$, 3, above, it will begin immediately

Additional Notes on John 18 / 1081

after the death of each believer ; and, whether this interpretation be given to that particular verse or not, a union with Christ from that time onward is indicated in other passages in the New Testament. The full blessedness of the believer, however, and the most perfect beholding of the glory of Christ, may perhaps not be enjoyed until after the Parousia. The perfection of unity in and among themselves on earth, and the union with Himself in a dwelling together in heaven, are the two gifts which Jesus asks for all His followers in all ages.—3. The glory spoken of in ver. 24 is apparently that which is referred to in vv. 1, 5—the glory which is bestowed upon Christ as the reward of His earthly work, and which involves a restoration to that glory which He had with the Father even before the creation of the world. It is spoken of as given to Him, because it is viewed as the reward of His work. As it is, however, the glory mentioned in ver. 5, there can be no reason for doubting that the words *thou didst love me before the foundation of the world* involve the idea of Christ's pre-existence, which is clearly set forth in ver. 5.

4. Vv. 25, 26. These verses form a kind of conclusion of the whole prayer, and the thought seems to turn back to Himself and the apostles, with a declaration that they stand apart from the world, and an appeal to the righteousness of God to grant the requests because of this fact. There is evidently a contrast in these verses, not merely between the world and the apostles, but between the world, on the one side, and Himself and the apostles on the other. Jesus, however, places Himself here, as elsewhere in the chapter, not in precisely the same position in which He places them. He has the knowledge of the Father in and of Himself ; they reach the possession of it through Him. The καί following δίκαιε is quite difficult of explanation. It seems to the writer of this note that Meyer's view is probably correct—the words being uttered with a pause after δίκαιε, and the suggested thought being : *Yes, Thou art righteous ;* (the καί thus meaning *and yet ;*) and yet the world has not known Thee, but I have known thee, and these who are here with me on this last evening of my life have known Thee. Decide between the two parties according to Thy righteousness, and grant the petitions which I have offered. The objection which Meyer and Weiss make to the view of those who, with Bengel and Ebrard, regard the two καί as equivalent to the Latin *et . . . et*, seems decisive—namely, that it is inconsistent with "the antithetic character of the conceptions and with the manifest reference of the second καί to ἐγὼ δέ."

48

John 18

Vv. 1-11. 1. The word ἐξῆλθεν, for the reasons suggested in Note 38 para. 7, above, is to be understood as referring to the departure from the room. There can be no doubt that the place here indicated is the garden of Gethsemane, and thus that this Gospel represents Jesus and the apostles as going after the supper to this spot, which belonged probably to one of the friends of Jesus.—2. The σπεῖρα or detachment from the Roman cohort was called upon to accompany the officers of the Sanhedrim for the purpose, apparently, of intimidation, and of assistance in case of any attempt at rescue. They were thus a secondary and attendant body, and, after ver. 13, where Jesus was led to the house of Annas, they disappear. When Jesus was thus securely in the possession of the Jewish authorities, these Roman soldiers had accomplished their work, and they then returned, doubtless, to the place where they were stationed by the civil government. The body which went forth for the arrest took the lanterns and torches, as well as their arms, for the purpose of impression. The fact that the full moon was shining would make no difference in such a case.

3. Godet, Meyer and others think that ἐξῆλθεν of ver. 4 means that Jesus went out of the garden. This may be the meaning, but it cannot be regarded as certainly so. Weiss holds, and this is not improbably the right view, that He came forth from the depth of the garden, or, with perhaps less probability, from the circle of the disciples. Westcott thinks that the ἐξῆλθεν is opposed to the εἰσῆλθεν of ver. 1; this, however, is questionable. —4. There is a certain difficulty in bringing John's narrative in ver. 5 f. into accordance with Matt. xxvi. 49 f., but it may probably be due to the brevity of the narrative in the latter case, or even in both cases. The approach of Judas to Jesus with a kiss and the words of Jesus in answer must be placed before the allusion to Judas in ver. 5 of this chapter.—5. The "falling to the ground" which is mentioned in ver. 6 can scarcely be explained, except by some special influence exerted by Jesus' supernatural power. Roman soldiers would hardly have been thus prostrated by the mere dignified or innocent bearing of an ordinary man, or by the unexpected calmness of Jesus' demeanor.—6. The words of the 9th verse, when connected with those to which they refer in xvii. 12, must include more than the idea of a loss occasioned by arrest or death. The result of the arrest of the disciples, or any of them, He feared might be a danger to their faith and thus to their salvation, and so His mind turns again here to what had been His thought in the latter part of ch. xv. and elsewhere.—7. The last words of ver. 11 present a similar thought to that of the prayer in Gethsemane as recorded in the other Gospels. It seems not unnatural that the mind of Jesus should have been full of this thought on this last night.

49

Vv. 12–27. There are in this passage two great questions, one having reference to the examination of Jesus, and the other bearing upon Peter's denials. On these two questions the following brief suggestions may be offered :

I. The examination of Jesus. That this was not the one an account of which is given by the Synoptic Gospels is rendered probable by the following considerations :—(*a*) The fact that it was in the house of Annas. Ver. 24 cannot be satisfactorily explained except as indicating that Jesus was not sent to Caiaphas until after the examination here recorded. (*b*) The character of the examination itself. It was not of a judicial character. Jesus was simply inquired of as to His disciples and His teaching, as if in a conversation or an informal inquiry. In the Synoptic account, on the other hand, witnesses are called, and the whole proceeding is like that of a court, with the high-priest presiding as a judge. (c) If the two accounts are carefully compared, we find, in connection with what has been said under (b), that all the details are different in the two : the questions addressed to Jesus ; His answers ; the minor circumstances, and the persons participating in the scene. This is certainly the fact, with the possible exception that the high-priest who takes part in the two scenes was the same person, and that the blows inflicted upon Jesus by bystanders were given by the same persons. The latter supposition is neither necessary nor probable, for the language used by those who smote Him is not the same, nor to the same effect. As to the former supposition, see below. (d) It is altogether improbable that if John was present at the judicial trial recorded in the Synoptics, he would have given an account of only a part of it, and would have omitted the most important part—namely, that which contained the final result and decision. On the other hand, if what John relates was a more informal and private inquiry in the house of Annas, which preceded the judicial examination, it is very easy to believe that John was not admitted to the latter, and that he gives the account of what he heard, and passes over what he did not hear.

The question as to whether the high-priest mentioned in vv. 15–23 is Annas or Caiaphas is one of some difficulty. It is evident that Caiaphas is spoken of in this chapter, and elsewhere in this Gospel, as the high-priest, and that Annas is not thus spoken of, unless in these verses. It is also evident that Caiaphas was the actual high-priest at the time, and that Annas was not. Moreover, the allusion to the high-priest in ver. 15, following immediately as it does upon ver. 13, where Caiaphas is declared to be the high-priest, is such that, in the case of ordinary words, there would be no doubt that the reference in the two verses was the same. It is to be observed, however, on the other hand, that ver. 24, when compared with ver. 13, seems to separate Annas and Caiaphas altogether, and to limit what is said between ver. 15 and ver. 24 to the house and presence of Annas. Godet, as also Riggenbach, Ebrard, Hofmann, and others, suppose that the two lived in the same palace. The only improbability in such a supposition is, that they were dignitaries of such high position ; but this is removed, provided we regard them as occupying two palatial residences which were on opposite sides of a common interior court, and were thus, in reality, one great building surrounding the court. There would seem to be an improbability, however, that the actual high-priest himself, who was to preside at the trial, would have entered into such a conversation and inquiry just before the trial began. His judicial position and dignity might seem inconsistent with it. But that Annas should do so might well have been in the plan of the leaders. It might well be a part of the attempt to prepare for the trial by involving Jesus, if possible, in some difficulty or self-accusation. As Annas, therefore, is called high-priest by Luke, both in his Gospel and in the Acts, and as he had held the office and was unquestionably in a very exalted position in the public opinion, it is more probable that the title is given to him in the verses under consideration, and that he was the person who conducted this inquiry.

50

II. The denials of Peter. Vv. 15-27.—In respect to these there are two points of inquiry :

1. As to the place where they occurred. That the first denial occurred in the court of the house of Annas is certain, if Jesus was not sent to the house of Caiaphas until ver. 24. But, if this was the fact respecting the first denial, the connection of ver. 25 with ver. 18 furnishes the strongest proof that the second and third denials also occurred in the same court. The opening words of ver. 25 evidently resume the closing ones of ver. 18, and the absence of any expressed subject for the verb εἶπον of ver. 25 can only be explained in a natural way by supposing that the subject is intended by the author to be the same persons as those who are mentioned in the 18th verse. We may believe, therefore, that all the denials took place in one and the same court ; that this was the court of the house of Annas ; and that the last of the three denials coincided in point of time with the moment when Jesus went forth from the house of Annas on His way to that of Caiaphas. If we now suppose that the house of Caiaphas stood on the opposite side of the same court, so that the latter belonged equally to the two houses, the accounts of all the Gospels, so far forth as the place of Peter's denials is concerned, can be easily brought into harmony.

2. As to what was said by Peter, and as to those who addressed him. —That there were three denials, and three only, must be admitted as proved, beyond reasonable doubt, by the fact that Jesus predicted only three, and that each of the Gospels speaks of three only as having occurred. The attempt to escape the difficulties of the case by the supposition of two or three sets of denials, each consisting of two or more, is one which is contradictory to the impression produced by every one of the evangelists.—The most serious difficulties in the reconciling of the different narratives are, *first : with respect to the persons*, the fact that in the case of the second denial Mark represents the same person as speaking to Peter who had spoken to him in the first case, while the other Gospels represent that it was another person— another maid (Matthew), ἕτερος (Luke), the servants and officers (John). If the maid was actually another (and not, as Mark intimates, the same), and if she moved the servants, etc., to unite with her, the other three writers may be harmonized ;—*secondly : with respect to what was said to Peter*, the fact that John states that the kinsman of Malchus, in the case of the third denial, said, *Did I not see thee in the garden with him*, while the other evangelists represent that the words (spoken, according to Matthew and Mark, by *those who stood by*, and, according to Luke, by *another*) were, *Surely thou art one of them, for thou art a Galilean, and thy speech agreeth thereto*, or words substantially like these. This may be easily explained, if we suppose that immediately upon the latter words, which came from several of the bystanders this kinsman of Malchus pressed the matter home upon Peter

Additional Notes on John 18 / 1085

by saying, *Did I not see thee*, etc.;—*thirdly: with respect to the interval between the denials*, the fact that Luke represents that there was about an hour between the second and third, while, if we are to suppose any interval of this sort as indicated by John, it is apparently between the first and second. The differences in regard to what Peter said are scarcely worthy of notice. There would seem to be no need, therefore, of supposing any such multiplying of the number of denials as has been imagined by some writers. With regard to the time previous to which the three denials were, according to the prediction of Christ, to take place, it is the same undoubtedly in all the Gospels, for Mark means by the words *before the cock crows twice* precisely what the other writers mean by *before the cock crows*—namely, the end of the watch called ἀλεκτοροφωνία.

51

Vv. 28–40. The bearing of ver. 28 on the question as to whether Jesus died on the 14th or the 15th of the month Nisan, and, in connection with this, whether the Lord's Supper was instituted on the evening of the Jewish Passover supper, is dependent on whether the expression *to eat the Passover* can be, or probably is to be, referred to anything else than the Passover supper itself. The presentation of the facts of the case by Godet is sufficient to show two things: first, that the passages from the Old Testament which are relied on to prove the wider extension of meaning for the expression in question do not prove it. Indeed, the point to be proved is not simply an extension of meaning to cover the whole feast, but such an extension as would cover the rest of the feast, with the exclusion of the supper itself;—secondly, that there is no sufficient reason to believe that the words *that they might not be defiled* are not applicable to the 14th day.—It is doubtful whether it can be affirmed as beyond question that the words here used *must mean* that the Jewish Passover supper had not yet occurred. But this is nevertheless the more natural interpretation of the words, and the probabilities of the case point strongly in this direction.

2. If we may take John's account as giving the beginning of the trial of Jesus before Pilate, it would seem that the Jewish rulers supposed that the mere fact of their presenting Him before the Roman tribunal would secure a verdict in their favor. They must have supposed that this result would be secured either by the respect which Pilate, in such a case, would have for them as rulers among the Jews, or by the fact that the crime of blasphemy was one which might properly come under their jurisdiction, and that the resort to the Roman power was only to obtain permission to inflict the death-penalty which the crime deserved. Their first words to Pilate (ver. 30) in answer to his question of ver. 29 imply, apparently, that whatever charge they have against Jesus belongs within the sphere of their own law, rather than that of the Romans.

3. The simplest explanation of the question proposed by Pilate in ver. 33 is that the Jews, after ver. 31, brought forward the charge which is mentioned in Luke xxiii. 2: "We found this man perverting our nation, and

forbidding to give tribute to Cæsar, and saying that he himself is Christ, a King." This view of the matter is taken by Godet and others. Meyer denies this, and holds that John could not have omitted such an essential point. He thinks that Pilate must have known of this political accusation through the application of the Jews for the help of the σπεῖρα. Weiss, however, in his edition of Meyer's Commentary, declares these reasons of Meyer to be insufficient. The omission of the charge as something already known, and something that would be understood, is in consistency with what we find in John's Gospel in other cases. It is certainly difficult to account for Pilate's question unless there was some such charge, and the insertion of Luke xxiii. 2 here is not unnatural.

4. The explanation given by Godet in ver. 34 is also, in all probability, the true one. If we hold that Jesus intended to ask whether Pilate meant that He claimed to be a king in the Roman and political sense, or in the Jewish and Messianic sense, the course of the conversation and inquiry moves on in the most simple and natural way. If He claimed to be king in the former sense, there might be just ground of accusation against Him before the Roman tribunal, but if in the latter, there might be none. Pilate answers, "Am I a Jew?"—that is to say, I have nothing to do with Jewish questions. I mean, of course, king in the only sense of the word in which I, as a Roman judge, can consider it. This is a matter belonging wholly to the Jews : they have delivered thee to me, with a charge that thou claimest to be a king in opposition to Cæsar. I have to investigate this question only. Tell me what thou hast done.—Having drawn an answer to this effect from him, Jesus now, in His turn, gives a more definite reply—that He is a king, but not in the Roman sense—and He adds the most decisive proof of this negative: namely, that if He were a king or claimed to be one in the earthly meaning of the word, His servants would fight for Him, as they were evidently now not doing. Pilate then asks if He really means that He is a king, and Jesus answers : Yes—in the sphere of the truth. Truth is nothing to Pilate, and he goes out at once, and says, I find no crime in Him, and proposes to release Him. Nothing can be more simple and straightforward than this progress of thought, if the explanations of vv. 33 and 34 which have been suggested are adopted as correct.—5. The servants spoken of in ver. 6 are those who believe in the justice of His claims. They are, in one sense, His disciples, but the case is presented as a hypothetical one, and these adherents are accordingly conceived of as they would be if the circumstances were in accordance with the supposition.—6. The ουκουν of ver. 37 should have the circumflex accent on the last syllable, and the meaning is thus, "After all, then, thou art a king?" "Is it not true, then, that thou art a king?" The question is, so far as the progress of thought in the passage is concerned, merely a renewal of the one which had been suggested before. But it includes a certain ironical element, or an expression of surprise that one in the condition of Jesus should claim to be a king in any sense.—7. The phrase *Thou sayest* is, in substance, an affirmative answer. A. R. V. regards ὅτι as meaning *for*, and this is not improbably the true view of the sentence : Yes, for I am a king.

8. The question of Pilate, *What is truth?* undoubtedly indicates that he felt that there was no such thing, and that it was idle for a man to be dreaming of any such kingdom. Pilate's attitude towards Jesus was not that of enmity or of scorn. He was, apparently, impressed by His calmness, dignity and sincerity. He evidently believed Him guiltless, so far as any charge of crime against the Roman authority was concerned. He comprehended fully, we may believe, the bitterness and selfishness of the opposition of the Jews. He saw clearly that they had no foundation to rest upon, as they brought their case before him. He was disposed to discharge Him, and even tried to effect His release. But as related to "the truth," he was an intellectual sceptic. He believed that there was no such thing as truth. He had pity for Jesus, and regarded Him as a harmless enthusiast for what He called the truth ; but he meant to remind Him by his question, that it was a delusion for Him to give Himself to the search for it, or to suppose that He had discovered it. It was for this reason, as we may believe, that he did not wait for an answer to his question. It was presented with no desire for an answer.—9. Pilate had the Roman sense of justice, as Renan says in the sentence quoted by Godet, and hence, when he went out to the Jewish rulers (ver. 38), he distinctly declared that he discovered no criminality in Jesus, and therefore proposed to release Him. But Pilate was a time-serving politician, rather than a man of lofty character and boldness in obeying his sense of right. He had, also, a dangerous record behind him. He was like men of his class, when placed in his circumstances, in all ages of the world's history. It was certain, from the beginning, that he would yield to the Jews. The question was only whether his resistance would be longer or shorter. The Jewish rulers were far bolder men, and they knew well with whom they had to deal. They pressed him gradually but steadily, and were ready with a new charge whenever the one already presented failed of its effect. The story of the two parties in this judicial attempt to put Jesus to death is so life-like, that it bears the strongest evidence of its truthfulness.— 10. This life-like character of the narrative makes it probable that the author was an ear and eye-witness of what he relates, and, as Weiss ed. Mey. remarks, this seems not impossible when the publicity of the Roman judicial trials is borne in mind. That John should have had admission to the examination before Annas, by reason of his acquaintance with him, and to the trial before Pilate, because of the custom of admitting persons in such cases to the judgment-hall, but should have been excluded from the trial in the house of Caiaphas before the Sanhedrim, may easily be supposed—and the supposition is in harmony with the facts of the narrative as we find them: namely, the insertion of the story of what took place before Annas and Pilate, and the omission of the scene in the house of Caiaphas.

52

John 19

Vv. 1–16. 1. The action of Pilate in connection with the scourging of Jesus and the giving Him up to the insults of the soldiers was evidently, as we see from vv. 4–6, with the design of inducing the Jewish leaders to yield with respect to the demand for His death. The words of ver. 4, "Behold, I bring him out to you, that you may know that I find no crime in Him," indicate anew his belief in Jesus' innocence and appeal to the sense of justice in the Jews. Those of ver. 5, "Behold the man," appeal to their compassion. If there be anything more than this appeal, it is probably what Meyer supposes, "This suffering one cannot be the usurper of a throne." It suggests, therefore, the unreasonableness of their course, the groundlessness of their severity. Finally, the words of ver. 6 are spoken with indignation, as Pilate finds that his effort is unsuccessful and that their answer to his appeal is only in the outcry, "Crucify, crucify." At this point Pilate approaches to the very borders of the boldness of real courage. It was the point which men of his character sometimes reach under great provocation, and where only a step is needed to transform them into men of true nobility or even heroes. But the step is not taken. To any one who has, in his own experience with men, seen a character of the order of Pilate subjected to a test of a similar kind—who has seen the struggle, the impulse to do the right act, the indignation at the unyielding opposition and pressure, the seemingly courageous refusal to violate the sense of justice in the soul, let the enemies do what they will, and then the submission, at the end, through fear inspired by the consciousness of a past career which it is dangerous to have investigated or made public—to any one who has seen this, the story of Pilate leading up to this point will prove that the author who tells it was either the witness of the facts, or that he had the creative imagination of the higher order of writers of fiction. But the author of this Gospel, whatever else he may have possessed, certainly did not have this creative imagination.

2. The Jewish rulers, finding Pilate dangerously near to a refusal of their demands, are driven to the use of the last two means at their command—the excitement of his fear of disregarding their law, which the Roman power, according to its policy towards conquered nations, would respect, and of his fear of the Roman emperor, in case he seemed to protect one who was guilty of treason. They try to awaken the former fear first. The resort to personal intimidation, in the strictest sense of the words, was so base a thing that they would reserve it for the final moment, the moment of absolute necessity.—In their appeal to their own law, we see once more that the charge against Jesus was blasphemy. They understood Him to place Himself on an equality with God.—3. The effect of what they said was evidently different from that which they expected. Pilate's fears were awakened, but in another line. The sceptic became superstitious. The movement of Pilate's mind here was most natural. The intellectual, as well as the careless, doubter, when he is aroused by some thought of the possi-

Additional Notes on John 19 / 1089

bility that the belief of those about him may, after all, be true, easily passes, for the moment, into the sphere of superstition, or what is like it. This must have been the case, in a peculiar degree perhaps, with men of this class in the age when Pilate lived. As he hears the expression, *Son of God*, and thinks of the wonderful bearing of Jesus and His remarkable words, he seems to question whether He may not be, indeed, something more than an ordinary man, some Divine messenger or being who has appeared on earth.—4. The reason why Jesus gave no answer to Pilate's question suggested by his fear : *Whence art thou ?* we may believe to have been His knowledge that Pilate's condition of mind and heart was such that an answer would have accomplished no good. The sceptic of Pilate's class, whether he is rejecting truth as having no reality, or, under the influence of some sudden fear, is turning towards superstition—whether he is ready to say, *What is truth?* or, *Whence art thou?*—is best treated as Jesus treated Pilate. He asks his question with no desire or intention to be moved in his inner life if the true answer is given—and silence is the only answer that may, by a possibility, awaken his conscience.

5. Pilate now assumes the dignity of his office, and calls the attention of Jesus to the power which he possesses over Him. To this Jesus replies. In the words of Jesus (ver. 11) there are apparently two suggestions : first, in the way of rebuke to Pilate, reminding him that all his power is dependent on God; and, secondly, in the way of lenity, admitting that his sin is less than that of the Jewish rulers. The verse, in its details, bears especially on this latter point. Because the authority over Jesus in the present case was given to Pilate of God—that is, because he was in a Divinely assigned station, according to the providential arrangement, where he must judicially try all persons brought before his tribunal, his sin was less than that of those who, by their own voluntary action, brought Him before that tribunal. His act in conducting the trial was a part of his official work ; theirs was a wilful violation of all justice. There was an involuntary element in his relation to the matter, but not in theirs. This fact lessened his sin. Whatever Pilate's sin might be in his final yielding to the pressure of the Jews, it would not equal that voluntary, selfish, bitter enmity which originated the whole movement against Jesus, and carried it forward even to the point of bringing Him before the Roman governor and demanding His crucifixion.

6. The words of ver. 12—whether we understand them, with Godet and most commentators, as implying a succession of further efforts to persuade the Jews and release Jesus with their consent, or, with Weiss, as meaning that he attempted to release Him at once, but was prevented by the renewed outcry of the Jews—show that Pilate was much affected by the words of Jesus (ver. 11) and His silence (ver. 9). Pilate was not, indeed, moving towards belief in Jesus ; he was not in a condition of mind to receive honestly and heartily the answer which Jesus must have given, had He broken His silence in ver. 9. But he was conscious of the injustice of treating Him as a criminal, and apprehensive, perhaps, of the vengeance of the Divine power, or of some divinity represented in or by Jesus, if he

gave Him up to His enemies. He attempted anew, therefore, to release Him.

7. The Jews bring forward the appeal to Pilate's personal fears as related to the Roman emperor. These fears were, doubtless, due to two causes : first, the well-known suspiciousness of the emperor; and, secondly, his own bad record in the past. The latter point was the one of greatest importance. Resistance became hopeless from this moment, for he could not face the possibility of a charge against him at Rome, which should involve, perhaps, the investigation of his past career. He succumbed to the enemy—notwithstanding his conviction of the innocence of Jesus and his insight into the baseness and deadly hatred of the Jews—because he was unable to meet the threatened danger to himself.

8. The words, *Behold your King* (ver. 14), may, perhaps, have been intended in part to convey a final appeal to the Jews to consent to His release, and in part to express his own bitter feeling by way of scorn. Or they may, perhaps, have been intended to intimate that he now brought Jesus out before them to pass the sentence upon him which they should demand. Behold your king—the one whom you charge with declaring Himself against Cæsar—what shall be done to Him ? They answer, *Crucify Him.* Pilate says, *Shall I crucify your King?* He means, thus, to make them assume the responsibility, and assume it on the ground on which they had made their last accusation (ver. 12). In this latter case, and not improbably this is the right view, Pilate's question in ver. 15 is, as it were, his washing his hands (comp. Weiss) ; and, we may add, the reply of the chief-priests, *We have no king but Cæsar*, is, in substance, their expression of readiness to take the responsibility : *His blood be upon us and upon our children.* This last act and word of Pilate, as given in Matthew's Gospel and John's, is as characteristic of the men of Pilate's class as are all the other words and acts of his which John records.

9. The phrase *Preparation of the Passover* (ver. 14) may possibly mean either Friday of the Passover week, or the hours or day of preparation for the Passover feast. That it, probably, has the latter meaning is indicated by the fact that, if the former idea had been in the mind of the author, it would have been unnecessary to add the words τοῦ πάσχα, for every reader would know that it was the Passover week. If we hold that the Friday on which Jesus was crucified was the day in the day-light hours of which the preparation for the Passover supper, occurring in the evening, was made, and thus could properly be called the Preparation of the Passover and, also, the Preparation of the Sabbath, we find the simplest explanation of the terms which are used in different places and which designate it in one way or another as the Preparation. In the brief space allowed for these Additional Notes it was evidently impossible to enter into a full discussion of the question as to the day of Jesus' death, whether the 14th or 15th. The writer of these notes has limited himself, therefore, to an indication of the probabilities, as they appear to his own mind, in the several verses of this Gospel which bear upon the question, and the suggestion of a very few points which have seemed worthy to be considered. There is no passage in John's

Additional Notes on John 19 / 1091

work which is absolutely decisive, but each of the several passages where a pointing in either direction can be discovered seems to point, to say the least, somewhat more strongly towards the 14th as the day, than the 15th. The Lord's Supper, if this be the true view, preceded by one day the Jewish Passover supper.

53

Vv. 17–30. 1. The title which was placed upon the cross was, according to Matthew, This is Jesus, the King of the Jews ; according to Mark, The King of the Jews ; according to Luke, This is the King of the Jews ; according to John, Jesus of Nazareth, the King of the Jews. The resemblances and variations in these forms given by the four evangelists are indicative of the character of their writings, and suggestive as to the view which is to be held respecting the relation of the Divine guidance to the words of the writers. That all the evangelists knew the substantial fact in the case is beyond question.—2. The fact that Pilate caused the title to be written, and the words which passed between him and the Jews in vv. 21, 22, are details of the history recorded by John alone, in consistency with his more graphic account of the whole matter. The life-like manifestation of Pilate's character appears even at the end of the story, in the title which he wrote, and especially in the words, " What I have written, I have written." These words exhibit the sort of apparent boldness and decision which seems to men like him to be a true assertion of themselves and truly courageous, notwithstanding their yielding to the pressure of the hostile party in the only vital point.—3. The recording of the two scenes which follow is, not improbably, intended to bring before the reader the same contrast at the scene of the crucifixion which is presented elsewhere in this Gospel. The soldiers, as the representatives of those on whom no impression at all had been made by the words and works of Jesus, appear as acting with the harshness and brutality of coarse men who were dealing with a criminal, and appropriating what the law allowed them, without sympathy. The explanation of the ἵνα clause in ver. 24 is the same with that which has been mentioned in other cases—namely, that the New Testament writers saw in Christ the meaning and end of the whole Old Testament, and, in view of this, carried the fulfilment of the latter into all its parts, wherever these corresponded with the experiences of Christ.—4. The reference to the fulfilment of the Old Testament passage indicates that, to the view of the evangelist, the action of these soldiers was, though unconsciously on their own part, a testimony to the Messiahship of Jesus. The story is thus brought within the plan of the Gospel in the matter of *proof* or (in the more extended sense of that word) of σημεῖα, as it is also introduced, as already remarked, in connection with the matter of *belief* and *unbelief*.—5. The question as to whether three or four women are mentioned in ver. 25 is one which cannot be decisively answered on either side. That there were four, however, is the more probable view. This view is favored by the following considerations : — (*a*) The fact that Jesus committed His mother to John, and that John's house became her home, is more easily explained if John's mother was the sister of the mother of Jesus. (b) The mother of John was present at the crucifixion scene, according to Mark xv. 40 and Matt. xxvii. 56, with Mary Magdalene and Mary the wife of Alphæus (Klopas). As she was associated with these women in a part of the scene, it is altogether probable that she may have been with them, also, throughout the whole. If, however, she was present at the time alluded to in ver. 25, there seems to be no reason why John should omit all reference to her. It would be rather in accordance with his custom when speaking of himself and his family, so far as we can judge, to mention or allude to her presence, while omitting her name. This would be what he does here, provided she is the one designated as *the sister of Jesus' mother*. (c) If we hold that Salome was in this relation to Jesus' mother, the request which she makes in Matt. xx. 20 ff. is most satisfactorily explained. (d) The supposition that Salome was the sister of Jesus' mother relieves us of the difficulty of supposing that two sisters had the name Mary. The only objection to this view which has any special weight is the one derived from the entire absence elsewhere in the Gospels of any distinct allusion to the existence of such a relationship. This objection must be admitted to be somewhat serious, but it may be questioned whether it can, by any means, overbalance the arguments which have just been presented.—6. The committing of Mary to the care of John cannot be accounted for simply on the ground that he was her nephew, for she had children of her own, or children of her husband by a former marriage, living with her, and these children were soon to be believers. John's relationship as nephew makes such an act on Jesus' part more natural than it would be otherwise, but there must have been something more than this in the case. There must have been a rising above all earthly relationships (see this on p. 510). The story becomes in this way an evidence of the living experience of the writer, and it enters into his plan as one of the things which marked the progress of his inner life. He tells his readers this fact which belonged to his own friendship with Jesus, believing that it would bear witness of what Jesus was in His union with individual souls, and would thus tend to bring them to seek after the life in and with Him. —7. The words "in order that the Scripture might be accomplished" are to be taken, according to Meyer, in connection with the previous clause, "that all things are now finished," but Weiss ed. Mey. agrees with Godet in connecting them with $\lambda\acute{\epsilon}\gamma\epsilon\iota$, $\Delta\iota\psi\omega$. The latter view is probably, though not certainly, the correct one.—8. Meyer holds that the words of Luke xxiii. 46, "Father, into thy hands I commend my Spirit," belong to "the enlarging representations of tradition." But it can hardly be considered inconsistent with the probabilities of the case that Jesus should have accompanied the word "It is finished," recorded in John, with these additional words addressed to His Father.

54

Vv. 31–42. 1. If the Sabbath referred to in ver. 31 was the 15th of Nisan, we have a very simple and satisfactory explanation of the expression that it was "a great day." In that case it was a weekly Sabbath, as being

Saturday, and also the feast Sabbath. This verse, therefore, points towards the conclusion that the day of Jesus' death was the 14th. The supposition that this Sabbath was the day of the sheaf-offering is far less probable. If the Sabbath mentioned was the 15th, the readers in Ephesus and its neighborhood, for whom John wrote, might be able to understand from the narrative itself and from the indications that all took place in connection with the Passover, how this day should be a Sabbath of a special character and special solemnity. But such a familiarity with the Jewish arrangements as to make them readily understand that the day of the sheaf-offering was referred to could hardly be supposed by him, so that he could allude to it without any more definite designation.—2. The reference in the words *he that has seen it* (ver. 35) is to what is mentioned in vv. 33, 34, and not merely to ver. 34b. This is indicated by the fact that the two quotations from the Old Testament point to vv. 33, 34a. The statement of ver. 34b can scarcely be regarded, therefore, as the one of sole prominence in connection with this scene.—3. With reference to the 35th verse as pointing to the author of the Gospel, see, in addition to Godet's note, the remarks in these pages 502, 503. A further consideration may be presented here, as connected with vv. 36, 37. These verses are so related to ver. 35 that they seem clearly to show that the witness referred to was confirmed in his belief by means of this fulfilment of prophecy. The allusion to this point corresponds, on the one hand, with what the author says elsewhere respecting the disciple whom Jesus loved—that is, himself—and, on the other, there is an additional improbability (in the line of that which is mentioned in Vol. I.) that he would bring forward the conviction of a person wholly unknown to the readers, and also unnamed, that a certain prophecy was true, as a matter of emphasis and importance.—The proof that the witness here is the author is found in every indication of the passage :—(*a*) in the valuelessness of the testimony as coming from an unknown person ; (*b*) in the statement that his testimony is ἀληθινή (that which corresponds to the true idea of testimony); (*c*) in the emphatic assertion, "he knows that he says what is true ;" (*d*) in the declaration that he bears the testimony to the end that you (the readers) may believe ; (*e*) in the matter of the quotation from the prophetic writings. How impossible that a witness, necessarily insignificant because utterly unknown to any one who read the book, should be thus introduced.—4. The action of Nicodemus, as recorded in ver. 39, is certainly indicative of love and devotion to Jesus. It is worthy of notice that the evangelist does not say of Nicodemus, as he does of Joseph of Arimathea, that he was "a disciple, but secretly for fear of the Jews." This fact, when brought into connection with the position which he is represented as taking in the meeting of the Sanhedrim in ch. vii., vv. 50, 51, is worthy of consideration in forming our estimate of the character of Nicodemus.

55
John 20

Vv. 1–18. 1. The other women who are represented in the Synoptics as going with Mary Magdalene to the sepulchre are not mentioned here, and the appearance to all the women which is spoken of by Matthew, xxviii. 9, 10, is omitted by John. The former difference between John and the others may be explained, with Weiss, on the ground that John introduces the story only with reference to the message which Mary alone carried to Peter and himself; or it may be explained by supposing, with Luthardt and others, that she hastened in going to the grave more rapidly than the others who had started with her, and thus arrived alone before them. The latter difference may, not improbably, be due to a mingling together in the narrative of Matthew of what happened to the other women (the appearance of the angel, etc.) with what happened to Mary alone (the appearance of Jesus); or there may have been an appearance to the other women on their return from the sepulchre, and after Mary had left them, which was altogether different from the appearance to Mary herself. The sameness of the words represented by Matthew as addressed by Jesus to the women (ver. 10), with those addressed to them by the angel (ver. 7), may point towards the former supposition as the correct one. In any case, there is no insuperable difficulty in reconciling the different Gospels here. The word οἴδαμεν (ver. 2), as Weiss holds, in opposition to Meyer, may fairly be taken as indicating that Mary had others with her at the tomb or as she went towards it.—2. The story of Peter and John, as also that of Mary, bears the evidence of its truthfulness, both in the striking character of its details, which would scarcely have been thought of by a later writer, and its accordance in some of these details with the peculiarities of the persons in question, as presented before us elsewhere.—3. The *belief* which "the disciple whom Jesus loved" is said to have had in consequence of what he saw in the tomb, is not to be understood as simply a belief in the fact that Jesus had risen from the dead, but —in accordance with the use of the verb throughout this Gospel—a belief in Jesus as the Christ, the Son of God. He attained a belief, at this time and in view of what he saw, which was beyond what he had had before, a belief which included an understanding that He must rise from the dead, and thus that He was, by a new manifestation, proved to be the Divine Logos.—4. The failure of Mary to recognize Jesus at first is to be explained in part, perhaps, by some peculiarity in dress, etc.; but, in part, by the fact that she did not think of His appearance before her alive, and in a bodily form, as a possibility. It is noticeable that Jesus was, in several instances, not immediately recognized by those to whom He appeared.—5. The best explanation of the difficult expression μή μου ἅπτου, with what follows it in ver. 17, is, in the view of the writer of this note, that which takes ἅπτου in the sense of *cling to*. Jesus bids her not to cling to Him as if He were now to be in a new communion with her and His other disciples, such as He had promised before His death, but to go and tell His disciples that this was to come afterwards, through and after His ascension. This is substantially the view of Godet, and it meets the demands of the words which follow as they are connected with this expression.—6. The story of Mary Magdalene, as here given, bears, in its first part (vv. 1, 2), wholly towards the faith of the two disciples; in its second part, it is evidently designed to present a proof of the resurrection of Jesus as tending to show that He is the Son of God. Testimony and experience come together, once more, in this place, and the author moves steadily towards the end which he has in view (vv. 30, 31). The incidents are selected and related, not for their own sake, but with a view to the great purpose of the book. But there is a new stage in the development here, which is evidently beyond what is found in the earlier chapters. The chronological progress, the progress in the testimony and proof, and the progress in faith, are seen to be united throughout the book in a very remarkable way. This union, in itself, bears witness that the whole narrative came from the author's own life and experience.

56

Vv. 19-29. 1. The appearance of Jesus when the doors were shut (vv. 19, 26) is a point which we are unable to explain. The evangelist has not stated the facts of the case with sufficient definiteness to make any conclusion absolutely certain. That Jesus had a body after His resurrection, which could be touched, and which bore the marks of the nails; that He could eat and walk, and could speak with the same voice as before His death; that He was seen and known to be the same person whom the disciples had been familiar with in their past association with Him, is evident from all the Gospel narratives. That, on the other hand, He appeared and disappeared at will, as He had not done before His death; that He was not recognized with the same immediateness, apparently, as He had been; that He even passed some hours with the disciples who were going to Emmaus, without any recognition on their part, seems equally clear. The mystery of His ascension may also be borne in mind in its relation to this question.—In the consideration of the particular words found in these verses (19, 26), two points are worthy of notice :—first, that we have no indication in other passages of any such thing as passing through the wood of closed doors—a thing which, in itself, would seem to be in the highest degree improbable; and, secondly, that we find the fact somewhat prominently suggested that, during the forty days, Jesus made Himself visible or invisible at will. May not these points, when taken together, indicate that Jesus here did not enter, at the time mentioned, into the room where the disciples were, but simply appeared to their view within it; that He appeared now as He disappeared at the close of His meeting with the disciples from Emmaus ?—2. In vv. 21-23 Jesus renews to the disciples their commission, or assures them again that they have it, and then bestows upon them the gift of the Holy Spirit. With respect to this gift it may be observed : (*a*) that it is, according to the natural interpretation of the words, an actual gift ; (*b*) that the distinction made by some writers between πνεῦμα ἅγιον and τὸ πνεῦμα ἅγιον can hardly be sustained, and the words must here designate the Holy Spirit in the same sense in which the latter phrase is used (comp. vii. 39, xvi. 13) ; (c) that the full gift of the Spirit seems to be placed in this Gospel, as in the Acts, after the glorification of Jesus. From these three considerations it follows that the gift here referred to was of the same nature, but not of the same measure, with that of the Day of Pentecost. It was, as Meyer remarks, an actual ἀπαρχή of the Holy Spirit.—3. The power of remitting and retaining sins which is spoken of in ver. 23 is not something bestowed as a mere official prerogative on the disciples, so that their mere word and will accomplish the end. Jesus Himself exercised forgiveness only on the conditions of faith and repentance, and in accordance with the will of the Father. The whole teaching of the New Testament shows that the apostles could, at the most, only pronounce the man who believed forgiven, and, as they did not possess omniscience, this pronouncing could not go beyond the point of declaring that the man was forgiven, provided he had the faith required. It was under the guidance and in accordance with the mind of the Spirit that they were to exercise this power, but not in any such sense that forgiveness depended on them or was to be determined by them alone.—4. The exclamation of Thomas, in ver. 28, is the final declaration of the faith of the apostles as given in this Gospel. Immediately after the record of it the writer closes his book. That this is a declaration of belief in the Divinity of Christ is proved by the words εἶπεν αὐτῷ, by which it is introduced—these words show that it is not a mere exclamation of surprise or astonishment ; by the fact that ὁ κύριός μου is most naturally used as referring to Jesus (see xiii. 13, xx. 13) ; by the connection of these words with vv. 30, 31 ; by the whole progress of faith and testimony in this Gospel, as leading up to the end. If it is such a declaration, the 29th verse shows that it was accepted by Jesus. At such a moment—indeed, at any moment, but especially at such a moment, when He was soon to send forth the apostles on their great mission in the world, in which they were to proclaim His message and even to expose themselves to the danger of death in His cause—He could not have allowed them to remain under a delusion and to believe Him to be Divine when He was not. He could not have pronounced a solemn benediction on all who believed what He knew to be untrue. These words of Thomas, therefore, together with those of Jesus which follow, become a fitting climax of the whole book, both with respect to the testimony of Jesus to Himself and the answering faith of His immediate disciples.

57

Vv. 30, 31. This passage is evidently the conclusion of the Gospel as it was originally written, and it sets forth the purpose which the author had in view. We may notice in connection with these verses the following points:—(a) The writer evidently shows that he prepares his book on a principle of selection (many others are not written, but these are written) ; (b) The selections which he makes are made with a view to the proving of some truth or doctrine or fact (σημεῖα) ; (c) The proofs are those which were given in the presence of the disciples—they depend for their force, therefore, in a special sense, upon the experience and personal witness-bearing of these disciples ; (d) The disciples are those whose first meeting with Jesus is recorded in the first chapter, and their companions in the apostolic company and the personal friends of Jesus ; (e) The doctrine or truth or fact to be proved is that Jesus is the Christ, the Son of God ; (f) This statement, when interpreted as it must be by the Prologue, from which the entire development of the proof begins, must mean that He is the Logos made flesh ; (g) The object in view in giving this proof and establishing this doctrine is that the readers may believe what the writer evidently believes ; (h) The final purpose is that, through thus believing, the readers may have life— that is, that eternal life of which the book speaks.

58

John 21

Vv. 1–14. The appearance of Jesus which is here recorded as taking place in Galilee is so entirely different in all its details from that which is mentioned in Matt. xx. 16 f., so far as any details are there given, that it must be regarded as a different appearance. Whether it occurred before or after the one in Matthew, cannot be determined. Godet supposes that the appearance recorded in Matthew coincides with the one to which Paul alludes in 1 Cor. xv. 6, where Jesus manifested Himself to more than five hundred of the believers. From the order of Paul's list of the appearances, however, and the form of expression which he uses respecting the appearance to the Twelve and that to all the apostles, it is more probable that the appearance to the five hundred occurred in Jerusalem during the week which intervened between the Sunday on which Jesus rose and the following Sunday. In the account in Matthew no distinct mention is made of any but the eleven, and, though it is possible that others may have been present, it is hardly to be supposed that so many as five hundred could be passed over without any allusion.—2. The object of the author in the introduction of this story of Jesus' appearance to the disciples seems to have been, not the appearance itself as proving the resurrection, or as suggesting the lesson which the miracle may be supposed to have carried within it, but as preparing the way for the conversation with Peter respecting himself and John which follows. This was the occasion on which the conversation took place. That Jesus intended, however, to teach some lesson of dependence on His wisdom and guidance as related to the future work of the apostles, and as, in some sense, preparatory for what was to be said to Peter, is to be regarded as probable.—3. The word τρίτον (ver. 14) must be understood as referring to the third appearance before a company of the apostles, etc., which is recorded in this Gospel, and as having no further bearing.

59

Vv. 15–23. In the words addressed to Peter there are two parts : first, those which bear upon his re-instatement in office, as it may be called; and, secondly, those which relate to his death.—1. The words which are found in vv. 15–17 introduce the matter of Peter's re-instatement by calling attention to his former protestations of love, with respect to which he had so signally failed and fallen. The readiness of Jesus to forgive and to restore is thus more tenderly manifested here than anywhere else in the Gospel narrative. The passage exhibits Jesus, in this regard, in His relation to His own friends. Following upon the words which restore Peter to his place and position in the great work and kingdom, Jesus utters a word of prophecy, in which He proclaims, as it were, to the two friends among the apostles who stood nearest to Him in His love, and who were to continue in life for many years, as James was not, the future which they must expect. The testimony of Jesus to Himself, in His relation of love to the individual disciple, is thus brought out in this appended chapter, which by reason of this characteristic, as well as its many forms of expression, manifests a truly Johannean type.—2. That the word *these* (τούτων) in ver. 15 refers to the other disciples, and thus carries the thought back to Peter's protestation in xiii. 37, "I will lay down my life for thee," and the similar protestation in Mark xiv. 29 (comp. Matt. xxvi. 33), "Although all shall be offended, yet will not I," is generally admitted now by the best writers, and there can be but little doubt that this is the correct view.—3. As to the distinction between the words ἀγαπᾶν and φιλεῖν, it is undoubtedly intended to be a marked one in this place. Otherwise the use of the two words can hardly be satisfactorily accounted for. The former word has in it the moral element, and is more appropriate to express the relation of man towards God and Christ, while the latter is here used of the affection of friendship. Weiss, however, thinks that the occurrence of the latter word in the third question put by Jesus to Peter makes it doubtful whether any such distinction is intended.—4. That the reference of the prophetic words of Jesus respecting Peter's future is to the manner of his death, is affirmed by the evangelist, and there is nothing in the language used to make this reference in any way improbable. The language, however, only indicates death by violence, and is not sufficiently definite to show that Peter was to be crucified. The parallelisms of the expressions are such as to make it evident that the words *thou shalt stretch forth thy hands and another shall gird thee* form *as a whole* the contrast to *thou girdedst thyself.* The stretching forth the hands, therefore, does not follow the girding or binding, but precedes it and is incidental to it ;—it must accordingly refer to that forced submission which pertains to the prisoner or criminal who is bound and led out to execution. —5. The word ἔρχομαι in vv. 22, 23 is one which presents some difficulty. That it cannot mean *come for him at death* is evident, because all men— Peter as well as John—tarry till this coming. It cannot refer to the coming in and through the Spirit, for both of the disciples alike were to live beyond that period. For the same reason, it cannot mean the return for the forty days. Both of these latter events, also, were so near at hand that no such expression would have been used respecting them. The ordinary reference of the word to the Parousia escapes these objections ; but as Jesus appears to have been free from any idea that the Parousia was to take place in the near future, there seems to be a kind of extravagance in the expression, as thus explained, which bears with it a certain improbability. This last view is that which is pressed upon us by the usage of the word, and, if it is adopted, the explanation of the meaning suggested by the evangelist is the one which must be regarded as correct—namely, that the emphasis is on the *if*. Luthardt holds that the contrast which the evangelist makes, as he claims, between the dying of the disciple and his tarrying until Jesus should come, shows that, at the time of writing the words, Jesus had already come. The coming began, according to his view, with the judgment upon Israel and Jerusalem. Alford has substantially the same view. Weiss holds (see his notes on xiv. 3, xxi. 22) that Jesus is represented by John as having thought, like the apostles, that the Parousia would be in the near future.

60

Vv. 24, 25. It is worthy of notice that the most full and complete designation of the disciple who is nowhere mentioned by name in this Gospel is given in this place, and this is immediately followed by the words, "This is the disciple who wrote," etc. We have, therefore, in this verse the strongest affirmation that this disciple is the writer of the book. If the contrast in the tenses of the two participles γράψας and μαρτυρῶν, which Godet presses, is to be insisted upon, the evidence of the sentence is very strong that the author of the Gospel was still living when this verse was written. It will follow from this understanding of the words, also, that the verse was either written by the author himself, designating himself by the use of the third person as in other places, or by contemporaries who could say of his testimony, "We know that it is true." Weiss, however, claims that ὁ μαρτυρῶν determines nothing as to this question, and Westcott says that it may not determine the point. The position of Westcott may be admitted. But the passage i. 15, to which both of these writers appeal—"John bears witness (μαρτυρεῖ) and has cried (κέκραγεν), saying," etc.—is hardly altogether parallel. The perfect κέκραγε in that passage may, not improbably, be used in the sense of the present (see Meyer on that verse), and the propositional present form is adapted to the character of the statements in the Prologue. Here, however, there is a natural contrast, as in xix. 35 between μεμαρτύρηκεν and οἶδεν ὅτι λέγει, and if there were a reference to a permanent testimony in the book, it would more naturally be set forth either by putting the expression in such a form as to declare it distinctly, or at least by placing the participle which speaks of testimony after (instead of before) that which speaks of the preparation of the book.—That the disciple whom Jesus loved was the author of this Gospel is proved without this passage, as we have seen. This passage only adds, at the most, a definite and distinct declaration of what is contained elsewhere in incidental references or statements, and is suggested, above all, by the manifold evidence of his personality and his remembered experience, which we find throughout the entire history which is presented before us.

61

Concluding Note

If we now briefly review the book and observe its progress from the beginning to the end, we find the first chapter (following the Prologue) introducing to us the earliest disciples—the persons in the story who are, in a peculiar sense, the representatives of the disciples mentioned in xx. 30. The proofs given to these disciples begin at once to be set forth. They consist in works and words. The evidence from *the works* is carried forward from ch. ii. to ch. xii. It is, in many cases, accompanied by that of the words, but the works have a certain special prominence. Beginning with ch. xiii. the evidence from *the words alone* is presented. In this section of the book, however, we have at last the great miracle of the resurrection, as the final σημεῖον. The section in which *the works* are made prominent contains the discoursings with the people and the Jewish rulers—with unbelievers, as well as believers. That in which *the words* alone are brought before the reader has relation only to the inmost circle of believers (chs. xiii.-xvii.). The order of the great proofs is thus the natural one.

Of the miracles, the one at Cana was an exercise of power for the purpose of confirming the five or six disciples in their first faith ; that in which the nobleman's son was healed manifested the power of Jesus as working at a distance ; that of Bethesda, as effective in the case of a man who had been suffering from his malady for nearly forty years ; that of the walking on the sea and the multiplication of the loaves displayed His power over the elements and the unlimited character of it ; that in the case of the man who had been blind from birth exhibited the power of remedying maladies even to the utmost limit, and that of the raising of Lazarus the power even over death ; finally, the great miracle of His own resurrection showed the endless life-force inherent in Himself. Here is no repetition, but steady progress—following the chronological order of Jesus' life, indeed, but manifestly guided, in the author's choice of his materials, by the desire of presenting a continually growing and strengthening proof of the truth.

The proofs and testimonies also which are connected with the miracles, and are given in conversations and discourses, move on in the natural order. They are sometimes clear and decisive ; sometimes suggestive, but penetrating the depths of Christian truth far more deeply than the disciples could then understand. The testimony to Nicodemus is of the new spiritual birth and of the Divine provision for bringing men to the true life through the lifting up of the Only-begotten Son. That of the fifth chapter is of the relation of the Son to the Father as connected with judgment and the resurrection, together with the evidences which establish this. That of ch. vi. takes up and unfolds the eternal life as founded upon the Son and upon belief in Him. That of chs. viii., x. enters more fully into the nature of the Son, His pre-existence, His equality with God. Those of chs. xiii.–xvi. relate to what He is and does for the inmost life and needs of His disciples, and speak of the very deepest things in the personal relations of the believer and His Lord.

Of the steady growth of faith in the minds of the disciples, the examination of the chapters, as we have discussed them in these notes, has shown constant evidence. The weak beginning in the words "We have found the Messiah," which needed the miracle at Cana to establish it, so that it could grow in the coming time, turns at the end into the declaration of the Deity of Christ, which is uttered by the one who was slowest to believe, and which bears witness of the existence of a faith in the whole company that could never pass away.

The suggestions of these brief notes have been largely devoted to the setting forth of this progress and development of *testimony* and *belief* within the limits imposed by the *biographical* character of the book. They have been necessarily partial and imperfect. But it is believed that a careful study of this Gospel by any candid scholar, uninfluenced by a preconceived theory, will tend to convince him the more fully, as he pursues his investigation more thoroughly, of the error of those who claim that the book only repeats the same idea from one end to the other—that there is no orderly movement—that it is the work of a speculative philosopher creating his facts to suit his theory, or subordinating the development of proof as moving along the line of biography to the ever-renewed statement of an alleged truth. The writer was not a speculative philosopher, but a man who wrote from the joyful recollections of his own personal experience and inner life.

That the writer was the disciple whom Jesus loved is proved by the peculiar manner in which this disciple is brought before the reader's notice from time to time ; by the evident indications that this disciple was the unnamed companion of Andrew who came to Jesus on the day mentioned in ch. i., vv. 35–40 ; by the words of ch. xix., ver. 35, according to the only explanation which can be given of them as introduced for the purpose which the author evidently has in view ; by the distinct and positive declaration of ch. xxi., ver. 24, provided this verse was written by the author of the Gospel or by contemporaries who knew him ; and in the most impressive way for the mind which opens itself to receive what comes from such a source, by the constant and manifest evidence which the book bears within itself that it is the outgrowth of an intimate friendship with Jesus while He was on the earth.

That the disciple whom Jesus loved was the apostle John is placed beyond reasonable doubt by all the proofs which show that he belonged to the apostolic company; that, if belonging to that company, he must have been one of the three to whom the Lord gave His deepest and strongest affection; and that of these three we cannot suppose him to be Peter, since he is clearly distinguished from that apostle, or James, because of James' early death. As we move, therefore, from the central and inmost recesses of the book outward until we come to the most distinct statements which it makes in words, we find, everywhere and at every step of our progress, the evidence that it is the work of John and that it is the record not only of Jesus' life, but also of his own life with Jesus.

THE END

INDEX

A

Abbott, Ezra, on authorship of St. John's Gospel, 26, 237, 238, 280, 281.
Abraham, Seed of, 666, 669, 672, 679; claim of pure blood, 673, 1036, 1037; Christ greater than, 681, 1038.
"According to" κατά, Meaning of, 238, 239.
"Acts of Paul and Thecla," 206; Acta Pauli, 377.
Aeluis Aristides, 327.
Aenon, 404, 405.
Alogi, in second century, 20, 171.
Amen ἀμήν, frequent use by St. John, 336, 682, 701, 1007.
American Editor, Preface of, ix; introductory suggestions of on the internal evidence, 493-512; additional notes by, on chs. 1-5, 513-559; on chs. 6-21, 1017-1102.
Andrew, The Apostle, 31, 32, 33, 38, 90, 92, 327, 329, 567, 717-719, 1017.
Angel of the Lord, on the Presence, etc., 177, 288.
Anicetus, 40.
Annas and Caiaphas, 63, 70, 72, 73, 82, 501, 914-917, 1082-1084.
ἄνωθεν, Meaning of, as used by the Lord, 376-379.
Antiochus Epiphanes, 717.
Apocalypse of St. John, 16, 17, 23, 39, 49, 53, 182, 183-185, 188-190, 217, 218, 336, 473, 941, 943, 985, 1065.
Apollinaris, quoted, 143, 965, 967, 968, 971.
Apollonius, 40, 49.
Apollos. and Epistle to the Hebrews, 14; Gospel of St. John ascribed to, 14, 204; one of John the Baptist's disciples, 214.
Apostolical Constitutions, 359, 380, 643.
Arimathaea, 956, 957.
Aristion, 18, 1000, 1014.

Arnaud, on plan of St. John's Gospel, 226.
Artemidorus, 377.
Ascension of the Lord (ch. 3:13), 388-389, 603, 605, 998, 1024, 1025.
"Assumption of Moses," 324.
Astié, on St. John's Gospel, 24.
Athanasius, 281, 970.
Athenogoras, 139, 144.
Augustine, referred to or quoted, 50, 51, 267, 273, 350, 357, 389, 407, 605, 622, 643, 653, 659, 707, 744, 826, 841, 887, 1003, 1007.

B

Baptism with water, appointed by the Lord, 379, 380, 543, 544.
Barabbas, 931, 932
Barnabas, Epistle of, 17, 27.
Basilides, 157-160, 186.
Bath-Kol, 785
Bauer, B., on authenticity of St. John's Gospel, 11, 12, 22, 580.
Baumgarten-Crusius, 223, 376.
Baur, F.C., on St. John's Gospel, 12, 13, 14, 17, 22; against Thiersch and Ewald, 23, 24; on conduct of the apostles, 36, 37; on historical value of the Fourth Gospel, 66, 74, 123; date of the Gospel, 140, 141; author of the Gospel, 181, 182, 199, 204; on the Logos, 291, 292; on baptism of Jesus, 322; on miracle at Cana, 354; on miracle of opening eyes of the blind, 695; on resurrection of Lazarus, 759-760.
Bengel, Gnomon of, (now reprinted as *New Testament Word Studies*, Kregel Publications), 222, 224, 258, 279, 345, 385, 410, 618, 649, 702, 797, 867, 940.
Bertholdt, Introduction to New Testament, 21
Bethany, 309, 730, 737; the supper at, 762, 1034.
Bethlehem, 640.

Bethsaida, 331, 357, 564.
Beyschlag, on authenticity of St. John's Gospel, 26.
Biedermann, on St. John's Gospel, 54.
Bindemann, on the Gospel histories, 23.
Bleek, Introduction to New Testament, 17, 23, 24.
Boanerges, 33, 34.
Body of the Lord, after the resurrection, 952, 977-980, 992, 993, 1095.
Bread, from Heaven, 581-583, 593, 594; the Lord Himself, 593, 594, 599, 1021, 1022.
Brethren or brothers of Jesus, who these were, 357-361, 510; Godet's view, 357-360, 614.
Bretschneider, on authenticity of St. John's Gospel, 9, 10, 21.
Bunsen, on St. John's Gospel, 24.
Buxtorf, 324.

C

Caesar (Tiberius), 937, 938.
Caiaphas, the high priest, 751-755, 914-917, 918-922, 942, 1051, 1083.
Cana of Galilee, Miracle of Jesus at, 342-355, 444, 551, 999.
Capernaum, 355, 356, 361, 444, 445, 565, 571, 572.
Cedron, 852, 884, 909, 910.
Celsus, against Christianity, 145, 146.
Cephas. See Peter.
Cerinthus and St. John, 148, 171, 209, 211.
Chiliasm and St. John's Gospel, 133, 134.
Christ. See Messiah.
Christology, 185, 467-469.
Chronicon Paschale, 965.
Chrysostom, referred to or quoted, 235, 236, 276, 281, 335, 340, 385, 453, 469, 478, 485, 487, 603, 605, 618, 644, 653, 659, 702, 707, 743, 797, 808, 832, 838, 867, 948, 959, 977, 995.
Church, The, in Gospel and Apocalypse, 187, 188; history of, 788, 854, unity of, 901, 902.
Chuza, 444.
Circumcision, 625, 626.
Clement of Alexandria referred to or quoted, 41, 48, 50, 139, 141, 168, 209, 236, 280, 357, 595.
Clement of Rome, 139, 204.
Clementine Homilies, 14, 139, 144, 153, 964, 965.
Clopas, 358-360; Mary, wife of, 360, 361, 946.
Coming of the Lord, 1010, 1015. See Parousia.
Cousins of the Lord Jesus, 357-361.
Credner, on authenticity of St. John's Gospel, 21; Introduction to the New Testament, 197.
Crome, on St. John's Gospel, 21.
Crown of thorns, 933, 934.
Crucifixion of the Lord, Day of, 78, 958-960; Friday, April 7, A.D. 30, 967, 1052, 1090, 1091.
Crux interpretum, 442, 443.
Cureton and Syriac Version of New Testament, 236, 237, 575.
Cyril of Alexandria, 1003.

D

Daniel, Prophecy of, 339, 340.
Davidson, on authenticity of St. John's Gospel, 17.
Dedication, Feast of, 711-718.
Déramey, on authenticity of St. John's Gospel, 25.
De Rougemont, on plan of St. John's Gospel, 227; on the Gnostics, 295.
De Saulcy, 454.
Devil, The, a murderer, 674, 676, 1037.
De Wette, on authenticity of St. John's Gospel, 10, 21; on plan of the Gospel, 222-225.
Diaspora, 16.
Diatessaron, 149, 717.
Didymus, i.e., Thomas, 200, 736, 737, 983, 999.
Diognetus, Letter to, 139, 154, 204.
"Disciple whom Jesus loved," i.e., St. John, 12, 31-35, 190-193, 203, 501-503, 815, 816, 946, 1001, 1008, 1093, 1101, 1102, "that other disciple," 918, 974, 975, 1101.
Docetas, 380, 953.
Docetism, and St. John's Gospel, 133, 202, 422, 684.
Domitian, Emperor, 217.
Doorkeepers, Female, commonly, 918, 919.
Dualism, and St. John's Gospel, 132.
D'Uechtritz, on St. John's Gospel, 17, 18.
Dwight, Professor T. See American Editor.

E

Eating and drinking the flesh and

Index / 1105

blood of the Lord, 593, 602.
Ebionitism, 211, 213.
Ebrard, on Gospel history, 22; on plan of St. John's Gospel, 224.
Eckermann, on authenticity of St. John's Gospel, 9.
Egyptian versions of the New Testament, 234.
Eichhorn, Introduction to the New Testament, 21, 222.
Emmaus, 973, 980, 983, 986, 987.
"End, to the," Meaning of, 804, 1055, 1060.
Enoch, Book of, 289, 340.
Ephesians, Epistle to the, 713.
Ephesus, St. John in, 38, 39.
Ephraim, City of, 755.
Ephrem Syrus, 149.
Epiphanius, referred to or quoted, 8, 50, 157, 171.
Eschatology of Gospel and Apocalypse, 188-190, 473, 480.
Eusebius, referred to or quoted, 40, 41, 43, 49, 141, 186, 209, 281, 357, 358, 645, 939, 959, 969.
Evanson, on dissonance of the evangelists, 9, 21.
"Evil, The," 895, 896; American Editor prefers "the evil one,"1079.
Ewald, on authenticity of St. John's Gospel, etc., 24, 367, 447.
Excommunication, 694, 695.

F

Father, the Subordination of the Son to, 291, 297; Father of Christ, 461-467, 652, 654, 655, 662, 678, 680, 713, 714, 720, 726, 747, 799, 849, 872, 880, 888, 889, 893, 1018, 1046, 1072.
Fathers, The, mode of quoting from the New Testament, 234, 235.
Faustus, the Manichaean, 238.
"Feast," a, or the, i.e., Purim, or Passover, or Pentecost, or Tabernacles, 452, 453, 552, 553.
Flesh and blood, Meaning of words, 596, 1023.
Frommann, on authenticity of Gospel histories, 22.

G

Galilee and Galileans, 416, 441-447, 550, 551, 642, 643, 999, 1000, 1097.
Gerizim, 426-428.
Gess, on Person and Work of Christ, 25, 296, 341, 592, 620, 637, 719, 798, 822, 832, 836, 845, 859, 905.
Gethsemane, 850, 851, 853, 884, 898, 906, 909, 910, 1054, 1055, 1081.
Gfroerer, on authenticity of St. John's Gospel, 22; on miracle at Cana, 353, 354.
Gieseler, on origin of Gospels, 21.
Gnosticism and Gnostics, 12, 13, 17, 39, 127, 133, 140, 155, 173, 211, 295, 320, 469, 706.
Good Friday, 958, 960.
Gospel literature, Formation of, 3-8.
Gospel, The Fourth, discussion of authenticity of, 8; adversaries of authenticity, 8-20; defenders of, 20-26; advocates of intermediate positions, 26-28; analysis of, 54-65; characteristics, 66-138; epoch or date, 139-167; author of, 167-208; place of writing, 208, 209; occasion and aim, 209-219; introduction to commentary, 221; plan of the Gospel of St. John, 221-230; preservation of the text, 230-237; MSS., 230-233; ancient versions, 233, 234; the fathers' quotations from, 234, 235; text in general, 235-237; title of the Gospel, 238, 239; prologue (ch. 1:1-18) exegesis of, 240-298; the Logos, unbelief, faith, 243-283; plan and intention of prologue, 283, 286; idea and term Logos, 286, 298; importance of prologue, 291-298; exegesis of first part, ch. 1:19-4:54, 299-447; exegesis of second part, ch. 5:1-47, 448-492; 6:1-12:50, 561-800; exegesis of third part, ch. 13:1-17:26, 801-907; exegesis of the fourth part, ch. 18:1-19:42, 908-971; exegesis of the fifth part, ch. 20:1-29, 972-993; exegesis of ch. 20:30,31, 994-996; exegesis of appendix, ch. 21:1-25, 997-1016.
Gospel, Aim of writer of each, 212; testimony of St. John to first three, 995.
"Great Unknown," author of the Fourth Gospel, 204; genius of, 505-512.
Greeks (ch. 7:35), 633 (ch. 7:20); 777-784, 1054.
Guericke, Introduction to the New Testament, 22.

H

Hades, 657.

1106 / Index

Harvest in Palestine, Sowing and reaping, 434-440.
Hase, Life of Jesus and on St. John's Gospel, 19, 20, 24, 28, 86, 87, 171, 181, 204.
Hasert, "the anonymous Saxon," 23.
Hauff, on St. John's Gospel, 21, 23.
Heaven, 388-390.
Hebrews, Epistle to the, 112, 113, 205, 215, 395.
Hegesippus, 30, 357-359.
Hengstenberg, Commentary on St. John's Gospel, 24, 343, 347, 351, 376, 384, 397, 404, 405, 453, 478, 620, 730, 824, 837,859, 999, 1001.
Heracleon, 235, 250, 277, 425.
Heretics, Ancient, quote on St. John's Gospel, 144.
Hermas, 27, 139.
Herod Antipas, 444; 931, 941.
Herod the Great, 369.
Hilgenfeld, on St. John's Gospel, 14, 16; Introduction to New Testament, 17, 27; criticisms, etc., 64, 196, 406, 439, 453, 463, 480, 823, 841.
Hippolytus, on the Alogi, and St. John's Gospel, 20; philosophumena of, 139, 155, 380, 967.
Holtzmann, on St. John's Gospel, 17, 27, 32, 75; on death of St. John, 52; on St. John and synoptics, 77, 80; on baptism of Jesus, 322, 323; on name "Son of man," 341, 342.
Holy Spirit, 638-640, 838-843, 846, 847;procession of, 864, 865; work of, 869-872, 1068, 1069, 1072, 1074, 1075, 1076.
Hort. *See* Westcott.
"Hour" of Jesus, 630, 656, 1027, 1060.
Hug, Introduction to New Testament, 21.
"Hundred, a, and fifty-three," Meaning of, 1003.

I

"I am," our Lord's assertion of eternal existence, 682,683.
Ignatius, 27; Epistles of, 41, 42, 164-166, 204, 359, 600.
Incarnation of Christ, 263, 264, 267-270.
Inspiration of the Gospels, 872.
Internal evidence of St. John's Gospel, 197-204; suggestions on, by American Editor, 493-512, 1066.
Irenaeus, referred to or quoted, 8, 31, 37, 38, 39, 46, 48, 49, 51, 139, 142, 144, 168, 186, 266, 280, 380, 447, 453, 508, 967, 969.
Itala, Latin Version of the New Testament, 140, 234, 280, 281, 687, 831, 838.

J

Jacob's well, 420, 421, 435.
James, brother of John, 29, 30, 31, 328, 525, 526; martyrdom of, 35; in catalogue of the apostles, 203; at the Sea of Tiberias, with the Lord, 999, 1098, 1101.
James, brother of the Lord, 357-359, 614, 987, 988.
James, son of Alphaeus, or Clopas, 358, 360.
Jerome, referred to or quoted, 51, 209, 357, 643, 707, 970, 1003.
Jerusalem, 362, 371, 448, 449, 487, 628, 1026, 1029.
Jerusalemites, 628, 1029.
Jesus Christ, 887, 888.
Jesus, the Lord, loved John, 31-35; entrusts His mother to John, 35; passion of, 63, 64; resurrection of, 64; day of crucifixion, 78; the Logos of God, 94-97; discourses of, according to St. John, 97-123; human life of, 292-296; gift received in baptism, 319-321; calls the first disciples, 325-330; calls Philip and Nathanael, 331-336; designates Himself "Son of man," 336, 338-342; miracle at Cana, 342-355; brethren of, 357-361; in the temple, 361-369; prophesies His death and resurrection, 365-368; "must be lifted up," 392, 393; interview with Nicodemus, 374-403; in the country of Judaea, 403-415; in Samaria, 415 seq.; discourses with woman of Samaria, and result, 421-432; with the Samaritans, 440, 441; heals nobleman's son, 444-447; miracle at Pool of Bethesda, 454-458; asserts His divinity as "Son of God," 461-467, 554, 555; condemns unbelief,448- 492; remains in Galilee, 561, 562; miracle of loaves and fishes, 565-568; plot to make Him a king, 569-571; walks on the water, 571-574; discourses in the synagogue at Capernaum, 574-608; pre-existence of, 586; reference to the holy supper, 600, 601; followers of desert, 607-608; sojourn in

Galilee, 612-619; goes up to Jerusalem, 619, 620; teaches in the temple, 621-633; true origin of, 628-631; approaching departure, 631-633; the true source, 634-643; the light of the world, 649, 656; further teaching, 656-665; testifies against Jewish unbelief, 665-684; miracle wrought on the blind man, 685-691; parable of the shepherd, 699-705; of the door, 705-708; of the good shepherd, 709-713; address at feast of dedication, 718-728; sojourn beyond Jordan, 728; raises Lazarus from the dead, 729-750; Jews resolve to put to death, 754; sojourn in Ephraim, 755; the supper at Bethany, 762-771; enters Jerusalem, 711-776; last scene in the temple, 776-790; Greeks wish to see, 777-784; washes the disciples' feet, 807-811; sends away Judas Iscariot, 814, 815; discourses to His disciples on separation from them, on outpouring of the Spirit, etc., and bids them farewell, 823-883; prayer of, 883-907, 1077-1081; arrest of, 909-913, 1082; trial before the Sanhedrim, 914-923, 1082-1084; trial before Pilate, 923-942, 1085-1090; crucifixion of, 942-956; burial, 972-993; resurrection, 998-1012; interview with the disciples, 1097, 1098.

Job, Book of, 205.

Johannean discussion. *See* Gospel, the Fourth.

John Baptist, 55, 104-106, 117, 203, 255, 257, 274-277; testimonies to Jesus, 300; first, 300-309; second, 310-321; third, 321-325; questions as to the testimonies, 322-325, 385; not yet in prison, 405; questions proposed to and answers, 406-414; spirit of John's disciples, 407; testimony of the Lord to, 483, 484; testimonies to the Lord, 523-526.

John the apostle, in his father's house, 29, 30; a follower of Jesus, 30-35; at head of Jewish Church, 35-38; in Asia Minor, 38-50; death of, 51, 52; character of, 52, 53; charges against, by Baur, etc., 127-128; Greek style of Gospel, 134-138; time of writing, 140-167; author of Fourth Gospel, 167-208; "the disciple whom Jesus loved," 190-193; First Epistle of, 201; writes in Ephesus, 208, 209; aim and occasion of Fourth Gospel, 209-219; plan of Gospel traced, 221-230; prologue to the Gospel, 240-298; first part, ch. 1:19-4:54, 299-447; second part, ch. 5:1-12:50, 448-492, 561-800; third part, ch. 13:1-17:26, 801-907; fourth part ch. 18 1:19:42, 908-971; fifth part, ch. 20:1-29, 972-993; conclusion, 994-996; appendix, 997-1016; did he, or did he not, die? 1011, 1098, 1099.

John, Gospel of. *See* Gospel, the Fourth.

John, The presbyter, 14, 17, 20, 25, 207, 1000.

Joseph of Arimathaea, 956, 957.

Joseph, husband of Mary, 357, 359, 470; reputed father of Jesus, 589.

Josephus, 184, 369, 416, 426, 431, 634, 717, 752, 919, 923, 925, 927, 930.

Judas, or Jude, 845.

Judas Iscariot, the traitor, 58, 60, 71, 81, 86, 200, 570, 606, 609, 610, 768, 769, 805, 814, 817-819, 822, 894, 909-912, 1025, 1053, 1062, 1064.

Judas Maccabaeus, 718.

Judgment of mankind, 469-473, 536, 537, 556; moral, 473-475, 477-479, 1074.

Julian, the apostate, 845.

Justification, Means of, 185, 186.

Justin Martyr, 23, 40, 139, 147, 149-153, 183, 186, 600, 628, 933.

K

Keerl, on "Son of man," 341.

Keil, on St. John's Gospel, criticisms, etc., 275, 314, 335, 343, 391, 423, 436, 462, 484, 565, 582, 594, 626,824, 830, 837, 865, 939, 940, 949, 980, 1079.

Keim, History of Jesus, 15, 16, 26; on death of St. John, 52; on author of the Fourth Gospel, 167; on the baptism of Jesus, 322; on miracle at Cana, 354; on cleansing the temple, 370; on the narrative, ch. 18:10, 913; on Caiaphas, 920; on the crucifixion, 943; on the resurrection of the Lord, 990, 992.

Koestlin, on pseudonymous literature in the early Church, 13.

Krenkel, on St. John's Gospel, 17.

L

Lampe, Commentary on St. John's

Gospel, 21, 221, 222.
Lange, Commentary on St. John's Gospel, and life of Jesus, 24, 227, 297, 401, 578, 710, 997.
Lazarus, and his sisters, 60; resurrection of, 80, 84, 87, 89; narrative of the resurrection of, 730-750; effect produced by this miracle, 750-756, 1047; at the supper in Bethany, 762, 765, 770; death of planned by the Jews, 770.
Labbaeus. See Judas or Jude.
Le Clerc, answers the deists, 21.
Leimbach, 25, 43.
Leuschner, on St. John's Gospel, 26.
"Life" ζωή, Meaning of, 250, 251.
"Light" φῶς, Force of word, in St. John. 252-256, 258, 259, 517, 518; Jesus, light of the world, 641-656, 685, 688.
Lightfoot, 581, 767, 932.
Logos, The, 12, 54, 55, 82, 87, 92, 93, 94-97, 125; doctrine of the, 173-180; term, 180, 181; exegesis of the name, 243-253, 283; idea and term, 286-291, 467, 476, 503, 504, 513-515, 703, 745, 880.
Lord's Supper, 600, 601, 605, 814, 1023, 1024; when instituted, 819-822, 1058, 1059, 1063, 1090, 1091.
Lucian, 826.
Lücke, Commentary on St. John's Gospel, 21, 22, 221, 276, 285, 330, 367, 401.
Ludemann, on Papias, 27.
Luthardt, Commentary on St. John's Gospel, 24, 26, 221, 226, 426, 450, 659, 661, 694, 783, 826, 863.
Lützelberger, on authenticity of St. John's Gospel, 11, 12, 16, 204.

M

Maimonides, 926.
Malchus, 92, 200.
Mangold, on St. John's Gospel, 17, 167.
Manuscripts of the New Testament, 230-233; majuscules, three groups, 230-233; minuscules, 233.
Marcion, 139, 147, 154-157.
Martha and Mary, 60, 74, 77, 80, 81, 89, 730; send word to Jesus that Lazarus is sick, 731; interview of the sisters with the Lord, 738, 739-743, 1049, 1050; Mary's adoring homage to the Saviour, 765-767.

Mary, mother of Jesus, 29, 35, 343-349, 510, 618; near the cross, 946, 947; in St. John's house, 974, 1091, 1092.
Mary, wife of Clopas, 360, 361, 946.
Mary Magdalene, 736, 946; goes to the sepulchre, 972, 973, 975; Jesus appears to, 976-979, 980, 986, 987, 1004, 1094, 1095.
Melito, 967.
Memar, Memra, 178, 289. See Logos.
Messiah, or Christ, 55, 327, 328, 431, 432, 478, 488-490, 498, 558, 559, 615-617, 633, 640, 689, 703, 789, 853, 863, 887, 888, 928, 975, 976, 996, 999, 1019, 1033-1035, 1101.
Messiahs, False, 489, 707.
Meyer, Commentary on St. John's Gospel, 24, 226, 397, 422, 437, 443, 453, 460, 484, 621, 690, 710, 765, 887, 943, 985, 1001, 1049, 1050, 1055, 1070, 1071, 1086.
Milligan, Professor, on John the presbyter, 25; Commentary on St. John's Gospel, 229, 242, 534, 1022, 1055, 1079.
Ministry of Christ, Length of, 452, 453. See Passover.
Minutius, Felix, 826.
Miracles, in general, On, 353.
Montanism, 12, 13, 15, 147, 211, 990.
Moses, Law of, 279; testimony of to the Messiah, 489, 490, 492, 681; Moses and the law, 624, 625, 1027, 1028; disciples of, 693.
Muratori, Discovery of, 146, 148, 168, 209, 1014.

N

Nard, 766, 767.
Nathanael, 32, 128, 200; called by the Master, 331-336, 526, 999.
Nazareth, 331-333, 344, 355, 356, 442, 443.
Neander, Life of Jesus, 22; on "the Son of man," 342; on the miracle at Cana, 350; on return of the Lord, 830.
Nice, Council of, on the paschal controversy, 969, 970.
Nicodemus, 56, 71, 90, 91, 98-100, 120, 373; interview with the Lord, 374-403; Godet's judgment on, 402, 403; American Editor's judgment, 530-533; in Sanhedrim, 642, 1031, 1093.
Nicolas, M., on St. John's Gospel, 14, 207.

Niermeyer, on St. John's Gospel and the Apocalypse, 23, 184.
Noack, Wild speculations of, 216.
Norton, on the authenticity of the Gospels, 22.
Nyegaard, on the authenticity of St. John's Gospel, 26.

O

Old Testament, as quoted by the Lord, 584, 591; fulfilled in the New, 1061.
Olshausen, on St. John's Gospel, 21, 222, 410, 439, 830.
Ophites, 674.
Origen, referred to or quoted, 52, 141, 145, 235, 274, 277, 302, 308, 309, 376, 380, 434, 595, 644, 830, 838.

P

Palm day (Sunday or Monday), 763, 771, 772, 786, 1052.
Papias, 25, 27, 183; epoch of, 42-45, 160-163, 204, 645, 1014, 1015.
Parable παροιμία in St. John's Gospel, 699, 988, 1043.
Paraclete, 107, 838, 839, 841, 846, 869, 874, 877, 879, 1068, 1069.
Paradise, 661, 947.
Parousia, 475, 480, 661, 830, 841, 903, 989, 1010, 1066, 1081, 1098, 1099.
Pascal, 399, 400.
Paschal controversy, 13, 15, 16, 23, 140, 172, 182, 967-971.
Passover, 55, 552; first in our Lord's ministry, 362, 369, 371; second (probably), 452, 453; third (or second), 564; fourth (or third) 763, 802; meaning of "eating the passover," 924-926, 1085.
Paul, the apostle, 35-37, 297, 346, 381, 395, 396, 439, 461, 479, 580, 623, 640, 792, 794, 866, 963, 987, 988, 990, 991.
Paulus, referred to or quoted, 340, 345, 353, 569, 683, 758, 990, 1008.
Pentecost, a feast of the Jews, 453; coming of the Holy Ghost on, 836, 840, 844, 876, 879, 905, 981, 982, 1010.
People, The common, despised, 641, 642, 697.
Peraea, 728, 729.
Peschito, Syriac Version of New Testament, 140, 146, 233, 234, 575, 687, 831, 838.
Peter, Simon, 29, 31, 35-37, 53, 61, 63, 65, 92, 191, 192, 327-329; confesses the Lord, 608, 609, 703, 808, 809, 815, 816, 827, 866, 913; denies the Lord, 918, 922, 923, 1064, 1084, 1085; at the sepulchre, 974-975, 988; at the Sea of Tiberias, 998-1012; the Lord's words to, 1005-1008, 1098; martyrdom of, 1007, 1008, 1098.
Pharisees, 305, 306, 374, 631, 641, 645, 651, 652, 691, 697, 698, 705, 706, 710, 750, 751, 796, 909.
Philip, 35, 38, 90, 92, 331, 565-567, 777-779, 863, 1017, 1067.
Philo, Doctrine of the Logos, 173-177, 180, 181, 287, 288, 297, 298, 927, 944.
Pilate, Pontius, 200; wife of, 911, 935; trial of the Lord before, 923-942, 1085-1090; life and career of, 923, 927, 964, 1087-1090.
Plato, and Socrates, 126, 127.
Polycarp, 16, 27, 38, 39, 40-42, 44, 46, 48, 49, 163, 164, 169, 170, 204, 327, 508, 967, 969.
Polycrates, 31, 32, 40, 46, 50, 51, 168, 969, 971.
Porphyry, 619.
Praetorium, or judgment hall, 924, 925, 934.
Pre-existence of souls, 1039.
Preliminary chapters on the Gospel literature and Johannean discussion, 1-28; on the life and career of the Apostle John, 29-53; on the Fourth Gospel, analysis, etc., 54-138; on origin, author, etc., of the Fourth Gospel, 139-219.
"Preparation" of the Passover, 938, 939, 957, 1090.
Pressensé, De, on the Johannean question, 24; on St. John, 53; on the Passover, 966; on the Lord's appearance to the disciples, 980; on the Lord's body after the resurrection, 990, 991.
Priestley, answers Evanson, 21.
πρός, Force of preposition in John 1:1, 245-247.
Protevangelium Jacobi, 359.
Pseudonymous literature in the early Church, 13.
Ptolemy, the Valentinian, 168, 280.
Purim, a feast of the Jews, 452, 453, 458, 552, 1017.

Q

Quarto-decimans, 970.

R

Rambert, on St. John's Gospel, 27.
Regeneration, 379-383.
Renan, Life of Jesus, criticisms, difficulties, etc., 18, 28, 43, 64, 65, 74, 76, 79, 97, 108, 140, 159, 190, 199, 200, 205, 238, 291, 324, 339, 343, 354, 355, 368, 414, 491, 569, 684, 692, 757, 759, 760, 917, 935, 951, 975, 978.
Resurrection, 469-471; spiritual, 473-475; of life and of judgment, 479, 991, 992.
Rettig, on authenticity of St. John's Gospel, 10.
Reuss, on St. John's Gospel, 18, 19, 28, 66-68, 75; theory of the Logos, 74, 94-97, 123; date and author of St. John's Gospel, 140, 170, 193-196, 202, 213; plan of the Gospel, 222-225; meaning of $κατά$, 238, 239; $τὰ ἴδια$, 262, 263; on "Son of God," 291; on the Lord's interview with the Samaritan woman, 422; on the divinity of Christ, 467-470; on the resurrection, 470, 471, 480; on "the last day," 587; discourses of Jesus and the Jews, 684; resurrection of Lazarus, 757; on the Christ of St. John, 784; words of Jesus, 912; on Pilate's conduct, 942; on close of St. John's Gospel, 1012, 1013.
Reuterdahl, on authenticity of St. John's Gospel, 10, 16.
Reville, on St. John's Gospel, 15; on the Logos, 123; on the Fourth Gospel and criticism, 492.
Riggenbach, on St. John's Gospel, 24, 25.
"Righteous Father," 904, 905, 1081.
Robinson, E., 343, 455, 456.
Roman Soldiers, Band of, arrest the Lord, 910-917, 1082; break the legs of the malefactors, 951, 952.
Rulers of the Jews who believed, 665, 666, 796.

S

Sabatier, on St. John's Gospel and the Apocalypse, 18, 19, 70, 140, 190, 201, 991, 992.
Sabbath, Observance of, 459-463, 624-628, 691, 692, 950, 951, 1092, 1093.
Sadducees, The, 752.
Salome, mother of St. John, 29, seq.; at the crucifixion of the Lord, 203, 531, 532.
Samaria, Woman of, Discourse of Jesus with, 421-432, 544-548.
Samaritans, Origin of the, 422, 423, 426.
Sanday, on the Fourth Gospel, 26.
Sanhedrim,, 631, 632, 641, 642, 645, 656, 665, 691, 751, 914, 922, 924, 927, 937, 939, 1051.
Satan, enters Judas Iscariot, 817, 819, 1063. See Devil.
Schenkel, on St. John's Gospel, 27.
Schleiermacher, on John's Gospel, 21
Scholten, on St. John's Gospel, 15, 17, 26.
Schott, on St. John's Gospel, 21.
Schurer, on St. John's Gospel, 171.
Schwegler, on authenticity of St. John's Gospel, 13.
Schweizer, on St. John's Gospel, 27, 28, 223.
Scourging, cruel torture, 933, 934.
Scribes, The, 647, 710.
Sea of Tiberias, 526, 564, 574, 575, 998.
"Seed of the woman," i.e., Jesus the Lord, 342.
Semisch, on Gospel histories, 23.
Shekinah, 177, 270.
"Signs which Jesus did," 995, 1058.
Siloam, Pool of, 688, 689.
Simon. See Peter.
Simon of Cyrene, 943.
Simpson, answers the diests, 21.
Sin, of parents, or one's own, and suffering, 685, 686, 1039, 1040.
Slavery, Ancient, 666-669.
Socinus, and Socinian Catechism, 683, 888, 984.
Socrates, and his genius or daemon, 463.
"Son of God," "equal with God" (see Father of Christ), 461-467, 554, 695, 696, 724, 935, 994, 1045, 1046, 1061.
"Son of man," Meaning, etc., of designation, 338-342, 476, 477, 695, 696, 789, 823, 824, 1061.
Spinoza, and resurrection of Lazarus, 761.
Spirit of truth, 871. See Holy Spirit.
Stap and Tübingen School, 14, 70, 72.

Steitz, on the paschal controversy, 23; on St. John in Asia, 25.
Stier, "Words of Jesus," 374, 424, 618, 637, 668, 702, 820, 929, 960.
Storr, answers the deists, 21.
Strauss, Life of Jesus criticisms, objections, etc., 10, 11, 22, 323, 349, 353, 354, 379, 380, 426, 491, 569, 611, 733, 736, 745, 749, 758, 759, 908, 909, 913, 946, 952, 964, 975, 980, 986, 988, 1003.
Stroud, W., on the death of Christ, 952.
"Supernatural Religion," Author of, on St. John's Gospel, 17, 154.
Süskind, answers the deists, 21.
Sychar, 416, 419, 420, 436.
Synagogue, Meetings in, 602.
"Synoptic" Gospels, 7, 10, 961-967.
Syriac Version of the New Testament. See Peschito.

T

Tabernacles, Feast of, 613, 614, 651, 715-717, 1026.
Talmud, 960, 963.
Tatian, 149, 717.
Temple at Jerusalem, Jesus drives out the money-changers, etc., 361-365; second driving out, 370.
Tertullian, referred to or quoted, 50, 139, 142, 266, 280, 281, 457, 469, 644.
Thaddaeus. See Judas or Jude.
Theodoret, on John 1:18, 281.
Theophilus, of Antioch, 142, 143, 168.
Thiersch, against Baur's views, 22, 23, 38.
"Thieves and robbers," i.e., the Pharisees, 705, 706.
Tholuck, Commentary on St. John's Gospel, 21; on credibility of Gospel history, 22.
Thomas, 200. See Didymus; 831, 977, 983-985, 987, 1096.
Tiberias, On the Lake, 564, 574, 1020; Sea of, 998.
Tiberius, Emperor of Rome, 937, 938.
"Till I come," Meaning of, 1010, 1098, 1099. See Parousia.
Time, Mode of reckoning, 326, 327, 421, 446, 939, 940, 1052.
Tischendorf, 24, 335; Sinaitic manuscript and readings, 231, 390, 393, 833, 850, 857, 872, 880.
Trinity, Doctrine of the, 903, 904, 1075.
Tubingen School of critics, 14, 36, 66, 140, 206, 284, 421, 705, 961, 975.

U

Unbelief, Reason of, 399; of the Jews, 791-796; consequences of, 796-800.

V

Valentinian heresy, 14.
Valentinus, The heretic, 144, 147, 154, 157.
Van Goens, on St. John's Gospel, 27.
"Via Dolorosa," 925.
Vine and vine-dressing in Palestine, 856.
Vogel, on authenticity of St. John's Gospel, 9.
Volkmar, on authenticity of St. John's Gospel, 13, 14, 15.
Vulgate, Latin Version of the New Testament, 234.

W

Wabnitz, on St. John in Asia, 25; on name, "Son of man," 339, 342.
Washing the feet of the disciples, by the Lord, 807-811, 1060; rite based on this, 811.
Wegscheider, on St. John's Gospel, 21.
Weiffenbach, on Papias, 27.
Weiss, B., on authenticity of St. John's Gospel, criticisms, etc., 26, 208, 216, 368, 391, 397, 462, 467, 827, 830, 842, 864, 873, 912, 991, 1013, 1079, 1086, 1099.
Weisse, C.H., on authenticity of St. John's Gospel, 11, 26, 27, 28; on the resurrection of the Lord, 992.
Weitzel, on the paschal controversy, 23.
Weizsacker, on the Gospel, 15, 27, 28, 182, 414, 968, 969, 1013.
Westcott, Professor, Commentary on St. John's Gospel, 26, 229, 241, 242; Westcott and Hort, critical text of the New Testament, 236, 237, 280; Westcott on John 1:41, 42, 327; on the title "the son of man," 342; heaven, 390; on our Lord's interview with the Samaritan woman, 423, 424; on the

divinity of the Son, 462; on resurrection and judgment, 474; on ch. 3:16-21, 534, 535; on 6:51, 594; on St. Peter's confession, 612; Dissertation of, 849; on the Lord's charge to Peter, 1067.
Wieseler, 29, 30.
Wilke, on authenticity of St. John's Gospel, 11.
Wisdom, Book of, 289.
Witness or testimony of the Lord to Himself, 651-655, 1032, 1033. *See* note, p. 557, 558.
Wittichen, on St. John in Asia, 25.
Wolfenbuttel Fragments, 988.
Woman held in low esteem among ancient Jews, 432, 433.
Woman, The, taken in adultery, 643-649; Godet holds the story to be an interpolation; American Editor's note upon, 1031, 1032.
Word of God. *See* Logos.
World $κόσμος$ 582, 651; judgment of, 787; conviction of by the Spirit, 869, 870.

X

Xenophon, and Socrates, 126.

Z

Zahn, on John, the presbyter, 25; on Papias, 43; on the Diatessaron, 717.
Zebedee, and family, 29, 30.
Zeller, on authenticity of St. John's Gospel, 13; on Philo, 179.

DATE DUE